T0205288

Lecture Notes in Computer Science 12046

More information about this series at http://www.springer.com/series/7412

Shivakumara Palaiahnakote ·
Gabriella Sanniti di Baja ·
Liang Wang · Wei Qi Yan (Eds.)

Pattern Recognition

5th Asian Conference, ACPR 2019
Auckland, New Zealand, November 26–29, 2019
Revised Selected Papers, Part I

Editors
Shivakumara Palaiahnakote
University of Malaya
Kuala Lumpur, Malaysia

Gabriella Sanniti di Baja
Consiglio Nazionale delle Ricerche, ICAR
Naples, Italy

Liang Wang
Chinese Academy of Sciences
Beijing, China

Wei Qi Yan
Auckland University of Technology
Auckland, New Zealand

ISSN 0302-9743 ISSN 1611-3349 (electronic)
Lecture Notes in Computer Science
ISBN 978-3-030-41403-0 ISBN 978-3-030-41404-7 (eBook)
https://doi.org/10.1007/978-3-030-41404-7

LNCS Sublibrary: SL6 – Image Processing, Computer Vision, Pattern Recognition, and Graphics

This Springer imprint is published by the registered company Springer Nature Switzerland AG
The registered company address is: Gewerbestrasse 11, 6330 Cham, Switzerland

Preface

Our heartiest welcome to ACPR 2019, the 5th Asian Conference on Pattern Recognition, held in Auckland, New Zealand, during 26–29 November, 2019. It is truly an honor to host our premier conference in the business capital of New Zealand; the first time that this conference has been hosted in this part of the world. Auckland is New Zealand's largest city and most important economic region. It is host to some of the most picturesque seaside views in New Zealand as well as fantastic shopping and dining opportunities. Auckland is a true multicultural city – it has the largest Polynesian population of any city in the world as well as a significant percentage of Maori and Asian peoples. We did our best to prepare every aspect of this conference and hope that you enjoyed your stay in Auckland.

ACPR was initiated to promote the scientific exchanges and collaborations of pattern recognition researchers in the Asia-Pacific region, and it also welcomed participation from other regions of the world. The fifth ACPR followed the previous editions, ACPR 2011 in Beijing, China, ACPR 2013 in Okinawa, Japan, ACPR 2015 in Kuala Lumpur, Malaysia, and ACPR 2017 in Nanjing, China. For ACPR 2019, there was not only a well-presented technical program, but we also invited participants to experience the diverse culture of the city of Auckland.

ACPR 2019 received 214 full submissions from 37 countries. The program chairs invited 68 Program Committee members and 54 additional reviewers to review the submitted papers. Each paper received at least two reviews, and most papers received three reviews. Based on the reviews, the Program Committee accepted a total of 125 papers, leading to an oral paper acceptance rate of 16.82% and for posters a 41.58% acceptance rate. The technical program included nine oral sessions, three poster spotlights, three poster sessions, and three keynotes. The keynote speeches were given by three internationally renowned researchers active in pattern recognition and computer vision. They are:

- Professor Andrea Cavallaro of Queen Mary University of London, UK, "Multimodal Learning for Robust and Privacy Preserving Analytics"
- Professor Yihong Wu of the Chinese Academy of Sciences, China, "Possibility to Localize a Camera without Matching"
- Professor Dacheng Tao of the University of Sydney, Australia, "AI at Dawn - Opportunities and Challenges"

A large event like ACPR depends almost exclusively on a team of volunteers who work hard on the program, infrastructure, and facilities. We would like to thank the chairs of the different committees for their help and support. Our special thanks to our workshop chairs for arranging six workshops in this iteration of ACPR. We gratefully acknowledge the financial support of our sponsors which helped to reduce costs and provide various awards including best paper awards. We would like to thank sponsorship chairs and the AUT Professional Conference Organizer for helping us with this event. Our sincere thanks to all the researchers who have shown an interest in ACPR 2019 by sending contributed papers, workshop and tutorial proposals, and by participating. Thanks also to the Program Committee members, reviewers, and Local Organizing Committee members for their strong support and active participation. Finally, we would like to express our deep appreciation for the valuable guidance of the ACPR Advisory Board.

We hope you found your stay to be fruitful and rewarding, and that you enjoyed the exchange of technical and scientific ideas during ACPR 2019, as well as the flavor of the diverse and beautiful city of Auckland.

November 2019

Reinhard Klette
Brendan McCane
Umapada Pal
Shivakumara Palaiahnakote
Gabriella Sanniti di Baja
Liang Wang

Organization

Steering Committee

Seong-Whan Lee	Korea University, South Korea
Cheng-Lin Liu	Chinese Academy of Sciences, China
Sankar K. Pal	Indian Statistical Institute, India
Tieniu Tan	Chinese Academy of Sciences, China
Yasushi Yagi	Osaka University, Japan

General Chairs

Reinhard Klette	Auckland University of Technology, New Zealand
Brendan McCane	University of Otago, New Zealand
Umapada Pal	Indian Statistical Institute, India

Program Chairs

Gabriella Sanniti di Baja	Institute of High Performance Computing and Networking, Italy
Shivakumara Palaiahnakote	University of Malaya, Malaysia
Liang Wang	Chinese Academy of Sciences, China

Publication Chair

Wei Qi Yan	Auckland University of Technology, New Zealand

International Liaison Chairs

Chokri Ben Amar	University of Sfax, Tunisia
Wang Han	Nanyang Technology University, Singapore
Edwin Hancock	University of York, UK
Anil K. Jain	University of Michigan, USA
Domingo Mery	Pontificia Univerisdad Catolica, Chile

Workshop Chairs

Michael Cree	University of Waikato, New Zealand
Fay Huang	National Ilan University, Taiwan
Junsong Yuan	State University of New York at Buffalo, USA

Tutorial Chairs

Michael Blumenstein	University of Technology Sydney, Australia
Yukiko Kenmochi	French National Centre for Scientific Research, France
Ujjwal Maulik	Jadavpur University, India

Sponsorship Chair

Koichi Kise	Osaka University, Japan

Local Organizing Chair

Martin Stommel	Auckland University of Technology, New Zealand

Organizing Committee

Terry Brydon	Auckland University of Technology, New Zealand
Tapabrata Chakraborty	University of Otago, New Zealand
Gisela Klette	Auckland University of Technology, New Zealand
Minh Nguyen	Auckland University of Technology, New Zealand

Web Manager

Andrew Chen	The University of Auckland, New Zealand

Program Committee

Alireza Alaei	Griffith University, Australia
Fernando Alonso-Fernandez	Halmstad University, Sweden
Mahmoud Al-Sarayreh	Auckland University of Technology, New Zealand
Yasuo Ariki	Kobe University, Japan
Md Asikuzzaman	University of New South Wales, Australia
George Azzopardi	University of Groningen, The Netherlands
Donald Bailey	Massey University, New Zealand
Nilanjana Bhattacharya	Bose Institute, India
Saumik Bhattacharya	IIT Kanpur, India
Partha Bhowmick	IIT Kharagpur, India
Michael Blumenstein	University of Technology Sydney, Australia
Giuseppe Boccignone	University of Milan, Italy
Phil Bones	University of Canterbury, New Zealand
Gunilla Borgefors	Uppsala University, Sweden
Murk Bottema	Flinders University, Australia
Alfred Bruckstein	Technion, Israel
Weidong Cai	The University of Sydney, Australia
A. Campilho	University of Porto, Portugal
Virginio Cantoni	Università di Pavia, Italy

Sukalpa Chanda	Uppsala University, Sweden
Chiranjoy Chattopadhyay	IIT Jodhpur, India
Songcan Chen	Nanjing University of Aeronautics and Astronautics, China
Li Cheng	University of Alberta, Canada
Hsiang-Jen Chien	Auckland University of Technology, New Zealand
Michael Cree	University of Waikato, New Zealand
Jinshi Cui	Peking University, China
Zhen Cui	Nanjing University of Science and Technology, China
Dao-Qing Dai	Sun Yat-sen University, China
Daisuke Deguchi	Nagoya University, Japan
Andreas Dengel	German Research Center for Artificial Intelligence, Germany
Alberto del Bimbo	University delgi Studi di Firenze, Italy
Eduardo Destefanis	Universidad Tecnológica Nacional, Spain
Claudio de Stefano	Università degli studi di Cassino e del Lazio Meridionale, Italy
Changxing Ding	South China University of Technology, China
Jihad El-Sana	Ben Gurion University of the Negev, Israel
Miguel Ferrer	Universidad de Las Palmas de Gran Canaria, Spain
Robert Fisher	University of Edinburgh, UK
Gian Luca Foresti	University of Udine, Italy
Huazhu Fu	Inception Institute of Artificial Intelligence, UAE
Fei Gao	Hangzhu Dianzi University, China
Guangwei Gao	Nanjing University of Posts and Telecommunications, China
Edel Bartolo Garcia Reyes	Academy of Sciences of Cuba, Cuba
Andrew Gilman	Massey University, New Zealand
Richard Green	University of Canterbury, New Zealand
Yi Guo	Western Sydney University, Australia
Michal Haindl	Czech Academy of Sciences, Czech Republic
Takatsugu Hirayama	Nagoya University, Japan
Shinsaku Hiura	University of Hyogo, Japan
Kazuhiro Hotta	Meijo University, Japan
Du Huynh	The University of Western Australia, Australia
Ichiro Ide	Nagoya University, Japan
Masaaki Iiyama	Kyoto University, Japan
Yoshihisa Ijiri	OMRON, Japan
Atsushi Imiya	IMIT Chiba University, Japan
Koichi Ito	Tohoku University, Japan
Yumi Iwashita	Kyushu University, Japan
Motoi Iwata	Osaka Prefecture University, Japan
Yunde Jia	Beijing Institute of Technology, China
Xiaoyi Jiang	University of Münster, Germany
Xin Jin	Beijing Electronic Science and Technology Institute, China

Kunio Kashino	NTT Labs, Japan
Rei Kawakami	University of Tokyo, Japan
Yasutomo Kawanishi	Nagoya University, Japan
Hiroaki Kawashima	Kyoto University, Japan
Jinman Kim	The University of Sydney, Australia
Akisato Kimura	NTT Labs, Japan
Nahum Kiryati	Tel Aviv University, Israel
Itaru Kitahara	University of Tsukuba, Japan
Takumi Kobayashi	Tokyo Institute of Technology, Japan
Arjan Kuijper	Technical University of Darmstadt, Germany
Takio Kurita	Hiroshima University, Japan
Steven Le Moan	Massey University, New Zealand
Seong-Whan Lee	Korea University, South Korea
Hua Li	Chinese Academy of Sciences, China
Zechao Li	Nanjing University of Science and Technology, China
Alan Wee-Chung Liew	Griffith University, Australia
Xianglong Liu	Beihang University, China
Weifeng Liu	China University of Petroleum, China
Daniel Lopresti	Lehigh University, USA
Brian Lovell	The University of Queensland, Australia
Huimin Lu	Kyushu Institute of Technology, Japan
Jianfeng Lu	Nanjing University of Science and Technology, China
Yasushi Makihara	Osaka University, Japan
Maria de Marsico	Sapienza University of Rome, Italy
Takeshi Masuda	National Institute of Advanced Industrial Science and Technology, Japan
Tetsu Matsukawa	Kyushu University, Japan
Stephen Maybank	Birkbeck College, UK
Yoshito Mekada	Chukyo University, Japan
Domingo Mery	Catholic University of Chile, Chile
Dan Mikami	NTT Labs, Japan
Steven Mills	University of Otago, New Zealand
Ikuhisa Mitsugami	Hiroshima City University, Japan
Daisuke Miyazaki	Hiroshima City University, Japan
Yoshihiko Mochizuki	Waseda University, Japan
Olivier Monga	IRD, France
Kazuaki Nakamura	Osaka University, Japan
Yuta Nakashima	Osaka University, Japan
Naoko Nitta	Osaka University, Japan
Mark Nixon	University of Southampton, UK
Shohei Nobuhara	Kyoto University, Japan
Wataru Ohyama	Saitama Institute of Technology, Japan
Kazunori Okada	San Francisco State University, USA
Fumio Okura	Osaka University, Japan
Srikanta Pal	Griffith University, Australia
Jaehwa Park	Chung-Ang University, South Korea

Contents – Part I

Classification

Action and Video and Motion

Object Detection and Anomaly Detection

Adversarial Learning and Networks

Computational Photography

Learning Theory and Optimization

Contents – Part II

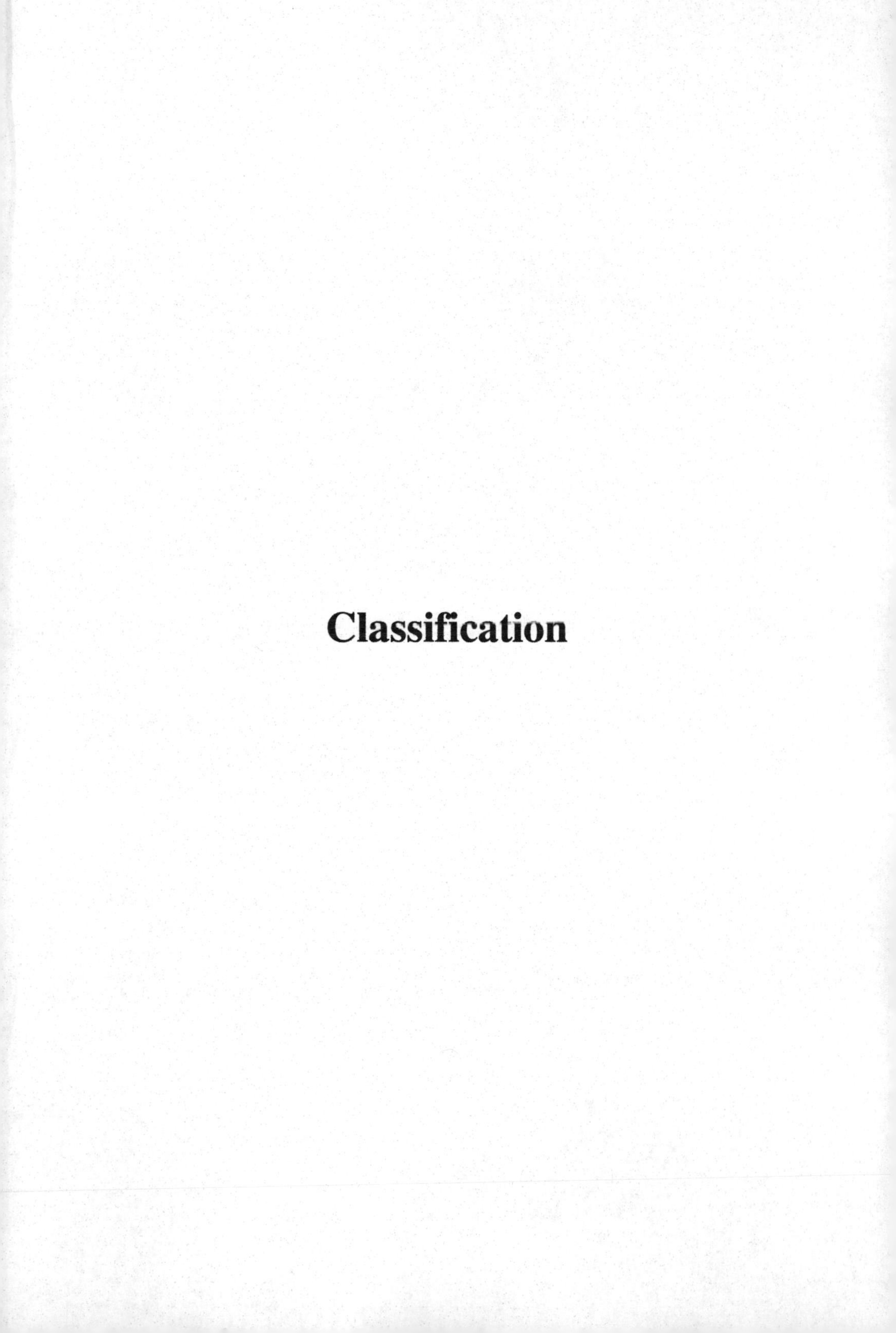

Classification

Integrating Domain Knowledge: Using Hierarchies to Improve Deep Classifiers

Clemens-Alexander Brust[1(✉)] and Joachim Denzler[1,2]

[1] Computer Vision Group, Friedrich Schiller University Jena, Jena, Germany
clemens-alexander.brust@uni-jena.de

[2] Michael Stifel Center Jena, Jena, Germany

Abstract. One of the most prominent problems in machine learning in the age of deep learning is the availability of sufficiently large annotated datasets. For specific domains, *e.g.* animal species, a long-tail distribution means that some classes are observed and annotated insufficiently. Additional labels can be prohibitively expensive, *e.g.* because domain experts need to be involved. However, there is more information available that is to the best of our knowledge not exploited accordingly.

In this paper, we propose to make use of preexisting class hierarchies like WordNet to integrate additional domain knowledge into classification. We encode the properties of such a class hierarchy into a probabilistic model. From there, we derive a novel label encoding and a corresponding loss function. On the ImageNet and NABirds datasets our method offers a relative improvement of 10.4% and 9.6% in accuracy over the baseline respectively. After less than a third of training time, it is already able to match the baseline's fine-grained recognition performance. Both results show that our suggested method is efficient and effective.

Keywords: Class hierarchy · Knowledge integration · Hierarchical classification

1 Introduction

In recent years, convolutional neural networks (CNNs) have achieved outstanding performance in a variety of machine learning tasks, especially in computer vision, such as image classification [15,25] and semantic segmentation [27]. Training a CNN from scratch in an end-to-end fashion not only requires considerable computational resources and experience, but also large amounts of labeled training data [35]. Using pre-trained CNN features [33], adapting existing CNNs to new tasks [17] or performing data augmentation can reduce the need for labeled training data, but may not always be applicable or effective.

For specific problem domains, *e.g.* with a long-tailed distribution of samples over classes, the amount of labeled training data available is not always sufficient for training a CNN to reasonable performance. When unlabeled data

S. Palaiahnakote et al. (Eds.): ACPR 2019, LNCS 12046, pp. 3–16, 2020.
https://doi.org/10.1007/978-3-030-41404-7_1

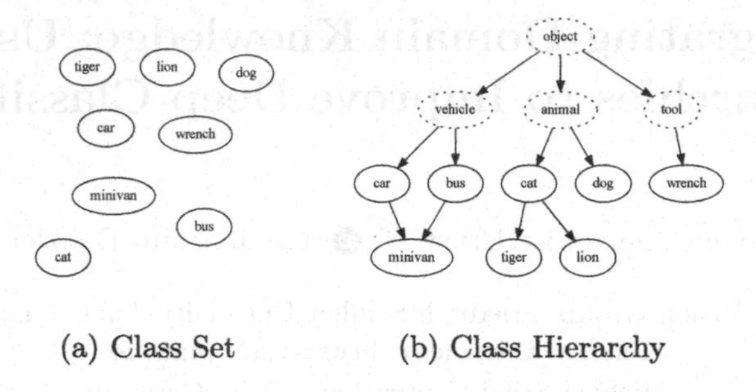

(a) Class Set (b) Class Hierarchy

Fig. 1. Comparison between a loose set of independent classes and a class hierarchy detailing inter-class relations.

already exists, which is not always the case, active learning [32] to select valuable instances for labeling may be applied. However, labels still have to be procured which is not always feasible.

Besides information from more training data, domain knowledge in the form of high-level information about the structure of the problem can be considered. In contrast to annotations of training data, this kind of domain knowledge is already available in many cases from projects like iNaturalist [38], Visual Genome [23], Wikidata [41] and WikiSpecies[1].

In this paper, we use class hierarchies, *e.g.* WordNet [11], as an example of domain knowledge. In contrast to approaches based on attributes, where annotations are often expected to be per-image, class hierarchies offer the option of domain knowledge integration on the highest level with the least additional annotation effort. We encode the properties of such a class hierarchy into a probabilistic model that is based on common assumptions around hierarchies. From there, we derive a special label encoding together with a corresponding loss function. These components are applied to a CNN and evaluated systematically.

Our main **contributions** are: (i) a deep learning method based on a probabilistic model to improve existing classifiers by adding a class hierarchy which (ii) works with any form of hierarchy representable using a directed acyclic graph (DAG), *i.e.* does not require a tree hierarchy. We evaluate our method in experiments on the CIFAR-100 [24], ImageNet and NABirds [37] datasets to represent problem domains of various scales.

2 Related Work

Hierarchical methods have been subject of extensive research in image categorization. A given class hierarchy can be used explicitly to build a hierarchical classifier [20,28], to regularize a preexisting model [12,34], to construct an embedding space [2,10,13,21], in metric learning-based methods [20,40,44] or, to construct a probabilistic model [7,14].

[1] https://species.wikimedia.org/wiki/Main_Page.

Leveraging external semantic information for performance improvements, also called knowledge transfer, has been studied in the context of text categorization [3] as well as visual recognition [19,30,42]. Attributes are also considered as a knowledge source in [21]. While improvements are generally expected when using such methods, disagreements between visual and semantic similarity may introduce new errors [5]. Alternatively, visual hierarchies can be learned [1,43] or used implicitly [4,8]. An extreme case of knowledge transfer is zero-shot learning, where some categories have zero training examples [18,31].

Our work is most closely related to [28] in that we consider similar individual classification problems. However, instead of their step-by-step approach using binary classifiers, our probabilistic model is evaluated globally for inference. A similar approach is also used in [7], where a relations between classes such as subsumption and mutual exclusion are extracted from a hierarchy and then used to condition a graphical model.

Hierarchical Data. Typical image classification datasets rarely offer hierarchical information. There are exceptions such as the iNaturalist challenge dataset [38] where a class hierarchy is derived from biological taxonomy. Exceptions also include specific hierarchical classification benchmarks, *e.g.* [29,36] as well as datasets where the labels originate from a hierarchy such as ImageNet [6]. The Visual Genome dataset [23] is another notable exception, with available metadata including attributes, relationships, visual question answers, bounding boxes and more, all mapped to elements from WordNet.

To augment existing non-hierarchical datasets, class hierarchies can be used. For a typical object classification scenario, concepts from the WordNet database [11] can be mapped to object classes. WordNet contains nouns, verbs and adjectives that are grouped into *synsets* of synonymous concepts. Relations such as hyponymy (**is-a**), antonymy (**is-not**), troponymy (**is-a-way-of**) and meronymy (**is-part-of**) are encoded in a graph structure where synsets are represented by nodes and relations by edges respectively. In this paper, we use the hyponymy relation to infer a class hierarchy.

3 Method

In this section, we propose a method to adapt existing classifiers to hierarchical classification. We start by acquiring a hierarchy and then define a probabilistic model based on it. From this probabilistic model, we derive an encoding and a loss function that can be used in a machine learning environment.

3.1 Class Hierarchy

For our model, we assume that a hierarchy of object categories is supplied, *e.g.* from a database such as WordNet [11] or WikiSpecies. It is modeled in the form of a graph $W = (S, h)$, where S denotes the set of all possible object categories, called *synsets* in the WordNet terminology. These are the nodes of the graph.

Note that S is typically a superset of the dataset categories $C \subseteq S$, since parent categories are included to connect existing categories, *e.g.* `vehicle` is a parent of `car` and `bus`, but not originally part of the dataset.

A hyponymy relation $h \in S \times S$ over the classes, which can be interpreted as directed edges in the graph, is also given. For example, $(s, s') \in h$ means that s' is a hyperonym of s, or s is a hyponym of s', meaning s **is-a** s'. In general, the **is-a** relation is transitive. However, WordNet only models direct relationships between classes to keep the graph manageable and to represent different levels of abstraction as graph distances. The relation is also irreflexive and asymmetric.

For the following section, we assume that W is a directed acyclic graph (DAG). However, the WordNet graph is commonly reduced to a tree, for example by using a voting algorithm [36] or selecting task-specific subsets that are trees [6]. In this paper, we work on the directed acyclic graph (DAG) directly.

3.2 Probabilistic Model

Elements of a class hierarchy are not always mutually exclusive, *e.g.* a `corgi` is also a `dog` and an `animal` at the same time. Hence, we do not model the class label as one categorical random variable, but assume multiple independent Bernoulli variables $Y_s, s \in S$ instead. Formally, we model the probability of any class s occurring independently (and thus allowing even multi-label scenarios), given an example x:

$$P(Y_s = 1|X = x), \tag{1}$$

or, more concisely,

$$P(Y_s^+|X). \tag{2}$$

The aforementioned model on its own is overly flexible considering the problem at hand, since it allows for any combination of categories co-occurring. At this point, assumptions are similar to those behind a one-hot encoding. However, from the common definition of a hierarchy, we can infer a few additional properties to restrict the model.

Hierarchical Decomposition. A class s can have many independent parents $S' = s'_1, \ldots, s'_n$. We choose $Y_{S'}^+$ to denote an observation of at least one parent and $Y_{S'}^-$ to indicate that no parent class has been observed:

$$\begin{aligned} Y_{S'}^+ &\Leftrightarrow Y_{s'_1}^+ \vee \ldots \vee Y_{s'_n}^+ \Leftrightarrow Y_{s'_1} = 1 \vee \ldots \vee Y_{s'_n} = 1, \\ Y_{S'}^- &\Leftrightarrow Y_{s'_1}^- \wedge \ldots \wedge Y_{s'_n}^- \Leftrightarrow Y_{s'_1} = 0 \wedge \ldots \wedge Y_{s'_n} = 0. \end{aligned}$$

Based on observations $Y_{S'}$, we can decompose the model from Eq. (2) in a way to capture the hierarchical nature. We start by assuming a marginalization of the conditional part of the model over the parents $Y_{s'}$:

$$\begin{aligned} P(Y_s^+|X) = &P(Y_s^+|X, Y_{S'}^+)P(Y_{S'}^+|X) \\ &+ P(Y_s^+|X, Y_{S'}^-)P(Y_{S'}^-|X). \end{aligned} \tag{3}$$

The details of this decomposition are given in the supplementary material.

Simplification. We now constrain the model and add assumptions to better reflect the hierarchical problem. If none of the parents $S' = s'_1, \ldots, s'_n$ of a class s occur, we assume the probability of s being observed for any given example to be zero:

$$P(Y_s^+|X, Y_{S'}^-) = P(Y_s^+|Y_{S'}^-) = 0. \tag{4}$$

This leads to a simpler hierarchical model, omitting the second half of Eq. (3) by setting it to zero:

$$P(Y_s^+|X) = P(Y_s^+|X, Y_{S'}^+)P(Y_{S'}^+|X). \tag{5}$$

Parental Independence. To make use of recursion in our model, we require the random variables $Y_{s'_1}, \ldots, Y_{s'_n}$ to be independent of each other in a naive fashion. Using the definition of $Y_{S'}^+$, we derive:

$$P(Y_{S'}^+|X) = 1 - \prod_{i=1}^{|S'|} 1 - P(Y_{s'_i}^+|X). \tag{6}$$

Parentlessness. In a non-empty DAG, we can expect there to be at least one node with no incoming edges, *i.e.* a class with no parents. In the case of WordNet, there is exactly one node with no parents, the root synset `entity.n.01`. A marginalization over parent classes does not apply there. We assume that all observed classes are children of `entity` and thus set the probability to one for a class without parents:

$$P(Y_s^+|X, S' = \emptyset) = 1. \tag{7}$$

Note that this is not reasonable for all hierarchical classification problems. If the hierarchy is composed of many disjoint components, $P(Y_s^+|X, S' = \emptyset)$ should be modeled explicitly. Even if there is only a single root, explicit modeling could be used for tasks such as novelty detection.

3.3 Inference

The following section describes the details of the inference process in our model.

Restricted Model Outputs. Depending on the setting, when the model is used for inference, the possible outputs can be restricted to the classes C that can actually occur in the dataset as opposed to all modeled classes S including parents that exist only in the hierarchy. This assumes a known class set at test time as opposed to an open-set problem. We denote this setting *mandatory labeled node prediction (MLNP)* and the unrestricted alternative *arbitrary node prediction (ANP)*.

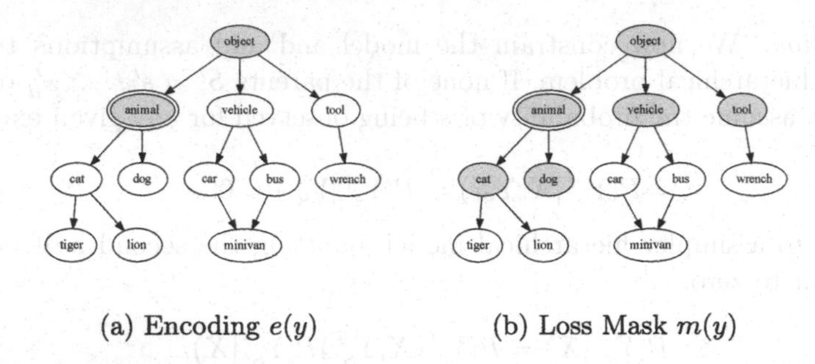

(a) Encoding $e(y)$ (b) Loss Mask $m(y)$

Fig. 2. Hierarchical encoding and loss mask for $y = \texttt{animal}$. Shaded nodes represent 1 and light nodes 0 respectively.

Prediction. To predict a *single* class s given a specific example x, we look for the class where the joint probability of the following observations is high: (i) the class s itself occurring (Y_s^+) and (ii) none of the children $S'' = s_1'', \ldots, s_m''$ occurring ($Y_{S''}^-$):

$$s(x) = \underset{s \in C \subseteq S}{\operatorname{argmax}} P(Y_s^+|X) P(Y_{S''}^-|X, Y_s^+). \tag{8}$$

Requiring the children to be pairwise independent similar to Eq. (6), inference is performed in the following way:

$$s(x) = \underset{s \in C \subseteq S}{\operatorname{argmax}} P(Y_s^+|X) \prod_{i=1}^{|S''|} 1 - P(Y_{s_i''}^+|X, Y_s^+). \tag{9}$$

Because $P(Y_s^+|X)$ can be decomposed according to Eq. (3) and expressed as a product (cf. Eq. (6)), we infer using:

$$s(x) = \underset{s \in C \subseteq S}{\operatorname{argmax}} P(Y_s^+|X, Y_{S'}^+) \cdot \underbrace{(1 - \prod_{i=1}^{|S'|} 1 - P(Y_{s_i'}^+|X))}_{\text{Parent nodes } S'} \cdot \underbrace{\prod_{i=1}^{|S''|} 1 - P(Y_{s_i''}^+|X, Y_s^+)}_{\text{Child nodes } 'S}. \tag{10}$$

Again, $P(Y_{s_i'}^+|X)$ can be decomposed. This decomposition is performed recursively following the scheme laid out in Eq. (3) until a parentless node is reached (cf. Eq. (7)).

3.4 Training

In this section, we describe how to implement our proposed model in a machine learning context. Instead of modeling the probabilities $P(Y_s^+|X)$ for each class s directly, we want to estimate the conditional probabilities $P(Y_s^+|X, Y_{S'}^+)$. This changes each individual estimator's task slightly, because it only needs to discriminate among siblings and not all classes. It also enables the implementation of the hierarchical recursive inference used in Eq. (10).

The main components comprise of a label encoding $e : S \rightarrow \{0,1\}^{|S|}$ as well as a special loss function. A label $y \in S$ is encoded using the hyponymy relation $h \in S \times S$, specifically its transitive closure $\mathcal{T}(h)$, and the following function:

$$e(y)_s = \begin{cases} 1 & \text{if } y = s \text{ or } (y,s) \in \mathcal{T}(h), \\ 0 & \text{otherwise.} \end{cases} \tag{11}$$

A machine learning method can now be used to estimate encoded labels directly. However, a suitable loss function needs to be provided such that the conditional nature of each individual estimator is preserved. This means that, given a label y, a component s should be trained only if one of its parents s' is related to the label y by $\mathcal{T}(h)$, or if y is one of its parents. We encode this requirement using a *loss mask* $m : S \rightarrow \{0,1\}^{|S|}$, defined by the following equation:

$$m(y)_s = \begin{cases} 1 & y = s \text{ or} \\ & \exists (s,s') \in h : y = s' \text{ or } (y,s') \in \mathcal{T}(h), \\ 0 & \text{otherwise.} \end{cases} \tag{12}$$

Figure 2 visualizes the encoding $e(y)$ and the corresponding loss mask $m(y)$ for a small example hierarchy. Using the encoding and loss mask, the complete loss function $\mathcal{L}$ for a given data point (x,y) and estimator $f : X \rightarrow \{0,1\}^{|S|}$ is then defined by the the masked mean squared error (alternatively, a binary cross-entry loss can be used):

$$\mathcal{L}_f(x,y) = m(y)^T (e(y) - f(x))^2. \tag{13}$$

The function $f(x)_s$ is then used to estimate the conditional probabilities $P(Y_s^+|X, Y_{S'}^+)$. Applying the inference procedure in Sect. 3.3, a prediction is made using the formula in Eq. (10) and substituting $f(x)_s$ for $P(Y_s^+|X, Y_{S'}^+)$.

4 Experiments

We aim to assess the effects of applying our method on three different scales of problems, using the following datasets:

CIFAR-100. For our experiments, we want to work with a dataset that does not directly supply hierarchical labels, but where we can reasonably assume that an underlying hierarchy exists. The CIFAR-100 dataset [24] fulfills this requirement. Because there are only 100 classes, each can be mapped to a specific synset in the WordNet hierarchy without relying on potentially faulty automation. Direct mapping is not always possible, *e.g.* `aquarium_fish`, which doesn't exist in WordNet and was mapped to `freshwater fish.n.01` by us. This process is a potential error source.

The target hierarchy is composed in three steps. First, the synsets mapped from all CIFAR-100 classes make up the foundation. Then, parents of the synsets are added in a recursive fashion. With the nodes of the graph complete, directed edges are determined using the WordNet hyponymy relation. Mapping all classes to the WordNet synsets results in 99 classes being mapped to leaf nodes and one class to an inner node (`whale`). In total, there are 267 nodes as a result of the recursive adding of hyperonyms.

ImageNet. Manually mapping dataset labels to WordNet synsets is a potentional source of errors. An ideal dataset would use WordNet as its label space. Because of WordNet's popularity, such datasets exist, *e.g.* ImageNet [6] and 80 Million Tiny Images [36]. We use ImageNet, specifically the dataset of the 2012 ImageNet Large Scale Visual Recognition Challenge. It contains around 1000 training images each for 1000 synsets. All 1000 synsets are leaf nodes in the resulting hierarchy with a total of 1860 nodes.

NABirds. Quantifying performance on object recognition datasets such as CIFAR and ImageNet is important to prove the general usefulness of a method. However, more niche applications such as fine-grained recognition stand to benefit more from improvements because the availability of labeled data is much more limited. We use the NABirds dataset [37] to verify our method in a fine-grained recognition setting. NABirds is a challenge where 555 categories of North American birds have to be differentiated. These categories are comprised of 404 species as well as several variants of sex, age and plumage. It contains 48,562 images split evenly into training and validation sets. Annotations include not only image labels, but also bounding boxes and parts. Additionally, a class hierarchy based on taxonomy is supplied. It contains 1010 nodes, where all of the 555 visual categories are leaf nodes.

4.1 Experimental Setup

Convolutional Neural Networks. For our experiments on the CIFAR-100 dataset, we use a ResNet-32 [15] in the configuration originally designed for CIFAR. The network is initialized randomly as specified in [15].

We use a minibatch size of 128 and the adaptive stochastic optimizer Adam [22] with a constant learning rate of 0.001 as recommended by the authors. Although SGD can lead to better performance of the final models, its learning rate is more dependent on the range of the loss function. We choose an adaptive optimizer to minimize the influence of different ranges of loss values.

In our NABirds and ImageNet experiments, we use a ResNet-50 [15,16] because of the larger image size and overall scale of the dataset. The minibatch size is reduced to 64 and training is extended to $120,000$ steps for NABirds and $234,375$ steps for ImageNet. We crop all NABirds images using the given bounding box annotations and resize them to 224×224 pixels.

All settings use random shifts of up to 4 pixels for CIFAR-100 and up to 32 pixels for NABirds and ImageNet as well as random horizontal flips during training. All images are normalized per channel to zero mean and standard deviation one, using parameters estimated over the training data. Code will be published along with the paper. We choose our ResNet-50 and ResNet-32 baselines to be able to judge effects across datasets, which would not be possible when selecting a state-of-the-art method for each dataset individually. Furthermore, the moderately sized architecture enables faster training and therefore more experimental runs compared to a high performing design such as PNASNet [26].

Evaluation. We report the overall accuracy, not normalized w.r.t class instance counts. Each experiment consists of six random initializations per method for the CIFAR-100 dataset and three for the larger-scale NABirds and ImageNet datasets, over which we report the average. We choose to compare the methods using a measure that does not take hierarchy into account to gauge the effects of adding hierarchical data to a task that is not normally evaluated with a specific hierarchy in mind. Using a hierarchical measure would achieve the opposite: we would measure the loss sustained by omitting hierarchical data.

4.2 Overall Improvement—ImageNet

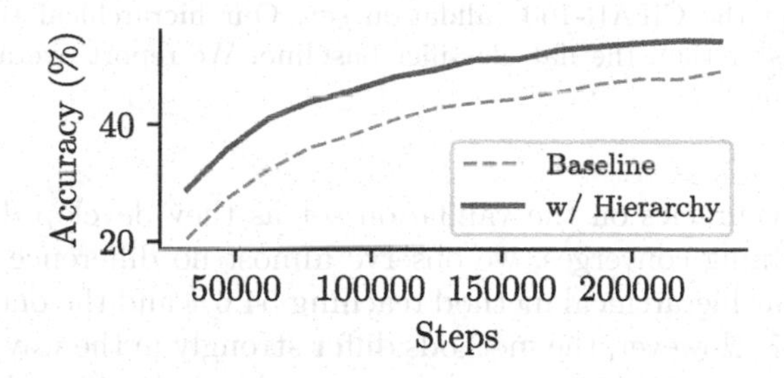

Fig. 3. Accuracy on the ImageNet validation set over time. Our hierarchical training method gains accuracy faster than the flat classifier baseline. We report overall classification accuracy in percent.

In this experiment, we quantify the effects of using our hierarchical classification method to replace the common combination of one-hot encoding and mean squared error loss function. We use ImageNet, specifically the ILSVRC2012 dataset. This is a classification challenge with 1000 classes whose labels are taken directly from the WordNet hierarchy of nouns.

Figure 3 shows the evolution over time of accuracy on the validation set. After around 240,000 gradient steps, training converges. The one-hot baseline reaches a final accuracy of 49.1%, while our method achieves 54.2% with no changes to training except for our loss function and hierarchical encoding. This is a relative improvement of 10.4%.

While an improvement of accuracy at the end of training is always welcome, the effects of hierarchical classification more drastically show in the change in accuracy over time. The strongest improvement is observed during the first training steps. After training for 31250 steps using our method, the network already performs with 28.9% accuracy. The one-hot baseline matches this performance after 62500 gradient steps, taking twice as long. The baseline's final accuracy of 49.1% is matched by our method after only 125,000 training steps, resulting in an overall training speedup of 1.88x.

4.3 Speedup—CIFAR-100

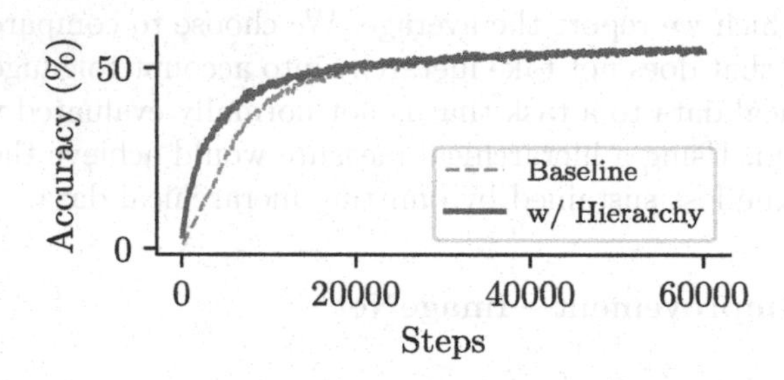

Fig. 4. Results on the CIFAR-100 validation set. Our hierarchical training method gains accuracy faster than the flat classifier baseline. We report overall classification accuracy in percent.

We report the accuracies on the validation set as they develop during training in Fig. 4. As training converges, we observe almost no difference between both methods, with our hierarchical method reaching 54.6% and the one-hot encoding baseline at 55.4%. However, the methods differ strongly in the way that accuracy is achieved. After the first 500 steps, our hierarchical classifier already predicts 10.7% of the validation set correctly, compared to the baseline's 2.8%. It takes the baseline another 1600 steps to match 10.7%, or 4.2 times as many steps.

This advantage in training speed is very strong during initial training, but becomes smaller over time. After the first half of training, the difference between both methods vanishes almost completely.

4.4 Fine-Grained Recognition—NABirds

To evaluate the performance of our hierarchical method in a more specific setting, we use the NABirds dataset [37], a fine-grained recognition challenge where the task is to classify 555 visual categories of birds. A hierarchy is given by the dataset. We observe results similar to the ImageNet dataset (see Sect. 4.2), where our method leads to an improvement in both training speed and overall accuracy. The one-hot baseline converges to an accuracy of 56.5%. Our hierarchical classifier reaches 61.9% after the full 120,000 steps of training. It already matches the baseline's final accuracy at 39,000 iterations, reducing training time to less than a third. The relative improvement with full training is 9.6%.

Table 1. Results overview.

Dataset	# of classes	Accuracy (%)		Speedup w/Hierarchy	
		Baseline	w/Hierarchy	Overall	Initial
CIFAR-100	100	**55.4** $\pm$ 0.84	54.6 $\pm$ 1.03	—	7.00
NABirds	555	56.5 $\pm$ 0.49	**61.9** $\pm$ 0.27	3.08	10.00
ILSVRC2012	1000	49.1 $\pm$ 0.33	**54.2** $\pm$ 0.04	1.88	—

4.5 Overview and Discussion

Table 1 provides the most important facts for each dataset. We report the accuracy at the end of training for the one-hot baseline as well as our method. Overall speedup indicates how much faster in terms of training steps our hierarchical method achieves the end-of-training accuracy of the baseline. Initial speedup looks at the accuracy delivered by our method after the first validation interval. We then measure how much longer the baseline needs to catch up.

On all 3 datasets, the initial training is faster using our method. However, we only observe an improvement in classification accuracy on ImageNet and NABirds. With CIFAR-100, the benefits of adding hierarchical information are limited to training speed. There are a few possible explanations for this:

First, the CIFAR-100 dataset is the only dataset that requires a manual mapping to an external hierarchy, whereas the other datasets either supply one or have labels directly derived from one. The manual mapping is a possible error source and as such, could explain the observation, as could the small image size.

The second possible reason lies in the difference between semantic similarity and visual similarity [5,9]. Semantic similarity relates two classes using their meaning. It can be extracted from hierarchies such as WordNet [11], for example by looking at distances in the graph. Visual similarity on the other hand relates images that look alike, regardless of the meaning behind them. When classifying, we group images by semantics, even if they share no visual characteristics. Adding information based on only semantics can thus lead to problems.

5 Conclusion

We present a method to modify existing deep classifiers such that knowledge about relationships between classes can be integrated. The method is derived from a probabilistic model that is itself based on our understanding of the meaning of hierarchies. Overall, it is just one example of the integration of domain knowledge in an otherwise general method. One could also consider our method a special case of learning using privileged information [39].

Our method can improve classifiers by utilizing information that is freely available in many cases such as WordNet [11] or WikiSpecies. There are also datasets which include a hierarchy that is ready to use [6,37].

Further research should focus on the data insufficiency aspect and quantify the data reduction made possible by our method on small datasets, and compare the sample efficiency to the baseline for artificially reduced datasets as well as alternatives such as data augmentation.

References

1. Bart, E., et al.: Unsupervised learning of visual taxonomies. In: IEEE Conference on Computer Vision and Pattern Recognition, pp. 1–8 (2008)
2. Barz, B., Denzler, J.: Hierarchy-based image embeddings for semantic image retrieval. In: 2019 IEEE Winter Conference on Applications of Computer Vision (WACV), pp. 638–647, January 2019
3. Benkhalifa, M., Mouradi, A., Bouyakhf, H.: Integrating WordNet knowledge to supplement training data in semi-supervised agglomerative hierarchical clustering for text categorization. Int. J. Intell. Syst. **16**(8), 929–947 (2001)
4. Bilal, A., et al.: Do convolutional neural networks learn class hierarchy? IEEE Trans. Vis. Comput. Graph. **24**(1), 152–162 (2018)
5. Brust, C.-A., Denzler, J.: Not just a matter of semantics: the relationship between visual similarity and semantic similarity. arXiv:1811.07120 [cs], 17 November 2018
6. Deng, J., et al.: Imagenet: a large-scale hierarchical image database. In: Computer Vision and Pattern Recognition (CVPR), pp. 248–255 (2009)
7. Deng, J., et al.: Large-scale object classification using label relation graphs. In: Fleet, D., Pajdla, T., Schiele, B., Tuytelaars, T. (eds.) ECCV 2014. LNCS, vol. 8689, pp. 48–64. Springer, Cham (2014). https://doi.org/10.1007/978-3-319-10590-1_4
8. Deng, J., Berg, A.C., Li, K., Fei-Fei, L.: What does classifying more than 10,000 image categories tell us? In: Daniilidis, K., Maragos, P., Paragios, N. (eds.) ECCV 2010. LNCS, vol. 6315, pp. 71–84. Springer, Heidelberg (2010). https://doi.org/10.1007/978-3-642-15555-0_6
9. Deselaers, T., Ferrari, V.: Visual and semantic similarity in imagenet. In: Computer Vision and Pattern Recognition (CVPR), pp. 1777–1784 (2011)
10. Faghri, F., et al.: VSE++: improving visual-semantic embeddings with hard negatives. arXiv:1707.05612 [cs], 18 July 2017
11. Fellbaum, C.: WordNet. Wiley Online Library (1998)
12. Fergus, R., Bernal, H., Weiss, Y., Torralba, A.: Semantic label sharing for learning with many categories. In: Daniilidis, K., Maragos, P., Paragios, N. (eds.) ECCV 2010. LNCS, vol. 6311, pp. 762–775. Springer, Heidelberg (2010). https://doi.org/10.1007/978-3-642-15549-9_55
13. Frome, A., et al.: DeViSE: a deep visual-semantic embedding model. In: Burges, C.J.C., et al. (eds.) Advances in Neural Information Processing Systems 26, pp. 2121–2129. Curran Associates Inc. (2013)
14. Gaussier, E., Goutte, C., Popat, K., Chen, F.: A hierarchical model for clustering and categorising documents. In: Crestani, F., Girolami, M., van Rijsbergen, C.J. (eds.) ECIR 2002. LNCS, vol. 2291, pp. 229–247. Springer, Heidelberg (2002). https://doi.org/10.1007/3-540-45886-7_16
15. He, K., et al.: Deep residual learning for image recognition. In: Computer Vision and Pattern Recognition (CVPR) (2016)
16. He, K., Zhang, X., Ren, S., Sun, J.: Identity mappings in deep residual networks. In: Leibe, B., Matas, J., Sebe, N., Welling, M. (eds.) ECCV 2016. LNCS, vol. 9908, pp. 630–645. Springer, Cham (2016). https://doi.org/10.1007/978-3-319-46493-0_38

17. Hoffman, J., et al.: LSDA: large scale detection through adaptation. arXiv preprint arXiv:1407.5035, 18 July 2014
18. Huo, Y., Ding, M., Zhao, A., Hu, J., Wen, J.-R., Lu, Z.: Zero-shot learning with superclasses. In: Cheng, L., Leung, A.C.S., Ozawa, S. (eds.) ICONIP 2018. LNCS, vol. 11303, pp. 460–472. Springer, Cham (2018). https://doi.org/10.1007/978-3-030-04182-3_40
19. Hwang, S.J.: Discriminative object categorization with external semantic knowledge. Ph.D. thesis, August 2013
20. Hwang, S.J., Grauman, K., Sha, F.: Learning a tree of metrics with disjoint visual features. In: Shawe-Taylor, J., et al. (eds.) Advances in Neural Information Processing Systems 24, pp. 621–629. Curran Associates Inc. (2011)
21. Hwang, S.J., Sigal, L.: A unified semantic embedding: relating taxonomies and attributes. In: Advances in Neural Information Processing Systems 27, p. 9 (2014)
22. Kingma, D.P., Ba, J.: Adam: a method for stochastic optimization. In: International Conference for Learning Representations (ICLR), 22 December 2014. arXiv: 1412.6980v9
23. Krishna, R., et al.: Visual genome: connecting language and vision using crowdsourced dense image annotations. Int. J. Comput. Vis. (IJCV) **123**(1), 32–73 (2017)
24. Krizhevsky, A., Hinton, G.: Learning multiple layers of features from tiny images. Technical report, University of Toronto (2009)
25. Krizhevsky, A., Sutskever, I., Hinton, G.E.: ImageNet classification with deep convolutional neural networks. In: Advances in Neural Information Processing Systems (NIPS), pp. 1097–1105 (2012)
26. Liu, C., et al.: Progressive neural architecture search. arXiv preprint arXiv:1712.00559 (2017)
27. Long, J., Shelhamer, E., Darrell, T.: Fully convolutional networks for semantic segmentation. In: Computer Vision and Pattern Recognition (CVPR) (2015). arXiv: 1411.4038v2
28. Marszalek, M., Schmid, C.: Semantic hierarchies for visual object recognition. In: 2007 IEEE Conference on Computer Vision and Pattern Recognition, pp. 1–7, June 2007
29. Partalas, I., et al.: LSHTC: a benchmark for large-scale text classification. arXiv preprint arXiv:1503.08581 (2015)
30. Rodner, E., Denzler, J.: One-shot learning of object categories using dependent Gaussian processes. In: Goesele, M., Roth, S., Kuijper, A., Schiele, B., Schindler, K. (eds.) DAGM 2010. LNCS, vol. 6376, pp. 232–241. Springer, Heidelberg (2010). https://doi.org/10.1007/978-3-642-15986-2_24
31. Rohrbach, M., Ebert, S., Schiele, B.: Transfer learning in a transductive setting. In: Burges, C.J.C., et al. (eds.) Advances in Neural Information Processing Systems 26, pp. 46–54. Curran Associates Inc. (2013)
32. Settles, B.: Active learning literature survey. Technical report 1648, University of Wisconsin-Madison (2009)
33. Sharif Razavian, A., et al.: CNN features off-the-shelf: an astounding baseline for recognition. In: Computer Vision and Pattern Recognition Workshops (CVPR-WS) (2014)
34. Srivastava, N., Salakhutdinov, R.R.: Discriminative transfer learning with tree-based priors. In: Burges, C.J.C., et al. (eds.) Advances in Neural Information Processing Systems 26, pp. 2094–2102. Curran Associates Inc. (2013)
35. Sun, C., et al.: Revisiting unreasonable effectiveness of data in deep learning era. In: International Conference on Computer Vision (ICCV), pp. 843–852 (2017)

36. Torralba, A., Fergus, R., Freeman, W.T.: 80 million tiny images: a large data set for nonparametric object and scene recognition. Trans. Pattern Anal. Mach. Intell. (PAMI) **30**(11), 1958–1970 (2008)
37. Van Horn, G., et al.: Building a bird recognition app and large scale dataset with citizen scientists: the fine print in fine-grained dataset collection. In: Computer Vision and Pattern Recognition (CVPR), pp. 595–604 (2015)
38. Van Horn, G., et al.: The iNaturalist challenge 2017 dataset. arXiv preprint arXiv:1707.06642 (2017)
39. Vapnik, V., Vashist, A.: A new learning paradigm: learning using privileged information. Neural Netw. **22**(5–6), 544–557 (2009)
40. Verma, N., et al.: Learning hierarchical similarity metrics. In: 2012 IEEE Conference on Computer Vision and Pattern Recognition, pp. 2280–2287, June 2012
41. Vrandecic, D., Krötzsch, M.: Wikidata: a free collaborative knowledgebase. Commun. ACM **57**(10), 78–85 (2014)
42. Wu, Q., et al.: Image captioning and visual question answering based on attributes and external knowledge. IEEE Trans. Pattern Anal. Mach. Intell. **40**(6), 1367–1381 (2018)
43. Yan, Z., et al.: HD-CNN: hierarchical deep convolutional neural networks for large scale visual recognition. In: 2015 IEEE International Conference on Computer Vision (ICCV), Santiago, Chile, pp. 2740–2748. IEEE, December 2015
44. Zhang, X., et al.: Embedding label structures for fine-grained feature representation, pp. 1114–1123 (2016)

Label-Smooth Learning for Fine-Grained Visual Categorization

Xianjie Mo[1], Tingting Wei[1], Hengmin Zhang[2], Qiong Huang[1], and Wei Luo[1](✉)

[1] College of Mathematics and Informatics, South China Agricultural University, Guangzhou 510642, GD, People's Republic of China
cedricmo.cs@gmail.com, {weitingting,qhuang}@scau.edu.cn, cswluo@gmail.com
[2] Key Laboratory of Advanced Control and Optimization for Chemical Processes of Ministry of Education, East China University of Science and Technology, Shanghai 200237, People's Republic of China
zhanghengmin@126.com

Abstract. Fine-Grained Visual Categorization (FGVC) is challenging due to the superior similarity among categories and the large within-category variance. Existing work tackles this problem by designing self-localization modules in an end-to-end DCNN to learn semantic part features. However the model efficiency of this strategy decreases significantly with the increasing of the number of categories, because more parts are needed to offset the impact of the increasing of categories. In this paper, we propose a label-smooth learning method that improves models applicability to large categories by maximizing its prediction diversity. Based on the similarity among fine-grained categories, a *KL* divergence between uniform and prediction distributions is established to reduce model's confidence on the ground-truth category, while raising its confidence on similar categories. By minimizing it, information from similar categories are exploited for model learning, thus diminishing the effects caused by the increasing of categories. Experiments on five benchmark datasets of mid-scale (CUB-200-2011, Stanford Dogs, Stanford Cars, and FGVC-Aircraft) and large-scale (NABirds) categories show a clear advantage of the proposed label-smooth learning and demonstrate its comparable or state-of-the-art performance. Code is available at https://github.com/Cedric-Mo/LS-for-FGVC.

Keywords: Fine-Grained Visual Categorization · Deep convolutional neural networks · Label-smooth learning

1 Introduction

The Fine-Grained Visual Categorization (FGVC) task focuses on differentiating between subordinate categories, e.g., distinguishing wild bird species [33], vehicle makes or varieties [16], etc. With a decade study on FGVC, the community is still struggling to learn robust features to handle the large intra-class and small inter-class variance in FGVC. Although many methods have been proposed, ranging

S. Palaiahnakote et al. (Eds.): ACPR 2019, LNCS 12046, pp. 17–31, 2020.
https://doi.org/10.1007/978-3-030-41404-7_2

from strongly supervised learning [37] to weakly supervised learning [6,30], and to unsupervised learning [38,41], the increasing of the number of fine-grained categories, the variance of object scales, and the imbalance between categories pushes the challenge beyond the ability of current models. Actually, the increasing of object variance and category imbalance is usually with the increasing of category numbers. Therefore, the difficulty of FGVC can be escalated easily by solely increasing the number of categories.

Existing studies on FGVC are almost neglecting the difficulties caused by the increasing of category numbers, and tackle the FGVC problem mainly from two aspects. Much work embraces the viewpoint that semantic parts should be first localized and then extracting discriminative features from them for categorization, since the differences between categories are subtle and difficult to be localized [29,39,45]. This line of research has recently shifted to combine the two operations together to learn better task relevant features [3,23,46]. Another line of research attempts to learn discriminative features by exploring the label relationships, e.g., label hierarchical structures [8,44], label semantic distance [25], etc. However, these methods are constrained in their learning efficiency due to the increasing difficulty of part detection and label relationships construction with the increasing of category numbers. Normally, more parts or more complicated label relationships are required to achieve a good performance in the case of large categories.

In this paper, we propose label-smooth learning, a simple yet effective approach that exploits the similarity information among categories in the learning stage to address the inefficiency of model learning in large categories. Our approach regularizes model learning by applying a KL constraint to the uniform and model prediction distribution. It forces models to reduce its probability mass on the mostly probably correct category, and elevates its probability on the mostly probably correct *top*-K categories, thus resulting in a more even output distribution. Such a design is based on the superior similarity between fine-grained categories in visual appearance and structure, which is a kind of useful information can be exploited to guide the learning of common features existed among those similar categories, while encouraging information from the ground-truth category to focus more on the fine and discriminative feature learning. Therefore, by minimizing the KL divergence, label-smooth learning integrates information from non-ground-truth categories, especially from those similar categories, to improve models feature learning ability, thus alleviating the inefficiency of models caused by the increasing of category numbers. To demonstrate the effectiveness of our proposal, a ResNet-50 [10] with cross-category cross semantic (C^3S) module [3] is instantiated in this paper. However, notice that the label-smoothing learning can be implemented as an independent module to plug into any network with softmax outputs. Experiments on datasets of large categories, e.g., NABirds, show a clear advantage of the label-smooth learning over those without it. In addition, we also observe its positive effects on datasets of mid-scale categories, e.g., Stanford Dogs, etc. Generally, we make the following contributions in this paper:

- We propose a label-smooth learning approach for FGVC. Label-smooth learning regularizes model learning by minimizing the KL divergence between uniform and prediction distributions, thus implicitly integrating prediction probabilities from other categories to improve the efficiency of model learning.
- We demonstrate the advantage of label-smooth learning over those without it on datasets of large categories and provide ablation studies to validate its effectiveness. Extensive experiments on datasets of mid-scale categories also show its general applicability.

The reminder of the paper is organized as follows: We review the related work in Sect. 2. The label-smooth learning is detailed in Sect. 3, together with a review of the C^3S regularizer. Comparison to state-of-the-arts and ablation studies are presented in Sect. 4. We conclude our work of this study in Sect. 5.

2 Related Work

2.1 Fine-Grained Visual Categorization

Research in Fine-Grained Visual Categorization has shifted from multistage framework with strongly supervised learning [2,9,37,43] to multistage framework based on weakly supervised learning [29,36,45], and then to end-to-end learning framework [6,30,38,41]. Localization-classification sub-networks [6,14,17,20,40,42] usually first localize object parts by using a localization network such as a variant of R-CNN [8], FCN (Fully Convolutional Network) [22] and STN (Spatial Transformer network) [14], and then extract part-specific feature for classification by using a recognition network. More recent advances recursively learn the location/scale of the object parts using a recurrent localization network such as LSTM [17] or a specifically designed recurrent architecture [6]. End-to-end learning frameworks [6,7,21,35,39,46] utilize the final objective to optimize both part localization and fine-grained classification at the same time. The classical benchmark, Bilinear-CNN [21] uses a symmetric two-stream network architecture and a bilinear module that computes the outer product at each location of the image to obtain the second-order information. [7] further observed that similar performance can be achieved using compact bilinear representation derived through kernelized analysis of bilinear pooling. The work in [30] proposes a metric learning framework with multi-attention multi-excitation constraint that exploits the relationships among attention features to guide corresponding features learning. More recent work [23] further utilizes a cross-category cross-semantic regularizer and a cross-layer regularizer to guide the attention features learning. Exploring the label relationships such as label hierarchical structures [8,44] and label semantic distance [25] has also been explored. Combining visual and textual information and supplementing training data also achieve significant improvements. Our work in this paper explores the direction of exploiting the similarity information among categories to improve its applicability to large scale categories. Further, our method focuses on the the classification task by maximizing model's prediction diversity, and thus can be easily integrated into these models.

2.2 Label-Smooth Leaning

Lable-smooth learning has been explored successfully to improve the performance of deep learning architectures across a series of tasks, from image classification and speech recognition to machine translation. The training of a deep neural network is sensitive to the objective that is optimized. Shortly after Rumelhart et al. [28] deduced backpropagation for the quadratic loss function, more recent works show that higher accuracy and faster convergence could be achieved by performing gradient descent to minimize cross entropy [1,19]. However, in the early stages of neural network research, there were indications that other more peculiar objectives could outperform the standard cross entropy loss [11]. More recently, Szegedy et al. [31] originally introduced a notion of label-smooth leaning that improved the generalization of the Inception architecture on the ImageNet dataset. The idea of label-smooth leaning has been explored in different state-of-the-art image classification architectures ever since [13,27,47]. In speech recognition, Chorowski and Jaitly [4] utilized label-smooth leaning to alleviate the overconfidence in its predictions on the Wall Street Journal dataset. In machine translation, Vaswani et al. [32] improves accuracy and BLEU score through label-smooth leaning, but hurts perplexity since the model learns to be more unsure. However, utilizing the label-smooth leaning in context of Fine-Grained Visual Categorization has largely been unexplored. We also note the related idea of maximum-entropy learning [26], which tries to maximize the entropy of the output probability distribution and shows improved generalization in fine-grained image categorization problems. Compared to [26], our method applies a KL constraint to optimize the probability mass between different categories, and thus address the inefficiency of model learning in large categories.

3 Approach

In this section, we present our label-smooth leaning learning for FGVC. The key idea behind this approach is to prevent models from assigning massive prediction probability to one class and guide it to output relatively even prediction probabilities among possibly correct categories, thus information from similar categories can be integrated to improve the efficiency of models in large categories. Notably, our method is model independent and can be easily integrated into DCNNs. In particular, we employ ResNet-50 with cross-category cross-semantic (C^3S) module as instantiation to demonstrate the effectiveness of our method. An overview of our approach is depicted in Fig. 1.

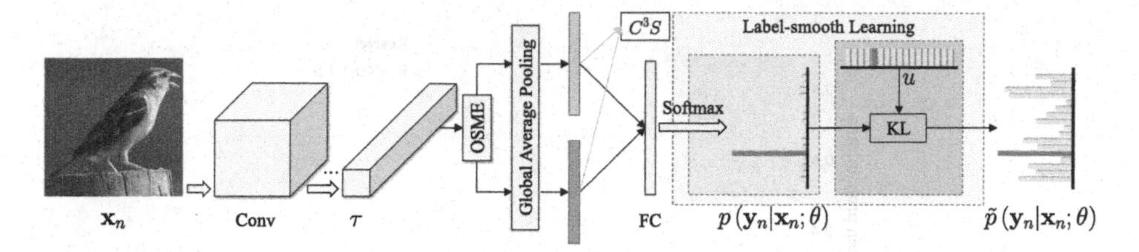

Fig. 1. An overview of our approach. Label-smooth learning (blue box) improves model efficiency by minimizing an KL divergence between the model output distribution, $p(\mathbf{y}_n|\mathbf{x}_n;\theta)$, and an uniform distribution, u. In the learning stage, the cross entropy loss (red box) and the label-smooth loss (gray box) are minimized to optimize the model. $\tilde{p}(\mathbf{y}_n|\mathbf{x}_n;\theta)$ is the final predictions. (Color figure online)

3.1 Label-Smoothing Learning

The softmax function couples with cross-entropy loss becomes the *de facto* operation in image recognition for model learning. Although its simplicity, it on the other hand discards much useful information, e.g., prediction probability, from non-groud-truth categories for model learning. However, such information may play an important role to improve model's efficiency. In FGVC, which is orders of complexity than ordinary image recognition to figure out effective features, simple softmax and cross-entropy combination usually needs a very long time to make learning converge. In the case of large fine-grained categories, this learning strategy lacks operability. To this end, we study a label-smooth learning method, which exploits the prediction probabilities from other categories, especially from those similar categories, to improve the efficiency of model learning.

Specifically, in a multi-class classification setting over K output classes and N training examples. Given an image $\mathbf{x}$, a FGVC network outputs a conditional probability distribution $p(\mathbf{y}|\mathbf{x};\theta)$ over classes, $\mathbf{y}$, through a softmax function. Label-smooth learning regularizes the classifier layer by preventing its output probabilities from over-concentrated on one class through matching a prior distribution, thus information from other categories can be integrated for model learning. In the case of the prior label distribution is uniform, label-smooth learning is equivalent to computing the Kullback-Liebler (KL) divergence between the uniform distribution u and the network's predicted distribution p_θ

$$\mathcal{L}_{LS} = \frac{1}{N}\sum D_{KL}\left(u \| p\left(\mathbf{y}_n|\mathbf{x}_n;\theta\right)\right). \tag{1}$$

By removing the term unrelated to the model parameters we get the regularized optimization criterion

$$\tilde{\mathcal{L}}_{LS} = -\frac{1}{N}\sum_{n=1}^{N}\sum_{k=1}^{K}\frac{1}{K}\log\left(p\left(y_{nk}|\mathbf{x}_n;\theta\right)\right). \tag{2}$$

The above regularization term can be understood as a measurement of the dissimilarity between the prediction distribution and the uniform distribution.

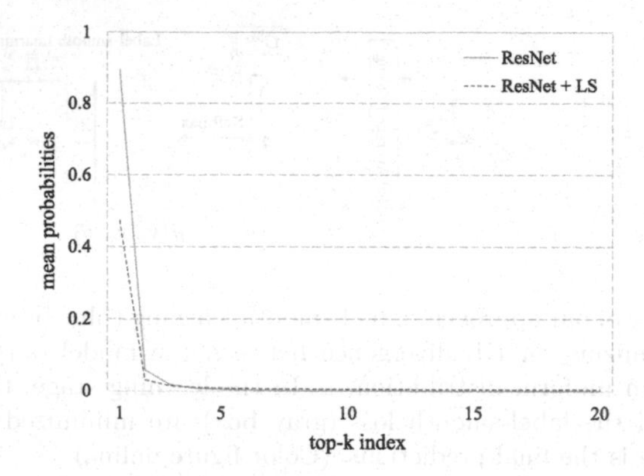

Fig. 2. A line graph of the mean probabilities of *top*-K categories. On CUB-200-2011 dataset for ResNet architecture, the model employing label-smooth learning outputs a more even prediction distribution when compared with the model that directly minimizes cross entropy.

For instance, if the output probability distribution has all the mass concentrated at a particular class k, then an infinite value will be returned. Conversely, if the output probability distribution reaches equal mass ratio among all K classes, the minimum value $\log(K)$ can be reached, which will be canceled by the constant term in Eq. 1. In FGVC, where samples coming from different categories are extremely similar in visual appearance and structure, it is reasonable to prevent the classifier from being over-confident in its predicted distribution (Fig. 2).

3.2 Cross-Category Cross-Semantic Regularization

We choose a FGVC framework, ResNet-50 with C^3S [3,23], to demonstrate the effectiveness of the proposed label-smooth learning. For completeness, we briefly describe C^3S in this section. C^3S is an unsupervised feature learning module that exploits relationships between categories, and between semantics to learn robust part-specific attention features. Given a network with P output feature maps, $\mathbf{U}^p, p \in 1 \cdots P$, which can be realized by inserting an OSME module with P excitations [30] into the last convolutional layer of a network, C^3S maximizes the correlations between features from the same excitation and minimizes those between features from different excitations. Specifically, it first generates a feature vector, $\mathbf{f}^p \in \mathbb{R}^C$, for every feature map, $\mathbf{U}^p$, by performing a global average pooling, followed by ℓ_2 normalization ($\mathbf{f}^p \leftarrow \mathbf{f}^p / \|\mathbf{f}^p\|$). Then the correlations between all pairs of excitation module p and p' construct a matrix S:

$$S_{[p,p']} = \frac{1}{N^2} \sum \mathbf{F}^{p\mathrm{T}} \mathbf{F}^{p'}, \tag{3}$$

where $S_{[p,p']}$ represents a matrix element, N is the batch size, T is the transpose operator and $\mathbf{F}^p = [\mathbf{f}_1^p, \cdots, \mathbf{f}_N^p] \in \mathbb{R}^{C \times N}$ is a matrix storing the feature vectors from excitation module p for total samples in the batch.

The C^3S regularization loss is then constructed from two key components: (1) maximizing the diagonal of S to maximize the correlation between same-excitation features and (2) minimizing the non-diagonal of S to minimize the correlation between different-excitation features:

$$\mathcal{L}_{C^3S}(S) = \frac{1}{2}[\sum S - \mathrm{tr}\,(S)] + [P - \mathrm{tr}\,(S)] = \frac{1}{2}[\sum S - 3\mathrm{tr}\,(S) + 2P] \quad (4)$$

where $\mathrm{tr}(S)$ indicates the sum of the elements on the main diagonal of S. P represents the number of excitation modules.

Putting all together, the objective is optimized by minimizing:

$$\mathcal{L} = \mathcal{L}_s + \gamma\mathcal{L}_{C^3S} + \lambda\tilde{\mathcal{L}}_{LS}, \quad (5)$$

where L_s is the softmax loss, γ and λ are weights that balance the contribution of different losses. Our framework can be trained end-to-end by using stochastic gradient descent (SGD).

4 Experiments

4.1 Fine-Grained Visual Categorization (FGVC) Datasets

Wildlife Species Categorization. We comprehensively evaluate our method on several widely used FGVC datasets. The Caltech-UCSD Birds (**CUB-200-2011**) dataset [33] contains 5,994 training and 5,794 testing images across 200 species of North-American birds. The **NABirds** dataset [12] includes 23,929 training and 24,633 testing images over 555 visual categories, encompassing 400 species of birds, containing separate classes for male and female birds in some cases. The **Stanford Dogs** dataset [15] consists of 12,000 training, 8,580 testing images across 120 breeds of dogs around the world.

Vehicle Model/Variety Categorization. We evaluate our method on two common vehicle categorization datasets, The **Stanford Cars** dataset [16] contains 8,144 training and 8,041 testing images over 196 car categories. The subordinate categories are defined as car make, model and year. The **FGVC-Aircraft** dataset [24] includes 6,667 training images and 3,333 testing images across 100 categories, where subordinate categories represent aircrafts of different varieties.

These FGVC datasets contain (i) large intra-class variation, (ii) subtle inter-class difference, and (iii) significantly imbalanced in terms of images per category. In addition, some of these datasets provide manual object part annotations, which we do not utilize in our experiments. The detailed statistics with categories number and data splits are summarized in Table 1.

Table 1. Statistics of benchmark datasets.

Datasets	#class	#train	#test
FGVG-Aircraft	100	6,667	3,333
Standford Dogs	120	12,000	8,580
Standford Cars	196	8,144	8,041
CUB-200-2011	200	5,994	5,794
NABirds	555	23,929	24,633

4.2 Implementation

We experiment our model with ResNet-50 [10] over 2 NVIDIA Tesla K80 GPUs in PyTorch. We train our model with the batch size of 32 and momentum 0.9 by SGD [18]. The initial learning rate is 0.01 except for the experiments on Stanford Dogs dataset where 0.001 is used. We train our model for 30 epoch and decayed the learning rate by 0.1 every 16 epochs. For datasets that consist of bird species, the images are first resized to 600 × 600 and then randomly cropped a region of size 448 × 448 as the input with a horizontal flipping probability of 0.5, while a center crop of 448 × 448 without horizontal flipping is used in testing. For the rest of datasets, the images are first resized to 448 × 448 and flipped horizontally with a probability of 0.5, while a resized region of 448 × 448 without horizontal flipping is used in testing. The balance weight γ is empirically set to 1 as it achieves consistently good performances, and λ is set to 0.65 except for CUB-200-2011 dataset where 0.8 is used.

4.3 Ablation Studies

Table 2. Ablation studies on five benchmark datasets.

	Aircraft	Dogs	Cars	CUB	NABirds
ResNet (P = 1)	90.5	88.3	92.9	85.6	83.2
ResNet (P = 2)	90.2	87.6	92.4	84.5	82.5
ResNet + C^3S (P = 2)	91.5	87.8	93.4	86.1	83.4
ResNet + LS (P = 1)	91.7	88.5	94.1	86.8	**85.7**
ResNet + C^3S + LS (P = 2)	**92.6**	**88.5**	**94.2**	**87.6**	85.6

Effectiveness of C^3S and LS: The effectiveness of our regularization is studied in Table 2. All compared method use ResNet-50 model for Fine-Grained Visual Categorization, but with different regularization setting. We find the performance of ResNet with OSME block is slightly worse than original ResNet on all datasets (ResNet (P = 1) vs. ResNet (P = 2)), since the training difficulties increase when employing the OSME block for multiple attention features.

Employing the C^3S module can bring systematic performance improvement on all datasets (ResNet (P = 2) vs. ResNet + C^3S (P = 2)). This validates the effectiveness of the C^3S that exploiting relationships between categories, and between semantics to learn robust part-specific attention features for better classification. As we expected, label-smooth learning can effectively encourages the model to reduce its confidence on the mostly probable category and elevate its confidence on the mostly probable *top*-K categories thus resulting in performance increase on all datasets (ResNet (P = 1) vs. ResNet + LS (P = 1) and ResNet + C^3S (P = 2) vs. ResNet + C^3S + LS (P = 2)). An interesting observation is that the performance of ResNet with LS on NABirds dataset is better than that of the ResNet with both C^3S and LS, this signifies that the effectiveness of C^3S decreases with the increasing of the number of categories while our label-smooth leaning method improves models applicability to large categories by maximizing its prediction diversity.

4.4 Comparison with State-of-the-Art

Baselines: We compare the performance of our approach against various state-of-the-art methods for FGVC without utilizing manual object part annotations. For fair comparison, we mainly compare with the results using ResNet-50 as their backbone structure and include the best results of DenseNet based methods as well. Unless particularly specified, all results reported in the following are from models based on ResNet-50. All the baselines are listed as following:

- **RA-CNN** [6]: recurrent attention convolutional neural network which recursively learns discriminative regions and region-based feature representation at multiple scales.
- **DFL-CNN** [34]: discriminative filter bank approach that learns a bank of convolutional filters to capture class-specific discriminative patches.
- **NTS-Net** [39]: navigator-teacher-scrutinizer network finds highly informative regions via multi-agent cooperation.
- **PC-CNN** [5]: optimization procedure approach that improve generalization ability by encouraging confusion in output activations.
- **MaxEnt-CNN** [26]: maximum entropy approach provides a training routine that maximizes the entropy of the output probability distribution for FGVC.
- **MAMC-CNN** [30]: metric learning framework with multi-attention multi-excitation constraint that exploits the relationships among attention features to guide corresponding features learning.

Results on FGVC-Aircraft: Table 3 reports the classification accuracy on FGVC-Aircraft. Our approach obtains the best result among methods reporting results on this dataset, even compared to those based on more advanced network architectures. This dataset is different from the rest of datasets in the larger within-category variance due to the variety of aircraft structures, this result indicates that our method is applicable to classification problems with relatively large inter-class structural variation. PC-CNN and MaxEnt-CNN can respectively achieve 89.2% and 89.8% when implemented with DenseNet-161 as reported in their work, however, still a bit lower than ours.

Table 3. Performance evaluation on FGVC-Aircraft.

Method	1-stage	Accuracy
PC-CNN [5]	√	83.4%
MaxEnt-CNN [26]	√	89.9%
DFL-CNN [34]	√	92.0%
NTS-Net [39]	√	91.4%
ResNet + C^3S (P = 2)	√	91.5%
ResNet + $C^3S + LS$ (P = 2)	√	**92.6%**

Table 4. Performance evaluation on Stanford Dogs.

Method	1-stage	Accuracy
PC-CNN [5]	√	73.3%
MaxEnt-CNN [26]	√	73.6%
RA-CNN [6]	×	87.3%
MAMC-CNN [30]	√	84.8%
ResNet + C^3S (P = 2)	√	87.8%
ResNet + $C^3S + LS$ (P = 2)	√	**88.5%**

Results on Stanford Dogs: The classification results on Stanford Dogs dataset are summarized in Table 4. Our reimplementation of ResNet-50 obtains a comparable results to that of RA-CNN which first learns informative parts and then extracts part-based features at multiple scales. PC-CNN and MAMC-CNN respectively improve to 83.8% and 85.2% when implemented with DenseNet-161 and ResNet-101 as reported in their papers. ResNet-50 with C^3S suffers from more images per category and relatively fewer categories, resulting in a slight drop in their performance. Our method with label-smooth leaning can offset the impact of this problem and outperform it by 0.7%. This signifies that our method could effectively exploits the prediction information on all categories to achieve better performance.

Results on Stanford Cars: The classification results for Stanford Cars are presented in Table 5. Our method achieves the state-of-the-art performance on this dataset, even compared to those utilizing multi-scale crops. Notice that DFL-CNN needs a non-random layer initialization to prevent the model learning from degeneration and NTS-Net combines multi-scale features for prediction, while our approach only needs to feedforward a single scale input once without any specialized initialization. Compared to RA-CNN, which adapt a two-stage strategy to recursively learns discriminative regions and region-based feature representation at multiple scales, our method outperforms it by 1.7%. The improvement implies that our method is applicable to regularize model learning by maximizing its prediction diversity.

Table 5. Performance evaluation on Stanford Cars.

Method	1-stage	Accuracy
PC-CNN [5]	√	93.4%
MaxEnt-CNN [26]	√	93.9%
RA-CNN [6]	×	92.5%
MAMC-CNN [30]	√	93.0%
DFL-CNN [34]	√	93.8%
NTS-Net [39]	√	93.9%
ResNet + C^3S (P = 2)	√	93.4%
ResNet + $C^3S + LS$ (P = 2)	√	**94.2%**

Table 6. Performance evaluation on CUB-200-2011.

Method	1-stage	Accuracy
PC-CNN [5]	√	80.2%
MaxEnt-CNN [26]	√	80.4%
RA-CNN [6]	×	85.3%
MAMC-CNN [30]	√	86.2%
DFL-CNN [34]	√	87.4%
NTS-Net [39]	√	87.5%
ResNet + C^3S (P = 2)	√	86.1%
ResNet + $C^3S + LS$ (P = 2)	√	**87.6%**

Results on CUB-200-2011: Table 6 shows the classification performance on CUB-200-2011. Our method achieves the state-of-the-art performance on this dataset, even though DFL-CNN and NTS-Net employ non-random layer initialization and multi-scale crops, respectively. Compared to MAMC-CNN, which employs a metric learning framework with the OSME block to mine semantics features, our method outperform it by 1.4%. The improvement indicates the effectiveness of our proposed method to regularizes model learning by maximizing its prediction diversity. Our reimplementation of ResNet-50 gets an accuracy of 85.6%, which is better than more sophisticated pairwise confusion regularization PC-CNN (80.2%) and the maximum entropy regularized MaxEnt-CNN (80.4%). PC-CNN improves to 86.9% when implemented with DenseNet-161. This shows the benefits brought by more advanced network architectures. However, our method can further outperform it by 0.7% with a relative simple ResNet-50 architecture, which indicates the effectiveness of our approach.

Results on NABirds: Most previous methods do not conduct experiments on this datasets, since the model efficiency of them decrease significantly with the increase of the number of categories. Our approach scales well to large categories by maximizing the model's prediction diversity. Table 7 compares our results to

Table 7. Performance evaluation on NABirds.

Method	1-stage	Accuracy
PC-CNN (ResNet-50) [5]	√	68.1%
PC-CNN (DenseNet-161) [5]	√	82.8%
MaxEnt-CNN (ResNet-50) [26]	√	69.2%
MaxEnt-CNN (DenseNet-161) [26]	√	83.0%
ResNet + C^3S (P = 2)	√	83.4%
ResNet + $C^3S + LS$ (P = 2)	√	**85.6%**

previous published results, which are all optimized on single-crop inputs. PC-CNN and MaxEnt-CNN respectively obtain 68.1% and 69.2% when coupled with ResNet-50 as reported in their papers. Surprisingly, our reimplementation of ResNet-50 obtains a comparable result to that of MaxEnt-CNN coupled with DenseNet-161. An interesting observation is that the ResNet-50 with C^3S loss outperforms ResNet-50 by only 0.2%; this signifies that the efficiency of C^3S decreases with the increasing of the number of categories on this large dataset. However, our method with label-smooth learning further surpasses it in performance by a relative 2.2%. The improvement indicates the effectiveness of our method to improves models applicability to large categories by maximizing its prediction diversity.

5 Conclusion

In this paper, we propose a label-smooth leaning method for the FGVC problem, which address the inefficiency of model learning arising from the increasing of category numbers. The proposed label-smooth learning improves the efficiency of model learning by exploiting similarity information among categories through minimizing a KL divergence between uniform and prediction distributions, thus maximizing the prediction diversity. Comparable or state-of-the-art performance on datasets of either mid-scale or large categories with 30 training epochs validates the effectiveness of our method. An ablation study is also provided to demonstrate the advantage brought independent by the label-smooth learning. In the future, we plan to integrate it into other label relationship induced learning for a better performance.

Acknowledgements. This work was supported in part by the National Natural Science Foundation of China under Grant 61702197, in part by the Natural Science Foundation of Guangdong Province under Grant 2017A030310261.

References

1. Baum, E.B., Wilczek, F.: Supervised learning of probability distributions by neural networks. In: NIPS (1988)
2. Chai, Y., Lempitsky, V., Zisserman, A.: Symbiotic segmentation and part localization for fine-grained categorization. In: ICCV (2013)
3. Chen, Y., Mo, X., Liang, Z., Wei, T., Luo, W.: Cross-category cross-semantic regularization for fine-grained image recognition. In: Lin, Z., et al. (eds.) PRCV 2019. LNCS, vol. 11857, pp. 110–122. Springer, Cham (2019). https://doi.org/10.1007/978-3-030-31654-9_10
4. Chorowski, J., Jaitly, N.: Towards better decoding and language model integration in sequence to sequence models. arXiv preprint arXiv:1612.02695 (2016)
5. Dubey, A., Gupta, O., Guo, P., Raskar, R., Farrell, R., Naik, N.: Pairwise confusion for fine-grained visual classification. In: Ferrari, V., Hebert, M., Sminchisescu, C., Weiss, Y. (eds.) ECCV 2018. LNCS, vol. 11216, pp. 71–88. Springer, Cham (2018). https://doi.org/10.1007/978-3-030-01258-8_5
6. Fu, J., Zheng, H., Mei, T.: Look closer to see better: recurrent attention convolutional neural network for fine-grained image recognition. In: CVPR (2017)
7. Gao, Y., Beijbom, O., Zhang, N., Darrell, T.: Compact bilinear pooling. In: CVPR (2016)
8. Girshick, R., Donahue, J., Darrell, T., Malik, J.: Rich feature hierarchies for accurate object detection and semantic segmentation. In: CVPR (2014)
9. Gosselin, P.H., Murray, N., Jégou, H., Perronnin, F.: Revisiting the Fisher vector for fine-grained classification. Pattern Recogn. Lett. **49**, 92–98 (2014)
10. He, K., Zhang, X., Ren, S., Sun, J.: Deep residual learning for image recognition. In: CVPR (2016)
11. Hertz, J.A.: Introduction to the Theory of Neural Computation. CRC Press, Boca Raton (2018)
12. Horn, G.V., et al.: Building a bird recognition app and large scale dataset with citizen scientists: the fine print in fine-grained dataset collection. In: CVPR (2015)
13. Huang, Y., et al.: GPipe: efficient training of giant neural networks using pipeline parallelism. arXiv preprint arXiv:1811.06965 (2018)
14. Jaderberg, M., Simonyan, K., Zisserman, A., Kavukcuoglu, K.: Spatial transformer networks. In: NIPS (2015)
15. Khosla, A., Jayadevaprakash, N., Yao, B., Li, F.F.: Novel dataset for fine-grained image categorization. In: First Workshop on Fine-Grained Visual Categorization (FGVC) at CVPR (2011)
16. Krause, J., Stark, M., Deng, J., Li, F.F.: 3D object representations for fine-grained categorization. In: 4th IEEE Workshop on 3D Representation and Recognition at ICCV (2013)
17. Lam, M., Mahasseni, B., Todorovic, S.: Fine-grained recognition as HSnet search for informative image parts. In: CVPR (2017)
18. LeCun, Y., Bottou, L., Bengio, Y., Haffner, P.: Gradient based learning applied to document recognition. Proc. IEEE **86**(11), 2278–2324 (1998)
19. Levin, E., Fleisher, M.: Accelerated learning in layered neural networks. Complex Syst. **2**, 625–640 (1988)
20. Lin, D., Shen, X., Lu, C., Jia, J.: Deep LAC: deep localization, alignment and classification for fine-grained recognition. In: CVPR (2015)
21. Lin, T.Y., RoyChowdhury, A., Maji, S.: Bilinear CNN models for fine-grained visual recognition. In: ICCV (2015)

22. Long, J., Shelhamer, E., Darrell, T.: Fully convolutional networks for semantic segmentation. In: CVPR (2015)
23. Luo, W., Yang, X., Mo, X., Lu, Y., Davis, L.S., Lin, S.N.: Cross-X learning for fine-grained visual categorization. In: ICCV (2019)
24. Maji, S., Rahtu, E., Kannala, J., Blaschko, M., Vedaldi, A.: Fine-grained visual classification of aircraft. In: arXiv preprint arXiv:1306.5151 (2013)
25. Mo, X., Zhu, J., Zhao, X., Liu, M., Wei, T., Luo, W.: Exploiting category-level semantic relationships for fine-grained image recognition. In: Lin, Z., et al. (eds.) PRCV 2019. LNCS, vol. 11857, pp. 50–62. Springer, Cham (2019). https://doi.org/10.1007/978-3-030-31654-9_5
26. Naik, N., Dubey, A., Gupta, O., Raskar, R.: Maximum entropy fine-grained classification. In: NIPS (2018)
27. Real, E., Aggarwal, A., Huang, Y., Le, Q.V.: Regularized evolution for image classifier architecture search. In: AAAI (2019)
28. Rumelhart, D.E., Hinton, G.E., Williams, R.J., et al.: Learning representations by back-propagating errors. Cogn. Model. **5**(3), 1 (1988)
29. Simon, M., Rodner, E.: Neural activation constellations: unsupervised part model discovery with convolutional networks. In: ICCV (2015)
30. Sun, M., Yuan, Y., Zhou, F., Ding, E.: Multi-attention multi-class constraint for fine-grained image recognition. In: Ferrari, V., Hebert, M., Sminchisescu, C., Weiss, Y. (eds.) ECCV 2018. LNCS, vol. 11220, pp. 834–850. Springer, Cham (2018). https://doi.org/10.1007/978-3-030-01270-0_49
31. Szegedy, C., Vanhoucke, V., Ioffe, S., Shlens, J., Wojna, Z.: Rethinking the inception architecture for computer vision. In: CVPR (2016)
32. Vaswani, A., et al.: Attention is all you need. In: NIPS (2017)
33. Wah, C., Branson, S., Welinder, P., Perona, P., Belongie, S.: The caltech-UCSD birds-200-2011 dataset. Technical report, California Institute of Technology (2011)
34. Wang, Y., Morariu, V.I., Davis, L.S.: Learning a discriminative filter bank within a CNN for fine-grained recognition. In: CVPR (2018)
35. Wu, C.Y., Manmatha, R., Smola, A.J., Krahenbuhl, P.: Sampling matters in deep embedding learning. In: Proceedings of the IEEE International Conference on Computer Vision, pp. 2840–2848 (2017)
36. Xiao, T., Xu, Y., Yang, K., Zhang, J., Peng, Y., Zhang, Z.: The application of two-level attention models in deep convolutional neural network for fine-grained image classification. In: CVPR (2015)
37. Xu, Z., Huang, S., Zhang, Y., Tao, D.: Augmenting strong supervision using web data for fine-grained categorization. In: ICCV (2015)
38. Yang, S., Bo, L., Wang, J., Shapiro, L.G.: Unsupervised template learning for fine-grained object recognition. In: NIPS (2012)
39. Yang, Z., Luo, T., Wang, D., Hu, Z., Gao, J., Wang, L.: Learning to navigate for fine-grained classification. In: Ferrari, V., Hebert, M., Sminchisescu, C., Weiss, Y. (eds.) Computer Vision – ECCV 2018. LNCS, vol. 11218, pp. 438–454. Springer, Cham (2018). https://doi.org/10.1007/978-3-030-01264-9_26
40. Zhang, H., et al.: SPDA-CNN: unifying semantic part detection and abstraction for fine-grained recognition. In: CVPR (2016)
41. Zhang, J., Zhang, R., Huang, Y., Zou, Q.: Unsupervised part mining for fine-grained image classification. In: arXiv preprint arXiv:1902.09941 (2019)
42. Zhang, N., Donahue, J., Girshick, R., Darrell, T.: Part-based R-CNNs for fine-grained category detection. In: Fleet, D., Pajdla, T., Schiele, B., Tuytelaars, T. (eds.) ECCV 2014. LNCS, vol. 8689, pp. 834–849. Springer, Cham (2014). https://doi.org/10.1007/978-3-319-10590-1_54

43. Zhang, N., Farrell, R., Iandola, F., Darrell, T.: Deformable part descriptors for fine-grained recognition and attribute prediction. In: ICCV (2013)
44. Zhang, X., Zhou, F., Lin, Y., Zhang, S.: Embedding label structures for fine-grained feature representation. In: CVPR (2016)
45. Zhang, X., Xiong, H., Zhou, W., Lin, W., Tian, Q.: Picking deep filter responses for fine-grained image recognition. In: CVPR (2016)
46. Zheng, H., Fu, J., Mei, T., Luo, J.: Learning multi-attention convolutional neural network for fine-grained image recognition. In: ICCV (2017)
47. Zoph, B., Vasudevan, V., Shlens, J., Le, Q.V.: Learning transferable architectures for scalable image recognition. In: CVPR (2018)

ForestNet – Automatic Design of Sparse Multilayer Perceptron Network Architectures Using Ensembles of Randomized Trees

Dalia Rodríguez-Salas[1(✉)], Nishant Ravikumar[2], Mathias Seuret[1], and Andreas Maier[1]

[1] Pattern Recognition Lab, Friedrich-Alexander-Universität Erlangen-Nürnberg, Martensstr. 3, 91058 Erlangen, Germany
{dalia.rodriguez,mathias.seuret,adreas.maier}@fau.de
[2] School of Computing, University of Leeds, Leeds LS2 9JT, UK
n.ravikumar@leeds.ac.uk
https://www5.cs.fau.de,
https://www.leeds.ac.uk

Abstract. In this paper, we introduce a mechanism for designing the architecture of a Sparse Multi-Layer Perceptron network, for classification, called *ForestNet*. Networks built using our approach are capable of handling high-dimensional data and learning representations of both visual and non-visual data. The proposed approach first builds an ensemble of randomized trees in order to gather information on the hierarchy of features and their separability among the classes. Subsequently, such information is used to design the architecture of a sparse network, for a specific data set and application. The number of neurons is automatically adapted to the dataset. The proposed approach was evaluated using two non-visual and two visual datasets. For each dataset, 4 ensembles of randomized trees with different sizes were built. In turn, per ensemble, a sparse network architecture was designed using our approach and a fully connected network with same architecture was also constructed. The sparse networks defined using our approach consistently outperformed their respective tree ensembles, achieving statistically significant improvements in classification accuracy. While we do not beat state-of-art results with our network size and the lack of data augmentation techniques, our method exhibits very promising results, as the sparse networks performed similarly to their fully connected counterparts with a reduction of more than 98% of connections in the visual tasks.

Keywords: Multilayer perceptron · Random forest · Randomized trees · Sparse neural networks · Network architecture

This research was partially funded by The German Academic Exchange Service (DAAD—German: Deutscher Akademischer Austauschdienst) and the Emerging Field Initiative project of FAU Erlangen-Nürnberg: Big-Thera.

S. Palaiahnakote et al. (Eds.): ACPR 2019, LNCS 12046, pp. 32–45, 2020.
https://doi.org/10.1007/978-3-030-41404-7_3

1 Introduction

Diverse complicated learning tasks have been successfully solved using Multi-Layer Perceptron (MLP) networks, including those that involve visual recognition. A traditional approach to solve these tasks using MLP networks is to extract hand-crafted features from each visual sample and use the resulting feature vectors to train the network parameters. However, this requires the design and/or use of feature extractors, that gather useful information and remove useless variability, which in turn is a difficult task. An alternative approach would be to directly use the raw data/pixel information (in visual tasks) to train the MLP network, which intrinsically extracts representative features within its hidden layers [8].

Two drawbacks of using raw visual data to train MLP networks were highlighted in [9]: (a) related to thc number of parameters and the complexity of the network. Since visual data are normally high-dimensional, the first hidden layer alone would have a large number of parameters to be learned, and consequently, a large number of samples would be required for training, leading to high memory requirements; and (b) MLP networks completely ignore the topology of visual data, and consequently, are unable to learn spatial relationships, and representations that are invariant to translations and/or local distortions in the input data. Additionally, we define a third drawback of MLP networks, not specific to visual data alone: (c) the difficulty associated with deciding on the number of hidden layers and the number of hidden units in each layer (i.e. the overall network complexity). In this paper we present a model to build MLP networks to tackle drawbacks (a) and partially (c).

In order to automatically define the architecture of a MLP network, we built an ensemble of randomized trees and used the information given on each of their branches. The network is built such that each hidden neuron corresponds to one of the trees' branches; a neuron is only fed with the inputs associated to the features which define its corresponding branch, and similarly, its outputs are only connected to the classes associated with the same branch. Thus, the resulting network has a structure matching the forest's. As a result, we obtain an easy-to-interpret highly sparse network capable of handling high-dimensional data, including visual data.

The main contributions of our work are:

- A model which enables automatic design of network architecture and complexity, i.e. the appropriate number of hidden neurons per layer, and the connections between layers of MLP networks.
- Foundation for developing easy-to-interpret models or architectures of Artificial Neural Networks (ANN), which either use or are based on MLP networks, such as Convolutional Neural Networks (CNNs).

The paper is organized as follows: in the next section we present the related work, followed by a description of our model in the subsequent section. Sections 4 and 5 describe the experiments conducted to validate our approach and their corresponding results, respectively. The final section summarizes our findings and discusses future directions for research.

2 Related Work

The most relevant study [19], which relates decision trees to ANNs was published three decades ago, in what the author calls *Perceptron Trees.* These trees have the characteristic of comprising Rossenblatt's perceptrons on their leaves. Subsequently, in [16], the first algorithm to map decision trees to partially connected MLP networks, with two hidden layers, was presented. Such notworks were referred to as *Entropy Nets.* In [15], the mapped MLP networks from decision trees consisted of only one hidden layer, and achieved comparable classification performance to *Entropy Nets*, whilst having significantly fewer connections and hidden units.

More recent works show that the idea of designing MLP networks using decision trees has been getting attention. For example, in [1], the mapping of a Random Forest to two different models of MLP networks was introduced, for regression tasks. Such a mapping was based on the concatenation of networks comprising two hidden layers, mapped from distinct trees, into a wide 2 or 3 hidden layer network. Lastly, in [7], an ensemble of MLP networks is built such that each network is derived from a tree in a forest, and it contains as many layers as levels in its respective tree. However, the method was only tried with low-dimensional and non-visual data using shallow trees with maximum-depths of 3, 4, and 5.

Other approaches to automatically define the architectures of ANNs have been developed, for example, in [17], the authors use an evolution algorithm, called NEAT, to select the architecture of Recurrent Neural Networks. NEAT has been recently adapted to evolve the architecture of deep neural networks in [11]. However, its main drawback is that it is extremely computationally expensive. Decision trees and ANNs have also been related in [5], where a mapping of the knowledge acquired by a CNN into a soft decision tree was performed, in order to provide a means for interpreting the decisions taken by the network. In [4], the authors present a top-down method for creating sparse ANN by iterating training phases, network pruning, and reset of the initial weights of the remaining connections. They obtain smaller networks performing at least as good as their fully-connected versions.

3 Model to Build a Sparse Multilayer Pereceptron Network

Consider a single binary decision tree which is built using the training data X. Given two terminal nodes which are siblings l_{left} and l_{right}, each has an associated class-label y_{left} and y_{right}. In order to decide if a sample belongs to either y_{left} or y_{right}, only the features on the path from the root node to the father of l_{left} and l_{right} are required. In other words, there exists a subset of training samples whose class can be determined by using just a *small* subset of the available features. Thus each pair of siblings define their own subspace. Since two siblings have only one father, we can say that the number of sub-spaces defined by a single tree is equal to the total number of fathers of terminal nodes. Thus, the maximum number of sub-spaces defined by a tree grows exponentially with the depth of the tree.

The formulation of our model is based on the idea of designing a network in such a manner that, the information of the sub-spaces found by each tree in an ensemble, is provided to the network in terms of defining its architecture. This is based on the underlying hypothesis that once the network is trained, it can learn better boundaries than the random forest, as the latter produce axis-aligned boundaries [7].

Our approach consist of three main steps; building the ensemble of randomized trees, defining the Sparse Multilayer Pereceptron (SMLP) network architecture and the initialization of the weights.

3.1 Building the Ensemble of Randomized Trees

Given training data X for a classification problem, with m features and targets y, an ensemble of randomized trees can be built to identify suitable decision boundaries for the associated classes. Although the algorithm (or algorithms) used to build such trees would result in different network architectures, a broad analysis of such algorithms is out of the scope of this study. Nonetheless, it is important to highlight that such algorithms should consider only a random subset of candidate features during the construction of each tree. This is because one of the main ideas of mapping an ensemble of trees rather than a single tree to a network is that high-dimensional data can be handled. Random Forest [2] and Extremely Randomized Trees (ERT) [6] algorithms are an example of tree ensembles which use only a random subset of candidate features, wherein $\sqrt{m}$ is a common default value used to determine the number of features considered within the subset.

When an ensemble of randomized trees is used for classification, the number of trees determines the model complexity and is thereby associated with either under- or over-fitting to the data. The role of this hyper-parameter, however, is different with respect to our model. Ideally, the size of the forest should be *just enough* to cover the whole data space, while the network architecture derived from the forest helps to prevent over-fitting by incorporating sparsity in its associated weights.

3.2 Defining the SMLP Network Architecture

As the aim is to capture all the information of the sub-spaces found by the ensemble of trees, our architecture considers one hidden neuron per node parent of at least one leaf, where only the features involved in the sub-spaces defined by the leaves are considered as inputs to the neuron. Similarly, the output of each of these hidden neurons will only feed the output neurons which are associated with the classes that the sub-space separates, as the other classes are not involved. These two architectural designs lead to the sparse connections of the MLP, both in the inputs of the hidden layer and the ones of the output layer. The network architecture obtained with this methodology consists of 3 layers; input-,hidden-, and output-layers.

Henceforth, the SMLP networks derived from ensembles of randomized trees, using our approach, will be referred to as *ForestNet*.

The pseudo-code to build a ForestNet for a dataset (X, y) given an already built tree ensemble for the same dataset is shown in Algorithm 1.

Algorithm 1. Pseudo-code to build a *ForestNet* given a tree ensemble.

```
Input: Tree ensemble ET built using the training set (X, y), Training
       matrix X, and Labels y
Output: ForestNet FN
leaves ⟵ getLeaves(ET);
nodeList ⟵ unique(getFathersOfAll(leaves));
numHiddenUnits ⟵ size(nodeList);
numOutputUnits ⟵ countUniqueValues(y);
numSamples ⟵ countSamples(X);
FN ⟵ emptyForestNet(numHiddenUnits, numOutputUnits);
i ⟵ 0;
for node ∈ nodeList do
    neuronInputs ⟵ featuresOnThePath(ET, node) ;
    neuronOutputs ⟵ getLeavesAndLabels(node) ;
    connectHiddenNeuron(FN, i, neuronInputs, neuronOutputs) ;
    i ⟵ i + 1;
end
```

The network creation process is illustrated in Fig. 1, where a tree ensemble of size 3 is mapped to a *ForestNet* for a classification problem with 3 classes ("red", "blue", and "green") and 8 features ($x_1, x_2 \dots x_8$). In the figure, each of the 6 fathers of terminal nodes in the ensemble has a corresponding hidden neuron on the *ForestNet.* For instance, the gray-shadowed branch in the leftmost tree contains a father of terminal nodes and corresponds to the hidden neuron at the top in the network (both colored black). In the ensemble, the highlighted branch defines a sub-space with the features x_4 and x_5, where only objects that belong to classes "red" and "green" can be separated. This is mapped to the *ForestNet* and is depicted as the highlighted part of the network. This mapping from the tree branch to the network is achieved by only connecting features x_4 and x_5 to the corresponding hidden neuron, which in turn is connected to the output neurons that correspond to the classes "red" and "green".

The subset of features associated with each sub-space found by a tree, will always contain the feature associated with the root node of that tree. Thus, let x_k be the feature associated with the root node of such a tree, which is fully grown to a depth D; the feature x_k will be in all 2^{D-1} sub-spaces. Analogously, the features associated with the two nodes in the first level will be in 2^{D-2} sub-spaces, the four features on the second level will be 2^{D-3}, and, so on. Therefore,

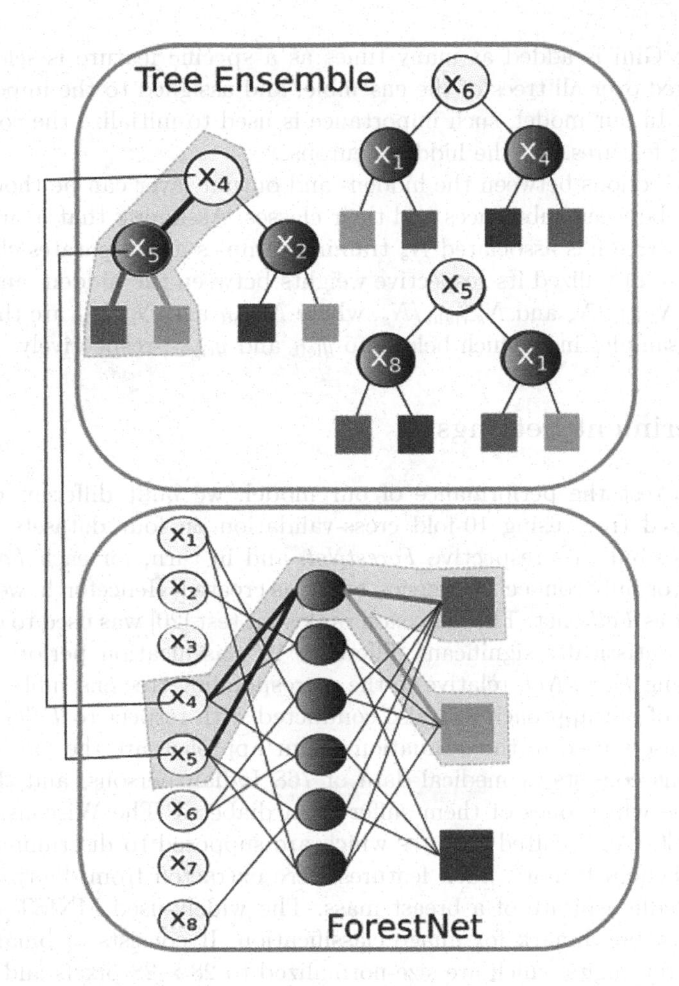

Fig. 1. Mapping of a Tree Ensemble to a *ForestNet* for a problem with 8 features and 3 classes. The 6 fathers of leaves have a corresponding hidden neuron in the network. The gray-shadowed branch on the ensemble corresponds to the gray-shadowed part on the network. (Color figure online)

the deeper a node is on the tree, the fewer the sub-spaces that its feature will be involved in. Through its architecture, a *ForestNet* also reflects the hierarchy of the features on a tree, as the deeper a node is on the tree, fewer are the number of hidden neurons that the associated feature is connected to, as inputs.

3.3 Initialization of the Weights

A feature, associated to a tree's internal node, is selected among others if the training samples which reached that node are splitted at a given threshold and the classes' impurity is reduced the most. The Gini is often used for the measurement of such impurity. In [18], weighted by the proportion of samples in a node, the Gini is added as many times as a specific feature is selected in a tree, averaged over all trees of the ensemble, and assigned to the importance of the feature. In our model, such importance is used to initialize the connections between the features and the hidden neurons.

The connections between the hidden- and output-layer can be thought of as connections between sub-spaces and their classes. Assuming that a sub-space S defined by a tree has associated N_s training samples and separates classes y_{left} and y_{right}, we initialized its respective weights between the hidden- and output-layer to be $N_{s\text{-left}}/N_s$ and $N_{s\text{-right}}/N_s$, where $N_{s\text{-left}}$ and $N_{s\text{-right}}$ are the amount of training samples in S which belong to y_{left} and y_{right}, respectively.

4 Experiment Settings

In order to test the performance of our model, we built different ensembles of randomized trees using 10-fold cross-validation on four datasets. For each ensemble, we built its respective *ForestNet*, and in turn, for each *ForestNet* a non-sparse (or fully connected) version of it was created. Henceforth, we will refer to the latter as *Fully* net. The Wilcoxon rank sum test [20] was used to determine whether a statistically significant difference in classification performance was achieved using *ForestNet*, relative to the corresponding tree ensemble. A similar comparison of our approach was also conducted with respect to *Fully* net.

The datasets used in the evaluation of our approach are the following. The Pima Indians consists of medical data of 768 Indian persons, and the goal is to determine which ones of them suffer from diabetes. The Wisconsin dataset consists of 30 hand-crafted features which are supposed to discriminate malignant from benign tumors. Such features were extracted from digitized images of a fine needle aspirate of a breast mass. The widely-used MNIST dataset is a well known benchmark for image classification. It consists of binary images of handwritten digits which are size-normalized to 28×28 pixels and centered. The SVHN, or Street View House Numbers, dataset consists of 32×32 pixels images of digits cropped from house numbers photos. There is a large variety of styles for the digits, and, because of the position of the camera, there are also some perspective distortions as well. Numeric information about the datasets are given in Table 1.

4.1 Hyperparameter Settings for Tree Ensembles

Per each dataset, four ensembles of randomized trees with $3, 6, 9$, and 12 trees were created, respectively. The algorithm used to build each ensemble was the ERT [6] as implemented in [14] using $\sqrt{m}$ randomly selected features per tree, where m is the number of available features. The maximum depth of the trees was set to 10 since a depth of 11 did not show a significant improvement. We attributed this to the idea that 10 is a sufficient depth for partitioning the given datasets since a fully-grown tree with depth 10 gives the possibility to explore 2^9 sub-spaces.

Table 1. Brief description of the datasets used on the experiments

Dataset ID	No. of samples	No. of features	No. of classes	Visual ?	Pre-processing	Source
Pima Indians	768	8	2	No	Nomalization	[3]
Wisconsin	569	30	2	No	Nomalization	[3]
MNIST	60000	784	10	Yes	Nomalization	[10]
SVHN	73257	3072[a]	10	Yes	Nomalization, Gray-scale	[12]

[a]Only 1024 were used as a result of the Gray-scale pre-processing step.

4.2 Hyperparameter Settings for Networks

Most of the hyper-parameters associated with both the *ForestNet* and the *Fully* net, were derived from the tree ensemble. However, the activation functions as well as the optimizer used to train the parameters for each network, need to be defined. In our experiments we used the Rectified Linear Unit (ReLU) in the hidden-layer and log-softmax in the output layer. The Adam optimizer, with a learning rate of 1×10^{-2}, and cross-entropy loss, were used for all experiments. Both *ForestNet* and its *Fully* net were trained using early stopping with a patience of 35.

All networks were implemented and trained on [13] (PyTorch). For the case of our *ForestNet*, parameters that were not required (i.e. due to the sparse nature of the derived network), were set to zero before each forward pass and their respective gradients were also set to zero in the backward pass, in order to enforce sparsity.

5 Results and Discussion

In this section we present firstly the results on classification accuracy of the three evaluated models. Secondly, the amount of connections and of hidden neurons used by both *ForestNet* and *Fully* net. Lastly, we show the behavior of the training and validation loss during the training process for both network models.

5.1 Classification Accuracy

The classification accuracy of the proposed approach was evaluated using the Pima Indians, Wisconsin, MNIST, and SVHN datasets, and compared with ERT and *Fully* net. These results are summarized in Table 2. The columns are organized according to the number of trees used, and it is indicated in the second row of the table. The mean and standard deviation of the classification accuracy achieved across 10-fold cross validation, using each approach, are presented separately in the table.

Table 2. Average accuracy and standard deviation of using 10-Fold Cross-Validation on four datasets with ERT, its respective ForestNet and its Fully version. The maximum depth of the trees is indicated along the name (ERT-10). The amount of trees in the ensemble is indicated in the second row of the table.

Classifier	Accuracy				Standard Deviation			
	3-trees	6-trees	9-trees	12-trees	3-trees	6-trees	9-trees	12-trees
Pima Indians								
ForestNet	0.764	0.767	0.768	0.759	0.046	0.042	0.052	0.014
ERT-10	0.717	0.717	0.747	0.741	0.030	0.048	0.064	0.011
Fully net	0.766	0.770	0.779	0.767	0.043	0.046	0.046	0.010
Wisconsin								
ForestNet	0.977	0.975	0.970	0.974	0.019	0.022	0.025	0.006
ERT-10	0.928	0.958	0.956	0.953	0.037	0.020	0.032	0.002
Fully net	0.977	0.975	0.974	0.975	0.019	0.018	0.018	0.005
MNIST								
ForestNet	0.966	0.971	0.973	0.973	0.002	0.002	0.002	0.002
ERT-10	0.845	0.890	0.908	0.914	0.006	0.005	0.006	0.002
Fully net	0.976	0.977	0.975	0.974	0.002	0.003	0.003	0.003
SVHN								
ForestNet	0.829	0.846	0.850	0.852	0.003	0.002	0.003	0.008
ERT-10	0.393	0.449	0.464	0.473	0.014	0.007	0.013	0.008
Fully net	0.835	0.831	0.833	0.826	0.006	0.007	0.008	0.012

Results in Table 2 show that the accuracy achieved by ERT tends to improve as the number of trees used is increased. However, the same trend is only true for our *ForestNet* when using the visual data (MNIST and SVHN), whereas for the non-visual data and for the *Fully* when using both visual and non-visual data, we can see that increasing network complexity does not improve classification accuracy, and in some cases even has a detrimental effect, decreasing the overall accuracy. This tendencies are clear to see on the results obtained when using SVHN dataset (last tree rows in the table).

In order to determine whether the classification performance of our *ForestNet* is significantly different to the other two approaches, measurements on *ForestNet* accuracy obtained during the 10-folds cross-validation experiments were compared against those obtained using ERT and *Fully* net, separately. In Table 3, the small p-values for the Wilcoxon signed-rank when comparing our model against ERT show a clear statistical significant difference with 3, 6, 9, and 12 trees. When comparing it against its fully connected version, the p-values show that, at a significance level of 0.05, the difference on classification accuracy is no significant for those networks built using ERT with 6, 9 or 12 trees.

Table 3. The two-sided p-values for the Wilcoxon signed-rank test applied to compare the gotten accuracies by ForestNet against those gotten by ERT and Fully net, respectively.

Compared pairs	3-trees	6-trees	9-trees	12-trees
ForesNet - ERT	1.29E−07	1.34E−07	2.09E−06	1.41E−06
ForesNet - Fully net	0.031	0.461	0.683	0.150

From the results in Tables 2 and 3, we can conclude that *ForestNet* significantly outperformed on classification accuracy the ERT, independently of the amount of trees used to build them. Furthermore, at a significance level of 0.05%, the sparse networks performed similarly to their *Fully* counterparts when built using ERT with 6, 9 or 12 trees, whilst having the main advantage of using significantly less parameters due to their sparse nature.

5.2 Amount of Connections

An important and desired effect of our approach is that it produces MLPs with very sparse connections. This is shown in Table 4, where the average amount of connections for both *ForestNet* and its corresponding *Fully* net obtained on a 10-fold cross-validation are given. As expected, the amount of connections increases proportionally to the amount of trees the networks were built with. In all experiments, the percentage of connections was greatly reduced by our method. From this table, we can also notice that for the two visual datasets, MNIST and SVHN, more than 98% of the connections were discarded by our approach. Thus, our method produces sparse networks with a small yet sufficient amount of connections without hindering the accuracy when compared to fully connected versions of the networks.

5.3 Amount of Hidden Neurons

As seen in Sect. 3, a tree of depth D can produce up to 2^D neurons. Thus, a *ForestNet* built with t trees could have up to $t \cdot 2^D$ neurons. We measured the amount of neurons in the hidden layer of *ForestNets*, and reported these values in Table 5. For the MNIST and SVHN datasets, which have high-dimensional inputs, the networks had in average roughly 80% of this maximum amount of neurons, while the two other datasets had only 11% of this amount. We can note that for the two visual datasets, the amount of neurons are very similar, while they differ much for the two other datasets.

The amount of neurons is not only linked to the dimensionality of the data but seems to as well related to class separability. Indeed, the trees in the random forest will have fewer nodes if the classes can be separated in a simple way rather than with difficulties.

Table 4. Average amount of connections when using 10-Fold Cross-Validation on four dataset with ForestNet and its Fully version. The amount of trees in the ensemble the networks were built with is indicated in the second row of the table.

Classifier	Amount of connections			
	3-trees	6-trees	9-trees	12-trees
Pima Indians				
ForestNet	1942	3900	5643	7380
Fully net	3012	6044	8859	11638
Reduction (%)	35.52	35.48	36.31	36.59
Wisconsin				
ForestNet	7934	1674	2379	3178
Fully net	3081	6529	9259	12502
Reduction (%)	74.23	74.36	74.30	74.59
MNIST				
ForestNet	16882	33449	51150	66953
Fully net	1078030	2140150	3266267	4283231
Reduction (%)	98.43	98.44	98.43	98.44
SVHN				
ForestNet	16961	34209	51562	67099
Fully net	1402849	2828355	4261105	5557650
Reduction (%)	98.79	98.79	98.79	98.79

Table 5. Average amount of hidden neurons when using 10-Fold Cross-Validation on four datasets. The amount of trees in the ensemble the networks were built with is indicated in the second row of the table.

Dataset	Amount of hidden neurons			
	3-trees	6-trees	9-trees	12-trees
Pima Indians	251	504	738	970
Wisconsin	93	198	281	379
MNIST	1356	2692	4109	5388
SVHN	1355	2733	4117	5370

Thus, increasing the depth of the trees does not increase exponentially the actual size of the hidden layers, therefore the maximal depth of the trees is not a critical parameter of our method.

5.4 Training and Validation Losses

The *Fully* nets and the *ForestNets* have different behaviors during their training. Typical examples of the training and validation losses are shown in Fig. 2.

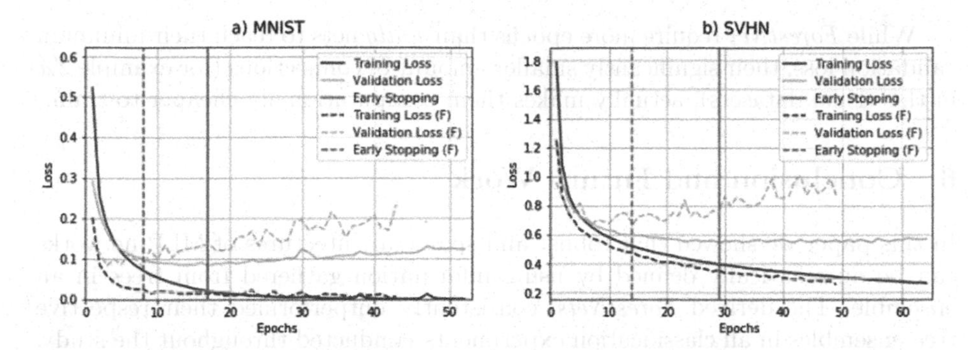

Fig. 2. Training and validation loss on the MNIST and SVHN datasets. We used a middle-sized ForestNet obtained with 9 trees, and its fully-connected version. The exhibited behavior is typical of what we observed with other networks, regardless of the amount of trees used to create them.

The vertical lines correspond to early stopping of the training. We can see that the *Fully* net has his lower validation loss roughly twice faster than the *ForestNet.* This is due to the over-fitting which is clearly visible, as the validation loss of the *Fully* net increases after having quickly reached a minimum. The *ForestNet* exhibits substantially less over-fitting.

Additionally, the evolution of its validation loss is less chaotic, thus the exact time the training is stopped is less critical.

5.5 Discussion

On comparing *ForestNet* against its fully connected counterparts, the statistical significance tests indicate that our approach performs similar to *Fully* net with only a fraction of its number of parameters. We also saw that the amount of neurons in the hidden layer of *ForestNets* does not depend only on the amount or depth of the trees, but also on properties of the data itself – our method can produce layers much smaller than their theoretical maximum size. Thus, although deeper trees are able to produce larger hidden layers, their size is adapted to the datasets' requirements. Furthermore, *Fully* nets exhibit the adverse effects of over-fitting, due to their higher network complexity, as highlighted by the results shown in Table 4 and Fig. 2, for the SVHN and MNIST datasets.

Our results clearly show a lower accuracy in SVHN than on MNIST. One of the main differences between these two datasets is that the first one is composed of cropped digits from photographies, while the latter one is composed of digits written on a tablet pen and centered in a patch. Thus, there is little location variability in the MNIST data. The lower performance of both the *Fully* net and *ForestNet* is due to an inherent property of non-convolutional neural networks: they struggle with input offset.

In a tree, the nodes close to the root are involved in more sub-spaces than nodes closer to the leaves. This property is matched by our method, as it produces more connections corresponding to the first nodes than to the latter ones.

While *ForestNet* require more epochs than *Fully* nets to reach their minimum validation loss, their significantly smaller amount of connections (for example 2% in the visual datasets), actually makes them computationally cheaper to train.

6 Conclusion and Future Work

In this paper we showed that robust and sparse architectures of MLP networks can be automatically defined by using information gathered from trees in an ensemble. The derived *ForestNets*, consistently outperformed their respective tree ensembles in all classification experiments conducted throughout the study. Furthermore, the sparse and compact nature of the derived networks, helps reduce memory requirements, and could aid in reducing energy consumption, which might be especially relevant to mobile devices.

As future work, we are planning investigations in two domains. First, while our approach is able to work on visual data, it is unable to achieve invariance/equivariance to translations and scaling. However, we believe that the presented work can be adapted to network structures, such as CNNs, able to deal with this kind of data. Second, as the network structure is based on the initial ensemble of trees, the outputs of a *ForestNet* can potentially be explained by using the rules produced by the trees. We intend to investigate automatic methods providing justifications or explanations for these outputs.

References

1. Biau, G., Scornet, E., Welbl, J.: Neural random forests. Sankhya A **81**, 347–386 (2019)
2. Breiman, L.: Random forests. Mach. Learn. **45**(1), 5–32 (2001). https://doi.org/10.1023/A:1010933404324
3. Dheeru, D., Karra Taniskidou, E.: UCI machine learning repository (2017). http://archive.ics.uci.edu/ml
4. Frankle, J., Carbin, M.: The lottery ticket hypothesis: finding sparse, trainable neural networks. In: International Conference on Learning Representations (2019). https://openreview.net/forum?id=rJl-b3RcF7
5. Frosst, N., Hinton, G.: Distilling a neural network into a soft decision tree. arXiv preprint arXiv:1711.09784 (2017)
6. Geurts, P., Ernst, D., Wehenkel, L.: Extremely randomized trees. Mach. Learn. **63**(1), 3–42 (2006). https://doi.org/10.1007/s10994-006-6226-1
7. Humbird, K.D., Peterson, J.L., Mcclarren, R.G.: Deep neural network initialization with decision trees. IEEE Trans. Neural Netw. Learn. Syst. **30**(5), 1286–1295 (2019). https://doi.org/10.1109/TNNLS.2018.2869694
8. LeCun, Y., Bengio, Y., Hinton, G.: Deep learning. Nature **521**(7553), 436 (2015)
9. LeCun, Y., Bottou, L., Bengio, Y., Haffner, P.: Gradient-based learning applied to document recognition. Proc. IEEE **86**(11), 2278–2324 (1998)
10. LeCun, Y., Cortes, C.: MNIST handwritten digit database (2010) . http://yann.lecun.com/exdb/mnist/
11. Miikkulainen, R., et al.: Evolving deep neural networks. In: Artificial Intelligence in the Age of Neural Networks and Brain Computing, pp. 293–312. Elsevier (2019)

12. Netzer, Y., Wang, T., Coates, A., Bissacco, A., Wu, B., Ng, A.Y.: Reading digits in natural images with unsupervised feature learning (2011)
13. Paszke, A., et al.: Automatic differentiation in pytorch (2017)
14. Pedregosa, F., et al.: Scikit-learn: machine learning in Python. J. Mach. Learn. Res. **12**, 2825–2830 (2011)
15. Rodríguez-Salas, D., Gómez-Gil, P., Olvera-López, A.: Designing partially-connected, multilayer perceptron neural nets through information gain. In: The 2013 International Joint Conference on Neural Networks (IJCNN), pp. 1–5, August 2013. https://doi.org/10.1109/IJCNN.2013.6706991
16. Sethi, I.K.: Entropy nets: from decision trees to neural networks. Proc. IEEE **78**(10), 1605–1613 (1990)
17. Stanley, K.O., Miikkulainen, R.: Evolving neural networks through augmenting topologies. Evol. comput. **10**(2), 99–127 (2002)
18. Steinberg, D., Colla, P.: CART: classification and regression trees. In: The Top Ten Algorithms in Data Mining, vol. 9, p. 179 (2009)
19. Utgoff, P.E.: Perceptron trees: a case study in hybrid concept representations. Connect. Sci. **1**(4), 377–391 (1989)
20. Wilcoxon, F.: Individual comparisons by ranking methods. Biometrics Bull. **1**(6), 80–83 (1945)

Clustering-Based Adaptive Dropout for CNN-Based Classification

Zhiwei Wen, Zhiwei Ke, Weicheng Xie(✉), and Linlin Shen

Computer Vision Institute, School of Computer Science and Software Engineering,
Guangdong Laboratory of Artificial Intelligence and Digital Economy (SZ),
Guangdong Key Laboratory of Intelligent Information Processing,
Shenzhen University, Shenzhen 518060, China
wcxie@szu.edu.cn

Abstract. Dropout has been widely used to improve the generalization ability of a deep network, while current dropout variants rarely adapt the dropout probabilities of the network hidden units or weights dynamically to their contributions on the network optimization. In this work, a clustering-based dropout based on the network characteristics of features, weights or their derivatives is proposed, where the dropout probabilities for these characteristics are updated self-adaptively according to the corresponding clustering group to differentiate their contributions. Experimental results on the databases of Fashion-MNIST and CIFAR10 and expression databases of FER2013 and CK+ show that the proposed clustering-based dropout achieves better accuracy than the original dropout and various dropout variants, and the most competitive performances compared with state-of-the-art algorithms.

Keywords: Feature and weight clustering · Feature derivative dropout · Self-adaptive dropout probability · Facial expression recognition

1 Introduction

To improve the generalization ability of deep networks, regularizer and batch normalization [1] and sparse deep feature learning [2] were proposed to reduce the possibility of over-fitting. Dropout [3] that randomly drops network hidden units or weights, has been also applied to many object recognition problems [4]. Motivated from the hidden unit dropout, connection (weight) dropout [5] was proposed dropout weight elements randomly. *Khan et al.* [6] proposed to perform dropout for the spectral transformation of a feature map, where three different variants corresponding to the reshaped dimension of the feature map were introduced.

The work was supported by Natural Science Foundation of China under grants no. 61602315, 61672357 and U1713214, the Science and Technology Project of Guangdong Province under grant no. 2018A050501014, the Tencent "Rhinoceros Birds"-Scientific Research Foundation for Young Teachers of Shenzhen University, the School Startup Fund of Shenzhen University under grants no. 2018063.

S. Palaiahnakote et al. (Eds.): ACPR 2019, LNCS 12046, pp. 46–58, 2020.
https://doi.org/10.1007/978-3-030-41404-7_4

However, the hidden units or weights in the traditional dropout are suppressed element by element, which may neglect the structural information implied in the element block. *Tompson et al.* [7] proposed spatial dropout to drop one entire feature map, i.e. the hidden units in one feature map are all dropped or retained simultaneously. Poernomo and Kang [8] divided the features into two groups with equal size according to the magnitudes of hidden unit responses [9], and assigned a dropout probability to each group. Meanwhile, an additional cross-map dropout [8] was proposed, where the elements at the same coordinate on different feature maps are dropped or retained simultaneously. However, two groups are not large enough to differentiate the contributions among different features, more groups should be devised. *Rohit et al.* [10] proposed the guided dropout by dropping nodes according to the strength of each node. *Zhang et al.* [11] proposed the region dropout to use the combination of the salient regions for training. However, the relative positions and sizes of the regions are fixed, which are not flexible enough. *Zhang et al.* [12] proposed grid dropout to reduce the searching space to facilitate the exploration of the global feature. However, the elements in the same grid may be significantly different from each other, the same dropout probability assigned to the entire grid may not work well for the significantly different elements in the same grid.

For the **characteristics (hidden unit, feature or weight)** grouping for dropout, the state-of-the-art dropout variants do not partition these characteristics with enough flexibility and diversity. Actually, for network back propagation, even adjacent elements in feature map and weight matrix contribute largely differently to the network loss. For example, Fig. 1 shows the active regions of the feature maps of an expression image with ResNet18 [13], where different feature maps are categorized into three different levels of importance, i.e. insignificant, fair and significant according to the heat maps response. Intuitively, the magnitude of the characteristic element response should be negatively correlated with the probability of the dropout probability. However, traditional dropout and the state-of-the-art variants can not gather these insignificant feature maps or elements distributed on an entire map for dropout. In this work, network element clustering is introduced in dropout to group the similar elements to share the same dropout probability. Thus, with the proposed clustering, the insignificant elements can be suppressed simultaneously by assigning the corresponding group with a large dropout probability.

For the dropout probability setting, the fixed dropout probability throughout the network training may neglect the dynamic influences of different parts for the network optimization. *Wager et al.* [14] treated the dropout training as a form of adaptive regularization with the approximation of second-order derivative. Ba and Frey [15] proposed a self-adaptive dropout by updating a probability mask matrix according to matrix elements' performance. In this work, the dropout probabilities are updated dynamically according to the clustering group of average characteristic response.

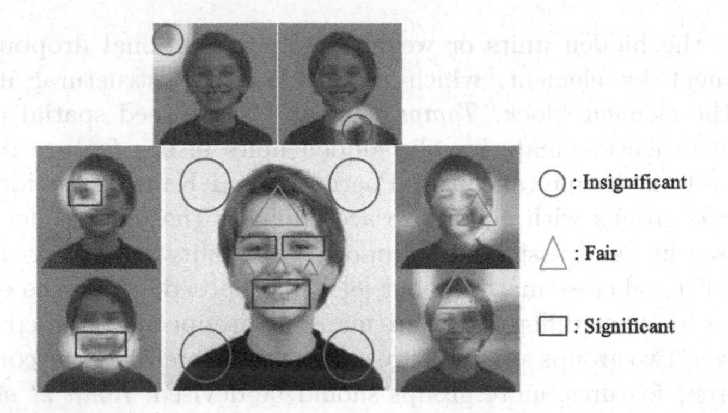

Fig. 1. Six of the 512 feature maps of an example expression in the last convolution layer of the residual network (ResNet18) [13]. According to the effect of the areas of interest on the RaFD database, the feature maps can be divided into different importance levels, i.e. insignificant, fair and significant.

To consider the characteristic for dropout, the fully connected (FC) layer features (i.e. layer input) and weight matrix in a deep network are often used as the discriminative features to determine the recognition performance. Consequently, FC features, the weights, together with their derivatives are used as the characteristics for the clustering.

The main contributions of this work are summarized as follows

- A new dropout based on the clustering of FC features, weights or their derivatives is proposed;
- Self-adaptive renewal of dropout probabilities is proposed based on the response magnitude of each group of feature, weight or derivative clustering;
- Competitive performances are achieved on the databases of Fashion-MNIST and CIFAR10, and expression databases of FER2013 and CK+.

This paper is structured into the following sections. The proposed clustering-based dropout is introduced in Sect. 2. The experimental results and the corresponding illustrations are demonstrated in Sect. 3. Finally, the conclusions and a discussion are presented in Sect. 4.

2 The Proposed Algorithm

In this section, the difference between the proposed dropout and the traditional version [3] is first illustrated, then the framework of the proposed algorithm is introduced. Finally, the related network configuration and loss function are presented.

Figure 2 shows the difference between the traditional dropout and the proposed clustering-based dropout. Compared with the traditional dropout (a) that the FC features are dropped with an uniform dropout probability, the proposed

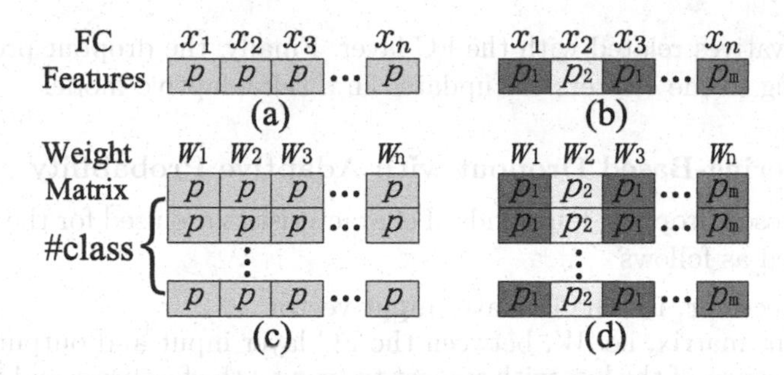

Fig. 2. The traditional dropout [3] ((a), (c)) and the proposed dropout based on clustering ((b), (d)). p, $\{p_1, ..., p_m\}$ are the assigned dropout probabilities. $\#class$ denotes the number of classes, $x = \{x_1, ..., x_n\}$ denotes the FC input, n is the feature dimension, $W = \{W_1, ..., W_n\}$ denotes the weight matrix.

dropout (b) takes into account the variation among different feature elements. As shown in Fig. 2(d), clustering is performed on the column vectors of a 2D weight matrix, in this way, the elements of each weight vector share the same dropout probability. Based on the network element clustering, different dropout probabilities are assigned to the corresponding groups to differentiate their different contributions.

The framework of the proposed dropout is presented in Fig. 3, where the convolution layers are followed by an average pooling layer and a FC layer, then the dropout is performed on the network characteristics, i.e. features, weights

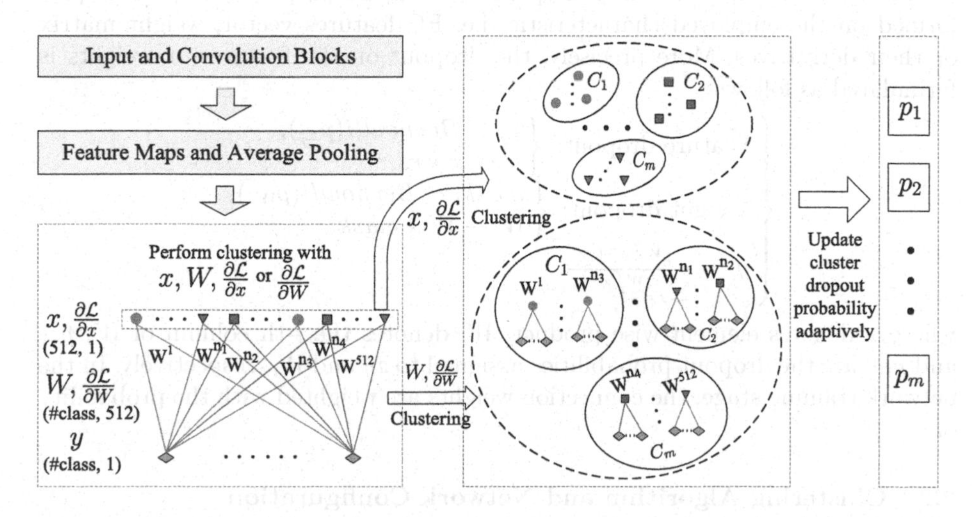

Fig. 3. The framework of the proposed clustering-based dropout. Notations x, W, $\mathcal{L}$ and y are the features input, weight matrix, network loss and output of the FC layer, $\mathcal{L}$ is the network loss function, p_i is the dropout probability assigned to the i-th cluster C_i.

or their derivatives related with the FC layer. Finally, the dropout probabilities corresponding to the clusters are updated in a self-adaptive mode.

2.1 Clustering-Based Dropout with Adaptive Probability

For the proposed dropout, four kinds of characteristics are used for the clustering and presented as follows

- Feature vector x, i.e. the FC layer input vector;
- The weight matrix, i.e. W, between the FC layer input and output y;
- The derivatives of the loss with respect to (w.r.t.) the feature x and the weight matrix W, i.e. $\frac{\partial \mathcal{L}}{\partial x}$, $\frac{\partial \mathcal{L}}{\partial W}$;

With the clustering of the FC features, weights or their derivatives, the self-adaptive renewal algorithm of the dropout probabilities is proposed as follows.

$$\begin{cases} \gamma_i = \frac{1}{\#C_i} \sum_{t \in C_i} ||t||_1, \\ \gamma_{min} = \min_i \gamma_i, \gamma_{max} = \max_i \gamma_i, \\ tp_i = p_{min} \frac{\gamma_{max} - \gamma_i}{\gamma_{max} - \gamma_{min}} + p_{max} \frac{\gamma_i - \gamma_{min}}{\gamma_{max} - \gamma_{min}}, \\ p_i = 1 - tp_i. \end{cases} \tag{1}$$

where the user-defined parameters $p_{min} = 0.2$, $p_{max} = 0.8$ are the minimal and maximal dropout probabilities, γ_i is the average of the L_1-norm values of the i-th cluster C_i. p_i is the dropout probability assigned to the i-th cluster C_i. For feature or feature derivative, variable t is a scalar element of the average response of a batch of elements; for weight or weight derivative clustering, t denotes one of their column vector with the dimension of $\#class$.

Based on the updated dropout probabilities, the proposed dropout is performed on the employed characteristic, i.e. FC features vector, weight matrix or their derivatives. More precisely, the dropout on the features or weights is formulated as follows

$$\begin{cases} \text{Feature dropout:} & \begin{cases} r_j \sim Bernoulli(p_{x_j}), \\ x \leftarrow x \star r, \end{cases} \\ \text{Weight dropout:} & \begin{cases} mask_i \sim Bernoulli(p_{W_i}), \\ W \leftarrow W \star mask, \end{cases} \\ y_i = \frac{e^{W_i^T x + b_i}}{\sum_j e^{W_j^T x + b_j}}. \end{cases} \tag{2}$$

where $\star$ denotes element-wise product, W_i denotes the i-th column of W, p_{x_j} and p_{W_i} are the dropout probabilities assigned to x_j and W_i, respectively. In the network training stage, the connection weights are weighted with the probability of $1 - p_i$.

2.2 Clustering Algorithm and Network Configuration

For the network element clustering, k-means algorithm is employed, which is formulated as following equations in an iterative mode

$$\begin{cases} c_i = \frac{1}{\#C_i} \sum_{t \in C_i} t, \\ l_t = argmin_{1 \le i \le m} ||c_i - t||_2^2. \end{cases} \tag{3}$$

where m is the number of clusters, c_i is the center vector of the i-th cluster C_i, and $\#C_i$ denotes the number of samples, l_t is the updated label of the sample t, variable t is defined in Eq. (1).

For the characteristics of the derivatives w.r.t. the features and weights, the similar clustering in Eq. (3) are performed by replacing x or W with $\frac{\partial \mathcal{L}}{\partial x}$ or $\frac{\partial \mathcal{L}}{\partial W}$, then the features or weights based on the results of derivative clustering are used for the dropout in Eq. (2).

The residual network (ResNet18) [13] is used for the training and evaluation. ResNet18 fits the residual mapping $\mathcal{F}$ and then appends it to the identity mapping im to estimate the output $\mathcal{H} = \mathcal{F} + im$, rather than fitting the output $\mathcal{H}$ directly. ResNet18 was reported to be able to decrease the possibility of weight gradient vanishing when the network is very deep. The configuration of the ResNet18 network is presented in Fig. 4.

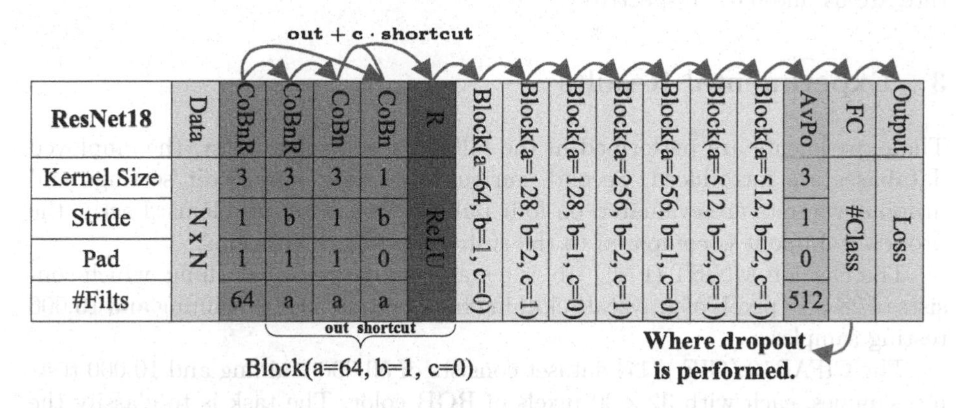

Fig. 4. The network structure of ResNet18. $N \times N$ denotes the image size. Co, Bn, R, $AvPo$ and FC denote the convolution, batch normalization, ReLU, average pooling and fully connected layers, respectively. $\#Filts$ and $\#class$ denote the numbers of feature maps and classes, respectively.

The cross entropy softmax function is used as the network discrimination loss, which is formulated as follows

$$\mathcal{L} = -ln \frac{e^{W_{l_i}^T x} + b_{l_i}}{\sum_j e^{W_j^T x + b_j}}, \tag{4}$$

where l_i is the label of the i-th sample. The derivatives of the loss $\mathcal{L}$ w.r.t. the feature x and weights W, i.e. $\frac{\partial \mathcal{L}}{\partial x}$, $\frac{\partial \mathcal{L}}{\partial W}$ are calculated automatically with network back propagation. For clarity, the proposed dropout is presented in Algorithm 1.

2.3 Implementation Details

We perform the experiments using four-kernel Nvidia TITAN GPU Card and the Pytorch platform. The learning rate is updated with cosine annealing and

Algorithm 1. The proposed dropout.

1: Initialize the network parameters and cluster number m.
2: **for** $s = 0, \cdots, MaxIter$ **do**
3: Select a combination of the characteristics (x, W, $\frac{\partial \mathcal{L}}{\partial x}$ and $\frac{\partial \mathcal{L}}{\partial W}$) for clustering with k-means algorithm.
4: Update the dropout probability of the features x or weights W in each cluster with equation (1) with the interval of $IntBat$ batches.
5: Perform dropout on the features x or weights W with equation (2).
6: **end for**
7: Output the trained network model for testing.

SGD optimizer is employed. $IntBat = 1$, $m = 10$, the batch size and learning rate are 64 and 0.01, respectively.

3 Experimental Results

The experiments are performed in the following sequence. First, the employed databases are introduced; Second, various clustering parameter settings and dropout variants are evaluated on four public recognition problems; Lastly, the proposed dropout is compared to the state-of-the-art algorithms.

The Fashion-MNIST (FM.) [16] is a standard dataset of clothing, which consists of 28×28 pixels of grayscale clothing images with 60,000 training and 10,000 testing samples.

The CIFAR10 (CIF.) [17] dataset consists of 50,000 training and 10,000 testing samples, each with 32×32 pixels of RGB color. The task is to classify the images into 10 different objects.

The FER2013 (FER.) [18] database consists of 35887 grayscale face images with size 48×48, which is collected from the internet and used for a challenge. The faces were labeled with one of seven categories, i.e. angry, disgust, fear, happy, sad, surprise and neutral. The training, public test (validation) and final test (testing) sets consist of 28,709, 3,589 and 3,589 examples, respectively.

The CK+ [19] database consists of 593 expression sequences from 123 subjects, where 327 sequences are labeled with one of seven expressions, i.e. six basic and 'contempt' expressions. Five non-neutral images sampled from each expression sequence are used for testing. The person-independent strategy with ten-fold setting is employed for CK+ testing. The example samples of the four databases are presented in Fig. 5.

To evaluate different model settings in the proposed dropout, three independent trails are performed for each parameter or model setting. Table 1 presents the average recognition accuracies and their standard variances using different network characteristics. For the dropout fusing with two characteristics in the last two columns of Table 1, the clustering with each characteristic is weighted by 0.5 for the dropout probability update in Eq. (1).

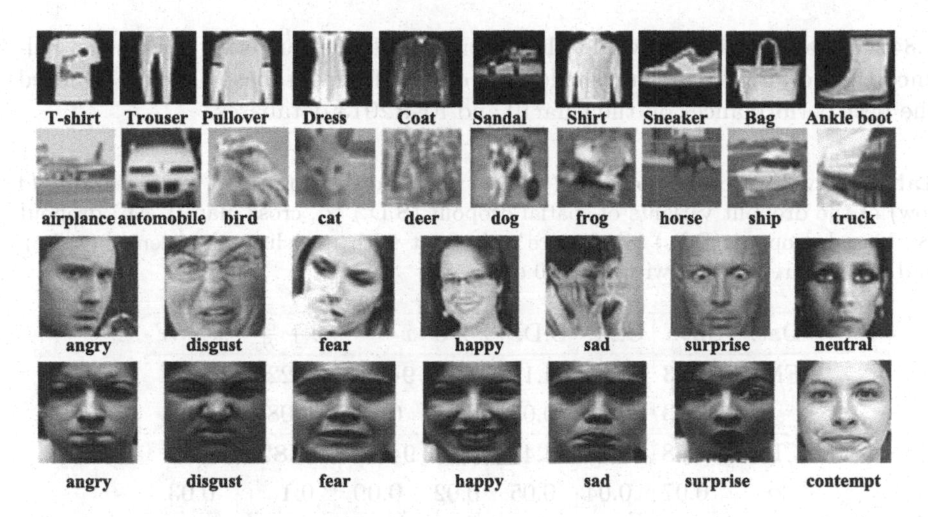

Fig. 5. Example images and the corresponding labels of the Fashion-MNIST, CIFAR10, FER2013 and CK+ databases.

Comparing the 4th and 5th (or 6th and 7th) columns in Table 1, the proposed algorithm with the clustering of FC features generally achieves better performance than that of weight matrix. Comparing the 3rd column with 4th-9th columns, one can observe that the proposed dropout significantly outperforms the original dropout with the significance level of 0.05 on the four databases, especially for FER2013 and CK+ databases, large improvements of 0.35% and

Table 1. Average recognition rates (%, even row) and their standard variances (odd row) of different parameter settings on the four databases. Notations of 'data.', 'Non' and 'Ori.' are the abbreviations of 'database', 'non dropout' and 'original dropout', respectively. For the original dropout, the best performances are achieved when the dropout probability is set as 0.5. † means that the proposed dropout is significantly better than the original dropout with Student's t-Test [20] under the significance level of 0.05.

Dat.	Non	Ori.	x	W	$\frac{\partial L}{\partial x}$	$\frac{\partial L}{\partial W}$	$x+\frac{\partial L}{\partial x}$	$x+W$
FM.	94.08	94.03	94.27†	**94.28**†	94.21	94.16	94.22†	94.25†
	0.08	0.03	0.01	0.06	0.12	0.09	0.08	0.05
CIF.	94.5	94.48	94.72†	94.62	94.65†	94.59†	**94.82**†	94.68†
	0.09	0.11	0.09	0.09	0.06	0.01	0.1	0.03
FER.	72.68	72.87	73.08	73.08	72.95	73.19†	73.13	**73.22**†
	0.13	0.15	0.36	0.05	0.23	0.03	0.3	0.1
CK+	96.64	96.53	**98.37**†	97.76†	98.17†	97.55†	98.16†	98.27†
	0.01	0.35	0.14	0.29	0.23	0.25	0.25	0.14

1.84% are achieved. Meanwhile, the fusion of multiple clustering results can balance the performances with single ones on the four databases, which achieved the best performances on the Cifar10 and FER2013 databases.

Table 2. Average recognition rates (%, even row) and their standard variances (%, odd row) of the dropout variants of spatial dropout (S.D.) [7], cross map (C.M.) dropout [8], biased dropout (B.D.) [8], feature x dropout with two-cluster clustering (x 2-c), and our feature dropout with $m = 10$ clusters.

Dat.	S.D.	C.M.	B.D.	x 2-c	x	$x + \frac{\partial L}{\partial x}$	$x + W$
FM.	94.03	94.04	94.12	94.17	**94.27**	94.22	94.25
	0.03	0.09	0.08	0.15	0.01	0.08	0.05
CIF.	94.58	94.63	94.48	94.69	94.72	**94.82**	94.68
	0.07	0.04	0.05	0.02	0.09	0.1	0.03
FER.	72.92	72.95	72.74	72.92	73.08	73.13	**73.22**
	0.19	0.25	0.11	0.14	0.36	0.3	0.1
CK+	97.15	97.35	97.25	97.96	**98.37**	98.16	98.27
	0.64	0.18	0.53	0.38	0.14	0.25	0.14

To compare the proposed dropout with other dropout variants, Table 2 shows the accuracies and their standard variances of five dropout variants. For the dropout probability update with two groups [8], biased dropout (B.D.) and 2-cluster clustering (x 2-c), the characteristic of FC features are employed.

Comparing the 4th and the 5th columns, Table 2 shows that feature clustering outperforms the feature equipartition [8] on the four databases, which illustrates the effectiveness of the clustering employed in the proposed dropout. When the same clustering is employed, 10-cluster setting (6th column) still performs better than 2-clusters (5th column) on the four databases, which reveals that 10-cluster clustering matches the variations of FC features better than 2-cluster clustering.

To study the variations of the dropout probabilities with the proposed dropout, Fig. 6 presents the numbers of FC features elements in 10 clusters with different iteration epochs. One can observe that the elements with large response values after training account for a small proportion of the number of the entire FC features. More precisely, the feature elements are mostly concentrated in the cluster with small response value. This observation is similar to that of the network compression [21] and L_2-normalization on FC feature for generalization ability improvement. Meanwhile, large difference among the numbers of feature neurons in different clusters is observed, which implies the diverse contributions of different feature groups for network training. By taking into account this difference, the proposed dropout with the feature clustering can better differentiate the feature contribution than the original dropout during network training.

Regarding to the runtime of the proposed algorithm, the time complexity of the k-means algorithm for FC features is $O(n)$ (n is the feature dimension),

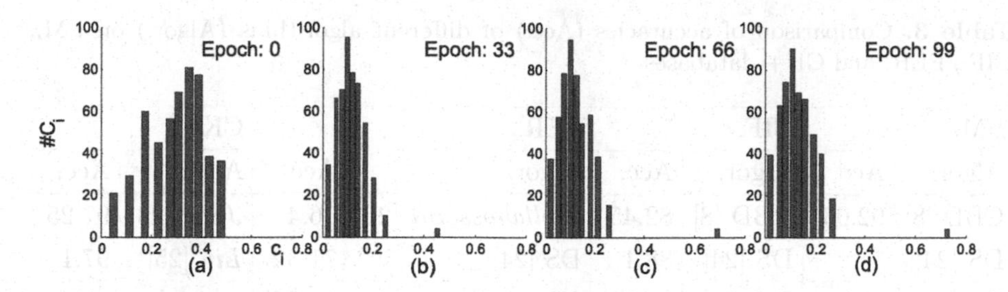

Fig. 6. The number of feature elements of 10 clusters with different iteration epochs on the FER2013 databases, where the FC feature average is used to label the corresponding cluster.

which is almost negligible compared with the network training. For the clustering with weights or weight derivatives, the runtime of the k-means is $O(n \cdot \#class)$. To reduce the runtime cost of the weight clustering in the proposed training, the clustering is performed periodically after a interval of $IntBat$ batches. Meanwhile, the testing performances of the proposed algorithm against the number of interval batches, i.e. $IntBat$ are presented in Fig. 7. Figure 7 shows that a even better performance can be achieved by the proposed algorithm with the fine tuning of the number of interval batches, i.e. $IntBat = 10$. Thus, a slightly large number of interval batches help clustering not only save the runtime cost, but also learn more stable information to contribute to the performance improvement.

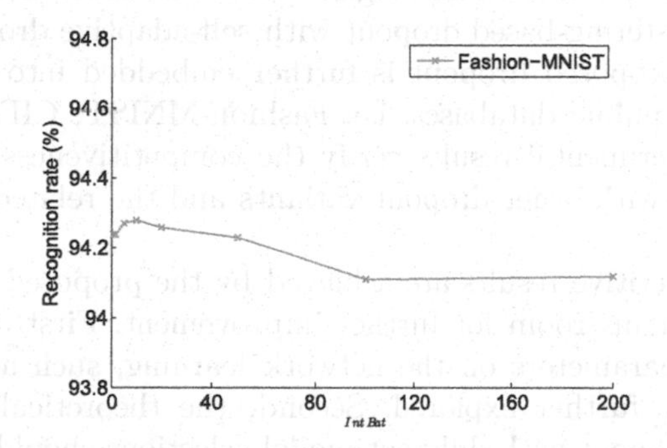

Fig. 7. The performances of the proposed algorithm with different setting of the interval batches ($IntBat$) on the Fashion-MNIST database.

To compare the performance of the proposed algorithm with other state-of-the-art approaches, Tables 3 compares the testing recognition rates of the proposed algorithm with those reported in eight state-of-the-art works on the four databases, where 10-cluster clustering of feature and feature derivative is employed in the proposed dropout. For the CK+ database, the works using the same seven expressions as this paper are included for the comparison.

Table 3. Comparison of accuracies (Acc.) of different algorithms (Algor.) on FM., CIF., FER. and CK+ databases.

FM.		CIF.		FER.		CK+	
Algor.	Acc.	Algor.	Acc.	Algor.	Acc.	Algor.	Acc.
CBD [8]	92.03	CBD [8]	82.45	*Mollahosseini* [22]	66.4	*Jung* [23]	97.25
DS [24]	–	DS [24]	88.1	DS [24]	71.32	*Liu* [25]	97.1
BC [26]	–	BC [26]	91.73	*Wen* [27]	69.96	–	–
GD [10]	–	GD [10]	94.12	–	–	–	–
Ours	**94.27**	Ours	**94.82**	Ours	**73.22**	Ours	**98.37**

Tables 3 show that the proposed algorithm achieves the consistently best performances on the four databases among the state-of-the-art algorithms, where large improvements of 2.24%, 0.7%, 1.9% and 1.12% are achieved by the proposed algorithm on the Fashion-MNIST, CIFAR10, FER2013 and CK+ databases, respectively. The competitive performances verify the effectiveness of the proposed dropout with the clustering of FC feature and weight matrix.

4 Conclusion

To take into account that the elements in the fully connected (FC) features, weights, derivatives of features and weights contribute differently to the network optimization, a clustering-based dropout with self-adaptive dropout probability is proposed. The proposed dropout is further embedded into the FC layer of ResNet18 for four public databases, i.e. Fashion-MNIST, CIFAR10, FER2013 and CK+, the experimental results verify the competitiveness of the proposed dropout compared with other dropout variants and the related state-of-the-art algorithms.

Although competitive results are achieved by the proposed clustering-based dropout, there remains room for further improvement. First, the influences of introduced hyper-parameters on the network learning, such as the number of clusters, should be further explored. Second, the theoretical analysis of the clustering-based dropout with different model selections should be deeply studied. Lastly, the proposed dropout should be applied in more models and tasks.

References

1. Liu, S., Deng, W.: Very deep convolutional neural network based image classification using small training sample size. In: 2015 3rd IAPR Asian Conference on Pattern Recognition (ACPR), pp. 730–734 (2015)
2. Xie, W., Jia, X., Shen, L., Yang, M.: Sparse deep feature learning for facial expression recognition. Pattern Recogn. (PR) **96**, 106966 (2019)

3. Srivastava, N., Hinton, G., Krizhevsky, A., Sutskever, I., Salakhutdinov, R.: Dropout: a simple way to prevent neural networks from overfitting. J. Mach. Learn. Res. (JMLR) **15**, 1929–1958 (2014)
4. Wang, H., Wang, L.: Learning robust representations using recurrent neural networks for skeleton based action classification and detection. In: International Conference on Multimedia Expo Workshops (ICMEW), pp. 591–596, July 2017
5. Wan, L., Zeiler, M., Zhang, S., Cun, Y.L., Fergus, R.: Regularization of neural networks using DropConnect. In: Proceedings of International Conference on Machine Learning (ICML), vol. 28, pp. 1058–1066, June 2013
6. Khan, S., Hayat, M., Porikli, F.: Regularization of deep neural networks with spectral dropout. Neural Netw. **110**, 82–90 (2019)
7. Tompson, J., Goroshin, R., Jain, A., LeCun, Y., Bregler, C.: Efficient object localization using convolutional networks. In: IEEE Conference on Computer Vision and Pattern Recognition (CVPR), pp. 648–656 (2014)
8. Poernomo, A., Kang, D.K.: Biased dropout and crossmap dropout: learning towards effective dropout regularization in convolutional neural network. Neural Netw. **104**, 60–67 (2018)
9. Han, S., Pool, J., Tran, J., Dally, W.: Learning both weights and connections for efficient neural network. In: Advances in Neural Information Processing Systems (NIPS), pp. 1135–1143 (2015)
10. Rohit, K., Richa, S., Mayank, V.: Guided dropout. In: AAAI Conference on Artificial Intelligence (AAAI) (2019)
11. Zhang, X., Yang, Y., Feng, J.: ML-LocNet: improving object localization with multi-view learning network. In: Ferrari, V., Hebert, M., Sminchisescu, C., Weiss, Y. (eds.) ECCV 2018. LNCS, vol. 11207, pp. 248–263. Springer, Cham (2018). https://doi.org/10.1007/978-3-030-01219-9_15
12. Zhang, C., Zhu, C., Xiao, J., Xu, X., Liu, Y.: Image ordinal classification and understanding: grid dropout with masking label. In: 2018 IEEE International Conference on Multimedia and Expo (ICME), pp. 1–6, July 2018
13. He, K., Zhang, X., Ren, S., Sun, J.: Deep residual learning for image recognition. In: IEEE Conference on Computer Vision and Pattern Recognition (CVPR), pp. 770–778 (2016)
14. Wager, S., Wang, S., Liang, P.S.: Dropout training as adaptive regularization. In: Advances in Neural Information Processing Systems (NIPS), pp. 351–359 (2013)
15. Ba, J., Frey, B.: Adaptive dropout for training deep neural networks. In: Advances in Neural Information Processing Systems (NIPS), pp. 3084–3092 (2013)
16. Xiao, H., Rasul, K., Vollgraf, R.: Fashion-MNIST: a novel image dataset for benchmarking machine learning algorithms. arXiv preprint arXiv:1708.07747 (2017)
17. Krizhevsky, A., Hinton, G.: Learning multiple layers of features from tiny images. Master's thesis, Department of Computer Science, University of Toronto (2009)
18. Goodfellow, I.J., et al.: Challenges in representation learning: a report on three machine learning contests. In: Lee, M., Hirose, A., Hou, Z.-G., Kil, R.M. (eds.) ICONIP 2013. LNCS, vol. 8228, pp. 117–124. Springer, Heidelberg (2013). https://doi.org/10.1007/978-3-642-42051-1_16
19. Kanade, T., Cohn, J.F., Tian, Y.: Comprehensive database for facial expression analysis. In: Proceedings Fourth IEEE International Conference on Automatic Face and Gesture Recognition (FG), pp. 46–53 (2000)
20. De Winter, J.C.: Using the student's t-test with extremely small sample sizes. Pract. Assess. Res. Eval. **18**(10), 1–12 (2013)

21. Han, S., Mao, H., Dally, W.J.: Deep compression: compressing deep neural networks with pruning, trained quantization and Huffman coding. arXiv preprint arXiv:1510.00149 (2015)
22. Mollahosseini, A., Chan, D., Mahoor, M.H.: Going deeper in facial expression recognition using deep neural networks. In: 2016 IEEE Winter Conference on Applications of Computer Vision (WACV), pp. 1–10 (2016)
23. Jung, H., Lee, S., Yim, J., Park, S., Kim, J.: Joint fine-tuning in deep neural networks for facial expression recognition. In: Proceedings of the IEEE International Conference on Computer Vision (ICCV), pp. 2983–2991 (2015)
24. Tang, Y.: Deep learning using support vector machines. In: Proceedings of International Conference on Machine Learning (ICML) (2013)
25. Liu, X., Vijaya Kumar, B., You, J., Jia, P.: Adaptive deep metric learning for identity-aware facial expression recognition. In: Proceedings of the IEEE Conference on Computer Vision and Pattern Recognition Workshops (CVPRW), pp. 20–29 (2017)
26. Courbariaux, M., Bengio, Y., David, J.P.: BinaryConnect: training deep neural networks with binary weights during propagations. In: Advances in Neural Information Processing Systems (NIPS), pp. 3123–3131 (2015)
27. Wen, G., Hou, Z., Li, H., Li, D., Jiang, L., Xun, E.: Ensemble of deep neural networks with probability-based fusion for facial expression recognition. Cogn. Comput. **9**(5), 597–610 (2017)

Action and Video and Motion

Real-Time Detection and Tracking Using Hybrid DNNs and Space-Aware Color Feature: From Algorithm to System

Liang Feng[1(✉)], Hiroaki Igarashi[2], Seiya Shibata[2], Yuki Kobayashi[2], Takashi Takenaka[2], and Wei Zhang[1]

[1] Hong Kong University of Science and Technology, Kowloon, Hong Kong
{lfengad,wei.zhang}@ust.hk
[2] NEC Corporation, Kawasaki,Kanagawa, Japan
h-igarashi@hf.jp.nec.com, s-shibata@ax.jp.nec.com,
y-kobayashi@hq.jp.nec.com, takenaka@aj.jp.nec.com

Abstract. Object detection and tracking are vital for video analysis. As the development of Deep Neural Network (DNN), multiple object tracking is recently performed on the detection results from DNN. However, DNN-based detection is computation-intensive. In order to accelerate multiple object detection and tracking for real-time application, we present a framework to import the tracking knowledge into detection to allow a less accurate but faster DNN for detection and recover the accuracy loss. By combining different DNNs with accuracy-speed trade-offs using space-aware color information, our framework achieves significant speedup (6.8×) and maintains high accuracy. Targeting NVIDIA Xavier, we further optimize the implementation from system and platform level.

Keywords: DNN · Object detection · Tracking · GPU

1 Introduction

Multiple object detection and tracking is a key technology for video interpretation. Tracking-by-detection has become the leading paradigm in multiple object tracking due to the recent progress in object detection. Objects are detected each frame as bounding boxes and tracked by matching detections for the same object across frames. Deep neural networks (DNN) for object detection proposed in recent years, such as Faster-R-CNN [18], SSD [15], Yolo [17], Mask-R-CNN [11], etc., provide highly accurate detections, and thus allow simpler but more efficient tracking-by-detection approaches. However, such computation-intensive large DNNs are not fast enough to satisfy the real-time processing, especially when with limited computing power like in embedded systems. Therefore, in addition to these large DNNs, smaller DNN structures are explored for high-speed detection, such as Tiny-Yolo [17], Tiny-SSD [21], etc., although their accuracy is too low to satisfy the detection and tracking requirement.

S. Palaiahnakote et al. (Eds.): ACPR 2019, LNCS 12046, pp. 61–75, 2020.
https://doi.org/10.1007/978-3-030-41404-7_5

To simultaneously achieve high speed of the small DNN and high accuracy of the large DNN, we creatively combine both DNNs with different speed-accuracy trade-offs in a time-interleaving way. Relying on the tracking knowledge, the accurate information from large DNN is used to recover the accuracy loss from small DNN. By importing tracking knowledge into detection, the accuracy requirement for detection is relaxed to allow the high-speed small DNN used in most video frames. In this way, both good accuracy and high speed are achieved simultaneously in our framework.

To match detections across frames for tracking, their similarity needs to be measured. Intersection over union (IOU), feature description neural network (NN), etc. are used in recent works [4–6,20,24] for similarity measurement. However, they are either not accurate enough or with high computation complexity. We propose a space-aware color feature for more accurate similarity measurement by extracting both color and space information with high accuracy and low computation complexity. Such a distinguishable feature also allows re-identifying the same object after occlusion and works well in recovering the accuracy of small DNN detections. By combining many novel techniques in detection matching and accuracy recovering, our framework achieves state-of-the-art detection and tracking accuracy at high speed. The framework can also be used in detection-only case to speed up detection while maintaining high accuracy.

Our key contribution is combining hybrid DNNs with different speed-accuracy trade-offs in a time-interleaving way and importing the tracking knowledge into detection, which result in both high accuracy and high speed. The novel usage of the space-aware color feature is another main contribution. In addition, many new techniques are designed to fit these novel concepts. Besides algorithm level, we also perform optimization at system and platform level for a higher-speed implementation, by exploring architectural heterogeneity, multi-core parallelism, data precision, clock frequency, etc., targeting the underlying NVIDIA Xavier. In summary, we design a complete detection and tracking framework with both high accuracy and high speed, from the algorithm level to the system and platform level, from software to hardware. We achieve a high speed at 55.2 FPS for the whole real-time multiple object detection and tracking task, which is 6.8× faster with similar level high accuracy than the traditional large DNN only method on NVIDIA Xavier.

2 Related Work

2.1 Multiple Object Tracking

MOT can be formulated as a global optimization problem that processes entire video batches at once, which cannot be used in real-time applications, such as flow network formulations-based [25] and probabilistic graphical models-based MOT works [23]. Multiple Hypothesis Tracking (MHT) [13] and Joint Probabilistic Data Association (JPDA) filters [9] used in traditional MOT are still impractical for real-time processing due to the large delay from high combinatorial complexity. Some tracking works build appearance models [3,22] through online learning, which are quite complex. Relying on accurate DNN detection, recent works adopt simple IOU to match detections from frames using Hungarian or greedy algorithm [4–6]. Although with high speed, these works show low accuracy in many scenarios due to little object feature extraction. Further, some works use additional DNNs to describe object feature for matching [20,24], where the feature description NN brings high computation complexity and is hard to train for different scenarios. We propose a simple but efficient space-aware color feature with new matching algorithms to achieve simpler usage, higher speed and even better accuracy. Moreover, current DNN detection-based MOT works only consider one large detection DNN with low speed, which cannot satisfy real-time requirement especially when with limited computing power as in embedded applications. We creatively combine hybrid DNNs for detection to achieve both superior speed and accuracy.

2.2 Color Feature

Color feature distinguishes object efficiently. Many works describe object for tracking using color histogram [1,16]. More complex color features have been proposed, like color naming [19], color attributes [7]. Color feature has also been combined with other well engineered features like gradient [8], HOG [26], correlation filters [7], etc. Due to the power of DNN detection in our work, color histogram is a good choice with simple computation to distinguish objects. Because color feature is most discriminative for objects within the same class from DNN, while other features like edges, etc., have already been included by DNN. Different from existing color features, our novel space-aware color feature uses partial histograms to include space information for better discrimination.

3 Whole Framework

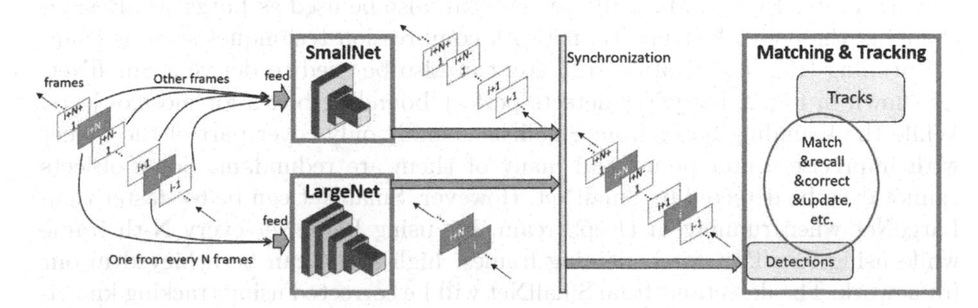

Fig. 1. Whole framework

The framework is based on NVIDIA DeepStream on Jetson Xavier platform. As in Fig. 1, there are three stages, LargeNet, SmallNet and Matching&Tracking (M&T). Each stage is implemented as a pipeline stage in DeepStream and handled by different threads for high parallelism and full resource usage. The stages

(a) LargeNet Detection (b) SmallNet Detection

Fig. 2. Detection example for ADL-Rundle-6 from 2D MOT15 benchmark

execute different video frames simultaneously in a pipeline fashion. A synchronization mechanism ensures the frames from SmallNet and LargeNet enter M&T in order. LargeNet uses a large DNN for object detection with low speed and high accuracy, while SmallNet adopts a small DNN for detection with high speed and low accuracy. Among every N frames, only the first frame goes to LargeNet for detection, while the following N-1 frames all go to SmallNet. N is the network switching interval. M&T receives the detection results for each frame in order and performs the tracking. It matches current detections with existing tracks. SmallNet and LargeNet execute on GPU while M&T executes on CPU to fully utilize the heterogeneous architecture.

4 Detection

While LargeNet gives accurate detections, detections from SmallNet are usually with bad bounding boxes and imprecise positions. We use Yolo as the LargeNet and Tiny-Yolo as the SmallNet. Other detection neural networks such as SSD, Faster-RCNN, Mask-RCNN, etc. can also be used as LargeNet. Besides changing the network structure, network compression techniques such as channel pruning [10], quantization [12], etc. can also be used to derive a SmallNet. As shown in Fig. 2, LargeNet detects perfect bounding boxes for most objects. While the bounding boxes from SmallNet usually only cover part of the object with imprecise center point, and many of them are redundant. Some objects cannot even be detected by SmallNet. However, SmallNet can be 6× faster than LargeNet when running in DeepStream. By using LargeNet every N-th frame while using SmallNet for remaining frames, high speed can be achieved in our framework. The detections from SmallNet will be corrected using tracking knowledge with previous LargeNet detections to recover the accuracy. Due to the low quality of SmallNet, a high detection confidence threshold will lose detection of many objects causing a high false negative number. Therefore in practice, the confidence threshold for a valid detection in SmallNet should be set low to provide more candidate SmallNet detections although imprecisely. More candidates mean more opportunities to find the exact matching of the same object to existing tracks. And the imprecision can be corrected using tracking knowledge with previous LargeNet detections.

5 Matching and Tracking

5.1 Similarity Sorting-Based Matching

The aim of tracking is to match the detections for current frame with existing tracks. Unlike previous IOU based matching [4–6], we rely on both space-aware color feature and IOU for matching. We denote the detections and tracks to be matched as D and T, respectively. A similarity distance s_{ij} is derived for every pair of $t_i \in T$ and $d_j \in D$ based on the space-aware color feature and IOU, where a smaller distance indicates a larger similarity between the detection and track. The smaller the similarity distance is, the more likely the detection should be matched to the track. Therefore, we propose a sorting-based matching to match the most similar pairs with priority as in Algorithm 1. All s_{ij} are sorted in ascending order. From the smallest s_{ij}, we match d_j to t_i if both have not been matched before. Besides, matching is performed only if the similarity distance is small enough ($< Th_{sim}$). $Assign_i$ reflects which detection is matched to track t_i. $Assign_i$ as -1 means no matched detection, while other value j means matching detection d_j to t_i.

Algorithm 1. Similarity Sorting-based Matching

```
   Input: D of size m, T of size n
   Output: Assign of size n
1  Function SortMatching(D, T):
2      all Assign ← -1;
3      foreach t_i ∈ T do
4          foreach d_j ∈ D do
5              s_ij ⟵ SimilarityDistance(t_i, d_j);
6          end foreach
7      end foreach
8      sort {s_ij | 0 ≤ i < n, 0 ≤ j < m} in ascending order;
9      foreach s_ij in ascending order do
10         if Assgin_i = −1 && ∀Assign ≠ j && s_ij < Th_sim then
11             Assign_i ⟵ j;
12         end if
13     end foreach
14     return Assign.
15 End Function
```

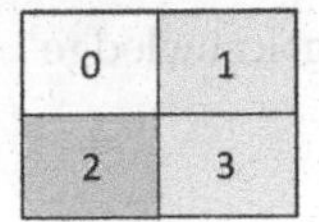

Fig. 3. Partial Histogram Calculation

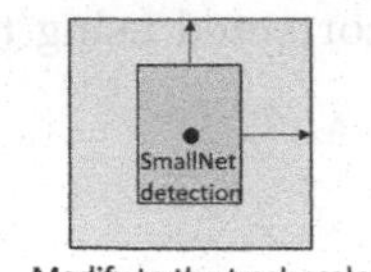

Fig. 4. Scaling for SmallNet Detection

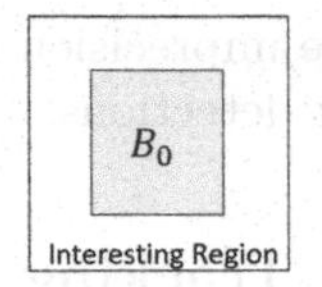

Fig. 5. Interesting Region

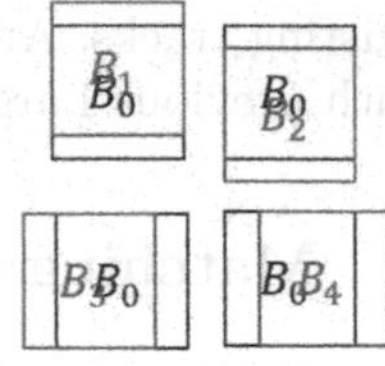

Fig. 6. Bounding Box Derivation

Space-Aware Color-Based Similarity Distance. The similarity distance s_{ij} between track t_i and detection d_j is defined as Eq. 1. If the last bounding box of t_i and the bounding box of d_j have no overlap (IOU = 0) or the detection class of d_j from LargeNet differs from the track class of t_i, s_{ij} is set to a large value MAX to disable matching since t_i and d_j are unlikely to be the same object. Otherwise, the color histograms of t_i and d_j will be used for calculating s_{ij} to check their similarity using space-aware color feature. Each detection or track has 5 color histograms $h_0 \sim h_3$ and H. H is the color histogram of the whole bounding box, while $h_0 \sim h_3$ are the color histograms of four partial boxes $0 \sim 3$ as in Fig. 3, respectively. Lab color space is used for calculating the color histograms by considering all three channels. For a track and a detection, correlation distances between them for H and $h_0 \sim h_3$ are calculated, respectively, before summed up with different weights α_0 (0.1) and α_1 (0.6). Correlation distance is 1 minus the correlation $Corr$ between two histograms. In this way, both color and space information are considered as a space-aware color feature to estimate the similarity with much better accuracy. All 5 histograms of a track t_i are updated in the same way every time a LargeNet detection d_j is matched to it as in Eq. 2, where part of history information is kept for stability. Since SmallNet detection is inaccurate, it will not update the histograms of a track. The class of a track is set as the class of its associated LargeNet detections because the class prediction from LargeNet is usually true. We still check the color histograms for a SmallNet detection even if its class differs from the track, since they are still possible to be the same object due to the frequent wrong classification of SmallNet.

$$s_{ij} = \begin{cases} MAX\ , \text{ if } IOU(t_i, d_j) = 0 \ || \ LargeNet\ class\ differs \\ \sum_{k=0}^{3} \alpha_0 (1 - Corr(h_{k_{t_i}}, h_{k_{d_j}})) + \alpha_1 (1 - Corr(H_{t_i}, H_{d_j})), \\ \qquad \text{otherwise} \end{cases} \quad (1)$$

$$H_{t_i} = (1 - \beta) H_{t_i} + \beta H_{d_j} \quad (2)$$

$$(width\ or\ height)_{t_i} = (1 - \gamma)(width\ or\ height)_{t_i} + \gamma (width\ or\ height)_{d_j} \quad (3)$$

SmallNet Detection Scaling. SmallNet detections usually hold wrong bounding box scale (width and height), and thus we perform scaling to them. Each track holds a scale, which is only updated when a LargeNet detection is matched to it since only scale from LargeNet detection is accurate. The scale is updated as Eq. 3 to consider the history information for stability. The scale can also be updated using a Kalman filter although which performs not stably in real applications. When calculating the similarity distance between a SmallNet detection and a track, only the center point of the detection is kept while the scale of the detection is replaced by the scale of the track to form a new detection bounding box as in Fig. 4. The calculation for color histograms of the detection and IOU will follow the new bounding box. Every SmallNet detection will perform different scaling for calculating the similarity distance with different tracks. In this way, the scale inaccuracy of SmallNet detections can be corrected by the accurate scale from LargeNet detections.

5.2 Space-Aware Color-Based Bounding Box Refinement

Although the center point (position) of SmallNet detection is usually close to the ground truth, but not highly precise. We use space-aware color feature to refine the position of the SmallNet detections which have been matched to a track. The bounding box of the SmallNet detection first performs scaling as in Sec. SmallNet Detection Scaling to change its scale to the track scale. This bounding box is the root bounding box B_0. We consider an Interesting Region centering at center of B_0 with larger scale ($K\times$ width and height, K can be 2) as in Fig. 5. Inside this region, we are aimed at finding a new bounding box position with larger similarity to the matched track, which should be more precise than B_0. The ground truth bounding box is usually near B_0, thus only the Interesting Region needs to be considered. B_0 is moved one small step to four directions, up, down, left and right, respectively, to derive four new bounding boxes $B_1 \sim B_4$, as in Fig. 6. B_0 is parent and $B_1 \sim B_4$ are child bounding boxes. One step for up or down directions and for left or right directions are calculated as $height_{B_0}/M$ and $width_{B_0}/M$, respectively. M is the granularity for refinement and using higher M is more accurate with more computation. M can be set to 8. From each newly derived bounding box, four child bounding boxes of it are further derived. In this way, a graph can be formulated as in Fig. 8. A bounding box stops deriving its child bounding boxes if it is outside the Interesting Region or has appeared

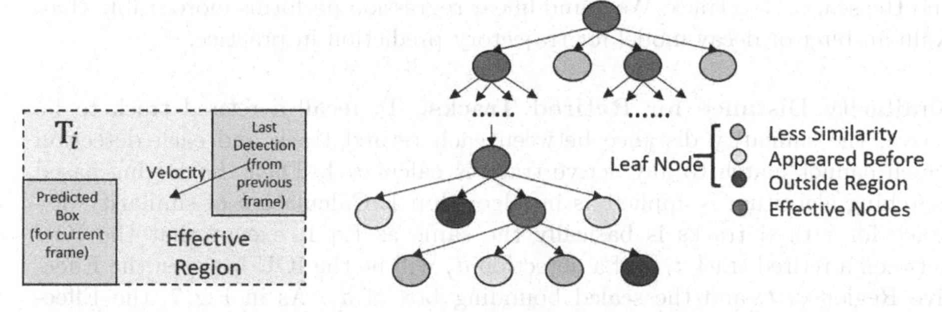

Fig. 7. Effective region **Fig. 8.** Bounding box graph

before, so it becomes the leaf node in the graph. If the similarity distance to the matched track of a bounding box increases compared to the distance to the track of its parent bounding box, it also becomes the leaf node; since it indicates a bad direction with less similarity and thus any exploration along this direction is no need and pruned. In this way, the space of the bounding boxes to be searched is reduced for saving computation. Either breath-first-search (BFS) or depth-first-search (DFS) is performed to traverse the graph. During traverse, the similarity distance to the track of each bounding box is calculated as in Sec. Space-aware Color-based Similarity Distance. After traverse, the bounding box with the smallest similarity distance will be chosen as the refined bounding box since it matches the track best. The bounding box of both the SmallNet detection and the track at this frame will be updated as this refined bounding box. The refinement is only performed to a SmallNet detection when its detection confidence is less than Th_{ref} (0.8). The bounding box position is usually highly precise for a SmallNet detection with very high confidence, thus we only refine the detections with low confidence for saving computation. The refinement is only performed for a completed matching while the scaling is needed for calculating the similarity distance as the base of matching.

5.3 Retire-Recall Mechanism

Targeting the occlusion case, we propose a retire-recall mechanism. A newly instantiated track is active and it will become retired if not matched with any detection for Th_{ret} frames. A retired track is permanently deleted if not matched with any detection for Th_{del} ($Th_{del} > Th_{ret}$) frames. Only active tracks are valid and output for the detection and tracking task, while a retired track can be recalled to become active if a detection without matching in active tracks has large similarity to it.

Trajectory Prediction. For each track, the trajectory is recorded as {center point.x, center point.y, frame number} for all its matched detections. Linear regression is applied to the last L trajectory records to calculate the slope as the velocity, in x and y directions, respectively. The center pointer of the track in one frame can be predicted based on its last detected center point and the velocity, and its bounding box can be predicted by combining the predicted center point and the scale of the track. We found linear regression performs more stably than Kalman filter or decay model for trajectory prediction in practice.

Similarity Distance for Retired Tracks. To recall a retired track to be active, the similarity distance between each retired track and each detection which cannot match to any active track is calculated. Then the sorting-based matching algorithm is applied as in Algorithm 1. Calculation of similarity distance for retired tracks is basically the same as Eq. 1, except that the IOU between a retired track t_i and a detection d_j will be the IOU between the Effective Region of t_i and the scaled bounding box of d_j. As in Fig. 7, the Effective Region of t_i is the rectangle covering the bounding box of t_i from its last matched detection and the linear regression-predicted bounding box for t_i at current frame. The object has high possibility to re-appear between its last appeared position and its predicted current position, thus only the detections in the Effective Region should be focused on. In this way, the number of detections requiring color histogram and correlation calculation is reduced for saving computation.

5.4 Whole Matching and Tracking Algorithm

Combining all above techniques, the whole matching and tracking algorithm for M&T stage is as in Algorithm 2. First, the similarity sorting-based matching guided by the space-aware color-based similarity distance as in Algorithm 1 is performed to the detections from current frame and the existing active tracks from last frame, for a largely improved tracking accuracy. Second, for remaining unmatched detections and active tracks, IOU-based Hungarian matching similar to previous works [4,5] is applied to find additional matchings with large overlap, where a matching is valid only if its IOU is large enough ($> Th_{iou}$). In this way, our new space-aware color guided matching is combined with IOU-based matching to take advantages of both. Third, the space-aware color guided similarity sorting-based matching as in Algorithm 1 is applied again to the remaining unmatched detections and existing retired tracks to recall some retired tracks to become active for the retire-recall mechanism as in Sect. 5.3 and match them with corresponding detections. Next, a new active track is created for each remaining unmatched detection from LargeNet, while a new active track is created for a remaining SmallNet detection only if its detection confidence is larger than a high threshold Th_{crt} (0.8). Because only a SmallNet detection with high confidence indicates an object accurately. Then, according to the number of frames each track has not been matched with any detection for, some active tracks retire and some retired tracks are deleted as in Sect. 5.3 for the retire-recall mechanism. The bounding box at current frame of an matched active track will be updated as the bounding box of its matched detection, after scaling and refinement if necessary. Then, for an unmatched active track, traditional tracker such as KCF is applied to decide its bounding box at current frame as a supplement. If KCF fails, its current bounding box will be updated using the trajectory prediction as in Sec. Trajectory Prediction as a further supplement. The updated bounding boxes at current frame of all active tracks with their track IDs will finally output from the whole framework. Algorithm 2 is performed for each frame. We eliminate the re-calculation of the same color histogram and correlation if calculated before by keeping them to reduce the computation. To better utilize the multi-core CPUs, OpenMP is used in many steps along the execution for multi-threading, including similarity distance calculation, bounding box scaling and refinement, trajectory prediction, KCF, etc. The calculation for different tracks or detections are mostly independent and thus suitable for multi-threading with high parallelism.

Algorithm 2. Whole Matching and Tracking Algorithm at Each Frame

Input: current frame detections D, existing active tracks T_a, existing retired tracks T_r

Output: updated active tracks T_a, updated retired tracks T_r

1 Similarity sorting-based matching to D & T_a;
2 IOU-based Hungarian matching to remaining unmatched D & T_a;
3 Similarity sorting-based matching to remaining unmatched D & T_r to recall some retired tracks to become active tracks ($T_r \rightarrow T_a$);
4 Initiate new active tracks in T_a for remain unmatched D from SmallNet with confidence > Th_{crt} or from LargeNet;
5 Delete tracks from T_r and move tracks from $T_a \rightarrow T_r$ according to the number of frames a track has not been matched with any detection for;
6 Update T_a using its matched D after necessary scaling and refinement;
7 Update T_a without matching using KCF or trajectory prediction.
8 **return** T_a,T_r for current frame.

Table 1. Overall MOT metrics

	MOTA↑	**FPS**↑	IDsw↓	FM↓	FP↓	FN↓	MOTP↑
Large-IOU	**47.0**	**8.1**	1733	1178	7663	11717	73.9
Large-Ours	**50.5**	**8.1**	367	1168	7661	11715	74.0
Small-Ours	**−17.3**	**46.3**	85	407	10347	36401	75.8
Hybrid-Ours	**44.5**	**37.2**	513	1308	4626	17024	71.1

6 Experiment Evaluation

The framework is implemented on NVIDIA Xavier platform based on DeepStream, TensorRT, OpenCV, etc. We test the performance on diverse videos in a real-time execution scenario, where 11 videos are generated from the training set of 2D MOT15 benchmark [14]. Yolo-v3 pre-trained on COCO dataset is used as LargeNet and Tiny-Yolo-v3 pre-trained on COCO dataset is used as SmallNet. The neural network switching interval N is set to 10. All experiments are performed on Xavier for a fair comparison.

6.1 Overall Performance

We use standard MOT metrics, whose details are in [2], to evaluate the performance of the detection and tracking task as in Table 1. ↑ in the table means the larger is the better while ↓ on the contrary. MOTA is the overall score to evaluate the detection and tracking accuracy, while FPS reflects the speed. The other MOT metrics are not important for the whole detection and tracking task compared to MOTA and most of them have been covered in MOTA. Large-IOU adopts LargeNet at each frame with IOU-based tracking, similar to previous works [4–6]. Large-Ours applies LargeNet at each frame with all our proposed techniques except bounding box scaling and refinement. Small-Ours uses SmallNet at each frame with our techniques. Hybrid-Ours is our proposed complete framework using hybrid neural networks in a time-multiplexing way with all our proposed techniques. All methods are implemented on Xavier for a fair comparison. Only using SmallNet gives an extremely bad accuracy but with a high speed. While only using LargeNet achieves good MOTA accuracy but with low speed, which cannot satisfy real-time requirement. Our framework with hybrid networks achieves both good MOTA and high speed. It increases the speed by 4.6× to LargeNet-only case, but maintains the similar level MOTA. By importing LargeNet information, it corrects the totally messy results of SmallNet-only case but still maintains a high speed. Furthermore, Large-Ours increases MOTA by 3.5 than Large-IOU and reduces ID switches (IDsw) by 78.8%, which shows our techniques, including space-aware color-based similarity, sorting-based matching, retire-recall mechanism, etc., achieve better tracking ability. Because the space-aware color feature used is more distinguishable and the retire-recall works well for occlusion case. Although targeting on different videos, the MOTA we achieve is at the similar level with other state-of-the-art works and even larger than the best 2D MOT 2015 results on the MOT Challenge website. Our method achieves state-of-the-art accuracy and high speed satisfying real-time requirement.

6.2 Technique Effect

Table 2. Effect of techniques

	MOTA↑	**FPS↑**	IDsw↓	FM↓	FP↓	FN↓	MOTP↑
No-partial-color	**38.5**	**38.2**	514	1733	6074	17942	70.1
No-refinement	**40.5**	**38.3**	600	1547	5369	17721	70.4
No-recall	**44.0**	**37.3**	660	1308	4627	17024	71.1
All(Hybrid-Ours)	**44.5**	**37.2**	513	1308	4626	17024	71.1
Merge	**44.5**	**17.0**	513	1308	4626	17024	71.1
No-OMP	**44.5**	**31.2**	513	1308	4626	17024	71.1

Algorithm Level. To see the effect of different algorithm level techniques we propose, three variations are derived from the complete framework. No-partial-color only uses one whole color histogram H to calculate the similarity distance. No-refinement does not apply the bounding box refinement as in Sect. 5.2. No-recall does not recall any retired tracks. All, the same as Hybrid-Ours, means our complete framework with all proposed techniques. As in Table 2, MOTA is decreased by 6, 4 and 0.5 without partial color histograms, bounding box refinement and retire-recall, respectively. Our novel usage of partial color histograms brings the largest benefit since both the space and color information can be considered into similarity estimation. Bounding box refinement also brings large benefit by correcting the SmallNet detection position. Retire-recall mechanism shows the largest effect in reducing ID switches, by 22.3% since it can recall retired tracks with an existing ID. All these techniques benefit the accuracy but with only little speed overhead and maintain the same level FPS.

System Level. At the system level, we design a highly pipelined structure as in Fig. 1 for the whole framework. If we merge the LargeNet, SmallNet and M&T into the same pipeline stage, the average speed will degrade to 17.0 FPS as Merge in Table 2. Our highly pipelined design brings 2.2× speedup by exploring the parallelism and fully utilizing all computing resources. In addition, we use OpenMP for multi-threading in the CPU execution as in Sect. 5.4. After disabling OpenMP, the average speed degrades to 31.2 FPS as No-OMP in Table 2. Using OpenMP brings 19.2% speedup by fully utilizing multi-core CPUs.

6.3 Platform-Specific Exploration

Table 3. FPS regarding platform-specific exploration

GPU-FP32 (Default)	GPU-INT8	GPU-FP16	DLA-FP16	Best-version	Default+HF-mode	Best-version+HF-mode
37.2	48.7	46.0	45.8	48.9	40.0	55.2

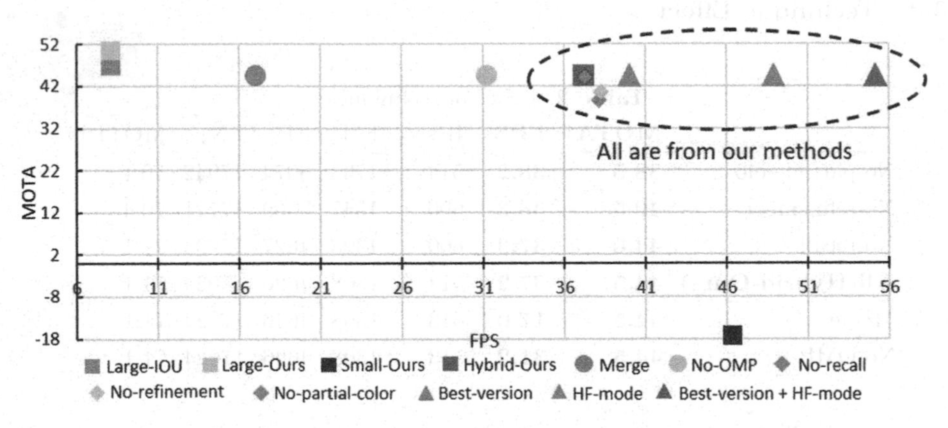

Fig. 9. Accuracy (MOTA) vs Speed (FPS)

Implementation Alternatives. TensorRT on Xavier platform provides different data precisions, including FP32, FP16 and INT8. Besides GPU, the neural network can also be implemented on the Deep Learning Accelerator (DLA) although only some layers supported. For both LargeNet and SmallNet, we try four implementations, GPU-FP32, GPU-FP16, GPU-INT8 and DLA-FP16. The default implementation in previous sections is GPU-FP32. The TensorRT we use only supports FP16 for DLA and the DLA-unsupported layers are executed on GPU. Calibration is used in GPU-INT8 to minimize the information loss. MOTA maintains at the same level as the implementation changes. Because

FP16 is enough to keep most information of the neural network and the calibration for INT8 is effective to minimize the information loss. Using low precisions, the speed is improved due to simpler computation. The highest achievable speed when varying the network implementations for each video respectively is 48.9 FPS on average, denoted as Best-version case, increased by 31.5% compared to the default GPU-FP32 case. The LargeNet is the speed bottleneck since varying the SmallNet implementation does not change the speed obviously while varying the LargeNet does. The average speed of whole framework is 37.2, 46.0, 48.7 and 45.8 FPS, when LargeNet adopts GPU-FP32, GPU-FP16, GPU-INT8 and DLA-FP16, respectively, as in Table 3. Using INT8 gives the largest speedup and two FP16 cases also show large speedup. GPU-FP16 is slightly better than DLA-FP16, since GPU executes faster than DLA and additional data transfer between layers executed on DLA and GPU occurs in DLA-FP16. When only using LargeNet at each frame, the average speed is 15.2, 15.4 and 16.8 FPS for DLA-FP16, GPU-FP16 and GPU-INT8, respectively. When only using SmallNet at each frame, the average speed is 47.9, 52.3, 59.3 FPS for DLA-FP16, GPU-FP16 and GPU-INT8, respectively. Our LargeNet-SmallNet hybrid framework achieves close speed to SmallNet-only case even for DLA-FP16, GPU-FP16 and GPU-INT8. The highest average speed for LargeNet-only case is 16.8 FPS from GPU-INT8, which is still outperformed by our hybrid framework by 2.9×.

High Frequency Mode. Xavier platform provides high frequency (HF) mode with higher clock frequency for computing engines. At this mode, our framework with default case, where both LargeNet and SmallNet adopt GPU-FP32, can achieve 40.0 FPS with a 2.8 FPS improvement as in Table 3. The Best-version case FPS can achieve 55.2 at HF mode with a 6.3 FPS improvement. Considering HF mode and different implementations of the networks, our framework can achieve 55.2 FPS while maintaining the MOTA of about 44.5, which is 6.8× faster than the LargeNet-only baseline with similar level high MOTA. Such a high FPS is beyond the real-time requirement and outperforms most existing works. From the MOT Challenge website, the speed we achieve ranks 12% among all state-of-the-art 2D MOT 2015 results and only 3 out of 89 state-of-the-art MOT 2016 results are faster than us. And we achieve much better accuracy than the works faster than us. Although targeting on different videos from these results, we can conclude that our framework achieves both state-of-the-art speed and accuracy.

6.4 Discussion

The detection and tracking accuracy in terms of MOTA and the speed in terms of FPS for most above evaluated cases are plotted in Fig. 9. All points in the top right are from our methods, which means our proposed methods achieve both high speed and accuracy, especially compared to the LargeNet-only and SmallNet-only cases as Large-IOU, Small-Ours, etc. Even though disabling some techniques, our framework still achieves a large improvement compared to the

SmallNet-only and LargeNet-only cases considering both accuracy and speed, as in No-recall, No-partial-color and No-refinement. Combining all proposed techniques, our complete framework, Hybrid-Ours, achieves high accuracy at high speed without typical drawbacks. Considering platform-specific optimizations as in Sect. 6.3, our framework, as in Best-version+HF-mode, achieves even higher FPS while maintaining the same level high MOTA. Our method, combining hybrid neural networks using many novel and useful techniques, achieves both state-of-the-art accuracy and speed.

The detection and tracking performance is highly dependent on the detection network. Yolo series used here is less accurate than some networks such as Faster-RCNN, Mask-RCNN, etc. Changing the networks is potential to further improve the performance like MOTA. The key of our method is combining networks with different accuracy-speed trade-offs in a time-interleaving way for both good accuracy and high speed. The LargeNet and SmallNet choices are not limited. The current network switching interval N is 10. Different N is allowed for speed-accuracy trade-offs. A larger N can show larger FPS but lower MOTA. It is also possible to not use any network at some frame to skip the detection and tracking but directly keep the results from the last frame. Such frame skip can be combined with our method to achieve a higher speed while sacrificing accuracy. Moreover, our method is able to mitigate to other platforms than Xavier.

7 Conclusion

We present a novel framework to combine hybrid DNNs with different accuracy-speed trade-offs in a time-multiplexing way for real-time multi-object detection and tracking. By import the tracking knowledge into detection, we allow an inaccurate but fast small DNN for detection in most frames and successfully recover its accuracy loss. By combining different DNNs with space-aware color information, we achieve both state-of-the-art high speed and accuracy. Targeting NVIDIA Xavier, we further optimize the implementation from system and platform level. We achieve 6.8× speedup with similar level high accuracy compared to the traditional large DNN only method on Xavier.

References

1. Abdelali, H.A., et al.: Fast and robust object tracking via accept-reject color histogram-based method. J. Vis. Commun. Image Represent. **34**, 219–229 (2016)
2. Bernardin, K., Stiefelhagen, R.: Evaluating multiple object tracking performance: the CLEAR MOT metrics. J. Image Video Process. **2008**, 1 (2008)
3. Bewley, A., et al.: Alextrac: affinity learning by exploring temporal reinforcement within association chains. In: ICRA, pp. 2212–2218. IEEE (2016)
4. Bewley, A., et al.: Simple online and realtime tracking. In: ICIP, pp. 3464–3468. IEEE (2016)
5. Bochinski, E., et al.: High-speed tracking-by-detection without using image information. In: AVSS, pp. 1–6. IEEE (2017)

6. Bochinski, E., et al.: Extending IOU based multi-object tracking by visual information. In: AVSS, pp. 1–6. IEEE (2018)
7. Danelljan, M., et al.: Adaptive color attributes for real-time visual tracking. In: CVPR, pp. 1090–1097 (2014)
8. Dollár, P., et al.: Fast feature pyramids for object detection. TPAMI **36**(8), 1532–1545 (2014)
9. Hamid Rezatofighi, S., et al.: Joint probabilistic data association revisited. In: ICCV, pp. 3047–3055 (2015)
10. Han, S., et al.: Learning both weights and connections for efficient neural network. In: Advances in Neural Information Processing Systems, pp. 1135–1143 (2015)
11. He, K., et al.: Mask R-CNN. In: ICCV, pp. 2961–2969 (2017)
12. Hubara, I., et al.: Quantized neural networks: training neural networks with low precision weights and activations. J. Mach. Learn. Res. **18**(1), 6869–6898 (2017)
13. Kim, C., et al.: Multiple hypothesis tracking revisited. In: ICCV, pp. 4696–4704 (2015)
14. Leal-Taixé, L., et al.: Motchallenge 2015: towards a benchmark for multi-target tracking. arXiv:1504.01942 (2015)
15. Liu, W., et al.: SSD: single shot MultiBox detector. In: Leibe, B., Matas, J., Sebe, N., Welling, M. (eds.) ECCV 2016. LNCS, vol. 9905, pp. 21–37. Springer, Cham (2016). https://doi.org/10.1007/978-3-319-46448-0_2
16. Possegger, H., et al.: In defense of color-based model-free tracking. In: CVPR, pp. 2113–2120 (2015)
17. Redmon, J., Farhadi, A.: YOLOv3: an incremental improvement. arXiv:1804.02767 (2018)
18. Ren, S., et al.: Faster R-CNN: towards real-time object detection with region proposal networks. In: Advances in Neural Information Processing Systems, pp. 91–99 (2015)
19. Van De Weijer, J., et al.: Learning color names for real-world applications. TIP **18**(7), 1512–1523 (2009)
20. Wojke, N., et al.: Simple online and realtime tracking with a deep association metric. In: ICIP, pp. 3645–3649. IEEE (2017)
21. Womg, A., et al.: Tiny SSD: a tiny single-shot detection deep convolutional neural network for real-time embedded object detection. In: CRV, pp. 95–101. IEEE (2018)
22. Xiang, Y., et al.: Learning to track: Online multi-object tracking by decision making. In: ICCV, pp. 4705–4713 (2015)
23. Yang, B., Nevatia, R.: An online learned CRF model for multi-target tracking. In: CVPR, pp. 2034–2041. IEEE (2012)
24. Yu, F., Li, W., Li, Q., Liu, Y., Shi, X., Yan, J.: POI: multiple object tracking with high performance detection and appearance feature. In: Hua, G., Jégou, H. (eds.) ECCV 2016. LNCS, vol. 9914, pp. 36–42. Springer, Cham (2016). https://doi.org/10.1007/978-3-319-48881-3_3
25. Zhang, L., et al.: Global data association for multi-object tracking using network flows. In: CVPR, pp. 1–8. IEEE (2008)
26. Zhu, G., et al.: MC-HOG correlation tracking with saliency proposal. In: 30th AAAI (2016)

Continuous Motion Numeral Recognition Using RNN Architecture in Air-Writing Environment

Adil Rahman[1(✉)], Prasun Roy[2], and Umapada Pal[2]

[1] Department of Information Technology,
Heritage Institute of Technology, Kolkata, India
adil.rahman.it20@heritageit.edu.in

[2] Computer Vision and Pattern Recognition Unit,
Indian Statistical Institute, Kolkata, India
prasunroy.pr@gmail.com, umapada@isical.ac.in

Abstract. Air-writing, defined as character tracing in a three dimensional free space through hand gestures, is the way forward for peripheral-independent, virtual interaction with devices. While single unistroke character recognition is fairly simple, continuous writing recognition becomes challenging owing to absence of delimiters between characters. Moreover, stray hand motion while writing adds noise to the input, making accurate recognition difficult. The key to accurate recognition of air-written characters lies in noise elimination and character segmentation from continuous writing. We propose a robust and hardware-independent framework for multi-digit unistroke numeral recognition in air-writing environment. We present a sliding window based method which isolates a small segment of the spatio-temporal input from the air-writing activity for noise removal and digit segmentation. Recurrent Neural Networks (RNN) show great promise in dealing with temporal data and is the basis of our architecture. Recognition of digits which have other digits as their sub-shapes is challenging. Capitalizing on how digits are commonly written, we propose a novel priority scheme to determine digit precedence. We only use sequential coordinates as input, which can be obtained from any generic camera, making our system widely accessible. Our experiments were conducted on English numerals using a combination of MNIST and Pendigits datasets along with our own air-written English numerals dataset (ISI-Air Dataset). Additionally, we have created a noise dataset to classify noise. We observe a drop in accuracy with increase in the number of digits written in a single continuous motion because of noise generated between digit transitions. However, under standard conditions, our system produced an accuracy of 98.45% and 82.89% for single and multiple digit English numerals, respectively.

Keywords: Air writing · Handwritten character recognition · Human-computer interaction · Long short term memory · Recurrent Neural Network

S. Palaiahnakote et al. (Eds.): ACPR 2019, LNCS 12046, pp. 76–90, 2020.
https://doi.org/10.1007/978-3-030-41404-7_6

1 Introduction

Recent advancements in gesture recognition and motion tracking have opened up new avenues in human-computer interaction. Most conventional devices use a keyboard, mouse or a touchscreen as their input medium. In some cases, however, these input options may not be available or suitable. Gesture and motion tracking algorithms have introduced simpler and more advanced interaction mechanisms for the user, involving simple patterns in the form of hand gestures that the user memorizes as shortcuts to certain commands. These simple patterns, however, are not sufficient for the detection of complex string input.

"Air-writing", referred to as the writing of characters using free hand movements in three-dimensional space utilizing six degrees of freedom, is a promising advancement towards equipment-independent human-computer interaction. This bears its own set of challenges for identification of characters, and gets more complex for a string of characters. The initial challenge is to track the motion of an object (finger, pen, etc.) using which the user writes on an imaginary surface. Air-writing lacks haptic feedback. Two dimensional input space has the benefit of concrete anchor points and pen-up/pen-down delimiters to separate consecutive characters. These advantages are lost when the characters are drawn in a three dimensional free space. With the recent advent of advanced motion tracking devices with depth sensors like LEAP Motion [2] and Kinect [1], equivalents of the pen-up and pen-down gestures may be captured, even in three-dimensional space. However, these ancillary sensors are expensive and not available in most of the common devices, inhibiting general accessibility to such systems. Almost all smart devices are equipped with a camera these days. It is thus far more feasible to relay the input directly to a generic device camera for recognition.

The challenge persists for recognition of a string of characters which requires character segmentation. There is an absence of delimiters between characters, since device cameras lack stereoscopic information that is crucial for decent recognition accuracy. Presence of redundant strokes between characters, along with stray marker movements, contributes to the noise present in the air-written input. Moreover, some characters might be sub-shapes of other characters. For instance, 0 is a sub-shape of 9. This makes it hard to determine if a character has been completely constructed and the user is ready to move on to the next

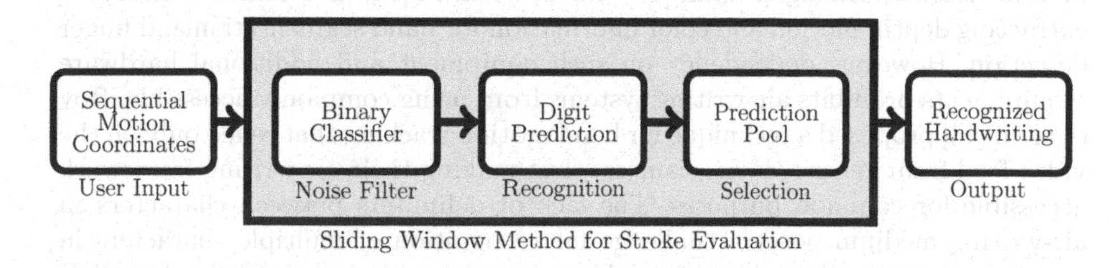

Fig. 1. Air-writing numeral recognition system overview

character or if the character is still being traced by the user. For words that are constructed from alphabets corresponding to a particular language, recognition accuracy is often boosted by referring a language model [5,6] that corrects the recognized word to the most likely word. However, this technique is impractical in case of numbers due to the lack of a language model that predicts what the numbers are most likely to be.

Our present work employs marker-based segmentation as introduced by Roy et al. in [13]. Requiring only a simple device camera input, they have made the need for expensive hardware equipment redundant. For the purpose of efficient segmentation, we have incorporated a sliding window approach in our Long-Short Term Memory (LSTM) model. LSTM is a promising neural network model for spatio-temporal data like air-writing. We have incorporated a dual-network architecture for noise elimination and numeral recognition. We have introduced a novel priority scheme to tackle the problem of recognizing digits which involve sub-shapes of other digits. An overview of our system is presented in Fig. 1. Our method eliminates the use of language models which are inherently unsuitable for certain forms of input like numbers, names and alpha-numeral entries. We instead present a language-independent model that focuses on character-wise recognition, as opposed to word recognition. We have performed our experiments on English numerals, training our recognition model using Pendigits, MNIST, and ISI-Air, which is our custom English numeral air-writing dataset. For noise elimination, we have created a noise dataset using various possible combinations of digits and stray motions in our air-writing environment.

The rest of this paper is organized as follows. The next section explores the research previously done in this field. Section 3 outlines our proposed methodology. The experimental results have been provided and discussed in Sect. 4. Section 5 concludes the paper.

2 Related Works

Hardware support has been the crux of most air writing approaches that rely on tracking hand movements and gestures. Amma et al. [3] wirelessly captured hand gestures by attaching motion sensors with accelerometers and gyroscopes to the back of the user's hand. Chen et al. in [6] came up with a controller-free technique where they used LEAP motion capture device for continuous finger motion tracking. Zhang et al. in [15] and Ye et al. in [14] used Kinect sensors for extracting depth, motion and color information for hand segmentation and finger detection. However, dependency on such equipment and additional hardware requirements prohibits air-writing systems from being commonly accessible. Roy et al. in [13] proposed a technique for hand motion tracking that relied only on the video feed from generic device camera, thus making their air-writing framework accessible for common purposes. The lack of delimiters between characters in air-writing medium poses a challenge for recognition of multiple characters in a continuous flow. To tackle this problem, several authors have defined explicit manual delimiters to distinguish each character from the next. Kim et al. [10]

have solved the lack of distinction between pen-ups and pen-downs by using a 3D handwriting ligature model that describes the shapes of pen-up motions. Huang et al. [8] defined explicit hand gestures to signify character segmentation. Roy et al. [13] have used Convolutional Neural Network (CNN) as the character recognition model where they defined a velocity threshold criterion to indicate the end of a character. Oh et al. in [12] used Fisher Discriminant Analysis for character recognition. However, these works remain limited to recognizing single unistroke characters only and fail in case of multiple characters drawn in a continuous motion. A window-based algorithm has been adopted in previous works [4,6] but the window properties and operations are based on empirically decided time or velocity constants, both of which are user-dependent factors and thus may not function universally. Amma et al. in [3,4] used Hidden Markov Model (HMM) for continuous text recognition in air writing, as have Chen et al. in [6] and Lee et al. in [11]. Junker et al. [9] have used a similarity search method for the initial stage in continuous gesture recognition, and have used HMM in the second phase for further classification. These works take advantage of the spatio-temporal property of the input for multiple character recognition. HMM has been a popular choice in continuous writing recognition models, given its effectiveness in working with temporal data and implicit segmentation abilities.

To the best of our knowledge, there hasn't been any previous consideration to a character being a sub-shape of its successor in a string. Moreover, most of these works rely on expensive hardware equipment that are not commonly available. In our work, we use video feed from the generic webcams, with Recurrent Neural Network (RNN) as the recognition model, which is more efficient than HMM for spatio-temporal data. Prediction is done using only sequential coordinate information. Details like velocity and time taken to write haven't been taken into consideration owing to its variability among different users, making it a poor classification feature. An additional priority scheme tackles the issue of recognition of digits which have some other digit as their sub-shape.

3 Proposed Methodology

3.1 Motion Tracking Method

We have adopted this method from the previous work of Roy et al. [13] for detecting and tracking the input coordinates from the video feed. To avoid the complexities of the range of variability of skin tone for finger tracking, a simple marker of a fixed color has been used for tracing characters. The visible portion of the marker can then be segmented from the background using a color segmentation technique. The segmented binary image thus obtained is used for identifying the marker by eliminating the noise. If the color of the marker can be distinctly demarcated from the background, the contour with the largest area in the segmented image is considered to be the marker, with its tip as the topmost point on the contour boundary with the lowest y-coordinate value. The air-writing input coordinates consist of a sequential set of points. The number of frames rendered per second is estimated as $N_{FPS} = \frac{1}{t_{update}}$, where t_{update} is the time taken to process the last video frame. Let the changes in the position of the marker between two consecutive frames in the x and y directions be Δ_x andΔ_y, respectively. The normalized instantaneous velocity of the tip of the marker is computed as:

$$dx = \frac{1}{N_{FPS}} \sum_{t}^{t+N_{FPS}} \Delta_x \quad \text{and} \quad dy = \frac{1}{N_{FPS}} \sum_{t}^{t+N_{FPS}} \Delta_y$$

In order to interpret when the user has finished writing a string of characters, a velocity threshold v_t is used. If both dx and dy are less than v_t, it is assumed that the marker is static and the user has finished tracing the string of characters. The trajectory of the marker for the input string of characters is approximated as straight line segments between marker tip positions in each consecutive video frame while the tip is in motion.

3.2 Numeral Recognition

In case of a single digit being traced out in a three-dimensional environment, digit prediction can be done simply by passing the final frame to a recognition model. However, in the case of string of digits written continuously one after the other in a three-dimensional environment, i.e., without the presence of delimiters, it becomes challenging to isolate and recognize the digits from the input. Therefore, for predicting such types of inputs, we need to analyze the entire motion in which the digits have been traced out.

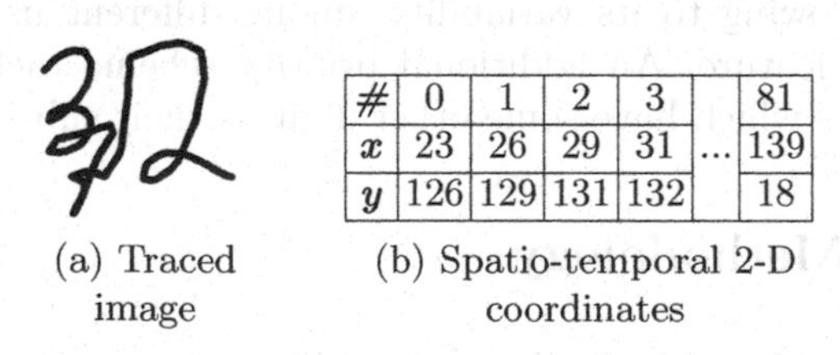

#	0	1	2	3		81
x	23	26	29	31	...	139
y	126	129	131	132		18

(a) Traced image (b) Spatio-temporal 2-D coordinates

Fig. 2. Air-writing gestures recorded as sequential coordinates

The input to our system is thus in the form of a spatio-temporal series of data as seen in Fig. 2. The data is solely in the form of a sequential set of points, as traced by the marker tip in the video frames. Other information like velocity of the marker tip and time taken by the user to draw the stroke is not recorded as input to our system, owing to the variability of writing speeds of different people and the frame lag in different video capturing devices.

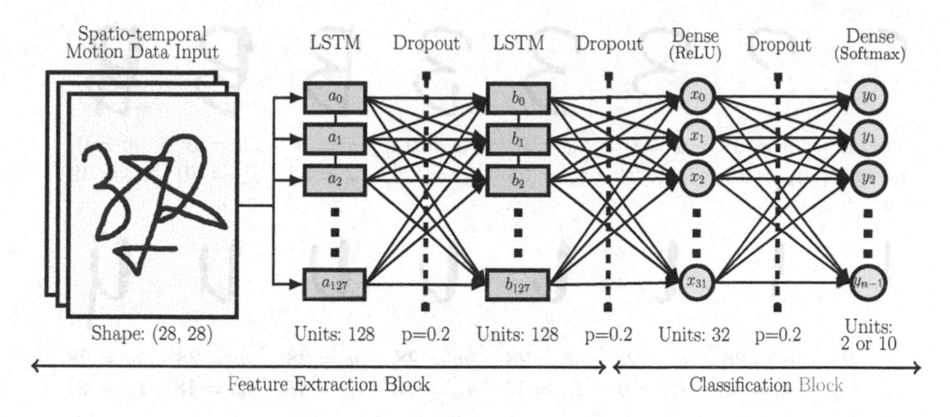

Fig. 3. RNN-LSTM architecture employed in our methodology

Dual Network Configuration: Upon analyzing the input, we observe a lot of noisy signals derived from the presence of stray hand motion and overlapping digits written in a continuous motion. This noise hinders numeral prediction. Thus, to overcome this problem, we propose a dual network configuration. The dual network removes noise and subsequently detects digits. It consists of a binary classifier for noise filtration and another 10-class classifier for digit recognition. Owing to the temporal nature of the input, we have decided to use RNN-LSTM architecture as illustrated in Fig. 3 for both the networks, given their suitability for such types of inputs.

The architecture of the employed network (Fig. 3) consists of a feature extraction block followed by a classification block. A 28×28 grayscale serves as the input for the feature extraction block which is passed through two consecutive LSTM layers. Both LSTM layers have 128 hidden units and use rectified linear units (ReLU) as their activation function. The classification layer comprises of two fully connected layers having 32 and n neurons, respectively, where n is 2 in case of binary classifier and 10 in case of 10-class digit classifier. The two fully connected layer use ReLU and softmax as their activation functions, respectively. A dropout layer with a p-value of 0.2 has been employed between every layer in our network to minimize the possibility of overfitting.

Sliding Window: Since the input data is in the form of a continuous motion, we need to isolate parts of the motion to detect the digits. Lack of delimiters between digits necessitates the scanning of motion from the very beginning, until the first digit is identified. Upon identification of the first digit, we record the detected digit and discard all motion data till that point. A fresh scan is started there onward and the process is repeated until the entire motion has been analyzed. We have employed a sliding window-based approach in conjunction with our dual network configuration to facilitate this process. To prevent scanning the entire motion data repeatedly, the sliding window isolates parts of the motion data for analysis, thus improving performance. The sliding window is characterized by

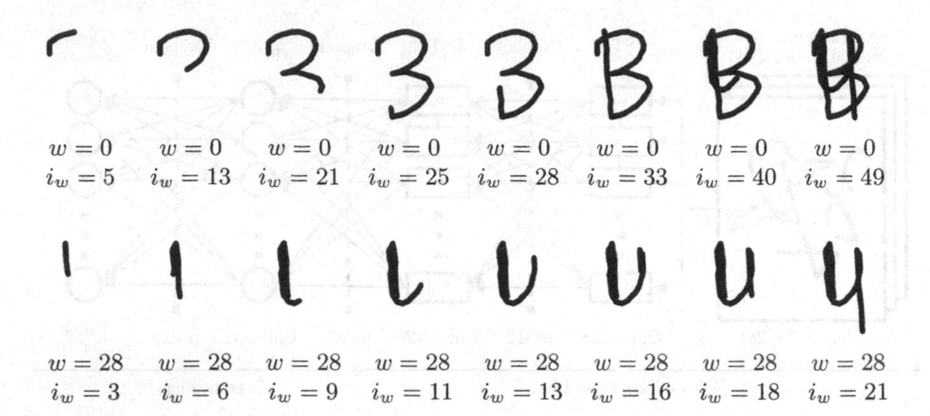

Fig. 4. Example of sliding window with a split at the 28th index, where w denotes the starting index and i_w denotes the index of the frame relative to w

four properties - window index, window size, split index and point threshold. Window index (w), initialized as 0, is a variable which determines the starting point of the window relative to the first motion data point. Window size (W) is a constant defining the number of consecutive data points to be analyzed at any particular instance from the entire motion data. A large window size affects performance whereas a small window size affects recognition. Empirically, an optimal value of 40 has been determined. Split index (s) is defined as the index of the point relative to the sliding window where a digit has been detected. The split index is responsible for shifting the window by modifying the value of the window index as $w' = w + s$, where w' is the new window index. In case no digit is detected in the window, the split index defaults to 5 and consequently, the window shifts by 5 data points. Point threshold (θ) is a constant which can be defined as the minimum number of data points required for the sliding window to function. For our experiments, we empirically found 10 to be the optimal point threshold value. This property defines the termination criterion as $n - w \leq \theta$, where n is the total number of data points. A sliding window example is provided in Fig. 4.

Priority Scheme: In a string of digits, a digit might be a sub-shape of the next digit, like 0 is a sub-shape of 9 and 2 is a sub-shape of 3. Also, since all the digits are traced in a single continuous stroke, the transition between two digits may create an undesirable intermediate digit. For instance, if a '2' is drawn after a '6' in the air-writing environment, the resultant trace may first resemble a '6' and then an '8'. The substring '62' could thus be mispredicted as '8' since it is the final prediction, as demonstrated in Fig. 5. Such scenarios may challenge how digit predictions are made in the sliding window methods.

Our approach capitalizes on the way digits are generally written. We use both our custom air-writing dataset and Pendigits dataset which contain the sequential motion coordinate information of each digit. We pass these coordinates as

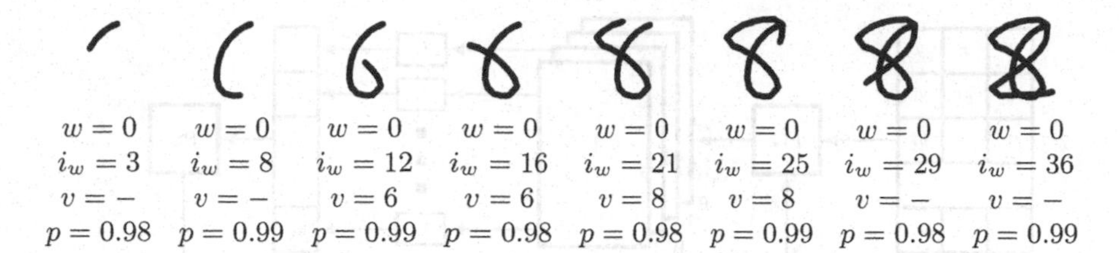

Fig. 5. 2D Trajectory traced out for the string '62' by the user, where w denotes the starting index of the window, i_w denotes the index of the frame relative to w, v denotes the predicted value, and p denotes the prediction confidence

inputs to our sliding-window based classifier, and then obtain the possible classifications that formation of any digit can give (for example: when drawing '3', the sequential classification may first recognize '0', then '2', and then finally '3'). Such results are recorded for each and every digit in our dataset. Using a statistical model, we extracted the possible digits that may occur before a desired digit is drawn and projected it in a *Priority Matrix (PM)*, as illustrated in Fig. 6. Each element in the priority matrix can have 3 values: $+1$ if digit x is a sub-shape of digit y $(x \neq y)$, 0 if $x = y$ and -1 otherwise. If $PM[x, y]$ for two consecutive digits is $+1$, then the resultant prediction gets updated from x to y. At the end of the window, the values from the classifier and the priority function are passed as the final results.

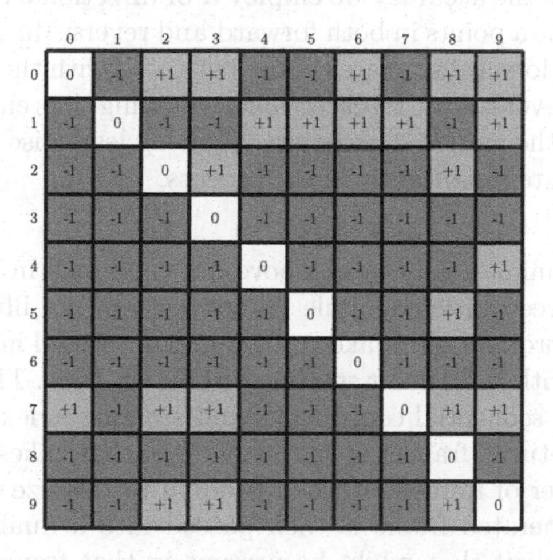

	0	1	2	3	4	5	6	7	8	9
0	0	-1	+1	+1	-1	-1	+1	-1	+1	+1
1	-1	0	-1	-1	+1	+1	+1	+1	-1	+1
2	-1	-1	0	+1	-1	-1	-1	-1	+1	-1
3	-1	-1	-1	0	-1	-1	-1	-1	-1	-1
4	-1	-1	-1	-1	0	-1	-1	-1	-1	+1
5	-1	-1	-1	-1	-1	0	-1	-1	+1	-1
6	-1	-1	-1	-1	-1	-1	0	-1	-1	-1
7	+1	-1	+1	+1	-1	-1	-1	0	+1	+1
8	-1	-1	-1	-1	-1	-1	-1	-1	0	-1
9	-1	-1	+1	+1	-1	-1	-1	-1	+1	0

Fig. 6. Priority matrix for English numerals

Bi-directional Scan: When digits are written in a continuous motion, transitional strokes between digits start adding up as noise. With an increase in the number of digits drawn in a single continuous motion, the noise accumulates, making it increasingly difficult to detect digits as we progress along the air-written string

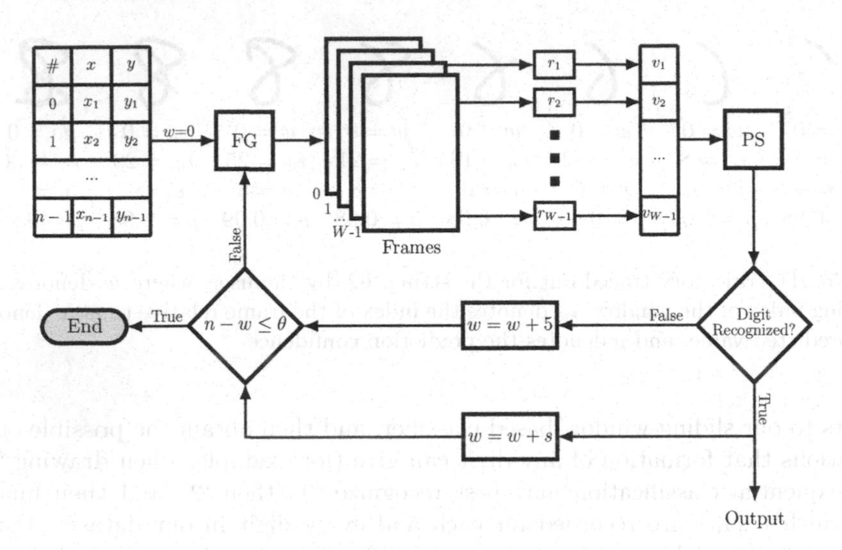

Fig. 7. Pipeline of our system. r_i and v_i denote classifier and predicted value for the ith frame respectively. W denotes the size of the sliding window, w denotes the starting index of the sliding window, s is the split index, θ is the point threshold, and n is the total number of data points. FG and PS stand for Frame Generator and Priority Scheme respectively.

of digits. To improve the accuracy we employ a bi-directional scanning technique where we scan the data points in both forward and reverse directions. The results of the second half of forward scan are then substituted with the reversed results of the first half of the reverse scan. Bi-directional scanning thus employs two starting points for scanning the motion data points, allowing less noise to accumulate and reducing the error rate significantly in the process.

Pipeline: The techniques delineated above are combined in a pipeline to facilitate the numeral recognition module of our system, as illustrated in Fig. 7. Spatio-temporal coordinates are taken as inputs and passed into the Frame Generator (FG) along with the default starting index (w) value. The frame generator takes in two inputs: sequential coordinates and starting index value for the sliding window, and returns frames of motion traces that takes place inside that window. The number of frames returned is equal to the size of the sliding window (W). Each generated frame is then passed into a dual-network classifier which predicts the digit that might be present in that frame. All such predictions along with their frame indices are stored in an array which we refer to as *Prediction Pool.* The prediction pool is then analyzed using the Priority Scheme (PS). If a digit is recognized, it is considered an output, and the window index is updated using the split index value. If no digit is recognized, then the window index is updated by a default value of 5. Termination criteria is checked, and if not met, the updated window index is passed on to the frame generator and the process is repeated.

4 Results and Discussion

4.1 Data Collection

To the best of our knowledge, there is no publicly available standard air-writing dataset. For this project, we developed ISI-Air, a custom English numeral air-writing dataset with 8000 samples recorded by 16 persons, each recording 50 samples per digit. The numerals were traced in three dimensional space with a uniformly colored marker and the data was recorded using a generic video camera. The marker was segmented, the marker tip was identified and its trajectory was approximated. The recorded trajectory coordinates were tagged with their numerical labels and saved. Pendigits is a standard online handwritten English numeral dataset, consisting of 5120 samples of online handwritten English numerals. However, its data samples were recorded using a digital pen on a pressure-sensitive tablet which comes with pen-up/pen-down motion. We have tweaked the Pendigits dataset to remove every pen-up and pen-down instance by connecting the coordinates before and after the pen-up and pen-down motion, respectively, thus emulating the air-writing environment. We have also used the MNIST dataset in our experiments, given its ubiquitous usage and owing to the similarity between handwritten and air-written numerals and for exhaustive benchmarking purposes. It comprises 70000 samples of handwritten English numerals. All the aforementioned datasets are split into training and test sets. The dataset distribution, as used in our experiments, is shown in Table 1.

Table 1. Dataset distribution for English numerals

Index	Type	Source dataset	#Sample	#Training	#Test
DS-1	Offline, Handwritten	MNIST	70000	60000	10000
DS-2	Online, Handwritten	Pendigits	5120	2560	2560
DS-3	Online, Air-Written	ISI-Air	8000	5000	3000

Noise Dataset: Noise elimination is crucial for obtaining better recognition accuracy in an air-writing environment. While certain stray motions which add to the overall noise in the system are random in nature, a majority of the noise can be attributed to the extra motion in the data while making transitions from one digit to another. To counter this issue, we used the same method as the creation of our air-writing dataset and recorded transitions between every pair of English numerals (00, 01, 02, up to 99). We then extracted the frames of each transition from the point at which the first digit was traced completely and the second digit had started to overlap the first digit, as illustrated in Fig. 8. The composition and distribution of our noise dataset is shown in Table 2. Training an LSTM network with this noise dataset yielded a validation accuracy and loss of 99.16% and 0.0245, respectively.

Fig. 8. Some noise samples

Table 2. Composition and distribution of the noise dataset

Index	Type	Source	Class	#Sample	#Training	#Test
–	Noise	Air-Writing	Positive	10000	6000	4000
–	English numerals	DS-1, DS-2, DS-3	Negative	10000	6000	4000
NZ-1	Collective noise dataset	–	–	20000	12000	8000

4.2 Experimental Setup

An LSTM network was trained for noise elimination using the noise dataset (NZ-1). For numeral recognition, an evaluation set (EVAL) was made by combining the test splits from DS-1, DS-2 and DS-3. A second LSTM network was trained and tested using various combinations of the datasets as follows:

1. Training with DS-1 and testing on EVAL
2. Training with DS-1 and DS-2 combined and testing on EVAL
3. Training with DS-1 and DS-3 combined and testing on EVAL
4. Training with DS-1, DS-2 and DS-3 combined and testing on EVAL

Given the widespread usage and the volume of the MNIST dataset (DS-1), we have maintained it as a baseline and is thus a constant in all training sets.

4.3 Result

We have tabulated the results from our experiments on set EVAL in Table 3, obtained using the aforementioned combinations of datasets for training and validation. We observe maximum validation accuracy and minimum validation loss for training set TS-D.

The final tests on the trained models have been performed on single digits from our ISI-Air dataset and the results have been tabulated in Table 4. Here too, we observe the highest single digit recognition accuracy on training set TS-D which stands at 98.45%. Owing to the difference in evaluation methods and lack of a standardized dataset, the results of our system is not directly comparable with those of previous works. However, under comparable evaluation conditions, the results obtained for the model trained on TS-D when tested with isolated digits from ISI-Air outperforms the recognition accuracy values for isolated English numerals achieved by Roy et al. in [13] by 0.75% and that achieved by Dash et al. [7] by 6.75%.

Table 3. Validation accuracy for various training sets

Index	Training set	Test set	Accuracy	Loss
TS-A	DS-1	EVAL	87.74%	0.6817
TS-B	DS-1 + DS-2	EVAL	96.72%	0.1279
TS-C	DS-1 + DS-3	EVAL	96.43%	0.1496
TS-D	**DS-1 + DS-2 + DS-3**	**EVAL**	**98.07%**	**0.0682**

Table 4. Test accuracy for single digit English numeral recognition

Training set	TS-A	TS-B	TS-C	TS-D
Accuracy	65.35%	90.09%	98.20%	**98.45%**

Table 5. Test accuracy for multi-digit English numeral recognition

Digit count	Test sample	Training set	Forward scan accuracy	Bi-directional scan accuracy
2	100	TS-A	51.50%	59.50%
		TS-B	79.00%	88.50%
		TS-C	84.00%	96.50%
		TS-D	**84.50%**	**97.00%**
3	100	TS-A	40.33%	48.00%
		TS-B	65.00%	77.33%
		TS-C	72.67%	86.67%
		TS-D	**73.33%**	**87.67%**
4	100	TS-A	31.75%	39.25%
		TS-B	55.00%	66.25%
		TS-C	63.75%	71.50%
		TS-D	**64.50%**	**72.25%**

For our experiments on multi-digit recognition, we have considered 100 samples of numeral strings of length 2, 3 and 4 each, and we present the results for both forward and bi-directional scanning of these in Table 5. The cumulative average accuracy achieved for multi-digit English numeral recognition is 82.89%.

4.4 Error Analysis

The confusion matrices derived from our experiments have been shown in Fig. 9. The performance of our recognition model improves significantly when the air-writing dataset is incorporated for training. Using a combination of parts of MNIST, Pendigits and our own air-written dataset in EVAL for fine tuning purposes ensures versatility of our system in the kind of data it can handle. As can

Table 6. Some misclassified noise samples

Sample					
Actual Class	Noise	Noise	Noise	Noise	Noise
Predicted Class	5	8	7	6	4
Confidence	97.85%	97.94%	98.85%	97.12%	99.35%

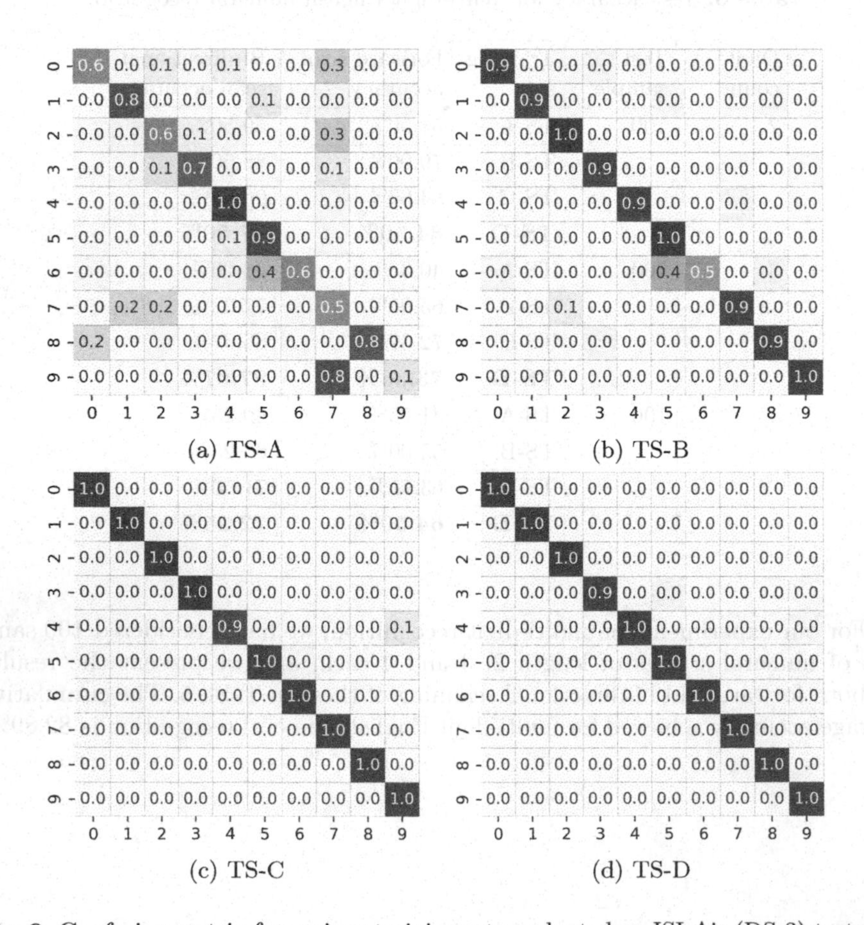

(a) TS-A (b) TS-B

(c) TS-C (d) TS-D

Fig. 9. Confusion matrix for various training sets evaluated on ISI-Air (DS-3) test set

be observed from Table 4, recognition accuracy is very poor for the model that has only been trained on handwritten digits (TS-A), and improves significantly upon incorporation of Pendigits in TS-B, and further upon using ISI-Air in TS-C and TS-D. In Table 5, we observe a decrease in the recognition accuracy with increase in number of digits in a single stroke. This gradual decrease in accuracy is attributed to noise accumulation. Bi-directional scanning boosts performance by scanning the string in reverse as well to avoid too much noise accumulation by the time the last few digits in the string are reached. The focus of our work is a demonstration of identification of split points in numerals without the use of sensors. As can be observed from the confusion matrices, our framework achieves a fairly robust recognition of air-written numerals in real time. Some noise samples misclassified as digits have been presented in Table 6.

5 Conclusion

In this study, a robust and hardware-independent framework is proposed for multi-digit unistroke air-written numeral recognition. While the tests are performed on English numerals, the proposed methodology is language-independent. To make the framework universally applicable, usage of language models have been avoided since they are redundant for some input forms. The priority scheme proposed in our methodology avoids recognition of any undesirable digit in a unistroke motion and resolves the issue of recognition of digits which are sub shapes of their succeeding digits. In our experiments, the proposed methodology achieved an accuracy of 98.45% and 82.89% for the recognition of single and multi-digit numerals, respectively. The work is independent of any external motion tracking or depth sensing hardwares like Kinect and LEAP motion, making it highly accessible. Our custom online air-written English numeral dataset ISI-Air is freely available for research purposes at https://github.com/adildsw/ISI-Air. We are presently working on improving the accuracy for lengthier strings and eliminating the need of dedicated noise datasets for individual languages by analyzing the sub-strokes involved in tracing numerals.

References

1. Leap Motion Inc. LEAP Motion (2010). https://www.leapmotion.com/
2. Microsoft Corporation. Kinect (2010). https://developer.microsoft.com/en-us/windows/kinect/
3. Amma, C., Gehrig, D., Schultz, T.: Airwriting recognition using wearable motion sensors. In: Proceedings of the 1st Augmented Human International Conference, p. 10. ACM (2010)
4. Amma, C., Georgi, M., Schultz, T.: Airwriting: hands-free mobile text input by spotting and continuous recognition of 3D-space handwriting with inertial sensors. In: 2012 16th International Symposium on Wearable Computers, pp. 52–59. IEEE (2012)

5. Chen, M., AlRegib, G., Juang, B.H.: Air-writing recognition–Part I: modeling and recognition of characters, words, and connecting motions. IEEE Trans. Hum.-Mach. Syst. **46**(3), 403–413 (2015)
6. Chen, M., AlRegib, G., Juang, B.H.: Air-writing recognition–Part II: detection and recognition of writing activity in continuous stream of motion data. IEEE Trans. Hum.-Mach. Syst. **46**(3), 436–444 (2015)
7. Dash, A., et al.: Airscript-creating documents in air. In: 2017 14th IAPR International Conference on Document Analysis and Recognition (ICDAR), vol. 1, pp. 908–913. IEEE (2017)
8. Huang, Y., Liu, X., Jin, L., Zhang, X.: Deepfinger: a cascade convolutional neuron network approach to finger key point detection in egocentric vision with mobile camera. In: 2015 IEEE International Conference on Systems, Man, and Cybernetics, pp. 2944–2949. IEEE (2015)
9. Junker, H., Amft, O., Lukowicz, P., Tröster, G.: Gesture spotting with body-worn inertial sensors to detect user activities. Pattern Recogn. **41**(6), 2010–2024 (2008)
10. Kim, D.H., Choi, H.I., Kim, J.H.: 3D space handwriting recognition with ligature model. In: Youn, H.Y., Kim, M., Morikawa, H. (eds.) UCS 2006. LNCS, vol. 4239, pp. 41–56. Springer, Heidelberg (2006). https://doi.org/10.1007/11890348_4
11. Lee, H.K., Kim, J.H.: An hmm-based threshold model approach for gesture recognition. IEEE Trans. Pattern Anal. Mach. Intell. **10**, 961–973 (1999)
12. Oh, J.K., et al.: Inertial sensor based recognition of 3-D character gestures with an ensemble classifiers. In: Ninth International Workshop on Frontiers in Handwriting Recognition, pp. 112–117. IEEE (2004)
13. Roy, P., Ghosh, S., Pal, U.: A CNN based framework for unistroke numeral recognition in air-writing. In: 2018 16th International Conference on Frontiers in Handwriting Recognition (ICFHR), pp. 404–409. IEEE (2018)
14. Ye, Z., Zhang, X., Jin, L., Feng, Z., Xu, S.: Finger-writing-in-the-air system using kinect sensor. In: 2013 IEEE International Conference on Multimedia and Expo Workshops (ICMEW), pp. 1–4. IEEE (2013)
15. Zhang, X., Ye, Z., Jin, L., Feng, Z., Xu, S.: A new writing experience: finger writing in the air using a kinect sensor. IEEE Multimedia **20**(4), 85–93 (2013)

Using Motion Compensation and Matrix Completion Algorithm to Remove Rain Streaks and Snow for Video Sequences

Yutong Zhou(✉) and Nobutaka Shimada

Ritsumeikan University, 1-1-1 Noji-higashi, Kusatsu, Shiga 525-8577, Japan
zhou@i.ci.ritsumei.ac.jp

Abstract. The current outdoor surveillance equipment and cameras are vulnerable to be influenced by rain, snow, and other inclement weather, reducing the performance of the surveillance systems. In this paper, we propose a method to detect and remove rain streaks even snow artifacts from video sequences, using motion compensation and low-rank matrix completion method. First, we adopt the optical flow estimation method between consecutive frames to get a warped frame and obtain an initial binary rain map. We further use morphological component analysis method to dilate the tiny rain streaks. Then we employ the online dictionary learning for sparse representation technique and SVM classifier to refine the rain map by getting rid of parts which are not rain streaks. Finally, we reconstruct the video sequence by using low-rank matrix completion techniques. The experimental results demonstrate the proposed algorithm and perform qualitatively as well as quantitatively better in terms of PSNR/SSIM.

Keywords: Rain streaks removal · Motion compensation · Sparse representation technique · Block matching estimation

1 Introduction

In today's informatization of society, computer vision systems are widely applied in intelligent transportation, public safety, sports performance analysis and other fields. However, images and videos were taken in fog, sandstorms, haze, rain, snow and so on are easily affected by adverse weather [8], which not only greatly reduces the quality of images but also interferes with nearby pixels [10], affects the effectiveness of computer vision algorithms, such as stereo correspondence, navigation applications [3], object detection [6], object tracking [24], object recognition [18], critical weather conditions detection, weather observation, video-surveillance systems [3] *etc.* Thus, researchers have extensively studied on poor visibility affected by bad weather for images and video sequences in recent years, and proposed several methods as a preprocessing to increase the accuracy of computer vision algorithms.

S. Palaiahnakote et al. (Eds.): ACPR 2019, LNCS 12046, pp. 91–104, 2020.
https://doi.org/10.1007/978-3-030-41404-7_7

Rain and snow are extremely common weather conditions in our daily lives. Garg *et al.* [7] firstly raised a simple and efficient algorithm that defined rain streak pixels which are brighter than the other pixels in every frame for detecting and removing rain streaks from videos. There are a variety of published approaches to remove rain streaks from images or video sequences. However, most of the rain streaks removal methods mainly paid attention to the physical characteristics, *e.g.*, photometric appearance [3,6,7], chromatic consistency [16] and spatio-temporal configurations [22] of rain streaks. Recently, Wei *et al.* proposed a method that takes into account object motions and formulates rain as a patch-based mixture of Gaussian(P-MoG) [24]. Wei's method has demonstrated superiority over other methods. However, it cannot process video sequences captured with moving camera [24].

In this paper, we propose a method by using motion compensation and matrix completion algorithm to remove rain streaks and snow for video sequences. To summarize, our contributions of this work are:

1. We have the prior knowledge that rain streaks appear randomly and move faster than the other objects in every adjacent frame [7]. We obtain an initial rain map from the differences between the current frame and the previous frame warped by using Liu's algorithm [15] from adjacent pixels between two consecutive frames.
2. Due to illumination variation between consecutive frames or incorrect detection, the initial rain map includes some outliers. We adopt SVM classifier to separate rain streaks from outliers.
3. A video sequence may contain some moving objects or be captured with a moving camera. Instead of related works, this work makes the most of the temporal information from video sequences. Thus, we search for the most similar blocks from each of the adjacent frames by using block matching method and adopt low-rank matrix completion technique to restore the detected rain streaks pixels.

2 Challenges

Recently, the research works on rain streaks removal found in the literature have been mainly focused on image-based approaches that exploit deep learning neural network [14,20,23]. Each of the neural networks has to assemble a series of rain streaks images and without rain streaks images to learn these network parameters. Though these image-based methods can handle rain removal for video sequences in a frame-by-frame way, the extra utilization of temporal information always makes the video-based methods work better than image-based ones [12].

In the past few years, many studies have attempted to remove rain streaks for video sequences. These methods can handle rain video sequences with static and/or moving background [21]. And these video sequences can be captured with a static camera [6,12,16,22,24] or a moving camera [3,7].

Specifically, studies on rain streak removal for video sequences with a moving background by utilizing the temporal relationship between the video frames are still limited. Furthermore, removal raindrops adhered to glass of windows, heavy rain and water splashes caused by rain drop are also significant challenges.

3 The Proposed Method

3.1 Rain Streaks Detection

Rain streaks appear randomly and when they pass through one pixel, the pixel value will become brighter than its original form [7]. The optical flow estimation algorithm can find dense motion fields between two consecutive frames [15]. For captured video sequences by outdoor surveillance equipment, situations of dynamic objects in the background or moving cameras are always included, in order to compensate for these discrepancies between consecutive frames, we adopt the two-frame version of Liu's algorithm [15] to warp the previous frame into the current frame by estimating the optical flow field between each frame.

Figure 1(a) and (b) show the current *8th* frame and the previous *7th* frame captured in the "Waterfall" video sequence, (c) is the result of the method of optical flow using motion compensation and (d) is a difference image between the current frame and the warped previous frame by using optical flow method, which can be used to roughly estimate the position of rain streaks. Since the pixels containing rain streaks have larger luminance value than pixels without

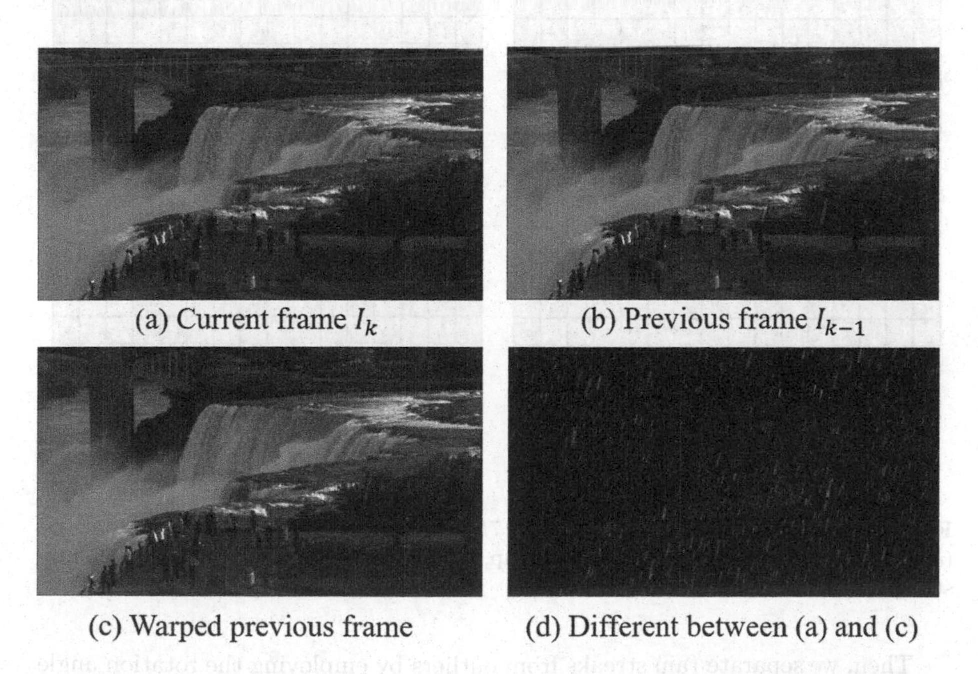

Fig. 1. Initial rain map detection on *7th* frame in the "Waterfall" video sequence

rain streaks, we only use the luminance components of rain streaks and adopt adaptive thresholding method to get the binary initial rain map.

3.2 Rain Map Refinement

As shown in Fig. 1(d), since some areas are not rain streaks, we employ the directionality of rain streaks to refine the initial rain map. Rain streaks generally tend to have elliptical or linear shapes and the direction of rain streaks is mainly consistent with the direction of the long axis [2]. Conversely, an erroneously detected outlier normally has an arbitrary shape and random direction. Therefore, we adopt one of the typical applications of sparse representation technique – morphological component analysis (MCA) [5,9], in order to separate the rain streaks into basis vectors, and reconstruct rain streaks by employing selected basis vectors only [11]. Then, we adopt Mairal *et al.*'s algorithm [17] to establish a dictionary for each initial rain map that is associated with each frame in the rainy video sequence. To reconstruct the basis vectors dictionary, we get each patch's structure and update the best matching kernel in each patch by using the singular value decomposition (SVD) method [4].

Figure 2(a) demonstrates basis vectors in the dictionary selected from the initial rain map of the $7th$ frame in the "Waterfall" video sequence. The basis vectors have diverse directional structures, dimensions of 256, and are visualized as 16×16 patches.

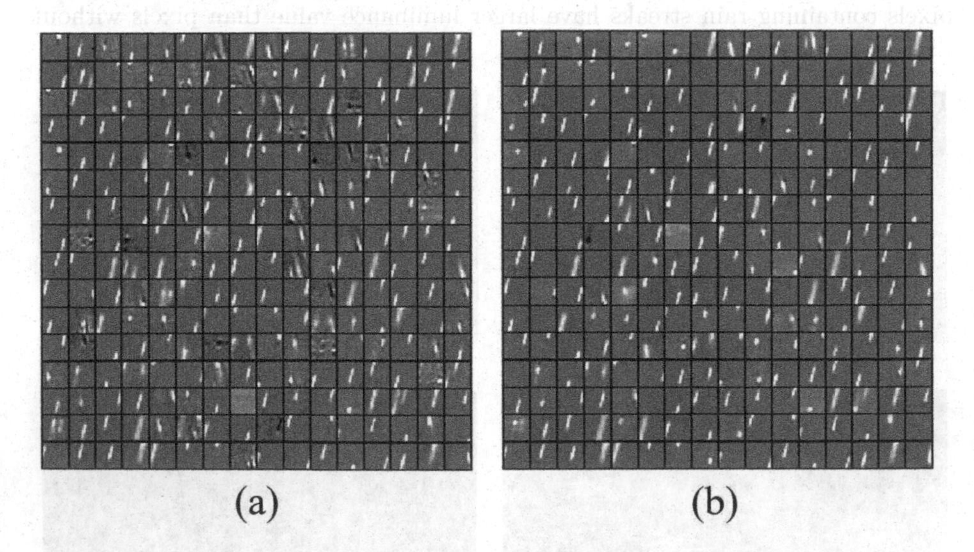

Fig. 2. Visualization of basis vectors of the $7th$ frame in the "Waterfall" video sequence: (a) The basis vectors of the initial rain map, (b) The basis vectors of the effective rain streaks in initial rain map.

Then, we separate rain streaks from outliers by employing the rotation angle and eigenvalues of kernels. We exploit SVM classifier by taking deviation angle between the base vector, the horizontal direction and the kernel scales along the major axes and minor axes. The new dictionary is shown in Fig. 2(b).

Figure 3 illustrates the initial binary rain map and the result of rain map refinement processing.

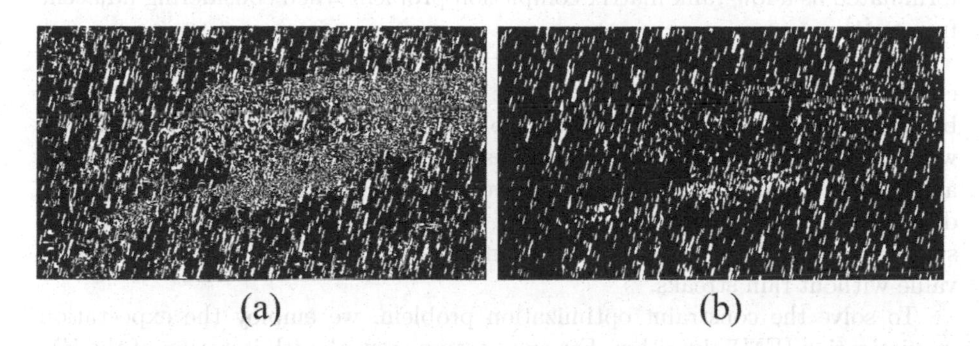

Fig. 3. SVM processing of refining initial binary rain map of the *7th* frame in the "Waterfall" video sequence: (a) The initial binary rain map before processing, (b) The initial binary rain map after processing.

In addition, some tiny rain streaks have not been detected in the initial rain map, some thick rain streak boundaries have been distorted, so we create structuring element of rain streaks to dilate the initial rain map. The improved parts are highlighted in orange and blue in Fig. 4(a) and (b).

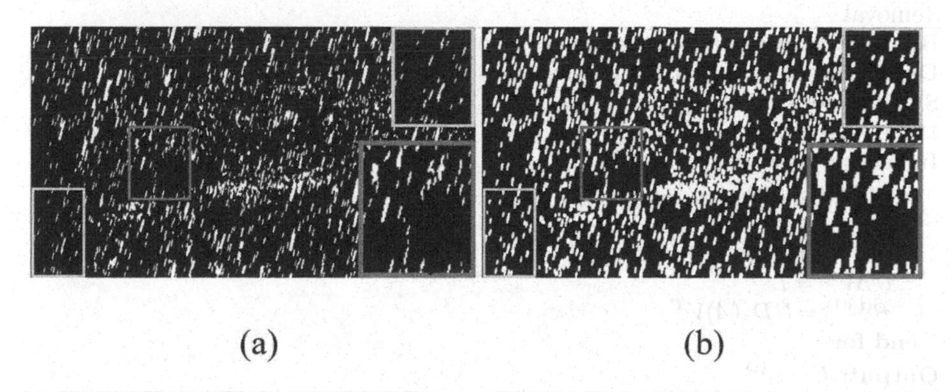

Fig. 4. Dilate processing of refining initial binary rain map of the *7th* frame in the "Waterfall" video sequence: (a) The initial binary rain map before processing, (b) The initial binary rain map after processing. (Color figure online)

3.3 Rain Streaks Reconstruction

By using the correlation between the spatio-temporal of adjacent frames, it is possible to restore the detected rain streak pixel values of rain streaks. Specifically, rain/snow distortion is sparse in nature. Thus, rain streak removal can be formulated as a low-rank matrix completion problem when considering adjacent frames [1].

Block matching (BM) motion estimation plays a very important role in video coding. For block matching approach, we divide each frame into several disjoint l blocks. For each block, we search for $4l$ blocks from each of four adjacent frames which belong to the same area. To measure the similarity between two blocks and reduce the amount of calculation, we only compute the sum of the squared differences(SSD) between pixels without rain streaks. We also use another constraint that the pixel value contains rain streaks that are larger than the pixel value without rain streaks.

To solve the constraint optimization problem, we employ the expectation maximization (EM) algorithm. For expectation step, the tth iteration of the EM algorithm is calculated by taking the elements of the input matrix L as pixels without rain streaks and the elements of the current estimate to obtain the filled matrix $L^{(t)}$. For maximization step, update current estimate $R^{(t)}$ to a low-rank approximation of the filled matrix $L^{(t)}$, and minimize the sum of the singular values of the matrix L (nuclear norm $||L||_*$). Finally, we replace the rain streak pixel values in the block matrix B with the corresponding elements of the final filled matrix $\tilde{L}$. The analysis of the algorithm is as Algorithm 1.

Algorithm 1. EM-Based Low-Rank Matrix Completion for Rain Streak Removal

---

Require: blocks matrix B and binary rain mask matrix M
Define: low-rank matrix L, minimize $||L||_*$
Subject to: $(1 - M) \circ L = (1 - M) \circ B$
$M \circ L \leq M \circ B$
Initialize: $t = 0$ and $R^{(1)} = B$
  for t=1:t_{max} **do**
    $t = t + 1$
    $L^{(t)} = (1 - M) \circ B + M \circ (R^{(t)} \wedge B)$
    $U \Lambda V^T = L^{(t)}$
    $R^{(t+1)} = U D_\tau(\Lambda) V^T$
  end for
Output: $\tilde{L} = L^{(t)}$

Definition 1. *"$\circ$" denotes the element-wise multiplication. "$\wedge$" denotes the element-wise minimum operator to return the minimum between two elements. "$D_\tau(\Lambda)$" means applying the soft-thresholding rule to shrink the singular values which are under the threshold(τ = 2000) towards zero. The number of t_{max} in this paper is set to 200 times.*

4 Experimental Results

In this section, we show experimental results and evaluate the performance of synthetic video sequences and real video sequences. Experimental results of rain removal compared method just include Wei *et al.* [24] have been published in ICCV2017 which only considers static scenes without camera motions. That is because Wei's method had already efficiently reconstructed the real scene more faithfully than other related works of removing rain streaks in static scenes [24], and the proposed method also demonstrates the powerful superiority of processing in the moving background. Furthermore, the proposed method proves the effectiveness of removal linear raindrops on window glass and splashes caused by heavy rain drop in real video sequences. We compare the performance of raindrops removal with Qian's method [19] which specializes in raindrops on window glass removal. More results are available as supplementary materials in YouTube[1].

4.1 Synthetic Video Sequences

Figures 5 and 6 show one frame of the light rain scene while some thick rain streaks. Both the "Golf" video sequence and "Tennis" video sequence are static background video sequences, which means the camera is not moving. It is obvious

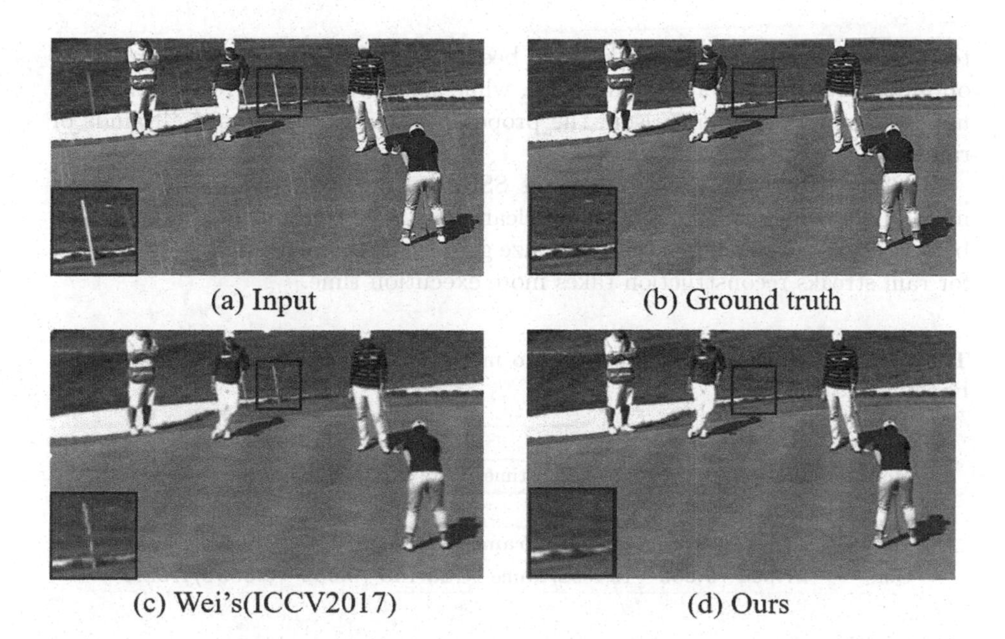

Fig. 5. Result of the proposed rain streaks removal algorithm on the 29th frame in the "Golf" video sequence.

[1] https://youtu.be/hnKFMUQvmNw.

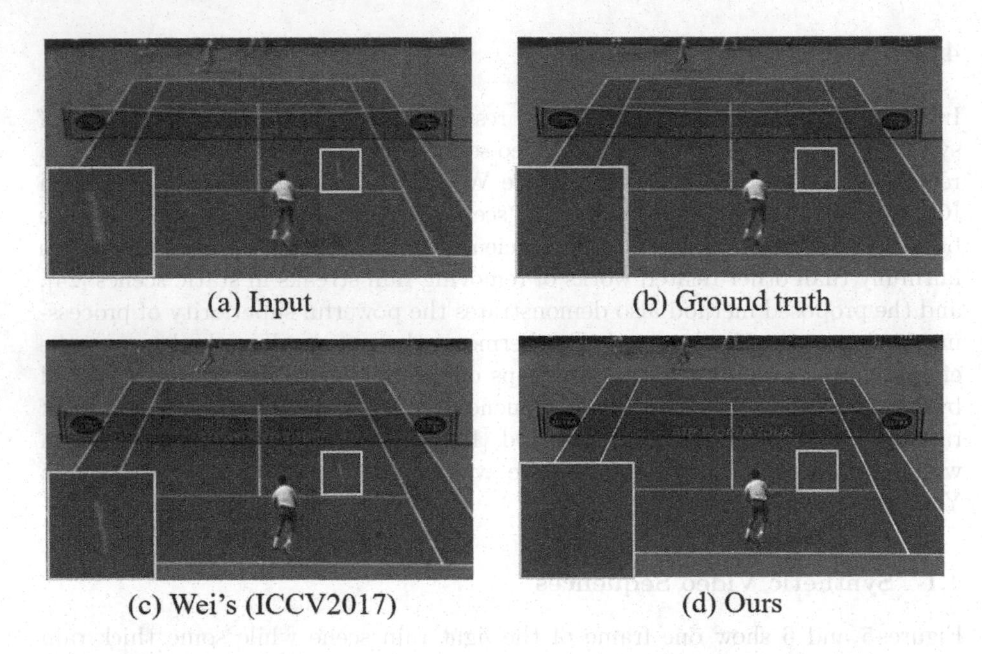

(a) Input (b) Ground truth

(c) Wei's (ICCV2017) (d) Ours

Fig. 6. Result of the proposed rain streaks removal algorithm on the 19th frame in the "Tennis" video sequence.

to observe that tiny rain streaks have been removed in the rain removal maps obtained by Wei *et al.*'s algorithm [24], while some thick rain streaks still could not be removed. In comparison, the proposed method can remove all kinds of rain streaks clearly.

In this paper, we use PSNR and SSIM to evaluate the result of Wei's method [24] and ours. In Table 1, it is clearly observed that our method attained better results. However, as the image size get larger, the block matching method for rain streaks reconstruction takes more execution time.

Table 1. Performance comparison of two methods on synthetic video sequences of PSNR and SSIM.

Dataset	"Golf" (320 × 640)			"Tennis" (240 × 320)		
Metrics	PSNR ↑	SSIM ↑	Execution time ↓	PSNR ↑	SSIM ↑	Execution time ↓
Input	21.909	0.714	–	29.210	0.907	–
Wei's [24]	25.896	0.856	**11.404 s/frame**	32.894	0.935	11.249 s/frame
Ours	**27.054**	**0.863**	12.153 s/frame	**33.146**	**0.952**	**9.053 s/frame**

4.2 Real Video Sequences

Since Wei *et al.* mentioned that their method still can not experiment with a moving camera of video sequences [24], we only do comparisons between input frames and our results.

Figure 7 shows three frames randomly selected from the proposed rain streak removal algorithm on the "Movie" video sequence. This video sequence is a movie clip of "Four Weddings and a Funeral", which contains thin rain streaks, sometimes with thick rain streaks and are captured under a moving background, while the protagonists are sometimes not still.

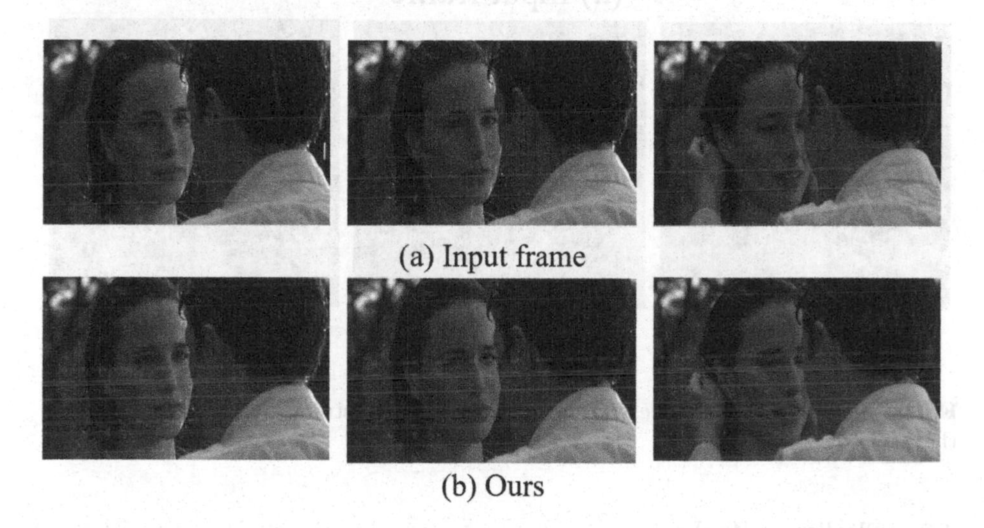

(a) Input frame

(b) Ours

Fig. 7. Rain removal results of the proposed rain streaks removal algorithm on the "Movie" video sequence.

It is important to note that Wei's method so far could not solve the rain removal problem with a moving background [24]. Wei *et al.* propose a Gaussian Model initialization to modeling the background layer. The premise of this method is the foreground objects are present continuously, the background model needs to be initialized and the background data should accumulate over multiple frames [15]. What is different from Wei's method is that we employ the block matching method to match the most similar blocks of size 32×32 for detecting moving objects. After that, we explore a low-rank matrix completion method to fill in rain streak pixels, in order to remove rain streaks from video sequences. It is obvious to be seen that the proposed method can keep the details of the background and remove rain streaks faithfully.

Figure 8 shows three frames randomly selected from the result of the proposed rain streak removal algorithm on the "Snow" video sequence. This video sequence contains snowflakes and a moving protagonist captured under a moving camera.

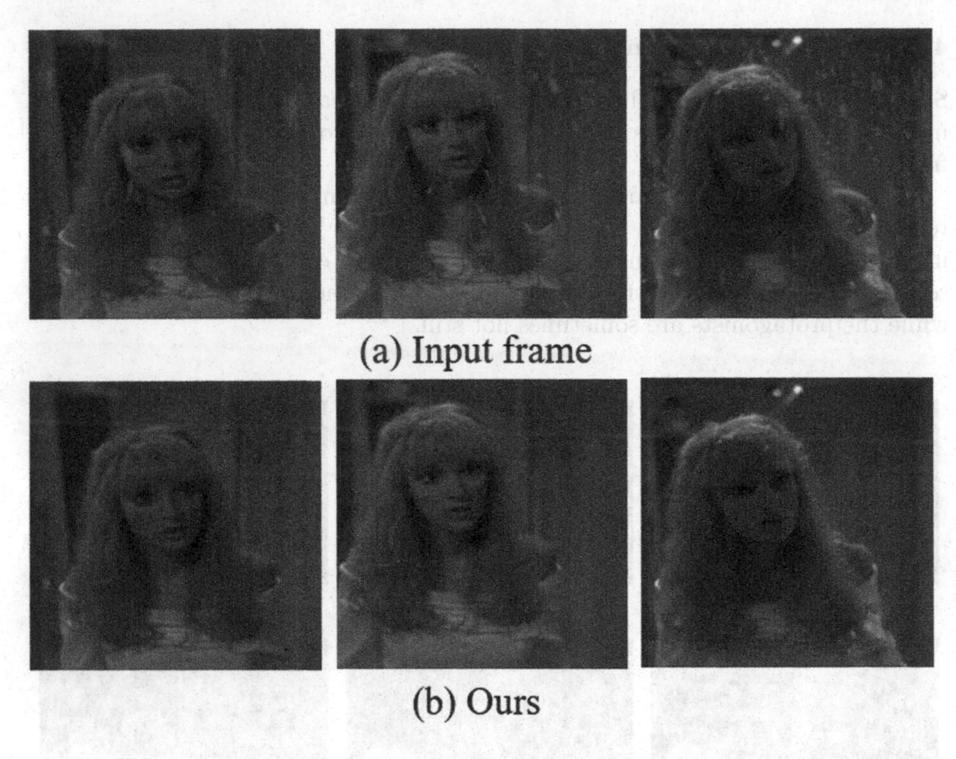

Fig. 8. Snowflakes removal results of the proposed rain streaks removal algorithm on the "Snow" video sequence.

4.3 Challenge Tasks

Furthermore, our proposed method also presents experimental results of two unique challenges for real video sequences:

- **Linear raindrops on window glass removal**

Raindrops flow down the window glass can seriously hinder the visibility of a background scene and degrade an image considerably [19]. Since raindrops are transparent, attach to the glass and have several uncertain shapes, removing raindrops on window glass is a great challenge. The raindrops on window glass can be classified into three types according to different directions of the wind and rainy severity, which are shown in Fig. 9. The Fig. 9(a) shows the most similar shape to rain streaks, so we attempt to use the proposed method to remove rain streaks and linear raindrops on window glass together.

In Fig. 10, we present the results of two certain frames selected from the sequence "Raindrop" by the method of Qian *et al.* [19] and ours respectively. The comparison results are highlighted in yellow, red and green. It is obvious that our method can remove not only rain streaks outside of the window but also most of the linear raindrops on the window faithfully, which are hard to remove

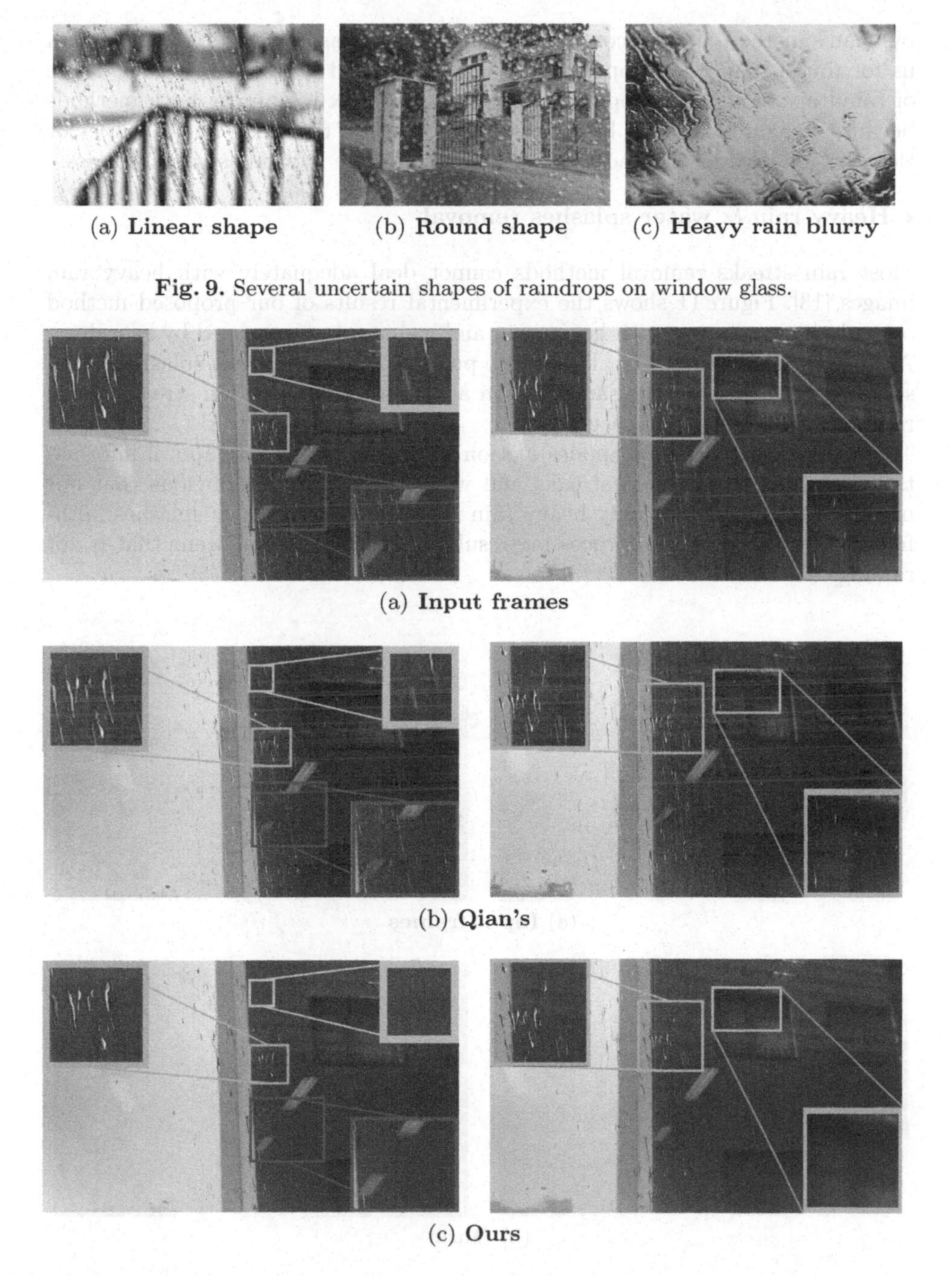

(a) **Linear shape** (b) **Round shape** (c) **Heavy rain blurry**

Fig. 9. Several uncertain shapes of raindrops on window glass.

(a) **Input frames**

(b) **Qian's**

(c) **Ours**

Fig. 10. Rain removal results of the proposed rain streaks removal algorithm on the "Raindrop" video sequence. (Color figure online)

by Qian's method. On the contrary, Qian's method has better performance than us for round shape raindrops because Qian's method is trained for such shape of raindrops. Some raindrops highlighted in gray box remain by both methods because they are excluded by SVM classifier due to their non-linear shapes or they are modeled as the background due to the same motion as window glass.

- **Heavy rain & water splashes removal**

Most rain streaks removal methods cannot deal adequately with heavy rain images [13]. Figure 11 shows the experimental results of our proposed method on real video sequence with heavy rain and water splashes caused by rain drop. Assume that heavy rain streaks fall into puddles and cause water splashes, these splashes of water have the same motion and linear shape as rain streaks which randomly distributed in space.

Our method efficiently applies motion compensation and temporal information to remove heavy rain streaks and water splashes. It is obvious that our method can remove not only heavy rain streaks but also water splashes faithfully, and then makes the processing results approach the real scene that is not raining.

(a) **Input frames**

(b) **Ours**

Fig. 11. Rain removal results of the proposed rain streaks removal algorithm on the "Heavy-rain" video sequence.

5 Conclusion

We propose a rain streak detection and removal method, which exploits motion compensation of each frame in a video sequence based on the low-rank matrix completion. The proposed algorithm firstly obtains an initial rain map by using optical flow method. Then we use sparse representation technique to refine the rain map. Finally, we remove the rain streaks by using a low-rank matrix completion method. Experimental results indicate that our method can detect and remove rain streaks reliably while preserving the original scene. For future work, we consider employing other more efficient block matching algorithm for rain streaks reconstruction. Also, we intend to fully utilize the proposed algorithm to process underwater data-sets, aiming to remove impurities in the water and sand suddenly kicked up by underwater robots.

References

1. Abdel-Hakim, A.E.: A novel approach for rain removal from videos using low-rank recovery. In: 2014 5th International Conference on Intelligent Systems, Modelling and Simulation, pp. 351–356. IEEE (2014)
2. Barnum, P.C., Narasimhan, S.G., Kanade, T.: Analysis of rain and snow in frequency space. Int. J. Comput. Vision **86**, 256–274 (2008)
3. Bossu, J., Hautière, N., Tarel, J.P.: Rain or snow detection in image sequences through use of a histogram of orientation of streaks. Int. J. Comput. Vision **93**(3), 348–367 (2011)
4. Elad, M., Aharon, M.: Image denoising via sparse and redundant representations over learned dictionaries. IEEE Trans. Image Process. **15**(12), 3736–3745 (2006)
5. Fadili, M.J., Starck, J.L., Bobin, J., Moudden, Y.: Image decomposition and separation using sparse representations: an overview. Proc. IEEE **98**(6), 983–994 (2009)
6. Garg, K., Nayar, S.K.: Detection and removal of rain from videos. In: Proceedings of the 2004 IEEE Computer Society Conference on Computer Vision and Pattern Recognition, CVPR 2004, vol. 1, p. I (2004)
7. Garg, K., Nayar, S.K.: When does a camera see rain? In: Tenth IEEE International Conference on Computer Vision (ICCV 2005) Volume 1, vol. 2, pp. 1067–1074 (2005)
8. Garg, K., Nayar, S.K.: Vision and rain. Int. J. Comput. Vision **75**, 3–27 (2006)
9. George, J., Bhavani, S., Jaya, J.: Certain explorations on removal of rain streaks using morphological component analysis. Int. J. Eng. Res. Technol. (IJERT) **2** (2013). ISSN: 2278-0181
10. Jiang, T.X., Huang, T.Z., Zhao, X.L., Deng, L.J., Wang, Y.: FastDeRain: a novel video rain streak removal method using directional gradient priors. IEEE Trans. Image Process. **28**, 2089–2102 (2018)
11. Kim, J.H., Sim, J.Y., Kim, C.S.: Video deraining and desnowing using temporal correlation and low-rank matrix completion. IEEE Trans. Image Process. **24**, 2658–2670 (2015)
12. Li, M., et al.: Video rain streak removal by multiscale convolutional sparse coding. In: 2018 IEEE/CVF Conference on Computer Vision and Pattern Recognition, pp. 6644–6653 (2018)

13. Li, R., Cheong, L.F., Tan, R.T.: Heavy rain image restoration: integrating physics model and conditional adversarial learning. arXiv abs/1904.05050 (2019)
14. Li, X., Wu, J., Lin, Z., Liu, H., Zha, H.: Recurrent squeeze-and-excitation context aggregation net for single image deraining. In: Ferrari, V., Hebert, M., Sminchisescu, C., Weiss, Y. (eds.) ECCV 2018. LNCS, vol. 11211, pp. 262–277. Springer, Cham (2018). https://doi.org/10.1007/978-3-030-01234-2_16
15. Liu, C., et al.: Beyond pixels: exploring new representations and applications for motion analysis. Ph.D. thesis, Massachusetts Institute of Technology (2009)
16. Liu, P., Xu, J., Liu, J., Tang, X.: Pixel based temporal analysis using chromatic property for removing rain from videos. Comput. Inf. Sci. **2**, 53–60 (2009)
17. Mairal, J., Bach, F.R., Ponce, J., Sapiro, G.: Online learning for matrix factorization and sparse coding. J. Mach. Learn. Res. **11**, 19–60 (2010)
18. Mukhopadhyay, S., Tripathi, A.K.: Combating bad weather part i: rain removal from video. Synth. Lect. Image Video Multimedia Process. **7**(2), 1–93 (2014)
19. Qian, R., Tan, R.T., Yang, W., Su, J., Liu, J.: Attentive generative adversarial network for raindrop removal from a single image. In: 2018 IEEE/CVF Conference on Computer Vision and Pattern Recognition, pp. 2482–2491 (2017)
20. Ren, D., Zuo, W., Hu, Q., Zhu, P., Meng, D.: Progressive image deraining networks: a better and simpler baseline. In: The IEEE Conference on Computer Vision and Pattern Recognition (CVPR), June 2019
21. Tripathi, A.K., Mukhopadhyay, S.: Removal of rain from videos: a review. SIViP **8**, 1421–1430 (2014)
22. Tripathi, A., Mukhopadhyay, S.: Video post processing: low-latency spatiotemporal approach for detection and removal of rain. IET Image Proc. **6**(2), 181–196 (2012)
23. Wang, T., Yang, X., Xu, K., Chen, S., Zhang, Q., Lau, R.W.: Spatial attentive single-image deraining with a high quality real rain dataset. In: The IEEE Conference on Computer Vision and Pattern Recognition (CVPR), June 2019
24. Wei, W., Yi, L., Xie, Q., Zhao, Q., Meng, D., Xu, Z.: Should we encode rain streaks in video as deterministic or stochastic? In: 2017 IEEE International Conference on Computer Vision (ICCV), pp. 2535–2544 (2017)

Assessing the Impact of Video Compression on Background Subtraction

Poonam Beniwal(✉), Pranav Mantini, and Shishir K. Shah

University of Houston, 4800 Calhoun Road, Houston, TX 77204, USA
pbeniwal@uh.edu, pmantini@cs.uh.edu, sshah@central.uh.edu

Abstract. Video cameras are deployed in large numbers for surveillance. Video is compressed and transmitted over bandwidth limited communication channels. Researches have increasingly focused on automated analysis algorithms to understand video. This raises the question "Does compression have an effect on automated analysis algorithms?". This is a vital question in understanding the reliability of automated analysis algorithms. In this paper, we evaluated background subtraction algorithm's performance on videos acquired using a typical surveillance camera under different scenarios. The videos in the dataset are collected from an IP-based surveillance camera and compressed using different bitrates and quantization levels. The experimental results provide insights on the different compression settings and their impact on the expected performance of background subtraction algorithms. Furthermore, we train a classifier that utilizes video quality to predict the performance of an algorithm.

Keywords: Video surveillance · Video compression · Background subtraction · H.264/AVC · Video quality

1 Introduction

Video surveillance cameras are deployed in large numbers for safety and security. For example, a large university can have up to 1500 cameras, an international airport can have up to 3000 cameras, and a large casino can have well over 5000 cameras. It is impossible for humans to manually search, and analyze these videos. This has increased the demand for automated video surveillance systems. A wide variety of computer vision algorithms are available for automated analysis.

In a typical networked camera surveillance system, videos captured from multiple cameras are sent to a centralized location for storage, viewing, and automated analysis. They are transmitted over bandwidth limited channels, and this is accomplished using video compression. Most camera systems adopt the H.264 compression algorithm for video encoding, which exploits spatial and temporal redundancy. A video frame is divided into blocks of fixed size. This is done based on the fact that blocks that are spatially and temporally close

S. Palaiahnakote et al. (Eds.): ACPR 2019, LNCS 12046, pp. 105–118, 2020.
https://doi.org/10.1007/978-3-030-41404-7_8

are highly correlated. Compression algorithms use this correlation for removing spatial and temporal redundancy. While compression helps in efficient transmission of a large amount of video data, the methods for compression are designed mostly to optimize quality based on human perception. In turn, the loss of data due to compression can have a different effect on computer vision algorithms that are not necessarily designed by taking perceptual quality of videos into consideration.

Typically, computer vision algorithms are developed and evaluated on uncompressed and high quality data. It is important to understand the impact of compression on computer vision algorithms to determine their reliability for automated video surveillance. Recently, the impact of compression have been investigated on face detection, recognition, and object detection [8,15] algorithms. However, these algorithms use object-level information and do not provide an understanding of the effects of compression on individual pixels. Since compression is inherently encoding small blocks of pixels using spatial and temporal redundancies, we choose to study background subtraction as an application, which leverages methods that model individual and small blocks of pixels.

Background subtraction algorithms classify each pixel in the video as one belonging to the background or foreground. Numerous algorithms have been developed for background subtraction that use individual pixel or its neighboring pixels for making the background/foreground decision. All approaches perform temporal analysis of individual pixels for background modeling. We evaluate three popular background subtraction algorithms ViBe [2], PBAS [11] and Wren [24] to ascertain the effects of compression on their performance.

Quantifying and understanding the performance of different algorithms on compressed videos can be used as a guidance for setting compression parameters. Furthermore, in many computer vision applications, videos are collected from different sources and have varying quality. It is important to predict a lower bound on the performance to ensure the reliability of different algorithms. Because compression parameters are unknown, video quality can be used to predict a bound on performance. We utilize video quality as a feature to predict the performance of an algorithm.

Our contributions are: (1) We evaluate three background subtraction algorithm to study the impact of compression. (2) We identify perceptual quality metrics that correlate with the performance of background subtraction algorithms. (3) We identify compression parameters that result in a bounded loss in performance of background subtraction algorithms. (4) We build a classifier to predict the performance of an algorithm based on video quality.

The paper is organized as follows: Sect. 2 presents related work. Problem formulation is given in Sect. 3. Experimental design is described in Sect. 4. Experimental results are reported in Sect. 5.

2 Related Work

H.264 achieves a high level of compression and is the standard for media, and video surveillance. The compression is achieved by eliminating redundant spatial and temporal information in the video. Redundancy is defined with respect to the human visual system, and the quality of the compressed video is often assessed under the same criterion. There are numerous studies that measure and evaluate the perceptual quality of the H.264 compressed video [4,5,18]. However, there are only a handful of methods that objectively evaluate the quality of compressed video with respect to computer vision algorithms.

Delac *et al.* [8] studied image compression effects on face recognition algorithms. They compressed images at various bitrates, and explored the results on 12 different algorithms. The experiments showed that compression degrades the performance of algorithms, but in some cases it slightly improves the performance.

Korshunov *et al.* [15] studied the impact of compression on face detection [22] and object tracking algorithm [3] on the MIT/CMU [12] dataset. Face detection was evaluated on images that were compressed using different JPEG quality parameters. Object tracking algorithm was evaluated using different frame drop pattern, and compression quality. Results showed that videos can be compressed significantly without degrading accuracy of computer vision algorithms. Following this work, Korshunov and Ooi [16] studied the impact of compression on face detection [19,22], face recognition [17], and object tracking algorithms. The experiment demonstrated that vision algorithms can tolerate a degradation in video quality without affecting vision algorithms accuracy.

Klare *et al.* [14] studied the impact of H.264 compression on face recognition algorithms. Videos were compressed using nine different bitrates from 8 kbs to 2048 kbs with H.264 standard profile. In their experiment, two popular face recognition algorithms were used in surveillance and mobile video scenarios. The experiment showed that videos can be compressed up to 128 kbps without a significant drop in performance.

Cozzolino *et al.* [7] studied the effects of MJPEG compression on motion tracker used in metro railway surveillance. The focus was on investigating the cause of false alarm in surveillance system. They collected uncompressed videos, and then applied MJPEG compression using different compression factors. The experiment demonstrated that at low compression there was a reduction in number of objects detected, which results in less number of false positives.

Aqqa *et al.* [1] studied the effect of compression on object detection algorithms. They focused on effect of compression on different object categories, object sizes, and object aspect ratios. The experiment demonstrated that performance drop in algorithms is dominated by false negatives.

The findings presented in some of the previous works is based on the use of images/videos that are already compressed. So, when low compression is applied to these videos, the loss in information and the corresponding drop in performance is minimal. Furthermore, these papers study the effects at an object-level, and do not explain how decision on individual pixel is impacted due to compression. In this paper, we focus on background subtraction algorithms that make decision at a pixel-level. Background subtraction algorithm output is often used as input to object-level algorithms [20]. Hence investigating the impact on background subtraction can help to better understand the impact on object-level algorithms.

3 Problem Formulation

The first objective of the study is to ascertain the change in the performance of computer vision algorithms on compressed videos. Let v_o be a video from a surveillance camera and v_c be the corresponding video obtained under compression parameter Θ ($\Theta = \{\theta_1, \theta_2, ..., \theta_n\}$), where n represents different parameters used for compression . Let l_π be the drop in performance of the computer vision algorithm on v_c (compressed) from v_o (original), using π as the performance metric. We would like to quantify $P(L_\pi \leq l_\pi | \Theta = \{\theta_1, \theta_2, ..., \theta_n\})$, where P is probability, and L_π is a random variable that takes the value of change in performance of the algorithm.

Let q be a quantifiable quality metric that can be computed on videos. Let q_o and q_c be the quality of v_o and v_c respectively, due to compression parameters. Let l_q be percentage loss in perceptual quality defined as:

$$\%l_q = \frac{q_c - q_o}{q_o} \tag{1}$$

Let $P(L_q \leq l_q | \Theta = \{\theta_1, \theta_2, ..., \theta_n\})$ be the probability of loss in quality metric q given the compression parameters ($\Theta = \{\theta_1, \theta_2, ..., \theta_n\}$), and L_q be a random variable that takes the values of the change in the quality metric q. Using chain rule we can write:

$$P(L_\pi \leq l_\pi, L_q \leq l_q | \Theta) = P(L_\pi \leq l_\pi | L_q \leq l_q, \Theta) \tag{2}$$

$$\times P(L_q \leq l_q | \Theta) \tag{3}$$

Then we have:

$$P(L_\pi \leq l_\pi | L_q \leq l_q, \Theta) = \frac{P(L_\pi \leq l_\pi, L_q \leq l_q | \Theta)}{P(L_q \leq l_q | \Theta)} \tag{4}$$

The value of l_q that corresponds to l_π is unknown. Let there exist a function $R : \Re \rightarrow \Re$, such that $l_\pi = R(l_q)$. If R is either a non-decreasing or a non-increasing function then the inverse exist, s.t. $l_q = R^{-1}(l_\pi)$. Then we can estimate:

$$P(L_\pi \leq l_\pi | L_q \leq R^{-1}(l_\pi), \Theta) = \frac{P(L_\pi \leq l_\pi, L_q \leq R^{-1}(l_\pi) | \Theta)}{P(L_q \leq R^{-1}(l_\pi) | \Theta)} \tag{5}$$

We use this to compute the probability of having a bounded loss on the performance, conditioned on the loss in quality defined by the relationship function R and compression parameter. This problem can be solved by:

1. Identifying a quality metric q, that correlates with the performance (π) of the computer vision algorithm, such that $l_\pi = R(l_q)$, and R is a monotonic function.

2. Estimating the probability $P(L_q \leq l_q|\Theta)$.
3. Estimating the probability $P(L_\pi \leq l_\pi, L_q \leq l_q|\Theta)$.

The second objective of our study is to predict the performance on videos when compression parameters are unknown. Let q be the quality and π be the performance of a video. Videos are grouped into different classes based on performance of the algorithms. Let c_i be class containing videos whose performance is bounded by a_i and b_i ($a_i < \pi \leq b_i$). We cast this as a multi-class classification problem. Given q as the quality of a video, performance class can be predicted using the following equation:

$$c = argmax_{i=1,\dots,k}((w^{\mathrm{i}})^{\mathrm{T}} q + d^{\mathrm{i}}) \tag{6}$$

where w^{i} and d^{i} are weight and bias parameters, respectively, for i_{th} class, k is number of classes and c is the predicted class. The model parameters are learned by training a classifier using quality as a feature.

4 Study Design

4.1 Background Subtraction

Background subtraction is often an initial step for many high-level computer vision algorithms. General schema of a background subtraction process is shown in Fig. 1. The goal of background subtraction is to identify pixels that belong to the foreground. Most methods focus on building a background model (the complement of which is the foreground). The process starts with the initialization of a background model from fixed number of frames. After the initialization, corresponding pixel in current frame and background model are compared to make decision. Background model is updated based on current frame to allow changes made by moving objects to integrate in the background model. Each pixel in the background model is updated based on; (1) the past values of the pixel (temporal information), and (2) the neighborhood values of the pixels (spatial information). We selected three popular background subtraction algorithms from the BGSLibrary [21], one of which models temporal information, and others model both spatial and temporal information.

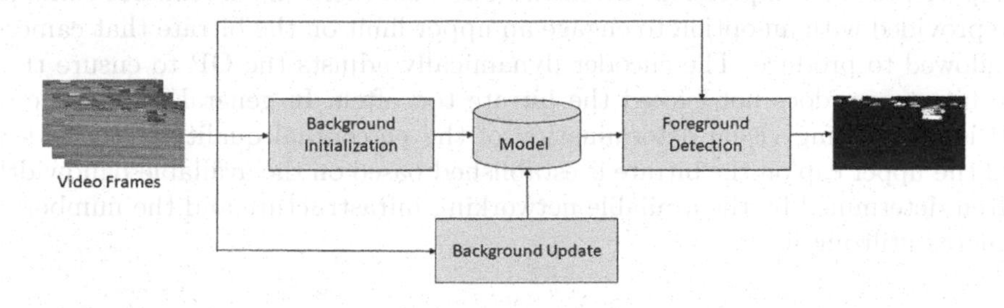

Fig. 1. Block diagram of a typical background subtraction process.

Wren [24] models the temporal information of each pixel to create a background model. Each pixel is modeled independently as a Gaussian distribution using constant numbers of pixels from the past. Pixels in the current frame are compared to their corresponding pixel in the background model, and classified as background or foreground based on a decision threshold. Background model is updated by taking the running average of pixels.

ViBe [2] models temporal and spatial information of each pixel to create a background model. Each background pixel is modeled using a set of pixels from the past. Background decision on individual pixel is made by comparing the pixel with corresponding neighborhood of pixels from background model. Pixels in the neighborhood are highly correlated, and are updated at each step to maintain spatial consistency.

PBAS [11] uses similar approach to ViBE and models spatial and temporal information for each pixel to create a background model. In addition, the algorithm establishes a different threshold for each pixel, and is updated according to a per-pixel learning rate.

4.2 Dataset

We collected videos in indoor and outdoor environments using an AXIS P3227-LVE network camera. Real-world surveillance scenarios have different viewpoints, and contain objects of different sizes that are moving at varying speeds. Khan *et al.* [13] reported that contents of video effects the compression level in the video with rapid movements causing more compression. We collect a dataset that is reflective of such characteristics.

In H.264 compression, the amount of compression is dictated by the quantization step. The quantization step reduces the overall precision of the integer coefficients and tends to eliminate high frequency coefficients while maintaining perceptual quality. A quantization parameter (QP), usually a value between 1 and 51, is used to control the quantization. QP used for encoding is dependent on the quantization level and bitrate, along with the content in the scene (that cannot be quantified). Most camera manufacturers provide options to control the encoding settings. The camera allows one to select the average QP value the encoder should use. However, the bandwidth limitation imposed by the network is a critical concern that could create congestion and higher loss in information compared to the compression. Often times the encoders on surveillance cameras are provided with an option to engage an upper limit on the bitrate that camera is allowed to produce. The encoder dynamically adjusts the QP to ensure that the bit stream does not exceed the bitrate too often. In general, the choice of QP is made using visual determination of the perceptual quality of the video, and the upper cap on the bitrate is established based on the available bandwidth (often determined by the available networking infrastructure and the number of cameras utilizing it).

Most surveillance cameras record videos at a resolution of 1080p, and a frame rate of 10–30 fps. The cameras are set to capture video that have a QP value between 30 and 35. Each camera is assigned an upper limit of 1 Mb/s to 2 Mb/s. To simulate these scenarios, we used *ffmpeg* tool to compress videos in the constant rate factor (CRF) mode with the video buffering verifier (bitrate upper limit) enabled. This simulates a compression that is similar to the encoder in a surveillance camera. We used four different bitrates (2 Mb/s, 1.5 Mb/s, 1 Mb/s, 0.5 Mb/s) and five different CRF (23, 29, 35, 41, 47) values to compress videos. The combination results in 20 videos for an uncompressed video. The compression effects videos that have sufficient variability among macro blocks over time. Encoder uses a higher QP value to meet bandwidth constraints. Videos that are not undergoing sufficient compression are removed from the dataset by analyzing the QP value used between variants. The final dataset has 30 original videos and 600 compressed videos.

4.3 Quality Metrics for Videos

While one could study the relation between QP and the performance of an algorithm, QP is not an intuitive indicator of the quality of a video. The chosen QP value is the cause, and the effect is the visual artifact that is manifested in compressed video due to loss in information. We choose to compute perceptual quality metrics on compressed video that are intuitive.

- **Structural Similarity Index Metric (SSIM):** This metric is based on the Human Visual System and evaluates the perceptual quality of images. The structural distortion [23] in an image is used as a measure of perceptual quality. This metric focuses on the texture components of the image. Higher values of SSIM implies that compressed image is more similar to original image.
- **PSNR:** This is the ratio of the maximum luminance value and mean squared error between the original and compressed image. It gives a rough estimate of human perception. A higher PSNR indicates higher similarity between original and compressed images. We use maximum PSNR value as a metric for the video.
- **Noise:** As suggested by [9,10], this metric utilizes the local mean and variance of pixel luminance. It is based on the fact that noise variance of an image can be estimated by the local variance of a flat area. According to this work, the most convenient method for noise estimation is to identify homogeneous image areas and use them to compute noise statistics.
- **Blur:** This artifact is introduced by compression algorithms that are based on Discrete Cosine Transform (DCT). The reason behind this artifact is the removal of high frequency components and de-blocking filters. It is the loss of spatial details in the image, and reduction in the sharpness of the edges. Higher value means higher blur. The details of the metric are given in [6].
- **Contrast:** It is the difference in luminance that makes an object distinguishable. Higher value indicates higher contrast.

- **Blockiness:** It is defined as the ratio of absolute difference in luminance of the intra-pairs (pixels in the same block) and inter-pairs (pixels in different blocks). The details of the metric are given in [18]. This artifact is introduced by the compression algorithms that uses various block sizes for coding.

4.4 Performance Metric for Background Subtraction Algorithms

As the objective is to ascertain the relative loss in performance due to compression, the output from each background subtraction algorithm applied on the uncompressed version of the video is used as the groundtruth. This eliminates the bias towards algorithms that inherently perform better than others. We use F1-measure as a performance metric. F1-measure is defined as the harmonic mean of precision and recall, and is a better measurement of performance in class imbalance problems.

$$F_1 = 2\frac{PPV.TPR}{PPV + TPR} = \frac{2TP}{2TP + FP + FN} \tag{7}$$

Background is the positive class, and foreground is the negative class, where TP = True Positive, FP = False Positive, FN = False Negative, PPV = Positive Predictive Value (Precision), TPR = True Positive Rate (Recall).

5 Results

5.1 Relation Between Percentage Drop in Quality and Performance

Some quality metrics can have a direct relation to performance of the algorithms, while others may not. To find the correlation, we compute perceptual quality metrics over the entire dataset (30 original and 600 compressed videos). For each compressed video, we compute the percentage of change in perceptual quality. Figure 2 presents the change in each of the quality metric ($\%l_q$) against the drop in F1-measure ($\%l_\pi$) of algorithms. As SSIM and PSNR are full reference metrics, we take maximum value in our dataset for these metrics to compute percentage drop. From Fig. 2, we infer the following:

- A degradation in perceptual quality may not always imply a degradation in the performance of the background subtraction algorithms. For example, noise is a common perceptual quality metric; An increase in noise may not always degrade the performance of the background subtraction algorithm. The noise metric assigns a low value for images with high amount of noise. A change in the metric from −7.5% to −10%, indicates a 2.5% increase in noise. In fact for this dataset, the plots show that an increase in the noise within this range has no effect on the performance of the algorithms.
- The relation between blur, contrast, and noise; and the performance of the algorithm is convoluted. A loss in one of these perceptual qualities may not always predict a loss in the performance of the algorithms. These functions are not monotonic in nature, and hence $l_q = R^{-1}(l_\pi)$, does not exists.

- Blockiness, PSNR, and SSIM show a correlation with the performance of the background subtraction algorithm, and display a monotonic nature. SSIM, shows some fluctuation, and is not strictly monotonic. We assume this is due to the discrete nature of the computations.
- A 2% loss in blockiness, or a 25% loss in PSNR, or a 3% loss in SSIM results in about 10% loss in the performance of algorithm.

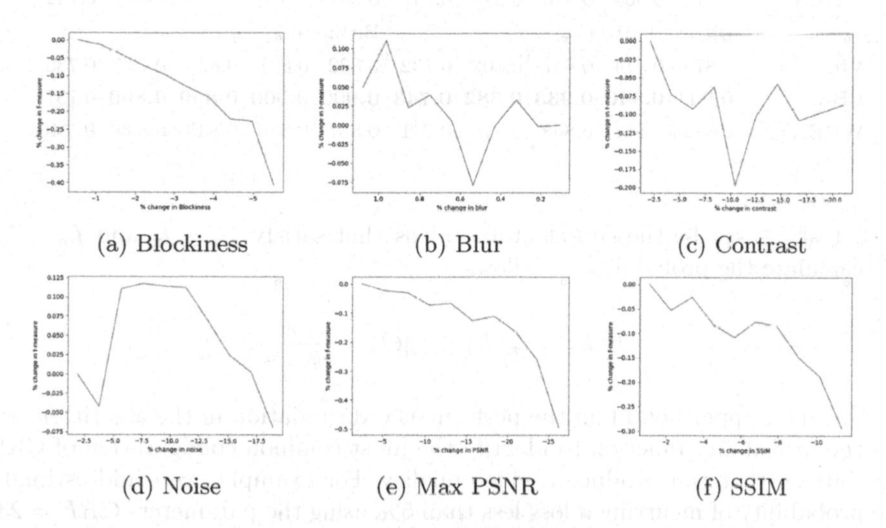

(a) Blockiness (b) Blur (c) Contrast

(d) Noise (e) Max PSNR (f) SSIM

Fig. 2. Plots of different perceptual quality metrics against the performance of the algorithm. The x-axis shows the percentage change in perceptual quality of a compressed video compared to the perceptual quality of the original videos, and y-axis shows the amount of drop in performance corresponding to the drop in perceptual quality.

5.2 Identify the Encoding Parameters to Employ in Surveillance Scenarios

Our objective is to find the encoding parameters that can compress the video significantly without affecting the performance of the algorithms. To find these parameters, we form groups of compressed video based on the amount of percentage loss in perceptual quality. We study the performance of background subtraction algorithms on these groups of videos so that we can select encoding parameters. The average F1-measure for all algorithms on different bitrate and CRF is shown in Table 1.

Let $s_{b,c}$ be the set of all videos in the dataset that are encoded using different parameters where b and c represent bitrate and CRF. Let $s^q_{b,c}$ be a set of videos in the dataset that satisfy $L_q \leq l_q$. For each metric that shows a correlation with the performance, we calculate the probability. If $|.|$ is the cardinality of the set, the probability is calculated as follows:

$$P(L_q \leq l_q|\Theta) = \frac{|s^q_{b,c}|}{|s_{b,c}|} \tag{8}$$

Table 1. The table shows average F1-measure for ViBe, PBAS, and WREN on 4 bitrate and 5 CRF values.

Model/CRF	Bitrate 2 Mb/s					Bitrate 1.5 Mb/s				
	23	29	35	41	47	23	29	35	41	47
ViBe	0.904	0.899	0.865	0.802	0.734	0.893	0.893	0.864	0.802	0.734
PBAS	**0.968**	**0.957**	**0.939**	**0.883**	**0.744**	**0.953**	**0.951**	**0.938**	**0.882**	**0.744**
WREN	0.914	0.908	0.876	0.818	0.742	0.901	0.899	0.875	0.818	0.742
	Bitrate 1 Mb/s					Bitrate 0.5 Mb/s				
ViBe	0.875	0.874	0.857	0.802	0.732	0.832	0.831	0.828	0.797	0.735
PBAS	**0.941**	**0.940**	**0.933**	**0.882**	**0.743**	**0.900**	**0.900**	**0.899**	**0.869**	0.737
WREN	0.882	0.881	0.868	0.818	0.741	0.837	0.836	0.835	0.808	**0.740**

Let $s^{\pi}_{b,c} \in s_{b,c}$ be the subset of all videos that satisfy $L_{\pi} \leq l_{\pi}$ and $L_q \leq l_q$. We calculate the probability as follows:

$$P(L_{\pi} \leq l_{\pi}, L_q \leq l_q | \Theta) = \frac{|s^{\pi}_{b,c}|}{|s_{b,c}|} \tag{9}$$

Given an upper bound on the performance degradation in the algorithm, we use the probability function to identify the most common configuration of CRF and bitrate that can produce a video quality. For example, we could estimate the probability of incurring a loss less than 5% using the parameters $CRF = 23$, and $Bitrate = 2.00$ Mb/s by computing.

$$P(L_{\pi} \leq 5\% | L_q \leq 7.5\%, \{23, 2.00\}) = \frac{P(L_{\pi} \leq 5\%, L_q \leq 7.5\% | \{23, 2.00\})}{P(L_q \leq 5\% | \{23, 2.00\})} \tag{10}$$

We compute probabilities under three different scenarios of maximum loss of 5%, 10%, and 15% that are shown in Fig. 3. The corresponding values for the loss in quality are inferred from the relationships established in the previous subsection. We infer the following:

- Blockiness, maxPSNR and SSIM show approximately equal confidence for 10% and 15% drop in performance. SSIM shows more confidence at higher bitrate and lower CRF values for 5% drop in performance.
- The plot shows that using a CRF value of less than 29, we can decrease the bitrate from 2.00 Mb/s to 1.50 Mb/s, while staying in the 80–100% confidence range that the drop in performance would be bounded by 10%. In general, the plot indicates that choosing to lower the bitrate, has lower impact on the performance of the algorithm, over choosing a higher value for CRF.
- Using any quality metric to predict the performance of the algorithm, we can predict with 100% confidence that encoding a video with CRF value less than 35, and a bitrate greater than 1.00 Mb/s, would result in a percentage loss of less than 15%.

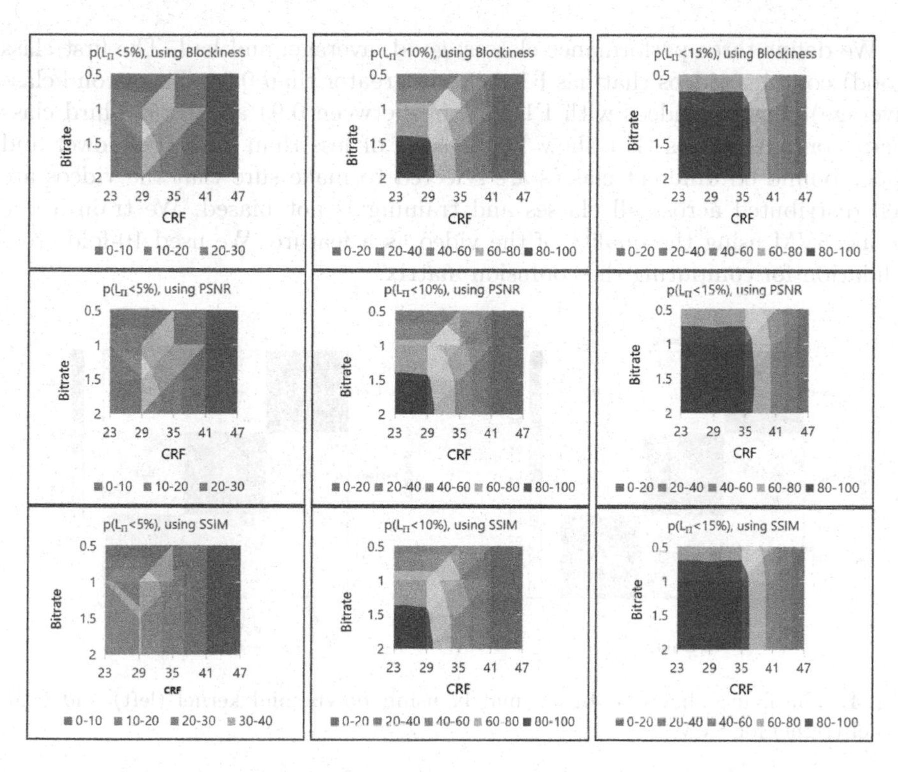

Fig. 3. Contour plots using Blockiness, PSNR, and SSIM (top to bottom) to show confidence score in 5%, 10%, 15% performance drop (left to right).

- Most surveillance systems today operate with a CRF value of 30–35, and bandwidth, of 1.50 Mb/s to 2.00 Mb/s. Using PSNR as a metric, this indicates, that the percentage loss in performance of algorithm would be bounded by 10%, with 60%–80% confidence.

5.3 Predicting Performance Based on Video Quality

To predict the performance of an algorithm, we build a classifier using video quality as a feature. Figure 2 shows a correlation between performance and three video quality metrics: PSNR, SSIM, and Blockiness. SSIM and PSNR are full reference metrics, i.e the original video is required to compute these values. Building a classifier based on these metrics have limited applicability in the real-world, as the original uncompressed video is generally not available. Blockiness is a no-reference metrics and correlates well with performance. So, we train a classifier that uses blockiness as a feature to predict the performance of the videos. PBAS [11] has shown to be more robust to compression compared to VIBE [2] and Wren [24]. We choose to build a classifier that predicts the performance of PBAS background modeling algorithm for a given video.

We define three performance classes: good, average, and bad. The first class (good) contains videos that has F1-measure greater than 0.94. The second class (average) contains videos with F1-measure between 0.94 and 0.85. Third class (bad) contains videos that show F1-measure of less than 0.85. The lower and upper bound on different classes are selected to make sure that the videos are well distributed across all classes and training is not biased. We train a one vs one SVM using the quality of the video as a feature. We used 10-fold cross validation for computing the confusion matrix.

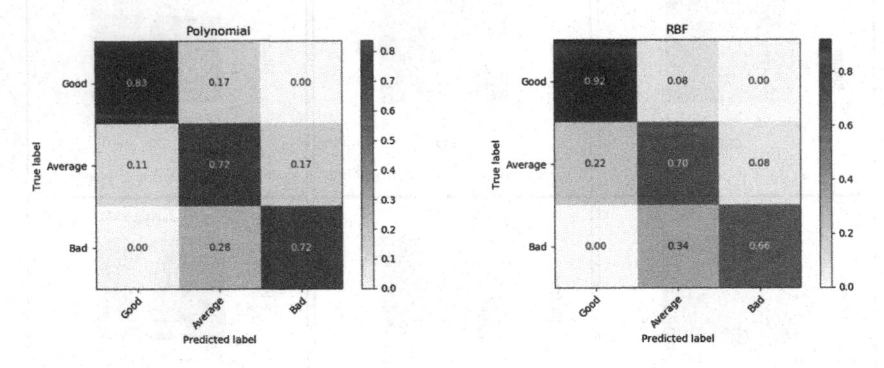

Fig. 4. The figure shows confusion matrix using polynomial kernel (left) and RBF kernel (right) for SVM

Figure 4 shows confusion matrices for SVM trained with polynomial and radial basis function (RBF) kernel. The resulting can be inferred as:

- The average accuracy of two models are similar. RBF kernel has an accuracy of 76% and polynomial kernel has accuracy of 75.6% across the three classes. However, the accuracy of classifying the good class using the RBF kernel (92%) is better than the using the polynomial kernel (83%).
- The performance for average class is nearly same for both classifiers. However, using the polynomial kernel the classifier tends to confuse the average class with bad class more often, while using the RBF kernel it tends to confuse it with the good class.
- The implications of the results are application dependent. Some application require to predict a lower bound on the algorithms. So, these applications only get effected when the actual performance is less than predicted. In RBF kernel SVM, 22% of the average class is predicted as good (actual performance is less than predicted), while for polynomial kernel only 11% of the class are classified as good. So in this case, the polynomial kernel has a desirable performance over the RBF kernel.

6 Conclusion

In this paper, we evaluated the impact of video compression on different background subtraction algorithms. Our experiment shows that performance of all algorithms is impacted by compression. PBAS is more robust to compression at lower CRF values in comparison to other algorithms. The drop in performance at higher CRF value is approximately same for all algorithms. We found that choosing a lower value for the bitrate has lower impact on the performance of algorithm over choosing a higher CRF value. The results can be used to determine the best compression parameters to minimize bitrate usage and maximize performance.

We also find the relation between video quality metrics and performance of different algorithms. Our result shows that blockiness, PSNR, SSIM show a correlation with the drop in performance of algorithms. Finally, a classifier is designed to predict the drop in performance of an algorithm using blockiness as the video quality metrics.

Acknowledgment. This work was performed in part through the financial assistance award, Multi-tiered Video Analytics for Abnormality Detection and Alerting to Improve Response Time for First Responder Communications and Operations (Grant No. 60NANB17D178), from U.S. Department of Commerce, National Institute of Standards and Technology.

References

1. Aqqa, M., Mantini, P., Shah, S.K.: Understanding how video quality affects object detection algorithms. In: 14th International Conference on Computer Vision Theory and Applications VISAPP (2019)
2. Barnich, O., Van Droogenbroeck, M.: ViBe: a universal background subtraction algorithm for video sequences. IEEE Trans. Image Process. **20**(6), 1709–1724 (2011)
3. Bradski, G.: Computer vision face tracking as a component of a perceptual user interface. In: Proceedings of the IEEE Workshop Applications of Computer Vision, pp. 214–219 (1998)
4. Brandão, T., Queluz, M.P.: No-reference quality assessment of H.264/AVC encoded video. IEEE Trans. Circ. Syst. Video Technol. **20**(11), 1437–1447 (2010)
5. Chaabouni, A., Gaudeau, Y., Lambert, J., Moureaux, J.M., Gallet, P.: Subjective and objective quality assessment for H264 compressed medical video sequences. In: 2014 4th International Conference on Image Processing Theory, Tools and Applications (IPTA), pp. 1–5. IEEE (2014)
6. Choi, M.G., Jung, J.H., Jeon, J.W.: No-reference image quality assessment using blur and noise. Int. J. Comput. Sci. Eng. **3**(2), 76–80 (2009)
7. Cozzolino, A., Flammini, F., Galli, V., Lamberti, M., Poggi, G., Pragliola, C.: Evaluating the effects of MJPEG compression on motion tracking in metro railway surveillance. In: Blanc-Talon, J., Philips, W., Popescu, D., Scheunders, P., Zemčík, P. (eds.) ACIVS 2012. LNCS, vol. 7517, pp. 142–154. Springer, Heidelberg (2012). https://doi.org/10.1007/978-3-642-33140-4_13
8. Delac, K., Grgic, M., Grgic, S.: Effects of JPEG and JPEG2000 compression on face recognition. In: Singh, S., Singh, M., Apte, C., Perner, P. (eds.) ICAPR 2005. LNCS, vol. 3687, pp. 136–145. Springer, Heidelberg (2005). https://doi.org/10.1007/11552499_16

9. Dosselmann, R., Yang, X.D.: A prototype no-reference video quality system. In: Fourth Canadian Conference on Computer and Robot Vision, pp. 411–417. IEEE (2007)
10. Farias, M.C., Mitra, S.K.: No-reference video quality metric based on artifact measurements. In: IEEE International Conference on Image Processing, ICIP 2005, vol. 3, pp. III–141. IEEE (2005)
11. Hofmann, M., Tiefenbacher, P., Rigoll, G.: Background segmentation with feedback: the pixel-based adaptive segmenter. In: 2012 IEEE Computer Society Conference on Computer Vision and Pattern Recognition Workshops (CVPRW), pp. 38–43. IEEE (2012)
12. Huang, G.B., Mattar, M., Berg, T., Learned-Miller, E.: Labeled faces in the wild: a database for studying face recognition in unconstrained environments. In: Workshop on faces in 'Real-Life' Images: Detection, Alignment, and Recognition (2008)
13. Khan, A., Sun, L., Ifeachor, E.: Impact of video content on video quality for video over wireless networks. In: Fifth International Conference on Autonomic and Autonomous Systems, ICAS 2009, pp. 277–282. IEEE (2009)
14. Klare, B., Burge, M.: Assessment of H.264 video compression on automated face recognition performance in surveillance and mobile video scenarios. In: Biometric Technology for Human Identification VII, vol. 7667, p. 76670X. International Society for Optics and Photonics (2010)
15. Korshunov, P., Ooi, W.T.: Critical video quality for distributed automated video surveillance. In: Proceedings of the 13th Annual ACM International Conference on Multimedia, pp. 151–160. ACM (2005)
16. Korshunov, P., Ooi, W.T.: Video quality for face detection, recognition, and tracking. ACM Trans. Multimedia Comput. Commun. Appl. (TOMM) **7**(3), 14 (2011)
17. Lu, J., Plataniotis, K.N., Venetsanopoulos, A.N.: Regularized discriminant analysis for the small sample size problem in face recognition. Pattern Recogn. Lett. **24**(16), 3079–3087 (2003)
18. Romaniak, P., Janowski, L., Leszczuk, M., Papir, Z.: Perceptual quality assessment for H.264/AVC compression. In: 2012 IEEE Consumer Communications and Networking Conference (CCNC), pp. 597–602. IEEE (2012)
19. Rowley, H.A., Baluja, S., Kanade, T.: Neural network-based face detection. IEEE Trans. Pattern Anal. Mach. Intell. **20**(1), 23–38 (1998)
20. Saravanakumar, S., Vadivel, A., Ahmed, C.S.: Multiple human object tracking using background subtraction and shadow removal techniques. In: 2010 International Conference on Signal and Image Processing, pp. 79–84. IEEE (2010)
21. Sobral, A.: BGSLibrary: an OpenCV C++ background subtraction library. In: IX Workshop de Visão Computacional (WVC 2013), Rio de Janeiro, Brazil, June 2013. https://github.com/andrewssobral/bgslibrary
22. Viola, P., Jones, M.J.: Robust real-time face detection. Int. J. Comput. Vision **57**(2), 137–154 (2004)
23. Wang, Z., Lu, L., Bovik, A.C.: Video quality assessment based on structural distortion measurement. Sig. Process. Image Commun. **19**(2), 121–132 (2004)
24. Wren, C.R., Azarbayejani, A., Darrell, T., Pentland, A.P.: Pfinder: real-time tracking of the human body. IEEE Trans. Pattern Anal. Mach. Intell. **7**, 780–785 (1997)

Object Detection and Anomaly Detection

Learning Motion Regularity for Temporal Video Segmentation and Anomaly Detection

Fatima Zohra Daha and Shishir K. Shah(✉)

University of Houston, 4800 Calhoun Road, Houston, TX 77204, USA
fdaha@uh.edu, sshah@central.uh.edu

Abstract. Detecting anomalous events in a long video sequence is a challenging task due to the subjective definition of "anomalous" as well as the duration of such events. Anomalous events are usually short-lived and occur rarely. We propose a semi-supervised solution to detect such events. Our method is able to capture the video segment where the anomaly happens via the analyses of the interaction between the spatially co-located interest points. The evolution of their motion characteristics is modeled and abrupt changes are used to temporally segment the videos. Spatiotemporal and motion features are then extracted to model standard events and identify the anomalous segments using a one-class classifier. Quantitative and qualitative experiments on publicly available anomaly detection dataset capturing real-world scenarios show that the proposed method outperforms state-of-the-art approaches.

1 Introduction

With the increasing number of indoor and outdoor surveillance cameras as well as the different events that would be of concern for public safety, scene understanding and anomaly detection have gained significant attention from the computer vision community. Anomaly detection (so-called outliers detection) is basically the identification of anything that deviates from the norm. Anomalies can be subjective and depend on many aspects. They could represent irregular behaviors (e.g. fights, crimes), illegal activities (e.g. illegal U-turn) or natural disasters (e.g. earthquakes), just to cite a few. Detecting anomalies in videos from public space cameras facilitates continuous video monitoring to improve first responder communications and operations while reducing the workload on human operators, therefore reducing the scale of mishaps.

Over the past several years, considerable attempts have been made towards video analytics for monitoring, e.g. analytics for left object (baggage) detection or line (perimeter) crossing are common today. However, these tools require extensive human involvement to initialize or define parameters for effective utilization. The anomaly detection task still remains very challenging and is not completely solved because of the vague definition of anomaly, its wide range

S. Palaiahnakote et al. (Eds.): ACPR 2019, LNCS 12046, pp. 121–135, 2020.
https://doi.org/10.1007/978-3-030-41404-7_9

of activities, the lack of annotated data, the duration of the anomaly and the different characteristics of the scene (e.g. day/night, indoor/outdoor).

In this paper, we propose a graph-based semi-supervised learning approach to identify anomalous segments in videos from surveillance cameras. Semi-supervised video segmentation is performed to identify significant changes in the observed scene. This is based on coherent motion detection and dominant motion extraction using graph modeling. From each segment of the video, spatiotemporal features are extracted to model the observed scene. A one-class classification model is finally used to detect anomalous segments.

The remainder of this paper is organized as follows. In the next section, we discuss some of the previous work on anomaly detection. Section 3 provides detailed discussions and explanation of the proposed anomaly detection and temporal video segmentation approaches. Experimental results on real-world dataset are presented in Sect. 4. In the conclusion section, we briefly elaborate other worthy investigation applications for further research.

2 Related Work

Anomaly Detection: Many surveillance systems have been proposed in recent years [7,16,17,30]. Some of them focus on specific types of anomalies. Kelathodi Kumaran *et al.* [9] present a survey where they explore various anomaly detection techniques that can be applied on roads, such as traffic accident detectors. Violence has also attracted many researchers [6,7,18]. In [6], a method based on optical flow energy characteristics is presented for pedestrian violence detection. Mohammadi *et al.* [18] identify violence by describing the cognitive processes that gives rise to the behavioral patterns observed in crowd scenes using heuristics. More recently, Hansaon *et al.* [7] leverage long-range information in both temporal directions of the video via a Spatiotemporal Encoder. Panic scenarios have also been addressed by many researchers. Mehran *et al.* [17] suggested using Social Force models to capture the dynamics of the crowd behavior and detect the escaping crowd. Besides approaches that try to solve specific anomaly scenarios, several techniques have been utilized to learn normal motion patterns. Among those, Mixture of Dynamic Textures (has been used to detect temporal abnormality [13,16]. Wu *et al.* [2] model crowded scenes using particle trajectories then use chaotic dynamics to characterize the motion. Zhu *et al.* [30] capture the anomaly using context-aware model.

Following the success of deep learning based methods [3,8,22,26] in many computer vision and semantic understanding tasks, [8,26] used autoencoders to learn a generative model for regular motion patterns. Sultani *et al.* [22] used deep multiple instance ranking framework to learn the anomaly. However, all these anomaly detection techniques either require annotated data for training, which is a challenging task, or they are based on the reconstruction of normal training data using deep neural networks. These models assume that abnormal events would correspond to larger reconstruction errors, but due to their generalization ability, this assumption often fails. Our approach aims at overcoming both the issues of labeled data and generalization capacity of deep neural networks and to further boost the performance of the anomaly detection systems.

Temporal Video Segmentation: One of the main modules in our approach is temporal video segmentation, which aims at dividing a video into temporal volumes that share semantically related content. This task is different from spatiotemporal segmentation [5,12], which helps accomplishing other video analysis tasks such as image classification, scene reconstruction and object tracking. A vast majority of temporal video segmentation techniques are developed to solve the problem of structured video summarization [4,28] or video action segmentation. These works generally focus on videos related to a specific domain e.g. cooking [10,11] or sports [15]. Therefore, it's usually hard to extend these techniques to general video sequences.

Many types of visual attributes have been used for temporal video segmentation. In [20], Simakov *et al.* propose a bi-directional similarity measure between visual data. Chasanis *et al.* [1] create a bag of visual words for each shot. In [27], pixels comparison have been used to accomplish this task. In [4], Potapov *et al.* apply low level visual features to detect kernel-based change points. Our approach is significantly different from these methods. We use pixel level motion to cluster interest points based on motion coherency.

3 Anomaly Detection Method

Our anomaly detection approach is summarized in Fig. 1. First, we use our temporal video segmentation module to divide the video into segments based on motion coherency of interest points. Every resultant segment shares semantically related content with consistent evolution of motion over time. Then, spatiotemporal features (C3D) are extracted for every segment using a pre-trained model [23]. We introduce another attribute computed from the video segmentation module to model motion transformation over video sequences.

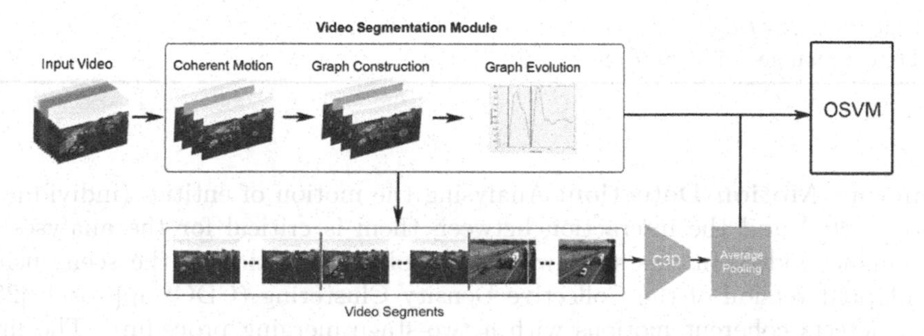

Fig. 1. The flow diagram of the proposed approach. First, the videos are temporally segmented according to interest points motion and interaction. Then, features for every video segment are extracted. Finally, a one-class classifier is trained to learn normal events.

Using segments from normal videos, we train a unary classifier that learns normal patterns. This avoids the need for having annotated abnormal videos to detect anomalies.

3.1 Temporal Video Segmentation

To temporally segment our videos, we cluster interest points based on motion coherency using pixel level motion. Constructing a graph model of our clusters, we extract the dominant motion in the scene and its characteristics (e.g. orientation, magnitude, position). Our hypothesis is that the interaction between the spatially co-located interest points exhibit similar motion characteristics. The evolution of this motion is modeled, and sudden changes are used to temporally segment the videos.

From the temporal perspective, entities in a group share a common goal, resulting in motion consistency in spatial domain. The evolution of this motion over time allows us to segment the videos based on meaningful events happening in the scene without supervision. The operational flow of the proposed system is explained in the pseudo code as listed in Algorithm 1.

Algorithm 1. Temporal Video Segmentation

```
Input: Video with n frames
Output: Frame IDs where change occurred
1  initialize step                              // number of successive frames
2  sceneRep is an array                              // scene representation
3  for i = 0; i < n − step/2; i = i + step/2 do
4  |   Track interest points (IPs)
5  |   Cluster IPs based on motion
6  |   Construct graph
7  |   Refine the graph
8  |   Form feature vector featVec
9  |   Append featVec to sceneRep
10 Smooth sceneRep
11 Detect changes in sceneRep
```

Coherent Motion Detection: Analysing the motion of entities (individuals, objects, etc.) and the interaction between them is critical for the analyses of surveillance video. In this step, we detect coherent motion in the scene using an adapted version of the Collective Density Clustering (CDC) approach [25]. CDC detects coherent motions with a two-stage merging procedure. The first stage consists of identifying local collective subgroups with entities having similar behavior. This behavior is estimated by factors such as spatial position and orientation of moving particles. These particles are extracted from the scene as interest points using the generalized KLT tracker [29]. The second stage focuses on characterizing the global consistency by merging collective subgroups. This stage is helpful in situations of extremely low density (e.g. off-peak traffic), which leads to the clustering of entities into subgroups because they are spatially far from each other even if their motion is coherent. The distribution of orientation of the adjacent sets in these subgroups determines whether they should be merged. To adapt this approach to our situation, we include a condition about the distribution of magnitude of the adjacent sets as well. The coherent motion based scene segmentation is treated as a clustering process of interest points.

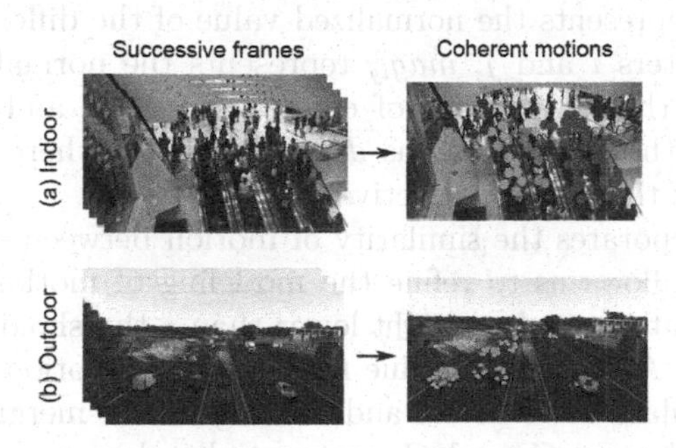

Fig. 2. Coherent motion detection via CDC approach. The color of every interest point represents its assignment to a cluster. The "+" in red represent outliers. (Color figure online)

The advantage of this approach compared to others [24] is its ability to detect coherent motions of varying densities and arbitrary shapes. The illustrations of collective clustering algorithm for indoor and outdoor scenes are shown in Fig. 2(a) and (b), respectively. Points with different colors indicate that they belong to different clusters of coherent motion. Entities in (a) represent people, while in (b) they represent vehicles. The "+" in red represents outliers, i.e. clusters with one interest point only. These outliers are resulting from low quality of videos and tracking. Given their characteristics, they will be clustered independently with a single point.

Graph Representation of Motion: The coherent motions detected in the above step are represented as clusters. Interactions between different clusters play an important role in further refining the clusters and capturing the topological structure of these interactions. To do so, we propose to model the structure as a graph $G = (V, E)$ as shown in Fig. 3.

Let $G = (V, E)$ be an undirected fully connected graph whose vertices are centroids of the clusters and edges are factors representing similarities of motion (i.e. orientation and magnitude) between the clusters. A fully connected graph ensures that we capture the motion information occurring between every pair of clusters. A scene with n different coherent motions may be represented with a graph of n vertices. To capture the exact structure of the motion in the scene and to track its spatial evolution over time, the pixel coordinates of each vertex are the spatial position of its associated cluster's centroid.

Let V_i and V_j be two vertices, and E_{ij} be the edge between them. The edge's weight w_{ij} is the Euclidean norm of their velocities and orientations as in Eq. (1). According to the definition of the edge weight, a larger value of w_{ij} indicates that the two clusters C_i and C_j have inconsistent motion i.e. different orientation, different magnitude, or both.

$$w_{ij} = \sqrt{ori_{ij} + mag_{ij}} \tag{1}$$

where, $ori_{ij} = \frac{|ori_j - ori_i|}{\pi}$ and $mag_{ij} = \frac{|mag_j - mag_i|}{d}$.

In Eq. 1, ori_{ij} represents the normalized value of the difference between the orientations of clusters i and j, mag_{ij} represents the normalized value of the difference between the magnitudes of clusters i and j, and d represents the diagonal length of the scene given as $d = \sqrt{h^2 + w^2}$, where h and w are the height and width of the video, respectively.

The graph incorporates the similarity of motion between every pair of clusters (nodes). This allows us to refine the modeling of motion in the scene by merging clusters that have edge weight lower than a threshold and are spatially close to each other. A lower edge value reveals higher motion coherency of two clusters. We recalculate the centroid and the edges after merging. As illustrated in Fig. 3, the two clusters C_2 and C_4 are spatially close to each other and the motion similarity between them is very high, represented by a thin edge with a weight lower than the cut_off value cut_w, specifically $w_{24} < cut_w$. Therefore, they are considered as coherent subgroups and have been grouped together. After merging, we recompute the edges between every pair of clusters as in Eq. (1). The empirical value of cut_w is set to 0.1.

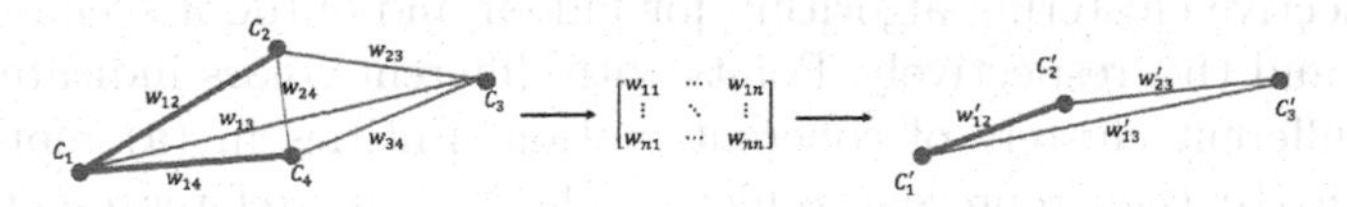

Fig. 3. Graph refining based on the similarities between clusters properties. The width of an edge is proportional to its weight. Clusters C_2 and C_4 have been merged, therefore creating a new cluster C'_2.

The graph evolves over time from one set of frames to another. We quantify the relationships in the graph and its evolution over time to detect anomalies. Our hypothesis is that the graph keeps similar overall motion from one set to another if the events happening in the scene are uniform. A change in motion or abrupt transitions would result in a significant change in the graph-based motion representation. We generate a feature vector for every set of frames $featVec = [m, p, l, e, a]$ to represent the motion in the scene. In our feature representation, we mainly consider the dominant motion in the scene and some characteristics of the graph-based motion representation:

- m is the number of nodes in the graph,
- p is the number of interest points,

- l is the $l2$-norm of the matrix representing the graph weights,
- e is the average of the matrix eigenvalues,
- a is the area where motion is concentrated in the scene. To compute a, we construct a convex hull of a set of points P, with P representing the nodes of the graph. Then we compute the area of this convex hull.

Every element in the feature vector is normalized by its maximum value across the whole video using the following function $\phi(x) = \frac{x}{\max_{j \in N}\{x_j\}}$, with N representing the number of frame sets (segments) in the video.

Change Detection: Given the feature vector generated from the previous steps, we compute the Euclidean distance between every consecutive element. A time series X is therefore generated as in Eq. 2.

$$x_i = \sqrt{\sum_{n=1}^{5}(featVec_{n,i} - featVec_{n,i+1})^2}, \forall i \in N \tag{2}$$

We identify changes in the resulting time series X. Our idea is that the evolution of the signal would not change if semantically related events are happening in the scene. We find the points in X at which the root-mean-square level of the signal changes most significantly. Figure 4 illustrates this step. The x-coordinates of the blue lines indicate the points where changes occur. Therefore, we partition the time series X into 3 regions separated by the blue lines.

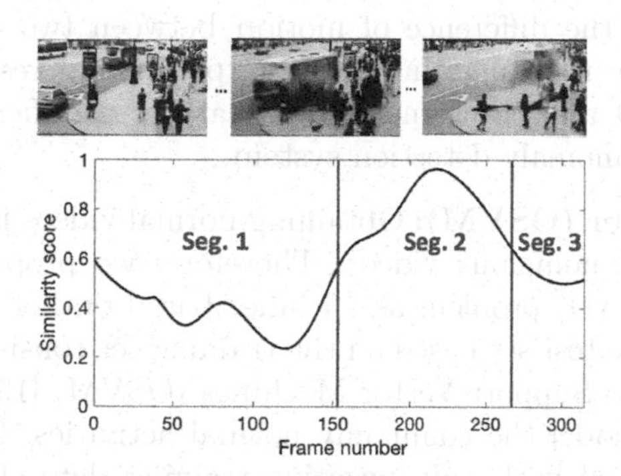

Fig. 4. Example of video segmentation. Each blue line represents a break-point that delineates segments with different motion characteristics. (Color figure online)

3.2 Anomaly Detection

Having obtained temporally segmented videos with each segment representing semantically consistent content. Our goal is to find features representing each of these segments and then train a one-class SVM (OSVM) to learn regular patterns. The intuition behind this approach is that the built classification model will learn regularities in video sequences. In other words, it will learn a decision function that classifies new data as similar to the training data (normal segments) or different from it (abnormal segments).

Video Segment Representation: Most existing work only considers handcrafted features, such as Histogram of Oriented Gradients (HOG) or Histogram of Optical Flow (HOF) [8] to learn regularities in video sequences. Our hypothesis is that the combination of spatial, temporal and motion features can help improve the modeling of regularities.

C3D architecture was originally designed for action recognition tasks. Such C3D networks have a useful attribute that models both appearance and motion. They preserve the temporal information of the input signal via the time dimension that is not present in 2D ConvNets. The resulting features of 3D ConvNets have proved to be powerful for many other tasks. We use a ResNet model pre-trained on UCF101 dataset [21]. The input of C3D is a short video clip of 16 successive frames. The output from the pooling layer for every 16-frame clip is a 512-dimensional feature. To obtain features for a video segment, we take the average of all 16-frame clip features within that segment [22] followed by $l2$ normalization. Then, we use PCA for dimensionality reduction. We refer to this representation as C3D video descriptor in the remaining of this work.

We also use an additional attribute computed from the signal representing the graph similarity between every consecutive frame sets. We compute the range of the signal for every segment, $range = highest\_value - lowest\_value$. As illustrated in Fig. 5, when the event happening in a given segment is normal, the range is low. In contrast, when something sudden or abnormal happens during the video sequence, the difference of motion between two consecutive graphs is different, therefore the range increases. Experimental results show how the combination of C3D and the signal range features significantly improves the performance of our anomaly detection system.

One-Class Classifier (OSVM): Obtaining normal videos is an easy task compared to gathering anomalous videos. Therefore, we propose to address the anomaly detection (AD) problem as an inlier-based outlier detection task, i.e. finding outliers in the test set based on the training set consisting only of inliers. We train a One-Class Support Vector Machines (OSVM) [19] with only normal training videos to model the commonly normal activities. OSVM is an SVM-based detector trained with only negative training data. Its basic idea is to separate data samples $\{x_k\}_{k=1}^{n}$ into outliers and inliers by a hyperplane. In our context, due to the complexity of our data, we apply the Gaussian Radial Basis Function (RBF) kernel for the OSVM. We control its sensitivity by adjusting the number of support vectors.

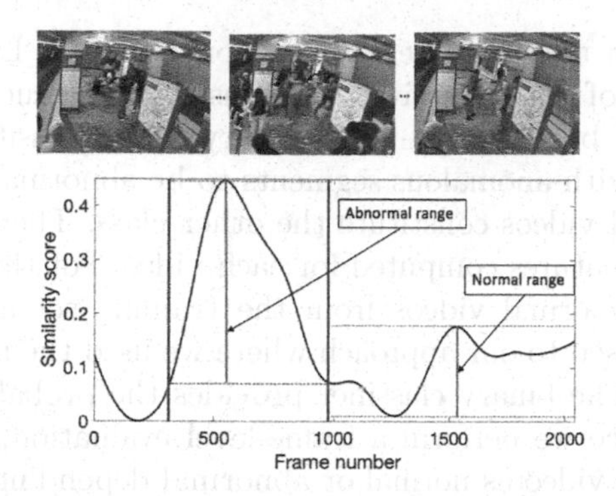

Fig. 5. Illustration of range values for a normal video segment versus an abnormal video segment. For anomalous segments, the range is usually higher due to abrupt changes in motion. Blue vertical lines delimit consecutive video segments. (Color figure online)

4 Experiments

In this section, we first describe the dataset used to evaluate our framework. Then, we specify the implementation details. Finally, we present the performance of our method versus the baseline and state-of-the-art approaches. We also report the performance of our temporal video segmentation module separately.

4.1 Dataset

We conducted our experiments on the UCF Crime dataset [22] which consists of real-world surveillance videos. This dataset contains normal activities as well as 13 types of anomalies: *Abuse, Accident, Arrest, Arson, Assault, Burglary, Explosion, Fighting, Robbery, Shooting, Shoplifting, Stealing and Vandalism.*

This dataset has video-level labels, i.e. normal or abnormal, for the training set that consists of 800 normal and 810 abnormal videos. The testing set however has temporal annotations, i.e. the start and ending frames of the anomalous event, and it includes 150 normal and 140 abnormal videos.

Since our method requires normal videos only for training, we use the 800 normal videos from the training set to train OSVM.

4.2 Implementation Details

For our one-class classifier, we used grid-search to find the optimal hyperparameters. We use momentum $\mu = 0.04$ and $\gamma = 0.5$. The C3D feature vector computed is of 512-dimension. We use PCA for dimensionality reduction. For the best performance, the number of component is set to 4.

We evaluate our pipeline against three state-of-the-art methods [8,14,22]. Sultani *et al.* [22] proposed a deep multiple instance ranking framework to learn anomalies. Hasan *et al.* [8] proposed a fully convolutional deep autoencoder to learn a generative model for regular motion patterns. Lu *et al.* [14] learns sparse combinations of normal activities and used reconstruction errors to identify anomalies. As a baseline, we use a binary SVM classifier. In essence, we consider the videos with anomalous segments to be abnormal, thus constituting one class and normal videos constitute the other class. Then we train the classifier with the C3D features computed for each video. For this baseline method, both normal and abnormal videos from the training set are used to train a binary SVM as opposed to our approach where we used the normal set from the training data only. The binary classifier provides the probability of each video to be abnormal. Since we perform a frame-level evaluation, we classify all the frames of a classified video as normal or abnormal depending on the video-level classification provided by the binary SVM.

4.3 Results

Quantitative Evaluation: The performance of our method is evaluated using frame-level receiver operating characteristic (ROC) curve and area under the curve (AUC). A higher AUC indicates better performance. For frame-level evaluation, we alter frame abnormality threshold to produce the ROC curve shown in Fig. 6. The AUC of different methods is listed in Table 1. We can see that our method outperforms all existing methods, which demonstrates the effectiveness of our approach. Moreover, it's important to note that our method learns normal behavior from normal video sequences only, therefore avoiding the need of annotated abnormal videos for the training process.

In video surveillance systems, reducing the false alarm rate has received significant attention. A false alarm happens when normal behaviour is marked as anomalous. A system with high false alarm rate results in an overwhelming manual validation workload for the operators, especially since in real-life system, a considerable part of surveillance videos is normal and only sometimes abnormal events happen. We measure the false alarm rate by counting false-positives on the subset from UCF Crime dataset representing normal videos only and we compare the performance of our approach to other methods. We report the results in Table 2. Our model achieves lower FAR compared to other methods, which reduces significantly the human intervention rate.

Qualitative Evaluation: Some success and failure cases for our anomaly detection method are shown in Fig. 7. In (a), (b) and (c), we successfully identified the segment where the anomaly happened. In the case of (d), all the frames of a normal video have been successfully identified as normal. However, we misdetect the anomaly in (e) due to the lack of scene context. The person committing the burglary crime in this video appears to be a resident of the house. The darkness of the scene and the extremely low motion cause our system to fail in detecting the anomaly. In the case of (f), a false alarm is caused by a group of people who start running suddenly in the street. It's actually quite challenging for humans as well to determine whether an abnormal event is happening in the scene.

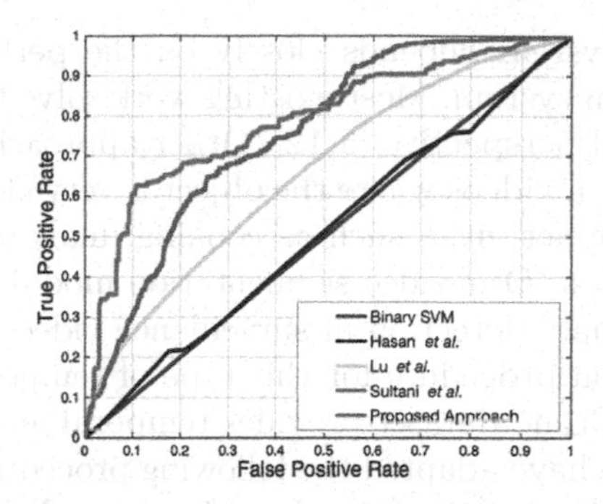

Fig. 6. Performance comparison (ROC) of various methods on UCF Crime dataset. Our approach achieves 78.3% on AUC and outperforms state-of-the-art by 3%

Table 1. Performance comparison (AUC) of various methods on UCF Crime dataset.

Method	AUC
Binary SVM	50.0
Hasan *et al.* [8]	50.6
Lu *et al.* [14]	65.5
Sultani *et al.* [22]	75.4
Proposed method	**78.3**

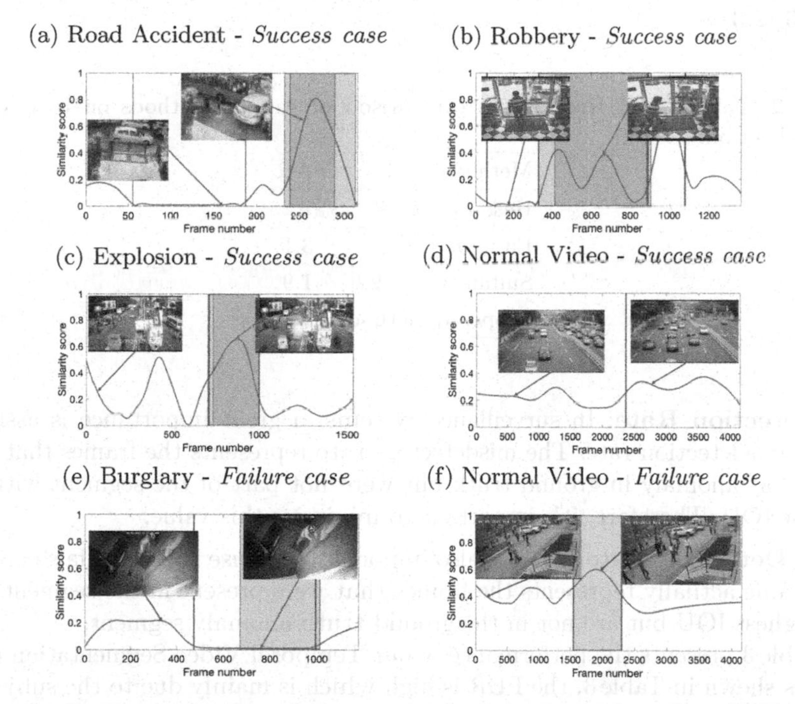

Fig. 7. Qualitative evaluation of our approach on testing videos from UCF Crime dataset. Red colored window indicates ground truth anomalous segment. Blue colored window shows the anomalous segment detected using our method. Blue vertical lines partitions the video into regions. (Color figure online)

4.4 Analysis of the Impact of Temporal Video Segmentation

Our key idea is to temporally segment the video based on the events happening in the scene. Every segment should contain consistent motion. Therefore, the performance of our anomaly detection system depends closely on the performance of our temporal video segmentation system. Most existing work solve the video segmentation work from the spatial perspective [5,12]. Other approaches that leverage temporal information focus on videos where the object is very close to the camera, and they focus on specific activities such as cooking, make up, etc. for the purpose of video summarization. Our video segmentation module is based on motion and is oriented for anomaly detection in surveillance videos.

Since there is no established evaluation procedure for this type of temporal video segmentation, and since the UCF Crime dataset provides temporal annotation for the anomalous segment only, we have adapted the following procedure. We compute the misdetection rate (MDR) and the false detection rate (FDR) between the anomalous segment in ground truth and the obtained segment from our temporal video segmentation module that has the highest Intersection Over Union (IOU) with the GT anomalous segment. For example, in the case of Fig. 8, MDR and FDR will be computed between the GT anomalous segment and segment 3 (s_3).

Table 2. False Alarm Rate (FAR) comparison of various methods on UCF Crime **normal** set only.

Method	FAR
Hasan *et al.* [8]	27.2
Lu *et al.* [14]	3.1
Sultani *et al.* [22]	1.9
Proposed method	**1.0**

Misdetection Rate: In surveillance systems, a great importance is assigned to the misdetection rate. The misdetection rate represents the frames that were labeled as anomaly in ground truth but were not part of the segment with the highest IOU. Therefore, it's important to minimize this value.

False Detection Rate: FDR is also important because it creates false alarms. This value actually represents the frames that were present in the segment with the highest IOU but are not in the ground truth anomaly segment.

Table 3 presents the performance of our Temporal Video Segmentation module. As shown in Table 3, the FDR is high which is mainly due to the subjectivity of the anomaly definition. In the temporal annotation provided along with the UCF Crime dataset, the anomalous segments are usually short, some videos even have two anomalous segments separated by less than 5 s. This ground truth temporal annotation gives more weight to the beginning of the anomalous event, while our segmentation system identifies the video clip beginning with the frame where the anomaly started until the end of the anomaly. Basically, when an anomalous event happens in the scene, atypical behaviors last until the scene goes back to normal. This subjectivity in the definition of the anomalous segment results in higher MDR and FDR.

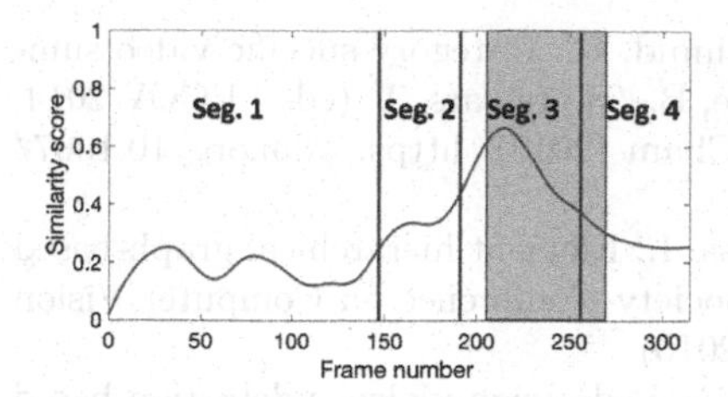

Fig. 8. Example of anomalous segment selection based on IOU. Red colored window represents the ground truth anomalous segment (s_gt). Blue lines delimit video segments. (s_gt) intersects with two of our resulting segments (s_3 and s_4), but $IOU(s\_gt, s\_3) > IOU(s\_gt, s\_4)$. (Color figure online)

Table 3. Performance of our Temporal Video Segmentation approach on the anomalous videos from UCF Crime test set.

Method	MDR	FDR
Proposed method	9.2	27.3

5 Conclusion

In this paper, we propose a semi-supervised motion-based model that learns motion regularity from surveillance videos. Our method can be used to temporally segment videos based on motion coherency. Moreover, it has the ability to identify video segments where abnormalities happen. Experiments on real-world video surveillance dataset show that our approach outperforms state-of-the-art methods while reducing the false alarm rate. Moreover, we overcome the need of anomalous dataset to train our model which is a laborious and challenging task. Our approach has various potential applications and extensions to be explored in future work. It can be used for action recognition. The extended model also has the potential to identify different anomaly scenes. Furthermore, the improvement of the temporal video segmentation module will lead to a better performance on anomaly detection task.

Acknowledgement. This work was performed in part through the financial assistance award, Multitiered Video Analytics for Abnormality Detection and Alerting to Improve Response Time for First Responder Communications and Operations (Grant No. 60NANB17D178), from U.S. Department of Commerce, National Institute of Standards and Technology.

References

1. Chasanis, V., Kalogeratos, A., Likas, A.: Movie segmentation into scenes and chapters using locally weighted bag of visual words (2009)
2. Cui, X., Liu, Q., Gao, M., Metaxas, D.N.: Abnormal detection using interaction energy potentials. In: CVPR 2011, pp. 3161–3167 (2011)
3. Daha, F., Hewavitharana, S.: Deep neural architecture with character embedding for semantic frame detection, pp. 302–307 (2019)

4. Potapov, D., Douze, M., Harchaoui, Z., Schmid, C.: Category-specific video summarization. In: Fleet, D., Pajdla, T., Schiele, B., Tuytelaars, T. (eds.) ECCV 2014. LNCS, vol. 8694, pp. 540–555. Springer, Cham (2014). https://doi.org/10.1007/978-3-319-10599-4_35
5. Grundmann, M., Kwatra, V., Han, M., Essa, I.: Efficient hierarchical graph-based video segmentation. In: IEEE Computer Society Conference on Computer Vision and Pattern Recognition, pp. 2141–2148 (2010)
6. Guo, Z., Wu, F., Chen, H., Yuan, J., Cai, C.: Pedestrian violence detection based on optical flow energy characteristics. In: 2017 4th International Conference on Systems and Informatics (ICSAI), pp. 1261–1265 (2017)
7. Hanson, A., PNVR, K., Krishnagopal, S., Davis, L.: Bidirectional convolutional LSTM for the detection of violence in videos. In: Leal-Taixé, L., Roth, S. (eds.) ECCV 2018. LNCS, vol. 11130, pp. 280–295. Springer, Cham (2019). https://doi.org/10.1007/978-3-030-11012-3_24
8. Hasan, M., Choi, J., Neumann, J., Roy-Chowdhury, A.K., Davis, L.S.: Learning temporal regularity in video sequences. In: 2016 IEEE Conference on Computer Vision and Pattern Recognition (CVPR), pp. 733–742 (2016)
9. Kelathodi Kumaran, S., Dogra, D., Roy, P.: Anomaly detection in road traffic using visual surveillance: a survey (2019)
10. Lea, C., Flynn, M.D., Vidal, R., Reiter, A., Hager, G.D.: Temporal convolutional networks for action segmentation and detection. In: 2017 IEEE Conference on Computer Vision and Pattern Recognition (CVPR), pp. 1003–1012 (2017)
11. Lea, C., Reiter, A., Vidal, R., Hager, G.D.: Segmental spatiotemporal CNNs for fine-grained action segmentation. In: Leibe, B., Matas, J., Sebe, N., Welling, M. (eds.) ECCV 2016. LNCS, vol. 9907, pp. 36–52. Springer, Cham (2016). https://doi.org/10.1007/978-3-319-46487-9_3
12. Lezama, J., Alahari, K., Sivic, J., Laptev, I.: Track to the future: spatio-temporal video segmentation with long-range motion cues. In: CVPR, pp. 3369–3376 (2011)
13. Li, W., Mahadevan, V., Vasconcelos, N.: Anomaly detection and localization in crowded scenes. IEEE Trans. Pattern Anal. Mach. Intell. **36**(1), 18–32 (2014)
14. Lu, C., Shi, J., Jia, J.: Abnormal event detection at 150 FPS in MATLAB. In: 2013 IEEE International Conference on Computer Vision, pp. 2720–2727, December 2013
15. Lu, J., Xu, R., Corso, J.J.: Human action segmentation with hierarchical supervoxel consistency. In: CVPR, pp. 3762–3771 (2015)
16. Mahadevan, V., Li, W., Bhalodia, V., Vasconcelos, N.: Anomaly detection in crowded scenes. In: 2010 IEEE Computer Society Conference on Computer Vision and Pattern Recognition, pp. 1975–1981 (2010)
17. Mehran, R., Oyama, A., Shah, M.: Abnormal crowd behavior detection using social force model. In: 2009 IEEE Conference on Computer Vision and Pattern Recognition, pp. 935–942 (2009)
18. Mohammadi, S., Perina, A., Kiani, H., Murino, V.: Angry crowds: detecting violent events in videos. In: Leibe, B., Matas, J., Sebe, N., Welling, M. (eds.) ECCV 2016. LNCS, vol. 9911, pp. 3–18. Springer, Cham (2016). https://doi.org/10.1007/978-3-319-46478-7_1
19. Schölkopf, B., Williamson, R., Smola, A., Shawe-Taylor, J., Platt, J.: Support vector method for novelty detection. In: Proceedings of the 12th International Conference on Neural Information Processing Systems, NIPS 1999, pp. 582–588 (1999)

20. Simakov, D., Caspi, Y., Shechtman, E., Irani, M.: Summarizing visual data using bidirectional similarity. In: 2008 IEEE Conference on Computer Vision and Pattern Recognition, pp. 1–8 (2008)
21. Soomro, K., Roshan Zamir, A., Shah, M.: UCF101: a dataset of 101 human actions classes from videos in the wild. CoRR (2012)
22. Sultani, W., Chen, C., Shah, M.: Real-world anomaly detection in surveillance videos. In: Conference on Computer Vision and Pattern Recognition (2018)
23. Tran, D., Bourdev, L., Fergus, R., Torresani, L., Paluri, M.: Learning spatiotemporal features with 3D convolutional networks. In: 2015 IEEE International Conference on Computer Vision (ICCV), pp. 4489–4497 (2015)
24. Wang, S., Wang, D., Li, C., Li, Y., Ding, G.: Clustering by fast search and find of density peaks with data field. Chin. J. Electron. **25**(3), 397–402 (2016)
25. Wu, Y., Ye, Y., Zhao, C.: Coherent motion detection with collective density clustering. In: Proceedings of the 23rd ACM International Conference on Multimedia, MM 2015, New York, NY, USA, pp. 361–370 (2015)
26. Xu, D., Ricci, E., Yan, Y., Song, J., Sebe, N.: Learning deep representations of appearance and motion for anomalous event detection. In: Computer Vision and Image Understanding (2015)
27. Zhang, H., Kankanhalli, A., Smoliar, S.W.: Automatic partitioning of full-motion video. Multimedia Syst. **1**(1), 10–28 (1993)
28. Zhang, S., Zhu, Y., Roy-Chowdhury, A.K.: Context-aware surveillance video summarization. IEEE Trans. Image Process. **25**(11), 5469–5478 (2016)
29. Zhou, B., Tang, X., Zhang, H., Wang, X.: Measuring crowd collectiveness. IEEE Trans. Pattern Anal. Mach. Intell. **36**(8), 1586–1599 (2014)
30. Zhu, Y., Nayak, M., Roy-Chowdhury, K.: Context-aware activity recognition and anomaly detection in video. IEEE J. Sel. Top. Signal Process. **7**(1), 91–101 (2013)

A New Forged Handwriting Detection Method Based on Fourier Spectral Density and Variation

Sayani Kundu[1], Palaiahnakote Shivakumara[2], Anaica Grouver[2], Umapada Pal[1], Tong Lu[3](✉), and Michael Blumenstein[4]

[1] Computer Vision and Pattern Recognition Unit, Indian Statistical Institute, Kolkata, Kolkata, India
sayani.frndz@gmail.com, umapada@isical.ac.in

[2] Faculty of Computer Science and Information Technology, University of Malaya, Kuala Lumpur, Malaysia
shiva@um.edu.my, anaicagrouver@gmail.com

[3] National Key Lab for Novel Software Technology, Nanjing University, Nanjing, China
lutong@nju.edu.cn

[4] Faculty of Engineering and Information Technology, University of Technology, Sydney, Ultimo, Australia
Michael.Blumenstein@uts.edu.au

Abstract. Use of handwriting words for person identification in contrast to biometric features is gaining importance in the field of forensic applications. As a result, forging handwriting is a part of crime applications and hence is challenging for the researchers. This paper presents a new work for detecting forged handwriting words because width and amplitude of spectral distributions have the ability to exhibit unique properties for forged handwriting words compared to blurred, noisy and normal handwriting words. The proposed method studies spectral density and variation of input handwriting images through clustering of high and low frequency coefficients. The extracted features, which are invariant to rotation and scaling, are passed to a neural network classifier for the classification for forged handwriting words from other types of handwriting words (like blurred, noisy and normal handwriting words). Experimental results on our own dataset, which consists of four handwriting word classes, and two benchmark datasets, namely, caption and scene text classification and forged IMEI number dataset, show that the proposed method outperforms the existing methods in terms of classification rate.

Keywords: Handwriting recognition · Forgery detection · Fourier spectrum · Spectral distributions · Forged handwriting word detection

1 Introduction

Due to rapid advancements in life and technology, crime rates are increasing exponentially in the world [1]. At the same time, techniques to find a solution to crime or forensic issues are also advancing in the research field. For example, the methods based on biometric features to protect properties from various crimes [2], are popular and successful

S. Palaiahnakote et al. (Eds.): ACPR 2019, LNCS 12046, pp. 136–150, 2020.
https://doi.org/10.1007/978-3-030-41404-7_10

in the market. However, sometimes, these systems are not reliable due to the creation of fake inputs and open environments [3]. Besides, the systems are computationally expensive. To overcome such limitations, systems use handwriting as a part of verification because handwriting can help us in identifying persons, persons' behaviors, gender or ages, document verification, authentication, fraud document identification, etc. [3]. In contrast to biometric feature based methods, handwriting process does not consume high processing time. Therefore, the number of applications and importance of handwriting increases. In the meantime, forging, tampering and creating fake writing also increases. Hence, detecting forged handwriting words is an unsolved issue for the researchers in the field of image processing and pattern recognition. The variations in handwriting make the problem more complex and challenging.

Forgery detection in images and videos, fraud document identification, printer identification and signature verification are all well-known topics in the literature [4]. There are several methods for addressing challenges of the above-mentioned topics. It is noted from the methods developed in the past that they work based on the fact that forgery operation introduces noises [5]. It is valid but noises can exist due to blurring, and flaws in devices or writing style in case of handwriting. Therefore, the methods developed in the past may not work for forged handwriting detection. Hence, we consider forged handwriting detection as a four-class classification problem in this work. The classification problem includes classes of Forged words created by copy-paste, insertion and deletion operations, Normal words (any word without forgery operation), Blurred words (we manually add Gaussian blur) and Noisy words (we add Gaussian noise to the words) as the sample images are shown in Fig. 1. Figure 1 shows that it is hard to identify a forged word from the normal one with our naked eyes. The proposed work aims to detect forged handwriting words irrespective of blur and noise.

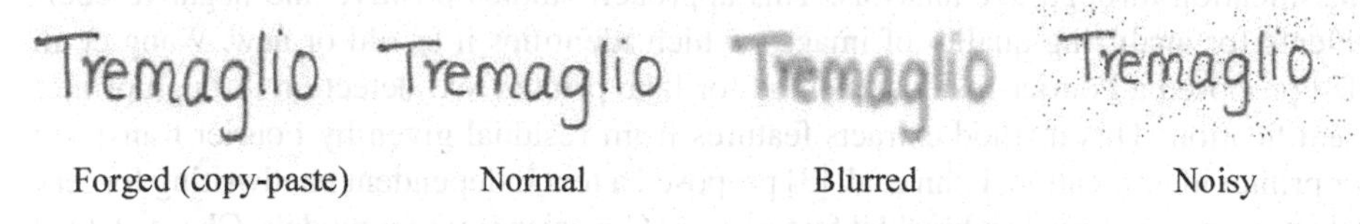

Fig. 1. Examples for four classes of handwriting words.

2 Related Work

As per our knowledge, there are not many methods for forged handwriting detection in literature. Therefore, we consider the methods that address forged caption text detection in video images, printer identification and fraud document identification as related work for reviewing.

In case of forged caption text detection in video images, caption text can be considered as tampered since it is edited. Shivakumara et al. [6] proposed caption text detection as a classification problem. The method works based on the combination of Canny and Sobel edge images along with ring radius transform. Xu et al. [7] proposed a method for detecting caption texts in videos by exploring Eigen values of input images. Roy et al. [8] proposed caption text detection by exploring DCT coefficients. In a similar way, Bhardwaj and Pankajakshan [9] explored tampered features using DCT coefficients in compression domain for detecting caption texts in video images. Recently, Roy et al. [10] proposed a method for caption text detection using video information. Shivakumara et al. [1] proposed a method for detecting forged IMEI (International Mobile Equipment Identity) based on RGB color channels and fusion concept.

It is observed from the above methods that the scope of the methods is to detect forgery in natural scene or video images. Since texts in these images appear as printed, the method may not be adequate to address the issue of handwriting texts in document images. There are methods for handwriting and printed texts in document images. Barbosa et al. [11] proposed text fraud detection in documents written with ballpoint pens. This method uses ink of ballpoint pens as features for fraud text identification. Elkasrawi and Shafait [12] proposed printer identification using supervised learning for document forgery detection. This approach explores prints based on noises produced by different printers for fraud document classification. Ahmed and Shafait [13] proposed forgery detection based on intrinsic document contents. This method explores similarity between blocks of an image to identify forged document identification. Khan et al. [14] proposed automatic ink mismatch detection for forensic document analysis. This method analyzes ink of different pens to find fraud documents. Luo et al. [15] proposed localized forgery detection in hyperspectral document images. This is an improved version of the above method, which explores ink quality in hyperspectral for fraud document identification. Bertrand et al. [16] proposed a system based on intrinsic features for fraudulent document detection. This approach extracts features or characters to match with the ground truth for fraud estimation. Based on mismatch scores, the method identifies fraud documents. Raghunandan et al. [17] proposed Fourier coefficients for fraud handwritten document classification through age analysis. This approach studies positive and negative coefficients for analyzing quality of images, which identifies it as old or new. Wang et al. [18] proposed a Fourier-residual method for fake printed text detection through printer identification. This method extracts features from residual given by Fourier transform for printer identification. Fahn et al. [3] proposed a text independent handwriting forgery detection system based on brachlet features and Gaussian mixture models. Cha et al. [19] proposed automatic detection of handwriting forgery. The method studies the contour of handwriting for forgery detection.

From the above discussion, it is noted that none of the methods considers blurred and noisy images for detecting forgery in images. This shows that the methods consider distortion, like noises created during forgery operation, as the main basis for achieving results. Therefore, the methods may not work well for images affected by forgery operation, blur and noises. Hence, this work explores new cues for detecting forged handwriting texts from images of blur and noises. The main intuition for the proposed method is the inconsistency caused in writing by forgery operation like creating fake characters using software, copy-paste, insertion and deletion compared to normal writing, blurred and noisy texts. This is because it is difficult to mimic dynamic aspects, such as speed and acceleration [19]. This results in wiggly, inconsistency and irregularity in writing. On the other hand, one can expect some regularity in case of blurriness and noisiness because blur degrades images with some consistency and noises introduced by scanning and devices do not affect contours of characters as they are isolated. Since noises are isolated, they do not create problems for studying consistency and inconsistency in writing. In order to extract such unique observations, we introduce spectral densities and distributions. Motivated by the method [20] where it is stated that width and amplitude of spectrum directions have the ability to measure the quality of images affected by haze and blur, we explore the same spectral directions in a different way for classifying forged handwriting from blur, noise and clear images. The proposed work studies distribution of frequency coefficients and corresponding spectral densities for detecting forged handwriting words.

3 Proposed Method

As mentioned in the previous section, the inconsistency introduced by forgery operation is unique compared to blur, noise created by device, scanning process, normal images. It is true that the shape of spectral distribution is prominent for extracting such distinct features to detect forged handwriting images [20]. To study the shape of spectral distribution, the proposed method classifies high values of the spectrum into one cluster, which is called Max cluster, and low values into another cluster, which is called Min cluster. This is due to the relationship between high values, which generally represent edges (text), and low values, which represent background. Since the considered problem is complex, studying the shape of the whole spectrum alone may not be adequate for achieving successful results. Therefore, the proposed method finds a unique relationship between the spectrums of text and background information. To make the features invariant to rotation and scaling, the proposed method estimates the principal axis for the binarized spectrum of Max and Min clusters. With respect to principal axis, the proposed method draws parallel and vertical lines over the Max and Min cluster spectrums. For the pixels of each parallel and vertical line of the spectrum of Max and Min clusters, the proposed method counts the number of white pixels and calculates the mean of intensity values as spectral density and spectral variations, respectively. To extract width and amplitude of the spectrum, the proposed method draws a line graph for the number of lines vs respective number of white pixels, which results in spectral density histogram. Similarly, the proposed method performs histogram operation for the mean intensity values of Max and Min cluster spectrums, which results in spectral variation histogram. The proposed method extracts statistical information from the spectral density and variation histograms. The extracted statistical features from the histograms of Max and Min cluster spectrums are further concatenated and fed to a Neural Network classifier for classification.

3.1 Fourier Spectral Distributions

For each input image, the proposed method obtains Fourier spectrum as defined in Eq. (1)

$$Y_{p+1,q+1} = \sum_{j=0}^{m-1} \sum_{k=0}^{n-1} X_{j+1,k+1} \omega_n^{kq} \omega_m^{jp} \tag{1}$$

where, Y denotes Fourier spectrum matrix for the m-by-n image matrix X, ω_m and ω_n are complex root of unity. The spectrums for four types of handwriting word images are shown in Fig. 2(a), where the spectrum for each image appears different though the content is the same. This is a cue for us to explore the features for detecting forged handwriting words from blurred, noise and normal word images. The same cue is clearly visible in binary form of the spectrum of respective spectrums as shown in Fig. 2(b), where it is evident that the spectral distribution is unique for each type of word images. For obtaining the binary form of spectrum, we use well-known Otsu thresholding [21] as it is good for separating foreground and background for plain document images.

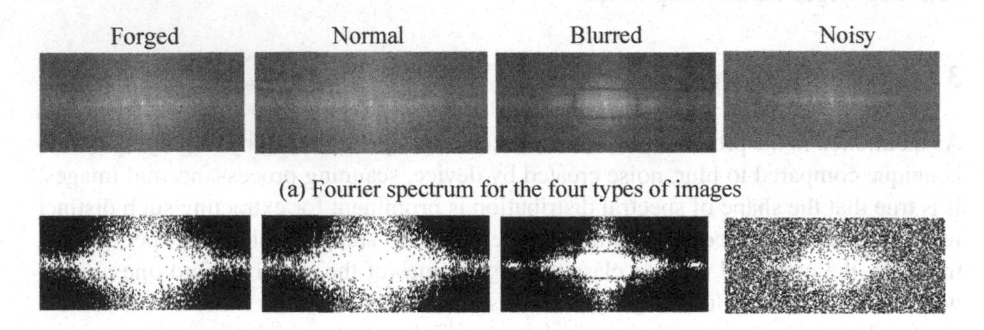

(a) Fourier spectrum for the four types of images

(b). Binary form of Fourier spectrum for the four types of images

Fig. 2. Fourier spectrum distribution for classification.

3.2 Spectral Density and Variance Based Features for Forged Handwriting Classification

For the frequency coefficient values of corresponding white pixels in the spectrum, the proposed method performs K-means clustering for classifying high frequency coefficients into Max and low frequency coefficients into Min cluster. The spectrum in binary form is obtained for the Max and Min cluster frequency coefficients as respectively shown in Fig. 3(a) and (b) for all the four type of texts. It is noted from Fig. 3(a) and (b) that shapes of spectrum differ from one image to another. This observation motivated us to study the shape of the spectrum of Max and Min clusters. For this purpose, the proposed method estimates the principal axis and draws parallel and vertical lines with respect to principal axis as shown in Fig. 3(a) and (c) for parallel lines and Fig. 3(b) and (d) for vertical lines. For pixels of parallel and vertical lines of Max and Min clusters, the proposed method counts the number of white pixels as spectral density features and calculates the mean of intensity values as spectral variation features as defined in Eq. (2). As mentioned in the Proposed Method Section, to extract width and amplitude of spectrum, the proposed method draws line graphs for the number of lines vs respective the number of white pixels of max and min clusters, which results in spectral density histogram as shown in Fig. 4(a) on the left, where the line graph is drawn for the number of parallel lines and their number of white pixels. Then the proposed method finds the average value of the spectral density histogram and considers it as a reference as shown in Fig. 4(a) on the left where we can see center thick dark line. The deviations from the reference to the lowest value either on side of the reference line are calculated as shown in Fig. 4(a) on the left where deviation is calculated from reference line. This results in two features for the spectral density histogram of parallel lines of Max clusters, and two more features for spectral density histogram of vertical lines of Max cluster. In the same way, for the spectral density histograms of parallel and vertical lines of Min cluster, the proposed method obtains four more features. In total, 8 features are extracted as spectral density features.

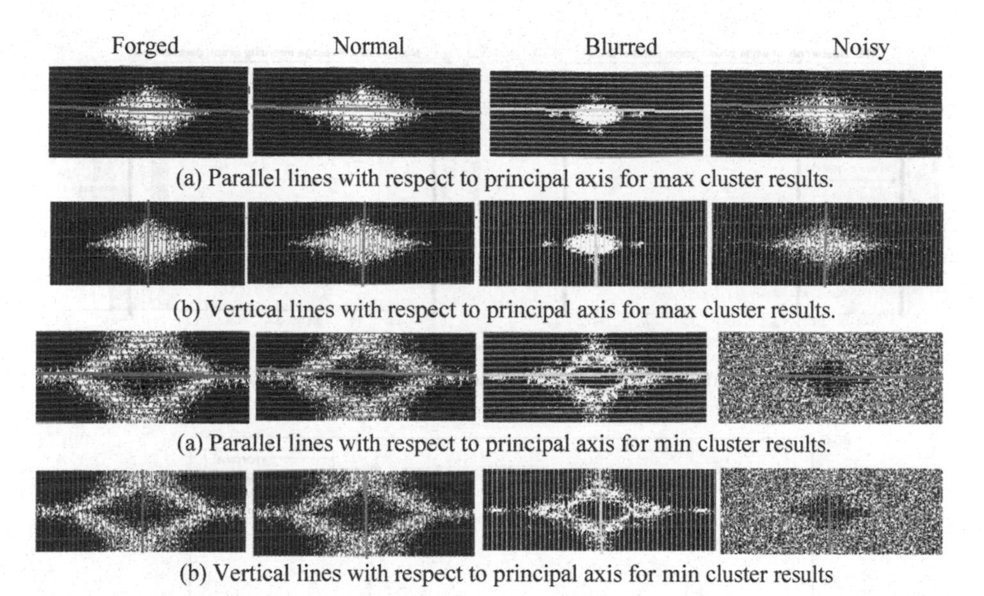

Fig. 3. Parallel and vertical lines with respect to principal axis for the spectrum of max and min cluster.

Similarly, the proposed method performs histogram operations for the mean intensity values which are extracted from the input images corresponding to white pixels of parallel lines of the Max cluster spectrum as shown in Fig. 4(b) on the right. The proposed method finds average value of the histogram peaks and considers it as a reference line and it estimates deviation of the minimum peaks on either side of the reference line as shown in Fig. 4(b) on the right, where it can be seen dark lines and calculations. This results in two features. In addition to these features, the proposed method considers value at the reference line as one more feature as it represents spatial variations in images. This gives three features for the spectral variation histogram of parallel lines of max cluster. In the same way, three features using spectral variation of histogram of parallel lines of min cluster, which gives total 6 features. In total, the proposed method extract 12 features which includes 6 more features from spectral variation histograms of vertical lines of max and min clusters. In total, the proposed method extracts 20 features from input images. The effect of 20 features can be seen in Fig. 4(b) where graph is drawn for 20 features for the four types of input images. Figure 4(b) shows that the line graphs of respective feature vectors of the four types behave differently. This shows that the extracted features have a discriminative power for classifying forged handwriting word from blurred, noise and normal words images.

$$AV = \frac{\sum_{i=1}^{Nwp} n_i}{Nwp} \tag{2}$$

where, Nwp is the number of white pixels on that particular line, and n_i is the intensity of that pixel of the Fourier spectrum.

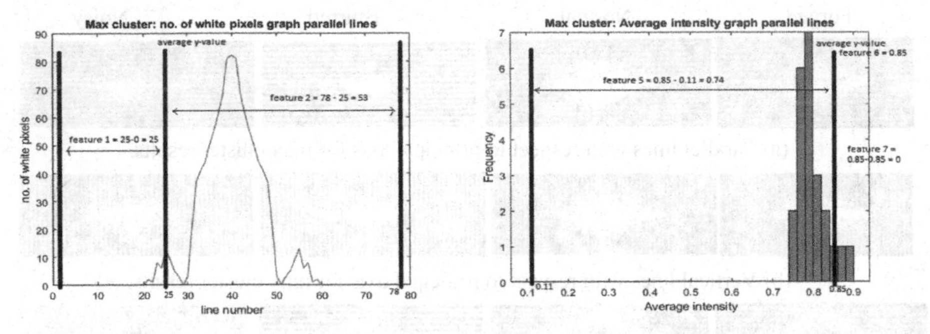

(a) Illustration for extracting features from spectral density and variations histograms.

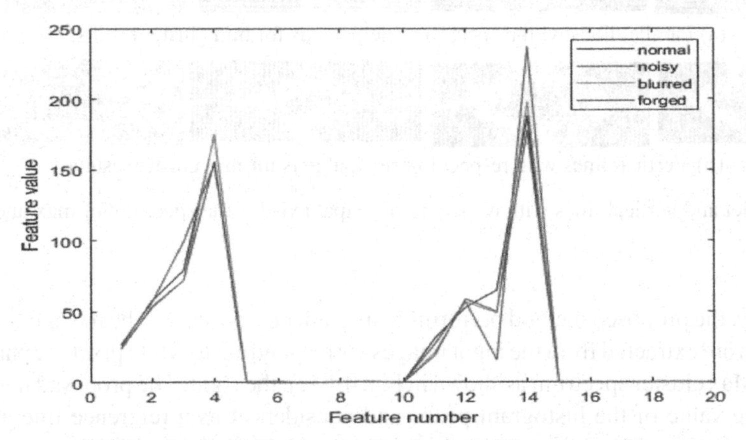

(b) The extracted 20 features distribution of four types of images.

Fig. 4. Feature extraction for classification of forged handwriting word from blurred, noisy and normal word images.

For classification, we propose to use a neural network classifier in this work because as discussed the previous section, the features are good enough to distinguish forged handwriting words from the other images. Therefore, we prefer to use a simple classifier. The proposed method uses a feed-forward neural network with 20 hidden layers. For determining weights and updating, the proposed method uses the Levenberg-Marquardt back-propagation procedure to update weights and bias terms of the model. The error is calculated using the mean squared error and the process of training stops when the maximum number of epochs is reached or the performance is minimized to the goal. For experiments, we divide the dataset into 80% of samples for training, 10% for testing and 10% for validation. The process of training and the structure of neural networks are shown in Fig. 5, where we can see how the proposed work trains parameter values for classification experiments.

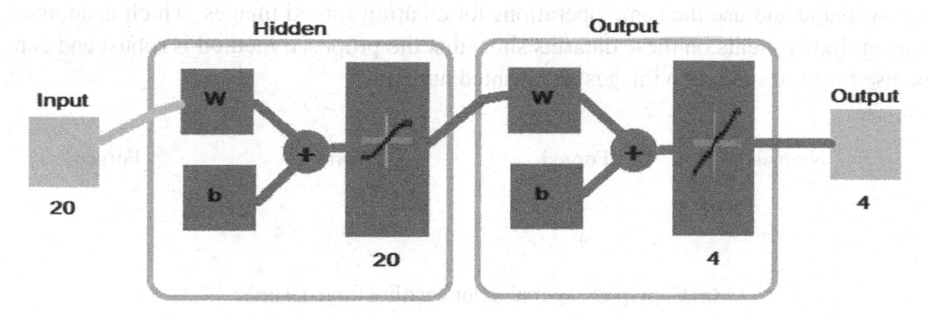

Fig. 5. Structure of the training neural network classifier for classification

4 Experimental Results

For evaluating the performance of the proposed method, since this is the first work for forged handwriting word detection, there are no standard datasets available in literature. We thus create our own dataset, which includes 200 images for each class and hence the size of our dataset is 800 images. We use the handwriting dataset created for writer identification and words spotting by the method [22] for creating forged dataset in this work. For forgery, we follow standard operations, namely, copy-paste which copies words/characters from one source to a target place, deletion which erases a few characters in the words, and insertion which adds character words to the original text. Sample images for each operation are shown in Fig. 6(a)–(c), respectively, where one can see the effect of forgery operation for each case. If we compare forged words with normal words, it is hard to notice the change in content without any knowledge of dataset and problem. Besides, the words written by different writers make the created dataset more challenging. Therefore, we believe the created dataset is good enough for evaluating the performance of the proposed forged handwriting word detection. To make sure that the proposed method does not consider the basis which the existing methods consider for forgery detection, we created two more classes of blurred and noise images as shown in Fig. 6(d) and (e), respectively. For creating blurred and noisy images, we use Gaussian functions for adding blur and pepper-salt noise function for adding noises at some different levels. Therefore, the considered problem is a four-class classification problem instead of two-class classification.

In order to test the objectiveness of the proposed method, we also consider two standard datasets, namely, forged caption text detection [8] in video images which consists of 1075 images, and forged IMEI number detection [1] which consists of 1000 images.

In total, 2875 images are considered for experimentation in this work. In case of caption and scene text dataset, caption text images are considered as forged images as they are edited, and scene text images are considered as normal ones as these are part of images. In case of forged IMEI number dataset, images of forged IMEI numbers are one class, and the original images are considered as another class. Although these data are not handwritten, the reason to choose these two datasets as the standard datasets for experimentation is show how our work behaves on printed text. Also these datasets are available and use the same operations for creating forged images, which is another reason. Experiments on these datasets show that the proposed method is robust and can be used for texts in video images and printed numerals.

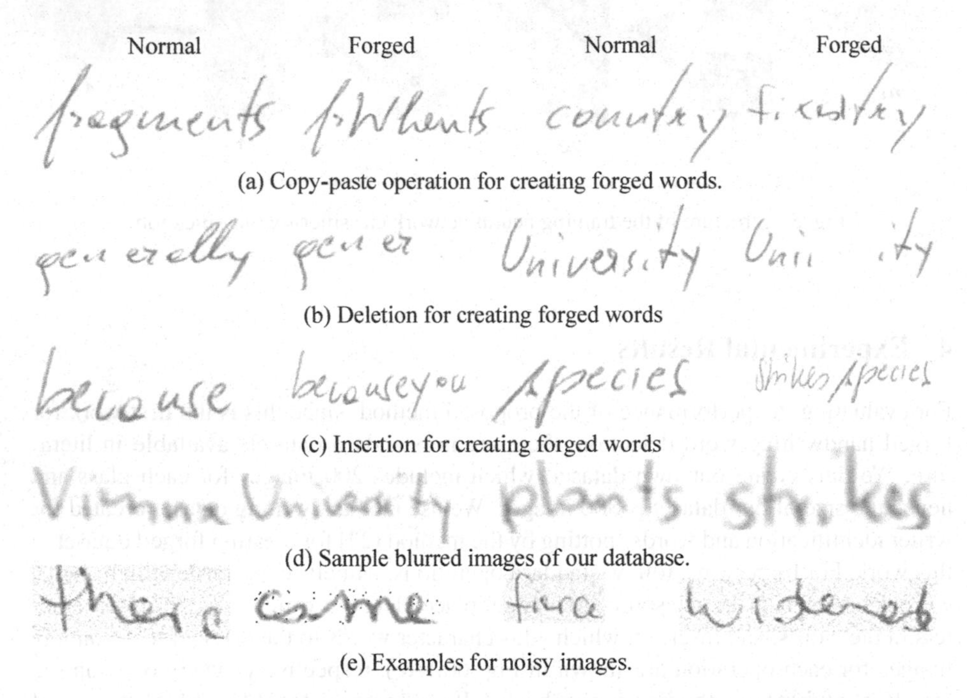

(a) Copy-paste operation for creating forged words.

(b) Deletion for creating forged words

(c) Insertion for creating forged words

(d) Sample blurred images of our database.

(e) Examples for noisy images.

Fig. 6. Sample images for forged, blurred and noisy handwriting word images

To show the usefulness of the proposed method, we implement three existing methods to compare with the results of the proposed method. Wang et al. [18] proposed Fourier-residual for printer identification, which extracts statistical, spatial and texture features for residual images given by Fourier reconstructed images. Elkasrawi and Shafait [12] proposed printer identification using supervised learning for document forgery detection, and they use residual in a different way. Bhardwaj et al. [9] proposed a method for forged caption text detection in video images. The reason to choose the first two methods is that the objective of these methods is forgery detection in document images including handwriting also, which is the same as the proposed method. Besides, to show that the methods which use noise created by forgery operation as the main basis for forgery detection is not adequate for the proposed forgery detection. This is due to confusion between images affected by forgery operation, noise and blur. The third one is to show that the methods, which are developed for forged caption text detection in video, may not be suitable for forged handwriting word detection. In addition, the method, which uses distortion created by forgery operation as the main basis for forgery detection, may not work well for forged handwriting word detection from blurred, and noisy word images. Note that since the methods [12, 18] used classifiers for forgery detection in images, we can extend the same classifier for the proposed four classes. Therefore, we run these two methods on our four-class dataset as well as the two-class dataset of our dataset and the standard datasct. However, the method [9] uses threshold for two-class classification because it is developed for two-class problem. Hence, we run this method on two classes of our dataset and the standard dataset for comparative study in this work but not for three classes. For measuring the performances of the proposed and existing methods, we use standard measures, namely, confusion matrix and classification rate as defined in Eq. (3), which is the mean of all the diagonal elements of the confusion matrix. For all the above three datasets, since there is no ground truth, we count manually for calculating measures in this work.

$$CR = \frac{TP}{N_{total}} \times 100 \tag{3}$$

where, *TP* are the total images labeled correctly and N_{total} are the total number of test images.

4.1 Experiments on Forged Handwriting Word Detection

Quantitative results of the proposed and existing methods for four-class classification are reported in Table 1, where it is noted that the proposed method is better than two existing methods in terms of Classification Rate (CR). When we compare the two existing methods, Wang et al. score the better results compared to Elkasrawi and Shafait. This is due to the lack of discriminative power in feature extraction in case of Elkasrawi and Shafait's method. At the same time, Wang et al. take advantage of statistical, texture and spatial features for forged document identification compared to Elkasrawi and Shafait's method. However, the extracted features may not be robust to cope with the challenges posed by different writing styles and variations compared to printed texts in document images, and hence the existing method [18] reports poor results for forged handwriting word detection from blurred and noise words. In addition, the existing methods are developed based on the fact that noises created by different operations or sources exhibit different natures. This is not necessarily true for the proposed problem, which includes noises created by blur and different noise levels. The same thing is true for the other existing method [12]. In order to test the ability of the proposed method for two classes, we conduct experiments on two classes, namely, Forged *vs* Normal, Forged *vs* Blurred and Forged *vs* Noise as reported in Table 2. Table 2 shows that the proposed method is the best at classification rate compared to the existing methods for forged *vs* blur and forged *vs* noise classes. However, out of three types, the proposed method scores high classification rate for forged *vs* blur and forged *vs* noise compared to forged *vs* normal. This is possible because the aim of the proposed method is to classify the four classes. As result, the extracted features may not fit for two classes, which may leads to overfitting.

It is observed from Table 2 that Bhardwaj and Pankajakshan [9] fail to achieve better results compared to the other existing methods and the proposed method for all three combinations. The main reason is the fixing of a constant threshold because a fixed threshold may not be optimal for all different combinations and datasets. It is expected that the proposed and the existing methods score better results for two classes compared to four classes reported in Table 1. Interestingly, it is noted from Table 2 that for Forged *vs* Noise classes, Wang et al. and the proposed method achieve 100% classification rate. It is evident that these two methods have the ability to differentiate between the distortions created by noises and forgery operation, while the other methods do not.

Table 1. Classification rates of the proposed and existing methods on forged handwriting dataset for four classes (in %).

Methods	Proposed method				Wang et al. [18]				Elkasrawi and Shafait [12]			
Classes	Forged	Normal	Blur	Noise	Forged	Normal	Blur	Noise	Forged	Normal	Blur	Noise
Forged	85.7	4.8	9.5	0.0	71.4	25	1.8	1.8	81.8	3.6	5.5	9.1
Normal	20.0	70.0	10.0	0.0	25	57.8	7.8	9.4	0	58.2	5.5	36.3
Blurred	15.8	15.8	63.2	5.2	1.8	9	78.2	11	4.8	9.5	60.3	25.4
Noisy	0.0	0.0	10.0	90.0	8	14.3	1.5	76.2	3.25	14	26.5	56.25
CR	77.5				70.1				64.14			

Table 2. Classification rates of the proposed and existing methods on forged handwriting dataset for two classes (in %).

Methods	Proposed		Bhardwaj et al. [9]		Wang et al. [18]		Elkasrawi and Shafait [12]	
Classes	Forged	Normal	Forged	Normal	Forged	Normal	Forged	Normal
Forged	72.2	27.8	66.0	34.0	90.6	9.4	70.3	29.7
Normal	18.2	81.8	72.0	28.0	20	80	25.5	74.5
CR	77.5		49.7		85.3		72.4	
Classes	Forged	Blur	Forged	Blur	Forged	Blur	Forged	Blur
Forged	95.8	4.2	66.0	34.0	94	6	96.4	3.6
Blur	0.0	100	0.0	100.0	22.82	77.18	6.25	93.75
CR	97.5		83		87.6		95	
Classes	Forged	Noise	Forged	Noise	Forged	Noise	Forged	Noise
Forged	100	0.0	66.0	34.0	100	0.0	70.3	29.7
Noise	0.0	100.0	95.0	5.0	0.0	100	23.6	76.4
CR	100		35.50		100.0		73.35	

4.2 Experiments on Forged Caption Text Detection in Video Images

As mentioned in Experimental Section, to test the proposed method on different dataset, we conduct experiments on forged caption text detection from scene texts in video images. Sample successful classification images for caption and scene texts in videos can be seen in Fig. 7(a), where it can be seen that the distortion created by editing over video is not visible in case of caption texts, while we can see blur and degradations created by perspective distortion in case of scene texts. As a result, this dataset is challenging as the proposed dataset. Quantitative results reported in Table 3 for the proposed and existing methods show that the proposed method is better than the existing methods in terms of classification rate. It is noted from Table 3 that though the method proposed by Bhardwaj and Pankajakshan [9] is developed for forged caption text detection in video, it fails to achieve the best results. This shows that fixing threshold for all the three different datasets is not easy. Therefore, one cannot expect consistent results from the Bhardwaj and Pankajakshan's [9] method. However, the other two existing methods report reasonable results compared to the proposed method. Overall, one can argue that the proposed method is robust to different datasets and different numbers of classes.

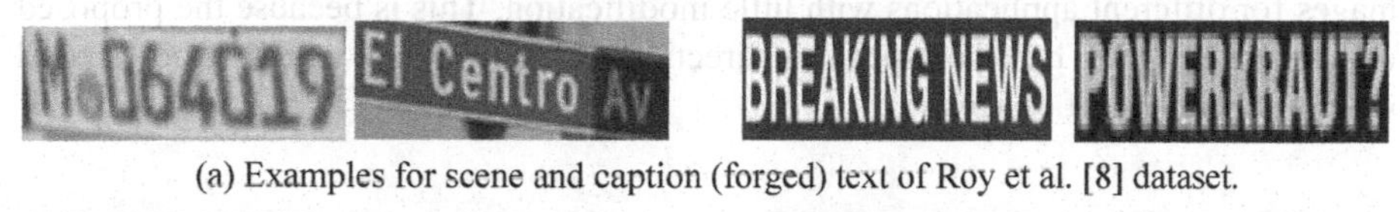

(a) Examples for scene and caption (forged) text of Roy et al. [8] dataset.

(b) Examples for normal and forged words IMEI number of Shivakumara et al dataset [1].

Fig. 7. Successful classification of the proposed method on scene-caption and IMEI number images

Table 3. Classification rates of the proposed and existing methods on scene text dataset for two classes (in %).

Methods	Proposed		Bhardwaj et al. [9]		Wang et al. [18]		Elkasrawi and Shafait [12]	
Classes	Scene	Caption	Scene	Caption	Scene	Caption	Scene	Caption
Scene	100	0	46.7	53.3	93.3	6.7	87.6	12.4
Caption	3.5	96.5	72.8	27.2	3.6	96.4	15.3	84.7
CR	98.1		36.9		94		86.15	

4.3 Experiments on Forged IMEI Number Detection

Sample successful results of the proposed method are shown in Fig. 7(b), where it is noted that there is no visible evidence to differentiate forged IMEI number from the normal IMEI number. As a result, the distortion created by forgery operation may overlap with the distortions in normal images because the scope is limited to only numerals. In addition, the dataset includes images of forging only a few numerals but not the whole of images unlike forged caption text detection and forged handwriting word detection. Therefore, this dataset is complex compared to the other two datasets. It is confirmed from the results reported in Table 4 that the proposed and existing methods score poor results compared to the other two datasets in spite of having two classes. This is due to overfitting problem. However, Elkasrawi and Shafait [12] score the best for this dataset compared to the proposed and the other existing methods. This shows that the method [12] is not consistent for different datasets when we compare the performances of the proposed and Wang et al.'s methods. Overall, though the proposed method is developed for forged handwritten word detection from blurred and noisy words, it achieves the best result for almost all the experiments of different datasets. Therefore, we can conclude that the proposed method is robust, generic and can be extended to more classes and more images for different applications with little modification. This is because the proposed features are extracted based on spectrum direction and distribution, which do not depend on specific content of images.

Table 4. Classification rates of the proposed and existing methods on forged IMEI number dataset for two classes (in %).

Methods	Proposed		Bhardwaj et al. [9]		Wang et al. [18]		Elkasrawi and Shafait [12]	
Classes	Original	Forged	Original	Forged	Original	Forged	Original	Forged
Original	57.8	42.2	10.2	89.8	47.8	52.1	45.2	54.8
Forged	41.8	58.2	5.8	94.2	41.0	59.0	27.0	73
CR	58.0		51.5		53.5		59.1	

Sometimes, due to the large variations in writing style, there is a chance of misclassification as the shown sample misclassified images in Fig. 8(a) and (b). This is valid because the proposed features are extracted based on the global information, which may not be robust when images do not contain enough characters. Therefore, there is a scope for improvement and the method can be extended to overcome this limitation by exploring the combination of local and global information.

(a) Normal words as forged words (b) Normal words as blurred words

Fig. 8. Unsuccessful classification of the proposed method for some cases.

5 Conclusion and Future Work

In this work, we have proposed a new method for forged handwriting word detection from blurred, noisy and normal (clear) words. The proposed method explores spectral density and variations for extracting features based on the fact that width and amplitude of spectrum direction are sensitive to distortion created by forged operation, blur and noises. To extract such an observation, the proposed method divides high and low frequency coefficients to study the unique relationship between text and background information in input images. The extracted features are fed to a neural network classifier for classification. To evaluate the proposed method, we have tested the proposed method on forged handwriting, forged caption text and forged IMEI number datasets. Experimental results on different datasets show that the proposed method is robust to different datasets and different number of classes compared to the existing methods. As pointed out in the experimental section, there is a scope for the improvement and extension to overcome the limitations by exploring combination of local and global information in the future.

References

1. Shivakumara, P., Basavaraja, V., Gowda, H.S., Guru, D.S., Paland, U., Lu, T.: A new RGB based fusion for forged IMEI number detection in mobile images. In: Proceedings of the ICFHR, pp. 386–391 (2018)
2. Ferrer, M.A., Morales, A., Vargas, J.F., Lemos, I., Quintero, M.: Is it possible to automatically identify who has forged my signature? Approaching to the identification of static signature forger. In: Proceedings of the DAS, pp. 175–179 (2012)
3. Fahn, C.S., Lee, C.P., Chen, H.I.: A text independent handwriting forgery detection system based on branchlet features and Gaussian mixture models. In: Proceedings of the PST (2016)
4. Ghanim, T.M., Nabil, A.M.: Offline signature verification and forgery detection approach. In: Proceedings of the ICCES, pp. 293–298 (2018)
5. Kumar, R., Pal, N.R., Chanda, B., Sharma, J.D.: Forensic detection of fraudulent alterations in ball point pen strokes. IEEE Trans. IFS **7**(2), 809–820 (2012)
6. Shivakumara, P., Kumar, N.V., Guru, D.S., Tan, C.L.: Separation of graphics (superimposed) and scene text in videos. In: Proceedings of the DAS, pp. 344–348 (2014)
7. Xu, J., Shivakumara, P., Lu, T., Phan, T.Q., Tan, C.L.: Graphics and scene text classification in video. In: Proceedings of the ICPR, pp. 4714–4719 (2014)
8. Roy, S., Shivakumara, P., Pal, U., Lu, T., Tan, C.L.: New tampered features for scene and caption text classification in video frame. In: Proceedings of the ICFHR, pp. 36–41 (2016)
9. Bhardwaj, D., Pankajakshan, V.: Image overlay text detection based on JPEG truncation error analysis. IEEE Signal Process. Lett. **23**(8), 1027–1031 (2016)

10. Roy, S., Shivakumara, P., Pal, U., Lu, T., Wahab, A.W.B.A.: Temporal integration of word-wise caption and scene text identification. In: Proceedings of the ICDAR, pp. 350–355 (2017)
11. Barbosa, R.D.S., Lins, R.D., Lira, E.D.F.D., Camara, A.C.A.: Later added strokes of text fraud detection in documents written with ballpoint pens. In: Proceedings of the ICFHR, pp. 517–522 (2014)
12. Elkasrawi, S., Shafait, F.: Printer identification using supervised learning for document forgery detection. In: Proceedings of the DAS, pp. 146–150 (2014)
13. Ahmed, A., Shafait, F.: Forgery detection based on intrinsic document features. In: Proceedings of the DAS, pp. 252–256 (2014)
14. Khan, Z., Shafait, F., Mian, A.: Automatic ink mismatch detection for forensic document analysis. Pattern Recogn. **48**, 3615–3626 (2015)
15. Luo, Z., Shafait, F., Mian, A.: Localized forgery detection in hyperspectral document images. In: Proceedings of the ICDAR, pp. 496–500 (2015)
16. Bertrand, R., Kramer, P.G., Terrades, O.R., Franco, P., Ogier, J.M.: A system based on intrinsic features for fraudulent document detection. In: Proceedings of the ICDAR, pp. 106–110 (2013)
17. Raghunandan, K.S., et al.: Fourier coefficients for fraud handwritten document classification through age analysis. In: Proceedings of the ICFHR, pp. 25–30 (2016)
18. Wang, Z., Shivakumara, P., Lu, T., Basavanna, M., Pal, U., Blumenstein, M.: Fourier-residual for printer identification. In: Proceedings of the ICDAR, pp. 1114–1119 (2017)
19. Cha, S.H., Tappert, C.C.: Automatic detection of handwriting forgery. In: Proceedings of the IWFHR (2012)
20. Wang, R., Li, W., Li, R., Zhang, L.: Automatic blur type classification via ensemble SVM. Sig. Process. Image Commun. **71**, 24–35 (2019)
21. Otsu, N.: A threshold selection method from gray-level histograms. IEEE Trans. Man Cybern. **9**(1), 62–66 (1979)
22. Kleber, F., Fiel, S., Diemand, M., Sablatnig, R.: CVL-database: an off-line database for writer retrieval, writer identification and word spotting. In: Proceedings of the ICDAR, pp. 560–564 (2013)

Robust Pedestrian Detection: Faster Deployments with Fusion of Models

Chan Tong Lam(✉), Jose Gaspar, Wei Ke, Xu Yang, and Sio Kei Im

School of Applied Sciences, Macao Polytechnic Institute, Macao S.A.R., China
{ctlam,p1204726,wke,xuyang,marcusim}@ipm.edu.mo

Abstract. Pedestrian detection has a wide range of real-world critical applications including security and management of emergency scenarios. In critical applications, detection recall and precision are both essential to ensure the correct detection of all pedestrians. The development and deployment of object detection vision-based models is a time-consuming task, depending on long training and fine-tuning processes to achieve top performance. We propose an alternative approach, based on a fusion of pre-trained off-the-shelf state-of-the-art object detection models, and exploit base model divergences to quickly deploy robust ensembles with improved performance. Our approach promotes model reuse and does not require additional learning algorithms, making it suitable for rapid deployments of critical systems. Experimental results, conducted on PASCAL VOC07 test dataset, reveal mean average precision (mAP) improvements over base detection models, regardless of the set of models selected. Improvements in mAP were observed starting from just two detection models and reached 3.53% for a fusion of four detection models, resulting in an absolute fusion mAP of 83.65%. Moreover, the hyperparameters of our ensemble model may be adjusted to set an appropriate tradeoff between precision and recall to fit different recall and precision application requirements.

Keywords: Deep learning · Pedestrian detection · Fusion · Ensemble learning

1 Introduction

Pedestrian detection, as a canonical instance of object detection, has a vast range of real-world applications including surveillance, security, venue management, crowd monitoring and control, behavior monitoring, action detection, semantic scene analysis, pedestrian tracking, smart-city management, and management of emergency scenarios. Some applications, including smart-city management, pedestrian flow monitoring, and management of emergency scenarios, rely on accurate pedestrian detection systems to drive appropriate management decisions to improve citizens' quality of live and contribute for efficient and effective life-saving rescue operations.

The multiple achievements in deep learning vision-based object detection triggered a world-wide race to develop accurate real-world systems. However, deep learning systems often rely on large training datasets and specific hyperparameter fine-tuning processes to achieve top performance, slowing down deployments. Pre-trained object detectors, however, have greatly accelerated the deployment of real-world applications with tight time-to-market constraints. In this paper, we propose a quickly deployable post-processing

S. Palaiahnakote et al. (Eds.): ACPR 2019, LNCS 12046, pp. 151–163, 2020.
https://doi.org/10.1007/978-3-030-41404-7_11

method, based on the fusion of predictions of multiple off-the-shelf detection models and improve the overall recall and precision rates.

Succinctly, our work provides the following contributions: (i) we explore intrinsic divergences among state-of-the-art pre-trained generic object detectors, (ii) combine predictions from a set of detectors to improve the overall performance, and (iii) add a post-processing stage to merge overlapped detections.

2 Related Works

Generic Object Detectors. Object detection is a multi-step process composed by localization of object region proposals, feature extraction and classification. The localization process identifies object region proposals within an image, the classification process extracts representative and distinguishable features from object proposals and, finally, a classifier predicts the object class.

Early machine learning object detectors relied on handcrafted descriptors to extract object features from images, feeding them to a classifier for class prediction. Such approaches, pursued by Viola-Jones detection framework (HAAR features) [1], Scale-invariant feature transform (SIFT features) [2], Histogram of oriented gradients (HOG) features [3], and Aggregate Channel Features (ACF) framework [4], achieved limited performance partially due to the difficult task of selecting optimal object representative features.

Recent object detectors, based on deep learning, capture the most representative and distinguishable features, based on a hierarchal layered structure, where basic features are captured by low-level layers and grouped into higher layers to predict the object class. Some examples of popular detectors include Faster R-CNN [5], SSD [6], YOLO v.2 [7], and YOLO v.3 [8], most of which relying on deep learning backbone feature extraction networks inspired in Alexnet [9], VGG [10], Google Inception v.1 [11], Inception v.2 [12], Inception v.3 [13], Inception v.4 [14], or ResNet [15].

State-of-the-art detectors rely on large training datasets and deep neural networks which require long train and fine-tune times to achieve superior accuracy. However, pre-trained models reuse network parameters, learned from previous training processes, significantly reducing the deployment time of new object detection systems.

Despite the remarkable progresses achieved over the past decades, object detection and classification are still considered complex and challenging computer vision problems due to large intra-class variations, including pose, illumination, viewpoint, scale, and background. These variations increase the hypothesis space and become partially responsible for accuracy and precision limitations of state-of-the-art object detectors.

Dietterich [16] identified three performance limitation factors: (i) Statistical limitations attributed to a large hypothesis space and limited training data. (ii) Computational limitations attributed to models which become stuck in a local optima, even in the presence of a large training dataset, and (iii) Representational limitation attributed to the inability of representing a hypothesis within the hypothesis space.

Ensemble Learning. Ensemble learning meta-algorithms have been widely explored in object classification tasks, combining weak base classifiers trained with divergent datasets to improve the generalization ability and classification performance. The authors in [17] offer a comprehensive study and discussion of widely used ensemble methods, including bagging [18], boosting [19], stacking [20, 21], and mixture of experts [22]. **Bagging** [18], commonly known as bootstrap aggregation, combines weak base classifiers trained with datasets collected from a main training dataset, with replacement. **Boosting** [19] adds incorrectly classified object instances to a new classifier along with additional training instances, making the final prediction based on a voting mechanism. **Stacking** [20, 21] trains an combiner algorithm to combine predictions of base classifiers, trained with the available dataset. **Mixture of experts (MoE)** [23, 24] relies on a set of base expert learners and a gating algorithm which selects the most appropriate learner according to the input data.

The ensemble learning methods above rely on training processes which eventually delay system deployments. In addition, they are designed for classification tasks, requiring modified versions to handle object detection.

3 Methods

In this paper, we fuse object detectors, pre-trained with PASCAL VOC0712 trainval dataset [25], and exploit the divergences among base models to improve the performance of pedestrian detectors. We use ChainerCV [26] computer vision deep learning library which unifies a set of classification and detection algorithms and provides pre-trained models fine-tuned for top mean average precision (mAP).

3.1 State-of-the-Art Object Detectors

We select a small set of pre-trained models, based on detection time and precision, to achieve a top performing fusion of models. We selected Faster R-CNN [5], SSD 300 [6], SSD 512 [6], YOLO v.2 [7], and YOLO v.3 [8] models which are briefly described below.

Faster R-CNN [5] is an evolution of the R-CNN [27] detector, with applications in the pedestrian detection [28] domain, which introduces significant speed improvements achieved by the introduction of a region proposal network (RPN), reducing the number of region proposals presented and processed by the classifier.

SSD 300 and SSD 512 [6] Single Shot Multibox Detectors (SSD) are single-stage object detectors, with applications in the pedestrian detection [29] domain, which eliminate the need of a region proposal network, incorporate multi-scale feature maps, and use default boxes, resulting in faster and accurate detections using low-resolution images. A high-resolution SSD version further improves the mAP with a detection speed penalty.

YOLO v.2 [7] is the second generation of the popular, single shot, You Only Look Once (YOLO) [30] family of fast object detectors, with applications in the pedestrian detection [31] domain. This version improves mAP by adding multiple improvements including batch normalization, a high-resolution classifier, convolutional anchor box detection, k-means clustering of box dimensions, direct location prediction, fine-grained features, multi-scale training, and a light-weighted base model.

YOLO v.3 [8] is the third generation of the popular, single shot, YOLO family of fast object detectors, with applications in the pedestrian detection [32] domain. This incremental version introduces a new feature extractor implemented in a deeper network model, along with multi-scale detections, and a logistic classifier for every class which enables multi-label classification.

3.2 Non-maxima Suppression

Most state-of-the-art object detectors generate redundant detections which severely degrade the precision rate. As a result, a non-maximum suppression (NMS) [33, 34] post-processing stage is added to the end of the detection pipeline to suppress low-score redundant detections and output exactly one detection per object. The NMS determines the intersection over union (IoU) overlap ratio of all pairwise combinations of detection bounding boxes, and keeps the detection with the highest confidence score among overlapped detections matching or exceeding a prefixed overlap ratio threshold NMS_t.

The best-performing NMS threshold depends on the complexity and object density of input image datasets. Therefore, we evaluate the mean average precision (mAP) of each detector $D = \{FRCNN, SSD300, SSD512, YOLO2, YOLO3\}$, based on a range of thresholds $t = \{0.05, 0.10, \ldots, 0.95\}$, and determine the best-performing threshold $NMS_t = arg\ \max_t\left[1/|D| \cdot \sum_{i \in D} mAP(D_i, t)\right]$ which delivers the highest mean mAP among all detectors, as demonstrated in Table 1. Figure 1 plots the variation of mAP across a wide range of NMS thresholds. Our evaluation reveals a maximum mean mAP when the NMS threshold is set to 0.45. Hence, we use it in all our experiments.

Table 1. Object detector mAP for different NMS thresholds

Detector mAP (%)	NMS threshold									
	0.05	0.15	0.25	0.35	0.45	0.55	0.65	0.75	0.85	0.95
Faster RCNN	70.39	72.81	74.55	75.54	**75.37**	73.46	68.62	58.98	43.03	28.42
SSD 300	72.46	74.67	76.18	76.99	**77.61**	77.34	76.25	73.90	66.68	41.16
SSD 512	73.82	77.34	78.75	79.45	**79.65**	79.49	78.51	76.05	68.38	38.09
YOLO v.2	69.75	73.14	74.32	75.43	**75.79**	75.76	74.88	71.74	62.11	49.45
YOLO v.3	73.84	76.36	78.13	79.47	**80.12**	79.90	77.90	71.76	55.97	43.34
Mean	*72.05*	*74.86*	*76.39*	*77.38*	***77.71***	*77.19*	*75.23*	*70.49*	*59.23*	*40.09*

3.3 Detectors Divergences

A fusion of detection models may improve the overall performance by combining a set of base detectors with divergent training datasets, hyperparameters, or models. Thus, the divergence among base detectors is fundamental to obtain performance improvements from a fusion of models. The authors in [35] provide an analysis of multiple diversity measures. We adopt a classical approach to measure pairwise diversities between detection models, based on a disagreement measure [36, 37] which is simpler to interpret

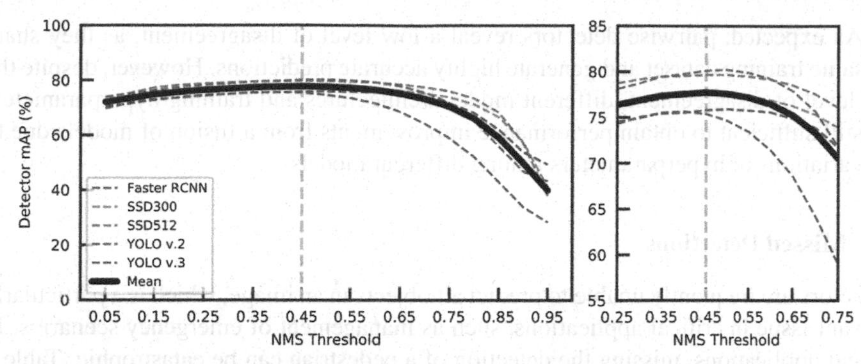

Fig. 1. Comparison of mAP of different detectors, and the mean mAP, for a full range of NMS thresholds (left), and a view for a limited range of thresholds (right). Detector's mAP depends on a prefixed NMS threshold and, if not properly selected, penalizes the detection precision.

than the popular Cohen's Kappa-statistic [38, 39]. Let $\{(x_1, y_1), (x_2, y_2), \ldots, (x_n, y_n)\}$ be the set of binary detections D where x denotes a ground truth object and $y \in \{0, 1\}$ denotes a detection outcome. Table 2 shows a contingency table for a pair of detectors d_i and d_j, with basic detection agreements denoted by a and d, and disagreements denoted by b and c.

Table 2. Contingency table of detectors d_i and d_j.

		Detector d_j	
		Detected (1)	Undetected (0)
Detector d_i	Detected (1)	a	c
	Undetected (0)	b	d

Let m denote the total detections $a + b + c + d$. The disagreement measure between the pair of detectors d_i and d_j, expressed as $dis_{i,j} = (b + c)/m$, reveals the proportion of examples with divergent predictions. Given the set of base detectors $\{FRCNN, SSD300, SSD512, YOLO2, YOLO3\}$, denoted by D, and the number of base detectors $|D|$ denoted by n, we determine the mean disagreement measure $\overline{dis} \in [0, 1]$ by $\{2/[n(n-1)]\} \cdot \sum_{i=1}^{n} \sum_{j=i+1}^{n} dis_{i,j}$. Table 3 displays the complete set of pairwise disagreement measures and the mean disagreement measure $\overline{dis}$ used for overall disagreement evaluation.

Table 3. Disagreement measures of all combinations of pairwise detectors. Disagreement measures range from 0, for equal detectors, to 1, for independent detectors.

Detectors d_i, d_j	FRCNN, SSD300	FRCNN, SSD512	FRCNN, YOLO2	FRCNN, YOLO3	SSD300, SSD512	SSD300, YOLO2	SSD300, YOLO3	SSD512, YOLO2	SSD512, YOLO3	YOLO2, YOLO3	$\overline{dis}$
$dis_{i,j}$	0.0683	0.0658	0.1075	0.1021	0.0364	0.1114	0.1006	0.1164	0.0969	0.1187	**0.0924**

As expected, pairwise detectors reveal a low level of disagreement, as they share the same training dataset and generate highly accurate predictions. However, despite the low level of disagreement, different model architectures and training hyperparameters are still sufficient to obtain performance improvements from a fusion of models due to the variations of hyperparameters among different models.

3.4 Missed Detections

Detectors are frequently unable to predict all objects in an image, which is a particularly relevant issue in critical applications, such as management of emergency scenarios. In critical applications, missing the detection of a pedestrian can be catastrophic. Table 4 reveals the number of objects undetected by base detectors, as well as the number of objects undetected by different fusion of models of size n, composed by models selected from a set of detectors $D = \{FRCNN, SSD300, SSD512, YOLO2, YOLO3\}$. Figure 2 emphasizes observed variances for each size of the fusion of models, resulting from the set of all k combinations of base detectors D, where $k = {}_{|D|}C_n$.

Table 4. Comparison of undetected objects against the size of the fusion of models. As the fusion size increases, the variance and the number of objects undetected reduces substantially, suggesting that a fusion of detection models can improve the overall performance. PASCAL VOC07 test dataset, used in comparison, includes 12032 object instances.

Size of fusion of models	1 (No fusion)			2			3			4			5		
	Min	Mean	Max	Min	Mean	Max	Min	Mean	Max	Min	Mean	Max	Min	Mean	Max
Obj. undetected	288	848	1460	124	292	663	74	146	321	64	88	119	59	59	59

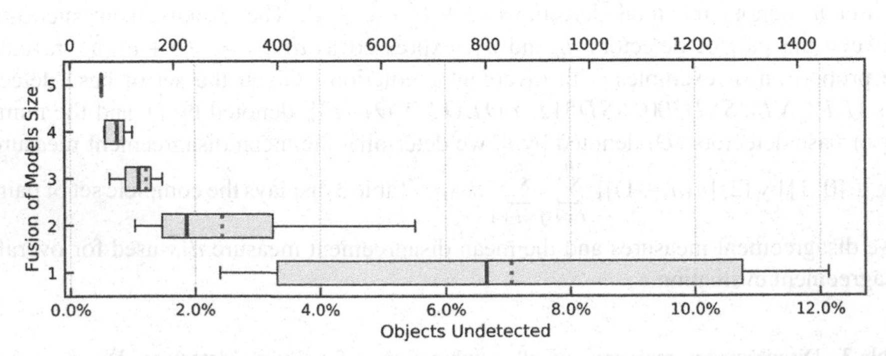

Fig. 2. Comparison of undetected objects against the size of the fusion of models. The top and bottom scales show the absolute number and the percentage of objects undetected, respectively. Dotted red lines denote mean missed objects. Solid blue lines denote median missed objects. (Color figure online)

3.5 Proposed Architecture for Fusion of Models

Preliminary empirical studies from previous section suggest that we can benefit from a fusion of detectors due to existing divergences among models and a reduction of the number of undetected objects. We propose a fusion of detection models for pedestrian detection which does not require additional training and hence may be quickly deployed. Figure 3 illustrates our proposed architecture, composed by: (i) Detection Combiner, (ii) Confidence Score Filter, (iii) Inter-Detector NMS Filter, and (iv) Selected Overlaps Re-scorer.

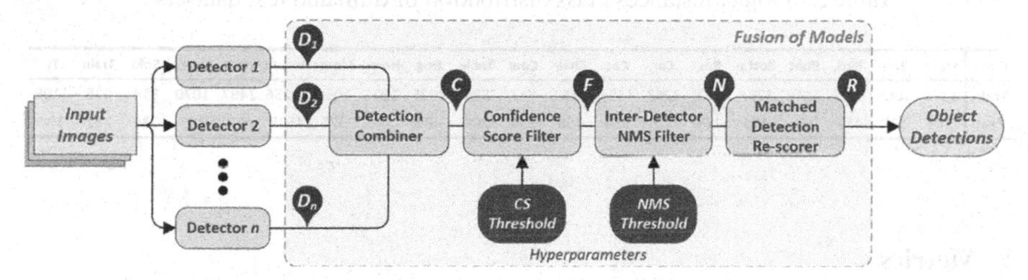

Fig. 3. Architecture of the fusion of detection models.

A fusion of models is a multi-stage process with specific functions described below:

1. **Detection Combiner** concatenates predictions from base detectors into a single large set of detection instances $C = \bigcup_{i=1}^{n} D_i$, where D_i is the ith detector prediction.
2. **Confidence Score Filter** discards low-score detections which do not exceed a cs confidence score threshold, from the set of all combined detection instances C.
3. **Inter-Detector NMS Filter** computes the IoU of all combinations of pairwise predictions from different detectors, identifies overlapped matching predictions with an $IoU \geq NMS\, threshold$, and discards all low-score overlap predictions, keeping only the overlap prediction with the highest confidence score.
4. **Selected Overlaps Re-scorer** updates the confidence score of overlapped detections selected by the inter-detector NMS filter. The confidence score of the selected prediction is updated with a joint score determined based on both selected and discarded detections, as expressed by Eq. 1.

$$cs = 1 - \prod_i (1 - C_i), \tag{1}$$

where $cs \in [0, 1]$ is the rescored confidence of the selected detection, and $C_i \in [0, 1]$ is the confidence score of an overlapped prediction from base detector i.

4 Experiments and Results

4.1 Datasets

In this paper, object detectors are pre-trained and evaluated with the publicly available, 20-class, PASCAL VOC dataset [25]. Detectors are pre-trained with VOC0712 trainval dataset containing 40058 non-difficult objects across 16551 images, resulting from the combination of VOC07 train, VOC07 validation, VOC12 train, and VOC12 validation datasets. Evaluations are conducted with VOC07 test dataset containing 12032 non-difficult objects across 4952 images. VOC dataset has a significant prevalence of person instances, corresponding to 33.1% of VOC0712 trainval and 37.6% of VOC2007 test dataset, making it appropriate for pedestrian detection tasks. Table 5 shows the object instance distribution among classes for training and testing datasets.

Table 5. Object instances class distribution of train and test datasets.

Class	Plane	Bike	Bird	Boat	Bottle	Bus	Car	Cat	Chair	Cow	Table	Dog	Horse	Motor	Person	Plant	Sheep	Sofa	Train	Tv
Train	1171	1064	1605	1140	1764	822	3267	1593	3152	847	824	2025	1072	1052	13256	1487	1070	814	925	1108
Test	285	337	459	263	469	213	1201	358	756	244	206	489	348	325	4528	480	242	239	282	308

4.2 Metrics

In this paper, we use standard, generally accepted, detection and localization evaluation metrics enumerated below:

- *Intersection over Union (IoU)* measures the overlap ratio between bounding boxes.
- *Recall (R)* and *Mean Recall (mR)* measure the detector's ability to predict all ground-truth objects.
- *Precision (P)* and *Mean Precision (mP)* measure the detector's ability to correctly identify objects.
- *F1-Score (F1)* represents the harmonic mean of precision and recall metrics.
- *Mean Average Precision (mAP)* measures the performance, evaluated according to VOC07 challenge development kit, ignoring objects marked as difficult and using interpolated average precision.

Baseline Performance Metrics. Absolute performance metrics are unable to reveal improvements over existing algorithms. We use the metrics of the best-performing base model within a fusion of models, as baseline performance metrics in our comparisons. Table 6 displays detectors' baseline performance metrics as well as metrics of corresponding individual object classes. Class metrics are used in class performance comparisons whereas detector metrics are used in detector performance comparisons.

Performance Evaluation. We conduct a standard performance evaluation of object detectors based on PASCAL VOC07 challenge [25] and using VOC07 test dataset. We use class average precision AP and detector mean average precision mAP as fundamental metrics to assess and compare the accuracy of base and fusion of models. We evaluate a fusion of SSD 300, SSD 512, YOLO v.2, and YOLO v.3 base models and set a detection confidence score cs threshold $= 0.005$ to remove low-score detections. The low confidence score filter reduces significantly the evaluation time with negligible impact on evaluation metrics. We present, in Table 7, the absolute AP of each object

Table 6. Baseline performance metrics of base detectors. The upper section shows class-level AP metrics whereas the lower section shows detector-level mAP metrics.

AP (%)	Plane	Bike	Bird	Boat	Bottle	Bus	Car	Cat	Chair	Cow	Table	Dog	Horse	Motor	Person	Plant	Sheep	Sofa	Train	Tv
FRCNN	74.5	80.8	72.8	65.8	64.0	80.5	85.9	86.2	59.7	81.1	70.6	83.7	86.1	81.4	82.6	49.7	77.6	70.3	80.4	74.2
SSD 300	80.0	83.9	76.0	69.5	50.7	86.7	85.8	88.4	60.5	81.2	75.3	86.2	87.5	83.9	79.6	52.7	79.0	79.5	87.8	77.9
SSD 512	85.5	85.8	81.2	73.0	58.4	87.9	88.4	87.7	64.1	85.5	73.1	86.2	87.3	83.9	82.7	55.3	80.9	79.3	86.6	80.2
YOLO2	78.0	83.5	75.2	65.3	52.1	82.4	80.0	88.4	58.5	80.0	78.0	86.6	84.5	82.0	77.8	52.3	73.4	76.8	86.0	75.0
YOLO3	87.0	85.6	78.3	71.2	67.2	85.6	87.5	89.0	64.6	84.9	73.6	87.1	87.1	87.2	83.4	56.8	82.1	79.1	85.9	79.3

Detector	FRCNN	SSD 300	SSD 512	YOLO2	YOLO3
mAP (%)	75.37	77.61	79.65	75.79	80.12

Table 7. AP absolute metrics of each object class, based on a fusion of SSD 300, SSD 512, YOLO v.2, and YOLO v.3 base detectors. The AP upper table section shows the class-level absolute AP metrics and the improvements of our method over the corresponding base detection models. The mAP lower table section shows the absolute mAP of our method and the improvements of our method over base detection models. The baseline performance, YOLO3, is underlined.

AP (%)	Plane	Bike	Bird	Boat	Bottle	Bus	Car	Cat	Chair	Cow	Table	Dog	Horse	Motor	Person	Plant	Sheep	Sofa	Train	Tv
Our Method	**87.0**	**87.6**	**84.3**	**77.5**	**70.9**	**88.8**	**89.3**	**89.7**	**71.6**	**87.7**	**79.8**	**89.1**	**89.0**	**88.0**	**85.4**	**63.0**	**86.2**	**84.8**	**88.0**	**85.4**
SSD 300	6.9	3.7	8.4	8.0	20.2	2.1	3.5	1.3	11.1	6.6	4.4	2.9	1.5	4.1	5.8	10.3	7.2	5.2	0.2	7.5
SSD 512	1.5	1.8	3.1	4.5	12.5	0.9	0.9	2.0	7.4	2.3	6.7	2.9	1.7	4.1	2.7	7.7	5.3	5.5	1.4	5.2
YOLO2	9.0	4.0	9.1	12.2	18.9	6.4	9.3	1.3	13.0	7.7	1.8	2.5	4.5	6.0	7.7	10.7	12.8	8.0	2.0	10.4
YOLO3	0.0	2.0	6.0	6.3	3.7	3.2	1.8	0.7	7.0	2.9	6.2	2.0	1.9	0.7	2.1	6.2	4.2	5.7	2.1	6.1

mAP (%)	Our Method	SSD 300	SSD 512	YOLO2	YOLO3 (Baseline)
	83.65	6.04	4.00	7.86	3.53

class and the absolute mAP of our fusion method along with class-level and detector-level improvements over corresponding base detection models.

A bar chart, displayed in Fig. 4, offers a cleaner visualization of class AP improvements of our fusion method.

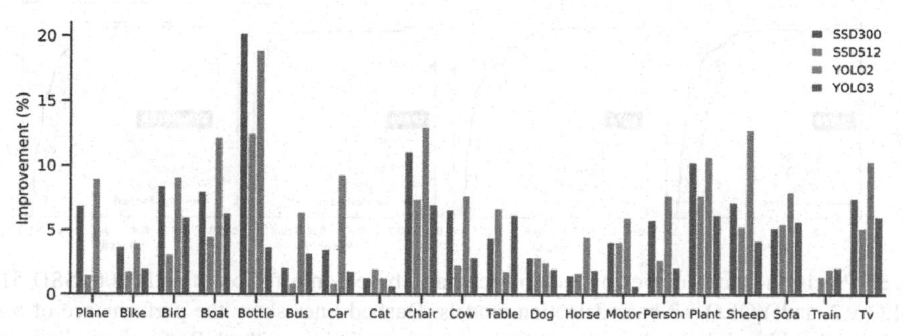

Fig. 4. Class AP percentage improvements of our fusion method with SSD 300, SSD 512, YOLO v.2, and YOLO v.3 base detectors.

Figure 5 displays classic precision-recall curves of each object class, based on a fusion of SSD 300, SSD 512, YOLO v.2, and YOLO v.3 base detection models. The curves of our fusion method, represented by solid black lines, outperform the corresponding base models, achieving an absolute mAP of 83.65% which represents an improvement of 3.53% over the baseline absolute mAP of 80.12%, set by YOLO v.3 detection model.

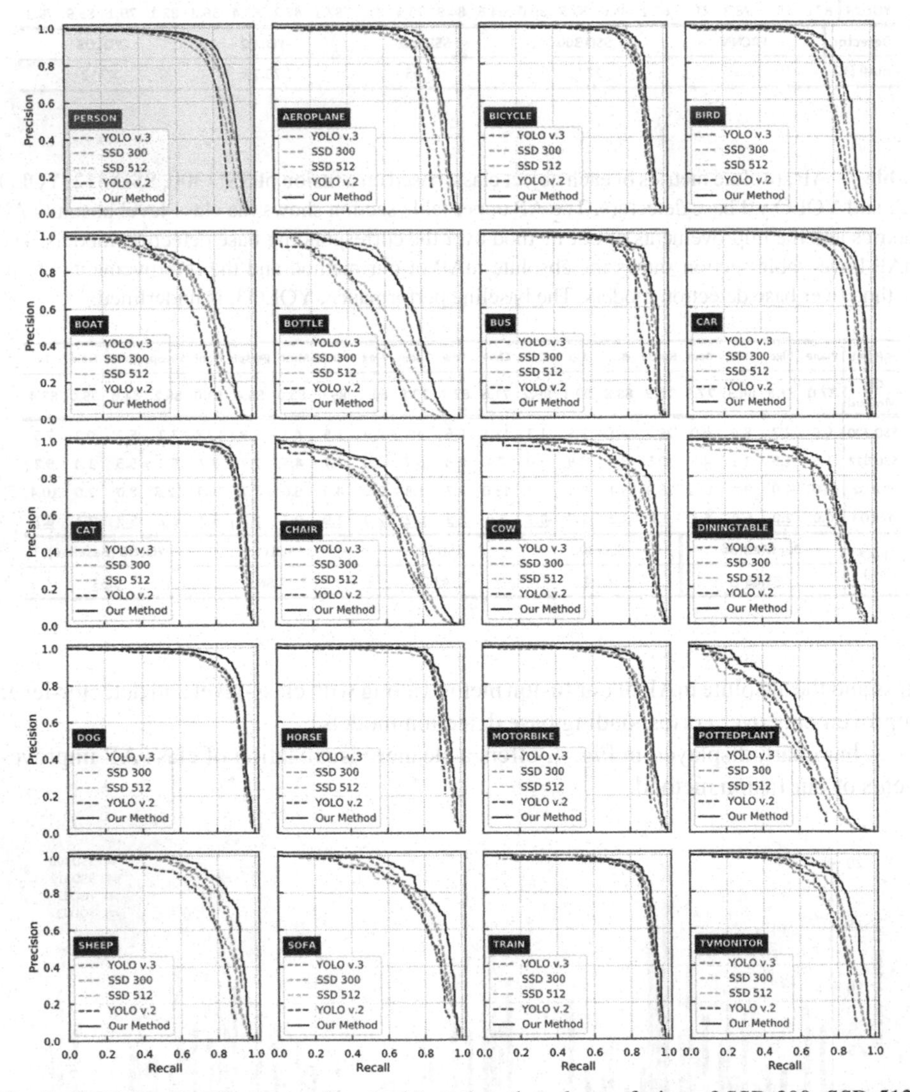

Fig. 5. Precision-Recall curves of each object class, based on a fusion of SSD 300, SSD 512, YOLO v.2, and YOLO v.3 base detection models. Dashed lines show the performance of base detectors. Solid black lines show the performance of our fusion method. Performance improvements are not limited to pedestrian detection, extending across a wide range of object classes, making fusion of models also applicable to generic object detection applications.

Fusion Size vs. Overall Performance. Increasing the size of a fusion of models does not always improve the overall performance, as observed in our experiments and summarized in Table 8. Our experimental results show a significant improvement of the maximum mAP for a fusion of two models, followed by diminished improvements as additional base detectors are added. Therefore, two to three models should be sufficient for significant improvements.

Table 8. Comparison of maximum mAP for different fusion sizes. The maximum mAP of a particular fusion size corresponds to the best-performing combination among base detectors.

Fusion size	1 *(No Fusion)*	2	3	4	5
Maximum mAP (%)	**80.12**	**83.20**	**83.63**	**83.65**	**83.33**

5 Conclusion

A post-processing method has been presented in this paper to fuse pre-trained off-the-shelf object detectors and exploit intrinsic model divergences to improve the detection mAP, recall, and precision of pedestrian detection. The proposed method can improve detection mAP and enable fast deployments of pedestrian detection systems, without re-training models. Our method combines predictions from different detectors, discards low-score overlap predictions, and rescores selected overlapped detections. Experiments reveal improvements starting from a fusion of just two models. Despite the additional system complexity, our method is still very important for critical applications such as security and management of emergency scenarios, where any undetected pedestrian results in substantial losses. Experimental results show improvements across a wide range of object classes, with the fusion of two to three models, demonstrating that our method can be applied in generic object detection. In future works, additional comprehensive experiments may be conducted to evaluate the robustness of the proposed method across a range of base object detection settings. Additionally, contextual and temporal information may be inferred from video streams and exploited to improve, even more, the overall detection performance.

Acknowledgments. This work was funded by the Science and Technology Development Fund of Macau SAR (File no. 138/2016/A3).

References

1. Viola, P., Jones, M.: Rapid object detection using a boosted cascade of simple features. In: Proceedings of the 2001 IEEE Computer Society Conference on Computer Vision and Pattern Recognition, CVPR 2001, vol. 1, pp. I-511–I-518 (2001). https://doi.org/10.1109/CVPR.2001.990517
2. Lowe, D.G.: Object recognition from local scale-invariant features. In: Proceedings of the Seventh IEEE International Conference on Computer Vision, vol. 2, pp. 1150–1157 (1999). https://doi.org/10.1109/ICCV.1999.790410

3. Dalal, N., Triggs, B.: Histograms of oriented gradients for human detection. In: IEEE Computer Society Conference on Computer Vision and Pattern Recognition, CVPR 2005, pp. 886–893 (2005). https://doi.org/10.1109/CVPR.2005.177
4. Dollar, P., Appel, R., Belongie, S., Perona, P.: Fast feature pyramids for object detection. IEEE Trans. Pattern Anal. Mach. Intell. **36**, 1532–1545 (2014). https://doi.org/10.1109/TPAMI.2014.2300479
5. Ren, S., He, K., Girshick, R., Sun, J.: Faster R-CNN: towards real-time object detection with region proposal networks. IEEE Trans. Pattern Anal. Mach. Intell. **39**, 1137–1149 (2017). https://doi.org/10.1109/TPAMI.2016.2577031
6. Liu, W., et al.: SSD: single shot multibox detector. In: Leibe, B., Matas, J., Sebe, N., Welling, M. (eds.) ECCV 2016. LNCS, vol. 9905, pp. 21–37. Springer, Cham (2016). https://doi.org/10.1007/978-3-319-46448-0_2
7. Redmon, J., Farhadi, A.: YOLO9000: better, faster, stronger (2016). https://doi.org/10.1109/CVPR.2017.690
8. Redmon, J., Farhadi, A.: YOLOv3: an incremental improvement (2018). https://doi.org/10.1109/CVPR.2017.690
9. Krizhevsky, A., Sutskever, I., Hinton, G.E.: ImageNet classification with deep convolutional neural networks. Adv. Neural Inf. Process. Syst., 1–9 (2012). https://doi.org/10.1016/j.protcy.2014.09.007
10. Simonyan, K., Zisserman, A.: Very deep convolutional networks for large-scale image recognition. arXiv:1409.1556 (2015). https://doi.org/10.1016/j.infsof.2008.09.005
11. Szegedy, C., et al.: Going deeper with convolutions. In: Proceedings of the IEEE Computer Society Conference on Computer Vision and Pattern Recognition, 7–12 June 2015, pp. 1–9 (2015). https://doi.org/10.1109/CVPR.2015.7298594
12. Ioffe, S., Szegedy, C.: Batch normalization: accelerating deep network training by reducing internal covariate shift. arXiv:1502.03167 (2015)
13. Szegedy, C., Vanhoucke, V., Ioffe, S., Shlens, J., Wojna, Z.: Rethinking the inception architecture for computer vision (2015). https://doi.org/10.1109/CVPR.2016.308
14. Szegedy, C., Ioffe, S., Vanhoucke, V.: Inception-v4, inception-ResNet and the impact of residual connections on learning. arXiv:1602.07261 (2016). https://doi.org/10.1016/j.patrec.2014.01.008
15. He, K., Zhang, X., Ren, S., Sun, J.: Deep residual learning for image recognition. In: Proceedings of the IEEE Computer Society Conference on Computer Vision and Pattern Recognition, pp. 770–778 (2016). https://doi.org/10.1109/CVPR.2016.90
16. Dietterich, T.G.: Ensemble methods in machine learning. In: Kittler, J., Roli, F. (eds.) MCS 2000. LNCS, vol. 1857, pp. 1–15. Springer, Heidelberg (2000). https://doi.org/10.1007/3-540-45014-9_1
17. Opitz, D., Maclin, R.: Popular ensemble methods: an empirical study. **11**, 169–198 (2016). https://doi.org/10.1613/jair.614
18. Breiman, L.: Bagging predictors. Mach. Learn. **24**, 123–140 (1996). https://doi.org/10.1007/BF00058655
19. Freund, Y., Schapire, R.E.: A short introduction to boosting. J. Japanese Soc. Artif. Intell. **14**, 771–780 (1999)
20. Wolpert, D.H.: Stacked generalization. Neural Netw. **5**, 241–259 (1992). https://doi.org/10.1016/S0893-6080(05)80023-1
21. Breiman, L.: Stacked regressions. Mach. Learn. **24**, 49–64 (1996). https://doi.org/10.1007/bf00117832
22. Jacobs, R.A., Jordan, M.I., Nowlan, S.J., Hinton, G.E.: Adaptive mixtures of local experts. Neural Comput. **3**, 79–87 (2008). https://doi.org/10.1162/neco.1991.3.1.79
23. Masoudnia, S., Ebrahimpour, R.: Mixture of experts: a literature survey. Artif. Intell. Rev. **42**, 275–293 (2014). https://doi.org/10.1007/s10462-012-9338-y

24. Yuksel, S.E., Wilson, J.N., Gader, P.D.: Twenty years of mixture of experts. IEEE Trans. Neural Networks Learn. Syst. **23**, 1177–1193 (2012). https://doi.org/10.1109/TNNLS.2012.2200299
25. Everingham, M., Van Gool, L., Williams, C.K.I., Winn, J., Zisserman, A.: The PASCAL visual object classes (VOC) challenge. Int. J. Comput. Vis. **88**, 303–338 (2010). https://doi.org/10.1007/s11263-009-0275-4
26. Niitani, Y., Ogawa, T., Saito, S., Saito, M.: ChainerCV: a library for deep learning in computer vision, pp. 2–5 (2017). https://doi.org/10.1145/3123266.3129395
27. Girshick, R., Donahue, J., Darrell, T., Malik, J.: Rich feature hierarchies for accurate object detection and semantic segmentation. In: Proceedings of the IEEE Computer Society Conference on Computer Vision and Pattern Recognition, pp. 580–587 (2014). https://doi.org/10.1109/CVPR.2014.81
28. Zhao, X., Li, W., Zhang, Y., Gulliver, T.A., Chang, S., Feng, Z.: A faster RCNN-based pedestrian detection system. In: IEEE Vehicular Technology Conference (2017). https://doi.org/10.1109/VTCFall.2016.7880852
29. Wu, Q., Liao, S.: Single shot multibox detector for vehicles and pedestrians detection and classification. DEStech Trans. Eng. Technol. Res., 22–28 (2018). https://doi.org/10.12783/dtetr/apop2017/18705
30. Redmon, J., Divvala, S., Girshick, R., Farhadi, A.: You only look once: unified, real-time object detection. In: Proceedings of the IEEE Conference on Computer Vision and Pattern Recognition, pp. 779–788 (2016). https://doi.org/10.1016/j.nima.2015.05.028
31. Liu, Z., Chen, Z., Li, Z., Hu, W.: An Efficient pedestrian detection method based on YOLOv2. Math. Probl. Eng. **2018** (2018). https://doi.org/10.1155/2018/3518959
32. Qiu, S., Wen, G., Deng, Z., Liu, J., Fan, Y.: Accurate non-maximum suppression for object detection in high-resolution remote sensing images. Remote Sens. Lett. **9**, 237–246 (2018). https://doi.org/10.1080/2150704X.2017.1415473
33. Felzenszwalb, P.F., Girshick, R.B., Mcallester, D., Ramanan, D.: Object detection with discriminatively trained part-based models. IEEE Trans. Pattern Anal. Mach. Intell. **32**, 1627–1645 (2009). https://doi.org/10.1109/TPAMI.2009.167
34. Devernay, F.: A non-maxima suppression method for edge detection with sub-pixel accuracy. INRIA Res. Rep. 2724 (1995)
35. Tang, E.K., Suganthan, P.N., Yao, X.: An analysis of diversity measures. Mach. Learn. **65**, 247–271 (2006). https://doi.org/10.1007/s10994-006-9449-2
36. Skalak, D., et al.: The sources of increased accuracy for two proposed boosting algorithms. In: Proceedings of the American Association for Artificial Intelligence, AAAI-96, Integrating Multiple Learned Models Workshop, vol. 1129, p. 1133. Citeseer (1996)
37. Ho, T.K.: The random subspace method for constructing decision forests. IEEE Trans. Pattern Anal. Mach. Intell. **20**, 832–844 (1998). https://doi.org/10.1109/34.709601
38. Cohen, J.: A coefficient of agreement for nominal scales. Educ. Psychol. Meas. **20**, 37–46 (1960). https://doi.org/10.1177/001316446002000104
39. Margineantu, D.D., Dietterich, T.G.: Pruning adaptive boosting. In: Proceedings of the Fourteenth International Conference on Machine Learning, pp. 211–218. Morgan Kaufmann Publishers Inc., San Francisco (1997)

Perceptual Image Anomaly Detection

Nina Tuluptceva[1,3(✉)], Bart Bakker[2], Irina Fedulova[1], and Anton Konushin[3]

[1] Philips Research, Moscow, Russia
{nina.tuluptceva,irina.fedulova}@philips.com
[2] Philips Research, Eindhoven, The Netherlands
bart.bakker@philips.com
[3] Lomonosov Moscow State University, Moscow, Russia
anton.konushin@graphics.cs.msu.ru

Abstract. We present a novel method for image anomaly detection, where algorithms that use samples drawn from some distribution of "normal" data, aim to detect out-of-distribution (abnormal) samples. Our approach includes a combination of encoder and generator for mapping an image distribution to a predefined latent distribution and vice versa. It leverages Generative Adversarial Networks to learn these data distributions and uses perceptual loss for the detection of image abnormality. To accomplish this goal, we introduce a new similarity metric, which expresses the perceived similarity between images and is robust to changes in image contrast. Secondly, we introduce a novel approach for the selection of weights of a multi-objective loss function (image reconstruction and distribution mapping) in the absence of a validation dataset for hyperparameter tuning. After training, our model measures the abnormality of the input image as the perceptual dissimilarity between it and the closest generated image of the modeled data distribution. The proposed approach is extensively evaluated on several publicly available image benchmarks and achieves state-of-the-art performance.

Keywords: Anomaly detection · Out-of-distribution detection · Deep learning · Generative Adversarial Networks

1 Introduction

Anomaly detection is one of the most important problems in a range of real-world settings, including medical applications [15], cyber-intrusion detection [13], fraud detection [2], anomaly event detection in videos [11] and overgeneralization problems of neural networks [26]. Anomaly detection tasks generally involve the use of samples of a "normal" class, drawn from some distribution, to build a classifier that is able to detect "abnormal" samples, i.e. *outliers* with respect to the aforementioned distribution. Although anomaly detection is well-studied in a range of domains, image anomaly detection is still a challenge due to the complexity of distributions over images.

S. Palaiahnakote et al. (Eds.): ACPR 2019, LNCS 12046, pp. 164–178, 2020.
https://doi.org/10.1007/978-3-030-41404-7_12

Generative Adversarial Networks (GANs) [8] present one of the new promising deep anomaly detection approaches. One network called *the generator* is trained to transform latent vectors, drawn from a latent distribution, to images in such a way that the second network, *the discriminator*, cannot distinguish between real images and generated ones. Thus after training, the generator performs a mapping of the latent distribution to the data distribution. This property has been used [6,19,24,29,30] to estimate the likelihood of abnormality for an input: if there is a vector in latent space, which after passing through the generator could reconstruct the input object, the object is normal, otherwise it is not. The difference between an input and its closest reconstruction (*reconstruction error*) is used as *an anomaly score* for this object.

Although there is a scope of methods that use GAN for anomaly detection, none of them were directly developed for anomaly detection on images. Usually, they apply the L1-norm or Mean Squared Error (MSE) between the pixels to compute a reconstruction error, which does not correspond to human understanding of the similarity between two images. Another problem of GAN-based approaches is how to find the latent vector that, after passing through the generator, recovers the input object. Previously, it was performed by a gradient descent optimization procedure [6,24], co-training the generator and *the encoder* that recovers the latent vector [19,29,30]. However, existing techniques are either time-consuming [6,24] or difficult to train [29,30], or consist of complex multi-step learning procedures [19]. Another problem is that the complete loss function consists of a sum of many components with weighting coefficients as hyperparameters. The lack of a validation set (we do not have anomaly examples during training), makes it difficult to choose these coefficients.

(a) Perc: 4.29
Rel-perc-L1: 0.52

(b) Perc: 3.36
Rel-perc-L1: 0.49

(c) Perc: 2.58
Rel-perc-L1: 0.47

Fig. 1. Dependence of perceptual loss (*perc*) and proposed relative-perceptual-L1 loss (*rel-perc-L1*) on a contrast of images (on an example of LSUN datasets [28]). Each column presents a pair of images: the bottom image is shifted by 5 pixels on both axes relative to the top image. (a) Pair of images with original contrast. (b), (c) Pairs of images with decreased contrast (by histogram stretching with reduced dynamic range).

In our work we propose solutions for each of these three problems:

1. We developed a new metric that measures the similarity between the perception of two images. Our metric, called *relative-perceptual-L1 loss*, is based on perceptual loss [10], but is more robust to noise and changes of contrast of images (Fig. 1).
2. We propose a new technique for training an encoder, which predicts a latent vector corresponding to an input image, jointly with the generator. We construct a loss function in such a way that the encoder predicts a vector *belonging to the latent distribution*, and that the image reconstructed from this vector by the generator *is similar to the input.*
3. We propose a way to choose the weighting coefficients in the complete loss functions for the encoder and the generator. We base our solution on the norm of the gradients (with respect to network parameters) of each loss function, to balance the contribution of all losses during the training process.

The proposed approach, called Perceptual Image Anomaly Detection (PIAD), allows us to improve performance on several well-known datasets. We experimented with MNIST [14], Fashion MNIST [27], COIL-100 [17], CIFAR-10 [12], LSUN [28] and CelebA [16] and made an extensive comparison with a wide range of anomaly detection approaches of different paradigms.

2 Related Work

Anomaly detection has been extensively studied in a wide range of domains [4]. However, anomaly detection on image data is still challenging. Classical approaches such as explicit modeling of latent space using KDE [18] or One-Class SVM [5] which learns a boundary around samples of a normal class, show poor quality when applied to *image* anomaly detection tasks. Due to the problem of the curse of dimensionality, these algorithms are weak in modeling complex high-dimensional distributions.

Deep autoencoders play an important role among anomaly detection methods [3,23,31]. Autoencoders that perform dimension reduction (or create sparse representations) learn some common factors inherent in normal data. Abnormal samples do not contain these factors and thus cannot be accurately reconstructed by autoencoders. However, image anomaly detection is still challenging for autoencoders, and usually they are applied only on simple abnormal samples, when the variability of normal images is low.

There are also "mixed" approaches that use autoencoders or other deep models for representation learning. *GPND* [20] leverages an adversarial autoencoder to create a low-dimensional representation and then uses a probabilistic interpretation of the latent space to obtain an anomaly score. The method described in [1] models a latent distribution obtained from a deep autoencoder using an auto-regressive network. In *Deep SVDD* [21], Ruff *et al.* show how to train a one-class classification objective together with deep feature representation.

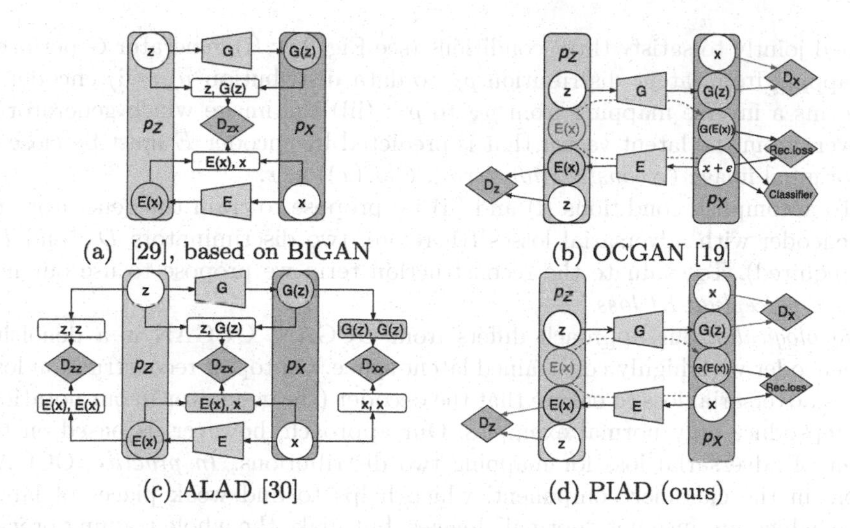

(a) [29], based on BIGAN (b) OCGAN [19]

(c) ALAD [30] (d) PIAD (ours)

Fig. 2. Comparison of anomaly detection approaches. G denotes the generator, E the encoder, D_* the discriminators, "Rec. loss" is a reconstruction loss. p_Z denotes the latent distribution, and z its sample. In the same way, p_X is the data distribution and x is data sample, ϵ is noise.

GANs [8] created a new branch in the development of image anomaly detection. GAN-based approaches [6,19,24,29,30] differ in two parts: (i) how to find latent vectors that correspond to the input images, (ii) how to estimate abnormality based on the input image and the reconstructed one. For the second problem, methods use a linear combination of the L1-norm or the MSE between the input image and the reconstruction (*reconstruction error*), and the discriminator's prediction of the reality of the reconstructed image. For the first problem, approaches AnoGAN [24] and ADGAN [6] propose to use time-consuming gradient descent optimization of a latent vector. Other approaches train an encoder to predict a latent vector for each image. Figure 2 demonstrates the differences between the existing approaches. ALAD [30] and method [29] train the encoder adversarially: the adversarial loss computed by the discriminator, which takes pairs (image, vector), forces the encoder to predict a latent vector that reconstructs the input image. However, discriminators of such models train with a cross-entropy loss function, which causes an unstable training process. The OCGAN model trains a denoising autoencoder. To improve the quality of mapping, authors added two discriminators: D_X and D_Z, and a classifier which searches for hard negative examples (bad generated images).

3 Perceptual Image Anomaly Detection

Conceptually the idea of *PIAD* follows the OCGAN. We apply the power of GANs two times, once for building a mapping from the latent space to the image space, and again to create an inverse mapping. A generator and an encoder are trained jointly to satisfy three conditions (see Fig. 2d): (i) generator G performs a mapping from latent distribution p_Z to data distribution p_X; (ii) encoder E performs a inverse mapping from p_X to p_Z; (iii) the image which generator G recovers from the latent vector that is predicted by encoder E must be close to the original image (*reconstruction term*): $G(E(x)) \approx x$.

To accomplish conditions (i) and (ii) we propose to train the generator and the encoder with adversarial losses (therefore, two discriminators D_X and D_Z are required). To evaluate the reconstruction term we propose to use our new *relative-perceptual-L1 loss*.

Ideologically, our approach differs from OCGAN. OCGAN is a denoising autoencoder with highly constrained latent space. On top of reconstruction loss, it uses adversarial loss to ensure that the decoder (the generator in our notation) can reproduce only normal examples. Our approach, however, is based on the power of adversarial loss for mapping two distributions. *In practice*, OCGAN differs in the classifier component, which helps to find weak places of latent space, which produce not "normal" images, but make the whole training process much complicated and multi-steps. Also, we do not add noise to image x before passing it through the encoder.

In order to train the encoder and the generator to minimize a multi-objective loss function, we propose a new way of setting the weights of the loss functions that equalizes the contribution of each loss in the training process. Due to the fact that our approach relies on gradients of the loss functions, we called it *gradient-normalizing weights policy*.

After training the proposed model on samples of a normal class, we suggest to predict *the abnormality* $A(x)$ of a new example x by evaluating the relative-perceptual-L1 loss between the input x and $G(E(x))$:

$$A(x) = L_{rel-perc-L1}(x, G(E(x))). \tag{1}$$

We consider the relative-perceptual-L1 loss in more detail in Sect. 3.1, the procedure for training models in Sect. 3.2 and the gradient-normalizing weights policy in Sect. 3.3.

3.1 Relative-perceptual-L1 Loss

Features obtained by a neural network, trained on a large dataset for the task of object recognition, can capture high-level image content without binding to exact pixel locations [7]. In [10] Johnson *et al.* proposed *content* distance between two images, called *perceptual loss*: this metric computes the MSE between features taken at a deep level of a pre-trained neural network.

Let $f(x)$ be a feature map obtained from some deep layer of the network on image x, and $C \times H \times W$ the shape of this feature map. Then the *perceptual loss* between image x and y is determined as:

$$L_{perc}(x, y) = \frac{\|f(x) - f(y)\|_2^2}{C \times H \times W}. \tag{2}$$

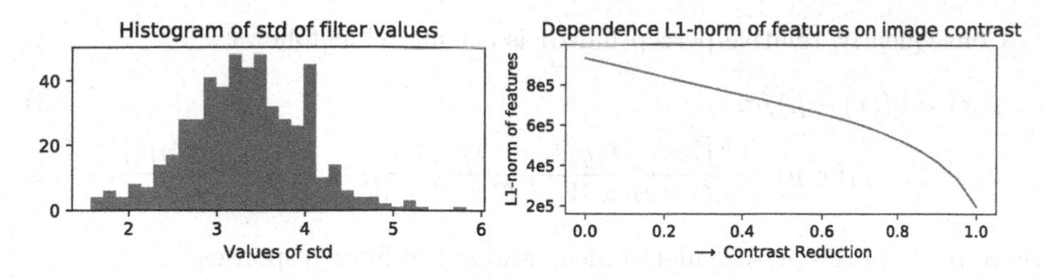

Fig. 3. (left) Histogram of std of responses of 512 filters of a VGG19 [25] layer (the 2nd conv. of the 4-th block), computed over Imagenet [22]. (right) Dependence of the L1-norm of the VGG19 features (the 2nd conv. of 4-th block) on image contrast. Dependence is shown on an image of LSUN dataset (Fig. 1). On the x axis, 0.0 is the original image, 1.0 is completely grey image, between them contrast is linearly decreased (0.2 is corresponds to Fig. 1b, 0.4 to Fig. 1c).

However, perceptual loss is very sensitive to changes in image contrast. Figure 1 shows three pairs of images: pairs Fig. 1b and c have lower contrast than Fig. 1a. Perceptual loss drops by 22% for images Fig. 1b compared to Fig. 1a, although for human supervision the pair Fig. 1b differs from the pair Fig. 1a very little. In this way, if we used perceptual loss for computing anomaly score, the model would tend to predict lower contrast images as less abnormal. Another problem is that perceptual loss applies the MSE over features, but the MSE penalizes the noise in the obtained feature values very heavily.

We tackled these problems and propose *relative-perceptual-L1* loss, which is robust to contrast and noise. First of all, we noticed that features obtained at different filters can have a different scatter of values. As an example, Fig. 3 (left) shows the standard deviations of filter responses of some deep layer of VGG-19 [25], computed over Imagenet [22]. We visualize the standard deviations since they indicate the overall value of the features, which are themselves distributed around zero. Standard deviations differ by a factor of 2-3, which means that the contributions per filter vary by a factor 2-3 as well. Therefore, as the first step of relative-perceptual-L1, we propose to normalize the obtained deep features by the mean and std of filter responses which are pre-calculated over the large dataset, like Imagenet. Secondly, we propose to use the L1-norm instead of the MSE, since the L1-norm is more robust to noise. Thirdly, to make the loss more resistant to contrast, we research how feature values behave under changes of contrast. Figure 3 (right) illustrates this behavior: during the reduction of image contrast, the L1-norm of feature values decreases. In this way, the absolute error (the difference between features), which is used in perceptual loss, decreases as well for each pair of lower contrast images. Therefore, we propose not to use absolute error, but *relative error*, which measures the ratio of the absolute error of features to the average values of these features.

Consequently, relative-perceptual-L1 is calculated as follows:

$$\tilde{f}(x) = (f(x) - \mu)/\sigma, \tag{3}$$

$$L_{rel-perc-L1}(x, y) = \frac{\|\tilde{f}(x) - \tilde{f}(y)\|_1}{C \times H \times W} / \frac{\|\tilde{f}(x)\|_1}{C \times H \times W} = \frac{\|\tilde{f}(x) - \tilde{f}(y)\|_1}{\|\tilde{f}(x)\|_1}, \tag{4}$$

where μ, σ are the pre-calculated mean and std of filter responses.

3.2 Training Objective

To train both discriminators we used the Wasserstein GAN with a Gradient Penalty objective (WGAN-GP) [9]. The training of a Wasserstein GAN is more stable than a classical GAN [8] (which was used in [19,29,30]), it prevents mode collapse, and does not require a careful searching schedule of generator/discriminator training. Thus, the discriminator D_X learns by minimizing the following loss:

$$L_{disc}(D_X) = \mathbb{E}_{z \sim p_Z}[D_X(G(z))] - \mathbb{E}_{x \sim p_X}[D_X(x)] + \lambda \cdot GP(D_X), \tag{5}$$

where GP is Gradient Penalty Regularization [9] and λ is a weighting parameter. In the same way, D_Z minimizes $L_{disc}(D_Z)$. Adversarial loss of the generator is

$$L_{adv}(G) = \mathbb{E}_{x \sim p_X}[D_X(x)] - \mathbb{E}_{z \sim p_Z}[D_X(G(z))]. \tag{6}$$

Adversarial loss of the encoder $L_{adv}(E)$ is computed in the same way. Reconstruction loss is measured using the proposed *relative-perceptual-L1* loss:

$$L_{rec}(G, E) = \mathbb{E}_{x \sim p_X}[L_{rel-perc-L1}(x, G(E(x)))]. \tag{7}$$

Thus, the total objectives for the encoder and generator are as follows:

$$L_{total}(G) = L_{adv}(G) + \gamma_G L_{rec}(G, E), \tag{8}$$

$$L_{total}(E) = L_{adv}(E) + \gamma_E L_{rec}(G, E), \tag{9}$$

where γ_G and γ_E are weighting parameters. The training process consists of alternating n_{dis} steps of optimization of the discriminators and one step of optimization of the generator together with the encoder. Parameters γ_G and γ_E change every n_{param} iterations following our *gradient-normalizing weights policy.* The full training procedure is summarized in Algorithm 1. (Steps *"update gradient history"* and *"select weighting parameter"* are explained in detail in the next section).

3.3 Gradient-Normalizing Weight Policy

Our objective function consists of the sum of multiple losses. To find weighting parameters for these losses, we cannot use cross-validation, because no anomaly examples are available to calculate anomaly detection quality. The work [19] chooses weights empirically based on reconstruction quality. However, it requires a person to manually evaluate quality and then select the coefficients for each experiment, and it is not objective and reproducible.

In order to choose weighting parameters automatically, we need to base our solution on measured values of an experiment. Let $\bar{w} = [w_1, \ldots, w_n]$ be a vector of network parameters, $l_1(w)$, $l_2(w)$ are losses calculated for this network, and $L_{total}(w) = l_1(w) + \gamma l_2(w)$. Then $\frac{\partial L_{total}(w)}{\partial w_i} = \frac{\partial l_1}{\partial w_i} + \gamma \frac{\partial l_2}{\partial w_i}$. Depending on the nature of the loss functions l_1 and l_2, the norms of $\|\frac{\partial l1}{\partial w_i}\|$ and $\|\frac{\partial l_2}{\partial w_i}\|$ can differ by a factor of ten or even a hundred. Coefficient γ regulates the relative influence of the loss functions in the total gradient with respect to this parameter w_i. To make the contribution of the loss functions equal, we can choose coefficient γ in the following way: $\|\frac{\partial l1}{\partial w_i}\| = \gamma \|\frac{\partial l_2}{\partial w_i}\|$. However, due to using stochastic optimization, gradients are very noisy during training. To make this process more robust and stable, we propose to average the γ coefficients over all network parameters and over their previous values (*history information*). Our approach is summarized in Algorithms 2 and 3.

In short: for each loss, we calculate the derivative (backpropagate loss) wrt each network weight w_i (see in Algorithm 1), and for each convolutional layer of the network, we compute the L2-norm of the derivative wrt the weight matrix

---

Algorithm 1. Training procedure of PIAD. *"Reset gradients"* zeros all stored gradients of network parameters. *"Backpropagate* loss" computes gradients of loss wrt network parameters and sums them to current stored gradients. *"Update* net" performs one step of gradient descent using stored gradients.

Require: N, the total number of iterations. n_{dis}, the number of iterations of training the discriminators. n_{weight}, frequency of change of γ_G and γ_E.
1: **for** $iter = 0, ..., N$ **do**
2:   **for** $t = 0, ..., n_{dis}$ **do**
3:     Sample $\{x\} \sim p_X$, $\{z\} \sim p_Z$.
4:     Compute $L_{disc}(D_X)$, $L_{disc}(D_Z)$.
5:     Reset gradients; backpropagate $L_{disc}(D_X)$, $L_{disc}(D_Z)$; update D_X, D_Z.
6:   **end for**
7:   Sample $\{x\} \sim p_X$, $\{z\} \sim p_Z$.
8:   Compute $L_{adv}(G)$, $L_{adv}(E)$, $L_{rec}(G, E)$.
9:   **if** $iter \ \% \ n_{weight} == 0$ **then**
10:     **for** $loss \in \{L_{adv}(G), L_{adv}(E), L_{rec}(G, E)\}$ **do**
11:       Reset gradients; backpropagate $loss$; update gradient history of $loss$.
12:     **end for**
13:     Select weighting parameter γ_G; select weighting parameter γ_E.
14:   **end if**
15:   Reset gradients.
16:   Backpropagate $L_{rec}(G, E)$; multiply gradients of G by γ_G, E by γ_E.
17:   Backpropagate $L_{adv}(G)$, $L_{adv}(E)$.
18:   Update G, E.
19: **end for**

Algorithm 2. Update gradient history (of some $loss$ function)

Require: *net*, the neural network, with pre-calculated gradients of the $loss$ function. *history*, the dictionary with previous values of gradient norm.

1: **for** *layer* $\in$ *net* **do**
2: *history[layer.name]* $\leftarrow$ *history[layer.name]* $\cup$ *L2-norm(layer.weight.grad)*
3: **end for**

Algorithm 3. Select weighting parameter

Require: M, *net*, the number of historical points and the neural network involved in the calculations. *history_1*, *history_2*, historical information of 1'st and 2'nd loss.

1: γ*_per_layer* = new_list()
2: **for** *layer* $\in$ *net* **do**
3: *values_1* $\leftarrow$ select_last_M(M, exp_smoothing(*history_1[layer.name]*))
4: *values_2* $\leftarrow$ select_last_M(M, exp_smoothing(*history_2[layer.name]*))
5: γ*_per_layer* $\leftarrow$ γ*_per_layer* $\cup$ mean(*values_1/values_2*)
6: **end for**
7: $\gamma \leftarrow$ mean(γ*_per_layer*)
8: **return** γ

Table 1. Statistics of the image datasets

	MNIST	fMNIST	COIL-100	CIFAR-10	LSUN (bedr.)	CelebA
# classes	10	10	100	10	1	40 attrib.
# instances	70,000	70,000	7,200	60,000	3,033,342	202,599

and store it (Algorithm 2). This is done after every n_{weight} iterations in training, and all previously calculated values are kept, thus creating a gradient history per loss, per layer. We calculate the L2-norm per layer (but not per each weight w_i) to reduce the size of the stored information. Computing the norm over all network parameters would lose too much information since the last layers usually have more parameters, and hence information about gradients from the first layers would be lost. Firstly, the coefficient γ is calculated per layer (Algorithm 3): we perform exponential smoothing of the historical values of each loss (to make values robust to noise), and then calculate the average ratio between the last M entries in the gradient history for $loss_1$ and the same for $loss_2$. The final value for γ is computed as the average over the γ-s per layer.

Our approach simply generalizes to a loss function consisting of more than two contributions. It also leaves room for research on which norm to use and how to compute the final weights.

4 Experiments

We show the effectiveness of the proposed approach by evaluation on six publicly available datasets and compare our method with a diverse collection of state-of-the-art methods for out-of-distribution detection, including state-of-the-art GAN-based approaches.

Datasets. For evaluation we use the following well-known datasets (Table 1): **MNIST** [14] and **Fashion MNIST (fMNIST)** [27], **COIL-100** [17], **CIFAR-10** [12], **LSUN** [28] (we used only the *bedrooms* and *conference room* classes), and face image attributes dataset **CelebA** [16] (*aligned & cropped* version).

In all experiments, images of MNIST, fMNIST and COIL-100 were resized to 32×32, examples of the LSUN dataset were downscaled to size 64×64 and for images of CelebA we made a 140×140 central crop and then downscaled to size 64×64.

Competing Methods. As shallow baselines we consider standard methods such as *OC-SVM* [5] and *KDE* [18]. We also test the performance of our approach against four state-of-the-art GAN-based methods: *AnoGAN* [24], *ADGAN* [6], *OCGAN* [19] and *ALAD* [30]. Finally, we report the performance of three deep learning approaches from different paradigms: *Deep SVDD* [21], *GPND* [20], and

Table 2. ROC AUC for anomaly detection on MNIST and CIFAR-10. Each row presents an experiment in which this class was considered as normal data. For each line, the best result is shown in bold, and the second best result is underlined.

		Shallow		GAN-based methods				Deep methods		PIAD
		OC-SVM	KDE	AnoGAN	ADGAN	OCGAN	ALAD	LSA	Deep SVDD	(our)
MNIST	0	0.988	0.885	0.926	**0.999**	0.998	-	0.993	0.980	0.996
	1	**0.999**	0.996	0.995	0.992	**0.999**	-	**0.999**	0.997	**0.999**
	2	0.902	0.710	0.805	0.968	0.942	-	0.959	0.917	**0.985**
	3	0.950	0.693	0.818	0.953	0.963	-	0.966	0.919	**0.981**
	4	0.955	0.844	0.823	0.960	**0.975**	-	0.956	0.949	0.960
	5	0.968	0.776	0.803	0.955	**0.980**	-	0.964	0.885	0.976
	6	0.978	0.861	0.890	0.980	0.991	-	0.994	0.983	**0.995**
	7	0.965	0.884	0.898	0.950	0.981	-	0.980	0.946	**0.984**
	8	0.853	0.669	0.817	0.959	0.939	-	0.953	0.939	**0.982**
	9	0.955	0.825	0.887	0.965	0.981	-	0.981	0.965	**0.989**
	avg	0.951	0.814	0.866	0.968	0.975	-	0.975	0.948	**0.985**
CIFAR-10	airplane	0.630	0.658	0.708	0.661	0.757	-	0.735	0.617	**0.837**
	car	0.440	0.520	0.458	0.435	0.531	-	0.580	0.659	**0.876**
	bird	0.649	0.657	0.664	0.636	0.640	-	0.690	0.508	**0.753**
	cat	0.487	0.497	0.510	0.488	**0.620**	-	0.542	0.591	0.602
	deer	0.735	0.727	0.722	0.794	0.723	-	0.761	0.609	**0.808**
	dog	0.500	0.496	0.505	0.640	0.620	-	0.546	0.657	**0.713**
	frog	0.725	0.758	0.707	0.685	0.723	-	0.751	0.677	**0.839**
	horse	0.533	0.564	0.471	0.559	0.575	-	0.535	0.673	**0.842**
	ship	0.649	0.680	0.713	0.798	0.820	-	0.717	0.759	**0.867**
	truck	0.508	0.540	0.458	0.643	0.554	-	0.548	0.731	**0.849**
	avg	0.586	0.610	0.592	0.634	0.657	0.607	0.641	0.648	**0.799**

the Latent Space Autoregression approach [1] (results will be reported under the name *LSA*). All these methods have been briefly described in Sect. 2.

For ADGAN [6], OCGAN [19], ALAD [30], GPND [20], *LSA* [1] we used results as reported in the corresponding publications. Results for OC-SVM, KDE, AnoGAN were obtained from [1].

Evaluation Protocol. To test the methods on classification datasets, we use a one-vs-all evaluation scheme, which has recently been increasingly used in anomaly detection papers [1,6,19–21,30]: to simulate out-of-distribution condition, one class of a dataset is considered as normal data while images of other classes are considered as abnormal. We evaluate results quantitatively using the area under the ROC curve (ROC AUC), which is a standard metric for this task.

Implementation Details. In all experiments we used pre-activation residual blocks to build our generator, encoder, and discriminator; for computing relative-perceptual-L1 loss we used VGG-19 [25] network, pre-trained on Imagenet [22].

4.1 Results

MNIST and CIFAR-10. Following [1,6,19,21,30] we evaluated our approach on MNIST and CIFAR-10 using a train-test dataset split, where the training split of the known class is used to train the model and the test split (of known and unknown classes) is used for testing. We run each experiment 3 times with different initializations and present the averaged ROC AUC in Table 2.

Since the MNIST dataset is easy, all methods work well. However, our approach allows to improve performance on several tricky digits (like 3 and 8) and outperforms all other approaches on average over the dataset. On the more diverse and complex CIFAR-10, the superiority of the proposed method is even more noticeable. This dataset contains 10 image classes with extremely high intra-class variation and the images are so small that even a human cannot always distinguish the kind of object on the image. Our approach based on the perceptual similarity of images can better capture class-specific information of an image, and hence, improves performance of anomaly detection in almost all experiments.

Table 3. (left) Average ROC AUC for anomaly detection on fMNIST and COIL-100. (center) ROC AUC of anomaly detection against several anomaly classes on CelebA dataset. (right) Ablation study: average ROC AUC on CIFAR-10.

	fMNIST	COIL-100
GPND	0.933	0.979
OCGAN	0.924	0.995
PIAD	**0.949**	**1.000**

	ROC AUC
Bald	0.506
Mustache	0.561
Bangs	0.650
Eyeglasses	0.777
Wearing_Hat	0.916

Model	ROC AUC
baseline	0.609
+ gr-norm w	0.608
+ gr-norm w + perc	0.701
+ gr-norm w + perc-L1	0.724
+ gr-norm w + rel-perc-L1	**0.799**

fMNIST and COIL-100. The work of *GPND* [20] uses another train-test separation to evaluate performance. For a fair comparison, we repeat their evaluation scheme. The model trains on 80% randomly sampled instances of a normal class. The remaining 20% of normal data and the same number of randomly selected anomaly instances are used for testing. We report the average performance of GPND and PIAD on the fMNIST and COIL-100 datasets in Table 3 (left), along with OCGAN since they came out the second best on the previous datasets, and they report fMNIST/COIL-100 results in the same evaluation scheme as well. For the COIL-100 dataset we randomly selected one class to be used as normal, and repeated this procedure 30 times (as it was done in [20]). The comparison shows that PIAD excels on both datasets.

LSUN. We also compare PIAD with the ADGAN approach on the LSUN dataset, training a model on images of bedrooms and treating images of the conference room class as anomaly. We achieve a ROC AUC of 0.781 against 0.641 with ADGAN.

CelebA. In order to test our approach in conditions that are closer to a real-world use case, we experimented on the CelebA dataset, where we use attributes (Bald, Mustache, Bangs, Eyeglasses, Wearing_Hat) to split the data into normal/anomaly cases. We train our model on 'normal' images where one of these attributes is *not* present and test against anomaly images, where that same attribute *is* present. Table 3 (center) shows the results.

Anomaly attributes Eyeglasses and Wearing_Hat are the easiest for PIAD. As shown in Fig. 4c (4th and 5th examples), passing image x through the encoder and the generator $G(E(x))$ removes glasses and hat from the images. Anomalies Mustache and Bangs are more of a challenge, but we noticed that our model removes the mustache as well, and makes bangs more transparent. However, our model failed to recognize the Bald anomaly. This may be a result of the complexity of the anomaly (see Fig. 4c first image, where indeed the man is not completely bald) and also inexact annotation (on Fig. 4c the first image is annotated as bald, but the second is not).

4.2 Ablation Study

We also performed an ablation study on the CIFAR-10 dataset to show the effectiveness of each proposed component of PIAD. We considered 5 scenarios:

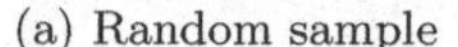

(a) Random sample (b) Reconst. of normal (c) Reconst. of anomaly

Fig. 4. CelebA experiments. In (c) for Celeba each anomaly case is presented in sequence (from left to right): Bald, Mustache, Bangs, Eyeglasses, Wearing_Hat.

(a) MSE: 0.481 (b) Perc. loss: 0.644 (c) Rel-perc-L1 loss: 0.878

Fig. 5. The least (top) and the most (bottom) anomalous images for *car* class of CIFAR-10. Results are presented with ROC AUC.

baseline, i.e. our model with MSE as reconstruction error during training and as anomaly score, with empirically chosen weighting parameters by human supervision of the quality of generated examples and reconstructions; **+ gr-norm w**, the same, but with gradient-normalizing weights policy; **+ perc**, where we further changed from MSE to perceptual loss; **+ perc-L1**, where we added normalization on μ, σ in perceptual loss and used L1-norm over features instead of MSE, **+ rel-perc-L1**, where we used the proposed loss of Sect. 3.1. We present the average ROC AUC over CIFAR-10 in Table 3 (right).

We note that our proposed gradient-normalizing weight policy shows the same result as carefully found weights through parameter selection by a human after running the model several times. Each further modification improved results as well. Figure 5 shows examples of images that were seen as the least and the most likely to be an anomaly with respect to class *car*, for different reconstruction losses. We note that only relative-perceptual-L1 loss is not prone to select monochrome images as the least anomalous, and furthermore, this loss selected classes that are closest to the *car* class as less anomalous: *truck*, *ship*.

5 Conclusion

We introduced a deep anomaly detection approach, built directly for the image domain and exploiting knowledge of perceptual image similarity. For the latter, we proposed a new metric that is based on perceptual loss, but is more robust to noise and changes of contrast of images. As a part of our work we proposed an approach for selecting weights of a multi-objective loss function, which makes a contribution of all losses equal in the training process. We demonstrated the superiority of our approach against state-of-the-art GAN-based methods and deep approaches of other paradigms on a diverse collection of image benchmarks. In the future, we plan to perform a more extensive evaluation of our method on higher resolution image data, like medical images.

References

1. Abati, D., Porrello, A., Calderara, S., Cucchiara, R.: Latent space autoregression for novelty detection. In: Proceedings of the IEEE Conference on Computer Vision and Pattern Recognition, pp. 481–490 (2019)
2. Abdallah, A., Maarof, M.A., Zainal, A.: Fraud detection system: a survey. J. Netw. Comput. Appl. **68**, 90–113 (2016)
3. An, J., Cho, S.: Variational autoencoder based anomaly detection using reconstruction probability. Special Lecture on IE 2015-2, pp. 1–18 (2015)
4. Chalapathy, R., Chawla, S.: Deep learning for anomaly detection: a survey. arXiv preprint arXiv:1901.03407 (2019)
5. Chen, Y., Zhou, X.S., Huang, T.S.: One-class SVM for learning in image retrieval. In: ICIP, vol. 1, pp. 34–37. Citeseer (2001)
6. Deecke, L., Vandermeulen, R., Ruff, L., Mandt, S., Kloft, M.: Image anomaly detection with generative adversarial networks. In: Berlingerio, M., Bonchi, F., Gärtner, T., Hurley, N., Ifrim, G. (eds.) ECML PKDD 2018. LNCS (LNAI), vol. 11051, pp. 3–17. Springer, Cham (2019). https://doi.org/10.1007/978-3-030-10925-7_1
7. Gatys, L., Ecker, A.S., Bethge, M.: Texture synthesis using convolutional neural networks. In: Advances in Neural Information Processing Systems, pp. 262–270 (2015)
8. Goodfellow, I., et al.: Generative adversarial nets. In: Advances in Neural Information Processing Systems, pp. 2672–2680 (2014)
9. Gulrajani, I., Ahmed, F., Arjovsky, M., Dumoulin, V., Courville, A.C.: Improved training of Wasserstein GANs. In: Advances in Neural Information Processing Systems, pp. 5767–5777 (2017)
10. Johnson, J., Alahi, A., Fei-Fei, L.: Perceptual losses for real-time style transfer and super-resolution. In: Leibe, B., Matas, J., Sebe, N., Welling, M. (eds.) ECCV 2016. LNCS, vol. 9906, pp. 694–711. Springer, Cham (2016). https://doi.org/10.1007/978-3-319-46475-6_43
11. Kiran, B., Thomas, D., Parakkal, R.: An overview of deep learning based methods for unsupervised and semi-supervised anomaly detection in videos. J. Imaging **4**(2), 36 (2018)
12. Krizhevsky, A., Hinton, G.: Learning multiple layers of features from tiny images. Technical report, Citeseer (2009)
13. Kwon, D., Kim, H., Kim, J., Suh, S.C., Kim, I., Kim, K.J.: A survey of deep learning-based network anomaly detection. Cluster Comput. **22**, 949–961 (2019)
14. LeCun, Y., Cortes, C., Burges, C.: MNIST handwritten digit database **2**, 18 (2010). AT&T Labs. http://yann.lecun.com/exdb/mnist
15. Litjens, G., et al.: A survey on deep learning in medical image analysis. Med. Image Anal. **42**, 60–88 (2017)
16. Liu, Z., Luo, P., Wang, X., Tang, X.: Deep learning face attributes in the wild. In: Proceedings of International Conference on Computer Vision, December 2015
17. Nene, S.A., Nayar, S.K., Murase, H.: Columbia object image library: COIL-100. Technical report, CUCS-006-96 (1996)
18. Parzen, E.: On estimation of a probability density function and mode. Ann. Math. Stat. **33**(3), 1065–1076 (1962)
19. Perera, P., Nallapati, R., Xiang, B.: OCGAN: one-class novelty detection using GANs with constrained latent representations. In: Proceedings of the IEEE Conference on Computer Vision and Pattern Recognition, pp. 2898–2906 (2019)

20. Pidhorskyi, S., Almohsen, R., Doretto, G.: Generative probabilistic novelty detection with adversarial autoencoders. In: Advances in Neural Information Processing Systems, pp. 6822–6833 (2018)
21. Ruff, L., et al.: Deep one-class classification. In: International Conference on Machine Learning, pp. 4390–4399 (2018)
22. Russakovsky, O., et al.: Imagenet large scale visual recognition challenge. Int. J. Comput. Vis. **115**(3), 211–252 (2015)
23. Sakurada, M., Yairi, T.: Anomaly detection using autoencoders with nonlinear dimensionality reduction. In: Proceedings of the MLSDA 2014 2nd Workshop on Machine Learning for Sensory Data Analysis, p. 4. ACM (2014)
24. Schlegl, T., Seeböck, P., Waldstein, S.M., Schmidt-Erfurth, U., Langs, G.: Unsupervised anomaly detection with generative adversarial networks to guide marker discovery. In: Niethammer, M., et al. (eds.) IPMI 2017. LNCS, vol. 10265, pp. 146–157. Springer, Cham (2017). https://doi.org/10.1007/978-3-319-59050-9_12
25. Simonyan, K., Zisserman, A.: Very deep convolutional networks for large-scale image recognition. In: International Conference on Learning Representations (2015)
26. Spigler, G.: Denoising autoencoders for overgeneralization in neural networks. arXiv preprint arXiv:1709.04762 (2017)
27. Xiao, H., Rasul, K., Vollgraf, R.: Fashion-MNIST: a novel image dataset for benchmarking machine learning algorithms. arXiv preprint arXiv:1708.07747 (2017)
28. Xiao, J., Hays, J., Ehinger, K.A., Oliva, A., Torralba, A.: Sun database: large-scale scene recognition from abbey to zoo. In: 2010 IEEE Computer Society Conference on Computer Vision and Pattern Recognition, pp. 3485–3492. IEEE (2010)
29. Zenati, H., Foo, C.S., Lecouat, B., Manek, G., Chandrasekhar, V.R.: Efficient GAN-based anomaly detection. arXiv preprint arXiv:1802.06222 (2018)
30. Zenati, H., Romain, M., Foo, C.S., Lecouat, B., Chandrasekhar, V.: Adversarially learned anomaly detection. In: 2018 IEEE International Conference on Data Mining (ICDM), pp. 727–736. IEEE (2018)
31. Zhou, C., Paffenroth, R.C.: Anomaly detection with robust deep autoencoders. In: Proceedings of the 23rd ACM SIGKDD International Conference on Knowledge Discovery and Data Mining, pp. 665–674. ACM (2017)

Segmentation, Grouping and Shape

Deep Similarity Fusion Networks for One-Shot Semantic Segmentation

Shuchang Lyu(✉), Guangliang Cheng, and Qimin Ding

Sensetime, Beijing, China
{lvshuchang,chengguangliang,dingqimin}@sensetime.com

Abstract. One-shot semantic segmentation is a new challenging task extended from traditional semantic segmentation, which aims to predict unseen object categories for each pixel given only one annotated sample. Previous works employ oversimplified operations to fuse the features from query image and support image, while neglecting to incorporate multi-scale information that is essential for the one-shot segmentation task. In this paper, we propose a novel one-shot based architecture, Deep Similarity Fusion Network (DSFN) to tackle this issue. Specifically, a new similarity feature generator is proposed to generate multi-scale similarity feature maps, which can provide both contextual and spatial information for the following modules. Then, a similarity feature aggregator is employed to fuse different scale feature maps in a coarse-to-fine manner. Finally, a simple yet effective convolutional module is introduced to create the final segmentation mask. Extensive experiments on $PASCAL-5^i$ demonstrate that DSFN outperforms the state-of-the-art methods by a large margin with mean IoU of 47.7%.

Keywords: Deep Similarity Fusion Network · One-shot learning · Semantic segmentation

1 Introduction

In recent years, convolutional neural networks (CNN) have shown powerful performance on image recognition tasks [15–18,20,30,31]. Different to assigning the whole image with one predefined label in the image recognition task, semantic segmentation aims at recognizing per-pixel object categories for the image. Fully convolutional networks (FCNs) [22] is the first architecture to tackle the semantic segmentation task in an end-to-end manner. Afterwards, many other architectures [2,5,6,9,21,27] with complex design have been proposed to improve the segmentation performance. However, all these networks require large amount of annotated samples, which are costly and tedious to annotate.

To overcome the limitations of strong dependence on annotations, one-shot semantic segmentation task is introduced to predict unseen-categories with only

Supported by organization Sensetime.

S. Palaiahnakote et al. (Eds.): ACPR 2019, LNCS 12046, pp. 181–194, 2020.
https://doi.org/10.1007/978-3-030-41404-7_13

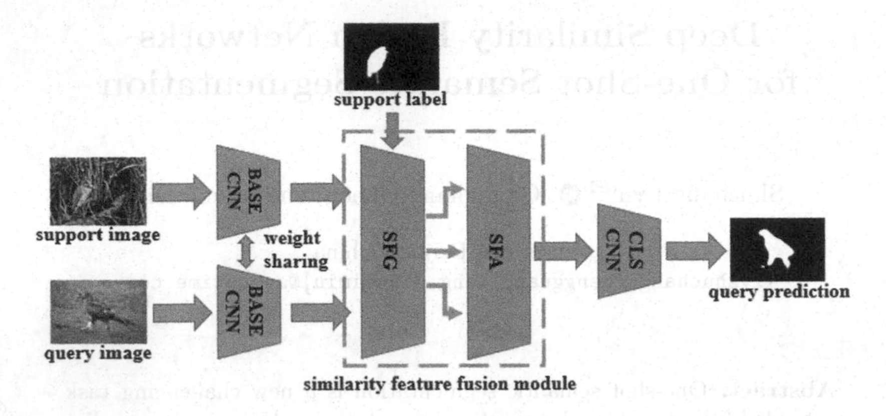

Fig. 1. The Overview of Deep Similarity Fusion Network (DSFN) for one-shot semantic segmentation. It mainly consists of three modules: weight sharing "BASE CNN", similarity feature fusion module and "CLS CNN".

one single training example for each category. Shaban et al. [29] introduce a two-branch architecture, OSLSM [29], to undertake this task for the first time. It produces the final segmentation binary mask by measuring the "dot-similarity" between the feature vector created from conditioning branch and feature maps generated in segmentation branch. Like OSLSM, SG-One [33] also adopts a two-branch structure. It uses cosine distance in guidance branch to generate a similarity feature map which will then be treated as the guidance of segmentation branch.

Currently, two-branch architecture is widely used in some state-of-the-art algorithms to tackle one-shot semantic segmentation task in an end-to-end manner. However, there are still some existing weaknesses. In this paper, we mainly address two problems: (1). Existing approaches apply dot operation or cosine-distance to measure the similarity between the representative vector extracted from support image and the vector at each pixel of the feature map created from query image. The output similarity map is a one-channel feature map. If is used as prior knowledge to determine the categories of each pixel, we find that it is far from enough to provide discriminating information. (2). Previous works (e.g. OSLSM and SG-One) overlook multi-scale information in their two-branch architectures. In the support branch, it only produces one vector from the support image, which is not rich enough to represent the image. Meanwhile, they also neglect to extract multi-scale feature maps in segmentation branch, which will miss a lot of hidden information in feature maps with different scales.

In this paper, we propose a Deep Similarity Fusion Network (DSFN) to solve the above problems. The overview of DSFN is shown in Fig. 1. We first adopt a weight-sharing CNN as a basic feature extractor for both the query image and support image. Then their feature maps together with the support label are pushed into the similarity feature generator (SFG) to generate similarity map. In this module, we first use masked average pooling to generate feature vectors of support image, then we directly apply element-wise multiplication operation between the support vectors and the feature maps of query image. Thus, the final output similarity features are multi-channel feature maps. Compared to previous method, we keep the channel-wise similarity information, which is much more flexible and reasonable. Moreover, SFG is also designed to generate multi-scale similarity features to provide abundant information for the segmentation part. Following SFG, a similarity feature aggregator (SFA) is proposed to fuse the multi-scale similarity features in a fancy cascade structure. Finally, we employ a classification CNN (CLS CNN) to map the similarity feature into a two-channel feature map for producing binary segmentation mask.

In general, our main contributions are listed as follows: (1) We first propose to generate multi-channel similarity features which can provide abundant similarity information among channels. (2) Our architecture focuses on extracting multi-scale features in both support branch and segmentation branch to explore the useful information in features with different scales. (3) We design a cascade fusion module to aggregate similarity feature maps with different scales. (4) The architecture, DSFN achieves much better results than existing state-of-the-art works with mean IOU of 47.7% on PASCAL – 5^i.

2 Related Work

One/Few-shot Learning aims to recognize objects with a limited amount of annotated samples. In this field, metric learning [19,23] is widely adopted as an interpretable approach. Koch et al. [19] propose a siamese architecture which has achieved great performance on k-shot image classification tasks. Meta learning [1] focuses on enabling machines to quickly acquire useful prior information from limited labeled samples. Additionally, Model-Agnostic [12] and Meta-learning LSTM [28] methods utilize recurrent neural network (RNN) for the representation of prior information to solve the few-shot problem.

Semantic Segmentation has been extensively studied and many new methods have been proposed in recent years. Its goal is to predict a semantic label for each pixel in image. Fully convolutional networks (FCN) [22] utilize convolutional layers to replace fully connected layers, which is the pioneer to achieve end-to-end semantic segmentation. SegNet [2] and UNet [27] adopt an "encoder-decoder" structure by mapping the high-level feature maps to the same spatial size as original image. Based on these end-to-end segmentation architectures, many new models are designed to improve the aggregation of contextual information, such as PSPNet [35], which integrates pyramid pooling module into baseline backbones to incorporate contextual information from different scales by employing different-sized kernels. Chen et al. [4,7] utilize dilated convolution to increase the receptive field and have achieved state-of-the-art performance. Meanwhile, PSANet [36] and DANet [13] focus more on the attention mechanism. In addition, ICNet [34], ContextNet [24], BiSeNet [32] and Fast-SCNN [25] concentrate on integrating the multi-scale information. However, all above architectures require a large amount of annotations on training process that costs much to obtain.

One-shot Semantic Segmentation aims at performing dense pixel-wise classification for the image that contains some unseen classes. Caelles et al. [3] propose an effective approach to achieve one-shot video segmentation, which fine-tunes a pretrained segmentation network with few annotated images from unseen categories. But the fine-tuning process tends to overfit and will bring some extra computational cost. Shaban et al. [29] are the first pioneers to define the one/few-shot semantic segmentation problem officially. Rakelly et al. [26] and Dong et al. [10] extend two-branch based approach and achieve better performance than OSLSM. Zhang et al. [33] propose an architecture named SG-One, which achieves state-of-the-art results in the one-shot semantic segmentation task. In this paper, we mainly compare our model with these two architectures, OSLSM and SG-One.

3 Problem Setup

We follow the notations and settings from Shaban et al. [29]. The training set, test set and support set are respectively represented as $D_{train} = \{(I_j^{train}, Y_j^{train})\}_{j=1}^{N}$, $D_{test} = \{(I_j^{test}, Y_j^{test})\}_{j=1}^{M}$ and $S = \{(I_j^S, Y_j^S(l))\}_{j=1}^{k}$. Let L_{train}, L_{test} and $L_{support}$ denote the label of training, test and support set. The aim of one-shot semantic segmentation is to learn a model that produces a binary mask $\widehat{M_q}$ for the new semantic category l when given a support set S and query image I_q.

During the training procedure, each annotation Y_j^{train} from D_{train} is a binary mask regarding the specific class as foreground and others as background. During testing procedure, I_q only contains unseen semantic categories, i.e. $L_{train} \bigcap L_{test} = \phi$. Compared to traditional segmentation task that the training set L_{train} shares the same categories with test set L_{test}, one-shot segmentation task focuses on predicting the unseen categories in training set.

The problem definition of k-shot semantic segmentation is similar to the one-shot segmentation problem. Following the existing works, we choose $k = 5$ to handle the 5-shot semantic segmentation task.

Table 1. The fold partitions of test classes on PASCAL – 5^i

Fold num (i)	Test classes
PASCAL – 5^0	aeroplane, bicycle, bird, boat, bottle
PASCAL – 5^1	bus, car, cat, chair, cow
PASCAL – 5^2	diningtable, dog, horse, motorbike, person
PASCAL – 5^3	potted plant, sheep, sofa, train, tv/monitor

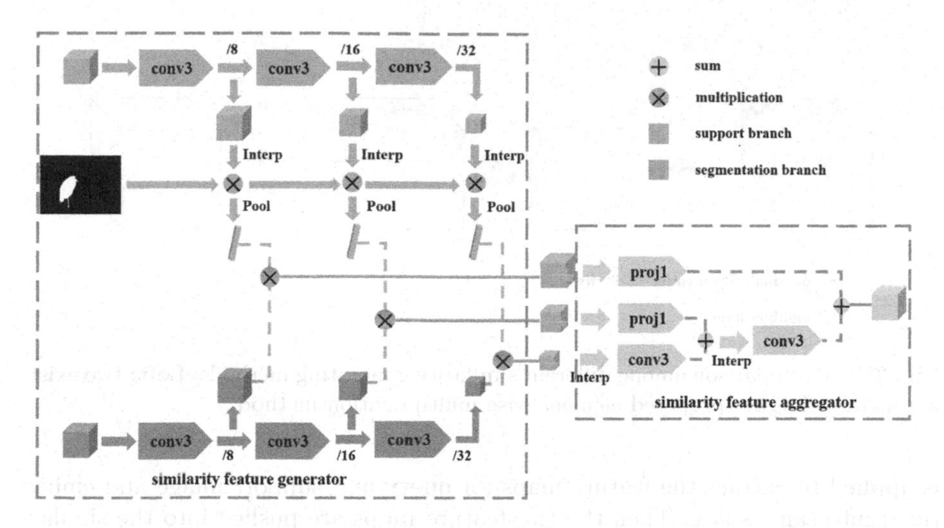

Fig. 2. The structure of similarity feature fusion module. It consists of two main parts, similarity feature generator (SFG) and similarity feature aggregator (SFA). Specifically, the "conv3" block in both two branches of SFG contains structure like [conv3 × 3 - ReLU - maxpooling]. The "conv3" block in SFA only contains one 3 × 3 convolutional layer and the "proj1" represents a 1×1 convolutional layer.

4 Method

4.1 Dataset and Metric

Dataset: We evaluate our method on the $\mathrm{PASCAL} - 5^i$ dataset, which consists of PASCAL VOC 2012 [11] and SDS [14]. Following the settings applied in OSLSM [29], the 1000 test pairs are randomly picked from the validation set from PASCAL VOC 2012. The training set contains the images from SDS and PASCAL VOC 2012, excluding the overlapping samples that have existed in test set. Table 1 shows the category distribution of $\mathrm{PASCAL} - 5^i$ in the test set. In this paper, we divide the 20 categories into 4 groups and train the model with other 15 categories, and evaluate the model with the rest 5 unseen classes.
Metric: we apply the mIoU (mean Intersection over Union) as our metric to evaluate our model. For a specific class i, its IoU is formulated as $IoU_i = \frac{tp_i}{tp_i+fp_i+fn_i}$, where tp_i, fp_i, fn_i denote true positive, false positive and false negative, respectively. The mIoU is the mean value of all the IoU_i in different test folds.

4.2 Deep Similarity Fusion Network

To maintain the channel-wise similarity information and utilize abundant multi-scale features from both query and support images, we propose DSFN to handle the one-shot semantic segmentation task. DSFN mainly consists of "BASE CNN", similarity feature fusion module and the "CLS CNN". The overview of our architecture is illustrated in Fig. 1. The weight sharing module "BASE CNN"

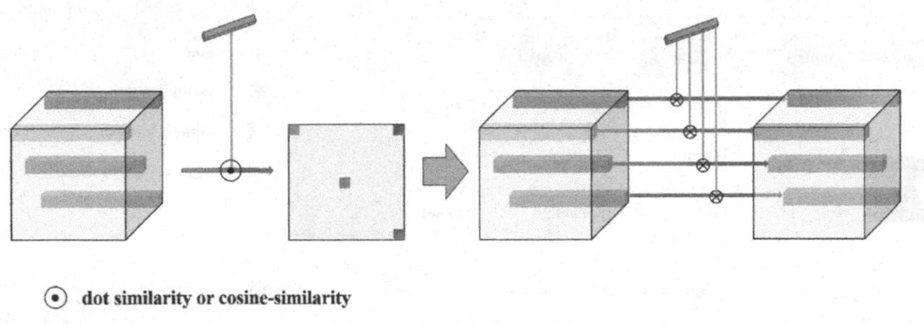

Fig. 3. The comparison among different similarity generating methods: **Left:** two existing method **Right:** proposed element-wise multiplication method.

is applied to extract the feature maps for query and support image and embed them into same space. Then the two feature maps are pushed into the similarity feature fusion module, which is the core module in DSFN. This module is designed to combine the information of two feature maps by generating several multi-channel similarity feature maps with different scales. Then with a fusion module, those different-scaled similarity features are integrated and will be sent to "CLS CNN", which is used to represent the similarity feature as a two-channel feature map for the final segmentation.

4.3 Similarity Feature Fusion Module

Similarity Feature Fusion Module is the key module in DSFN which consists of two sub-modules: SFG and SFA. The former is used to generate multi-channel similarity features with different scales and the latter is to fuse those features. The structure of similarity feature fusion module is shown in Fig. 2.

SFG: Previous works always neglect to extract multi-scale features. In SFG, we first design a group of convolutional blocks with pooling layers to create multi-scale feature maps for both query image and support image. Figure 2 shows that the support and query feature maps are first extracted into three different scales by three "conv3" blocks. Then, the feature maps in support branch are used to generate feature vectors under the guidance of support label. In segmentation branch, feature maps are prepared to generated similarity features.

Previous methods treat the support feature vector as a prior knowledge and measure the similarity between support feature vector and the feature vector at each pixel on query feature map. The output one-channel similarity feature produced by dot operation or cosine-distance is then utilized to predict the final binary mask [29] or to guide the feature map on segmentation branch [33]. However, the one-channel feature is inefficient and rough to represent the similarity. Motivated by improving the similarity generating method, we propose SFG. In Fig. 2, element-wise multiplication is adopted to combine the multi-scale feature maps in segmentation branch with those feature vectors from support branch to generate multi-channel feature maps in different scales.

In SFG, we propose element-wise multiplication other than "dot operation" and "cosine-distance" which is shown in Fig. 3. To theoretically prove that our idea is effective and interpretable, we analyze the three methods. First, we denote the support vector as $\mathbf{v}$, and the query feature map as F, where $\mathbf{v} = \{v_i\}$ and $F = \{F^{x,y}\}$, and C denotes the channel number of query feature map. Then, the dot operation ($\odot$), cosine-distance and element-wise multiplication ($\otimes$) is formulated respectively in Formulas 1, 2 and 3.

$$S_{dot}^{x,y} = \mathbf{v} \odot F^{x,y} = \sum_{i=1}^{C} v_i F_i^{x,y}, \qquad S_{dot} = \{S_{dot}^{x,y}\} \tag{1}$$

$$S_{cos}^{x,y} = \frac{\mathbf{v} \odot F^{x,y}}{\|\mathbf{v}\|_2 \|F^{x,y}\|_2} = \frac{\sum_{i=1}^{C} v_i F_i^{x,y}}{\|\mathbf{v}\|_2 \|F^{x,y}\|_2}, \qquad S_{cos} = \{S_{cos}^{x,y}\} \tag{2}$$

$$S_{mul}^{x,y} = \mathbf{v} \otimes F^{x,y}, \qquad S_{mul} = \{S_{mul}^{x,y}\} \tag{3}$$

Here, S_{dot} and S_{cos} refer to the one-channel similarity feature. S_{mul} denotes the multi-channel similarity feature, which is composed of $x * y$ vectors. If we add 1×1 convolutional layer and 3×3 convolutional layer (the weight is denoted as $\mathbf{w} = \{w_i\}$) after element-wise multiplication, the result is respectively shown in Formulas 4 and 5.

$$S_{mul}^{x,y\,'} = \sum_{i=1}^{C} w_i v_i F_i^{x,y}, \qquad S_{mul}{}' = \{S_{mul}^{x,y\,'}\} \tag{4}$$

$$S_{mul}^{x,y\,''} = \sum_{i=1}^{C} \sum_{m=x-1,n=y-1}^{x+1,y+1} w_i^{m,n} v_i^{m,n} F_i^{m,n}, \qquad S_{mul}{}'' = \{S_{mul}^{x,y\,''}\}, \qquad m > 0, n > 0 \tag{5}$$

The output of Formulas 4, 5 are denoted as $S_{mul}{}'$ and $S_{mul}{}''$. After convolution operation, both of the outputs are transformed into one-channel feature. From Formula 4, it is clear that, using 1×1 convolutional layer after element-wise multiplication is equal with dot operation and cosine distance adding a channel-wise weight constraint. Moreover, from Formula 5, we can obtain that, the operation using 3×3 convolutional layer after element-wise multiplication not only adds a channel-wise weight constraint but also integrates other similarity information in the 3×3 neighboring grids.

In summary, element-wise multiplication for generating similarity feature has the following advantages: (1). It preserves channel-wise similarity information which means one feature vector instead of one scalar is used to represent the similarity at each pixel. (2). Utilizing element-wise multiplication can be regarded as adding channel-wise attention to the query feature map. With this method, the query feature map can be guided in a more flexible way. (3). Multi-channel similarity features can be further represented by adding some convolutional layers after it.

SFA: In SFA, we design a cascade structure (Fig. 2) to fuse the similarity features with different scales in a coarse-to-fine manner. Inspired by Formulas 4 and 5,

Table 2. The Mean IoU results (%) comparison of one-shot segmentation on datasets PASCAL – 5^i.

Methods	$PASCAL - 5^0$	$PASCAL - 5^1$	$PASCAL - 5^2$	$PASCAL - 5^3$	Mean
1-NN	25.3	44.9	41.7	18.4	32.6
LogReg	26.9	42.9	37.1	18.4	31.4
Siamese	28.1	39.9	31.8	25.8	31.4
OSVOS [3]	24.9	38.8	36.5	30.1	32.6
OSLSM [29]	33.6	55.3	40.9	33.5	40.8
co-FCN [26]	36.7	50.6	44.9	32.4	41.1
SG-One [33]	40.2	**58.4**	48.4	38.4	46.3
DSFN	**43.1**	57.8	**49.8**	**39.9**	**47.7**

the large scale features will be first fed into 1×1 convolutional layer and the small scale features will be upsampled to a larger spatial size first and then pass through 3×3 convolutional layer. The final output similarity feature contains different scales and neighbor grid information, which is much more abundant for the final segmentation.

5 Experiments

5.1 Implement Details

In DSFN, the "BASE CNN" borrows the first five convolution layers from VGG-16 [30], which is pretrained on ImageNet 2012 dataset [8]. We remove the max-pooling layer of "conv4" and "conv5" to adapt to the resolution constraints of feature map. In SFG and SFA (Fig. 2), all 3×3 and 1×1 convolutional layers have 512 output channels. At the end of the network, the "CLS CNN" consists of three bottleneck blocks, each of which is composed of a 1×1 convolutional layer, ReLU and 3×3 convolutional layer. One shortcut structure is employed between each bottleneck to enable the similarity information flow among different layers.

To train this network, we choose the SGD optimizer with the momentum of 0.9. The initial learning rate is set to 0.001 and the weight decay 0.0005. All networks are trained and tested on one NVIDIA TITAN XP GPU with 12GB memory. The batch size is set to 1.

5.2 Results

One-Shot Results Comparison: We evaluate our architectures on PASCAL – 5^i. The results are shown in Table 2. The mean IoU of DSFN reaches 47.7%, which surpasses the SG-One [33] by 1.4% and OSLSM [29] by 6.9% and achieves the new state-of-the-art. On PASCAL – 5^0, DSFN surpasses SG-One by about 3%.

Table 3. The Mean IoU results (%) comparison of five-shot segmentation on datasets PASCAL – 5^i.

Methods	$PASCAL-5^0$	$PASCAL-5^1$	$PASCAL-5^2$	$PASCAL-5^3$	Mean
1-NN	34.5	53.0	46.9	25.6	40.0
LogReg	35.9	51.6	44.5	25.6	39.3
Siamese	25.1	28.9	27.7	26.3	27.1
OSVOS [3]	35.9	58.1	42.7	39.1	43.9
OSLSM [29]	33.6	55.3	40.9	33.5	40.8
co-FCN [26]	37.5	50.0	44.1	33.9	41.4
SG-One-max [33]	40.8	57.2	46.0	38.5	45.6
SG-One-avg [33]	41.9	**58.6**	48.6	39.4	47.1
DSFN	**43.1**	58.5	**50.2**	**40.6**	**48.1**

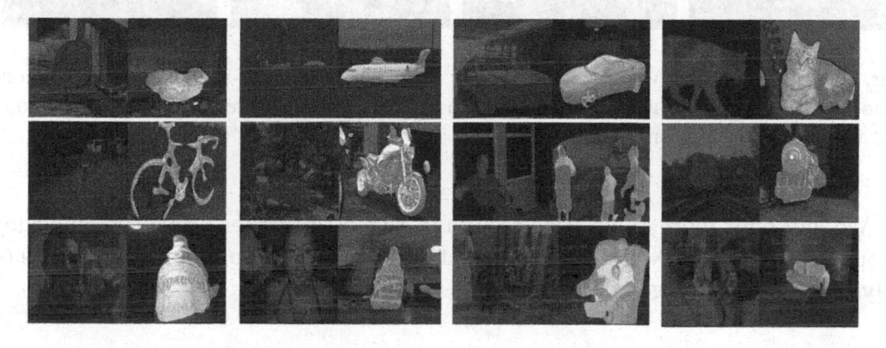

Fig. 4. The visualization of segmentation results. The left and right image of each pair respectively represents the support image and the query prediction. The first row includes "easy" samples. We specifically select the eight relatively "hard" samples in next two rows to show the robust performance of our proposed model.

K-Shot Results Comparison: We follow the approach in [29] to evaluate DSFN with k support images. We take one query image with k support images as a group and then fuse the k segmentation outputs with a logical OR operation. Comparison results are listed in Table 3. Under the guidance of five support images, DSFN could achieve 48.1% of mean IoU score which is better than SG-One by 1% and OSLSM by 7.3%.

Visualization Results: To intuitively observe the segmentation results of DSFN, we provide some qualitative visualization results on one-shot segmentation task. In Fig. 4, the four query images in the first row are relatively easy samples. The target objects in support images and query images are always clear and easy to distinguish. The next eight images in the following two rows are much more difficult, because target objects in support/query images are small or occluded by other objects. The visualization results prove that DSFN has strong ability to deal with the easy instances and is also robust on hard instances.

Fig. 5. The qualitative visualization results from DSFN on one-shot semantic segmentation. The left and right image of each pair respectively represents the support image and the query prediction.

We will offer more qualitative results in Fig. 5 to further prove the efficiency of our proposed DSFN. All query predictions are created under the guidance of only one support image.

5.3 Ablation Study

Element-Wise Multiplication vs Dot Operation and Cosine-Distance: In Fig. 2, we adopt element-wise multiplication to generate a multi-channel similarity features. To evaluate the efficiency of element-wise multiplication, we design "DSFN-dot" which uses dot operation to replace the element-wise multiplication (Fig. 6). In SGA, we replace the element-wise multiplication with dot operation. Therefore, the output similarity features are changed from multi-channel into only one-channel. Because of this, we have to change the structure of SFA. In Fig. 6, the "conv3" and "proj1" in similarity feature aggregator all have only one input channel and one output channel. The output feature of SFA is also a one-channel similarity feature. Besides, DSFN-dot still applies the "BASE CNN" as the same design of DSFN. However, due to the changes of the SFA's output feature, we have to remove the "CLS CNN", which means the SFA's output is the final output.

We evaluate this model on one-shot segmentation task where the result is listed in Table 4 **Left**. From the result comparison we can see that adopting element-wise multiplication has big advantages. We also try to use cosine-distance but the result is far poor.

Fusion Method: To obtain the integrated similarity features from similarity features with different scales, we use a cascade structure. To prove our design

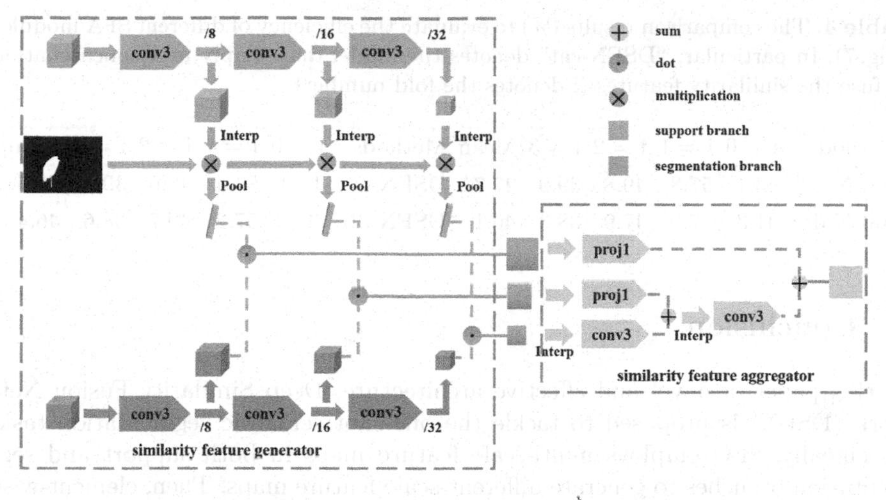

Fig. 6. The similarity feature fusion module of DSFN-dot.

is reasonable, we propose two models named "DSFN-cat" and "DSFN-3b". The "BASE CNN", SFG and "CLS CNN" in these two architectures are the same as DSFN. Detailed structures are shown in Fig. 7. In DSFN-cat (Fig. 7(a)), feature maps with small kernel size are first upsampled. And then, three feature maps with same size are directly concatenated together. The following "proj1" and "conv3" is respectively a 1×1 convolutional layers and 3×3 convolutional layer. Both of them have 512 output channels. In DSFN-3b (Fig. 7(b)), three feature maps are separately fed into the "proj1" and "conv3". The three output feature maps are fused together by sum operation.

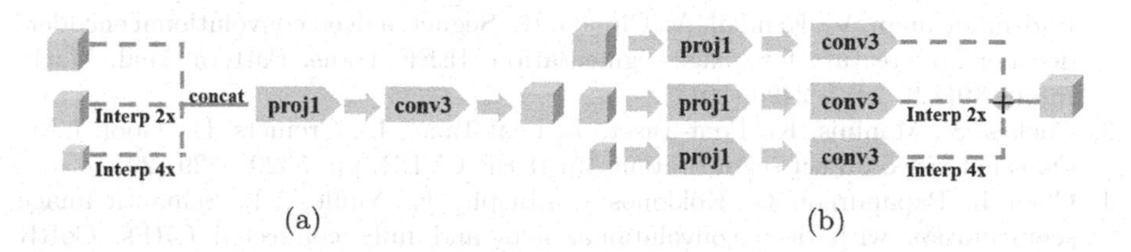

Fig. 7. (a): The SFA of DSFN-dot; **(b):** The SFA of DSFN-3b.

From the comparison results in Table 4 **Right**, we can see the two models not perform better than DSFN. It is because that directly fusing the naive similarity feature together will bring in too much noise and applying three separate branches will result in lacking communication among different similarity features.

Table 4. The comparison results (%) to evaluate the efficiency of different SFA modules (Fig. 7). In particular, "DSFN-cat" denotes the model that simply uses concatenation to fuse the similarity features (i denotes the fold number).

Methods	i = 0	i = 1	i = 2	i = 3	Mean	Methods	i = 0	i = 1	i = 2	i = 3	Mean
DSFN	43.1	57.8	49.8	39.9	47.7	DSFN-cat	41.0	57.4	48.6	39.0	46.5
DSFN-dot	41.3	57.0	47.9	38.3	46.1	DSFN-3b	40.1	57.2	49.7	38.6	46.4

6 Conclusion

In this paper, a novel and effective architecture, Deep Similarity Fusion Network (DSFN) is proposed to tackle the one-shot semantic segmentation task. Specifically, SFG employs multi-scale feature maps in both support and segmentation branches to generate different-scale feature maps. Then, element-wise multiplication is utilized to bridge the information from the two branches to generate multi-channel similarity features with different scales. SFA employs cascaded structure to fuse different-scale similarity features together. Extensive experiments show that our proposed network outperforms the previous works and achieves a new state-of-the-art result on the one-shot segmentation task. In addition, theoretically analysis proves that our proposed structures are interpretable and visualization results further show the robust performance of our proposed architecture intuitively.

References

1. Adam, S., Sergey, B., Matthew, B., Daan, W., Timothy, L.: Meta-learning with memory-augmented neural networks. In: ICML, pp. 1842–1850 (2016)
2. Badrinarayanan, V., Kendall, A., Cipolla, R.: Segnet: a deep convolutional encoder-decoder architecture for image segmentation. IEEE Trans. Pattern Anal. Mach. Intell. **39**(12), 2481–2495 (2017)
3. Caelles, S., Maninis, K., Pont-Tuset, J., Leal-Taixé, L., Cremers, D., Gool, L.V.: One-shot video object segmentation. In: IEEE CVPR, pp. 5320–5329 (2017)
4. Chen, L., Papandreou, G., Kokkinos, I., Murphy, K., Yuille, A.L.: Semantic image segmentation with deep convolutional nets and fully connected CRFs. CoRR abs/1412.7062 (2014). http://arxiv.org/abs/1412.7062
5. Chen, L., Papandreou, G., Kokkinos, I., Murphy, K., Yuille, A.L.: Deeplab: semantic image segmentation with deep convolutional nets, atrous convolution, and fully connected CRFs. IEEE Trans. Pattern Anal. Mach. Intell. **40**(4), 834–848 (2018)
6. Chen, L., Papandreou, G., Schroff, F., Adam, H.: Rethinking atrous convolution for semantic image segmentation. CoRR abs/1706.05587 (2017). http://arxiv.org/abs/1706.05587
7. Chen, L.-C., Zhu, Y., Papandreou, G., Schroff, F., Adam, H.: Encoder-decoder with atrous separable convolution for semantic image segmentation. In: Ferrari, V., Hebert, M., Sminchisescu, C., Weiss, Y. (eds.) ECCV 2018, Part VII. LNCS, vol. 11211, pp. 833–851. Springer, Cham (2018). https://doi.org/10.1007/978-3-030-01234-2_49

8. Deng, J., Dong, W., Socher, R., Li, L., Li, K., Li, F.: Imagenet: a large-scale hierarchical image database. In: IEEE CVPR, pp. 248–255 (2009)
9. Ding, H., Jiang, X., Shuai, B., Liu, A.Q., Wang, G.: Context contrasted feature and gated multi-scale aggregation for scene segmentation. In: IEEE CVPR, pp. 2393–2402 (2018)
10. Dong, N., Xing, E.: Few-shot semantic segmentation with prototype learning. In: BMVC, p. 79 (2018)
11. Everingham, M., Eslami, S.M.A., Gool, L.J.V., Williams, C.K.I., Winn, J.M., Zisserman, A.: The pascal visual object classes challenge: a retrospective. IJCV **111**(1), 98–136 (2015)
12. Finn, C., Abbeel, P., Levine, S.: Model-agnostic meta-learning for fast adaptation of deep networks. In: ICML, pp. 1126–1135 (2017)
13. Fu, J., Liu, J., Tian, H., Fang, Z., Lu, H.: Dual attention network for scene segmentation. CoRR abs/1809.02983 (2018)
14. Hariharan, B., Arbeláez, P., Girshick, R., Malik, J.: Simultaneous detection and segmentation. In: Fleet, D., Pajdla, T., Schiele, B., Tuytelaars, T. (eds.) ECCV 2014, Part VII. LNCS, vol. 8695, pp. 297–312. Springer, Cham (2014). https://doi.org/10.1007/978-3-319-10584-0_20
15. He, K., Zhang, X., Ren, S., Sun, J.: Deep residual learning for image recognition. In: IEEE CVPR, pp. 770–778 (2016)
16. He, K., Zhang, X., Ren, S., Sun, J.: Identity mappings in deep residual networks. In: Leibe, B., Matas, J., Sebe, N., Welling, M. (eds.) ECCV 2016, Part IV. LNCS, vol. 9908, pp. 630–645. Springer, Cham (2016). https://doi.org/10.1007/978-3-319-46493-0_38
17. Hu, J., Shen, L., Sun, G.: Squeeze-and-excitation networks. In: IEEE CVPR, pp. 7132–7141 (2018)
18. Huang, G., Liu, Z., van der Maaten, L., Weinberger, K.Q.: Densely connected convolutional networks. In: IEEE CVPR, pp. 2261–2269 (2017)
19. Koch, G., Zemel, R., Salakhutdinov, R.: Siamese neural networks for one-shot image recognition. In: ICML Deep Learning Workshop, vol. 2 (2015)
20. Krizhevsky, A., Sutskever, I., Hinton, G.E.: Imagenet classification with deep convolutional neural networks. In: NIPS, pp. 1106–1114 (2012)
21. Lin, G., Milan, A., Shen, C., Reid, I.D.: Refinenet: Multi-path refinement networks for high-resolution semantic segmentation. In: IEEE CVPR, pp. 5168–5177 (2017)
22. Long, J., Shelhamer, E., Darrell, T.: Fully convolutional networks for semantic segmentation. In: IEEE CVPR, pp. 3431–3440 (2015)
23. Oriol, V., Charles, B., Timothy, L., Daan, W., et al.: Matching networks for one shot learning. In: Advances in Neural Information Processing Systems, pp. 3630–3638 (2016)
24. Poudel, R.P.K., Bonde, U., Liwicki, S., Zach, C.: Contextnet: Exploring context and detail for semantic segmentation in real-time. In: BMVC, p. 146 (2018)
25. Poudel, R.P.K., Liwicki, S., Cipolla, R.: Fast-SCNN: Fast semantic segmentation network. CoRR abs/1902.04502 (2019). http://arxiv.org/abs/1902.04502
26. Rakelly, K., Shelhamer, E., Darrell, T., Efros, A., Levine, S.: Conditional networks for few-shot semantic segmentation. In: ICLR Workshop (2018)
27. Ronneberger, O., Fischer, P., Brox, T.: U-Net: convolutional networks for biomedical image segmentation. In: Navab, N., Hornegger, J., Wells, W.M., Frangi, A.F. (eds.) MICCAI 2015, Part III. LNCS, vol. 9351, pp. 234–241. Springer, Cham (2015). https://doi.org/10.1007/978-3-319-24574-4_28
28. Sachin, R., Hugo, L.: Optimization as a model for few-shot learning. In: ICLR (2016)

29. Shaban, A., Bansal, S., Liu, Z., Essa, I., Boots, B.: One-shot learning for semantic segmentation. In: BMVC (2017)
30. Simonyan, K., Zisserman, A.: Very deep convolutional networks for large-scale image recognition. CoRR abs/1409.1556 (2014). http://arxiv.org/abs/1409.1556
31. Szegedy, C., et al.: Going deeper with convolutions. In: IEEE CVPR, pp. 1–9 (2015)
32. Yu, C., Wang, J., Peng, C., Gao, C., Yu, G., Sang, N.: BiSeNet: bilateral segmentation network for real-time semantic segmentation. In: Ferrari, V., Hebert, M., Sminchisescu, C., Weiss, Y. (eds.) ECCV 2018, Part XIII. LNCS, vol. 11217, pp. 334–349. Springer, Cham (2018). https://doi.org/10.1007/978-3-030-01261-8_20
33. Zhang, X., Wei, Y., Yang, Y., Huang, T.: Sg-one: Similarity guidance network for one-shot semantic segmentation. CoRR abs/1810.09091 (2018). http://arxiv.org/abs/1810.09091
34. Zhao, H., Qi, X., Shen, X., Shi, J., Jia, J.: ICNet for real-time semantic segmentation on high-resolution images. In: Ferrari, V., Hebert, M., Sminchisescu, C., Weiss, Y. (eds.) ECCV 2018, Part III. LNCS, vol. 11207, pp. 418–434. Springer, Cham (2018). https://doi.org/10.1007/978-3-030-01219-9_25
35. Zhao, H., Shi, J., Qi, X., Wang, X., Jia, J.: Pyramid scene parsing network. In: IEEE CVPR, pp. 6230–6239 (2017)
36. Zhao, H., et al.: PSANet: point-wise spatial attention network for scene parsing. In: Ferrari, V., Hebert, M., Sminchisescu, C., Weiss, Y. (eds.) ECCV 2018, Part IX. LNCS, vol. 11213, pp. 270–286. Springer, Cham (2018). https://doi.org/10.1007/978-3-030-01240-3_17

Seeing Things in Random-Dot Videos

Thomas Dagès(✉), Michael Lindenbaum, and Alfred M. Bruckstein

Technion - Israel Institute of Technology, 3200003 Haifa, Israel
thomas.dages@cs.technion.ac.il

Abstract. The human visual system correctly groups features and can even interpret random-dot videos induced by imaging natural dynamic scenes. Remarkably, this happens even if perception completely fails when the same information is presented frame by frame. We study this property of surprising dynamic perception with the first goal of proposing a new detection and spatio-temporal grouping algorithm for such signals when, per frame, the information on objects is both random and sparse. The algorithm is based on temporal integration and statistical tests of unlikeliness, the a contrario framework. The striking similarity in performance of the algorithm to the perception by human observers, as witnessed by a series of psychophysical experiments, leads us to see in it a simple computational Gestalt model of human perception.

Keywords: A contrario · Object detection · Random-dot videos · Human visual system

1 Introduction

Some imaging processes yield highly noisy and difficult to interpret signals. For instance, ultrasound imaging or Fluorescence Photoactivation Localization Microscopy (FPALM) heavily rely on sophisticated post-processing to remove noise and retrieve useful information. We will here consider random-dot videos, where visible dots randomly appear in each frame with a slightly higher dot density on object boundaries than elsewhere. The increase in density is too low to see any meaningful structure on each frame, however, humans manage to effortlessly "see" the moving object or static outlines when frames are presented in succession as a video. We design an algorithm, based on the a contrario framework, applied to integrated frames of a video to process such signals. A contrario is a statistical test of unlikeliness, under randomness assumptions, that controls the expected number of false alarms. We then propose the algorithm to model the human visual system, since this model nicely explains the empirical human performance.

Our contributions consist in designing an algorithm based on an a contrario decision applied to time integrated images, in predicting its performance on random-dot video data, in proposing it as a simple model of human perception, and in carrying out psychophysical experiments to challenge this model. All the details on this work, along with demos, are presented in the technical report [2].

S. Palaiahnakote et al. (Eds.): ACPR 2019, LNCS 12046, pp. 195–208, 2020.
https://doi.org/10.1007/978-3-030-41404-7_14

The paper is structured as follows. We first define the signals we work on in Sect. 2. Then, we briefly review the relevant literature in Sect. 3 and then present the a contrario framework in Sect. 4. We define the a contrario based algorithm for detecting lines in noisy random-dot video signals in Sect. 5. We then mathematically analyse its expected performance in Sect. 6, and compare the estimated and empirical performances in Sect. 7. We then observe human performance and compare it with our a contrario algorithm in Sect. 8. We finish the paper with concluding remarks in Sect. 9.

2 Signal Modelling

Our signals consist of a noisy degraded version of a black and white video of moving objects in a stationary scene. We call foreground the edges of the object and the background the rest of the image, inside or outside the objects. A sensor example could be one that computes and thresholds gradient magnitudes. Since sensors are not ideal, the underlying signal is corrupted with noise. This results in noisy gradients and hence very noisy dotted outputs. We thus have two dot densities, one for the background (a pixel is white with probability p_0) and one for the foreground, respectively p_1 (see Fig. 1). In some cases the gap between p_0 and p_1 is so small that in a single image we cannot "see" the foreground contours, but large enough so that we can easily "see" them when presented with a video that displays the successive independently acquired random outputs of the noisy sensors. We here work with simulated data. For mathematical simplicity, we formulated the degradation process as follows. From the clean image I we first generate an image where each pixel value is drawn independently, Bernoulli with parameter p_b, and a foreground image that is 0 everywhere in the background but each pixel of the foreground is drawn independently, Bernoulli with parameter p_f. We then merge both images using a pixel-wise logical OR operation to get the simulated degraded image. Both formulations are rigorously equivalent if:

$$p_0 = p_b \qquad \text{and} \qquad p_1 = p_b + p_f - p_b p_f \iff p_f = \frac{p_1 - p_b}{1 - p_b} \tag{1}$$

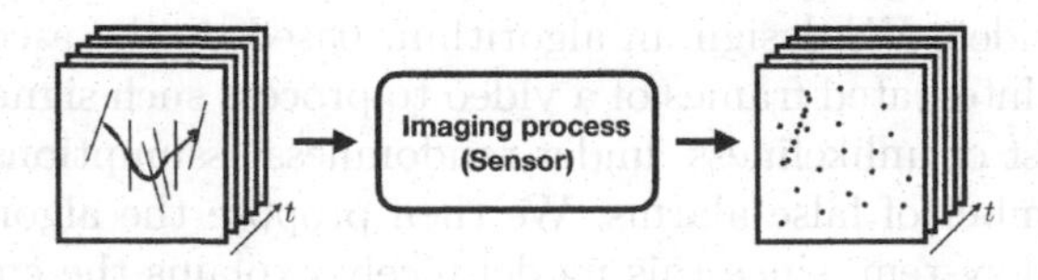

Fig. 1. Data acquisition model for a video containing a moving line segment.

3 Literature Review

Our problem falls under the general topic of spatio-temporal grouping in noisy video data. It is a particular example of Gestalt effect [15] that integrates multiple cues in emergent perception phenomena that characterises human vision. Early experiments of Johansson [8] strikingly demonstrated the effect that the human brain can easily group and interpret illuminated features that, attached to joints of a human body in total darkness, generate familiar motion. In our case, the human visual system is called upon to detect and perceive familiar contours in extremely noisy random-dot images, where dots do not persist in time for more than one frame in a video sequence. The only source of information is a slightly higher probability of dots appearing along consistent, but generally moving, contours.

Mathematical theories were put forth to explain several Gestalt grouping phenomena, leading to the possibility to predict and analyse observed grouping laws. Along such lines, we only mention the probabilistic Hough transform [10] and the a contrario framework [3–5]. The a contrario framework is deeply rooted in statistical decision theory and provides a beautiful explanation for structure detection in very noisy images, while modelling human visual processes [1] based on extensive search of highly unlikely configurations under randomness assumptions.

Here, we adapt the a contrario theory to our spatio-temporal grouping problem and provide a novel performance analysis of such a contrario processes.

4 The A Contrario Framework

A nice way to formalise the Gestalt theory into a mathematical framework was proposed by Desolneux, Moisan and Morel [3,4]. The framework adapts to any detection task. The idea is to assume that most of the observed data was due to some unstructured random distribution H_0 and under this distribution to search for unlikely patterns to be detected as objects of interest.

To illustrate the concept of a contrario, we provide a simple example, inspired by von Gioi [14]. Consider a long sequence of bits, where each bit takes the value 1 with probability 0.5, except on a contiguous subsequence of length L where it takes the value 1 with higher probability. The task is to detect the location of this subsequence of length L, that should have a higher density of 1s compared to the rest of the sequence. The background model (the hypothesis H_0) is that each bit is independently drawn to be 1 with probability 0.5. Under this assumption, all subsequences of length L have the same probability: 1111111111 and 1001101001 are equally probable, although the first pattern is clearly very special while the other one looks compatible with H_0. Thus, rather than looking at the probability of specific subsequences, the idea is to associate some reasonable measure to an observation and then look at how likely this measure is. Here, a natural measure would be the count of 1s in the subsequence. Let c_i be a candidate, i.e. a subsequence of length L, within the observed long sequence x. Denote the count value by $k(c_i, x)$. The problem now boils down to defining some threshold k_i for each candidate subsequence providing a decision between being acceptable under H_0 (i.e. no detection) and rejection of H_0 (i.e. detecting something of interest). Note that k_i could explicitly depend or not on the candidate location c_i. Rather than choosing k_i to be a decision level with a prespecified α-confidence value, the powerful key idea of the a contrario framework is to consider the expected number of false alarms. Under H_0, x is a realisation of a random variable X, and a false alarm will be a detection by the a contrario algorithm. We denote the number of false alarms as d, which is a random variable depending on X. The total number of false alarms is given by a sum of indicator functions:

$$d(x) = \sum_{i=1}^{N_T} \mathbb{1}_{k(c_i,x) \geq k_i} \tag{2}$$

where N_T is the number of candidates (here subsequences) also called the number of tests. The expected number of false alarms is:

$$\mathbb{E}_{H_0}(d(X)) = \sum_{i=1}^{N_T} \mathbb{P}_{H_0}(k(c_i, X) \geq k_i) \tag{3}$$

We choose the values k_i so that $\mathbb{E}_{H_0}(d(X))$ is upper bounded by a level ε. While there are many possibilities to choose from, a uniform splitting of ε is often chosen:

$$k_i = \min_{\widetilde{k}} \mathbb{P}_{H_0}(k(c_i, X) \geq \widetilde{k}) \leq \frac{\varepsilon}{N_T} \tag{4}$$

Equality can be reached in this definition for sufficient continuity assumptions [14]. Note that, in our simple example, all the $\mathbb{P}_{H_0}(k(c_i, X))$ are identical, due to the fixed length L and iid modelling under H_0. This implies that all thresholds could be equal, say to k_{th}, and the expected number of false alarms is then a sum of identical terms. Here, as previously discussed, we can choose k_{th} to correspond to the level $\frac{\varepsilon}{N_T}$, which here gives the same threshold value as in Eq. 4, and this will enforce the expected number of false alarms to be at most ε.

The a contrario test for a candidate region c_i (i.e. a possible detection location) is simply testing whether the measured value $k(c_i, x)$ is greater than the threshold k_i. In practice we equivalently look at the right tail distributions instead. The test now becomes, thanks to the definition of the threshold k_i at level $\frac{\varepsilon}{N_T}$, to see whether $N_T \mathbb{P}_{H_0}\Big(k(c_i, X) \geq k(c_i, x)\Big)$ is smaller than ε:

$$k(c_i, x) \geq k_i \iff N_T \mathbb{P}_{H_0}\Big(k(c_i, X) \geq k(c_i, x)\Big) \leq \varepsilon \tag{5}$$

In the second formulation, we do not have to explicitly compute k_i, which requires to invert the cumulative distribution, but only the right tail of the distribution, which is easier to handle. The quantity:

$$\mathcal{N}_{FA}(c_i, x) = N_T \mathbb{P}_{H_0}\Big(k(c_i, X) \geq k(c_i, x)\Big) \tag{6}$$

is traditionally called the Number of False Alarm score in the a contrario literature. Usually, ε is chosen to be 1. If the number of tests is large, for example of order 10^4, then allowing one false alarm seems reasonable. The dependency of the decisions on ε is slow and can be shown in specific cases to be logarithmic [3]. Empirically, such a choice gives good and coherent results for traditional detection problems [1,3,5].

5 A Contrario on Random-Dot Videos

From now on we assume that we know what we are looking for and have a precise model for it. In practice, we worked on videos where the clean foreground was an edge of known length L and width w_e in a smooth Euclidean movement (rotation and translation) with a small displacement between frames. We also fix the frame-rate to 30 frames per second. For further simplicity we assume we also know the background parameter p_b of the degradation process although it is possible to estimate it locally [11].

5.1 A Merging Strategy for Temporal Integration

Should we run an a contrario algorithm on a single frame of a video, then we would fail to detect the edge. Recall that we assume that p_b and p_f are such that it is nearly impossible to detect objects per-frame. We propose a simple way of using temporal information at each time step by merging n_f neighbouring frames, which consists in the pixel-wise logical OR operation: if a pixel is white in any of the n_f frames, it is white in the merge of frames. Taking the OR operation rather than, for example, an averaging operation, allows us to stay within the boolean domain and also handles well cases when the edge moves between frames by at least one pixel, as in this case, averaging pixel values will not yield much information since the pixels are not on the foreground of many frames. We work with a centred time neighbourhood for the frames, so that at the considered time step the pixels on the object will be centred (for uniform object trajectories) in a cloud of pixels that are on the foreground at neighbouring times.

5.2 Designing the A Contrario Algorithm

We now need to spatially search through the merged image in order to find an unlikely structure corresponding to the edge. Target candidates are chosen as rectangles of length L and width w, which is not necessarily the edge width in order to take into account alignment tolerance and edge displacement, since in a merge of frames the edge covers a larger area than in one frame. We can try N_w different widths, usually sampled in logarithmic scale. We use the sparse strategy for sampling candidates [4]: a candidate line is supported by two white pixels in the image. If M is the number of white pixels, then the number of candidate positions is $\frac{M(M-1)}{2}$. We have removed the length constraint in the estimation of the size of the candidate space since we cannot truly enforce humans to limit themselves to only a specific length, and we later want to compare this algorithm to human performance. The number of tests is therefore:

$$N_T = N_w \frac{M(M-1)}{2} \tag{7}$$

At run-time, we run through all candidates. If the supporting points are distant from each other from more than L we discard the candidate, otherwise we look at all sliding rectangles of length L supported by the two chosen points. For each rectangle we perform the a contrario test and keep the one giving the lowest a contrario score. To speed-up the algorithm, and inspired by the RANSAC algorithm [6] and the probabilistic Hough transform [10], we only run through a random subset, about a tenth of all candidates: since the foreground is denser than the background, it is likely to have at least one random candidate sample that fits to the true position of the line, thus giving the algorithm the opportunity to decide to detect at the considered position. Note that using this speed-up does not allow us to redefine the number of tests N_T. For further details on the sampling strategy see [2]. The output is chosen as the rectangle giving the smallest $\mathcal{N}_{FA}$ score that is smaller than ε. In particular, if all rectangles have scores larger than ε, then the algorithm does not detect anything.

We summarise the a contrario process in Fig. 2.

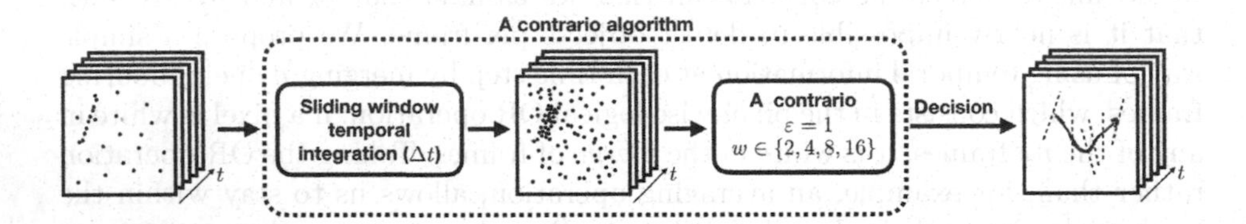

Fig. 2. Model for the a contrario algorithm for random-dot videos.

6 A Priori Analysis of A Contrario Performance

To better understand the a contrario procedure and design psychophysical experiments, we analyse the decision algorithm and provide an estimate of the expected a priori performance of the algorithm.

In the sequel, we further simplify the dynamics of the edge for the sake of avoiding non essential details. The edges will either be static or will move orthogonally to their direction at a uniform velocity of 1 pixel/frame, where pixel distance is the side size of a pixel. We will also consider single-width a contrario algorithms, justified by our model for human perception, presented in Sect. 8.

In this Section, we consider noisy images of a line at random locations of length L and width w_e, that can be seen as merged frames of a video of a line of width 1 pixel. Since the expected false alarm rate of the a contrario algorithm is controlled (the key idea of a contrario to have on average at most ε false alarms) and is small, we will only attempt to predict the hit performance of the decision process. In a given degraded frame with (p_b, p_f) parameters, the question is whether we expect to detect the true line or not? We expect the result to be relevant for human performance too. The task is to find what is the critical transition region in the (p_b, p_f) plane between expected success to detect the true edge and expected failure to detect it. Therefore, we are only interested in the decision done when, during the exhaustive search, the candidate rectangle fits the true position of the edge, and shall consider the a contrario score for this rectangle. Note that there could be redundant detections for other candidate regions overlapping with the true position of the edge but not perfectly fitting to it but we forget about them in the a priori performance estimation.

If the scene in the video is a static edge, with per-frame degradation parameters (p_b, p_f), then by merging frames we increase the background and foreground densities. A rigorous analysis shows [2] that a merge of n_f frames, is characterised by the new parameters $((p_b^M)_{n_f}, (p_f^M)_{n_f})$ associated to the merged frame:

$$(p_b^M)_{n_f} = 1 - (1 - p_b)^{n_f} \qquad \text{and} \qquad (p_f^M)_{n_f} = 1 - (1 - p_f)^{n_f} \tag{8}$$

We can estimate a priori what is the hit performance of an a contrario algorithm, working with candidate rectangle width w, on an image generated with arbitrary parameters (p_b, p_f). For this, we use a plugin estimator of the a contrario score for the candidate rectangle c_i^* at the true location of the edge $\widehat{\mathcal{N}_{FA_w}^*}(p_b, p_f)$, where we use the expectation of N_T and the expectation of the number of white points in the rectangle conditionally to the true distribution of pixel values in the ideal candidate c_i^* (see [2] for details). The estimated score $\widehat{\mathcal{N}_{FA_w}^*}(p_b, p_f)$ is, for each candidate rectangle width w, simply a function of (p_b, p_f), for which we are interested in the contour level ε. This is the decision curve splitting the plane into two configuration regions: one where we predict to fail to detect the true edge (below the curve) and the other where we predict to succeed in detecting it (above the curve). If we are now studying a video of a static edge, with per-frame degradation parameters (p_b, p_f), and considering a single-width a contrario algorithm working on width w on a merge of n_f frames, then, to predict whether or not the static edge in the video will be detected, we look at whether the point $((p_b^M)_{n_f}, (p_f^M)_{n_f})$ given by Eq. 8 is above or below the detection curve with width w.

We do a similar analysis in the dynamic case. If we consider a video of a moving edge, with the type of movement we have previously defined, and with per-frame degradation parameters (p_b, p_f), then by merging n_f frames we increase the background and foreground densities, with a smaller increase of the foreground density than before, but with a foreground that is now thicker as the edge has moved. For simplicity, in the rest of this study, we fix p_b, on the per-frame basis in a video, to be $p_b^{(1)}$. A rigorous analysis shows [2] that, up to negligible digitisation effects, we can derive new parameters $((p_b^M)_{n_f}, (p_f^M)_{n_f})$ associated to the merge of n_f frames:

$$(p_b^M)_{n_f} = 1 - (1 - p_b)^{n_f} \qquad \text{and} \qquad (p_f^M)_{n_f} = p_f \tag{9}$$

We can again perform a plugin estimation of the a contrario test score $\widehat{\mathcal{N}^*_{FAw}}((p_b^M)_{n_f}, p_f)$ at the ideal candidate rectangle location c_i^*, by replacing random a priori variables by their expectations, and where $(p_b^M)_{n_f}$ is given by Eq. 9 and corresponds to considering n_f merged frames. Note that the width of the edge in the merged image is now n_f. When studying an a contrario algorithm, with candidate rectangle width w, applied to a video of a dynamic edge with per-frame degradation parameters $(p_b^{(1)}, p_f)$, we simply look at whether the point $((p_b^M)_{n_f}, (p_f^M)_{n_f})$ is below (predicted miss of the true edge) or above (predicted hit of the true edge) the theoretical detection curve for this w.

A plot of the predicted curves in each case can be found in Fig. 4.

7 Empirical Results of the A Contrario Algorithm

We first put to an empirical test the theoretical detection performances.

7.1 Static Edge Case

We generated a random dataset of 620 degraded images of a single straight line of length L and width 1 pixel with various (p_b, p_f) parameters. We used our a priori analysis of the algorithms to define the interesting area for sampling the (p_b, p_f) space.

We submitted the dataset to four single-width a contrario algorithms, with $w \in \{2, 4, 8, 16\}$. We defined an empirical decision threshold curve, that for each value p_b passes at ordinate p_f such that there are as many empirical hits below p_f than misses above p_f, and to be compared to the predicted a priori contour level. We found that it was similar to the theoretical predictions (see [2]), which shows that our predictions are good and relevant.

7.2 Dynamic Edge Case

Similarly to the static case, we generated a random dataset of 600 degraded images of a single straight line of length L and width $t \in \{1, ..., 10\}$ pixels, with various (p_b, p_f) parameters. For images of an edge of width t, we are considering the context of t merged frames and so p_b was taken to be $(p_b^M)_t$ as given by Eq. 9, with the p_b for one frame being the chosen $p_b^{(1)}$. We used our a priori analysis of the algorithms to define the interesting area for sampling the (p_b, p_f) space.

We ran on the dataset four single-width a contrario algorithms, with $w \in \{2, 4, 8, 16\}$. We defined an empirical decision threshold curve as in the static case. We found that it was similar to the theoretical predictions (see [2]), which again shows how good and relevant our predictions are.

8 Human Performance Versus the A Contrario Process

We first found that the a contrario algorithms performed similarly to humans on preliminary observations. We thus defined a simple computational model for human perception and put it to an exhaustive test in psychophysical experiments. The model consists in a succession of a time integrator over Δt time, doing logical OR operations, followed by a statistical spatial search using a single-width a contrario algorithm working on candidate rectangular windows of width θ in visual angle. For a fixed video frame-rate, the time integration is then equivalent to a number of frames n_f to merge, and for a fixed distance of visualisation and angle of the display, the visual angle is then equivalent to a width w in pixels. The task is thus to find n_f and w such that humans perform similarly to the corresponding single-width a contrario algorithm applied to merged frames. See Fig. 3 for a summary of the proposed model.

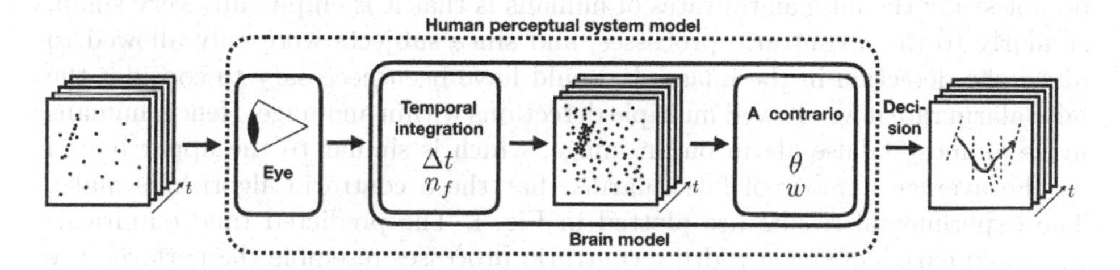

Fig. 3. Model of the human visual system based on the a contrario algorithm.

All the experiments detailed here were approved by the Ethics committee of the Technion as conforming to the standards for performing psychophysics experiments on volunteering human subjects.

8.1 Evaluating the Visual Angle

To recover θ, we worked on the same static images as those described in the previous Section for the a contrario algorithms. Recall that they could be considered as merges of degraded frames or a degradation of a single image with higher parameters. The task is to compute empirically the human performance on the static and dynamic edge image datasets and see whether the human decision level fits for each set to one of the four single-width a contrario algorithm levels. The level of the a contrario algorithm, working on the best width w, will provide us the visual angle of humans for our model.

Static Edge Experiments on Images. We here present the first psychophysical experiment, done on images corresponding to the static edge case.

Brief Description of the Experiment. The stimuli is the random-dot static edge image dataset (620 images) we have previously described, shown in random order. Subjects were seated in a well-lit room, about 70 cm in front of a screen, displaying images of size 10.4 cm × 10.4 cm. Subjects were the first author and thirteen other subjects, who were unfamiliar with psychophysical experiments and were unaware of the aim of our study. All subjects had normal or corrected to normal vision. Subjects knew that each image consists in random points with an alignment of points somewhere forming a straight line of length two thirds of the horizontal image size. They were told to try and detect it, within a 10 second duration, by clicking on distant locations approximately corresponding to the extremities of the edge, or subpart of the edge, they saw. If they could not see it, they clicked on a button to pass to the next image. They were encouraged to click on the image if the detection was "obvious" for them, without giving them a definition of "obvious". For more details please refer to [2].

Discussion. We once again only consider the hit performance. The reasons we do not study the false alarm rates of humans is that it is empirically very small, similarly to the a contrario processes, and since subjects were only allowed to make one detection in the image. It would have been necessary to consider the false alarm rate if we allowed multiple detections within an image. Hence, humans make at most 1 false alarm on an image, which is similar to the upper bound on the average number of false alarms that the a contrario algorithms make. The experimental results are plotted in Fig. 4. The predicted (and empirical) threshold curves of single-width a contrario processes resemble the performance of humans. The a contrario algorithm with candidate rectangle of width 8 pixels (or equivalently a visual angle θ of 0.23°) is a good candidate for modelling human performance when looking at random-dot static data corresponding to an image of a static edge. This result provides the parameter θ in our model for human perception.

Dynamic Edge Experiments on Images. We next present the second psychophysical experiment, done on images corresponding to the dynamic edge case.

Brief Description of the Experiment. The stimuli is the random-dot dynamic edge image dataset (600 images) we have previously described, shown in random order. The apparatus and subjects were the same as in the static edge experiment. The procedure is also the same, up to the fact that subjects were told that this time the width of the line could change, and thus that they were looking for a thick line of maximal width less than half a centimetre wide. For more details and a traditional format for the description of the psychophysical experiment, please refer to [2].

Discussion. For the same reason as previously, we only consider the hit performance. The experimental results are plotted in Fig. 4. The predicted (and empirical) threshold curves of single-width a contrario processes seem relevant to the performance of humans. The a contrario algorithm with candidate rectangle of width 8 pixels is again a good candidate for modelling human performance when looking at random-dot data corresponding to a dynamic edge. For the results on each subject and further discussion see [2].

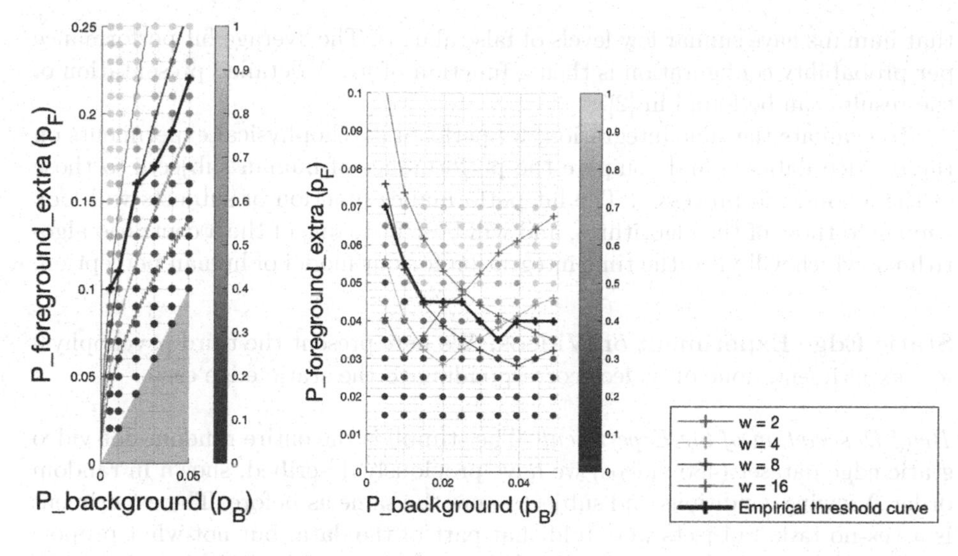

Fig. 4. Average empirical subject performance versus the predicted decision curves of single-width a contrario algorithms. Dots are sampled probability configurations, their colour is the average human performance for that configuration. The red, green, blue, and pink curves are the predicted detection curves of the algorithms, working on width 2, 4, 8, and 16 pixels in this order. The black curve is the empirical human decision curve. Left: results on the static edge case. Right: results on the dynamic edge case. (Color figure online)

8.2 Evaluating the Time Integration

We have found θ for our model. We still need to determine the time integration Δt. For this we used video datasets, for both the static an dynamic edge case.

For both datasets, we fixed the background degradation parameter p_b, per frame, to be 0.005, to be consistent with our previous choice in the static image dataset corresponding to the dynamic edge case, and sampled various p_f. The position of the edge was chosen at random. However, in order to avoid long term memory reinforcements, we randomly repositioned the line, i.e. made it randomly "jump", every 16 frames (0.53 s), which is a good compromise between short display and lengthy duration for detecting the line (see [2] for a discussion on the time between jumps). Therefore, in the static edge dataset, the line randomly jumps every 16 frames but does not move between jumps, whereas in the dynamic edge dataset the line randomly jumps every 16 frames but also moves between jumps. We then doubled the size of each dataset by adding to them purely white noise videos with background degradation parameter p_b.

We ran, for each time integration measured in frames to merge $n_f \in \{1, ..., 10\}$, an a contrario algorithm on these datasets with candidate rectangle width of 8 pixels. We found that the false alarms of the algorithms are consistent between each algorithm and very low, as expected, and we then focus on the hit performance. Further justification for forgetting about the false alarm rate is that humans have similar low levels of false alarms. The average hit performance per probability configuration is then a function of p_f. A detailed presentation of the results can be found in [2].

To evaluate the time integration, we perform psychophysical experiments on these video datasets and compare the performance of human subjects to those of the a contrario processes. The hit performance function of subjects will look similar to those of the algorithms, and will best fit to one of the a contrario algorithms, which will yield the time integration for our model of human perception.

Static Edge Experiment on Videos. We here present the third psychophysical experiment, done on videos corresponding to the static edge case.

Brief Description of the Experiment. The stimuli is the entire random-dot video static edge dataset (480 videos) we have previously described, shown in random order. Viewing conditions and subjects were the same as before. The experiment is a yes-no task. Subjects were told that part of the data, but not what proportion, was just random noise whereas the rest of it were videos of a jumping edge. If they believed the video was edge data (resp. white noise) they had to click on a large green YES (resp. red NO) button, and had to decide in less than 10 s. For more details please refer to [2].

Discussion. We found that the false alarm rate of humans is very low, close to the a contrario algorithm rates, justifying to look only at the hit performance (see [2]). Just like the algorithms, the average human hit performance per probability configuration defines a function of p_f. Its looks similar to those obtained by the a contrario processes, and we compared them using the L_2 distance measure. We found that time integrations, measured in number of merged frames, of $n_f \in [6, 8]$ frames fit similarly and best in L_2 distance. We hence get the time integration $n_f \in [6, 8]$ frames, corresponding to $\Delta t \in [0.2, 0.27]$ s, in our model for human perception. For the results on each subject see [2].

Dynamic Edge Experiment on Videos. We here present the fourth psychophysical experiment, done on videos corresponding to the dynamic edge case.

Brief Description of the Experiment. The stimuli is the entire random-dot video dynamic edge dataset (480 videos) we have previously described, shown in random order. The apparatus, subjects and procedure is the same as in the previous experiment. For more details see [2].

Discussion. We here again found that the false alarm rate of humans is very low, close to the a contrario algorithm rates, justifying to look only at the hit performance (see [2]). Once again, the average human hit performance per probability configuration is a function of p_f, with similar shape to those obtained by a contrario processes, and to be compared with using the L_2 distance measure. We found that the time integrations, measured in number of merged frames, of

$n_f \in [4, 10]$ frames fit similarly and best in L_2 distance (Fig. 5). We hence get the time integration $n_f \in [4, 10]$ frames, corresponding to $\Delta t \in [0.13, 0.33]$ s, in our model for human perception. For the results on each subject see [2].

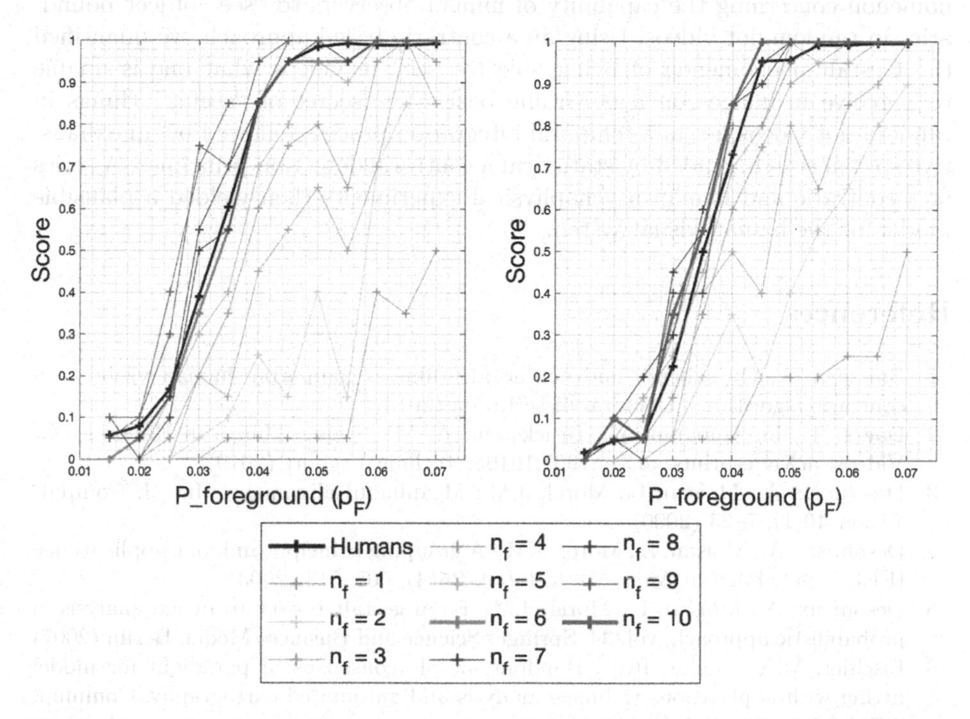

Fig. 5. Hit performances of humans versus single-width a contrario algorithms working on width w of 8 pixels and on $n_f \in \{1, ..., 10\}$ frames. The black curve corresponds to the average human hit performance. Left: results on videos of a static edge. Right: results on videos of a dynamic edge. The a contrario performance curve closest to the human performance is thicker than the other ones.

Discussion on Both Video Experiments. The video experiments suggest that the sequential time integration by merging images and then performing a single-width a contrario algorithm working on a candidate rectangle width of 8 pixels (or 0.23° in terms of visual angle) is reasonable if we select $n_f \in [6, 8]$ frames for the static edge and $n_f \in [4, 10]$ for the dynamic edge. However, in our model, the time integration should not depend on the dynamics of the edge, thus by taking the intersection of both good candidate regions for the time integration we get that the time interval of $n_f \in [6, 8]$ frames, i.e. $\Delta t \in [0.2, 0.27]$ s, is a good candidate for the time integration in our model. This time integration is comparable to the time necessary to group and understand dynamic biological point light displays [9] but is closer to eye fixation durations than the low level integration time [7, 12]. Furthermore, the visual angle, θ, of 0.23° or equivalently of 13.8 arc minutes, is consistent with some psychophysical experiments [13].

9 Concluding Remarks

In this work, we dealt with analysing an interesting visual perception phenomenon concerning the capability of human observers to "see" object boundaries in random-dot videos. Using an a contrario based approach, we quantified the Gestalt phenomenon of being able to "see" in videos what one is unable to perceive in images on a per-frame basis. The secret of "seeing" things in random-dot videos lies in a temporal integration process followed by an exhaustive spatial search, guided by statistical a contrario detection principles. A series of a contrario and human psychophysical experiments then yielded a plausible model for the human visual system.

References

1. Blusseau, S.: On salience and non-accidentalness: comparing human vision to a contrario algorithms, Doctoral dissertation (2015)
2. Dagès, T., Lindenbaum, M., Bruckstein, A. M.: Seeing Things in Random-Dot Videos, arXiv e-prints, arXiv:1907.12195, Technical report (2019)
3. Desolneux, A., Moisan, L., Morel, J.M.: Meaningful alignments. Int. J. Comput. Vision **40**(1), 7–23 (2000)
4. Desolneux, A., Moisan, L., Morel, J.M.: A grouping principle and four applications. IEEE Trans. Pattern Anal. Mach. Intell. **25**(4), 508–513 (2003)
5. Desolneux, A., Moisan, L., Morel, J.M.: From gestalt theory to image analysis: a probabilistic approach, vol. 34. Springer Science and Business Media, Berlin (2007)
6. Fischler, M.A., Bolles, R.C.: Random sample consensus: a paradigm for model fitting with applications to image analysis and automated cartography. Commun. ACM **24**(6), 381–395 (1981)
7. Hooge, I.T.C., Erkelens, C.J.: Adjustment of fixation duration in visual search. Vision Res. **38**(9), 1295-IN4 (1998)
8. Johansson, G.: Visual perception of biological motion and a model for its analysis. Percept. Psychophys. **14**(2), 201–211 (1973)
9. Johansson, G.: Spatio-temporal differentiation and integration in visual motion perception. Psychol. Res. **38**(4), 379–393 (1976)
10. Kiryati, N., Eldar, Y., Bruckstein, A.M.: A probabilistic Hough transform. Pattern Recogn. **24**(4), 303–316 (1991)
11. Lezama, J., Morel, J.M., Randall, G., Von Gioi, R.G.: A contrario 2D point alignment detection. IEEE Trans. Pattern Anal. Mach. Intell. **37**(3), 499–512 (2014)
12. Martinez-Conde, S., Macknik, S.L., Hubel, D.H.: The role of fixational eye movements in visual perception. Nat. Rev. Neurosci. **5**(3), 229–240 (2004)
13. Unuma, H., Hasegawa, H., Kellman, P.J.: Spatiotemporal integration and contour interpolation revealed by a dot localization task with serial presentation paradigm. Jpn. Psychol. Res. **52**(4), 268–280 (2010)
14. Grompone von Gioi, Rafael: A Contrario Line Segment Detection. Springer, New York (2014). https://doi.org/10.1007/978-1-4939-0575-1
15. Wertheimer, M.: Laws of organization in perceptual forms. In: Ellis, W.D. (ed.) A Source Book of Gestalt Psychology, pp. 71–88. Kegan Paul, Trench, Trubner and Company, London (1938)

Boundary Extraction of Planar Segments from Clouds of Unorganised Points

Zezhong Xu[1], Cheng Qian[1], Xianju Fei[1], Yanbing Zhuang[1], Shibo Xu[2], and Reinhard Klette[3](✉)

[1] Changzhou Institute of Technology, no. 666 Liaohe Road, Changzhou, China
{xuzz,qianc,feixj,zhuangyb}@czu.cn

[2] Changsha High-tech Engineering School, no. 607 Dongfang Road, Changsha, China
1744424368@qq.com

[3] Auckland University of Technology, 34 St. Paul Street, Auckland, New Zealand
rklette@aut.ac.nz

Abstract. Planar segment detection in 3D point clouds is of importance for 3D registration, segmentation or analysis. General methods for planarity detection just detect a planar segment and label the 3D points; a boundary of the planar segment is typically not considered; spatial position and scope of coplanar 3D points are neglected. This paper proposes a method for detecting planar segments and extracting boundaries for such segments, all from clouds of unorganised points. Altogether, this aims at describing completely a set of 3D points: If a planar segment is detected, not only the plane's normal and distance from the origin to the plane are detected, but also the planar segments boundary. By analysing Hough voting (from 3D space into a Hough space), we deduce a relationship between a planar segment's boundary and voting cells. Cells that correspond to the planar segments boundary are located. Six linear functions are fitted to the voting cells, and four vertices are computed based on the coefficients of fitted functions. The bounding box of the planar segment is determined and used to represent the spatial position and scope of coplanar 3D points. The proposed method is tested on synthetic and real-world 3D point clouds. Experimental results demonstrate that the proposed method directly detects planar segment's boundaries from clouds of unorganised points. No knowledge about local or global structure of point clouds is required for applying the proposed technique.

Keywords: Planar segment detection · 3D clouds of points · Bounding box

1 Introduction

Planarity detection in clouds of unorganised 3D points is a fundamental task in 3D computer vision applications, such as 3D building modelling [30] or robot navigation [6], and also important for 3D segmentation [8] or 3D registration [26]. Planarity detection has been studied in digital geometry assuming that given

S. Palaiahnakote et al. (Eds.): ACPR 2019, LNCS 12046, pp. 209–222, 2020.
https://doi.org/10.1007/978-3-030-41404-7_15

3D points are restricted to be at 3D grid point positions and, ideally, forming a digitised surface [2,10,20]. In this paper, *unorganised* points are not limited to be at grid point positions, and their density in 3D space may vary.

Many methods have been proposed for planarity detection in clouds of 3D points. They can be categorised into three types [16], region-growing methods, random sample consensus (RANSAC) fitting methods, and Hough voting methods.

Region growing methods [19,24] start with an initial seed and merge neighbouring points using neighbourhood information. After region growing, parameters are estimated for the estimated plane assumed to be incident with the clustered points. For range images, points may be considered to be distributed on a surface in 3D space, and the extraction of neighbourhood information may follow this assumption. For unorganised points, an octree [23] may be exploited to extract neighbouring information. Region growing methods are more suitable for somehow organised clouds of points. In addition, region growing methods have problems of over-growing or under-growing.

RANSAC methods [7,12,14,29] iteratively generate and evaluate hypothetical planes until an optimal plane model, which has the most inliers, is fitted to a given cloud of 3D points. The RANSAC fitting methods are developed [21,25] to deal with multiple-plane detection. RANSAC methods are robust. However, the approach is time consuming due to the iterative scheme. The computation time depends on the number of planes and number of iterations.

Hough voting methods [9,22] have manifold applications, and can also be used for planarity detection in range images or 3D point clouds. A 3D Hough transform is defined based on the Hough voting scheme. The Hough space is designed as an accumulator ball [1]. Plane detection from 3D point clouds becomes a peak seeking problem in the accumulator space. Each point in a given point cloud votes for a sinusoidal surface in the Hough space. After voting, local maxima are searched in the Hough space and considered as a plane. In order to improve the performance of the 3D Hough transform, different variants of 3D Hough transforms [4,5,13,27] for plane detection are proposed. Hough voting methods are robust to outliers in point clouds. Computational and storage requirements are huge, thus causing a substantial problem for applying these methods.

Recently, **deep leaning** techniques have also been used for 3D segmentation of sets of 3D points [11,15,18]. By designing and training the network models, a cloud of points is segmented into different regions using local or global features. Voxelisation is usually implemented as a preprocessing step. These methods still need to demonstrate their inherent benefits in comparison to the three classes mentioned before.

So far, approaches for plane detection just estimate the plane's normal and the distance from the origin to the plane. Segmented 3D points are then labelled by different colours (one for each plane) for visualisation. However, in order to describe a set of coplanar 3D points, the boundaries of the planar segments need to be extracted further. For example, by using structure information in a range image [17] or regular grid locations [2,10,20], a set of boundary points is detected by exploiting neighbouring edge information. This kind of method is not suitable for clouds of unorganised points.

In order to detect and represent a set of coplanar 3D points, not only the plane parameters but also some kind of a bounding box of a planar segment should be extracted. By analysing Hough voting in this paper, we deduce a corresponding relationship between voting cells and boundaries for planar segments. Six linear functions are fitted and four vertices are determined with the coefficients of the fitted functions. Upper or bottom, and left or right boundaries are computed directly in the Hough space.

The remainder of the paper is organized as follows. Section 2 describes the corresponding relationship between the boundary of a cloud of points and the voting cells. Section 3 presents plane boundary extraction by fitting six linear functions. Section 4 tests the proposed methods using synthetic and real-world point clouds. Section 5 concludes.

2 Hough Voting Analysis

A plane in 3D space can be defined in different ways. A common definition of a plane uses four parameters which are the normal and the distance between origin and plane:

$$\rho = N_x \cdot x + N_y \cdot y + N_z \cdot z \tag{1}$$

where $(N_x, N_y, N_z)^\top$ is the plane's normal, and ρ is the distance.

In order to implement efficiently a Hough transform for plane detection from a cloud of points, a 3-parameter definition is used to describe a 3D plane instead of a 4-parameter definition.

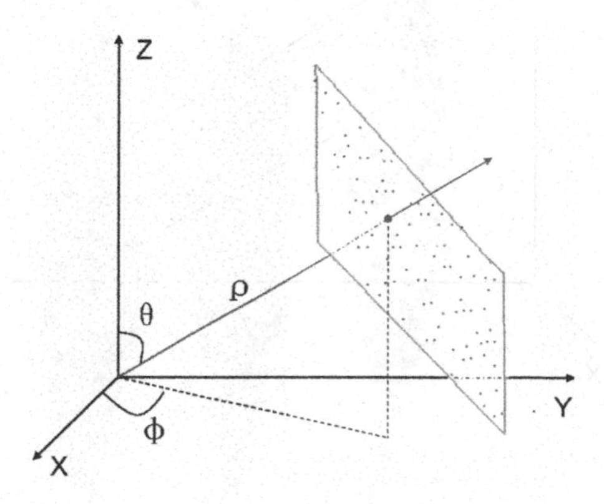

Fig. 1. A plane defined by parameters θ, ϕ, and ρ. The arrow diagonally up illustrates the plane's normal.

2.1 Hough Space

An accumulator ball, which is used commonly for plane detection, is selected to define the Hough space. Thus, a plane is defined by three parameters θ, ϕ, and ρ:

$$\rho = x \cdot \cos\phi \sin\theta + y \cdot \sin\phi \sin\theta + z \cdot \cos\theta \tag{2}$$

where, θ is the angle between the normal and the Z axis, with $\theta \in [0, \pi]$, ϕ is the angle between the projected normal and the X axis, with $\theta \in [0, 2\pi)$, and ρ is the distance from the origin to the plane, with $\rho \geq 0$.

Given θ, ϕ, and ρ, the plane parameters, the normal can also be computed. This is illustrated in Fig. 1. Therefore, the Hough space is defined by a 3-dimensional accumulator array which corresponds to θ, ϕ, and ρ.

Any 3D point in a given cloud of points votes for all possible cells in the 3D accumulator. Our method is robust against discretisation errors; θ and ϕ are quantised in relatively large intervals.

2.2 Voting Analysis

For voting angles θ_i and ϕ_i, there is a set of parallel slices which intersects with the given cloud of points. Different slices correspond to different voting distances ρ. This is illustrated in Fig. 2. When θ_i and ϕ_i are close to the actual real parameters of the plane, the count of intersecting parallel slices is minimal, and the corresponding voting values are maximal.

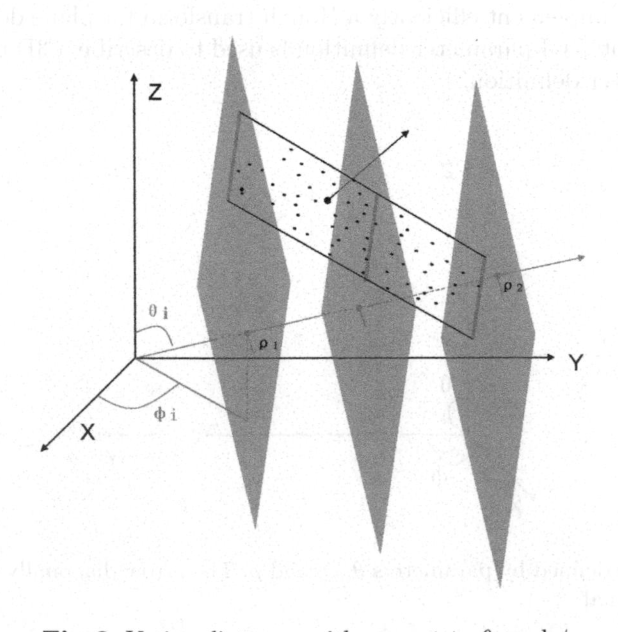

Fig. 2. Voting distances with respect to θ_i and ϕ_i.

Given voting angles θ_i and ϕ_i, the voting distance ρ ranges from ρ_1 to ρ_2; both values are determined by the coplanar 3D points, and can be used to compute the boundaries of the planar segment. For example, when ϕ_i is close to the actual ϕ of the detected plane, ρ_1 and ρ_2 are related to the voting from the top-boundary and the bottom-boundary of the approximated set of points.

Similarly, if θ_i is close to the actual θ of the detected planar segment, the computed voting distances ρ_1 and ρ_2 are determined by the left-boundary and right-boundary of the approximated set of points, and can be used to compute the left and right boundaries in return.

3 Plane Boundary Extraction

The initial peak is found by searching for a local maximum in the 3D accumulator array. In order to reduce the time requirements, the 3D accumulator is discretised using relatively large quantisation intervals.

In our implementation, voting angles θ and ϕ are quantised with steps of 0.04 rad, and the quantisation of the voting distance ρ depends upon the spatial resolution of the given clouds of points. The initial peak is denoted by $(\theta_{peak}, \phi_{peak}, \rho_{peak})$, which can be considered to be a plane without boundaries in 3D space.

3.1 Top and Bottom Boundary Detection

If the voting angle ϕ equals ϕ_{peak}, the voting distribution, corresponding to different voting angles θ_i, is illustrated in Fig. 3.

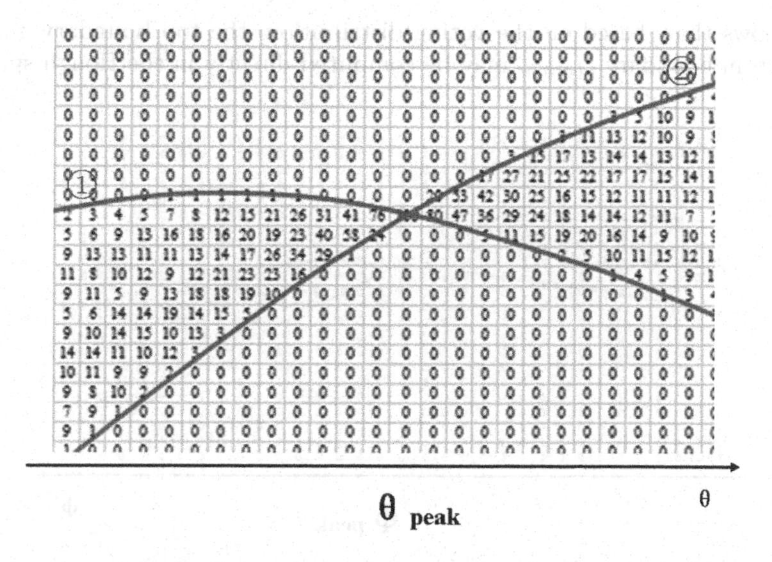

Fig. 3. Voting distribution around an initial peak if ϕ is fixed.

Curve 1 in Fig. 3 comes from the voting of the top-boundary of the coplanar point cloud. Therefore,

$$\rho = x \cdot \cos\phi_{peak} \sin\theta + y \cdot \sin\phi_{peak} \sin\theta + z_{top} \cdot \cos\theta \tag{3}$$

This can be linearised by the following transform:

$$\rho/\cos\theta = (x \cdot \cos\phi_{peak} + y \cdot \sin\phi_{peak}) \cdot \tan\theta + z_{top} \tag{4}$$

Using the different ρ and θ coordinates of cells where Curve 1 passes through, a linear function f is fitted as follows:

$$\begin{aligned} f : \rho/\cos\theta &= f(\tan\theta) \\ &\triangleq f_1 \cdot \tan\theta + f_0 \end{aligned} \tag{5}$$

According to Eqs. (4) and (5), the top-boundary of the coplanar set of 3D points is given by:

$$z_{top} = f_0 \tag{6}$$

Similarly, using the different ρ and θ coordinates of cells where Curve 2 passes through, a linear function g is fitted as follows:

$$\begin{aligned} g : \rho/\cos\theta &= g(\tan\theta) \\ &\triangleq g_1 \cdot \tan\theta + g_0 \end{aligned} \tag{7}$$

The bottom-boundary of the coplanar 3D points is now given by:

$$z_{bottom} = g_0 \tag{8}$$

This shows that, based on the voting distribution, the top boundary z_{top} and the bottom boundary z_{bottom} may be computed directly in the Hough space.

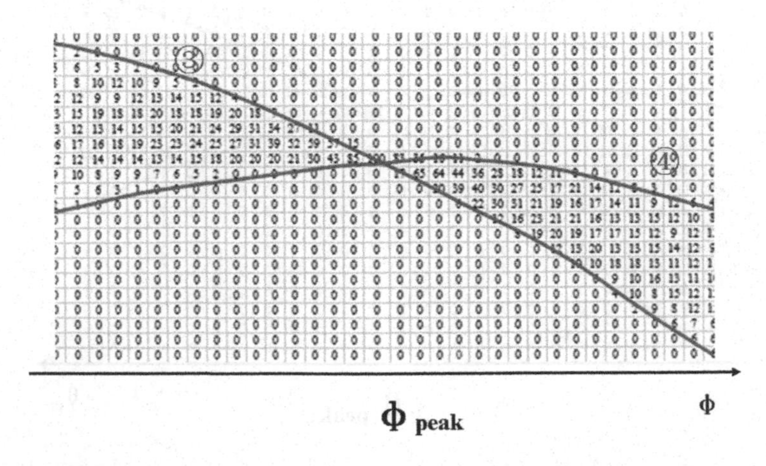

Fig. 4. Voting distribution around an initial peak if θ is fixed.

3.2 Left and Right Boundary Detection

If voting angle θ equals θ_{peak}, the voting distribution of different ϕ values is shown in Fig. 4.

Curve 3 in Fig. 4 originates from the voting of the left-boundary of the given point cloud. Thus,

$$\rho = x \cdot \cos\phi \sin\theta_{peak} + y \cdot \sin\phi \sin\theta_{peak} + z \cdot \cos\theta_{peak} \tag{9}$$

This is again linearized by the following transform in order to fit a function conveniently:

$$(\rho - z \cdot \cos\theta_{peak})/(\sin\theta_{peak} \cdot \cos\phi) = y \cdot \tan\phi + x \tag{10}$$

Let $z = z_{top}$, and consider the different ρ and ϕ coordinates of cells where Curve 3 passes through. A linear function a is fitted to those as follows:

$$a : (\rho - z_{top} \cdot \cos\theta_{peak})/(\sin\theta_{peak} \cdot \cos\phi) \triangleq a_1 \cdot \tan\phi + a_0 \tag{11}$$

According to Eqs. (10) and (11), the left-top vertex P_{lt} has the following coordinates:

$$\begin{aligned} x_{lt} &= a_0 \\ y_{lt} &= a_1 \\ z_{lt} &= z_{top} \end{aligned} \tag{12}$$

Let $z = z_{bottom}$, and consider the different ρ and ϕ coordinates of cells where Curve 3 passes through. A linear function b is fitted:

$$b : (\rho - z_{bottom} \cdot \cos\theta_{peak})/(\sin\theta_{peak} \cdot \cos\phi) \triangleq b_1 \cdot \tan\phi + b_0 \tag{13}$$

According to Eqs. (10) and (13), the left-bottom vertex P_{lb} has the following coordinates:

$$\begin{aligned} x_{lb} &= b_0 \\ y_{lb} &= b_1 \\ z_{lb} &= z_{bottom} \end{aligned} \tag{14}$$

Similarly, Curve 4 in Fig. 4 originates from the voting of points in the right-boundary of the given point cloud. Let $z = z_{top}$ and $z = z_{bottom}$; respectively, two linear functions c and d are fitted as follows:

$$c : (\rho - z_{top} \cdot \cos\theta_{peak})/(\sin\theta_{peak} \cdot \cos\phi) \triangleq c_1 \cdot \tan\phi + c_0 \tag{15}$$

and

$$d : (\rho - z_{bottom} \cdot \cos\theta_{peak})/(\sin\theta_{peak} \cdot \cos\phi) \triangleq d_1 \cdot \tan\phi + d_0 \tag{16}$$

Then, the right-top vertex P_{rt} has the following coordinates:

$$\begin{aligned} x_{rt} &= c_0 \\ y_{rt} &= c_1 \\ z_{rt} &= z_{top} \end{aligned} \tag{17}$$

and those of the right-bottom vertex P_{rb} are given by

$$\begin{aligned} x_{rb} &= d_0 \\ y_{rb} &= d_1 \\ z_{rb} &= z_{bottom} \end{aligned} \tag{18}$$

Thus, based on the voting distribution, the left boundary and right boundary have been determined. By fitting four linear functions, four vertices are computed using the coefficients of the fitted functions. After those four vertexes have been computed, the parameters of the plane may be refined by recalculating the plane's normal and the distance.

4 Experimental Results

Synthetic 3D point clouds and real-world point clouds are used for testing the proposed method for boundary detection of planar segments.

4.1 Test on Synthetic Point Clouds

We generate randomly synthetic clouds of points whose 3D points are "nearly" coplanar. The coordinates of those 3D points are randomly disturbed. Two examples are shown in Fig. 5. The one on the left consists of a set of 3D "nearly" coplanar 3D points, and the one on the right consists of two sets of 3D points.

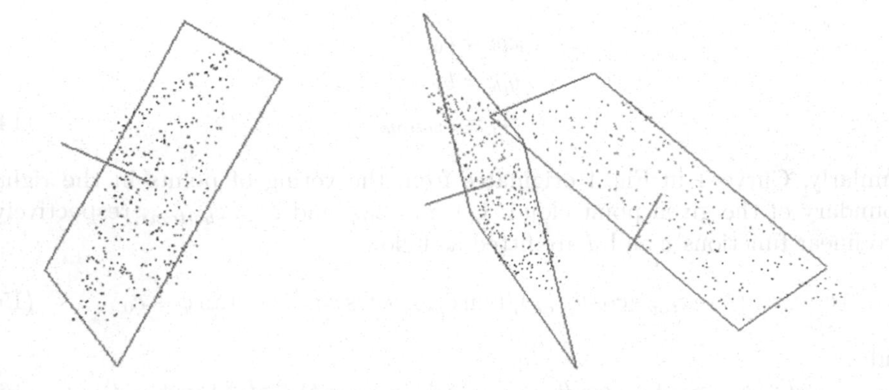

Fig. 5. Planes detection from "nearly" coplanar unorganised points.

Table 1. Comparison of detection accuracies.

Detection error		RANSAC fitting	Region growing	HT for boundary
N_x	Mean	0.029	0.017	0.024
	Std	0.030	0.015	0.017
N_y	Mean	0.018	0.017	0.016
	Std	0.020	0.016	0.015
N_z	Mean	0.014	0.010	0.015
	Std	0.014	0.008	0.014
ρ	Mean	0.915	0.533	1.037
	Std	0.828	0.506	0.972

With the method described above, not only the plane's parameters are detected from the set of "nearly" coplanar unorganised points, but also the bounding boxes are extracted of the unorganised point clouds.

In order to verify the performance, the detected plane's normals and distances are compared with those obtained by the RANSAC fitting or region growing methods. For the RANSAC fitting method, the plane's parameters are directly fitted using the common RANSAC technique. For the region growing method, point clustering followed by least-median-square fitting is implemented. We processed 100 3D clouds of unorganised points. The mean detection errors and the root-mean-square errors are listed in Table 1.

With the proposed Hough voting method, the detected plane's normals and distances are close to those of RANSAC fitting and region growing plus least-median-squares fitting. Besides the plane's normal and distance, the bounding box of unorganised 3D points is also extracted.

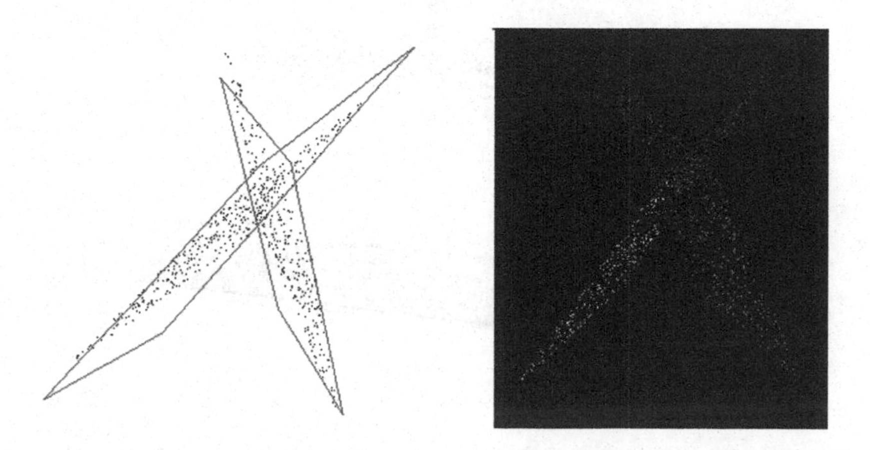

Fig. 6. Two intersecting "nearly" coplanar point clouds.

The region growing method is the most accurate because the 3D points are clustered before fitting plane parameters. But the region growing method would have a problem of under-growing if two coplanar point clouds intersect or are adjacent. An example that consists of intersecting "nearly" coplanar point clouds is shown in Fig. 6. The proposed method can detect two planes and their bounding boxes while the region growing method would segment the point clouds into three regions.

4.2 Test on Real-World Point Clouds

In this section, for testing the proposed method, we use two real-world 3D point clouds which are publicly available (and may thus be used for comparative testing) and one point cloud of a road-surface project regarding pothole detection. For the publicly available point clouds, only 25% of given 3D points are sampled randomly from the raw point clouds in order to improve computational efficiency.

The first is a public point cloud named as *table_scene_lms400.pcd*, available on GitHub. The raw point cloud and detection results are shown in Fig. 7. The detected plane normals and bounding boxes are drawn together with the given raw point cloud. With the proposed method, two main planes are detected, and the corresponding bounding boxes are extracted. (The algorithm could continue with detecting smaller planar segments by accepting smaller peaks in Hough space.)

The second point cloud is from the dataset [28]. Farther away 3D points are ignored. The extracted planes and the raw point cloud are shown in Fig. 8. With the proposed method, four planes are extracted. Each plane corresponds to a set of "nearly" coplanar 3D points. The normals describes the direction of each set

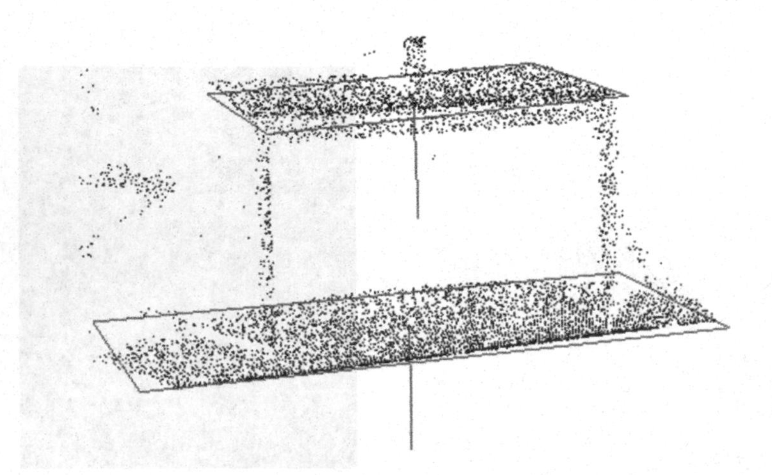

Fig. 7. Plane detection and boundary extraction from real point cloud *table_scene_lms400.pcd*.

of coplanar points in 3D space; the bounding boxes describe the spatial position and scope of these coplanar 3D points.

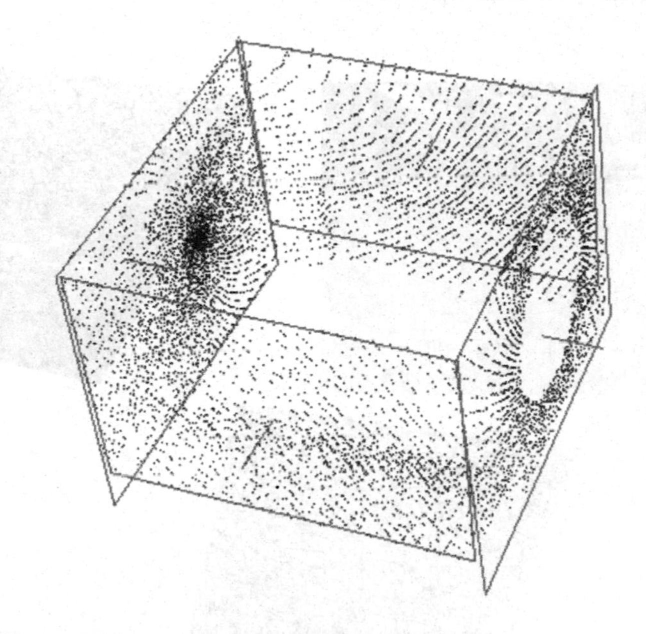

Fig. 8. Plane and boundary detection for a real point cloud provided by [28].

Experiments show that the proposed method can not only detect the plane, but also extract the plane boundary from unorganised point clouds. With the bounding box, the spatial position and scope of a set of coplanar points in 3D space is represented efficiently.

A third point cloud for this discussion is from our road surface application (see [3]). A set of 3D points are generated by stereo vision (stereo road images are recorded in a driving car for the purpose of road surface inspection, e.g. pothole detection). One image of a recorded stereo pair and the generated (by stereo matching) 3D point cloud are shown in Fig. 9, *top*. For applying our method, only those 3D points are retained whose Z coordinate is less or equal to 10 (metres), others are filtered out.

For this situation, the proposed method detects two planes as approximations of the road surface. Their boundaries are computed. The detected bounding boxes of both planes are drawn in Red in Fig. 9, *bottom*.

The initial peak in the Hough space represents the plane Π with the most coplanar 3D points. 3D points being below Π are extracted; they form another unorganized point cloud. By plane approximation and bounding box calculation, we have candidates for potholes (below Π); those still need to be evaluated whether of "sufficient size", not just forming a minor artefact.

With the extracted normal and bounding box, the spatial position and scope of a set of 3D points can be determined. Experiments showed that this is a way for estimating the pose and depth of potholes.

Fig. 9. Plane detection for a road-surface application. *Top*: Example of an input image (of a stereo pair) and corresponding point cloud. *Bottom*: Detected road surface Π and pothole. (Color figure online)

5 Conclusions

In order to describe efficiently and completely a set of unorganised 3D points, a method for plane detection and boundary extraction (of planar segments) is proposed. Both the plane parameters and the segment boundaries (i.e. bounding boxes) are extracted based on Hough voting techniques.

By analysing Hough voting, the relationship between the boundary of coplanar point segments in 3D space and voting cells in Hough space are deduced. The voting cells that correspond to the top, bottom, left and right boundaries are located. By fitting six linear functions to corresponding voting cells, the four vertices of the bounding box may be directly determined using the coefficients of the fitted functions in Hough space.

The bounding box, detected from unorganized points, describes the pose of a set of 3D points. The proposed method is time efficient and robust against positional noise of 3D points.

Acknowledgement. This work was supported by the National Natural Science Foundation of China (61602063), Jiangsu Collaborative Innovation Center for Cultural Creativity (XYN1705), the Natural Science Foundation of Jiangsu Higher Education Institute (18KJB520004), and Changzhou Science and Technology Project (CE20175023). Authors thank Amita Dhiman for providing 3D road surface data.

References

1. Borrmann, D., Elseberg, J., Lingemann, K., Nüchter, A.: The 3D Hough transform for plane detection in point clouds: a review and a new accumulator design. 3D Res. **2**, 1–13 (2011)
2. Brimkov, V., Coeurjolly, D., Klette, R.: Digital planarity - a review. Discrete Appl. Math. **155**(4), 468–495 (2007)
3. Dhiman, A., Klette, R.: Pothole detection using computer vision and learning. IEEE Trans. Intell. Transp. Syst. (2019). https://doi.org/10.1109/TITS.2019.2931297
4. Drost, B., Ilic, S.: Local Hough transform for 3D primitive detection. In: IEEE International Conference on 3D Vision, pp. 398–406 (2015)
5. Dube, D., Zell, A.: Real-time plane extraction from depth images with the randomized Hough transform. In: IEEE International Conference on Computer Vision Workshops, pp. 1084–1091 (2011)
6. Harati, A., Gachter, S., Siegwart, R.: Fast range image segmentation for indoor 3D-SLAM. In: IFAC Symposium Intelligent Autonomous Vehicles, pp. 475–480 (2007)
7. Fischler, M.A., Bolles, R.C.: Random sample consensus: a paradigm for model fitting with applications to image analysis and automated cartography. Commun. ACM **24**, 381–395 (1981)
8. Hoover, A., Jean-Baptiste, G., Jiang, X., et al.: An experimental comparison of range image segmentation algorithms. IEEE Trans. Pattern Anal. Mach. Intell. **18**, 673–689 (2002)
9. Hulik, R., Spanel, M., Smrz, P., et al.: Continuous plane detection in point-cloud data based on 3D Hough transform. J. Vis. Commun. Image Represent. **25**(1), 86–97 (2014)
10. Klette, R., Rosenfeld, A.: Digital Geometry. Morgan Kaufmann, San Francisco (2004)
11. Landrieu, L., Simonovsky, M.: Large-scale point cloud semantic segmentation with superpoint graphs. In: IEEE Conference on Computer Vision Pattern Recognition (2018)
12. Li, L., Yang, F., Zhu, H., et al.: An improved RANSAC for 3D point cloud plane segmentation based on normal distribution transformation cells. Remote Sens. **9**(5), 433 (2017)

13. Limberger, F.A., Oliveira, M.M.: Real-time detection of planar regions in unorganized point clouds. Pattern Recogn. **48**(6), 2043–2053 (2015)
14. Luchowski, L., Kowalski, P.: Using RANSAC for 3D point cloud segmentation. Theor. Appl. Inform. **25**(20), 105–117 (2013)
15. Luo, L., Tang, L., Yang, Z.: Learning combinatorial global and local features on 3D point clouds. In: IEEE SmartWorld Ubiquitous Intelligence Computing, pp. 1956–1961 (2018)
16. Nguyen, A., Le, B.: 3D point cloud segmentation: a survey. In: IEEE Robotics Automation Mechatronics, pp. 12–15 (2013)
17. Poppinga, J., Vaskevicius, N., Birk, A., Pathak, K.: Fast plane detection and polygonalization in noisy 3D range images. In: IEEE/RSJ International Conference on Intelligent Robots Systems, pp. 3378–3383 (2008)
18. Qi, C.R., Su, H., Mo, K., et al.: PointNet: deep learning on point sets for 3D classification and segmentation. In: IEEE Conference on Computer Vision Pattern Recognition, pp. 77–85 (2017)
19. Sekiguchi, H., Sano, K., Yokoyama, T.: Interactive 3-dimensional segmentation method based on region growing method. Syst. Comput. Jpn. **25**(1), 88–97 (2010)
20. Sivignon, I., Coeurjolly, D.: Minimum decomposition of a digital surface into digital plane segments is NP-hard. Discrete Appl. Math. **157**, 558–570 (2009)
21. Trevor, A., Rogers, J., Christensen, H.: Planar surface slam with 3D and 2D sensors. In: IEEE International Conference on Robotics Automation, pp. 3041–3048 (2012)
22. Vera, E., Lucio, D., Fernandes, L.A.F., et al.: Hough transform for real-time plane detection in depth images. Pattern Recogn. Lett. **103**, 8–15 (2018)
23. Vo, A.V., Truong-Hong, L., Laefer, D.F., et al.: Octree-based region growing for point cloud segmentation. ISPRS J. Photogramm. Remote Sens. **104**, 88–100 (2015)
24. Wang, X., Xiao, J., Wang, Y.: Research of plane extraction methods based on region growing. In: International Conference on Virtual Reality Visualization, pp. 298–303 (2016)
25. Weingarten, J., Gruener, G., Siegwart, R.: A fast and robust 3D feature extraction algorithm for structured environment reconstruction. In: International Conference on Advanced Robotics, pp. 390–397 (2003)
26. Weinmann, M.: Point cloud registration. Reconstruction and Analysis of 3D Scenes, pp. 55–110. Springer, Cham (2016). https://doi.org/10.1007/978-3-319-29246-5_4
27. Woodford, O.J., Pham, M.T., Atsuto, M., et al.: Demisting the Hough transform for 3D shape recognition and registration. Int. J. Comput. Vis. **106**(3), 332–341 (2014)
28. Xiao, J., Zhang, J., Adler, B., et al.: Three-dimensional point cloud plane segmentation in both structured and unstructured environments. Robot. Auton. Syst. **61**(12), 1641–1652 (2013)
29. Xu, B., Jiang, W., Shan, J., Zhang, J., Li, L.: Investigation on the weighted RANSAC approaches for building roof plane segmentation from LiDAR point clouds. Remote Sens. **8**(1), 5 (2015)
30. Zhang, M., Jiang, G., Wu, C., et al.: Horizontal plane detection from 3D point clouds of buildings. Electron. Lett. **48**(13), 764–765 (2012)

Real-Time Multi-class Instance Segmentation with One-Time Deep Embedding Clustering

Yu-Chi Chen[1], Chia-Yuan Chang[1], Pei-Yung Hsiao[2], and Li-Chen Fu[1](✉)

[1] National Taiwan University, Taipei, Taiwan, ROC
{r06922093,lichen}@ntu.edu.tw

[2] National University of Kaohsiung, Kaohsiung, Taiwan, ROC

Abstract. In recent years, instance segmentation research has been considered as an extension of object detection and semantic segmentation, which can provide pixel-level annotations on detected objects. Several approaches for instance segmentation exploit object detection network to generate bounding box and segment each bounding box with segmentation network. However, these approaches need more time consumption due to two independent networks as their framework. On the other hand, some approaches based on clustering transform each pixel into unique representation and produce instance mask by postprocessing. Nevertheless, most clustering approaches have to cluster all instances of each class individually, which contribute to additional time consumption. In this research, we propose a fast clustering method called one-time clustering with single network aiming at reducing time consumption on multi-class instance segmentation. Moreover, we present a class-sensitive loss function that allows the network to generate unique embedding which contains class and instance information. With the informative embeddings, we can cluster them only once instead of clustering for each class in other clustering approaches. Our approach is up to 6x faster than the state-of-the-art UPSNet [1], which appeared in CVPR 2019, and get about 25% lower AP performance on Cityscape dataset. It achieves significantly faster speed and great segmentation quality while having an acceptable AP performance.

Keywords: Deep learning · Real-time instance segmentation · Multi-class instance segmentation · One-time clustering

1 Introduction

In recent years, more and more computer vision technologies have been used to build more reliable systems in Autonomous Driving Systems (ADS) and Advanced Drive Assistance Systems (ADAS), such as object detection, semantic segmentation and instance segmentation. The primary purpose of these computer vision technologies is to provide the system with information about the surrounding environment.

Object detection technique which locate the detected objects with a set of bounding boxes is an important application in ADAS and ADS, such as Faster-RCNN [2], YOLO [3]. With this technique, the system can detect obstacles in front of the vehicle, thereby

S. Palaiahnakote et al. (Eds.): ACPR 2019, LNCS 12046, pp. 223–235, 2020.
https://doi.org/10.1007/978-3-030-41404-7_16

preventing the vehicle from colliding with obstacles. However, object detection technique is not good at handling too complicated situations, such as object occlusion. In addition, it cannot separate the foreground object from the background in a bounding box.

On the other hand, semantic segmentation technique, such as FCN [4] and SegNet [5], can provide class labels for each pixel, so using this technique can easily distinguish between background pixel and foreground object pixel. However, semantic segmentation techniques cannot distinguish between different objects even though they have ability to separate background and foreground objects.

As we have mentioned, object detection and semantic segmentation both have drawbacks. Instance segmentation techniques which can provide pixel-level annotation on detected object are able to handle this issue. In the recent years, most of state-of-the-art instance segmentation methods are based on the object proposal framework [6–8] which have high time consumption, but they can achieve high accuracy on several dataset. However, for real-world application, time consumption is a key consideration we must consider. Therefore, some research [9–11] does not apply object proposal framework, they use the Deep CNN to convert raw image pixels into embeddings and use clustering methods to cluster embeddings to get instance segmentation result. These methods are faster than the methods based on object proposal framework because they do not have to waste time on object proposal. However, these methods tend to treat different class separately and they can't handle multi-class at once. Due to this factor, time consumption increases as the number of classes increases.

In this research, we present an efficient instance segmentation method which combines a confidence map and embeddings with instance information to handle multi-class instance segmentation through one-time clustering. To validate our work, we evaluate it on Cityscapes datasets [12] which contains instances in different classes. The experimental results show that our method can achieve real-time speed in multi-class case while remaining an acceptable performance.

In this paper, the remaining parts are composed as follows. In Sect. 2, we mention related work about CNN based networks to achieve instance segmentation task. In Sect. 3, we introduce the proposed method in detail. In Sect. 4, we present our experiments on Cityscape dataset. In Sect. 5, we give a conclusion of our proposed method.

2 Related Works

In the last few years, there are many CNN-based instance segmentation approaches. We can divide these approaches into three categories by their process pipeline. They are based on object detection, based on recurrent network and based on clustering approaches. In the following section, we'll cover some of the work based on these methods and discuss the difference between our method and those methods.

Instance Segmentation Based on Object Detection Framework. Methods based on object detection can be seen as a multi-stage pipeline. They first use an object proposal network to generate object proposals, then classify and segment them to produce instances. The performance of this pipeline depends on the quality of object proposal network. If the quality of object proposal is good, then no instance will be lost. In 2017,

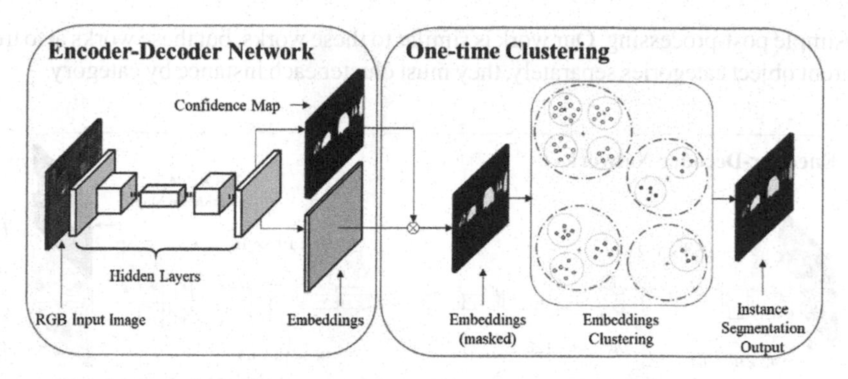

Fig. 1. Overview of the proposed one-time clustering instance segmentation

He et al. [6] propose Mask R-CNN which is a framework based on object detection. They first use Faster R-CNN [2] as an object detection network to generate object proposals, and add a segmentation head to extract instance masks from object proposals. Their framework has inspired many works. For example, PANet proposed by Liu et al. [7] is a framework based on Mask R-CNN. They replace each component in Mask R-CNN with a more powerful version, such as replacing ResNet [13] with FPN [14] for extracting better features. Different from these methods, our method which does not depend on object proposal network considers the entire image, not just a small proposal region. This strategy is shown to be useful for handling occlusions. In addition, we do not use the object proposal network, so that we can reduce the time consumption of object proposal process.

Instance Segmentation Based on Recurrent Neural Network (RNN). Some works use recurrent neural networks (RNN) to sequentially generate instances. Romera-Paredes et al. [15] propose an instance segmentation paradigm which can sequentially find objects and their segmentations one at a time. Further, they use an end-to-end recurrent neural network with convolutional LSTM [16] to produce binary segmentation mask for each instance. Inspired by their work, Ren et al. [17] add an attention mechanism to recurrent neural network to produce detailed instance segmentations. However, methods based on RNN only consider a single object category. If there are many object categories, they have to train a different network for each category. In contrast to these works, our method handles different instances between different categories at the same time.

Instance Segmentation Based on Clustering Post-processing. Another works is based on clustering, which uses CNN to learn a specific representation for each pixel and then cluster these representations to obtain discrete instances. In 2018, Watanabe et al. [9] presents a mathematical representation of instances that treats each individual instance as a combination of a center of mass and a field of vectors pointing to it. Bai et al. [10] use deep neural networks to learn the energy of the watershed transform such that each basin corresponds to a single instance, then each instance can be extracted by a cut at a single energy level. De Brabandere et al. [11] transform each pixel into a point in high-dimensional feature space by a discriminative loss function, and then their method can cluster each instance by a simple post-processing. Our work is similar to these works, but these works also treat different object categories separately, they must cluster each instance by category.

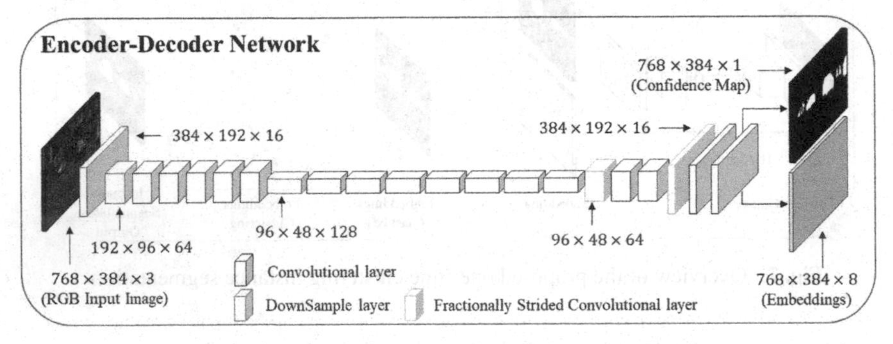

Fig. 2. The architecture of encoder-decoder network

3 One-Time Clustering Method

In this chapter, we will introduce our proposed one-time clustering instance segmentation method in detail. First, we will describe the network architecture which generates a foreground mask and embeddings. Then, we will explain the loss function which contains the proposed class-sensitive loss function that makes our network transform the pixel to the embedding with instance information. Lastly, we will describe the one-time clustering algorithm we use to cluster the embeddings into instances. The method we propose is a two-stage pipeline. The overall pipeline of the proposed method is illustrated in Fig. 1.

3.1 Encoder-Decoder Network

Our encoder-decoder network is based on ERFNet [18] which is a CNN-based semantic segmentation network. The network architecture is illustrated in Fig. 2. In order to obtain information about individual instances, our main idea consists of two steps. In the first step, we want to know the location of the instance, that is, whether there is an instance on the pixel. To achieve this goal, we use a fractionally strided convolutional layer to generate a confidence map. Each cell on the confidence map represents the confidence score which is a probability of an instance appearing. In addition, to give each pixel in the input image a confidence score, the size of the confidence map is same as the input image. With the confidence map, we can filter out pixels that don't contain the instance. In the second step, we want to separate each individual instance from the confidence map. Our proposed network outputs embedding to provide more information for distinguishing instance. Each embedding is a point in high-dimensional feature space transformed from each RGB and has a particular relationship with other embeddings. The relationship is that two embeddings are close if they belong to the same instance. Through this particular relationship, we can use a clustering method to gather embeddings belonging to the same instance, that is, we now can know each individual instance. To make the embedding has this particular relationship, we propose a class-sensitive loss function.

3.2 Loss Function

As mention above, our proposed encoder-decoder network will output a confidence map and embeddings. Our total loss function is composed with two loss function, one is confidence map loss function, and the other is class-sensitive loss function, as shown in Eq. (1).

$$L_{total} = L_{confi\_map} + L_{class\_sen} \tag{1}$$

For confidence map, the goal is to know if the pixel contains an instance or not. This goal can be thought of as a pixel-wise classification, that is, determine the probability that a pixel is an instance. For each cell on the confidence map, there is a scalar indicated the probability that a pixel is an instance. We use a binary cross-entropy loss function as shown in Eq. (2) to calculate the loss. For each location of pixel (x, y), we calculate the loss between the ground truth $G(x, y)$ and the prediction of the probability $P(x, y)$

$$L_{confi\_map} = -\frac{1}{N}\sum_{x=1}^{W}\sum_{y=1}^{H} G(x, y)log(P(x, y)) \tag{2}$$

where W is the width of ground truth, H is the height of ground truth, and N is the number of ground truth.

Our intuition to separating different instances from different classes in one-time is that embeddings from the same instance should be close together in n-dimensional feature space, while embeddings from different instances should be far apart in n-dimensional feature space, and different classes should have their own space in n-dimensional feature space so that instances from the same class can be in their own class space.

The loss function proposed by De Brabandere *et al.* [11] has two terms to achieve the relationship of embeddings between instances. One term draws embeddings of the same instance towards the mean embedding of the instance and the other term pushes the mean embedding of different instances away from each other. With these two terms, the relationship between embedding and instance can be handled. However, these two terms cannot handle the relationship between instance and class. In our loss function, we will handle the relationship between embedding and instance, and the relationship between instance and class at the same time. Therefore, we formulate our class-sensitive loss function in terms of a pull force within instance, a push force between instance and a pull force between instance and class, as shown in Eq. (3).

$$L_{class\_sen} = \alpha * L_{intra\_ins} + \beta * L_{inter\_ins} + \gamma * L_{intra\_class} \tag{3}$$

The notation α, β and γ are hyper-parameters to balance the effect of each term. We will introduce each term of our loss function in the following paragraphs.

For embeddings belonging the same instance, they should gather together in n-dimensional feature space and each embedding should be close enough to the mean embedding of the instance, that is to say, the distance between each embedding and the mean embedding should be small enough. The mean embedding can be seemed as the center of the instance. When the distance between the embedding and the center of the instance is too far, there is an intra-instance force which can be seen as a pull-force between the embedding and the center of the instance. Inspired by De Brabandere *et al.* [11], to make the network easier to converge, our pull force will only trigger when the distance is greater than a threshold δ_{intra_ins}. The intra-instance force is written as follows:

$$L_{intra\_ins} = \frac{1}{I}\sum_{i=1}^{I}\frac{1}{N_i}\sum_{j=1}^{N_i}\max\left(0, \left\|\mu_i - x_j^i\right\|_2 - \delta_{intra\_ins}\right)^2 \tag{4}$$

where I is the number of instances in the ground truth, N_i is the number of pixels in the instance i, x_j^i is the embedding of the pixel j of the instance i. μ_i is the mean embedding of the instance i, $\|\cdot\|_2$ is the L2 distance, and δ_{intra_ins} is the threshold of the distance for intra-instance force.

For the centers of different instances, they should be kept at a certain distance so that the embedding belonging to different instances does not mix together, that is, the distance between the mean embeddings of different instances will be greater than the threshold. When two centers are too close, there is an inter-instance force which can be seen as a push-force to push them away from each other. As mention above, in order to make the network easier to converge, when the distance between the two centers is greater than the threshold δ_{inter_ins}., the push-force stops working. The intra-instance force is written as follows:

$$L_{inter\_ins} = \frac{1}{I(I-1)}\sum_{\substack{i_A = 1 \\ i_A \neq i_B}}^{I}\sum_{i_B=1}^{I} max\left(0, 2\delta_{inter\_ins} - \|\mu_{i_A} - \mu_{i_B}\|_2\right)^2 \tag{5}$$

where I is the number of instances, δ_{inter_ins} is the threshold of the distance for inter-instance force, μ_i is the mean embedding of the instance i, and $\|\cdot\|_2$ is the L2 distance.

For the instances of the same class, they should be close to the center of the class. The distance between the center of the instance and the center of the class should be small enough. In order to handle different classes at the same time, each class has its own center. The center of the class is also an embedding in n-dimensional feature space. The center of each class is set a certain distance so that the instances belonging to different classes will not be mixed together. When the instance is too far away from the center of the class, there is an inter-class force which can be seen as a pull-force between the instance and the center of the class. We only draw the center of the instance towards the center of class because we have the intra-instance force which makes embeddings close to the center of the instance, so the center of the instance can represent all embeddings within the instance. Therefore, we can just use the distance between the instance center and the class center to determine if the instance is close enough to the center of the class. The pull-force activates up at a certain distance δ_{intra_class}, so the network does not need to pull all instances to the class center. The intra-class term is written as follows:

$$L_{intra\_class} = \frac{1}{C}\sum_{k=1}^{C}\frac{1}{N_k}\sum_{j=1}^{N_k} max\left(0, \left\|m_k - \mu_j^k\right\|_2 - \delta_{inter\_class}\right)^2 \tag{6}$$

where C is the number of classes, N_k is the number of instances belonging to the class k, m_k is the class center embedding,μ_j^k is the mean embedding of the instance j, and δ_{inter_class} is the threshold of the distance.

3.3 One-Time Clustering Algorithm

In the second step of our proposed instance segmentation, we use the confidence map and embeddings to obtain each individual instance. First, the embeddings which contains instances is our only concern, so we use the confidence map as a mask to filter out the embeddings that does not contain instances. For each embedding, the embedding will be set to zero if the probability on the corresponding position in the confidence map is below the threshold.

After thresholding, we collect non-zero embeddings and use one-time clustering algorithm to group them. When we train our network with class-sensitive loss function, we set $\delta_{inter\_ins} > 2\delta_{intra\_ins}$. After training, the embedding has the following properties, the distance between embeddings belonging to same instance and its instance center is lower than a threshold δ_{intra_ins}, the distance between each instance center is greater than a threshold δ_{inter_ins}, and the distance between instance center and the class center it belong to is below a threshold δ_{inter_class}.

According to these properties, one embedding is closer to the embeddings belonging to the same instance rather than the embeddings belonging to a different instance. Thus, we set a distance threshold and use this threshold to determine the instance to which the embedding belonging, that is, we can select any embedding and calculate the distance with other embeddings, and if the distance is lower than threshold, we regard it as belonging to the same instance as the select embedding. After grouping the embeddings, a group of embeddings can be seen as an instance, then we calculate the mean embedding of the grouped embeddings, and calculate its distance from each class center embedding to determine which class the instance belongs to. When all embeddings are grouped, the clustering algorithm is completed.

4 Experiments

In this chapter, we will evaluate our method by conducting three experiments on Cityscapes dataset. First, we will describe Cityscapes dataset and evaluation metric. Then, we show the experimental results, including the comparison with other state-of-the-art methods.

4.1 Cityscapes Dataset

Cityscapes dataset [12] is the most challenge and authoritative dataset for semantic understanding of urban street scenes. There is a benchmark for pixel-level and instance-level semantic segmentation in it. For pixel-level semantic segmentation benchmark, the goal is to correctly classify each pixel, which is a general semantic segmentation task. On the other hand, instance-level semantic segmentation has to not only correctly classify each pixel, but also distinguish each individual instance. There are 8 classes in

Cityscapes dataset. Our method focuses on distinguishing instances, so we evaluate our method on instance-level semantic segmentation benchmark.

For fair comparison with other instance segmentation methods, we use only the image with fine-grained annotation in Cityscapes dataset to evaluate our method. The image with fine-grained annotation, there are three sets, one is training set containing 2975 images, another is validation set containing 500 images and the other is test set containing 1525 images. The training and validation sets are provided with ground truth annotation. The test set contains the image only. Furthermore, results on test set need to be uploaded to evaluation server. We train our model on training set and report our results on validation set.

4.2 Evaluation Metrics

Each prediction result of instance segmentation will be evaluated by their intersection-over-union (*IOU*) with ground truth first. The prediction result is considered correct only when the *IOU* is above the threshold. Each instance will calculate its own *IOU*, which is using the pixels of prediction instance and the pixels of ground truth instance, as shown in Eq. (7).

$$IOU = \frac{TP}{TP + FP + FN} \tag{7}$$

In the IOU calculation, true positive (TP) indicates the number of pixels annotated in the ground truth and the prediction result, false negative (FN) indicates the number of pixels annotated in the ground truth, but is not annotated in the prediction result, false positive (FP) indicates the number of pixels annotated in the prediction result, but is not annotated in the ground truth.

$$\text{Precision} = \frac{\text{TP}}{\text{TP} + \text{FP}} \tag{8}$$

$$\text{Recall} = \frac{\text{TP}}{\text{TP} + \text{FN}} \tag{9}$$

In recall and precision calculations, the formula is as in Eqs. (8) and (9). True positive (TP) indicates the number of instances in which the *IOU* of the prediction and the ground truth is higher than the threshold, and false positive (FP) indicates the number of predictions that are not paired with any ground truth ($IOU <$ threshold), and false negative (FN) indicates the number of ground truth that are not paired with any predictions ($IOU <$ threshold). If a ground truth is paired with many predictions, it will only treat the prediction with the highest IOU as true positive and the remaining predictions are seemed as false positives.

In public dataset, Average Precision (AP) is a widely used evaluation metrics to evaluate the performance of instance segmentation method. It can evaluate the overall performance of an instance segmentation method by calculating the area under precision-recall curve which means the precision under different recalls. In general, Average Precision (AP) is calculated with the *IOU* threshold from 50% to 95% in steps of 0.05 and take the average. In addition to mean Average Precision (AP), there is another evaluation metrics called AP0.5 which only considers IOU threshold 50%.

The Average Precision (AP) metrics can evaluate the performance of detection instances in image. In addition to evaluate the detection performance, we also evaluate the quality of our segmentation result. We use segmentation quality (SQ) metrics defined in [19]. The segmentation quality (SQ) metrics is defined as:

$$\mathrm{SQ} = \frac{\sum_{(p,g)\in TP} IOU(p,g)}{|TP|} \quad (10)$$

where p is the prediction, g is the ground truth, and $|TP|$ is the number of predictions whose IOU with ground truth is higher than 0.5. The segmentation quality (SQ) metrics is used to evaluate the quality of segmentation, that is, if the IOU between ground truth and prediction is higher, the performance is better.

4.3 Training Environment Setup

Our method is trained and tested on personal computer with a single NVIDIA RTX 2080Ti GPU, Intel Core i7-8700 3.20 GHz CPU, 32G Memory, and Ubuntu 16.04 operation system. The deep learning framework we used is PyTorch developed by Facebook. PyTorch integrates NVIDIA Cuda and cudnn toolkit, which allow us to utilize strong GPU acceleration.

Table 1. Comparison of runtime speed and performance with other state-of-the-art approaches

Method	AP	AP0.5	FPS	Input resolution
R-CNN+MCG [12]	4.6	12.9	0.017	512 × 256
Mask R-CNN [6]	26.2	49.9	5	2048 × 1024
PANet [7]	31.7	57.1	–	2048 × 1024
UPSNet [1]	**33.0**	**59.6**	4.4	2048 × 1024
ISVDC [20]	2.3	3.7	5	512 × 256
De Brabandere *et al.* [11]	17.5	35.9	15	512 × 256
Ours	7.6	13.8	**33**	512 × 256

We train the model with 600 epochs and each mini-batch has 1 image. The starting learning rate is $1e^{-3}$, and when the minimum loss is not updated for 20 epochs, the learning rate drops to one tenth. To reduce the high computational cost of the encoder-decoder network, we downsample the training images from 2048 × 1024 to 768 × 384. The subsampling transformation has an impact on our final results because we have to upsample the final results to the original resolution for evaluation which adds some noise to it. The hyper-parameters in our class-sensitive loss is set as follows: $\delta_{intra\_ins} = 0.5$, $\delta_{inter\_ins} = 1.5$, $\delta_{intra\_class} = 5$, and the dimension of embedding is 8.

Table 2. Comparison of speed with other state-of-the-art method

Method	FPS	Input resolution	GPU
R-CNN+MCG [12]	0.017	512 × 256	–
Mask R-CNN [6]	5	2048 × 1024	Nvidia Tesla M40 GPU
UPSNet [1]	4.4	2048 × 1024	Nvidia GTX 1080 Ti
ISVDC [20]	5	512 × 256	Nvidia GTX 1070
De Brabandere *et al.* [11]	15	512 × 256	Nvidia Titan X
Ours	**33**	512 × 256	Nvidia GTX 1080 Ti

The hyper-parameters are determined by performance of validation set, and the dimension of embedding is according to the number of classes in the dataset. The embedding of each class center is in 8-dimension. The ith element in the class center embedding is 7 and others are 0, where i is the class number.

4.4 Result and Discussion

We compare the inference time and performance to other state-of-the-art instance segmentation approaches in Table 1. Compared to UPSNet [1], our runtime speed is six times faster and our performance is around four times lower. We compare to PANet [7] which performance is better than us four times, but we suppose that their runtime speed is slower than us. PANet is based on Mask R-CNN [6] and they replace each component in Mask R-CNN. For example, they add a fully connected layer combined with original convolutional layer at the mask branch. These replacements can improve their performance, but they will increase their time consumption. Therefore, the runtime of PANet is slower than Mask R-CNN. Our approach is faster than Mask R-CNN, so we are faster than PANet. In the following paragraph, we will compare the runtime and the performance with other approaches, respectively.

Fig. 3. Instance segmentation visual results of Cityscapes dataset.

Compared to object detection-based approaches [1, 6, 7], the runtime speed of our method is faster. Because our method only uses one network for generating result, the object detection-based approaches have to go through a proposal network and a segmentation network to obtain the result. Therefore, the time consumption from network computation can be reduced in our method. On the other hand, our method is quite faster than methods based on clustering [11, 20]. As mention previously, we operate instance from different classes in one time to obtain result, so the runtime will not increase when we handle multi-class instance segmentation. The comparison of runtime speed is shown in Table 2.

In Table 1, we compare the performance between ours and other approaches. To achieving high runtime speed, our approach has to downsample the input image first, so some information about small object will lose, which harm our performance. Thus, the detection-based approaches [1, 6, 7] which has a strong feature extractor have better performance than us, but they have to sacrifice the runtime speed. To handle different class at the same time, some instances belonging to same class are misclassified. Therefore, compared to clustering-based approaches [11, 20], our method achieves acceptable performance, but it can still be improved.

In Table 3, we use segmentation quality (SQ) metrics to evaluate our method and compare with Mask R-CNN [6] and UPSNet [1] which are the state-of-the-art instance segmentation methods. Compared to Mask R-CNN and UPSNet, our method has the information from the whole image to generate our instance segmentation, and they use only the information in the bounding box to generate instance segmentation, so the segmentation in our instance segmentation prediction can have better result.

Table 3. Comparison of segmentation quality (SQ)

Method	Segmentation quality (SQ)
Mask R-CNN [6]	78.7
UPSNet [1]	79.7
Ours	**80.1**

In Fig. 3, we show the instance segmentation results on Cityscapes dataset. The different color in our prediction represents different label for each individual instance. In most of scenarios, our method can identify the individual instances. As shown in the first column, the cars are close to each other, but our method still can separate them. In another scenario, our method can handle that a car in front of the bus, as shown in the third column of Fig. 3, because we have a push force in our class-sensitive loss that make the embeddings of two nearby instances far away from each other. Our confidence map also plays an important role, as shown in the second column, there is a road sign in front of the bus, and our confidence mask filter out the road sign. In addition, there are few instances belonging to different class that be merged into a single instance because the instances belonging to different class has its own class center.

Some failure cases, such as incorrect merging of neighboring instance, or splitting a single instance into multiple instances, happen in our example. Some instances belonging to same class, such as person, as shown in the fourth column of Fig. 3, are merged into same instance because our class-sensitive loss function forces them close to the same center. Although our confidence map finds most of instance in the image, there are still some instances are not detected. Most of not detected instances are small, so their probability in the confidence map are low, which make them be filter out. Therefore, the quality of foreground mask also effects the instance segmentation result.

5 Conclusion

In this paper, we proposed an efficient clustering-based method for instance segmentation. It exploits the class-sensitive loss function to help our encoder-decoder generate unique embedding for each pixel with class and instance information. With those informative embeddings, we can handle multi-class instance segmentation and reach real-time speed at the same time. Empirical results on Cityscapes shows that our method achieves significantly faster speed compared to other approaches while remaining acceptable performance. Moreover, the class-sensitive loss function can be easily applied to recent encoder-decoder architecture. We believe that our loss function can be useful to future research in instance segmentation. Due to the fixed threshold in clustering which is set from training dataset, we would like to explore the learnable threshold in our future work.

References

1. Xiong, Y., et al.: UPSNet: a unified panoptic segmentation network. In: Proceedings of the IEEE Conference on Computer Vision and Pattern Recognition, pp. 8818–8826 (2019)
2. Ren, S., He, K., Girshick, R., Sun, J.: Faster R-CNN: towards real-time object detection with region proposal networks. In: Advances in Neural Information Processing Systems, pp. 91–99 (2015)
3. Redmon, J., Divvala, S., Girshick, R., Farhadi, A.: You only look once: unified, real-time object detection. In: Proceedings of the IEEE Conference on Computer Vision and Pattern Recognition, pp. 779–788 (2016)
4. Long, J., Shelhamer, E., Darrell, T.: Fully convolutional networks for semantic segmentation. In: Proceedings of the IEEE Conference on Computer Vision and Pattern Recognition, pp. 3431–3440 (2015)
5. Badrinarayanan, V., Kendall, A., Cipolla, R.: SegNet: a deep convolutional encoder-decoder architecture for image segmentation. IEEE Trans. Pattern Anal. Mach. Intell. **39**, 2481–2495 (2017)
6. He, K., Gkioxari, G., Dollár, P., Girshick, R.: Mask R-CNN. In: Proceedings of the IEEE International Conference on Computer Vision, pp. 2961–2969 (2017)
7. Liu, S., Qi, L., Qin, H., Shi, J., Jia, J.: Path aggregation network for instance segmentation. In: Proceedings of the IEEE Conference on Computer Vision and Pattern Recognition, pp. 8759–8768 (2018)
8. Huang, Z., Huang, L., Gong, Y., Huang, C., Wang, X.: Mask scoring R-CNN. In: Proceedings of the IEEE Conference on Computer Vision and Pattern Recognition, pp. 6409–6418 (2019)
9. Watanabe, T., Wolf, D.: Distance to center of mass encoding for instance segmentation. In: 2018 21st International Conference on Intelligent Transportation Systems (ITSC), pp. 3825–3831. IEEE (2018)

10. Bai, M., Urtasun, R.: Deep watershed transform for instance segmentation. In: Proceedings of the IEEE Conference on Computer Vision and Pattern Recognition, pp. 5221–5229 (2017)
11. De Brabandere, B., Neven, D., Van Gool, L.: Semantic instance segmentation with a discriminative loss function (2017)
12. Cordts, M., et al.: The cityscapes dataset for semantic urban scene understanding. In: Proceedings of the IEEE Conference on Computer Vision and Pattern Recognition, pp. 3213–3223 (2016)
13. He, K., Zhang, X., Ren, S., Sun, J.: Deep residual learning for image recognition. In: Proceedings of the IEEE Conference on Computer Vision and Pattern Recognition, pp. 770–778 (2016)
14. Lin, T.-Y., Dollár, P., Girshick, R., He, K., Hariharan, B., Belongie, S.: Feature pyramid networks for object detection. In: Proceedings of the IEEE Conference on Computer Vision and Pattern Recognition, pp. 2117–2125 (2017)
15. Romera-Paredes, B., Torr, P.H.S.: Recurrent instance segmentation. In: Leibe, B., Matas, J., Sebe, N., Welling, M. (eds.) ECCV 2016. LNCS, vol. 9910, pp. 312–329. Springer, Cham (2016). https://doi.org/10.1007/978-3-319-46466-4_19
16. Hochreiter, S., Schmidhuber, J.: Long short-term memory. Neural Comput. **9**, 1735–1780 (1997)
17. Ren, M., Zemel, R.S.: End-to-end instance segmentation with recurrent attention. In: Proceedings of the IEEE Conference on Computer Vision and Pattern Recognition, pp. 6656–6664 (2017)
18. Romera, E., Alvarez, J.M., Bergasa, L.M., Arroyo, R.: ERFNet: efficient residual factorized convnet for real-time semantic segmentation. IEEE Trans. Intell. Transp. Syst. **19**, 263–272 (2017)
19. Kirillov, A., He, K., Girshick, R., Rother, C., Dollár, P.: Panoptic segmentation. In: Proceedings of the IEEE Conference on Computer Vision and Pattern Recognition, pp. 9404–9413 (2019)
20. van den Brand, J., Ochs, M., Mester, R.: Instance-level segmentation of vehicles by deep contours. In: Chen, C.-S., Lu, J., Ma, K.-K. (eds.) ACCV 2016. LNCS, vol. 10116, pp. 477–492. Springer, Cham (2017). https://doi.org/10.1007/978-3-319-54407-6_32

Face and Body and Biometrics

Multi-person Pose Estimation with Mid-Points for Human Detection under Real-World Surveillance

Yadong Pan(✉) and Shoji Nishimura(✉)

NEC Biometrics Research Laboratories, Tokyo, Japan
{panyadong,nishimura}@nec.com

Abstract. This paper introduces the design and usage of a multi-person pose estimation system. The system is developed targeting some challenging issues in real-world surveillance such as (i) low image resolution, and (ii) people captured in crowded situation. Under such conditions, we evaluated the system's performance on human detection by comparing to other state-of-art algorithms. The leading results by using the proposed system are accomplished by several features in the system's design: (i) training and inference of mid-point, which is the center of two body region points defined in human pose, (ii) core-of-pose which is association of a plurality of body region points, and used as root of each individual person during parsing multiple people under crowded situation. The proposed system is also fast and has the potential for industrial use.

Keywords: Industrial image analysis · Pose estimation · Human detection · Real-world surveillance

1 Introduction

Human pose estimation is recently attracting a great attention and has been studied extensively in action recognition [2,3,25], online human tracking [16,23], person re-identification [20], human-object interaction [6] and human parsing [4]. As to human detection, which is an important task in real-world surveillance, using pose estimation to determine the human bounding area is becoming a more practical way, compared to directly using a human detector such as faster R-CNN [18], SSD [13] or YOLO [17]. This is because in real-world surveillance, especially in public spaces where people often appear in a crowd, (i) some people's bodies are under partial occlusion, and (ii) because of the distance between camera and people, and the requirements of real-time data processing, images and people captured are often with low resolution. These two facts would lead to inaccuracy when using human detector [7]. For example, in the task of recognizing suspicious persons near two countries' border (Fig. 1(left)), animals or even shaking trees are often recognized as human; In surveillance of a pedestrian crossing like Fig. 1(right), it happens a lot that multiple people in a crowd are

S. Palaiahnakote et al. (Eds.): ACPR 2019, LNCS 12046, pp. 239–253, 2020.
https://doi.org/10.1007/978-3-030-41404-7_17

Fig. 1. Examples of real-world surveillance: The left one shows a wide-range surveillance near two countries' border (Getty image). The right one is surveillance of a pedestrian crossing (MOT dataset [14]).

recognized as a single person. To solve such problems, a practical way is to implement bottom-up approach, which means to first detect body region points (each region point represents a certain part of human body), then to build association among those region points in order to get a pose vector for each individual person.

State-of-the-art bottom-up approach include recent works such as OpenPose [1], Art-Track [15] and Associative Embedding [10]. OpenPose uses a part-affinity-field to train the area between each pairwise body region points. Art-Track trains the geometric relationship between head and each of other body regions. Associative Embedding uses a neural network to estimate a person-index-number for each detected body region. In this paper, we designed a bottom-up pose estimation system called NeoPose, and compared NeoPose to those state-of-the-art algorithms for human detection task. The comparisons were conducted on MHP (Multi-Human Parsing) dataset [11], which contains many cases of dense people in the images. We resized all images to smaller size to make the test under low image resolutions. NeoPose gained leading results in the task.

The design of NeoPose is featured by two concepts: mid-point and core-of-pose. Mid-point is the center of two body region points defined in human pose (Fig. 2). We trained and inferred mid-points to help in the association of body region points. In OpenPose [1], the idea of mid-point was mentioned but denied due to concerns of crowded situation. In this paper, we explained when and how to use mid-points. Firstly, we point out that mid-point would be suitable for pose estimation under low image resolution. This was referred to a problem of part-affinity-field, which was used in OpenPose. Second, we used mid-point after human parsing, and supplemented it with a reference of body size. The human parsing and the estimation of body size were realized by what we called core-of-pose.

Core-of-pose is the combination of a plurality of upper body's region points and the links among them (Fig. 5(a)). It is defined on each individual person, and used as root to associate other body region points of the person. What's more, body size of a person could be estimated by referring to the length of links in core-of-pose, and could be used as a criterion for other region points' association. Such criterion helps to reduce the region points' association that crosses different persons. In this paper, we explained the algorithm of building core-of-pose. Compared to a previous work [21] that used a single region point (the head point) as root of each person, and length of head as reference size of human body, our algorithm, using multiple links to build the core, and functioned with the help of mid-points, would thereby reduce the risk of errors under low image resolution and crowded situation.

Overall, targeting real-world surveillance, this paper provides two directions for the design of bottom-up pose estimation and human detection system. (i) training mid-points in order to better support the association of body region points under low image resolution, (ii) using core-of-pose which consists of upper body's region points to parse multiple persons, and to estimate a reference size of each person's body in order to supplement the region points' association among multi-person under crowded situation.

2 Methodology

In this research, human pose is defined as in Fig. 2. Totally 18 body region points are associated to build up one person's pose. During pose estimation, there might be some region points which are not detected, thereby we defined the pose vector of one person as a subset of the 18 body region points. The 10 mid-points are defined according to 10 pairs of region point, each pair of which are physically connected on human body. Mid-points are not involved in pose vector, but help to associate the body region points and to determine the pose vector.

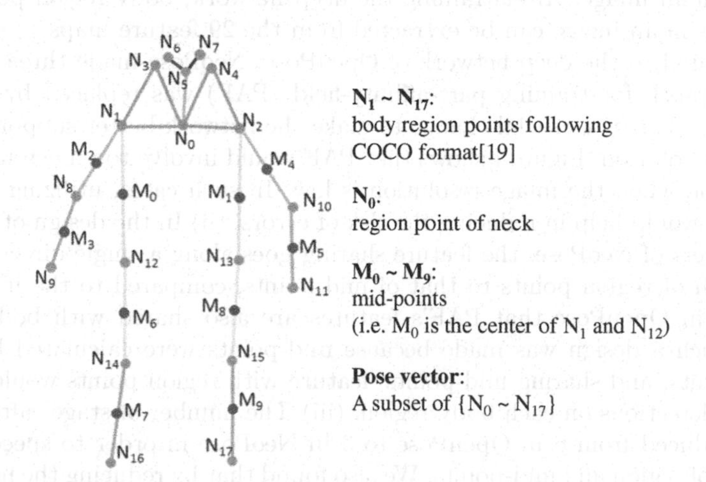

Fig. 2. Human pose defined by body region points and mid-points. N_0:neck, N_1:right shoulder, N_2:left shoulder, N_3:right ear, N_4:left ear, N_5:nose, N_6:right eye, N_7:left eye, N_8:right elbow, N_9:right wrist, N_{10}:left elbow, N_{11}:left wrist, N_{12}:right hip, N_{13}:left hip, N_{14}:right knee, N_{15}:left knee, N_{16}:right ankle, N_{17}:left ankle.

Given an image that contains one or multiple persons, pose estimation and human detection by NeoPose are achieved through three steps: (i) generating body region points and mid-points, (ii) generating core-of-pose, and (iii) generating pose vectors and human bounding boxes.

2.1 Generating Body Region Points and Mid-Points

Based on COCO dataset [12], we trained 18 body region points, 10 mid-points as well as a background channel using the deep network defined in Fig. 3(a). Ground truth of body region points except the region point of neck (defined as center of two shoulders) were provided by COCO dataset, and they were used to calculate the ground truth for the region point of neck as well as 10 mid-points. The network starts with a pre-defined VGG-19 [19], followed by two branches, each of which consists of three stages. The output of each stage in the first branch includes 19 channels (18 region points and one for background), while the second branch generates 10 channels for the mid-points after each stage. Concatenation layers between the stages share the features from VGG to the first branch, and from the first to the second branch. After the second and the third stages, all 29 feature maps from two branches are concatenated and used to calculate loss:

$$Loss = \sum\nolimits_{T} \sum\nolimits_{C} \sum\nolimits_{P} W(P) \cdot \parallel S_P^T(P) - S_P^G(P) \parallel_2^2$$

In the loss function, T stands for the second and the third stages, C refers to the 29 channels, and P represents all pixels in the feature map. S_P^T is the score generated from the deep network and S_P^G is the ground truth. W is a binary weight, which returns a value 0 when the annotation is missing at the current location in an image. After training the deep network, body region points and mid-points in an image can be extracted from the 29 feature maps.

Compared to the deep network of OpenPose, NeoPose made three changes: (i) The branch for training part-affinity-field (PAF) was replaced by training mid-points. This is a crucial change to make the network better support images with low resolution. Figure 4 shows that PAF would involve too much unreliable information when the image resolution is low. In such cases, utilizing a simple mid-point would help in reducing the risk of errors. (ii) In the design of concatenation layers of NeoPose, the feature sharing goes along a single direction from the branch of region points to that of mid-points, compared to the interactive structure in OpenPose that PAF's features are also shared with body region points. Such a design was made because mid-points were calculated based on region points, and sharing mid-points' feature with region points would lead to multiple detections on each body region. (iii) The number of stages after VGG-19 was reduced from 6 in OpenPose to 3 in NeoPose in order to speed up the inference of region and mid-points. We also found that by reducing the number of stages, the network could recognize more region and mid-points under crowded situation. Such phenomenon was studied in [24], which suggested that repeating the process of convolution would make the network focus more on features of the whole scene rather than individual object/person.

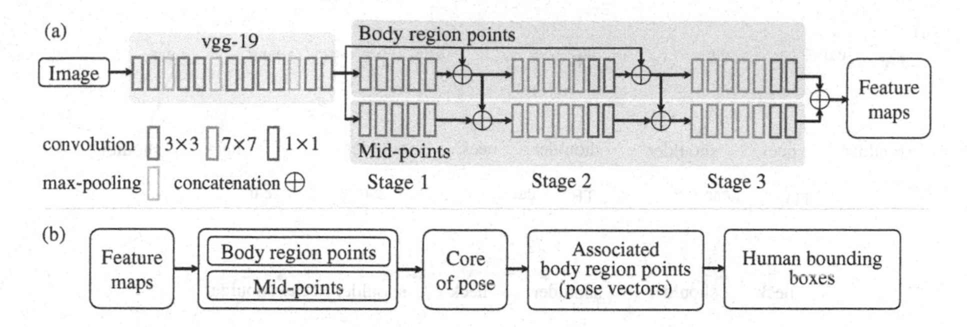

Fig. 3. Architecture of NeoPose. (a) the deep network, (b) the flowchart of data processing after the deep network.

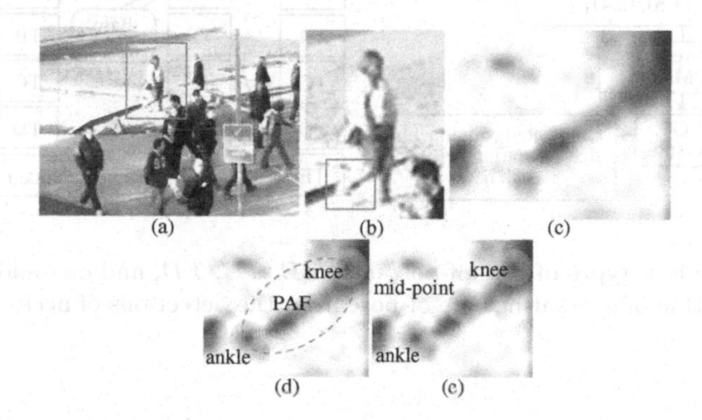

Fig. 4. Description of mid-point. (a, b, c) image, person and body region with low resolution, (d) part-affinity-field (PAF), which is used by OpenPose [1], (e) concept of mid-point used in this research.

2.2 Generating Core-of-Pose

Core-of-pose is defined based on region points of neck, shoulder and ear. These body parts are selected because they are highly spatially correlated on human body, and they are more likely to be captured in real-world surveillance even if people are in a crowd. Six types of link can be included in the core: neck and left shoulder, neck and left ear, left shoulder and left ear, neck and right shoulder, neck and right ear, right shoulder and right ear. Figure 5(a) shows the four types of core (TA, TB, TC, TD) and one midterm format (TE). TA is the full core which has two triangles corresponding to the neck. TB, TC and TD has one triangle. TE is a midterm format and can be converted to TB and TC by excluding the link in the middle of the path between two neck points.

The algorithm for generating core-of-pose (Fig. 5(b)) starts with a graph G and V. G includes all detected body region points of neck, shoulders and ears in the image. V is called full mapping links that consists of all allowable types of link among the region points in G. A pairwise matching algorithm (PMA) is then performed on G and V to filter each type of the link. Assuming that

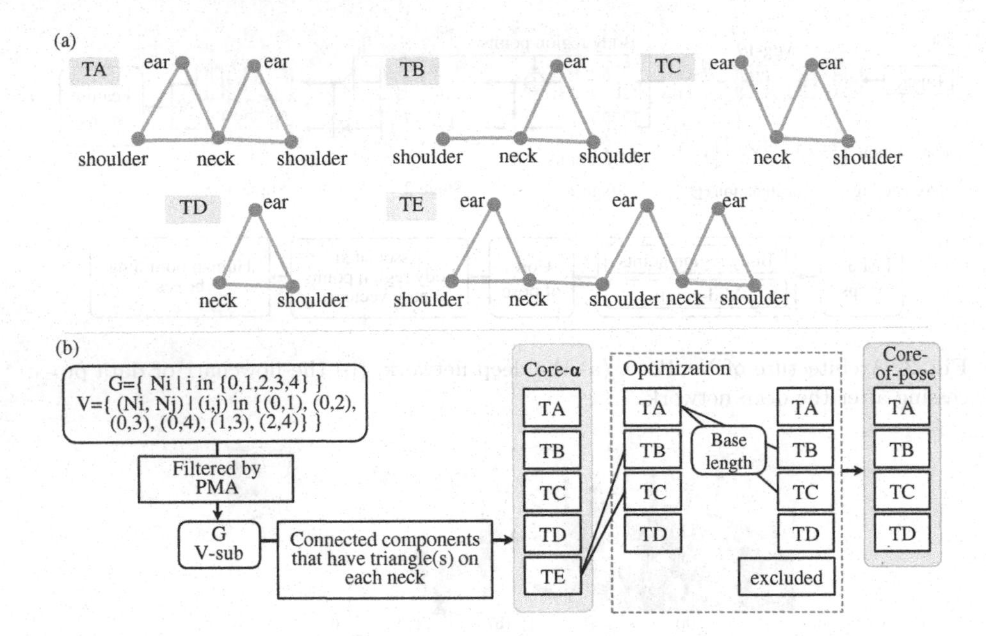

Fig. 5. (a) The four types of core-of-pose TA, TB, TC, TD, and one midterm format TE. (b) Algorithm of generating core-of-pose from the detections of neck, shoulder and ear region points.

a type of link is between two kinds of region points RX and RY, the PMA first accepts only the shortest link for each of RX among its multiple links and removes all other links. Then for each of RY, PMA also accepts the shortest link from its remaining links and removes other links. After performing PMA, the graph G with the filtered links (V-sub) will contain a plurality of connected components. Among all connected components, those which include at least one triangle according to each neck point are accepted and called core-α. TA, as well as TB, TC, TD and TE, are the only five possible types of core-α.

Core-α is not the completed format of core-of-pose. Two steps of optimization are performed on core-α. (Step 1) TE is converted to TB and TC by excluding the link in the middle of the path between two neck points. By doing this, all core-α are aligned with having one neck point. (Step 2) A base length for each core-α is calculated:

$$L_a = \begin{cases} min(|(N_0, N_1)|, |(N_0, N_2)|) & (N_1 \text{ and } N_2 \text{ exist}) \\ |(N_0, N_1)| & (N_2 \text{ does not exist}) \\ |(N_0, N_2)| & (N_1 \text{ does not exist}) \end{cases}$$

$$L_b = \begin{cases} min(|(N_0, N_3)|, |(N_0, N_4)|) & (N_3 \text{ and } N_4 \text{ exist}) \\ |(N_0, N_3)| & (N_4 \text{ does not exist}) \\ |(N_0, N_4)| & (N_3 \text{ does not exist}) \end{cases}$$

$$L_c = \begin{cases} min(|(N_0, M_0)|, |(N_0, M_1)|) & (M_0 \text{ and } M_1 \text{ exist}) \\ |(N_0, M_0)| & (M_1 \text{ does not exist}) \\ |(N_0, M_1)| & (M_0 \text{ does not exist}) \\ L_a + L_b + 1 & (M_0 \text{ and } M_1 \text{ do not exist}) \end{cases}$$

Among multiple detections of M_0 and M_1, we used the closest ones to N_0 for calculating L_c.

$$Base\ length = \begin{cases} L_c & (L_c \leq L_a + L_b, L_b \leq L_a \times 2) \\ L_c \times 1.17 & (L_c \leq L_a + L_b, L_b > L_a \times 2) \\ L_a + L_b & (L_c > L_a + L_b, L_b \leq L_a \times 2) \\ L_b \times 1.7 & (L_c > L_a + L_b, L_b > L_a \times 2) \end{cases}$$

1.17 and 1.7 are fixed referring to $1/\sin 60°$ and $\tan 60°$, assuming that in the core-of-pose of a front-view person, each triangle is an equilateral triangle.

The base length is used to exclude some region points and links in core-α. In a core-α, when the distance between a region point R and the neck point N is over the base length of the current core-α, point R as well as any link associated to it will be excluded from the current core-α. With such process, some of TA will be converted to TB or TC, and some of TB, TC and TD will lose their triangle. Those core-α without a triangle will be excluded and not be used anymore. Throughout two steps of optimization, a plurality of core-of-pose are obtained. We assume that all body region points included in the same core-of-pose are located on the same person.

2.3 Generating Pose Vectors and Human Bounding Boxes

Having core-of-pose, the next step is to associate other types of body region point detected in the image to each core. The association follows an order described in Table 1. Each step of association shares the same algorithm as shown in Fig. 6. Taking the "right shoulder-right elbow" link as an example, PX in Fig. 6 corresponds to right shoulder which is already associated (in core-of-pose), and PY represents right elbow which is to be associated. The algorithm first generates full mapping links between all associated region points of right shoulder and all detected region points of right elbow. The full mapping links are then filtered by two criteria. (i) Length of link should be no more than the allowable maximum length of the current type of link. The allowable maximum length is related to the base length calculated from core-of-pose, and varies according to each type of link (Table 1). The varied length according to type of link is determined based on human's body context [9]. (ii) A mid-point with its type corresponding to the link should be detected in a middle area of the link. As shown in Fig. 7, the middle area is an ellipse area centered on a mid-point M' between two region points N_i and N_j. In this research, R_{major} of the middle area is set to $|(N_i, N_j)| \times 0.35$, and the R_{minor} is set to $R_{major} \times 0.75$. The algorithm excludes the links in which no mid-point exists in the middle area. Note that for those links located on the head, filtering by mid-point is not required. After filtering the links by maximum length and mid-point, the pairwise matching algorithm is performed to optimize the association. As a result, the region points of right elbow on the remaining links are accepted and associated to the right shoulders.

Following the order of region points' association described in Table 1, the full association is completed after hands, feet and eyes are associated to core-of-pose. In case that some types of region point are not detected or not satisfying the proposed criteria, the full association may not be completed. Figure 8 shows some examples of multi-person pose estimation using NeoPose. For each person, body region points, mid-points and core-of-pose are rendered on the image. Having estimated the pose, the human bounding box could be created by enclosing all the region points of a person.

Table 1. Rules for association of body region points based on core-of-pose

Order	Association	Requiring mid-point	Maximum length
1	Shoulder and elbow	Yes	1.5 × base length
2	Elbow and wrist	Yes	1.5 × base length
3	Shoulder and hip	Yes	2.0 × base length
4	Hip and knee	Yes	2.0 × base length
5	Knee and ankle	Yes	2.0 × base length
6	Neck and nose	No	1.0 × base length
7	Nose and eye	No	0.5 × base length

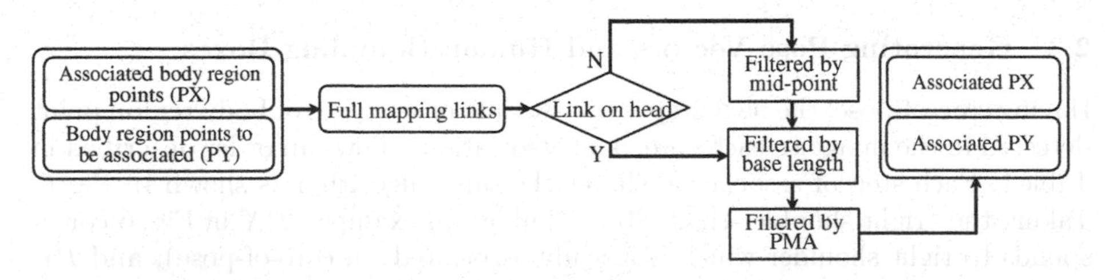

Fig. 6. Algorithm of associating two types of body region point which are physically connected on human body. (e.g. PX is right shoulder and PY is right hip)

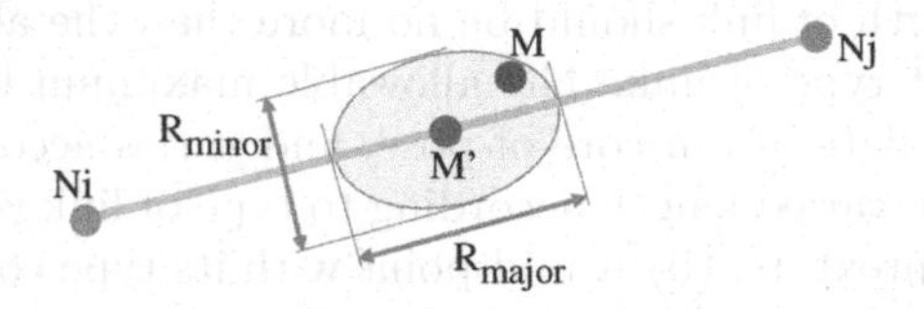

Fig. 7. Mid-point and the middle area. M': ground-truth of mid-point. M: detected mid-point. N_i and N_j: two body region points.

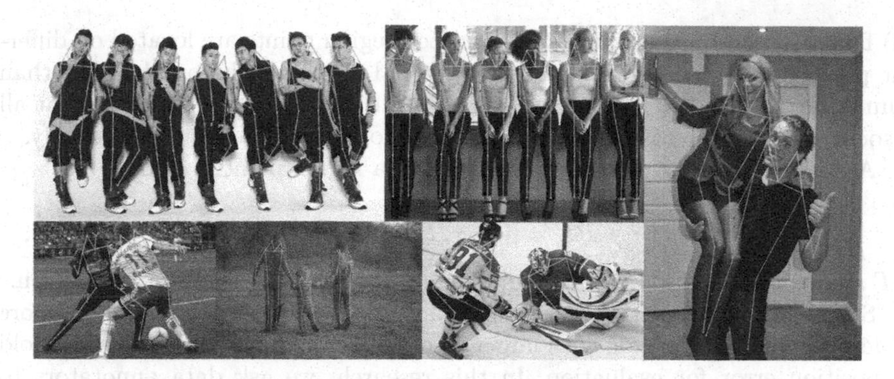

Fig. 8. Multi-person pose estimation by NeoPose on images in MHP dataset [11]. Body region points, mid-points and core-of-pose are rendered for each person.

Fig. 9. Three categories of human detection: (left) correct association, (middle) false association, (right) ghost association.

3 Evaluation

To evaluate the quality of NeoPose's human detection function, we performed a quantitative analysis on MHP dataset [11]. MHP dataset contains many cases of dense people in the images, and a variety of different poses in real-life scenes. Its original mission is for testing human parsing algorithms. We considered that MHP is a good dataset to simulate the situation of crowded people in real-world surveillance. What's more, before evaluation, we resized all images in the dataset to a fixed height (120 pixels) without changing the aspect ratio, and used the resized images as input to NeoPose's deep network. By doing this, we simulated the situation of analyzing low resolution images.

We used NeoPose to perform pose estimation on all images in MHP dataset (merging training set with validation set). Figure 8 shows some images in MHP dataset rendered with estimated poses. To evaluate human detection function, we extracted those estimated pose vectors which have at least 10 body region points associated (including the region points in core-of-pose), rendered the region points on the image with color according to different type, and extracted the person's image along with his/her bounding box. We asked two data annotators to manually check those extracted images and classify them into three categories as shown in Fig. 9: (i) correct association, which means all associated region points are located on one person's body without an obvious position error,

(ii) false association, which means associated region points are located on different persons, or some region points are located on the background rather than human body, and (iii) ghost association, which stands for the situation that all associated region points are located on background rather than human body.

Assuming that the position error (PE) of a region point is defined like:

$$PE = |(P_{DT}, P_{GT})|/Hp$$

DT stands for detection and GT for ground-truth. Hp is height of the person.

Since the fluctuation of PE on person with low resolution would be more violent than that on person with larger resolution, it is difficult to fix a threshold of position error for evaluation. In this research, we ask data annotators to manually judge whether the body region points are correctly located or not.

We also performed the same evaluation using state-of-art algorithms including OpenPose, Art-Track [10] and Associative Embedding (AE) [15] under the same criteria. Based on the results of three categories, we computed precision and recall for each algorithm. For NeoPose and OpenPose, we also compared the system's processing speed on MHP since they were implemented under the same framework (assuming OpenPose's speed is 1). Table 2 summarizes the results. The results suggests that OpenPose and Art-Track's precisions are close to NeoPose (difference within 1%). However, NeoPose's recall is much higher than OpenPose and Art-Track. On the other hand, AE and NeoPose's recalls are on the same level (with a 0.7% difference), but AE's precision is 2.4% less than NeoPose. Overall, NeoPose performs the best in the evaluation.

Table 2. Results of human detection on MHP dataset using different algorithms

	GT	Correct	False	Ghost	Precision	Recall	Speed
OpenPose	12319	8762	1499	5	85.3%	71.1%	1
Art-Track	12319	6878	1190	2	85.2%	55.8%	–
AE	12319	9372	1738	125	83.4%	76.0%	–
NeoPose	12319	9284	1516	9	85.8%	75.3%	1.6

4 Discussion

4.1 Associating Parts Rather Than Detecting the Whole Target

In the evaluation of NeoPose, we focused on how it can succeed in correctly associating more than 10 region points for each individual person. This is a practical way of evaluation especially for industrial use. Taking the task in Fig. 1(left) as an example, when the task is to recognize suspicious persons near two countries' border, what is the most important is to confirm that the target recognized is indeed a person. With low resolution of person in the image and a complex environment around the person, human detection directly using a human detector often fails because of the existence of animals, the texture of ground, or even the shaking trees. For such tasks, to first recognize parts of human body as a plurality of distributed evidence, and to check whether they could be associated together, helps in generating more reliable detection result.

4.2 Training Mid-Points

In the deep network of NeoPose, mid-points use the shared features from body region points, which include information of both appearance and location in the image. Considering that the appearance of a mid-point may not have significant difference compared to its nearby points, we assume that the location information of body region points is the dominant factor learnt by the network for inference of mid-points. Such theory of training might have extensions on machine learning of human-object/human-human interaction.

4.3 Triangles in Core-of-Pose

The process of generating core-of-pose contains a criterion that at least one triangle corresponding to the region point of neck should exist. Since each link in the triangle is obtained by performing pairwise matching algorithm that scans all the links of that type in the image, a triangle could thereby suggest that each pair of the three region points are spatially close to each other. Based on such strong spatial correlation, we could assume that the three region points are located on a same person, and use such spatial correlation to parse multiple persons before associating other body region points.

5 Conclusion and Future Work

In this paper, we introduced the design, field-of-use and evaluation of NeoPose. The design of NeoPose - implementing mid-points and core-of-pose - helps the system deal with the difficulties under real-world surveillance. Firstly, training mid-points reduces the risk of errors compared to training part-affinity-field under low image resolution. Secondly, core-of-pose benefits in two ways: (i) using upper body's information - which is more likely to be captured even under crowded situation - to parse multiple persons, (ii) providing a reference size of each individual person's body, and utilizing the size to supplement the association of body region points. These features of NeoPose provide good directions in designing systems for pose estimation and human detection under real-world surveillance.

Using pose estimation for human detection is a practical way for industrial problems. In this paper, the evaluation of human detection on MHP dataset attempted to simulate a variety of different poses under low image resolution and crowded situation. The leading results by using NeoPose compared to other state-of-art methods also suggests that NeoPose has potential industrial use. Currently the use of NeoPose is limited to general road surveillance cameras which are not 360-degree vision or drone-based.

Future work is to test the system in a wide scope of industrial issues depending on customers' need, such as recognizing suspicious person/behavior in public spaces, sports training, worker's skill assessment on production line, animals' behavior analysis on the farm, etc.

Appendix: Human Detection and Pose Estimation on Industrial Scene

As an early result of future work, we tested NeoPose's performance on the surveillance of a pedestrian crossing(from MOT dataset [14]), and compared it to using OpenPose and a human detector Faster-RCNN. Besides human detection, we compared the quality of pose estimation by using the three algorithms as well. For pose estimation, Faster R-CNN was used together with a pose detector called MS Pose [22]. Such kind of approach that estimates pose based on human detection was implemented in some recent researches [5,8]. For both the tasks, the resolution of the image input to the deep network was (width: 768 pixels, height: 576 pixels), and the height of each person was less than 120 pixel as we did in the evaluation based on MHP dataset.

Figure 10 shows some typical examples of the results. Regarding human detection, there happened a lot in cases of using OpenPose or Faster-RCNN that multiple persons who were in a crowd were recognized as an individual person, or an object that occluded a person was recognized as part of the person (Fig. 10(a)), while such mistakes were much fewer in case of NeoPose. A second issue is that OpenPose generated lots of false detection of region point especially on the ground (Fig. 10(b)). Those false detections would make the association of region points much slower. Another issue in MS Pose is that under crowded situation and with low resolution, many body region points were not correctly located (Fig. 10(b)). Similar issues also happened in other surveillance scenes in MOT dataset. These early results reveal NeoPose's potential in solving both human detection and pose estimation under low resolution and crowded situation.

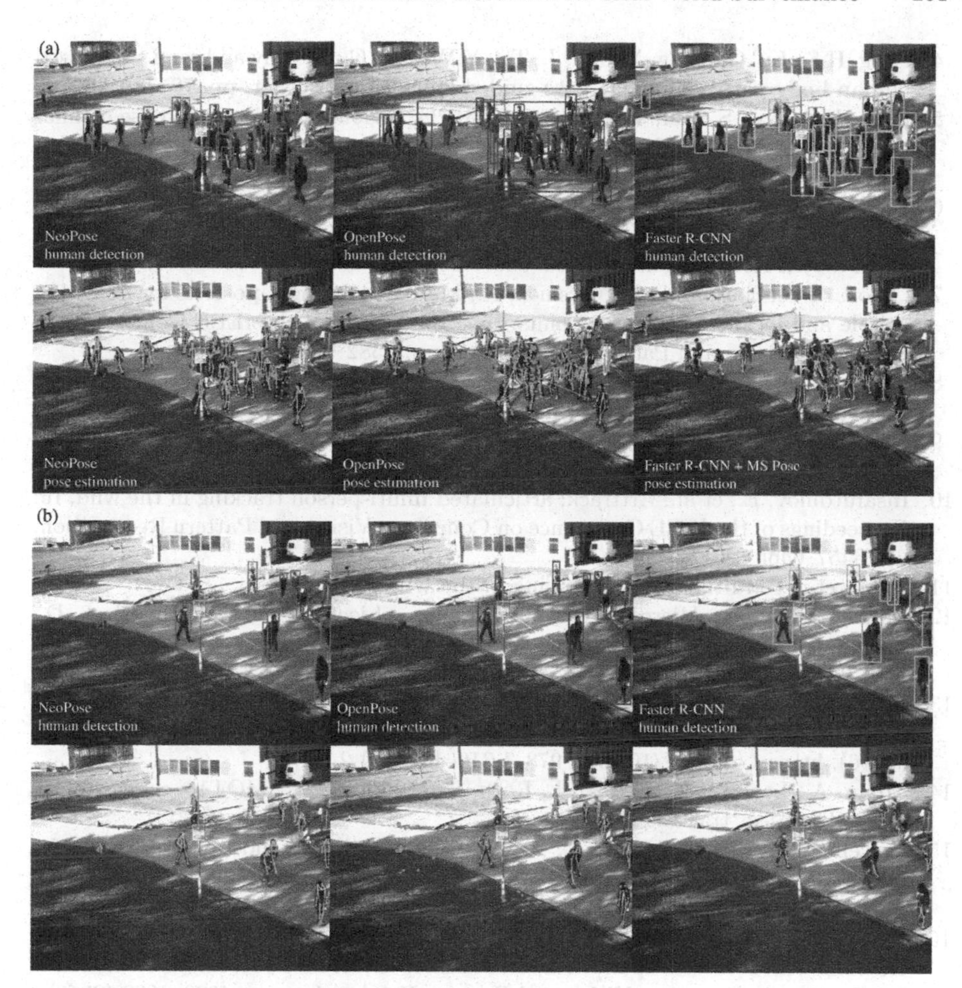

Fig. 10. Comparisons of human detection and pose estimation on surveillance images of a pedestrian crossing (MOT dataset) using different algorithms. (a) and (b) are two representative moments.

References

1. Cao, Z., Simon, T., Wei, S.E., Sheikh, Y.: Realtime multi-person 2D pose estimation using part affinity fields. In: Proceedings of the IEEE Conference on Computer Vision and Pattern Recognition, pp. 7291–7299 (2017)
2. Choutas, V., Weinzaepfel, P., Revaud, J., Schmid, C.: Potion: pose motion representation for action recognition. In: Proceedings of the IEEE Conference on Computer Vision and Pattern Recognition, pp. 7024–7033 (2018)
3. Demisse, G.G., Papadopoulos, K., Aouada, D., Ottersten, B.: Pose encoding for robust skeleton-based action recognition. In: Proceedings of the IEEE Conference on Computer Vision and Pattern Recognition Workshops, pp. 188–194 (2018)

4. Fang, H.S., Lu, G., Fang, X., Xie, J., Tai, Y.W., Lu, C.: Weakly and semi supervised human body part parsing via pose-guided knowledge transfer, pp. 70–78 (2018)
5. Fang, H.S., Xie, S., Tai, Y.W., Lu, C.: RMPE: regional multi-person pose estimation. In: Proceedings of the IEEE International Conference on Computer Vision, pp. 2334–2343 (2017)
6. Gkioxari, G., Girshick, R., Dollár, P., He, K.: Detecting and recognizing human-object interactions. In: Proceedings of the IEEE Conference on Computer Vision and Pattern Recognition, pp. 8359–8367 (2018)
7. Gkioxari, G., Hariharan, B., Girshick, R., Malik, J.: Using k-poselets for detecting people and localizing their keypoints. In: Proceedings of the IEEE Conference on Computer Vision and Pattern Recognition, pp. 3582–3589 (2014)
8. He, K., Gkioxari, G., Dollár, P., Girshick, R.: Mask R-CNN. In: Proceedings of the IEEE International Conference on Computer Vision, pp. 2961–2969 (2017)
9. Herman, I.P.: Physics of the Human Body. BMPBE. Springer, Cham (2016). https://doi.org/10.1007/978-3-319-23932-3
10. Insafutdinov, E., et al.: Arttrack: articulated multi-person tracking in the wild. In: Proceedings of the IEEE Conference on Computer Vision and Pattern Recognition, pp. 6457–6465 (2017)
11. Li, J., et al.: Multiple-human parsing in the wild (2017)
12. Lin, T.-Y., et al.: Microsoft COCO: common objects in context. In: Fleet, D., Pajdla, T., Schiele, B., Tuytelaars, T. (eds.) ECCV 2014. LNCS, vol. 8693, pp. 740–755. Springer, Cham (2014). https://doi.org/10.1007/978-3-319-10602-1_48
13. Liu, W., et al.: SSD: single shot multibox detector. In: Leibe, B., Matas, J., Sebe, N., Welling, M. (eds.) ECCV 2016. LNCS, vol. 9905, pp. 21–37. Springer, Cham (2016). https://doi.org/10.1007/978-3-319-46448-0_2
14. Milan, A., Leal-Taixe, L., Reid, I., Roth, S., Schindler, K.: MOT16: a benchmark for multi-object tracking (2016)
15. Newell, A., Huang, Z., Deng, J.: Associative embedding: end-to-end learning for joint detection and grouping. In: Advances in Neural Information Processing Systems, pp. 2277–2287 (2017)
16. Raaj, Y., Idrees, H., Hidalgo, G., Sheikh, Y.: Efficient online multi-person 2D pose tracking with recurrent spatio-temporal affinity fields. In: Proceedings of the IEEE Conference on Computer Vision and Pattern Recognition, pp. 4620–4628 (2019)
17. Redmon, J., Divvala, S., Girshick, R., Farhadi, A.: You only look once: unified, real-time object detection. In: Proceedings of the IEEE Conference on Computer Vision and Pattern Recognition, pp. 779–788 (2016)
18. Ren, S., He, K., Girshick, R., Sun, J.: Faster R-CNN: towards real-time object detection with region proposal networks. In: Advances in Neural Information Processing Systems, pp. 91–99 (2015)
19. Simonyan, K., Zisserman, A.: Very deep convolutional networks for large-scale image recognition. In: International Conference on Learning Representations (2015)
20. Su, C., Li, J., Zhang, S., Xing, J., Gao, W., Tian, Q.: Pose-driven deep convolutional model for person re-identification. In: Proceedings of the IEEE International Conference on Computer Vision, pp. 3960–3969 (2017)
21. Varadarajan, S., Datta, P., Tickoo, O.: A greedy part assignment algorithm for real-time multi-person 2D pose estimation. In: 2018 IEEE Winter Conference on Applications of Computer Vision (WACV), pp. 418–426 (2018)
22. Xiao, B., Wu, H., Wei, Y.: Simple baselines for human pose estimation and tracking. In: Proceedings of European Conference on Computer Vision (2018)

23. Xiu, Y., Li, J., Wang, H., Fang, Y., Lu, C.: Pose flow: efficient online pose tracking. In: Proceedings of British Machine Vision Conference (2018)
24. Zhou, B., Bau, D., Oliva, A., Torralba, A.: Interpreting deep visual representations via network dissection. IEEE Trans. Pattern Anal. Mach. Intell. **41**(9), 2131–2145 (2019)
25. Zolfaghari, M., Oliveira, G.L., Sedaghat, N., Brox, T.: Chained multi-stream networks exploiting pose, motion, and appearance for action classification and detection. In: Proceedings of the IEEE International Conference on Computer Vision, pp. 2904–2913 (2017)

Gaze from Head: Gaze Estimation Without Observing Eye

Jun'ichi Murakami[(✉)] and Ikuhisa Mitsugami

Hiroshima City University, Hiroshima, Japan
murakami@sys.info.hiroshima-cu.ac.jp, mitsugami@hiroshima-cu.ac.jp
http://www.sys.info.hiroshima-cu.ac.jp

Abstract. We propose a gaze estimation method not from eye observation but from head motion. This proposed method is based on physiological studies about the eye-head coordination, and the gaze direction is estimated from observation of head motion by using the eye-head coordination model trained by preliminarily collected data of gaze direction and head pose sequence. We collected gaze-head datasets of from people who walked around under real and VR environments, constructed the eye-head coordination models from those datasets, and evaluated them quantitatively. In addition, we confirmed that there was no significant difference between the models from the real and VR datasets in their estimation accuracy.

Keywords: Gaze estimation · Eye-head coordination · Virtual realty

1 Introduction

When we observe a person at a distance, we can often predict their gaze direction, regardless of whether their eyes are clearly observed or totally hidden. Thus, we can estimate gaze direction even without observing the eyes directly. Why is it possible? What do we observe in fact to do it?

When a person gazes in a particular direction, they rotate both the head and the eyeballs. Physiological research has revealed several types of coordination between the eyeballs and head. For example, Fang *et al.* reported a significant linear relationship between the rotation angles of the eyeballs and head [1,2]. Besides, in a further study, Okada *et al.* reported that the same relationship is present even while walking [3]. The vestibulo-ocular reflex (VOR) [4] is another well-known type of eye-head coordination. VOR is an unconscious reflex that enables the stabilization of images on the retinas during head movement by producing eye movements in the direction opposite to head movement, maintaining the image at the center of the visual field. During natural vision, we unconsciously control the eyeballs and head using these coordination functions. Thus, implicit knowledge about eye-head coordination may also be unconsciously applied during the estimation of the gaze direction of others, utilizing information about the position of the head.

S. Palaiahnakote et al. (Eds.): ACPR 2019, LNCS 12046, pp. 254–267, 2020.
https://doi.org/10.1007/978-3-030-41404-7_18

There are several existing methods for estimating gaze, which can be categorized into the following two approaches: model-based and appearance-based. The model-based methods use 2-D or 3-D geometric eye models. Studies based on corneal reflection-based methods [5–8] use 3-D models. In addition, several methods have been developed for extracting features, including techniques that extract pupil center or iris edges from 2-D eye images [9–12]. These methods generally require comparatively high-resolution images, and so are not robust for lower resolution images like those captured by commonly used surveillance cameras. On the other hand, appearance-based methods use eye images directly. Compared with the model-based methods, these approaches tend to be more robust at lower resolutions. Early appearance-based methods were based on several assumptions, such as a fixed head position [13–17]. Recently developed methods have less reliance on such assumptions by simultaneously estimating 3D head pose [18–21]. All those methods are based on the measurement or estimation of gaze by observing the eyes. However, the resolution and quality of images captured by commonly-used surveillance methods are insufficient for appearance-based methods to process accurately. Thus, to our knowledge, no previous gaze estimation method is appropriate for use with surveillance images.

In this paper, therefore, we propose a method for estimating gaze not from eye appearance but from head motion because usually the head pose can be estimated more easily than the gaze direction due to a difference in their physical sizes. Such an approach is valid also when the eyes cannot be observed since a person wears glasses or is captured by the camera from his/her back. Moreover, it would be used complementarily even when the eyes can be observed. To realize such a method, we utilize physiological findings; there is an unconscious coordination mechanism between the eye and head motions. The proposed method trains this eye-head coordination by collecting dataset of the eye and head motions and applying machine learning techniques. More concretely, the gaze direction at a particular moment is estimated from the head motion around that moment using the Gradient Boosting Regression [22]. To collect the gaze-head datasets, we constructed two environments; real and VR environments. The real one is a corridor-like space, where a participant wore eye-tracker and repeatedly walked while gazing at several targets. As the VR one, we constructed an eye-tracking VR system that has a participant wearing a VR goggle feel as if he/she was in various scenes. We collected the gaze and head motion from multiple participants to construct datasets, and quantitatively evaluated the gaze estimation accuracy using the datasets and the proposed method. The experimental results revealed that the eye-head coordination actually existed and the proposed method relying on the coordination was effective for the gaze estimation.

2 Eye-Head Coordination

When a person shifts his/her gaze direction, he/she typically moves the head as well as the eyeballs. Physiological researchers have reported a strong relationship between head and eyeball motions. Thus, in natural behavior, the head and

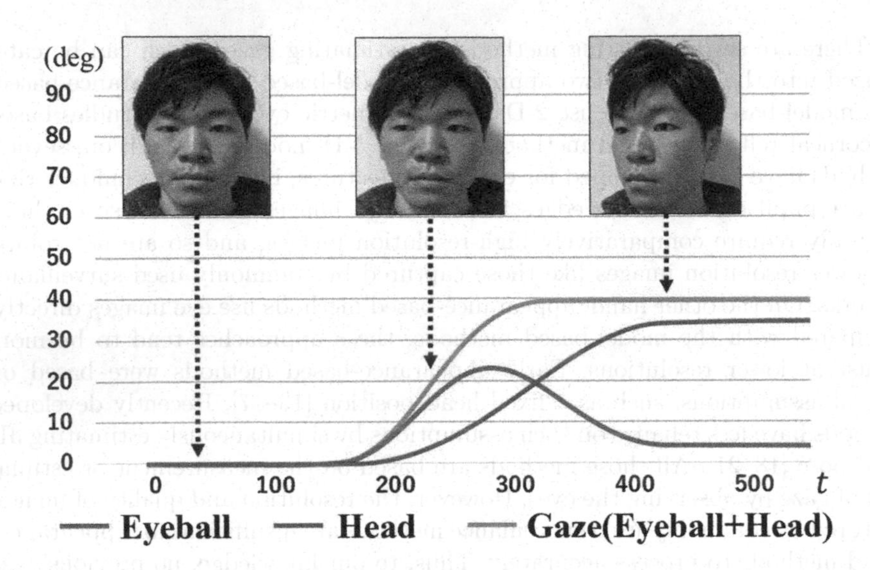

Fig. 1. Eye-head coordination (Color figure online)

eyeballs do not move independently, but in a coordinated way, known as human eye-head coordination [23,24].

Fang *et al.* reported that the rotation angles of the head and eyes exhibited a significant linear relation [1,2]. In a further study, Okada *et al.* reported that the same relationship was present while subjects walked [3].

The vestibulo-ocular reflex (VOR) [4] is another well-known coordination system. VOR is an unconscious reflex that stabilizes images on the retinas during head movement by producing eye movements in the opposite direction to head movement, maintaining the image at the center of the visual field. Figure 1 shows a typical example of VOR. The red and blue curves denote the motion of the eyeball and head, respectively, and the orange curve denotes the gaze direction, which corresponds to the summation of the eyeball and head rotation angles. When a person changes their attention to the right, the eyeballs initially move quickly to the right. This motion (i.e., a saccade) captures an image of the target in the center of the retinas. The head then follows the direction of movement, moving less quickly than the eyeballs. During the head motion to the right, the eyeballs turn to the left for stabilizing images on the retinas. This phenomenon can be seen as a crossing of the red (eyeball) and blue (head) curves in the figure. As a result, the head movement and gaze exhibit sigmoid-like curves.

3 Methods

To estimate gaze from the head movement, we need to define a model that describes the eye-head coordination. While several studies have described such models as control diagrams, however, they are too complicated to deduce a

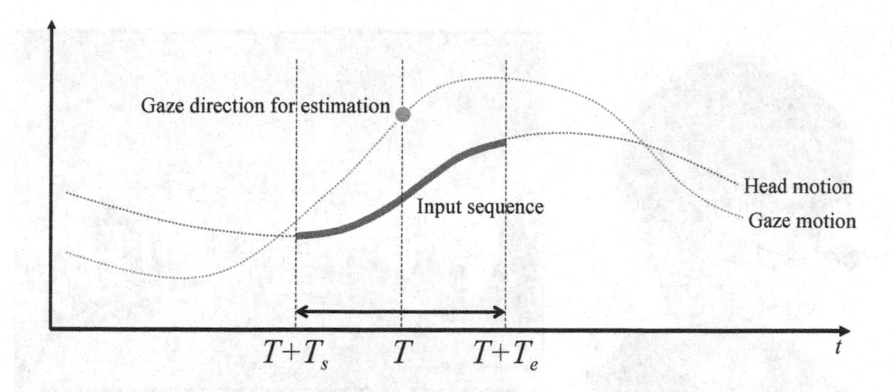

Fig. 2. The proposed method.

formulation analytically or are solely conceptual. Besides, as a fundamental limitation of this approach, even complicated control diagrams cannot cover every possible movement of the eyes and head, because of the high degree of variance within and between participants.

Considering the drawbacks mentioned above of those top-down modeling, it would be more useful to obtain the eye-head coordination using a bottom-up approach that does not rely on examining the mechanisms of the eye-head coordination. The proposed method thus trains the coordination as the relationship between gaze direction at a particular moment T and a sequence of head direction $[T + T_s : T + T_e]$ around that moment, as shown in Fig. 2. Gradient Boosting Regression [22] is then applied to construct a model that estimates the gaze direction from the head motion.

4 Datasets

For evaluation of the proposed method, we collected two types of gaze-head datasets.

4.1 Real Dataset

Considering the aim and expected applications of the proposed method, it would be appropriate to evaluate our approach using surveillance images. It is difficult to obtain ground truth information about the gaze direction of a person without an eye-tracking device. However, if a person is wearing an eye-tracker, surveillance images may look unnatural and affect the estimation of head pose. In this paper, therefore, for quantitative evaluation we used a wearable eye-tracker, and head pose was obtained not from surveillance images but using a camera position estimation technique with a head-mounted camera that was part of the eye-tracker (Fig. 3).

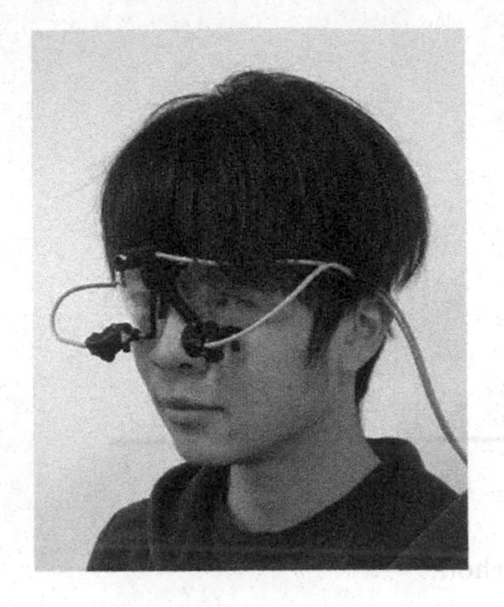

Fig. 3. EMR-9

Fig. 4. Sight of EMR-9 camera.

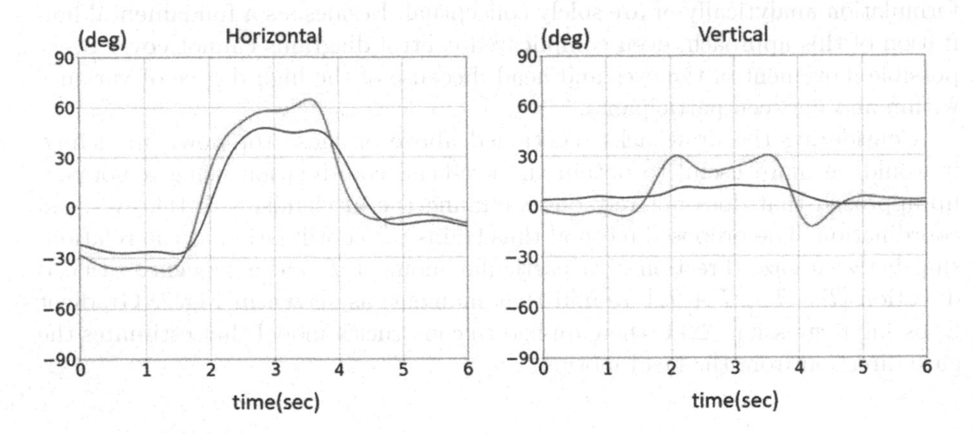

Fig. 5. Real dataset. The black lines denote the measured head motion. The red lines denote the measured gaze. (Color figure online)

We collected data of gaze and head motion from people who walk around under the real environment. We used NAC Inc. EMR-9 eye-tracker [25]. This device is a binocular eye-tracker based on a pupil corneal reflection method [26]. With this system, binocular eye directions are described as points on the image plane of the egocentric camera. Details of calibration for this device have been described by Mitsugami *et al.* [27]. Figure 4 shows an image captured by the camera. Each participant walked back and forth along a straight 8 m corridor, where 60 AR markers were located at various positions and orientations, enabling us to obtain positions and poses of the cameras located anywhere in the environment. There were also several gaze targets, and the participant was asked to repeatedly gaze at each of them in accord with verbal instructions.

Fig. 6. Experimental environment using VR system [28].

The camera positions in the global coordinate system were estimated from captured videos using AR marker-based position estimation. Using the camera position and its intrinsics, we transformed the gaze directions measured by the eye-tracker into the global coordinate system. The gaze/head angles in the global coordinate system were then transformed again into the person coordinate where Z axis denotes their walking direction, which was obtained as a differential of the camera trajectory. The videos had a frame-rate of 30 frames per second.

Figure 5 shows examples of the gaze and head motions captured in this system. We observed the gaze direction changes faster than head movement. We also confirmed that this dataset contained more gaze and head changes in the horizontal direction than in the vertical direction due to the locations of the targets. Using this system, we collected the gaze and head motions from 8 participants.

4.2 VR Dataset

On the other hand, to evaluate our method with more datasets, we collected data of gaze and head motion from people who walk around under the VR environment. We used an eye-tracking VR system that can simultaneously measure gaze direction and head position/poses from a user who experiences 6-DoF VR scenes [28]. As shown in Fig. 6, a participant worn an eye-tracking VR goggle and two controllers. The goggle is connected to a PC, and is calibrated using software offered by its providers. Once the calibration finished, the position and pose of the head, positions of both shoulders, and gaze direction were obtained in the global coordinate system. The gaze and head pose were then transformed again into the person coordinate system where Z axis denotes their chest direction, which was obtained from positions of both shoulders.

We designed user experience so as that we could efficiently construct a large dataset containing frequent gaze shifts and adequately long sequences of gaze behaviors and head motions of many participants in various scenes. For maintaining the scene variation, we implemented three realistic CG scenes, as shown

(a) Library (b) Shop (c) Class Room

Fig. 7. Variation of CG scenes.

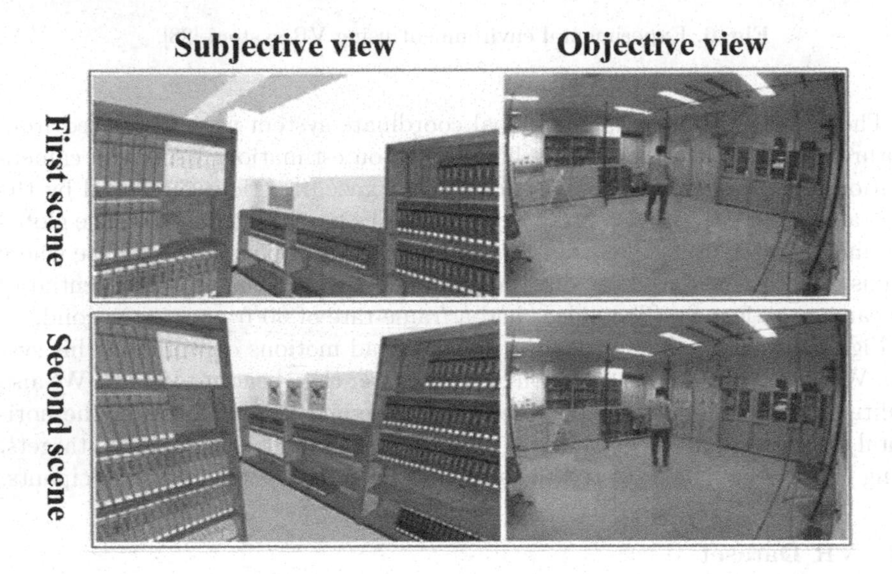

Fig. 8. The spot-the-difference trials.

in Fig. 7, where each participant was able to walk freely within the field of $2\,\mathrm{m}^2$. To collect unconstrained and natural data of the gaze and head motion, we asked each participant to do the spot-the-difference tasks, as shown in Fig. 8. In the first stage, a participant browsed a base scene walking freely to remember the scene for a minute. In the second stage, a participant then browsed the same scene but containing just a difference (e.g., a poster pasted on a wall, or a book eliminated from a bookshelf), and tried to find the difference as quickly as possible. Although his/her chest, head, and gaze directions were measured in both the first scene and the second scene, we used only the first scene data for training and evaluation of the eye-head coordination modeling. This is because, in the case of the second scene, the participant tends to move his/her eyeballs and head faster than usual by the intention to search for a different part quickly, and were

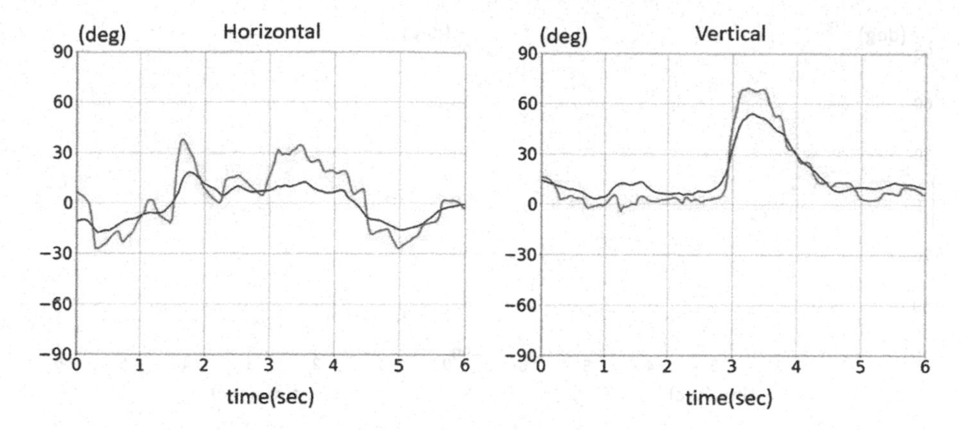

Fig. 9. VR dataset. The black lines denote the measured head motion. The red lines denote the measured gaze. (Color figure online)

considered unsuitable for acquiring natural coordination. The chest, head, and gaze directions were measured with a frame-rate of 90 frames per second (fps) by this system. They were resampled to 30 fps to match the real dataset.

Figure 9 shows examples of the captured gaze-head data in the VR system. In addition, we confirmed that the VR dataset contained data of greater gaze/head direction changes in the vertical direction than the real dataset. Thanks to this system, it is easy to have participants experience various scenes, so that it is easier to increase the number of participants, which is vital to make the coordination model more robust and general. We collected data from 16 participants.

5 Experiment

We constructed the eye-head coordination models by applying the proposed method to the real and VR datasets and evaluated their performances. In this experiment, $T_s = -30$(frame) (i.e., -1(s)) and $T_e = 30$(frame) (i.e., 1(s)).

To confirm the gaze estimation performance of those models, we adopted leave-one-subject-out cross-validation; we selected a participant for testing, and used the other participants for training. We used Gradient Boosting for the regression.

5.1 Qualitative Evaluation

Figure 10 show examples of the gaze estimation using the real and VR datasets; the left and right graphs show the real and VR datasets, respectively. In both graphs, the dotted blue curves (the estimated gaze direction) are close to the red curves (the measured (ground truth) gaze direction).

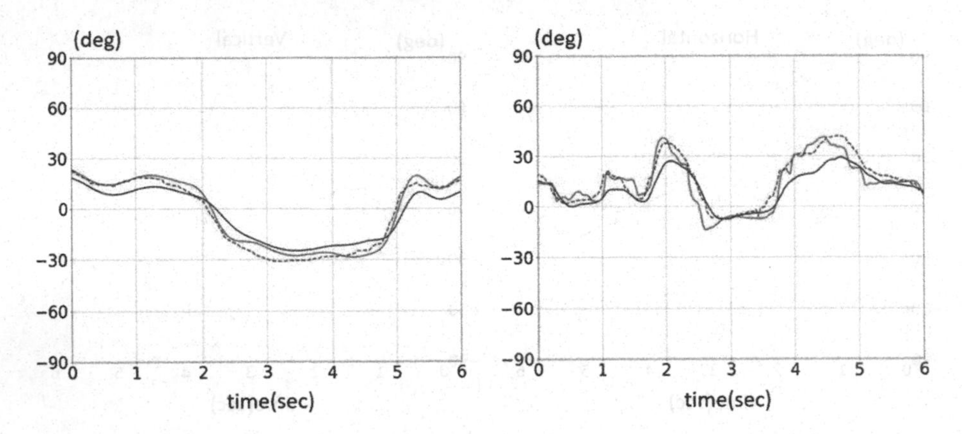

Fig. 10. Examples of the gaze estimation using the real and VR datasets (Left: real, Right: VR). The black lines denote head motion. The dotted blue and red lines denote the estimated gaze and ground truth, respectively. (Color figure online)

5.2 Quantitative Evaluation

To quantitatively evaluate the gaze estimation performance, we adopted leave-one-subject-out cross-validation; we used a participant for testing, and the others for training.

Tables 1 and 2 show the mean absolute error (MAE) of the estimated gaze direction. Tables 1 and 2 show the mean absolute error (MAE) of the estimated gaze direction using only the real and VR datasets, respectively. The MAE values in the table are similar among different people, with no extremely large or small values. Thus, it was not necessary to adjust parameters for each person, enabling us to use a consistent trained model. Our method was thus able to estimate gaze direction across different people, which is a favorable characteristic considering the use in real-world surveillance applications.

Table 1. The performance of model using the real dataset.

ID	MAE (deg)	
	Horizontal	Vertical
01	8.0	8.2
02	6.5	6.6
03	7.4	8.6
04	8.7	8.6
05	6.9	6.9
06	7.6	7.9
07	8.3	8.0
08	6.4	6.4
Average	7.5	7.7

Table 2. The performance of model using the VR dataset.

ID	MAE (deg)	
	Horizontal	Vertical
09	7.8	6.6
10	8.0	6.9
11	9.8	7.9
12	8.3	8.6
13	8.5	7.7
14	10.0	8.9
15	8.1	6.7
16	7.7	6.8
17	8.2	7.3
18	7.7	7.6
19	8.4	7.5
20	7.5	5.2
21	7.3	6.5
22	9.1	7.6
23	7.6	9.8
24	8.1	7.5
Average	8.3	7.4

In addition, for evaluating the effectiveness of the proposed method, Tables 3 and 4 show the performance of the case in which head direction was simply regarded as the estimated gaze direction, referred to as the "baseline" method. As shown in both tables, the proposed method outperformed the baseline.

Table 3. Quantitative evaluation: the model using the real dataset.

Methods	MAE (deg)	
	Horizontal	Vertical
Baseline (Assuming gaze dir. = head dir.)	9.3	9.2
Proposed (Gradient Boosting Machine)	7.5	7.7

Table 4. Quantitative evaluation: the model using the VR dataset.

Methods	MAE (deg)	
	Horizontal	Vertical
Baseline (Assuming gaze dir. = head dir.)	9.9	8.9
Proposed (Gradient Boosting Machine)	8.3	7.4

5.3 Compatibility of the Real and VR Datasets

To confirm compatibility between the real and VR datasets, we used different datasets for training and testing; estimating the real data using a model trained by the VR data, and vice versa.

Table 5. The performance of models. Test data was the real dataset and training data was the VR dataset.

ID	MAE (deg)	
	Horizontal	Vertical
01	8.4	11.2
02	6.4	9.8
03	7.4	9.3
04	8.5	8.8
05	7.0	9.7
06	7.3	12.0
07	6.9	5.5
08	6.5	9.9
Average	7.3	9.5

Table 6. The performance of models. Test data was the VR dataset and training data was the real dataset.

ID	MAE (deg)	
	Horizontal	Vertical
09	8.6	9.8
10	8.2	10.2
11	10.1	10.0
12	8.8	10.7
13	9.1	9.0
14	10.0	10.5
15	8.6	10.8
16	8.3	8.4
17	8.8	10.5
18	8.8	9.0
19	9.0	9.4
20	7.8	10.1
21	7.9	10.1
22	9.6	11.1
23	7.9	10.9
24	8.9	11.2
Average	8.8	10.1

Table 7. Comparison of real and VR datasets (horizontal)

		Test data	
		Real	VR
Training data	Real	17.5	18.8
	VR	17.3	18.3

Table 5 shows the results when using the real dataset for testing and the VR dataset for training, and Table 6 vice versa. We confirmed that the errors in the vertical direction are larger than those in Tables 1 and 2. This fact indicates that the coordination models in the vertical direction obtained from the real and VR datasets are not consistent. We consider, however, it is mainly because of the difference in location of the gaze targets; in the real environment the targets were located at similar heights, while in the VR environment the participant saw widely in the horizontal and vertical directions. As for the horizontal direction, on the other hand, there is no large difference between the errors in Tables 1, 2, 5 and 6, which are summarized in Table 7. We then applied the t-test to check whether there was a significant difference between the real and VR datasets. As a result, there was no significant difference ($p > 0.05$).

6 Conclusion

In this paper we proposed a novel approach for gaze estimation from head motion, by exploiting the eye-head coordination function revealed by physiological research. To analyze eye-head coordination, we propose a learning-based method that implicitly learns the eye-head coordination from collected gaze and head trajectories. By experiments using the datasets collected from people who walked around under real and VR environments, we quantitatively confirmed that our approach was effective for gaze estimation. This result indicated that the eye-head coordination actually existed and thus the proposed method relying on the coordination was effective for the gaze estimation. It was also important findings that there was no significant difference between the models from the real and VR datasets in their estimation accuracy.

As future work, we plan to increase the number of participants and variations of scenes/tasks to analyze consistency or differences of the eye-head coordination in order to construct a general coordination model. In addition, we need to find the optimum values for T_s and T_e. It is also an interesting topic to extend consumer VR goggles to those equipped with gaze estimation function. If the gaze information can be obtained in those goggles, it gets possible to subjectively present high-quality scenes by allocating resources preferentially to the scene ahead of his/her gaze direction even in environments with limited graphic resources, as described in [29].

Acknowledgment. This work was supported by JSPS KAKENHI Grant Numbers JP18H03312 and JP19H00635.

References

1. Fang, Y., Emoto, M., Nakashima, R., Matsumiya, K., Kuriki, I., Shioiri, S.: Eye-position distribution depending on head orientation when observing movies on ultrahigh-definition television. ITE Trans. Media Technol. Appl. **3**(2), 149–154 (2015)
2. Fang, Y., Nakashima, R., Matsumiya, K., Kuriki, I., Shioiri, S.: Eye-head coordination for visual cognitive processing. PLoS One **10**(3), e0121035 (2015)
3. Okada, T., Yamazoe, H., Mitsugami, I., Yagi, Y.: Preliminaly analysis of gait changes that correspond to gaze direcions. In: 2013 2nd IAPR Asian Conference on Pattern Recognition, pp. 788–792, November 2013
4. Steen, J.: Vestibulo-ocular reflex (VOR). In: Encyclopedia of Neuroscience, pp. 4224–4228 (2009)
5. Morimoto, C.H., Amir, A., Flickner, M.: Detecting eye position and gaze from a single camera and 2 light sources. In: International Conference on Pattern Recognition, pp. 314–317 (2002)
6. Shih, S.-W., Liu, J.: A novel approach to 3-D gaze tracking using stereo cameras. IEEE Trans. Syst. Man Cybern. Part B: Cybern. **34**(1), 234–245 (2004)
7. Yoo, D.H., Chung, M.J.: A novel non-intrusive eye gaze estimation using cross-ratio under large head motion. Comput. Vis. Image Underst. **98**(1), 25–51 (2005)
8. Hennessey, C., Noureddin, B., Lawrence, P.: A single camera eye-gaze tracking system with free head motion. In: ACM International Symposium on Eye Tracking Research & Applications, pp. 87–94 (2006)
9. Ishikawa, T., Baker, S., Matthews, I., Kanade, T.: Passive driver gaze tracking with active appearance models. In: 11th World Congress on Intelligent Transportation Systems (2004)
10. Chen, J., Ji, Q.: 3D gaze estimation with a single camera without IR illumination. In: International Conference on Pattern Recognition, pp. 1–4 (2008)
11. Yamazoe, H., Utsumi, A., Yonezawa, T., Abe, S.: Remote gaze estimation with a single camera based on facial-feature tracking without special calibration actions. In: ACM International Symposium on Eye Tracking Research & Applications, pp. 245–250 (2008)
12. Valenti, R., Sebe, N., Gevers, T.: Combining head pose and eye location information for gaze estimation. IEEE Trans. Image Process. **21**(2), 802–815 (2012)
13. Baluja, S., Pomerleau, D.: Non-intrusive gaze tracking using artificial neural networks. Technical report, DTIC Document (1994)
14. Tan, K.-H., Kriegman, D.J., Ahuja, N.: Appearance-based eye gaze estimation. In: Winter Conference on Applications of Computer Vision, pp. 191–195 (2002)
15. Williams, O., Blake, A., Cipolla, R.: Sparse and semisupervised visual mapping with the S3GP. In: IEEE Conference on Computer Vision and Pattern Recognition, pp. 230–237 (2006)
16. Sewell, W., Komogortsev, O.: Real-time eye gaze tracking with an unmodified commodity webcam employing a neural network. In: ACM CHI Conference on Human Factors in Computing Systems, pp. 3739–3744 (2010)
17. Lu, F., Sugano, Y., Okabe, T., Sato, Y.: Adaptive linear regression for appearance-based gaze estimation. IEEE Trans. Pattern Anal. Mach. Intell. **36**(10), 2033–2046 (2014)

18. Lu, F., Okabe, T., Sugano, Y., Sato, Y.: Learning gaze biases with head motion for head pose-free gaze estimation. Image Vis. Comput. **32**(3), 169–179 (2014)
19. Zhang, X., Sugano, Y., Fritz, M., Bulling, A.: Appearance-based gaze estimation in the wild. In: IEEE Conference on Computer Vision and Pattern Recognition, pp. 4511–4520 (2015)
20. McMurrough, C.D., Metsis, V., Rich, J., Makedon, F.: An eye tracking dataset for point of gaze detection. In: ACM International Symposium on Eye Tracking Research & Applications, pp. 305–308 (2012)
21. Choi, J., Ahn, B., Parl, J., Kweon, I.S.: Appearance-based gaze estimation using kinect. In: 10th International Conference on Ubiquitous Robots and Ambient Intelligence, pp. 260–261 (2013)
22. Friedman, J.H.: Greedy function approximation: a gradient boosting machine. Ann. Stat. 1189–1232 (2001)
23. Maesako, T., Koike, T.: Measurement of coordination of eye and head movements by sensor of terrestrial magnetism. Japan. J. Physiol. Psychol. Psychophysiol. **11**(2), 69–76 (1993)
24. Jones, G.M., Guitton, D., Berthoz, A.: Changing patterns of eye-head coordination during 6h of optically reversed vision. Exp. Brain Res. **69**(3), 531–544 (1988)
25. Eye Mark Recorder EMR-9, NAC Inc. http://www.nacinc.com/
26. Jian-nan, C., Peng-yi, Z., Si-yi, Z., Chuang, Z., Ying, H.: Key techniques of eye gaze tracking based on pupil corneal reflection. In: Proceedings of the 2009 WRI Global Congress on Intelligent Systems, vol. 02, pp. 133–138 (2009)
27. Mitsugami, I., Ukita, N., Kidode, M.: Estimation of 3D gazed position using view lines. In: 12th International Conference on Image Analysis and Processing (2003)
28. Murakami, J., Mitsugami, I.: VR-based eye and head motion collection for modeling their coordination. In: IEEE 8th Global Conference on Consumer Electronics (2019)
29. Xiao, L., Kaplanyan, A., Fix, A., Chapman, M., Lanman, D.: DeepFocus: learned image synthesis for computational displays. In: ACM SIGGRAPH Asia (2018)

Interaction Recognition Through Body Parts Relation Reasoning

Mauricio Perez(✉), Jun Liu, and Alex C. Kot

Nanyang Technological University, 50 Nanyang Avenue, Singapore 639798, Singapore
{mauricio001,jliu029,eackot}@ntu.edu.sg

Abstract. Person-person mutual action recognition (also referred to as interaction recognition) is an important research branch of human activity analysis. It begins with solutions based on carefully designed local-points and hand-crafted features, and then progresses to deep learning architectures, such as CNNs and LSTMS. These solutions often consist of complicated architectures and mechanisms to embed the relationships between the two persons on the architecture itself, to ensure the interaction patterns can be properly learned. Our contribution with this work is by proposing a more simple yet very powerful architecture, named Interaction Relational Network, which utilizes minimal prior knowledge about the structure of the data. We drive the network to learn to identify how to relate the body parts of the persons interacting, in order to better discriminate among the possible interactions. By breaking down the body parts through the frames as sets of independent joints, and with a few augmentations to our architecture to explicitly extract meaningful extra information from each pair of joints, our solution is able to achieve state-of-the-art performance on the traditional interaction recognition dataset SBU, and also on the mutual actions from the large-scale dataset NTU RGB+D.

Keywords: Action recognition · Pose information · Relational reasoning

1 Introduction

Recognition of human interaction (mutual actions) in videos is an important computer vision task, which can help us to develop solutions for a range of applications, such as surveillance, robotics, human-computer interface, content-based retrieval, and so on. Although there have been lots of works during the past decades [17,22,27], it is still a challenging problem, especially when the videos offer unconventional conditions, such as unusual viewpoints and cluttered background.

A. C. Kot—This research was carried out at the Rapid-Rich Object Search (ROSE) Lab at the Nanyang Technological University, Singapore. The ROSE Lab is supported by the National Research Foundation, Singapore, and the Infocomm Media Development Authority, Singapore.

S. Palaiahnakote et al. (Eds.): ACPR 2019, LNCS 12046, pp. 268–280, 2020.
https://doi.org/10.1007/978-3-030-41404-7_19

Most of the previous works focused on mutual action recognition using RGB videos [1,15,17,25]. These solutions comprise approaches going from hand-crafted local features to data-driven feature extraction [1,4,16,20,28]. Some methods try to implicitly learn the information from the poses of the persons interacting [15,22]. These solutions often operate over the pixel data, making use of manually annotated regions or poselet labels to focus on these specific regions on the frame or to add extra ad-hoc information. However, they fail to explicitly model the relationships between the interacting body parts of the involved persons, crucial information for interaction recognition.

With the development of more advanced capturing devices that can also capture depth and extract pose information from the people in the scene (e.g., Microsoft Kinect [29]), a more accurate and valuable description for the human pose can be directly used by new solutions. Besides, very recently, techniques that can estimate poses from regular RGB videos have improved significantly [2]. This allows us to apply reliable pose-based solutions to mutual action recognition in the RGB videos.

The availability of explicit pose representation of the humans in the videos led to a new branch of interaction recognition techniques focusing on this type of data [7,8,26,27]. These solutions usually involve hand-crafted features and a classification technique that theoretically incorporates the different body-parts' relationships, and then generate a rigid architecture highly dependent on what is believed to be the prior knowledge over the human skeleton structure.

There also exists solutions, using pose information, that target general action recognition [5,12,13,30], i.e. they include actions performed by a single individual as well. Majority of more recent approaches are based on LSTMs and CNNs, usually ad-hoc network architectures, extra regularization or losses, which tries to better model the spatial and temporal dynamics of the poses during the action. Although these works achieve promising results on general actions, they lack means of leveraging the relationship information between the poses of the two persons when dealing with interactions, under-performing in those cases.

Our contribution involves designing a novel architecture, based on the powerful Relational Network (RN) [18], for explicitly reasoning over the relationships present at human interactions. Although simple, RNs proved to be highly efficient at learning what are the important relationships between pair of objects. Santoro et al. [18] proposed RNs as a simple architecture to deal with problems that require relational reasoning, obtaining state-of-the-art performance on tasks such as visual and text-based question answering, as well as understanding the dynamic of physical systems that included motion data. To the best of our knowledge, no one before have developed a solution based on Relational Network with the purpose of interaction recognition, nor with explicit body information.

On this work we propose Interaction Relational Network (IRN), summarized in Fig. 1. This approach consist on initially re-structuring the poses across the video, representing the joints as independent objects, comprising the coordinates from multiple frames for each joint separately. Then we consciously pair up the joints based on what type of relationship do we want our Relation Modules to model.

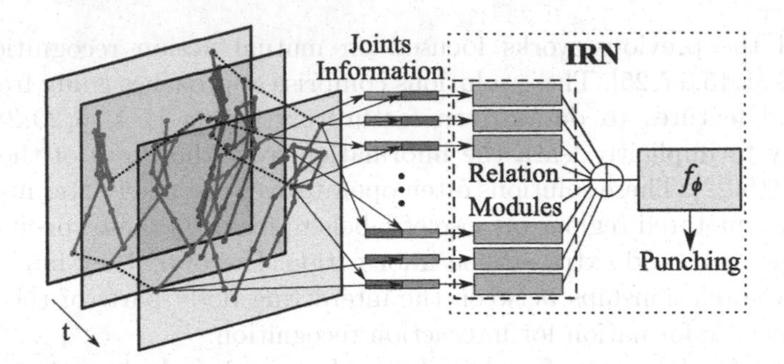

Fig. 1. Overview of the proposed Interaction Relational Network (IRN). Joints of the persons are separately paired up, and then fed to the independent relation modules. The outputs are then aggregated for final human interaction recognition.

For our problem we propose two relationships mapping: one inter-person, pairing the joints from one body to the joints from the other body; and another intra-person, where the joints from the same body are paired up with each other. The Relation Modules from the same relationship mapping share the same weights, and should learn from the data which relations exists between the joints, and which are important for interaction recognition. The description generated from all the Relation Modules will then be pooled and fed to a module, which will learn how to interpret this arrangement of relations, and classify accordingly. We also designed different ways to fuse these two types of relationships defined by us here, leveraging both types of information and therefore leading to a more accurate recognition. We demonstrate the importance of appropriately choosing a fusion architecture, and initializing it with the right models prior to training.

We validate our approach through experiments on a traditional dataset for human interaction recognition: SBU [27]. On which we obtain state-of-the-art performance. Also, for further validating our IRN, we run experiments on a larger-scale dataset: NTU RGB + D [19]. Although this dataset initial purpose is for general human action recognition, it contains many classes with mutual actions, which by itself constitute a substantial subset of interactions samples.

Our contribution can be summarized in the following manner:

- A novel approach to Human Interaction Recognition, using the different body parts from the pose information as independent objects, and modeling their relationship pairwise.
- We evaluate and design effective ways to fuse different types of relationships, leveraging their complementary for an improved performance.
- A new and efficient paradigm for interaction recognition, based on relational networks, as an alternative to the CNN/RNN/GCN architectures that currently dominate the field.

These contributions constitute the novel architecture Interaction Relational Network, which is simple yet effective and efficient. We validate on important datasets that contains human interactions under different conditions, achieving state-of-the-art performance, demonstrating the strength of our technique.

2 Related Work

2.1 Action Recognition

The problem of human interaction recognition is in fact a sub-field from the more general task of action recognition, which also takes into consideration actions performed by a single person. Previous work with methods using solely RGB videos usually rely on spatio-temporal local features description [23] or CNN architectures for processing appearance and motion separately [21,24]. Here we will focus more on the previous work that also used explicit pose information, and have as well evaluated their methods on the SBU interaction dataset.

Most of the latest works using pose information have moved to solutions involving Deep Learning, specially LSTMs [5,12,13,30]. Du et al. [5] designed a hierarchical structure using Bidirectional Recurrent Neural Networks (BRNNs), which initially process the joints separately by body part, then fuses these parts step-by-step at subsequent layers, until whole body is covered. Zhu et al. [30] introduced a regularization in their LSTM to learn the co-occurrence features from the joints – i.e. learn the discriminative joint connections related to human parts. Liu et al. [11] proposed a spatio-temporal LSTM architecture, where the network would unroll not only in the temporal domain, with sequential frames, but also in the spatial, with a pre-defined traversal order of the joints following the human skeleton structure.

Since these works focus on general actions, which mostly are performed by a single person, they do not include in their solutions any approach to model the relationship between the interacting persons when it is a mutual action. Therefore disregarding the additional information coming from the interaction itself, which our experiments demonstrate to be invaluable when dealing with two-person action recognition.

2.2 Human Interaction Recognition

Most of early work on human interaction recognition is based on hand-crafted local features, following a bag-of-words paradigm, and often using SVM for the final classification [15–17,22,28]. More recent and successful approaches rely on Convolutional Neural Networks for feature extraction, usually combining it with Recurrent Neural Networks (e.g., Long-short Term Memory) for more complex temporal reasoning over the interactions [1,4,9,20].

Some of these approaches allegedly focus on pose [15,22], or try to embed human structural knowledge on their solution [9]. Vahdat et al. [22] requires pre-computed person trajectories for their solution, initially they employ a pedestrian detector to obtain bounding boxes around the individuals on the first frame, then subsequently apply a tracker to find the trajectory in the later frames.

These bounding boxes are used to retrieve the input information for their solution: spatial location, time of the pose and the cropped image within this region. On the work of Rapitis et al. [15], the authors have labeled pre-defined poselets on some of the frames. They create templates from these poselets by extracting local-features on the cropped image around these annotations. Based on these poselets features, their max-margin framework would then select key-frames to model an action.

Another branch of works do use explicit pose information with the purpose of interaction recognition [7,8,26,27]. For example Yun et al. [27] proposed features coming from different geometric relations between the joints intra-person and inter-person, as well as intra-frames and inter-frames, then using these features as input to an SVM for classification. Ji et al. [8] grouped joints that belonged to the same body part to create poselets, for describing the interaction of these body parts from both individuals, subsequently generating a dictionary representation from these poselets, which will then be fed to an SVM. Differently from the above mentioned approaches, our proposed architecture does not need the prior knowledge about the skeleton structure – we do not use the edge information on our architecture, and the input is invariant to the joint order – therefore learning the existing and important relationships by itself.

2.3 Relational Network

Relational networks have been recently introduced by Santoro et al. [18], targeting to improve relational reasoning over a different range of tasks. Roughly speaking, it consists of a simple architecture, on which the problem is initially reduced to individual objects, and modeling how do they relate to each other in a pair-wise form, then subsequently using the general view from all the relationships to solve the problem at hand. The authors demonstrated the versatility of these networks by applying their method on three tasks: visual question answering (QA), text-based question answering and complex reasoning about dynamic physical systems. Which covered not only distinct purposes – question-answering and physical modeling – but also different types of input data – visual, textual and spatial state-based.

Expanding RNs to Video QA, Chowdhury et al. [3] proposed Hierarchical Relational Attention. On which the authors connected attention modules over VGG and C3D features to hierarchical relational modules, nested by input question query token. Ibrahim et al. [6] also employed Hierarchical RNs, but this time for group activity recognition. They start from CNN features from each individual, then input these features to hierarchically stacked multiple layers of relational modules, each one with their own parameters and relationships graph, which dictates the pairwise relationships to be made. The graphs are based on domain knowledge of the problem, in their case volleyball games, and goes from initially connecting only those players from the same team and same position (offense or defense), then moving to connecting all the players from the same team, and finally connecting all players in the game. Their results indicates that using domain specialized graphs did not necessarily helped at improving the performance, with their best resulting coming from all-pairwise relationships mapping.

As far as we know, none of the previous work have designed relational networks that use pose information or for the purpose of Human Interaction Recognition, with our work being the first one to extend RNs for this domain and application.

3 Relational Network Overview

The Relational Network proposed by Santoro et al. [18] can be simplified through the following equation:

$$RN(O) = f_\phi \left(\sum_{i,k} g_\theta \left(o_i, o_k \right) \right) \quad (1)$$

Where O is a set of objects $\{o_1, o_2, ..., o_N\}$, on which any i^{th} object is represented by an arbitrary $\mathbb{R}^m$ vector containing the properties of that object. The function g, with learnable parameters θ, is responsible by modeling the relationships for each pair of input objects independently, therefore being also referred to as Relational Module. Meanwhile function f, with trainable parameters ϕ, is in charge for reasoning from the merger of the relationships inferred by g_θ.

It is a versatile formulation, which can have as input different types of data describing the objects – such as CNN/LSTM features or even physical states – and allows simple modifications to accommodate extra input information, or additional relationships types, as long as the objects are fed in pairs to the relational module with shared weights.

4 Interaction Relational Network

We designed an architecture adapted to our problem for processing directly the joints data (coordinates) through a Interaction Relational Network. The power of the relational networks lies on breaking down the problem into separate interacting objects, and learning specific parameters for describing how each object relate to each other, before merging this information for the classification of the whole. In the case of pose information and action recognition, we can define each joint j_i as an object, using as their low-level feature its coordinates along the frames, together with integers to identify to which joint and body part does it belong: $j_i = (x_1, y_1, x_2, y_2, ..., x_T, y_T, i, b)$, where x_t and y_t are the 2D coordinates of the joint i belonging to the body part b at the frame t, and T is the desired sampling of frames to be used. As previous work have done [5,13,19], we considered five body parts: torso, left hand, right hand, left leg, and right leg. Each person p will therefore have a set of joints for each video, which can be defined as: $P_p = \{j_1^p, j_2^p, ..., j_N^p\}$, where N is the total number of

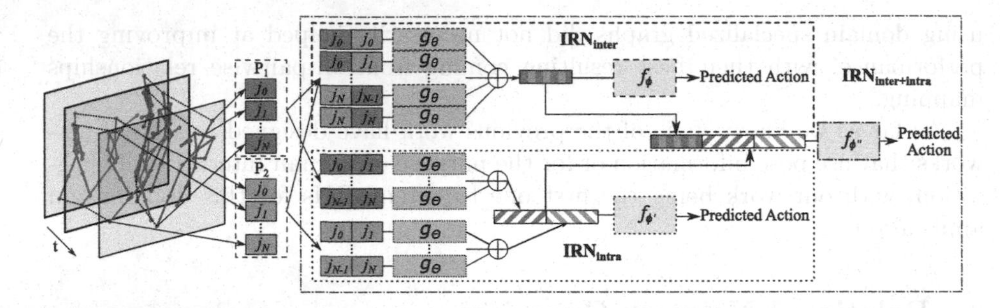

Fig. 2. Illustration of the IRN architecture for human interaction recognition. First, we extract the information across frames from each joint separately (j_n). Then we use the set of joints from both persons (P_p) as input to our different architectures, IRN_{inter} and IRN_{intra}. Each architecture models different relationships between the joints, and can be used independently to predict the action. Furthermore, the models can be fused as $IRN_{inter+intra}$, this way using the knowledge from both types of relationships for a more accurate prediction.

joints provided by the pose data. Figure 2 contains a visual representation of our IRN. For a more informative input to our relational module, we also added to our IRN mechanisms for automatically extracting the distance and motion information [26, 27] of the paired joints, and using this information alongside the raw coordinates j_i and j_k.

Inter-person Relationships. Since we are dealing with interaction recognition, it is desired to map the relation between the joints inter-person. Therefore, all joints from one individual will be paired with all joints from the other individual, bi-directionally, so that it can be order-invariant (in the case of active/passive actions such as kicking). For that purpose, inspired by the formulation (1), we derive the following equation:

$$IRN_{inter}(P_1, P_2) = f_\phi \left(\sum_{i,k} g_\theta \left(j_i^1, j_k^2\right) \oplus \sum_{i,k} g_\theta \left(j_i^2, j_k^1\right) \right) \tag{2}$$

Where f_ϕ and g_θ can be Multi-Layer Perceptrons (MLPs), with learnable parameters ϕ and θ respectively. In theory $\sum$ and $\oplus$ can be any pooling operation, such as sum, max, average or concatenate, but from our experiments, we decided to use average because it gives the best results.

Intra-person Relationships. Since the intra-person relationship of the joints can be highly informative as well, we also propose another architecture, where the joints from each person will be paired with the other joints from the same person. For this case there is no need to pair bi-directionally, since the paired joints are from the same person, what would only add unnecessary redundancy to our model – in fact our preliminary experiments demonstrated that it can lead to overfitting in some cases. The pooled output from each individual is concatenated ($\frown$) before going through function f with trainable parameters ϕ'.

$$IRN_{intra}(P_1, P_2) = f_{\phi'}\left(\sum_{i=1}^{N}\sum_{k=i+1}^{N} g_{\Theta}\left(j_i^1, j_k^1\right) \frown \sum_{i=1}^{N}\sum_{k=i+1}^{N} g_{\Theta}\left(j_i^2, j_k^2\right)\right) \quad (3)$$

Fusing Relations. Conclusively, we propose an architecture that fuses both types of relationships under the same function f (parameters ϕ''), by concatenating the pooled information from each function g, each with its own parameters θ and Θ:

$$\begin{aligned} &IRN_{inter+intra}(P_1, P_2) = \\ &f_{\phi''}\left(\sum_{i,k} g_{\theta}\left(j_i^1, j_k^2\right) \oplus \sum_{i,k} g_{\theta}\left(j_i^2, j_k^1\right) \frown \right. \\ &\left. \sum_{i=1}^{N}\sum_{k=i+1}^{N} g_{\Theta}\left(j_i^1, j_k^1\right) \frown \sum_{i=1}^{N}\sum_{k=i+1}^{N} g_{\Theta}\left(j_i^2, j_k^2\right)\right) \quad (4) \end{aligned}$$

5 Experiments

5.1 Datasets

SBU [27] is a dataset for two-person interaction recognition, created using Kinect, providing reliable RGBD data for each video. It consists of eight interactions (approaching, departing, pushing, kicking, punching, exchanging objects, hugging, and shaking hands), seven different participants (pairing up to 21 different permutations), on a total of 282 short videos – around 2–3 s each, with a frame rate of 15 frames per second (FPS). Recording was done in a single laboratory environment. Pose information is provided by means of 3D coordinates over 15 joints per person, at each frame. Coordinates are not entirely accurate, containing noise and incorrect tracking at some cases. We followed the 5-fold cross validation protocol defined by the authors, reporting the average accuracy.

NTU RGB+D [19] is a dataset with a wide range of actions, and it is the largest available dataset for human action recognition with RGBD data. It is not a dataset exclusively for interaction recognition, however it contains 11 classes of mutual actions (punch/slap, pat on the back, giving something, walking towards, kicking, point finger, touch pocket, walking apart, pushing, hugging, handshaking), more than SBU. Moreover, this subset with interaction-only classes, contains a total of 10,347 videos, which were collected with the more precise Kinect (V2) and under more challenging conditions, with 40 different subjects and large variation in viewpoints, by using three cameras recording the same action. The length of the videos range from 1 to 7 seconds, with a frame rate of 30 FPS. The dataset contains the 3D coordinates from 25 joints per person for all frames. For evaluation, the authors proposed two protocols: Cross Subject (CS), on which 20 pre-defined actors are used for training, and the remaining for testing; and Cross View (CV), where two-cameras are reserved for training, and the third one for testing. Because of these characteristics (large scale and more challenging conditions), although this is not a dataset specifically for Human Interaction Recognition, we believe that experimenting over this dataset mutual-only classes can be highly valuable at validating our methods.

5.2 Implementation Details

MLPs Configuration. Hyperparameters detailed here were tuned during preliminary experiments. The IRN is implemented as an MLP, where g_θ consists of four fully-connected layers, the first three with 1000 units and the last with 500. Meanwhile, f_ϕ contains a dropout layer for the input (dropout rate of 0.10 for IRN_{inter} and 0.25 for IRN_{intra} and $IRN_{inter+intra}$), followed by three fully-connected layers with 500, 100 and 100 units respectively, connected to a softmax layer to perform the video classification. Training was performed with Adam optimizer, learning rate value of 1e-4 and weight initialization following a truncated normal distribution with zero mean and 0.045 standard deviation.

Training Procedure. To improve generalization during training, we randomly swap the input order between the persons' joints set ($P_1 \rightleftharpoons P_2$), this was significantly beneficial for the IRN_{intra} architecture to avoid bias on the order of the concatenated feature generated after g_Θ. $IRN_{inter+intra}$ parameters θ and Θ are fine-tuned from the weights obtained previously by training IRN_{inter} and IRN_{intra} separately, meanwhile ϕ is randomly initialized.

Joints and Frames Subsampling. Although the poses for NTU RGB+D contains 25 joints, we sampled only 15 of them, analogous to what is provided by SBU data. As for the parameter T, regarding the frame sampling, we used different values for each dataset. For SBU, since the videos are shorter and the frame-rate is lower (15 FPS), we used the central 10 consecutive frames as a sampling for our input feature. Considering NTU RGB+D have longer videos and higher frame-rate (30 FPS), we first sample half of the frames, in an alternately fashion, then we sample the central 32 frames. This gives a higher temporal range to our input. We have chosen to sample the central frames because most likely they contain the more relevant parts of the interaction.

5.3 Experimental Results

To better evaluate the impact of each part from our proposed methodology, we first discuss our results at the SBU dataset, reported in Table 1.

Table 1. Comparison of our results with previous work on SBU.

Method	Acc
Yun et al. [27]	80.3%
Ji et al. [8]	86.9%
HBRNN [5] (reported by [30])	80.4%
CHARM [10]	83.9%
CFDM [7]	89.4%
Co-occurrence LSTM [30]	90.4%
Deep LSTM (reported by [30])	86.0%
ST-LSTM [12]	93.3%
Wu et al. [26]	91.0%
Two-stream GCA-LSTM [13]	94.9%
IRN_{inter}	93.6%
IRN_{intra}	95.8%
Averaging scores	94.3%
Random-$IRN_{inter+intra}$	92.5%
$IRN_{inter+intra}$	**96.1%**

Our baseline architectures, IRN_{inter} and IRN_{intra}, already obtained 93.6% and 95.8% of accuracy respectively, demonstrating that our approach was able to successfully map the different types of relationships present in the problem of interaction recognition. Attempting to fuse our two different models, we show that only averaging the scores obtained by each part does not work, with a performance lower than using only IRN_{intra}. On the other hand, our approach fusing the models into a single architecture ($IRN_{inter+intra}$) managed to better correlate the distinct type of relationships, leading to a slightly improvement in performance. However, only when fine-tuned starting from the models pre-trained separately, as demonstrated by our experiment with random initialization of weights (Random-$IRN_{inter+intra}$), which performed worst than any of the models separately.

SBU. Now comparing our best results for SBU dataset in Table 1 with previous works results, it can be seen that our approach, $IRN_{inter+intra}$, obtained significantly better accuracy than previous work. It is paramount to highlight that the input of our approach is currently bound to a fixed number of sampled frames – we used only 10 for SBU. On the other hand, most of the other approaches can make use from all the frames in the videos. Therefore, using more information than our solution.

NTU RGB+D. Our experiments over the interaction classes of this dataset are present at Table 2. Differently than with SBU dataset, our IRN_{inter} architecture had superior performance than IRN_{intra}, and with a significant contrast: 3–4%

more. This might have happened because of the scale of the dataset, or because of the nature of the extra interaction classes it has (e.g., pat on the back, touch pocket, etc). Nonetheless, fusing the architectures is still beneficial, specially for the more challenging protocol of Cross Subject. The $IRN_{inter+intra}$ fusion architecture is able to outperform previous works on both protocols.

Table 2. Results from our proposed methods on the subset of NTU RGB+D dataset, containing only the mutual action classes.

Method	Mutual actions	
	CS	CV
ST-LSTM [11]	83.0%	87.3%
GCA-LSTM [14]	85.9%	89.0%
IRN_{inter}	84.7%	90.8%
IRN_{intra}	80.2%	87.8%
$IRN_{inter+intra}$	85.4%	91.0%

6 Conclusion

Through the proposal of the novel Interaction Relational Network in this work, we demonstrated the high value of this type of architecture for two-person action recognition, using pose information to reason about the different body-parts relationships during the action. Our solution obtained state-of-the-art performance on the traditional interaction dataset SBU, and it also obtained the highest performance on the NTU RGB+D dataset subset with mutual actions only. Moreover this approach can be improved through different means. For example by finding a way to feed the IRN with all the frames from videos with different lengths, not only a fixed number of the central frames. It is also likely that providing the IRN with an higher-level information could also improve the results, such as a features coming from an LSTM or Graph Convolutional based solution.

References

1. Aliakbarian, M.S., Saleh, F.S., Salzmann, M., Fernando, B., Petersson, L., Andersson, L.: Encouraging LSTMs to anticipate actions very early. In: IEEE International Conference on Computer Vision (ICCV), pp. 280–289 (2017)
2. Cao, Z., Simon, T., Wei, S.E., Sheikh, Y.: OpenPose: realtime multi-person 2D pose estimation using part affinity fields, pp. 1–14. arXiv preprint arXiv:1812.08008 (2018)
3. Chowdhury, M.I.H., Nguyen, K., Sridharan, S., Fookes, C.: Hierarchical relational attention for video question answering. In: IEEE International Conference on Image Processing (ICIP), pp. 599–603 (2018)

4. Donahue, J., et al.: Long-term recurrent convolutional networks for visual recognition and description. In: IEEE Conference on Computer Vision and Pattern Recognition (CVPR), pp. 2625–2634 (2015)
5. Du, Y., Wang, W., Wang, L.: Hierarchical recurrent neural network for skeleton based action recognition. In: IEEE Conference on Computer Vision and Pattern Recognition (CVPR), pp. 1110–1118 (2015)
6. Ibrahim, M.S., Mori, G.: Hierarchical relational networks for group activity recognition and retrieval. In: Springer European Conference on Computer Vision (ECCV), pp. 721–736 (2018)
7. Ji, Y., Cheng, H., Zheng, Y., Li, H.: Learning contrastive feature distribution model for interaction recognition. J. Vis. Commun. Image Represent. **33**, 340–349 (2015)
8. Ji, Y., Ye, G., Cheng, H.: Interactive body part contrast mining for human interaction recognition. In: IEEE International Conference on Multimedia and Expo Workshops (ICMEW), pp. 1–6 (2014)
9. Ke, Q., Bennamoun, M., An, S., Sohel, F., Boussaid, F.: Leveraging structural context models and ranking score fusion for human interaction prediction. IEEE Trans. Multimedia (TMM) **20**(7), 1712–1723 (2018)
10. Li, W., Wen, L., Chuah, M.C., Lyu, S.: Category-blind human action recognition: a practical recognition system. In: IEEE International Conference on Computer Vision (ICCV), pp. 4444–4452, December 2015
11. Liu, J., Shahroudy, A., Xu, D., Kot, A.C., Wang, G.: Skeleton-based action recognition using spatio-temporal LSTM network with trust gates. IEEE Trans. Pattern Anal. Mach. Intell. **40**(12), 3007–3021 (2018)
12. Liu, J., Shahroudy, A., Xu, D., Wang, G.: Spatio-temporal LSTM with trust gates for 3D human action recognition. In: Leibe, B., Matas, J., Sebe, N., Welling, M. (eds.) ECCV 2016. LNCS, vol. 9907, pp. 816–833. Springer, Cham (2016). https://doi.org/10.1007/978-3-319-46487-9_50
13. Liu, J., Wang, G., Duan, L.Y., Abdiyeva, K., Kot, A.C.: Skeleton-based human action recognition with global context-aware attention LSTM networks. IEEE Trans. Image Process. (TIP) **27**(4), 1586–1599 (2018)
14. Liu, J., Wang, G., Duan, L.Y., Hu, P., Kot, A.C.: Global context-aware attention LSTM networks for 3D action recognition. In: IEEE Conference on Computer Vision and Pattern Recognition (CVPR), pp. 1647–1656 (2017)
15. Raptis, M., Sigal, L.: Poselet key-framing: a model for human activity recognition. In: IEEE Conference on Computer Vision and Pattern Recognition (CVPR), pp. 2650–2657 (2013)
16. Ryoo, M.S.: Human activity prediction: early recognition of ongoing activities from streaming video. In: IEEE International Conference on Computer Vision (ICCV), pp. 1036–1043 (2011)
17. Ryoo, M.S., Aggarwal, J.K.: Spatio-temporal relationship match : video structure comparison for recognition of complex human activities. In: IEEE International Conference on Computer Vision (ICCV), pp. 1593–1600 (2009)
18. Santoro, A., et al.: A simple neural network module for relational reasoning. In: Advances in Neural Information Processing Systems (NIPS), pp. 4967–4976 (2017)
19. Shahroudy, A., Liu, J., Ng, T.T., Wang, G.: NTU RGB+D: a large scale dataset for 3D human activity analysis. In: IEEE Conference on Computer Vision and Pattern Recognition (CVPR), pp. 1010–1019 (2016)
20. Shi, Y., Fernando, B., Hartley, R.: Action anticipation with RBF kernelized feature mapping RNN. In: Ferrari, V., Hebert, M., Sminchisescu, C., Weiss, Y. (eds.) ECCV 2018. LNCS, vol. 11214, pp. 305–322. Springer, Cham (2018). https://doi.org/10.1007/978-3-030-01249-6_19

21. Simonyan, K., Zisserman, A.: Two-stream convolutional networks for action recognition in videos. In: Advances in Neural Information Processing Systems (NIPS), pp. 568–576 (2014)
22. Vahdat, A., Gao, B., Ranjbar, M., Mori, G.: A discriminative key pose sequence model for recognizing human interactions. In: IEEE International Conference on Computer Vision, pp. 1729–1736 (2011)
23. Wang, H., Schmid, C.: Action recognition with improved trajectories. In: IEEE International Conference on Computer Vision (ICCV), pp. 3551–3558 (2013)
24. Wang, L., et al.: Temporal segment networks: towards good practices for deep action recognition. In: Leibe, B., Matas, J., Sebe, N., Welling, M. (eds.) ECCV 2016. LNCS, vol. 9912, pp. 20–36. Springer, Cham (2016). https://doi.org/10.1007/978-3-319-46484-8_2
25. Wang, X., Ji, Q.: Hierarchical context modeling for video event recognition. IEEE Trans. Pattern Anal. Mach. Intell. (TPAMI) **39**(9), 1770–1782 (2017)
26. Wu, H., Shao, J., Xu, X., Ji, Y., Shen, F., Shen, H.T.: Recognition and detection of two-person interactive actions using automatically selected skeleton features. IEEE Trans. Hum.-Mach. Syst. **48**(3), 304–310 (2018)
27. Yun, K., Honorio, J., Chattopadhyay, D., Berg, T.L., Samaras, D.: Two-person interaction detection using body-pose features and multiple instance learning. In: IEEE Conference on Computer Vision and Pattern Recognition Workshops (CVPRW), pp. 28–35 (2012)
28. Zhang, Y., Liu, X., Chang, M.-C., Ge, W., Chen, T.: Spatio-temporal phrases for activity recognition. In: Fitzgibbon, A., Lazebnik, S., Perona, P., Sato, Y., Schmid, C. (eds.) ECCV 2012. LNCS, vol. 7574, pp. 707–721. Springer, Heidelberg (2012). https://doi.org/10.1007/978-3-642-33712-3_51
29. Zhang, Z.: Microsoft kinect sensor and its effect. IEEE Multimedia **19**(2), 4–10 (2012)
30. Zhu, W., et al.: Co-occurrence feature learning for skeleton based action recognition using regularized deep LSTM networks. In: AAAI, vol. 2, pp. 3697–3703 (2016)

DeepHuMS: Deep Human Motion Signature for 3D Skeletal Sequences

Neeraj Battan(✉), Abbhinav Venkat, and Avinash Sharma

International Institute of Information Technology, Hyderabad (IIIT-H), Hyderabad, India
{neeraj.battan,abbhinav.venkat}@research.iiit.ac.in, asharma@iiit.ac.in

Abstract. 3D Human Motion Indexing and Retrieval is an interesting problem due to the rise of several data-driven applications aimed at analyzing and/or re-utilizing 3D human skeletal data, such as data-driven animation, analysis of sports bio-mechanics, human surveillance etc. Spatio-temporal articulations of humans, noisy/missing data, different speeds of the same motion etc. make it challenging and several of the existing state of the art methods use hand-craft features along with optimization based or histogram based comparison in order to perform retrieval. Further, they demonstrate it only for very small datasets and a few classes. We make a case for using a learned representation that should recognize the motion as well as enforce a discriminative ranking. To that end, we propose, a 3D human motion descriptor learned using a deep network. Our learned embedding is generalizable and applicable to real-world data - addressing the aforementioned challenges and further enables sub-motion searching in its embedding space using another network. Our model exploits the inter-class similarity using trajectory cues, and performs far superior in a self-supervised setting. State of the art results on all these fronts is shown on two large scale 3D human motion datasets - NTU RGB+D and HDM05.

Keywords: 3D Human Motion Retrieval · Self-supervised learning · 4D indexing · MoCap analysis

1 Introduction

3D Human Motion Retrieval is an emerging field of research due to several attractive applications such as data-driven animation, athletic training, analysis of sports bio-mechanics, human surveillance and tracking etc. Performing such analysis is challenging due to the high articulations of humans (spatially and temporally), noisy/missing data, different speeds of the same action etc. Recent research in pose estimation, reconstruction [28,29], as well as the advancement in

Link for Code: https://github.com/neerajbattan/DeepHuMS.
Link for Project Video: https://bit.ly/31B1XY2.

S. Palaiahnakote et al. (Eds.): ACPR 2019, LNCS 12046, pp. 281–294, 2020.
https://doi.org/10.1007/978-3-030-41404-7_20

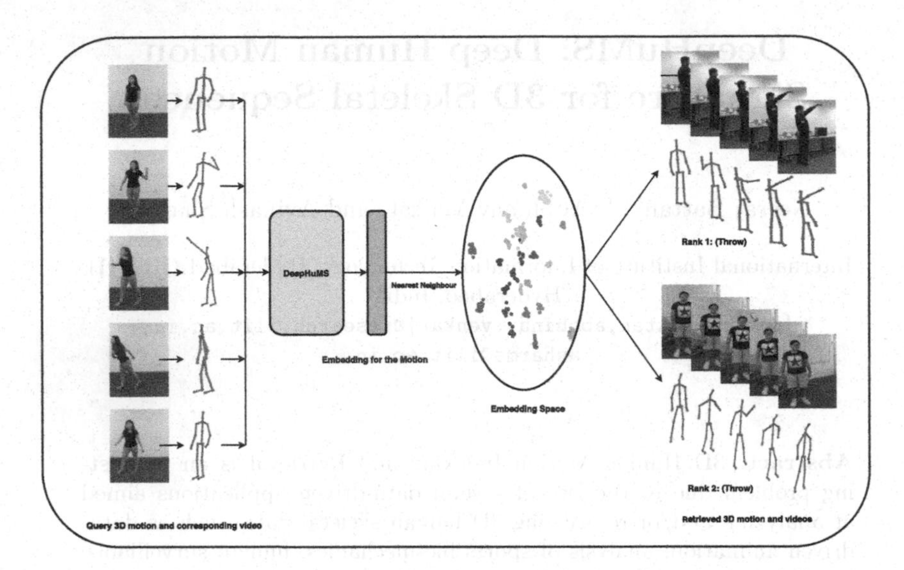

Fig. 1. Motivation of 3D Human Motion Retrieval. Given a query 3D skeletal motion sequence, we retrieve the top-k most similar sequences. A major motivation is that the corresponding videos of the retrieved results are view, appearance and background invariant.

motion capture systems has now resulted in a large repository of human 3D data that requires processing. Moreover, since the procurement of new motion data is a time-consuming and expensive process, re-using the available data is of primary importance. To that end, we solve the problem of 3D Human Motion Retrieval and address several of the aforementioned challenges, using, a 3D human motion descriptor learned using a deep learning model (Fig. 1).

While 3D human motion recognition is a commonly researched field, 3D human motion retrieval is much less explored. The task of human motion retrieval consists of two parts - building the feature representation and then the retrieval algorithm. Therefore, it requires recognizing the action as well as, importantly, enforcing a ranking i.e., a "low-dimensional" "recognition-robust" and "discriminative" feature embedding that is capable of fast retrieval is desirable.

Aiming at incorporating several of these properties, several hand crafted features from skeleton sequences have been developed [8]. There has also been considerable research in the direction of improving the retrieval algorithm [5] and having better similarity metrics for comparison [10]. For retrieval purposes, one common method is to solve an optimization problem, which is however slow and susceptible to local minimas [12]. Alternatively, a few others perform a histogram/code-book matching. However, these methods are affected by noisy data, different lengths and variable frame rates of sequences, etc. Moreover, they all demonstrate their retrieval accuracy over a very small number of sequences and classes. Hence, we would like to move towards learnable representations that can account for several of these shortcomings, while still maintaining minimal supervision.

A closely related problem to retrieval in which learnable representations have been widely explored is 3D action/motion recognition. In the last few years, several deep learning model innovations have been made to better exploit the spatial and temporal information available in skeleton data [19–21]. While these models do a respectable job in recognition, they perform poorly in retrieval due to not having a discriminative enough embedding space. Further, several of them highly depend on the availability of class labels. The number of class labels available in existing datasets is fairly limited, and such supervised models are incapable of exploiting similar sub-actions amongst various classes. Hence, the requirement of a more generalized model is in order.

Therefore, in this paper, we would like to propose a discriminative learnable representation, DeepHuMS, for retrieval, which produces instantaneous retrieval with a simple nearest neighbour search in the repository. To summarize, our contributions are:

- We propose a novel deep learning model that makes use of trajectory cues, and optionally class labels, in order to build a discriminative and robust 3D human motion descriptor for retrieval.
- Further, we perform sub-motion search by learning a mapping from sub-sequences to longer sequences in the dataset by means of another network.
- Experiments are performed, both, with and without class label supervision. We demonstrate our model's ability to exploit the inter-class motion similarity better in the unsupervised setting, thus, resulting in a more generalized solution.
- Our model is learned on noisy/missing data as well as motions of different speeds and its robustness in such scenarios indicates its applicability to real world data.
- A comparison of our retrieval performance with the publicly available state of the art in 3D motion recognition as well as 3D motion retrieval on 2 large scale publicly available datasets is done to demonstrate the state-of-the-art results of the proposed model.

2 Related Work

Most approaches on the 3D human motion retrieval have focused on developing hand crafted features to represent the skeleton sequences [8,12,17]. In this section, we broadly categorize them by the method in which they engineer their descriptors. Some existing methods use objective function [12], few others use codebook or histogram comparisons [5,18] to obtain hand-crafted features. The traditional frame based approaches extract out features for every frame. [10] proposed a geometric pose feature to encode pose similarity. [18] used joints' orientation angles and angles-forward differences as local features to create a codebook and generate a Bag of Visual Words to represent the action. [7,22] suggest hand drawn sketch based skeleton sequence retrieval methods. On the

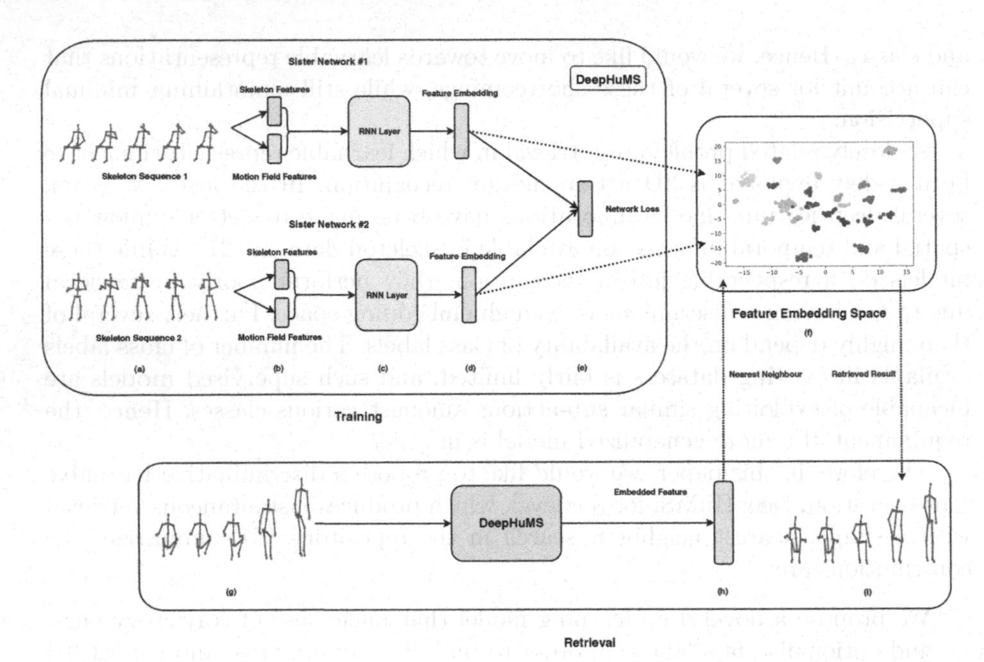

Fig. 2. Overview of our model - DeepHuMS. Given two skeleton sequences (a), we first extract the 3D joint locations (i.e., skeletal features) and motion field between consecutive frames (i.e., motion field features) to represent the spatio-temporal data (b). The two are concatenated together and given to an RNN [19] to model the 4D data (c). The resulting embeddings (d) are compared based using (e) contrastive loss (and optionally classification loss) to make them "discriminative" and "recognition-robust". Similarity is enforced based on the full sequence's motion distance and motion field. At the time of retrieval, given a 3D sequence to the network (g), with the resultant embedding, a nearest neighbour search is done in the embedding space (f) generated from the training data.

other end of the spectrum, sequence based motion features utilize global properties of the motion sequence [3,6,11]. Muller et al. [11] presented the motion template (MT) in which motions of the same class can be represented by an explicit interpretable matrix using a set of boolean geometric feature. To tolerate the temporal variance in the training process, dynamic time warping (DTW) was employed in their work. [13] created a temporal motion model using HMM and a histogram of 3D joints descriptors after creating the dictionary. [9] applied a Gaussian Mixture Model to represent character poses, wherein the motion sequence is encoded, then they used DTW and a string matching to find similarities between two videos. Recently many graph based models have been proposed to exploit the geometric structure of the skeleton data [14–16]. The spatial features are represented by the edges connecting the body joints and temporal features are represented by the edges connecting the same body joint in adjacent frames.

For the task of retrieval, [27] proposed a simple auto-encoder that captures high-level features. However, their model doesn't explicitly use a temporal construct for motion data. Primarily, learnable representations from 3D motion data have been used for other tasks. [19,23] are a few amongst many who used deep learning models for 3D motion recognition. Similarly, [26] adopts a unidirectional LSTM to encode the skeleton frames within the hidden network states and learn what subsequences of encoded frames belong to the specified action classes.

Broadly, the existing methods are affected by noisy data, the length and variable frame rates of sequences, and are slow at retrieval. Further, they lack a learned discriminative embedding which is capable of performing sub-sequence retrieval.

3 DeepHuMS: Our Method

In order to build a 3D human motion descriptor, we need to exploit the spatio-temporal features in the skeletal motion data. Briefly, we have three key components - (i) the input skeletal location and joint level motion trajectories to the next frame, (ii) an RNN to model this temporal data and (iii) a novel trajectory based similarity metric (explained below) to project similar content together using a Siamese architecture. We use two setups to train our model - (a) self-supervised, with a "contrastive loss" given by Eq. 1 to train our Siamese model and (b) supervised setup, with a cross entropy on our embedding, in addition to the self-supervision. Refer to Fig. 2 for a detailed architecture explanation.

$$L_{contrastive} = (1-Y)\frac{1}{2}(D_w^2) + (Y)\frac{1}{2}\{max(0, m - D_w\}^2 \tag{1}$$

In Eq. 1, Dw is the distance function (e.g., "Euclidean distance"), m is the margin for similar and dissimilar samples and Y is if the label value (1 for similar samples and 0 for dissimilar).

$$L_{crossentropy} = \sum_{n=1}^{M} y_{o,c} log(p_{o,c}) \tag{2}$$

In Eq. 2, y indicates (0 or 1) if class label c is the correctly classified, given o, the observation. M is the number of classes and p is the predicted probability, given an observation o of class c.

Similarity Metric. Two 3D human motion sequences are said to be similar if both the joint-wise "Motion Field" and joint-wise "Motion Distance" across the entire sequence are similar. The motion field depicts the direction of motion as well as the importance of the different joints for that specific sequence. The motivation behind this is evident in Fig. 3 in which the hand and elbow joints are more important for *waving*. However, the motion field can end up being zero as shown in Fig. 3. Therefore, we couple it with the joint-wise motion distance in order to build a more robust similarity metric. It is to be noted that having such a full video trajectory based similarity makes it difficult to directly retrieve sub-sequences of similar content. We handle this scenario in Sect. 4.5 using a second network.

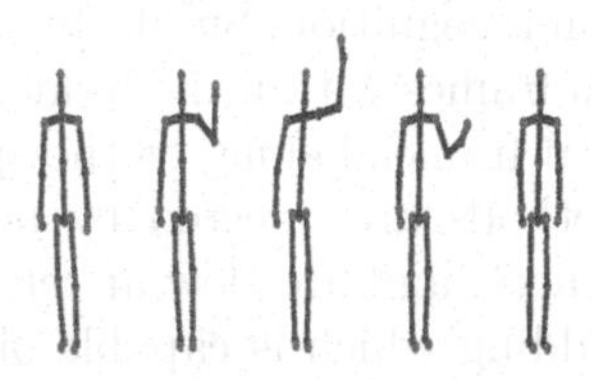

Fig. 3. Hand and elbow are important joints while waving, due to higher motion distance.

Equation 3 gives the motion field MF between two frames i and j. It is to be noted that we used motion field in two ways - one between every pair of frames on the input side, and the second between the first and last frame (whole video), for the similarity loss in Siamese network. Here $F[i]$ contains the 3D joints for ith frame in the skeleton sequence. Similarly, Eq. 4 gives the motion distance of the entire sequence. $MD[j]$ is the total distance covered by j^{th} joint and N is the number of frames in the 3D skeleton sequence.

$$MF[i,j] = F[i] - F[j] \tag{3}$$

$$MD[j] = \sum_{i=1}^{N-1} \|F[i+1][j] - F[i][j]\| \tag{4}$$

Different Number of Frames. In case of sequences that have different speeds of motion or sampling rate, but similar content, the information available at the input is different, but, the resulting motion field and motion distance across the entire sequence is the same. Hence, we augment our data and enforce such sequences to be projected together in our embedding space using the contrastive loss. In other words, we map sequences with less information to the same location to sequences with more information, in the embedding space (See Sect. 4.5 for more on implementation details).

4 Experiments

4.1 Datasets

We use two commonly used large scale public MoCap datasets to evaluate our method for human 3D motion retrieval.

NTU RGB+D [2]: This dataset provides RGB, depth, infra red images and 3D locations of 25 Joints on the human body. It consists of around 56,000 sequences from 60 different classes acted by 40 performers. We use the given performer wise split for learning from this dataset.

HDM05 [1]: This dataset provides RGB images and 3D locations of 31 Joints in human body. There are around 2300 3D sequences of 130 different classes performed by 5 performers in this dataset. We follow [12] for evaluation and therefore combine similar classes (for e.g. *walk2StepsLstart* and *walk2StepsRstart*) to get a total of 25 classes. We follow a performer-wise split with the first 4 performers for training and the last one for testing.

4.2 Implementation Details

All of the trained models, code and data shall be made publicly available, along with a working demo. Please refer to our supplementary video for more results.

Data Pre-processing & Augmentation. In order to make it performer/character invariant, we normalized the 3D joint locations based on the bone length of the performer. To diversify our datasets, for every 3D sequence, we create two more sequences - a faster and a slower one. The faster sequence is created by uniformly sampling every other frame, and the slower sequence is created by interpolating between every pair of frames.

Network Training. We use Nvidias GTX 1080Ti, with 11GB of VRAM to train our models. A batch size of 128 is used for NTU RGB+D dataset, and a batch size of 8 is used for training the HDM05 dataset. We use the ADAM optimizer with an initial learning rate of 10^{-3}, to get optimal performance on our setup. The training time for NTU RGB+D dataset is 6 h and HDM05 is 1 h. Each dataset is trained individually from scratch.

4.3 Evaluation Metrics

Retrieval Accuracy. This is a class-specific retrieval metric. In "top-n" retrieval accuracy, we find out how many of the "n" retrieved results belong to the same class as the query motion.

Dynamic Time Warping (DTW) Distance. Inspired from [10], we use Dynamic Time Warping as a quantitative metric to find out the similarity between two sequences based on distance. Two actions with different labels can be very similar, for example, drinking and eating. Likewise, the same class of actions performed by two actors can have very different motion. Hence using only the class-wise retrieval accuracy as metric doesn't provide the complete picture, and therefore, we use DTW as well.

4.4 Comparison with State of the Art

Since all of the existing state of the art methods use supervision, we compare our supervised setup with them in two ways - (a) with existing 3D Human Motion Retrieval models and (b) with 3D Human Motion Recognition embeddings. Class-wise retrieval accuracy of the top-1 and top-10 results are reported for the same.

3D Human Motion Retrieval. Most of the existing retrieval methods [6,24,25] show results on only up to 10 classes, and on very small datasets. [12] uses the same number of class labels as us, and we therefore, compare with them in Fig. 4a. As shown in Fig. 4a, the area under the PR curve is far larger for our method, and we have learned a much more robust 3D human motion descriptor.

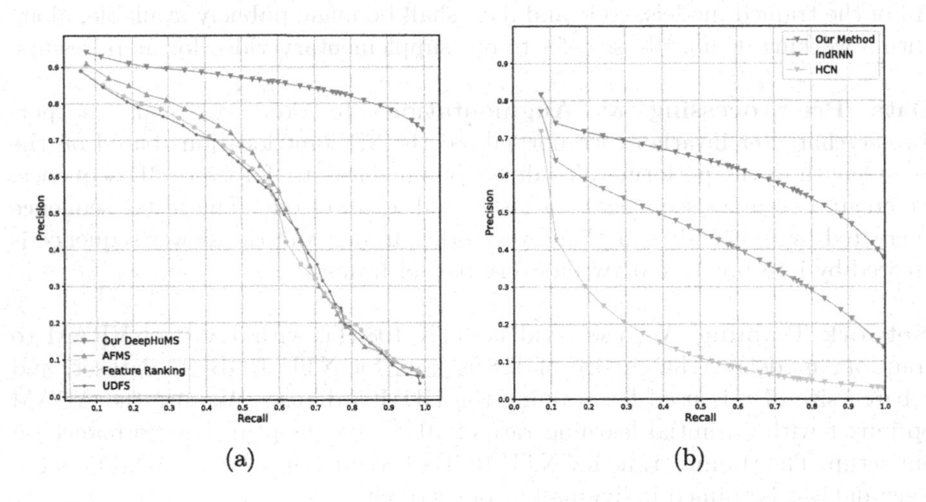

Fig. 4. A comparison of retrieval accuracy using PR curves for (a) 3D Motion Retrieval on HDM05 and (b) 3D Motion Recognition on NTU RGB+D

Table 1. Retrieval accuracy with 3D motion recognition on NTU RGB+D

Method	Top 1 ret. acc.	Top 10 ret. acc.
HCN [23]	0.61	0.56
IndRNN [19]	0.69	0.62
DeepHuMS (ours)	**0.78**	**0.753**

3D Human Motion Recognition. We compare with learned representations from 3D Motion recognition. The results for the recognition models in Table 1 and Fig. 4b are computed using their embeddings trained on our datasets.

Retrieval v/s Recognition. Figure 5 shows how our model produces a more clustered and therefore, discriminative space, suitable for retrieval, in comparison with the embedding space of [19], a state of the art 3D motion recognition algorithm. Recognition algorithms only focus on learning a hyperplane that enables them to identify limited motion classes. Adding a generalized similarity metric enforces an implicit margin in the embedding space - a motion trajectory based clustering.

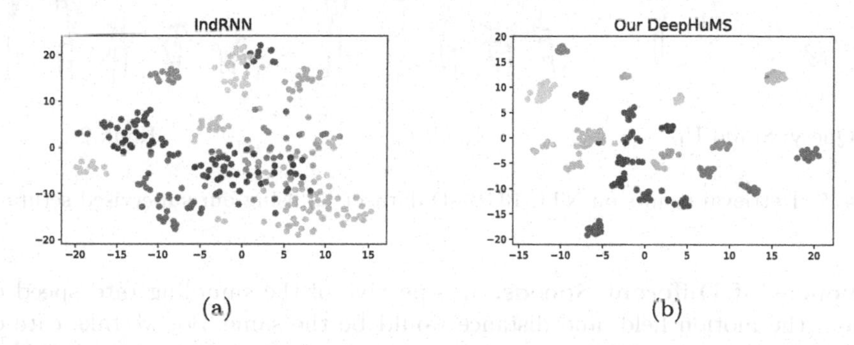

Fig. 5. A comparison of the t-SNE representation of Motion Recognition [19] with our method on NTU-RGB+D dataset [2]

4.5 Discussion

The results and inferences reported below are consistent for all datasets. For more detailed results, please see our supplementary video. Given a query, we show the top-2 ranked results in Figs. 6, 7, 9 and 11.

Results of Self-supervision. Going beyond class labels, we are able to exploit inter-class information when trained with only self-supervision; therefore, the resulting retrieved motions are more closer to the query motion than the supervised setup, in terms of per frame error after *DTW - 34 mm of supervised v/s 31 mm of unsupervised.* This is a promising result, particularly because existing datasets have a very limited number of labels and it enables us to exploit 3D sub-sequence similarity and perform retrieval in a label-invariant manner.

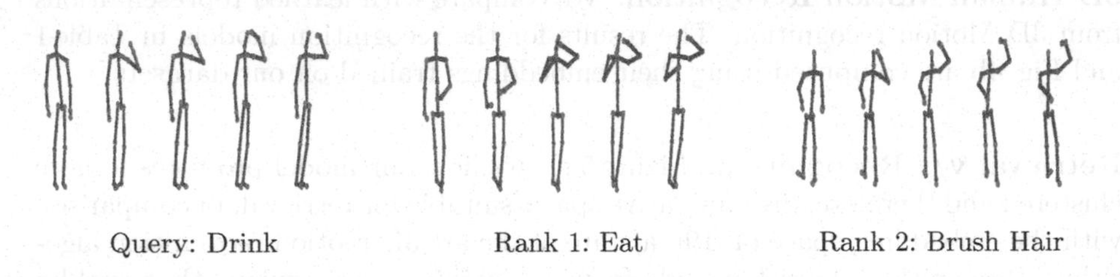

Fig. 6. Retrieval results for self-supervised setup, which shows that we exploit inter-class similarity

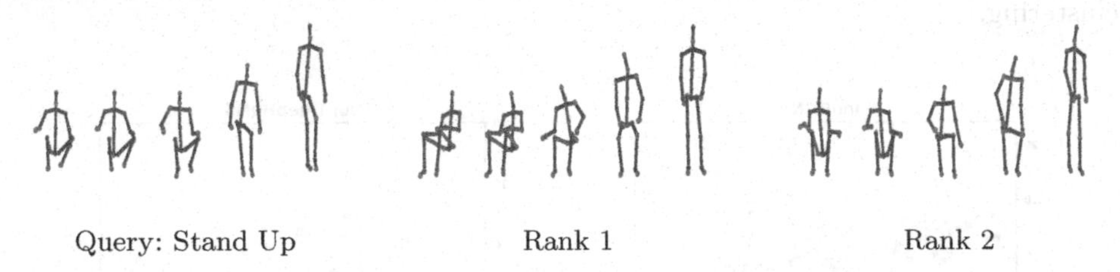

Fig. 7. Retrieval results on NTU-RGB+D dataset [2] using our supervised setup.

Sequences of Different Speeds. Irrespective of the sampling rate/speed of motion, the motion field, and distance would be the same. So, we take care of motions performed at different speeds by minimizing all to the same embedding. We do this by simulating a sequence that is twice as slow and twice as short by interpolation and uniform sampling respectively and training a Siamese over them. Figure 8a and b shows that more the number of frames, more amount of information is given to the network, and therefore, better the results. We handle short to very long sequences ranging in length from 15 to 600 frames.

Noisy/Missing Data. To prove the robustness of our method towards noisy data, we trained and tested out model with missing data - random 20% of joints missing from all frames of each sequence. This scenario simulates sensor noise or occlusions while detection of 3D skeletons. As shown in Fig. 8c, we still achieve an impressive retrieval accuracy in scenarios where optimization based state of the art methods would struggle.

Sub Motion Retrieval. Sub Motion retrieval becomes important when we would like to search for a smaller action/motion in longer sequences. But it is a very challenging task due to the variations in length and actions in sub sequences. Moreover, our similarity metrics, in their current form can't account for sub sequences directly. To address this, we follow the model shown in Fig. 10. Using this simple model, we retrieve the whole sequence it is a part of. This is a

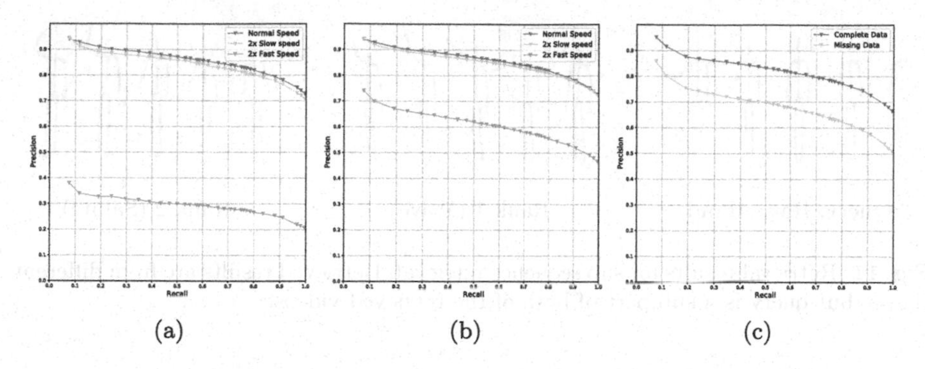

Fig. 8. A comparison of our precision recall curves **(a)** before training for different speeds on HDM05 dataset, **(b)** after training for different speeds on HDM05 dataset and **(c)** with noisy data.

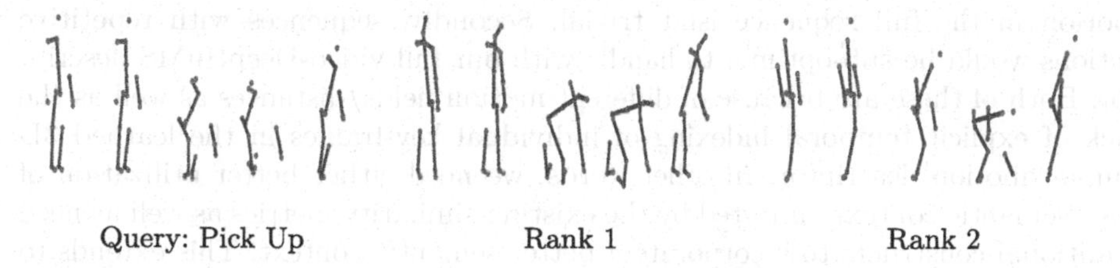

Fig. 9. Retrieval results for noisy data

good starting point for the community and we believe that better solutions can be developed that directly incorporate sub-sequence information in the motion descriptor.

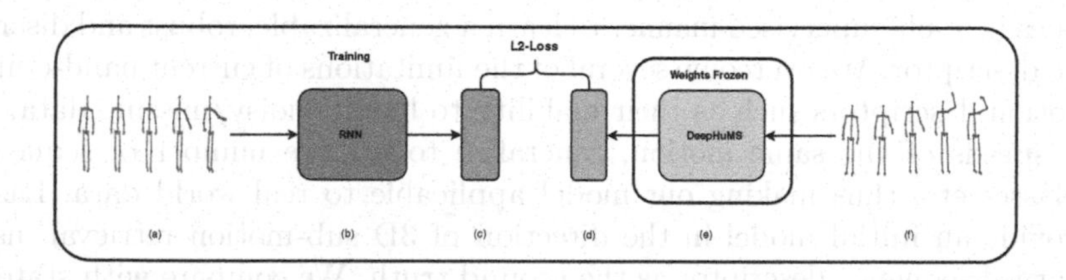

Fig. 10. Given a subsequence (a) as the input, we use another RNN (b) to learn an embedding (c). This is minimized with L2 loss w.r.t the ground truth (d) generated from DeepHuMS (e) trained on long sequences (f)

Retrieval Time. We have a fairly low dimensional embedding of size 512, and perform a simple nearest neighbour search throughout the training dataset. This yields an average retrieval time for the test set to be 18 ms for NTU RGB+D and 0.8 ms for HDM05 dataset. The retrieval time is proportional to the dataset size, and one could use more advanced algorithms such as tree based searching.

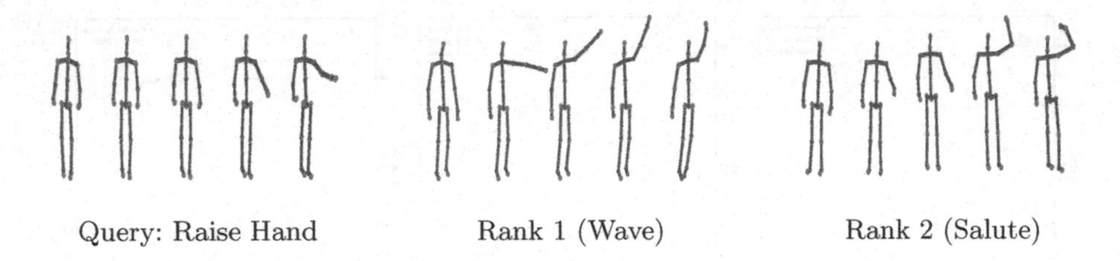

Fig. 11. Retrieval results for sub sequence retrieval. Retrieved results are from different classes but query is a sub part of both of the retrieved videos.

4.6 Limitations

Although our current model demonstrates impressive results, there exist some shortcomings in terms of generalisability and design. Firstly, indexing the submotion in the full sequence isn't trivial. Secondly, sequences with repetitive actions would be sub-optimal to handle with our full video-DeepHuMS descriptor. Both of these are because of different motion fields/distances as well as the lack of explicit temporal indexing of individual key-frames in the learned 3D human motion descriptor. In other words, we need either better utilization of the "semantic context" injected by the existing similarity metrics as well as need additional constructs to incorporate a better semantic context. This extends to a larger discussion about how to design models to learn in an unsupervised manner.

5 Conclusion

In this paper, we make a case for using a learned representation for 3D Human Motion retrieval by means of a deep learning based model. Our model uses trajectory cues in a self-supervised manner to learn a generalizable, robust and discriminative descriptor. We overcome several of the limitations of current hand-crafted 4D motion descriptors such as their inability to handle noisy/missing data, different speeds of the same motion, generalize to a large number of sequences and classes etc, thus making our model applicable to real world data. Lastly, we provide an initial model in the direction of 3D sub-motion retrieval, using the learned sequence descriptor as the ground truth. We compare with state-of-the-art 3D motion recognition as well as 3D motion retrieval methods on two large scale datasets - NTU RGB+D and HDM05 and demonstrate far superior performance on all fronts - class-wise retrieval accuracy, time and frame level distance.

References

1. Müller, M., Röder, T., Clausen, M., Eberhardt, B., Krüger, B., Weber, A.: Documentation mocap database HDM05. Technical report, No. CG-2007-2, Universität Bonn (June 2007). ISSN 1610–8892

2. Shahroudy, A., Liu, J., Ng, T.-T., Wang, G.: NTU RGB+ D: a large scale dataset for 3D human activity analysis. In: Computer Vision and Pattern Recognition, pp. 1010–1019 (2016)
3. Junejo, I., Dexter, E., Laptev, I., Perez, P.: View-independent action recognition from temporal self-similarities. IEEE Trans. Pattern Anal. Mach. Intell. **33**, 172–185 (2010)
4. Müller, M., Baak, A., Seidel, H.-P.: Efficient and robust annotation of motion capture data. In: Eurographics Symposium on Computer Animation, pp. 17–26 (2009)
5. Liu, X., He, G., Peng, S., Cheung, Y., Tang, Y.: Efficient human motion retrieval via temporal adjacent bag of words and discriminative neighborhood preserving dictionary learning. IEEE Trans. Human-Mach. Syst. **47**, 763–776 (2017)
6. Ramezani, M., Yaghmaee, F.: Motion pattern based representation for improving human action retrieval. Multimedia Tools Appl. **77**, 26009–26032 (2018)
7. Choi, M.G., Yang, K., Igarashi, T., Mitani, J., Lee, J.: Retrieval and visualization of human motion data via stick figures. Comput. Graph. Forum **31**(7), 2057–2065 (2012)
8. Xiao, Q., Li, J., Wang, Y., Li, Z., Wang, H.: Motion retrieval using probability graph model. In: International Symposium on Computational Intelligence and Design, vol. 2, pp. 150–153 (2013)
9. Qi, T., et al.: Real-time motion data annotation via action string. Comput. Anim. Virtual Worlds **25**, 293–302 (2014)
10. Chen, C., Zhuang, Y., Nie, F., Yang, Y., Wu, F., Xiao, J.: Learning a 3D human pose distance metric from geometric pose descriptor. IEEE Trans. Visual. Comput. Graph. **17**, 1676–1689 (2010)
11. Müller, M., Röder, T.: Motion templates for automatic classification and retrieval of motion capture data. In: Proceedings of the 2006 Eurographics Symposium on Computer animation, pp. 137–146. Eurographics Association (2006)
12. Wang, Z., Feng, Y., Qi, T., Yang, X., Zhang, J.: Adaptive multi-view feature selection for human motion retrieval. Signal Process. **120**, 691–701 (2016)
13. Xia, L., Chen, C.-C., Aggarwal, J.K.: View invariant human action recognition using histograms of 3D joints. In: Computer Vision and Pattern Recognition Workshops, pp. 20–27. IEEE (2012)
14. Li, M., Chen, S., Chen, X., Zhang, Y., Wang, Y., Tian, Q.: Actional-structural graph convolutional networks for skeleton-based action recognition. In: Computer Vision and Pattern Recognition, pp. 3595–3603 (2019)
15. Shi, L., Zhang, Y., Cheng, J., Lu, H.: Skeleton-based action recognition with directed graph neural networks. In: Conference on Computer Vision and Pattern Recognition, pp. 7912–7921 (2019)
16. Yan, S., Xiong, Y., Lin, D.: Spatial temporal graph convolutional networks for skeleton-based action recognition. In: Thirty-Second AAAI Conference on Artificial Intelligence (2018)
17. Wang, J., Liu, Z., Wu, Y., Yuan, J.: Learning actionlet ensemble for 3D human action recognition. IEEE Trans. Pattern Anal. Mach. Intell. **36**, 914–927 (2013)
18. Kapsouras, I., Nikolaidis, N.: Action recognition on motion capture data using a dynemes and forward differences representation. J. Vis. Commun. Image Represent. **25**, 1432–1445 (2014)
19. Li, S., Li, W., Cook, C., Zhu, C., Gao, Y.: Independently recurrent neural network (IndRNN): building a longer and deeper RNN. In: 2018 Conference on Computer Vision and Pattern Recognition (2018)

20. Li, Q., Qiu, Z., Yao, T., Mei, T., Rui, Y., Luo, J.: Action recognition by learning deep multi-granular spatio-temporal video representation (2016)
21. Tang, Y., Tian, Y., Lu, J., Li, P., Zhou, J.: Deep progressive reinforcement learning for skeleton-based action recognition. In: Computer Vision and Pattern Recognition, pp. 5323–5332 (2018)
22. Chao, M., Lin, C., Assa, J., Lee, T.: Human motion retrieval from hand-drawn sketch. IEEE Trans. Visual. Comput. Graph. **18**, 729–740 (2011)
23. Li, C., Zhong, Q., Xie, D., Pu, S.: Co-occurrence feature learning from skeleton data for action recognition and detection with hierarchical aggregation. In: International Joint Conference on Artificial Intelligence (2018)
24. Ofli, F., Chaudhry, R., Kurillo, G., Vidal, R., Bajcsy, R.: Sequence of the most informative joints (SMIJ): a new representation for human skeletal action recognition. J. Vis. Commun. Image Represent. **25**, 24–38 (2014)
25. Gowayyed, M., Torki, M., Hussein, M., El-saban, M.: Histogram of oriented displacements (HOD): describing trajectories of human joints for action recognition. In: International Joint Conference on Artificial Intelligence, pp. 1351–1357 (2013)
26. Carrara, F., Elias, P., Sedmidubsky, J., Zezula, P.: LSTM-based real-time action detection and prediction in human motion streams. Multimedia Tools Appl. **78**, 27309–27331 (2019)
27. Wang, Y., Neff, M.: Deep signatures for indexing and retrieval in large motion databases. In: Conference on Motion in Games, pp. 37–45 (2015)
28. Venkat, A., et al.: HumanMeshNet: polygonal mesh recovery of humans. arXiv preprint arXiv:1908.06544 (2019)
29. Venkat, A., Jinka, S.S., Sharma, A.: Deep textured 3D reconstruction of human bodies. arXiv preprint arXiv:1809.06547 (2018)

Adversarial Learning and Networks

Towards a Universal Appearance for Domain Generalization via Adversarial Learning

Yujui Chen, Tse-Wei Lin, and Chiou-Ting Hsu(✉)

Department of Computer Science, National Tsing Hua University, Hsinchu, Taiwan
e124874356@yahoo.com.tw, shockshandian@gmail.com, cthsu@cs.nthu.edu.tw

Abstract. Domain generalization aims to learn a generalized feature space across multiple source domains so as to adapt the representation to an unseen target domain. In this paper, we focus on two main issues of domain generalization for image classification. First, instead of focusing on aligning data distributions among source domains, we aim to leverage the generalization capability by explicitly referring to image content and style from different source domains. We propose a novel appearance generalizer to learn a universal appearance, which captures domain-invariant content but exhibits various styles. Second, to tackle the class-discriminative issue, we resort to the prominent adversary learning and impose an additional constraint on the discriminator to boost the class-discriminative capability. Experimental results on several benchmark datasets show that the proposed method outperforms existing methods significantly.

Keywords: Domain generalization · Appearance generalizer · Adversarial learning · Image classification · Gaussian mixture models

1 Introduction

With the rapid advance of deep learning, domain adaptation grows increasingly critical to many applications in computer vision. Through domain adaptation, we can learn a common feature space (i.e., latent vector space) from the "labeled" data (source domain) to adapt the task (e.g., classification) to the "unlabeled" testing data (target domain). Since there usually exists a domain shift between the source and target domains, achieving a satisfactory task on the unlabeled target domain is very challenging. Many efforts have been conducted to minimize the domain shift so as to alleviate the need of data labeling, which is time-consuming and costly. Recently, several work takes advantage of adversarial learning to bring the source and target domains to become indistinguishable [4,21,26]. For example, in [4], Ganin et al. used a domain classifier to reduce the domain difference between the source and target domains.

Similar to the problem of domain adaptation, domain generalization aims to find a generalized feature representation through multiple labeled source domains

S. Palaiahnakote et al. (Eds.): ACPR 2019, LNCS 12046, pp. 297–311, 2020.
https://doi.org/10.1007/978-3-030-41404-7_21

so as to tackle the task on an unseen target domain. The main difference between these two problems is that, in domain generalization, target domain data is totally "*invisible*" during the training stage. Unlike domain adaptation, where the distribution of target data is available and can be used to minimize the domain shift [4,21,26], domain generalization can only rely on source domains to find a domain-invariant representation [1,3,6,14,17,19,24]. Existing methods can be divided into two groups. The first group learns a generalized feature space by establishing one branch for each individual source domain [3,6,19]. Ghifary et al. [6] proposed a multi-task autoencoder with several separated branches in the final layer to relate to their corresponding source domains. Ding et al. [3] designed a set of domain-specific networks and one domain invariant network, and adopted a low-rank reconstruction to align the two types of networks. Rahman et al. [19] proposed a network using multiple GANs to transfer input images to other source domains and then used the generated images to train the network. On the other hand, the other group of methods attempts to minimize the discrepancy between source domains in terms of different metrics, e.g. maximum mean discrepancy (MMD), low-rank constraint [3,14,19], and etc. In [14], the adversarial learning combined with MMD loss minimization is adopted to increase the generalization ability of the learned features while aligning the distributions among multiple source domains.

Nevertheless, existing methods are subject to several limitations. For example, the first group of methods, which include multiple branches for the source domains, will have increased number of branches along with the number of source domains. As to the second group of methods, it is still unsatisfactory to find a well-generalized representation by merely aligning distributions among multiple source domains. Therefore, in this paper, we focus on image classification application and propose a Universal Appearance for Domain Generalization via Adversarial Learning (UAAL) model to tackle the above-mentioned limitations. The proposed UAAL model consists of an appearance generalizer and a deep encoder through adversarial learning. The appearance generalizer, introducing the concept of appearance transferring, learns a universal appearance by preserving the image content but adopting the styles learned from all the available source domains. As to the deep encoder, we propose a novel prior in the adversarial learning model to constrain the distribution of the learned latent space. Our experiments verify that the latent space is not only domain-invariant but also class-discriminative.

Our contributions are summarized as follows:

- We propose a novel appearance generalizer to capture a universal appearance among multiple source domains.
- Through adversarial learning, the proposed UAAL model learns not only domain-invariant but also class-discriminative latent space.
- Extensive experiments have been conducted to show that our method achieves state-of-the-art results.

2 Related Work

Domain Adaptation. With deep layers and enormous training data, deep learning-based methods tremendously outperform traditional methods on many tasks. Considering the cost of data collection and labeling, researchers [4,21,23, 25,26] have paid special attention to try to minimize the domain gap between source and target datasets. Ganin et al. [4] used a discriminator to learn indistinguishable features between source and target domains via a gradient reversal layer. Tzeng et al. [23] proposed an adversarial discriminative domain adaptation (ADDA) model with three stages. Firstly, ADDA pre-trains an encoder (i.e., source CNN encoder) and a classifier on the source domain data. Next, the model constrains another encoder (i.e., target CNN encoder) with a discriminator to minimize the domain gap. The target data are then encoded by the target CNN encoder and classified by the source classifier. Sankaranarayanan et al. [21] proposed to use a generator to yield source-like images from two domains and utilized an auxiliary classifier to predict true or fake images and also predict the class labels. Wang et al. [25] proposed to align data distributions between the source and target domains by focusing on the transferable regions of images through several local discriminators.

Domain Generalization. Domain generalization aims to capture shared information among multiple source domains so as to generalize to unseen target data. The main challenge of this scenario comes from the unavailability of the target domain data during the training stage. Many methods have been proposed to tackle this problem [1,3,6,12–17,19,24]. Ghifary et al. [6] proposed a multi-task autoencoder with three layers, where the latent representation is designed to learn universal information among the source domains and the output layer has multiple branches corresponding to different source domains. Ding and Fu [3] designed a set of domain-specific networks and a domain-invariant network to learn shared feature space under low-rank constraint. Rahman et al. [19] took advantage of Generative Adversarial Network (GAN) to generate synthetic data and to minimize the Maximum Mean Discrepancy (MMD) between synthetic images and generated images so as to generalize to unseen target data. Li et al. [14] used the adversarial autoencoder to prevent the model from overfitting on source domains and also relied on minimizing the MMD loss to capture a domain-invariant representation. Li et al. [15] proposed a conditional invariant adversarial network to learn domain invariant representation by matching the joint distributions of source domains. Carlucci et al. [1] designed a network by using self-supervised signals to learn jigsaw puzzles and spatial information from source domains. To tackle the large domain shift problem, Wang et al. [24] designed a two-branch neural network, where the first and the second branches first extract intensity and texture features respectively, and then tried to learn a generalized representation irrelevant to texture changes.

3 Proposed Method

3.1 Problem Statement and Motivations

Let X be the set of input images and Y be its corresponding ground truth labels of L categories. During the training stage, K source domains $(X^{S_i}, Y^{S_i}) = \{(x_1^{S_i}, y_1^{S_i}), (x_2^{S_i}, y_2^{S_i}), ..., (x_{n_i}^{S_i}, y_{n_i}^{S_i})\}$, $i \in \{1, 2, ..., K\}$ are given; whereas in the testing stage, only n unlabeled images in the target domain $X^T = \{x_1^T, x_2^T, ..., x_n^T\}$ are available. Under the assumption that the source domain distribution $S_i(x, y)$, $i \in \{1, 2, ..., K\}$ and the target domain distribution $T(x, y)$ are different, our main goal is to find a function (encoder E) to project the input image $x \in X$ into a feature space (latent vector space) Z which can fully characterize the feature representation of the K source domains. As mentioned in Sects. 1 and 2, recent domain generalization methods either rely on building multiple models for the source domains or focusing on aligning the distributions of different source domains without explicitly modeling the dependency between domains and classes. Therefore, once the unknown test domain behaves very differently from these source domains, the generalization ability of these methods becomes doubtful.

In this paper, we aim to maximize the generalization capability during the training stage so as to better adapt the learned representation to an unknown target domain. We propose a deep generalization network by including a novel appearance generalizer into the adversarial learning framework. Inspired by the idea of style transfer [5], we develop an appearance generalizer A by integrating the content and style derived from different source domains to learn a generalized appearance. With the increased number of source domains, we believe that the set of appearance generalized images can largely promote the generalization and can help the network learn a domain-invariant representation. We then use an encoder E to encode the input and the generalized images into a latent space. To enforce the latent space to be class-discriminative, we impose an additional constraint on the latent space via the discriminator D. With the appearance generalizer A and the constraint on the discriminator D, we encourage the encoder E to learn a universally generalized as well as class-discriminative representation.

3.2 Network Architecture

Figure 1 shows the overview of the proposed adversarial learning network and Fig. 2 is the proposed appearance generalizer. We first use the appearance generalizer A to construct an augmented dataset $(X^U, Y^U) = (X^S, Y^S) \cup (X^{\bar{S}}, Y^{\bar{S}})$, where X^S is the set of images from all the source domains $S = \{S_1, S_2, ..., S_K\}$, and $X^{\bar{S}}$ is its generalized set of images by preserving the image content of a certain domain but referring to the image style from all the source domains S. As shown in Fig. 1, we encode each input image $x \in X^U$ by the encoder E to derive its domain-invariant latent vector $\mathbf{z}$:

$$\mathbf{z} = E(x, \theta_E). \tag{1}$$

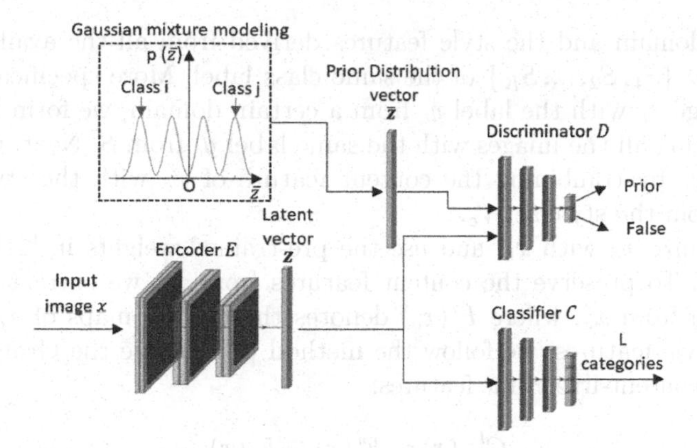

Fig. 1. Architecture of the proposed UAAL network.

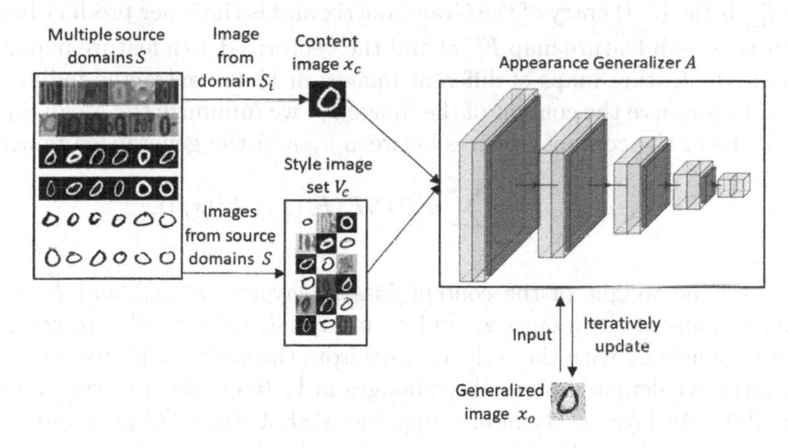

Fig. 2. Illustration of the proposed appearance generalizer.

Next, we use a discriminator D and a classifier C via adversarial learning to constrain the learned latent space to be class-discriminative.

3.3 Appearance Generalizer

Figure 2 shows our proposed appearance generalizer A. In order to learn a universal appearance across all the available source domains, we refer to the idea of Appearance Adaptation network (AAN) [28], which was originally developed for semantic segmentation and aimed to bridge the domain gap between synthetic data and realistic data. Unlike in [28], our goal is not to minimize the domain gap. Instead, under the scenario of domain generalization, our goal is to learn a universal representation which not only preserves the discriminative information in the sources domains but also generalizes well to the unseen target domain.

Given the labeled images in the source domains (X^S, Y^S), we propose to generate a set of new images $(X^{\bar{S}}, Y^{\bar{S}})$ by combining the content features from one source domain and the style features derived from all the available source domains $S = \{S_1, S_2, ..., S_K\}$ of the same class label. More specifically, given a content image x_c with the label y_c from a certain domain, we form its style set V_c by collecting all the images with the same label y_c from S. Next, we generate an images x_o by combining the content feature of x_c with the style features extracted from the style set V_c.

We initialize x_o with x_c, and use the pre-trained weights in [21] to extract the features. To preserve the content features from x_c, we extract the feature maps $F^l(x_c)$ from x_c, where $F^l(x_c)$ denotes the feature maps of x_c in layer l. As to the style features, we follow the method [5] and use the Gram matrix to extract the content-irrelevant features:

$$G^l_{i,j}(x) = F^l_i(x) \odot F^l_j(x), \tag{2}$$

where $G^l_{i,j}$ is the (i, j) entry of the Gram matrix and is the inner product between the vectorized i-th feature map $F^l_i(x)$ and the vectorized j-th feature map $F^l_j(x)$. Note that, the feature maps of different images in V_c are extracted individually.

Next, to preserve the content of the image x_c, we minimize the Mean Squared Error (MSE) of the content features between x_c and the generalized image x_o:

$$L_{CT}(x_o, x_c) = \sum_l w^l_c MSE(F^l(x_o), F^l(x_c)), \tag{3}$$

where w^l_c is the weight of the content loss in layer l, $F^l(x_o)$ and $F^l(x_c)$ are the feature maps of the images x_o and x_c in layer l, respectively. To render the generalized image x_o with the style features from the style set V_c, we average the Gram matrices calculated from all the images in V_c to obtain the averaged Gram matrix $G^l(V_c)$ in layer l. By minimizing the MSE between $G^l(x_o)$ and $G^l(V_c)$, we encourage the generalized image x_o to resemble the style of V_c:

$$L_S(x_o, V_c) = \sum_l w^l_s MSE(G^l(x_o), G^l(V_c)), \tag{4}$$

where w^l_S is the weight of the style loss in layer l.

By combining the content loss L_{CT} and the style loss L_S, we learn a generalized image x_o for each source image x_c by minimizing the appearance generalizing loss L_{AG}:

$$L_{AG}(x_o, x_c, V_c) = \beta L_{CT}(x_o, x_c) + L_S(x_o, V_c). \tag{5}$$

The generalized image x_o is iteratively updated by gradient descent:

$$x_o \leftarrow x_o - \eta \frac{\partial L_{AG}}{\partial x_o}, \tag{6}$$

where η is the learning rate of the appearance generalizer.

3.4 Adversarial Learning

The idea of adversarial learning has been popularly studied in domain adaption problems, where a discriminator D is designed to match the distributions between source and target domains so as to minimize their domain shift. However, unlike in domain adaptation, domain generalization usually assumes that the target domain data are unavailable during the training stage. Therefore, it is impossible to estimate the target distribution from the target domain data themselves. Nevertheless, as the goal of the discriminator is to minimize the discrepancy between source and target distributions, we may still enforce the source data to approximate certain pre-defined distributions.

Moreover, learning a domain-invariant representation is far from enough to tackle the classification task in the target domain. We also expect the learned representation to be class-discriminative. Thus, we propose to leverage the generalized source data (X^U, Y^U) to pre-determine the distribution priors. Without loss of generality, we assume the latent feature representation of each class follows a Gaussian distribution and then model the latent space as a mixture of L Gaussians. We uniformly sample L values as the Gaussians means within $(-B, B]$ by

$$u_i = 2B \cdot (\frac{i}{L} - \frac{1}{2}), \tag{7}$$

where B is a positive constant number and $i \in \{1, 2, ..., L\}$ represents the i th class in the source data (X^U, Y^U). Thus, we assign each class of the source data to one specified Gaussian distribution $\mathbf{\bar{z}_i} \sim \mathcal{N}(\mu_\mathbf{i}\mathbf{1}, \sigma\mathbf{I})$, where σ is the standard deviation and $\mathbf{u_i}$ is determined according to Eq. 7. Our prior constraint is then formulated as a Gaussian mixture model:

$$p(\mathbf{\bar{z}}) = \sum_{i=1}^{L} \phi_i \mathcal{N}(\mu_\mathbf{i}\mathbf{1}, \sigma\mathbf{I}), \tag{8}$$

where $\sum_{i=1}^{L} \phi_i = 1$, $0 \leq \phi_i \leq 1$. Using the pre-determined Gaussian mixture source models, we develop an adversarial learning network to guide the distribution of the latent space. Our goal is two-fold: one is to constrain the network to capture shared information among multiple source domains (that is, to encode the data into a domain-invariant latent space), and the other is to constrain the latent distribution to follow the pre-defined Gaussian mixture distribution (that is, to encourage the latent vector to be class-discriminative). By imposing the constraint on the latent space, we encourage the unseen target data to map to the Gaussian mixture priors and to promote the discriminability between different classes. We follow the idea in adversarial learning [7] and let $D(x)$ be the probability that x comes from the Gaussian priors. We then define the adversarial loss by

$$L_A(\mathbf{\bar{z}}, X^U) = \frac{1}{N} \sum_{i=1}^{L} \mathbb{1}(i = y_j) \sum_{j=1}^{N} (log(D(\mathbf{\bar{z}_i})) + log(1 - D(E(x_j))), \tag{9}$$

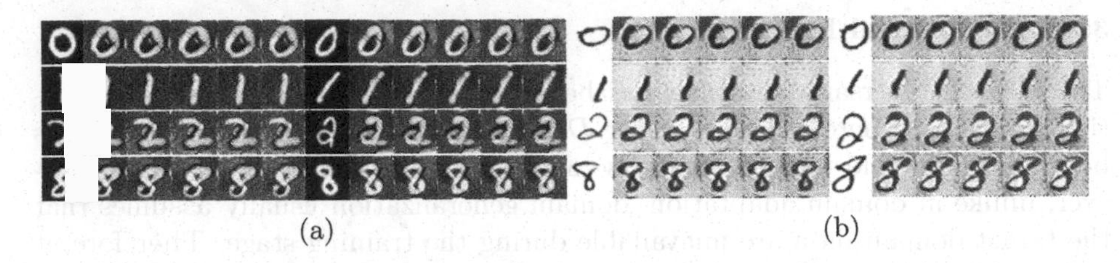

Fig. 3. Visualization results of appearance generalizer on handwritten digit datasets MINST (M) and USPS (U), by using (a) M, and (b) U as content images, respectively. The style set for both cases is $V_c = \{M, U\}$. In (a) and (b), the leftmost column shows the original content images, and the rest columns are the generalized results after 200 and 400 iterations, respectively.

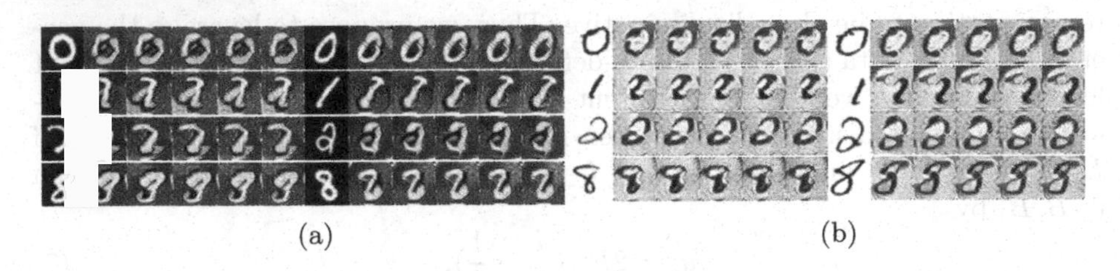

Fig. 4. Comparisons of the generalized images by referring to the style set collected from all the class labels, i.e., digits 0–9. The images are generated using (a) M, and (b) U as content images, respectively; but using all the class labels data in the style set.

where N denotes the number of training samples in one batch, and $\bar{\mathbf{z}}_i$ is the Gaussian priors that the encoder $E(x_j)$ should learn to approximate. Through the min-max game, the encoder E gradually learns to generate a latent vector $\mathbf{z}$ to fool the discriminator D; whereas the discriminator D learns to better distinguish between the Gaussian prior vector $\bar{\mathbf{z}}$ and the generated vector $\mathbf{z} = E(x_j)$.

In addition, to include the available label information of multiple source domains, we incorporate a classifier C in our network and define the classification loss L_H by,

$$L_H(X^U, Y^U) = -\frac{1}{N}\sum_{j=1}^{N} y_j[\log(C(E(x_j)))]. \tag{10}$$

Finally, our objective function is defined as,

$$L = L_H(X^U, Y^U) + \lambda_1 L_A(\bar{\mathbf{z}}, X^U), \tag{11}$$

where λ_1 is set as 0.1 in our experiment.

4 Experiment

To evaluate the performance of the proposed model, we conduct experiments on three cross-domain benchmark datasets: Office-31 [20], PACS [13] and MUS-10. We use the notation $\{W, D\} \rightarrow A$ to represent that the model is trained on the labeled source domains W and D, and is tested on the target domain A.

Office-31 consists of 3 different domains, including *Amazon* (A), *Webcam* (W), and *Dslr* (D). Each domain contains 31 categories, and the whole dataset contains 4,652 images. Images in the domain *Amazon* are download from Amazon.com and are of intermediate resolution with simple background. *Webcam* and *Dslr* domains contain images captured in office using webcam and digital SLR camera, respectively. Three experimental settings are conducted: $\{W, D\} \rightarrow A$, $\{W, A\} \rightarrow D$, and $\{A, D\} \rightarrow W$. The images in W and D are visually similar; but are much different from the domain A. Therefore, the setting $\{W, D\} \rightarrow A$ is the most challenging one in this dataset.

PACS was a recently proposed dataset with four domains (i.e., *Photo* (P), *Art painting* (A), *Cartoon* (C), and *Sketch* (S)), and each domain contains 7 categories (i.e. dog, elephant, giraffe, guitar, horse, house and person). This dataset is quite challenging because there exists large domain shift between different domains. In the experiment, we use three domains as training datasets and the remaining one as the testing dataset.

MUS-10: MNIST (M) [11] and USPS (U) are hand-written digit datasets; SVHN (S) [18] is a street-view house number digit dataset. Each domain contains 10 categories (i.e., digits 0–9). Three experimental settings are conducted: $\{M, U\} \rightarrow S$, $\{M, S\} \rightarrow U$, and $\{U, S\} \rightarrow M$. In this dataset, $\{M, U\} \rightarrow S$ is the most challenging one, because M and U are visually similar to each other but are quite different from S.

Training Strategies. We use VGG-19 pre-trained on ILSVRC-2012 dataset [22] to develop the appearance generalizer. The learning rate of our appearance generalizer η is set to $1e^{-4}$. The parameter setting for the content weights w_c^l on conv4_2 layer is 10^3, and 0 on the other layers. The style weights on conv1_1, conv2_1, conv3_1, conv4_1 and conv5_1 are set as $10^3/64^2$, $10^3/128^2$, $10^3/256^2$, $10^3/512^2$, and $10^3/512^2$, respectively; and are set as 0 on the other layers. β is set as 1.5, 0.8 and 1 on Office-31, PACS and MUS-10, respectively.

As to the encoder E, we use ResNet-18 [8] and AlexNet structure [10] pre-trained on ImageNet dataset [2] for the experiment on Office-31 and PACS datasets, respectively. For the experiment on MUS-10 dataset, we exploit CNN structures [1]. Throughout our experiment, we use Adam optimizer [9] with initial learning rate $5e^{-5}$ to train our network with batch size 64, 50, and 128 for Office-31, PACS and MUS-10, respectively. B is set as 10 in Eq. 7.

4.1 Evaluation of Appearance Generalizer

We first show the results of appearance generalizer on the two hand-written digit datasets: MNIST (M) [11] and USPS (U). Figure 3(a) and (b) show the

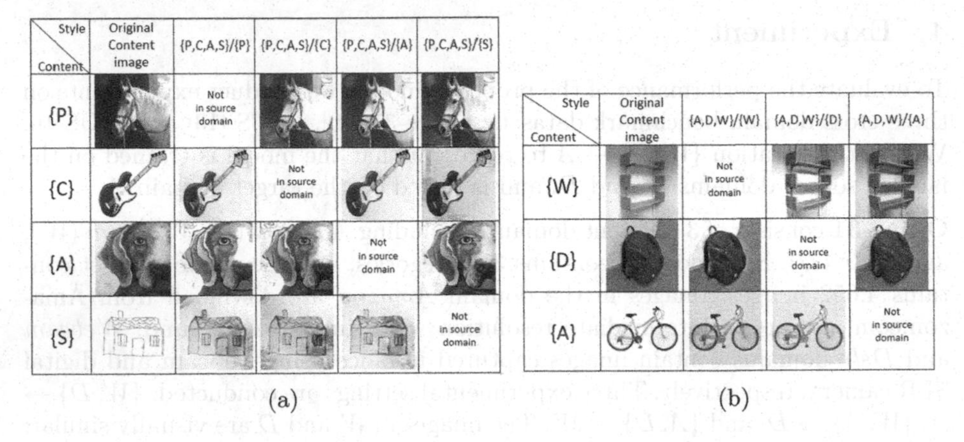

Fig. 5. Results of our appearance generalizer on (a) PCAS and (b) Office-31 datasets. We use $\{P, C, A, S\}/\{P\}$ to denote that the style set is collected from all the domains except the domain P.

Table 1. Recognition accuracy (%) on Office-31 dataset.

Unseen domain	LRE-SVM [27]	MTAE [6]	DGLRC [3]	MCIT [19]	ResNet-18	UAAL
Amazon	44.14	43.67	45.36	51.73	51.97	**54.42**
Webcam	93.98	94.21	**95.28**	94.03	92.33	93.46
DSLR	98.84	98.97	**99.44**	97.87	97.99	98.59
Average	78.99	78.95	80.02	81.21	80.08	**82.16**

generalized images by combining the content from M and U with the style from $V_c = \{M, U\}$, respectively. These results verify that the generalized images not only exhibit various styles from other domains but also preserve the class-discriminative content features.

Furthermore, in Fig. 4, we generate images by referring to style features extracted from all the class labels for comparison. For example, given a content image with label 0, we use only the source data with label 0 to build its style set V_c in Fig. 3, but use the data with labels $\{0, 1, ..., 9\}$ to build its style set in Fig. 4. In other words, in Fig. 4, we use the whole source domain data as the style set. As shown in Fig. 4, the generalized images no longer retain the class-discriminative content; whereas in Fig. 3, when referring to class-specific style features, the generalized images have various styles but still capture class-discriminative content. Therefore, in the domain generalization scenario, it is advisable to refer to the same class label to generate the class-specific appearance.

Table 2. Recognition accuracy (%) on PACS dataset.

Unseen domain	AlexNet	MLDG [12]	Fusion [16]	CIDDG [15]	Adv [24]	UAAL
Photo	84.25	88.00	**90.20**	78.65	88.20	85.39
Art	62.50	66.23	64.10	62.70	64.90	**66.89**
Cartoon	61.39	66.88	66.80	**69.73**	69.60	67.32
Sketch	61.01	58.96	60.10	**64.45**	56.30	63.22
Average	67.29	70.01	70.30	68.88	69.75	**70.71**

Table 3. Recognition accuracy (%) on MUS-10 dataset.

Unseen domain	Baseline	UAAL
USPS	38.53	**48.40**
SVHN	30.13	**36.48**
MNIST	72.01	**76.13**
Average	46.89	**53.67**

Table 4. Ablation study on Office-31 dataset.

Unseen domain	UAAL/A	UAAL/D	UAAL
Amazon	53.04	53.60	**54.42**
Webcam	91.07	**93.58**	93.46
DSLR	**98.59**	98.19	**98.59**
Average	77.69	81.79	**82.16**

In Fig. 5, we give some examples of the generalized images in PCAS and Office datasets. These results again show that, even using the same content image, the proposed appearance generalizer is able to generate images with various styles, according to different settings for collecting the style set.

4.2 Comparison with Existing Methods

Evaluation on Office-31. Table 1 shows the classification accuracy on Office-31 dataset of our method (denoted by UAAL) and compares with existing methods LRE-SVM [27], MTAE [6], DGLRC [3], MCIT [19] and ResNet-18 (which is a baseline model only with the classification loss in Eq. 10). The classification rates of these methods are cited from their original papers. As we expected, the setting $\{W, D\} \rightarrow A$ is the most challenging one and results in the lowest accuracy. Nevertheless, our method still largely outperforms the other methods.

Evaluation on PACS. Table 2 shows the results on PACS dataset. For fair comparison with the other methods [12,15,16,24], we use AlexNet with pre-trained weights [2] as the backbone of our encoder. We compare our method with AlexNet (with pre-trained weights and then fituned on PACS dataset), MLDG [12], Fusion [16], CIDDG [15] and Adv [24]. As shown in Table 2, our method achieves comparable results with these methods.

Table 5. Ablation study on PACS dataset.

Unseen domain	UAAL/A	UAAL/D	UAAL
Photo	84.61	85.21	**85.39**
Art	66.21	63.98	**66.89**
Cartoon	66.08	64.93	**67.32**
Sketch	63.60	**64.49**	63.22
Average	70.12	69.65	**70.71**

Table 6. Ablation study on MUS-10 dataset.

Unseen domain	UAAL/A	UAAL/D	UAAL
USPS	45.66	44.73	**48.40**
SVHN	30.98	33.89	**36.48**
MNIST	73.51	72.99	**76.13**
Average	44.76	50.54	**53.67**

Evaluation on MUS-10. Table 3 shows the results on MUS-10 dataset. Because there is no reported result on MUS-10 from other domain generalization work, we implement a baseline model based on CNN structures [1] for comparison. As shown in Table 3, our method outperforms the baseline model in all settings and verifies that the appearance generalizer and adversarial learning indeed help to learn a domain-invariant and class-discriminative latent vector space.

4.3 Ablation Study

To further verify the effectiveness of the proposed appearance generalizer and adversarial learning, we conduct experiments using models with different settings:

- UAAL: the proposed network, using the generalized dataset (X^U, Y^U) for training
- UAAL/A: the proposed network, using only the original source domains (X^S, Y^S) for training (i.e., without the appearance generalizer)
- UAAL/D: the proposed network without the discriminator, using (X^U, Y^U) for training

The experiments on Office-31 dataset are shown in Table 4. In the case $\{W, D\} \rightarrow A$, because of the similarities between W and D, the appearance generalizer little improves this case; nevertheless, our method still achieves the best result in all settings. The experiments on PACS dataset are shown in Table 5, where the results show that the best-averaged performance is obtained when including both the appearance generalizer and adversarial learning. The experiments on MUS-10 dataset are given in Table 6, where the adversarial learning improves significantly in this challenging case $\{M, S\} \rightarrow U$ and the appearance generalizer improves the case $\{M, U\} \rightarrow S$. With our prior constraint in the adversarial learning, we successfully encourage the latent space to be class-discriminative. In addition, the result shows that the appearance generalizer works well by learning a well-generalized appearance from different source domains.

Evaluation of Different Priors. To further explore the impact of using different priors, we show the results on PACS dataset in Table 7 using single Gaussian

Table 7. Evaluation of different priors on PACS dataset. B denotes the positive number in Eq. 7

Unseen domain	single Gaussian $\bar{z} \sim \mathcal{N}(0.707, 1^2)$	Gaussian mixture $B=5$ $\sigma=1$	Gaussian mixture $B=10$ $\sigma=1$
Photo	82.51	85.03	**85.39**
Art painting	56.25	64.60	**65.19**
Cartoon	64.93	63.35	**67.32**
Sketch	59.58	59.25	**63.22**
Average	65.82	68.06	**70.28**

distribution and Gaussian mixture distributions with different settings. Table 7 shows that single Gaussian prior yields the worst performance and that Gaussian mixture prior indeed encourages the representation to retain the class-discriminative nature.

5 Conclusion

In this paper, we propose a deep generalization framework UAAL to tackle the domain generalization problem for image classification. The proposed method includes a novel appearance generalizer to augment the training dataset with universal appearance learned from multiple source domains. Through an adversarial learning network under the Gaussian mixture prior assumption, our model successfully learns a domain-invariant and class-discriminative latent space. Our experiments on several benchmark cross-domain datasets show that our method outperforms existing methods.

References

1. Carlucci, F.M., D'Innocente, A., Bucci, S., Caputo, B., Tommasi, T.: Domain generalization by solving jigsaw puzzles. In: Proceedings of the IEEE Conference on Computer Vision and Pattern Recognition (CVPR) (2019)
2. Deng, J., Dong, W., Socher, R., Li, L.J., Li, K., Li, F.F.: ImageNet: a large-scale hierarchical image database. In: Proceedings of the IEEE Conference on Computer Vision and Pattern Recognition (CVPR) (2009)
3. Ding, Z., Fu, Y.: Deep domain generalization with structured low rank constraint. IEEE Trans. Image Process. **27**(1) (2018)
4. Ganin, Y.: Domain-adversarial training of neural networks. J. Mach. Learn. Res. **17**(59), 1–35 (2016)
5. Gatys, L.A., Ecker, A.S., Bethge, M.: Image style transfer using convolutional neural networks. In: Proceedings of the IEEE Conference on Computer Vision and Pattern Recognition (CVPR) (2016)
6. Ghifary, M., Kleijn, W.B., Zhang, M., Balduzzi, D.: Domain generalization for object recognition with multi-task autoencoders. In: Proceedings of the IEEE International Conference on Computer Vision (ICCV) (2015)

7. Goodfellow, I.J., et al.: Generative adversarial nets. In: Advances in Neural Information Processing Systems (NIPS) (2014)
8. He, K., Zhang, X., Ren, S., Sun, J.: Deep residual learning for image recognition. In: Proceedings of the IEEE Conference on Computer Vision and Pattern Recognition (CVPR) (2016)
9. Kingma, D.P., Ba, J.: Adam: a method for stochastic optimization (2014). arXiv preprint arXiv:1412.6980
10. Krizhevsky, A.: One weird trick for parallelizing convolutional neural networks (2014). arXiv:1404.5997
11. Lecun, Y., Bottou, L., Bengio, Y., Haffner, P.: Gradient-based learning applied to document recognition. Proc. IEEE **86**(11), 2278–2324 (1998)
12. Li, D., Yang, Y., Song, Y.Z., Hospedales, T.M.: Learning to generalize: meta learning for domain generalization. In: AAAI Conference on Artificial Intelligence (2018)
13. Li, D., Yang, Y., Song, Y.Z., Hospedales, T.: Deeper, broader and artier domain generalization. In: Proceedings of the IEEE International Conference on Computer Vision (ICCV) (2017)
14. Li, H., Pan, S.J., Wang, S., Kot, A.C.: Domain generalization with adversarial feature learning. In: Proceedings of the IEEE Conference on Computer Vision and Pattern Recognition (CVPR) (2018)
15. Li, Y., et al.: Deep domain generalization via conditional invariant adversarial networks. In: Ferrari, V., Hebert, M., Sminchisescu, C., Weiss, Y. (eds.) ECCV 2018. LNCS, vol. 11219, pp. 647–663. Springer, Cham (2018). https://doi.org/10.1007/978-3-030-01267-0_38
16. Mancini, M., Bulo, S.R., Caputo, B., Ricci, E.: Best sources forward: domain generalization through source-specific nets. In: IEEE International Conference on Image Processing (ICIP) (2018)
17. Muandet, K., Balduzzi, D., Schölkopf, B.: Domain generalization via invariant feature representation. In: Proceedings of the IEEE International Conference on Machine Learning (ICML) (2013)
18. Netzer, Y., Wang, T., Coates, A., Wu, B., Ng, A.Y.: Reading digits in natural images with unsupervised feature learning. In: Advances in Neural Information Processing Systems, January 2011
19. Rahman, M.M., Fookes, C., Baktashmotlagh, M., Sridharan, S.: Multi-component image translation for deep domain generalization. In: IEEE Winter Conference on Applications of Computer Vision (WACV) (2019)
20. Saenko, K., Kulis, B., Fritz, M., Darrell, T.: Adapting visual category models to new domains. In: Daniilidis, K., Maragos, P., Paragios, N. (eds.) ECCV 2010. LNCS, vol. 6314, pp. 213–226. Springer, Heidelberg (2010). https://doi.org/10.1007/978-3-642-15561-1_16
21. Sankaranarayanan, S., Balaji, Y., Castillo, C.D., Chellappa, R.: Generate to adapt: aligning domains using generative adversarial networks. In: Proceedings of the IEEE Conference on Computer Vision and Pattern Recognition (CVPR) (2018)
22. Simonyan, K., Zisserman, A.: Very deep convolutional networks for large-scale image recognition (2014). arXiv:1409.1556
23. Tzeng, E., Hoffman, J., Saenko, K., Darrell, T.: Adversarial discriminative domain adaptation (2017). arXiv preprint arXiv:1702.05464
24. Wang, H., He, Z., Lipton, Z.C., Xing, E.P.: Learning robust representations by projecting superficial statistics out. In: Proceedings of the International Conference on Learning Representation (ICLR) (2019)
25. Wang, X., Li, L., Ye, W., Long, M., Wang, J.: Transferable attention for domain adaptation. In: AAAI Conference on Artificial Intelligence (2019)

26. Wei, K.Y., Hsu, C.T.: Generative adversarial guided learning for domain adaptation. In: Proceedings of the British Machine Vision Conference (BMVC) (2018)
27. Li, W., Xu, Z., Xu, D., Dai, D., Gool, L.V.: Domain generalization and adaptation using low rank exemplar SVMs. IEEE Trans. Pattern Anal. Mach. Intell. **40**(5), 1114–1127 (2017)
28. Zhang, Y., Qiu, Z., Yao, T., Liu, D., Mei, T.: Fully convolutional adaptation networks for semantic segmentation. In: IEEE Conference on Computer Vision and Pattern Recognition (CVPR) (2018)

Pre-trained and Shared Encoder in Cycle-Consistent Adversarial Networks to Improve Image Quality

Runtong Zhang[1(✉)], Yuchen Wu[1(✉)], and Keiji Yanai[2(✉)]

[1] University of Electronic Science and Technology of China, Chengdu, China
3313560262@qq.com, wuyuchen1234567890@gmail.com
[2] The University of Electro-Communications, Tokyo, Japan
yanai@cs.uec.ac.jp

Abstract. Images generated from Cycle-Consistent Adversarial Network (CycleGAN) become blurry especially in areas with complex edges because of loss of edge information in downsampling of encoders. To solve this problem, we design a new model called ED-CycleGAN based on original CycleGAN. The key idea is using a pre-trained encoder: training an Encoder-Decoder Block (ED-Block) at first in order to get a difference map, which we call an edge map and is produced by the subtraction of input and output of the block. Then, the encoder part of a generator in CycleGAN share the parameters with the trained encoder of ED-Block and they will be frozen during training. Finally, by adding the output from a generator to the edge map, higher quality images can be produced. This structure performs excellently on "Apple2Orange", "Summer2Winter" and "blond-hair2brown-hair" datasets. We use SSIM and PSNR to evaluate resolution of results and our method achieved the highest evaluation scores among CycleGAN, Unit and DiscoGAN.

Keywords: ED-Block · Edge map · Pre-trained encoder · Cycle-consistent adversarial networks

1 Introduction

CycleGAN [10] realizes domain translation in the absence of paired data. The structure of two generators consists of three parts: an encoder, a transformer and a decoder. The size of images shrinks in the encoder, stays constant in the transformer, and expands again in the decoder. Because of downsampling process realized by stride-2 convolution layers of encoder, the information of edges in original images are lost. After being processed by the transformer, the images expands in the decoder but only a part of edge information are restored. Therefore, the output images will be blurry. Especially for some complex pictures, edges are mixed and it is difficult to distinguish object shapes.

Our contribution is to suppose a new network based on CycleGAN to improve image quality with appropriate amount of parameters and time expense.

S. Palaiahnakote et al. (Eds.): ACPR 2019, LNCS 12046, pp. 312–325, 2020.
https://doi.org/10.1007/978-3-030-41404-7_22

This network works well on “Apple2Orange” and “Summer2Winter” datasets provided by Zhu et al. [10] and also performs well on “blond-hair2brown-hair” datasets, which we collected from celebA dataset provided by [8]. Our network can be easily trained by only the highly successful backpropagation and model freezing. This method need high texture similarity between input and output and focus on color translation. Therefore, it can be used in enhancement of domain translated images, virtual makeup, hair-color changing and so on, all of which need color translation and high quality images.

2 Related Work

2.1 Cycle-Consistent Adversarial Networks

CycleGAN [10] realizes unpaired training data in image-to-image translation. This network consists of two Generative Adversarial Networks (GANs) [1] and inputs are two images in different domains. One input is translated from domain X to domain Y and the other is from Y to X. The key to CycleGAN's success is cycle-consistency loss, which represents cycle consistency and guarantees that the learned function can map an individual input to a desired output. The structure of two generators adopted from Johnson et al. [3] is the encoder-transformer-decoder: the input images will be shrunk in the encoder and expanded in the decoder. Information of edges are lost in this processing since downsampling is irreversible and transposed convolution layers cannot totally restore edge information in the decoder part. So when observing the output from CycleGAN, we can find some areas in images are blurry and indistinct. To solve this problem, our method is adding a new block called ED-Block in CycleGAN, which can extract edge map from input image. In this way, the edge information is protected from being lost in the encoder. By adding the edge map to the output from the generator, we can get the much clearer image as an output.

2.2 Super-Resolution

Super-Resolution (SR) refers to the reconstruction of corresponding high-resolution images from observed low-resolution images, which has important application value in monitoring equipment, satellite images and medical imaging. Super-Resolution Generative Adversarial Network (SRGAN) [6] is a SR problem method based on deep learning, using GAN [1]. The key point is that: since traditional method cannot make results enough smooth when the magnification of images is too large, SRGAN uses GAN to generate appropriate edge information to improve image resolution. But the generated edge information is irrelevant to input. Hence, when we zoom in the results, we can observe that although the generated edges have a good holistic visual feeling in whole image, they are visually meaningless in small visual field.

Therefore, we propose ED-Block, which can extract edge information of input, to remain the relevance between edge information and input images.

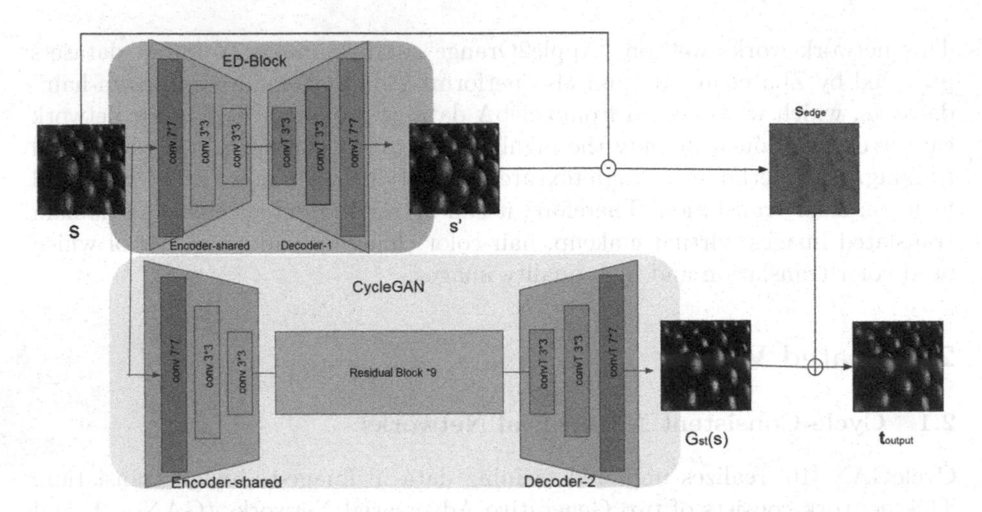

Fig. 1. The structure of our proposed network. The orange part is ED-Block consisting of only an encoder and an decoder. The gray part is original CycleGAN. ED-Block and CycleGAN share the same frozen encoder but their decoders are different.

In this way, we need not to train a GAN network to generate edge information, which costs too much time expense and memory cost, and we can get highly relevant edge information, which will be added to output to improve image quality.

3 Proposed Method

Edge information will be lost in the encoder because of irreversible downsampling and cannot be fully restored in the decoder. The key to our idea is extracting edge map of original input by a Encoder-Decoder Block (ED-Block) and adding them to the output from generator to restore the edge information.

3.1 Encoder-Decoder Block

Structure of Encoder-Decoder Block. The architecture of ED-Block is shown in Fig. 1 and is adopted from the generator of CycleGAN. First, an input image will be processed by a convolution layer followed by an instance normalization layer to transfer from 3 to 64 channels and kernel size is 7×7. Then, the image will be shrunk two times in the encoder, of which the downsampling is realized by two convolution layers using stride 2. Both of them are followed by an instance normalization layer and a ReLu layer. In the decoder, feature maps are expanded by two transpose convolution layers to original size. Both of two layers are followed by an instance normalization and a ReLu layer. Finally, feature maps are processed by a convolution layer to transfer to 3 channels and the kernel size of the layer is also 7×7 as that in the encoder. After Tanh operation, the recovered image are output to be used in subtraction.

Training Encoder-Decoder Block. ED-Block is trained in advance and then it will be frozen before training CycleGAN part. The work of ED-Block is to restore the input as much as possible even though restoring the original edge information is very difficult. In order to guarantee that the output is similar enough to input, we propose recover loss $\mathcal{L}_{recover}$ to train the ED-Block, which is L1 loss to measure the difference between recovered image s' and the original image s. This process can be shown below:

$$\mathcal{L}_{recover}(s, s') = ||s - s'||_1 \tag{1}$$

After the ED-Block has been trained well, the main visual difference between output images from it and input images are the edges and boundaries. Therefore, if we subtract the output images s' to the original input s, we can get edge map s_{edge}, which saves the necessary edge information. This process can be shown as Eq. 2.

$$s_{edge} = s - s' \tag{2}$$

The number of training ED-Block epoch is very significant. If the epoch is set too high, the edge map we get cannot has enough edge information. Since by more developed block, recovered images are more detailed and less information can be extracted by subtraction. Besides, if the epoch is set too small, it is difficult for block to reconstruct the image and some color information will be remained in edge map, which is not needed. We set the training epoch of ED-Block to 200 in our experiment and the reason will be illustrated in Sect. 4.2.

Comparison with CycleGAN with Skip-Connection. Skip-connection proposed in U-Net [9] realizes the effective use of feature maps of each layer in subsequent calculations by transmitting data of low-level layers directly, which improves accuracy of semantic segmentation. Therefore, CycleGAN with skip-connection can also avoid data lost caused by encoding process. However, the transmitted data in skip-connection channel not only includes edge information, but also includes color information of images. Because our ED-Block can selectively only extract edge information, the performance of CycleGAN with skip-connection cannot be better than ours. To make comparison, we design a CycleGAN with skip-connection structure, in which convolution layers of the encoder and the decoder with the same input sizes are connected by skip-connection channel to transmit data to the other end of network. Tables 2, 3 and 4 show the evaluation scores of ours and CycleGAN with skip-connection, which are symbolized as "Ours" and "CycleGAN-Skip" separately. The output images of CycleGAN-Skip are shown in the Fig. 6.

3.2 Partly Frozen CycleGAN

Structure of Generator. The generator has three parts: an encoder, a transformer and a decoder. The architecture is adopted from Johnson et al. [3]. Therefore, the encoder part is the same as that in Encoder-Decoder Block in order to share parameters while training. The transformer consists of nine residual blocks and each residual block consists of two stride-1 convolution layers, two instance normalization layers and a ReLu layer.

Structure of Discriminator. For the discriminator networks, we use 16×16 PatchGANs [2] aiming to distinct whether 94×94 overlapping image patches are real or fake. This PatchGANs consists of five convolution layers using stride-4 followed by instance normalization and Leaky ReLu layers.

Training CycleGAN. First, we apply the parameters of the pre-trained encoder of ED-Block to two generators in CycleGAN and freeze them. With the same frozen parameters in the encoder, the lost edge information are the same in both ED-Block and the generator. Therefore, the extracted edge information from ED-Block can have high relevance to the output from the generator. The initialization of rest parameters of the other layers are using Gaussian distribution $N(0, 0.02)$.

We adopt adversarial losses [1] and cycle consistency loss [10] to train CycleGAN. For adversarial loss, G_{st} aims to transfer image s of source domain into image $G_{st}(s)$ of target domain to fake D_T, while D_T aims to correctly identify the real image t and fake image, which is integration of G_{st}(s) and s_{edge} calculated by Eq. 2. Equation 3 is the adversarial loss, which G_{st} tries to minimize but D_T tries to maximize.

$$\mathcal{L}^s_{adv}(G_{st}, D_T) = \mathbb{E}_{t \sim P_T(t)}[\log D_T(t)] + \mathbb{E}_{s \sim P_S(s)}[\log(1 - D_T(G_{st}(s) + s_{edge}))] \quad (3)$$

According to Zhu et al. [10], input s can be mapped to any random permutation of images since it is hard to guarantee the learned mapping function only with adversarial loss. Therefore, cycle consistency loss is used to further reduce the space of possible mapping functions. G_{st} aims to transfer input to target domain and G_{ts} aims to transfer fake images, which combines $G_{st}(s)$ with s_{edge}, back to source domain, which is shown in Eq. 4. The final recovered image s'' will be calculated with original input s to get the difference to back propagation. This process is shown in Eq. 5.

$$s'' = G_{ts}\big(G_{st}(s) + s_{edge}\big) + s_{edge} \quad (4)$$

$$\mathcal{L}^s_{cyc}(s, s'') = ||s - s''||_1 \quad (5)$$

Moreover, s'' is got from G_{ts} plus s_{edge} rather than plus t_{edge} in Eq. 4. Because s_{edge} is extracted from input s and t_{edge} is from the generated image in the target domain, the edge information of s_{edge} is better than that of t_{edge}. Hence, we choose s_{edge} rather than t_{edge} in cycle consistency process. Besides, we shows the evaluation scores of using s_{edge} and t_{edge} separately, which are symbolized as "Ours" and "Ours (with t_{edge})" in Tables 2, 3 and 4. The output images of "Ours (with t_{edge})" are shown in the Fig. 6.

Finally, we combine the adversarial and cycle-consistency losses for both source and target domains to optimize the final energy, which is shown below:

$$\mathcal{L}(G_{st}, G_{ts}, D_s, D_t) = \mathcal{L}^s_{adv} + \mathcal{L}^t_{adv} + \lambda(\mathcal{L}^s_{cyc} + \mathcal{L}^t_{cyc}) \quad (6)$$

We use the loss hyper-parameters λ=10 in our experiments. The optimal parameters of $\mathcal{L}$ are obtained by solving the minimax optimization problem:

$$G^*_{st}, G^*_{ts}, D^*_s, D^*_t = \underset{G^*_{st}, G^*_{ts}}{argmin}\Big(\underset{D^*_s, D^*_t}{argmax}\mathcal{L}\big(G^*_{st}, G^*_{ts}, D^*_s, D^*_t\big)\Big) \quad (7)$$

4 Experiments

4.1 Training Setting

The usage of s_{edge} needs high texture similarity between output and input. Therefore, the domain translation should not translate the object textures and edges but only translate color. To ensure this premise, we use "Apple to Orange" and "Summer to Winter" datasets provided by Zhu et al. [10] and "blond-hair2brown-hair" datasets including about 3000 blond and brown hair images from celebA dataset provided by [8] to train models and we adopt CycleGAN's notation to illustrate our structures. For example, "c7s1-k-R" means a 7×7 convolution layer with stride 1 and k filters, followed by a ReLU activation and "ct3s2 k-LR" means a 3×3 transposed convolution layer with stride 2 and k filters, followed by a LeakyReLU activation with slop 0.2. "rk" denotes a residual block with k filters. A tanh activation is indicated by 'T'. Moreover, we apply instance normalization after all convolution layers and transposed convolution layers except the first convolution layer of discriminator and the last convolution layers of decoder and discriminator. The structures of our model are shown below:

ED-Block structure is: c7s1-64-R, c3s2-128-R, c3s2-256-R, ct3s2-128-R, ct3s2-64-R, c7s1-3-T.

Residual Block structure is: c3s1-256-R, c3s1-256

Generator structure is: c7s1-64-R, c3s2-128-R, c3s2-256-R, r256, r256, r256, r256, r256, r256, r256, r256, r256, ct3s2-128-R, ct3s2-64-R, c7s1-3-T.

Discriminator structure is: c4s2-64-LR, c4s2-128-LR, c4s2-256-LR, c4s2-512-LR, c4s1-1

All batch sizes of ours and other models for comparison are 4 and we use Adam solver [5] to optimize parameters and initial learning rate is 0.0002, which will decrease in each epoch after 100 epochs. We use GPU Intel Core i7-4790 (3.60 GHz) to train models.

4.2 Training Epoch of ED-Block

The epoch of training ED-Block should be proper to reconstructed the input image better with smaller loss $\mathcal{L}_{recover}$ and less time expense. Figure 2 shows the generated results when the number of training epochs are 10, 50, 100, 200, and 500. We can observe that in the results of 10, 50, 100 epochs, there are a little needless remaining color information and its amount decreases by epochs. In the edge maps of 200 and 500 epochs, the color information is eliminated. Therefore, the ED-Block should be trained in enough epochs to get rid of color influence. Figure 3 shows the graph of $\mathcal{L}_{recover}$ during training. We can observe that $\mathcal{L}_{recover}$ in 500 epochs is only a little lower than that in 200 epochs but with much higher time expense. Based on Fig. 2 and Fig. 3, we set training epoch of ED-Block to 200.

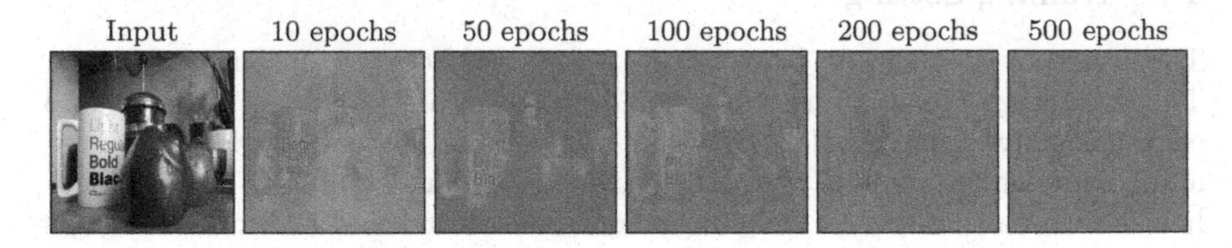

Fig. 2. The results of ED-Block by different training epochs. In the lower training epochs, such as 10, 50, 100 epochs, color information remains in edge map. The higher training epochs, the less color residues. In 200 and 500 epochs, remained color information is not visually obvious. (Color figure online)

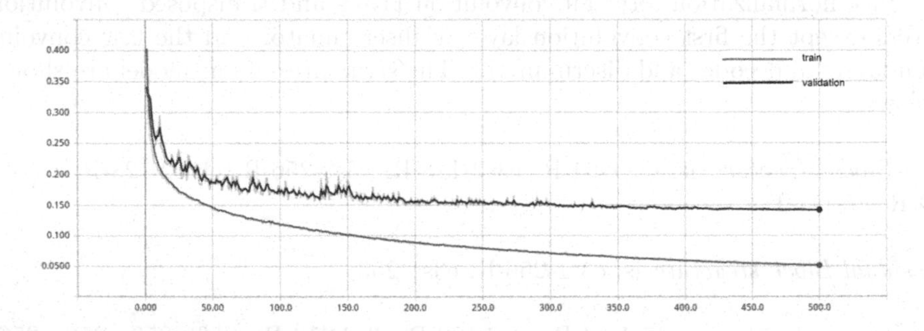

Fig. 3. The graph of $\mathcal{L}_{recover}$ during 500 training epochs. Loss function drops rapidly in first 100 epochs and tends to be gentle later.

4.3 Results

Figure 4 represents the generator loss decrease during 200 training epochs. Because the encoder is pre-trained and frozen and only the transformer and the decoder part need to be trained, our models has much faster convergence speed compared with CycleGAN. Figure 5 shows the results from ours, original CycleGAN, Unit [7] and DiscoGAN [4] in 200 training epochs. Figure 6 shows the results from our model, our model using t_{edge} in cycle consistency equation, CycleGAN and CycleGAN with skip-connection channels. We can observe that our model remains much more edge information so that the results are far clearer and have more texture compared with other results, which are obviously blurry. Therefore, our network has achieved a great progress in improving the image quality.

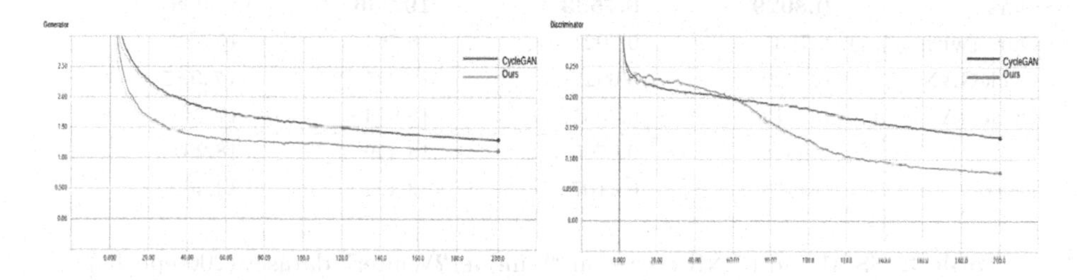

Fig. 4. The left side graph shows loss value of two generators and right side graph shows loss value of two discriminator during 200 epochs.

4.4 Evaluation and Discussion

Table 1 shows the comparison on quantity of parameters and time training expense on "Apple2Orange" dataset. The amount of parameters of our model is same as CycleGAN and much less than DiscoGAN while Unit has least parameters. The time expenses of ours, CycleGAN and DiscoGAN do not have large difference and much less than that of Unit. To summarize, our model has a compromise between the amount of parameters and training time expense.

We use SSIM and PSNR, of which input are real images and cycle consistency image shown in Fig. 7 and Fig. 8, to evaluate image resolution. Table 2, Table 3 and Table 4 show the SSIM and PSNR scores of Ours, Ours (with t_{edge}), CycleGAN, CycleGAN-Skip, Unit [7] and DiscoGAN [4] after 200 training epochs on "Apple2Orange", "Summer2Winter" and "blond-hair2brown-hair" datasets.

Our model achieves the highest scores among them except PSNR score of consistent-orange. Ours (with t_{edge}) achieves the second highest SSIM scores on "apple2orange" and "Summer2Winter" datasets and only a little lower than CycleGAN on "blond-hair2brown-hair" dataset but PSNR scores are not ideal.

Table 1. Models comparison.

Model	Parameters (10^5)	Time expense (hours)
ED-Block	7.56	1.533
Our-CycleGAN	275.30	16.898
CycleGAN	282.86	15.35
Unit	270.66	21.198
Disco	598.1	16.844

Table 2. SSIM and PSNR scores on "Apple2Orange" dataset.(200 epochs)

Model	SSIM		PSNR(dB)	
	consistent-apple	consistent-orange	consistent-apple	consistent-orange
Ours	**0.8029**	**0.7503**	**19.266**	17.068
Ours (with t_{edge})	0.7535	0.7021	16.764	15.582
CycleGAN	0.7329	0.6927	19.035	**17.985**
CycleGAN-Skip	0.7412	0.7061	18.654	17.743
Unit	0.6948	0.6705	18.449	18.297
Disco	0.4403	0.4107	13.424	14.462

Table 3. SSIM and PSNR scores on "Summer2Winter" dataset.(200 epochs)

Model	SSIM		PSNR(dB)	
	consistent-summer	consistent-winter	consistent-summer	consistent-winter
Ours	**0.8410**	**0.8318**	**21.267**	**20.622**
Ours (with t_{edge})	0.8059	0.8089	19.433	19.314
CycleGAN	0.7842	0.7911	20.259	20.013
CycleGAN-Skip	0.7726	0.7850	19.903	20.054
Unit	0.7025	0.7188	19.031	18.878
Disco	0.6688	0.6699	18.765	18.124

Table 4. SSIM and PSNR scores on "Blond-hair2Brown-hair" dataset.(200 epochs)

Model	SSIM		PSNR(dB)	
	consistent-blond	consistent-brown	consistent-blond	consistent-brown
Ours	**0.8682**	**0.8903**	**24.679**	**24.744**
Ours (with t_{edge})	0.8189	0.8283	22.188	20.731
CycleGAN	0.8222	0.8554	22.799	23.553
CycleGAN-Skip	0.6821	0.6910	17.028	16.206
Unit	0.7889	0.8046	22.521	22.583
Disco	0.7637	0.7924	20.539	21.248

Fig. 5. Image translation results from "Apple2Orange", "Summer2Winter" and "Blond-hair2Brown-hair" datasets in 200 epochs. From top to bottom is apple to orange, orange to apple, summer to winter, winter to summer, blond hair to brown hair and brown hair to blond hair.

Since PSNR realizes image evaluation based on the mean-square error between corresponding pixels and does not take into account the visual characteristics of human eyes, the ability to capture perceptually relevant differences is very

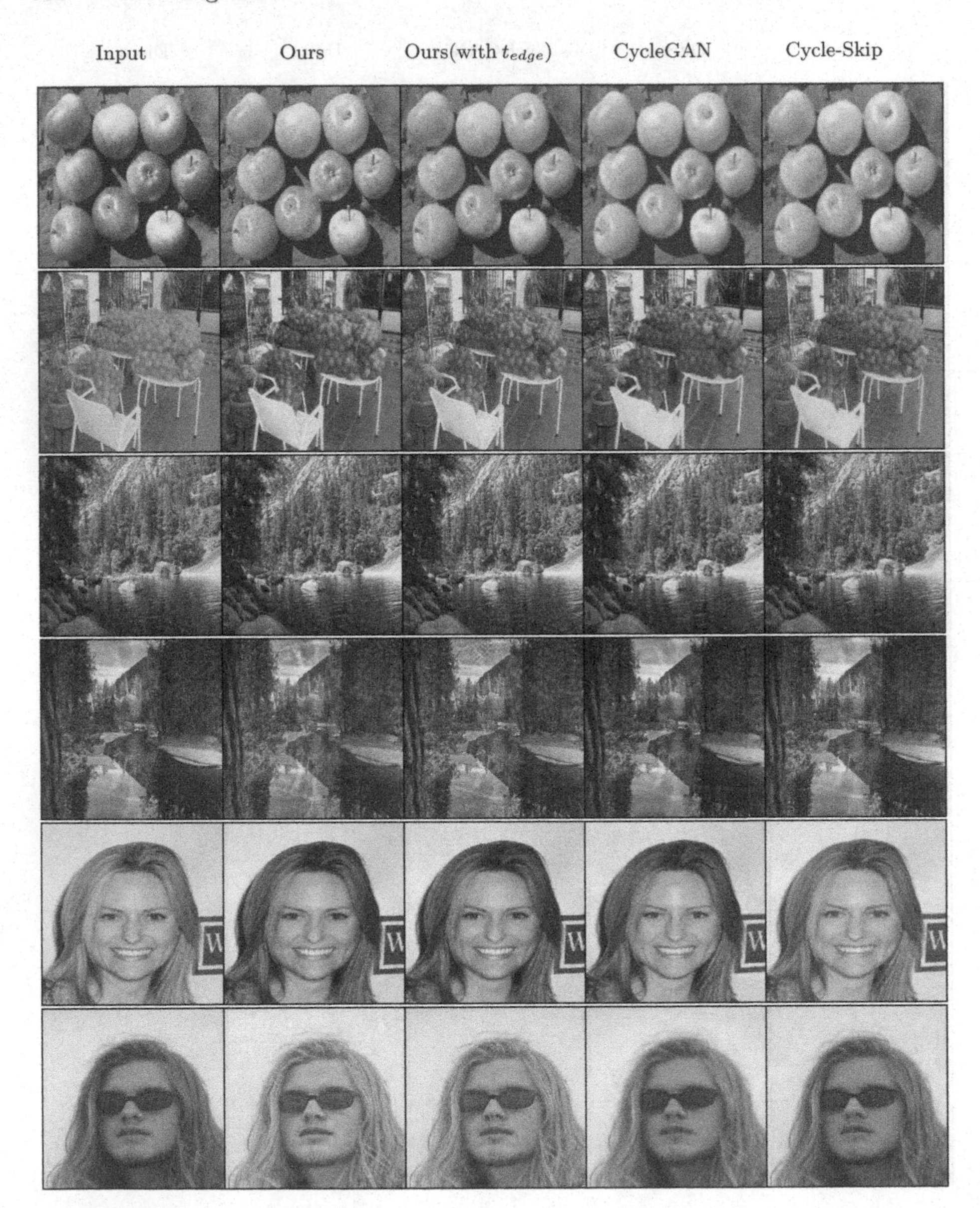

Fig. 6. Image translation results from "Apple2Orange", "Summer2Winter" and "Blond-hair2Brown-hair" dataset in 200 epochs. From top to bottom is apple to orange, orange to apple, summer to winter, winter to summer, blond hair to brown hair and brown hair to blond hair.

limited and it is acceptable that the score is inconsistent with people's subjective feelings in some cases. But in Figs. 7 and 8, we can observe that our cycle-consistency orange image is really clearer than those of other models. CycleGAN

Fig. 7. The cycle consistency images in 200 epochs of Ours, CycleGAN, Unit and DiscoGAN. The results from our models has less artifacts and are much clearer and more similar to input.

and CycleGAN-Skip get similar evaluation scores on "apple2orange" and "summer2winter" datasets but have a large disparity on "blond-hair2brown-hair" dataset, which illustrates that only adding skip-connection channel to generators cannot improve images quality greatly since transmitted data consists of not only edge information but also color information. The transmitted color

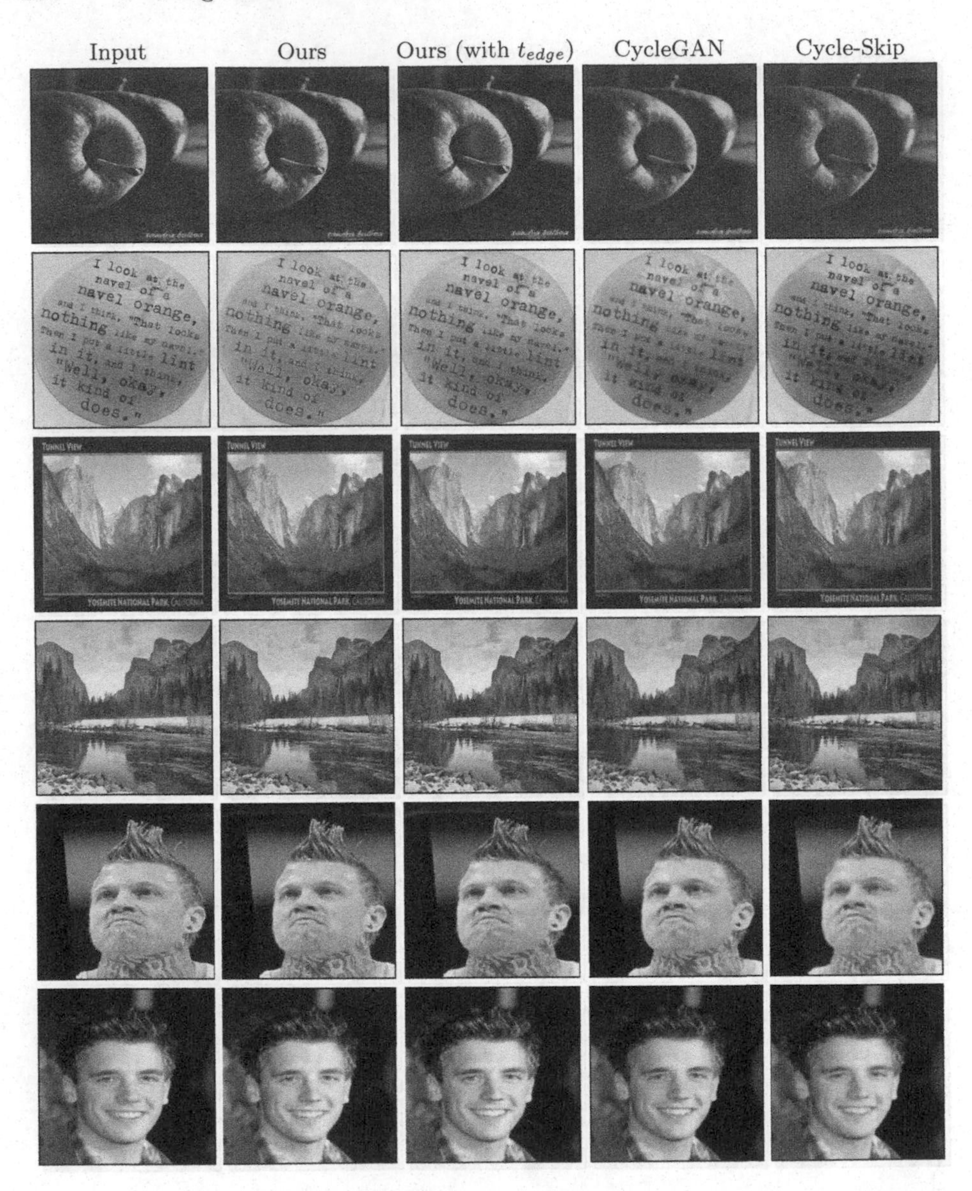

Fig. 8. The cycle consistency images in 200 epochs of Ours, Ours (with t_{edge}), CycleGAN, and CycleGAN with skip-connection. The results from our models has less artifacts and are much clearer and more similar to input.

information even have a bad perceptual effect on cycle consistent images to cause low evaluation score. Finally, DiscoGAN obtains the lowest scores among them on "apple2orange" and "Summer2Winter" datasets and also performs not well on "blond-hair2brown-hair" dataset because of deeper convolution layers in encoder without any solution to protect edge information. To summarize, our model have achieved the highest evaluation scores and our results are visually excellent.

5 Conclusions

In this paper, we proposed ED-CycleGAN to improve the image quality of CycleGAN. The ED-Block extracts edge maps of input firstly to prevent edge information from being destroyed in the encoder processing. Then two generators of CycleGAN share the pre-trained and frozen encoder of ED-Block during training. And finally processed images are integrated with edge maps as final outputs of generator. Our model, ED-CycleGAN, improves the image quality of generators with less time expense and get highest SSIM and PSNR scores compared with CycleGAN, Unit and DiscoGAN.

References

1. Goodfellow, I., et al.: Generative adversarial nets. In: Ghahramani, Z., Welling, M., Cortes, C., Lawrence, N.D., Weinberger, K.Q. (eds.) Advances in Neural Information Processing Systems, vol. 27, pp. 2672–2680. Curran Associates, Inc. (2014)
2. Isola, P., Zhu, J.Y., Zhou, T., Efros, A.A.: Image-to-image translation with conditional adversarial networks. In: 2017 IEEE Conference on Computer Vision and Pattern Recognition (CVPR) (2017)
3. Johnson, J., Alahi, A., Fei-Fei, L.: Perceptual losses for real-time style transfer and super-resolution. In: Leibe, B., Matas, J., Sebe, N., Welling, M. (eds.) ECCV 2016. LNCS, vol. 9906, pp. 694–711. Springer, Cham (2016). https://doi.org/10.1007/978-3-319-46475-6_43
4. Kim, T., Cha, M., Kim, H., Lee, J.K., Kim, J.: Learning to discover cross-domain relations with generative adversarial networks. In: Proceedings of the 34th International Conference on Machine Learning, ICML 2017, vol. 70, pp. 1857–1865. JMLR.org (2017)
5. Kingma, D.P., Ba, J.: Adam: a method for stochastic optimization. arXiv preprint arXiv:1412.6980 (2014)
6. Ledig, C., et al.: Photo-realistic single image super-resolution using a generative adversarial network. In: CVPR (2017)
7. Liu, M.Y., Breuel, T., Kautz, J.: Unsupervised image-to-image translation networks. In: Guyon, I., et al. (eds.) Advances in Neural Information Processing Systems, vol. 30, pp. 700–708. Curran Associates, Inc. (2017)
8. Liu, Z., Luo, P., Wang, X., Tang, X.: Deep learning face attributes in the wild. In: Proceedings of International Conference on Computer Vision (ICCV), December 2015
9. Ronneberger, O., Fischer, P., Brox, T.: U-Net: convolutional networks for biomedical image segmentation. In: Navab, N., Hornegger, J., Wells, W.M., Frangi, A.F. (eds.) MICCAI 2015. LNCS, vol. 9351, pp. 234–241. Springer, Cham (2015). https://doi.org/10.1007/978-3-319-24574-4_28
10. Zhu, J.Y., Park, T., Isola, P., Efros, A.A.: Unpaired image-to-image translation using cycle-consistent adversarial networks. In: 2017 IEEE International Conference on Computer Vision (ICCV) (2017)

MobileGAN: Compact Network Architecture for Generative Adversarial Network

Tomoyuki Shimizu, Jianfeng Xu(✉), and Kazuyuki Tasaka

KDDI Research, 2-1-15 Ohara, Saitama 356-8502, Japan
{tomoyuki,ji-xu}@kddi-research.jp

Abstract. In this paper we introduce a compact neural network architecture for a generator of generative adversarial network (GAN), which reduces the number of weight parameters so that mobile devices can afford to download these parameters via cellular networks.

Network architecture of GAN generator usually consists of a fully-connected layer on top and succeeding convolutional layers with upscaling which extend picture characteristics to a larger image. Consequently, the GAN generator network is highly enlarged, and the size of its weight parameters becomes tens or hundreds of MBs, which is not preferable for transmission over cellular network or running on mobile or embedded devices.

Our approach named MobileGAN is based on layer decomposition technique like MobileNets. At a generator side, all convolutional layers except the bottom layer to output an RGB image are decomposed into pixelwise and depthwise convolutional layers to reduce the number of weight parameters. Also, the first fully-connected layer is decomposed into a couple of 1-dimensional convolution layers for the similar purpose. On the other hand, our approach does not modify any layers in discriminator network in order to maintain picture quality of output images generated by the decomposed generator network.

We evaluated the performance of MobileGAN generator network by Inception Score and Fréchet Inception Distance. As a result, we confirmed that MobileGAN can reduce the size of weight parameter into up to 20.5% of generator network of ResNet GAN with slight score degradation.

Keywords: Generative adversarial network · Compact network architecture · Decomposition

1 Introduction

Recent activities on Generative Adversarial Network (GAN) [1] have achieved great improvement on high-fidelity image generation. Network architecture of GAN is fundamentally based on convolutional neural network [2], and has been improved by a lot of efforts to improve picture quality of generated images [3–6]. A basic GAN structure consists of two convolutional networks, generator and discriminator. In a training process of GAN, a discriminator learns images in a training dataset as real images and images generated by a generator as fake images, and then the generator is trained to produce

S. Palaiahnakote et al. (Eds.): ACPR 2019, LNCS 12046, pp. 326–338, 2020.
https://doi.org/10.1007/978-3-030-41404-7_23

images so that the discriminator might misinterpret them as real images. The generator network architecture is typically constructed almost in a reversed network architecture of the generator; the discriminator network contains blocks of convolutional layers like ResNet [7] with downsampling or strides followed by vector conversion like global average pooling or fully-connected layer, while the generator network contains one or fully-connected layers on top and succeeding convolutional layers blocks with upsampling. In this scheme, both discriminator and generator require a larger amount of weight parameters to recognize and generate wider variety and deeper details of picture characteristics. Consequently, the size of weight parameters in discriminator and generator networks increases to tens or hundreds of megabytes.

Another challenge for practical use of deep neural networks (DNNs) is DNNs on mobile devices. Generally, running DNN models on user devices can eliminate network traffic and latency to transmit inference results and unwanted exchanges of privacy information with cloud servers. For instance, there have been well-known machine learning frameworks which run on mobile operating systems with hardware acceleration [8, 9], which enable mobile and embedded devices to run DNN applications like object classification, human pose estimation, semantic segmentation, etc. Machine learning processors for mobile devices have been rapidly evolving [10, 11] and have become capable of running larger and more advanced DNN applications. However, several practical issues for mobile DNN applications remains; storage and network usage for application installation. For these reasons, several network architecture for mobile devices have been proposed [12–14].

Our goal is to build a mobile application which utilizes a GAN generator, since GAN applications practically need a generator running on the device while discriminators are necessary only during training. Image generation on user devices has some advantages; it can suppress network traffic for image downloading and keep generated images private. In this paper, we propose compact network architecture of a generator convolutional neural network named MobileGAN, and introduce experimental results using several datasets.

2 Related Work

Evolution of deep convolutional neural network has been achieved by accumulation of convolutional layers [15, 16] and improvement on building block structure [7] during the past several years. Those advancement, however, has resulted in large increase of the number of convolutional layers or weight parameters. The size of GAN generator network is inevitably enlarged by increasing the number of channels in convolutional layers for further improvement on variety and details of picture quality. For instance, the number of weight parameters of generator network for images in 64×64 pixels are shown in Table 1 in detail. The architecture of ResBlockUp block used in the generator network is shown in Fig. 1.

The files size of those weight parameters in single-precision floating point becomes approximately 46.6 MB. This would imply that the files size of weight parameters of larger image generators could be tens or hundreds of MBs, which would not be preferable for storage in mobile devices or transmission over cellular network.

Table 1. Number of weight parameters in ResNet-based generator

Building block	# of parameters (incl. biases)
$z \in \mathbb{R}^{128} \sim \mathcal{N}(0, 1)$	
Dense → 4 × 4 × 1024	2,113,536 (=128 × 4 × 4 × 1,024 + 4 × 4 × 1,024)
ResBlockUp 1024	7,603,712
ResBlockUp 512	1,901,312
ResBlockUp 256	475,520
ResBlockUp 128	118,976
BN, Leaky ReLU, 3 × 3 Conv2D 3, Tanh	1,731 (=64 × 3 × 3 × 3 + 3)
Total	12,214,787

Note: # of parameters in ResBlockUp C equals to $C \times 3 \times 3 \times (C/2) + (C/2) + (C/2) \times 3 \times 3 \times (C/2) + (C/2) + C \times (C/2) + C/2$.

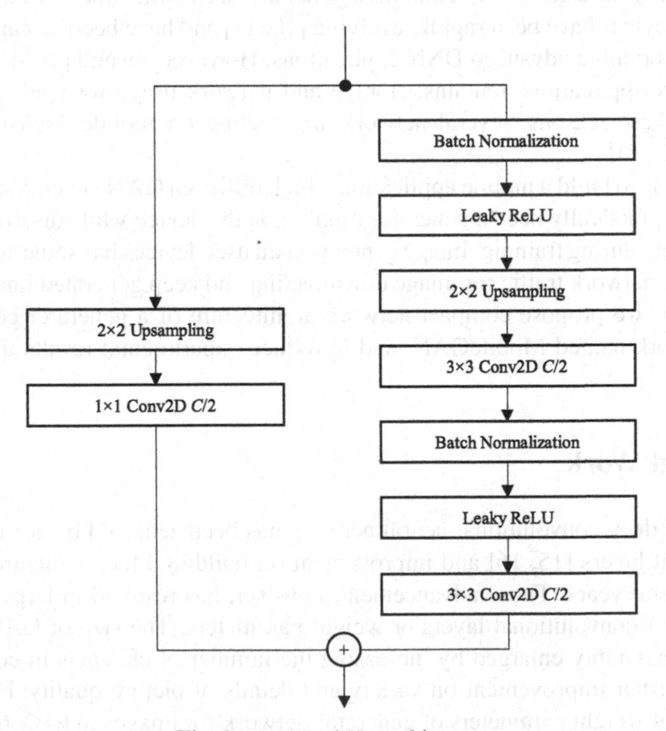

Fig. 1. ResBlockUp architecture

Most of those weight parameters belong to filter weights in convolutional layers. Therefore, we describe conventional weight parameter reduction schemes for convolutional layers in this section.

2.1 MobileNetV1: Separable Convolution

MobileNetV1 [12] introduces Separable Convolution as its key building block. For kernel size of $k \times k$, and the numbers of input and output channel dimensions C_{in}, C_{out}, Separable Convolution decomposes convolutional kernel $K \in \mathcal{R}^{k \times k \times C_{in} \times C_{out}}$ into depthwise convolutional kernel $K_{dw} \in \mathcal{R}^{k \times k}$ and pointwise convolutional kernel $K_{pw} \in \mathcal{R}^{C_{in} \times C_{out}}$. Depthwise convolution layer applies $k \times k$ convolution filter per channel, and then pointwise convolution layer applies 1×1 convolutional layer to extend channel dimension from C_{in} to C_{out}. This decomposition scheme reduces weight parameters of the filter from $k \times k \times C_{in} \times C_{out}$ to $k \times k + C_{in} \times C_{out}$, while it can empirically work as well as the regular convolutional layers at only small accuracy degradation (Fig. 2).

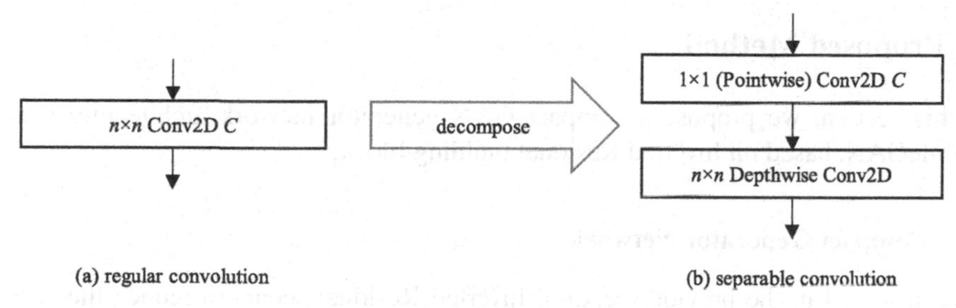

Fig. 2. Separable Convolution

Separable Convolution can reduce weight parameters if the kernel size k is larger than 1. In the case of ResBlockUp architecture, this scheme takes effect in two 3×3 Conv2D layers, while a single 1×1 Conv2D layer cannot be changed at all.

2.2 MobileNetV2: Inverted Residuals

In order to reduce channel dimension of the residual path, MobileNetV2 [13] proposes the Inverted Residuals architecture. A residual path in the regular ResNet architecture directly connects input to output. In this architecture, the number of weight parameter can be eliminated by applying the factor $1/t$ to the middle convolutional layer (Fig. 3(a)). However, larger dimensions of input and output channels still become bottleneck for weight parameter reduction.

On the other hand, MobileNetV2 offers more efficient architecture named Inverted Residuals (Fig. 3(b)). This building block has smaller dimensions of input and output channels, and the channel dimension is expanded for a depthwise convolutional layer in the middle of the building block. Its residual path now connects reduced input and output channel dimensions and the convolutional kernel of 1×1 Conv2D on the residual path becomes smaller than that of regular ResNet block. Although the input channel dimension of the middle depthwise convolution is expanded, the convolutional kernel of the depthwise convolution still remains $k \times k$.

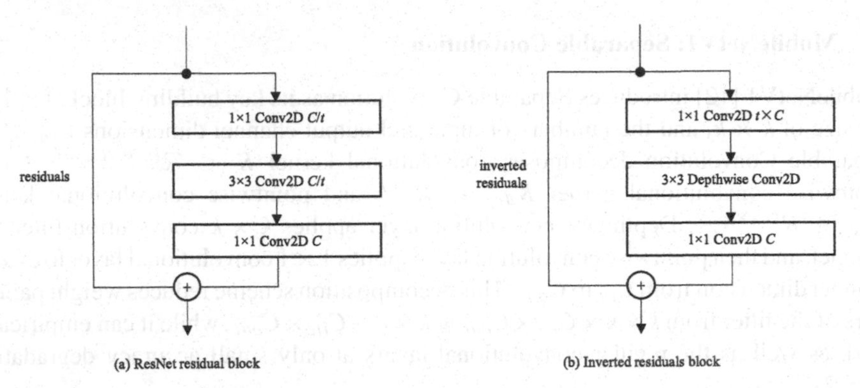

Fig. 3. Inverted Residuals

3 Proposed Method

In this section, we propose a compact GAN generator network architecture named MobileGAN, based on Inverted Residual building block.

3.1 Compact Generator Network

As considered in the previous section, Inverted Residual seems to reduce the size of weight parameters in ResBlockUp building efficiently with slight quality degradation.

On the other hand, typical GAN generator network architecture starts with a fully-connected layer with greatly large dimension of output channel. For instance, the 64 × 64-pixel generator network illustrated in Sect. 2 includes a fully-connected layer with approximately two million weight parameters as shown in Table 1. Critical difference from popular deep convolutional networks for image classification such as [7, 12, 13, 15, 16] is that channel dimension of a fully-connected layer on top of GAN generators depends on details and resolution of their output images and there is no equivalent vectorization technique without weight parameter like Global Average Pooling which is applicable for GAN generators. Therefore, weight parameter reduction scheme for fully-connected layer can also be a key feature for compact GAN generator.

3.1.1 Compact Residual Block

In MobileGAN, we apply CResBlockUp building block shown in Fig. 4 as a compact architecture of ResBlockUp.

CResBlockUp is modified architecture of Inverted Residuals optimized as an upsampling building block for GAN generator. Major difference between Inverted Residuals and CResBlockUp is that the CResBlockUp architecture includes two successive depthwise convolutional layers as an expansion part, because the regular ResBlockUp architecture shown in Fig. 1 contains two 3 × 3 Conv2D layers which can induce picture characteristic parameters for upsampled images per pixel from neighboring 5 × 5 regions.

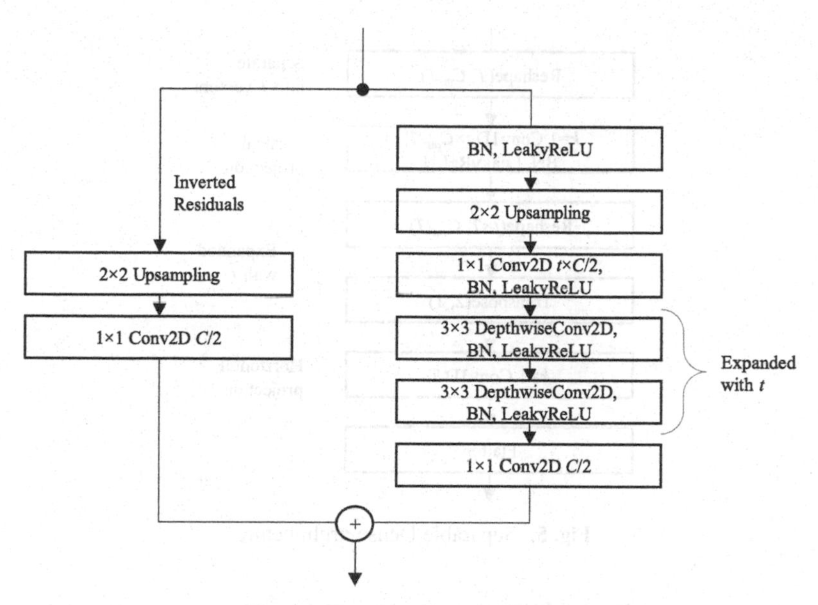

Fig. 4. CResBlockUp architecture

3.1.2 Separable Dense

For the purpose of further parameter reduction, we adopt another compact building block named Separable Dense shown in Fig. 5, as a replacement for a fully-connected layer on top.

A basic idea of Separable Dense is to decompose projection operation of a fully-connected layer into two stages by mapping C_{in}-dimensional input vector into 2-D tensor $(T, C_{in}/T)$ and decomposing the fully-connected projection into two stages, vertical and horizontal projection. These stages of decomposed projection perform fully-connected projection at every divided row or column vector parallelly. The vertical projection maps the tensor $(T, C_{in}/T)$ onto the tensor $(T, C_{out}/T)$, and the projected tensor is transposed into $(C_{out}/T, T)$, and then the horizontal projection maps the transposed tensor onto $(C_{out}/T, T)$, and finally the output tensor is flattened into C_{out}-dimensional vector. This decomposition technique can reduce the number of weight parameters from $C_{in} \times C_{out} + C_{out}$ to $(C_{in} \times C_{out}/T + C_{out}) + C_{out} \times (T + 1)$.

On the other hand, such a vector composition scheme is not commonly supported by typical neural network framework implementations. Instead of those two stages of parallel fully-connected projection, we apply 1-D convolutional layers with the kernel size of 1 to Separable Dense architecture for better compatibility with framework implementations and further weight parameter reduction. Also, weight parameter expansion with the factor t is adopted in a similar manner to Inverted Residuals for better projection representation.

Consequently, Separable Dense reduces the number into $(t \times C_{in} \times C_{out}/T^2 + t \times C_{out}/T) + (t \times T^2 + T)$. If $C_{in} = 128$ and $C_{out} = 4 \times 4 \times 1024$, as indicated in Table 1, and $t = T = 8$, the number of weight parameters is modified from 2,113,536 to 279,048 by Separable Dense architecture.

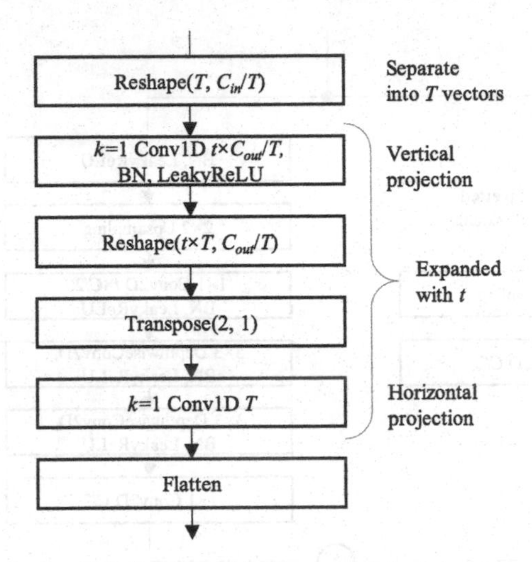

Fig. 5. Separable Dense architecture

3.2 Asymmetric GAN Architecture

We adopt asymmetric GAN architecture of discriminator and generator named MobileGAN shown in Table 2. The discriminator network architecture shown in Table 2, mainly consists of succeeding ResBlockDown building blocks shown in Fig. 6. Spectral Normalization [17] is applied to stabilize the training process of this discriminator. Please note that the generator network architecture does not adopt Spectral Normalization, though it is shown that applying Spectral Normalization to both discriminator and generator can stabilize GAN training even better [18]. The reason is that our network architecture is mainly intended for use on mobile and embedded environment and we need to restrict all layers to commonly used operations.

Table 2. MobileGAN network architecture

Discriminator	Generator
RGB image $x \in \mathbb{R}^{64\times64\times3}$	$z \in \mathbb{R}^{128} \sim \mathcal{N}(0, 1)$
ResBlockDown 64	Separable Dense → 4 × 4 × 1024
ResBlockDown 128	$t = 6$ CResBlockUp 192
ResBlockDown 256	$t = 6$ CResBlockUp 128
ResBlockDown 512	$t = 6$ CResBlockUp 96
ResBlockDown 1024	$t = 6$ CResBlockUp 72
ReLU	BN, Leaky ReLU, 3 × 3 Conv2D 3, Tanh
Global Average Pooling	
Spectral Norm Dense → 1	

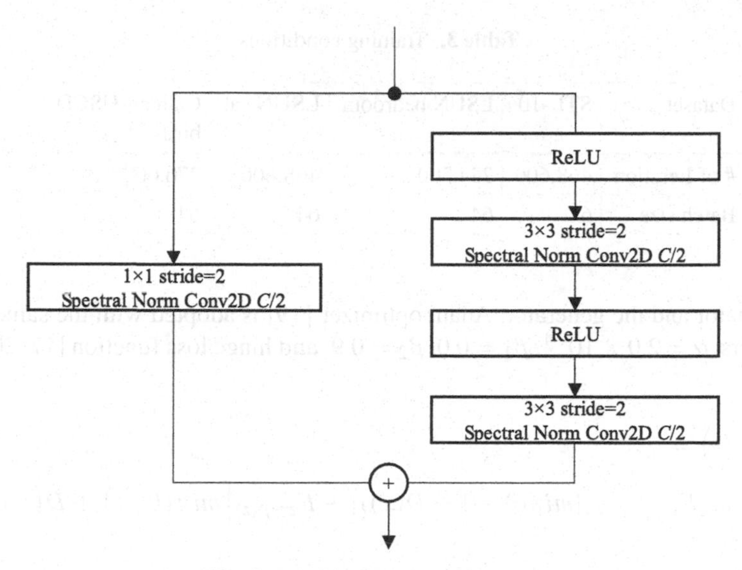

Fig. 6. ResBlockDown architecture

Although both discriminator and generator generally have symmetric network architecture, e.g. ResBlockDown-based and ResBlockUp-based, our approach modifies only the generator network architecture. This asymmetric architecture is intended to maintain picture quality of generated images regardless of weight parameter reduction on the generator.

The generator is trained to produce fake images so that the discriminator would misinterpret them as real images. In other words, the picture quality of generated images closely depends on how elaborately the discriminator becomes capable of distinguishing fake images from real images. For this reason, the discriminator preserves its network architecture so that the MobileGAN generator can be trained as hard as regular generators.

4 Experiments

We conducted a series of experiments of unsupervised image generation on STL-10 [21], LSUN [22], and Caltech-USCD Birds 200 [23], and compared our method MobileGAN with regular ResNet-based GAN Architecture, for the purpose of evaluation on picture quality degradation due to weight parameter reduction. As criteria for picture quality evaluation of generated images, we used Inception Score [3] and Fréchet Inception Distance (FID) [24]. Detailed training conditions for every dataset are indicated in Table 3.

Training procedure of discriminator and generator is almost the same as one illustrated in [17]. At each training step, the discriminator is fed with batches of real images and fake images produced by the generator at five times, and the generator is fed with a batch of random latent vectors to train the generator so that the discriminator would classify them as real images. These steps are iterated alternately. In training of the

Table 3. Training conditions

Dataset	STL-10	LSUN bedroom	LSUN cat	Caltech-USCD birds
# of Iteration	468,600	234,300	468,600	276,000
Batch size	64	64	64	64

discriminator and the generator, Adam optimizer [19] is adopted with the same hyper-parameters, $\alpha = 2.0 \times 10^{-4}$, $\beta_1 = 0.0$, $\beta_2 = 0.9$, and hinge loss function [17, 20] given by:

$$V_D\left(\hat{G}, D\right) = E_{x \sim q_{data}(x)}[min(0, -1 + D(x))] + E_{z \sim p(z)}\left[min\left(0, -1 + D\left(\hat{G}(z)\right)\right)\right] \quad (1)$$

$$V_G\left(G, \hat{D}\right) = -E_{z \sim p(z)}\left[\hat{D}(G(z))\right] \quad (2)$$

for the discriminator and the generator, respectively, where q_{data} is the data distribution, $z \in \mathbb{R}^{d_z}$ is a latent variable, and $p(z)$ is the standard normal distribution $\mathcal{N}(0, 1)$.

The number of weight parameters in each network architecture are listed in Table 4. In order to evaluate MobileGAN in detail, all combinations of ResBlockUp vs. CResBlockUp and regular fully-connected layer (Dense) vs. Separable Dense are compared. These results indicate that Separable Dense and CReesBlockUp can reduce 15.02% and 65.07% of weight parameters compared to regular ResNet-based generator.

Table 4. Number of weight parameters

Generator architecture	# of Parameters	Ratio to (a)
(a) Regular ResNet	12,214,787	100.00%
(b) ResBlockUp + Separable Dense	10,380,299	84.98%
(c) CResBlockUp + regular Dense	4,266,523	34.93%
(d) CResBlockUp + Separable Dense	2,432,035	19.91%

Inception Scores and FID resulted from experiments of unsupervised image generation are shown in Table 5, except that results from STL-10, which consists of images in 10 classes, are not presented because image generation of MobileGAN did not converge properly on STL-10. Each Inception Score is the average of values computed five times. Examples of generated images are illustrated in Fig. 7. While MobileGAN represents worse scores than regular ResNet in Table 5, Fig. 7 indicates slight difference between regular ResNet and MobileGAN.

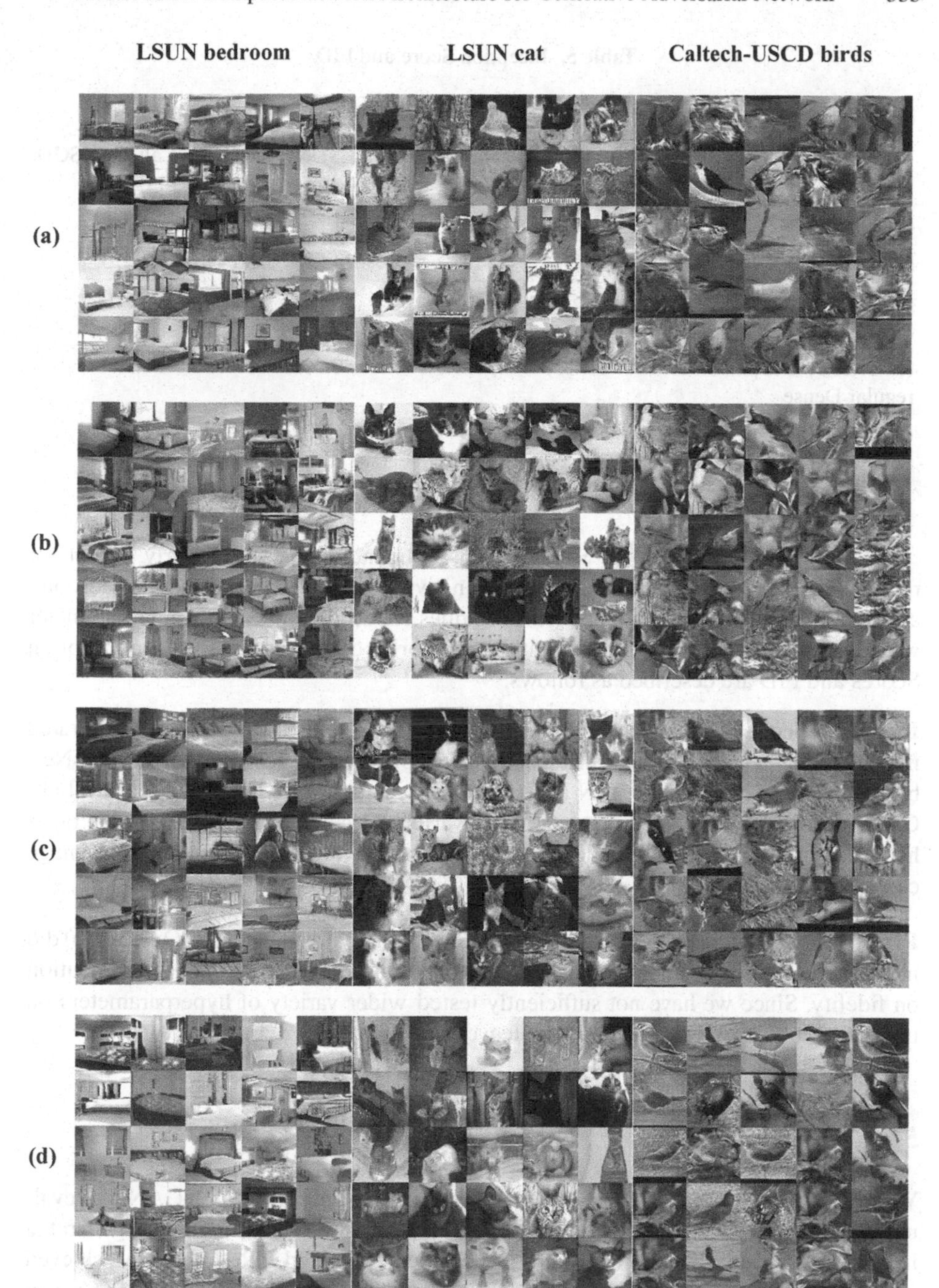

Fig. 7. Example generated images

Table 5. Inception Score and FID

Generator architecture	Inception score			FID		
	LSUN bedroom	LSUN cat	Caltech-USCD birds	LSUN bedroom	LSUN cat	Caltech-USCD birds
Real data	2.863	8.902	4.410			
(a) Regular ResNet	2.814	6.949	4.549	24.517	36.473	132.076
(b) ResBlockUp + Separable Dense	2.790	7.347	4.670	23.596	31.926	106.610
(c) CResBlockUp + regular Dense	3.318	6.859	4.518	40.200	39.156	81.234
(d) CResBlockUp + Separable Dense	3.233	6.634	5.206	47.952	40.285	116.926

Although training with the STL-10 dataset did not converge properly except for regular ResNet, we have confirmed that training with single-category datasets, bedroom, cat, and birds, successfully completed. It implies reduced number of weight parameter would be insufficient to reproduce multiple categories of images. Analysis on Inception Scores and FID are described as follows.

Inception Score. Higher value of Inception Score represents wider variety of generated images. Table 5 indicates that difference on Inception Score between regular ResNet-based GAN (a) and MobileGAN (b), (c), (d) is less than 0.7. It implies that Mobile-GAN technique could avoid degradation in variety of generated images. On the other hand, Inception Scores of MobileGAN (b), (c), (d) might represent unexpected image corruption.

FID. Lower value of FID represents higher fidelity of generated images. Overall, (b) did not degrade quality of generated images, while training (c) and (d) resulted in degradation on fidelity. Since we have not sufficiently tested wider variety of hyperparameters on training, MobileGAN architecture still leaves room for improvement.

5 Conclusions

We proposed new compact GAN generator architecture named MobileGAN and evaluated weight parameter reduction and its impact on variety and fidelity of generated images. Our compact building blocks Separable Dense and CResBlockUp achieved much less amount of weight parameters, while we confirmed that MobileGAN can maintain variety of generated images for single-category datasets. However, improving fidelity of images generated by MobileGAN and robustness on training with multiple-category datasets is still an important issue.

In recent years, more advanced techniques for GAN have been proposed and contributed to much higher picture fidelity, e.g. self-attention [18], large-batch training [5].

Although our interest is weight parameter reduction for mobile applications, we would like to explore another technique for fidelity improvement which can suppress weight parameter enlargement.

References

1. Goodfellow, I., et al.: Generative adversarial nets. In: Ghahramani, Z., Welling, M., Cortes, C., Lawrence, N.D., Weinberger, K.Q. (eds.) NIPS 2014, pp. 2672–2680 (2014)
2. Radford, A., Metz, L., Chintala, S.: Unsupervised representation learning with deep convolutional generative adversarial networks. In: ICLR 2016 (2016)
3. Salimans, T., Goodfellow, I., Zaremba, W., Cheung, V., Radford, A., Chen, X.: Improved techniques for training GANs. In: Lee, D.D., Sugiyama, M., Luxburg, U.V., Guyon, I., Garnett, R. (eds.) NIPS 2016, pp. 2234–2242. (2016)
4. Gulrajani, I., Ahmed, F., Arjovsky, M., Dumoulin, V., Courville, A.: Improved training of wasserstein GANs. In: Guyon, I., et al. (eds.) NIPS 2017, pp. 5767–5777 (2017)
5. Brock, A., Donahue, J., Simonyan, K.: Large scale GAN training for high fidelity natural image synthesis. In ICLR 2019 (2019)
6. Karras, T., Laine, S., Alia, T.: A style-based generator architecture for generative adversarial networks. In: IEEE CVPR 2019, pp. 4401–4410 (2019)
7. He, K., Zhang, X., Ren, S., Sun, J.: Deep residual learning for image recognition. In: IEEE CVPR 2016, pp. 770–778 (2016)
8. TensorFlow Lite | TensorFlow. https://www.tensorflow.org/lite. Accessed 22 July 2019
9. Core ML | Apple Developer Documentation. https://developer.apple.com/documentation/coreml/. Accessed 22 July 2019
10. IP Products | Arm ML Processor – Arm Developer. https://developer.arm.com/ip-products/processors/machine-learning/arm-ml-processor. Accessed 22 July 2019
11. iPhone XS | A12 Bionic | Apple. https://www.apple.com/iphone-xs/a12-bionic/. Accessed 22 July 2019
12. Howard, A.G., et al.: MobileNets: efficient convolutional neural networks for mobile vision applications. arXiv:1704.04861 (2017)
13. Sandler, M., Howard, A., Zhu, M., Zhmoginov, A., Chen, L.-C.: MobileNetV2: inverted residuals and linear bottlenecks. In: CVPR 2018, pp. 4510–4520 (2018)
14. Zhang, X., Zhou, X., Lin, M., Sun, J.: ShuffleNet: an extremely efficient convolutional neural network for mobile devices. In: IEEE CVPR 2018, pp. 6848–6856 (2018)
15. Krizhevsky, A., Sutskever, I., Geoffrey, E.H.: ImageNet classification with deep convolutional neural networks. In: Pereira, F., Burges, C.J.C., Bottou, L., Weinberger, K.Q. (eds.) NIPS 2012, pp. 1097–1105 (2012)
16. Simonyan, K., Zissermanar, A.: Very deep convolutional networks for large-scale image recognition. arXiv:1409.1556 (2014)
17. Miyato, T., Kataoka, T., Koyama, M., Yoshida, Y.: Spectral normalization for generative adversarial networks. In: ICLR 2018 (2018)
18. Zhang, H., Goodfellow, I., Metaxas, D., Odena, A.: Self-attention generative adversarial networks. In: ICML 2019, pp. 7354–7363 (2019)
19. Kingma, D.P., Ba, J.: Adam: a method for stochastic optimization. In: ICLR 2015 (2015)
20. Warde-Farley, D., Bengio, Y.: Improving generative adversarial networks with denoising feature matching. In: ICLR 2017 (2017)
21. Coates, A., Ng, A., Lee, H.: An analysis of single-layer networks in unsupervised feature learning. In: Proceedings of the Fourteenth International Conference on Artificial Intelligence and Statistics, pp. 215–223 (2011)

22. Yu, F., Zhang, Y., Song, S., Seff, A., Xiao, J.: LSUN: construction of a large-scale image dataset using deep learning with humans in the loop. arXiv preprint arXiv:1506.03365 (2015)
23. Welinder, P., et al.: Caltech-UCSD Birds 200 (2010). http://www.vision.caltech.edu/visipedia/CUB-200.html
24. Heusel, M., Ramsauer, H., Unterthiner, T., Nessler, B., Hochreiter, S.: GANs trained by a two time-scale update rule converge to a local nash equilibrium. In: Guyon, I., Luxburg, U.V., et al. (eds.) NIPS 2017, pp. 6626–6637 (2017)

Denoising and Inpainting of Sea Surface Temperature Image with Adversarial Physical Model Loss

Nobuyuki Hirahara[1(✉)], Motoharu Sonogashira[2], Hidekazu Kasahara[2], and Masaaki Iiyama[2]

[1] Graduate School of Informatics, Kyoto University, Kyoto, Japan
hirahara.nobuyuki.65c@st.kyoto-u.ac.jp
[2] Academic Center for Computing and Media Studies, Kyoto University, Kyoto, Japan

Abstract. This paper proposes a new approach for meteorology; estimating sea surface temperatures (SSTs) by using deep learning. SSTs are essential information for ocean-related industries but are hard to measure. Although multi-spectral imaging sensors on meteorological satellites are used for measuring SSTs over a wide area, they cannot measure sea temperature in regions covered by clouds, so most of the temperature data will be partially occluded. In meteorology, data assimilation with physics-based simulation is used for interpolating occluded SSTs, and can generate physically-correct SSTs that match observations by satellites, but it requires huge computational cost. We propose a low-cost learning-based method using pre-computed data-assimilation SSTs. Our restoration model employs *adversarial physical model loss* that evaluates physical correctness of generated SST images, and restores SST images in real time. Experimental results with satellite images show that the proposed method can reconstruct physically-correct SST images without occlusions.

Keywords: Image inpainting · Sea surface temperature · Adversarial loss

1 Introduction

Sea surface temperature (SST) is essential information for ocean-related industries such as the fishery industry. Multi-band sensors on satellites are used for measuring SSTs, covering a wide area in real time. However, such sensors cannot measure SSTs in regions covered by clouds, so most of the temperature data observed by satellites are partially occluded. Figure 1(a) shows an SST image observed by Himawari-8, a meteorological satellite. The regions shown in white and other colors indicate areas occluded by clouds and observed SSTs, respectively. As most SST images lack temperature data due to the clouds, estimating

S. Palaiahnakote et al. (Eds.): ACPR 2019, LNCS 12046, pp. 339–352, 2020.
https://doi.org/10.1007/978-3-030-41404-7_24

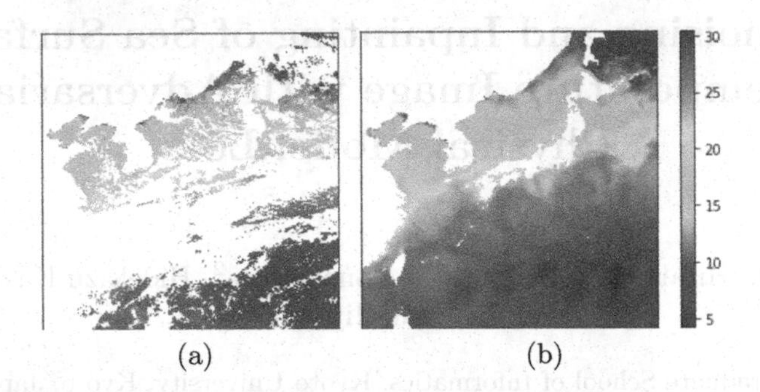

Fig. 1. (a) Partially occluded SST image observed by Himawari-8 satellite. White region corresponds to land or clouds. (b) Data-assimilation SST image [16] (Color figure online)

the temperature in such areas and restoring SST images is a useful technique for ocean-related applications.

One approach for this problem uses data assimilation. In this method, SSTs are simulated by combining observed information from sensors including satellite images and oceanographic physical models [16]. An SST image restored by data assimilation is shown in Fig. 1(b). Data assimilation is a method that estimates parameters of physical models considering with observations. So this method can generate physically-correct and noise-free SSTs that match observations by satellites. However, due to its huge computational cost, this approach is unsuitable for real-time applications.

To address the problem of the computational cost, we employ an idea of learning-based image inpainting. Pre-computed data-assimilation SST images of the past days are accumulated. They do not reflect the current SST but they are guaranteed to meet the physical correctness. Instead of computing SST with data assimilation, we use the pre-computed SST images as a training set for modeling the physical correctness.

Our method generates SST images matching observations under conditions of physical correctness by using data-assimilation images as real data, instead of directly estimating parameters of physical models. Specifically, we introduce the adversarial loss of generative adversarial networks (GANs) into restoration model as *adversarial physical model loss* which evaluates the physical correctness of reconstructed SST images. It is generally difficult to evaluate the physical correctness of given SST images because natural phenomena including sea temperature obey complicated physical laws. Using the synthesized SST images as *real* samples and constructing a discriminator that differentiates between the real samples (data-assimilation images) and fake samples generated by a neural network, our method generates physically-correct non-occluded SST images.

Contributions of this paper are as follows.

- A novel loss function, adversarial physical model loss, is proposed. This makes it possible to introduce complex physical models into the framework of deep learning.
- Our method can be considered as a new image inpainting method that can use noisy and partially occluded images as training samples.

Although this paper focuses on restoring SST images, our method is applicable to other application fields where noise-free data are difficult to collect through observation but available via simulation.

2 Related Work

2.1 Data Assimilation

To restore partially occluded SST data, data assimilation [16] estimates sea temperature by physical simulation using high-performance super computers. Since this simulation is based on an oceanographic physical model, a physically-correct sea temperature distribution is obtained as restoration results. However, the large computational cost of the simulation requires several days after the observation by satellites to complete the restoration. For the same reason, the spatial resolution of data-assimilation-based methods is limited. Thus, data assimilation is not suitable for cases where real-time restoration is required.

2.2 Image Restoration by Inpainting

Inpainting is a method of image processing for restoring partially occluded images, and various methods have been proposed. In its basic methods [2,4], occluded data is interpolated by estimation from structures or textures around missing regions in images. SST images are, as shown in Fig. 1, largely occluded due to clouds, and there are not suitable structures nor textures to be used for the interpolation in the images. Hence, these methods are ineffective for restoring SST images.

In learning-based inpainting methods, image restoration models are trained by using a large number of pairs containing partially occluded images and corresponding ground-truth images. In [1,3,11,17], the mean squared error (MSE) between the restored images and ground-truth images is minimized during the training. The loss function of such methods, called reconstruction loss, is typically given as follows:

$$\mathcal{L}_{rec} = \frac{1}{N}\sum_{n=1}^{N} \|x_n - G(\hat{x}_n)\|_2^2, \tag{1}$$

where N is the number of training images, x_n is the n-th ground-truth image, $\hat{x}_n$ is the occluded image corresponding to x_n, and G is the generator function that restores the occluded image. MSE minimization can restore partially occluded images with high accuracy, but the restored result is often over-smoothed.

To address the problem of over-smoothing, some inpainting methods employ GANs, which have been used in various tasks such as image generation [7] and translation [10]. The loss function of a GAN, called adversarial loss, is given as follows:

$$\mathcal{L}_{adv} = \log(1 - D(G(\hat{x}_n))) + \log D(x_n), \tag{2}$$

where D is the discriminator function. Image inpainting methods with a GAN [13,15,19] usually combine the reconstruction loss and adversarial loss. The adversarial loss helps to prevent restoration results from over-smoothing, and this method is able to obtain clear and photo-realistic images.

Shibata et al. proposed a method for restoring SST images by using the image inpainting with adversarial loss [14]. However, due to image noise on training images, discriminator classifies noisy images as real image, thus the generator reconstructs noisy images.

3 Our Method

To circumvent the computational cost of data assimilation, we propose a learning-based inpainting method using pre-computed data-assimilation images for training. Instead of directly performing simulation based on physical models, our method utilizes noise-free, physically-correct data-assimilation images for evaluating physical correctness. In addition, we use satellite images for matching restored images with observations.

Note that the data-assimilation images are only used for modeling physical correctness; the data-assimilation images are not required to be paired with satellite SST images, and past data-assimilation images can be reused for the training. We use two types of datasets, satellite images and data-assimilation images, and employ adversarial learning of GANs. Figure 2 provides an overview of our method. This comprises two components: the generator and the discriminator.

3.1 Loss Functions

We use two types of loss function to train the SST image restoring model: reconstruction loss and adversarial physical model loss.

Adversarial Physical Model Loss. While other GAN-based inpainting methods use non-occluded real images as true data, our method uses data-assimilation images as real data. Our discriminator is trained to regard the restored images by the generator as fake images, and the data-assimilation images based on physical models as real images. This means that the discriminator examines the physical correctness of the restored SST images. Consequently, the generator, which attempts to fool the discriminator, will generate noise-free and physically correct SST images similar to the data-assimilation images.

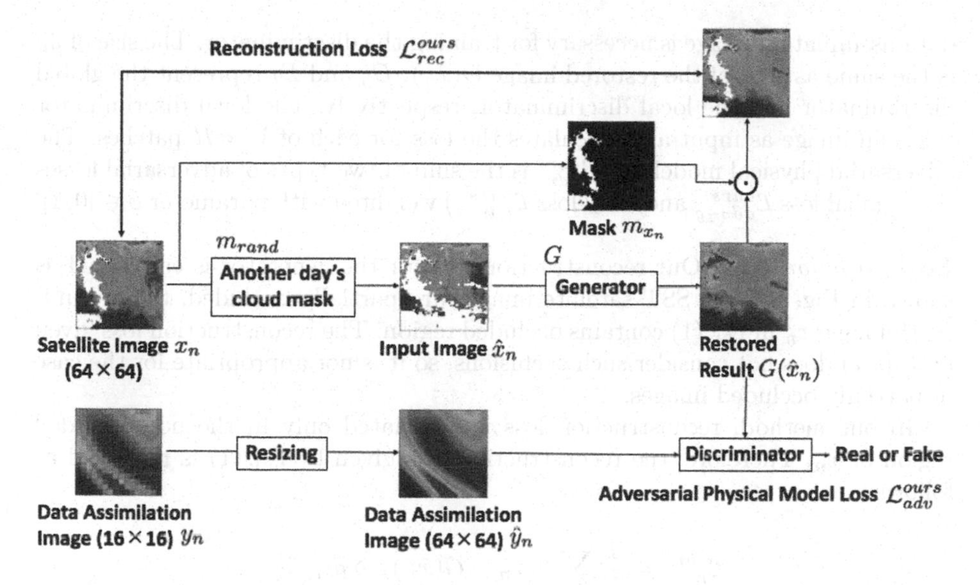

Fig. 2. Overview of our method.

The discriminator used in [13,14] is a network for examining whether the input image seems to be natural or not by using the global structure of the image. Whereas these methods are based on the global structure of the images, methods that simultaneously considering the local structures of images have shown better performance [8,18]. Therefore, following Demir and Unal [5], we build a multi-scale discriminator by employing a local discriminator in addition to the global discriminator. The global discriminator examines the global structure of the images, and the local discriminator examines the local structure of the images. For the local discriminator, we use the discriminator of PatchGAN [10]. This type of GAN divides the input image into small patches and calculates the loss locally in each patch. Training the generator using this multi-scale discriminator will enable it to generate clean restored images both globally and locally.

By employing the generator and the multi-scale discriminator, we redefine the adversarial loss as *adversarial physical model loss.*

$$\mathcal{L}_{adv-g}^{ours} = \frac{1}{N}\sum_{n=1}^{N}(\log(1 - D_g(G(\hat{x}_n))) + \log D_g(\hat{y}_n)), \tag{3}$$

$$\mathcal{L}_{adv-l}^{ours} = \frac{1}{N}\sum_{n=1}^{N}\frac{1}{VH}\sum_{i=1}^{V}\sum_{j=1}^{H}(\log(1 - D_l(G(\hat{x}_n))_{(i,j)}) + \log D_l(\hat{y}_n)_{(i,j)}), \tag{4}$$

$$\mathcal{L}_{adv}^{ours} = \beta\mathcal{L}_{adv-g}^{ours} + (1-\beta)\mathcal{L}_{adv-l}^{ours}, \tag{5}$$

Here, $\hat{y}_n$ is obtained by resizing original data-assimilation image y_n using bicubic interpolation. Note that resolution of data-assimilation images is lower than satellite images due to high computational cost of data assimilation, so resizing data-assimilation image is necessary for training the discriminator. The size of $\hat{y}_n$ is the same as that of the restored image $G(\hat{x}_n)$. D_g and D_l represent the global discriminator and the local discriminator, respectively. The local discriminator takes an image as input and calculates the loss for each of $V \times H$ patches. The adversarial physical model loss $\mathcal{L}_{adv}^{ours}$ is the sum of two types of adversarial losses (i.e., global loss $\mathcal{L}_{adv-g}^{ours}$ and local loss $\mathcal{L}_{adv-l}^{ours}$) weighted with parameter $\beta \in [0,1]$.

Reconstruction Loss. Our reconstruction loss for the generator is calculated as shown in Fig. 3. Since SST satellite images are partially occluded, the ground-truth image x_n in Eq. (1) contains occluded region. The reconstruction loss given by Eq. (1) does not consider such occlusions, so it is not appropriate for the case of partially occluded images.

In our method, reconstruction loss is calculated only in the non-occluded region of x_n. Therefore, the reconstruction loss given by Eq. (1) is redefined as follows:

$$\mathcal{L}_{rec}^{ours} = \frac{1}{N}\sum_{n=1}^{N} \|(x_n - G(\hat{x}_n)) \odot m_{x_n}\|_2, \tag{6}$$

$$m_{x_n}^{(i)} = \begin{cases} 0 & (x_n^{(i)} \text{ is occluded}) \\ 1 & (x_n^{(i)} \text{ is not occluded}), \end{cases} \tag{7}$$

$$\hat{x}_n = x_n \odot m_{rand}. \tag{8}$$

Here, m_{x_n} is a binary occlusion mask of x_n, in which both sizes are the same. Pixels whose values in m_{x_n} are 0 and 1 correspond to the occluded and non-occluded regions of x_n, respectively. In Eq. (7), $x_n^{(i)}$ and $m_{x_n}^{(i)}$ indicate the i-th pixel of x_n and m_{x_n}, respectively. In addition, m_{rand} is a randomly chosen occlusion mask from other SST images in a training dataset, which is applied to the ground truth image x_n for training as shown in Eq. (8). Our network is trained so that it restores the region masked by m_{rand}. While traditional image inpainting methods do not so much care about the shapes of missing (occluded) regions in the training set, we can make assumptions on the possible shapes of missing regions because occlusion in SST images is caused by cloud. We consider such a occlusion mechanism in generating masked training samples. Specifically, we prepare a cloud mask dataset by collecting cloud mask patterns from satellite images, and randomly choose the mask m_{rand} from this dataset.

Training. We use both the reconstruction loss ($\mathcal{L}_{rec}^{ours}$) and adversarial physical model loss ($\mathcal{L}_{adv}^{ours}$) to update the parameters of our network. The optimization problem is formulated as follows:

$$\min_{G}\max_{D} \left(\alpha\mathcal{L}_{rec}^{ours} + (1-\alpha)\mathcal{L}_{adv}^{ours}\right), \tag{9}$$

where $\alpha \in [0,1]$ is a weight parameter. The parameters of G and D are updated in an alternating manner.

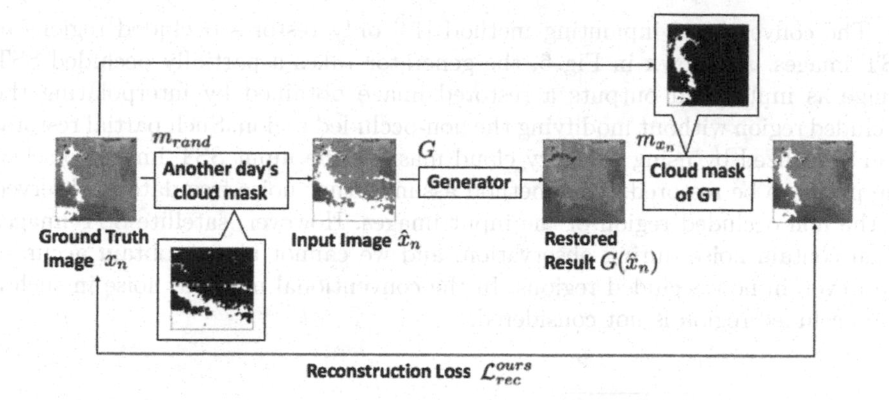

Fig. 3. Our reconstruction loss. The reconstruction loss is calculated only in the non-occluded region of the ground-truth image.

3.2 Using Spatio-Temporal SST Images

The speed of sea temperature flow is slower than that of cloud flow. For this reason, even if a certain region is occluded by clouds in an SST image one day, the same region is often not occluded in images going back several days, as shown in Fig. 4. Therefore, we use spatio-temporal SST image data for both training and restoration. Our model takes a three-dimensional volume consisting of SST images taken at the same location over three successive days as input. As a result, even when an SST image of current day has a large occlusion, our method achieves high quality restoration by using both one-day-before and two-days-before SST data.

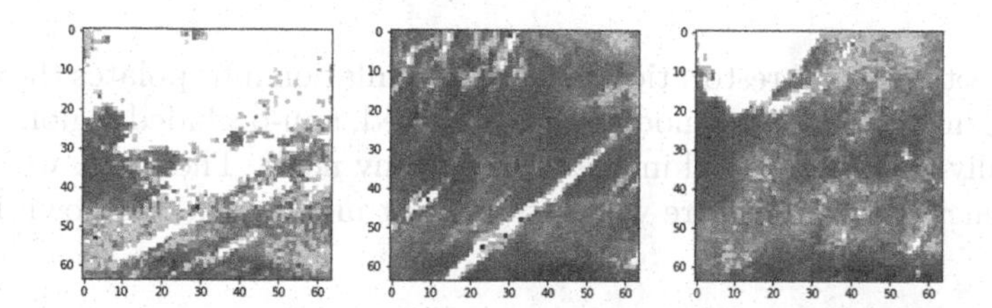

Fig. 4. Changes in SST images over three successive days. (Left) Current day. (Center) One day before. (Right) Two days before. All images are 64×64 and each pixel corresponds to $2\,\text{km} \times 2\,\text{km}$.

3.3 Generator Function

The generator in image inpainting acts as a restoration function; i.e., the input is partially occluded images and the output is restored results.

The conventional inpainting method [14] only restores occluded regions of SST images. As shown in Fig. 5, the generator takes a partially occluded SST image as input, and outputs a restored image obtained by interpolating the occluded region without modifying the non-occluded region. Such partial restoration is realized by using a binary cloud mask of the input SST image to select the pixels to be restored. This method assumes that noise-free data is observed in the non-occluded region of the input images. However, satellite SST images often contain noise during observation, and we cannot always obtain accurate data even in non-occluded regions. In the conventional method, noise in such a non-occluded region is not considered.

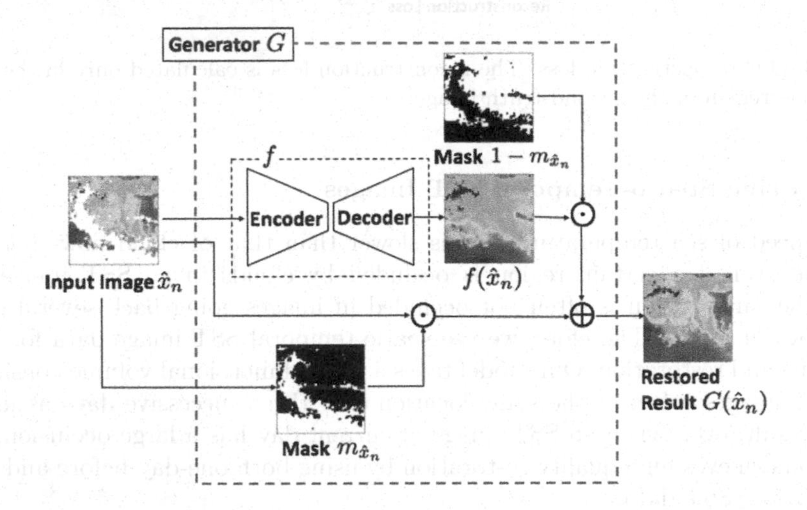

Fig. 5. Generator interpolating occlusions.

On the other hand, restoration by data assimilation interpolates the occluded region and in addition often modifies the observed, non-occluded region, resulting in physically-correct restored images without any noise. Therefore, we employ a simpler generator architecture without masking mechanism, as shown in Fig. 6.

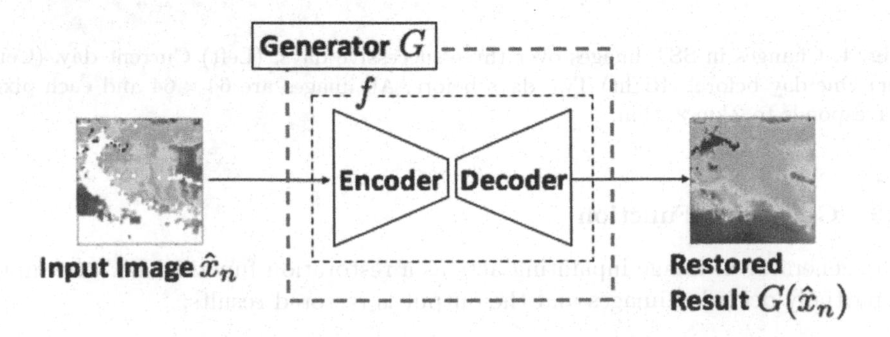

Fig. 6. Generator restoring an entire image.

3.4 Network Architecture

Generator Architecture. We employ U-Net-like architecture as shown in Fig. 7. It takes a $3 \times 64 \times 64 \times 2$ tensor as input, where the dimensions correspond to the number of days, vertical and horizontal numbers of pixels, and the number of channels (consisting of a SST image and a binary mask), respectively, and outputs a $3 \times 64 \times 64 \times 1$ tensor.

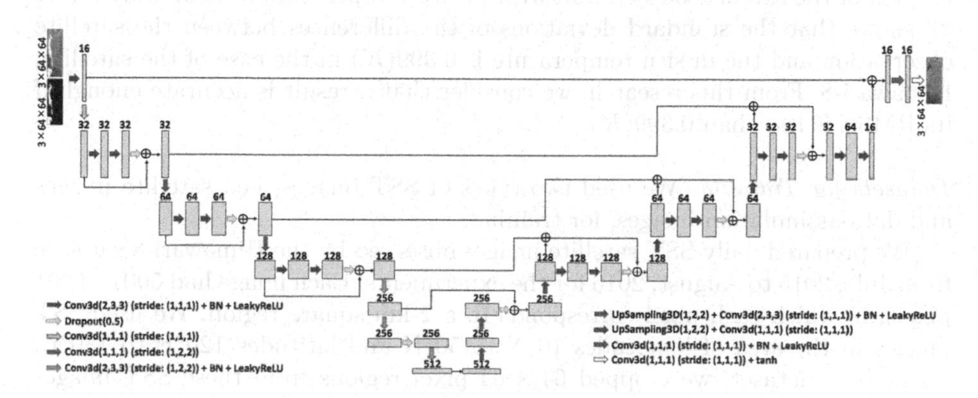

Fig. 7. Generator architecture.

Discriminator Architecture. Our global and local discriminator consist of 2D convolutional layers as shown in Fig. 8. Both of them take a $3 \times 64 \times 64$ tensor as input, while their outputs are a scaler and a 8×8 tensor, respectively.

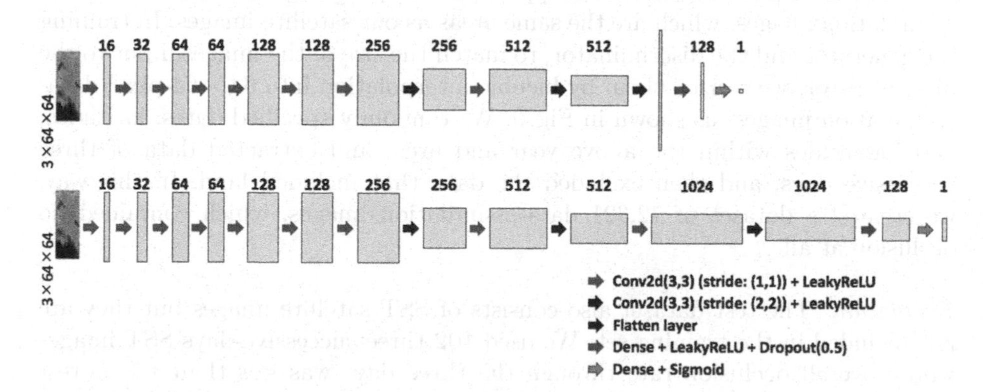

Fig. 8. Discriminator architecture. (Top) Global discriminator. (Bottom) Local Discriminator

4 Experiments

We conducted experiments to evaluate the effectiveness of our method. Note that satellite images contain noise, and ground truth of SST cannot be obtained unless it is measured directly by a buoy or ship. In our experiments, we used satellite images as ground truth for convenience and calculated root mean squared error (RMSE); therefore, methods that achieve low RMSE are not always good. Comparison of the satellite observation with in situ temperature measured by buoys [6] shows that the standard deviations of the differences between the satellite observation and the in situ temperature is $0.399(K)$ in the case of the satellite, Himawari-8. From this research, we consider that a result is accurate enough if its RMSE is less than $0.399(K)$.

Datasets for Training. We used two types of SST images, i.e., satellite images and data-assimilation images, for training.

We prepared daily SST satellite images observed by the Himawari-8 satellite from July, 2015 to August, 2016 for the experiments. Each image had 5001×6001 pixels, in which each pixel corresponds to a 2-km square region. We used SST images in the area of longitudes 10°N to 50°N and latitudes 120°E to 180°E. To make a dataset, we cropped 64×64 pixel regions from these SST images and extracted the data for three successive days in each area as a single spatio-temporal SST image volume. In this way, we created a dataset consisting of 124,521 satellite images, which contained partial occlusion.

SST images restored by data assimilation were accumulated before 2015. In this paper, we used the data-assimilation images in the same areas with our satellite image dataset from 2000 to 2015. In the data-assimilation images, one pixel corresponds to a 0.1-degree square in latitude and longitude, which is about a 9 to 10-km-square region. We cropped 16×16 pixel regions from these data-assimilation images, which are the same areas as our satellite images. In training the generator and the discriminator, to match the size of the images input to the discriminator, we resized them by bicubic interpolation into 64×64-pixel data-assimilation images, as shown in Fig. 9. We randomly specified dates, latitudes, and longitudes within the above year and area, and extracted data of three successive days, and then excluded the data that included land. In this way, we created a dataset of 72,321 data-assimilation images, which contained no occlusion at all.

Evaluation. The test dataset also consists of SST satellite images but they are not included in the training set. We used 102 three-successive-days SST images whose overall occlusion rate through the three days was less than 1% as test dataset. Generally, satellite images contain inaccurate pixels around the boundaries of the missing regions. This noise is due to cloud detection algorithms [9,12], and SST in the vicinity of thin clouds or edges of clouds tends to be measured lower than the surrounding SST. Hence, we removed the pixels with lower 5% SST from each satellite image in the test dataset.

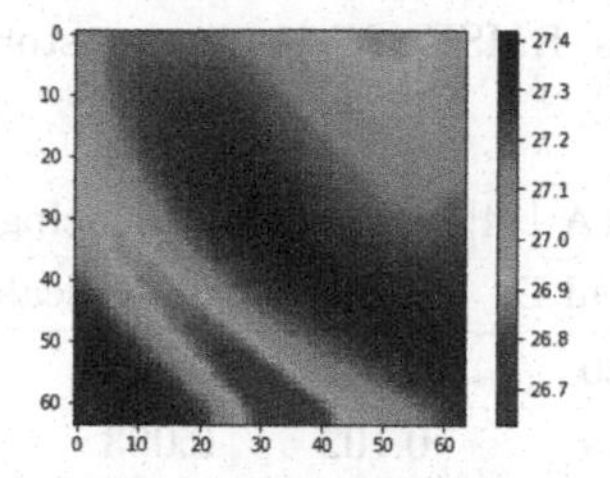

Fig. 9. Resized data-assimilation image (64 × 64) by bicubic interpolation.

For evaluating the accuracy of the inpainting, we synthesized partially occluded images by applying randomly chosen occlusion mask to the ground truth test images. We evaluated the accuracy with five levels of occlusion masks whose occlusion rates are 0%–20%, 20%–40%, 40%–60%, 60%–80%, and 80%–100%.

We restored the test images by using the following four types of inpainting methods and compared the restoration results. One of them is the state-of-the-art method proposed by Shibata et al. [14], which uses only SST satellite images and restored them by interpolating occluded regions only, not replacing non-occluded regions with model outputs. The other methods are versions of the proposed method, which uses both satellite and data-assimilation images for training. Two of them restore images by interpolating occluded regions only as in Shibata's method, but employ the global discriminator alone ($\beta = 1$ in Eq. (5)) and the multi-scale discriminator ($\beta = 0.5$ in Eq. (5)), respectively. The last method, i.e., the full version of the proposed method, restores entire images, and employs the multi-scale discriminator. We trained them with both the satellite and data-assimilation image datasets.

We used two evaluation metrics. First, restored SST images should be matched with the corresponding satellite images. This similarity can be measured by RMSE between the restored images and satellite images. We calculated RMSE only in non-occluded regions of partially occluded images in the test dataset. Second, our aim is to restore partially occluded SST images and obtain noise-free, physically-correct restoration results like the data-assimilation images; thus, we visualized the restored results and corresponding original satellite images, and compared them qualitatively, i.e., visually assessing whether the restoration reflected the physical correctness of the data-assimilation images.

Results. Quantitative results are shown in Table 1. They confirm that our methods (without replacing non-occluded region) achieved a competitive restoration error with the state-of-the-art method [14]. Although our entire restoration method scored relatively larger RMSE values than those of the other methods, the fluctuation in RMSE due to the occlusion rate was smaller than that of the other methods. In the case of the highest occlusion rate (80%–100%), this method could restore the SST images with smaller RMSE values than those in other methods.

Table 1. Quantitative results. RMSE (K) between restored results and original satellite images.

Occlusion rate (%)	SOTA [14]	Ours (w/o replacing)		Ours (w replacing)
	global D	global D	multi-scale D	multi-scale D
0–20	0.030	0.047	0.041	0.143
20–40	0.069	0.102	0.093	0.158
40–60	0.115	0.135	0.123	0.165
60–80	0.164	0.166	0.160	0.179
80–100	0.221	0.231	0.241	0.201

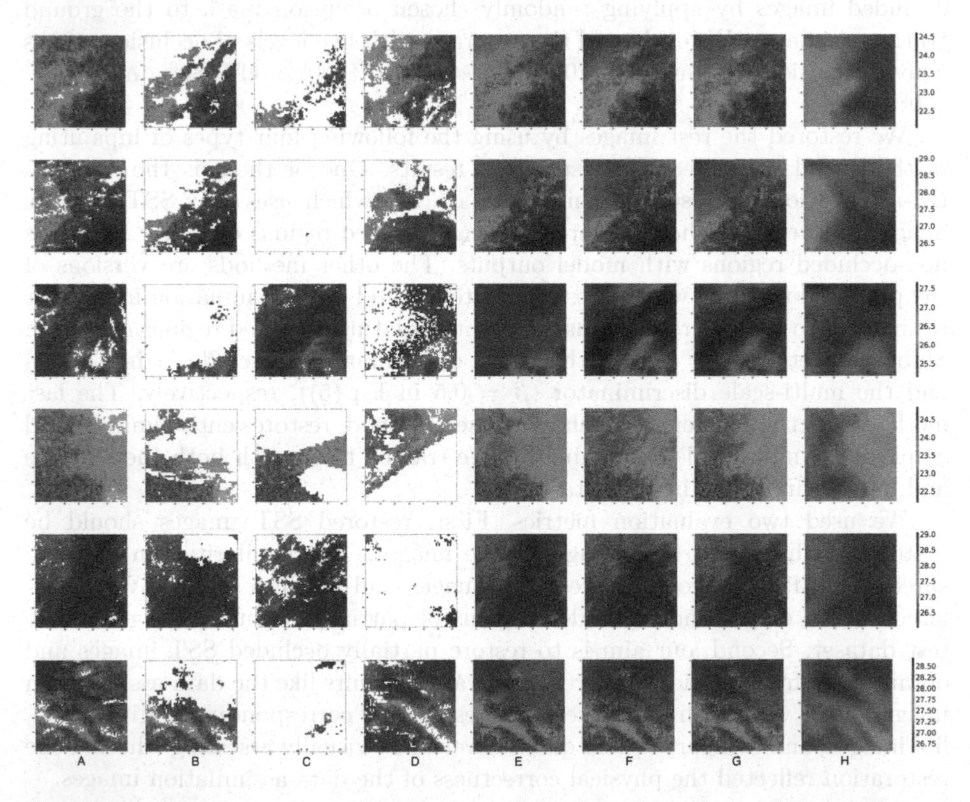

Fig. 10. Qualitative comparison with state-of-the-art method [14]. White pixels correspond to occluded regions. A is the original image in the test dataset. B is the input image to restore. C and D indicate one-day-before and two-days-before image of B, respectively. E to H indicate the restoration results using the state-of-the-art interpolating method [14], our interpolating method with the global discriminator, our interpolating method with the multi-scale discriminator, and our entire restoration method with the multi-scale discriminator, respectively.

Qualitative comparisons are shown in Fig. 10. They reveal that the proposed method yielded restoration results that are reflected features of typical data-assimilation images, i.e., noise-free SST images. The restoration results by the interpolating methods, including the state-of-the-art method, remained noisy especially in their non-modified regions. These noise were originally contained in the non-occluded regions of the satellite images. On the other hand, our entire restoration method obtained noise-free, more visually-plausible results (Fig. 10(row: H)) than those of the other methods, regardless to occlusion rate of satellite images. In addition, While data assimilation would have required huge computational resources, our method was so efficient that it even worked with a computer with a single GPGPU.

5 Conclusion

In this paper, we proposed a novel SST image inpainting method for the restoration of satellite SST images as an efficient alternative to computationally-expensive data assimilation. Since data assimilation takes several days to restore SST images, this approach is not suitable for real-time applications. Instead of directly estimating SSTs by using physical models, we employed a learning-based inpainting scheme to perform restoration quickly. We used pre-computed data-assimilation images to model physical correctness, and proposed *adversarial physical model loss* that evaluates the physical correctness of SST images. This loss allows the training images to contain noise and occlusions, and imposes physical constraints on the restoration process. Experimental results with satellite images show that our method can produce SST images closer to data-assimilation images in real time.

The work described in this paper is focused on restoring SST images of small regions. The restoration of SST images that cover a wider area would provide more useful data for ocean-related industries. This will be the subject of our future work.

References

1. Agostinelli, F., Anderson, M.R., Lee, H.: Adaptive multi-column deep neural networks with application to robust image denoising. In: Advances in Neural Information Processing Systems, pp. 1493–1501 (2013)
2. Bertalmio, M., Sapiro, G., Caselles, V., Ballester, C.: Image inpainting. In: Proceedings of the 27th Annual Conference on Computer Graphics and Interactive Techniques, pp. 417–424 (2000)
3. Cai, N., Su, Z., Lin, Z., Wang, H., Yang, Z., Ling, B.W.K.: Blind inpainting using the fully convolutional neural network. Vis. Comput. **33**(2), 249–261 (2017)
4. Criminisi, A., Perez, P., Toyama, K.: Region filling and object removal by exemplar-based image inpainting. IEEE Trans. Image Process. **13**(9), 1200–1212 (2004)
5. Demir, U., Unal, G.: Patch-based image inpainting with generative adversarial networks. arXiv preprint arXiv:1803.07422 (2018)

6. Ditri, A., Minnett, P., Liu, Y., Kilpatrick, K., Kumar, A.: The accuracies of himawari-8 and mtsat-2 sea-surface temperatures in the tropical Western Pacific ocean. Remote Sens. **10**(2), 212 (2018). https://doi.org/10.3390/rs10020212
7. Goodfellow, I., et al.: Generative adversarial nets. In: Advances in Neural Information Processing Systems, pp. 2672–2680 (2014)
8. Iizuka, S., Simo-Serra, E., Ishikawa, H.: Globally and locally consistent image completion. ACM Trans. Graph. (Proc. of SIGGRAPH 2017) **36**(4), 107:1–107:14 (2017)
9. Ishida, H., Nakajima, T.Y.: Development of an unbiased cloud detection algorithm for a spaceborne multispectral imager. J. Geophys. Res. (Atmos.) **114** (2009)
10. Isola, P., Zhu, J.Y., Zhou, T., Efros, A.A.: Image-to-image translation with conditional adversarial networks. In: Conference on Computer Vision and Pattern Recognition, pp. 5967–5976 (2017)
11. Mao, X.J., Shen, C., Yang, Y.B.: Image denoising using very deep fully convolutional encoder-decoder networks with symmetric skip connections. In: Advances in Neural Information Processing Systems, pp. 2810–2818 (2016)
12. McNally, A., Watts, P.: A cloud detection algorithm for high-spectral-resolution infrared sounders. Q. J. R. Meteorol. Soc. **129**(595), 3411–3423 (2003)
13. Pathak, D., Krahenbuhl, P., Donahue, J., Darrell, T., Efros, A.A.: Context encoders: feature learning by inpainting. In: Conference on Computer Vision and Pattern Recognition, pp. 2536–2544 (2016)
14. Shibata, S., Iiyama, M., Hashimoto, A., Minoh, M.: Restoration of sea surface temperature satellite images using a partially occluded training set. In: International Conference on Pattern Recognition (2018)
15. Song, Y., Yang, C., Lin, Z., Li, H., Huang, Q., Kuo, C.J.: Image inpainting using multi-scale feature image translation. CoRR abs/1711.08590 (2017). http://arxiv.org/abs/1711.08590
16. Usui, N., Ishizaki, S., Fujii, Y., Tsujino, H., Yasuda, T., Kamachi, M.: Meteorological research institute multivariate ocean variational estimaion (move) system: some early results. Adv. Space Res. **37**(4), 806–822 (2006)
17. Xie, J., Xu, L., Chen, E.: Image denoising and inpainting with deep neural networks. In: Advances in Neural Information Processing Systems, pp. 341–349 (2012)
18. Yang, C., Lu, X., Lin, Z., Shechtman, E., Wang, O., Li, H.: High-resolution image inpainting using multi-scale neural patch synthesis. In: Conference on Computer Vision and Pattern Recognition, pp. 4076–4084 (2017)
19. Yu, J., Lin, Z., Yang, J., Shen, X., Lu, X., Huang, T.S.: Generative image inpainting with contextual attention. CoRR abs/1801.07892 (2018). http://arxiv.org/abs/1801.07892

Computational Photography

Confidence Map Based 3D Cost Aggregation with Multiple Minimum Spanning Trees for Stereo Matching

Yuhao Xiao[1], Dingding Xu[2], Guijin Wang[1(✉)], Xiaowei Hu[1], Yongbing Zhang[2], Xiangyang Ji[3], and Li Zhang[1]

[1] Department of Electronic Engineering, Tsinghua University, Beijing 100084, China
wangguijin@tsinghua.edu.cn
[2] Graduate School at Shenzhen, Tsinghua University, Shenzhen 518055, China
[3] Department of Automation, Tsinghua University, Beijing 100084, China

Abstract. Stereo matching is a challenging problem due to the mismatches caused by difficult environment conditions. In this paper, we propose an enhanced version of our previous work, denoted as 3DMST-CM, to handle challenging cases and obtain a high-accuracy disparity map based on the ambiguity of image pixels. We develop a module of distinctiveness analysis to classify pixels into distinctive and ambiguous pixels. Then distinctive pixels are utilized as anchor pixels to help match ambiguous pixels accurately. The experimental results demonstrate the effectiveness of our method and reach state-of-the-art on the Middlebury 3.0 benchmark.

Keywords: Stereo matching · Distinctiveness analysis · 3D label

1 Introduction

Stereo matching has been one of the most active research areas in the fields of computer vision, artificial intelligence and multimedia for many years. Given a pair of images from the scene, the task of stereo matching is to compute the disparity of each pixel. Due to the diversity and uncertainty of the scene, stereo matching problem faces a great challenge in weakly-textured areas, discontinuities as well as other difficult environment conditions.

In the last decade, stereo matching has attracted a lot of attention. Zhang et al. [16] partitioned the input images into 2D triangles with shared vertices and then computed corresponding disparity values. They formulated a two-layer MRF model to handle the presence of depth discontinuities in their work. Kim and Kim [4] also focused on the case of near object boundaries and presented

D. Xu—Equally contributed to this work.

S. Palaiahnakote et al. (Eds.): ACPR 2019, LNCS 12046, pp. 355–365, 2020.
https://doi.org/10.1007/978-3-030-41404-7_25

a global algorithm based on texture and edge information. A novel global optimization framework for 3D label, which generates and fuses super-pixel proposals iteratively, was developed by Li et al. [6]. Shi et al. considered color dissimilarity, spatial relation and the pixel-matching reliability in support windows. They designed the confidence-based support window to solve the local plane fitting problem [11] and selected ground control points adaptively to regularize the ill-posed matching problem [12]. And a new move making scheme for stereo matching problem was introduced by Taniai et al. [13]. They used local expansion moves based on graph cuts to efficiently infer per-pixel 3D plane labels. Mozerov and van de Weijer [8] derived a fully connected model for the BP approach and applied it to the stereo matching problem. And they also proposed a solution that performs only one energy minimization process and avoids traditional left-right check procedure. Drouyer et al. [2] presented an algorithm that densifies sparse disparity map based on hierarchical image segmentation. Their method can be used as a post-processing step which is suitable for any stereo matching algorithm. With the rapid development of deep learning, more approaches have been proposed for stereo matching problem based on CNN. Ye et al. [14] proposed a feature ensemble network to perform matching cost computation and the disparity refinement using CNN. A novel pooling scheme of CNN was proposed by Park and Lee [9], which can handle a large image patch without losing the small details. Mao et al. [7] presented two CNN models for semi-dense stereo matching. They fed additional information into the matching-Net to effectively correct matches. And they designed the next evaluation-Net to label mismatches as post-processing.

An efficient 3D label cost-aggregation method (denoted as 3DMST) for stereo matching was proposed in our previous work [5]. We adopted 3D cost-aggregation methods which assign three continuous values to each pixel, representing the disparity and the surface normal direction simultaneously. Our previous work was able to calculate good disparity values. Nevertheless, this approach is not robust enough for handling challenging cases. If two features are similar in one image, it may be impossible to find their corresponding features in another image and this will cause a mismatch. 3DMST discovered mismatched pixels *post facto*, attempting to resolve challenging cases by imposing consistency constraints. This generate-and-test approach works hard to match corresponding pixels and then works harder to correct the bad ones.

In this paper, we propose an enhanced version of our previous work, denoted as 3DMST-CM, to handle challenging cases and obtain a high-accuracy disparity map based on the ambiguity of image pixels. We develop a module of distinctiveness analysis embedded in the stereo matching process which generates the confidence map to classify pixels into distinctive and ambiguous pixels. The high confidence pixels correspond to distinctive pixels, which can be precise anchor pixels for reliable match and then be utilized to handle challenging cases in subsequent processing. The experimental results show that the module of distinctiveness analysis can effectively distinguish distinctive areas in the image and then the high accuracy disparity map can be generated based on extracted distinctive pixels. The performance of our method (denoted as 3DMST-CM) on the Middlebury 3.0 benchmark greatly outperforms 3DMST [5] and for A95 error metric even ranks top first position.

2 Framework

The algorithm framework of our method is shown in Fig. 1. Our purpose is to find the 3D label $l = (a, b, c)^T \in \mathbb{R}^3$ with the minimum aggregated cost and then the best disparity value d_p for every pixel $p = (p_x, p_y)$ can be computed by $d_p = ap_x + bp_y + c$. Firstly, we adopt the tree structure filtering strategy for processing 3D labels in 3DMST [5], which is the "Generate Forest Structure" module. After constructing the forest structure, each pixel p is assigned a random 3D label l for initialization. Different from the previous work, we design the "Distinctiveness Analysis" module which generates the confidence map before later processing. The confidence map is used to indicate the ambiguity of image pixels and the disparity map only contains disparity values of distinctive pixels. Then we present another new "Anchored Rolling Refinement" module for disparity calculation of ambiguous pixels. Assuming that pixels in the same tree or nearby trees are more likely to share the same label, we utilize distinctive pixels as anchor pixels to propagate reliable disparity messages to ambiguous pixels iteratively in this module, which helps ambiguous pixels to match more accurately. Specific details will be discussed in the next section. The post-processing module we finally use is left-right consistency. The pixels that can not pass the left-right consistency check are refilled with nearest horizontal consistent 3D label.

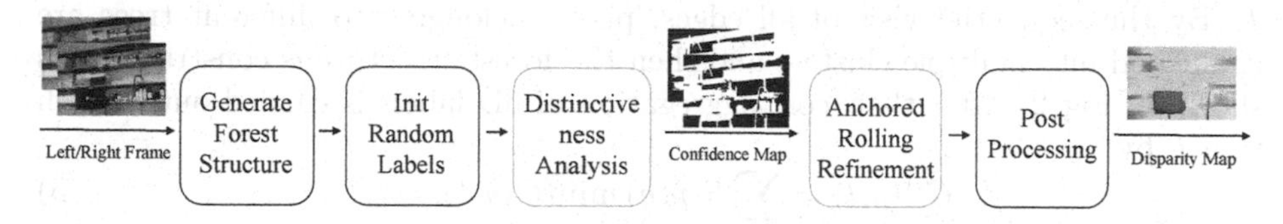

Fig. 1. The framework of our method. Given a pair of input images, the confidence map is generated after the "Distinctiveness Analysis" module and then is utilized to refine the disparity map using "Anchored Rolling Refinement" module. The black blocks represent the previous modules in 3DMST [5] and the blue blocks represent the newly proposed modules in this work. (Color figure online)

3 Proposed Method

In this section, we first review how to aggregate cost with forest structure in 3DMST, which plays an important role in later processing stages. Then we define a novel method to effectively measure the ambiguity of image pixels. With the classification of pixels, subsequent algorithm steps are optimized to process challenging areas more accurately, eventually generate a more precise disparity map.

3.1 3D Cost Aggregation with Forest Structure

As shown in Fig. 2, the image is regarded as a grid undirected graph. Each pixel is a node, and each four-neighboring pixel pair is connected with an edge. The weight of the edge connecting pixel p and q is defined as

$$w(p,q) = w(q,p) = \|I(p) - I(q)\|_1 \tag{1}$$

where $I(p)$ and $I(q)$ are color values of pixel p and q. $\|I(p) - I(q)\|_1$ is the l_1 distance between $I(p)$ and $I(q)$. With the preceding edge weights, a minimum spanning tree is extracted from the image grid. However, the computational complexity of cost aggregation on one single tree is too high when the number of 3D labels is huge. To remove the redundant computation in the 3D label case, we employ the strategy of [3] to construct the forest structure. In the initialization phase, each pixel is regarded as a separate tree. Then all edges $w(p,q)$ of the image grid are visited in weight-increasing order. The two trees connected by $w(p,q)$ are merged if

$$w(p,q) \leq min(Int(T_p) + \tau(T_p), Int(T_q) + \tau(T_q)) \tag{2}$$

where

$$Int(T) = \underset{e \in T}{max}(w(e)) \tag{3}$$

$$\tau(T) = \frac{\lambda}{|T|} \tag{4}$$

Here $Int(T)$ controls the maximum edge weight in each tree T and $\tau(T)$ controls the size of each tree T. λ is the balancing parameter and $|T|$ is the size of tree T. By the sequential visit of all edges, pixels belonging to different trees are connected into multiple clusters and then the forest structure is constructed, as shown in Fig. 2. After that, cost aggregation of 3D labels is carried out in each tree T by

$$C^A(p,l) = \sum_{q \in T} S(p,q) \min(C(q,l), \tau_{sim}) \tag{5}$$

where

$$S(p,q) = exp(\frac{-w(p,q)}{\gamma}) \tag{6}$$

Here $S(p,q)$ is the support weight between pixel p and q in the same minimum spanning tree, and parameter γ controls the support weight strength. Notably, for any two nonadjacent pixels p and q in the constructed tree structure, the edge weight $w(p,q)$ between them is defined as the sum of edge weights along their path. Parameter τ_{sim} is used to truncate the matching cost of pixels to increase robustness. $C(q,l)$ is the matching cost of pixel q and the corresponding pixel with disparity $aq_x + bq_y + c$ in another view based on the state-of-the-art method [15]. As discussed in the 3DMST, 3D cost aggregation on the forest structure achieves similar accuracy compared with the single MST, but has much lower computational complexity.

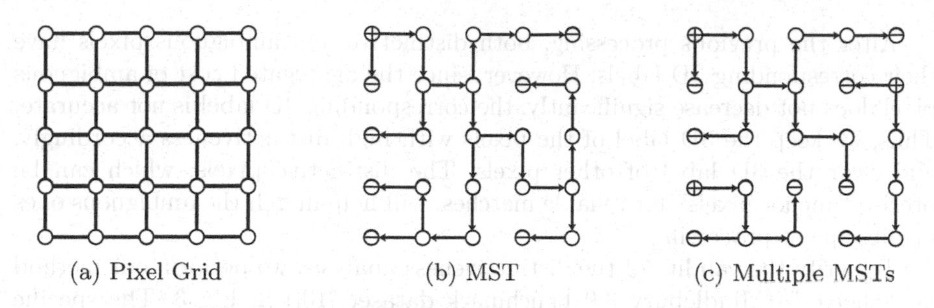

Fig. 2. Visual illustration of the forest structures in a 5 × 5 image: (a) Original image grid. The small circles represent pixels; (b) single MST generated from (a). "⊕" represents the root node and "⊖" represents leaf nodes. Arrows show the order form the root node to the leaf nodes; (c) multiple MSTs generated from (a).

3.2 Reliable Disparity Extraction with Distinctiveness Analysis

To improve our previous work, we first design a module to analyze the image pixels distinctiveness effectively. After that, pixels can be classified into distinctive and ambiguous pixels in the confidence map. The high confidence pixels correspond to distinctive pixels which will be used for label search and hole filling in the challenging areas and thus greatly improve the accuracy of the final disparity map.

In this work, we distinguish pixels' distinctiveness by iteratively calculating the aggregated cost of them. In the initialization phase of the iteration, we assign a random 3D label l_0 to each pixel p. We perform the cost aggregation with 3D labels on the forest structure as described before. Then we update the 3D label l by random search strategy to approximate the optimal value during the iteration. Since the cost of getting higher means that the wrong label is found, we don't record all aggregated costs in the process of iterations. In order to save storage space, we only record lower costs than before and update the corresponding 3D label of the pixel (*i.e.*, the better 3D label of the pixel). Hereby, the trend of recorded costs is monotonically decreasing and the 3D label of each pixel is the optimal value currently found. The aggregated cost decline of the pixel p during the iteration is taken as the distinctiveness measure, which is defined as

$$ACD(p) = \frac{|C^A(p, l_n) - C^A(p, l_0)|}{C^A(p, l_0)} \tag{7}$$

where $C^A(p, l_0)$ denotes the aggregated cost of the pixel p recorded for the first time and $C^A(p, l_n)$ denotes the aggregated cost recorded for the last time. Here l_n is the best 3D label found during the iteration. Since image pixels that have sufficient texture for matching are easier to find better labels, their aggregated cost decline will be greater than others. Thus, we can classify pixels into distinctive and ambiguous pixels by the ratio of aggregated cost decline during the iteration. On this basis, we define p as distinctive pixel if

$$ACD(p) < ACD_{TH} \tag{8}$$

where ACD_{TH} is the threshold preset by experiment.

After the previous processing, both distinctive and ambiguous pixels have their corresponding 3D labels. However, since the aggregated cost of ambiguous pixel does not decrease significantly, the corresponding 3D label is not accurate. Thus, we keep the 3D label of the pixels with high distinctiveness accordingly, and clear the 3D label of other pixels. The distinctive pixels, which can be precise "anchor pixels" for reliable matches, will help match the ambiguous ones in subsequent processing.

To verify the validity of the distinctiveness analysis, we perform our method on "Shelves" (Middlebury 3.0 benchmark dataset [10]) in Fig. 3. The specific scene of the data set is presented in Fig. 3(a). Texture-less area like the wall is generally considered as ambiguous area while characteristic area like the object is considered as distinctive area. We extract two typical pixels in these two areas, which are marked by red and blue respectively. Figure 3(c) shows the aggregated cost curve of these two pixels. The result of our method demonstrates the effectiveness of distinguishing between two different areas, which is shown in Fig. 3(b). The white regions represent distinctive areas, and the black regions represent ambiguous areas.

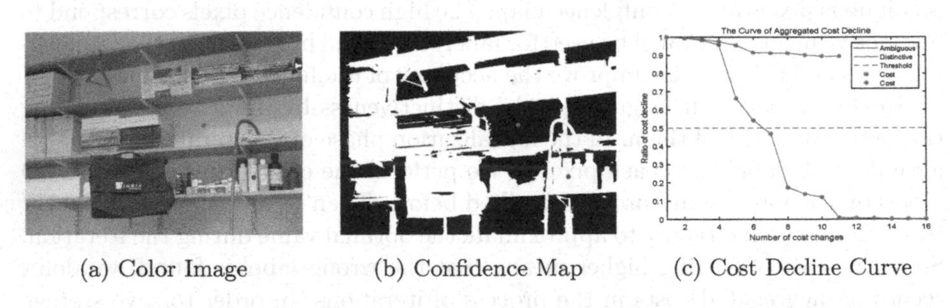

(a) Color Image (b) Confidence Map (c) Cost Decline Curve

Fig. 3. Result of distinctiveness analysis on "Shelves" data set. The red one denotes the ambiguous pixel, recording 11 aggregated cost changes in the iteration. The blue one denotes the distinctive pixel, recording 16 aggregated cost changes in the iteration. The threshold can effectively distinguish the ambiguity of two pixels by the ratio of cost decline. (Color figure online)

3.3 Anchored Rolling Refinement

Through the previous processing, only distinctive pixels have reliable 3D labels in the current disparity map, and ambiguous pixels do not. The purpose of this module is to guide ambiguous pixels to find optimal 3D labels with the help of distinctive pixels. Assuming that pixels in the same tree or nearby trees are more likely to share the same label, we formulate an anchored rolling refinement approach to find and test possible best 3D labels of ambiguous pixels from the infinite label space.

In the initialization phase of the refinement, we assign a random 3D label to each ambiguous pixel. Then we iteratively perform spatial propagation step and random refinement step to update the 3D label of each ambiguous pixel. 3D labels of distinctive pixels remain constant during the process.

For spatial propagation, we first process the ambiguous pixels which are near the distinctive pixels (*e.g.*, the ambiguous pixels and the distinctive pixels are in the same or nearby trees), and then from near to far until all ambiguous pixels are tested. The 3D labels of these distinctive pixels consist of the candidate label set C_i, which is then tested on the ambiguous pixels around. For each 3D label $l_i \in C_i$, we calculate the aggregated cost of ambiguous pixels on its tree T_i using Eq. (5). If the aggregated cost $C^A(p, l_i) < C^A(p, l_p)$, then we replace its current 3D label l_p with the new label l_i. For random refinement, we construct a refined label set R_i which adds decreasing random values to current 3D labels. Similar to the spatial propagation, we test the labels in R_i on T_i using Eq. (5) and update the current label of each ambiguous pixel if new aggregated cost is lower.

4 Experiments

We test our method on the Middlebury 3.0 benchmark, which contains 33 high-resolution image pairs [10]. 20 of the data set are used in the Middlebury Stereo Evaluation, 10 each for training and test sets. In this section, we first describe our experimental environment and parameters. Then we compare the accuracy of our method with the previous work (3DMST [5]) and other high ranking methods. Finally, we analyze the sensitivity of the algorithm to key parameters.

4.1 Parameter Setting

We run the experiments on a desktop computer equipped with i7-6700 3.4 GHz CPU, 32G memory. All methods are implemented using C++. The truncation threshold of CNN similarity cost τ_{sim} is set to 0.5 and the parameter γ to control the support weights is set to 50. The threshold of distinctiveness ACD_{TH} is set to 0.5 by experiment. And considering the accuracy of our method we iterate 200 times for both distinctiveness analysis and rolling refinement.

4.2 Evaluation Based on Middlebury 3.0 Benchmark

We compare our method against the previous work (3DMST) and other top-performing methods on the Middlebury 3.0 benchmark. To be fair, we test our method at half resolution which is the same as other state-of-the-art algorithms.

Our hierarchical stereo algorithm that matches distinctive pixels first minimizes the probability of mismatches and achieves better results than 3DMST for almost all metrics. Since our method is random in the search for 3D labels, there is no guarantee that each category of objects will go beyond the original method. However, the weighted average error is much lower than the original method can prove the effectiveness of our method. For "A95" metric our method (denoted as 3DMST-CM) outperforms all existing 121 methods and ranks top first position on the table. The result is provided in Fig. 4. The "A95" error metric is equivalent to 95-percent error quantile in pixels, which shows that our method provides more accurate disparities for the majority of the pixels and the average error over the 95-percent of the pixels with least error is very low. The pixels at the end of the error quantile are usually in the challenging areas and we achieve the best results in these local regions, indicating the effectiveness of our method for handling challenging cases. Besides this metric, our method also has good performances for other metrics. Since we use half-resolution images as inputs while the official evaluation is at full resolution, "bad 2.0" metric (*i.e.*, percentage of bad pixels whose error is greater than 2.0) equals to error threshold 1 pixel and "bad 1.0" metric (*i.e.*, percentage of bad pixels whose error is greater than 1.0) equals to error threshold 0.5 pixel. So they can measure pixel level accuracy and subpixel level accuracy for global image respectively. We provide the evaluation results in Fig. 5. The methods without references are anonymous submissions and unpublished work, while their results are available in [1]. The results demonstrate that the performance of our method greatly outperforms 3DMST and also achieve state-of-the-art for global region. Thus, to sum up the points which we have just indicated, our method can not only effectively deal with local challenging areas but also has a good performance for the global scene area. For more details, please view on the benchmark website [1].

Date	A95 (pixels) Name	Res	Weight Avg	Austr MP: 5.6 nd: 290 im0 im1 GT nonocc	AustrP MP: 5.6 nd: 290 im0 im1 GT nonocc	Bicyc2 MP: 5.6 nd: 250 im0 im1 GT nonocc	Class MP: 5.7 nd: 610 im0 im1 GT nonocc	ClassE MP: 5.7 nd: 610 im0 im1 GT nonocc	Compu MP: 1.5 nd: 256 im0 im1 GT nonocc	Crusa MP: 5.5 nd: 800 im0 im1 GT nonocc	CrusaP MP: 5.5 nd: 800 im0 im1 GT nonocc	Djemb MP: 5.7 nd: 320 im0 im1 GT nonocc	DjembL MP: 5.7 nd: 320 im0 im1 GT nonocc	Hoops MP: 5.7 nd: 410 im0 im1 GT nonocc	Livgrm MP: 5.9 nd: 320 im0 im1 GT nonocc	Nkuba MP: 5.5 nd: 570 im0 im1 GT nonocc	Plants MP: 5.6 nd: 320 im0 im1 GT nonocc	Stairs MP: 5.2 nd: 450 im0 im1 GT nonocc
03/09/19	3DMST-CM	H	**3.23** 1	1.57 10	1.31 10	1.38 2	1.43 14	5.37 13	**2.00** 1	1.58 2	1.70 7	1.26 18	6.80 6	4.17 5	**3.11** 1	11.7 18	2.32 11	7.40 15
01/24/17	3DMST	H	3.47 2	1.50 8	1.21 3	1.89 7	1.39 10	4.00 11	**2.00** 1	1.60 6	1.70 7	1.24 14	11.1 13	6.36 17	5.87 4	10.2 11	2.15 6	5.32 7
10/12/17	FEN-D2DRR	H	3.51 3	1.80 14	1.42 13	2.02 10	1.39 10	4.25 12	3.00 10	1.97 14	2.11 17	1.22 12	6.58 5	5.72 13	8.29 9	8.36 7	2.02 2	5.78 8
03/10/17	MC-CNN+TDSR	F	3.58 4	2.32 21	1.70 25	4.21 29	1.47 18	19.8 27	3.00 10	2.00 15	2.05 16	1.30 20	5.29 4	3.58 3	3.75 2	5.63 2	2.43 15	**3.33** 1
04/12/16	MeshStereoExt	H	4.05 5	1.69 11	1.49 15	2.15 13	1.48 19	5.80 14	3.00 10	1.89 12	1.93 14	1.46 26	8.96 11	6.61 19	6.88 6	12.0 19	3.82 23	6.10 10

Fig. 4. Middlebury 3.0 benchmark for the A95 metric. Our method achieves the current best error rate among 121 existing algorithms. Here we list current top five methods: 3DMST [5], FEN-D2DRR [14], MC-CNN+TDSR [2], MeshStereoExt [16] (Snapshot from website [1] on July 31, 2019)

The visual comparison between our method and 3DMST is provided in Fig. 6. We see that the proposed algorithm outperforms 3DMST and calculates more faithful disparities. Compared to 3DMST, our distinctiveness-utilization strategy works much better on the challenging areas, e.g., upper wall in the first row, areas around the stick in the second row and computer screen in the last row. To discuss the improvement in detail, we focus on "Shelves" data set in the second row. This data set contains lots of challenging areas in the scene, such as the background wall. 3DMST [5] can effectively handle most of the areas in the scene. However, the part of the wall near the objects tends to cause large errors. We use the red and blue boxes to indicate the areas that are obviously wrong.

Date	Name	Res	Avg	Austr MP: 5.6 nd: 290 im0 im1 GT nonocc	AustrP MP: 5.6 nd: 290 im0 im1 GT nonocc	Bicyc2 MP: 5.6 nd: 250 im0 im1 GT nonocc	Class MP: 5.7 nd: 610 im0 im1 GT nonocc	ClassE MP: 5.7 nd: 610 im0 im1 GT nonocc	Compu MP: 1.5 nd: 256 im0 im1 GT nonocc	Crusa MP: 5.5 nd: 800 im0 im1 GT nonocc	CrusaP MP: 5.5 nd: 800 im0 im1 GT nonocc	Djemb MP: 5.7 nd: 320 im0 im1 GT nonocc	DjembL MP: 5.7 nd: 320 im0 im1 GT nonocc	Hoops MP: 5.7 nd: 410 im0 im1 GT nonocc	Livgrm MP: 5.9 nd: 320 im0 im1 GT nonocc	Nkuba MP: 5.5 nd: 570 im0 im1 GT nonocc	Plants MP: 5.6 nd: 320 im0 im1 GT nonocc	Stairs MP: 5.2 nd: 450 im0 im1 GT nonocc
bad 1.0 (%)			Weight															
05/26/18	NOSS_ROB	H	**13.2** 1	9.63 9	7.80 11	9.18 4	8.96 9	24.4 13	8.78 3	11.9 4	**12.8** 1	6.91 7	20.6 2	**16.5** 1	14.6 2	25.8 19	15.2 7	14.6 2
03/06/18	NOSS	H	13.2 2	9.63 9	7.80 11	9.18 4	8.96 9	24.4 13	8.78 3	11.9 4	**12.8** 1	6.91 7	20.6 2	**16.5** 1	14.6 2	25.8 19	15.2 7	15.4 3
03/09/19	3DMST-CM	H	13.8 3	9.30 7	7.56 10	8.34 2	9.33 16	23.5 10	11.4 8	14.1 9	14.7 9	8.86 25	22.0 6	18.4 3	**12.5** 1	27.2 24	14.3 4	16.5 8
06/22/17	LocalExp	H	13.9 4	9.80 13	7.92 14	**7.41** 1	9.12 14	24.4 15	9.13 5	**11.7** 1	12.8 3	7.74 14	22.2 8	20.6 6	16.1 5	29.1 30	16.7 15	15.5 4
06/01/18	NaN_ROB	H	14.1 5	9.68 11	7.90 13	9.06 3	9.74 17	24.2 12	**8.70** 1	11.9 3	12.9 4	7.72 13	22.3 9	20.4 5	16.6 6	28.8 29	16.7 14	16.1 6
01/24/17	3DMST	H	14.5 6	8.97 5	7.03 8	10.0 10	9.18 15	23.0 7	11.1 7	13.7 6	14.9 10	8.53 22	24.2 12	23.2 9	17.1 7	28.0 27	14.1 3	15.7 5

(a) bad 1.0

Date	Name	Res	Avg	Austr MP: 5.6 nd: 290 im0 im1 GT nonocc	AustrP MP: 5.6 nd: 290 im0 im1 GT nonocc	Bicyc2 MP: 5.6 nd: 250 im0 im1 GT nonocc	Class MP: 5.7 nd: 610 im0 im1 GT nonocc	ClassE MP: 5.7 nd: 610 im0 im1 GT nonocc	Compu MP: 1.5 nd: 256 im0 im1 GT nonocc	Crusa MP: 5.5 nd: 800 im0 im1 GT nonocc	CrusaP MP: 5.5 nd: 800 im0 im1 GT nonocc	Djemb MP: 5.7 nd: 320 im0 im1 GT nonocc	DjembL MP: 5.7 nd: 320 im0 im1 GT nonocc	Hoops MP: 5.7 nd: 410 im0 im1 GT nonocc	Livgrm MP: 5.9 nd: 320 im0 im1 GT nonocc	Nkuba MP: 5.5 nd: 570 im0 im1 GT nonocc	Plants MP: 5.6 nd: 320 im0 im1 GT nonocc	Stairs MP: 5.2 nd: 450 im0 im1 GT nonocc
bad 2.0 (%)			Weight															
05/26/18	NOSS_ROB	H	**5.01** 1	3.57 4	2.84 3	3.99 4	**1.93** 1	**5.15** 1	3.34 2	3.32 2	**3.15** 1	2.32 5	8.55 2	**7.45** 1	7.06 3	12.5 3	5.20 3	9.06 5
03/06/18	NOSS	H	5.04 2	3.57 4	2.84 3	3.99 4	**1.93** 1	**5.15** 1	3.34 2	3.32 2	**3.15** 1	2.32 5	8.55 2	**7.45** 1	7.06 3	12.5 3	5.20 3	10.0 11
06/22/17	LocalExp	H	5.43 3	3.65 6	2.87 5	**2.98** 1	1.99 3	5.59 5	3.37 5	3.48 6	3.35 5	2.05 2	10.3 6	9.75 6	8.57 7	14.4 17	5.40 8	9.55 8
03/09/19	3DMST-CM	H	5.47 4	4.10 11	3.37 9	2.99 2	2.95 13	7.63 10	4.55 9	**3.26** 1	3.95 8	2.16 3	10.2 5	8.28 3	**6.37** 1	13.2 7	5.86 12	9.35 6
06/01/18	NaN_ROB	H	5.73 5	**3.41** 1	2.90 6	3.69 3	2.33 4	5.32 4	3.35 4	3.49 7	3.31 4	2.31 4	10.3 7	10.8 8	9.64 10	15.3 23	5.45 9	9.89 9
01/24/17	3DMST	H	5.92 6	3.71 8	2.78 2	4.75 7	2.72 7	7.36 9	4.28 7	3.44 4	3.76 6	2.35 8	12.6 12	11.5 10	8.56 6	14.0 15	5.35 7	8.87 4

(b) bad 2.0

Fig. 5. Middlebury 3.0 benchmark for the bad 1.0 and bad 2.0 metrics. Here we compare our method with the other top five methods: NOSS_ROB (unpublished work), NOSS (unpublished work), LocalExp [13], NaN_ROB (unpublished work) and 3DMST [5] (Snapshot from website [1] on July 31, 2019): (a)-result for the bad 1.0 metric;(b)-result for the bad 2.0 metric.

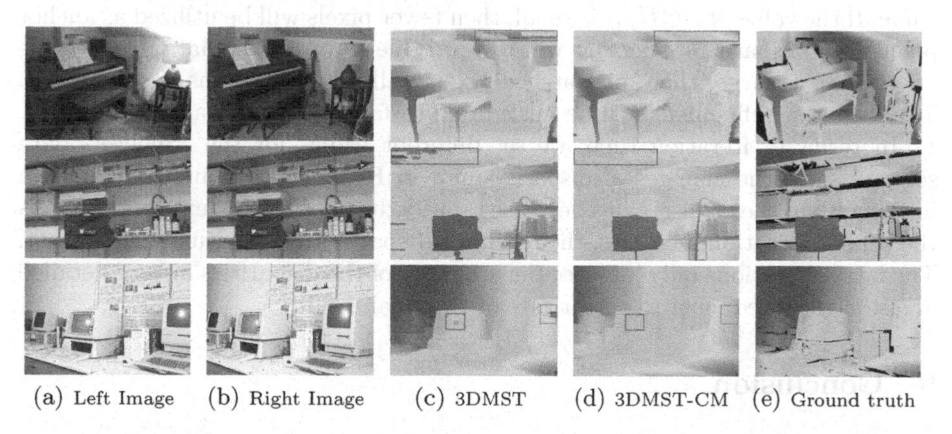

(a) Left Image (b) Right Image (c) 3DMST (d) 3DMST-CM (e) Ground truth

Fig. 6. Comparison of disparity maps of the proposed 3DMST-CM algorithm with those of the 3DMST method [5], together with the ground truth; see region highlighted. (Color figure online)

The red box indicates the wall near the shelf and the blue box indicates the wall near the stick. We can clearly notice the case of incorrect disparity filling in these areas. Our method can effectively solve this problem by distinguishing pixel distinctiveness first and then extracting the reliable disparity pixels for hole filling.

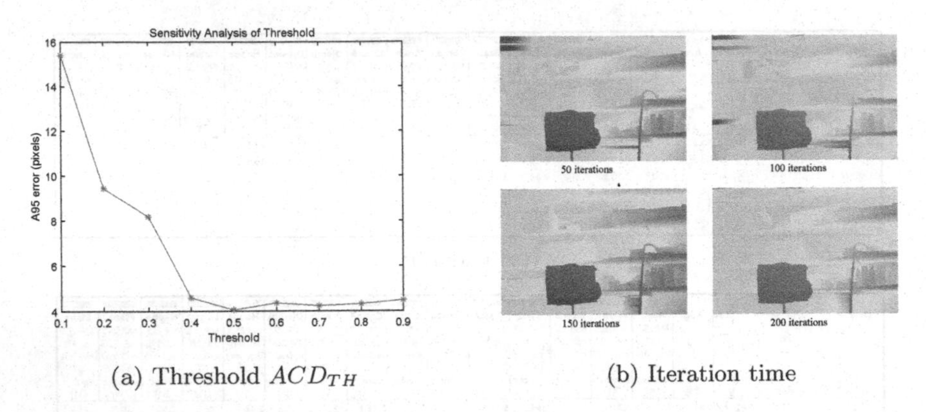

(a) Threshold ACD_{TH}

(b) Iteration time

Fig. 7. Sensitivity analysis of parameters: (a)-error rate for the threshold ACD_{TH}; (b)-disparity changes for the iteration time.

4.3 Parameter Analysis

We then evaluate the sensitivity of some key parameters in our method. Parameter ACD_{TH} controls the distinctiveness determination. Figure 7(a) shows the A95 errors when setting ACD_{TH} to different values for the middlebury training data set images. Our method is insensitive to ACD_{TH} in a middle region of the value. If the value of ACD_{TH} is small, then fewer pixels will be utilized as anchor pixels. The disparity refinement will be hard due to very little data. If the value of ACD_{TH} is large, then mismatched pixels will be mistaken as anchor pixels. The disparity refinement will be misled due to false data, the same as 3DMST.

In terms of iteration time, we set different values for the "Shelves" data set and show the changes of disparity map in Fig. 7(b). Starting rom random initialization, the error regions decrease rapidly during the first few iterations. As the time of iteration increases, the resultant disparity map is visually indifferent. The latter iterations only increase the accuracy of the disparities in very detailed areas, slightly reducing the error rate of the final result.

5 Conclusion

In this paper we propose a novel confidence map based stereo matching algorithm. We fuse the distinctiveness analysis in the stereo matching process and then propagate disparity messages from reliable areas to challenging areas through anchored rolling refinement. The distinctiveness-utilization strategy works much better on the challenging areas and provides more precise disparity values. The top first rank for A95 error metric on Middlebury 3.0 benchmark demonstrates that our algorithm is one of the most effective algorithms for the challenging areas. Beyond that, the results for other error metrics prove that our algorithm also reaches state-of-the-art for the global scene area. In the future, we will try to speed up the processing and continue to improve the accuracy in the challenging areas.

References

1. Scharstein, D., Szeliski, R.H.H.: Middlebury stereo evaluation. Version 3. http://vision.middlebury.edu/stereo/eval3/
2. Drouyer, S., Beucher, S., Bilodeau, M., Moreaud, M., Sorbier, L.: Sparse stereo disparity map densification using hierarchical image segmentation. In: Angulo, J., Velasco-Forero, S., Meyer, F. (eds.) ISMM 2017. LNCS, vol. 10225, pp. 172–184. Springer, Cham (2017). https://doi.org/10.1007/978-3-319-57240-6_14
3. Felzenszwalb, P.F., Huttenlocher, D.P.: Efficient graph-based image segmentation. Int. J. Comput. Vis. **59**(2), 167–181 (2004)
4. Kim, K.R., Kim, C.S.: Adaptive smoothness constraints for efficient stereo matching using texture and edge information. In: 2016 IEEE International Conference on Image Processing (ICIP), pp. 3429–3433. IEEE (2016)
5. Li, L., Yu, X., Zhang, S., Zhao, X., Zhang, L.: 3D cost aggregation with multiple minimum spanning trees for stereo matching. Appl. Opt. **56**(12), 3411–3420 (2017)
6. Li, L., Zhang, S., Yu, X., Zhang, L.: PMSC: PatchMatch-based superpixel cut for accurate stereo matching. IEEE Trans. Circuits Syst. Video Technol. **28**(3), 679–692 (2016)
7. Mao, W., Wang, M., Zhou, J., Gong, M.: Semi-dense stereo matching using dual CNNs. In: IEEE Winter Conference on Applications of Computer Vision, pp. 1588–1597 (2019). https://doi.org/10.1109/WACV.2019.00174
8. Mozerov, M.G., van de Weijer, J.: One-view occlusion detection for stereo matching with a fully connected CRF model. IEEE Trans. Image Process. **28**(6), 2936–2947 (2019)
9. Park, H., Lee, K.M.: Look wider to match image patches with convolutional neural networks. IEEE Signal Process. Lett. **24**(12), 1788–1792 (2016)
10. Scharstein, D., et al.: High-resolution stereo datasets with subpixel-accurate ground truth. In: Jiang, X., Hornegger, J., Koch, R. (eds.) GCPR 2014. LNCS, vol. 8753, pp. 31–42. Springer, Cham (2014). https://doi.org/10.1007/978-3-319-11752-2_3
11. Shi, C., Wang, G., Pei, X., He, B., Lin, X.: Stereo matching using local plane fitting in confidence-based support window. IEICE Trans. Inf. Syst. **95**(2), 699–702 (2012)
12. Shi, C., Wang, G., Yin, X., Pei, X., He, B., Lin, X.: High-accuracy stereo matching based on adaptive ground control points. IEEE Trans. Image Process. **24**(4), 1412–1423 (2015)
13. Taniai, T., Matsushita, Y., Sato, Y., Naemura, T.: Continuous 3D label stereo matching using local expansion moves. IEEE Trans. Pattern Anal. Mach. Intell. **40**(11), 2725–2739 (2018)
14. Ye, X., Li, J., Wang, H., Huang, H., Zhang, X.: Efficient stereo matching leveraging deep local and context information. IEEE Access **5**, 18745–18755 (2017)
15. Zbontar, J., LeCun, Y.: Computing the stereo matching cost with a convolutional neural network. In: Proceedings of the IEEE Conference on Computer Vision and Pattern Recognition, pp. 1592–1599 (2015)
16. Zhang, C., Li, Z., Cheng, Y., Cai, R., Chao, H., Rui, Y.: MeshStereo: a global stereo model with mesh alignment regularization for view interpolation. In: Proceedings of the IEEE International Conference on Computer Vision, pp. 2057–2065 (2015)

Optical Flow Assisted Monocular Visual Odometry

Yiming Wan[1,2], Wei Gao[1,2(✉)], and Yihong Wu[1,2]

[1] NLPR, Institute of Automation, Chinese Academy of Sciences, Beijing 100190, China
{yiming.wan,wgao,yhwu}@nlpr.ia.ac.cn

[2] School of Artificial Intelligence, University of Chinese Academy of Sciences, Beijing 100049, China

Abstract. This paper proposes a novel deep learning based approach for monocular visual odometry (VO) called FlowVO-Net. Our approach utilizes CNN to extract motion information between two consecutive frames and employs Bi-directional convolution LSTM (Bi-ConvLSTM) for temporal modelling. ConvLSTM can encode not only temporal information but also spatial correlation, and the bidirectional architecture enables it to learn the geometric relationship from image sequences pre and post. Besides, our approach jointly predicts optical flow as an auxiliary task in a self-supervised way by measuring photometric consistency. Experiment results indicate competitive performance of the proposed FlowVO-Net to the state-of-art methods.

Keywords: Visual odometry · ConvLSTM · Optical flow

1 Introduction

Visual odometry (VO) is the process of estimating camera poses solely from a sequence of images. It is a fundamental issue in robotics since it enables a robot to localize itself in various environments. In general, VO can be divided into two types in terms of the number of used cameras: stereo VO and monocular VO. Monocular VO uses only one camera, which often suffers from absolute scale drift, making it more challenging than stereo VO. To address this problem, a substantial amount of methods have been proposed during the last decades. However, there still exist many problems. For example, feature-based methods [19] are sensitive to illumination and require rich texture. Direct methods [4] are faster than feature-based methods but require the object has a small movement. Recently, convolution neural network (CNN) has made tremendous progress in various computer vision problems, such as object recognition, semantic segmentation and image classification. Due to these developments, it has made it possible to use deep learning to deal with VO problems. Most supervised methods

This work was supported in part by the National key R&D Program of China (2016YFB0502002) and in part by the Natural Sciences Foundation of China (61872361, 61836015).

S. Palaiahnakote et al. (Eds.): ACPR 2019, LNCS 12046, pp. 366–377, 2020.
https://doi.org/10.1007/978-3-030-41404-7_26

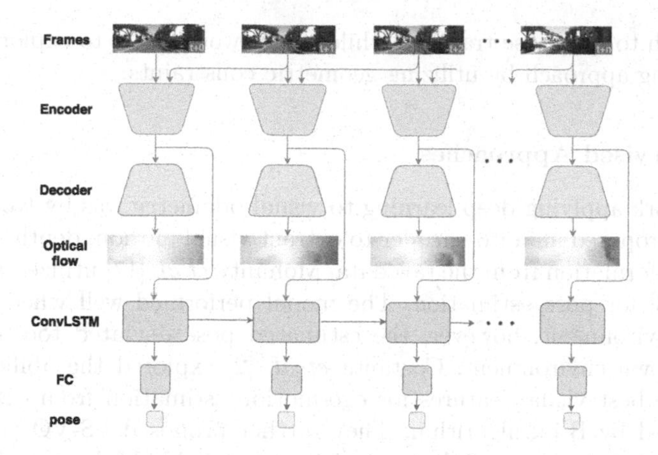

Fig. 1. The pipeline of our proposed FlowVO-Net. Inputs to our model are two images stacked through the third channel. Features extracted by CNN encoder part are delivered to ConvLSTM and CNN decoder part. CNN decoder outputs the optical flow of the two consecutive frames. The outputs of ConvLSTM are passed to FC layers to predict 6-DOF camera pose.

view this issue as a regression problem [1,2,12,18]. They utilize CNN to extract features of two consecutive frames and directly regress 6-DOF camera pose. The frames can be RGB images or optical flow images. Since VO often deals with a sequence of frames with temporal continuity, a great deal of pose information can be obtained by exploiting the temporal regularity. On this basis, some works explore the ability of CNN+RNN to learn ego-motion estimation [21,22]. Unsupervised methods do not need ground-truth pose labels, but leverage geometric constraints or visual information to supervise training process, such as depth, stereo images or optical flow [14,15,20,24,25]. In this paper, we propose a novel monocular VO system named FlowVO-Net. An overview of our pipeline can be seen in Fig. 1. Our main contributions are as follows:

- We utilize Bi-ConvLSTM to model sequential dependencies and complex motion dynamics, and leverage optical flow prediction to assist pose estimation.
- Optical flow prediction is self-supervised implemented by image warping. This auxiliary task makes it possible for our network to exploit the inner-task relationship between learning optical flow and regressing 6-DOF relative pose. We find this auxiliary task substantially improves the accuracy, especially for rotation estimation.

2 Related Work

In recent years, deep learning methods for visual odometry have attracted considerable attention. Early methods view it as a regression problem and need ground-truth to supervise training, while recent works start to explore unsupervised learning approach by utilizing geometric constraints.

2.1 Supervised Approaches

The first work applying deep learning to visual odometry was by Kondal *et al.* [12]. They proposed an auto-encoder to extract visual motion, depth, and finally odometry information from the raw data. Mohanty *et al.* [17] utilized pre-trained AlexNet [13] for pose estimation. The model performed well when testing on a known environment, however, the estimated pose deviated too much when in an unknown environment. Costante *et al.* [2] explored the ability of CNN to learn the best visual features for ego-motion estimation from dense optical flow obtained by Brox algorithm. They further proposed LS-VO [1] to find a non-linear representation of the optical flow manifold. Muller *et al.* proposed Flowdometry [18], which used FlowNet [3] to predict raw optical flow images. These raw flow images were used as input to the odometry network, which was based on the FlowNet architecture. Similar to Flowdometry, Wang *et al.* [22] utilized FlowNet features as input to Long Short-Term Memory(LSTM) [7] which enabled their network to exploit long term dependencies between monocular frames.

2.2 Unsupervised Approaches

Zhou *et al.* [25] presented an unsupervised learning framework to learn both monocular depth and camera motion from video sequences, which used view synthesis as the supervisory signal. Vijayanarasimhan *et al.* [20] further proposed SfM-Net to jointly predict depth, segmentation, camera, and rigid object motions. Li *et al.* [14] proposed UnDeepVO. They trained UnDeepVO by using stereo image pairs to recover the scale but tested it by using consecutive monocular images. Zhan *et al.* [24] also explored the use of stereo sequences for learning depth and visual odometry, however, they replaced the standard photometric warp loss with deep feature-based warping loss to solve the non-Lambertian problem. Mahjourian*et al.* [15] explicitly considered the inferred 3D geometry of the whole scene and enforced consistency of the estimated 3D point clouds and ego-motion across consecutive frames. Lyer *et al.* [8] proposed CTCs block(Composite Transformation Constraints), that automatically generate supervisory signals for training and enforce geometric consistency. However, their method needs a noisy teacher, which could be a standard VO pipeline.

3 Methodology

3.1 Overview

As shown in Fig. 1, our network receives two consecutive frames and outputs optical flow and relative pose at each time step. Generally, our model can be

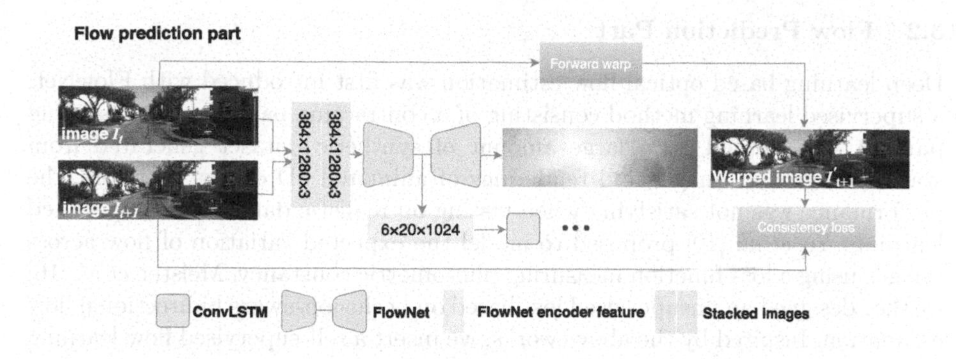

Fig. 2. Flow prediction part of our proposed FlowVO-Net.

divided into two part, the flow prediction part and the motion estimation part. The detailed implementation of the two parts is described in Figs. 2 and 3. For flow prediction part, as shown in Fig. 2, two consecutive frames stacked through the third channel are delivered to an encoder-decoder module to obtain raw optical flow. We adopt FlowNet [3] as our encoder-decoder model. The outputs of the encoder part contain rich motion information and are passed to ConvLSTM to regress camera motion. Given I_t and flow, we can synthesize I_{t+1} by forward warping. The photometric loss is computed as the difference between the warped image $I^{'}_{t+1}$ and the original I_{t+1}. For motion estimation part, as shown in Fig. 3, FlowNet features are delivered to Bi-ConvLSTM. Bi-ConvLSTM outputs are two groups of features(forward and backward) with the same size of input features but encapsulated with sequential dynamics information. The forward and backward features are concatenated through the last channel and after an average-pooling layer, two fully-connected layers are followed to regress the final 6-DOF motion vector.

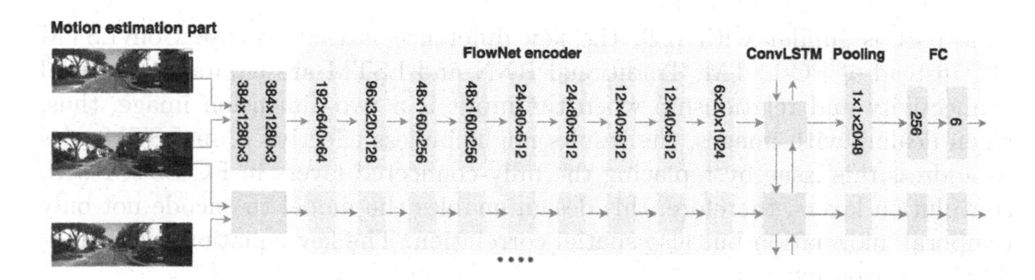

Fig. 3. Motion estimation part of our proposed FlowVO-Net.

3.2 Flow Prediction Part

Deep learning based optical flow estimation was first introduced with FlowNet, a supervised learning method consisting of a contracting part and an expanding part. It was trained on a large amount of synthetic dataset generated from static background images and renderings of animated 3D chairs, therefore, the performance was not satisfying when testing on realistic data. For unsupervised learning, Yu *et al.* [10] proposed to model the expected variation of flow across images using a loss function measuring photometric constancy. Meister *et al.* [16] further designed an unsupervised loss based on occlusion-aware bidirectional flow estimation. Inspired by the above works, we insert a self-supervised flow learning module based on photometric loss into our network.

Given two consecutive frames $I(x,y,t), I(x,y,t+1)$ and optical flow obtained by FlowNet, the photometric loss can be computed as the difference between the second image $I(x,y,t+1)$ and the forward warped first image $I^{'}(i,j,t+1)$:

$$L_{warp}(I_t, I_{t+1}) = \sum_{i,j} \left| I(i,j,t+1) - I^{'}(i,j,t+1) \right| \tag{1}$$

where $\boldsymbol{u}, \boldsymbol{v} \in \mathbb{R}^{H \times W}$ are the horizontal and vertical components of predicted flow field respectively. $I^{'}(i,j,t+1) = I(i+u_{i,j}, j+v_{i,j}, t)$. The forward warp is performed using the differentiable bilinear sampling mechanism proposed in the spatial transformer networks [9]. Given a sequence of images $I_1, I_2 ... I_T$, the loss for flow prediction is:

$$L_{photometric} = \frac{1}{T-1} \sum_{t=1}^{T-1} L_{warp}(I_t, I_{t+1}) \tag{2}$$

3.3 Motion Estimation Part

This part is similar with [22], the key difference is that we use ConvLSTM [23] instead of FC-LSTM. Traditional RNN and LSTM are ignorant of spatial connectivity and relationship when the input is a two-dimension image, thus, when dealing with images, the results might be less effective. ConvLSTM tries to address this issue by replacing the fully-connected layers in FC-LSTM with convolution layers, therefore, this design enables the model to encode not only temporal information but also spatial correlation. The key equations of ConvL-STM are given by:

$$\begin{aligned}
i_t &= \sigma(w_{xi} * x_t + w_{hi} * h_{t-1} + b_i) \\
f_t &= \sigma(w_{xf} * x_t + w_{hf} * h_{t-1} + b_f) \\
o_t &= \sigma(w_{xo} * x_t + w_{ho} * h_{t-1} + b_o) \\
c_t &= f_t \odot c_{t-1} + i_t \odot tanh(w_{xc} * x_t + w_{hc} * h_{t-1} + b_c) \\
h_t &= o_t \odot tanh(c_t)
\end{aligned} \tag{3}$$

Table 1. Motion estimation part configuration

Layers	Output size	Kernel size	Strides	Channels
Conv1	192 × 640	7 × 7	2	64
Conv2	96 × 320	5 × 5	2	128
Conv3	48 × 160	5 × 5	2	256
Conv3_1	48 × 160	3 × 3	1	256
Conv4	24 × 80	3 × 3	2	512
Conv4_1	24 × 80	3 × 3	1	512
Conv5	12 × 40	3 × 3	2	512
Conv5_1	12 × 40	3 × 3	1	512
Conv6	6 × 20	3 × 3	2	1024
Bi-ConvLSTM	6 × 20	1 × 1	1	1024
Average pooling	1 × 1	6 × 20	1	2048
FC1		256		
FC2		6		

where x_t represents input at time t, and i_t, f_t and o_t stands for input, forget and output gates, respectively. c_t, c_{t-1}, h_t and h_{t-1} are memory and output activations at time t and $t-1$. $*$ denotes convolution operation and $\odot$ element-wise multiplication. σ is the sigmoid activation function.

For each frame, its pose not only correlates with the last frame, but also the next one. To utilize the correlation, we adopt a Bidirectional architecture for ConvLSTM model. The structure of Bi-ConvLSTM network has two parallel layers propagating in two directions(forward and backward) to memorize the information from both directions. The forward and backward pass have the same state equations as in Eq. 3. Outputs of each step are two hidden states, The two states are then concatenated to give an overall output. In our work, we concatenate the two hidden states through the channel dimension.

As shown in Fig. 3, Flownet features are passed to Bi-ConvLSTM. The kernel size of ConvLSTM is 1×1. Stride is 1 and the number of output channel is 1024. After an average pooling layer, two FC with a hidden node of 256 and 6 are followed to regress 6-Dof relative pose. Detailed information can be found in Table 1. For relative pose regression, we employ the following loss function:

$$\begin{aligned} L_{trans} &= \frac{1}{T-1}\sum_{t=1}^{T-1} \|\widehat{\boldsymbol{p}_t} - \boldsymbol{p}_t\|_2^2 \\ L_{rot} &= \frac{1}{T-1}\sum_{t=1}^{T-1} \|\widehat{\boldsymbol{\varphi}_t} - \boldsymbol{\varphi}_t\|_2^2 \\ L_{motion} &= \alpha L_{trans} + \beta L_{rot} \end{aligned} \tag{4}$$

where $\widehat{p_t}$, $\widehat{\varphi_t}$ denotes the predicted relative translation and euler angles between frame t and $t+1$, respectively, and p_t, φ_t denotes the corresponding ground-truth. α and β are scale factors to balance translation and orientation.

3.4 Loss Function

Our final objective can be given by the following equation, where λ is the weighting for the flow prediction loss.

$$L = \alpha L_{trans} + \beta L_{rot} + \lambda L_{photometric} \tag{5}$$

By minimizing this function, our model can learn a valid VO model, however, it suffers from that it has to manually tune the hyper-parameter and α, β and λ. Recently, [11] proposed a novel loss function which was able to learn a weighting between different objective functions. In [11], the two different objective functions are global position and orientation while in our experiments, they are position, orientation, and photometric consistency. The final loss function is:

$$\begin{aligned} L_{final} = L_{trans} exp(-\hat{s}_x) + \hat{s}_x + L_{rot} exp(-\hat{s}_q) + \hat{s}_q \\ + L_{photometric} exp(-\hat{p}_x) + \hat{s}_p \end{aligned} \tag{6}$$

where $\hat{s}_x$, $\hat{s}_q$ and $\hat{s}_p$ are three learnable variables, which act as a weighting for the respective component in the loss function.

Table 2. testing results on sequence 03, 04, 05, 06, 07, 10

Method	Sequence											
	03		04		05		06		07		10	
	t_{rel}	r_{rel}	t_{rel}	r_{rel}	t_{rel}	r_{rel}	t_{rel}	r_{rel}	t_{rel}	r_{rel}	t_{rel}	r_{rel}
VISO2-S [6]	3.21	3.25	2.12	2.12	1.53	1.60	1.48	1.58	1.85	1.91	1.17	1.30
UnDeepVO [14]	5.00	6.17	5.49	2.13	3.40	1.50	6.20	1.98	3.15	2.48	10.63	4.65
Depth-VO-Feat [24]	15.58	10.69	2.92	2.06	4.94	2.35	5.80	2.07	6.48	3.60	12.45	3.46
VISO2-M [6]	8.47	8.82	4.69	4.49	19.22	17.58	7.30	6.14	23.61	19.11	41.56	32.99
SfMLearner [25]	10.78	3.92	**4.49**	5.24	18.67	4.10	25.88	4.80	21.33	6.65	14.33	3.30
DeepVO [21]	8.49	6.89	7.19	6.97	**2.62**	3.61	5.42	5.82	3.91	4.60	8.11	8.83
ESP-VO [22]	6.72	6.46	6.33	6.08	3.35	4.93	7.24	7.29	**3.52**	5.02	9.77	10.2
Ours	**4.46**	**1.67**	5.33	**2.04**	2.67	**1.00**	**4.88**	**1.92**	4.05	**2.25**	**5.73**	**2.39**

t_{rel}(%): average translational RMSE drift (%) on a length of 100–800 m.
r_{rel}(%): average rotational RMSE drift (°/100 m) on a length of 100–800 m.

4 Experiments

4.1 Datasets

We evaluate the proposed FlowVO-Net on the well-known KITTIVO/SLAM benchmark [5]. It contains 22 sequences of images. Sequence 00 – 10 are provided with ground truth while 11 − 21 only have raw sensor data. Since this dataset was recorded at 10 fps with many dynamic objects, it is challenging for monocular VO. In our experiments, the left RGB images are resized to 1280 × 384 for training and testing. We use Seq 00, 02, 08, 09 for training and Seq 03, 04, 05, 06, 07 and 10 for quantitative evaluation as it was done in [21].

4.2 Training Setup

We use pre-trained FlowNet weights to initialize flow prediction part and randomly initially the remaining weights. $\hat{s}_x$ and $\hat{s}_q$ and $\hat{s}_p$ is set to 0.0, −3.0 and 0.0 respectively in the experiments. The network is trained with Adam optimization with momentum fixed to (0.9, 0.999). The initial learning rate is 0.0001 and decreases by 2 times after 10 epochs. We train the model for a maximum of 100,000 iterations with a mini-batch of 2. All experiments are performed on one NVIDIA Titan X using Tensorflow.

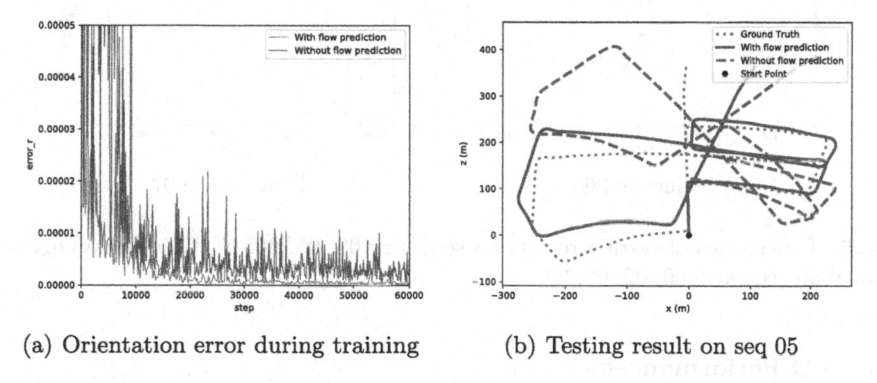

(a) Orientation error during training (b) Testing result on seq 05

Fig. 4. Training loss for rotation and VO results on seq 05 of models with and without flow prediction module.

4.3 How Our Flow Prediction Module Help VO Learning

We first present an experiment to show our flow prediction module helps VO learning. Specifically, we train our model with and without flow prediction module. Figure 4(a) shows the training loss of rotation error. It is clear that the model with flow prediction is able to fastly and stably converge compared with that without flow prediction. As shown in Fig. 4(b), after the same training iteration, the testing result with flow prediction is clearly better than that without flow prediction on sequence 05. This is because optical flow contains rich motion information and learning VO jointly with flow can promote our model exploiting the inter relationship between them. From another point, we employ a multi-task learning approach to assist VO learning and it can also alleviate the risk of over-fitting through weight sharing.

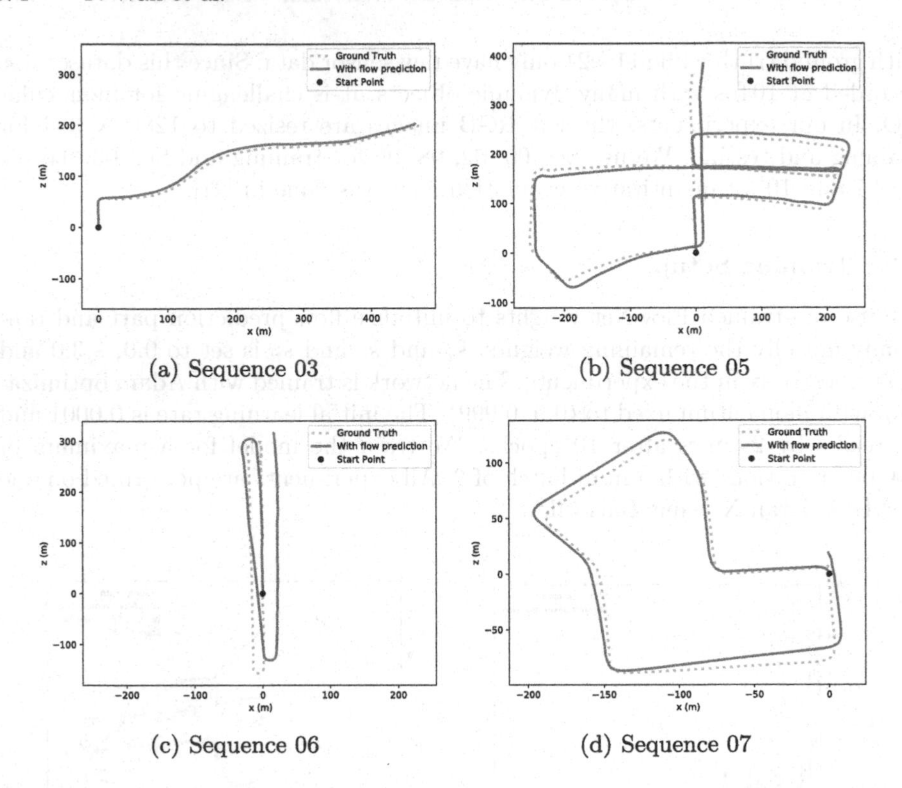

(a) Sequence 03 (b) Sequence 05

(c) Sequence 06 (d) Sequence 07

Fig. 5. Trajectories of testing results on sequence 03, 05, 06, 07. Our FlowVO-Net is trained on sequence 00, 02, 08, 09.

4.4 VO Performances

We compare our model with both traditional and learning-based monocular VO methods on KITTI. We evaluate results using standard KITTI VO evaluation metrics, computing translational and rotational errors for all possible sub-sequences of length (100, ..., 800) m.

Most monocular VO cannot recover absolute scale and VISO2-M [6] tried to deal with that through estimating scale according to the height of camera. However, our model is able to learn the scale through end-to-end learning. Table 2 indicates our model substantially exceeds VISO2-M [6] in terms of both translation and rotation. VISO2-S [6] utilizes stereo images to recover scale and achieve better performance. Our model, using monocular images, can still achieve competitive performance. Some qualitative results are shown in Fig. 5.

Besides, we compare our method against learning-based supervised approaches. It is noted our method significantly improves the accuracy of rotation compared with ESP-VO [22] and DeepVO [21], which are also CNN+LSTM based models. The biggest difference is that we employ the flow prediction module while ESP-VO and DeepVO not. This demonstrates leveraging the flow prediction module can substantially boost rotation learning as well as translation.

In addition, our method outperforms unsupervised monocular method SfM-Learner [25], as well as unsupervised stereo methods UnDeepVO [14] and Depth-VO-feat [24].

We also test our model on sequence 11–20. In this case, we train our model on all the training sequences. The testing results are shown in Fig. 6. It can be seen our FlowVO-net outperforms VISO2-M and is more similar to the stereo VISO2.

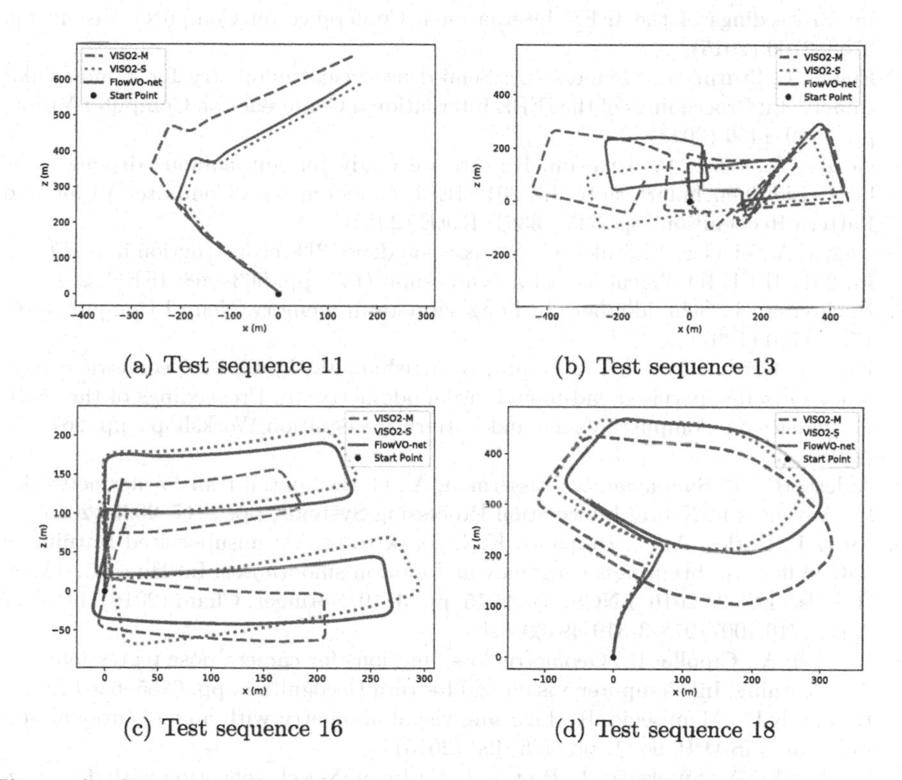

Fig. 6. Qualitative results of Sequence 11, 13, 16 and 18. Note ground truth is not available for these sequence and results of VISO2-S are used as reference.

5 Conclusions

In this paper, we propose FlowVO-Net, a CNN+Bi-ConvLSTM monocular system for motion estimation. In addition, we leverage multi-task learning, that is, learning optical flow through photometric consistency to help VO learning. Experiments indicate the optical flow prediction module is effective and evaluation results outperform current learning- and model-based model. Our future work will focus on integrating depth estimation into our model to construct more geometric constraints to help VO learning.

References

1. Costante, G., Ciarfuglia, T.A.: LS-VO: learning dense optical subspace for robust visual odometry estimation. IEEE Robot. Autom. Lett. **3**(3), 1735–1742 (2018)
2. Costante, G., Mancini, M., Valigi, P., Ciarfuglia, T.A.: Exploring representation learning with CNNs for frame-to-frame ego-motion estimation. IEEE Robot. Autom. Lett. **1**(1), 18–25 (2016)
3. Dosovitskiy, A., et al.: FlowNet: learning optical flow with convolutional networks. In: Proceedings of the IEEE International Conference on Computer Vision, pp. 2758–2766 (2015)
4. Engel, J., Sturm, J., Cremers, D.: Semi-dense visual odometry for a monocular camera. In: Proceedings of the IEEE International Conference on Computer Vision, pp. 1449–1456 (2013)
5. Geiger, A., Lenz, P., Urtasun, R.: Are we ready for autonomous driving? The kitti vision benchmark suite. In: 2012 IEEE Conference on Computer Vision and Pattern Recognition, pp. 3354–3361. IEEE (2012)
6. Geiger, A., Ziegler, J., Stiller, C.: StereoScan: dense 3D reconstruction in real-time. In: 2011 IEEE Intelligent Vehicles Symposium (IV), pp. 963–968. IEEE (2011)
7. Hochreiter, S., Schmidhuber, J.: Long short-term memory. Neural Comput. **9**(8), 1735–1780 (1997)
8. Iyer, G., Krishna Murthy, J., Gupta, G., Krishna, M., Paull, L.: Geometric consistency for self-supervised end-to-end visual odometry. In: Proceedings of the IEEE Conference on Computer Vision and Pattern Recognition Workshops, pp. 267–275 (2018)
9. Jaderberg, M., Simonyan, K., Zisserman, A., et al.: Spatial transformer networks. In: Advances in Neural Information Processing Systems, pp. 2017–2025 (2015)
10. Yu, J.J., Harley, A.W., Derpanis, K.G.: Back to basics: unsupervised learning of optical flow via brightness constancy and motion smoothness. In: Hua, G., Jégou, H. (eds.) ECCV 2016. LNCS, vol. 9915, pp. 3–10. Springer, Cham (2016). https://doi.org/10.1007/978-3-319-49409-8_1
11. Kendall, A., Cipolla, R.: Geometric loss functions for camera pose regression with deep learning. In: Computer Vision and Pattern Recognition, pp. 6555–6564 (2017)
12. Konda, K.R., Memisevic, R.: Learning visual odometry with a convolutional network. In: VISAPP, no. 1, pp. 486–490 (2015)
13. Krizhevsky, A., Sutskever, I., Hinton, G.E.: ImageNet classification with deep convolutional neural networks. In: Advances in Neural Information Processing Systems, pp. 1097–1105 (2012)
14. Li, R., Wang, S., Long, Z., Gu, D.: UnDeepVo: monocular visual odometry through unsupervised deep learning. In: 2018 IEEE International Conference on Robotics and Automation (ICRA), pp. 7286–7291. IEEE (2018)
15. Mahjourian, R., Wicke, M., Angelova, A.: Unsupervised learning of depth and ego-motion from monocular video using 3D geometric constraints. In: Proceedings of the IEEE Conference on Computer Vision and Pattern Recognition, pp. 5667–5675 (2018)
16. Meister, S., Hur, J., Roth, S.: Unflow: unsupervised learning of optical flow with a bidirectional census loss. In: Thirty-Second AAAI Conference on Artificial Intelligence (2018)
17. Mohanty, V., Agrawal, S., Datta, S., Ghosh, A., Sharma, V.D., Chakravarty, D.: DeepVO: a deep learning approach for monocular visual odometry. arXiv preprint arXiv:1611.06069 (2016)

18. Muller, P., Savakis, A.: Flowdometry: an optical flow and deep learning based approach to visual odometry. In: 2017 IEEE Winter Conference on Applications of Computer Vision (WACV), pp. 624–631. IEEE (2017)
19. Murartal, R., Montiel, J.M.M., Tardos, J.D.: ORB-SLAM: a versatile and accurate monocular slam system. IEEE Trans. Rob. **31**(5), 1147–1163 (2015)
20. Vijayanarasimhan, S., Ricco, S., Schmid, C., Sukthankar, R., Fragkiadaki, K.: SfM-Net: learning of structure and motion from video. arXiv preprint arXiv:1704.07804 (2017)
21. Wang, S., Clark, R., Wen, H., Trigoni, N.: DeepVO: towards end-to-end visual odometry with deep recurrent convolutional neural networks. In: 2017 IEEE International Conference on Robotics and Automation (ICRA), pp. 2043–2050. IEEE (2017)
22. Wang, S., Clark, R., Wen, H., Trigoni, N.: End-to-end, sequence-to-sequence probabilistic visual odometry through deep neural networks. Int. J. Robot. Res. **37**(4–5), 513–542 (2018)
23. Xingjian, S., Chen, Z., Wang, H., Yeung, D.Y., Wong, W.K., Woo, W.C.: Convolutional LSTM network: a machine learning approach for precipitation nowcasting. In: Advances in Neural Information Processing Systems, pp. 802–810 (2015)
24. Zhan, H., Garg, R., Saroj Weerasekera, C., Li, K., Agarwal, H., Reid, I.: Unsupervised learning of monocular depth estimation and visual odometry with deep feature reconstruction. In: Proceedings of the IEEE Conference on Computer Vision and Pattern Recognition, pp. 340–349 (2018)
25. Zhou, T., Brown, M., Snavely, N., Lowe, D.G.: Unsupervised learning of depth and ego-motion from video. In: Proceedings of the IEEE Conference on Computer Vision and Pattern Recognition, pp. 1851–1858 (2017)

Coarse-to-Fine Deep Orientation Estimator for Local Image Matching

Yasuaki Mori(✉), Tsubasa Hirakawa, Takayoshi Yamashita, and Hironobu Fujiyoshi

Chubu University, 1200 Matsumotocho, Kasugai, Aichi, Japan
{yasu071021,hirakawa}@mprg.cs.chubu.ac.jp,
{yamashita,fujiyoshi}@isc.chubu.ac.jp

Abstract. Convolutional neural networks (CNNs) have become a mainstream method for keypoint matching in addition to image recognition, object detection, and semantic segmentation. Learned Invariant Feature Transform (LIFT) is pioneering method based on CNN. It performs keypoint detection, orientation estimation, and feature description in a single network. Among these processes, the orientation estimation is needed to obtain invariance for rotation changes. However, unlike the feature point detector and feature descriptor, the orientation estimator has not been considered important for accurate keypoint matching or been well researched even after LIFT is proposed. In this paper, we propose a novel coarse-to-fine orientation estimator that improves matching accuracy. First, the coarse orientation estimator estimates orientations to make the rotation error as small as possible even if large rotation changes exist between an image pair. Second, the fine orientation estimator further improves matching accuracy with the orientation estimated by the coarse orientation estimator. By using the proposed two-stage CNNs, we can accurately estimate orientations improving matching performance. The experimental results with the HPatches benchmark show that our method can achieve a more accurate precision-recall curve than single CNN-based orientation estimators.

Keywords: Keypoint matching · Local image descriptor · Orientation estimation · HPatches

1 Introduction

Keypoint matching, which is the one of major problems in computer vision, is widely used for various applications such as large-scale image retrieval [13], image mosaicking [6], and simultaneous localization and mapping (SLAM) [2,7,12]. In these applications, the same points must be matched across images taken under different conditions (e.g., illumination, viewpoint, or rotation changes). Because of the development of convolutional neural networks (CNNs), several

S. Palaiahnakote et al. (Eds.): ACPR 2019, LNCS 12046, pp. 378–390, 2020.
https://doi.org/10.1007/978-3-030-41404-7_27

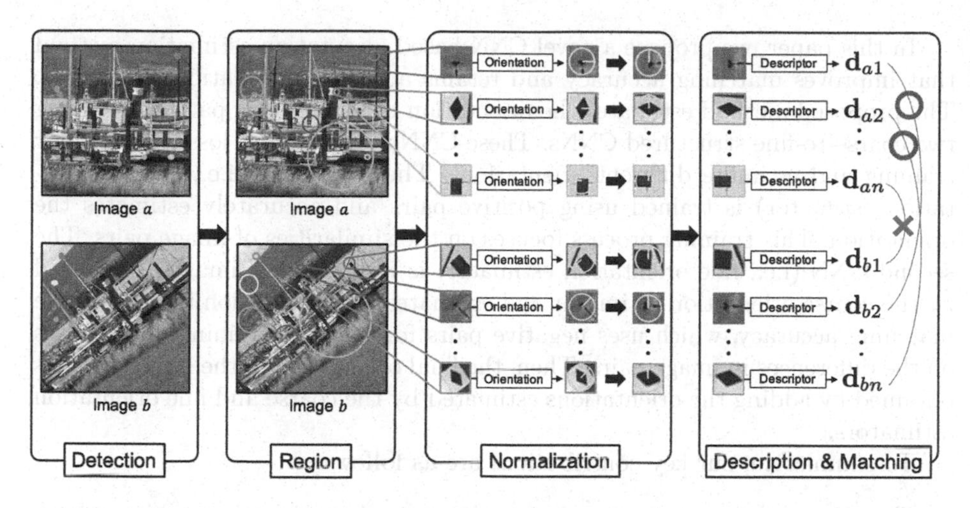

Fig. 1. Overview of keypoint matching. Keypoint matching is done by keypoint detection, region estimation, normalization, and feature description. The rotation change is dealt with by estimating orientation.

keypoint matching methods based on CNNs have been proposed [4,16,19,20] and have achieved higher performances than hand-crafted feature-based approaches [1,5,10,15].

Typical keypoint matching methods, e.g., Scale Invariant Feature Transform (SIFT) [10] or Learned Invariant Feature Transform (LIFT) [19], individually process detection, normalization, and description as shown in Fig. 1. If any of these processes have low accuracy, the final matching accuracy will deteriorate. The process of orientation estimation is only focusing on rotation differences. Although keypoint detection and feature description have been widely studied, orientation estimation has not despite its importance in keypoint matching.

Therefore, we focus on orientation estimation. SIFT [10], the representative method of keypoint matching, estimates the orientation by using the gradient information of the image. LIFT [19], a typical CNN-based method of keypoint matching, estimates the orientation on local image patches by inputting local image patches into a CNN. In this method, positive pairs are only used to training of the orientation estimator. The positive pairs mean a couple of local image patches of the same point taken under different conditions. The orientation estimator on LIFT estimates the angle of similar local image patches into the same orientation. However, when LIFT estimates the orientation between similar but different keypoint images, these are normalized into the same orientation, which increases the number of incorrect matching results. This problem is caused by the network training that focuses on only similarities. A practical approach to overcome this problem is triplet loss with negative pairs: a couple of local image patches of different points. Triplet loss is often used when training the distance between features such as in descriptor training. However, in orientation estimation, triplet loss may decrease orientation estimation accuracy.

In this paper, we propose a novel CNN-based orientation estimation method that improves matching accuracy and retains accurate orientation estimation. The proposed method estimates the orientation of local image patches by using two coarse-to-fine structured CNNs. These CNNs use different loss functions for training and estimate different orientations. The first CNN (i.e., coarse orientation estimator) is trained using positive pairs and accurately estimates the orientation. This training process focuses on the similarities of image pairs. The second CNN (i.e., fine orientation estimator) is input a local image normalized by the coarse orientation estimator and estimates the orientation improving the matching accuracy, which uses negative pairs for network training and focuses on the differences in image pairs. Then, the final orientation of the input image is obtained by adding the orientations estimated by the coarse and fine orientation estimators.

To summarize, our key contributions are as follows:

- The proposed two-stage structure estimates orientation that achieves both accurate orientation estimation and matching results.
- The fine orientation estimator can estimate the orientation improving the final matching accuracy by using the negative pairs for orientation training. Because the fine orientation estimator focuses on dissimilar points during training, our method can reduce incorrect matching results.

2 Related Work

Orientation estimation in keypoint matching has been considered less important than keypoint detection and feature description. Hence, the orientation estimation method of SIFT [10] is merely used for various local descriptors. However, the accuracy of orientation estimation greatly affects the performance of the descriptor. In this section, we introduce the orientation estimation in conventional keypoint matching.

2.1 Hand-Crafted Keypoint Detectors

SIFT [10] is the most common method in keypoint matching. SIFT uses the histograms of pixel gradients at estimates orientation and descriptions feature by voting. Speeded-up robust features (SURF) [5] computes Haar-wavelet response of sample points to extract the local image orientation. Oriented FAST and rotated BRIEF (ORB) [15] computes orientation by using image moments and the center of mass computed from pixel values in local image patches. Histogrammed intensity patches (HIPs) [17] estimate orientation by using intensity over a 16-pixel circle centered around the keypoint detected by FAST. These methods are design in a hand-crafted manner.

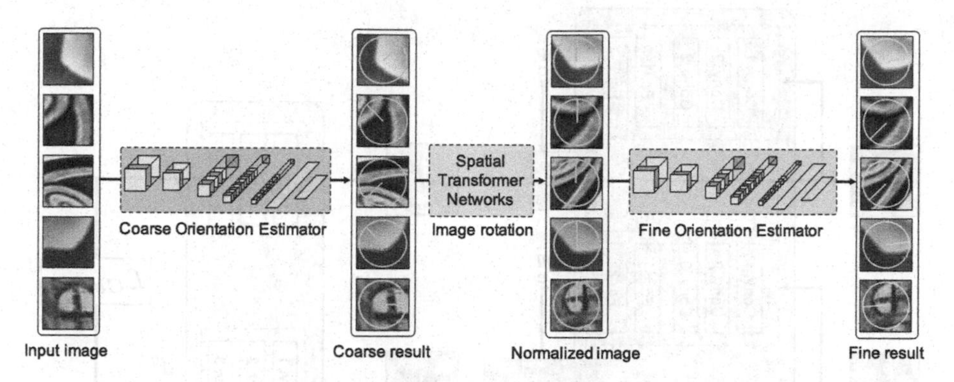

Fig. 2. Overview of the proposed method. Image patches are input to the coarse orientation estimator and then normalized by using the estimated orientation and the spatial transformer networks. The normalized image is input to the fine orientation estimator, and we obtain final results.

2.2 CNN-Based Methods

Although a number of CNN-based methods for keypoint matching have been proposed, few researches have focused on the CNN-based orientation estimation. In LIFT [19], different CNNs are used for keypoint detection, orientation estimation, and feature description. For orientation estimation, LIFT uses a CNN-based method proposed by Yi et al. [20]. This method estimates orientation of local image using a single CNN. LF-Net [14] is a CNN-based method that computes from keypoint detection to feature description in an end-to-end manner. This method outputs 4-channel feature maps from the CNN used for a keypoint detector. Then, the location, scale, and orientation of the keypoint are estimated simultaneously.

Because more accurate CNN-based orientation estimation has not been researched after these methods are proposed. In the latest keypoint matching methods based on CNN, orientation is often estimated by using either of these algorithms.

3 Proposed Method

The proposed method estimates orientation by using two CNNs. Figure 2 shows the overview of the proposed orientation estimation method. First, we input local images to the coarse orientation estimator to estimate the orientation. Second, the spatial transformer networks (STN) [8] normalizes the input image with result of coarse orientation estimator. Third, the normalized image is input to the fine orientation estimator, and we estimate the orientation. Finally, the orientation of the input image can be obtained by adding the orientations estimated by both the coarse and fine orientation estimators. Both CNNs have the same

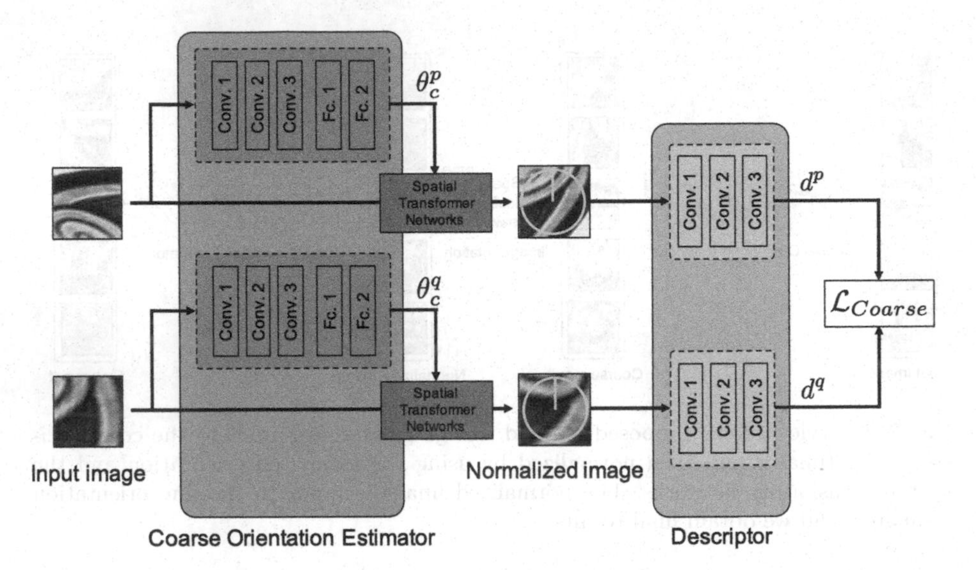

Fig. 3. The training process of the coarse orientation estimator. We train this network with positive pairs. The two coarse orientation estimators shown in this figure share parameters.

network structures but are trained independently by using different loss functions. Hereafter, we introduce the details of our proposed coarse-to-fine orientation estimator.

3.1 Coarse Orientation Estimator

For accurate keypoint matching, orientation estimation is also an important process. If keypoint matching has inaccurate orientation estimation, it might obtain indiscriminate features even for the same image pairs in feature descriptor. Therefore, orientation must be accurately estimated to improve keypoint matching. The coarse orientation estimator is the first process of our proposed method, as shown in Fig. 2. The coarse orientation estimator aims to estimate orientation exactly even if rotation changes exist between two local image patches. To achieve such orientation estimation, we train the coarse orientation estimator by using only positive pairs to make it focus on the similarities in patches.

Figure 3 shows the training process of the coarse orientation estimator. We use the distance between the described features of image patches to train the coarse orientation estimator. The reason is that it is difficult to prepare ground truth with respect to orientation as described by Yi et al. [20]. Although SIFT orientation could be used as ground truth, it may not necessarily be correct. Therefore, the distance between described features of normalized image patches leads to estimate orientation accurately in the coarse orientation estimator. In training of coarse orientation estimator, we use only positive pairs to focus on the similar points in the input image pair. Moreover, we rotate the input images

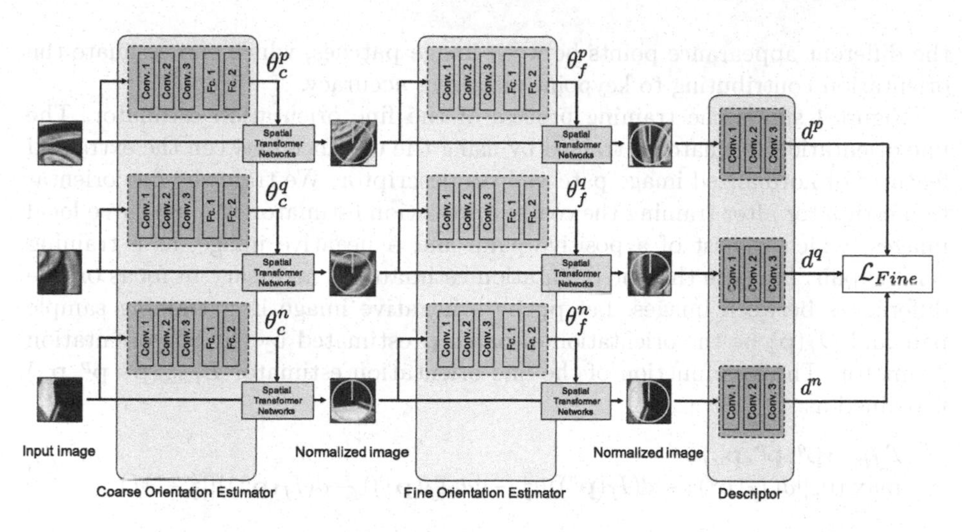

Fig. 4. The training process of the fine orientation estimator. The input images for the fine orientation estimator are normalized by the coarse orientation estimator. During the training, we update only the network parameter of the fine orientation estimator and not the other networks.

randomly to achieve robust orientation estimation. Here, let $\mathbf{p}^q$ and $\mathbf{p}^p$ be image patches of a positive pairs and $O_c(\mathbf{p})$ be the estimated orientation of patch $\mathbf{p}$ by coarse orientation estimator. We define the loss function of the coarse orientation estimator $L_{coarse}(\mathbf{p}^q, \mathbf{p}^p)$ as:

$$\mathcal{L}_{coarse}(\mathbf{p}^q, \mathbf{p}^p) = ||d(I_c(\mathbf{p}^q)) - d(I_c(\mathbf{p}^p))||_2^2, \tag{1}$$

where $d(\cdot)$ is a feature vector extracted by a descriptor. $I_c(\mathbf{p})$ is an image patch rotated by estimated orientation $O_c(\mathbf{p})$, which is formulated as follows:

$$I_c = t(\mathbf{p}, O_c(\mathbf{p})), \tag{2}$$

where $t(\mathbf{p}, O_c(\mathbf{p}))$ is computed by STN. The parameters of the descriptor are fixed and we do not train the descriptor during the training of the coarse orientation estimator. It mean that the network is attention to the similarities between positive pairs.

3.2 Fine Orientation Estimator

The coarse orientation estimator has a problem that the same orientation is estimated for different image patches having repetitive patterns or simple textures. This is caused that the coarse orientation estimator trains using only positive pairs. Therefore, we proposed auxiliary network as the fine orientation estimator. The fine orientation estimator is trained by using negative pairs to focus on the different appearance points between image patches, which can estimate the orientation contributing to keypoint matching accuracy.

Figure 4 shows the training process of the fine orientation estimator. The fine orientation estimator is trained by using the distance between the extracted features of normalized image patches by a descriptor. We train the fine orientation estimator after training the coarse orientation estimator. We use three local images, which consist of a positive pairs and a negative image, as a training sample pair. Because the fine orientation estimator is necessary to focus on the differences between images. Let $\mathbf{p}_n$ be a negative image in a training sample pair and $O_f(\mathbf{p})$ be the orientation of patch $\mathbf{p}$ estimated by the fine orientation estimator. The loss function of the fine orientation estimator $L_{fine}(\mathbf{p}^q, \mathbf{p}^p, \mathbf{p}_n)$ is defined as:

$$\begin{aligned} &\mathcal{L}_{fine}\left(\mathbf{p}^q, \mathbf{p}^p, \mathbf{p}_n\right) = \\ &\max\left(0, ||d(I_f(\mathbf{p}^q)) - d(I_f(\mathbf{p}^p))||_2^2 - ||d(I_f(\mathbf{p}^q)) - d(I_f(\mathbf{p}^n))||_2^2 + M\right), \end{aligned} \tag{3}$$

where M is a margin of triple loss. We set $M = 8.0$ in the experiments described below. $I_f(\mathbf{p})$ is an image patch rotated by estimated orientation $O_f(\mathbf{p})$, which is formulated as follows:

$$I_f = t(\mathbf{p}, O_f(I_c(\mathbf{p}))). \tag{4}$$

During the training of the fine orientation estimator, the parameters of the coarse orientation estimator and the descriptor are fixed to estimate orientation to accurately match keypoints.

3.3 The Calculation of Final Orientation

The orientation estimated by the fine orientation estimator is not the orientation for the original input local image since the input image is normalized by the coarse orientation estimator. Therefore, we compute the final orientation θ^{input} for an input image by adding the orientations estimated by the coarse and fine orientation estimators, which are defined as follows:

$$\theta^{input} = O_c + O_f. \tag{5}$$

4 Experiments

We evaluate the proposed method in terms how the orientation estimation accuracy affects the final keypoint matching accuracy.

4.1 Experimental Settings

Dataset. We use the HPatches dataset [3] to evaluate the proposed method. The HPatches dataset consists of local image patches extracted from six original images of the same scene under different conditions such as viewpoint and

Table 1. Results on HPatches benchmark. Orientation indicates the loss function used for training the coarse and fine orientation estimators. "L2" is Eq. (1), and "Tri" is triplet loss shown in Eq. (3).

Orientation		Patch verification	Image matching	Patch retrieval
Coarse	Fine			
L2	—	0.8332	0.2660	0.3734
Tri	—	0.8623	0.2754	0.3976
L2	L2	0.8366	0.2755	0.3859
Tri	L2	0.8299	0.2670	0.3745
Tri	Tri	0.8658	0.2976	0.4196
L2	Tri (Proposed)	**0.8680**	**0.3011**	**0.4232**

illumination changes. In total, the dataset contains 116 scenes. To detect image patches from the original images, the HPatches dataset used DoG, Hessian, and Harris detectors. On the basis of the difficulty of those changes, image patches are categorized into the three categories: easy, hard, and tough. We used 1,461,525 positive pairs for training and 892,980 positive pairs for evaluation. Additionally, we created negative pairs by selecting patches randomly and used them for training the fine orientation estimator. While training both the coarse and fine orientation estimators, we randomly rotated the image pairs and input them into the networks to obtain robustness to larger rotation changes.

Training Details. We input local image patches of 64×64 pixels into the proposed method. The coarse and fine orientation estimators have the same structure, which consists of three convolutional layers and two fully-connected layers. For the convolution layers, the first convolution layer use a filter size of 5×5 and 10 output channel with 3×3 max pooling, the second convolutional layer a filter size of 5×5 and 20 output channel with 4×4 max pooling, and third convolutional layer use a filter size of 3×3 and 50 output channel with 2×2 max pooling. The size of the output of the first fully connected layer is 100, with the second fully connected layer having two outputs. Then convert the output to radian. During the training, we used the Adam optimizer [9] to update network parameters. We set the learning rate as 0.001, mini-batch size as 128, and the number of training epochs is 300. The descriptor consists of three convolutional layers and extracts a 128-dimensional feature vector from 64×64 pixels patches. We train a descriptor by triplet loss with HPatches dataset. Also, we use a descriptor trained with easy samples on the HPatches dataset for training the fine orientation estimator. We train each network in the following order: descriptor, coarse orientation estimator, and fine orientation estimator.

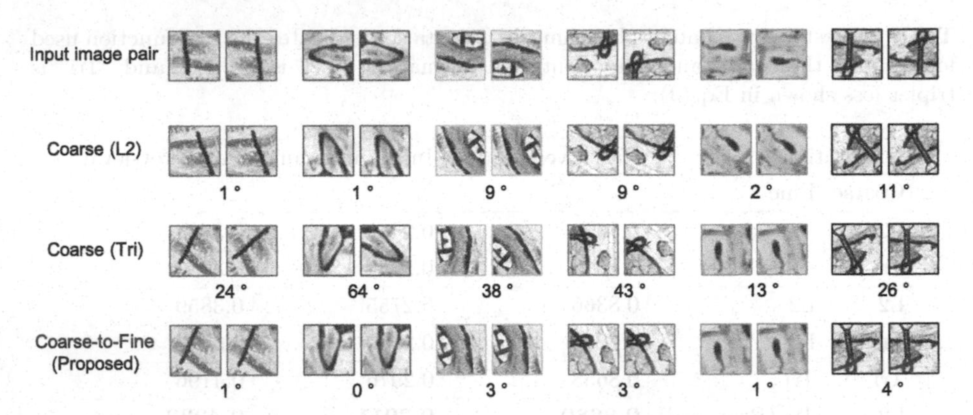

Fig. 5. Examples of orientation estimation accuracy. First row is input image pair, and the others are normalized images by orientation estimator. Input images are rotated by 180°. The red numbers below the pair are estimation errors. From second to fourth rows are results to different loss functions. "L2" is the loss shown in Eq. (1) and "Tri" is triplet loss shown in Eq. (3). (Color figure online)

4.2 Accuracies over Different Loss Functions

We compare the performance over different loss functions used for each orientation estimator. The HPatches benchmark evaluates the performance with respect to three metrics: patch verification, image matching, and patch retrieval. For more details about these metrics, please refer to Balntas et al. [3]. In this paper, due to we focus on the effect and performance of orientation estimation, we first randomly rotate image patches and normalize the patches by using estimated orientation. Then, we extract feature vectors from the normalized patches. The distance between extracted features is large even if we use positive pairs when the accuracy of orientation estimation is low. Therefore, accurate orientation estimator is required to obtain the highly accuracy in keypoint matching. In addition, we perform orientation normalization of patch pairs containing a rotation change of 180° and investigate estimation errors. For comparative methods, we use a single CNN, i.e., only coarse orientation estimator, and the proposed coarse-to-fine structured orientation estimator. Furthermore, we change the loss function used for each network training to investigate the effect on matching accuracy.

Table 1 shows results of each orientation estimation method on HPatches benchmark and Fig. 5 shows examples of the estimated orientation accuracies. From Table 1, when only the coarse orientation estimator is used, the triplet loss achieved higher accuracy than L2 loss. However, triplet loss has higher estimation errors than L2 loss as shown in Fig. 5. This result indicates that the estimated orientation affects the accuracy, and triplet loss function is robust to different patch pairs. And it can improves accuracy even when the estimation error is larger than L2 loss. In the proposed coarse-to-fine orientation estimation method, we employ triplet loss for the fine orientation estimator. Because

Table 2. Results for area under the precision-recall curve

Method	HP	Rot. 90	Rot. 180
LIFT	0.535	0.154	0.437
Coarse	0.540	0.182	0.511
Coarse-to-Fine (Proposed)	0.536	**0.232**	**0.513**

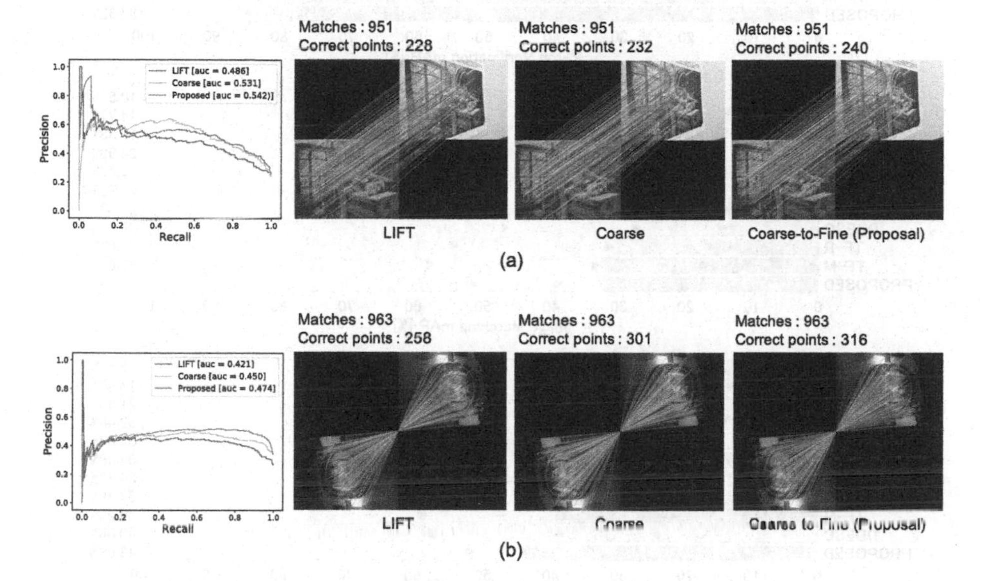

Fig. 6. Examples of matching results and precision-recall curve for (a) HP and (b) Rot. 180 conditions. From left to right: precision-recall curve, matching results of LIFT, only coarse orientation estimator, and the proposed method.

of it achieved the highest accuracy and smallest estimation error. Therefore, the proposed coarse-to-fine structured method effectively improves orientation estimation accuracy (Table 2).

4.3 Evaluation of Area Under the Precision-Recall Curve

In this section, we evaluate the performance on keypoint matching. In this experiment, we use HPatches full sequence [3], which consists of 116 sequences and 580 image pairs. We use the LIFT detector for keypoint detection and the scale estimation. We evaluate the performance under three different conditions. The first condition is keypoint matching with original image pairs (denoted as HP). In the second condition, we rotate reference images 90° (denoted as Rot. 90) and use them to conduct keypoint matching. In the third condition, we rotate the reference images 180° (denoted as Rot. 180).

We compare the performances of the proposed method, LIFT, and the coarse orientation estimator trained with positive pairs. Note that all methods use the

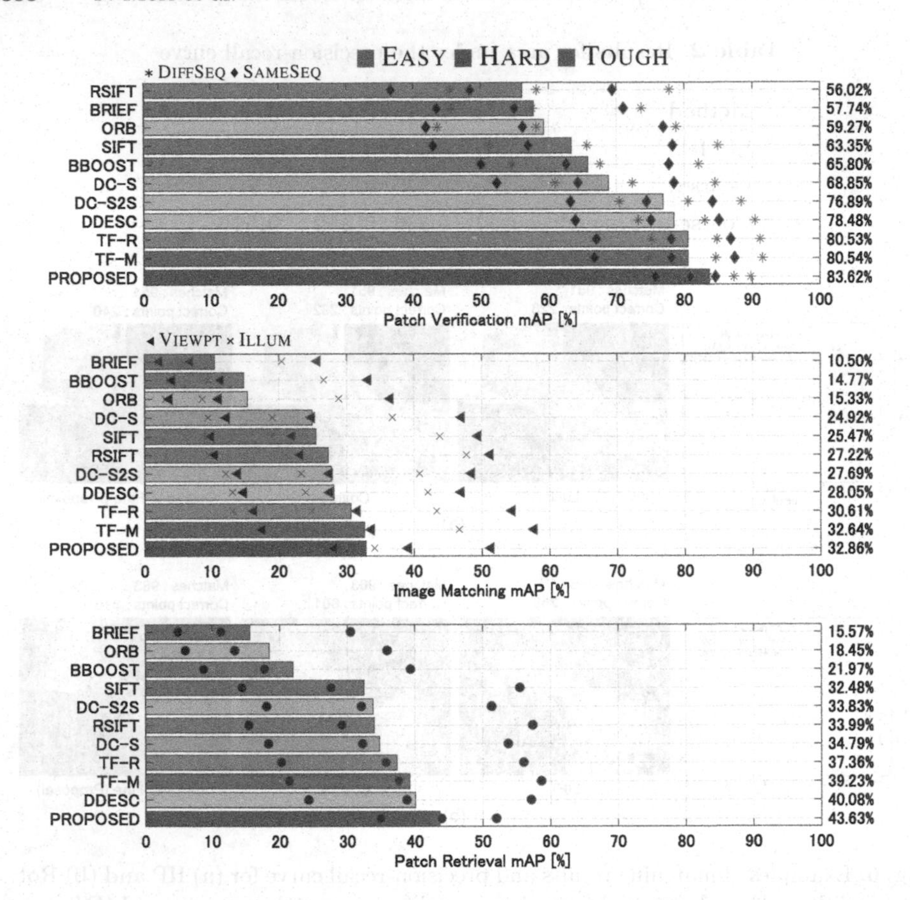

Fig. 7. The evaluation results on HPatches benchmark. Top to bottom: verification, matching and retrieval results. Marker color indicates the level of geometrical noise: easy, hard, and tough. DIFFSEQ and SAMESEQ show the scores of negative examples for the verification task. VIEWPT and ILLUM indicate the type of differences in image pairs in matching task.

same descriptor. For the evaluation metric, we use the area under the precision-recall curve (AUC).

Table 1 shows AUCs over different three conditions. The results of HP show that the proposed method can maintain the same matching accuracies as the other methods. Moreover, the proposed method achieved the highest accuracies for Rot. 90 and Rot. 180. Therefore, the proposed method can improve the matching when there are larger rotation changes. Figure 6 shows examples of matching results and precision-recall curves. The proposed method achieved a larger number of correct matches and a more accurate precision-recall curve than the other methods. Therefore, the orientation estimated by the proposed method contributes to keypoint matching.

4.4 Comparison with Other Local Feature Descriptors

We compare the performances of the proposed method and other local feature descriptors provided in the HPatches benchmark. For comparative methods, we use SIFT [10], RootSIFT [1], BRIEF [11], ORB [15], BinBoost [18], Siamese variants of DeepCompare [21], DeepDesc [16], TFeat margin*, and TFeat ratio* [4]. Patch pairs prepared in HPatches have at most a 30-degree rotation difference. The results of comparative methods are obtained by evaluating with this dataset. The proposed method first normalizes local image patches with estimated orientations and describes features from the normalized patches. Then, we evaluate for each task.

Figure 7 shows the evaluation results on the HPatches benchmark. The proposed method achieved the highest accuracies in all tasks. Moreover, for tough samples, the proposed method largely improves the performance. Therefore, our method efficiently normalizes rotation and describes features for image viewpoint changes.

5 Conclusion

In this paper, we proposed an orientation estimator using two convolutional neural networks (CNNs) that has a coarse-to-fine structure. The coarse orientation estimator is trained by using positive pairs and can estimate the orientations accurately. The fine orientation estimator is trained by triplet loss with negative pairs and can estimate orientation for accurate keypoint matching. We train each network with different loss functions, which enables us to achieve both accurate orientation estimation and accurate keypoint matching. The evaluation results demonstrate that our method achieved higher accuracy in all tasks on the HPatches benchmark than conventional hand-crafted approaches and CNN-based approaches. Moreover, our method achieved higher matching accuracy than single CNN-based orientation estimators. Consequently, the proposed method can estimate orientation that contributes to final keypoint matching accuracy. Our future work includes obtaining the invariance for projective changes.

References

1. Arandjelović, R., Zisserman, A.: Three things everyone should know to improve object retrieval. In: Conference on Computer Vision and Pattern Recognition, pp. 2911–2918 (2012)
2. Bailey, T., Durrant-Whyte, H.: Simultaneous localization and mapping (SLAM). Part II. Robot. Autom. Mag. **13**, 108–117 (2006)
3. Balntas, V., Lenc, K., Vedaldi, A., Mikolajczyk, K.: HPatches: a benchmark and evaluation of handcrafted and learned local descriptors. In: Computer Vision and Pattern Recognition, pp. 5173–5182 (2017)
4. Balntas, V., Riba, E., Ponsa, D., Mikolajczyk, K.: Learning local feature descriptors with triplets and shallow convolutional neural networks. In: British Machine Vision Conference, p. 119 (2016)

5. Bay, H., Tuytelaars, T., Gool, L.V.: SURF: Speeded-up robust features. Comput. Vis. Image Underst. **110**(3), 346–359 (2008)
6. Brown, M., Lowe, D.G.: Automatic panoramic image stitching using invariant features. Int. J. Comput. Vis. **74**(1), 59–73 (2007)
7. Durrant-Whyte, H., Bailey, T.: Simultaneous localization and mapping: part I. Robot. Autom. Mag. **13**(2), 99–110 (2006)
8. Jaderberg, M., Simonyan, K., Zisserman, A., Kavukcuoglu, K.: Spatial transformer networks. In: Neural Information Processing Systems, pp. 2017–2025 (2015)
9. Kingma, D.P., Ba, J.L.: Adam : a method for stochasic optimization. In: International Conference on Learning Representation (2015)
10. Lowe, D.G.: Object recognition from local scale-invariant features. In: International Conference on Computer Vision (1999)
11. Calonder, M., Lepetit, V., Strecha, C., Fua, P.: BRIEF: binary robust independent elementary features. In: Daniilidis, K., Maragos, P., Paragios, N. (eds.) ECCV 2010, Part IV. LNCS, vol. 6314, pp. 778–792. Springer, Heidelberg (2010). https://doi.org/10.1007/978-3-642-15561-1_56
12. Mur-Artal, R., Montiel, J.M.M., Tardos, J.D.: ORB-SLAM: a versatile and accurate monocular SLAM system. IEEE Trans. Robot. **31**(5), 1147–1163 (2015)
13. Nister, D., Stewenius, H.: Scalable recognition with a vocabulary tree. Comput. Vis. Pattern Recogn. **2**, 2161–2168 (2006)
14. Ono, Y., Trulls, E., Fua, P., Yi, K.M.: LF-Net: learning local features from images. In: Neural Information Processing Systems (2018)
15. Rublee, E., Rabaud, V., Konolige, K., Bradski, G.: ORB: an efficient alternative to SIFT or SURF. In: International Conference on Computer Vision, pp. 2564–2571 (2011)
16. Simo-Serra, E., Trulls, E., Ferraz, L., Kokkinos, I., Fua, P., Moreno-Noguer, F.: Discriminative learning of deep convolutional feature point descriptors. In: International Conference on Computer Vision, pp. 118–126 (2015)
17. Taylor, S., Drummond, T.: Binary histogrammed intensity patches for effcient and robust matching. Int. J. Comput. Vis. **94**, 241–265 (2011)
18. Trzcinski, T., Christoudias, M., Lepetit, V.: Learning image descriptors with boosting. Pattern Anal. Mach. Intell. **37**, 597–610 (2015)
19. Yi, K.M., Trulls, E., Lepetit, V., Fua, P.: LIFT: learned invariant feature transform. In: Leibe, B., Matas, J., Sebe, N., Welling, M. (eds.) ECCV 2016, Part VI. LNCS, vol. 9910, pp. 467–483. Springer, Cham (2016). https://doi.org/10.1007/978-3-319-46466-4_28
20. Yi, K.M., Verdie, Y., Fua, P., Lepetit, V.: Learning to assign orientations to feature points. In: Computer Vision and Pattern Recognition, pp. 107–116 (2016)
21. Zagoruyko, S., Komodakis, N.: Learning to compare image patches via convolutional neural networks. In: Computer Vision and Pattern Recognition, pp. 359–366 (2011)

Geometric Total Variation for Image Vectorization, Zooming and Pixel Art Depixelizing

Bertrand Kerautret[1] and Jacques-Olivier Lachaud[2](✉)

[1] Univ Lyon, Lyon 2, LIRIS, 69676 Lyon, France
bertrand.kerautret@liris.cnrs.fr
[2] Univ. Grenoble Alpes, Univ. Savoie Mont Blanc, CNRS, LAMA, 73000 Chambéry, France
jacques-olivier.lachaud@univ-smb.fr

Abstract. We propose an original method for vectorizing an image or zooming it at an arbitrary scale. The core of our method relies on the resolution of a geometric variational model and therefore offers theoretic guarantees. More precisely, it associates a total variation energy to every valid triangulation of the image pixels. Its minimization induces a triangulation that reflects image gradients. We then exploit this triangulation to precisely locate discontinuities, which can then simply be vectorized or zoomed. This new approach works on arbitrary images without any learning phase. It is particularly appealing for processing images with low quantization like pixel art and can be used for depixelizing such images. The method can be evaluated with an online demonstrator, where users can reproduce results presented here or upload their own images.

Keywords: Image vectorization · Image super-resolution · Total variation · Depixelizing pixel art

1 Introduction

There exist many methods for zooming into raster images, and they can be divided into two groups. The first group gathers "image super-resolution" or "image interpolation" techniques and tries to deduce colors on the zoomed image from nearby colors in the original image. These methods compute in the raster domain and their output is not scalable. The second group is composed of "image vectorization" approaches and tries to build a higher level representation of the image made of painted polygons and splines. These representations can be zoomed, rotated or transformed. Each approach has its own merits, but none perform well both on camera pictures and on drawings or pixel art.

This work has been partly funded by CoMEDiC ANR-15-CE40-0006 research grant.

S. Palaiahnakote et al. (Eds.): ACPR 2019, LNCS 12046, pp. 391–405, 2020.
https://doi.org/10.1007/978-3-030-41404-7_28

Image Interpolation/Super Resolution. These approaches construct an interpolated image with higher resolution. A common trait is that they see the image as a continuous function, such that we only see its sampling in the original image. Their diversity lies generally in the choice of the space of continuous functions. For instance linear/cubic interpolation just fits linear/cubic functions, but much more complicated spaces have been considered. For instance the method proposed by Getreuer introduces the concept of *contour stencils* [6,7] to accurately estimate the edge orientation. Roussos and Maragos proposed another strategy using a tensor driven diffusion [19] (see also [8]). Due to the increasing popularity of convolutional neural network (CNN), several authors propose super resolution networks to obtain super resolution image. For instance Shi *et al.* define a CNN architecture exploiting feature maps computed in low resolution space [22]. After learning, this strategy reduces the computational complexity for a fixed super-resolution and gives interesting results on photo pictures. Of course, all these approaches do not provide any vectorial representation and give low quality results on images with low quantization or pixel art images. Another common feature is their tendency to "invent" false oscillating contours, like in Fourier super-resolution.

Pixel Art Super-Resolution. A subgroup of these methods is dedicated to the interpolation of pixel art images, like the classic HqX magnification filter [23] where X represents the scale factor. We may quote a more advanced approach which proposes as well a full vectorization of pixel art image [13]. Even if the resulting reconstruction for tiny images is nice looking, the proposed approach is designed specifically for hand-crafted pixel art image and is not adaptable to photo pictures.

Image Vectorization. Recovering a vector-based representation from a bitmap image is a classical problem in the field of digital geometry, computer graphics and pattern recognition. Various commercial design softwares propose such a feature, like *Indesign*™, or Vector Magic [10] and their algorithms are naturally not disclosed. Vectorization is also important for technical document analysis and is often performed by decomposition into arcs and straight line segments [9]. For binary images, many vectorization methods are available and may rely on dominant points detection [16,17], relaxed straightness properties [1], multi-scale analysis [5] or digital curvature computation [11,15].

Extension to grey level images is generally achieved by image decomposition into level sets, vectorization of each level, then fusion (e.g. [12]). Extension to color images is not straightforward. Swaminarayan and Prasad proposed to use contour detection associated to a Delaunay triangulation [25] but despite the original strategy, the digital geometry of the image is not directly exploited like in above-mentionned approaches. Other methods define the vectorization as a variational problem, like Lecot and Levy who use the Mumford Shah piecewise smooth model and an intermediate triangulation step to best approximate the image [14]. Other comparable methods construct the vectorization from topological preservation criteria [24], from splines and adaptive Delaunay triangulation

[4] or from Bézier-curves-patch-based representation [26]. We may also cite the interactive method proposed by Price and Barrett that let a user edit interactively the reconstruction from a graph cut segmentation [18].

Our Contribution. We propose an original approach to this problem, which borrows and mixes techniques from both groups of methods, thus making it very versatile. We start with some notations that will be used thoughout the paper. Let Ω be some open subset of $\mathbb{R}^2$, here a rectangular subset defining the image domain. Let K be the image range, a vector space that is generally $\mathbb{R}$ for monochromatic images and $\mathbb{R}^3$ for color image, equipped with some norm $\|\cdot\|_K$. We assume in the following that gray-level and color components lie in $[0, 1]$.

First our approach is related with the famous Total Variation (TV), a well known variational model for image denoising or inpainting [20]. Recall that if f is a differentiable function in Ω, its total variation can be simply defined as:

$$\mathrm{TV}(f) := \int_{\Omega} \|\nabla f(x)\|_K \, \mathrm{d}x. \quad (1)$$

In a more general setting, the total variation is generally defined by duality. As noted by many authors [3], different discretizations of TV are not equivalent. However they are all defined locally with neighboring pixels, and this is why they are not able to fully capture the structure of images.

In Sect. 2, we propose a *geometric total variation*. Its optimization seeks the triangulation of lattice points of Ω that minimizes a well-defined TV corresponding to a piecewise linear function interpolating the image. The optimal triangulation does not always connect neighboring pixels and align its edges with image discontinuities. For instance digital straight segments are recognized by the geometric total variation.

In Sect. 3, we show how to construct a vector representation from the obtained triangulation, by regularizing a kind of graph dual to the triangulation. Section 4 shows a super-resolution algorithm that builds a zoomed raster image with smooth Bezier discontinuities from the vector representation. Finally, in Sect. 5 we compare our approach to other super-resolution and vectorization methods and discuss the results.

2 Geometric Total Variation

The main idea of our geometric total variation is to structure the image domain into a triangulation, whose vertices are the pixel centers located at integer coordinates. Furthermore, any triangle of this triangulation should cover exactly three lattice points (its vertices). The set of such triangulations of lattice points in Ω is denoted by $\mathcal{T}(\Omega)$.

Let s be an image, i.e. a function from the set of lattice points of Ω to K. We define the *geometric total variation* of s with respect to an arbitrary triangulation T of $\mathcal{T}(\Omega)$ as

$$\mathrm{GTV}(T, s) := \int_{\Omega} \|\nabla \Phi_{T,s}(x)\|_K \, dx, \quad (2)$$

where $\Phi_{T,s}(x)$ is the linear interpolation of s in the triangle of T containing x. Note that points of Ω whose gradient is not defined have null measure in the above integral (they belong to triangle edges of T).

And the Geometric Total Variation (GTV) of s is simply the smallest among all possible triangulations:

$$\mathrm{GTV}_{\mathcal{T}(\Omega)}(s) := \min_{T \in \mathcal{T}(\Omega)} \mathrm{GTV}(T, s). \tag{3}$$

In other words, the GTV of a digital image s is the smallest continuous total variation among all natural triangulations sampling s. Since $\mathcal{T}(\Omega)$ will not change in the following, we will omit it as subscript and write simply $\mathrm{GTV}(s)$.

One should note that classical discrete TV models associated to a digital image generally overestimate its total variation (in fact, the perimeter of its level-sets due to the co-area formula) [3]. Classical discrete TV models $\mathrm{TV}(s)$ are very close to $\mathrm{GTV}(T, s)$ when T is any trivial Delaunay triangulation of the lattice points. By finding more meaningful triangulation, $\mathrm{GTV}(s)$ will often be much smaller than $\mathrm{TV}(s)$.

Combinatorial Expression of Geometric Total Variation. Since $\Phi_{T,s}(x)$ is the linear interpolation of s in the triangle τ of T containing x, it is clear that its gradient is constant within the interior of τ. If $\tau = \mathbf{pqr}$ where $\mathbf{p}, \mathbf{q}, \mathbf{r}$ are the vertices of τ, one computes easily that for any x in the interior of τ, we have

$$\nabla \Phi_{T,s}(x) = s(\mathbf{p})(\mathbf{r} - \mathbf{q})^{\perp} + s(\mathbf{q})(\mathbf{p} - \mathbf{r})^{\perp} + s(\mathbf{r})(\mathbf{q} - \mathbf{p})^{\perp}. \tag{4}$$

We thus define the discrete gradient of s within a triangle $\mathbf{pqr}$ as

$$\boldsymbol{\nabla} s(\mathbf{pqr}) := s(\mathbf{p})(\mathbf{r} - \mathbf{q})^{\perp} + s(\mathbf{q})(\mathbf{p} - \mathbf{r})^{\perp} + s(\mathbf{r})(\mathbf{q} - \mathbf{p})^{\perp}, \tag{5}$$

where $\mathbf{x}^{\perp}$ is the vector $\mathbf{x}$ rotated by $\frac{\pi}{2}$. Now it is well known that any lattice triangle that has no integer point in its interior has an area $\frac{1}{2}$ (just apply Pick's theorem for instance). It follows that for any triangulation T of $\mathcal{T}(\Omega)$, every triangle has the same area $\frac{1}{2}$. We obtain the following expression for the GTV:

$$\begin{aligned}
\mathrm{GTV}(T, s) &= \int_{\Omega} \|\nabla \Phi_{T,s}(x)\|_K \, dx \\
&= \sum_{\mathbf{pqr} \in T} \int_{\mathbf{pqr}} \|\nabla \Phi_{T,s}(x)\|_K \, dx \qquad \text{(integral is additive)} \\
&= \sum_{\mathbf{pqr} \in T} \int_{\mathbf{pqr}} \|\boldsymbol{\nabla} s(\mathbf{pqr})\|_K \, dx \qquad \text{(by (4) and (5))} \\
&= \frac{1}{2} \sum_{\mathbf{pqr} \in T} \|\boldsymbol{\nabla} s(\mathbf{pqr})\|_K \qquad \text{(since Area}(\mathbf{pqr}) = \frac{1}{2}\text{)}
\end{aligned} \tag{6}$$

Table 1. Illustration of geometric total variation on a simple black and white image. Even if the pixel values of the image are the same (represented by black and white disks), different triangulations of the pixels yield different GTV. In this case, the right one is the optimal triangulation and is clearly more aligned with the underlying contour. Vectorizing or zooming the right triangulation will provide more interesting results.

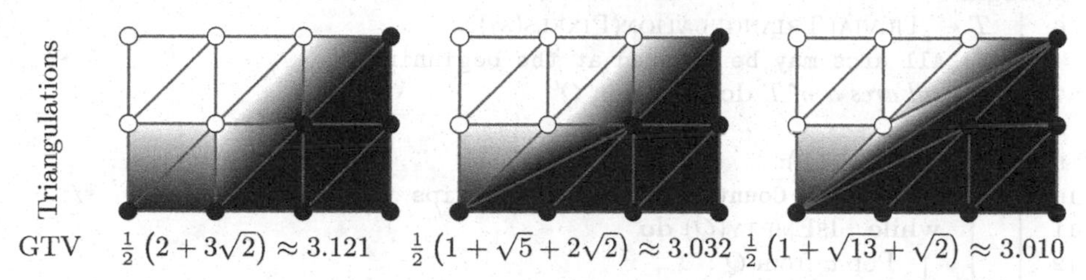

Minimization of GTV. Since we have a local combinatorial method to compute the GTV of an arbitrary triangulation, our approach to find the optimal GTV of some image s will be greedy, iterative and randomized. We will start from an arbitrary triangulation (here the natural triangulation of the grid where each square has been subdivided in two triangles) and we will flip two triangles whenever it decreases the GTV (Table 1).

This approach is similar in spirit to the approach of Bobenko and Springborn [2], whose aim is to define discrete minimal surfaces. However they minimize the Dirichlet energy of the triangulation (i.e. squared norm of gradient) and they show that the optimum is related to the intrinsic Delaunay triangulation of the sampling points, which can be reached by local triangle flips. On the contrary, our energy has not this nice convexity property and it is easy to see for instance that minima are generally not unique. We have also checked that there is a continuum of energy if we minimize the p-norm $\|\cdot\|_K^p$ for $1 \leq p \leq 2$. For $p = 2$ the optimum is trivially the Delaunay triangulation of the lattice points. When p is decreased toward 1, we observe that triangle edges are more and more perpendicular to the discrete gradient.

Table 1 shows the GTV of several triangulations in the simple case of a binary image representing an edge contour with slope $\frac{2}{3}$. It shows that the smaller the GTV the more align with the digital contour is the triangulation.

Algorithm 1 is the main function that tries to find a triangulation T which is as close as possible to $\mathrm{GTV}(s)$. It starts from any triangulation of s (line 6 : we just split into two triangles each square between four adjacent pixels). Then it proceeds by passes (line 7). At each pass (line 10), every potential arc is checked for a possible flip by a call to CheckArc (Algorithm 2) at line 13. The arc is always flipped if it decreases the GTV and *randomly* flipped if it does not change the GTV (line 14). Arcs close to the flip are queued (line 16) since their further flip may decrease the GTV later. The algorithm stops when the number of flips decreasing the GTV is zero (flips keeping the same GTV are not counted).

```
1  function OptimizeGTV( s : Image ) : Triangulation ;
2  var T : Triangulation /* the triangulation that is optimized       */;
3  var Q : Queue<Arc>/* the queue of arcs currently being checked */;
4  var Q' : Queue<Arc>/* the queue of arcs to be checked after    */;
5  begin
6      T ← TrivialTriangulation(Pixels(s));
       /* All arcs may be flipped at the beginning.                 */
7      for all arcs a of T do Push a in Q';
8      repeat
9          Swap(Q, Q');
10         n ← 0   /* Counts the number of flips that decrease GTV  */;
11         while ¬IsEmpty(Q) do
12             Pop a from Q ;
13             c ← CheckArc(s, T, a) ;
14             if c > 0 or (c = 0 and FlipCoin() = Heads) then
15                 if c > 0 then n ← n + 1;
16                 Push arcs of two faces around a in Q';
17                 Flip(T, a)   /* After, a represents the flipped arc  */;
18     until n = 0;
19     return T;
```

Algorithm 1. Function OptimizeGTV outputs a triangulation which is as close as possible to GTV(s). It builds a trivial triangulation of the pixels of s then optimize its GTV by flipping its edges in a greedy and randomized way.

Function CheckArc (Algorithm 2) checks if flipping some arc would decrease the GTV. It first checks if the arc/edge is flippable at line 3 (e.g. not on the boundary). Then it is enough to check only one arc per edge (line 5).

```
1  function CheckArc( s : Image, T : Triangulation, a : Arc ) : Integer ;
2  begin
3      if ¬isFlippable(T, a) then return -1;
4      P ← VerticesOfFacesAroundArc(T, a) ;
       /* P[0] is Tail(T, a), P[2] is Head(T, a), P[0]P[1]P[2] and
          P[0]P[2]P[3] are the two faces having a in common.         */
5      if P[0] < P[2] then return -1;
6      if ¬isConvex(P) then return -1;
7      E_cur = ||∇s(P[0]P[1]P[2])||_K + ||∇s(P[0]P[2]P[3])||_K ;
8      E_flip = ||∇s(P[0]P[1]P[3])||_K + ||∇s(P[1]P[2]P[3])||_K ;
9      if E_flip < E_cur then return 1;
10     else if E_flip = E_cur then return 0;
11     else return -1;
```

Algorithm 2. Function CheckArc checks if flipping the arc a of triangulation T decreases GTV(T, s) (returns 1), does not change GTV(T, s) (returns 0), or returns -1 in all the other cases.

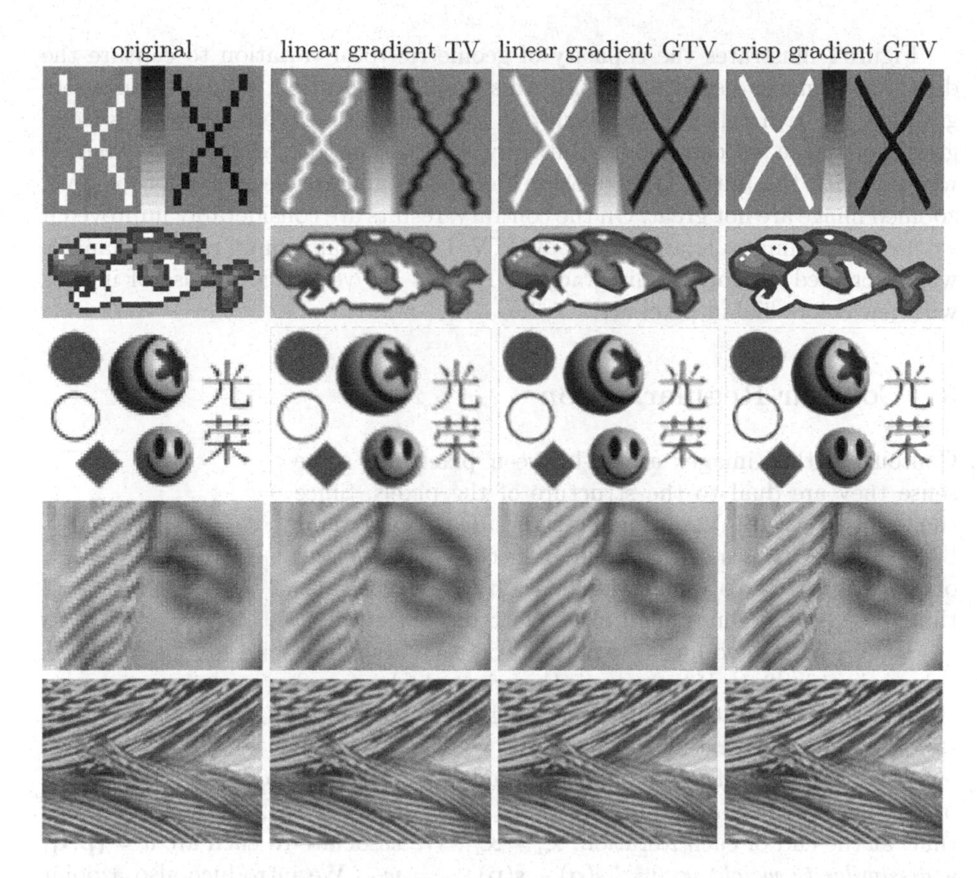

Fig. 1. Zoom ×16 of the images in leftmost column: (middle left) displaying the trivial triangulation given by a simple discretization of TV painted with induced linear gradient over each triangle, (middle right) displaying the triangulation after GTV optimization painted with induced linear gradient over each triangle, (rightmost) same as before except that triangles are painted with a crisped version of the same gradient.

Afterwards the edge may be flipped only if the four points surrounding the faces touching the edge form a strictly convex quadrilateron (line 6). Finally it computes the local GTV of the two possible decompositions of this quadrilateron using formula (6) and outputs the corresponding case (from line 7).

Note that the *randomization* of flips in the case where the energy GTV is not changed is rather important in practice. As said above, it is not a "convex" energy since it is easy to find instances where there are several optima (of course, our search space being combinatorial, convexity is not a well defined notion). Randomization helps in quitting local minima and this simple trick gives nice results in practice.

Figure 1 illustrates the capacity of geometric total variation to capture the direction of image discontinuities. In this simple application, we use the discrete gradient on each triangle to display it with the corresponding linear shaded gradient. Hence we can zoom arbitrarily any image. The results show that, if we stay with the initial triangulation (as does standard discretization of TV), zoomed image are not great. On the contrary, results are considerably improved if we use the optimized triangulation of GTV. Last, we can simply render triangles with a crisped version of this gradient. Results are very nice in case of images with few colors like in pixel art.

3 Contour Regularization

Contours within images are in-between pixels. In some sense they are dual to the structure of the pixels. Since the Geometric Total Variation has structured the relations between pixels, it is natural to define the contours as a kind of dual graph to the optimal triangulation T^*. We wish also that these contour lines align nicely with discontinuities.

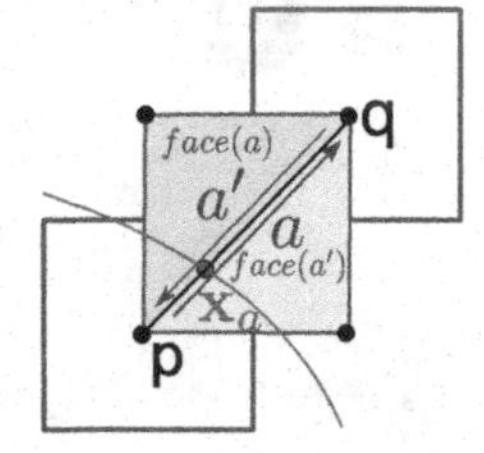

To do so, we introduce a variable t_a on each arc whose value is kept in $[0,1]$. If the arc a is the oriented edge $(\mathbf{p},\mathbf{q})$ then the position of the contour crossing this edge will be $\mathbf{x}_a = t_a\mathbf{p} + (1-t_a)\mathbf{q}$ (see the upper floating figure).

We denote by a' the arc opposite to a, i.e. $(\mathbf{q},\mathbf{p})$. The face that is to the left of a is denoted face(a) while the one to its right is face$'(a)$. We will guarantee that, at the end of each iteration, $\mathbf{x}_a = \mathbf{x}_{a'}$. We associate to each arc $a = (\mathbf{p},\mathbf{q})$ a *dissimilarity weight* $w_a := \|s(\mathbf{q}) - s(\mathbf{p})\|_K = w_{a'}$. We introduce also a point $\mathbf{b}_f$ for each face f of T, which will lie at a kind of weighted barycenter of the vertices of f.

Algorithm 3 regularizes these points and provides a graph of contours that is a meaningful vectorization of the input bitmap image s. Note that the function INTERSECTION$(a,\mathbf{y},\mathbf{z})$ returns the parameter t such that $\mathbf{x}_a$ lies at the intersection of straight line $(\mathbf{yz})$ and the arc a.

First it starts with natural positions for $\mathbf{x}$ and $\mathbf{b}$ (resp. middle of arcs and barycenter of faces) at line 3 and line 4. Then it proceeds iteratively until stabilization in the loop at line 8. Each iteration consists of three steps: (i) update barycenters such that they are a convex combination of surrounding contour points weighted by their dissimilarities (line 9), (ii) update contour points such that they lie at the crossing of the arc and the nearby barycenters (line 11), (iii) average the two displacements along each edge according to respective area (line 13), thus guaranteeing that $\mathbf{x}_a = \mathbf{x}_{a'}$ for every arc. The area AREA(a) associated to an arc a is the area of the quadrilateron formed by the tail of a, barycenters $\mathbf{b}_{\text{face}(a)}$ and $\mathbf{b}_{\text{face}'(a)}$ and $\mathbf{x}_a$. Note that the coefficients α and α' computed at line 14 have value 1 whenever the area is $\frac{1}{6}$.

Since this process is always computing convex combinations of points with convex constraints, it converges quickly to a stable point. In all our experiments,

```
 1 function RegularizeContours( s : Image, T : Triangulation );
   Result: Positions of contour points on arcs and barycenter on faces
 2 begin
 3    for every face f = pqr of T do b_f ← 1/3(p + q + r);
 4    for every arc a of T do
 5       if ¬isUpdateable(a) then t_a^(0) ← 1/2;
 6       else t_a^(0) ← Intersection(a, b_face(a), b_face'(a));
 7    n ← 0;
 8    repeat
 9       for every face f of T do /* Update barycenters */
10          b_f ← 1/2(b_f + Σ_{a∈∂f} w_a x_a / Σ_{a∈∂f} w_a);
11       for every arc a of T with isUpdateable(a) do /* Update contours */
12          t_a^(n) ← 1/2(t_a^(n) + Intersection(a, b_face(a), b_face'(a)));
         /* Average displacements along each edge according to area. */
13       for every arc a = pq of T with p < q and isUpdateable(a) do
14          (α, α') ← 1/2(1 + 1/(6Area(a)), 1 + 1/(6Area(a')));
15          t ← 1/2(α t_a^(n) + 1 − α' t_a'^(n));
16          (t_a^(n+1), t_a'^(n+1)) ← (t, 1 − t) ;
17       n ← n + 1;
18    until max_{arc a of T} |t_a^(n) − t_a^(n−1)| < ε;
19    return (x, b)
```

Algorithm 3. Function RegularizeContours iteratively moves contour points and barycenters such that they align with the edges of the triangulation that delineate image discontinuities.

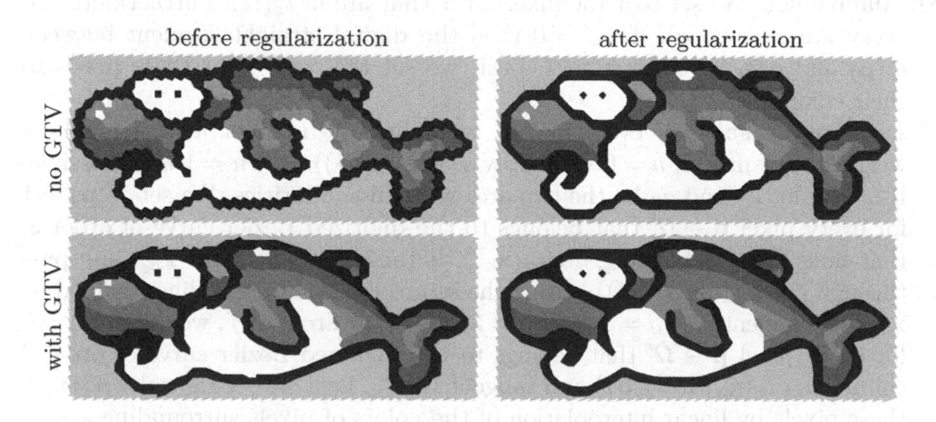

Fig. 2. Displays contour mesh: left column before regularization, right column after regularization with Algorithm 3. Top row shows contour meshes when using the initial trivial triangulation. Bottom row shows contour meshes when using the triangulation T^* that optimize GTV(s). Note that boundary triangles are displayed in white. (Color figure online)

we choose $\epsilon = 0.001$ and the process converges in a dozen of iterations. Figure 2 illustrates it. The *contour mesh* is defined simply as follows: there is one cell per pixel, and for each pixel $\mathbf{p}$, its cell is obtained by connecting the sequence of points $\mathbf{x}_{a_0}, \mathbf{b}_{\text{face}(a_0)}, \mathbf{x}_{a_1}, \mathbf{b}_{\text{face}(a_1)} \dots$ for every arc $a_0, a_1, \dots$ coming out of $\mathbf{p}$. Each cell of the contour mesh is displayed painted with the color of its pixel. It is clear that the contour mesh is much more meaningful after GTV optimization, and its further regularization remove some artefacts induced by the discretization. Last but not least, our approach guarantees that sample points always keep their original color.

4 Raster Image Zooming with Smooth Contours

Contour meshes as presented in Sect. 3 are easily vectorized as polylines. It suffices to gather cells with same pixel color as a regions and extract the common boundaries of these regions. Furthermore, these polylines are easily converted to smooth splines. We will not explore this track in this paper but rather present a raster approach with similar objectives and features.

From the image s with lattice domain Ω, we wish to build a *zoomed image* s' with lattice domain Ω'. If the zoom factor is the integer z and Ω has width w and height h, then Ω' has width $z(w-1)+1$ and height $z(h-1)+1$. The canonical injection of Ω into Ω' is $\iota_z : (x, y) \mapsto (zx, zy)$. We use two auxiliary binary images S (for similarity image) and D for (for discontinuity image) with domain Ω'. We also define the *tangent* $\mathbf{T}_a$ at an arc a as the normalization of vector $\mathbf{b}_{\text{face}(a)} - \mathbf{b}_{\text{face}'(a)}$.

The zoomed image s' is constructed as follows:

Similarity set. We set to 1 the pixels of S that are in $\iota_z(\Omega)$. Furthermore, for every arc $a = (\mathbf{p}, \mathbf{q})$, if $w_a = 0$ then the digital straight segment between $\iota_z(\mathbf{p})$ and $\iota_z(\mathbf{q})$ is also set to 1. Last, we set the color s' at these pixels to their color in s.

Discontinuity set. For every face f, we count the number n of arcs whose weight is not null. If $n = 0$ we simply set $D(\iota_z(\mathbf{b}_f)) = 1$. $n = 1$ is impossible. If $n = 2$, let a_1 and a_2 be the two arcs with dissimilarities. We set $D(\mathbf{p}) = 1$ for every pixel $\mathbf{p} \in \Omega'$ that belongs to the digitized Bezier curve of order 3, that links the points $\iota_z(\mathbf{x}_{a_1})$ to $\iota_z(\mathbf{x}_{a_2})$, is tangent to $\mathbf{T}_{a_1}$ and $\mathbf{T}_{a_2}$, and pass through point $\iota_z(\frac{1}{2}(\mathbf{b}_f + I))$, with I the intersection of the two lines defined by $\mathbf{x}_{a_i}$ and tangent $\mathbf{T}_{a_i}$, $i = 1, 2$. If $n = 3$, for every arc a of f, we set $D(\mathbf{p}) = 1$ for every pixel $\mathbf{p} \in \Omega'$ that belongs to the digitized Bezier curve of order 2 connecting $\iota_z(\mathbf{x}_a)$ to $\iota_z(\mathbf{b}_f)$ and tangent to $\mathbf{T}_a$. Last we set the color s' at all these pixels by linear interpolation of the colors of pixels surrounding s.

Voronoi maps. We then compute the voronoi map $\text{Vor}(S)$ (resp. $\text{Vor}(D)$), which associates to each pixel of Ω' the closest point $\mathbf{p}$ of Ω' such that $S(\mathbf{p}) = 1$ (resp. such that $D(\mathbf{p}) = 1$).

Image interpolation. For all pixel $\mathbf{p}$ of Ω' such that $S(\mathbf{p}) = 0$ and $D(\mathbf{p}) = 0$, let $\mathbf{q} = \text{Vor}(S)(\mathbf{p})$ and $\mathbf{q}' = \text{Vor}(D)(\mathbf{p})$. We compute the distances $d = \|\mathbf{q} - \mathbf{p}\|$

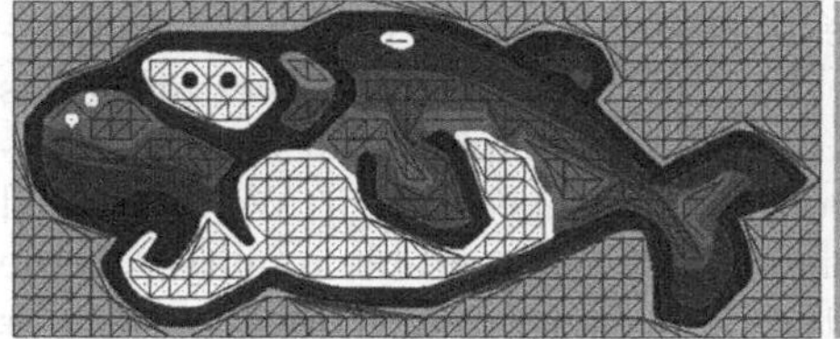

Fig. 3. Illustration of raster image zooming with smooth contours. On the left, similarity set is drawn in blue while discontinuity set is drawn in red. The final result is displayed on the right. (Color figure online)

and $d' = \|\mathbf{q}' - \mathbf{p}\|$. We use an amplification factor $\beta \in [0, 1]$: when close to 0, it tends to make linear shaded gradient while close to 1, it makes contours very crisp.

$$s'(\mathbf{p}) = \begin{cases} (1 - \frac{2d'}{d+d'})s'(\mathbf{q}') + \frac{2d'}{d+d'}(\beta s'(\mathbf{q}) + (1-\beta)s'(\mathbf{q}')) & \text{when } d' \leq d, \\ (1 - \frac{2d}{d+d'})s'(\mathbf{q}) + \frac{2d}{d+d'}(\beta s'(\mathbf{q}) + (1-\beta)s'(\mathbf{q}')) & \text{otherwise.} \end{cases}$$

In experiments, we always set $\beta = 0.75$ which gives good results, especially for image with low quantization. Of course, many other functions can be designed and the crispness could also be parameterized locally, for instance as a function of the GTV of the triangle.

Antialiasing discontinuities. To get images that are slightly more pleasant to the eye, we perform a last pass where we antialias every pixel $\mathbf{p}$ such that $D(\mathbf{p}) = 1$. We simply perform a weighted average within a 3×3 window, with pixels in S having weight 4, pixels in D having weight 0.25 and other pixels having weight 1.

Figure 3 illustrates this method of raster image zooming which provides crisp discontinuities that follow Bezier curves. Comparing with Fig. 2, image contours are no more polygonal lines but look like smooth curves. Last this method still guarantees that original pixel colors are kept.

5 Experimental Evaluation and Discussion

Our method can both produce vectorized image or make rasterized zoomed images, either from camera pictures or tiny image with low quantization like pixel art images. To measure its performance, several other super-resolution methods have been tested on the set of images given in the first column of Fig. 4, with parameters kept constant across all input images. First, we experimented the method based on geometric stencils proposed by Getreuer [6] with default parameters, which is implemented in the online demonstrator [7]. As shown in the second column of the figure, results appear noisy with oscillations near edges, which are well visible on pixel art images (e.g. x-shape or dolphin images). Such defaults are also visible on ara or barbara image near the white area.

Another super-resolution method was experimented which uses on a convolutional neural network [22]. Like the previous method, numerous perturbations are also visible both on pixel art images (x-shape or dolphin) but also in homogeneous areas close to strong gradients of ipol-coarsened image. We have tried different parameters but they lead to images with comparable quality. On the contrary, due to its formulation, our method does not produce false contours or false colors, and works indifferently on pixel art images or camera pictures.

Other comparisons are presented on Fig. 5 in order to give an overview of the behavior of five other methods. The two first methods complement the comparisons on pixel art image with respectively the depixelizing method proposed by Kopf and Lischinski [13] implemented in *Inkscape*, and a commercial software proposed by *Vector Magic Inc* [10]. Our method captures better the direction

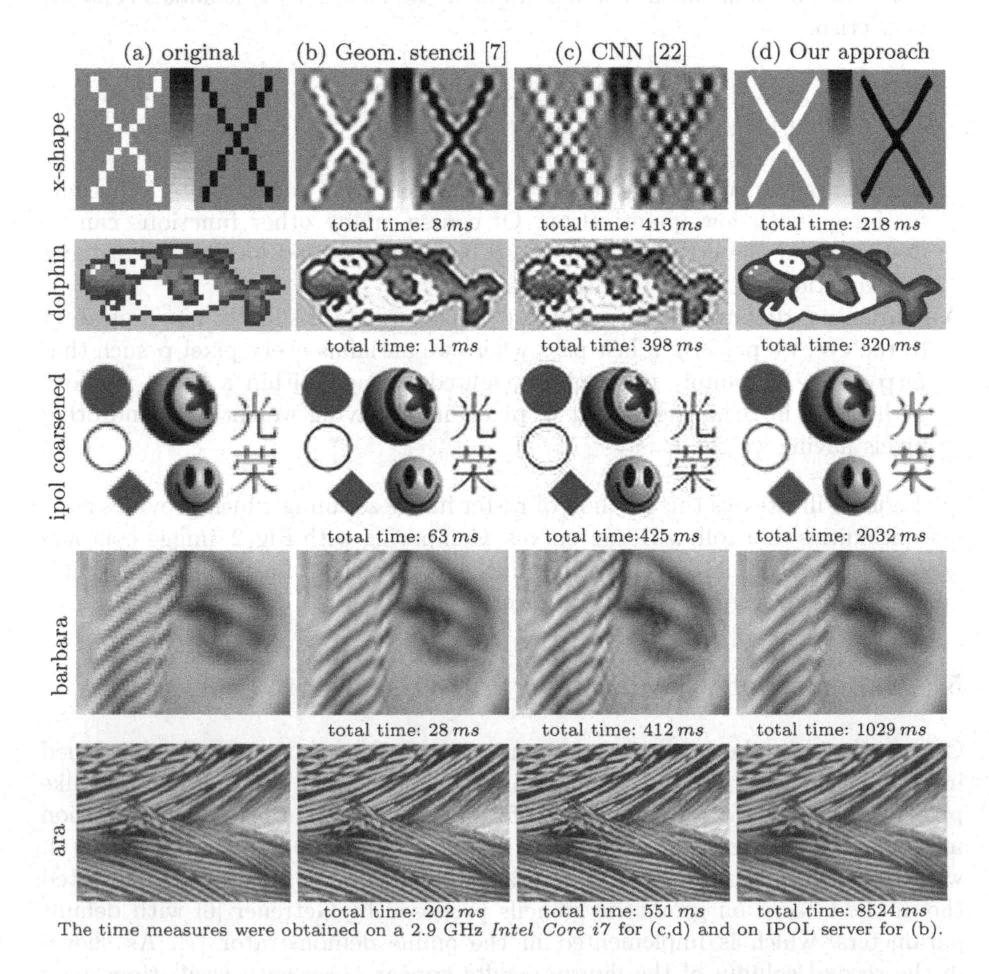

Fig. 4. Comparison of the proposed approach (d) with other methods on Geometric Stencils [7] (b) and based on Convolution Neural Network [22] (c).

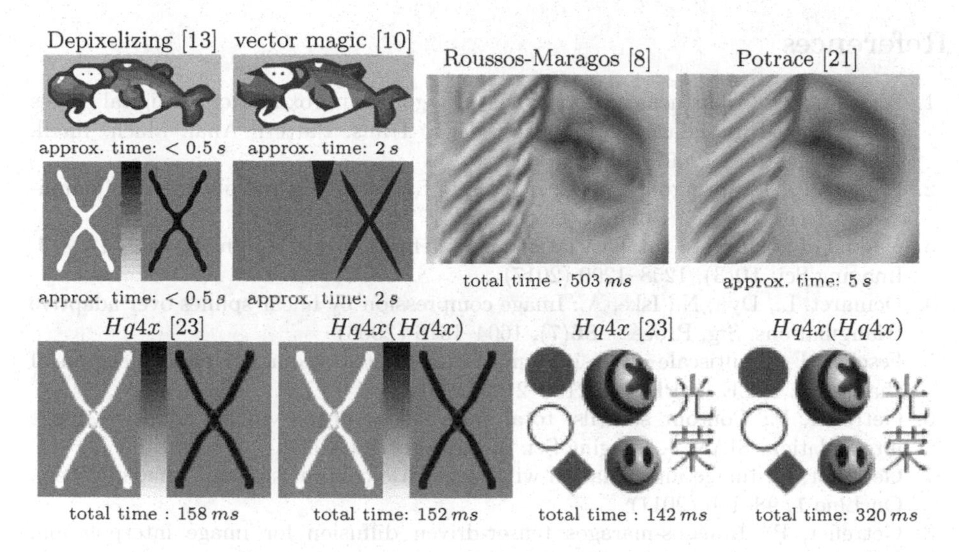

Fig. 5. Other complementary comparisons on five other approaches. The time measures were obtained on a 2.9 GHz *Intel Core i7* for all experiments expect Roussos-Maragos obtained on IPOL server. We use the default parameters expect for Potrace: we select 512 passes with color option.

of discontinuities of the underlying shape with less contour oscillations (see the border of dolphin or x-shape). Two other methods were tested on barbara image: Roussos and Maragos tensor-driven method [8] and Potrace vectorization software [21]. Again, results appear with oscillations around strong gradients with Roussos-Maragos algorithm, while Potrace software tends to smooth too much the image. Finally we also applied the Hqx magnification filter proposed by Stepin [23] that provides interesting zoom results but presents some artefacts (see for instance the X center of Hq4x) and limited scale factor (i.e. 4). Note that other comparisons can easily be done with the following online demonstrator: https://ipolcore.ipol.im/demo/clientApp/demo.html?id=280 and source code is available on a *GitHub* repository: https://github.com/kerautret/GTVimageVect.

6 Conclusion

We have presented an original approach to the problem of image vectorization and image super-resolution. It is based on a combinatorial variational model, which introduces geometry into the classical total variation model. We have compared our method both to state-of-the-art vectorization and super-resolution methods and it behaves well both for camera pictures and pixel art images. We have also provided an online demonstrator, which allows users to reproduce results or test our method with new images. In future works, we plan to compare quantitatively our method with state-of-the-art techniques, and also use our approach to train a CNN for zooming into pixel art images.

References

1. Bhowmick, P., Bhattacharya, B.B.: Fast polygonal approximation of digital curves using relaxed straightness properties. IEEE Trans. Pattern Anal. Mach. Intell. **29**(9), 1590–1602 (2007)
2. Bobenko, A.I., Springborn, B.A.: A discrete Laplace-Beltrami operator for simplicial surfaces. Discret. Comput. Geom. **38**(4), 740–756 (2007)
3. Condat, L.: Discrete total variation: new definition and minimization. SIAM J. Imaging Sci. **10**(3), 1258–1290 (2017)
4. Demaret, L., Dyn, N., Iske, A.: Image compression by linear splines over adaptive triangulations. Sig. Process. **86**(7), 1604–1616 (2006)
5. Feschet, F.: Multiscale analysis from 1D parametric geometric decomposition of shapes. In: IEEE, ICPR, pp. 2102–2105 (2010)
6. Getreuer, P.: Contour stencils: total variation along curves for adaptive image interpolation. SIAM J. Imaging Sci. **4**(3), 954–979 (2011)
7. Getreuer, P.: Image interpolation with geometric contour stencils. Image Process. On Line **1**, 98–116 (2011)
8. Getreuer, P.: Roussos-maragos tensor-driven diffusion for image interpolation. Image Process. On Line **1**, 178–186 (2011)
9. Hilaire, X., Tombre, K.: Robust and accurate vectorization of line drawings. IEEE TPAMI **28**(6), 890–904 (2006)
10. Vector Magic Inc. Vector magic (2010). http://vectormagic.com
11. Kerautret, B., Lachaud, J.-O., Naegel, B.: Curvature based corner detector for discrete, noisy and multi-scale contours. IJSM **14**(2), 127–145 (2008)
12. Kerautret, B., Ngo, P., Kenmochi, Y., Vacavant, A.: Greyscale image vectorization from geometric digital contour representations. In: Kropatsch, W.G., Artner, N.M., Janusch, I. (eds.) DGCI 2017. LNCS, vol. 10502, pp. 319–331. Springer, Cham (2017). https://doi.org/10.1007/978-3-319-66272-5_26
13. Kopf, J., Lischinski, D.: Depixelizing pixel art. In: ACM SIGGRAPH 2011 Papers, pp. 99:1–99:8. Vancouver, British Columbia (2011)
14. Lecot, G., Levy, B.: ARDECO: automatic region detection and conversion. In: 17th Eurographics Symposium on Rendering-EGSR 2006, pp. 349–360 (2006)
15. Liu, H., Latecki, L.J., Liu, W.: A unified curvature definition for regular, polygonal, and digital planar curves. Int. J. Comput. Vis. **80**(1), 104–124 (2008)
16. Marji, M., Siy, P.: Polygonal representation of digital planar curves through dominant point detection – a nonparametric algorithm. Pattern Recogn. **37**(11), 2113–2130 (2004)
17. Nguyen, T.P., Debled-Rennesson, I.: A discrete geometry approach for dominant point detection. Pattern Recogn. **44**(1), 32–44 (2011)
18. Price, B., Barrett, W.: Object-based vectorization for interactive image editing. Vis. Comput. **22**(9–11), 661–670 (2006)
19. Roussos, A., Maragos, P.: Vector-valued image interpolation by an anisotropic diffusion-projection PDE. In: Sgallari, F., Murli, A., Paragios, N. (eds.) SSVM 2007. LNCS, vol. 4485, pp. 104–115. Springer, Heidelberg (2007). https://doi.org/10.1007/978-3-540-72823-8_10
20. Rudin, L.I., Osher, S., Fatemi, E.: Nonlinear total variation based noise removal algorithms (1992)
21. Selinger, P.: Potrace (2001–2017). http://potrace.sourceforge.net
22. Shi, W., et al.: Real-time single image and video super-resolution using an efficient sub-pixel convolutional neural network. In: CVPR, pp. 1874–1883. IEEE, Las Vegas, June 2016

23. Stepin, M.: HQx magnification filter (2003). http://web.archive.org/web/20070717064839/www.hiend3d.com/hq4x.html
24. Sun, J., Liang, L., Wen, F., Shum, H.-Y.: Image vectorization using optimized gradient meshes. Trans. Graph. **26**, 11 (2007)
25. Swaminarayan, S., Prasad, L.: Rapid automated polygonal image decomposition. In: 35th Workshop AIPR 2006, pp. 28–28, October 2006
26. Xia, T., Liao, B., Yu, Y.: Patch-based image vectorization with automatic curvilinear feature alignment. Trans. Graph. **28**, 115 (2009)

Learning Theory and Optimization

Information Theory-Based Curriculum Learning Factory to Optimize Training

Henok Ghebrechristos(✉) and Gita Alaghband

University of Colorado, Denver, CO 80014, USA
{henok.ghebrechristos,gita.alaghband}@ucdenver.edu

Abstract. We present a new system to optimize feature extraction from 2D-topological data like images in the context of deep learning using correlation among training samples and curriculum learning optimization (CLO). The system treats every sample as 2D random variable, where a pixel contained in the sample is modelled as an independent and identically distributed random variable (i.i.d) realization. With this modelling we utilize information-theoretic and statistical measures of random variables to rank individual training samples and relationship between samples to construct syllabus. The rank of each sample is then used when the sample is fed to the network during training. Comparative evaluation of multiple state-of-the-art networks, including, ResNet, GoogleNet, and VGG, on benchmark datasets demonstrate a syllabus that ranks samples using measures such as Joint Entropy between adjacent samples, can improve learning and significantly reduce the amount of training steps required to achieve desirable training accuracy. We present results that indicate our approach can produce robust feature maps that in turn contribute to reduction of loss by as much as factors of 9 compared to conventional, no-curriculum, training.

Keywords: Deep learning · Curriculum learning · Convolutional neural network

1 Introduction

Humans and other organisms, as in supervised learning, can learn to acquire knowledge and perform tasks by observing a sequence of labelled concepts. Supervision is often accompanied with a curriculum in human teaching. Hence the order in which topics are presented is not random when a teacher uses curriculum to teach. The ordering is such that simple concepts are presented early, progressing through concepts with increasing difficulty. When used in supervised machine learning, curriculum-based training (Fig. 1) exposes samples to the learning system in a predetermined order. The basic idea is to present samples that have low complexity at the start of training and gradually increase complexity of samples fed to the network over the course of training. Hence, at core of this approach lies ranking (weighting) training samples based on their level of presumed difficulty.

Many techniques described in the literature consider difficulty level of a sample to be proportional to a chosen distance metric between the output label and the actual truth label of the sample [3, 5]. The distance metric is often provided by the *loss function* used

S. Palaiahnakote et al. (Eds.): ACPR 2019, LNCS 12046, pp. 409–423, 2020.
https://doi.org/10.1007/978-3-030-41404-7_29

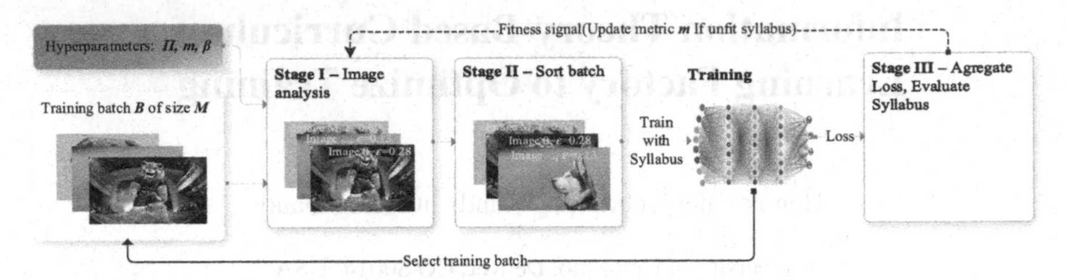

Fig. 1. Curriculum learning

by the learning algorithm, since it already attempts to minimize the distance between the expected and truth sample labels. In order to use this approach, one must employ two training passes: the first to measure the difference between the true label and predicted label value of each sample to get the presumed difficulty (or rank) of the sample. The training set is then ordered according to rank of each sample to form a curriculum used to train the network in the second training pass. Although one could potentially determine a good curriculum.

In contrast to the existing class of curriculum algorithms, our proposed method combines information theory tools (ITT) with curriculum learning to assess and adaptively order training samples to form an input path for training a network (Fig. 1). We utilize ITT-based image analysis techniques to assess each sample and its relationship with other samples to determine the time the sample is fed to the network.

A unique feature our approach is that the syllabus is generated, enforced and evaluated at training time using a node, curriculum factory, integrated into training pipeline. The node is designed to handle both online and batch training modes. When training using batches, a random subset (batch) of samples of size $\boldsymbol{M}$ from the training set is processed and the weights are updated based on the cumulative error. With online training, one sample is fed to the network at every iteration and weights are updated based on error corresponding to that sample. During batch training, the samples in a batch are ordered to form a syllabus corresponding to that batch. The primary means of ordering is a metric $\boldsymbol{m}$ that ranks a sample by measuring its content. The syllabus and batch are then supplied to the network to train via curriculum learning.

Supervised training seeks to minimize a global loss function that includes distance component as well as a regularization term. The distance component, that measures learning progress overtime, is used to evaluate the fitness of a syllabus. A syllabus deemed unfit is discarded and\or replaced in the early stages of training. A syllabus that incurs significant overhead to training time is also considered unfit and blacklisted. We report experimental results conducted using batch sizes of 8 and 16.

To summarize, this paper makes two main contributions. Currently there exists no methods in the literature that take characteristics of training data into account to expedite non-convex optimization via curriculum learning or other means. As the first contribution, we present a curriculum learning algorithm that reduces training loss at each iteration by ordering batches to form a syllabus. When used in stochastic gradient descent (SGD)-based training, our algorithm expedites training and reduces the overall loss by as much as a factor of 9 without compromising generalization performance. Second, we present results that showcase improved generalization performance of popular CNN models on benchmark datasets in comparison to baseline, state-of-the-art performance.

2 Related Work

Most work on curriculum learning utilize error-based correction [3] to uniformly sample from training set as a means to speed up training. Other methods have been proposed [4, 5] to sample, weigh and sort training samples to improve accuracy and expedite training. Most of these methods either require modification of the objective function with a term for sample valuation [6] or run training procedure twice to obtain accurate representation of sample effectiveness [7]. Use optimization loss to valuate and increase the replay probability of samples that have high expected-learning-progress. The authors use a weighted importance sampling method to counter bias of sampling. Similarly, [8] proposed to sample batches non-uniformly [5]. Proposed an automatic curriculum learning method for LSTM for the NLP application. They use a non-stationary multi-armed bandit algorithm of getting a reward signal from each training sample to define a stochastic syllabus [9]. Use influence functions from robust statistics to measure the effect of parameter changes or perturbations of the training data such as pixel values which was applied to debugging models, and training-set attack. In addition, [10] describes a pre-processing algorithm that divides each input image into patches (image regions) and constructs a new sample by reorganizing the patches according their statistical or content summary. The authors present results that support training a CNN network in this manner can aid feature extraction and produce networks that tolerate adversarial attacks.

Unlike these approaches, our curriculum was formed by presenting the training samples to the network in order of increasing similarity or dissimilarity, measured by the sample's statistical pixel (content) distribution. Our method takes advantage of similarity and image content measures to define and propose a stochastic syllabus. *During batch training, all samples within a batch are sorted in ascending order based on a standalone or mutual measure.* When a standalone measure is used, every sample in the batch is ranked according to an index that measures some characteristics of that sample. For instance, when entropy is used as a ranking metric, the batch is sorted based on the entropy value of each sample. If mutual or distance measure is employed, the entire batch is sorted based on similarity or dissimilarity to a reference sample. *Our results indicate that this approach* expedites a search for local minima which helps expedite the overall training.

3 Proposed Method

The goal of training CNNs is to try and determine optimal network weights to approximate target mapping $g : x_i \rightarrow y_i$ [11] where x_i is the input vector and y_i is the corresponding desired output taken from a training set,

$$T_s = \{(x_n, y_n) : 1 \leq n \leq N\}, \quad (1)$$

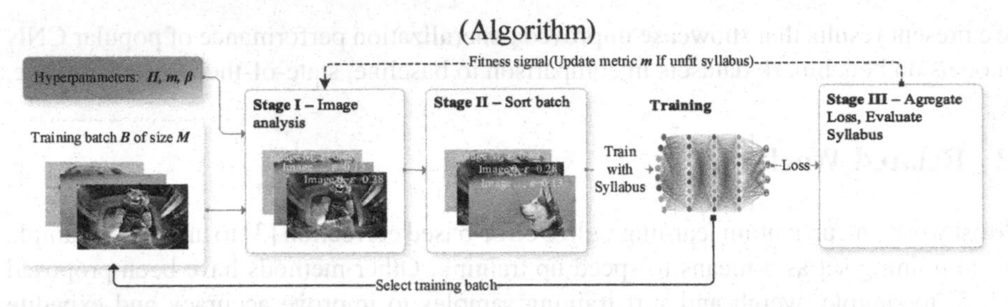

Fig. 2. Processing stages within *sp-module*. From left to right given batch B and hyperparameters read once at start: I. Rank each sample. II. Generate syllabus by ordering B according to rank of each sample which is then used to train a network. III. Evaluate syllabus using network loss.

consisting of N samples. If we consider a jth training batch $\boldsymbol{B}_j \subset \boldsymbol{T}_s$ containing $\boldsymbol{M}$ samples, a curriculum training syllabus, $\boldsymbol{Syllabus}_{\boldsymbol{B}_j}$ of $\boldsymbol{B}_j$ is generated by ranking and ordering every sample in the batch based on some *measure* $\boldsymbol{m}$. The syllabus is then applied to train the network. Note here, $\boldsymbol{M} = 1$ corresponds to online training where samples (not batches) are fed one by one. In our system, $M = 1$ is a special case where the syllabus corresponds to ordering of the entire training set.

Curriculum factory, an original feature of our proposal, is a system that generates ordering of samples of a selected batch during training. It comprises a syllabus proposal submodule (*sp-module*) that takes a batch of randomly ordered samples as input and returns an ordering of the samples that serves as a syllabus. Given $\boldsymbol{T}_s$ we denote the jth mini-batch containing $\boldsymbol{M} \ll \boldsymbol{N}$ samples by $\boldsymbol{B}_j = \{s_1, s_2, \ldots, s_M\}$. A training syllabus, $\boldsymbol{Syllabus}_{\boldsymbol{B}_j}$ is defined as an ordering of every sample, $s_k = (\boldsymbol{x}_i, \boldsymbol{y}_i) \in \boldsymbol{B}_j$ for$1 \le \boldsymbol{i} \le \boldsymbol{M}$, in ascending (*asc*) or descending (*dec*) order. Ordering is determined by the rank, $\boldsymbol{\varepsilon}$, of each sample as measured by a metric m taken from Table 1. Formally, $\boldsymbol{Syllabus}_{\boldsymbol{B}_j} = (\boldsymbol{s'}_1, \boldsymbol{s'}_2, \ldots, \boldsymbol{s'}_M)$ is a computationally found ordered set such that $\boldsymbol{\varepsilon}_{s'_1} \le \boldsymbol{\varepsilon}_{s'_1} \le \ldots \le \boldsymbol{\varepsilon}_{s'_M}$ if ordering is *asc* and $\boldsymbol{\varepsilon}_{s'_1} \ge \boldsymbol{\varepsilon}_{s'_1} \ge \ldots \ge \boldsymbol{\varepsilon}_{s'_M}$ if *dec*.

The *sp-module* is built using a three-step processing depicted in Fig. 2. In stage I, all samples of a batch are assessed and ranked using a prespecified metric $\boldsymbol{m}$ (Table 1). In stage II, the batch is ordered according to the rank of each sample. The ordered batch, or syllabus, is then supplied to the network for training. In stage III, the effectiveness of the syllabus is determined using the network's native loss function after training with a fixed number of batches. The number of batches used to control how often the syllabus is evaluated is a configurable hyperparameter. Below we discuss each stage in detail. The full recipe in an end-to-end training pipeline is presented in Table 1 (Algorithm).

3.1 Stage I: Assessing Content of Training Samples

CNNs learn patterns of features from training and use layer-wise superposition of these features to generalize to unseen samples. To enable robust feature extraction and ease the pattern discovery, we are interested in generating curricula based on how samples are related to each other. We consider two types of metrics to measure these relationships; *statistical* and *information-theoretic measures*. These measures are further categorized into *standalone* and *distance* depending on the input(s) to the measure. If a measure takes two samples as input and returns a single value that relates the two samples, then it is considered a distance measure. Otherwise, the measure is standalone and takes a single sample as input and returns a value that describes certain characteristics of the sample.

In order to use information-theoretic measures, we model all samples as 2D random variables where each pixel is an independent and identically distributed random variable *(i.i.d)* realization. With this model, we utilize information theoretic measures such as Entropy to quantify information content of training samples. Below we discuss few measures. A complete list is presented in Table 1.

Entropy. Let X be a discrete random variable with alphabet χ and a probability distribution function $p(x), x \in \chi$. The Shannon entropy [12] of χ is defined as

$$H(X) = \sum_{x \in \chi} p(x) \log \frac{1}{p(x)} \tag{2}$$

where $0 \log \infty = 0$ and the base of the logarithm determines the unit, e.g. if base 2 the measure is in *bits* [13]. The term $-log\ p(x)$ can be viewed as the amount of information gained by observing the outcome $p(x)$. Entropy is usually meant to measure the uncertainty of a continuous random variable. However, when applied to discrete images, this measures how much relevant information is contained within an image when representing the image as a discrete information source that is random [14]. Here, we construct probability distribution associated with each image by binning the pixel values into histograms. The normalized histogram can then be used as an estimate of the underlying probability of pixel intensities, i.e., $p(i) = b_s(i)/N$, where $b_s(i)$ denotes the histogram entry of intensity value i in s, and N is the total number of pixels of s. With this representation the entropy of an image s can be computed as:

$$E(s) = \sum_{i \in \chi, s \in T_s} b_s(i) \log \frac{N}{b_s(i)}, \tag{3}$$

where T_s (Eq. 1) is the training set and $\chi(s)$ represents the image as a vector of pixel values. While individual entropy is used to measure the standalone rank of a sample, we also used metrics that relate training samples. These include *joint entropy (JE), kl-divergence (KL), mutual information (MI), information variation (IV), conditional entropy (CE) and their variants such as normalized mutual information (MIN).* A complete list of the metrics used for this study are listed in Table 2. Readers are encouraged to refer to [14–16] for detailed treatment of these metrics and others.

Statistical metrics on the other had measure the similarity (dissimilarity) of samples and typically use statistical measurements such as mean μ and standard deviation σ. One such measure is the Structural Similarity Index (SSIM). SSIM is often used for predicting image quality using a reference image. Given two samples s_1 and s_2 the SSIM index [16] is given by:

$$SSIM(s_1, s_2) = \frac{(2\mu_{s_1}\mu_{s_2} + C_1)(2\sigma_{s_1 s_2} + C_2)}{(\mu_{s_1}^2 + \mu_{s_2}^2 + C_1)(\sigma_{s_1}^2 + \sigma_{s_2}^2 + C_2)} \tag{4}$$

Table 1. (Algorithm 1) Curriculum training of a CNN network η. Here, at least two m values, a primary measure and backup measures, from Table 2 are pre-specified. If no $\boldsymbol{m}$ *is* prespecified, *sp-module* picks a primary and backup measures randomly from the set of measures listed in Table 2.

Input: ***Training set*** $\boldsymbol{T_s}$, ***Metric*** $\boldsymbol{m}$, ***Order*** $\boldsymbol{o}$, β, π
Outputs: ***Trained model*** η (network weights)

1. *Initialize* iteration (training batch) counter *iter and* $\boldsymbol{\beta_{\eta \to S}}$ *to 0 and* $\boldsymbol{f_S}$ with *continue*
2. *Draw* training batch $\boldsymbol{B}$ of size $\boldsymbol{M}$ from $\boldsymbol{T_s}$
   For $\boldsymbol{i = 0}$ ***to*** $\boldsymbol{< M - 1}$
   1. ***Select input*** $\boldsymbol{s_i}$
   2. ***Compute rank*** $\boldsymbol{\varepsilon_{s_i}}$

   End

   Syllabus = *Sorted batch according to* $\boldsymbol{\varepsilon}$
3. ***Train network on B using Syllabus and increment*** *iter*
4. ***If*** *iter* **is equal to** π
   Calculate syllabus-to-baseline loss ratio ⍰ and set fitness signal $\boldsymbol{f_S}$
   If $\boldsymbol{f_S}$ *is* set to *continue*
   go-to step *2*
   If $\boldsymbol{f_S}$ *is* set to *replace*
   go-to step 1
   Otherwise Halt training

---

where the terms μ and σ are the mean and variances of the two vectors and $\sigma_{s_1 s_2}$ is the covariance of s_1 and s_2. The constant terms C_1 and C_2 are used to avoid a null denominator. We also use simple measures such as L_1 norm to compare the pixel histograms of two samples.

3.2 Stage II: Sorting Batches of Samples

A batch of training samples $\boldsymbol{B} = \{\mathbf{s}_1, \mathbf{s}_2, \ldots, \mathbf{s}_\mathbf{M}\} \subset \boldsymbol{T_s}$ is selected from the training set. Each sample $s_k \in \boldsymbol{B}$ is assigned a rank by analysing its pixel distribution using the specified metric $\boldsymbol{m}$. We use two types of metrics; *distance* and *standalone*. If $\boldsymbol{m}$ is a distance metric, a reference sample $\mathbf{s}_r \in \boldsymbol{B}$ is used to rank a moving sample $\mathbf{s}_m \in \boldsymbol{B}$. Initially, the reference sample is chosen at random. For instance, consider the following setup: let $\boldsymbol{m}$ be the mutual information (***MI***) measure, the algorithm first selects an initial reference sample, $\mathbf{s}_r = \mathbf{s}_1$ and computes the MI-index or rank ($\boldsymbol{\varepsilon}$) of every other sample, $\mathbf{s}_2, \ldots, \mathbf{s}_\mathbf{M}$, in the batch against $\mathbf{s}_r$. If *asc* ordering is used, the sample with the smallest $\boldsymbol{\varepsilon}$ value is promoted to become a reference sample. This is repeated until the last sample is promoted and a syllabus is proposed. Note here, the syllabus, $\boldsymbol{S_B}$, is an ordering of the samples according to their mutual information index. Given a proposed syllabus $\boldsymbol{S_B} = \left\{s'_1, s'_5, s'_{2,}, s'_8 \ldots, s'_M\right\}$, the network first sees the initial reference sample, then the sample having the smallest ε value is fed to the network. The overall behaviour is that adjacent samples are closer to each other than those that are not adjacent. Closeness in this context is measured by the metric in use. The smaller the value ε the closer the two samples are. When using a *standalone* metric, each sample is ranked. The entire batch is then sorted based on the specified ordering and the rank of each sample. m is pre-specified as a learning parameter and can be updated during training if corresponding syllabus is deemed unfit. We experimented with several metrics to observe their impact on training.

Table 2. List of measures used in this study

Metric	Category	Implementation - given samples $s_1, s_2 \in T_s$ where b_s is normalized histogram of pixel intensities and i is an index of a pixel value in a sample
Entropy	Standalone	Section 3.1
Joint Entropy (JE)	Distance	$JE(s_1, s_2) = \sum_i b_s(i) \log b_s(i),$
Mutual Information (MI)	Distance	$MI(s_1, s_1) = E(s_1) + E(s_1) - JE(s_1, s_2)$
KL-Divergence	Distance	$D_{k\|L}(s_1, s_2) = \sum_i s_{1i} \log \frac{b_{s1}(i)}{b_{s2}(i)}$
Information Variation (IV)	Distance	$IV(s_1, s_2) = E(s_1) + E(s_2) - 2MI(s_1, s_1)$
Conditional Entropy (CE)	Distance	$CE(s_1\|s_2) = E(s_1, s_2) - E(s_1)$, where $E(s_1, s_2)$ is the sum entropies of s_1 and s_2
L1 Norm (L1)	Distance	$L_1(s_1, s_2) = \|\|s_1 - s_2\|\| = \sum_{i=1} \|s_{1i} - s_{2i}\|$
L2 Norm (L2)	Distance	$L_2(s_1, s_2) = \|\|s_1 - s_2\|\|_2 = \sqrt{\sum_{i=1} (s_{1i} - s_{2i})^2}$
Max Norm (MN)	Distance	This is like L1norm where, instead of every entry, the maximum entries' magnitude is used to calculate the norm [17]
Peak-signal-to-noise ratio (PSNR)	Standalone	$PSNR = 20\log_{10}(\frac{MAX}{\sqrt{MSE(S_1, S_2)}}$ where, $MSE(a, b) = \frac{1}{N^2} \sum_i^N \sum_j^N (a_{ij} - b_{ij})^2$
Structural Similarity index (SSIM)	Distance	Section 3.1

3.3 Stage III: Syllabus Evaluation

We use the network's native loss function to determine the fitness of a given syllabus. The syllabus is evaluated after training for a fixed number of iterations. Fitness of a syllabus for a given network η and training set $\boldsymbol{T_s}$ is determined using two configurable hyperparameters; number of iterations (can also be number of batches) π and the baseline performance β of the network on $\boldsymbol{T_s}$ averaged over π. β is the threshold by which the syllabuses' s fitness is determined and is chosen to be the average baseline loss of the network over π number of iterations. Baseline performance of a network is the network's training performance without curriculum.

Syllabus Fitness Criteria. Once η is trained on $\boldsymbol{T_s}$ for π number of iterations using a syllabus $\boldsymbol{Syllabus}$, the losses are aggregated and the average loss,

$$\beta_{\eta \rightarrow Syllabus} = \frac{\sum_{i=0}^{\pi} loss(i)}{\pi}, \tag{5}$$

where ***loss(i)*** is the ith iteration training loss, of the network associated with $\boldsymbol{S}$ is computed. The syllabus-to-baseline loss ratio, $\omega = \beta_{\eta \rightarrow Syllabus}/\beta$, is then used as the sole criteria to determine the fitness of the syllabus. Depending on the value of ω, a fitness signal $\boldsymbol{f_S}$, that can take on one of three forms; *continue, stop* or *replace,* is propagated to the image analysis submodule. A syllabus is deemed fit if the ratio is less than or equal to **1** and $\boldsymbol{f_S}$ is set to *continue.* Otherwise $\boldsymbol{f_S}$ is set to *stop or replace* and the syllabus is considered unfit and discarded. If *replace* is propagated, the curriculum factory adaptively proposes a new syllabus using a prespecified backup metric. Here, we make a naive assumption that the syllabus's training performance is as good as the baseline if the ratio is close to 1.

4 Experiments

4.1 Datasets

Our method is implemented with the TensorFlow library [18] and training was done using a system equipped with four NVIDIA Tesla P100 GPUs. We present training and classification results obtained by training state-of-the-art image classification networks using different curriculum strategies described in Sect. 3 on CIFAR10, CIFAR100 [19] and ILSVRC-2015 ImageNet [20] datasets. Specifically, given the moderate cost of time associated with training a network using CIFAR10, CIFAR10 was used to perform an in-depth study of the proposed method using several network architectures. Based on the training trends on CIFAR10, we then perform repeatability study using CIFAR100. Finally, a syllabus that exhibits exceptional performance on those datasets is selected and compared with baseline performance on ImageNet.

4.2 Training

We trained several past and current state-of-the-art CNNs using open-source TensorFlow implementations. Each network is first evaluated on the corresponding datasets to create baseline reference performance metrics for comparison. For each network we used stochastic gradient descent optimizer with cross-entropy loss, fixed momentum of 0.9, batch size of 8, and an exponentially decaying learning rate with factor 0.94 starting at 0.01. For the rest of training, we used recommended configurations by respective authors. We report empirical results gathered by training each network for at least 100 thousand iterations. We ensure all learning parameters and environment are identical, with varying networks and learning methods, to rule out other factors of influence.

4.3 Networks

GoogleNet (Inception) versions 1 [21] and 4 [22] were two of the networks evaluated in this study. Inception V1 was placed number 1 in the 2014 ImageNet [23] competition for classification and detection challenges. It's a 22 layered network that comprises of basic units referred to as *inception cells*. For each cell, a set of 1×1, 3×3 and 5×5 filters are learned to extract features at different scales from the input. The architecture also consists of two auxiliary classifiers that prevent the middle part of the network from dying out. The auxiliary losses are weighted and added to the Softmax loss as a way to combat vanishing gradient problem and provide regularization [21]. Inception V4 [22] evolved from Inception V1 and has a more uniformly simplified architecture and more inception cells. Additional network architectures include ResNet [24], VGG [25] which placed top in ILSVRC 2015 and ILSVRC 2014 respectively as well as several version of the MobileNet [26] architecture which were designed for computational efficiency.

To observe the training trends, we use curriculum settings with varying measure $\boldsymbol{m}$, $\pi = 10000$, $\boldsymbol{o} = \boldsymbol{asc}$ and $\boldsymbol{\beta}$ value that is unique to each network and training set. To capture the classification results each network is trained for 500,000 iterations or until the learning curve is stable and the loss converges. Batch sizes of 8 and 16 were used for these experiments.

5 Results and Analysis

5.1 Training Trends

To capture the impact of the proposed approach on training, we trained all networks on CIFAR10 dataset. We use the total loss, which is the sum of cross-entropy and regularization losses as implemented in TensorFlow [27] framework as the primary evaluation criteria of the impact of the proposed method.

The training loss of select metrics and that of the baseline (blue) are depicted in Fig. 3. Clear trends can be observed from the plots. First, in all cases, curriculum-based training performs remarkably well in reducing training loss. For instance, when training GoogleNet using JE-based curriculum, it achieves a loss of 0.163 compared to 1.494 after training for only 100 K iterations. This is a loss reduction by a factor of 9. Similarly, MobileNet's loss is reduced by factor of 4. The second and most impressive

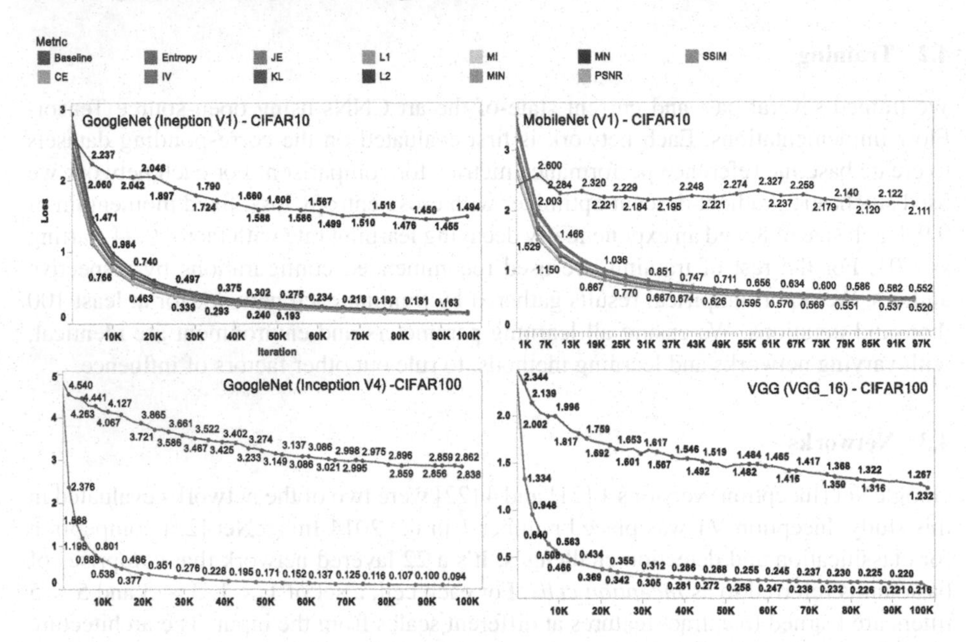

Fig. 3. Training loss of training MobileNet (top-right), GoogleNet V1 (top-left) on CIFAR10 using all metrics listed in Table 1, and GoogleNet V4 (bottom-left) and VGG (bottom-right) on CIFAR100 using the entropy measure. (Color figure online)

observation that highlights the effectiveness of the proposed technique is that the baseline performance is almost always inferior to any curriculum strategy throughout training. Only in few cases do we see a strategy produce higher loss. This is partly because our method removes variability due random shuffling using consistent input path with each batch as measured by the metric in use. Whilst these results are interesting, to ensure repeatability and confirm the efficacy of the best models, we performed additional experiments on CIFAR100. The bottom two plots of Fig. 3 show the training trends of GoogleNet and VGG on CIFAR100 using Entropy-based curriculum syllabus.

5.2 Regularization Loss

Regularization methods are supplementary techniques that are used to reduce test error and prevent overfitting. In neural networks and deep learning, the term is reserved solely for a penalty term in the loss function [28]. In all the networks used for this study, regularization is achieved by adding a regularize term R to the native loss function. Unlike the loss function, which expresses the deviation of the network output with labels, R is independent of the labels. Instead, it's used to encode *other properties* of the desired model to induce bias. These properties are rooted in assumptions other than consistency of network output with labels. The most common approaches are *weight decay* [29] and *smoothness* of the learned mapping. The regularization loss trends of training various networks on CIFAR10 and CIFAR100 using JE and IV curriculum strategies are depicted in Fig. 4.

5.3 Sparsity

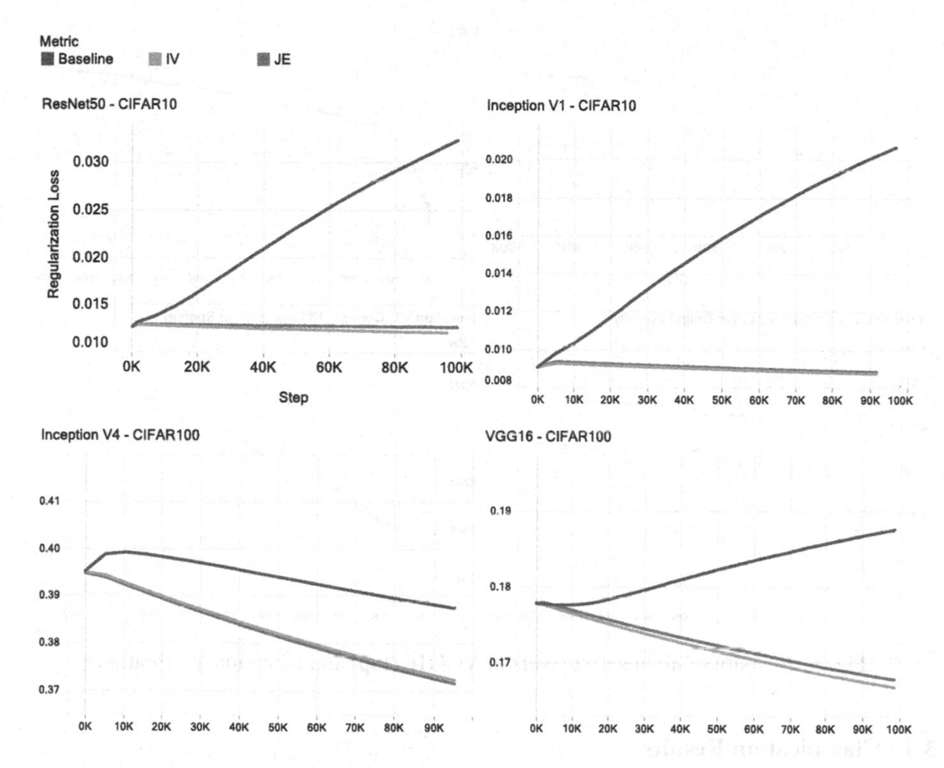

Fig. 4. Comparison of regularization loss of several curriculum strategies with the baseline on CIFAR10 (top) and CIFAR100 (bottom)

Output sparsity is in deep neural networks is highly desirable to reduce model training and inference costs. CNNs are highly sparse with many values involved in the calculations being zero or close to zero. Features map sparsity can be exploited to expedite training and reduce inference cost by skipping the values that are known to be zeros. Feature maps in CNN models usually have high sparsity. This is because convolution operation is immediately followed by an activation layer that turns all negative inputs into zeros. In addition, max-pooling layers only select a max value in a sub-region of the input and drop other values in the region. As shown in Fig. 5, we observe that the average feature-map and fully connected layer output sparsity scores are reduced much faster when training a network with the proposed method.

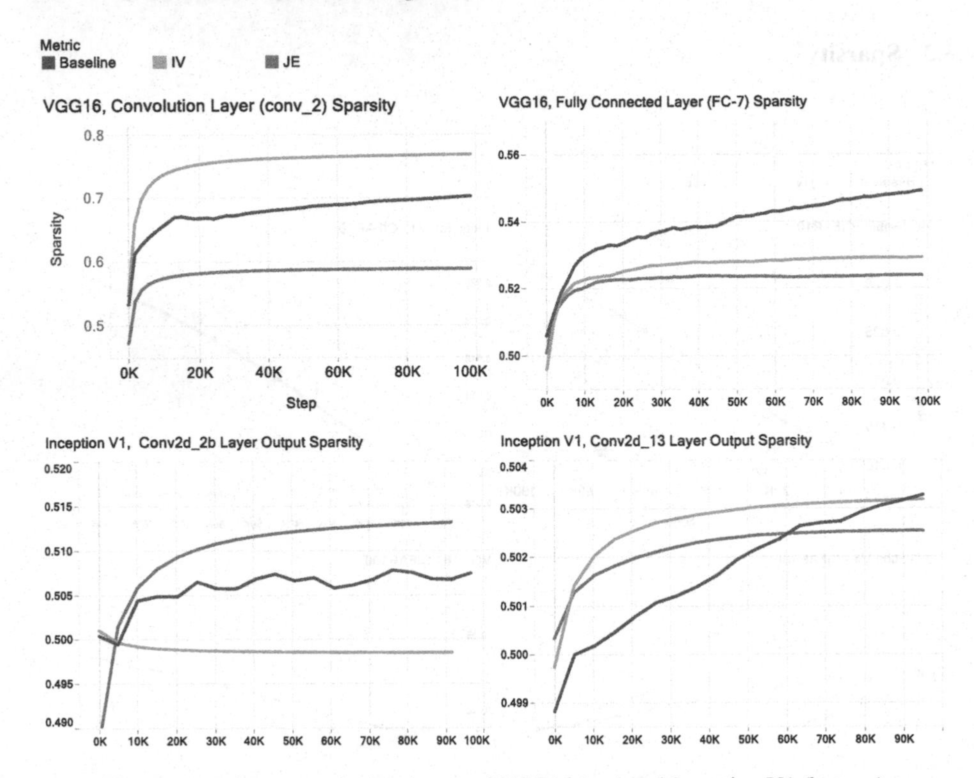

Fig. 5. Sparsity score of select layers of VGG16 (top) and Inception V1 (bottom)

5.4 Classification Results

Due to the lack of directly comparable techniques for curriculum-based training, we contrasted our techniques against the baseline generalization capabilities of a network on a given dataset. More specifically, we first trained the network to establish its baseline performance on the dataset. The same network is then trained using the proposed technique. The best performing weights are then chosen for performance comparison. The results on CIFAR10 and CIFAR100 datasets are presented below.

With most curriculum setups, the network's generalization capability is uncompromised and is within range of the baseline performance. However, depending on the dataset, several curriculum metrics produce networks that generalize better than the baseline. For instance, training GoogleNet (Table 3) using MI and IV based curriculum strategies perform better on CIFAR10, while IV and JE enabled syllabus performs better on CIFAR100 (Tables 4 and 5).

Table 3. Comparison of GoogleNet (Inception V1) network on CIFAR10 and CIFAR100. Reported is the test accuracy in percent of classification for network with and without the proposed training approach. Best results are highlighted in bold. The baseline performance is the first entry in the table.

Network	CIFAR10 (test acc. %)	CIFAR100 (test acc. %)	Curriculum
GoogleNet	0.528	0.433	
GoogleNet-MI	**0.615**	0.358	MI
GoogleNet-MIN	0.456	0.146	MIN
GoogleNet-IV	**0.671**	**0.456**	IV
GoogleNet-JE	0.586	**0.489**	JE

Table 4. Comparison of ResNet_V1_50 network on CIFAR10 and CIFAR100.

Network	CIFAR10 (test acc. %)	CIFAR100 (test acc. %)	Curriculum
VGG	0.922	0.645	
VGG-MI	**0.945**	0.512	MI
VGG-MIN	0.904	0.602	MIN
VGG-IV	0.897	**0.698**	IV
VGG-JE	**0.943**	0.631	JE

Table 5. Comparison of ResNet_16 network on CIFAR10 and CIFAR100.

Network	CIFAR10 (test acc. %)	CIFAR100 (test acc. %)	Curriculum
ResNet	0.954	0.791	
ResNet-MI	0.945	**0.842**	MI
ResNet-MIN	**0.973**	0.789	MIN
ResNet-IV	0.943	**0.849**	IV
ResNet-JE	0.924	**0.851**	JE

5.5 Conclusion

We have introduced a system for training CNNs using curriculum strategies. Our approach combines content measures taken from information theory with curriculum learning and alleviates the need to determine the presumed difficulty of training samples. Unlike previous works, we exploit information-theoretic and statistical relationship between training samples to propose a syllabus to guide training; we have shown that this improves training performance of CNNs. The results indicate that curriculum strategies reduce training loss faster without necessarily increasing the generalize performance compared to conventional training. Our intuition is that the proposed technique enables faster convergence by discovering optimal path that take to local minima. However, further analysis is required to fully test and prove our *hypothesis that the proposed method combined with SGD optimization expedites a search for local minima by creating an optimal path in input space.*

References

1. Graves, A., Bellemare, M.G., Menick, J., Munos, R., Kavukcuoglu, K.: Automated curriculum learning for neural networks (2017). 10 p.
2. Kim, T.-H., Choi, J.: ScreenerNet: learning self-paced curriculum for deep neural networks. arXiv:1801.00904 Cs, January 2018
3. Hinton, G.E.: To recognize shapes, first learn to generate images. Prog. Brain Res. **165**, 535–547 (2007)
4. Zhou, H.-Y., Gao, B.-B., Wu, J.: Adaptive feeding: achieving fast and accurate detections by adaptively combining object detectors. arXiv:1707.06399 Cs, July 2017
5. Graves, A., Bellemare, M.G., Menick, J., Munos, R., Kavukcuoglu, K.: Automated curriculum learning for neural networks. arXiv:1704.03003 Cs, April 2017
6. Kumar, M.P., Packer, B., Koller, D.: Self-paced learning for latent variable models. In: Lafferty, J.D., Williams, C.K.I., Shawe-Taylor, J., Zemel, R.S., Culotta, A. (eds.) Advances in Neural Information Processing Systems 23, pp. 1189–1197. Curran Associates, Inc. (2010)
7. Schaul, T., Quan, J., Antonoglou, I., Silver, D.: Prioritized experience replay. arXiv:1511.05952 Cs, November 2015
8. Loshchilov, I., Hutter, F.: Online batch selection for faster training of neural networks. arXiv:1511.06343 Cs Math, November 2015
9. Koh, P.W., Liang, P.: Understanding black-box predictions via influence functions. arXiv:1703.04730 Cs Stat, March 2017
10. Ghebrechristos, H., Alaghband, G.: Expediting training using information theory-based patch ordering algorithm (2018). 6 p.
11. Goodfellow, I., Bengio, Y., Courville, A.: Deep Learning. MIT Press, Cambridge (2016)
12. Shannon, C.E.: A mathematical theory of communication. Bell Syst. Tech. J. **27** (1948). 55 p.
13. Bonev, B.I.: Feature selection based on information theory (2010). 200 p.
14. Feixas, M., Bardera, A., Rigau, J., Xu, Q., Sbert, M.: Information theory tools for image processing. Synthesis Lectures on Computer Graphics and Animation, vol. 6, no. 1, pp. 1–164 (2014)
15. Cover, T.M., Thomas, J.A.: Elements of Information Theory. Wiley, Hoboken (2006). 774 p.
16. Horé, A., Ziou, D.: Image quality metrics: PSNR vs. SSIM, pp. 2366–2369 (2010)
17. Deming, W.E., Morgan, S.L.: The Elements of Statistical Learning. Elsevier, Amsterdam (1993)
18. Abadi, M., et al.: TensorFlow: a system for large-scale machine learning. arXiv:1605.08695 Cs, May 2016
19. Krizhevsky, A.: Learning multiple layers of features from tiny images (2009). 60 p.
20. Russakovsky, O., et al.: ImageNet large scale visual recognition challenge. arXiv:1409.0575 Cs, September 2014
21. Szegedy, C., et al.: Going deeper with convolutions. arXiv:1409.4842 Cs, September 2014
22. Szegedy, C., Vanhoucke, V., Ioffe, S., Shlens, J., Wojna, Z.: Rethinking the inception architecture for computer vision. arXiv:1512.00567 Cs, December 2015
23. ImageNet Large Scale Visual Recognition Competition (ILSVRC). http://image-net.org/challenges/LSVRC/. Accessed 29 Apr 2017

24. He, K., Zhang, X., Ren, S., Sun, J.: Deep residual learning for image recognition. In: 2016 IEEE Conference on Computer Vision and Pattern Recognition (CVPR), Las Vegas, NV, USA, pp. 770–778 (2016)
25. Simonyan, K., Zisserman, A.: Very deep convolutional networks for large-scale image recognition. arXiv:14091556 Cs, September 2014
26. Howard, A.G., et al.: MobileNets: efficient convolutional neural networks for mobile vision applications. arXiv:170404861 Cs, April 2017
27. TensorFlow: TensorFlow. https://www.tensorflow.org/. Accessed 14 Mar 2019
28. Bishop, C.M.: Neural Networks for Pattern Recognition. Oxford University Press, New York (1995). 498 p.
29. Lang, K.J., Hinton, G.E.: Dimensionality reduction and prior knowledge in E-set recognition (1990). 8 p.

A Factorization Strategy for Tensor Robust PCA

Andong Wang[1], Zhong Jin[1,2(✉)], and Jingyu Yang[1,2]

[1] School of Computer Science and Engineering,
Nanjing University of Science and Technology, Nanjing 210094, China
zhongjin@njust.edu.cn

[2] Key Laboratory of Intelligent Perception and System for High-Dimensional Information of Ministry of Education, Nanjing University of Science and Technology, Nanjing 210094, China

Abstract. Many kinds of real-world data, e.g., color images, videos, etc., are represented by tensors and may often be corrupted by outliers. Tensor robust principal component analysis (TRPCA) servers as a tensorial modification of the fundamental principal component analysis (PCA) which performs well in the presence of outliers. The recently proposed TRPCA model [12] based on tubal nuclear norm (TNN) has attracted much attention due to its superiority in many applications. However, TNN is computationally expensive, limiting the application of TRPCA for large tensors. To address this issue, we first propose a new TRPCA model by adopting a factorization strategy within the framework of tensor singular value decomposition (t-SVD). An algorithm based on the non-convex augmented Lagrangian method (ALM) is developed with convergence guarantee. Effectiveness and efficiency of the proposed algorithm is demonstrated through extensive experiments on both synthetic and real datasets.

Keywords: Robust tensor principle component analysis · Tensor SVD · Non-convex ALM

1 Introduction

PCA is arguably the most broadly applied statistical approach for high-dimensional data analysis and dimension reduction. However, it regards each data instance as a vector, ignoring the rich intro-mode and inter-mode correlations in the emerging multi-way data (tensor data). One the other hand, it is sensitive to outliers which are ubiquitous in real applications. By manipulating the tensor instance in its original multi-way form and attempting to work well against outliers, tensor robust PCA [5,11] is a powerful extension of PCA which can overcome the above issues. TRPCA finds many applications

This work is partially supported by the National Natural Science Foundation of China [Grant Nos. 61872188, U1713208, 61602244, 61672287, 61702262, 61773215, 61703209].

S. Palaiahnakote et al. (Eds.): ACPR 2019, LNCS 12046, pp. 424–437, 2020.
https://doi.org/10.1007/978-3-030-41404-7_30

likes image/video restoration, video surveillance, face recognition, to name a few [5,11].

An idealized version of TRPCA aims to recover an underlying tensor $\mathcal{L}^*$ from measurements $\mathcal{M}$ corrupted by outliers represented by tensor $\mathcal{S}^*$, that is,

$$\mathcal{M} = \mathcal{L}^* + \mathcal{S}^*. \tag{1}$$

Obviously, the above decomposition is impossible without additional assumptions on the underlying tensor $\mathcal{L}^*$ and the outlier tensor $\mathcal{S}^*$. Thus, TRPCA further assumes $\mathcal{L}^*$ is "low-rank" and $\mathcal{S}^*$ sparse. Mathematically, TRPCA tries to solve a minimization problem as follows

$$\min_{\mathcal{L},\mathcal{S}} \quad \text{rank}(\mathcal{L}) + \lambda \|\mathcal{S}\|_0 \quad \text{s.t.} \quad \mathcal{L} + \mathcal{S} = \mathcal{M}, \tag{2}$$

where rank$(\cdot)$ denotes the "rank function" of a tensor, $\|\cdot\|_0$ is the tensor l_0-norm (used as a sparsity measure), and $\lambda > 0$ is a regularization parameter. Problem (2) is numerically very challenging, since both the tensor rank function and l_0-norm are neither continuous nor convex, even in their simplest matrix versions.

A mainstream approach for tackling the numerical hardness of Problem (2) is to respectively replace the rank function and l_0-norm with their convex surrogates conv-rank$(\cdot)$ and l_1-norm, leading to the following convex version of Problem (2)

$$\min_{\mathcal{L},\mathcal{S}} \quad \text{conv-rank}(\mathcal{L}) + \lambda \|\mathcal{S}\|_1 \quad \text{s.t.} \quad \mathcal{L} + \mathcal{S} = \mathcal{M}. \tag{3}$$

The l_1-norm $\|\cdot\|_1$ in Problem (3) is widely used as a convex envelop of the l_0-norm in compressive sensing and sparse representation to impose sparsity [3].

In the 2-way version of Problem (3) where $\mathcal{L}, \mathcal{S}$ and $\mathcal{Y}$ are matrices, tensor Robust PCA degenerates to the Robust PCA [1]. In RPCA, the matrix nuclear norm $\|\cdot\|_*$ [2] is often chosen as the convex surrogate of matrix rank. However, for general K-way ($K \geq 3$) tensors, one may have multiple choices of conv-rank$(\cdot)$, since a tensor has many definitions of rank function due to different extensions of the matrix SVD. The most direct tensor extension of matrix rank is the tensor CP rank [6] which is the smallest number of rank-one tensors that a tensor can be decomposed into. Nevertheless, both the CP rank and its corresponding version of nuclear norm are NP hard to compute [4,7]. Due to its computational tractability, the Tucker rank [15] defined as a vector of ranks of the unfolding matrices along each mode, is the most widely used tensor rank. Its corresponding nuclear norm (denoted by SNN in this paper) [10] is defined as the (weighted) sum of nuclear norms of the unfolding matrices along each mode, and has been used in TRPCA [5]. However, SNN is not a tight convex relaxation of sum of the Tucker rank [14], and it models the underlying tensor as simultaneously low rank along each mode, which may be too strong for some real data tensors.

Recently, the low tubal rank models have achieved better performances than low Tucker rank models in many low rank tensor recovery tasks, like tensor completion [17,18,23], tensor RPCA [11,23], sample outlier robust tensor PCA [24] and tensor low rank representation [19,20], etc. At the core of these models is the tubal nuclear norm (TNN), a version of tensor nuclear norm defined within the framework of t-SVD [9]. Using TNN as the low-rank regularization in Problem (3), the recently proposed TNN-based TRPCA model has shown better performances than traditional models [11,12,23]. The rationality behind the superior performance of TNN-based models lies in that TNN is the tight convex relaxation of the tensor average rank, and the low average rank assumption is weaker than the low Tucker rank and low CP rank assumption [12].

Despite its broad use, TNN is computationally expensive since it requires full matrix SVDs. The high computational complexity limits the application of TNN-based models to scale to emerging high-dimensional tensor data. By exploiting the orthogonal invariance of TNN, we come up with a factorization based model for TRPCA which can powerfully accelerate the original TNN-based TRPCA model. Extensive experiments show the superiority and efficiency of the proposed algorithm. The main contributions of this paper are as follows:

- A new model for TRPCA named TriFac is proposed in Model (11).
- An ALM algorithm (Algorithm 1) is designed to efficiently solve it.
- Convergence of the proposed algorithm is shown in Theorem 2.

The rest of the paper proceeds as follows. In Sect. 2, some preliminaries of t-SVD are introduced. The problem formulation and the algorithm are presented in Sect. 3. Experimental results are shown in Sect. 4. Proofs of the theorems and lemmas are in the supplementary material[1].

2 Notations and Preliminaries

Notations. The main notations and abbreviations are listed in Table 1 for convenience. For a 3-way tensor, a *tube* is a vector defined by fixing indices of the first two modes and varying the third one; A *slice* is a matrix defined by fixing all but two indices; $\text{fft}_3(\cdot)$ denotes the *fast discrete Fourier transformation (FFT)* along *the third mode* of a 3rd order tensor, i.e., the command $\text{fft}(\cdot, [], 3)$ in Matlab; similarly, $\text{ifft}_3(\cdot)$ is defined. Let $\lceil a \rceil$ denote the closest integer to $a \in \mathbb{R}$ that is not smaller than a, and $\lfloor a \rfloor$ denotes the closest integer to $a \in \mathbb{R}$ that is not larger than a. Let $\mathbf{1}(\cdot)$ denote the indicator function which equals 1 if the condition is true and 0 otherwise. The spectral norm $\|\cdot\|$ and nuclear norm $\|\cdot\|_*$ of a matrix are the maximum and the sum of the singular values, respectively.

Tensor SVD. Some preliminaries of tensor SVD will be introduced.

Definition 1 (T-product [22]**).** *Let $\mathcal{T}_1 \in \mathbb{R}^{d_1 \times d_2 \times d_3}$ and $\mathcal{T}_2 \in \mathbb{R}^{d_2 \times d_4 \times d_3}$. The t-product of $\mathcal{T}_1$ and $\mathcal{T}_2$ is a tensor $\mathcal{T}$ of size $d_1 \times d_4 \times d_3$:*

$$\mathcal{T} := \mathcal{T}_1 * \mathcal{T}_2, \tag{4}$$

whose $(i,j)_{th}$ tube is given by $\mathcal{T}(i,j,:) = \sum_{k=1}^{d_2} \mathcal{T}_1(i,k,:) \bullet \mathcal{T}_2(k,j,:)$, where $\bullet$ denotes the circular convolution between two fibers [9].

[1] The supplementary material is available at https://github.com/pingzaiwang/hitensor/blob/master/supp-ACPR2019-25.pdf.

Table 1. List of notations and abbreviations

Notations	Descriptions	Notations	Descriptions
$\boldsymbol{T}$	A matrix	$\mathcal{L}^*$	True low-rank tensor
$\mathcal{T}$	A tensor	$\mathcal{S}^*$	Outlier tensor
$\widetilde{\mathcal{T}}$	$\mathrm{fft}_3(\mathcal{T})$	$\Vert\mathcal{T}\Vert$	$\Vert\overline{\boldsymbol{T}}\Vert$
$\overline{\boldsymbol{T}}$ or $\overline{\mathcal{T}}$	Block-diagonal matrix of $\widetilde{\mathcal{T}}$	$\Vert\mathcal{T}\Vert_*$	$\Vert\overline{\boldsymbol{T}}\Vert_*/d_3$
$\mathcal{T}_{ijk}$	$(i,j,k)_{th}$ entry of $\mathcal{T}$	$\Vert\mathcal{T}\Vert_{\mathrm{F}}$	$\sqrt{\sum_{ijk}\mathcal{T}_{ijk}^2}$
$\mathcal{T}(i,j,k)$	$\mathcal{T}_{ijk}$	$\Vert\mathcal{T}\Vert_1$	$\sum_{ijk}\lvert\mathcal{T}_{ijk}\rvert$
$\mathcal{T}(i,j,:)$	$(i,j)_{th}$ tube of $\mathcal{T}$	$\Vert\mathcal{T}\Vert_\infty$	$\max_{ijk}\lvert\mathcal{T}_{ijk}\rvert$
$\mathcal{T}(:,:,k)$	k_{th} frontal slice of $\mathcal{T}$	$\Vert\mathcal{T}\Vert_0$	$\sum_{ijk}\mathbf{1}(\mathcal{T}_{ijk}\neq 0)$
$r_{\mathrm{t}}(\cdot)$	Tensor tubal rank	$\langle\mathcal{A},\mathcal{B}\rangle$	$\sum_{ijk}\mathcal{A}_{ijk}\mathcal{B}_{ijk}$

Definition 2 (Tensor transpose [22]**).** *Let $\mathcal{T}$ be a tensor of size $d_1 \times d_2 \times d_3$, then $\mathcal{T}^\top$ is the $d_2 \times d_1 \times d_3$ tensor obtained by transposing each of the frontal slices and then reversing the order of transposed frontal slices 2 through d_3.*

Definition 3 (Identity tensor [22]**).** *The identity tensor $\mathcal{I} \in \mathbb{R}^{d_1\times d_1\times d_3}$ is a tensor whose first frontal slice is the $d_1 \times d_1$ identity matrix and all other frontal slices are zero.*

Definition 4 (F-diagonal tensor [22]**).** *A tensor is called f-diagonal if each frontal slice of the tensor is a diagonal matrix.*

Definition 5 (Orthogonal tensor [22]**).** *A tensor $\mathcal{Q} \in \mathbb{R}^{d_1\times d_1\times d_3}$ is orthogonal if $\mathcal{Q}^\top * \mathcal{Q} = \mathcal{Q} * \mathcal{Q}^\top = \mathcal{I}$.*

Based on the above concepts, the tensor singular value decomposition (t-SVD) can be defined as follows.

Definition 6 (T-SVD, Tensor tubal-rank [22]**).** *For any $\mathcal{T} \in \mathbb{R}^{d_1\times d_2\times d_3}$, the tensor singular value decomposition (t-SVD) of $\mathcal{T}$ is given as follows*

$$\mathcal{T} = \mathcal{U} * \underline{\boldsymbol{\Lambda}} * \mathcal{V}^\top, \tag{5}$$

where $\mathcal{U} \in \mathbb{R}^{d_1\times d_1\times d_3}$, $\underline{\boldsymbol{\Lambda}} \in \mathbb{R}^{d_1\times d_2\times d_3}$, $\mathcal{V} \in \mathbb{R}^{d_2\times d_2\times d_3}$, $\mathcal{U}$ and $\mathcal{V}$ are orthogonal tensors, $\underline{\boldsymbol{\Lambda}}$ is a rectangular f-diagonal tensor.

The tensor tubal rank of $\mathcal{T}$ is defined to be the number of non-zero tubes of $\underline{\boldsymbol{\Lambda}}$ in the t-SVD factorization, i.e.,

$$r_{\mathrm{t}}(\mathcal{T}) := \sum_i \mathbf{1}(\underline{\boldsymbol{\Lambda}}(i,i,:) \neq \mathbf{0}). \tag{6}$$

The definitions of TNN and tensor spectral norm will be given. The former has been applied as a convex relaxation of the tensor tubal rank in [11,23,24].

Definition 7 (Tubal nuclear norm, tensor spectral norm [12,22]**).** *For any $\mathcal{T} \in \mathbb{R}^{d_1\times d_2\times d_3}$, let $\overline{\boldsymbol{T}}$ denote the block-diagonal matrix of the tensor $\widetilde{\mathcal{T}} := \mathrm{fft}_3(\mathcal{T})$, i.e.,*

$$\overline{\mathcal{T}} := \begin{bmatrix} \widetilde{\mathcal{T}}(:,:,1) & & \\ & \ddots & \\ & & \widetilde{\mathcal{T}}(:,:,d_3) \end{bmatrix} \in \mathbb{C}^{d_1 d_3 \times d_2 d_3}.$$

The tubal nuclear norm $\|\mathcal{T}\|_\star$ *and tensor spectral norm* $\|\mathcal{T}\|$ *of* $\mathcal{T}$ *are respectively defined as the rescaled matrix nuclear norm and the (non-rescaled) matrix spectral norm of* $\overline{\mathcal{T}}$, *i.e.,*

$$\|\mathcal{T}\|_\star := \frac{\|\overline{\mathcal{T}}\|_*}{d_3}, \quad \text{and} \quad \|\mathcal{T}\| := \|\overline{\mathcal{T}}\|. \tag{7}$$

It has been shown in [12] that TNN is the dual norm of tensor spectral norm.

3 TriFac for Tensor Robust PCA

3.1 Model Formulation

TNN-Based TRPCA. The recently proposed TNN-based TRPCA model[2] [12] adopts TNN as a low rank item in Problem 3, and is formulated as follows

$$\min_{\mathcal{L},\mathcal{S}} \ \|\mathcal{L}\|_\star + \lambda\|\mathcal{S}\|_1 \quad \text{s.t.} \quad \mathcal{L} + \mathcal{S} = \mathcal{M}. \tag{8}$$

In [11,12], it is proved that when the underlying tensor $\mathcal{L}^*$ satisfy the tensor incoherent conditions, by solving Problem (8), one can exactly recover the underlying tensor $\mathcal{L}^*$ and $\mathcal{S}^*$ with high probability with parameter $\lambda = 1/\sqrt{\max\{d_1, d_2\}d_3}$.

To solve the TNN-based TRPCA in Eq. (8), an algorithm based on the alternating directions methods of multipliers (ADMM) is proposed [11]. In each iteration, it computes a proximity operator of TNN, which requires FFT/IFFT, and d_3 full SVDs of d_1-by-d_2 matrices when the observed tensor $\mathcal{M}$ is in $\mathbb{R}^{d_1 \times d_2 \times d_3}$. The one-iteration computation complexity of the ADMM-based algorithm is

$$O\big(d_1 d_2 d_3(\log d_3 + \min\{d_1, d_2\})\big), \tag{9}$$

which is very expensive for large tensors.

Proposed TriFac. To reduce the cost of computing TNN in Problem (8), we propose the following lemma, indicating that TNN is orthogonal invariant.

Lemma 1 (Orthogonal invariance of TNN). *Given a tensor* $\mathcal{X} \in \mathbb{R}^{r \times r \times d_3}$, *let* $\mathcal{P} \in \mathbb{R}^{d_1 \times r \times d_3}$ *and* $\mathcal{Q} \in \mathbb{R}^{d_2 \times r \times d_3}$ *be two semi-orthogonal tensors, i.e.,* $\mathcal{P}^\top * \mathcal{P} = \mathcal{I} \in \mathbb{R}^{r \times r \times d_3}$ *and* $\mathcal{Q}^\top * \mathcal{Q} = \mathcal{I} \in \mathbb{R}^{r \times r \times d_3}$, *and* $r \leq \min\{d_1, d_2\}$. *Then, we have the following relationship:* $\|\mathcal{P} * \mathcal{X} * \mathcal{Q}^\top\|_\star = \|\mathcal{X}\|_\star$.

Equipped with Lemma 1, we decompose the low rank component in Problem 8 as follows:

[2] Following [12], when saying "TRPCA", we refer to the TNN-based TRPCA (8).

$$\mathcal{L} = \mathcal{P} * \mathcal{C} * \mathcal{Q}^\top, \quad \text{s.t. } \mathcal{P}^\top * \mathcal{P} = \mathcal{I}_r, \ \mathcal{Q}^\top * \mathcal{Q} = \mathcal{I}_r, \tag{10}$$

where $\mathcal{I}_r \in \mathbb{R}^{r \times r \times d_3}$ is an identity tensor. Further, we propose the following model based on triple factorization (TriFac) for tensor robust PCA

$$\begin{aligned} &\min_{\mathcal{P},\mathcal{Q},\mathcal{C},\mathcal{S}} \|\mathcal{C}\|_\star + \lambda \|\mathcal{S}\|_1 \\ &\text{s.t.} \quad \mathcal{P} * \mathcal{C} * \mathcal{Q}^\top + \mathcal{S} = \mathcal{M}, \ \mathcal{P}^\top * \mathcal{P} = \mathcal{I}_r, \ \mathcal{Q}^\top * \mathcal{Q} = \mathcal{I}_r, \end{aligned} \tag{11}$$

where $\mathcal{I}_r := \mathcal{I} \in \mathbb{R}^{r \times r \times d_3}$, r is an upper estimation of tubal rank of the underlying tensor $r^* = r_t(\mathcal{L}^*)$ and we set $\lambda = 1/\sqrt{\max\{d_1, d_2\} d_3}$ as suggested by [12].

Different from Problem 8, the proposed TriFac is a non-convex model which may have many local minima. We establish a connection between the proposed model TriFac in Problem (11) with the TNN-based TRPCA model (8) in the following theorem.

Theorem 1 (Connection between TriFac and TRPCA). *Let $(\mathcal{P}_*, \mathcal{C}_*, \mathcal{Q}_*, \mathcal{S}_*)$ be a global optimal solution to TriFac in Problem (11). And let $(\mathcal{L}^\star, \mathcal{S}^\star)$ be the solution to TRPCA in Problem (8), and $r_t(\mathcal{L}^\star) \le r$, where r is the initialized tubal rank. Then $(\mathcal{P}_* * \mathcal{C}_* * \mathcal{Q}_*^\top, \mathcal{S}_*)$ is also the optimal solution to Problem (8).*

Theorem 1 asserts that the global optimal point of the (non-convex) TriFac coincides with solution of the (convex) TNN-based TRPCA which is guaranteed to exactly recover the underlying tensor $\mathcal{L}^*$ under certain conditions. This phenomenon means that the accuracy of the proposed model cannot exceed TPRCA, which will be shown numerically in the experiment section.

3.2 Optimization Algorithm

The partial augmented Lagrangian of Problem (11) is as follows:

$$\begin{aligned} &L_\mu(\mathcal{P}, \mathcal{C}, \mathcal{Q}, \mathcal{S}, \mathcal{Y}) \\ &= \|\mathcal{C}\|_\star + \lambda \|\mathcal{S}\|_1 + \langle \mathcal{Y}, \mathcal{P} * \mathcal{C} * \mathcal{Q}^\top + \mathcal{S} - \mathcal{M} \rangle + \frac{\mu}{2} \|\mathcal{P} * \mathcal{C} * \mathcal{Q}^\top + \mathcal{S} - \mathcal{M}\|_F^2, \\ &\text{s.t.} \quad \mathcal{P}^\top * \mathcal{P} = \mathcal{I}_r, \ \mathcal{Q}^\top * \mathcal{Q} = \mathcal{I}_r, \end{aligned} \tag{12}$$

where $\mu > 0$ is a penalty parameter, and $\mathcal{Y} \in \mathbb{R}^{d_1 \times d_2 \times d_3}$ is the Lagrangian multiplier. Based on the Lagrangian in Eq. (12), we update each variable by fixing the others.

The $\mathcal{P}$-subproblem. We update $\mathcal{P}$ by fixing other variables and minimize $L_\mu(\cdot)$:

$$\mathcal{P}_{t+1} = \operatorname*{argmin}_{\mathcal{P}^\top * \mathcal{P} = \mathcal{I}_r} L_{\mu_t}(\mathcal{P}, \mathcal{C}_t, \mathcal{Q}_t, \mathcal{S}_t, \mathcal{Y}_t) = \operatorname*{argmin}_{\mathcal{P}^\top * \mathcal{P} = \mathcal{I}_r} \frac{\mu_t}{2} \|\mathcal{P} * \mathcal{A} - \mathcal{B}\|_F^2 \tag{13}$$

where $\mathcal{A} = \mathcal{C}_t * \mathcal{Q}_t^\top$ and $\mathcal{B} = \mathcal{M} - \mathcal{S}_t - \mathcal{Y}_t/\mu_t$. We need the following lemma to solve Problem (13).

Lemma 2. *Given any tensors $\mathcal{A} \in \mathbb{R}^{r \times d_2 \times d_3}, \mathcal{B} \in \mathbb{R}^{d_1 \times d_2 \times d_3}$, suppose tensor $\mathcal{B} * \mathcal{A}^\top$ has t-SVD $\mathcal{B} * \mathcal{A}^\top = \mathcal{U} * \underline{\boldsymbol{\Lambda}} * \mathcal{V}^\top$, where $\mathcal{U} \in \mathbb{R}^{d_1 \times r \times d_3}$ and $\mathcal{V} \in \mathbb{R}^{r \times r \times d_3}$. Then, the problem*

$$\min_{\mathcal{P}^\top * \mathcal{P} = \mathcal{I}_r} \|\mathcal{P} * \mathcal{A} - \mathcal{B}\|_F^2 \tag{14}$$

has a closed-form solution as

$$\mathcal{P} = \mathfrak{P}(\mathcal{B} * \mathcal{A}^\top) := \mathcal{U} * \mathcal{V}^\top. \tag{15}$$

The $\mathcal{Q}$-subproblem. By fixing other variables, we update $\mathcal{Q}$ as follows

$$\begin{aligned} \mathcal{Q}_{t+1} &= \operatorname*{argmin}_{\mathcal{Q}^\top * \mathcal{Q} = \mathcal{I}_r} L_{\mu_t}(\mathcal{P}_{t+1}, \mathcal{C}_t, \mathcal{Q}, \mathcal{S}_t, \mathcal{Y}_t) \\ &= \operatorname*{argmin}_{\mathcal{Q}^\top * \mathcal{Q} = \mathcal{I}_r} \frac{\mu_t}{2} \|\mathcal{A}' * \mathcal{Q}^\top - \mathcal{B}\|_{\mathrm{F}}^2 \\ &= \operatorname*{argmin}_{\mathcal{Q}^\top * \mathcal{Q} = \mathcal{I}_r} \frac{\mu_t}{2} \|(\mathcal{Q} * \mathcal{A}'^\top) - \mathcal{B}^\top\|_{\mathrm{F}}^2 \\ &= (\mathfrak{P}(\mathcal{B}^\top * \mathcal{A}'))^\top, \end{aligned} \tag{16}$$

where $\mathcal{A}' = \mathcal{P}_{t+1} * \mathcal{C}_t$ and $\mathcal{B} = \mathcal{M} - \mathcal{S}_t - \mathcal{Y}_t/\mu_t$, and $\mathfrak{P}(\cdot)$ is defined in Lemma 2. The last equality holds because of Eq. (15) in Lemma 2.

The $\mathcal{C}$-subproblem. We update $\mathcal{C}$ as follows

$$\begin{aligned} \mathcal{C}_{t+1} &= \operatorname*{argmin}_{\mathcal{C}} L_{\mu_t}(\mathcal{P}_{t+1}, \mathcal{C}, \mathcal{Q}_{t+1}, \mathcal{S}_t, \mathcal{Y}_t) \\ &= \operatorname*{argmin}_{\mathcal{C}} \|\mathcal{C}\|_\star + \frac{\mu_t}{2} \|\mathcal{P}_{t+1} * \mathcal{C} * \mathcal{Q}_t^\top + \mathcal{S}_t - \mathcal{M} + \mathcal{Y}/\mu_t\|_{\mathrm{F}}^2 \\ &= \operatorname*{argmin}_{\mathcal{C}} \|\mathcal{C}\|_\star + \frac{\mu_t}{2} \|\mathcal{C} - \mathcal{P}_{t+1}{}^\top * (\mathcal{M} - \mathcal{S}_t - \mathcal{Y}/\mu_t) * \mathcal{Q}_{t+1}\|_{\mathrm{F}}^2 \\ &= \mathfrak{S}_{1/\mu_t}(\mathcal{P}_{t+1}{}^\top * (\mathcal{M} - \mathcal{S}_t - \mathcal{Y}/\mu_t) * \mathcal{Q}_{t+1}) \end{aligned} \tag{17}$$

where $\mathfrak{S}_\tau(\cdot)$ is the proximity operator of TNN [16]. In [16], a closed-form expression of $\mathfrak{S}_\tau(\cdot)$ is given as follows:

Lemma 3 (Proximity operator of TNN [16]). *For any 3D tensor $\mathcal{A} \in \mathbb{R}^{d_1 \times d_2 \times d_3}$ with reduced t-SVD $\mathcal{A} = \mathcal{U} * \underline{\boldsymbol{\Lambda}} * \mathcal{V}^\top$, where $\mathcal{U} \in \mathbb{R}^{d_1 \times r \times d_3}$ and $\mathcal{V} \in \mathbb{R}^{d_2 \times r \times d_3}$ are orthogonal tensors and $\underline{\boldsymbol{\Lambda}} \in \mathbb{R}^{r \times r \times d_3}$ is the f-diagonal tensor of singular tubes, the proximity operator $\mathfrak{S}_\tau(\mathcal{A})$ at $\mathcal{A}$ can be computed by:*

$$\mathfrak{S}_\tau(\mathcal{A}) := \operatorname*{argmin}_{\mathcal{X}} \tau\|\mathcal{X}\|_\star + \tfrac{1}{2}\|\mathcal{X} - \mathcal{A}\|_F^2 = \mathcal{U} * \mathrm{ifft}_3(\max(\mathrm{fft}_3(\underline{\boldsymbol{\Lambda}}) - \tau, 0)) * \mathcal{V}^\top.$$

The $\mathcal{S}$-subproblem. We update $\mathcal{S}$ as follows

$$\begin{aligned} \mathcal{S}_{t+1} &= \operatorname*{argmin}_{\mathcal{S}} L_{\mu_t}(\mathcal{P}_{t+1}, \mathcal{C}_{t+1}, \mathcal{Q}_{t+1}, \mathcal{S}, \mathcal{Y}_t) \\ &= \operatorname*{argmin}_{\mathcal{S}} \lambda\|\mathcal{S}\|_1 + \frac{\rho}{2}\|\mathcal{P}_{t+1} * \mathcal{C}_{t+1} * \mathcal{Q}_{t+1}^\top + \mathcal{S} - \mathcal{M} + \frac{\mathcal{Y}_t}{\mu_t}\|_{\mathrm{F}} \\ &= \mathfrak{T}_{\lambda/\rho}(\mathcal{M} - \mathcal{P}_{t+1} * \mathcal{C}_{t+1} * \mathcal{Q}_{t+1}^\top - \frac{\mathcal{Y}_t}{\mu_t}) \end{aligned} \tag{18}$$

Algorithm 1. TriFac implemented by inexact non-convex ALM

Input: Observation $\mathcal{M} \in \mathbb{R}^{d_1 \times d_2 \times d_3}$, initialized rank r, and parameter λ.

1: Initialize $t = 0$, $\rho = 1.1$, $\varepsilon \leq 1e-7$, $\mu_0 = \|\mathcal{M}\|^{-1}$, $\mathcal{P}_0 = \mathbf{0} \in \mathbb{R}^{d_1 \times r \times d_3}$, $\mathcal{C}_0 = \mathbf{0} \in \mathbb{R}^{r \times r \times d_3}$, $\mathcal{Q}_0 = \mathbf{0} \in \mathbb{R}^{r \times d_2 \times d_3}$, $\mathcal{S}_0 = \mathbf{0} \in \mathbb{R}^{d_1 \times d_2 \times d_3}$, $\mathcal{Y}_0 = \mathcal{Y}_0^1 = \mathcal{Y}_0^2 = \mathcal{Y}_0^3 = \mathbf{0} \in \mathbb{R}^{d_1 \times d_2 \times d_3}$.

2: **while** not converged **do**

3: Update $\mathcal{P}_{t+1}$ by Eq. (13);

4: Update $\mathcal{Q}_{t+1}$ by Eq. (16);

5: Update $\mathcal{C}_{t+1}$ by Eq. (17);

6: Update $\mathcal{S}_{t+1}$ by Eq. (18);

7: Update the following variables $\mathcal{Y}_{t+1}, \mathcal{Y}_{t+1}^1, \mathcal{Y}_{t+1}^2, \mathcal{Y}_{t+1}^3$:

$$\begin{aligned} \mathcal{Y}_{t+1} &= \mathcal{Y}_t + \mu_t(\mathcal{P}_{t+1} * \mathcal{C}_{t+1} * \mathcal{Q}_{t+1}^\top + \mathcal{S}_{t+1} - \mathcal{M}); \quad (19)\\ \mathcal{Y}_{t+1}^1 &= \mathcal{Y}_t + \mu_t(\mathcal{P}_{t+1} * \mathcal{C}_{t+1} * \mathcal{Q}_{t+1}^\top + \mathcal{S}_t - \mathcal{M}); \\ \mathcal{Y}_{t+1}^2 &= \mathcal{Y}_t + \mu_t(\mathcal{P}_{t+1} * \mathcal{C}_t * \mathcal{Q}_{t+1}^\top + \mathcal{S}_t - \mathcal{M}); \\ \mathcal{Y}_{t+1}^3 &= \mathcal{Y}_t + \mu_t(\mathcal{P}_{t+1} * \mathcal{C}_t * {\mathcal{Q}_t}^\top + \mathcal{S}_t - \mathcal{M}). \end{aligned}$$

8: Update the penalty parameter $\mu_{t+1} = \rho\mu_t$;

9: Check the convergence conditions $\mu_t^{-1}\|\mathcal{Y}_{t+1} - \mathcal{Y}_t\|_\infty \leq \varepsilon$, $\mu_t^{-1}\|\mathcal{Y}_{t+1} - \mathcal{Y}_{t+1}^1\|_\infty \leq \varepsilon$, $\mu_t^{-1}\|\mathcal{Y}_{t+1}^1 - \mathcal{Y}_{t+1}^2\|_\infty \leq \varepsilon$.

10: $t = t + 1$.

11: **end while**

where $\mathfrak{T}_\tau(\cdot)$ is the proximity operator of tensor l_1-norm given as follows:

$$\mathfrak{T}_\tau(\mathcal{A}) := \operatorname*{argmin}_{\mathcal{X}} \tau\|\mathcal{X}\|_1 + \frac{1}{2}\|\mathcal{X} - \mathcal{A}\|_{\mathrm{F}}^2 = \operatorname{sign}(\mathcal{A}) \circledast \max\{(|\mathcal{A}| - \tau, 0\},$$

where $\circledast$ denotes the element-wise tensor product.

Complexity Analysis. In each iteration, the update of $\mathcal{P}$ involves computing FFT, IFFT and d_3 SVDs of $r \times d_2$ matrices, having complexity of order $O\big(rd_2d_3 \log d_3 + r^2 d_2 d_3\big)$. Similarly, the update of $\mathcal{Q}$ has complexity of order $O\big(rd_1d_3 \log d_3 + r^2 d_1 d_3\big)$. Updating $\mathcal{C}$ involves complexity of order $O\big(r^2 d_3 (r + \log d_3)\big)$. Updating $\mathcal{S}$ costs $O\big(d_1 d_2 d_3\big)$. So one iteration cost of Algorithm 1 is

$$O\left(d_3\big(d_1 d_2 \log d_3 + r^2(r + d_1 + d_2 + \log d_3) + r(d_1 + d_2) \log d_3\big)\right).$$

When $r \ll \min\{d_1, d_2\}$, the above cost is significantly lower than the one-iteration cost of ADMM-based TRPCA [12] in Eq. (9). Consider an extreme case in high dimensional settings where $r_{\mathrm{t}}(\mathcal{L}^*) = O(1)$, i.e., the tubal rank of the underlying tensor $\mathcal{L}^*$ scales like a small constant. By choosing the initialized rank $r = 2r_{\mathrm{t}}(\mathcal{L}^*) = O(1)$, the one-iteration cost of Algorithm 1 scales like

$$O(d_1 d_2 d_3 \log d_3), \quad (20)$$

which is much cheaper than $O(d_1 d_2 d_3 \min\{d_1, d_2\})$ of ADMM-based algorithm in high dimensional settings.

Convergence Analysis. The following theorem shows that Algorithm 1 is convergent.

Theorem 2. *Letting $(\mathcal{P}_t, \mathcal{C}_t, \mathcal{Q}_t, \mathcal{S}_t)$ be any sequence generated by Algorithm 1, the following statements hold*

(I) The sequences $(\mathcal{C}_t, \mathcal{P}_t * \mathcal{C}_t * \mathcal{Q}_t^\top, \mathcal{S}_t)$ are Cauchy sequences respectively.
(II) $(\mathcal{P}_t, \mathcal{C}_t, \mathcal{Q}_t, \mathcal{S}_t)$ is a feasible solution to Problem (11) in a sense that

$$\lim_{t \to \infty} \|\mathcal{P}_t * \mathcal{C}_t * \mathcal{Q}_t^\top + \mathcal{S}_t - \mathcal{M}\|_\infty \leq \varepsilon. \tag{21}$$

4 Experiments

In this section, we experiment on both synthetic and real datasets to verify the effectiveness and the efficiency of the proposed algorithm. All codes are written in Matlab and all experiments are performed in Windows 10 based on Intel(R) Core(TM) i7-8565U 1.80-1.99 GHz CPU with 8G RAM.

4.1 Synthetic Data Experiments

In this subsection, we compare Algorithm 1 (TriFac) with the TNN-based TRPCA [11] in both accuracy and speed on synthetic datasets. Given tensor size $d_1 \times d_2 \times d_3$ and tubal rank $r^* \ll \min\{d_1, d_2\}$, we first generate a tensor $\mathcal{L}_0 \in \mathbb{R}^{d_1 \times d_2 \times d_3}$ by $\mathcal{L}_0 = \mathcal{A} * \mathcal{B}$, where the elements of tensors $\mathcal{A} \in \mathbb{R}^{d_1 \times r^* \times d_3}$ and $\mathcal{B} \in \mathbb{R}^{r^* \times d_2 \times d_3}$ are sampled from independent and identically distributed (*i.i.d.*) standard Gaussian distribution. We then form $\mathcal{L}^*$ by $\mathcal{L}^* = \sqrt{d_1 d_2 d_3}\mathcal{L}_0 / \|\mathcal{L}_0\|_\mathrm{F}$. Next, the support of $\mathcal{S}^*$ is uniformly sampled at random. For any $(i, j, k) \in \mathrm{supp}(\mathcal{S}^*)$, we set $\mathcal{S}^*_{ijk} = \mathcal{B}_{ijk}$, where $\mathcal{B}$ is a tensor with independent Bernoulli ± 1 entries. Finally, we form the observation tensor $\mathcal{M} = \mathcal{L}^* + \mathcal{S}^*$. For an estimation $\hat{\mathcal{L}}$ of the underlying tensor $\mathcal{L}^*$, the relative squared error (RSE) is used to evaluate its quality [11].

Effectiveness and Efficiency of TriFac
We first show that TriFac can exactly recover the underlying tensor $\mathcal{L}^*$ from corruptions faster than TRPCA. We first test the recovery performance of different tensor sizes by setting $d_1 = d_2 \in \{100, 160, 200\}$ and $d_3 = 30$, with $(r_\mathrm{t}(\mathcal{L}^*), \|\mathcal{S}^*\|_0) = (0.05d, 0.05d^2 d_3)$. Then, a more difficult setting $(r_\mathrm{t}(\mathcal{L}^*), \|\mathcal{S}^*\|_0) = (0.15d, 0.1d^2 d_3)$ is tested. The results are shown in Table 2. It can be seen that TriFac can perform as well as TRPCA in the sense that both of them can exactly recover the underlying tensor. However, TriFac is much faster than TRPCA.

To further show the efficiency of the proposed TriFac, we consider a special case where the size of the underlying tensor $\mathcal{L}^*$ increases while the tubal rank is fixed as a constant. Specifically, we fix $r_\mathrm{t}(\mathcal{L}^*) = 5$, and vary $d \in \{100, 150, \cdots, 500\}$

Table 2. Comparison with TRPCA in both accuracy and speed for different tensor sizes when the outliers follow *i.i.d.* Bernoulli distribution.

Outliers from Ber(1, −1), observation tensor $\mathcal{M} \in \mathbb{R}^{d\times d\times d_3}$, $d_3 = 30$ $r_t(\mathcal{L}^*) = 0.05d$, $\|\mathcal{S}^*\|_1 = 0.05d^2d_3$, $r = \max\{\lfloor 2r_t(\mathcal{L}^*)\rfloor, 15\}$							
d	$r_t(\mathcal{L}^*)$	$\|\mathcal{S}^*\|_0$	Algorithm	$r_t(\hat{\mathcal{L}})$	$\frac{\|\hat{\mathcal{L}}-\mathcal{L}^*\|_F}{\|\mathcal{L}^*\|_F}$	$\frac{\|\hat{\mathcal{S}}-\mathcal{S}^*\|_F}{\|\mathcal{S}^*\|_F}$	Time
100	5	1.5e4	TRPCA	5	8.39e−9	3.75e−8	20.45
			TriFac	5	1.10e−8	2.44e−8	**2.37**
160	8	3.84e4	TRPCA	8	8.06e−9	3.58e−8	53.88
			TriFac	8	1.26e−8	2.82e−8	**6.65**
200	10	6e4	TRPCA	10	7.97e−9	3.56e−8	103.14
			TriFac	10	1.81e−8	3.99e−8	**9.16**
Outliers from Ber(1, −1), observation tensor $\mathcal{M} \in \mathbb{R}^{d\times d\times d_3}$, $d_3 = 30$ $r_t(\mathcal{L}^*) = 0.15d$, $\|\mathcal{S}^*\|_1 = 0.1d^2d_3$, $r = \lfloor 1.5r_t(\mathcal{L}^*)\rfloor$							
d	$r_t(\mathcal{L}^*)$	$\|\mathcal{S}^*\|_0$	Algorithm	$r_t(\hat{\mathcal{L}})$	$\frac{\|\hat{\mathcal{L}}-\mathcal{L}^*\|_F}{\|\mathcal{L}^*\|_F}$	$\frac{\|\hat{\mathcal{S}}-\mathcal{S}^*\|_F}{\|\mathcal{S}^*\|_F}$	Time
100	15	3e4	TRPCA	15	1.08e−7	7.28e−8	23.46
			TriFac	15	9.56e−8	4.87e−8	**7.16**
160	24	7.68e4	TRPCA	24	1.06e−7	6.85e−8	63.64
			TriFac	24	6.12e−8	4.97e−8	**21.86**
200	30	1.2e5	TRPCA	30	1.02e−7	6.30e−8	106.14
			TriFac	30	1.21e−8	6.01e−10	**34.57**

with $d_3 = 20$. We set the parameter of initialized rank r of TriFac in Algorithm 1 by $r = 30$. We test each setting 10 times and compute the averaged time. In all the runs, both TRPCA and TriFac can recover thc underling tensor with RSE smaller than 1e−6. The plot of averaged time versus the tensor size (shown in d) is given in Fig. 1. We can see that the time cost of TRPCA scales super-linearly with respect to d, whereas the proposed TriFac has approximately linear scaling.

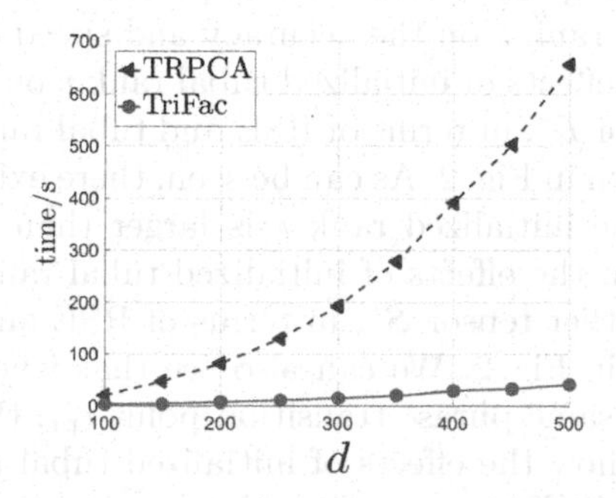

Fig. 1. Computation time of TRPCA [12] and the proposed TriFac versus $d \in \{100, 150, \cdots, 500\}$ with $d_3 = 20$, when the tubal rank of the underlying tensor is 5. The RSEs of TNN and TriFac in all the setting are smaller than 1e−6.

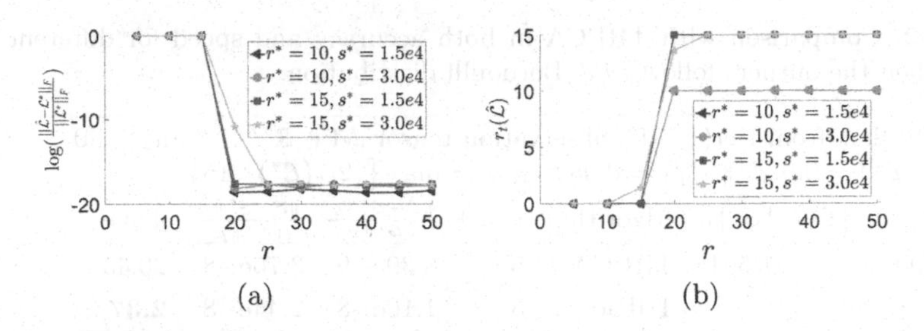

Fig. 2. Effects of initialized tubal rank r in Algorithm 1 on the recovery performance of the underlying tensor $\mathcal{L}^* \in \mathbb{R}^{100\times100\times30}$. (a): RSE of $\hat{\mathcal{L}}$ versus r in log scale; (b): tubal rank of $\hat{\mathcal{L}}$ versus r.

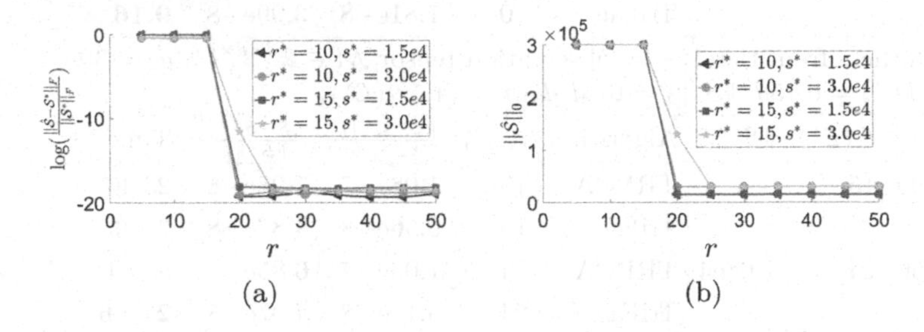

Fig. 3. Effects of initialized tubal rank r in Algorithm 1 on the estimation performance of the outlier tensor $\mathcal{S}^* \in \mathbb{R}^{100\times100\times30}$. (a): RSE of $\hat{\mathcal{S}}$ in log scale versus r; (b): l_0-norm of $\hat{\mathcal{S}}$ versus r.

Effects of the Initialized Tubal Rank r. The performance of TriFac heavily relies on the choice of initialized tubal rank r in Model (11). Here, we explore the effects of initialized tubal rank on the accuracy and speed of TriFac. Specifically, we consider tensors of size $100 \times 100 \times 30$ with four different settings of tubal rank $r^* = r_t(\mathcal{L}^*)$ and sparsity $s^* = \|\mathcal{S}^*\|_0$ as $(r^*, s^*) \in \{(10, 1.5e4), (10, 3e4), (15, 1.5e4), (10, 3e4)\}$, where the elements outliers follow *i.i.d.* $\mathcal{N}(0, 1)$. By varying the initialized $r \in \{5, 10, \cdots, 50\}$, we test the effects of the initialized tubal rank r on the accuracy and speed of TriFac.

We first report the effects of initialized tubal rank r on the recovery accuracy of the underlying tensor $\mathcal{L}^*$, in terms of RSE and tubal rank of the final solution $\hat{\mathcal{L}}$. The results are shown in Fig. 2. As can be seen, there exists a phrase transition point r_{pt} that once the initialized rank r is larger than it, the RSE of $\hat{\mathcal{L}}$ will decrease rapidly. Then, the effects of initialized tubal rank r on the estimation performance of the outlier tensor $\mathcal{S}^*$, in terms of RSE and l_0-norm of the final solution $\hat{\mathcal{S}}$ are shown in Fig. 2. We can also see that when the initialized rank r gets larger than the same phrase transition point r_{pt}, the RSE of $\hat{\mathcal{S}}$ will soon vanishes. Finally, we show the effects of initialized tubal rank r on the running time of TriFac in Fig. 4. We can see that the running time will increase, if the initialized rank r gets larger, the underlying tensor gets more complex (i.e.,

r^* gets greater), or the corruption gets heavier (i.e., s^* gets larger). That is consistent with our intuition (Fig. 3).

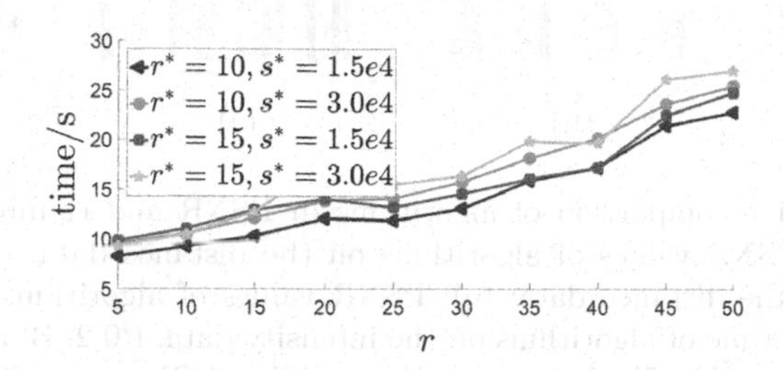

Fig. 4. Effects of initialized tubal rank r on the running time of TriFac for problem size $100 \times 100 \times 30$.

4.2 Real Data Experiments

In this section, the efficiency of the proposed TriFac compared with TRPCA [12] is evaluated on real-world datasets. Specifically, we carry out tensor restoration experiments on point cloud data and brain MRI data. For an estimation $\hat{\mathcal{L}}$ of the underlying tensor $\mathcal{L}^*$, the peak signal-to-noise ratio (PSNR) [11] is applied to evaluate the quality of $\hat{\mathcal{L}}$.

Point Cloud Data. We conduct experiments on a point cloud data set acquired by a vehicle-mounted Velodyne HDL-64E LiDAR[3] [13]. We extract the first 32 frames, transform and upsample the data to form two tensors in $\mathbb{R}^{512 \times 800 \times 32}$ representing the distance data and the intensity data, respectively. Given a data tensor, we uniformly choose its indices with probability $\rho_s \in \{0.2, 0.4\}$. We then corrupt the chosen positions with element-wise outliers from *i.i.d.* symmetric Bernoulli Ber$(-1, +1)$ or $\mathcal{N}(0, 1)$. The proposed algorithm is also compared with SNN [8] and RPCA [1]. RPCA works on each frontal slice individually. The parameters of RPCA is set by $\lambda = 1/\sqrt{\max\{d_1, d_2\}}$ [1]. The weight parameters $\boldsymbol{\lambda}$ of SNN are chosen by $\lambda_k = \sqrt{\max\{d_k, \prod_{k' \neq k} d_{k'}\}}/3$. We set the initialized tubal rank $r = 196$ in Algorithm 1.

We report the PSNR values and running time of each algorithm on the distance and intensity data in Fig. 5. It can be seen that TNN-based TRPCA has the highest PSNR values in all the settings, which is consistent with the results of tensor completion on this data that TNN outperforms SNN [17]. The proposed TriFac algorithm performs slightly worse than TNN, but it has the lowest running time. As is shown in Theorem 1, the proposed model in Eq. 11 can not outperform TNN-based RPCA model in Eq. (8) since they have the same global optimal solutions but the proposed model is non-convex. This explains why TriFac cannot achieve better performances than TRPCA.

[3] http://www.mrt.kit.edu/z/publ/download/velodynetracking/dataset.html.

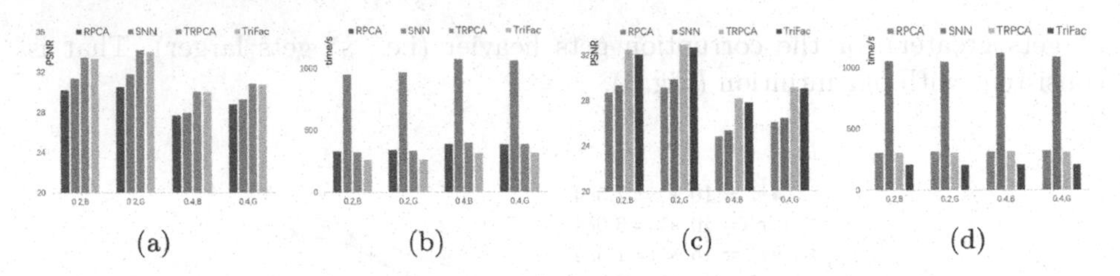

Fig. 5. Quantitative comparison of algorithms in PSNR and running time on point cloud data. (a): PSNR values of algorithms on the distance data; (b): running time of algorithms on the distance data; (c): PSNR values of algorithms on the intensity data; (d): running time of algorithms on the intensity data. ('0.2, B' means 20% of the positions are corrupted by $\text{Ber}(-1,+1)$ outliers, and '0.4,G' means 40% of the positions are corrupted by $\mathcal{N}(0,1)$ outliers).

Brain MRI Data. To show the efficiency of the proposed TriFac, we also use the 3-way MRI data set analyzed in [21] which has good low-rank property. We extract the first 15 slices, each having a size of 181×217. To further show the efficiency of TriFac, we resize the data with scale parameter $\kappa \in \{1, 1.5, 2, 2.5, 3\}$ to form tensors in $\mathbb{R}^{\lceil 181\kappa \rceil \times \lceil 217\kappa \rceil \times 15}$. Then, we randomly choose 20% of the elements in the rescaled tensor, and corrupts them by elements from *i.i.d.* Bernoulli distribution $\text{Ber}(-1,+1)$. We compare TriFac with TRPCA in both running time and recovery performance with respect to different sizes. The results are shown in Table 3. It can be seen that the proposed TriFac works almost as well as TRPCA but has faster speed.

Table 3. Comparison of TriFac with TRPCA in both PSNR values and running time on rescaled MRI data in $\mathbb{R}^{\lceil 181\kappa \rceil \times \lceil 217\kappa \rceil \times 15}$ with $\kappa \in \{1, 1.5, 2, 2.5, 3\}$.

Algorithm		$\kappa = 1$	$\kappa = 1.5$	$\kappa = 2$	$\kappa = 2.5$	$\kappa = 3$
TRPCA	PSNR	44.31	50.11	54.62	57.83	59.82
	Time/s	20.02	42.86	106.97	174.12	262.53
TriFac	PSNR	44.31	50.09	54.62	57.76	59.77
	Time/s	11.14	22.1	52.33	88.57	121.41
	Initial r	70	70	120	220	300

5 Conclusion

In this paper, a factorization-based TRPCA model (TriFac) is first proposed to recover a 3-way data tensor from its observation corrupted by sparse outliers. Then, we come up with a non-convex ALM algorithm (Algorithm 1) to efficiently solve it. Further, the convergence of the proposed algorithm is analyzed in Theorem 2. The effectiveness and efficiency of the proposed algorithm is demonstrated in experiments on both synthetic and real datasets.

References

1. Candès, E.J., Li, X., Ma, Y., Wright, J.: Robust principal component analysis? JACM **58**(3), 11 (2011)
2. Fazel, M.: Matrix rank minimization with applications. Ph.D. thesis, Stanford University (2002)
3. Foucart, S., Rauhut, H.: A Mathematical Introduction to Compressive Sensing, vol. 1. Birkhäuser, Basel (2013)
4. Friedland, S., Lim, L.: Nuclear norm of higher-order tensors. Math. Comput. **87**(311), 1255–1281 (2017)
5. Goldfarb, D., Qin, Z.: Robust low-rank tensor recovery: models and algorithms. SIAM J. Matrix Anal. Appl. **35**(1), 225–253 (2014)
6. Harshman, R.A.: Foundations of the PARAFAC procedure: models and conditions for an "explanatory" multi-modal factor analysis (1970)
7. Hillar, C.J., Lim, L.: Most tensor problems are NP-hard. J. ACM **60**(6), 45 (2009)
8. Huang, B., Mu, C., Goldfarb, D., Wright, J.: Provable models for robust low-rank tensor completion. Pac. J. Optim. **11**(2), 339–364 (2015)
9. Kilmer, M.E., Braman, K., Hao, N., Hoover, R.C.: Third-order tensors as operators on matrices: a theoretical and computational framework with applications in imaging. SIAM J. Matrix Anal. Appl. **34**(1), 148–172 (2013)
10. Liu, J., Musialski, P., Wonka, P., Ye, J.: Tensor completion for estimating missing values in visual data. IEEE TPAMI **35**(1), 208–220 (2013)
11. Lu, C., Feng, J., Chen, Y., Liu, W., Lin, Z., Yan, S.: Tensor robust principal component analysis: exact recovery of corrupted low-rank tensors via convex optimization. In: CVPR, pp. 5249–5257 (2016)
12. Lu, C., Feng, J., Liu, W., Lin, Z., Yan, S., et al.: Tensor robust principal component analysis with a new tensor nuclear norm. IEEE TPAMI (2019)
13. Moosmann, F., Stiller, C.: Joint self-localization and tracking of generic objects in 3D range data. In: ICRA, pp. 1138–1144. Karlsruhe, Germany, May 2013
14. Romera-Paredes, B., Pontil, M.: A new convex relaxation for tensor completion. In: NIPS, pp. 2967–2975 (2013)
15. Tucker, L.R.: Some mathematical notes on three-mode factor analysis. Psychometrika **31**(3), 279–311 (1966)
16. Wang, A., Jin, Z.: Near-optimal noisy low-tubal-rank tensor completion via singular tube thresholding. In: ICDM Workshop, pp. 553–560 (2017)
17. Wang, A., Lai, Z., Jin, Z.: Noisy low-tubal-rank tensor completion. Neurocomputing **330**, 267–279 (2019)
18. Wang, A., Wei, D., Wang, B., Jin, Z.: Noisy low-tubal-rank tensor completion through iterative singular tube thresholding. IEEE Access **6**, 35112–35128 (2018)
19. Wu, T., Bajwa, W.U.: A low tensor-rank representation approach for clustering of imaging data. IEEE Signal Process. Lett. **25**(8), 1196–1200 (2018)
20. Xie, Y., Tao, D., Zhang, W., Liu, Y., Zhang, L., Qu, Y.: On unifying multi-view self-representations for clustering by tensor multi-rank minimization. Int. J. Comput. Vis. **126**(11), 1157–1179 (2018)
21. Xu, Y., Hao, R., Yin, W., Su, Z.: Parallel matrix factorization for low-rank tensor completion. Inverse Prob. Imaging **9**(2), 601–624 (2015)
22. Zhang, Z., Aeron, S.: Exact tensor completion using T-SVD. IEEE TSP **65**(6), 1511–1526 (2017)
23. Zhang, Z., Ely, G., Aeron, S., Hao, N., Kilmer, M.: Novel methods for multilinear data completion and de-noising based on tensor-SVD. In: CVPR, pp. 3842–3849 (2014)
24. Zhou, P., Feng, J.: Outlier-robust tensor PCA. In: CVPR (2017)

Speeding up of the Nelder-Mead Method by Data-Driven Speculative Execution

Shuhei Watanabe[1,2](✉), Yoshihiko Ozaki[1,3], Yoshiaki Bando[1], and Masaki Onishi[1]

[1] AI Research Center, AIST, Tokyo, Japan
{shuhei.watanabe,ozaki-y,y.bando}@aist.go.jp, onishi@ni.aist.go.jp
[2] The University of Tokyo, Tokyo, Japan
[3] GREE, Inc., Tokyo, Japan

Abstract. The performance of machine learning algorithms considerably depends on the hyperparameter configurations. Previous studies reported that the Nelder-Mead (NM) method known as a local search method requires a small number of evaluations to converge and that these properties enable achieving considerable success in the hyperparameter optimization (HPO) of machine learning algorithms for image recognition. However, most evaluations using the NM method need to be implemented sequentially, which requires a large amount of time. To alleviate the problem that the NM method cannot be computed in parallel, we propose a *data-driven speculative execution* method based on the statistical features of the NM method. We analyze the behaviors of the NM method on several benchmark functions and experimentally demonstrated that the NM method tends to take certain specific operations. The experimental results show that the proposed method reduced the elapsed time by approximately 50% and the number of evaluations by approximately 60% compared to the naïve speculative execution.

Keywords: Nelder-Mead method · Hyperparameter optimization · Parallel computing

1 Introduction

Machine learning algorithms such as ResNet [9] or DenseNet [10] have demonstrated excellent performance on benchmark datasets. However, the performance of such algorithms is heavily influenced by the hyperparameter configurations. To automatically find proper configurations, several approaches for *hyperparameter optimization* (HPO) [5] have been proposed, such as random search [1], covariance matrix adaptation evolution strategy (CMA-ES) [8,16] and Bayesian optimization (BO) [3,17]. When the relation between hyperparameters and performance cannot be described in an analytic form, we opt for black-box optimization (BBO). HPO for machine learning algorithms is a BBO problem, in which the evaluation of the objective function is expensive. Therefore, a substantial

S. Palaiahnakote et al. (Eds.): ACPR 2019, LNCS 12046, pp. 438–452, 2020.
https://doi.org/10.1007/978-3-030-41404-7_31

amount of time is required to find good configurations, and efficient algorithms automating the configuration are necessary.

Recently, it was reported that the Nelder-Mead (NM) [19] method is superior to Gaussian process (GP)-based BO, CMA-ES, and random search for finding good configurations for convolution neural networks (CNNs) in a small number of evaluations [21]. The NM method is a derivative-free optimization and optimizes the objective function by transforming and moving an n-dimensional simplex using several rules, where n is the number of hyperparameters. One of the characteristics of the NM method is that there are fewer control parameters, comparing to BO and CMA-ES and this characteristic makes the method manageable for users while identifying good configurations well.

The major requirement of HPO is to converge to satisfactory configurations quickly. One of the solutions for this is processor scalability, and it is difficult for the NM method known as a sequential method to benefit from adding other computer resources. In particular, when optimizing deep-learning models, which require several hours to days to evaluate, sequential evaluations require several months to years to obtain satisfactory configurations. Therefore, it is necessary to propose a speculative execution to accelerate the NM method more effectively. Several methods have been proposed to speed up the NM method. One method is to evaluate all the possible configurations in an iteration in parallel [4] and another method is to choose the probable configurations by a GP [20].

In this paper, we propose a speculative execution method for the NM method. We hypothesize several statistical characteristics of the NM method. Analysis of an experiment on benchmark functions show that the NM method tends to take certain specific operations. We develop a parallel method for the NM method using the result of the analysis. This method uses the probabilities that each configuration will be evaluated in future iterations according to the statistical analysis. This allows us to avoid evaluating improbable future iterates and arrive at the termination conditions earlier.

The contributions of this paper include finding the trait of the NM method in terms of the frequency of each operation and significantly speeding up the NM method based on statistical analysis. Specifically, given the probabilities of each operation, the NM method evaluates the corresponding probable configurations.

2 Related Work

2.1 Problem Setting of Hyperparameter Optimization

In this paper, we optimize only supervised learning algorithms; therefore, we describe the problem setting of HPO for supervised learning algorithms. Given a machine learning algorithm A and a set $\mathcal{D} = \{(x_1, t_1), \cdots, (x_m, t_m)\}$ where x are input data and t is a label for the data x, we solve the problem of optimizing the configuration $y = \{y_1, \cdots, y_n\} \in Y$, where there are n given hyperparameters $y_1, \cdots, y_n$. The performance of a hyperparameter configuration y is the validation loss for $\mathcal{D}_{\text{valid}}$ by training with $\mathcal{D}_{\text{train}}$. The goal of HPO is to identify

$$y^* = \text{argmin}_{y \in Y} \ \mathcal{L}(A, y, \mathcal{D}_{\text{train}}, \mathcal{D}_{\text{valid}}) \tag{1}$$

where $\mathcal{L}(A, y, \mathcal{D}_{\text{train}}, \mathcal{D}_{\text{valid}})$ is the validation loss on $\mathcal{D}_{\text{valid}}$ obtained by A when trained on $\mathcal{D}_{\text{train}}$.

2.2 Parallel HPO Methods

The most naïve parallel HPO algorithm is a random search [1]. Random search is advantageous with respect to its processor scalability. Because it does not require previous data points, its search efficiency is proportional to the number of computer resources. This method has been broadly studied and hyperband [15] is a well-known application of random search. Hyperband focuses on speeding up random search through adaptive resource allocation and early-stopping. However, these methods are inefficient because new configurations are generated without using observations.

CMA-ES and BO such as TPE [2], SMAC [11], and spearmint [22], greatly improve the HPO performance using observations. CMA-ES can evaluate N points in parallel, where N is the number of individuals in each generation. In addition to its processor scalability, CMA-ES [8] achieved the best performance in black-box optimization competitions [7]. BO offers the prospects of a relationship between the observations and the performances of previously unseen regions. In fact, BO is intrinsically not suitable for parallel computation; however, there are some BO methods for parallel computing, including batch BO [6,12]. One of the batch BO is the BO via Thompson sampling (BOTS) which uses a GP surrogate for the objective function and samples multiple points via Thompson sampling.

The NM method uses simplex to find good configurations. The NM method uses five types of operations to transform simplex and produce points to evaluate. Let *iterates* be the points evaluated throughout an optimization by the NM method. There are two types of parallel computation for the NM method. One approach is to modify the algorithm of the NM method to make better use of additional computer resources. The other approach focuses on evaluating possible future iterates in advance. The former approach includes methods assigning iterates obtained by reflecting the i-th worst vertex over the centroid of the simplex to the i-th processor at each iteration and evaluating the iterates in parallel [14]. Such evaluations encourage the method to explore in good directions but not to speed up the original NM method. The latter approach includes methods evaluating all the possible iterates at each iteration [4] and methods evaluating the future iterates obtained by a GP surrogate [20]. These methods evaluate some points taken from all the possible iterates and can accelerate the original NM method. However, these methods evaluate many points not produced by the original NM method.

2.3 The Nelder-Mead (NM) Method

The NM method uses an n-dimensional simplex Δ composed of $n+1$ vertices, denoted as $(y^0\ y^1\ \cdots\ y^n) \in \mathbb{R}^{n\times(n+1)}$. This simplex transforms its shape based

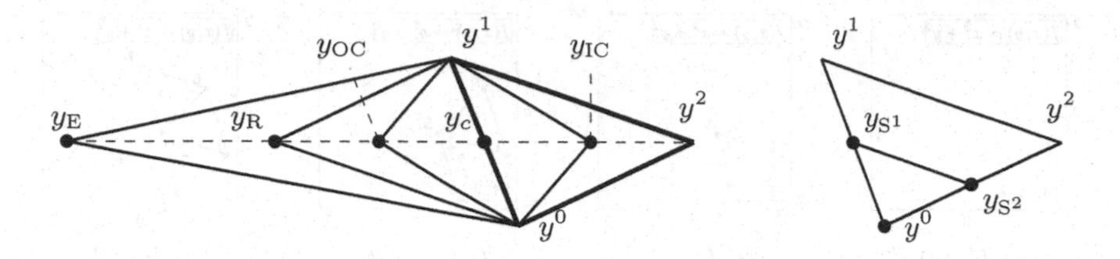

Fig. 1. Picture of each operation in the NM method.

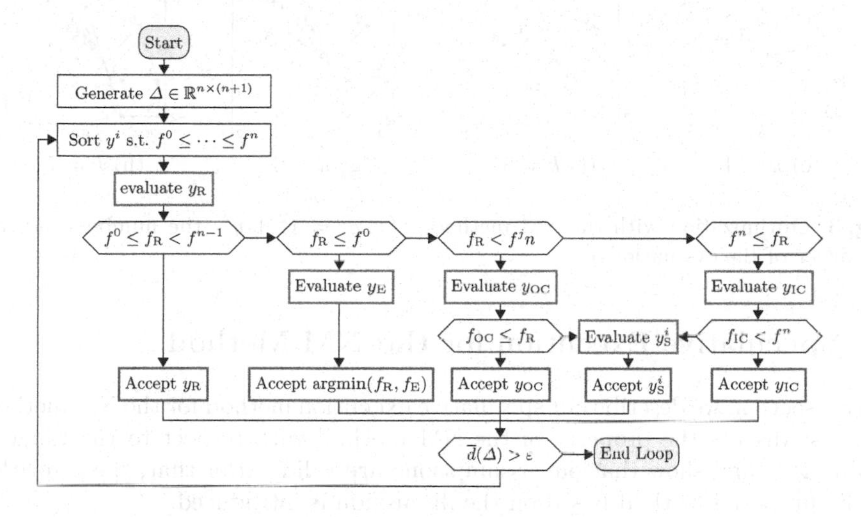

Fig. 2. Flowchart of the NM method. Note that $f(y_O^i) = f_O^i$.

on five types of operations, *Reflect* ($\mathcal{R}$), *Expand* ($\mathcal{E}$), *Inside Contract* ($\mathcal{IC}$), *Outside Contract* ($\mathcal{OC}$), and *Shrink* ($\mathcal{S}$) (Fig. 1), subsequent to initialization. All of these operations have their own coefficients denoted as

$$-1 < \delta_{IC} < 0 < \delta_{OC} < \delta_R < \delta_E,\ 0 < \delta_S < 1. \tag{2}$$

The iterate constructed by the operation $\mathcal{O}$ is described as $y_O = y_c + \delta_O(y_c - y^n)$ and the iterates obtained by shrinkage are written as $y_{S^i} = y_c + \delta_S(y_c - y^i)$ for $i = 1, \cdots, n$. The algorithm continues as long as the termination criterion $\overline{d}(\Delta) < \varepsilon$ is not met where $\overline{d}(\Delta)$ is the maximum distance between $\overline{y^0}$ and $\overline{y^i}$ and ε is an arbitrary positive number. $\overline{y^i}$ is calculated by normalizing each element of y^i. Each operation is performed according to Fig. 2. The coefficients for each operation are usually $(\delta_s, \delta_{ic}, \delta_{oc}, \delta_r, \delta_e) = \left(\frac{1}{2}, -\frac{1}{2}, \frac{1}{2}, 1, 2\right)$ [19] and we chose the same coefficients for our experiments. Figure 3 describes an example of optimization with the NM method.

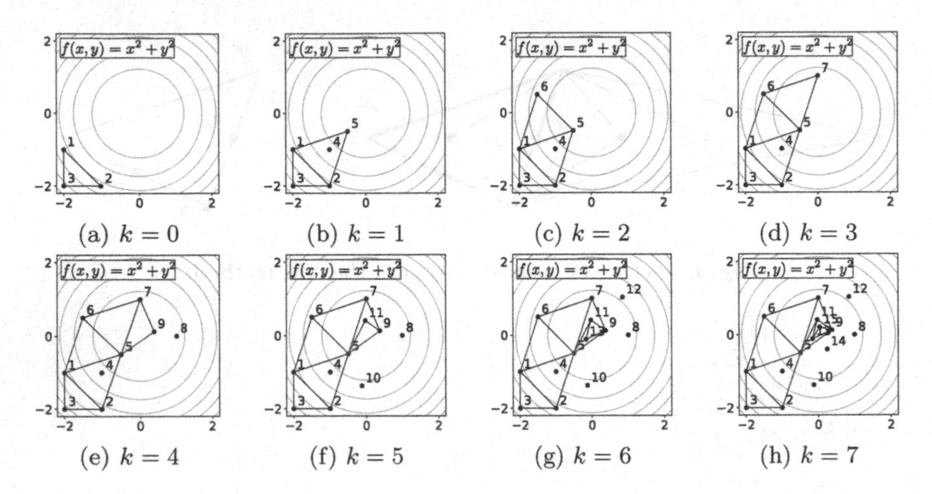

(a) $k = 0$ (b) $k = 1$ (c) $k = 2$ (d) $k = 3$

(e) $k = 4$ (f) $k = 5$ (g) $k = 6$ (h) $k = 7$

Fig. 3. Optimization with the NM method: $f(x, y) = x^2 + y^2$ (the numbers indicate the order of the evaluations)

3 Speculative Execution for the NM Method

In this section, we describe our speculative execution method for the NM method. We first discuss the property of the NM method with respect to the range of evaluations and show that our assumptions are valid. After that, the algorithm of the proposed method based on the discussion is introduced.

3.1 The Future Iterates of the NM Method

Even though the NM method is sequential except the iterates obtained by $\mathcal{S}$, the NM method can be computed in parallel due to its determinism. Let $y_{\mathrm{R-O}}$ be the future iterate that is produced when the NM method takes the action $\mathcal{O}$ after $\mathcal{R}$ (Fig. 4). Future iterates of the NM method can be reproduced if the ranking of the evaluations at each vertex and the operations taken at each iteration are given. When the NM algorithm samples a new iterate y_{R}, the rankings of $y^1, y^2, \cdots, y^n$ are already given. There are four possible next iterates: $y_{\mathrm{R-E}}$, $y_{\mathrm{R-R}}$, $y_{\mathrm{R-OC}}$, and $y_{\mathrm{R-IC}}$. These iterates are produced when the ranking of y_{R} in the simplex Δ is first for $y_{\mathrm{R-E}}$, from second to n-th for $y_{\mathrm{R-R}}$, $n+1$-th for

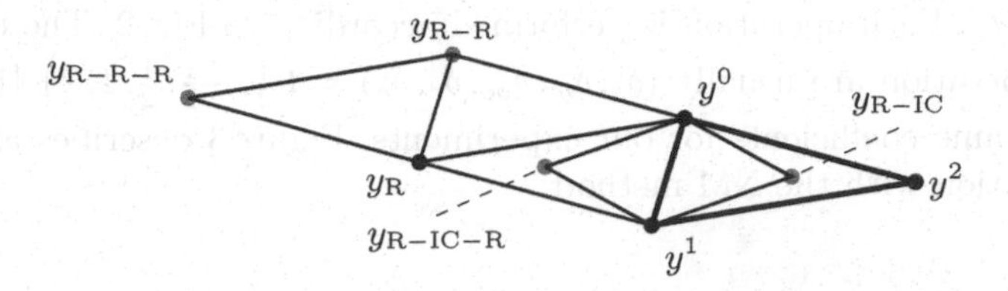

Fig. 4. Picture of the future iterates. Red points are future iterates. (Color figure online)

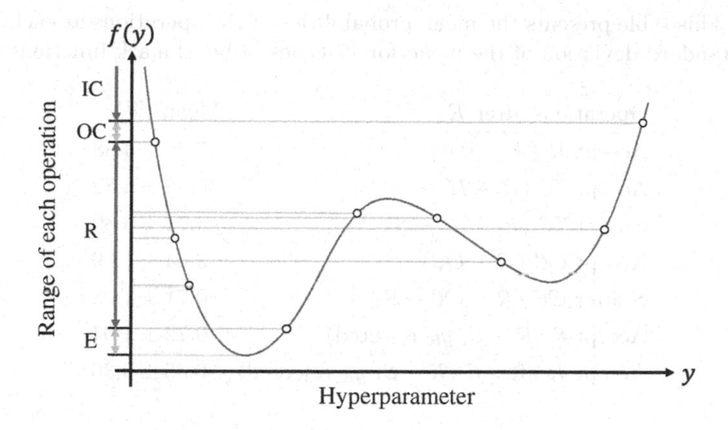

Fig. 5. The range of evaluations each operation occurs. An 8-dimensional hyperparameter space is conceptually projected to a 1-dimensional space.

y_{R-OC}, and worst for y_{R-IC} respectively (Fig. 2). Speculative execution literally evaluates the future iterates, such as y_{R-IC}, as if the ranking of y_R were already provided.

While it is possible to speed up the NM method by evaluating future iterates in advance, the patterns of future possible iterates increase exponentially as the future iterations continue. To effectively narrow down the candidates for future iterates, we consider three assumptions and give a visual example in Fig. 5.

- **Assumption 1:** y_{R-R} would occur with a high probability.
- **Assumption 2:** y_{R-IC} would occur with a high probability.
- **Assumption 3:** The evaluation of future iterates would not be close to that of the worst iterates in the current simplex.

y_{R-R} occurs when the ranking of y_R is from second to n-th and this range of ranking is the widest. y_{R-IC} occurs when the ranking of y_R is the worst and the quality of vertices in the simplex keeps improving throughout the optimization and it could lead to the wider range of evaluations between the worst evaluation in the simplex and the upper bound of the objective function. These characteristics lead to Assumption 1 and 2. As shown in Fig. 5, the range of evaluations for y_{R-R} and y_{R-IC} would be wider than that of others. The range between the best and the third-worst evaluation in simplex tends to be wider than the range between the third-worst and the worst evaluation in a 10-dimensional space when the evaluations follow a uniform distribution. We apply this fact to the range of evaluations in simplex and introduce Assumption 3. To accelerate the NM method, we use three assumptions to reduce candidates for future iterates.

3.2 The Frequency of Each Operation

To test our three assumptions, we performed an experiment. In this experiment, the NM method optimized 17 types of benchmark functions and the probabilities

Table 1. This table presents the mean probabilities of the operations at each iteration and the standard deviation of the mean for 17 types of benchmark functions.

Operations after $\mathcal{R}$	Mean (%)
Accept $\mathcal{R}$ ($\mathcal{R}-\mathcal{R}$)	47.28 ± 4.88
Accept $\mathcal{IC}$ ($\mathcal{R}-\mathcal{IC}$)	36.59 ± 6.82
$\mathcal{S}$ after $\mathcal{IC}$ ($\mathcal{R}-\mathcal{IC}-\mathcal{S}$)	4.71 ± 3.80
Accept $\mathcal{OC}$ ($\mathcal{R}-\mathcal{OC}$)	3.64 ± 1.69
$\mathcal{S}$ after $\mathcal{OC}$ ($\mathcal{R}-\mathcal{OC}-\mathcal{S}$)	0.71 ± 1.02
Accept $\mathcal{E}$ ($\mathcal{R}-\mathcal{E}$, y_{R} rejected)	0.72 ± 1.04
Accept $\mathcal{R}$ after $\mathcal{E}$ ($\mathcal{R}-\mathcal{E}$, y_{E} rejected)	6.36 ± 3.30

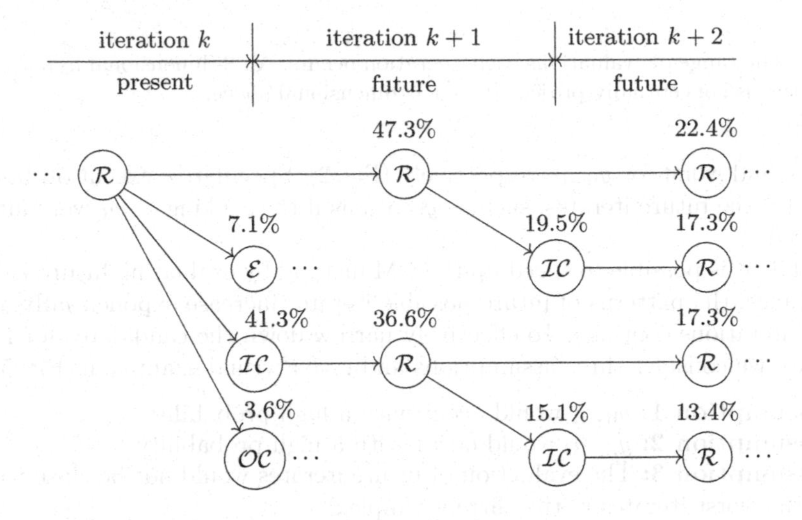

Fig. 6. The data-driven transitional probability of future operations

of each operation were measured. To imitate the machine learning optimization conditions, observational noise $\epsilon \sim \mathcal{N}(0, 0.0173^2)$, which was measured on the model shown in Table 2 over 40 runs, was added to the benchmark functions.

The result is shown in Table 1. This result shows that either accept $\mathcal{R}$ or accept $\mathcal{IC}$ occur with approximately 90% and it is reasonable to evaluate probable future points as a priority. Based on the experimental results, we take the probability of accepting $\mathcal{R}$ as to be 47.3%, that of evaluating $\mathcal{IC}$ as to be 41.3%, that of accepting $\mathcal{IC}$ as to be 36.6%, that of evaluating $\mathcal{OC}$ as to be 3.6% and that of evaluating $\mathcal{E}$ as to be 7.1%. Then, the approximate probabilities of future operations are presented in Fig. 6. For example, when the next operation at the beginning of the next step is $\mathcal{R}$, $y_{\mathrm{R-IC}}$ will occur with a probability of 41.3% and accepting $\mathcal{R}$ and moving on to the next iteration will occur with a probability of 47.3%. This result shows that operations other than evaluating $\mathcal{IC}$ and accepting $\mathcal{R}$ rarely occur. However, future iterates depend not only on operations taken in an iteration but also on which vertices are removed from the future simplex. The NM method removes the worst vertex at each iteration. Therefore, we measured the ranking of the new vertex at each iteration and approximately 85% of the new vertices are better than the third-worst vertex. This means that new vertices will not be removed within three iterations with a probability of more than 85%. Consequently, it is more computationally efficient to speculate that new vertices are relatively better out of existing vertices.

3.3 The Data-Driven Speculative NM Method

Here, we present a speculative execution method for the NM method. On the basis of the discussion, the following three rules are formulated for the parallel speculation:

- **Rule1:** Evaluate the iterates to be evaluated by the NM method first.
- **Rule2:** Evaluate the points whose transitional probabilities are as high as possible if computing resources are still available.
- **Rule3:** Regard the rankings of the new vertices as being the best in the future simplex.

The statistical probability to transition from the current state to other states is given in Table 1, and we denote it as the *transitional probability.* We use transitional probability to speed up the NM method. For example, at the beginning of an iteration k, each operation is taken with the probabilities shown in Fig. 6. We define the probable operations based on the transitional probabilities as transitional operations and denote them as op_{tr}, where the probability of occurring op_{tr}^{i} is lower than that of occurring op_{tr}^{i-1} and higher than that of occurring

---

Algorithm 1. The Speculative Nelder-Mead Method

Input: $P, B_{\text{total}}, \varepsilon, op_{tr} \leftarrow \{op_{tr}^{0}, op_{tr}^{1}, \cdots, op_{tr}^{B-1}\}$
Initialize: $S \leftarrow \{y^0, y^1, \cdots, y^n\}$. Evaluate each vertices. $op_{\text{next}} \leftarrow \mathcal{R}$
while $t < B_{\text{total}}$ and $\overline{d}(\Delta) > \varepsilon$ **do**
  for $i = 0, 1, \cdots, B-1$ **do** ▷ See Fig. 7 to know how to choose op
    if $op_{\text{next}} \neq \mathcal{R}$ **then**
      if $i \neq 0$ **then** $op \leftarrow \{op_{\text{next}}, op_{tr}^{i-1}\}$
      else $op \leftarrow op_{\text{next}}$
    else $op \leftarrow op_{tr}^{i}$
    Calculate y_{tr}^{i} by transforming Δ using op
  Compute $f(y_{tr}^{i})$ (for $i = 0, 1, \cdots, B-1$) in parallel, $t \leftarrow t + B$
  while $f(y_{\text{new}})$ is available **do**
    $f_{\text{new}} \leftarrow f(y_{\text{new}})$, get op_{next} in accordance with the NM method
    Get y_{new} by transforming Δ according to op_{next} and f_{new}.
    Renew the simplex S
  if $op_{\text{next}} = \mathcal{S}$ **then**
    Shrink: Apply shrinkage to Δ and evaluate each iterate
      $op_{\text{next}} \leftarrow \mathcal{R}$, $t \leftarrow t + n$

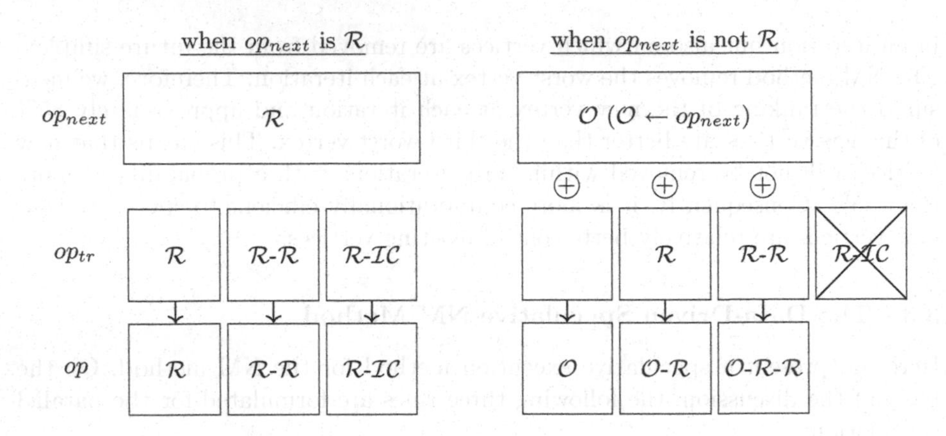

Fig. 7. An example of the transitional operations when $P = 3$.

Table 2. The architecture of naïve CNN

Components	Output size	Kernel type
Convolution 1	$32 \times 32 \times C_1$	5×5 conv $\times C_1$, Padding 2
Max pooling	$15 \times 15 \times C_1$	3×3, Stride 2
Convolution 2	$15 \times 15 \times C_2$	5×5 conv $\times C_2$, Padding 2
Average pooling	$7 \times 7 \times C_2$	3×3, Stride 2
Convolution 3	$7 \times 7 \times C_3$	5×5 conv $\times C_3$, Padding 2
Average pooling	$3 \times 3 \times C_3$	3×3, Stride 2
Full connected layer	$C_4 \times 1$	C_4 D fully-connected
Classification layer	100×1	100D fully-connected, softmax

op_{tr}^{i+1}. To explain, let us define one parallel computation as a step. For example, when there are four processors and 10 steps have passed, $4 \times 10 = 40$ different configurations have been evaluated. At every step, the proposed method takes transitional operations as presented in Fig. 7 and evaluates the points obtained by transforming the simplex as shown in Fig. 4 in parallel. After the evaluations, the iteration of the NM method proceeds and the next step begins. The algorithm of the proposed method is illustrated in Algorithm 1 where P is the number of parallel computing resources, and B_{total} is the total number of evaluations.

Both our method and previous studies [4,20] maintain the reproducibility of the convergence point of the original method. That is why the performance of our method is the same as or better than that of the original NM method. The major difference is that the proposed method cuts off improbable iterates based on a statistical analysis beforehand, while previous studies have tried to take candidates from all the possible iterates, including those statistically unlikely to occur. If there were cheap-to-evaluate proxies providing precisely the same evaluation as the objective function, it would be better to quantify all

Table 3. The hyperparameters of naïve CNN.

Hyperparameters	Type	Distribution	Range
Batch size	int	Log uniform	[32, 256]
Learning rate	float	Log uniform	[5.0e−3, 0.5]
Momentum	float	Uniform	[0.8, 1.0]
Weight decay	float	Log uniform	[5.0e−6, 5.0e−2]
# of feature maps in conv C_1, C_2, C_3	int	Log uniform	[16, 128]
# of feature maps in FC1 C_4	int	Log uniform	[16, 128]
Dropout rate	float	Uniform	[0, 1.0]

Table 4. The architecture of WRN

Components	Output size	Kernel type
Convolution	$32 \times 32 \times k_1$	3×3 conv $\times$ 16
Residual block 1	$32 \times 32 \times k_1$	$\begin{pmatrix} 3 \times 3 \text{ conv} \times 16k_1 \\ 3 \times 3 \text{ conv} \times 16k_1 \end{pmatrix} \times 4$
Residual block 2	$16 \times 16 \times k_2$	$\begin{pmatrix} 3 \times 3 \text{ conv} \times 32k_2 \\ 3 \times 3 \text{ conv} \times 32k_2 \end{pmatrix} \times 4$
Residual block 3	$8 \times 8 \times k_3$	$\begin{pmatrix} 3 \times 3 \text{ conv} \times 64k_3 \\ 3 \times 3 \text{ conv} \times 64k_3 \end{pmatrix} \times 4$
Average pooling	1×1	8×8
Classification layer	100×1	100D fully-connected, softmax

the possibilities. However, the objective function of HPO for machine learning algorithms suffers from observational noise and a surrogate requires an enormous amount of observations to predict an accurate value for the objective in a high-dimensional space. Therefore, it is difficult to pinpoint the proper ranking of a new vertex, especially in a high-dimensional space, due to the uncertainty of the prediction. Conversely, data-driven speculative execution is expected to evaluate approximately three to four iterates required by the original NM method on average at every step beginning by $\mathcal{R}$ when using 10 processors.

4 Experimental Evaluation

4.1 Experimental Conditions

We compared the NM method with random search and the BOTS [12] on HPO of naïve CNNs shown in Table 2 and validate the effectiveness of the NM method on HPO. Here, we chose the number of parallel computing resources $P = 4$. Then, the NM method was applied to wide residual network (WRN) [24] which is the more expensive-to-evaluate deep-learning algorithm. Finally, we conducted experiments to show how quickly the proposed method can be implemented.

Table 5. The hyperparameters of WRN.

Hyperparameters	Type	Distribution	Range
Batch size	int	Log uniform	[64, 256]
Learning rate	float	Log uniform	[1.0e−4, 1.0]
Learning rate decay	float	Log uniform	[1.0e−2, 1.0]
Momentum	float	Uniform	[0.8, 1.0]
Weight decay	float	Log uniform	[5.0e−6, 5.0e−2]
Widening factor k_1, k_2, k_3	int	Log uniform	[4, 16]
Dropout rate in res block 1, 2, 3	float	Uniform	[0, 0.5]

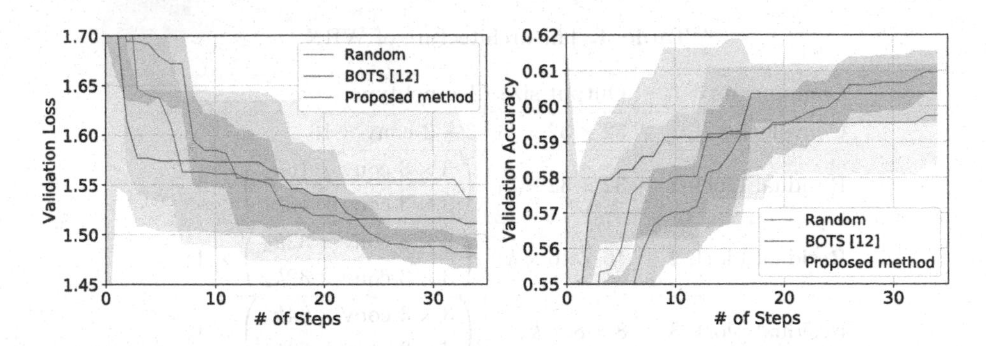

Fig. 8. The convergence speed of major parallel HPO methods for naïve CNN.

For the experiments, we chose CIFAR-100 image classification datasets [13] and performed the same data augmentation as that in [24]. The architectures of these two models are illustrated in Tables 2 and 4. It takes approximately 15 min to evaluate a naïve CNN and 4 h to evaluate a WRN using an NVIDIA Tesla V100 for NVLink. The hyperparameters are presented in Tables 3 and 5.

As reported in [23], the effective initialization of the NM method is the latin hypercube sampling (LHS) [18]. Accordingly, LHS was chosen as the initial sampling method for the experiments. Discrete hyperparameters were rounded off after a transformation of simplex.

We compared the proposed method with three different types of the NM parallel methods. Baseline 1 is a method computing only the initialization and iterates produced by $\mathcal{S}$ in parallel. The naïve parallel NM (NPNM) method is the naïve speculative execution suggested by [4]. The GP based parallel NM (GPPNM) method is the parallel method based on a GP surrogate proposed by [20]. We repeated the experiments four times for each deep-learning model. We chose $B_{total} = 150$ for naïve CNN and $B_{total} = 100$ for WRN, and $\varepsilon = 10^{-2}$, $P = n+1$ for the proposed method, Baseline 1, and the GPPNM and $P = n+4$ for the NPNM in the simulation.

Note that the iterates produced only by the sequential NM method were required to measure the effects of the proposed method comparing to the other

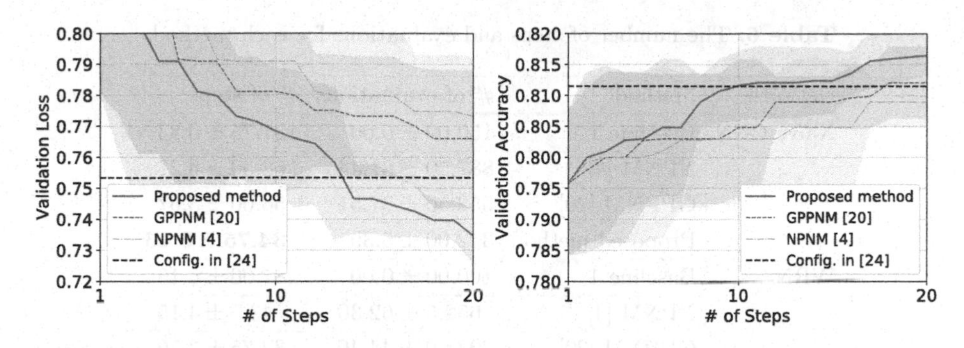

Fig. 9. The convergence speed of major parallel NM methods for WRN-28-10 [24].

methods; therefore, we did not evaluate iterates not produced by the sequential NM method in the experiment and the number of configurations the proposed method evaluated was less than that of configurations the BOTS and random search evaluated.

4.2 The Comparison with Parallel HPO Methods

The HPO results for naïve CNNs are presented in Fig. 8. The solid lines are the mean and the shadows are the standard deviation of the mean over four runs. According to the Fig. 8, the NM method successfully yields better configurations in 35 steps. In the early stage, the BOTS outperformed the proposed method, but the NM method obtained better configurations in 25 steps. This result shows that the performance will be further improved by starting with the BOTS and then switching to the NM method after several steps.

4.3 The Comparison with Other Parallel NM Methods

The HPO results for WRN illustrated in Fig. 9 shows that the proposed method converged to better configurations earlier than three conventional parallel methods and obtained better configurations than that in [24] which achieves 81.15% validation accuracy on CIFAR100. Table 6 summarizes the number of steps and the number of evaluations to reach the termination conditions.

Compared to the NPNM, the proposed method is nearly twice faster and requires 70% less computation. both accept $\mathcal{R}$ and accept $\mathcal{IC}$ occur with a probability of approximately 40% and both were the dominant operations in the optimization of each deep-learning model. The probabilities for the two operations were nearly the same as those shown in Table 1, and our strategies were effective in the experiments.

The NPNM evaluated all the possible iterates, including the n iterates produced by $\mathcal{S}$, even though $\mathcal{S}$ rarely occurs statistically. This led to three times as much computation as in Baseline 1. Conversely, the proposed method does not include the improbable iterates and reduced the computation by nearly 60%

Table 6. The number of steps and evaluations for each method.

Network	Method	# of evaluations	# of steps
Naïve CNN	Baseline 1	150.00 ± 0.00	137.75 ± 0.83
	NPNM [4]	887.50 ± 81.44	68.50 ± 6.27
	GPPNM [20]	552.50 ± 37.51	56.00 ± 3.67
	Proposed method	342.00 ± 5.39	$\mathbf{34.75 \pm 0.43}$
WRN	Baseline 1	100.00 ± 0.00	87.00 ± 6.16
	NPNM [4]	652.5 ± 62.30	43.5 ± 4.15
	GPPNM [20]	393.00 ± 44.40	32.75 ± 3.70
	Proposed method	240.00 ± 14.70	$\mathbf{20.00 \pm 1.22}$

compared to the NPNM. In terms of the elapsed time, the proposed method evaluated 100 hyperparameter configurations in approximately 40% of steps required by the NPNM. This means that the proposed method could shorten experiments on WRN by approximately 250 h. Further, the result experimentally demonstrated that data-driven parallel method outperforms a ranking prediction using GP. To achieve considerable success in speeding up the NM method, GP cannot make any error larger than the range of the best vertex and the worst vertex in simplex. However, GP samples include uncertainty and therefore it is difficult to prevent errors from being larger than 10% which is especially difficult in a high-dimensional space.

5 Conclusions

In this paper, we proposed a speculative execution for the NM method. This method introduces parallel computing based on statistical data obtained in an experiment with benchmark functions. The experimental results show that our method successfully reduces the elapsed time without increasing the number of evaluations compared to the conventional parallel NM methods. The proposed method tended to reduce the elapsed time by approximately 50% compared to the NPNM without increasing the number of evaluations. Since the proposed method evaluates the iterates produced by the original NM method as a priority, the proposed guarantee outperforms the original NM method even in the possible worst-case scenarios. Moreover, the proposed method reached the termination conditions with approximately 40% the number of evaluations required by the NPNM. Because the proportion of operations varies with the target functions and the number of dimensions, the proposed method can be improved by renewing the transitional probabilities with online learning or depending on the dimensionality. The NM method tends to utilize accept $\mathcal{R}$ and accept $\mathcal{IC}$ in the experiments with benchmark functions and deep-learning algorithms. Therefore, we plan to create a classifier to separate the future points into accept $\mathcal{R}$ or accept $\mathcal{IC}$ groups. The comparison with the BOTS and the NM method showed that the BOTS is better in an early stage and the NM method is better after a while. To find good configurations, we plan to study the combination of the BOTS and the NM method.

References

1. Bergstra, J., Bengio, Y.: Random search for hyper-parameter optimization. J. Mach. Learn. Res. **13**(Feb), 281–305 (2012)
2. Bergstra, J.S., Bardenet, R., Bengio, Y., Kégl, B.: Algorithms for hyper-parameter optimization. In: Advances in Neural Information Processing Systems, pp. 2546–2554 (2011)
3. Brochu, E., Cora, V.M., De Freitas, N.: A tutorial on Bayesian optimization of expensive cost functions, with application to active user modeling and hierarchical reinforcement learning. arXiv preprint arXiv:1012.2599 (2010)
4. Dennis, J., Torczon, V.: Parallel implementations of the Nelder-Mead simplex algorithm for unconstrained optimization. In: High Speed Computing, vol. 880, pp. 187–192. International Society for Optics and Photonics (1988)
5. Feurer, M., Hutter, F.: Hyperparameter optimization. In: Hutter, F., Kotthoff, L., Vanschoren, J. (eds.) Automated Machine Learning. TSSCML, pp. 3–33. Springer, Cham (2019). https://doi.org/10.1007/978-3-030-05318-5_1
6. González, J., Dai, Z., Hennig, P., Lawrence, N.: Batch Bayesian optimization via local penalization. In: Artificial Intelligence and Statistics, pp. 648–657 (2016)
7. Hansen, N., Auger, A., Ros, R., Finck, S., Pošík, P.: Comparing results of 31 algorithms from the black-box optimization benchmarking BBOB-2009. In: Proceedings of the 12th Annual Conference Companion on Genetic and Evolutionary Computation, pp. 1689–1696. ACM (2010)
8. Hansen, N., Ostermeier, A.: Completely derandomized self-adaptation in evolution strategies. Evol. Comput. **9**(2), 159–195 (2001)
9. He, K., Zhang, X., Ren, S., Sun, J.: Deep residual learning for image recognition. In: Proceedings of the IEEE Conference on Computer Vision and Pattern Recognition, pp. 770–778 (2016)
10. Huang, G., Liu, Z., Van Der Maaten, L., Weinberger, K.Q.: Densely connected convolutional networks. In: Proceedings of the IEEE Conference on Computer Vision and Pattern Recognition, pp. 4700–4708 (2017)
11. Hutter, F., Hoos, H.H., Leyton-Brown, K.: Sequential model-based optimization for general algorithm configuration. In: Coello, C.A.C. (ed.) LION 2011. LNCS, vol. 6683, pp. 507–523. Springer, Heidelberg (2011). https://doi.org/10.1007/978-3-642-25566-3_40
12. Kandasamy, K., Krishnamurthy, A., Schneider, J., Póczos, B.: Parallelised Bayesian optimisation via Thompson sampling. In: International Conference on Artificial Intelligence and Statistics, pp. 133–142 (2018)
13. Krizhevsky, A., Hinton, G.: Learning multiple layers of features from tiny images. Technical report, Citeseer (2009)
14. Lee, D., Wiswall, M.: A parallel implementation of the simplex function minimization routine. Comput. Econ. **30**(2), 171–187 (2007)
15. Li, L., Jamieson, K., DeSalvo, G., Rostamizadeh, A., Talwalkar, A.: Hyperband: a novel bandit-based approach to hyperparameter optimization. arXiv preprint arXiv:1603.06560 (2016)

16. Loshchilov, I., Hutter, F.: CMA-ES for hyperparameter optimization of deep neural networks. Network **1**, 1–5 (2016)
17. Močkus, J.: On Bayesian methods for seeking the extremum. In: Marchuk, G.I. (ed.) Optimization Techniques 1974. LNCS, vol. 27, pp. 400–404. Springer, Heidelberg (1975). https://doi.org/10.1007/3-540-07165-2_55
18. Navid, A., Khalilarya, S., Abbasi, M.: Diesel engine optimization with multi-objective performance characteristics by non-evolutionary Nelder-Mead algorithm: sobol sequence and Latin hypercube sampling methods comparison in DoE process. Fuel **228**, 349–367 (2018)
19. Nelder, J.A., Mead, R.: A simplex method for function minimization. Comput. J. **7**(4), 308–313 (1965)
20. Ozaki, Y., Watanabe, S., Onishi, M.: Accelerating the Nelder-Mead method with predictive parallel evaluation. In: 6th ICML Workshop on Automated Machine Learning (2019)
21. Ozaki, Y., Yano, M., Onishi, M.: Effective hyperparameter optimization using Nelder-Mead method in deep learning. IPSJ Trans. Comput. Vis. Appl. **9**(1), 20 (2017)
22. Snoek, J., Larochelle, H., Adams, R.P.: Practical Bayesian optimization of machine learning algorithms. In: Advances in Neural Information Processing Systems, pp. 2951–2959 (2012)
23. Wessing, S.: Proper initialization is crucial for the Nelder-Mead simplex search. Opt. Lett. **13**, 847–856 (2018)
24. Zagoruyko, S., Komodakis, N.: Wide residual networks. In: Proceedings of the British Machine Vision Conference (BMVC), pp. 87.1–87.12. BMVA Press (2016)

Efficient Bayesian Optimization Based on Parallel Sequential Random Embeddings

Noriko Yokoyama(✉), Masahiro Kohjima, Tatsushi Matsubayashi, and Hiroyuki Toda

NTT Service Evolution Laboratories, NTT Corporation, Kanagawa, Japan
{noriko.yokoyama.ad,masahiro.kohjima.ev,tatsushi.matsubayashi.tb, hiroyuki.toda.xb}@hco.ntt.co.jp

Abstract. Bayesian optimization, which offers efficient parameter search, suffers from high computation cost if the parameters have high dimensionality because the search space expands and more trials are needed. One existing solution is an embedding method that enables the search to be restricted to a low-dimensional subspace, but this method works well only when the number of embedding dimensions closely match the that of effective dimensions, which affects the function value. However, in practical situations, the number of effective dimensions is unknown, and embedding into a low dimensional subspace to save computation cost often results in a search in a lower dimensional subspace than the effective dimensions. This study proposes a Bayesian optimization method that uses random embedding to remain efficient even if the embedded dimension is lower than the effective dimensions. By conducting parallel search in an initially low dimensional space and performing multiple cycles in which the search space is incrementally improved, the optimum solution can be efficiently found. An experiment on benchmark problems shows the effectiveness of the proposed method.

Keywords: Expensive black-box optimization · Bayesian optimization · Random embedding

1 Introduction

Black-box optimization schemes have been proposed to tackle various machine learning and artificial intelligence problems. This is because the input-output relation of the objective function, e.g., hyperparameters and its classification performance of deep neural nets [1], internal parameters of multi agent simulator and its data assimilation accuracy [2], is hidden or too complicated to clarify; the common solution is to treat the function as a black-box function. Therefore, methods that support black-box objective functions are widely used and Bayesian optimization (hereinafter referred to as BO) is the dominant black-box optimization method [1,3,4].

S. Palaiahnakote et al. (Eds.): ACPR 2019, LNCS 12046, pp. 453–466, 2020.
https://doi.org/10.1007/978-3-030-41404-7_32

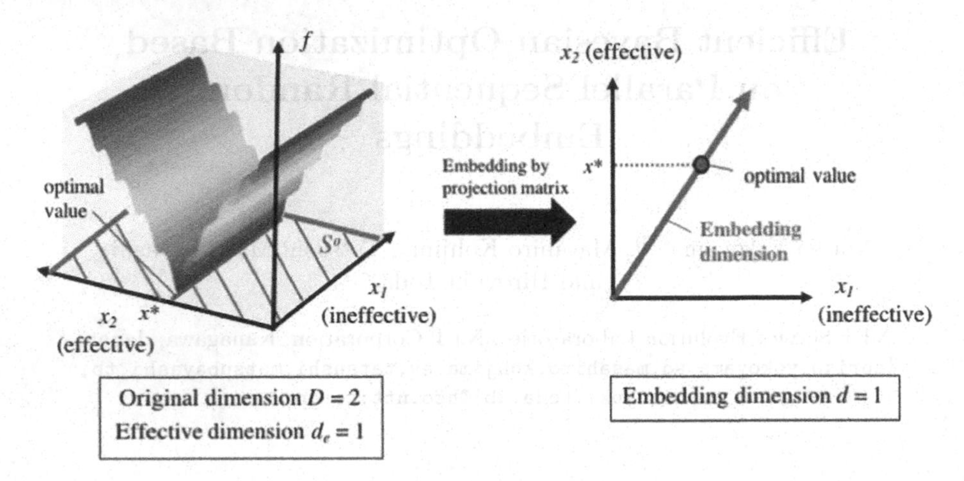

Fig. 1. Image of random embedding (RE). This shows an example of searching for two-dimensional functions (original dimension $D = 2$). Since only x_2 affects the function (effective dimension $d_e = 1$), the one-dimensional subspace (embedding dimension $d = 1$) also includes the optimum value making it possible to search for the optimum value more efficiently.

BO is a method of finding the optimum value (maximum value or minimum value) of a black-box objective function based on the posterior distribution of the function given observed data. The function is usually modeled by Gaussian processes [5] (GP) and the posterior distribution is constructed using matrix inversion. It is known that BO can more efficiently find the optimum values than random search since it determines the next search point based on the posterior.

However, standard BO suffers from low estimation accuracy and high computation cost, especially when the search space has very high dimensionality. This is because as the dimension rises, the number of observation points required for accurate estimation increases exponentially [6]. This characteristic also makes the cost of computing the posterior distribution too expensive. Therefore, developing Bayesian optimization methods that can work in high dimensional search spaces is important.

Random embedding (RE) is regarded as promising solution [10]. This method uses a randomly generated projection matrix, embeds the search space into low dimensional subspaces, and applies BO in the subspace. If the main search space contains many redundant dimensions that *do not* affect the function value and the number of embedding dimensions almost match the that of effective dimensions which *does* affect function value, RE works well both theoretically and experimentally (see Fig. 1).

However, in real world situations, the number of effective dimensions is unknown, and the number of embedding dimensions may be larger or smaller (see Fig. 2). When the number of embedding dimensions is large (see Fig. 2(a)), the number of calculations required becomes excessive it is proportional to the

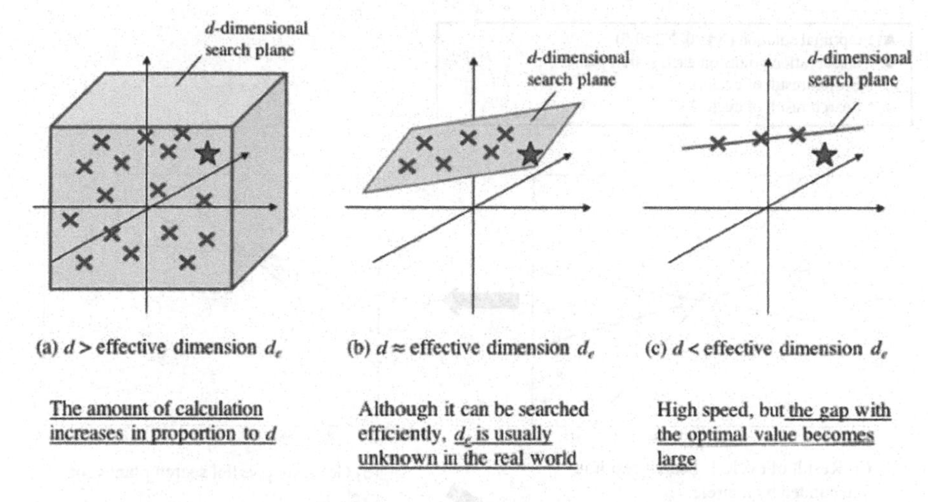

Fig. 2. Problems of existing low-dimensional embedding methods (Organization based on low dimensional size d).

number of embedding dimensions d. Accordingly, the number of embedding dimensions should be as small as possible. However, if the number of embedding dimensions is small (see Fig. 2(c)), there is a problem that the deviation from the optimum value becomes large. Therefore, it is necessary to construct a method that can work well even when the embedding dimension is smaller than the effective dimension.

In this study, we propose a Bayesian optimization method that uses random embedding; it remains efficient even if the embedded dimension is lower than the (unknown) effective dimension. Our method generates multiple search planes to permit searching in low-dimensional subspaces in parallel with incremental search plane refinement. This approach allows us to (i) decrease the probability of missing the optimum value (and its vicinity) by generating and examining search planes in parallel, and to (ii) reduce the deviation from the optimum value by updating the search plane incrementally. Thus, it can be expected to find an optimal solution efficiently even with arbitrary numbers of dimensions. Figure 3 is an example of searching for the optimal solution in one dimension for functions whose number of apparent dimensions is 100 while the effective number of dimensions is 2. It can be confirmed that the search approaches the optimum solution efficiently.

In evaluation experiments, we apply the proposed method to two benchmark problems, and confirm its validity from the viewpoints of whether it can identify the optimum value even when using lower dimensionality planes as well as its increase in convergence speed.

The contributions of this paper are summarized as follows.

- We propose parallel sequential random embedding; it realizes efficient search through the use of lower dimensionality subspaces.

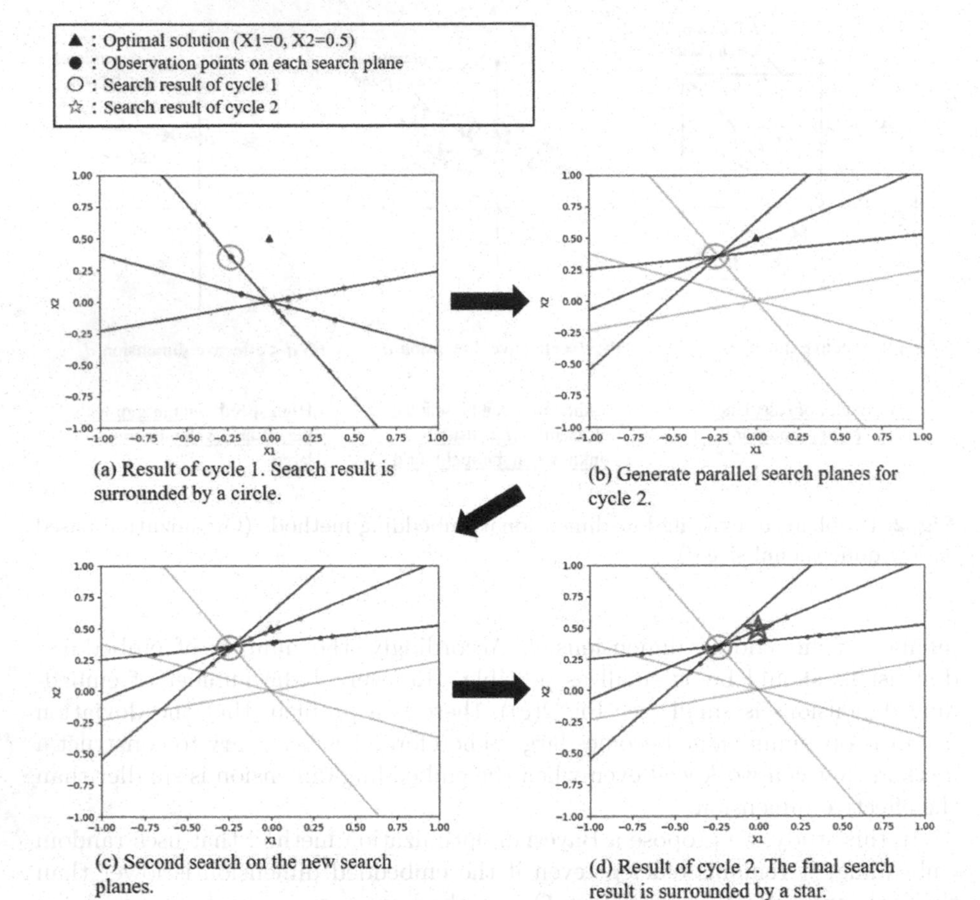

Fig. 3. Image of the proposed method (parallel sequential random embedding). This shows an example of searching for the optimal solution in one dimension for a black-box function whose number of apparent dimensions is 100; number of effective dimensions is 2. In the first cycle, search is performed on three axes in parallel, and the axis passing through the optimum value is taken as the search axis in the second cycle. This shows that the search rapidly approaches the optimal solution.

- In the evaluation experiment, we show the effectiveness of the method from the viewpoints of accuracy and convergence speed.

The structure of this paper is as follows. Section 2 introduces related work and Sect. 3 explains the problem setting and Random embedding, which is the basis of our method. Section 4 describes the proposed method and Sect. 5 details an evaluation experiment; a summary is given in Sect. 6.

2 Related Works

BO methods that deal with high dimensionality by converting the parameter space into low dimensional subspaces can be classified into two types: decomposition and embedding. By reducing the dimensionality, we can expect to find optimal solutions with fewer observation points (number of searches).

A decomposition method assumes that the function is decomposable into several low-dimensional partial functions, and optimizes each of the subordinate functions [8,9]. However, its use depends on the decomposability of the function, and its adaptation range is limited.

Embedding methods embed the search space into low dimensional subspaces, and apply BO in the subspace. Random embedding [6] is the basis of our method. However, as stated in Sect. 1, the number of embedding dimensions must exceed the effective dimensionality number, d_e. The method of [10], based on [6], sequentially performs random embeddings. It defines a new effective dimension d_ϵ, which makes it possible to conduct the search in a lower dimension. However, when using embedding dimensions less than the number of effective dimensions, it is conceivable that a large number of search numbers are required, depending on how the search plane (transformation matrix) is structured.

Parallelized processing is a widely used method for achieving significant speed enhancement. One parallelized BO method assigns tasks to M workers and executes BO in parallel [7]. By performing asynchronous parallel processing, efficient search is enabled. For example, if 100 searches are conducted in parallel using M = 4 workers, speed can be increased by about 4 times. However, parallel processing by itself is insufficient when the search space has high dimensionality.

Therefore, in this research, we focus on a low dimensional method that solves the high dimensional problems directly. We start by adopting the use of embedding to speed up BO processing [6,10], and then add parallel knowledge; the goal is to realize efficient search at lower embedding dimensions.

3 Settings and Random Embedding

Parameter search using BO can be formulated as the optimization problem of finding x^* of Eq. (1).

$$x^* = \arg\min_x G(x) \tag{1}$$

In Random Embedding [6], the input parameters are transformed into low dimensional subspaces using randomly generated transformation matrix A; this yields efficient searches. If input space x has a search dimension that does not affect $G(x)$, or there are some x that have a linear relationship to each other, there are A and w that yield $G(x) = G(Aw)$. In that case, we can convert the optimization problem of Eq. (1) into an optimization problem in a lower dimensionality space. According to [6], let D and $d(>$ EFFECTIVE DIMENSION $d_e)$ be the number of original dimensions and the number of embedding dimensions, respectively. Then, given $x \in R^D$, $A \in R^{D\times d}$, there exists a $w \in R^d$ such that $G(x) = G(Aw)$. That is, for $x^* \in R^D$ there exists a $w^* \in R^d$ such that $G(x^*) = G(Aw^*)$.

Therefore, if $L(w) = G(Aw)$, we can recast the problem as the problem of optimizing Eq. (2) for w^* in low dimensional subspaces.

$$w^* = \arg\min_{w} L(w) \tag{2}$$

We note that Sequential Random Embedding [6] based on [10] is a method that performs random embeddings sequentially. Let $L(w) = G(A_p w + x_{prior})$ in Eq. (1) and let the plane passing through the optimal value of the previous cycle be the search plane of the next cycle. In this way, by sequentially executing random embeddings for multiple cycles, it is possible to reduce the deviation, generated by random embedding, from the true optimum value.

4 Proposed Method

Our proposal of PSRE (parallel sequential random embedding), is based on a method that uses embeddings in low dimensional subspaces [6,10]. As PSRE performs parallel processing and multiple search cycles in low dimensional subspaces, it suppresses the increase in the number of searches depending on how the search plane is structured (transformation matrix) [10], and efficient search for the optimal solution becomes possible even when the number of embedding dimension $d < d_e$.

PSRE consists of three steps as shown in Fig. 4.

Step 1. P parallel transformation matrices, $A_p \in \mathbb{R}^{D\times d}$, are randomly generated and search planes $S_p = \{A_p w + x_{prior} | w \in \mathbb{R}^d\}$ are determined. Here, $x_{prior} = 0$ is set in the initial cycle.

Step 2. For all search planes, GP-based BO is implemented in parallel. Let $x = A_p w + x_{prior}$ and $L(w) = G(A_p w + x_{prior})$, and let $w_p^* = \operatorname{argmin}_w L(w)$ be the search result of each plane.

Step 3. The observation results from each search plane executed in parallel are integrated, and the optimum value x^* satisfying Eq. (1) is determined. Then, setting $x_{prior} = x^*$, the plane considered to have the highest probability of including the optimum value is adopted as the search plane in the next cycle.

Repeat the above steps for C cycles and search for the optimal solution. (i) the probability of including the optimum value (and its vicinity) is increased with each of the search planes generated in parallel, and (ii) the deviation from the optimum value is steadily decreased with each search plane update. A more detailed processing procedure is shown in Algorithm 1.

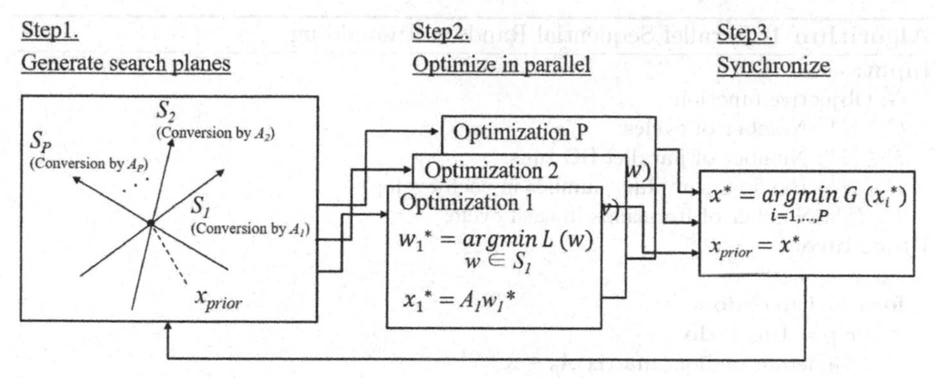

Fig. 4. Outline of parallel sequential random embedding

Here, in Step 2, GP [5] is used for BO. In this case, the posterior probability of the output variable y_* of the unknown input variable w_* under $y = L(w)$ is given by the Gaussian distribution of Eq. (3).

$$\begin{aligned} P(y_*|y) &= N(y_*|\mu(w_*), \sigma^2(w_*)), \\ \mu(w) &= k_w^T C_{nn}^{-1} y, \\ \sigma^2(w) &= k(w,w) - k_w^T C_{nn}^{-1} k_w, \end{aligned} \tag{3}$$

Here, we define $C_{nn} = K_{nn} + \sigma^2 I_n$, where I_n represents an $n \times n$ identity matrix. K_{nn} is the variance covariance matrix of $n \times n$ and the (d, d') element $k_{dd'}$ is represented by $k(w_d, w'_d)$ using kernel function $k(\cdot,\cdot)$. As the kernel function, we use the commonly used Gaussian kernel of Eq. (4).

$$k\left(w_d, w'_d\right) = \exp\left(-a\left\|w_d - w'_d\right\|^2\right), \text{ and } a > 0. \tag{4}$$

While several functions have been proposed as acquisition functions, we adopt the widely used EI (Expected Improvement) [11–13]; it is given by Eq. (5).

$$\alpha\left(w; D\right) = \left(\mu\left(w\right) - \tau\right) \Phi\left(\gamma\left(w\right)\right) + \sigma\left(w\right) \phi\left(\gamma\left(w\right)\right), \ \gamma\left(w\right) = \frac{\mu\left(w\right) - \tau}{\sigma\left(w\right)}, \tag{5}$$

Here, Φ and ϕ are CDF and PDF of the standard normal distribution, respectively; τ is the past optimal value w_{best}.

Algorithm 1. Parallel Sequential Random Embedding

Input:
G: Objective function;
$C \in \mathbb{N}^+$: Number of cycles;
$P \in \mathbb{N}^+$: Number of parallel BO runs;
$R \in \mathbb{N}^+$: Random sampling number in each cycle;
$I \in \mathbb{N}^+$: Number of iterations in each cycle;

Procedure:
$x_{prior} \leftarrow 0$
for $c = 1$ to C **do**
  for $p = 1$ to P **do**
    Generate random matrix $A_p \in \mathbb{R}^{D \times d}$
    Define $x = A_p w + x_{prior}, L(w) = G(A_p w + x_{prior})$
    Generate $\{(w^{(r)} \in \mathbb{R}^d | r = 1, ..., R\}$ by random sampling
    $D_p^{(R)} \leftarrow \{(w^{(r)}, x^{(r)}, L(w^{(r)}) | r = 1, ..., R\}$
    for $i = R + 1$ to $R + I$ **do**
      $w^{(i)} \leftarrow \text{argmax}_{w \in \mathbb{R}^d} \alpha(x; D)$
      $D_p^{(i+1)} \leftarrow D_p^{(i)} \cup (w^{(i)}, x^{(i)}, L(w^{(i)}))$
    end for
  end for
  $D \leftarrow \{D_p | p = 1, ..., P\}$
  $w^*, x^* \leftarrow \text{argmin}_{w \in D} L(w)$
  $x_{prior} \leftarrow x^*$
end for
return x^*

5 Experiment

Experiments on two benchmark problems were conducted to confirm the validity of the proposed method. We evaluate the method from the viewpoints of whether it can find the optimum value even though low dimensional subspaces are used, and where the process can be speeded up.

5.1 Experimental Method

For the experiment, we use the convex Sphere function and the non-convex Ackley function. These are also used in [10], and often used as benchmark functions.

We use the Sphere function given by Eq. (6) where D is the number of input dimensions (original dimensions) and d_e is the number of effective dimensions.

$$f_1(x) = \sum_{i=1}^{d_e} (x_i - 0.1 \times i)^2 \tag{6}$$

The Ackley function is given by Eq. (7), where D is the number of input dimensions (original dimensions) and d_e is the number of effective dimensions.

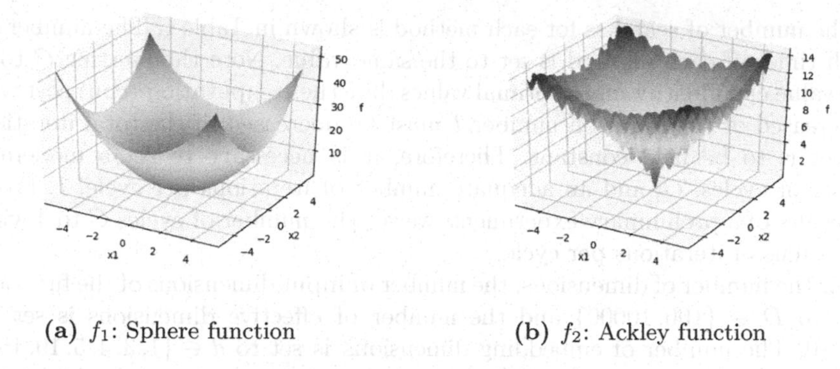

(a) f_1: Sphere function (b) f_2: Ackley function

Fig. 5. Benchmark problems used in experiments. The case of $d_e = 2$ is shown.

$$
\begin{aligned}
f_2(x) = &-20 \exp\left(-\frac{1}{5}\sqrt{\frac{1}{d_e}\sum_{i=1}^{d_e}(x_i - 0.1 \times i)^2}\right) \\
&- \exp\left(\frac{1}{d_e}\sum_{i=1}^{d_e}\cos 2\pi\left(x_i - 0.1 \times i\right)\right) + e + 20
\end{aligned}
\tag{7}
$$

Both functions have optimum values of $[0.1, 0.2, ..., 0.1 \times d_e]$. The functions shown in Fig. 5 are for the case of $d_e = 2$.

We compare the proposed method with the following optimization methods.

Random. An array of dimension D is randomly generated.
BO. BO is performed on the original dimension D.
RE. Using Random Embedding, BO is performed on the subspace of embedding dimension d. This method is proposed in [6].
SRE. BO with the number of low dimension d using Random Embedding is sequentially executed in C cycles by changing the search plane. This method is proposed in [10].
PSRE (proposed method). BO in the subspace of embedding dimension d using Random Embedding is executed in parallel with iterated search plane improvement, and C cycles are executed sequentially.

In the Random method, search points are generated by uniform distribution in a range $[-5, 5]^D$. The elements of transformation matrix $A \in \mathbb{R}^{D \times d}$ used in RE, SRE, PSRE are generated from a standard normal distribution $N(0, 1)$.

The number of searches for each method is shown in Table 1. The number of search times of each method is set to the same value. Note that setting C to a large value can identify more optimal values, but the computation (cpu) cost will be increased or the iteration number I must be decreased, if the total iteration number is to be held constant. Therefore, it is necessary to set a moderate number of cycles, C, and an adequate number of iterations per cycle, I. From the results of a preliminary experiment, we set the number of cycles C to 4 with several tens of iterations per cycle.

For the number of dimensions, the number of input dimensions of the function is set to $D \in \{100, 10000\}$ and the number of effective dimensions is set to $d_e = 10$. The number of embedding dimensions is set to $d \in \{1, 3, 4, 5, 10, 15\}$. BO is executed only when $D = 100$. In each experiment, we conducted 50 runs.

Table 1. Experimental method.

Method	Random sampling [R]	BO iteration [I]	Cycle [C]	Parallel [P]
Random	180	–	1	1
BO	60	120	1	1
RE	60	120	1	1
SRE	15*	30*	4	1
PSRE	15*	30*	4	3

*values are for each cycle.

5.2 Results and Discussion

Evaluation of the Number of Embedding Dimensions. Figure 6 shows the effect of the number of embedding dimensions on the search result. The values were obtained by conducting 50 runs with different seed values and averaging the optimum values returned. Figure 6(a)(b) shows that PSRE found a lower optimum value (smaller optimal value is better) than BO for all numbers of embedding dimensions examined. We can also confirm that optimum values can be found even if the number of embedding dimensions is low, i.e., $d < d_e$. Moreover, PSRE can also be applied to high-dimensional problems that BO cannot (Fig. 6(c)(d)). Figures 6(a)(b)(c)(d) show that PSRE achieved a lower optimum value than all of the other embedding methods (RE, SRE) regardless of the number of embedding dimensions. Although RE and SRE also employ low-dimensional subspaces, PSRE outperforms existing methods as it changes the search space in parallel and incrementally.

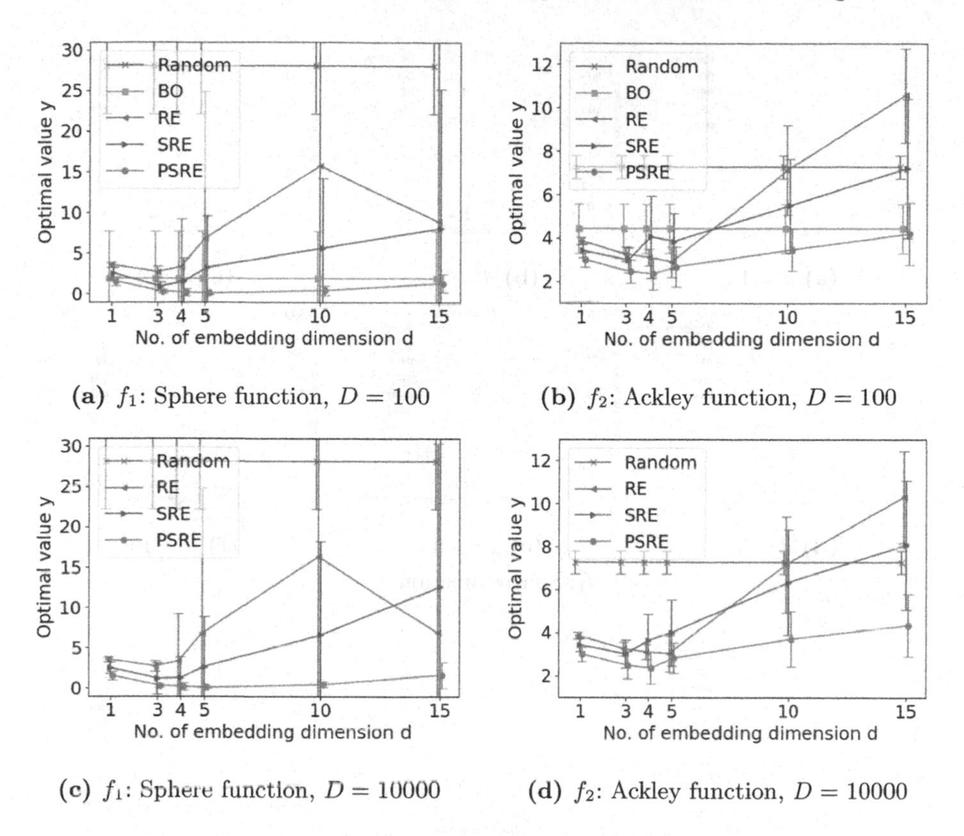

(a) f_1: Sphere function, $D = 100$

(b) f_2: Ackley function, $D = 100$

(c) f_1: Sphere function, $D = 10000$

(d) f_2: Ackley function, $D = 10000$

Fig. 6. Optimum values obtained varying the number of embedding dimensions. The average and standard deviation for 50 runs are shown. Random and BO show a constant value because their performance is not affected by the number of embedding dimensions.

Evaluation of Convergence Speed. Next, the results with regard to convergence speed (when $D = 100$) are shown in Fig. 7. We can confirm that PSRE has faster convergence speed than the other embedding methods (smaller optimal values at each search number are better). Thus, even if the number of iterations is limited, the proposed method achieves better optimal values than the other methods[1]. Although the result of $D = 10000$ is omitted due to space limitations, a similar result was obtained.

[1] We also checked the processing time of each method. PSRE and SRE have similar times, while RE is slower and BO is about ten times slower than PSRE.

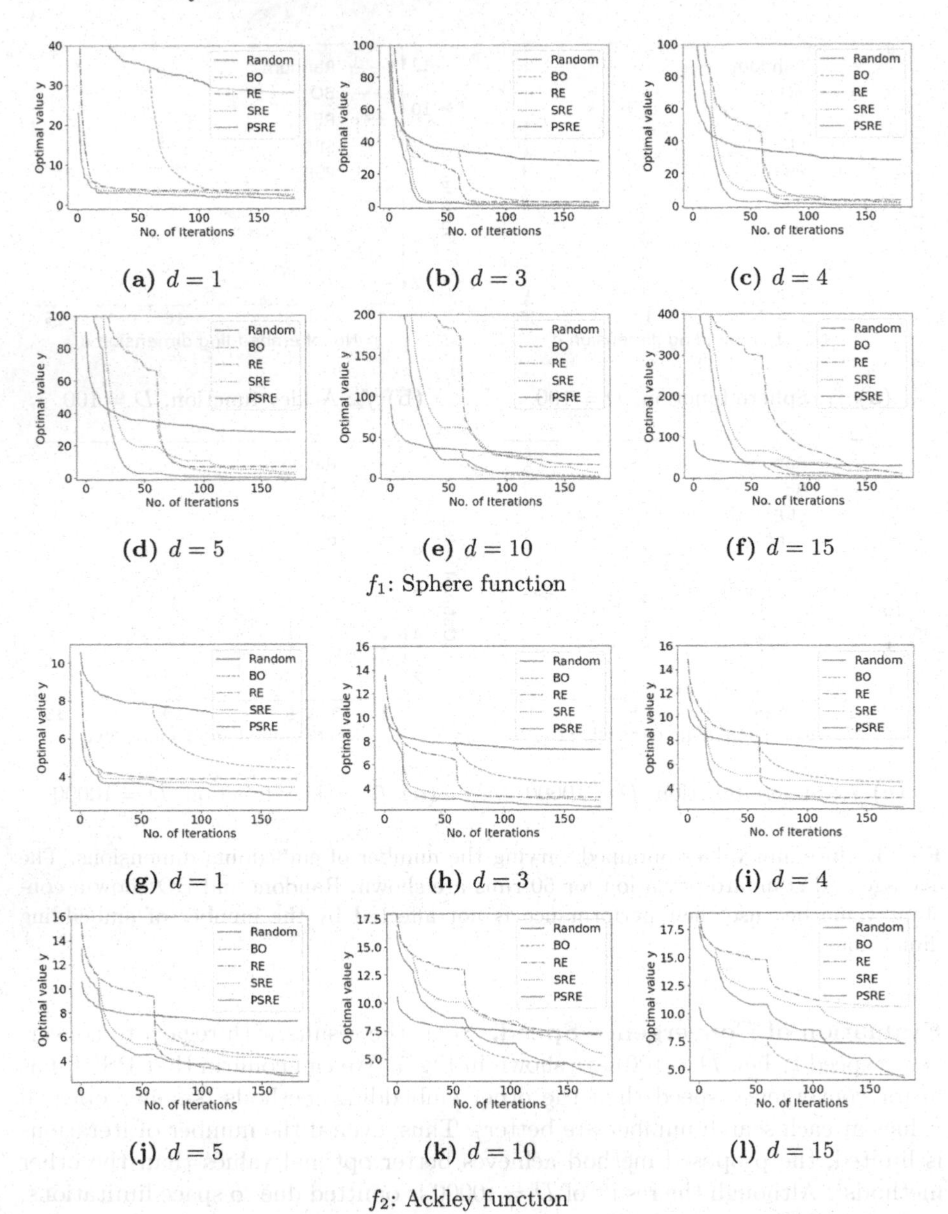

Fig. 7. Convergence speed (when $D = 100$). Values obtained by averaging 50 trial results with different seed values.

6 Conclusion

This study proposed PSRE (parallel sequential random embedding) to accelerate Bayesian optimization in high dimensional spaces. PSRE generates multiple search planes and searches low dimensional subspaces (embedding dimension) in parallel with incremental improvement. Experiments on two benchmark problems showed that the proposed method can efficiently identify the optimal value even if the embedded dimension is lower than the effective dimension. A great merit of PSRE is that optimization can be carried out without concern for d_e. PSRE can be applied to other BO methods, as well as other black box optimization methods than BO. Examples include the genetic algorithm (GA) [14] and the evolution strategy (ES) [15,16] which involves metaheuristic search.

References

1. Snoek, J., Larochelle, H., Adams, R.P.: Practical Bayesian optimization of machine learning algorithms. In: Advances in Neural Information Processing Systems (NIPS), pp. 2951–2959. Curran Associates Inc. (2012)
2. Kiyotake, H., Kohjima, M., Matsubayashi, T., Toda, H.: Multi agent flow estimation based on Bayesian optimization with time delay and low dimensional parameter conversion. In: Miller, T., Oren, N., Sakurai, Y., Noda, I., Savarimuthu, B.T.R., Cao Son, T. (eds.) PRIMA 2018. LNCS (LNAI), vol. 11224, pp. 53–69. Springer, Cham (2018). https://doi.org/10.1007/978-3-030-03098-8_4
3. Brochu, E., Cora, V.M., de Freitas, N.: A tutorial on Bayesian optimization of expensive cost functions, with application to active user modeling and hierarchical reinforcement learning (2010). http://arXiv.org/abs/1012.2599
4. Jones, D., Schonlau, M., Welch, W.: Efficient global optimization of expensive black-box functions. J. Global Optim. **13**(4), 455–492 (1998)
5. Rasmussen, C.E., Williams, C.K.: Gaussian Process for Machine Learning. MIT Press, Cambridge (2006)
6. Wang, Z., Hutter, F., Zoghi, M., Matheson, D., de Freitas, N.: Bayesian optimization in a billion dimensions via random embeddings. J. Artif. Intell. Res. (JAIR) **55**, 361–387 (2016)
7. Kandasamy, K., Krishnamurthy, A., Schneider, J., Poczos, B.: Parallelised Bayesian optimisation via Thompson sampling. In: Proceedings of the Twenty-First International Conference on Artificial Intelligence and Statistics (AISTATS), vol. 84, pp. 133–142. PMLR (2018)
8. Kandasamy, K., Schneider, J., Poczos, B.: High dimensional Bayesian optimisation and bandits via additive models. In: Proceedings of the 32nd International Conference on Machine Learning (ICML), vol. 37, pp. 295–304 (2015)
9. Rolland, P., Scarlett, J., Bogunovic, I., Cevher, V.: High dimensional Bayesian optimization via additive models with overlapping groups. In: International Conference on Artificial Intelligence and Statistics (AISTATS), pp. 298–307 (2018)
10. Qian, H., Hu, Y., Yu, Y.: Derivative-free optimization of high-dimensional non-convex functions by sequential random embeddings. In: Proceedings of the Twenty-Fifth International Joint Conference on Artificial Intelligence (IJCAI), pp. 1946–1952. AAAI Press, New York (2016)

11. Bull, A.D.: Convergence rates of efficient global optimization algorithms. J. Mach. Learn. Res. **12**(Oct), 2879–2904 (2011)
12. Vazquez, E., Bect, J.: Convergence properties of the expected improvement algorithm with fixed mean and covariance functions. J. Stat. Plann. Infer. **140**(11), 3088–3095 (2010)
13. Mockus, J.: Bayesian Approach to Global Optimization: Theory and Applications, vol. 37. Springer, Dordrecht (2012)
14. Davis, L.: Handbook of Genetic Algorithms. Van Nostrand Reinhold, New York (1991)
15. Hansen, N., Muller, S.D., Koumoutsakos, P.: Reducing the time complexity of the derandomized evolution strategy with covariance matrix adaptation (CMA-ES). Evol. Comput. **11**(1), 1–18 (2003)
16. Hansen, N., Auger, A., Ros, R., Finck, S., Posik, P.: Comparing results of 31 algorithms from the black-box optimization benchmarking BBOB-2009. In: Proceedings of the 12th Annual Conference Companion on Genetic and Evolutionary Computation (GECCO), pp. 1689–1696. ACM, New York (2010)

Applications, Medical and Robotics

Fundus Image Classification and Retinal Disease Localization with Limited Supervision

Qier Meng[1(✉)], Yohei Hashimoto[2], and Shin'ichi Satoh[1]

[1] Research Center for Medical Bigdata, National Institute of Informatics, Chiyoda City, Japan
qiermeng@nii.ac.jp

[2] Department of Ophthalmology, Graduate School of Medicine and Faculty of Medicine, The University of Tokyo, Bunkyo City, Japan

Abstract. Image classification using deep convolutional neural networks (DCNN) has a competitive performance with other state-of-the-art methods. Fundus image classification into disease types is also a promising application domain of DCNN. Typically fundus image classifier is trained using fundus images with labels showing disease types. Such training data is relatively easy to obtain, but a massive number of training data is required to achieve adequate classification performance. If classifier can concentrate the evidential regions attached to training images, it is possible to boost the performance with a limited number of the training dataset. However, such regions are very hard to obtain, especially for fundus image classification because only professional ophthalmologist can give such regions and selecting such regions by GUI is very time-consuming. To boost the classification performance with significantly light ophthalmologist intervention, we propose a new method: first, we show evidential heatmaps by DCNN to ophthalmologists, and then obtained their feedback of selecting images with reasonable evidential regions. This intervention is far very easy for opthalmologist compared to drawing evidential regions. Experiments using fundus images revealed that our method improved accuracy from 90.1% to 94.5% in comparison with the existing method. We also found that the attention regions generated by our process are closer to the GT attention regions provided by ophthalmologists.

Keywords: Deep learning · Gradient classification activation map · Attention mining · Fundus image

1 Introduction

Retinal diseases, such as age-related macular degeneration (AMD), diabetic retinopathy (DR), and glaucoma (GLA), are the leading causes of blindness in people aged 60 years and older. Population growth and ageing will have an

S. Palaiahnakote et al. (Eds.): ACPR 2019, LNCS 12046, pp. 469–482, 2020.
https://doi.org/10.1007/978-3-030-41404-7_33

impact on the number of people with vision impairments. AMD is a condition affecting older people and involves the loss of a person's central field of vision. It occurs when the macular retina develops degenerative lesions. It is thought that circulatory insufficiency, with a reduction in blood flow to the macular area, also plays a part. AMD ranks third globally as a cause of blindness. As ageing is one of the significant risk factors for AMD, the number of patients suffering from it may grow in the future as society ages [1]. It is estimated that 196 million people worldwide will have AMD by 2020, 5–15% of which would progress to the advanced stage of the disease [2]. DR is a leading cause of vision loss in middle-aged and older adults worldwide. According to the World Health Organization (WHO), it is estimated that DR accounts for 4.8% of the number of cases of blindness (37 million) worldwide [3]. The first stage of DR, called non-proliferative diabetic retinopathy (NPDR), has no symptoms in the patient. The only way to detect NPDR is by fundus photography, in which microaneurysms can be seen [4,5]. Early detection of NPDR can make for a successful treatment over time. Glaucoma can be regarded as a group of diseases that have as a common point a characteristic optic neuropathy that is determined by both structural changes and functional deficits [6]. Over 12% of blindness cases worldwide are caused by glaucoma [7]. The primary risk factor is caused by ageing and genetic predisposition. Glaucoma is a chronic and irreversible eye disease. The majority of glaucoma patients are asymptomatic until the disease reaches an advanced stage, and the number of ophthalmologists is not sufficient to diagnose patients before the symptoms present themselves. All of these retinal diseases are leading causes of blindness. Therefore, early detection and prompt treatment would allow prevention of retinal-related diseases.

However, the detection of these three kinds of retinal diseases is difficult due to its irregular shape and always has no clear boundary. Automatic disease-related location detection algorithms have been developed to assess retinal images of patients in developing countries that lack equipment and professional personnel [4,5,9–15]. Recent approaches based on weakly supervised learning show good performance [16–18]. [19] proposed a method that utilizes deep learning for localizing discriminative features in DR. Normally fundus image classifier is trained using fundus images with labels showing disease types. Such training data is relatively easy to obtain, but a huge number of training data is required to achieve sufficient classification performance. If classifier can concentrate the evidential regions attached to training images, it is possible to boost the performance with a limited number of the training dataset (e.g., Guided Attention Inference Network (GAIN) [20]). However, such regions are very hard to obtain, especially for fundus image classification because only professional ophthalmologists can give such regions and selecting such regions by GUI is very time-consuming. To boost the classification performance with significantly light ophthalmologist intervention, we propose a new method: first, we show evidential heatmaps by DCNN to ophthalmologists, and then obtained their feedback of selecting images with reasonable evidential regions. This intervention is far very easy for ophthalmologist compared to drawing evidential regions.

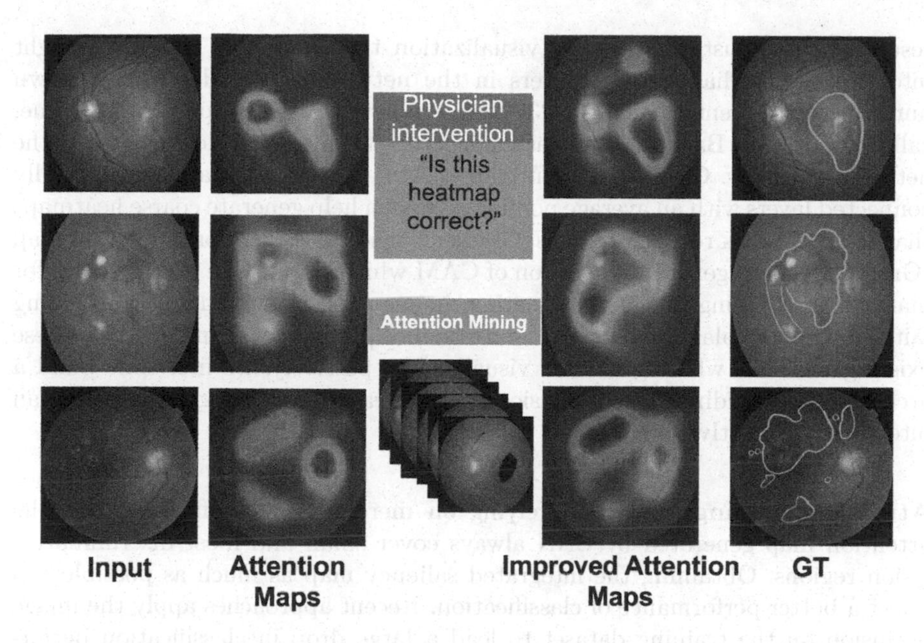

Fig. 1. Framework of the proposed method. The left-most column shows the input images. The second column shows the input images overlaid with heatmaps generated by Grad-CAM [8]. The third column image shows the input images overlaid with heatmaps generated by the proposed method. The right-most images show the ground-truth (GT). The upper and middle cases are examples of the occurrence of AMD and lower cases show an example of the occurrence of DR.

Experiments using over 3,000 fundus images for classification into four disease types revealed that our method improved accuracy from 90.1% (without intervention) to 94.5% (with intervention, for only randomly chosen 20% training images). We also found that the updated evidential regions generated by our process are closer to the ground truth attention regions provided by ophthalmologists (Fig. 1).

2 Related Work

Weakly-Supervised Classification for Object Localization. Weakly supervised learning for object localization has recently acquired much attention due to its high performance. In medical imaging domain, it becomes to a practical solution to address the problem of annotation scarcity [21]. Due to the heavy workload, it is quite difficult to obtain the fully annotation from physicians. Class-specific attention is recently popular as it can be useful in many aspects and applications. With only image-level labels information, attention maps can be for a given input with back-propagation on a Convolutional Neural Network (CNN) [22]. The value of the pixel on the attention map reveals how much the pixel in the original image contributes to the final classification result. [16,17] illustrates a novel visualization technique that give the insight into the intermediate feature layers in the network. Inspired by a top-down human visual attention model, [23] proposes a new back-propagation scheme, called Excitation Backprop, to pass along top-down signals downwards in the network hierarchy. Class activation map (CAM) [22] shows that replacing fully connected layers with an average pooling layer can help generate coarse heatmaps that highlight task relevant regions. Gradient-based classification activation map (Grad-CAM) is a generalized version of CAM which is available architectures for many task including image classification, image captioning and VQA providing faithful visual explanation for model decision [8]. However, comparing to these existing methods which generates visualization passively, we first time build a architecture providing the supervision on the heatmap by integrating physician intervention directly.

Attention Mining. However, relying on merely the classification loss, the attention map generated by CNN always cover small and most discriminative lesion regions. Obtaining the integrated saliency map as much as possible can boost a better performance of classification. Recent approaches apply the image occlusion on the training dataset to lead a large drop in classification performance in CNN, which forces the classifier to memorize other parts belong to the corresponding categories. [24] proposed a method that hiding patches randomly during the training phase to make the network to remember the relevant parts. [25] proposed a method which iteratively train a sequence of model for weakly-supervised semantic segmentation. [26] combines multiple attention maps from a network through iterative erasing steps and consolidate them. GAIN [20] proposed a method that erasing the discriminative part by using Grad-CAM, and used an attention mining loss function to detect the relevant part for classification as much as possible. Our work is closely related to the GAIN, but our work doesn't need the pixel-wise annotation which is time-consuming and difficult to be obtained. Another difference with [20] is our proposed method integrated the physician intervention to study the lesion region by selecting the better heatmaps generated by the model, which is far lighter than providing the pixel-wise annotation.

Learning from Human Feedback. Recently, the human in the loop approach is used by lots of AI developers. The reason for this is that no matter how great your model accuracy, there will always be some extreme cases that are too difficult for the algorithm to handle. It's very difficult to improve on this without human intervention. In medical imaging domain, the feedback from physicians can be important. Obtaining the full annotation from physician is quite difficult due to the heavy workload. In this work, we provide the heatmaps to physicians and get the feedback from them directly and integrated their feedback into the model which can reduce the workload and improve model accuracy effectively.

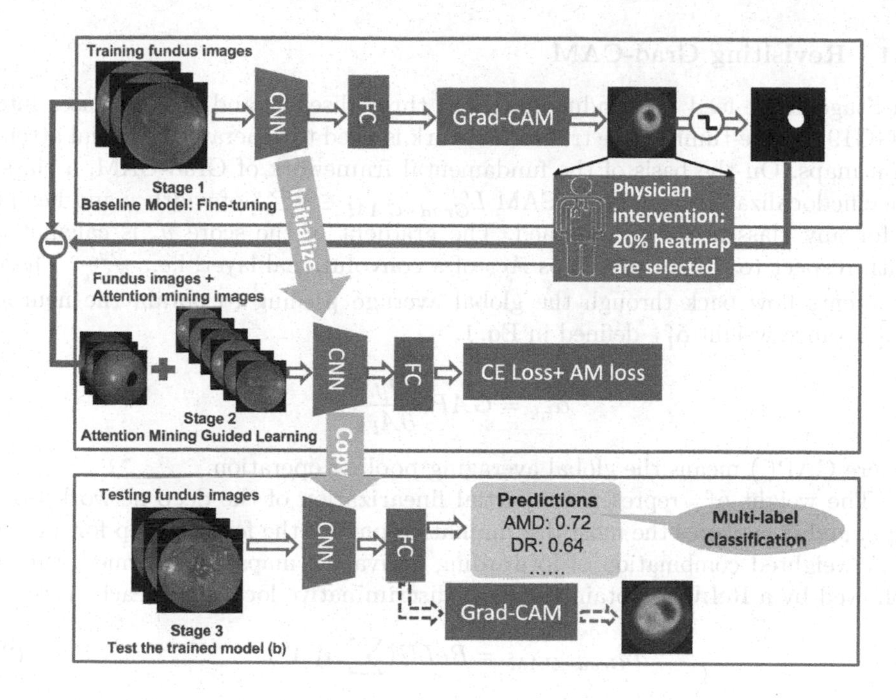

Fig. 2. Flowchart of the proposed method.

3 Method

The attention map reflects the lesion regions of different diseases in fundus images. A typical classifier always detects the discriminative part in the lesion region. Thus, the lesion regions are incomplete. Here, we propose a mechanism that triggers the network to detect integrated lesion regions. Figure 2 shows the flowchart of our method. In Stage 1, we obtain the attention map of each image by using Grad-CAM [8]. An ophthalmologist checks small fraction of training images and selects the attention map that reflects the lesion regions. In Stage 1, attention mining is performed by thresholding the attention maps and erasing the obtained parts from the original images. The images that have been subjected to attention mining and other untouched images are fed into the CNN model for fine-tuning and Grad-CAM is applied again to obtain the attention map in Stage 2. In Stage 3, the test images are input to the trained model to obtain the classification result and the heatmap. Our method is closely related to the GAIN, which guides attention maps with self-exploration. However, unlike that method, our method adds a physician intervention step to select the heatmap during the training phase, which is easier than GAIN and still obtains good performance.

3.1 Revisiting Grad-CAM

In Stage 1, we feed the fundus images of three diseases and healthy cases into VGG19 for fine-tuning. The trained network is used to generate the initial attention maps. On the basis of the fundamental framework of Grad-CAM, a class-specific localization map Grad-CAM $L^c_{Grad-CAM} \in \mathbb{R}^{u \times v}$ of width u and height v for any class c can be obtained. The gradient of the score y_c is calculated with respect to the feature maps $A_{l,k}$ of a convolutional layer, i.e., $\frac{\partial y_c}{\partial A_{l,k}}$. These gradients flow back through the global average pooling to obtain the neuron importance weight $\alpha^c_{l,k}$ defined in Eq. 1.

$$\alpha^c_{l,k} = GAP(\frac{\partial y_c}{\partial A_{l,k}}) \tag{1}$$

where GAP(.) means the global averaging pooling operation.

The weight $\alpha^c_{l,k}$ represents a partial linearization of the deep network from $A_{l,k}$, and it captures the most discriminative part of the feature map for a class c. A weighted combination of forwarding activation maps is performed; this is followed by a ReLU to obtain the most discriminative location of each class:

$$L^c_{Grad-CAM} = ReLU(\sum \alpha^c_k A^k), \tag{2}$$

for unity, we call $L^c_{Grad-CAM}$ as H_g.

3.2 Heatmap Selection by Physician Intervention (PI)

After the attention maps are generated by Grad-CAM, we need to select those that reflect the lesion regions. Here, ophthalmologists classify the attention maps. Certain fraction of training images with attention maps are selected randomly (we found the performance using 20% of training images is optimal), and these images are checked by ophthalmologists. They are requested to select images with reasonable attention maps, and this task is far easy than drawing attention regions (required by [20]).

3.3 Guidance with Attention Mining

Attention mining is utilized in this step. This step is similar to GAIN. Here, GAIN integrates the attention mining part and image classification part. We simplified this method by removing the image classification part (we implemented it in the initial heatmap generation stage). The simplified version requires less memory and runs more efficiently. We experimentally confirmed that the simplified version sufficiently modifies the first heatmaps to reflect actual lesion regions better.

In Sect. 3.1, we use the attention map H_g to generate a mask to be applied to the original input image to obtain I^{*c} using Eq. 3 below, which represents the regions beyond the network's current attention for class c of each disease. This procedure is called attention mining.

$$I^{*c} = I - (T(H_g) \otimes I), \tag{3}$$

where $\otimes$ denotes the element-wise multiplication, $T(H_g)$ is a hard threshold operation to obtain discriminative regions according to the heatmap. We normalize H_g to the range of 0 to 1. When the H_g is larger than 0.5, the $T(H_g)$ is equal to 1, which corresponds to the discriminative regions detected by Grad-CAM. Otherwise, the $T(H_g)$ is equal to 0, which keeps the original input images. The definition of $T(H_g)$ is as follows:

$$T(H_g) = \begin{cases} 0, & H_g < 0.5, \\ 1, & H_g \geq 0.5. \end{cases} \tag{4}$$

In Stage 2, I^{*c} are used as the input of the next classification learning iteration. The second iteration of the training phase of the CNN is initialized using the same network parameters as in Fig. 2. Since our goal is to guide the network to discover all parts of the lesion regions, we force I^{*c} to contain as few features as possible belonging to the disease class. To achieve this goal, we use an attention mining loss (AM loss) function L_{am} that can help in mining attention:

$$L_{am} = \frac{1}{n} \sum_{n} s^c(I^{*c}), \tag{5}$$

where $s^c(I^{*c})$ denotes the prediction score of I^{*c} for class c. n is the number of the class labels for the diseases.

Our final loss function L is defined as the summation of the classification loss L_{cl} and L_{am}.

$$L_1 = L_{cl} + \lambda_1 L_{am}. \tag{6}$$

In experiment, we defined $\lambda_1 = 0.5$. After training, Grad-CAM is applied to generate the heatmap as H_{am}.

4 Experiments

To verify the efficacy of our proposed method, we perform quantitative evaluation of our proposed method for lesion regions localization in fundus image.

4.1 Datasets and Experimental Settings

Dataset Details. The network was trained with 3332 fundus images from a privately collected dataset composed of diseased (three diseases) and healthy cases. This dataset was compiled by thirteen universities, and multiple ophthalmologist experts annotated the images with image-level labels. 60% of the dataset was used for training, 20% of it was used for validation, and the remaining 20% was used for testing. Another 150 pieces of retinal images showing age-related macular degeneration, diabetic retinopathy and glaucoma cases with free-labeled annotations by one ophthalmologist were prepared for evaluating the results in qualitative object localization. For the evaluation of our proposed method in qualitative object localization results, two public dataset, the DiaretDB1 [27], and the e-ophtha [28] are also used in the experiment. DiaretDB1 contains 89 color fundus images with hand-craft labels by four experts for four different DR lesion types. In our evaluation of DiaretDB1, we only consider those pixels as ground truth whose confidence level of labeling exceeds an average of 75% between experts. The dataset e-ophtha-EX is a database of color fundus images specially designed for scientific research in Diabetic Retinopathy (DR) with exudates, which includes 47 color fundus images with hand-craft labels by one expert.

Evaluation Metrics. To evaluate our proposed method of localization, we generate the bounding box according to the heatmap. We normalize our heatmaps between 0 to 1, then empirically threshold the heatmap by a threshold value of 0.5, given as a predicted region P_i, where i enumerated the predicted regions. The corresponding bounding box is generated as B_{Pi}. The corresponding lesion's ground truth is indicated as G_j. The corresponding bounding box is generated as B_{Gj}, where j enumerated the ground truth regions.

There are three evaluation metrics to measure performance: (1) Localization accuracy with know ground truth (*Loc acc*): fraction of images for which the predicted class with the highest probability is the same as the ground truth class and the corresponding predicted bounding box B_{Gj} for the ground truth class has more than 50% IoU with the ground truth box B_{Gj}. (2) False Positives (*FPs/I*): after we calculate the mean Intersection over union (mIOU) for each B_{Pi} with covered B_{Gj}. If the mIOU value is less than 0.5, this region is considered as FP. (3) Classification accuracy (*Class Acc*) to measure the impact of the proposed method on image classification performance

Implementation Details. Before the training, we preprocessed the fundus images by cropping them to remove the black regions, because these regions contain no information. After that, we resized the images to 512 × 512 pixels. During the training phase, we augmented the dataset with randomly rotated and horizontally and vertically flipped images from the dataset. The network was implemented using Keras trained on a Quadro GV100 for 50 epochs for each iteration of training. The backbone of the network architecture was VGG19. We initially fine-tuned the VGG19 with ImageNet. A gradient descent optimizer was used with a momentum of 0.9. We trained our network with a batch size of 16 and an initial learning rate of 0.01. We gradually decrease the learning rate to 0.0001. During the physician intervention, 20% of the heatmaps are chosen for the guidance of attention mining. To obtained the binary map, 50% of the max value of the Grad-CAM is selected as the threshold in the attention mining.

4.2 Performance on Classification

We input the testing dataset to the model trained with images combined with I^{*c} (20%) and I (80%). We compared the classification results of the proposed

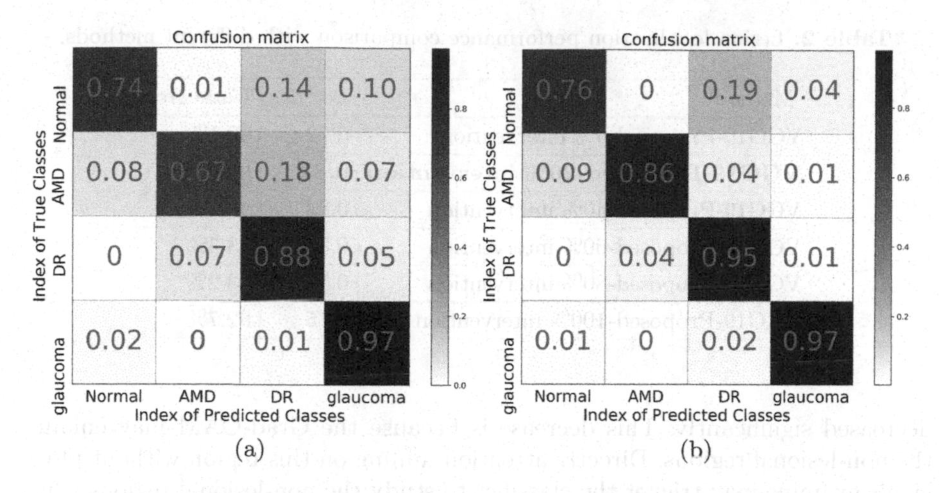

Fig. 3. Confusion matrix of the proposed method and VGG19.

Table 1. Lesion-level performance of the methods.

Method	AMD		DR		Glaucoma	
	Loc acc	*FPs/I*	*Loc acc*	*FPs/I*	*Loc acc*	*FPs/I*
CAM	0.60	2.17	0.64	3.64	0.63	1.89
Grad-CAM	0.62	2.04	0.67	3.14	0.66	1.64
Ours (no PI)	0.79	1.94	0.78	2.87	0.73	1.32
Ours	**0.83**	**1.83**	**0.81**	**2.17**	**0.85**	**1.24**

method and VGG19. Figure 3 shows the confusion matrixs. The total accuracy of VGG19 was 90.1%, the total accuracy of the method that 20% training dataset are fed to attention mining without physician intervention (Ours (no PI)) is 93.2%, whereas the total accuracy of the proposed method was around 94.5%, i.e., 4.4% higher than VGG19. According to Fig. 3, although the proposed method increased the percentage of correct classifications of the three diseases, it also misclassified some of the fundus images of the normal cases as abnormal. Here, we suppose that the attention mining sometimes misled the classifier. Table 1 compares the sensitivity (SE) and FP of different methods and our proposed method without physician intervention (Ours (no PI)). It shows that our method had fewer FPs than the other methods while achieving better results.

4.3 Physician Intervention Is Necessary

We present the experiment in Table 2, which compares the localization performance of 0% physician intervention, 20% physician intervention, 40% physician intervention, 60% physician intervention, 80% physician intervention and 100% physician intervention. According to Table 2, it can be seen that without physician intervention, the localization performance and classification performance is

Table 2. Lesion localization performance comparison with different methods.

Method	*Loc acc*	*Class Acc*
VGG19-Proposed-0% intervention	0.72	90.1%
VGG19-Proposed-20% intervention	**0.83**	**94.5%**
VGG19-Proposed-40% intervention	0.82	93.9%
VGG19-Proposed-60% intervention	0.80	93.5%
VGG19-Proposed-80% intervention	0.77	93.2%
VGG19-Proposed-100% intervention	0.75	92.7%

decreased significantly. This decrease is because the Grad-CAM may enhance the non-lesional regions. Directly attention mining on this region without physician's examine may trigger the classifier to study the non-lesional regions which decrease the performance. In general, the performance can be increased after adding physician intervention. But if the physician intervenes the heatmaps selection too much, it reduces the performance inversely. As we increase the amount of heatmap selection gradually from 0% to 100% by the step of 20%, we surprisingly find that the total localization accuracy and the overall classification accuracy is decreased accordingly. This decrease is because too much physician intervention may cause the overfit to the spurious attention mined regions. And to depart with the non-lesional area, the heatmap may be triggered to some marginal areas which increase the inaccuracy.

4.4 Qualitative Results on Lesion Localization

In Fig. 4, we visualize the gradient class activation map (Grad-CAM) and bounding box obtained by simply using VGG19 and our proposed method. We also visualize the bounding box obtained by our proposed and those obtained by VGG19-Grad-CAM on our privetely collected data and two public dataset the DiaretDB1 [27] and the e-ophtha [28]. In each image pair, the first image shows the predicted (green) and ground-truth (red) bounding box. The second images shows the corresponding Grad-CAM heatmaps. According to the Fig. 4, our proposed method can localize the lesion regions more accurately compare VGG19-Grad-CAM. The VGG19-Grad-CAM can only detect the most discriminative part of the lesion regions. Even in some cases, VGG19-Grad-CAM detect the incorrect regions. Our proposed method can more relevant lesion locations compare to VGG19-Grad-CAM.

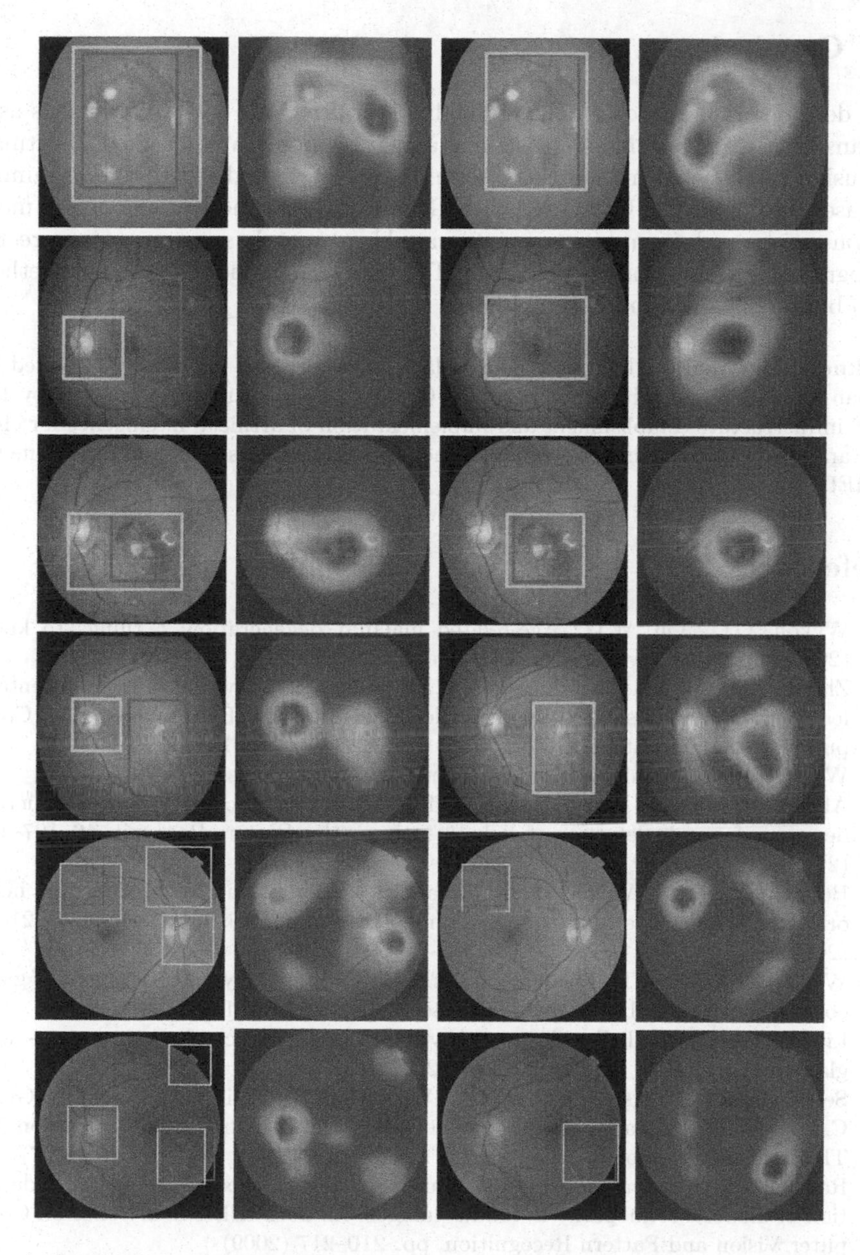

Fig. 4. Qualitative object localization results. We compare our approach with VGG19-Grad-CAM on our privetely collected data and two public dataset the DiaretDB1 [27] and the e-ophtha [28]. The first to fourth rows indicate the results of our privately collected dataset of AMD. The last two rows indicate the cases in DiaretDB1 and e-ophtha of disease of DR. For each image, we show the bounding box and Grad-CAM obtained by VGG19-Grad-CAM (left) and our proposed method (right). Compare to VGG19-Grad-CAM, our proposed method can detected more accurate and integrated lesion regions not only the most discriminative regions. (Color figure online)

5 Conclusion

We developed an approach that highlights lesion regions on retinal images as a means of assisting ophthalmologists in making diagnoses. We obtained a heatmap by using Grad-CAM, mined the discriminative part, and fed the new training dataset into the CNN. Compared with Grad-CAM, our method can detect more lesion regions and generate a more integrated heatmap. In some cases, incorrectly recognized heatmaps can be corrected. The experiment showed that our method also boosts classification performance.

Acknowledgement. The fundus image dataset is prepared and kindly provided by Japan Ocular Imaging Registry Research Group. This research is supported by the ICT infrastructure establishment and implementation of artificial intelligence for clinical and medical research from Japan Agency for Medical Research and development, AMED.

References

1. Wykoff, C.C., Ou, W.C.: Age-related macular degeneration: 5 things to know (2018). https://www.medscape.com/viewarticle/906221
2. Zhang, X., Wei, Y., Feng, J., Yang, Y., Huang, T.S.: Adversarial complementary learning for weakly supervised object localization. In: IEEE Conference on Computer Vision and Pattern Recognition, pp. 1325–1334 (2018)
3. World Health Organization: Global report on diabetes, January 2016
4. Akram, M., Khalid, S., Khan, S.: Identification and classification of microaneurysms for early detection of diabetic retinopathy. Pattern Recognit. **46**, 107–116 (2013)
5. Bortolin Júnior, S., Welfer, D.: Automatic detection of microaneurysms and hemorrhages in color eye fundus images. Int. J. Comput. Sci. Inf. Technol. **5**, 21–37 (2013)
6. Weinreb, R., Aung, T., Medeiros, F.: The pathophysiology and treatment of glaucoma a review. JAMA J. Am. Med. Assoc. **311**, 1901–1911 (2014)
7. Liu, Y., Allingham, R.R.: Major review: molecular genetics of primary open-angle glaucoma. Exp. Eye Res. **160**, 62–84 (2017)
8. Selvaraju, R.R., Cogswell, M., Das, A., Vedantam, R., Parikh, D., Batra, D.: Grad-CAM: visual explanations from deep networks via gradient-based localization. In: The IEEE International Conference on Computer Vision, pp. 618–626 (2017)
9. Ravishankar, S., Jain, A., Mittal, A.: Automated feature extraction for early detection of diabetic retinopathy in fundus images. In: 2012 IEEE Conference on Computer Vision and Pattern Recognition, pp. 210–217 (2009)
10. Zhou, W., Wu, C., Yu, X., Gao, Y., Du, W.: Automatic fovea center localization in retinal images using saliency-guided object discovery and feature extraction. J. Med. Imaging Health Inform. **7**, 1070–1077 (2017)
11. Muramatsu, C., Ishida, K., Sawada, A., Hatanaka, Y., Yamamoto, T., Fujita, H.: Automated detection of retinal nerve fiber layer defects on fundus images: false positive reduction based on vessel likelihood. In: Proceedings of the Medical Imaging 2016: Computer-Aided Diagnosis. SPIE, vol. 9785, p. 97852L (2016)

12. Waseem, S., Akram, M., Ahmed, B.: Drusen exudate lesion discrimination in colour fundus images. In: 2014 14th International Conference on Hybrid Intelligent Systems, HIS 2014, pp. 176–180 (2015)
13. Tang, L., Niemeijer, M., Reinhardt, J., Garvin, M., Abramoff, M.: Splat feature classification with application to retinal hemorrhage detection in fundus images. IEEE Trans. Med. Imaging **32**, 364–375 (2012)
14. Hatanaka, Y., et al.: CAD scheme to detect hemorrhages and exudates in ocular fundus images. In: Proceedings of the Medical Imaging 2007: Computer-Aided Diagnosis, vol. 6514, p. 65142M (2007)
15. Chen, X., Xu, Y., Yan, S., Wong, D.W.K., Wong, T.Y., Liu, J.: Automatic feature learning for glaucoma detection based on deep learning. In: Navab, N., Hornegger, J., Wells, W.M., Frangi, A.F. (eds.) MICCAI 2015. LNCS, vol. 9351, pp. 669–677. Springer, Cham (2015). https://doi.org/10.1007/978-3-319-24574-4_80
16. Simonyan, K., et al.: Deep inside convolutional networks: visualising image classification models and saliency maps. CoRR (2013)
17. Zeiler, M.D., Fergus, R.: Visualizing and understanding convolutional networks. In: Fleet, D., Pajdla, T., Schiele, B., Tuytelaars, T. (eds.) ECCV 2014. LNCS, vol. 8689, pp. 818–833. Springer, Cham (2014). https://doi.org/10.1007/978-3-319-10590-1_53
18. Pathak, D., Krahenbuhl, P., Darrell, T.: Constrained convolutional neural networks for weakly supervised segmentation. In: The IEEE International Conference on Computer Vision (ICCV), pp. 1796–1804 (2015)
19. Gondal, W.M., Köhler, J.M., Grzeszick, R., Fink, G.A., Hirsch, M.: Weakly-supervised localization of diabetic retinopathy lesions in retinal fundus images. In: 2017 IEEE International Conference on Image Processing (ICIP), pp. 2069–2073 (2017)
20. Li, K., Wu, Z., Peng, K.-C., Ernst, J., Fu, Y.: Tell me where to look: guided attention inference network. In: The IEEE Conference on Computer Vision and Pattern Recognition, pp. 9215–9223 (2018)
21. Hwang, S., Kim, H.-E.: Self-transfer learning for weakly supervised lesion localization. In: Ourselin, S., Joskowicz, L., Sabuncu, M.R., Unal, G., Wells, W. (eds.) MICCAI 2016. LNCS, vol. 9901, pp. 239–246. Springer, Cham (2016). https://doi.org/10.1007/978-3-319-46723-8_28
22. Zhou, B., Khosla, A., Lapedriza, A., Oliva, A., Torralba, A.: Learning deep features for discriminative localization. In: 2016 IEEE Conference on Computer Vision and Pattern Recognition (CVPR), Las Vegas, NV, pp. 2921–2929 (2016)
23. Zhang, J., Lin, Z., Brandt, J., Shen, X., Sclaroff, S.: Top-down neural attention by excitation backprop. In: Leibe, B., Matas, J., Sebe, N., Welling, M. (eds.) ECCV 2016. LNCS, vol. 9908, pp. 543–559. Springer, Cham (2016). https://doi.org/10.1007/978-3-319-46493-0_33
24. Singh, K.K., Lee, Y.J.: Hide-and-seek: forcing a network to be meticulous for weakly-supervised object and action localization. In: 2017 IEEE International Conference on Computer Vision (ICCV), pp. 3544–3553 (2017)
25. Zhang, X., Wei, Y., Feng, J., Yang, Y., Huang, T.S.: Adversarial complementary learning for weakly supervised object localization. In: The IEEE Conference on Computer Vision and Pattern Recognition, pp. 1325–1334 (2018)
26. Wei, Y., Feng, J., Liang, X., Cheng, M.-M., Zhao, Y., Yan, S.: Object region mining with adversarial erasing: a simple classification to semantic segmentation approach. In: The IEEE Conference on Computer Vision and Pattern Recognition, pp. 1568–1576 (2017)

27. Kauppi, T., et al.: DIARETDB1 diabetic retinopathy database and evaluation protocol. In: Proceedings of the Medical Image Understanding and Analysis (MIUA) (2007)
28. Decencire, E., et al.: TeleOphta: machine learning and image processing methods for teleophthalmology. IRBM **34**(2), 196–203 (2013)

OSTER: An Orientation Sensitive Scene Text Recognizer with CenterLine Rectification

Zipeng Feng[1,2], Chen Du[1,2], Yanna Wang[1], and Baihua Xiao[1(✉)]

[1] The State Key Laboratory of Management and Control for Complex Systems, Institute of Automation Chinese Academy of Sciences, Beijing, China
{fengzipeng2017,duchen2016,wangyanna2013,baihua.xiao}@ia.ac.cn
[2] University of Chinese Academy of Sciences, Beijing, China

Abstract. Scene texts in China are always arbitrarily arranged in two forms: horizontally and vertically. These two forms of texts exhibit distinctive features, making it difficult to recognize them simultaneously. Besides, recognizing irregular scene texts is still a challenging task due to their various shapes and distorted patterns. In this paper, we propose an orientation sensitive network aiming at distinguishing between Chinese horizontal and vertical texts. The learned orientation is then passed into an attention selective network to adjust the attention maps of the sequence recognition model, leading it working for each type of texts respectively. In addition, a lightweight centerline rectification network is adopted, which enables the irregular texts more readable while no redundant labels are needed. A synthetic dataset named SCTD is released to support our training and evaluate the proposed model. Extensive experiments show that the proposed method is capable of recognizing arbitrarily-aligned scene texts accurately and efficiently, achieving state-of-the-art performance over a number of public datasets.

Keywords: Scene text recognition · Arbitrarily-aligned Chinese texts · Attention selective network · Centerline rectification · Sequence-to-sequence

1 Introduction

Scene text recognition has attracted much interest in the computer vision field because of its various applications, such as intelligent driving and goods identification. Nowadays, text recognition methods based on convolutional neural networks [9] have gained large success, especially integrating convolutional neural networks with recurrent neural networks [20] and attention mechanisms [28].

However, the majority of the scene text recognition algorithms only cover English texts. According to our statistics, English vertical texts always have the same arrangement mode as horizontal ones, as Fig. 1(a) shows. But in China, horizontal and vertical texts usually have completely different arrangement modes.

S. Palaiahnakote et al. (Eds.): ACPR 2019, LNCS 12046, pp. 483–497, 2020.
https://doi.org/10.1007/978-3-030-41404-7_34

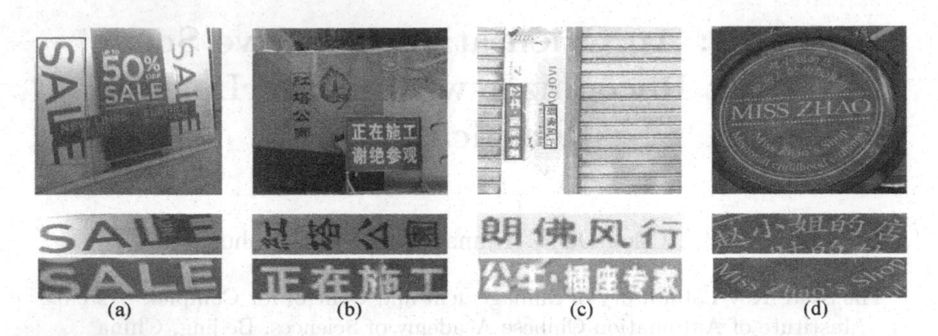

Fig. 1. Examples of arbitrarily-aligned scene texts. (a) Horizontal and vertical English texts generally have the same arrangement mode. (b) But Chinese scene texts have two different arrangement modes. (c) Identifying the arrangement modes of Chinese texts just by their aspect ratios may lead to terrible mistakes. (d) Curved and distorted patterns are popular in both Chinese and English scene texts.

If training them as a whole, the recognition network will learn entirely different features with the same label, which could puzzle the network, causing the training process slowly and inaccurately. In practice, we usually identify the orientation of texts depending on heuristic rules such as aspect ratio, but it is not enough to deal with scene texts which are arbitrarily-aligned. As Fig. 1(c) shows, some vertical texts have the same arrangement mode as horizontal texts, but they may be misclassified by merely aspect ratio. For these reasons, learning the orientation of texts is a more general approach.

Besides, irregular texts appear in natural scenes frequently owing to curved character placement, perspective distortion, etc. Recognizing texts with arbitrary shapes is an extremely difficult task because of unpredictable changeful text layouts. As illustrated in Fig. 1(d), both English and Chinese texts suffer from various irregular texts, causing additional challenges in recognition.

In this paper, we propose an orientation sensitive scene text recognition network (OSTER) to learn the orientation of texts automatically and deal with horizontal and vertical texts simultaneously. It consists of an orientation sensitive network (OSN), a centerline rectification network (CRN) and an attention selective sequence-to-sequence recognition network (ASN). The OSN judges the orientation of the input text images. As a result, the features of horizontal and vertical images could be learned respectively, helping the network to learn quickly and accurately. The CRN models the centerline of scene texts and corrects the distorted text to a regular one by fitting the equidistant sampling points with the centerline. The ASN generates entirely different attention maps for horizontal and vertical texts and predicts different character sequence according to the learned orientation weights. The whole network can be trained end-to-end by a multi-task learning manner.

The contributions of this paper can be summarized as follows:

- We propose an orientation sensitive network to learn the orientation of the input texts automatically, and an attention selective network to generate entirely different attention maps for horizontal and vertical texts, which improve the performance of the recognition network.
- We propose a centerline rectification network to correct the distorted text to a regular one by fitting the equidistant sampling points with the centerline.
- We establish a synthetic Chinese scene text dataset to train the proposed model, which includes half of horizontal texts and half of vertical texts.
- We develop an end-to-end trainable system that is robust to parameter initialization and achieves superior scene text recognition performance over a number of public datasets. To our knowledge, this paper is the first work to deal with different arrangement modes of Chinese texts.

2 Related Works

Recent years, scene text recognition has been widely researched and a variety of recognition methods have been proposed. The traditional character-level scene text recognition methods first generate multiple candidate character positions, and then applies the character classifier for recognition [2,26]. With the successful application of recurrent neural network (RNN) in sequence recognition, Shi [20] integrated convolutional neural networks (CNN) with RNN and proposed an end-to-end trainable network named CRNN. After that, Lee [13] proposed an attention mechanism, which can detect more discriminative regions in images, thus improving recognition performance. Facing the attention drift problem, Cheng [3] proposed the focusing attention network (FAN) to automatically adjust the attention weights. Liu [15] presented a binary convolutional encoder-decoder network (B-CEDNet). Combined with a bidirectional recurrent neural network, it can achieve significant speed-up. Although these approaches have shown attractive results, the irregular texts still can not be dealed with effectively. The main reason is that environments in scene texts are various, such as complicated backgrounds, perspective distortion and arbitrary orientation.

Due to these difficult cases, irregular text recognition has attracted more and more attention from researchers. Shi [21] applied the spatial transformer network (STN) [10] for text rectification, then put the rectified text images into the sequence-to-sequence recognition network to get the final result. To rectify the distorted text image better, Zhan [29] developed an iterative rectification framework, which can estimate and correct perspective distortion and text line curvature iteratively. Different from rectifying the entire distorted text image, Liao [14] presented a method called Character Attention FCN (CA-FCN), which modeled the irregular text images in a two-dimensional fashion. Although considerably improving the performance for irregular text recognition, it is still difficult to precisely locate the fiducial points which tightly bound the text regions, especially for severely distorted texts. This leads to errors in parameters estimation of the STN and causes the deformation of scene texts. Different from the existing methods, we model the centerline of texts and correct the distorted texts to straight lines, which is robust and flexible in scene text rectification.

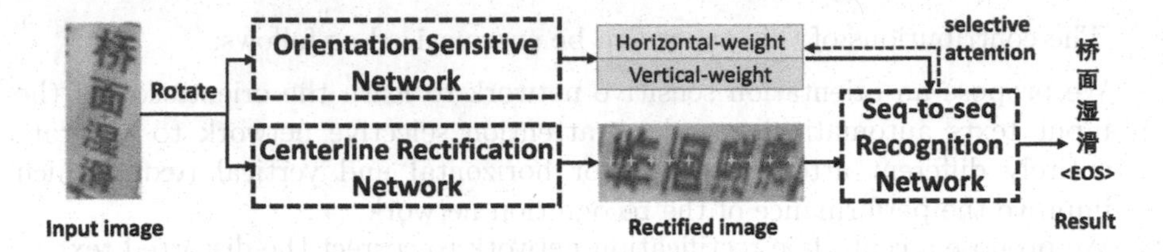

Fig. 2. Overview of the proposed OSTER. The centerline rectification network corrects the distorted text to a regular one; the orientation sensitive network perceives the arrangement mode of input images; the attention selective recognition network generate corresponding attention map at each time step for better recognition results.

At present, some methods process recognition task from the perspective of the orientation of texts. Cheng [4] devised an arbitrary orientation network (AON) to extract visual features of texts in four directions. Weighting the four-direction sequences of features, it can predict the orientation of rotated texts in an unsupervised learning method. However, the essence of AON is dealing with irregular texts caused by rotation, which is extremely different from learning arrangement modes of Chinese scene texts in this paper. Besides, the strategy of scaling word images to a square in AON will destroy the information of text lines, especially for Chinese texts whose aspect ratio are relatively large. For these reasons, we propose an orientation sensitive network to learn the orientation of the input texts automatically, and then pass the learned orientation into an attention selective network to deal with horizontal and vertical texts respectively.

3 Methodology

This section will present the proposed model including CRN, OSN and ASN. The overview of our proposed network is as Fig. 2.

3.1 Centerline Rectification Network

Recently, the STN based rectification methods have achieved great success in recognizing irregular texts, but there are still some problems to deal with. Firstly, it is still difficult to precisely locate the fiducial points which tightly bound the text region, especially for severely distorted text. Once the prediction of fiducial points deviates, the texts will often be incomplete, which will have a great impact on the recognition results. Our experiment shows that the background left at the text edges does not disturb the recognition results too much, but the real reason lies in that the character features in the distorted text line are significantly different from those of the horizontal text. Therefore, modeling the pose of texts and correcting the curved texts to straight lines should be paid more attention.

Some recent works [29] model the centerline of texts using the polynomial fitting method and have made great progress. But compared with predicting offsets of fiducial points, fitting polynomials is a more abstract task which needs

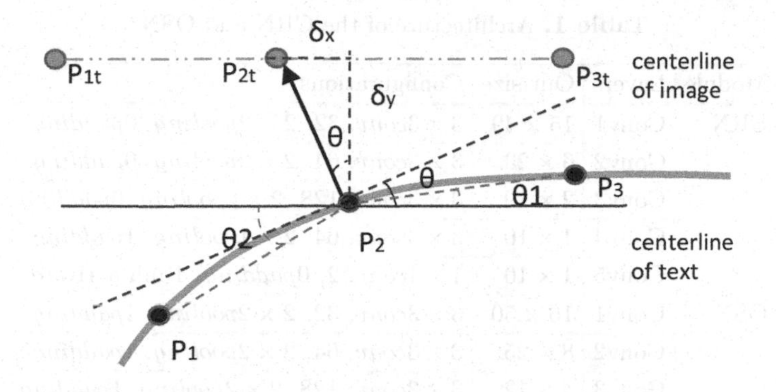

Fig. 3. Schematic of curved text correction.

greater learning cost. As a contrast, CRN predicts the offset from the centerline of texts to the centerline of the input images directly, which can correct the irregular texts at a small cost.

The CRN works as follows: firstly, it models the centerline of the texts and takes several points on it with equal sampling. As Fig. 3 shows, we predict N equal sampling points $(P_1, P_2, P_3, \ldots, P_N)$ on the centerline of the text. Their corresponding points on the centerline of image are $(P_{1t}, P_{2t}, P_{3t}, \ldots, P_{Nt})$. Each point $P_i(i = 1, \ldots, N)$ can be represented by (x_i, y_i).

In order to distribute the characters as evenly as possible, avoiding deformation due to compression and stretching, areas with more severe curved should be mapped for longer horizontal distances. Therefore, mapping along the normal direction is an ideal choice. Apparently, the y-coordinate of P_{it} is $h/2$, where h is the height of input image. The x-coordinate of P_{it} can be computed by

$$x_{it} = x_i - \Delta x_i \tag{1}$$

$$\Delta x_i = \Delta y_i \times \tan\theta_i \tag{2}$$

$$\Delta y_i = y_i - \frac{h}{2} \tag{3}$$

As can be seen from Fig. 3, θ_i can be approximated to $(\theta_{i1} + \theta_{i2})/2$, where

$$\tan\theta_{i1} = \left|\frac{y_{i+1} - y_i}{x_{i+1} - x_i}\right| \tag{4}$$

$$\tan\theta_{i2} = \left|\frac{y_i - y_{i-1}}{x_i - x_{i-1}}\right| \tag{5}$$

The CRN estimate the location of points by employing a network described in Table 1. Once the origin points and target points are determined, scene text distortions can then be corrected by a thin plate spline transformation (TPS) [22]. A grid can be generated within the distorted scene text, and a sampler is implemented to produce the rectified scene text image by using the determined

Table 1. Architecture of the CRN and OSN

Module	Layers	Out size	Configurations
CRN	Conv1	15×49	$3 \times 3 conv$, 32, $2 \times 2 pooling$, $0 padding$
	Conv2	6×23	$3 \times 3 conv$, 64, $2 \times 2 pooling$, $0 padding$
	Conv3	2×10	$3 \times 3 conv$, 128, $2 \times 2 pooling$, $0 padding$
	Conv4	1×10	$3 \times 3 conv$, 64, $2 \times 1 pooling$, $1 padding$
	Conv5	1×10	$1 \times 1 conv$, 2, $0 padding$, Tanh activate
OSN	Conv1	16×50	$3 \times 3 conv$, 32, $2 \times 2 pooling$, $1 padding$
	Conv2	8×25	$3 \times 3 conv$, 64, $2 \times 2 pooling$, $1 padding$
	Conv3	4×12	$3 \times 3 conv$, 128, $2 \times 2 pooling$, $1 padding$
	Conv4	1×5	$3 \times 3 conv$, 256, $2 \times 2 pooling$, $0 padding$
	FC1	64	Sigmoid activate
	FC2	1	Sigmoid activate

grid, where the value of the pixel p_t is bilinearly interpolated from the pixels near p within the distorted scene text image. It should be noted that the training of the localization network does not require any extra annotation but is completely driven by the gradients that are back-propagated from the recognition network. Only estimating the x-coordinate and y-coordinate of points, the total parameter number is just $2N$. In our trained network, 10 points are employed for scene text pose estimation.

3.2 Orientation Sensitive Network

The OSN is designed to judge the orientation of input text images, and pass the confidence of orientation to the subsequent recognition network. As a result, the horizontal image features and vertical image features could be learned respectively, which is beneficial to achieve better recognition performance.

Similar to the binary classification problem, the OSN can learn the orientation attributes of texts guided by the orientation label in the training stage. For every input scene text, the OSN can identify the orientation of it precisely. Compared with training all texts as a whole, it provides more discriminative features for recognition network, improving the recognition ability of the network. Compared with training horizontal and vertical texts respectively, it simplifies the recognition process and can handle abnormal cases as Fig. 1(c) shows, improving the robustness and convenience of the recognition network. The structure of OSN can be viewed as Table 1 too.

3.3 Attention Selective Sequence-to-Sequence Network

The recognition network employs a sequence-to-sequence model with an attention mechanism. It consists of a convolutional-recurrent neural network encoder and an attention-based recurrent neural network decoder.

Table 2. Architecture of the recognition network

Layers	Out size	Configurations
Block0	32×100	$3 \times 3 conv, 32, 1 \times 1 stride$
Block1	16×50	$\begin{bmatrix} 1 \times 1 conv, 32 \\ 3 \times 3 conv, 32 \end{bmatrix} \times 3, 2 \times 2 stride$
Block2	8×25	$\begin{bmatrix} 1 \times 1 conv, 64 \\ 3 \times 3 conv, 64 \end{bmatrix} \times 4, 2 \times 2 stride$
Block3	4×25	$\begin{bmatrix} 1 \times 1 conv, 128 \\ 3 \times 3 conv, 128 \end{bmatrix} \times 6, 2 \times 1 stride$
Block4	2×25	$\begin{bmatrix} 1 \times 1 conv, 256 \\ 3 \times 3 conv, 256 \end{bmatrix} \times 6, 2 \times 1 stride$
Block5	1×25	$\begin{bmatrix} 1 \times 1 conv, 512 \\ 3 \times 3 conv, 512 \end{bmatrix} \times 3, 2 \times 1 stride$
BiLSTM	25	256 hidden units
BiLSTM	25	256 hidden units
AttLSTM	-	256 hidden units, 256 attention units
AttLSTM	-	256 hidden units, 256 attention units

We employ a 31-layer ResNet to extract the sequence feature from the input image. A 2×2 stride convolution is implemented to down-sample feature maps in the first two residual blocks, which is changed to 2×1 stride in all following residual blocks. This helps to reserve more information along the horizontal direction and is very useful for distinguishing neighbor characters. To enlarge the feature context, we adopt a multi-layer bidirectional LSTM (BLSTM) network [5] over the feature sequence.

An attention-based decoder directly generates the target sequence from an input feature sequence. We trade T for the largest number of steps generated by the decoder and L for the length of the feature sequence. At time step t, the vector of attention weights $\alpha_{t,i}$ is as follows:

$$\alpha_{t,i} = exp(c_{t,i}) / \sum_{j=1}^{L} (exp(c_{t,j})) \tag{6}$$

$$c_{t,i} = w_1 \times e^h_{t,i} + w_2 \times e^v_{t,i} \tag{7}$$

The weights w_1 and w_2 indicate the possibilities of each orientation, which are predicted by OSN. Apparently, we have $w_1 + w_2 = 1$. The $e^h_{t,i}$ and $e^v_{t,i}$ denote the intermediate attention states of horizontal and vertical sequence separately. They are generated by two distinct learnable nonlinear transformations of activated value $e_{t,i}$. Each of the nolinear transformation is a full connection layer followed by a 1×1 convolution. And $e_{t,i}$ can be described as follow:

$$e_{t,i} = Tanh(W_s s_{t-1} + W_h h_i + b) \tag{8}$$

where s_{t-1} is the hidden state at previous time step $t-1$, and h_i indicates the sequential feature vectors generated by the convolutional-recurrent encoder. W_s, W_h and b are learnable parameters.

The target sequence can be described as $(y_1, ..., y_T)$. At time step t, the output y_t is:

$$y_t = softmax(W_{out}^T s_t + b_{out}) \tag{9}$$

where W_{out} and b_{out} are learnable parameters, too. s_t is the hidden state at time step t, which can be computed by:

$$s_t = RNN((f(y_{t-1}), g_t), s_{t-1}) \tag{10}$$

Normally, the RNN function above represents an LSTM network. $(f(y_{t-1}, g_t)$ indicates the concatenation of g_t and one-hot embedding of y_{t-1}. g_t can be computed by:

$$g_t = \sum_{i=1}^{L} (\alpha_{t,i} h_i) \tag{11}$$

From the description above, the attention value of decoder is bound to the orientation confidence at the time step scale. Thus the recognition network deals with horizontal and vertical texts respectively, avoiding the confusion of samples with different arrangements.

The decoder stops processing when it predicts an end-of-sequence token "EOS" [24]. We adopt beam search [22] while testing to achieve better performance. The architecture of the recognition network can be viewed as Table 2.

3.4 Training

We integrate the OSN, CRN and ASN into one network. Using word-level annotations and orientation labels, the whole network can be trained end-to-end by a multi-task learning manner. It's worth noting that random initialization will not affect the performance of this network. The loss consists of two partly losses:

$$Loss = L_w + \lambda L_o \tag{12}$$

where L_w and L_o denote the word prediction loss and orientation classification loss respectively. The word prediction loss function can be described as follows:

$$L_w = -\frac{1}{2} \sum_{l=1}^{L} (logp_1(y_l|I) + logp_2(y_l|I)) \tag{13}$$

where p_1 and p_2 are the predict possibility from left-to-right decoder and right-to-right decoder respectively. I denotes the input image, y_l indicates the l-th character of its text groundtruth whose length is L.

And L_o is binary cross entropy loss, whose labels are "horizontal" and "vertical". It can be described as follows:

$$L_o = -(ylog(p) + (1-y)log(1-p)) \tag{14}$$

where y indicates the true label of input text and p indicates the output of OSN. We set $\lambda = 1$ in our experiments.

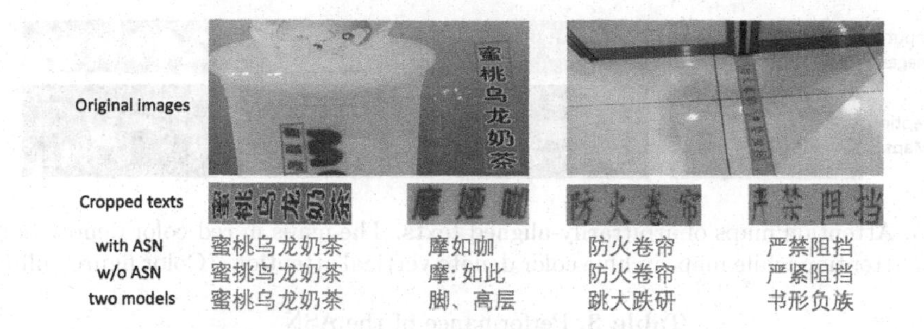

Fig. 4. Examples of recognition results of vertical texts. On one hand, the single model with ASN achieves much better results than the model without ASN. On the other hand, using "two models" method, we tend to select the vertical model via their aspect ratios information, which may return the totally wrong results.

4 Experiments

In this section we describe extensive experiments conducted on various datasets.

4.1 Datasets Setup

RCTW2017 and LSVT2019. They are representative Chinese scene text datasets [8,23], most images of which are natural images collected by phone cameras. In LSVT2019, we only use the fully annotated part. Because annotations of the test set are not public, so we random split the training set into two subsets following the ratio 3:1, and segment text strings from the original images based on annotations. Texts which are marked by the "difficult" flag are excluded.

It's worth noting that the orientation labels of public datasets are easy to generate. A simple approach is based on their aspect ratio, which is the most commonly used to distinguish the horizontally and vertically texts when training two independent models. Obviously, it can't handle the abnormal cases as Fig. 1 in our paper. The other approach is using our orientation-classification model pretrained on our dataset. It has been proved that the accuracy of direction discrimination can reach 98% on real scene texts.

SCTD. Compared with various English public datasets, existing Chinese scene text datasets do not provide sufficient data for deep network training. To overcome the problem, we generate a synthetic Chinese scene text dataset (SCTD) for training and evaluating the performance of the proposed method. It comprises half of the vertical texts and half of the horizontal texts. We adapt the framework proposed by Gupta et al. [6] to a multi-oriented setup.

Different from [6], our task does not involve text detection, thus we adopt a faster and simpler approach to establish our dataset. We generate bounding boxes randomly on the scene pictures and calculate the standard deviation of the

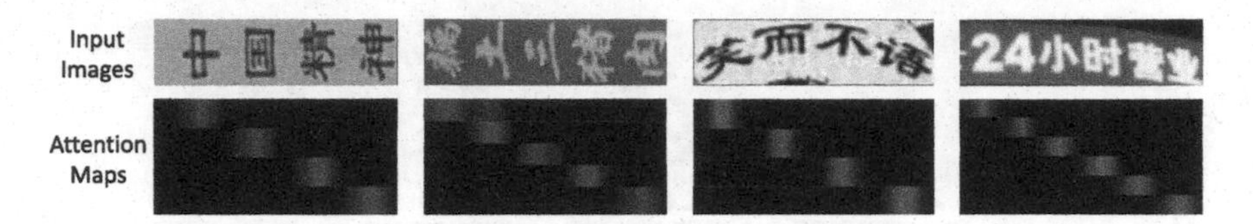

Fig. 5. Attention maps of arbitrarily-aligned texts. The maps in red color denote horizontal attention while maps in blue color denote vertical attention. (Color figure online)

Table 3. Performance of the ASN

Methods	PM on SCTD	PM on RCTW2017	PM on LSVT2019
Two models	70.4	53.1	51.9
OSTER (without ASN)	62.3	50.2	48.7
OSTER (with ASN)	69.5	52.5	51.3

Lab values of the regions, and select the regions whose standard deviation are less than the threshold for clipping (smaller standard deviation means the flatter color distribution). To increase sample diversity, we random add degrading strategies such as rotating, perspective transformation, brightness transformation. It includes 5 million training word images and 1,0000 testing word images. 5990 classes of Chinese characters are covered.

4.2 Implementation Details

Details about OSTER architecture are given in Tables 1 and 2 respectively. The number of hidden units of BLSTM in the decoder is 256. The recognition model outputs 5991 classes, including Chinese characters, digits, symbols, and a flag standing for "EOS". For vertical text images, we rotate them by 90°. After that, all images are resized to 32×100.

We adopt ADADELTA as the optimizer. The model is trained by batches of 64 examples. We set the learning rate to 1.0 at the beginning and decrease it to 0.1 after its convergence. We implement our method under the framework of PyTorch. Our model is GPU-accelerated with an NVIDIA GTX-1080Ti GPU, and CUDA 8.0 and CuDNN v7 backends are used.

4.3 Performance of the ASN

This part of the experiment is based on Chinese dataset. The OSTER is firstly trained on SCTD, then fine-tuned on the training subset of RCTW2017 and LSVT2019. We take perfect matching (PM) as the evaluation metric, which means the recognition results must be totally the same as the GT characters.

The accuracy of orientation discriminant can reach 99.8% on SCTD while 99.2% on RCTW2017 and 98.9% on LSVT2019. The recognition results are shown as Table 3. Compared with training all texts as a whole, the ASN improves

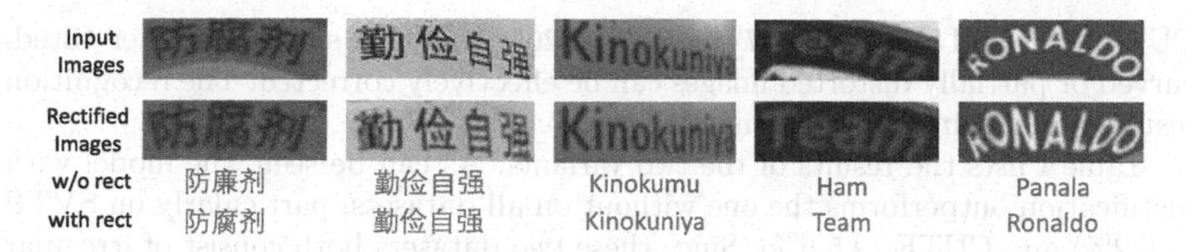

Fig. 6. Visualization of the source images, the rectified images and the recognition results. The results of rectified images is much better than that of source images.

Table 4. Performance of the CRN

Methods	SCTD	RCTW2017	LSVT2019	IC15	CUTE	IIIT5K	SVT	SVTP
Without CRN	65.7	49.4	48.7	74.2	76.2	91.2	84.7	74.2
With CRN	69.5	52.5	51.3	77.1	81.8	92.2	89.2	80.4

the recognition accuracy greatly. Compared with training two models separately, the ASN achieves similar performance with only a single model, which is a more general and simple approach. Figure 4 shows an example where OSTER can deal with arbitrarily-aligned texts easily while severe mistakes are made by the separately trained models.

Examples of attention heat maps when decoding individual characters are visualized in Fig. 5. The maps in red color denote horizontal attention while maps in blue color denote vertical attention, and they are quite different from each other. Although learned in a weakly supervised manner, the attention module can still localize characters being decoded precisely.

4.4 Performances of the CRN

We visualize the outcomes of the CRN to verify the ability of its distortion correction. We perform this part of the experiment on both the Chinese datasets and the English datasets. The test English datasets include ICDAR2015 [12],

Table 5. Comparison on public Chinese benchmarks

Methods	RCTW2017		LSVT2019	
	MED score	PM score	MED score	PM score
Shi et al. [20]	0.338	45.1	0.357	41.7
Lee et al. [13]	0.341	44.3	0.349	42.3
Wang et al. [25]	0.344	43.5	0.366	40.3
Luo et al. [16]	0.296	51.3	0.318	48.9
Shi et al. [20]	0.292	51.8	0.315	49.3
OSTER (without OSN)	0.293	51.7	0.318	49.2
OSTER (with OSN)	**0.270**	**53.3**	**0.296**	**50.9**

CUTE [18], IIIT5k-Words [17] and SVT [26]. As Fig. 6 shows, whether tilted, curved or partially distorted images can be effectively corrected. The recognition results are also improved dramatically.

Table 4 lists the results of the two variants. As can be seen, the model with rectification outperforms the one without on all datasets, particularly on SVTP (+6.2%) and CUTE (+5.6%). Since these two datasets both consist of irregular text, the rectification shows a significant effect.

4.5 Performances on Public Datasets

To prove the excellent performance of OSTER, We implement different open-source algorithms of text recognition on Chinese benchmarks. We keep the same aspect ratio as other methods (32 × 100) for fair comparison, rather than resizing the Chinese texts to a larger aspect ratio (32 × 160 for example) for higher accuracy. All images of the test subset of RCTW2017 are used.

The Mean Edit Distance (MED) [7] is also adopted as the evaluation metric. Lower MED and higher PM mean better performance. Table 5 lists the results of these methods. As can be seen, the OSTER outperforms the traditional methods on Chinese benchmarks either on MED or on PM metric.

To prove the generalization ability of OSTER, we conducted extensive experiments on various English benchmarks, including regular and irregular datasets. The training data consists of 8-million synthetic images released by Jaderberg [9] and 6-million synthetic images released by Gupta [6]. No extra data is used.

Table 6. Comparison on public English datasets

Method	IC13	IC15	CUTE	IIIT5k	SVT	SVTP
Jaderberg et al. [11]	81.8	-	-	-	71.7	-
Rodriguez et al. [19]	-	-	-	-	70.0	-
Lee et al. [13]	90.0	-	-	78.4	80.7	-
Shi et al. [20]	86.7	-	-	78.2	80.8	-
Shi et al. [21]	88.6	-	59.2	81.9	81.9	71.8
Cheng et al. [3]	89.4	66.2	63.9	83.7	82.2	71.5
Yang et al. [28]	-	-	69.3	-	-	75.8
Cheng et al. [4]	-	68.2	76.8	87.0	82.8	73.0
Bai et al. [1]	94.4	-	-	88.3	87.5	-
Liao et al. [14]	91.4	-	78.1	92.0	82.1	-
Luo et al. [16]	**92.4**	68.8	77.4	91.2	88.3	76.1
Shi et al. [20]	91.8	76.1	79.5	93.4	**93.6**	78.5
Zhan et al. [29]	91.3	76.9	83.3	93.3	90.2	79.6
Wang et al. [27]	91.3	74.0	**85.1**	93.3	88.1	80.2
OSTER (ours)	**92.4**	**77.1**	81.8	92.2	89.2	**80.4**

Because English datasets have rarely vertical texts, we set the orientation to be "horizontal" for every image. We only test lexicon-free case for SVT and IIIT5k. The training details are the same as training SCTD. Table 6 shows that OSTER achieves state-of-the-art performance over a number of public datasets.

5 Conclusion

In this paper, we propose an orientation sensitive scene text recognition network that is capable of recognizing horizontal and vertical scene texts simultaneously. The centerline rectification network corrects the distorted text to a regular one, the orientation sensitive network perceives the arrangement mode of input images, the attention selective recognition network generate corresponding attention map at each time step for better recognition results. The proposed network can be trained end-to-end and is robust to parameter initialization. Experiments over a number of public datasets demonstrate its superior performance in arbitrarily-aligned scene text recognition. The SCTD we established will be released to the public.

Acknowledgment. This work is supported by the Key Programs of the Chinese Academy of Sciences under Grant No. ZDBS-SSWJSC003, No. ZDBS-SSW-JSC004, and No. ZDBS-SSWJSC005, and the National Natural Science Foundation of China (NSFC) under Grant No. 61601462, No. 61531019, and No. 71621002.

References

1. Bai, F., Cheng, Z., Niu, Y., Pu, S., Zhou, S.: Edit probability for scene text recognition. In: Proceedings of the IEEE Conference on Computer Vision and Pattern Recognition, pp. 1508–1516 (2018)
2. Bissacco, A., Cummins, M., Netzer, Y., Neven, H.: PhotoOCR: reading text in uncontrolled conditions. In: Proceedings of the IEEE International Conference on Computer Vision, pp. 785–792 (2013)
3. Cheng, Z., Bai, F., Xu, Y., Zheng, G., Pu, S., Zhou, S.: Focusing attention: towards accurate text recognition in natural images. In: Proceedings of the IEEE International Conference on Computer Vision, pp. 5076–5084 (2017)
4. Cheng, Z., Xu, Y., Bai, F., Niu, Y., Pu, S., Zhou, S.: AON: towards arbitrarily-oriented text recognition. In: Proceedings of the IEEE Conference on Computer Vision and Pattern Recognition, pp. 5571–5579 (2018)
5. Graves, A., Schmidhuber, J.: Framewise phoneme classification with bidirectional LSTM and other neural network architectures. Neural Netw. **18**(5–6), 602–610 (2005)
6. Gupta, A., Vedaldi, A., Zisserman, A.: Synthetic data for text localisation in natural images. In: Proceedings of the IEEE Conference on Computer Vision and Pattern Recognition, pp. 2315–2324 (2016)
7. He, M., et al.: ICPR 2018 contest on robust reading for multi-type web images. In: 2018 24th International Conference on Pattern Recognition (ICPR), pp. 7–12. IEEE (2018)

8. ICDAR2019: ICDAR 2019 robust reading challenge on large-scale street view text with partial labeling. https://rrc.cvc.uab.es/?ch=16. Accessed 20 Apr 2019
9. Jaderberg, M., Simonyan, K., Vedaldi, A., Zisserman, A.: Synthetic data and artificial neural networks for natural scene text recognition. arXiv preprint arXiv:1406.2227 (2014)
10. Jaderberg, M., Simonyan, K., Zisserman, A., et al.: Spatial transformer networks. In: Advances in Neural Information Processing Systems, pp. 2017–2025 (2015)
11. Jaderberg, M., Vedaldi, A., Zisserman, A.: Deep features for text spotting. In: Fleet, D., Pajdla, T., Schiele, B., Tuytelaars, T. (eds.) ECCV 2014. LNCS, vol. 8692, pp. 512–528. Springer, Cham (2014). https://doi.org/10.1007/978-3-319-10593-2_34
12. Karatzas, D., et al.: ICDAR 2015 competition on robust reading. In: 2015 13th International Conference on Document Analysis and Recognition (ICDAR), pp. 1156–1160. IEEE (2015)
13. Lee, C.Y., Osindero, S.: Recursive recurrent nets with attention modeling for OCR in the wild. In: Proceedings of the IEEE Conference on Computer Vision and Pattern Recognition, pp. 2231–2239 (2016)
14. Liao, M., et al.: Scene text recognition from two-dimensional perspective. arXiv preprint arXiv:1809.06508 (2018)
15. Liu, Z., Li, Y., Ren, F., Yu, H.: A binary convolutional encoder-decoder network for real-time natural scene text processing. arXiv preprint arXiv:1612.03630 (2016)
16. Luo, C., Jin, L., Sun, Z.: MORAN: a multi-object rectified attention network for scene text recognition. Pattern Recogn. **90**, 109–118 (2019)
17. Mishra, A., Alahari, K., Jawahar, C.: Scene text recognition using higher order language priors. In: BMVC-British Machine Vision Conference. BMVA (2012)
18. Risnumawan, A., Shivakumara, P., Chan, C.S., Tan, C.L.: A robust arbitrary text detection system for natural scene images. Expert Syst. Appl. **41**(18), 8027–8048 (2014)
19. Rodriguez-Serrano, J.A., Gordo, A., Perronnin, F.: Label embedding: a frugal baseline for text recognition. Int. J. Comput. Vis. **113**(3), 193–207 (2015)
20. Shi, B., Bai, X., Yao, C.: An end-to-end trainable neural network for image-based sequence recognition and its application to scene text recognition. IEEE Trans. Pattern Anal. Mach. Intell. **39**(11), 2298–2304 (2017)
21. Shi, B., Wang, X., Lyu, P., Yao, C., Bai, X.: Robust scene text recognition with automatic rectification. In: Proceedings of the IEEE Conference on Computer Vision and Pattern Recognition, pp. 4168–4176 (2016)
22. Shi, B., Yang, M., Wang, X., Lyu, P., Yao, C., Bai, X.: ASTER: an attentional scene text recognizer with flexible rectification. IEEE Trans. Pattern Anal. Mach. Intell. **41**, 2035–2048 (2018)
23. Shi, B., et al.: ICDAR 2017 competition on reading Chinese text in the wild (RCTW-17). In: 2017 14th IAPR International Conference on Document Analysis and Recognition (ICDAR), vol. 1, pp. 1429–1434. IEEE (2017)
24. Sutskever, I., Vinyals, O., Le, Q.V.: Sequence to sequence learning with neural networks. In: Advances in Neural Information Processing Systems, pp. 3104–3112 (2014)
25. Wang, J., Hu, X.: Gated recurrent convolution neural network for OCR. In: Advances in Neural Information Processing Systems, pp. 335–344 (2017)
26. Wang, K., Babenko, B., Belongie, S.: End-to-end scene text recognition. In: 2011 International Conference on Computer Vision, pp. 1457–1464. IEEE (2011)

27. Wang, P., Yang, L., Li, H., Deng, Y., Shen, C., Zhang, Y.: A simple and robust convolutional-attention network for irregular text recognition. arXiv preprint arXiv:1904.01375 (2019)
28. Yang, X., He, D., Zhou, Z., Kifer, D., Giles, C.L.: Learning to read irregular text with attention mechanisms. In: IJCAI, pp. 3280–3286 (2017)
29. Zhan, F., Lu, S.: ESIR: end-to-end scene text recognition via iterative image rectification. In: Proceedings of the IEEE Conference on Computer Vision and Pattern Recognition, pp. 2059–2068 (2019)

On Fast Point Cloud Matching with Key Points and Parameter Tuning

Dániel Varga[1(✉)], Sándor Laki[1], János Szalai-Gindl[1], László Dobos[1], Péter Vaderna[2], and Bence Formanek[2]

[1] ELTE Eötvös Loránd University, Budapest, Hungary
{vaduaci,lakis,szalaigindl}@inf.elte.hu
dobox@complex.elte.hu
[2] Ericsson Research, Budapest, Hungary
{peter.vaderna,bence.formanek}@ericsson.hu

Abstract. Nowadays, three dimensional point cloud processing plays a very important role in a wide range of areas: autonomous driving, robotics, cartography, etc. Three dimensional point cloud registration pipelines have high computational complexity, mainly because of the cost of point feature signature calculation. By selecting keypoints and using only them for registration, data points that are interesting in some way, one can significantly reduce the number of points for which feature signatures are needed, hence the running time of registration pipelines. Consequently, keypoint detectors have a prominent role in an efficient processing pipeline. In this paper, we propose to analyze the usefulness of various keypoint detection algorithms and investigate whether and when it is worth to use a keypoint detector for registration. We define the goodness of a keypoint detection algorithm based on the success and quality of registration. Most keypoint detection methods require manual tuning of their parameters for best results. Here we revisit the most popular methods for keypoint detection in 3D point clouds and perform automatic parameter tuning with goodness of registration and run time as primary objectives. We compare keypoint-based registration to registration with randomly selected points and using all data points as a baseline. In contrast to former work, we use point clouds of different sizes, with and without noise, and register objects with different sizes.

Keywords: 3D point cloud · Keypoint detector · Point cloud registration

1 Introduction

With the advent of sensors capable of capturing 3D point clouds, numerous related applications have emerged. In addition to remote sensing, data sets recorded by LIDARs from the air, high resolution point clouds of entire buildings

---

Supported by organization x.

S. Palaiahnakote et al. (Eds.): ACPR 2019, LNCS 12046, pp. 498–511, 2020.
https://doi.org/10.1007/978-3-030-41404-7_35

(e.g. the Notre Dame) are also available. One of the most important steps of 3D point cloud processing is the registration if point set, i.e. the process of finding a spatial transformation that aligns two or more fully or partially overlapping point clouds. Registration also includes merging different scans of the same scene and it is a fundamental part of Simultaneous Localization and Mapping (SLAM) algorithms widely used in robotics.

We can distinguish local and global registration of 3D point clouds. In the local case, the two point clouds to be registered are recorded from nearby viewpoints and show significant overlap. When, for example, an autonomous robot is equipped with a point cloud capturing device (LIDAR or depth camera) and the capturing rate is faster than the speed of the robot, the majority of two consecutive records will overlap and, after transforming them into a common coordinate systems, they will be close to each other. This *a priori* information on the relationship of two or more point clouds is not available in global registration methods. Two families of registration algorithms are frequently used: Iterative Closest Point (ICP) and feature-based methods.

ICP-based methods aim at finding the rigid transformation that minimizes the least square distance of closest points after registration. There are a number of methods based on the ICP concept [1,3,4,12,18,21]. The two most frequently used ICP variants are the point-to-point and point-to-plane solutions [13]. Feature-based registration, on the other hand, relies on the idea of finding interesting points, called key points, in a point cloud. Each key point is described with its feature signature representing the local topology of the point. Then point-pair candidates (also known as correspondences) are identified in the feature space, usually by multi-dimensional proximity search. There may be many wrong point-pairs that have to be filtered out in a next step of the method which is usually called the rejection phase. Theoretically, three point pairs are enough for perfect registration but many more are necessary in real scenarios. The last step is to iteratively approximate or otherwise estimate the transformation that minimizes the distance between the corresponding point pairs in real space. As we will see later, not every registration pipeline applies all of these steps. Note, that feature-based and ICP methods are often used together where feature-based methods perform coarse registration only that can be further refined by ICP-based solutions.

In this paper, we focus on the special case of registration when a small point cloud is registered into a large point cloud where the large one covers the spatial volume of the small one. Consequently, the small point set can be considered as a query and the main task is to find it in the large data set (e.g., finding the locations of a specific object in a large building or localize a robot based on the local point cloud it captured in the large data set). Though this sub-problem can be solved by both global and local registration approaches, in this paper we propose a pipeline based on the widely used global registration method called Fast Global Registration (FGR) [24]. FGR generally provides good registration accuracy in the investigated subproblem, but as shown later in this paper require unnecessarily high computational complexity. To reduce the computational cost, we propose two modifications for the original FGR pipeline: (1) FGR originally uses each point of point clouds to be registered that significantly increases its computational costs. Instead, we propose the introduction of a key point selection phase and only apply FGR on key points to fasten registration speed. (2) As one of its key advantages, FGR is less sensitive to proper parameterization of the feature signatures, i.e. a good registration is usually possible with non-calibrated parameters. However, it only holds if all data points are used in the registration and the characteristic properties of the two point clouds are similar. When keypoints are used for registration, the accuracy provided by FGR varies in a wide range and optimization of keypoint detector parameters are necessary. In this paper, we show how a good trade-off between registration accuracy and computational cost can be achieved by using key point selection methods with appropriate number of key points and parameter tuning.

Let S and T be two point clouds such as $|S| \gg |Q|$ and Q represents the points of an object that also exists in point cloud S (e.g. Q and S come from independent recordings), showing an example where we aim at finding a small point set representing an object in a large point cloud describing, for instance, a room. The task is to find a rigid transformation T that minimizes the distance between the points of S and $T(Q)$:

$$d(S, T(Q)) = \sum_{p_i \in S} \sum_{p_j \in T(Q)} (p_i - p_j)^2 \tag{1}$$

A rigid transformation consists of a translation and a rotation, keeping the distance between any point pairs in the point cloud Q.

The paper is organized as follows: In Sect. 2 we discuss the related literature in this field. Section 3 describes the keypoint detection algorithms used. In Sect. 4 we present our registration pipeline and parameter tuning method. Finally, in Sect. 5 a comprehensive evaluation of the proposed pipeline is presented, followed by the conclusions.

2 Related Work

According to Mian et al. [11] the quality of a keypoint depends on three things. A point is a good keypoint if: (1) repeatable on different point clouds from the same object, (2) a local coordinate system can be defined based on the neighborhood of the point and, (3) the local environment of the point is highly distinctive and has unique information to describe the point. Repeatability is important to find real point pairs while uniqueness makes it easier to associate points in feature space. In the 2D case, it was considered a good key point that was "easy to track" [7].

Since key point detectors are widely used, many work has been focused on evaluating methods according to various aspects. Some work tested the invariance of repeatability under translation, rotation and scale changes [2]. In other papers [17], repeatability was also investigated, and the measurement noise of the points was also taken into account. One disadvantage of most former studies was that the default parameters specified in the implementations were used.

The novelty of our work is that keypoint detectors are not primarily assessed on the basis of repeatability and uniqueness as before. Instead, we examine the algorithms at a more abstract level and test whether the quality of the final point cloud registration is better. In contrast to previous work, parameter tuning was performed on algorithms rather than using defaults. We compare the result of the registration pipeline with keypoint detectors and with randomly selected points. We also consider how much time we can win without significant decrease in registration quality.

In the past two years deep learning-based 3D keypoint detectors have appeared. USIP [9] is one of the most impressive methods, using unsupervised learning for keypoint detection. The USIP detector out-performs the existing hand-crafted and other deep-learning based detectors, giving significantly better result on registration failure rate than hand-crafted solutions. An earlier deep learning-based method is the 3DFeat-Net [22] which promises better results than hand-crafted keypoint detectors. Other works also discuss the topic of interest points in 3D space [6,16,19,20]. Though there is an emerging trend of deep learning-based techniques, they require large number of training data and they are less widespread in real world applications, and thus we decided to not consider this family of methods in this paper.

3 Keypoint Selection

A wide range of keypoint detection algorithms have emerged in the past few years. In this paper, we only focus on the ones most widely used in practice and use the implementations available in the open source Point Cloud Library (PCL) [15].

3.1 ISS3D

Intrinsic Shape Signature 3D (ISS3D) [23] is one of the most popular 3D keypoint detection methods, having many good properties. ISS3D keypoints are viewpoint independent but not scale invariant which means that its parameters have to be tuned based on the resolution and other properties of the point cloud. For each point ISS3D defines a local coordinate system using the neighborhood of the point. It then calculates a 3×3 scatter matrix and determines its eigenvalues and eigenvectors. The points showing the largest variance along all the eigenvectors are selected as keypoints. For this, the method introduces constraints on the ratios of eigenvalues:

$$\lambda_2/\lambda_1 < \gamma_{21}$$

$$\lambda_3/\lambda_2 < \gamma_{32},$$

where λ_1, λ_2 and λ_3 are the eigenvalues of the scatter matrix in the order of decreasing magnitude and γ_{21}, γ_{32} are parameters specified by the user.

3.2 Harris3D

The Harris 3D keypoint detector was originally developed as a corner and edge detector in two dimension [5]. The original method could successfully be used to trace edges in 2D images. According to the PCL documentation, the 3D version of the algorithm uses the original idea, but instead of using image gradients, it works with surface normals.

3.3 SIFT

The Scale Invariant Feature Transform (SIFT) is another keypoint detection algorithm implemented in PCL. Like Harris, it was also developed for two-dimensional cases, and the 3D version also keeps the invariance of features under scaling and rotations [10].

4 Methodology

As mentioned previously, we extend the FGR pipeline with a keypoint detection phase in order to reduce the computational cost and keep the good registration accuracy. To better match keypoint detection to our requirements, we also perform automatic parameter tuning on the data sets tested which is not part of the pipeline but has to be performed for the certain instruments used to collect the data. Point clouds can be characterized by different properties influencing the performance of the proposed pipeline. Among them, point cloud resolution (*pcr*) is one of the most important that affects the parameters of both keypoint detection and registration methods. One can define *pcr* of point cloud Q as

$$pcr(Q) = \frac{\sum_{p \in Q} NN_Q(p)}{|Q|}, \tag{2}$$

where $p \in Q$ and $NN_Q(p)$ is the Euclidean distance between p and it's nearest neighbor in point cloud Q.

4.1 Keypoint Evaluation

Different algorithms executed with different parameters may lead to different keypoints for the same point cloud. Hence, finding the best keypoint detection algorithm and the best set of parameters is difficult and raises multiple questions:

- **Registration accuracy.** How many keypoints are needed to reach similar accuracy to the case when all the points are used for registration?
- **Registration time.** How can we reduce the time needed to achieve the same accuracy as in the case of using all the points for registration with the use of keypoints?

The trade-off between registration accuracy and time is obvious but the questions above are hard to answer on a theoretical basis since the answers depends on several factors such as robustness and consistency of the keypoint detection method used, the number of resulting keypoints which is a function of the parameters, the various characteristics of the point clouds to be registered, etc. As a consequence, in this study we chosen an empirical approach and attempt to test the algorithms and estimate the best parameters by applying them to real data.

Two metrics are introduced to verify the accuracy of the registration. One is the *fitness* and the other is root mean square error (*rmse*). Let D and Q be two already registered pointclouds. Then the *fit_set* of Q compared to D is a subset of Q, contains points which are close enough to points of D.

$$fit\_set_D(Q) = \{p | p \in Q \wedge NN_D(p) < 2 \cdot pcr(Q)\} \quad (3)$$

The *fitness* of Q compared to D means that how many points of Q fits on D.

$$fitness_D(Q) = \frac{|fit\_set_D(Q)|}{|Q|} \quad (4)$$

Finally, considering only the fitting points, the *rmse* shows the error of the registration.

$$rmse_D(Q) = \sqrt{\frac{\sum_{p \in fit\_set_D(Q)} NN_D(p)^2}{|fit\_set_D(Q)|}} \quad (5)$$

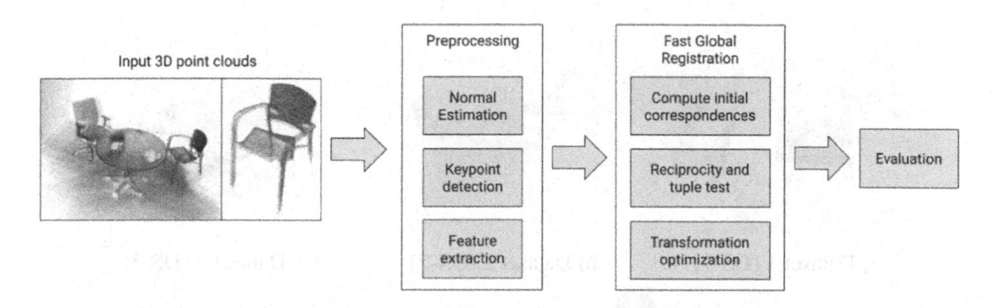

Fig. 1. Point cloud registration pipeline as used in this study. Steps listed below each other are performed in order. We improved Fast Global Registration by introducing a keypoint detection step with the purpose of reducing the number of feature signatures that need to be computed.

4.2 Registration Pipeline

To analyze how keypoint detection methods affect the accuracy of registration we chose the well-known global registration pipeline called Fast Global Registration (FGR) [24] and use its open source implementation throughout the study. For feature extraction, FGR uses Fast Point Feature Histograms (FPFH) [14] and feature signatures are computed for all points of both point cloud, without applying any keypoint detection method first. While this usually results in very good registration, run time is significantly impacted by the fact that calculating FPFH is associated with high computational cost. Once feature descriptors are computed for all the points, FGR determines the initial correspondences by finding nearest neighbors from both point clouds in feature space. Then it filters out spurious correspondences during a process often referred to as correspondence rejection. The following two tests are used during rejection:

1. **Reciprocity test.** A point pair fulfills the test if the two points are both nearest neighbors of each other in 3D space.
2. **Tuple test.** We test that three randomly picked correspondence pairs are compatible, i.e. they define approximately congruent triangles in the two point clouds. Mathematically [24]:

$$\forall i \neq j, \tau < \frac{\|p_i - p_j\|}{\|q_i - q_j\|} < 1/\tau$$

where $(p_1, q_1), (p_2, q_2), (p_3, q_3)$ are correspondence pairs and $\tau = 0.9$.

After the rejection step, the transformation between the two point clouds is determined from the remaining correspondences in an iterative manner.

FGR provides accurate registration but calculating the feature descriptors for each point in the cloud has high computational cost. Accordingly, it is ideal choice for demonstrating how the registration costs can be reduced by using keypoints.

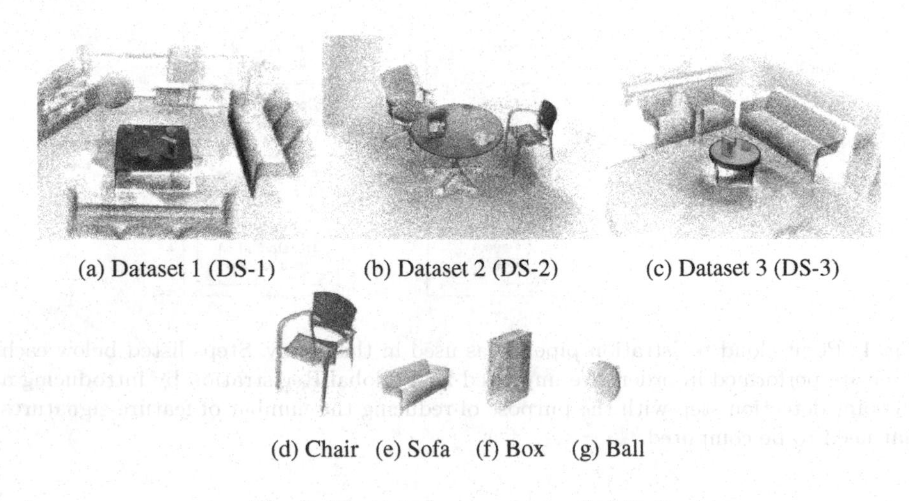

(a) Dataset 1 (DS-1) (b) Dataset 2 (DS-2) (c) Dataset 3 (DS-3)

(d) Chair (e) Sofa (f) Box (g) Ball

Fig. 2. Input indoor scenes and objects

During evaluation, we use the registration pipeline depicted in Fig. 1. First, we load the two point clouds and calculate the PCR. Then the preprocessing steps follow: (1) normal calculation, (2) keypoint detection, (3) computing the features signature descriptors. Feature descriptors are only calculated for keypoints but by using all data points of both point clouds. Then the registration is executed with the FGR algorithm. Finally, we evaluate the accuracy or registration. The same procedure is repeated for each keypoint detection methods tested and for a wide range of keypoint detection parameters.

4.3 Parameter Tuning

The registration pipeline, when used with FPFH as feature descriptor, has a number of parameters, including normal radius and feature radius, which values depend on the properties of the point cloud such as the PCR. Keypoint detectors also have a significant number of free parameters that need to be set correctly to achieve good results with registration. The use of default parameters, as defined in reference implementations, often leads to wrong results. Thus, some kind parameter tuning is necessary to compare their real performance. To find the optimal combinations, we performed a grid search over the parameters of FPFH: normal radius (1–15 cm with 1 cm steps), feature radius (1–20 cm with 1 cm steps). Parameters of keypoint detection methods were also tested in broad intervals (ISS: silent radius, non-max radius, gamma variables; Harris3D: radius, threshold; SIFT: min scale, number of octaves, number scales per octave, min contrast). On important result from parameter tuning for FGR is that when all points are used for registration, FPFH normal radius and feature radius do not play an important role (anything between 1 cm and 10 cm work just as well), which underlines the robustness of FGR.

Since feature computation dominates the run time of FGR, we randomly subsample the point clouds to find the minimum sampling rate that is necessary for acceptable registration. We note, that the sampling rate depends on the point density of the point clouds and the volume of the overlapping regions.

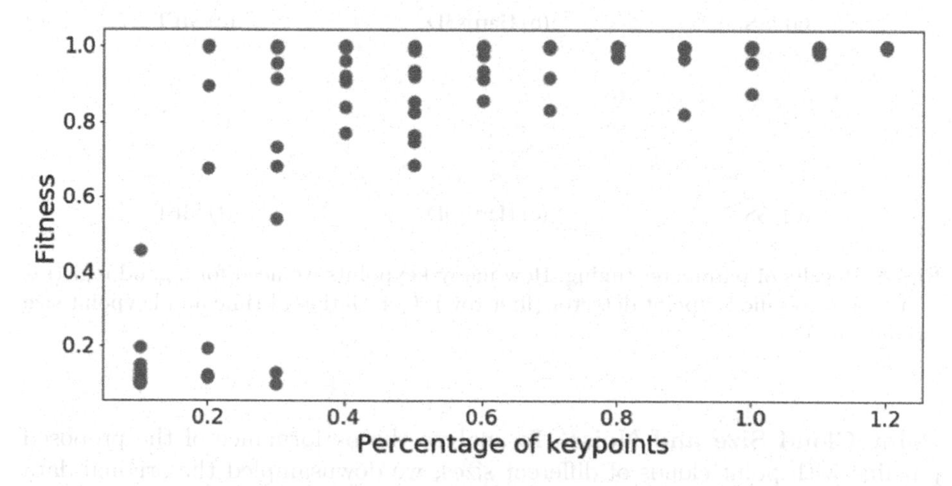

Fig. 3. Number of keypoints selected by random sampling vs registration accuracy

Number quoted here are for the particular data sets we used for the experiments. Figure 3 shows the case when registration with FGR is attempted by uniformly sampling data points from both point clouds to be registered. One can observe that selecting a minimum of 1.2% of the points selected is needed to obtain good registration accuracy with a high level of certainty. If the random sampling ratios is smaller the observed registration accuracy shows very high variance, leading to inconsistent and unpredictable performance.

5 Evaluation and Discussion

5.1 Data Sets

The proposed pipeline was evaluated on a freely available, high-quality indoor data set [8]. The data set contained several indoor scenes with objects of different sizes where each scene was recorded four times independently. Each point cloud had high resolution and consisted of about 1 million points. Our evaluation is based on three specific scenes of the large data set: (Fig. 2) (1) **DS-1:** Square table (objects: box and ball); Fig. (2a) (2) **DS-2:** Table with two chairs (objects: box and chair); Fig. (2b) (3) **DS-3:** Round table (objects: box and sofa). Fig. (2c)

Objects. Into all three clouds, we registered a smaller (box) and a few larger (sofa, chair, ball) objects. The point set of the object to be registered was always a cut-out from an independent recording of the same scene.

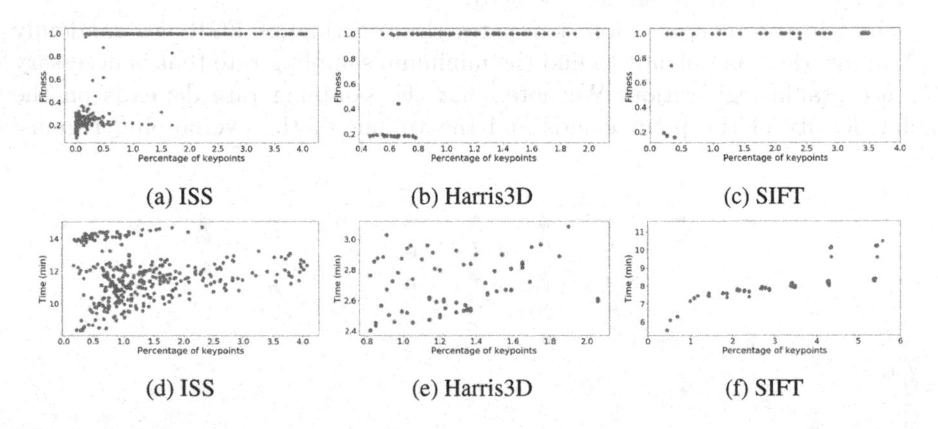

Fig. 4. Results of parameter tuning. How many keypoints we need for a good registration with a specific keypoint detector (first row). Correlation of time and keypoint size (second row).

Point Cloud Size and Noise. To analyze the performance of the proposed pipeline with point clouds of different sizes, we downsampled the original data sets, resulting in point sets of 1 million, 750k and 500k points. To investigate the robustness and noise tolerance, Gaussian-noise with different standard deviation was added to the point coordinates. The noise level was determined from the point cloud resolution (pcr) 2. Accordingly, we introduced three different noise levels with the following standard deviations: 0.0 (no noise), 0.3 pcr, 0.5 pcr, and 0.7 pcr. As a summary, there were six different registration scenarios with three point cloud sizes and four different levels of noise. Therefore, our evaluation consisted of $6 \times 3 \times 4 = 72$ registration scenarios in total.

5.2 Results

Figure 4 shows how the number of keypoints affects the registration accuracy (fitness) and the execution time of the entire pipeline with different keypoint detection methods. On can see that The execution times shows an increasing trend as the number of keypoints increases, while in the accuracy there is keypoint number that results in good registration performance and involving more keypoints cannot increase the observed fitness.

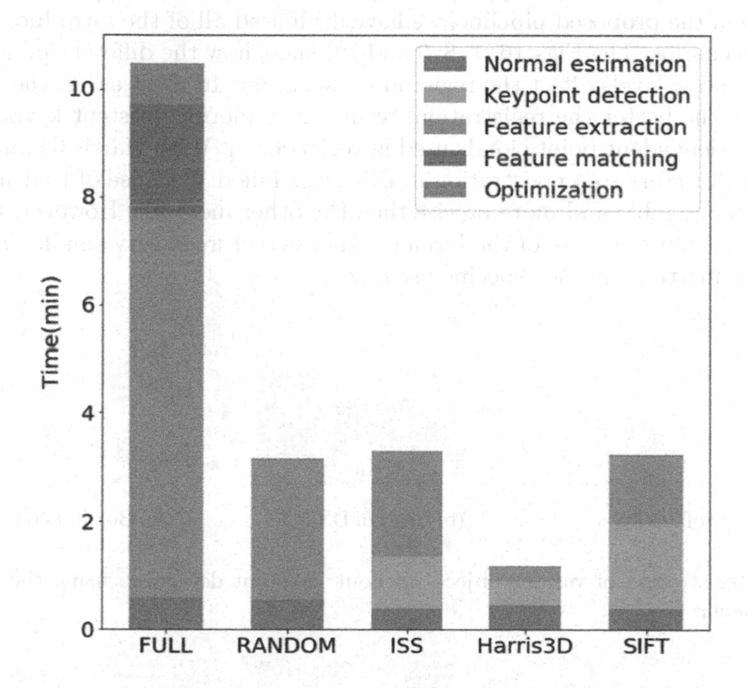

Fig. 5. Execution time of various processing phases with keypoint detectors (random, ISS, Harris3D, SIFT) and without them (based on dataset 3 that contains 1 million points, without noise and object sofa also without noise).

Figure 5 depicts the time consumption of various phases in the registration pipelines. The original FGR when all the points are used in the process the registration takes approx. 10 min. The most time consuming steps are feature extraction and feature matching. If randomly selected points are used as keypoints, keypoint detection time is basically zero, and the feature extraction time is significantly decreased, because of reduced size of point clouds to be processed. Note that feature matching and optimization steps have become negligible.

Using ISS as keypoint detector, feature extraction time was less than in the random case. But the keypoint detection step also took some time. Thus the total registration time of the random case and the ISS case was equal. Using the SIFT method, the total time was the same. The only difference is that key point detection took longer and feature counting took less time. For us, the Harris3D method gave the best result. Using Harris3D, the result is much better than any other case. Clearly, it was the fastest algorithm for our test cases.

It may seem that there is a contradiction between Figs. 4 and 5. Harris3D uses the most keypoint, still it is the fastest. This is because, in order for ISS and SIFT to use a fewer keypoints, they need bigger normal and feature radiuses, and longer running of keypoint detection algorithm. So overall registration would take longer. The Fig. 5 shows the case where the fastest registration was measured.

After determining the appropriate parameters for the keypoint detection methods in the proposed pipeline, we have evaluated all of the introduced registration scenarios. The Figs. (6, 7, 8, 9 and 10) show how the different point cloud sizes and noise levels affect the registration accuracy. In most cases, the smaller the noise, the better the registration, resulting in more consistent keypoints in the two independent point clouds used in registration. With Harris3D and SIFT keypoint detectors sofa registration in DS-1 was failed. Because of that it seems ISS is more reliable and more precise then the other methods. However, the difference between the *rmse* of the ISS and other detectors is very small. Thus this difference matters only for specific use cases.

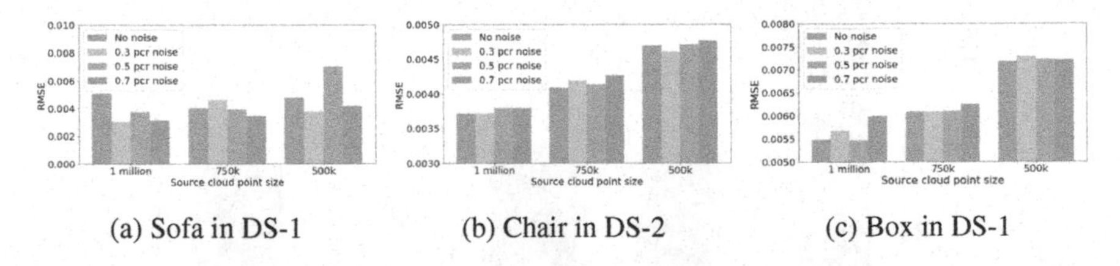

(a) Sofa in DS-1 (b) Chair in DS-2 (c) Box in DS-1

Fig. 6. Registration of various objects without keypoint detection, using the original FGR pipeline

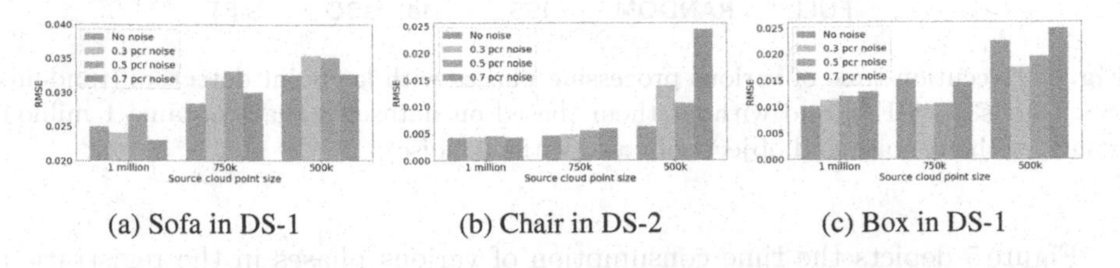

(a) Sofa in DS-1 (b) Chair in DS-2 (c) Box in DS-1

Fig. 7. Registration of various objects with random keypoint selection (baseline)

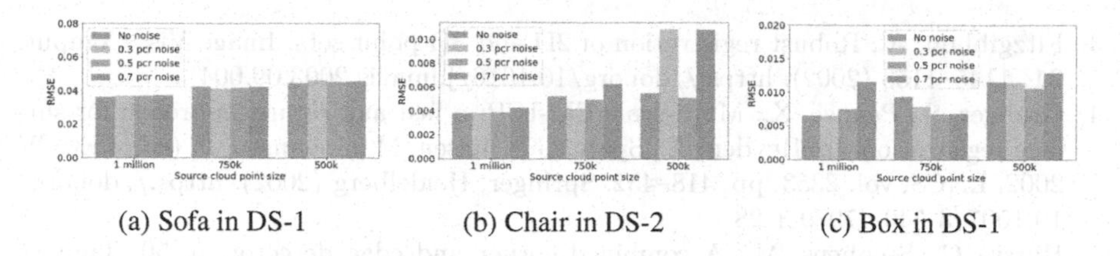

(a) Sofa in DS-1 (b) Chair in DS-2 (c) Box in DS-1

Fig. 8. Registration of various objects with ISS3D keypoint detection

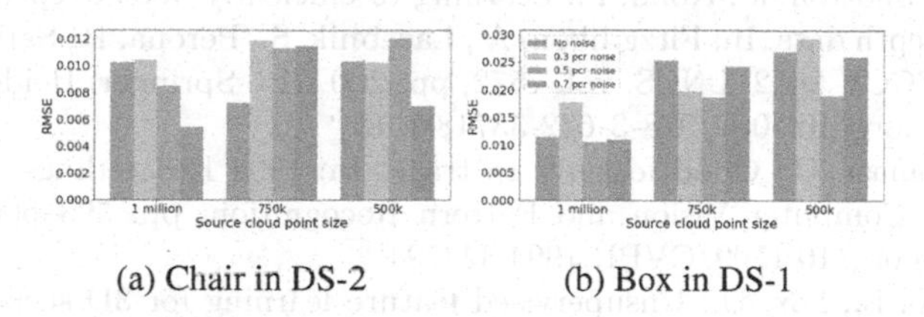

(a) Chair in DS-2 (b) Box in DS-1

Fig. 9. Registration of various objects with Harris3D keypoint detection

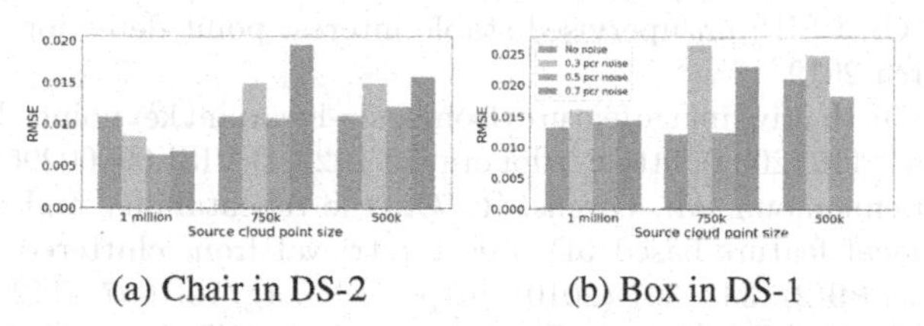

(a) Chair in DS-2 (b) Box in DS-1

Fig. 10. Registration of various objects with SIFT keypoint detection

6 Conclusion

In this paper we have compared hand-crafted 3D keypoint detectors according to their effect on accurate point cloud registration. It has been shown that based on our evaluation metrics, Harris3D gives the best results. With optimized parameters this method proved to be the fastest algorithm with the lowest number of keypoints. We have also shown that combining Harris3D and Fast Global Registration the running time can significantly be reduced, better than with any other methods, with negligible drop in the accuracy. Testing deep learning-based detectors and comparing them to the proposed solution are parts of our future plans.

References

1. Chetverikov, D., Stepanov, D., Krsek, P.: Robust Euclidean alignment of 3D point sets: the trimmed iterative closest point algorithm. Image Vis. Comput. **23**, 299–309 (2005). https://doi.org/10.1016/j.imavis.2004.05.007
2. Filipe, S., Alexandre, L.A.: A comparative evaluation of 3D keypoint detectors in a RGB-D object dataset. In: 2014 International Conference on Computer Vision Theory and Applications (VISAPP), vol. 1, pp. 476–483, January 2014

3. Fitzgibbon, A.: Robust registration of 2D and 3D point sets. Image Vis. Comput. **21**, 1145–1153 (2002). https://doi.org/10.1016/j.imavis.2003.09.004
4. Granger, S., Pennec, X.: Multi-scale EM-ICP: a fast and robust approach for surface registration. In: Heyden, A., Sparr, G., Nielsen, M., Johansen, P. (eds.) ECCV 2002. LNCS, vol. 2353, pp. 418–432. Springer, Heidelberg (2002). https://doi.org/10.1007/3-540-47979-1_28
5. Harris, C., Stephens, M.: A combined corner and edge detector, p. 50, January 1988
6. Holzer, S., Shotton, J., Kohli, P.: Learning to efficiently detect repeatable interest points in depth data. In: Fitzgibbon, A., Lazebnik, S., Perona, P., Sato, Y., Schmid, C. (eds.) ECCV 2012. LNCS, vol. 7572, pp. 200–213. Springer, Heidelberg (2012). https://doi.org/10.1007/978-3-642-33718-5_15
7. Shi, J., Tomasi, C.: Good features to track. In: 1994 Proceedings of IEEE Conference on Computer Vision and Pattern Recognition, pp. 593–600, June 1994. https://doi.org/10.1109/CVPR.1994.323794
8. Lai, K., Bo, L., Fox, D.: Unsupervised feature learning for 3D scene labeling. In: 2014 IEEE International Conference on Robotics and Automation (ICRA), pp. 3050–3057, May 2014. https://doi.org/10.1109/ICRA.2014.6907298
9. Li, J., Lee, G.: USIP: unsupervised stable interest point detection from 3D point clouds, March 2019
10. Lowe, D.G.: Distinctive image features from scale-invariant keypoints. Int. J. Comput. Vis. **60**(2), 91–110 (2004). https://doi.org/10.1023/B:VISI.0000029664.99615.94
11. Mian, A., Bennamoun, M., Owens, R.: On the repeatability and quality of keypoints for local feature-based 3D object retrieval from cluttered scenes. Int. J. Comput. Vis. **89**(2), 348–361 (2010). https://doi.org/10.1007/s11263-009-0296-z
12. Phillips, J.M., Liu, R., Tomasi, C.: Outlier robust ICP for minimizing fractional RMSD. In: Sixth International Conference on 3-D Digital Imaging and Modeling (3DIM 2007), pp. 427–434, August 2007. https://doi.org/10.1109/3DIM.2007.39
13. Pomerleau, F., Colas, F., Siegwart, R.: A review of point cloud registration algorithms for mobile robotics. Found. Trends® Robot. **4**, 1–104 (2015). https://doi.org/10.1561/2300000035
14. Rusu, R., Blodow, N., Beetz, M.: Fast point feature histograms (FPFH) for 3D registration, pp. 3212–3217, June 2009. https://doi.org/10.1109/ROBOT.2009.5152473
15. Rusu, R., Cousins, S.: 3D is here: point cloud library (PCL), May 2011. https://doi.org/10.1109/ICRA.2011.5980567
16. Salti, S., Tombari, F., Spezialetti, R., Stefano, L.D.: Learning a descriptor-specific 3D keypoint detector. In: 2015 IEEE International Conference on Computer Vision (ICCV), pp. 2318–2326, December 2015. https://doi.org/10.1109/ICCV.2015.267
17. Salti, S., Tombari, F., Stefano, L.D.: A performance evaluation of 3D keypoint detectors. In: 2011 International Conference on 3D Imaging, Modeling, Processing, Visualization and Transmission, pp. 236–243, May 2011. https://doi.org/10.1109/3DIMPVT.2011.37
18. Segal, A., Hähnel, D., Thrun, S.: Generalized-ICP, June 2009. https://doi.org/10.15607/RSS.2009.V.021
19. Teran, L., Mordohai, P.: 3D interest point detection via discriminative learning. In: Fleet, D., Pajdla, T., Schiele, B., Tuytelaars, T. (eds.) ECCV 2014. LNCS, vol. 8689, pp. 159–173. Springer, Cham (2014). https://doi.org/10.1007/978-3-319-10590-1_11

20. Tonioni, A., Salti, S., Tombari, F., Spezialetti, R., Stefano, L.D.: Learning to detect good 3D keypoints. Int. J. Comput. Vis. **126**(1), 1–20 (2018). https://doi.org/10.1007/s11263-017-1037-3
21. Yang, J., Li, H., Campbell, D., Jia, Y.: Go-ICP: a globally optimal solution to 3D ICP point-set registration. IEEE Trans. Pattern Anal. Mach. Intell. **38**, 2241–2254 (2015). https://doi.org/10.1109/TPAMI.2015.2513405
22. Yew, Z.J., Lee, G.H.: 3DFeat-Net: weakly supervised local 3D features for point cloud registration. In: Ferrari, V., Hebert, M., Sminchisescu, C., Weiss, Y. (eds.) ECCV 2018. LNCS, vol. 11219, pp. 630–646. Springer, Cham (2018). https://doi.org/10.1007/978-3-030-01267-0_37
23. Zhong, Y.: Intrinsic shape signatures: a shape descriptor for 3D object recognition, pp. 689–696, December 2009. https://doi.org/10.1109/ICCVW.2009.5457637
24. Zhou, Q.-Y., Park, J., Koltun, V.: Fast global registration. In: Leibe, B., Matas, J., Sebe, N., Welling, M. (eds.) ECCV 2016. LNCS, vol. 9906, pp. 766–782. Springer, Cham (2016). https://doi.org/10.1007/978-3-319-46475-6_47

Detection of Critical Camera Configurations for Structure from Motion Using Random Forest

Mario Michelini(✉) and Helmut Mayer

Institute of Applied Computer Science, Bundeswehr University Munich, Neubiberg, Germany
{mario.michelini,helmut.mayer}@unibw.de

Abstract. This paper presents an approach for the detection of critical camera configurations in unorganized image sets with (approximately) known internal camera parameters. Critical configurations are caused by an insufficient distance between cameras compared to the distance of the observed scene and can cause problems in triangulation-based structure from motion application.

We give a summary of existing techniques and propose a new approach for the detection of image pairs with a critical camera configuration based on classification using a random forest. To this end, several features characterizing the quality of the reconstructed 3D points as well as the estimated camera poses have been defined and evaluated for various configurations. The proposed approach is integrated into the structure from motion framework COLMAP demonstrating its potential on an independent real-world dataset.

Keywords: Structure from motion · Camera configuration · Classification · Random forest · Pure rotation · Weak baseline

1 Introduction

Structure from motion (SfM) methods based on the scene rigidity constraint assume a *general camera motion* [11], where the camera has been translated and/or rotated between image acquisitions. But if the camera does not undergo a translation (i.e., a missing baseline), *motion degeneracy* [25] occurs and the epipolar geometry is not defined. In case of uncalibrated cameras also *structure degeneracy* [25] may arise if the scene structure is planar and does not contain enough information to recover the epipolar geometry. However, in both cases the image correspondences are related by a homography.

If the internal camera parameters are known, the five-point algorithm [20] can be used to determine the epipolar geometry even for a planar scene structure, but motion degeneracy still remains a problem. In addition, due to inaccuracies in feature locations and internal camera parameters a general motion with small

S. Palaiahnakote et al. (Eds.): ACPR 2019, LNCS 12046, pp. 512–526, 2020.
https://doi.org/10.1007/978-3-030-41404-7_36

translations may be statistically indistinguishable from a motion degeneracy. This insufficient translation between images in relation to the distance to the observed scene is equivalent to a poor intersection geometry, which becomes undefined in case of pure rotation of the camera. We denote this as *critical camera configuration* and consider the corresponding image pair as unsuitable for triangulation-based geometry estimation.

For a reliable geometry estimation a sufficient baseline between the images is necessary for triangulation. An inappropriate handling of critical configurations may result in an incomplete, inaccurate or failed SfM determination. Additionally, a large number of feature correspondences is desirable for optimization. Unfortunately, larger baselines increase the distortion between images which makes occlusions more likely. As a consequence, a significant number of feature correspondences may be lost reducing redundancy, which is important for the optimization by means of *bundle adjustment* [11]. Thus, a compromise between a sufficiently large baseline and the number of correspondences needs to be found.

On the other hand seeking for a high number of correspondences only may prefer critical camera configurations. Image pairs comprising short baselines tend to have more overlap, to be less distorted relative to each other than images with larger baselines and, thus, lead to more feature correspondences. Therefore, an approach for the detection of critical camera configurations is highly desirable. In this way one can increase the image overlap by maximizing the number of feature correspondences, but at the same time also avoid image pairs with critical camera configurations.

To this end, we propose an approach for the detection of critical camera configurations based on classification using a random forest. By formulating the detection as binary classification problem, a reliable detection of motion degeneracy can be achieved. In addition, by taking the predicted class probabilities into account, we are able to detect also the remaining critical configurations comprising insufficient baselines.

The remainder of the paper is organized as follows: In Sect. 2, we give an overview of existing methods dealing with critical camera configurations. Our classification-based approach for the detection of critical configurations is described in Sect. 3. Section 4 presents an extensive evaluation to obtain an appropriate parametrization for the classifier on real-world datasets. Finally, in Sect. 5 conclusions are given.

2 Related Work

The problem of degeneracy was introduced in [15] in association with the estimation of the fundamental matrix and further discussed in [26]. A detailed description of geometric relations is given in [11].

2.1 Model Selection

The majority of methods dealing with critical configurations is based on model selection using the Geometric Robust Information Criterion – GRIC [24]

$$GRIC = \sum \rho\left(e_i^2\right) + \lambda_1 \, d \, n + \lambda_2 \, k, \tag{1}$$

where $\rho\left(e_i^2\right)$ is a robust function of the residuals:

$$\rho\left(e_i^2\right) = \min\left(\frac{e^2}{\sigma^2}, \lambda_3 (r - d)\right) \tag{2}$$

The result is a score for a model taking into account the number n of inlier plus outlier feature correspondences, the standard deviation σ of the measurement error, the number k of motion model parameters, the dimension r of the data, the residuals e_i and the dimension d of the structure. The remaining tuning parameters are usually set to $\lambda_1 = \log 4$, $\lambda_2 = \log 4n$ and $\lambda_3 = 2$ (cf. [25]).

The methods employing GRIC [5,19,23,25] are based on the assumption, that in case of a degeneracy the geometric relation between images can be better described by a homography instead of a fundamental or essential matrix. To this end, for each model GRIC is calculated and the model with the lower score is taken. The score itself provides the (negative) logarithm of the posterior probability, that the corresponding model is correct.

In [21] GRIC is approximated. A degenerate camera configuration is assumed if the ratio $\frac{N_H}{N_F}$ is above an empirically determined threshold, where N_H is the number of inliers supporting the estimated homography and N_F the number of inliers consistent with the estimated fundamental matrix. In case of known internal camera parameters, planar scenes and motion degeneracy are distinguished based on the median triangulation angle.

Other methods extend RANSAC [6] to select the appropriate model. In case of unknown internal camera parameters and structure degeneracy, DEGENSAC [3] employs the plane-and-parallax algorithm [13] to estimate the fundamental matrix. QDEGENSAC [8] does not require problem specific knowledge and is able to determine the underlying model automatically by using less and less constraints.

2.2 Conjugate Rotation

Mapping between image points can be described by a *homography*

$$\boldsymbol{H} = \alpha \boldsymbol{K}_2 \left(\boldsymbol{R} - \frac{\boldsymbol{t}\boldsymbol{n}^T}{d}\right) \boldsymbol{K}_1^{-1} \tag{3}$$

induced by a plane $\pi = (\boldsymbol{n}^T, d)^T$ with normal vector $\boldsymbol{n}$, distance d from the origin, calibration matrices $\boldsymbol{K}_i$, relative rotation matrix $\boldsymbol{R}$ and translation $\boldsymbol{t}$ between the images as well as an arbitrary scale factor α.

In case of motion degeneracy, the images are related by an *infinite homography*

$$\boldsymbol{H}_\infty = \lim_{d\to\infty} \boldsymbol{H} = \alpha \boldsymbol{K}_2 \boldsymbol{R} \boldsymbol{K}_1^{-1} \tag{4}$$

corresponding to a conjugate rotation [10] with the same eigenvalues[1] (up to scale) if $\boldsymbol{K}_1 = \boldsymbol{K}_2$.

For the detection of motion degeneracy between images, a homography is estimated and tested if it conforms with the conjugate rotation. This can be achieved by testing the eigenvalues of the homography for its complex conjugate form [25]. Alternatively, in [14] the test is based on the equivalence of the term $T = \boldsymbol{R} - \frac{\boldsymbol{t}\boldsymbol{n}^T}{d}$ from Eq. 3 and $\boldsymbol{R}$. The larger $\boldsymbol{t}$, the more T deviates from $\boldsymbol{R}$. A motion degeneration is assumed to be detected if the ratio of the largest to the smallest singular value of T is above an empirically determined threshold.

However, these methods fail if internal camera parameters have changed. In this case $\boldsymbol{K}_1 \neq \boldsymbol{K}_2$ and the homography does not correspond anymore to a conjugate rotation. But also a homography induced by a world plane can have the form of a conjugate rotation. If for example the translation $\boldsymbol{t}$ is perpendicular to the plane's normal $\boldsymbol{n}$, the term $(\boldsymbol{t}\boldsymbol{n}^T)$ in Eq. 3 becomes 0, which is not distinguishable from the case of pure rotation without translation (i.e., $\boldsymbol{t} = 0$).

2.3 Quality Measure

Many quality measures for image pairs were developed in the context of *keyframe selection*, where one seeks for an image pair (*keyframe*) with a good camera configuration for the initialization of an iterative or sequential reconstruction [1,5,22]. Keyframe selection does not allow direct degeneracy detection, but it ranks camera configuration with regard to the reconstruction according to the employed quality measure.

A quality measure for keyframe selection based on the uncertainty of the reconstructed scene points was proposed in [1]. For each reconstructed 3D point the eigenvalues λ_1, λ_2 and λ_3 of the corresponding covariance matrix are computed. The uncertainty of a 3D point is then given by the *roundness*

$$R = \sqrt{\frac{\lambda_3}{\lambda_1}} \tag{5}$$

of the corresponding error ellipsoid with $\lambda_1 \geq \lambda_2 \geq \lambda_3$. R lies between 0 and 1 and depends only on the relative geometry between cameras and image features. For coincident camera centers and correct feature correspondences, it is equal to zero. For each reconstructed point R is computed and the mean roundness is taken as the quality measure of the image pair.

[1] The eigenvalues of a rotation matrix are $(1, e^{i\theta}, e^{-i\theta})$, where the last two are complex conjugate with θ as the angle of rotation. The eigenvector corresponding to the eigenvalue 1 is the axis of rotation.

A similar measure based on ray divergence is proposed in [12]. The basic idea is to intersect rays

$$\boldsymbol{X}_{ij} = \boldsymbol{C}_i + \mu_{ij} \boldsymbol{R}_i \boldsymbol{K}_i^{-1} \boldsymbol{x}_{ij} \tag{6}$$

coming from camera centers $\boldsymbol{C}_i$ which go through corresponding pixels $\boldsymbol{x}_{ij}$. The ray direction is computed from the feature coordinates $\boldsymbol{x}_{ij} = (x_j \; y_j \; 1)^T$ in the image i, the internal camera parameters $\boldsymbol{K}_i$ and the camera rotation matrix $\boldsymbol{R}_i$. Due to inaccuracies in feature locations and camera parameters rays usually do not intersect. Therefore, the *ray divergence* is defined as the shortest Euclidean distance between the projection rays.

In [17], the detection of motion degeneracy was formulated as a binary classification problem, where properties of the reconstructed 3D points were used as features for an AdaBoost [9] classifier. Detection of critical camera configurations based on an empirically determined thresholds for the roundness from Eq. (5) was employed in [18].

3 Classification

The drawback of the methods based on model selection is the necessity of the computation of multiple models, which can be time-consuming and challenging. Methods employing the conformity with a conjugate rotation are not generally applicable. The classification-based approach [17] only detects motion degeneracy, but no critical configurations with an insufficient camera translation.

However, the analysis in [17] as well as the application in [18] have shown, that motion degeneracy can be detected using properties of the reconstructed 3D points. We extend this idea by formulating the detection as a classification problem using additional features. To this end, a random forest classifier [2] is employed, which is a popular machine learning method due to its relatively good accuracy and robustness.

By assuming (approximately) known internal camera parameters, the detection requires only the computation of a single model, namely the essential matrix. In addition, uncertainty information is required for the computation of some features. Thus, structure degeneracy is avoided using the five point algorithm [20] and the goal remains to detect critical configurations with an insufficient camera translation.

3.1 Features

The uncertainty of a reconstructed 3D point $\boldsymbol{X}$ is given by the covariance matrix $\boldsymbol{\Sigma}_x$. The corresponding error ellipsoid is defined by

$$(\boldsymbol{P} - \boldsymbol{X})^T \boldsymbol{\Sigma}_x^{-1} (\boldsymbol{P} - \boldsymbol{X}) = 1, \tag{7}$$

where $\boldsymbol{P}$ is a point on the ellipsoid. The eigenvectors of $\boldsymbol{\Sigma}_x$ define the directions and the eigenvalues $\lambda_1 \geq \lambda_2 \geq \lambda_3$ the squares of lengths a, b and c of the semi-axes of the ellipsoid:

$$a = \sqrt{\lambda_1} \quad b = \sqrt{\lambda_2} \quad c = \sqrt{\lambda_3} \tag{8}$$

Based on $\boldsymbol{\Sigma}_x$ or the shape of the error ellipsoid and the triangulation conditions, the following properties are derived for $\boldsymbol{X}$:

- Roundness of the error ellipsoid [1] (cf. Sect. 2.3):

$$R_x = \sqrt{\frac{\lambda_3}{\lambda_1}} \tag{9}$$

- Volume of the error ellipsoid [17]:

$$V_x = \frac{4}{3}\pi\, a\, b\, c = \frac{4}{3}\pi \sqrt{\lambda_1\, \lambda_2\, \lambda_3} \tag{10}$$

- Alternative roundness of the error ellipsoid [17] as the quotient of V_x and the volume of the circumscribed sphere with radius r:

$$K_x = \frac{\frac{4}{3}\pi\, a\, b\, c}{\frac{4}{3}\pi\, r^3} = \frac{a\, b\, c}{max(a, b, c)^3} = \frac{\sqrt{\lambda_2\, \lambda_3}}{\lambda_1} \tag{11}$$

- Total variance as the trace of the covariance matrix:

$$PTV_x = \mathrm{tr}(\boldsymbol{\Sigma}_x) \tag{12}$$

- Smallest depth D_x regarding camera centers
- Ray divergence RD_x [12]

In contrast to R_x, the properties V_x, K_x and PTV_x include the complete shape of the error ellipsoid. The total variance PTV_x of $\boldsymbol{\Sigma}_x$ is an overall measure of dispersion of the coordinates of the estimated point position. The assumption is that in case of a critical camera configuration the point localization will be less accurate. K_x correlates with R_x, but may be more expressive due to the additional eigenvalue it employs. A similar motivation lies behind the volume V_x, which in contrast to K_x has a lower correlation with R_x.

Properties D_x and RD_x are not derived from $\boldsymbol{\Sigma}_x$. The point depth D_x is proportional to the basis. Two cameras with a short baseline can undergo only a slight relative rotation or there will not be sufficient overlap between the images. This results in small angles between the intersection rays, which produce a higher depth (relative to the basis) of $\boldsymbol{X}$ in conjunction with a short basis. Therefore, for short baselines D_x shall differ significantly from the depth where cameras have undergone a larger translation. The usage of the smallest depth is motivated by the fact, that in case of a very large baseline (e.g., arising by combination of terrestrial with aerial images), the smallest depth is more meaningful concerning the camera configuration.

In addition to the point properties, we define several properties characterizing the quality of the estimated relative pose:

- Inlier rate *IR* as the number of feature correspondences supporting the estimated essential matrix.
- Mean reprojection error *MRE* in pixel

– Total variance as the trace of the covariance matrix $\boldsymbol{\Sigma}_p$ of the estimated projection matrix:

$$TV = \mathrm{tr}(\boldsymbol{\Sigma}_p) \tag{13}$$

In case of motion degeneracy, the fitted essential matrix $\boldsymbol{E}$ is under-constrained by the data [25]. Thus, it satisfies a family of epipolar geometries

$$\boldsymbol{E} = \boldsymbol{K}_2^T \, [\boldsymbol{e}_2]_x \, \boldsymbol{H}_\infty \, \boldsymbol{K}_1 \tag{14}$$

parametrized by the epipole $\boldsymbol{e}_2$, which is undetermined by feature correspondences related by the infinity homography $\boldsymbol{H}_\infty$ (cf. Sect. 2.2). Thus, the determination of $\boldsymbol{e}_2$ is arbitrary and depends on the largest consistent subset of wrong correspondences.

Based on this, we employ the inlier rate to examine whether a larger consistent subset of the correspondences indicates the correct model. We also expect a significant increase of the mean reprojection error MRE for pairs with a critical camera configuration.

Similar to PTV_x, the total variance TV measures the dispersion of the relative pose and is based on the uncertainty of the translation as well as the rotation. However, the rotation can be recovered reliably even in case of short baselines [4]. Therefore, it is expected, that the value of PTV_x is mostly determined by the uncertainty of the camera translation.

In summary, we employ properties IR, MRE, TV as well as the medians R, V, K, D, RD and PTV of the reconstructed point properties R_x, V_x, K_x, D_x, RD_x and PTV_x as features for the classification.

3.2 Detection

Detection of critical camera configurations is formulated as a binary classification problem. Image pairs comprising motion degeneracy belong to the positive and pairs with translated cameras to the negative class.

By this means, motion degeneracy can be detected but not critical configurations with an insufficient camera translation. An alternative would be to define three classes, i.e., using an additional class for pairs with an insufficient baseline. As discussed in Sect. 1, the problems arising from such configurations depend on several factors, which are usually application-specific. Thus, the generation of training data containing such pairs is very challenging, particularly because insufficient baselines are ill-defined.

Instead, we employ class probabilities to detect unsuitable pairs. First, pairs are classified into degenerate comprising motion degeneration (positive) and non-degenerate (negative). Then, a further subdivision of non-degenerate pairs is made into those with an insufficient baseline according to the prediction probability and an empirically determined threshold.

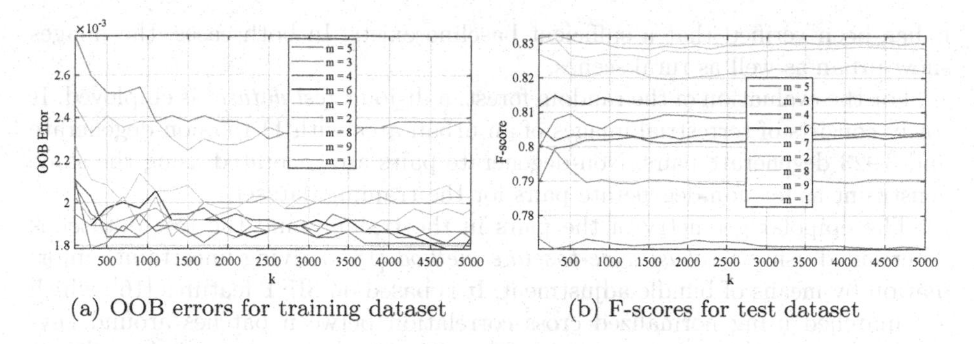

(a) OOB errors for training dataset (b) F-scores for test dataset

Fig. 1. Random forest performance for varying number of decision trees k and number of randomly selected features m using the complete feature set. The legends are ordered according to the OOB errors respectively F-scores.

4 Evaluation

We guide the training by means of the Out-of-Bag (OOB) error. The training of the random forest is based on *bagging*, where about 1/3 of the training samples are not used for training. This *OOB data* can be employed as test data to estimate the *OOB error* as a measure of the classifier's performance. The procedure corresponds to cross-validation and, thus, no explicit cross-validation is necessary [2].

The performance of the trained random forest is additionally evaluated on an independent test dataset (cf. Sect. 4.1) using the F-score. For imbalanced datasets such as our test dataset, precision and recall are good measures of an algorithm's performance. *Precision* specifies how many pairs classified as degenerate comprise motional degeneracy and *recall* gives the percentage of the detected degenerate pairs:

$$\text{precision} = \frac{\text{TP}}{\text{TP} + \text{FP}} \qquad \text{recall} = \frac{\text{TP}}{\text{TP} + \text{FN}}$$

The numbers of true positives (TP), false positives (FP) and false negatives (FN) refer to positive samples corresponding to degenerate pairs. The *F-score* combines precision and recall into a single score and is defined as their harmonic mean:

$$\text{F} = \frac{2 \cdot \text{precision} \cdot \text{recall}}{\text{precision} + \text{recall}} \tag{15}$$

In this way, we seek for a random forest minimizing the OOB error, but we are at the same time able to evaluate the performance on independent real-world data.

4.1 Datasets

Training is based on a *training dataset* comprising 18 242 non-degenerate and 18 734 degenerate pairs. The latter consist of terrestrial images with pure rotation. Non-degenerate pairs contain terrestrial, UAV and aerial images for which it has been verified that a sufficient baseline exists. In both cases, the images show urban as well as rural scenes.

For the evaluation of the random forest, a disjoint *test dataset* is employed. It solely consists of terrestrial images of an urban area with 11 155 non-degenerate and 3 923 degenerate pairs. Non-degenerate pairs are generated using the same constraint as for non-degenerate pairs for the training dataset.

The epipolar geometry of the pairs in the training and the test dataset is determined using a *robust wide-baseline method* [18] deriving uncertainty information by means of bundle adjustment. It is based on SIFT features [16], which are matched using normalized cross correlation between patches around keypoints. Potential matches are refined by affine least squares matching [7] to obtain sub-pixel positions including covariance information. Epipolar geometry is then estimated using a strategy similar to the Expectation Maximization algorithm based on the five-point algorithm [20] and refinement by means of robust bundle adjustment. To increase the number of samples and to simulate the matching on various resolutions, pairs are matched multiple times using three different image resolutions.

4.2 Analysis of Parameters

Crucial parameters of a random forest are the number k of decision trees and the number m of randomly selected features. Usually, parameter m is problem-dependent and, thus, m leading to the lowest classification error should be preferred [2].

To this end, we have trained multiple random forests using varying values for m and the complete set of features defined in Sect. 3.1. The resulting OOB errors for the training dataset and the corresponding F-scores for the test dataset are shown in Fig. 1. Except for $m = 1$ and $m = 9$, the random forest turns out to be not very sensitive regarding m and the OOB error.

Considering the constantly low OOB errors, the range $3 \leq m \leq 6$ seems to be optimal. However, the best classification performance on the test dataset in terms of the F-score is achieved for higher values of m. This could indicate a low importance of several features. If the percentage of relevant features is low, the probability of their selection during training decreases for decreasing m. Thus, weak features are often selected leading to a poorer classification performance. Therefore, we analyze the importance of features in the next section.

Due to the robustness of random forests concerning overfitting for an increasing k, the computational efficiency of the classification remains the primary criterion for its selection. As shown in Fig. 1 the performance doesn't improve anymore from k from above about 1 000 independent of m. The visible variations are regarded as purely random fluctuations resulting from the measurement of the OOB errors for each tree separately and the averaging over all trees afterwards.

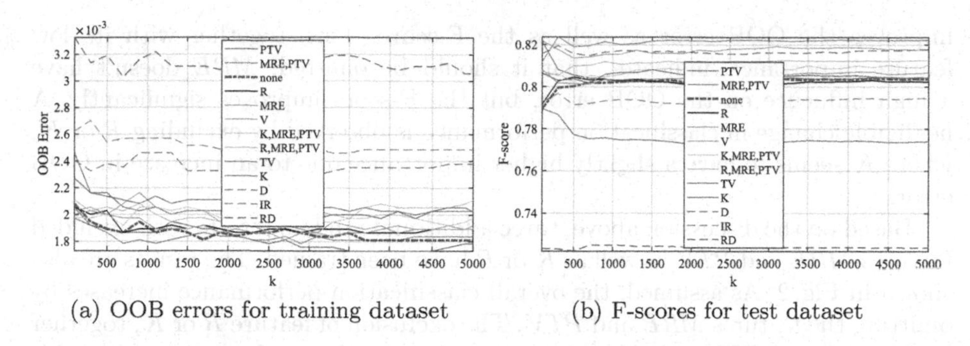

(a) OOB errors for training dataset (b) F-scores for test dataset

Fig. 2. Random forest performance for varying number of decision trees k, setting the number of randomly selected features $m = 5$, but excluding the features specified in the legend.

4.3 Analysis of Features

For a first overview of the characteristics of the features we employ the *variable importance* [2]. It measures the importance of a single feature in a random forest and is computed by means of OOB data (cf. Sect. 4) during training. A higher score means a higher contribution of a feature for the classification.

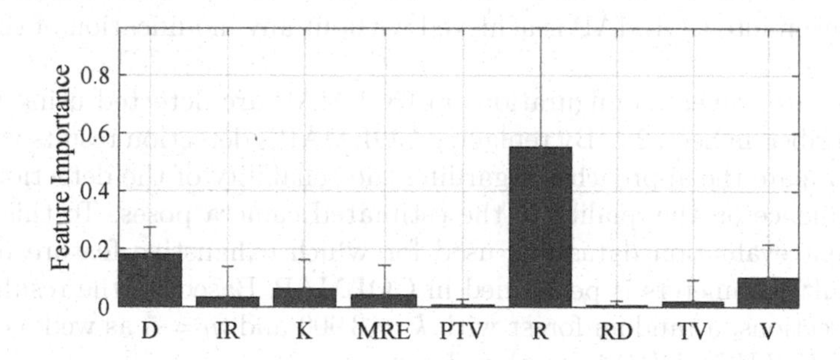

Fig. 3. Mean feature importances with extreme values (red lines) across random forests from Sect. 4.2 (Color figure online)

The mean variable importances are computed across all random forests from Sect. 4.2 and presented in Fig. 3. By far the most relevant feature is R, followed by D and V. Features R and K have similar properties and are correlated (correlation coefficient: 0.84), but K still has a lower importance. An explanation could be the higher information gain in R leading to a preferred selection during training.

Another method for characterizing features is to examine the influence of a single feature by leaving it out. For this, several random forests are trained without the feature as described in Sect. 4.2. Figure 2 shows OOB errors and F-scores of random forests per excluded feature. The exclusion of feature PTV

improves the OOB error as well as the F-score. This, together with its low feature importance, indicates, that it should be omitted. *MRE* doesn't have a high influence on the OOB error, but the F-score improves significantly. A negligible change in classification performance is observed by excluding R or K, where K seems to have a slightly higher importance due to an increase in OOB error.

Based on the discussion above, three additional random forests with excluded features *MRE* and *PTV* as well as K or R have been trained. The results are also shown in Fig. 2. As assumed, the overall classification performance increases by omitting the features *MRE* and *PTV*. The exclusion of feature R or K, together with *MRE* and *PTV*, results in a more or less similar performance. From this it can be concluded, that R is interchangeable with K and vice versa.

4.4 Integration into a Structure from Motion Framework

To demonstrate the practical applicability of the proposed approach, we have integrated our classification into the SfM framework COLMAP[2] [21] by modifying its database. The latter is used to cache the estimated models and camera configurations, which are then employed for the reconstruction. We rematch pairs contained in the database using the robust wide-baseline method described in Sect. 4.1 to obtain reliable uncertainty information, classify them as described in Sect. 3.2 and put the classification results back into the database. In this way, an integration into COLMAP is achieved without any modification of the source code.

Degenerate camera configurations in COLMAP are detected using the approach described in Sect. 2.1. By replacing COLMAP's detection results with ours, we can compare the approaches regarding the reliability of the detection as well as the influence on the quality of the estimated camera poses. To this end, an independent evaluation dataset is used for which exhaustive feature matching with default parameters is performed in COLMAP. Based on the results in the previous sections, a random forest with $k = 3\,000$ and $m = 5$ as well as features R, D, V, *IR*, *TV* and *RD* is employed.

Comparison of the classification performance is based on 6 965 ground truth pairs (of which 174 are degenerate) from the *evaluation dataset* shown in Fig. 4. Our approach is able to detect all degenerate pairs with 2.8 kHz classification frequency, but some of the non-degenerate pairs are wrongly classified (F-score: 0.383, precision: 0.237, recall: 1.0). On the other hand, COLMAP alone, i.e., without the integration of our classification, detects almost no degenerate pairs (F-score: 0.030, precision: 0.045, recall: 0.023).

The influence of the integration of our approach into COLMAP on the estimated camera poses is shown in Fig. 4. The ground truth camera poses form two circles without larger kinks and the positions of the cameras inside of the blue rectangles remain fixed due to the pure rotational movement. However, the estimated poses using the standard approach of COLMAP show some noticeable

[2] https://demuc.de/colmap, Version 3.5.

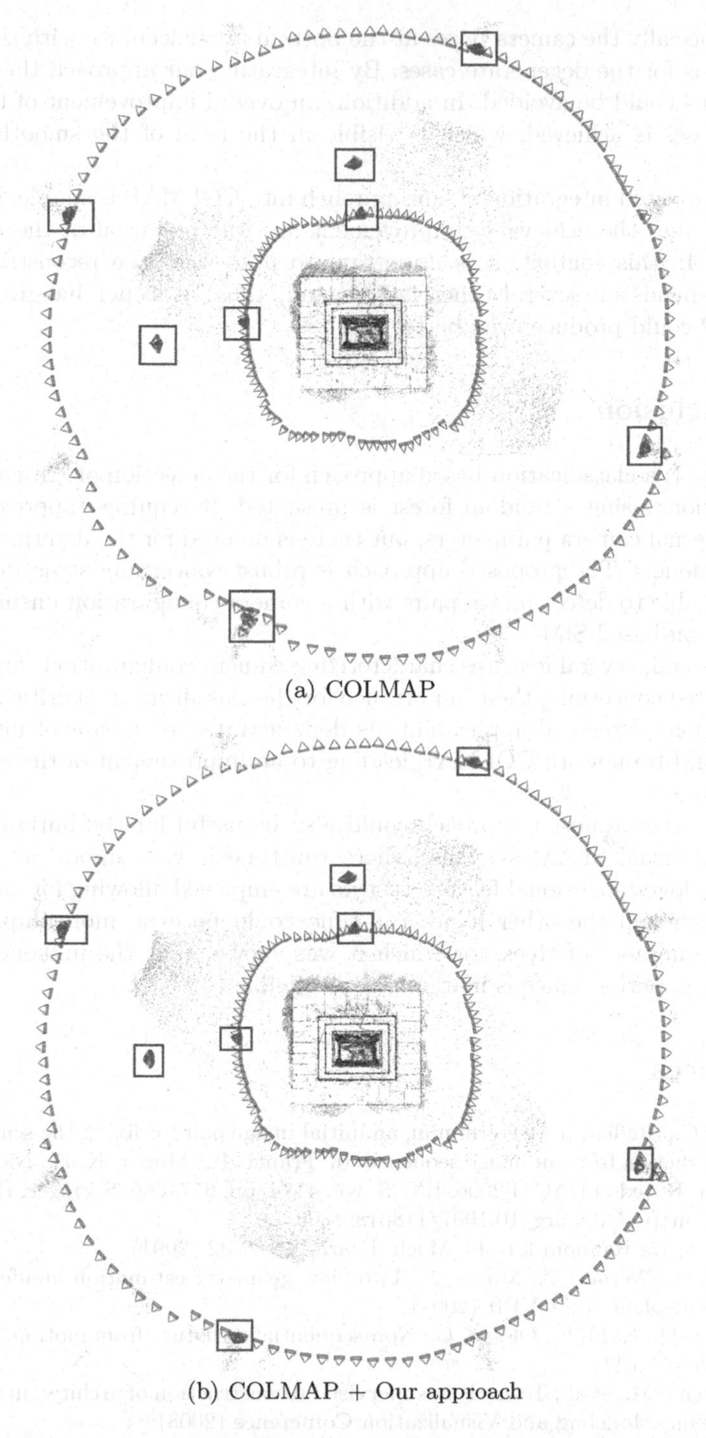

Fig. 4. Evaluation dataset containing 281 images reconstructed using COLMAP alone (a) and COLMAP with our approach (b). Degenerate configurations are marked by blue rectangles. (Color figure online)

kinks. Especially the camera poses at the bottom are inaccurate with significant translations for the degenerate cases. By integrating our approach these wrong translations could be avoided. In addition, an overall improvement of the outer camera poses is achieved, which is visible in the form of the smoother outer circle.

The presented integration of our approach into COLMAP is simple, but gives an insight into the achievable improvement and the potential of the proposed approach. In this context, it is important to note, that the reconstruction in general depends on several other factors and, thus, a deeper integration into COLMAP could produce even better results.

5 Conclusion

In this paper, a classification-based approach for the detection of critical camera configurations using a random forest is presented. It requires (approximately) known internal camera parameters, but there is no need for the determination of multiple models. The proposed approach is robust concerning structure degeneracy and able to detect image pairs with a camera configuration unsuitable for triangulation-based SfM.

To this end, several features characterizing camera configurations are defined and analyzed concerning their importance for the classification of critical camera configurations. Practical applicability is demonstrated by means of integration into the SfM framework COLMAP leading to an improvement of the estimated camera poses.

Finally, the proposed approach could also be useful for the initialization of monocular visual SLAM systems, where run-time is very important. On one hand, only low-dimensional feature vectors are employed allowing for an efficient classification. On the other hand, run-time could be even more improved by tuning the number of trees, for which it was shown, that the influence on the classification performance is marginal to negligible.

References

1. Beder, C., Steffen, R.: Determining an initial image pair for fixing the scale of a 3D reconstruction from an image sequence. In: Franke, K., Müller, K.-R., Nickolay, B., Schäfer, R. (eds.) DAGM 2006. LNCS, vol. 4174, pp. 657–666. Springer, Heidelberg (2006). https://doi.org/10.1007/11861898_66
2. Breiman, L.: Random forests. Mach. Learn. **45**, 5–32 (2001)
3. Chum, O., Werner, T., Matas, J.: Two-view geometry estimation unaffected by a dominant plane. In: CVPR (2005)
4. Enqvist, O., Kahl, F., Olsson, C.: Non-sequential structure from motion. In: ICCV Workshop (2011)
5. Farenzena, M., et al.: Towards unsupervised reconstruction of architectural models. In: Vision, Modeling and Visualization Conference (2008)

6. Fischler, M.A., Bolles, R.C.: Random sample consensus: a paradigm for model fitting with applications to image analysis and automated cartography. Commun. ACM **24**(6), 381–395 (1981)
7. Förstner, W.: Quality assessment of object location and point transfer using digital image correlation techniques. In: 25.3A, pp. 197–219 (1984)
8. Frahm, J.-M., Pollefeys, M.: RANSAC for (quasi-)degenerate data (QDEGSAC). In: CVPR (2006)
9. Freund, Y., Schapire, R.E.: A decision-theoretic generalization of on-line learning and an application to boosting. J. Comput. Syst. Sci. **55**(1), 119–139 (1997)
10. Hartley, R.I.: Self-calibration from multiple views with a rotating camera. In: Eklundh, J.-O. (ed.) ECCV 1994. LNCS, vol. 800, pp. 471–478. Springer, Heidelberg (1994). https://doi.org/10.1007/3-540-57956-7_52
11. Hartley, R., Zisserman, A.: Multiple View Geometry in Computer Vision. Cambridge University Press, Cambridge (2004)
12. Hess-Flores, M., Knoblauch, D., Duchaineau, M.A., Joy, K.I., Kuester, F.: Ray divergence-based bundle adjustment conditioning for multi-view stereo. In: Ho, Y.-S. (ed.) PSIVT 2011. LNCS, vol. 7087, pp. 153–164. Springer, Heidelberg (2011). https://doi.org/10.1007/978-3-642-25367-6_14
13. Irani, M., Anandan, P.: Parallax geometry of pairs of points for 3D scene analysis. In: Buxton, B., Cipolla, R. (eds.) ECCV 1996. LNCS, vol. 1064, pp. 17–30. Springer, Heidelberg (1996). https://doi.org/10.1007/BFb0015520
14. Kähler, O., Denzler, J.: Detection of planar patches in handheld image sequences. In: Photogrammetric Computer Vision (2006)
15. Kanatani, K.: Statistical Optimization for Geometric Computation: Theory and Practice. Elsevier, Amsterdam (1996)
16. Lowe, D.G.: Distinctive image features from scale-invariant keypoints. IJCV **60**(2), 91–110 (2004)
17. Michelini, M., Mayer, H.: Detection of critical camera configurations for structure from motion. In: ISPRS International Archives of the Photogrammetry, Remote Sensing and Spatial Information Sciences XL-3/W1, pp. 73–78 (2014)
18. Michelini, M., Mayer, H.: Efficient wide baseline structure from motion. In: ISPRS Annals of Photogrammetry, Remote Sensing and Spatial Information Sciences III-3, pp. 99–106 (2016)
19. Moulon, P., Monasse, P., Marlet, R.: Adaptive structure from motion with a contrario model estimation. In: Lee, K.M., Matsushita, Y., Rehg, J.M., Hu, Z. (eds.) ACCV 2012. LNCS, vol. 7727, pp. 257–270. Springer, Heidelberg (2013). https://doi.org/10.1007/978-3-642-37447-0_20
20. Nistér, D.: An efficient solution to the five-point relative pose problem. IEEE Trans. Pattern Anal. Mach. Intell. **26**(6), 756–777 (2004)
21. Schönberger, J.L., Frahm, J.-M.: Structure-from-motion revisited. In: CVPR (2016)
22. Thormählen, T., Broszio, H., Weissenfeld, A.: Keyframe selection for camera motion and structure estimation from multiple views. In: Pajdla, T., Matas, J. (eds.) ECCV 2004. LNCS, vol. 3021, pp. 523–535. Springer, Heidelberg (2004). https://doi.org/10.1007/978-3-540-24670-1_40

23. Toldo, R., et al.: Hierarchical structure-and-motion recovery from uncalibrated images. In: Computer Vision and Image Understanding 140.C, pp. 127–143 (2015)
24. Torr, P.H.S.: An assessment of information criteria for motion model selection. In: CVPR (1997)
25. Torr, P.H.S., Fitzgibbon, A.W., Zisserman, A.: The problem of degeneracy in structure and motion recovery from uncalibrated image sequences. IJCV **32**(1), 27–44 (1999)
26. Torr, P.H.S., Zisserman, A., Maybank, S.J.: Robust detection of degenerate configurations whilst estimating the fundamental matrix. Comput. Vis. Image Underst. **71**(3), 312–333 (1998)

Computer Vision and Robot Vision

Visual Counting of Traffic Flow from a Car via Vehicle Detection and Motion Analysis

Kevin Kolcheck[1], Zheyuan Wang[1], Haiyan Xu[2](✉), and Jiang Yu Zheng[1]

[1] Indiana University Purdue University Indianapolis, Indianapolis, IN 46202, USA
jzheng@iupui.edu
[2] Fukuoka Institute of Technology, Fukuoka, Japan
xu@fit.ac.jp

Abstract. Visual traffic counting so far has been carried out by static cameras at streets or aerial pictures from sky. This work initiates a new approach to count traffic flow by using populated vehicle driving recorders. Mainly vehicles are counted by a camera moves along a route on opposite lane. Vehicle detection is first implemented in video frames by using deep learning YOLO3, and then vehicle trajectories are counted in the spatial-temporal space called *motion profile*. Motion continuity, direction, and detection missing are considered to avoid multiple counting of oncoming vehicles. This method has been tested on naturalistic driving videos lasting for hours. The counted vehicle numbers can be interpolated as a flow of opposite lanes from a patrol vehicle for traffic control. The mobile counting of traffic is more flexible than the traffic monitoring by cameras at street corners.

Keywords: Computer vision · Vehicle detection · Motion analysis · YOLO3 · Traffic flow

1 Introduction

Understanding traffic flow by counting number of vehicles is important for traffic control and daily life in a smart city. Current traffic counting relies on wired press sensors on road or GPS of vehicles transmitted via cellar network to map services [1]. The former method is inconvenient to be set on every street. While the latter method based on measuring vehicle speed can find traffic jams but not traffic volume because not every vehicle is communicating with the servers at all time. For the visual counting of traffic, CCTV at street corners also counts number of vehicles [2] at static locations. Another way is to fly a helicopter to capture flow at busy locations [3, 4]. All these methods require some setting of infrastructures. Our new approach uses a camera on a patrol vehicle or driving recorders on many cars traveling on streets [5]. We are attempting to obtain traffic flow information from these mobile cameras with the minimum sensing and computing costs, and then collect compact data via communication network. It is very common that a car driving outside witnesses traffic situations on the road. Compared to traffic monitoring CCTV at limited locations such as intersections, a mobile camera will not miss any

S. Palaiahnakote et al. (Eds.): ACPR 2019, LNCS 12046, pp. 529–543, 2020.
https://doi.org/10.1007/978-3-030-41404-7_37

accident on a route in the opposite direction and give a complete traffic report on its path. Multiple vehicles can count traffic flows on the opposite roads at different times, and data are sent back to the map services. In general, your car is viewed by other cars on road more frequently than by sensors set on streets.

In driving video taken by a camera at the dashboard of a vehicle, we can recognize vehicles on all the lanes of current street by using YOLO3 (You Only Look Once) [6–8] with high detection accuracy. We focus the vehicle appearing regions of the opposite traffic in order to minimize the detection speed further on YOLO3. YOLOv3 real-time object detection system utilizes a single neural network to process a full image or frame. By comparison to classifier-based systems like R-CNN and Fast R-CNN, YOLO3 is much faster.

The YOLO3 detected vehicles have no detailed properties (e.g., vehicle face) associated with their motion direction. We further apply motion properties of vehicles such as direction and velocity for vehicle counting without tracking YOLO3 results overtime. To count traffic, however, we need to focus on vehicles on opposite lanes against current moving camera, because traffic in the same direction with the camera can be seen only locally in a limited range. Instead of recognizing vehicle faces such as front, back, and side [16], this work classifies the vehicle motion with respect to the camera. For the motion information processing of driving video, Kilicarslan et al. has proposed the motion profile as a spatio-temporal map to examine the vehicle trajectories [9] for vehicle identification [10], collision alarming [11, 12], and pedestrian detection [13, 14]. A motion trace longer than optical flow provides the stable motion of targets and can be used for object recognition because of the mechanical motion of vehicles, pedestrians, and static background.

The proposed method here only looks at opposite road. Assuming ego-vehicle moves on left lane and observes driving scenes as illustrated in Fig. 1. Oncoming vehicles through a road segment are all scanned in a period. Moreover, we only count those vehicles visible by the camera. Vehicles at farthest lane may be occluded completely by closer ones during traffic jam and they will be omitted. As a result, we can count vehicle in a good accuracy along road sections excluding intersection, roundabout, and one-way road.

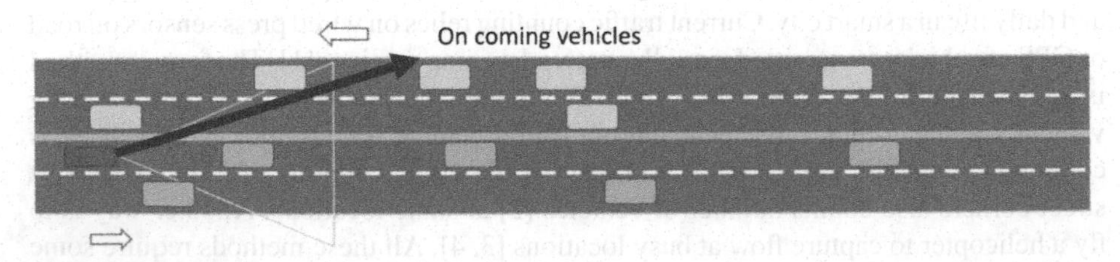

Fig. 1. A diagram to count vehicles on a route by a patrol vehicle (red) moving in the opposite direction. The observation vehicle can also be a normal car traveling on road. (yellow) oncoming vehicle from right two left, (green) vehicles moving in the same direction as the observing vehicle. (Color figure online)

In the following section, we will first solve spatial recognition in each frame by using deep learning YOLO3 in Sect. 2. Section 3 shows the vehicle traces across video and the counting of vehicles in opposite lanes. Section 4 discusses the traffic estimation by mobile cameras vs other ways of traffic monitoring. Section 5 addresses experiments and Sect. 6 gives a conclusion.

2 Vehicle Detection in Video Frame via YOLO3

As a vehicle moves forward, its forward camera can see surrounding vehicles moving in the same direction up to certain range, which is not effective for counting number of vehicles but can provide traffic flow information such as flow speed. On opposite lanes or road, the camera passes every oncoming vehicle and know the traffic flow along entire route. Oncoming vehicles appear from far away near the vanishing point of road and disappear on left margin as shown in Fig. 2. We can set the ROI only in left half of image to speed up the detection.

The default weights available on YOLO's website were trained on the COCO (Common Objects in Context) dataset and handle vehicle recognition out of the box. Among many objects YOLO3 can detect, vehicles are detected with a high accuracy viewed from street cameras and vehicle cameras. While YOLO3 does not provide any means of tracking objects from frame-to-frame, counting traffic is still possible beneficial from it due to YOLO's strong detection capabilities.

Fig. 2. A frame of driving video taken by a dashboard camera and detected vehicles by YOLO3 marked in bounding boxes.

The YOLO3 has been pretrained for detecting vehicles of various types such as car, truck, bus, etc. A bounding box is located approximately around an identified vehicle. The overall accuracy is over 90% on close vehicles without occlusion in our testing on naturalistic driving video. Even for partial occlusion between vehicles and by small obstacles such as fence and poles between the camera opposite roads, YOLO3 can still locate a box at the accuracy of 80% because of the underlying deep learning method looking at parts and their structure across different layers of the deep neural network. This maximumly helps the vehicle counting when an occlusion happens between vehicles on a wide road with multiple lanes. Figure 3 shows more results of vehicle detection under different illumination on several types of roads.

To count vehicles in opposition direction, we have to categorize all vehicles obtained by YOLO3 detection. Although the YOLO3 network can be retrained to find vehicle facing direction as for pedestrian facing direction [16], we employ the motion information to avoid a heavy training process of YOLO3, as the large dataset of vehicle samples have not been tagged with facing direction. Assume that ego-vehicle has a speed V_o and an observed vehicle has speed V. Their relative speed is then $S = V - V_o$.

Fig. 3. Results of vehicle recognition by YOLO3 under different illumination conditions.

Different moving vehicles thus have the following motion properties.

Front and Parallel Vehicles ($S \geq 0$): The front vehicle will not have long term negative relative speed in the visible range, otherwise it will cause a collision. Its position stays at frame center frequently. Multiple traces can be visible if more vehicles occupy several lanes and are moving in parallel to the camera. Their image velocity is low [10, 11].

Passed Vehicles ($S < 0$): If a vehicle with a lower speed than the ego-vehicle on a side lane is passed by the camera, the vehicle is moving in the video towards either side of the frame. The outward image velocity of such *passed vehicles* is larger than that of front vehicles.

Passing Vehicles ($S > 0$): If a *passing vehicle* overtakes the ego-vehicle or camera, its trajectory is moving from outside of video frame towards the frame center, because of the perspective projection of its speeding ahead motion. The inward image velocity has a different sign from that of a passed vehicle on the same side lane.

Stopped Vehicles ($S = -V_o$): For *stopped vehicles,* their image velocity is the same as those in static background, which diverges from the frame center [10].

Oncoming Vehicles ($S = -V - V_o) \ll 0$): The fastest image velocity in negative x direction happens at *oncoming* vehicles on the opposite lane or road because the relative speed between oncoming vehicles and the moving camera is almost doubled. Oncoming vehicles only appear on left side of the video for right side driving countries.

3 Motion Trace Generation and Vehicle Counting

3.1 Vehicles Motion Characteristics in Driving Video

To directly obtain motion of scenes, we generate a temporal image called *motion profile* [9] (MP) to record the trajectories of scenes in driving video. As seen in Fig. 4, a horizontal image belt (red) is located around the horizon projected into the video frame, which is almost invariant to the vehicle driving as long as the camera is set. All the vehicles, no matter how far or close, are covered by this belt completely or partially. We

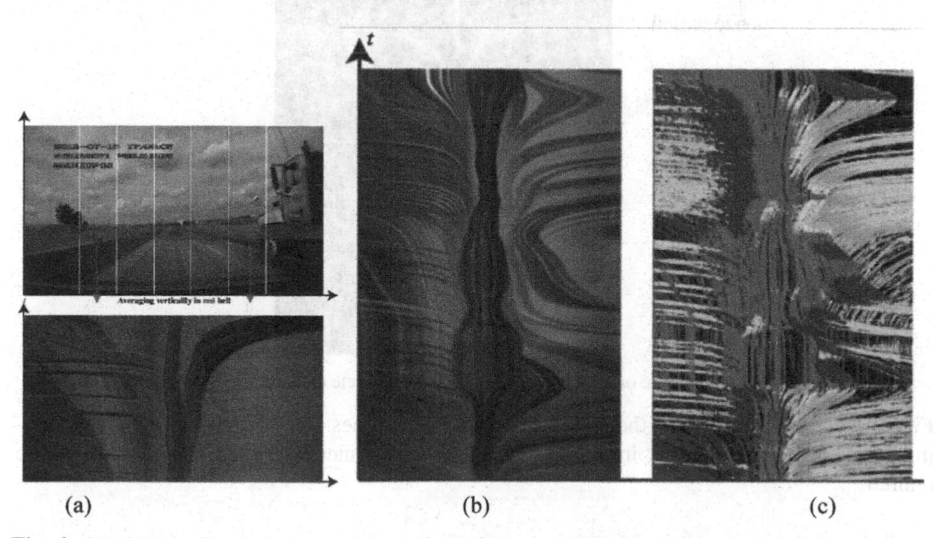

Fig. 4. Motion profile that shows the motion of scenes. Vehicles and background scenes have their motion traces appearing in the profile. The horizontal axis is the x axis of image and vertical axis is the time. The direction of motion traces can be calculated from the tangent of trace edges and colored accordingly. (a) frame belt and generation of motion profile, (b) a long motion profile with traces of vehicles, (c) traces in the motion profile are colored according to their orientation. (Color figure online)

average the pixel color vertically in the belt $B(x, y)$ and produce a line $L(x)$. The lines from consecutive frames form a spatio-temporal image $M(x, t)$ called *motion profile* [9]. The motion profile provides more stable image velocity of scenes than between-frame optical flow. The motion can be measured locally from the orientation of traces computed by pixel differentiation, which avoid tracking to obtain motion in the 2D image sequence.

To ignore the motion from background scenes for vehicle counting. We plot YOLO detected vehicles only into another image aligned with the motion profile. For each bounding box $b(x, y, w, h, t)$, it is projected to an image $m(x, t)$ as a line $l(x, w, t)$. The consecutive lines of bounding boxes form a trajectory in this spatiao-temporal image, named *vehicle motion profile* (VMP) as shown in Fig. 5. The trajectory of a vehicle is more vertical in $m(x, t)$, if its horizontal image velocity is low in the video, while the trajectory is more horizontal (slanted) when the vehicle image velocity is large.

It is visible from the vehicle traces that YOLO3 can achieve more than 90% detection rate for close vehicles. The failure parts include the vehicles close to the margin of view frame, because of the cut off vehicles by margin, a large occlusion of vehicle by some other vehicles at distance, and a far vehicle parked at roadside. Regardless of car overlap, the centroid of box is never overwritten if cars are detected.

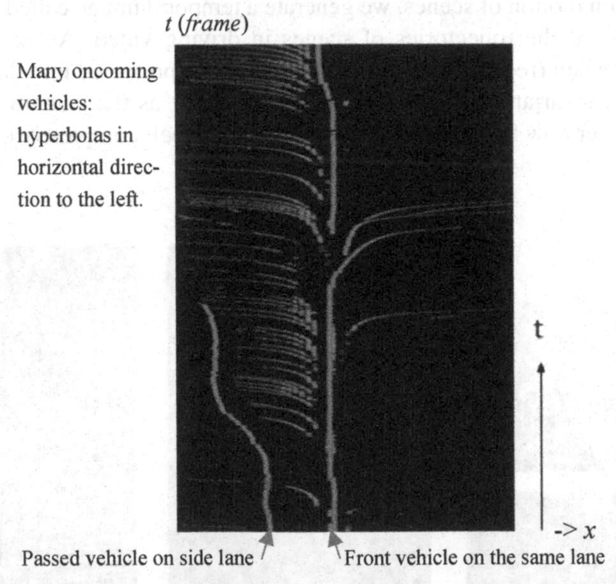

Fig. 5. Vehicle motion profile that shows the vehicle trajectories. The horizontal lengths of bounding boxes are colored in pink in that frame and the box center is a white point. (Color figure online)

The YOLO3 obtained boxes are not connected across frames. The maximum image velocity can be very large (negative) for oncoming vehicles. A general way to associate boxes along the time axis is to track boxes based on similar shapes of object. However, in our driving video, oncoming vehicle shape changes largely from front view near the image center (vanishing point) to sideview when it moves close to the frame margin.

Mover, the movement (image velocity) is large even if the video rate is 30 frame per second. If multiple vehicles are close to each other, they are easily confused because YOLO3 does not provide shape information in the output except the confidence value to be vehicles. Therefore, we focus on the local velocity of traces to avoid long term vehicle tracking to classify vehicles moving in different direction.

Let us examine the motion characters of vehicles around the moving camera. In the motion profile shown in Fig. 5, we can observe trajectories of detected vehicles along the time axis. These trajectories are from various vehicles. If the observing vehicle (ego-vehicle) is not moving on the leftist lane, it may also see stopped vehicles at roadside (parking, waiting for signal, in traffic jam, etc.). Also, the leftist lane may have vehicles passing the camera, or being passed by the camera, with their backside visible by the camera. They are all detected by YOLO3 without distinction in the left half of the video frame. To discriminate these vehicle traces from the oncoming vehicles, we examine their image velocities. Denote S be the relative speed of vehicle to the camera, and its position when captured is at (X, Z), it is not difficult to derive the image velocity

$$v = \partial x/\partial t = \partial(f X/Z)/\partial t = -xf S/Z \tag{1}$$

where f is the camera focal length, the two vehicles are moving in opposite direction, and detailed derivation can be found in [10]. We can further find that the relative speeds of different cars are

$$\begin{aligned} &S(oncoming) < S(stopping) < S(passed\, in\, same\, direction) \\ &< S(parallel\, in\, same\, direction) = 0 < S(passing\, in\, same\, direction) \end{aligned} \tag{2}$$

Their image velocities have the relation as

$$\begin{aligned} &v(oncoming) < v(stopping) < v(passed\, in\, same\, direction) \\ &< v(parallel) = 0 < v(passing\, in\, same\, direction) \end{aligned} \tag{3}$$

If the ego-vehicle with camera stops, i.e., $V = 0$, the relation of image velocity becomes

$$v(on\text{-}coming) < v(stopping) = 0 < v(passing\, in\, same\, direction) \tag{4}$$

These velocity constraints can be applied to relatively straight road only, but not at intersections or roundabouts where vehicles have no uniformed motion direction and the traffic flow there has uncertain transition between road segments. Based on these constraints, we filter out oncoming vehicles from all other vehicles detected by YOLO3 in the vehicle motion profile using the image velocity obtained in the motion profile.

3.2 Counting Vehicles Without Tracking Traces

How to count vehicles using trajectories? We have to either associate bounding boxes along the time axis as a unit, i.e., tracking vehicles, or just focus on a specific location in the frame for vehicle penetrating it. We employ the latter approach without tracking vehicles from frame to frame.

We set a vertical plane of sight from the camera in the 3D space as shown by the black arrow from the ego-vehicle in Fig. 1. It scans passing vehicles on opposite road at front side. In this direction, the vehicle size is relatively stable with the scale variation according to the number of opposite lanes from the camera. By examining the motion profile, vehicle motion traces can be counted for the number of vehicles on the opposite lanes. This is possible because cars that appear in the opposite lane produce a distinct "hook" shape in the VMP where they slowly come into view in the distance and then quickly leave the frame as they get closer as in Fig. 6.

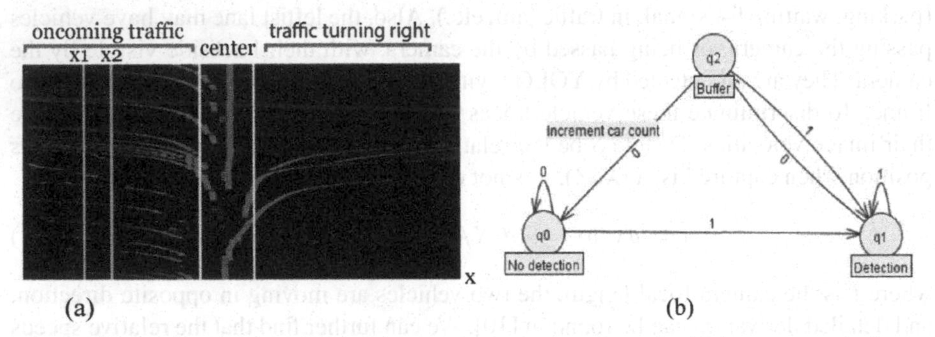

Fig. 6. Vehicle motion profile that shows the horizontal motion of vehicles on opposite lanes. The horizontal lengths of bounding boxes are colored in pink and the box center is a white point. (Color figure online)

The implementation to count the distinct oncoming vehicles is to define a scanning zone with two boundaries x_1 and x_2 in the motion profile as shown in Fig. 6(a) for the purpose of identify each centroid that passes through. This fixed zone $[x_1, x_2]$

(1) is set toward left side as much as possible for the leftward moving direction of oncoming vehicles, but a little away from the frame margin where vehicles may not be detected due to their partial shape excluded in the frame;
(2) is set away from the center of frame as much as possible where vehicles are small near the vanishing point. Also, this avoids the zone to cut a far road ahead possibly curved left, where the image velocity of vehicles becomes complex;
(3) is set enough wide to cover the fastest vehicle velocity. We estimate the maximum image velocity of oncoming vehicles even if for the road curved right. The width (x_1, x_2) guarantees that the fastest oncoming vehicle has the centroid captured once in the zone.

Searching the zone from x_1 to x_2 starting from beginning along the profile, we count each centroid in each frame and comparing the number to previous frames. It is possible to count how many vehicles passing through $[x_1, x_2]$.

To filter motion traces with a certain velocity from $v \ll 0$ to $v < 0$, we require the trace captured in the zone will not last too long, i.e., the duration of centroid within the zone is consecutively less than $(x_1 - x_2)/v$ frames. Assume the number of centroids is $n(t)$ at frame t. We count a vehicle in the total number $N(t)$ when $n(t)$ decreases (duration of a trace finishes). On the other hand, YOLO3 may still miss a frame or two along the trace due to various reasons including occlusion. A buffer of one frame is used so that, when the counted number of centroids in the zone changes relative to the previous frame, the total car count $N(t)$ is not immediately incremented until there has been no detections for two frames further in a row. This accounts for missing frames where YOLO3 fails to make a detection. Additional detections after the first missing frame are resolved and added to the total car count $N(t)$, after the row count $n(t)$ decreases from the previous frame count $n(t-1)$. We use an automaton to realize this counting as shown in Fig. 6(b).

A benefit of doing detection based on centroids rather than when encountering expected color of bounding box in the motion profile is that, in busier videos, it is possible to make distinctions between multiple cars that pass by around the same time. Some occasional traces of passed vehicle may also go through the zone but in a much slower velocity, i.e., $v < 0$, $|v|$ is small, and their trace is more vertically. But it will not add more count when its state keeps 1 in the automaton for too long. If ego-vehicle moves on the left lane, there is few chances that a passing vehicle will be observed on left side.

4 Dense Vehicle Counting for Traffic Flow Estimation

Here we introduce the nature of counting vehicles from mobile cars, and its potential application to traffic control. There is no method that can cover the real road traffic at the level of every car currently, except at some specific locations, at certain moment in a large area, or from a group of sampling cars. Figure 7(a) illustrates a traffic flow graph overtime [17] by depicting vehicle trajectories between two locations such as street intersections. According to different vehicle speeds, oncoming vehicles move from location 2 to location 1 (black traces). The observing vehicle (camera), however, moves from location 1 to location 2 inversely and its trajectory is depicted as a red trace. It will go across those oncoming vehicles at curved traces. Our vehicle moves in distance $d(t)$ on the road at time t. It counts the number of oncoming vehicles, $N(d, t)$ on opposite lanes. To monitor a route with many road segments and intersections, we can concatenate the flow graphs of all segments along the route as in Fig. 7(b), with on-coming vehicle traces appearing and disappearing at intersection. The number of vehicles (traces) gives the density in the traffic flow graph and the tangent of traces indicates the traffic speed.

A street camera monitoring a straight road obtain oncoming vehicles and their speed at different time, but the location is fixed as depicted by blue line in Fig. 7. A helicopter view is depicted in green line that captures a moment of road in a limited area. GPS based traffic monitoring, however, obtain multiple traces of vehicles equipped with GPS and wireless communication when the reporting function is turned on.

There are dense street cameras set in some cities for monitoring traffic flow, which has more blue vertical lines sampling the flow in Fig. 7. Through interpolation and vehicle reidentification, a dense flow chart can be generated based on statistical models such as Bayesian Network [15]. GPS based traces can also provide a vehicle flow such as flow speed around a reporting vehicle due to the constraint of a smooth traffic flow. Aerial views are usually taken for a short while if a helicopter takes off. Nevertheless, a patrol vehicle on the opposite road can observe more locations on a longer route than

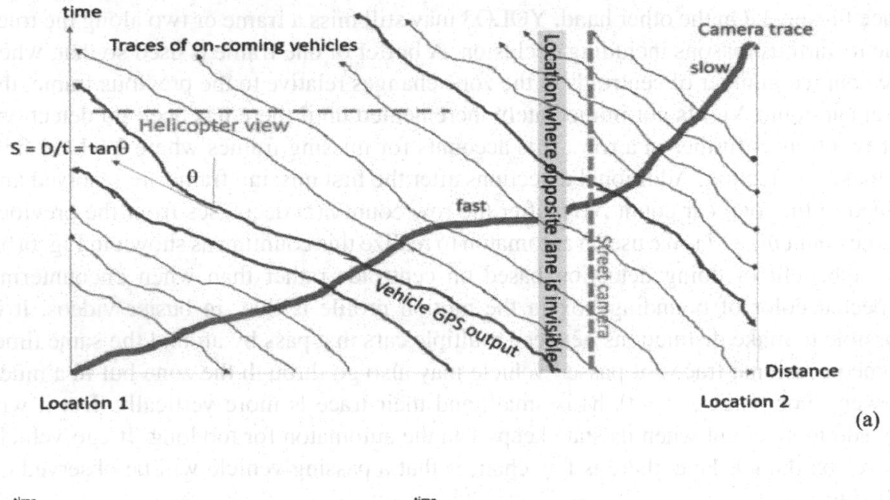

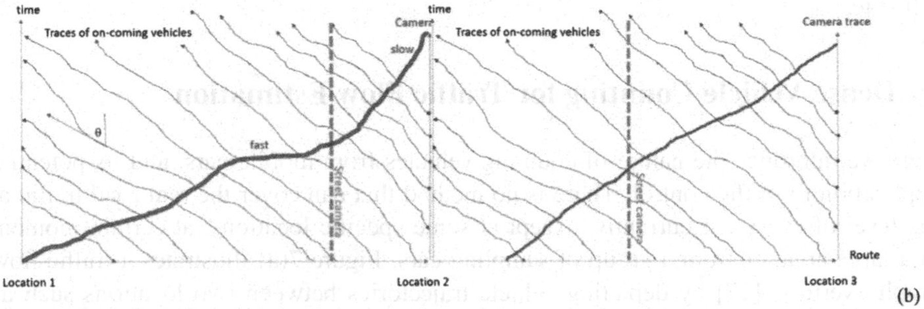

Fig. 7. Traffic flow chart changing over time along a road. The distance is along the horizontal axis and the time is vertically extended. (a) Traffic flow chart of one road segment. Oncoming vehicle trajectories are plotted in this distance-time space. (b) Traffic flow chart of consecutive road segments along a route. Two ego-vehicles are participating traffic flow counting. Oncoming vehicles may change the total number at street intersections (location *i*) because of the split and merge of traffic flow.

static cameras and aerial photos, since a traffic flow has a slow and incremental change, e.g., a traffic jam may be diminished after 10 min to one hour. Our method to assign the counting task to more observing vehicles can also interpolate traffic flow between them. Ultimately, the red curves of cameras can be dense enough to interpolate entire traffic flow, when observing vehicles have short intervals in between.

Our method using driving recorders to count oncoming vehicles may miss counting when the road center has some obstacles, trees, and separator to block the views of opposite lane. A splitting of two-way road to lanes apart from each other such as in tunnels or on highway makes this situation. Our data to detect vehicles are missing at such a road segment. In this sense, the traffic flow chart in Fig. 7(a) may have some hidden spots on road that causes blind belts vertically extended in the spatio-temporal flow chart of traffic.

5 Experiments

5.1 Naturalistic Driving Data for Testing

For the experiment, we started with 500 5-min long videos (1280 × 720) of dashcam footage from cars driving in a variety of weather, times of days, and road conditions. These videos were obtained from naturalistic driving on various roads in the City of Indianapolis [5]. The horizon of each video is manually specified once and then works for the entire clip. This allows us to locate ROI for car detection. We first sorted each video by road condition into three categories. The first is for videos of rural locations where the road is narrow, and traffic is low. The second category is local traffic, this would be busier locations, towns, etc. with roads that have more lanes than rural. The last category is highway and interstate footage. Some videos have overlap where they could technically fit in two categories, but we gave priority to which road type was most prominent. The videos were then subdivided into weather and time conditions [19], which are limited to sunny/cloudy, night, and rain/snow. We test our algorithm on naturalistic driving videos. Each clip results in 9000 frames in 30fps and they are passed to YOLO3 for vehicle detection. The detection achieved a high accuracy in sunny and cloudy days by using pretrained YOLO3 network.

YOLO3 is performed well on all sunny/cloudy videos but is not performed well on night or rainy/snowy footage. For the night footage, the issue is the default weights are not trained to recognize how vehicles look at nights, where cars are recognizable primarily by their headlights rather than vehicle shape like day-time video. The rainy and snowy footage was inconsistent due to water obscuring the windshield and concealing the shape of the vehicles, making frame to frame detections very spotty. After the motion profiles have been generated, we process them to count the motion traces present and export the results.

We processed the motion profiles in three separate batches, adjusting the size of the zone boundaries to widths 30 pixels, 75 pixels, and 125 pixels. A few observations: for a video with the dimensions of 1280 × 720, we found that 30 pixels was not wide enough to reliably spot the majority of passing vehicles. Depending on the exact x coordinates, many cars would stop being detected before passing through or would be detected after passing the boundaries. For 125 pixel zone width, on the other hand, was too large and more prone to counting cars multiple time due to a longer stretch of time required for a car to pass all the way through the boundaries, this made the counting algorithm more sensitive to inconsistent object detection. We found that 75 pixel boundary was the proper spot and tended to yield more accurate counts, more often, as in Fig. 8.

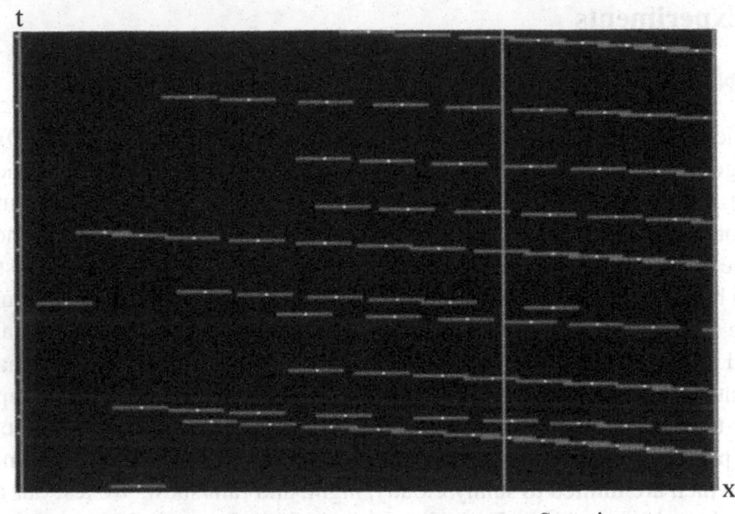

Fig. 8. Partial Vehicle Motion Profile on the left shows the horizontal motion of vehicles on opposite lanes. The horizontal length of bounding boxes is colored in pink and the box center is a white point. Two green lines bound a zone to scan oncoming vehicles. White dots on left column with orange time axis are the vehicle counting yielded in green zone. (Color figure online)

5.2 Counting Accuracy Along a Route

The detected vehicles are displayed with the motion profiles and the time (frame number) is marked on side. We can observe the correctness of counting in 5 min driving for many clips. Overall, the accuracy is summarized in Table 1. Recall, precision, and F_1 score are presented in *italic* and **bold** figures in the table for three types of road respectively. Over 30 videos are selected from busy clips on opposite road among 500 videos for testing. Figure 9 shows long time counting from routes lasting 5 min each, which are also selected from two local, a highway, and a rural road with the highest traffic density including short stopping time before street intersection. These data further contain some complex situations passing road interactions, which can be ignored using GPS data and are not included in our evaluation.

The false positive is a little large for local road because such roads also have parked cars in the opposite direction. The highway missed more vehicles than rural and local roads because of multiple lanes on separated opposite-road as well as possible occlusion of vehicles.

The real time consideration for the traffic flow counting demands us to reduce the computation cost and diminish the burden to the main tasks of camera such as road following, obstacle detection, and pedestrian avoidance. The following efforts can speed up the video.

Fig. 9. Vehicle motion profiles showing oncoming vehicle traces and their extracted counts.

Table 1. Accuracy of vehicle counting. The digits indicate counted vehicle numbers

	Rural 10 video			Local 10 video			Highway 10 video		
	True	False	Recall	True	False	Recall	True	False	Recall
Detected	194	21	*0.9*	600	78	*0.88*	668	24	*0.97*
Undetected	6			37			134		
Precision	*0.97*		**0.93**	*0.94*		**0.91**	0.83		**0.89**

(1) YOLO3 selects bounding box candidates on a grid, which is the key mechanism of YOLO3.
(2) Apply YOLO3 on left half of the frame, basically only around the belt and centered vertically around horizon.
(3) If YOLO3 was trained on vehicle attributes [16] to identify subclasses of front and rare vehicles including front-side and rare-side, it could omit the time to distinguish traffic flow of oncoming vehicles and vehicles in same direction based on motion.

The future work could be training of YOLO3 to respond vehicles in night, on which only headlights are visible, while the motion characteristics are the same as daytime. We will further investigate the possibility to filter the vehicle traces directly in the motion profiles so that YOLO3 based vehicle recognition can be omitted; the vehicle counting is only based trace recognition.

6 Conclusion

This paper explores a new approach to detect traffic flow by counting vehicles from a traveling vehicle in contrast to the existing methods to monitor traffic at static locations by wire or viewed by cameras at streets, to fly helicopter over jammed area, or to gain GPS from a subset of vehicles in the traffic flow. The key components are the vehicle detection in dense video frames, and non-redundant vehicle counting based on motion properties of vehicles. The motion trace in the motion profile has a longer time behavior than optical flow so that we can focus on a location specific motion velocity to sort out opposite vehicle flow. We have achieved good accuracy of counting oncoming vehicles. We also reduced computing time of detection so that it can be deployed to many vehicles to perform this additional function aside the main task of ADAS or autonomous driving.

References

1. Shi, W., Kong, Q.-J., Liu, Y.: A GPS/GIS integrated system for urban traffic flow analysis. In: IEEE International Conference on Intelligent Transportation Systems, pp. 844–849 (2008)
2. Bagheri, S., Zheng, J.Y., Sinha, S.: Temporal mapping of surveillance video for indexing and summarization. Comput. Vis. Image Underst. **144**, 237–257 (2016)
3. Ram, S., Rodriguez, J.: Vehicle detection in aerial images using multiscale structure enhancement and symmetry. In: International Conference on Image Processing (ICIP) (2016)

4. Ke, R., Li, Z., Kim, S., Ash, J., Cui, Z., Wang, Y.: Real-time bidirectional traffic flow parameter estimation from aerial videos. IEEE Trans. Intell. Transp. Syst. **18**(4), 890–901 (2017)
5. Tian, R., Li, L., Yang, K., Chien, S., Chen, Y., Sherony, R.: Estimation of the vehicle-pedestrian encounter/conflict risk on the road based on TASI 110-car naturalistic driving data collection. In: IEEE IV 2014, pp. 623–629 (2014)
6. Redmon, J., Divvala, S., Girshick, R., Farhadi, A.: You only look once: unified, real-time object detection. In: IEEE Computer Vision and Pattern Recognition (CVPR), pp. 779–788 (2016)
7. Redmon, J., Farhadi, A.: YOLO: better, faster, stronger. In: IEEE Conference on Computer Vision and Pattern Recognition. IEEE (2017)
8. Redmon, J.: YOLO: real-time object detection (n.d.). https://pjreddie.com/darknet/yolo. Accessed 16 Apr 2019
9. Kilicarslan, M., Zheng, J.Y.: Visualizing driving video in temporal profile. In: 2014 IEEE Intelligent Vehicles Symposium, pp. 1263–1269 (2014)
10. Jazayeri, A., Cai, H., Zheng, J.Y., Tuceryan, M.: Vehicle detection and tracking in car video based on motion model. IEEE Trans. Intell. Transp. Syst. **12**(2), 583–595 (2011)
11. Kilicarslan, M., Zheng, J.Y.: Predict vehicle collision by TTC from motion using a single video camera. IEEE Trans. Intell. Transp. Syst. **20**, 522–533 (2019)
12. Gao, Z., Liu, Y., Zheng, J.Y., Yu, R., Wang, X., Sun, P.: Predicting hazardous driving events using multi-modal deep learning based on video motion profile and kinematics data. In: 21st International Conference on Intelligent Transportation Systems (ITSC) (2018)
13. Kilicarslan, M., Zheng, J.Y., Raptis, K.: Pedestrian detection from motion. In: International Conference on Pattern Recognition, pp. 1–6 (2016)
14. Kilicarslan, M., Zheng, J.Y., Algarni, A.: Pedestrian detection from non-smooth motion. In: IEEE Intelligent Vehicle Symposium, pp. 1–6 (2015)
15. Wheeler, T.A., Kochenderfer, M.J., Robbel, P.: Initial scene configurations for highway traffic propagation. In: 2015 IEEE 18th International Conference on Intelligent Transportation Systems, pp. 279–284 (2015)
16. Sulistiyo, M.D., et. al.: Attribute-aware semantic segmentation of road scenes for understanding pedestrian orientations. In: IEEE International Conference on Intelligent Transportation Systems, pp. 1–6 (2018)
17. He, Z., Zheng, L., Song, L., Zhu, N.: A jam-absorption driving strategy for mitigating traffic oscillations. IEEE Trans. Intell. Transp. Syst. **18**(4), 802–813 (2017)
18. Porikli, F., Li, X.: Traffic Congestion estimation using HMM models without vehicle tracking. In: IEEE Intelligent Vehicles Symposium (2004)
19. Cheng, G., Wang, Z., Zheng, J.Y.: Modeling weather and illuminations in driving views based on big-video mining. IEEE Trans. Intell. Veh. **3**(4), 522–533 (2018)

Directly Optimizing IoU for Bounding Box Localization

Mofassir Ul Islam Arif(✉), Mohsan Jameel, and Lars Schmidt-Thieme

Information Systems and Machine Learning Lab (ISMLL), Univerity of Hildesheim, Hildsheim, Germany
{mofassir,mohsan.jameel,schmidt-thieme}@ismll.uni-hildesheim.de

Abstract. Object detection has seen remarkable progress in recent years with the introduction of Convolutional Neural Networks (CNN). Object detection is a multi-task learning problem where both the position of the objects in the images as well as their classes needs to be correctly identified. The idea here is to maximize the overlap between the ground-truth bounding boxes and the predictions i.e. the Intersection over Union (IoU). In the scope of work seen currently in this domain, IoU is approximated by using the Huber loss as a proxy but this indirect method does not leverage the IoU information and treats the bounding box as four independent, unrelated terms of regression. This is not true for a bounding box where the four coordinates are highly correlated and hold a semantic meaning when taken together. The direct optimization of the IoU is not possible due to its non-convex and non-differentiable nature. In this paper, we have formulated a novel loss namely, the Smooth IoU, which directly optimizes the IoUs for the bounding boxes. This loss has been evaluated on the Oxford IIIT Pets, Udacity self-driving car, PASCAL VOC, and VWFS Car Damage datasets and has shown performance gains over the standard Huber loss.

Keywords: Object detection · IoU loss · Faster RCNN

1 Introduction

Object detection is a multi-task learning problem with the goal of correctly identifying the object in the image while also localizing the object into a bounding box, therefore the end result of the object detection is to classify and localize the object. As with all machine learning models, the optimization is dictated by a loss that updates a loss towards a local optimum solution. The family of object detection models [5,9,15,16] is accompanied by multi-task [2] losses which are made up of a localization loss $\mathcal{L}_{loc}$ and a classification loss $\mathcal{L}_{cls}$, for each stage. For the first stage the $\mathcal{L}_{loc}$ is used to distinguish between the raw proposals from a Region Proposal Network (RPN) usually modeled by a Fully Convolutional Network (FCN) [10], and the ground truth bounding boxes. The aim here is to separate the background and the foreground, based on the bounding boxes, therefore, the classification loss $\mathcal{L}_{cls}$ becomes a binary classification

S. Palaiahnakote et al. (Eds.): ACPR 2019, LNCS 12046, pp. 544–556, 2020.
https://doi.org/10.1007/978-3-030-41404-7_38

problem between the foreground and the background. The output of this stage is passed to the second stage where second stage localization and classification losses are used. In the second stage, bounding box localization deals with the actual objects rather than the background and foreground. Similarly the second stage classification loss is now a K-way softmax where K is the number of classes. For each stage, these losses are jointly optimized during training by forming a linear combination of the two, therefore the total loss for each stage is:

$$\mathcal{L} = \mathcal{L}_{loc} + \mathcal{L}_{cls} \tag{1}$$

During training, ground-truth bounding boxes are used to train the model to learn the features of the objects that are present within the constraints of the boxes. Traditionally the two-stage methods rely on the Huber loss [1] for bounding box localization in both stages. Equation 2 shows the Huber loss, its popularity in R-CNN, Fast RCNN, Faster-RCNN, SSD and many others is due to its robustness against outliers. In our case, the outliers would be the bounding boxes that are very far away from the ground-truth.

$$L_{\delta}(z) = \begin{cases} \frac{1}{2}z^2, & \text{if } |z| < \delta \\ \delta|z| - \frac{1}{2}\delta^2, & \text{otherwise} \end{cases} \tag{2}$$

$$BB_{regression} = \min_{\theta} \mathcal{L}(\beta, \hat{\beta}(\theta)) \tag{3}$$

Here z is the L1 loss between the ground-truth and predicted bounding boxand δ is a threshold parameter. The bounding box localization therefore, is treated as a regression problem as seen in Eq. 3. Where β is the ground truth bounding box and $\hat{\beta}(\theta)$ is the prediction model, parametrized by θ which are the parameters learned during the training phase, the output is predicted bounding boxes. Each bounding box is a tuple $((x_1, y_1), (x_2, y_2))$ which represents the coordinates on the diagonal of the box. This regression problem deals with each of the four parameters of the bounding box as independent and unrelated items however semantically that is not the case since the four coordinates of the bounding box are highly correlated and need to be treated as a single entity.

Huber loss, used in bounding box localization, has a quadratic behavior for values $|z| < \delta$ which enables faster convergence when the difference (location, size, scale) between the ground-truth and predictions become small. For the regions where the difference between the boxes is greater than the threshold δ the Huber loss evaluates the L1 loss which has been shown to be less aggressive against outliers, this prevents exploding gradients due to large penalties, a behavior that is seen by the penalty incurred by the squared loss. While this loss has shown to be a good surrogate by casting the maximization of IoU between ground-truth and predicted bounding boxes as a four-point regression, it does not use the IoU information during optimization. Furthermore, as stated earlier, it conducts the bounding box regression without considering the parameters of a bounding box to be highly correlated items which hold a semantic meaning

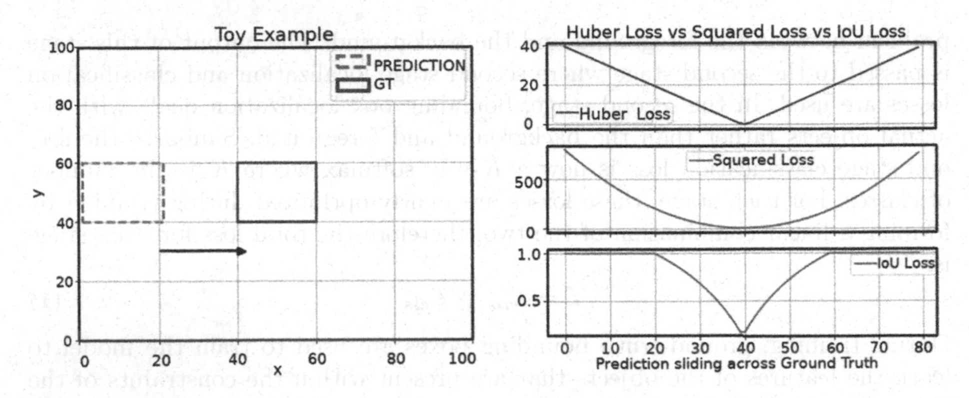

Fig. 1. The left figure mimicks the behaviour of a model predicting incrementally correct bounding boxes. The prediction is 'slid' over the ground-truth to examine the effect on the different losses. The figure on the right shows the behavior of the losses.

when taken together. Therefore, it stands to reason that the optimization of the object detection loss, more specifically the bounding box localization should involve a direct optimization of the IoU. The calculation of the IoU can be seen in Eq. 4. Here $\beta = ((x_1, y_1), (x_2, y_2))$ is the ground-truth bounding box and $\hat{\beta} = ((\hat{x}_1, \hat{y}_1), (\hat{x}_2, \hat{y}_2))$ is the predicted bounding box.

$$IoU = \frac{I_w \times I_h}{Area_1 + \hat{Area_2} - (I_w \times I_h)} \tag{4}$$

The areas for the bounding boxes are calculated as $Area = (x_2 - x_1) \times (y_2 - y_1)$. Converting the IoU measure into a loss function is trivial, since $\mathcal{L}_{IoU} = 1 - IoU$. The intersection term is calculated based on the region of overlap between the two boxes and it is as follows:

$$Intersection = I_w \times I_h \tag{5}$$

Here, $I_h = max(0, min_y - max_y)$ is the intersection height and where $min_y = min(y_2, \hat{y}_2)$ and $max_y = max(y_1, \hat{y}_1)$ are the minimum and maximum y-coordinates, respectively. Similarly, $I_w = max(0, min_x - max_x)$ is the intersection width with $min_x = min(x_2, \hat{x}_2)$ and $max_x = max(x_1, \hat{x}_1)$ as the minimum and maximum x-coordinates for the overlapping region, respectively. The product of I_h and I_w as in Eq. 5, yeilds the intersection. The denominator term for Eq. 4 shows the union term, here $Area_1$ and $Area_2$ are the ground-truth and predicted bounding box areas, respectively.

An examination of the behaviors for the different losses can be seen in Fig. 1. The example presented is designed to show the behavior of the losses as a model predicts bounding boxes that are translated over the ground-truth bounding box. The two boxes are not overlapping up until the point that the predicted bounding box reaches (20, 40). At this point, the overlap starts to occur and increases until the point (40, 40), at which the overlap is maximum and starts to decrease as the box continues moving to the right. The overlap drops to zero at point (60, 40). For the sake of simplicity of the illustration, we are limiting the movement of the box to the x coordinate only in Fig. 1.

For Huber loss, we can see a linear decrease as the predicted box approaches the ground-truth and conversely the loss linearly increases as the box starts to exit from the ground-truth. While inside some threshold δ it behaves quadratically, for areas with no overlap we can see the robustness of the Huber loss as it does not incur a large loss value. The L2 loss shows a similar (increase and decrease) behavior but is not bound by any δ parameter and is, therefore, quadratic throughout. This leads to a very high penalty around the area where the boxes do not overlap. These effects are obvious when we compare the scales of the losses.

Lastly, we can see the IoU loss plateauing outside the region where the two bounding boxes do not overlap. Here it can be seen that for the regions with no overlap between the two boxes the loss plateaus leading to zero gradients thus, effectively making the learning process impossible for all gradient-based learning methods. The areas outside the intersection offer no help in the learning process due to the fact that the IoU is bounded in [0, 1] and the worst case scenario i.e, no overlap always leads to a loss of 1, regardless of how far away the box is. From the loss profile, we can also see that the IoU loss is non-convex (due to the plateauing region violating Eq. 6) and non-differentiable.

$$f(tx_1 + (1-t)x_2) \leq tf(x_1) + (1-t)f(x_2) \tag{6}$$

The Huber loss does not suffer from these issues since the regression always returns the distance between the parameters of the bounding boxes. The shortcoming here is the inherent treatment of the parameters of the bounding boxes as independent and unrelated terms.

In this paper, we present a novel loss that addresses the shortcoming of the standard IoU loss, inherits the advantages of Huber loss, and enables a direct optimization of IoU for two-stage object detection networks. This is done by a proposed relaxation for the IoU loss which mitigates the non-differentiability and non-convexity of the loss without the need to sub-gradient or approximation methods [11]. We propose a dynamic loss, that leverages the gains of Huber loss while directly optimizing for IoU in bounding box localization. The main contributions of this paper are:

(a) A robust loss that can be integrated readily into the two-stage models.
(b) A performance guarantee that is lower bounded by the state-of-the-art performance.
(c) Empirical analysis of the proposed method on standard object detection datasets to show how optimizing for IoU can lead to better bounding boxes (higher IoU).

2 Related Work

The choice of losses in machine learning is dictated heavily by the convergence and convexity of the loss [17]. The Huber loss ensures a stable convergence due to its piece-wise quadratic and convex nature [25]. This enabled the loss to be adapted readily in the bounding box regression for the object detection tasks [5,9,16]. Similar to the Huber loss there is also an interest in using the squared loss for the bounding box regression [3,22]. This is however more susceptible to exploding gradients and is more sensitive to the learning rate and other such hyper-parameters [19]. In Fig. 1 we have demonstrated the behavior of these losses and how they, while suitable for regression, optimize for a proxy loss and a more direct approach for optimizing the IoU is needed. The disadvantage of the IoU loss stems from its non-differentiability and the disappearing gradients outside the regions of intersection. Attempts to addresses this problem by using the IoU loss by looking only at the pixel values inside the predictions and ground truth boxes with a non zero overlap [26]. They convert the IoU loss into a cross-entropy loss since $0 \leq IoU \leq 1$ by wrapping it in the natural log $\mathcal{L} = -ln(IoU)$. This conversion relies on using the IoU information after converting the tuple of four coordinates into a pixel map and then evaluating the IoU pixel-wise. Furthermore, they propose a novel architecture for their loss implementation thus might not be readily compatible with the other architectures used for the object detection tasks. Another related method looks at the complete replacement of the regression loss with their implementation of the IoU loss [14]. They approach the task of image segmentation and how the optimization of the IoU directly can serve to improve the overall performance of the model. They rely on a FCN which is a modified AlexNet [21] and present the work in light of how for the image segmentation task, the discrimination between the background and the foreground serves as an important step. However, optimizing for the overall accuracies could cause a model to encourage larger sized boxes. This can be the case when a larger portion (90%) of the image belongs to the background, in such a situation a naive algorithm can get 90% accuracy simply by predicting everything to be the background [26]. A case like this can be made for using the Huber loss for the bounding box regression which the Huber loss treats four independent and unrelated items during its optimization. The use of Bayesian decision theory has also been attempted by [12] where Conditional Random Field (CRF) is used to maximize the expected-IoU, they also use the pixel values and a greedy heuristic for the optimization of IoU. A pixel-wise approach is inherently slower since it is dictated by the number of pixels in the bounding box. A bounding boxwith size $P \times Q$ where P is the width and Q is the heigth would require $O(PQ)$ operations in order to calculate the IoU. Whereas, by treating the bounding box as a tuple and calculating IoU as in Eq. 4 the number of operations is constant regardless of the size.

3 Methodology

The IoU loss suffers from the plateauing phenomenon because of the unavailability of gradient information since $L_{IoU} \in [0, 1]$ where it is constant (1) outside the region of intersection as shown in Fig. 1. This gradient information in a standard Huber loss, for bounding box localization, is available throughout due to the regression between the four points of the ground-truth and predicted bounding box. The vanishing gradients of IoU loss for bounding boxes with no overlap hinder the learning process since two bounding boxes with no overlap present the same constant loss (zero gradients) regardless of how far they are from the ground-truth. A relaxation is needed for the IoU loss that will enable us to bring in the gradient information for the predicted bounding box in terms of the distance, and consequently guide the model in the correct direction. Albeit, this is needed only in the initial learning stage because once the predicted bounding boxes begin to overlap with the ground truth ones, non-zero overlap will address the plateauing behavior of the IoU loss. Standard object detection models treat the regression as an independent and unrelated four-way entity which is not true for a bounding box.

In order to optimize the true goal of object detection, we need to directly optimize for IoU in the bounding box localization loss. Our method proposes to morph the Huber loss in order to include the IoU information.

3.1 Smooth IoU Loss

A smooth stiched loss, named Smooth IoU is presented as an improvement on the Huber loss to enhances the localization of the bounding boxes while also overcoming the non-convexity issues (stemming from the IoU loss being bounded in $[0, 1]$) of the vanilla IoU loss, and is presented in Eq. 7.

$$\mathcal{L}_{SmoothIoU} = \lambda\mathcal{L}_{IoU} + (1 - \lambda)\mathcal{L}_{HuberLoss} \tag{7}$$

The first term of Eq. 7 is the IoU element which directly incorporates the IoU in the optimization process. The second term is the state-of-the-art Huber loss. The purpose of having the Huber loss is to make sure that the positional guidance can be made use when there is no overlap between the ground-truth and predicted bounding boxes, thus making gradient information available throughout the learning process. The two terms of the loss are linked by a scaling parameter λ. Naively, this term can be treated as a hyper-parameter that can be tuned for the best performance, however, doing so will be computationally expensive as well as time-consuming. Additionally, treating λ as a hyper-parameter will lead to having one λ for the entire retraining which was found to be detrimental to the overall performance. A mini-batch could have poor predictions and thus lead to bounding boxes with no overlap in which case the fixed value for λ would still try to make use of the non-existent gradients coming from the IoU element of Eq. 7. In order to prevent such outcomes, we propose to treat λ not as a hyper-parameter but rather scale it dynamically during training. λ is calculated based on the mean IoU of the minibatch under evaluation and used in scaling the loss between IoU and state-of-the-art Huber loss. This dynamic scaling enables us to remove the need to tune λ and allows the model to learn End-to-End. This enables the model to be trained faster and without the need for a problem specific set of hyper-parameters.

The loss profile for the Smooth IoU loss is presented in Fig. 2 (left). In order to distinguish our contribution from that state-of-the-art Huber loss,

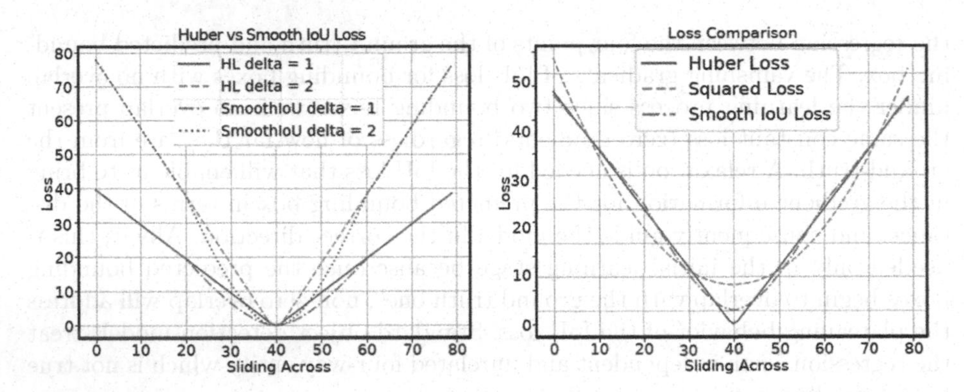

Fig. 2. (Right) Comparison of the Smooth IoU with Huber and Squared Loss, the losses have been scaled to highlight the profiles as they relates to the others. (Left) Behavior of Huber and Smooth IoU losses for varying values of δ. (see Eq. 2).

we are presenting the behavior of the losses for the same example as seen in Fig. 1 where a predicted bounding box is translated over the ground truth bounding box. The δ term is the cutoff threshold from Eq. 2 and is varied from 1–2 in order to show that the behavior of the Smooth IoU loss is not just a scaled variation of the inherent Huber loss cutoff behavior. Fig. 2 (left) shows the behavior of the Smooth IoU loss and highlights how it is purely a function of the overlap of the boxes. From the figure, it can be seen that the Smooth IoU loss introduces a quadratic behavior to the loss as soon as the overlap starts to occur at the point $(20, 40)$ (see the description of the example in the introduction). This quadratic behavior appears much later in the state-of-the-art Huber loss, which is governed by the δ and is not dynamic but rather fixed for each run. Outside of the areas of intersection, we are still maintaining the Huber loss which allows the loss to overcome the inherent shortcomings of the IoU loss, and localize the boxes better.

The Smooth IoU loss comes with a performance guarantee of the state-of-the-art in the worst case scenario i-e. the loss converges to the state-of-the-art performance if the modifications suggested in this method do not improve the bounding box localization. This can be shown as:

$$\lim_{\lambda \to 0} \mathcal{L}_{SmoothIoU} = \mathcal{L}_{HuberLoss} \tag{8}$$

$$\lim_{\lambda \to 1} \mathcal{L}_{SmoothIoU} = \mathcal{L}_{IoU} \tag{9}$$

This further highlights that the loss presented here is guaranteed to perform at the state-of-the-art level in the worst case scenario, making it a robust version of the Huber loss while introducing the IoU information into the optimization process. Additionally, this loss can be readily substituted into the current two-stage models without any architectural changes or case-specific modifications, making it modular.

Algorithm 1: Smooth IoU Loss

Data: predicted_boxes $P := \{p \in \mathbb{R}^{K\times 4} \mid p = \{y_1, x_1, h, w\}\}$, target_boxes $T := \{t \in \mathbb{R}^{K\times 4} \mid t = \{\bar{y}_1, \bar{x}_1, \bar{h}, \bar{w}\}\}$
Result: Smooth IoU Loss
1 **for** k = 1, . . . ,K **do**
2   P′= Transform (P_k);
3   T′= Transform (T_k);
4     $\mathcal{L}_{Huber_k}$ = Huberloss ($P_k{}'$,$T_k{}'$);
5   IoU_k = Calculate_IoU($P_k{}'$,$T_k{}'$);
6     $\mathcal{L}_{IoU_k}$ = 1 - IoU_k;
7 **end**
8 λ = mean($IoU_{1:K}$);
9 **for** k = 1, . . ., K **do**
10     $loss_{SmoothIoU_k} = \lambda \times \mathcal{L}IoU_k$ + (1- λ)$\mathcal{L}_{Huber_k}$;
11 **end**

Algorithm 1 shows the implemenetation of the Smooth IoU loss, lines 2–3 are used to transform the incoming points from $\{y_1, x_1, h, w\}$ representation to a $\{x_{min}, y_{min}, x_{max}, y_{max}\}$ representation. This is done in order to calculate the IoU of the bounding boxes. Line 10 shows the implementation of Eq. 7.

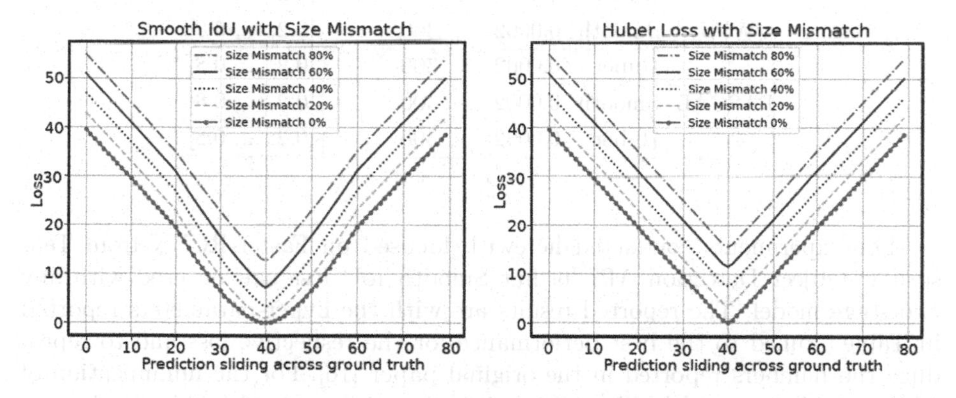

Fig. 3. Comparison of the losses with a size mismatch between the predicted and ground truth bounding boxes.

For the sake of completeness, the same example as seen in Fig. 1 is reproduced but this time with an introduced size mismatch between the prediction and ground truth bounding boxes. The loss profiles for both the Smooth IoU loss and Huber loss are shown in Fig. 3. The overall effect visible here is that even for the size mismatch between the two boxes the Smooth IoU loss tends to converge to a smaller loss value while leveraging the advantages of the Huber loss for non-overlapping regions. This smaller loss value will prevent the possibility of exploding gradients thus stabilizing the learning process.

4 Experiments

Having laid out the design of our new loss and its characteristics. We evaluated the performance on the object detection task using the Oxford-IIIT Pet Dataset [13], Udacity Self-Driving Car Dataset [24], PASCAL VOC [4], and Volkswagon Financial Services (VWFS) Damage Assessment dataset (propriety). The VWFS dataset is made up of images taken during an end-of-leasing damage assessment. The areas of interest in these images are the damaged parts that have been loosely annotated. The aim of this data is to serve as a foundation for training a model which is able to detect these damages automatically and estimate the damage costs at the end of the car lease period. The data has a very high variance in the number of images per class and suffers and from a long tail distribution. All experiments were conducted using Nvidia GTX 1080Ti, and Tesla P100 GPUs.

Table 1. Hyper-parameters used for the different datasets

		Initial LR	Proposals	Drop-out
Pets	Smooth	0.0002	300	[0.2, ..., 0.8]
	Huber	0.0002	300	[0.2, ..., 0.8]
Udacity	Smooth	0.002	300	[0.2, ..., 0.8]
	Huber	0.002	300	[0.2, ..., 0.8]
VWFS	Smooth	0.0002	300	[0.2, ..., 0.8]
	Huber	0.0002	300	[0.2, ..., 0.8]
PASCAL	Smooth	0.0002	300	[0.2, ..., 0.8]
	Huber	0.0002	300	[0.2, ..., 0.8]

The experiments conducted herewith focused on Faster-RCNN from Tensorflow Object Detection API [6] but Smooth IoU loss can be used with any two-stage model. The reported results are with the hyper-parameters reported in Table 1 tuned to the best performance for the respective loss and to reproduce the numbers reported in the original paper [16]. For the minimization of the loss we have used RMSProp [23], with a learning rate reduced by 10^{-1} every 50 K steps and a momentum term of 0.9. The underlying feature extractor was Inception_V2 [7], pre-trained on the COCO dataset [8]. This warm start enabled us to speed up training by leveraging the advantages offered by transfer learning and as it has been shown to be an effective method for initializing the network [5,6,16]. The baseline implementation [16] used VGG-16 [20] pre-trained on ImageNet [18] as the feature extractor. In all of our experiments, the models were retrained for 200k iterations and showed a smooth convergence behavior.

For the Udacity, and Pets datasets we have used a standard train/test split. For the VWFS dataset, a 80-20 split was created while for the PASCAL VOC dataset we have used the VOC2007 Train split for training the models and its performance is presented on the VOC2007 val split. VOC2012 was treated the same way. We have also used a merged PASCAL VOC dataset where the VOC++Train was created by merging the VOC2007 and VOC2012 train splits for training and we are presenting the results on the VOC2012 val dataset. Since the ground truth bounding box information was not available on the test set of PASCAL VOC datasets, we present the results on the validation set.

Table 2. Localization metrics: these highlight the results for the datasets under test. **VW** = VWFS, **UD** = Udacity, **2007** = VOC2007, **2012** – VOC2012, **VOC++** = VOC++Train. The IoU metric directly is reported here to show the quality of the bounding boxes. $\mathcal{L}_{S\_IoU}$ is optimized for the IoU directly. $\mathcal{L}_{HL}$ is the baseline Huber loss.

	Pets		UD		VW		2007		2012		VOC++	
$\mathcal{L}$	$\mathcal{L}_{HL}$	$\mathcal{L}_{S\_IoU}$	$\mathcal{L}_{HL}$	$\mathcal{L}_{S\_IoU}$	$\mathcal{L}_{HL}$	$\mathcal{L}_{S\_IoU}$	$\mathcal{L}_{HL}$	$\mathcal{L}_{S\_IoU}$	$\mathcal{L}_{HL}$	$\mathcal{L}_{S\_IoU}$	$\mathcal{L}_{HL}$	$\mathcal{L}_{S\_IoU}$
IoU	0.143	**0.162**	0.417	**0.425**	0.383	**0.388**	0.231	**0.263**	**0.275**	0.270	0.240	**0.244**

4.1 Evaluation and Discussion

We propose a new loss for the bounding box localization that takes into account the direct optimization of the IoU in order to improve the quality of the predicted bounding boxes. This localization loss ties in closely with the overall performance of the two-stage networks. Therefore, it is important to evaluate the IoU quality of the model as well as the accuracies in order to showcase the effectiveness of our method. Detection accuracies (mean average precision and average recall) measure the correct classification of the objects and do not directly take into account the quality of the predicted bounding boxes. This is because mAP scores are calculated for a subset of the predicted bounding boxes (that fall above a threshold of IoU). We want to demonstrate how the optimization of the IoU directly for bounding box localization helps in the overall learning process while simultaneously improving the accuracy over the state-of-the-art by proposing better bounding boxes. Furthermore, we would also like to showcase the robustness of the loss over varying levels of difficulty of the object detection tasks, hence the choice of datasets that range from low difficult (Pets) to high difficulty (PASCAL). As stated earlier, this loss comes with a performance guarantee of the state-of-the-art performance and that is shown in the results that follow. Faster RCNN with the standard Huber loss (for bounding box localization) becomes the baseline.

We break down the evaluation of the model into localization and classification performance. For the classification performance, we are using COCO detection metrics as they are readily available in the API and are also a favored metric for the object detection task. Localization is the primary focus here since we are optimizing it directly for the IoU. Table 2 presents the comparison of our proposed method against Huber loss for the different datasets. We are reporting the value of $IoU \in [0, 1]$, the values in bold show where our method is better than the baseline. We are evaluating the quality of the IoU against the ground-truth bounding boxes (higher value is better). The reported numbers here are all proposed boxes by the model, we are not discounting any boxes through post-processing, hence the values appear to be small. This is done to see the raw behavior of the model for the baseline and the proposed method. For the localization, it can be seen in Table 2 that our method outperforms the baseline in five out of six datasets that are under consideration. The results show that by optimizing for the IoU directly leads to better bounding boxes. Furthermore, the robustness of the loss is also verified by looking at the results for VOC2012 in Table 3. We underperform the baseline on the VOC2012 dataset in terms of the IoU however when we look at the overall performance for the classification Table 3, we can see that for the VOC2012 dataset our method is still better than the baseline. This indicates that the Smooth IoU loss can be used for directly optimizing the IoU and will not harm the overall performance in cases where it does not directly improve the IoU.

Table 3. Classification metrics: *$mAP@.50IoU$ is the PASCAL metric as set out in COCO Detections metrics, takes into account bounding boxeswith a 50% overlap with the ground-truth. Similarly, **$mAP@.75IoU$ takes into account 75% overlap. ***mAP takes into account overlap of 50% and higher. Average Recall (@1 and @10).

Dataset		mAP@.50IoU*	mAP@.75IoU**	mAP***	AR@1	AR@10
Wins	$\mathcal{L}_{HL}$	0	3	2	2	1
	$\mathcal{L}_{S\_IoU}$	**6**	3	**4**	**4**	**5**
Pets	$\mathcal{L}_{HL}$	89.94	80.46	66.03	75.59	76.63
	$\mathcal{L}_{S\_IoU}$	**93.91**	**87.19**	**72.09**	**79.68**	**80.35**
VW	$\mathcal{L}_{HL}$	64.3	37.01	37.03	**21.0**	45.42
	$\mathcal{L}_{S\_IoU}$	**64.79**	**37.33**	**37.4**	20.94	**45.63**
UD	$\mathcal{L}_{HL}$	78.23	**27.67**	**36.22**	37.14	50.68
	$\mathcal{L}_{S\_IoU}$	**78.36**	27.65	35.7	**37.15**	**51.13**
2007	$\mathcal{L}_{HL}$	65.94	**43.40**	**40.68**	**37.77**	**57.14**
	$\mathcal{L}_{S\_IoU}$	**66.29**	43.01	40.67	37.32	56.79
2012	$\mathcal{L}_{HL}$	69.14	**49.09**	44.20	39.63	59.82
	$\mathcal{L}_{S\_IoU}$	**69.31**	48.29	**44.41**	**40.26**	**60.04**
VOC++	$\mathcal{L}_{HL}$	70.47	49.68	44.19	39.81	59.39
	$\mathcal{L}_{S\_IoU}$	**70.52**	**50.08**	**45.17**	**39.96**	**59.58**

For the classification metrics in Table 3, the first row provides the total win/loss count for our proposed method and the baseline. As can be seen, our method outperforms the baseline for mAP@.50IOU, mAP, AR@1, and AR@10. We tie with the baseline for mAP@.75IOU. It should be noted here that we are not modifying the baseline classification optimization and show how directly optimizing the IoU can lead to gains in the mAP and recall as well. This lends credence to our proposed method shows it's usefulness. All the results highlight that there is a signal available in the IoU information of the bounding boxes and this information should be used during training. We experimentally showcase that the IoU driven loss variant proposed herewith can outperform the standard loss and it is lower-bounded to be at the state of the art level.

5 Conclusion

In this paper, we have presented a novel loss for the bounding box localization of two-stage models. The loss optimizes the IoU directly by treating the parameters of a bounding box as a single highly correlated item. Our loss is lower-bounded to perform at the state-of-the-art level. We demonstrate the efficacy of our model by replacing the Huber loss in Faster RCNN to show that optimizing for IoU directly in bounding box localization can lead to better bounding boxes and also improve the classification accuracy. Our method has shown to outperform the baseline in both localization and classification metrics. The modular and robust nature of the proposed loss makes it readily compatible with all two-stage models.

Acknowledgments. This work is co-funded by the industry project "Data-driven Mobility Services" of ISMLL and Volkswagen Financial Services. (https://www.ismll.uni-hildesheim.de/projekte/dna_en.html).

References

1. Box, G., Hunter, J.: Annals of mathematical statistics. Ann. Math. Stat. **27**(4), 1144–1151 (1956)
2. Caruana, R.: Multitask learning. Mach. Learn. **28**(1), 41–75 (1997)
3. Erhan, D., Szegedy, C., Toshev, A., Anguelov, D.: Scalable object detection using deep neural networks. In: Proceedings of the IEEE Conference on Computer Vision and Pattern Recognition, pp. 2147–2154 (2014)
4. Everingham, M., Van Gool, L., Williams, C.K.I., Winn, J., Zisserman, A.: The PASCAL visual object classes challenge 2012 (VOC2012) results. http://www.pascal-network.org/challenges/VOC/voc2012/workshop/index.html
5. Girshick, R.: Fast R-CNN. In: The IEEE International Conference on Computer Vision (ICCV), December 2015
6. Huang, J., et al.: Speed/accuracy trade-offs for modern convolutional object detectors. In: Proceedings of the IEEE Conference on Computer Vision and Pattern Recognition, pp. 7310–7311 (2017)
7. Ioffe, S., Szegedy, C.: Batch normalization: accelerating deep network training by reducing internal covariate shift. arXiv preprint arXiv:1502.03167 (2015)
8. Lin, T.-Y., et al.: Microsoft COCO: common objects in context. In: Fleet, D., Pajdla, T., Schiele, B., Tuytelaars, T. (eds.) ECCV 2014. LNCS, vol. 8693, pp. 740–755. Springer, Cham (2014). https://doi.org/10.1007/978-3-319-10602-1_48
9. Liu, W., et al.: SSD: single shot multibox detector. In: Leibe, B., Matas, J., Sebe, N., Welling, M. (eds.) ECCV 2016. LNCS, vol. 9905, pp. 21–37. Springer, Cham (2016). https://doi.org/10.1007/978-3-319-46448-0_2

10. Long, J., Shelhamer, E., Darrell, T.: Fully convolutional networks for semantic segmentation. In: Proceedings of the IEEE Conference on Computer Vision and Pattern Recognition, pp. 3431–3440 (2015)
11. Nedic, A., Bertsekas, D.P.: Incremental subgradient methods for nondifferentiable optimization. SIAM J. Optim. **12**(1), 109–138 (2001)
12. Nowozin, S.: Optimal decisions from probabilistic models: the intersection-over-union case. In: Proceedings of the IEEE Conference on Computer Vision and Pattern Recognition, pp. 548–555 (2014)
13. Parkhi, O.M., Vedaldi, A., Zisserman, A., Jawahar, C.V.: Cats and dogs. In: IEEE Conference on Computer Vision and Pattern Recognition (2012)
14. Rahman, M.A., Wang, Y.: Optimizing intersection-over-union in deep neural networks for image segmentation. In: Bebis, G., et al. (eds.) ISVC 2016. LNCS, vol. 10072, pp. 234–244. Springer, Cham (2016). https://doi.org/10.1007/978-3-319-50835-1_22
15. Redmon, J., Farhadi, A.: YOLO9000: better, faster, stronger. In: Proceedings of the IEEE Conference on Computer Vision and Pattern Recognition, pp. 7263–7271 (2017)
16. Ren, S., He, K., Girshick, R., Sun, J.: Faster R-CNN: towards real-time object detection with region proposal networks. In: Advances in Neural Information Processing Systems, pp. 91–99 (2015)
17. Rosasco, L., Vito, E.D., Caponnetto, A., Piana, M., Verri, A.: Are loss functions all the same? Neural Comput. **16**(5), 1063–1076 (2004)
18. Russakovsky, O., et al.: Imagenet large scale visual recognition challenge. Int. J. Comput. Vis. **115**(3), 211–252 (2015)
19. Schaul, T., Zhang, S., LeCun, Y.: No more pesky learning rates. In: International Conference on Machine Learning, pp. 343–351 (2013)
20. Simonyan, K., Zisserman, A.: Very deep convolutional networks for large-scale image recognition. arXiv preprint arXiv:1409.1556 (2014)
21. Sutskever, I., Hinton, G.E., Krizhevsky, A.: ImageNet classification with deep convolutional neural networks. In: Advances in Neural Information Processing Systems, pp. 1097–1105 (2012)
22. Szegedy, C., Reed, S., Erhan, D., Anguelov, D., Ioffe, S.: Scalable, high-quality object detection. arXiv preprint arXiv:1412.1441 (2014)
23. Tieleman, T., Hinton, G.: Rmsprop gradient optimization (2014). http://www.cs.toronto.edu/tijmen/csc321/slides/lecture_slides_lec6.pdf
24. Udacity: Self driving car (2017). https://github.com/udacity/self-driving-car/tree/master/annotations
25. Xu, Y., Lin, Q., Yang, T.: Stochastic convex optimization: faster local growth implies faster global convergence. In: Precup, D., Teh, Y.W. (eds.) Proceedings of the 34th International Conference on Machine Learning. Proceedings of Machine Learning Research, vol. 70, pp. 3821–3830. PMLR, International Convention Centre, Sydney, Australia, 06–11 August 2017. http://proceedings.mlr.press/v70/xu17a.html
26. Yu, J., Jiang, Y., Wang, Z., Cao, Z., Huang, T.S.: UnitBox: an advanced object detection network. CoRR abs/1608.01471 (2016). http://arxiv.org/abs/1608.01471

Double Refinement Network for Room Layout Estimation

Ivan Kruzhilov[1,2(✉)], Mikhail Romanov[1], Dmitriy Babichev[3], and Anton Konushin[1,4]

[1] Samsung AI Center, Lesnaya 5, 125047 Moscow, Russia
{i.kruzhilov,m.romanov,a.konushin}@samsung.com
[2] Moscow Power Engineering Institute, Krasnokazarmennay 14, 111250 Moscow, Russia
[3] Higher School of Economics, Myasnitskaya 20, 101000 Moscow, Russia
dobabichev@edu.hse.ru
[4] Lomonosov Moscow State University, Leninskie gory 1, 119991 Moscow, Russia

Abstract. Room layout estimation is a challenge of segmenting a cluttered room image into floor, walls and ceiling. We apply a Double Refinement Network (DRN) which has been successfully used to the monocular depth map estimation. Our method is the first not using encoder-decoder architecture for the room layout estimation. ResNet50 was utilized as a backbone for the network instead of VGG16 commonly used for the task, allowing the network to be more compact and faster. We introduced a special layout scoring function and layout ranking algorithm for key points and edges output. Our method achieved the lowest pixel and corner errors on the LSUN data set. The input image resolution is 224 * 224.

Keywords: Room layout · Algorithm · LSUN · Neural network · Pixel error · Room reconstruction · Segmentation

1 Introduction

Room layout estimation finds its application in different areas including augmented reality, robotics, indoor navigation [3].

The task is to find positions of the room corners and their connecting edges on a 2D room image. RGB images are often used as a standard input, although RGBD input is also possible [21]. The floor, ceiling and walls in a room are mutually orthogonal that sometimes is referred as 'Manhattan assumption'[4]. Furniture and other clutter in the room are the main challenge, as they make some key points and lines invisible. The two basic metrics for the room layout estimation are pixel and corner errors.

We estimate a room layout in two stages:

1. Key points and edges heat map estimation by a fully convolutional neural network.
2. Heat map post-processing.

S. Palaiahnakote et al. (Eds.): ACPR 2019, LNCS 12046, pp. 557–568, 2020.
https://doi.org/10.1007/978-3-030-41404-7_39

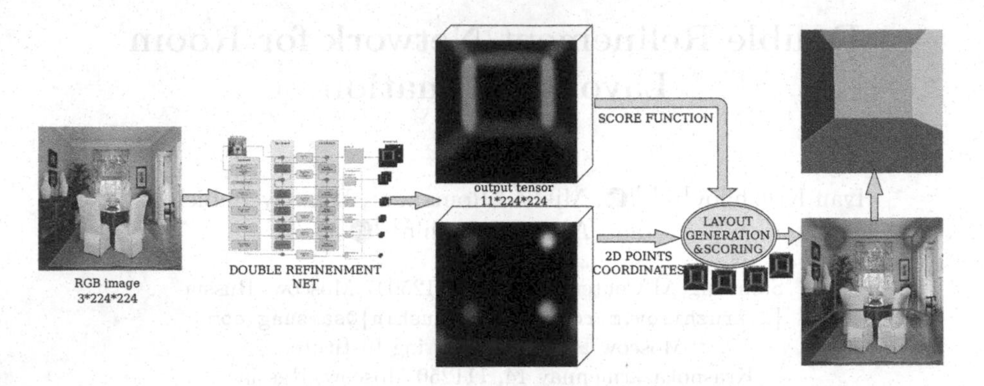

Fig. 1. Room layout estimation scheme

We used Double refinement net [7] with pretrained ResNet50 backbone for key points and edges heat maps estimation. The other room layout estimation methods [5,12,16,17] use encoder-decoder architecture predominantly with VGG16 backbone. The encoder-decoder architecture has a drawback of losing information on high-level features. For this reason, we decided to use an iterative refinement structure where low and high level features are analysed at different levels and then connected step-wise. This architecture is usually applied for segmentation task [14,18].

Double refinement network was initially proposed for the depth estimation, and we demonstrated that it could be applied for more complex tasks without major changes. Besides constructing an efficient network for the room layout estimation our purpose is to show that methods used for the depth estimation are applicable for other areas.

The chosen architecture allows to combine depth and layout estimation in one network which could be beneficial for robotics vision including odometry and re-localization mapping [13,15,23]. The other layout estimation methods use custom networks applied only for the specific task of layout estimation.

The novelty of our method involves the utilization of ResNet50 as a backbone in lieu of VGG16. ResNet50 is four times faster [2] than VGG16 (approx. 4 vs 15 GFLOPs) and has significantly less (25 million vs 138 million) parameters, making the network we use more compact and efficient than the architectures proposed in the state-of-the-art layout estimation methods.

Our post-processing algorithm is the first to construct the layout on both key points and edges heat maps. Edges heat maps were used in LayoutNet [25] for the regularization only. The post-processing algorithm is faster and simpler in implementation than the state-of-the-art handling with segmentation and edge maps [22].

We evaluate our results on the LSUN layout estimation benchmark and claim state-of-the-art results w.r.t pixel-wise errors for both corners and edges of the estimated layouts. When tested on Hedau dataset, the method achieved the second best results in pixel error.

The input image resolution is 224 * 224. The recent study [22] with the best state-of-the-art results used the same input image resolution.

2 Related Works

In this section we will focus on the recent (since 2015) room layout reconstruction methods. We refer to [1,6,20] to explore earlier methods.

Table 1. Room layout estimation algorithms characteristics

Net	Input resolution	Output semantic	Output tensors	Architecture	Loss	Layout construction
Mallya 2015 [16]	–	Edges	–	VGG16, pretrained on NYUDv2	Cross-entropy	Layout ranking
Delay 2016 [5]	321 × 321	Segment	405 × 321 × 321	Encoder-decoder, VGG16	Cross-entropy	Layout ranking
CFILE 2016 [17]	404 × 404	Segment edges	5 × 404 × 404 1 × 404 × 404	Encoder-decoder, VGG16, 2 branches	–	Layout ranking
Layout Net [25] 2018	512 × 512	Points edges room type	8 × 512 × 512 3 × 512×512 11	Encoder-decoder, 2 branches	Cross-entropy	Position based
Room Net [12] 2017	320 × 320	Points room type	48 × 320 × 320 11	Encoder-decoder, Segnet, recursive net	Euclidean distance	Position based
Edge seman-tic 2019 [22]	224 × 224	Segment edges	5 × 56×56 1 × 56×56	Encoder-decoder, VGG16 pretrained on ILSVRC, 2 branches	Cross-entropy	Layout ranking
DR (ours) 2019	224 × 224	Points edges	8 × 224 × 224 3 × 224 × 224 in one tensor	5-levels iterative refinement, ResNet50 pretrained on ImageNet	Cross-entropy	Layout ranking, without vani-shing lines

It a [9] a dataset of 308 cluttered room images was introduced. The dataset (also known as 'Hedau') became an important benchmark for the room layout reconstruction. The authors measured a first benchmark on the dataset by modeling the room space with a parametric 3D box and then by iteratively localizing clutter and refitting the box.

Mallya [16] showed that the fully connected neural network predicted edges better than the structured random forest. All layout reconstruction methods have shared the same pattern from that moment on. A fully connected neural network generates a heat map, and a layout is to be built on a post-processing stage. A summary of recent layout estimation methods is presented in Table 1.

There are 3 types of heat maps used for the room layout analysis namely segmentation, edges and key points heat maps. Each pixel of a heat map layer contains the probability that a pixel of the original image belongs to a certain class (e.g. the pixel lies in a room right upper corner). Segmentation heat map consists of 5 layers: two for a floor and a ceiling and three for the right, middle and left walls. Edge heat map consists of one or three layers. Three layers heat map allows to distinguish floor, walls and ceiling edges, whereas one layer heat map does not differentiate among them.

Key point is an intersection point between edges or between an edge and an image boundary. If key points are close enough their heat maps overlap which significantly deteriorates layout reconstruction and accuracy. For that reason, a key points heat map should contain multiple layers (one layer for each key point).

Most of the recent post-processing methods [5,16,17,22] use layout ranking procedure to construct a final layout. This procedure has two attributes: layouts generation and a scoring function. The methods [5,16,17] utilized vanishing points and lines approach. [22] uses in addition a predefined pool of 4000 layouts. Our approach is based on the analysis of all feasible key points combinations.

The only methods where layout ranking is not applied are RoomNet [12] and LayoutNet [25]. They predict a room type according to LSUN classification (Fig. 1 in [22] and Fig. 2 in [12]). RoomNet output tensor has 48 layers. The method does not require any complex post-processing, but the official code is not available, making the test impossible.

LayoutNet has only 8 layers which is a maximum number of points in a layout. The same layer may be associated in LayoutNet with key points for different room types, allowing to reduce the total number of output layers from 48 to 8. Zou [25] was the first introduced an edge heat map with different layers for the floor, wall and ceiling.

Although the details of post-processing are not described in [25] they may be found in the official GitHub repository [24]. The post-processing of LayoutNet does not need multiple layout generation or vanishing lines detection that was a serious progress. The complexity of key points post-processing is due an ambiguity between the right (left) and the middle wall.

The further development of the 2D room layout estimation is a 3D room reconstruction. Besides [25] the recent studies on the topic are [8,10,19].

3 Heat Map Estimation via Double Refinement Net

3.1 Network Architecture

A standard way of image key point representation is a heat map. Heat map has usually the same resolution as the original image, and the number of layers depends on the neural network structure. Ground truth points are to be projected on the map as a blur usually distributed under a Gaussian distribution.

We choose Double refinement network [7] for the heat map estimation. The network has proven to be efficient in depth estimation for RGB monocular image. The experiments [21] showed that employing depth reduces the layout error by 6% and the clutter estimation by 13% for NYUv2 data set. The architecture of the double refinement network adapted for our task is shown in Fig. 2.

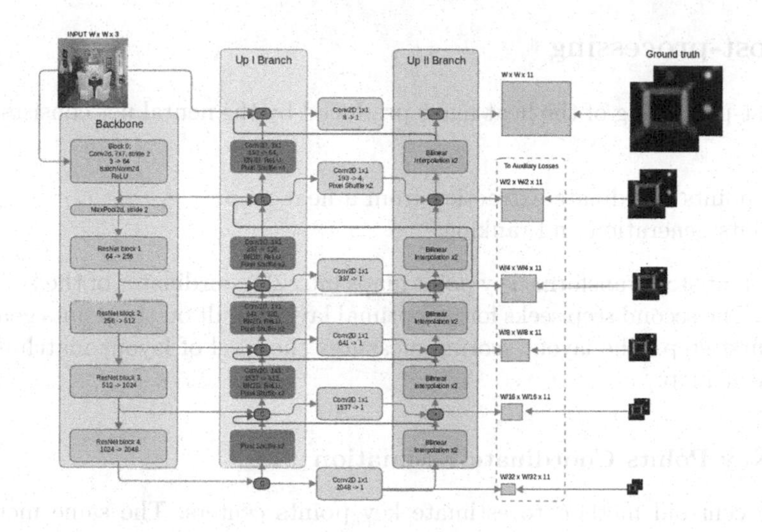

Fig. 2. Double refinement network [7] for the room layout estimation

We follow the same layout order for key points and edges while training as it was done in LayoutNet [25]. The Double refinement network architecture enables key points and edges heat map generation in one tensor. As our method does not use room type detection, we have only one output branch instead of three in LayoutNet.

The task of layout reconstruction from a heat map is ill-posed in Hadamard sense due to the fact that the layout does not depend continuously on a heat map and the solution is not unique. For this reason, cross-entropy and Euclidean distance are used as loss-functions. It is important to emphasize that the connection between loss function and basic metrics is complex and low loss on a validation set does not necessarily mean good metrics.

The net was trained with the following loss:

$$\mathcal{L} = \mathcal{L}_{points} + \lambda \mathcal{L}_{edges} \quad (1)$$

where $\lambda = 0.3$,

$$\mathcal{L}_{points} = CE_w(P, P_{GT}) \quad (2)$$

where p_{GT} is the ground truth heat map, p is the predicted heat map

$$\mathcal{L}_{edges} = CE(E, E_{GT}) \quad (3)$$

CE - cross entropy function, CE_w - weighted cross-entropy with weight w = 1.5,
P is a key points heat map estimated, $P =$ `output_tensor[:8,:,:]`,
E is an edges heat map estimated, $E =$ `output_tensor[8:,:,:]`,
`output_tensor` = 11 * 224 * 224 - a result from double refinement net,
P_{GT} - key points ground truth heat map, E_{GT} - edges ground truth heat map.

4 Post-processing

The post-processing of the heat maps produced by the neural net consists of two steps:

1. Key points coordinate extraction from a heat map.
2. Layouts generation and ranking.

The first step transforms key point maps into 2D coordinates of the key points centers. The second step seeks for an optimal layout built on the points generated at the first step. The layout scoring measures the level of layout matching with edges heat map.

4.1 Key Points Coordinate Estimation

We use centroid method to estimate key points centers. The same method is used when estimating star projection center for the satellite attitude estimation [11]. If corners heat maps estimation had a Gaussian distribution equal to their ground truth, then the maximum likelihood method [11] would be more efficient. However, in our case output corner heat maps are far from being Gaussian (e.g. key points in Fig. 1), so the centroid method is a better choice.

The centroid algorithm is to be applied for all layers 1, ..., 8 of `keyPointsHeatmap`. We ignore all heat map pixel having value lower than h. `SimpleBlobDetection` function using the cv2 package from the OpenCV library were applied for the initial heat map position estimation. The precise coordinates were estimated by the power centroid equation:

$$x = \frac{\sum_i i \sum_k \cdot \mathrm{w}_{ik}^{\gamma}}{\sum_i \sum_k \mathrm{w}_{ik}^{\gamma}} \tag{4}$$

$$y = \frac{\sum_j j \sum_k \cdot \mathrm{w}_{kj}^{\gamma}}{\sum_j \sum_k \mathrm{w}_{kj}^{\gamma}} \tag{5}$$

where w_{ij} - a corner heat map value of pixel i, j for a particular layer, $\gamma = 3.0$ is pow parameter (found empirically, the flatter is the key point energy distribution, the higher the parameter should be). i, j varies within a key point span.

If the distance between two points is less than `mergeDistance`, the points are to be merged and the coordinate of the result point is an average of two initial points.

Coordinates of heat maps lying near an image boundary should be treated specially, as one of their coordinates have to be equal zero to build a valid layout. At the same time, the centroid algorithm as well as other algorithms returns non-zero coordinates. One or both coordinates of a heat map are to be assigned to zero if the heat map is close enough to the image boundary.

4.2 Layout Ranking

Like most recent room layout estimation methods [5,16,17,22] we use layout ranking in post-processing. The layout ranking phase generates valid layouts which could be built on the points, ranks them according to a scoring function, and selects the best layout. Figure 3 illustrates 7 different layouts and their scores estimated by our method described below. A layout with the highest score (= 0.71) is an optimal one.

Our approach differs significantly from the methods based on segmentation map [17,22] which use vanishing point model, step-wise optimization of the layout and mean of all pixel coincided with a layout as a score function.

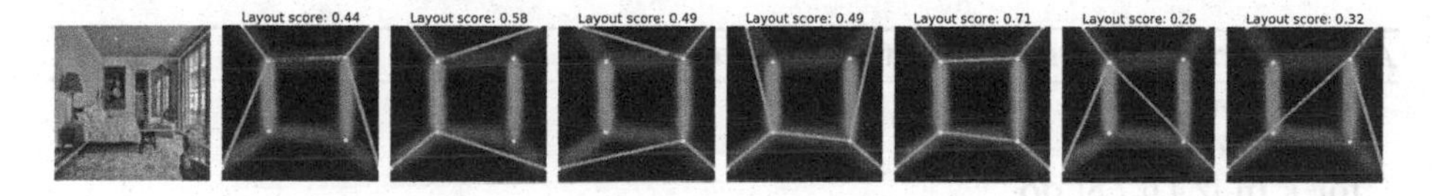

Fig. 3. Different layouts and their score.

A mean function as a score has a drawback of a poor optimization for cluttered rooms and rooms with nonstandard geometry that leads to inaccurate layout estimation.

An alternative to the mean value is a sum of all pixel coincided with a layout. The sum scoring function tends to select the most complex layouts. On the contrary, the mean function tends to select the most simple ones. To overcome the disadvantages of both scoring functions we suggest a special scoring function with two adjustable parameters $c_1, c_2 \in [0, 1]$ (the parameters were tuned on a LSUN validation data set).

The input for the layout ranking process is the extracted key points and edges heat map generated by the neural network. Edges heat map has three layers `ef`, `ew`, `ec` (a heat map of the floor, wall and ceiling edges respectively). Let us consider that ef_i, ew_i, ec_i are the pixel values of the corresponding edges heat map layers lying on the line between two points. We use the following measure to estimate whether there is an edge between two points:

$$p = \max(pf, pw, pc) \tag{6}$$

$$pf = \frac{\sum_i \mathrm{ef}_i}{nf^{c1}}, \quad pw = \frac{\sum_i \mathrm{ew}_i}{nw^{c1}}, \quad pc = \frac{\sum_i \mathrm{ec}_i}{nc^{c1}}, \tag{7}$$

where nf, nw, nc are number of pixels lying on the line between two points for each layer.

Consider we have a layout consisting of m lines with a measure p_j. The score s of the layout is:

$$s = \frac{\sum_j \mathrm{p}_j}{m^{c2}} \tag{8}$$

c_2 coefficient regulates preference of the complex or simple layout and c_1 regulates if smaller or bigger layout is preferable.

A formal description of the optimal layout selection Algorithm 1 is presented hereinafter.

Input:

points - 2D points from the 1st step of post-processing

edges - 3-layers heatmap tensor of edges 224 * 224

Output:

bestLayout = (*bestLayout.points*, *bestLayout.roomType*)

bestLayout.points - 2D points sorted in a specific order

bestLayout.roomType - layout type in [0, ..., 10]

Algorithm 1. Optimal layout algorithm

```
bestLayout = None
maxScore = 0
for k in [2,4,6,7,8] do
    for combination in combinations(points, k) do
        layout = Layout(combination)
        if layout.roomtype is not None then
            s = score(layout.points, layout.roomType, edges)
            if s > maxScore then
                maxScore = s
                bestLayout = layout
            end if
        end if
    end for
end for
```

Layout is a function which returns a corresponding room type for the set of points if it is possible to build a valid prospective layout of the points and *None* otherwise. It consists of numerous empirical rules determining whether the set of points corresponds to a certain room type. Most of the rules are simple comparison operations <,> or scalar product. That is why this approach is easier than vanishing points and lines estimation.

The proposed algorithm uses the combinatorical search, yet it is not critical since the number of points do not exceed 12 and therefore the number of combinations in the worst case is less than 4000.

Edge semantic post-processing algorithm [22] requires to analyze more than 4000 layouts (ray sampling + predefined pool) and estimates a score for all of them, whereas our algorithm estimates a score only for a small fraction of valid points combinations. Furthermore, edge semantic has a fine optimization step for the best 4 layouts, while our algorithm do not require any additional optimization.

Table 2. Room layout estimation algorithm benchmarks.

Method	Year	LSUN corner error	LSUN pixel error	Hedau pixel error
Mallya	2015	—	16.71%	12.83%
DeLay	2016	8.20%	10.63%	9.73%
CFILE	2016	7.95%	9.31%	8.67%
LayoutNet	2018	7.63%	11.96%	9.68%
RoomNet	2017	6.30%	9.86%	8.36%
Edge semantic	2019	5.16%	6.94%	**7.36%**
DR (ours)	2019	**5.11%**	**6.72%**	7.85%

Lower is better. For LSUN - numbers in italic are for the benchmarks on the test data set, normal font is for the benchmarks on the validation data set.

5 Results

The standard metrics for the room layout estimation are pixel and corner errors. Corner error is an average Euclidean distance between ground truth and predicted key points divided by the image diagonal. Pixel error is a pixel-wise error between the predicted surface labels and ground truth labels, i.e. the percentage of pixels that are labeled different from the ground truth. LSUN room layout toolkit provided by the authors of the LSUN layout competition addresses the labeling ambiguity problem by treating it as a bipartite matching problem solved using the Hungarian algorithm that maximizes the consistency of the estimated labels with the ground truth.

Table 2 compares efficacy of the recent (since 2015) room layout estimation algorithms on the standard benchmarks. The benchmarks for the earlier algorithms may be found e.g. in [22]. We tested our results on LSUN and Hedau datasets. We used 394 validation images on LSUN dataset and 105 test images on Hedau dataset. The pixel error for the whole Hedau dataset (train + val + test = 304 images) is 8.22%. Table 2 demonstrates that our layout estimation method achieved state-of-the-art results.

Figure 4 shows an example of room layouts reconstructed by our method. The last image in the second column is one of the most difficult cases in validation subset of LSUN dataset. Interestingly our approach and edge semantic method provide similar results (Fig. 11c in [22]), though we use different network architectures and our output maps also differ.

Fig. 4. An example of room layouts estimated by our algorithm for the LSUN dataset. *Green lines are for the ground truth layout, red lines are for the estimated layout.* (Color figure online)

6 Conclusions

We developed an efficient room layout estimation method based on a neural network with ResNet50 backbone and layout ranking post-processing. The outputs of the network are key points and edges heat maps. Our method is the second using this combination of outputs and the first using edges for the layout ranking in conjunction with key points.

Our method is also the first embedded ResNet50 backbone instead of VGG16 which is the common backbone in the encoder-decoder structure implemented in the other room layout estimation methods. ResNet50 is four times faster than VGG16 and has significantly less (25 million vs 138 million) parameters.

Our method outperforms state-of-the-art methods on both pixel and corner errors when tested on the LSUN dataset.

We also introduced a flexible score function for a layout ranking procedure allowing to choose what kind of layout is preferable.

References

1. Barinova, O., Konushin, V., Yakubenko, A., Lee, K.C., Lim, H., Konushin, A.: Fast automatic single-view 3-D reconstruction of urban scenes. In: Forsyth, D., Torr, P., Zisserman, A. (eds.) ECCV 2008. LNCS, vol. 5303, pp. 100–113. Springer, Heidelberg (2008). https://doi.org/10.1007/978-3-540-88688-4_8
2. Bianco, S., Cadene, R., Celona, L., Napoletano, P.: Benchmark analysis of representative deep neural network architectures. IEEE Access **6**, 64270–64277 (2018)
3. Boniardi, F., Valada, A., Mohan, R., Caselitz, T., Burgard, W.: Robot localization in floor plans using a room layout edge extraction network. arXiv preprint arXiv:1903.01804 (2019)
4. Coughlan, J.M., Yuille, A.L.: The Manhattan world assumption: regularities in scene statistics which enable Bayesian inference. In: Advances in Neural Information Processing Systems, pp. 845–851 (2001)
5. Dasgupta, S., Fang, K., Chen, K., Savarese, S.: DeLay: robust spatial layout estimation for cluttered indoor scenes. In: Proceedings of the IEEE Conference on Computer Vision and Pattern Recognition, pp. 616–624 (2016)
6. Del Pero, L., Bowdish, J., Fried, D., Kermgard, B., Hartley, E., Barnard, K.: Bayesian geometric modeling of indoor scenes. In: 2012 IEEE Conference on Computer Vision and Pattern Recognition, pp. 2719–2726. IEEE (2012)
7. Durasov, N., Romanov, M., Bubnova, V., Konushin, A.: Double refinement network for efficient indoor monocular depth estimation. arXiv preprint arXiv:1811.08466 (2018)
8. Fernandez-Labrador, C., Fácil, J.M., Pérez-Yus, A., Demonceaux, C., Civera, J., Guerrero, J.J.: Corners for layout: end-to-end layout recovery from 360 images. ArXiv abs/1903.08094 (2019)
9. Hedau, V., Hoiem, D., Forsyth, D.: Recovering the spatial layout of cluttered rooms. In: 2009 IEEE 12th International Conference on Computer Vision, pp. 1849–1856. IEEE (2009)
10. Howard-Jenkins, H., Li, S., Prisacariu, V.: Thinking outside the box: generation of unconstrained 3D room layouts. In: Jawahar, C.V., Li, H., Mori, G., Schindler, K. (eds.) ACCV 2018. LNCS, vol. 11361, pp. 432–448. Springer, Cham (2019). https://doi.org/10.1007/978-3-030-20887-5_27
11. Kruzhilov, I.: Minimization of point light source coordinates determination error on photo detectors. J. Opt. Commun. **32**(4), 201–204 (2011)
12. Lee, C.Y., Badrinarayanan, V., Malisiewicz, T., Rabinovich, A.: RoomNet: end-to-end room layout estimation. In: Proceedings of the IEEE International Conference on Computer Vision, pp. 4865–4874 (2017)
13. Li, R., Liu, Q., Gui, J., Gu, D., Hu, H.: Indoor relocalization in challenging environments with dual-stream convolutional neural networks. IEEE Trans. Autom. Sci. Eng. **15**(2), 651–662 (2018)
14. Lin, G., Milan, A., Shen, C., Reid, I.D.: RefineNet: multi-path refinement networks for high-resolution semantic segmentation. 2017 IEEE Conference on Computer Vision and Pattern Recognition (CVPR), pp. 5168–5177 (2017)
15. Lv, Z., Kim, K., Troccoli, A., Sun, D., Rehg, J.M., Kautz, J.: Learning rigidity in dynamic scenes with a moving camera for 3D motion field estimation. In: Proceedings of the European Conference on Computer Vision (ECCV), pp. 468–484 (2018)
16. Mallya, A., Lazebnik, S.: Learning informative edge maps for indoor scene layout prediction. In: Proceedings of the IEEE International Conference on Computer Vision, pp. 936–944 (2015)

17. Ren, Y., Li, S., Chen, C., Kuo, C.-C.J.: A coarse-to-fine indoor layout estimation (CFILE) method. In: Lai, S.-H., Lepetit, V., Nishino, K., Sato, Y. (eds.) ACCV 2016. LNCS, vol. 10115, pp. 36–51. Springer, Cham (2017). https://doi.org/10.1007/978-3-319-54193-8_3
18. Ronneberger, O., Fischer, P., Brox, T.: U-net: convolutional networks for biomedical image segmentation. In: Navab, N., Hornegger, J., Wells, W.M., Frangi, A.F. (eds.) MICCAI 2015. LNCS, vol. 9351, pp. 234–241. Springer, Cham (2015). https://doi.org/10.1007/978-3-319-24574-4_28
19. Sun, C., Hsiao, C.W., Sun, M., Chen, H.T.: HorizonNet: learning room layout with 1D representation and pano stretch data augmentation. ArXiv abs/1901.03861 (2019)
20. Wang, H., Gould, S., Roller, D.: Discriminative learning with latent variables for cluttered indoor scene understanding. Commun. ACM **56**(4), 92–99 (2013)
21. Zhang, J., Kan, C., Schwing, A.G., Urtasun, R.: Estimating the 3D layout of indoor scenes and its clutter from depth sensors. In: Proceedings of the IEEE International Conference on Computer Vision, pp. 1273–1280 (2013)
22. Zhang, W., Zhang, W., Gu, J.: Edge-semantic learning strategy for layout estimation in indoor environment. IEEE Trans. Cybern. 1–10 (2019) https://doi.org/10.1109/TCYB.2019.2895837
23. Zhou, H., Ummenhofer, B., Brox, T.: DeepTAM: deep tracking and mapping. In: Proceedings of the European Conference on Computer Vision (ECCV), pp. 822–838 (2018)
24. Zou, C.: Torch implementation for CVPR 18 paper: "layoutnet: Reconstructing the 3D room layout from a single RGB image" (2018). https://github.com/zouchuhang/LayoutNet
25. Zou, C., Colburn, A., Shan, Q., Hoiem, D.: LayoutNet: reconstructing the 3D room layout from a single RGB image. In: Proceedings of the IEEE Conference on Computer Vision and Pattern Recognition, pp. 2051–2059 (2018)

Finger Tracking Based Tabla Syllable Transcription

Raghavendra H. Bhalerao(✉), Varsha Kshirsagar, and Mitesh Raval

Institute of Infrastructure Technology Research and Management, Ahmedabad, India
{raghavendra.bhalerao,varsha.kshirsagar.19pe,
mitesh.raval.17me}@iitram.ac.in

Abstract. In this paper, a new visual-based automated tabla syllable transcription algorithm is proposed. The syllable played on the tabla depends on the manner in which various fingers strike the tabla. In the proposed approach, in first step fingers are tracked using SIFT features in all the frames. This path of fingers for various syllables are analyzed and rules are formulated. Then these rules are used to create a visual signature for different syllables. Finally, the visual signatures of all the frames are compared to the visual signature of the base frame and the frame is labeled to that syllable. Based on this the various signatures are classified into different syllables. Using the proposed method, we are able to transcript tabla syllables with 97.14% accuracy.

Keywords: Tabla · Music transcription · Tracking · SIFT

1 Introduction

Motion tracking is a method to estimate the location of the moving object in the consecutive frames of a video. Motion is a key attribute of a video, by analyzing it carefully we can extract information which is unique to the video. By observing we can define rules to operate any vision system in an uncontrolled environment. Motion captures the dynamic aspect of the scene under consideration. Extracting moving objects from a video is the basic crucial task in different applications of motion tracking in the field of computer vision. Status of motion is estimated by locating moving object in consecutive frames of the image sequence which finds its use in human-computer interaction, mobile robot platform to avoid the collision, to monitor the stability of drone, vehicle traffic control, musical instrument digital interface, visual tracking system for army, surveillance system, video games etc. One of the most popular forms of motion tracking is used in sports. Using motion tracking the event from many angles is observed and whenever required a decision is made.

The motion tracking can be classified into two main categories: static and dynamic. In static tracking, an object with a specific color and/or shape is detected in the consecutive frame by standard pattern matching techniques. In

S. Palaiahnakote et al. (Eds.): ACPR 2019, LNCS 12046, pp. 569–579, 2020.
https://doi.org/10.1007/978-3-030-41404-7_40

dynamic tracking, the target is first extracted from each video frame by and then tracked.

In the field of Human-Computer Interaction finger tracking plays a crucial role in different types of applications like sign language, virtual music instruments, music transcription, human-machine interface gesture, fingertip extraction in non-touch enable systems, gesture-based patient care system. The diversity of hand postures and self-movement of fingers make their detection very challenging for researchers. Finger tracking has a very important role in natural HCI. Results in the field of hand and finger tracking demonstrated that analyzing finger tracking can express much information about structural, interpretative and expressive issues.

Finger tracking finds an important application in music transcription. Generally, music transcription is carried out using audio signals but due to some limitations of audio signals classification recently some researchers used vision-based music transcription.

In the present research, we used vision-based methods to transcript the Tabla syllables also known as 'bols'. In the case of tabla it has to be tuned before playing and while tuning the same audio signatures can be from different syllables from different pitches, or in other words at different pitches the same syllable can have a different audio signature. This peculiar behavior of tabla makes it complicated for music transcription using audio-only. Therefore, in this paper, we are tracking finger movements to find the syllables played.

2 The Instrument

Tabla is a very important percussion instrument in Hindustani classical music. It is the most widely used instrument to control the rhythm by providing beats in classical music. It also controls the tempo of the music. In terms of Hindustani classical music, it gives 'taal' to the 'sur' of the music. It consists of two drums, namely 'dayan' and 'bayan'. These drums are also known as treble and bass drums. Figure 1 shows the tabla instrument. Different parts of the tabla instrument are described below.

The drum played by the right hand is called 'tabla' or 'dayan'. It has the diameter of 15 cm and a height of around 25 cm. It is made of wood. The drum played by the left hand is called 'dagaa' or 'bayan'. The bayan is approximately 20 cm in diameter and around 25 cm in height. It is made of metal. The word 'bayan' means 'left' and daya means right in hindi. The main parts of tabla which are responsible for various 'bols' are (1) Kinaar which is the outermost circular region of the tabla top made of goatskin (2) Maidaan which is the second ring after kinaar also made of goatskin and (3) Syahi which is the inner-most black circle of the tabla made by chemicals. The 'bol' produced by tabla depends in the manner by which a particular finger of the hand strikes the drum and the region where it strikes on the drum (Fig. 2).

Fig. 1. Tabla instrument.

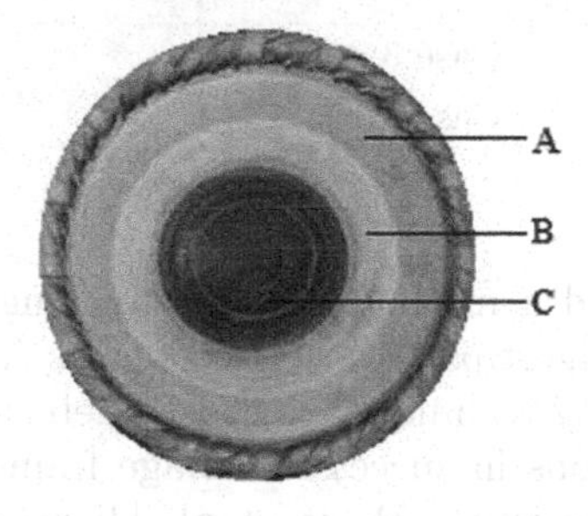

Fig. 2. Puri membrane along with its parts.

2.1 The Instrument Bols

The details of various tabla bols are detailed in Table 1.

3 Literature Survey

The proposed work is based on the finger tracking application to music transcription. In the following section, some of the important finger tracking works are discussed and then the specific work for finger tracking for music transcription is discussed. Yasuda et al. [1] proposed an online signature verification system. Where they used the Sequential Monto Carlo method for pen tracking. The signature data was collected from the images captured by webcams and then by tracking the pen tip is compared with the reference signature. Finally, the signature is classified as genuine or not. Neale et al. [2] developed a technique for determining the position and speed of objects visible in video footage captured with only one camera. Objects are tracked in the video footage based on the change in pixels that represent object moving. And PFTrack and Abode After Effects which contain automated pixel tracking features that record the position of the pixel overtime two-dimensionally using video resolution as a Cartesian coordinate system.

Table 1. Important Tabla *Bols*

S. No.	Dayan bols	Syahi	Maidan	Kinaar
1	Teh	Index	–	–
2	Tu	Index	–	–
3	Tin	Ring	Index	–
4	Ta	Ring	–	Index
5	Te	Index $\wedge$ Middle	–	–
	Bayan bols			
6	Ge	–	Index $\vee$ Middle	–
7	Ke	–	All	–
	Mixed bols			
8	Dha	Case 3 $\wedge$ 5		
9	Dhin	Case 2 $\wedge$ 5		

Oka et al. [3] proposed a method for locating fingertip locations in image frames and measuring fingertips trajectories across image frames for gesture detection. Here the filtering technique is used to detect fingertips in each frame to predict fingertip locations in successive image frames and verified predicted locations and detected fingertips. Haria et al. [4] proposed a vision and non-vision based approach for hand gesture recognition through the detection of finger movement with a pair of wired gloves. Overall the system contains three-module Camera, Detection and Interface Module. The image frames obtained are in the form of a video from a camera module given input to detection module after processing contour extraction is done and Haar cascade is used to detect the gesture. Finally, the Interface module is responsible for mapping the detected hand gestures to their related actions.

Chaudhary [5] developed a natural human-system interaction with the machine without gloves or any interfacing device. Fingertip extraction and motion tracking were done in Matlab with real-time constraints by cropping the image.

Hsu et al. [6] presents a new method of finger tracking designed based on Microsoft Kinect with an efficient algorithm is to track the detailed hand information including fingers using NITE hand Tracker. Finger region distribution is used to track the moving area of each finger using which the user could interact with music and graphics.

Gorodnichy and Yogeswaran [20] proposed a video recognition tool called C-MIDI which will track pianist hands and fingers using a video camera mounted on the top of the piano keyboard by locating crevices where two convex shapes meet. Which can be stored or transfer in terms of music pieces as a database.

MacRitchie [7] presents tracking of the pianist finger movement which contains information about the note. An optical motion capture system is described using a monocular camera set up to track passive UV paint markers placed directly onto the pianist's fingers. Tracking accuracy and 3D estimation algorithms are evaluated.

Paleri proposed a method to automatically transcript the guitar using hand tracking [8]. Gillet proposed a visual-based method for transcription of the drums [9]. Akbari et al. proposed an online visual-based system for transcription the piano [10]. In the present research, we are referring to the above three important works for transcription a different instrument 'tabla'. The tabla transcription work already exists but not is the visual domain. The important works that used audio signals for transcription can be referred in [9,11,12]. Based on these three works and their limitations we used feature-based tracking method to transcript one of the complex music syllables for tabla.

4 Dataset Used

For experimentation, we have acquired the dataset using a digital camera. The pixel resolution of the acquired frame is 1920 × 1080, and the frames are sampled at 50 frames per second. The tabla played at a tempo of 200 BPS for known tabla bol formations. The data is acquired for 1 min for 50 different patterns of tabla bols. We have thus 50 (fps) × 60 (min) × 50 (types) frames that captured 200 (Bps) × 50 (types) bols of 8 different syllable class. The movement of hand fingers is in 3D space and the images can only give information of 2D space. Freezing the camera position with respect to the instrument enables to convert 3D information to 2D without any loss. Therefore, the video is acquired for a fixed camera and instrument position. This enables to directly work on the image frame without geometrical transformations. Refer Fig. 3(A).

5 Proposed Methodology

In this section, the proposed methodology is explained. The unknown *bols* are identified by tracking the finger movement for known *bols* and then matching these bols' tracking patterns with the unknown *bols*. The first step is to track the fingers and then define the visual signature for each bol. The tracking is carried out by extracting the SIFT features [13] for the particular finger, then by matching them for the fingers in the next frame. The next step is to classify and label each frame to a bol.

Fig. 3. (A) Artificial markers (B) SIFT points

5.1 Feature Extraction and Processing

For better tracking, we used artificial markers and we marked each finger with these markers as shown in Fig. 3(A) and then captured the video. To track the finger's position SIFT features are extracted for these markers placed on the fingers. The feature extraction is carried out frame-wise. To begin with, the SIFT features for markers of left and right index middle and ring fingers are manually identified. And then the motion of the finger is tracked for the complete sequence as shown in Fig. 4.

5.2 Feature Classification

Once the features are extracted the 'x' and 'y' location of these features are plotted with respect to the frames. Figure 3 shows the plot of the index, middle and ring finger of the left and right hands. The syllables played for this plot are given. The 'x' location does not convey much information and the plots are for 'y' location of the finger in each frame.

Now using the plot of finger's 'y' location vs frame the pattern for a particular bol is identified and following observation as made -

1. The bols from the plot are played at the local maxima of any finger.
2. The difference between 2 bols are separated by 15 frames roughly. As the tempo is 200 BPS and the frame rate is 50 fps that means 3000 frames a minute, we expect a bol every 15th frame.
3. The gradient before the local maxima where a bol is played is 5 times as compared to the gradient after the local maxima.
4. Local maxima of right index finger tell a 'ta' 'tin' 'te' and 'tu'
   - To distinguish 'ta' and 'tin' with 'te' and 'tu' we used the information of right ring finger. This finger must be stable for 'ta' and 'tin'only.
   - To distinguish between 'ta' and 'tin' we used the distance of index finger with the ring finger, for 'ta' distance should be larger.
   - To distinguish between 'the' and 'tu' we observed the slope of these two syllables before and after the event. In the case of 'tu' the slope after the event is much higher.
5. Local maxima simultaneously for the right middle and ring finger simultaneously tells 'te'.
6. Local maxima simultaneously for the left index, middle and ring finger tells 'k'
7. Local maxima either for left index or middle finger tells 'g'
8. If 'g' and 'tin' are played simultaneously it is labeled as 'dhin'
9. If g' and 'ta' are played simultaneously it is labeled as 'dha'
10. Each 15th frame (roughly) is labeled with a syllable and all the other frames are labeled silent.

Based on the above observation we classified the different patterns of the fingers to different bols.

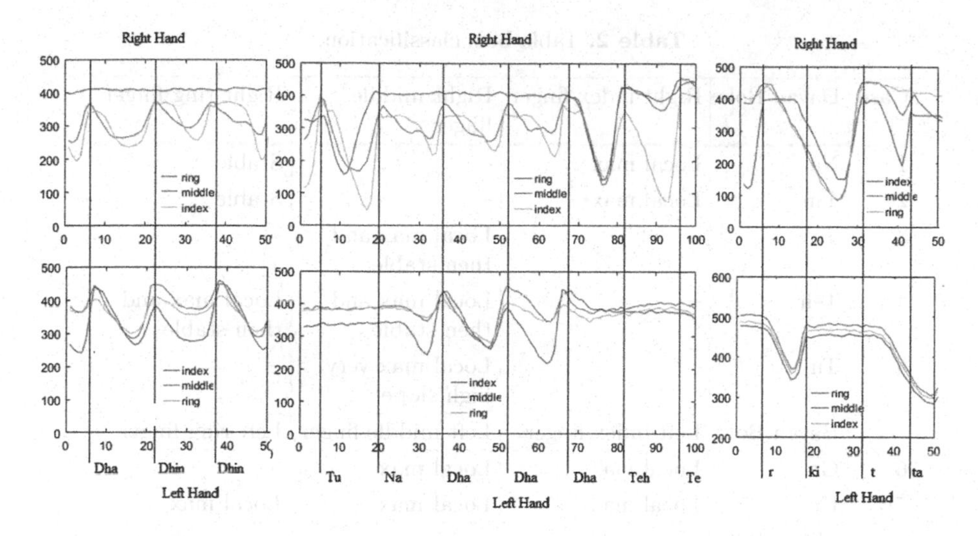

Fig. 4. Plot of left and right hand fingers for bols as indicated

Thus we have compared the profile of the tracked fingers of both the hands from the video frames with the test data we formulated above. Using the proposed method, we are proficiently able to transcript 97.14% of the tabla syllables correctly.

6 Results and Discussions

In this section, the performance of the proposed method is evaluated. To transcript each of the tabla syllables precisely, first of all, we captured videos for each syllable. Each finger of left and right hand involved in tabla playing is initially marked with the artificial marker and then SIFT features were detected for each finger. These marked initial features were tracked for all video frames and their position was noted. Reference database for finger motion for all the bols are created and compared with each incoming motion tracking data. Based on this the bols are classified.

The frames that satisfied the above conditions were labeled with the syllable. For validating the occurrence of a syllable, we iteratively validated each of the video frames manually. After the validation, we created a confusion matrix for each of the syllables.

Using this confusion matrix, we have computed the accuracy for each of the syllables as given in Table 3. The overall accuracy was calculated using the average of individual accuracies obtained for all the syllables. It is found to be 97.14%.

Table 2. Tabla bols classification.

Case	Dayan Bols	Right index finger	Right middle finger	Right ring finger
1	Na	Local max	–	Stable
2	Tin	Local max	–	Stable
3	Te	–	Local max and then stable	–
4	Teh	–	Local max and then stable	Local max and then stable
5	Tu	–	Local max very high slope	–
	Bayan Bols	Left index finger	Left middle finger	Left ring finger
6	Ge	Local max	Local max	–
7	Ke	Local max	Local max	Local max
	Mixed Bols	–	–	–
8	Dha	Condition 1 + 5		
9	Dhin	Condition 2 + 5		

Table 3. Performance evaluation of each of the syllables.

Syllable	Accuracy obtained (in %)	F1 score
Na	98.67	0.9922
Te	95.22	0.9688
Teh	98.78	0.9920
Tin	97.67	0.9856
Ge	98.56	0.9922
Ke	96.11	0.9533
Dha	98.67	0.9925
Dhin	98.56	0.9918
Tun	92.00	0.9466
Overall accuracy	97.14	0.98

This study aims for the automatic transcription of the tabla syllables using image processing techniques. In this study, automated transcription of tabla is done using the motion tracking of fingers. The presence of a finger for a syllable is determined by visual tracking. The performance by the proposed method has provided better transcription of the tabla syllables. The proposed method has exceeded the performance than the other existing transcribing techniques due to the following reasons:

1. Gillet et al. [9] have performed the automated transcription of the tabla signals using audio signal processing. They have done audio signal segmentation

in time-domain to separate the syllables produced on tabla while our proposed method presents the automated transcription of the table syllable using image processing techniques.
2. Since the tabla has to be tuned properly before playing, different tuning profiles produces varying audio tones for the syllables.
3. Gillet et al. [14] have used audio-visual information for the transcription of drums while we use image processing techniques to transcript tabla syllables.
4. Chordia [11] has used temporal features based on skewness, centroid and kurtosis while we have used SIFT features for generating the automated transcription of tabla syllables.
5. Akbari and Cheng [10] have used computer vision techniques for the automatic transcription of piano while we have used image processing techniques to transcript the tabla syllables.

Table 4. Comparison of various automated tabla transcription systems.

Author/year	Method adopted	Performance
Gillet et al. [9]	Audio signal segmentation in time-domain	93.6
Chordia [11]	Audio signal segmentation in time-domain with temporal Feed-Forward Neural Network (FFNN),	83%
	Probabilistic Neural Networks (PNN),	76%
	Multivariate Gaussian (MV Gauss)	76%
	Tree classifier	66%
Proposed method	SIFT features Visual Tracking	Overall accuracy = **97.14%**

7 Conclusion and Future Work

In the proposed method we used the visual tracking of the fingers to identify the tabla bols played. The tracking-based method is used for piano and guitar and drums but, for tabla, this is a method is a novel for transcription. The task is little simpler in the case of Guitar, and Piano because for these instruments the syllable only depends on the key or the wire pressed at a location. This is not true for Tabla which makes it complex as compared to these cases. Using the proposed methodology we have achieved an accuracy of 97.14%. In future work, we would like to increase the dataset and would like to work on better accuracy. The accuracy which we achieved is far better than the other audio-based methods for the same instrument.

Nowadays, a widely used state of the art uses deep learning methods. The ability of the deep learning methods in identifying multiple-class patterns with ease and accuracy has drawn the attention of numerous researchers [15]. The deep learning method uses a structure that functions similar to that of a human brain, known as artificial neural networks (ANN). Convolution neural networks (CNN) and recurrent neural networks (RNN) are some of the deep learning methods [16] which can be helpful. It is also found that CNN works better on unsaturated data like images and audio signals [17]. It does not require separate feature extraction, selection and classification processes. The advantage of using this is that it learns on its own and provides a better classification of multiple classes [18]. However, it requires large data for computation, thereby increasing the system complexity. Thus the requirement of fast computing CPUs and GPUs increases [19].

References

1. Yasuda, K., Muramatsu, D., Shirato, S., Matsumoto, T.: Visual-based online signature verification using features extracted from video. J. Netw. Comput. Appl. **33**(3), 333–341 (2010)
2. Neale, W.T., Hessel, D., Koch, D.: Determining position and speed through pixel tracking and 2D coordinate transformation in a 3D environment, April 2016
3. Oka, K., Sato, Y., Koike, H.: Real-time fingertip tracking and gesture recognition. IEEE Comput. Graph. Appl. **22**(6), 64–71 (2002)
4. Haria, A., Subramanian, A., Asokkumar, N., Poddar, S., Nayak, J.S.: Hand gesture recognition for human computer interaction. In: 7th International Conference on Advances in Computing and Communications, ICACC-2017, 22–24 August 2017, Cochin, India, vol. 115, pp. 367–374 (2017)
5. Chaudhary, A.: Finger-stylus for non touch-enable systems. J. King Saud Univ. - Eng. Sci. **29**(1), 35–39 (2017)
6. Hsu, M.H., Shih, T.K., Chiang, J.S.: Real-time finger tracking for virtual instruments. In: 2014 7th International Conference on Ubi-Media Computing and Workshops, pp. 133–138 (2014)
7. MacRitchie, J., Bailey, N.J.: Efficient tracking of pianists' finger movements. J. New Music Res. **42**(1), 79–95 (2013)
8. Paleari, M., Huet, B., Schutz, A., Slock, D.: A multimodal approach to music transcription. In: 2008 15th IEEE International Conference on Image Processing, pp. 93–96 (2008)
9. Gillet, O.: Automatic labelling of tabla signals (2003)
10. Akbari, M., Cheng, H.: Real-time piano music transcription based on computer vision. IEEE Trans. Multimed. **17**(12), 2113–2121 (2015)
11. Chordia, P.: Segmentation and recognition of tabla strokes. in: ISMIR (2005)
12. Sarkar, R., Singh, A., Mondal, A., Saha, S.K.: Automatic extraction and identification of bol from tabla signal. In: Chaki, R., Cortesi, A., Saeed, K., Chaki, N. (eds.) Advanced Computing and Systems for Security. AISC, vol. 666, pp. 139–151. Springer, Singapore (2018). https://doi.org/10.1007/978-981-10-8180-4_9
13. Lowe, D.G.: Distinctive image features from scale-invariant keypoints. Int. J. Comput. Vis. **60**(2), 91–110 (2004)

14. Gillet, O., Richard, G.: Automatic transcription of drum sequences using audiovisual features. In: IEEE International Conference on Acoustics, Speech, and Signal Processing, vol. 3, pp. iii/205–iii/208 (2005)
15. Hinton, G., LeCun, Y., Bengio, Y.: Deep learning. Nature **521**, 436–444 (2015)
16. Mallat, S.: Understanding deep convolutional networks. Philos. Trans. Roy. Soc. A: Math. Phys. Eng. Sci. **374**, 20150203 (2016)
17. Herremans, D., Chuan, C.-H.: The emergence of deep learning: new opportunities for music and audio technologies. Neural Comput. Appl. **32**, 913–914 (2019)
18. Jia, B., Lv, J., Liu, D.: Deep learning-based automatic downbeat tracking: a brief review. Multimed. Syst. **25**, 617–638 (2019)
19. Gad, A.F.: Convolutional Neural Networks. In: Gad, A.F. (ed.) Practical Computer Vision Applications Using Deep Learning with CNNs, pp. 183–227. Apress, Berkeley (2018). https://doi.org/10.1007/978-1-4842-4167-7_5
20. Gorodnichy, D.O., Yogeswaran, A.: Detection and tracking of pianist hands and fingers. In: The 3rd Canadian Conference on Computer and Robot Vision (CRV'06), pp. 63-63. Quebec, Canada (2006). https://doi.org/10.1109/CRV.2006.26

Dual Templates Siamese Tracking

Zhiqiang Hou[1,3], Lilin Chen[1,3(✉)], and Lei Pu[2]

[1] Institute of Computer, Xi'an University of Posts and Telecommunications, Xi'an 710121, China
ChenLilin_Linda@163.com

[2] Information and Navigation Institute of Air Force Engineering University, Xi'an 710077, China

[3] Shaanxi Key Laboratory of Network Data Analysis and Intelligent Processing, Xi'an University of Posts and Telecommunications, Xi'an 710121, China

Abstract. In recent years, Siamese networks which is based on appearance similarity comparison strategy has attracted great attention in visual object tracking domain due to its balanced accuracy and speed. However, most Siamese networks based tracking algorithms have not considered template updates. The fixed template may cause tracking matching error and can even cause failure of object tracking. In view of this deficiency, we proposed an algorithm based on dual templates Siamese network using difference hash algorithm to determine the template update timing. First, we kept the initial frame target with stable response map score as the base template z_r, using the difference hash algorithm to determine the dynamic template z_t. We analyzed the candidate targets region and the two template matching results, meanwhile the result response maps were fused, which could ensure more accurate tracking results. The experiment results on the OTB-2013 and OTB-2015 and VOT2016 datasets showed that the proposed algorithm has achieved satisfactory result.

Keywords: Siamese networks · Object tracking · Template update · Difference hash algorithm

1 Introduction

Object tracking research is an important topic in the field of computer vision, the main task is to automatically locate the target in a changing video sequence, which is widely applied in many fields such as intelligent monitoring, automatic driving, human-computer interaction, medical diagnosis, and Military targeting, and has high research value and practical significance [1]. With the advent of the artificial intelligence era, deep learning technology has been widely applied in the field of object tracking due to its robust feature expression, and various tracking algorithms based on different types of neural networks have emerged.

In recent years, the Siamese network based on the similarity comparison strategy has attracted great attention in the field of visual object tracking due

S. Palaiahnakote et al. (Eds.): ACPR 2019, LNCS 12046, pp. 580–593, 2020.
https://doi.org/10.1007/978-3-030-41404-7_41

to its good tracking performance. SINT [4], SiameseFC [5] and RASNet [6] takes the initial frame as a template to learn the similarity function of the priori depth Siamese network, and determines the candidate target by similarity comparison. SA-Siam [3] uses two branchs of Siamese networks: semantic branch and appearance branch. The shallow appearance branch correlation coefficient map and deep semantic branch correlation coefficient map added together in a certain proportion to obtain the final response map to realize feature fusion. FlowTrack [7] uses optical flow motion information in the Siamese network to improve feature representation and tracking accuracy. CFNet [8] and Dsiam [9] always takes the initial frame as input and learns to transform the target appearance matrix and background matrix through the ridge regression algorithm to achieve the purpose of adapting to the target time domain variation and suppressing the background change. EDCF [10] joins the deconvolution network after the SiameseFC feature layer, so that the feature network pays more attention to the detailed description of the target, and combines context-aware correlation filtering to suppress background interference. SiameseRPN [11], DaSiamRPN [12] and SiameseRPN++ [13] introduced detection methods in tracking, using ILSVRC [14] and Youtube-BB [15], these two large datasets to pretrain the template branch, and use the RPN network to detect targets.

While these tracking methods have nice accuracy and speed, most Siamese tracking methods does not allow for template updates. However, the appearance of the target and the angle of the scene tend to change during the tracking process. The fixed template will cause tracking matching error and scene adaptability decline, and may even lead to tracking failure. To solve this problem, we propose a Siamese dual-template tracking method based on differential hashing and background suppression. The initial frame target is selected as the base template z_r, which is regarded as the uncontaminated template to ensure the average performance of object tracking. The dynamic template z_t learns the apparent change of the target in the process of motion, which makes the tracking result more accurate. On the one hand, the dual template method can improve the correctness of the template and the support for tracking, and reduce the target drift; on the other hand, the adaptive update strategy used when selecting the dynamic template can reduce the number of updates, thereby ensuring the tracking speed. The proposed algorithm has advantages in tracking percision and success rate, and the computing speed on the GPU is real-time.

2 Related Works

In this section, we give a brief review on three aspects related to our work: Siamese networks, difference hash algorithm and background suppression.

2.1 SiameseFC Networks

SiameseFC network [5] removes the Padding layer and the full connection layer in the original Siamese network [4], and retains 5 convolution layers. In addition to the fifth convolution layer, there is a ReLU nonlinear activation layer behind each convolution layer, which is used to reduce the risk of over-fitting in the training process. The full convolution network makes it possible to input a large search region into the network, which can test all possible positions of the target in the new image, find the candidate region with the highest similarity with the target appearance, and thus predict the target position.

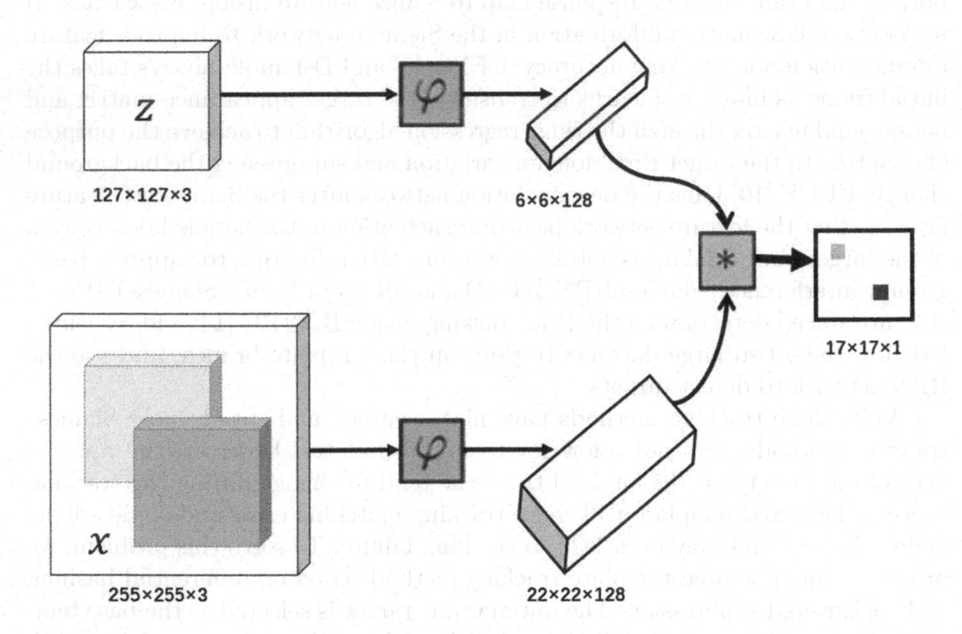

Fig. 1. SiameseFC network framework

As shown in Fig. 1, the SiameseFC network is used as a feature extractor to extract the features of the template z and the search region x, input them into the similarity function to calculate similarity, and return a score response map. The response map reflects similarity of the template x, template z and the candidate template x' with the same size as the template z in the search region: The score is high, x' is similar to z, and vice versa.

Because of its easy implementation, good performance and beyond real-time speed, the SiameseFC [4] algorithm brings the Siamese network to prosperity, and various improvements based on the SiameseFC tracker appear one after another [6–13]. However, due to the lack of online adaptation ability, SiameseFC tracking accuracy still has space for improvement.

2.2 Difference Hash Algorithm

Hash algorithm maps each value input to the hash function to the {0,1} space, thereby solving the problem of time consuming and excessive storage during data processing. It is usually applied to image retrieval and neighbor search [28–32].

The difference hash algorithm is an algorithm for generating a set of fingerprints based on image features and comparing the image fingerprints to determine the similarity of the images [16]. Applying this method to the target tracking field, it can quickly judge whether the target has deformation, occlusion and disappears. The difference hashing algorithm is better than the perceptual hash algorithm [17]. By calculating the difference between adjacent pixels of the image, it can obtain a more accurate tracking gradient, and the speed is much faster. The steps of the difference hash algorithm are as follows: (1) Convert to grayscale image. Convert input images to grayscale images to simplify calculations. (2) Resize the Image. Resize the Image to 17×16 to further simplify the calculation. (3) Calculate the difference. Calculate the difference between two adjacent pixels (from left to right), the positive number is 1, the negative number is 0, and the 256-bit image fingerprint is obtained. (4) Fingerprint comparison. Calculate the Hamming distance of a pair of image fingerprints and judge their similarity (Fig. 2).

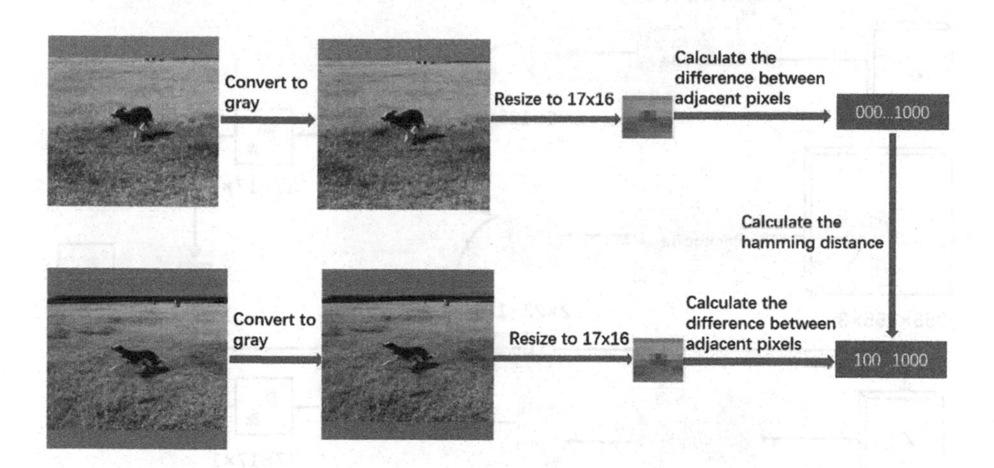

Fig. 2. Difference hash algorithm

3 The Proposed Approach

Although the Siamese network-based tracking method achieves good tracking accuracy and has a fast tracking speed, there are three problems [4–6]: First, most of the features used in the Siamese tracking method are shallow appearance features. Only the foreground and non-semantic background can be distinguished. Secondly, there is sample imbalance in Siamese network training. The lack of positive sample types leads to insufficient model generalization performance. Negative samples are too simple and most do not contain semantic information. Finally, most of Siamese tracking can't for template updating. Although, the simplicity of the tracking method based on the Siamese network led to the properties of high speed and a fixed model, the fixed template will cause tracking matching errors due to changes in the target appearance and scene perspective during the tracking process, the adaptability of the scene is degraded and may even lead to tracking failure. To address this last point, this paper mainly proposes a dual-template tracking algorithm based on Siamese network.

3.1 Dual Templates Siamese Networks

Base on SiameseFC framework, in this paper we proposed a double template tracking method: use the original frame target as a not contaminated base template z_r, with different hash algorithm to determine template update, get the dynamic templates z_t, two templates interact with each other, complement each other, similarity matching with the search region respectively, and get their own response, two response are weighted to get final response (Fig. 3).

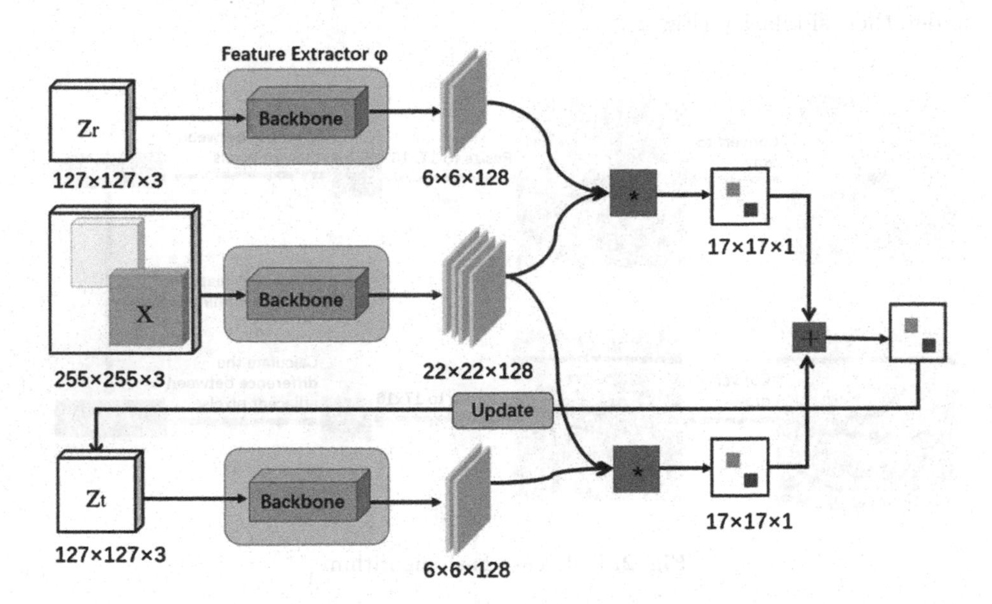

Fig. 3. Dual template tracking algorithm based on Siamese network

3.2 Similarity Estimate

Extracted features from template z_r, template z_t and search region x to $6 \times 6 \times 128$ feature map $\varphi(z_r)$, $\varphi(z_t)$ and $22 \times 22 \times 128$ feature map $\varphi(x)$ by using the feature mapping operation φ, b denotes a signal which takes value $b \in R$ in every location. $\varphi(z_r)$ and $\varphi(z_t)$ are calculated similarities with $\varphi(x)$, respectively. The function f, as the similarity function, calculates the similarity between the template and the search region to get a response map.

$$f(z; x) = \varphi(z) * \varphi(x) + b \tag{1}$$

We improved the SiameseFC network and the cross-correlation function, and merged the feature maps $\varphi(z_r)$ and $\varphi(z_t)$ obtained by the template z_r and the template z_t into a four-dimensional matrix ,then input the matrix together with the search region feature map $\varphi(x)$ to the cross-correlation layer, so we can obtain two response maps . Weighting the two response maps to obtain a new response map:

$$F(z_r, z_t; x) = \omega_1 \times f(z_r; x) + \omega_2 \times f(z_t; x) \tag{2}$$

In this way, it achieved the purpose of calculating similarity at the same time, improved the tracking speed effectively.

The determination of weight coefficient is very important. If ω_1 is too small will lead to a drift model, ω_2 is too small will make the updated template had little effect. Therefore, in the proposed algorithm, the base template is given a larger weight, and the dynamic template is given a smaller weight, that is, $\omega_1 \in [0.5, 1]$, $\omega_2 \in [0.2, 0.5]$. Under this principle, two response map values are analyzed synthetically to determine the specific value of weight parameters. After the weighting process, the position with the highest response value on the map is the position with the highest similarity. Multiply the position with the highest response value by the step size and plus the center offset to get the true position of the target in the next frame.

3.3 Adaptive Gaussian Background Suppression

During the object tracking process, it is often interfered by similar backgrounds, resulting in unsatisfactory tracking effect. Usually, we use background suppression to solve the similarity background interference. The general method of background suppression is that foreground extraction achieves a filtering effect on the background. A common background suppression method is to superimpose the window function on the image block to suppress the background clutter and noise interference and reduce the boundary effect. This method can not only suppress the background region, but also reduce the spectrum leakage.

The Siamese network based tracking algorithm usually adds a hanning window to the target [18] to suppress the background, but the hanning window has a fixed bandwidth and it is difficult to adapt to the target scale change. In order to overcome this shortcoming, the proposed algorithm adopts an adaptive Gaussian window [19] to avoid the lack of high-frequency details caused by the fixed bandwidth, and the low-frequency details are excessively sharpened, which causes damage to the edges of the image. Gaussian function is expressed as:

$$g(n, \sigma) = \exp(-\frac{1}{2}(\frac{i}{\sigma(n-1)})^2), 0 \leq i \leq n \tag{3}$$

The bandwidth of the gaussian filter is expressed by the parameter σ. The bigger the σ, the wider the bandwidth of the gaussian filter and the better the smoothness. The improved adaptive bandwidth gaussian window is defined as:

$$G(m, n, \sigma_w, \sigma_h) = g(m, \sigma_w) * g(n, \sigma_h) \tag{4}$$

The initial target size is $w \times h$, gaussian window size is $m \times n$. The sampling region is a square area, the side length of the square is $l = (w + 2p) \times (h + 2p)$, where p is the context margin $p = (w + h)/4$. The target size of frame t is $w_t \times h_t$,where $h_t = h \times s_t$, $w_t = w \times s_t$, s_t is the scale factor of frame t. The bandwidth of the gaussian filter of frame t is $\sigma_w = \theta \times \frac{w_t}{l_t}$, $\sigma_h = \theta \times \frac{h_t}{l_t}$, θ is bandwidth factor. This adaptive gaussian window avoids the problem that due to fixed bandwidth when the target becomes small, it contains a large amount of background information, while when the target becomes large, it lacks of target information. The adaptive gaussian window has the ability to adjust the bandwidth according to the target scale, optimize the extraction of foreground information, and has strong anti-interference ability.

3.4 Algorithm Flow

The main algorithm flow of the proposed algorithm is shown in Table 1.

Table 1. Dual templates tracking algorithm based on Siamese network.

Input: Image sequence: I_1, I_2, ..., I_n; Initial target position: $p_1 = (x_1, y_1)$, Initial target size: $s_1 = (w_1, h_1)$
Output: Estimate target position: $p_e = (x_e, y_e)$, Estimate target size: $s_e = (w_e, h_e)$
for t = 1, 2, 3, n, **do**:
1 Object tracking
1.1 The center position of the previous frame p_{t-1} crops the ROI (Region of Interest) in the t-th frame, and enlarges it into a search region;
1.2 Extracting features of the benchmark template z_r, the dynamic template z_t, and the search region x;
1.3 Using formula (2) to calculate the similarity between the two template features and the search region features to obtain the result response map, the highest response point in the response map is the estimated target position;
1.4 Update scale factor;
2 Template updating
2.1 Using the difference hash algorithm to calculate the similarity between the new target and the initial target, if the similarity is between 50% and 80%, update the dynamic template z_t;
Until End of image sequence

4 Experiments

We used MATLAB2018b + Visual Studio 2015 programming implementation to verify the performance of this algorithm, tested on the Intel(R) Core(TM) i7-6850k 3.6 GHZ processor, and accelerated with GPU (NVIDIA GTX 1080Ti). The experimental parameters of the algorithm are: the scale update sampling factor is 0.68, the bandwidth factor is 0.75, and the scale pyramid layer is 3.

4.1 OTB Datasets

The experiments were tested on OTB-2013 [20] and OTB-2015 [2] datasets, which contain challenging attributes of 11 manual markers: scale variation (SV), occlusion (OCC), illumination variation (IV), deformation (DEF), motion blur (MB), fast motion (FM), in-plane rotation (IPR), out-of-plane rotation (OPR), out-of-view (OV), background clutter (BC), and low resolution (LR) [2]. The OTB benchmark evaluates the tracking algorithm mainly in the two evaluation indicators which is central location error (CLE) and overlap rate (OR): the center location error refers to the Euclidean distance between the tracking result and the center position of the real target, if the center position error is lower than a given threshold, the target tracking is determined to be successful; the overlap rate refers to the overlap between the tracking result and the real target, if the current overlap rate exceeds a certain threshold, the target in the frame will be judged to be successfully tracked. Overlap rate and center location errors are reflected in the success rate map and the precision map respectively.

4.1.1 Qualitative Analysis

In order to make an intuitive analysis of the proposed algorithm, we analyze the 5 attributes of the 8 representative video sequences shown in Fig. 4:

(1) Deformation: In most video sequences, the tracking targets are deformed. Taking Bolt1 and Diving sequences as examples, the target deformation is severe. Due to the model update, the target can be continuously tracked by proposed algorithm.
(2) Occlusion: Taking the Soccer and Lemming video sequences as examples, the target is occluded for a short time. Although the target model is updated, continuous target tracking can be achieved because the base template is retained.
(3) Illumination variation: Taking the Shaking video sequence as an example, illumination changes in tracking, tracking algorithm is required to be robust to the illumination scene. The proposed algorithm has a good adaptability to illumination changes.

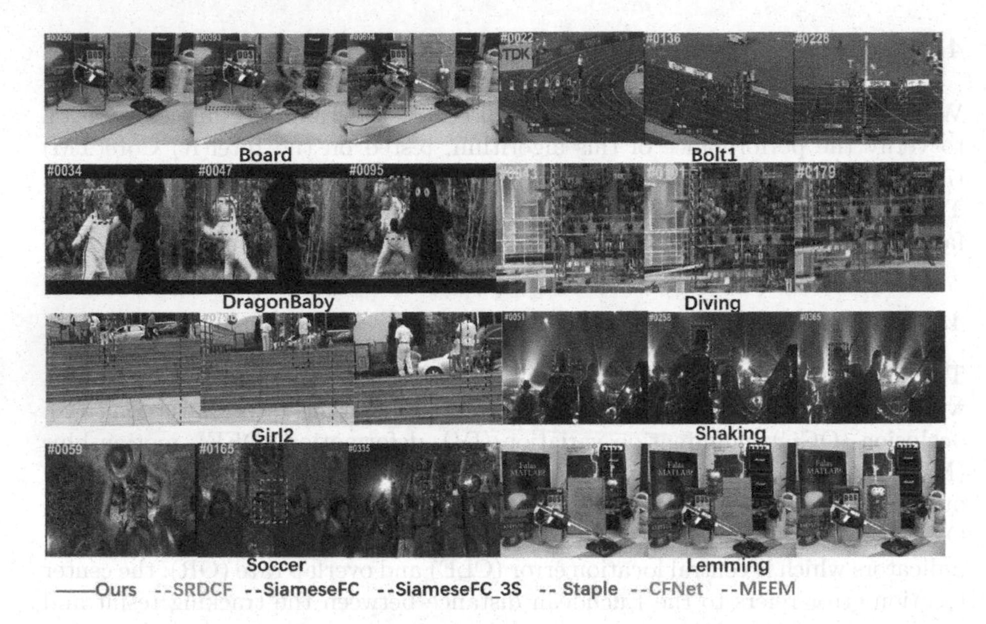

Fig. 4. Comparison partial results of 7 different algorithms on OTB dataset

(4) Target rotation: Taking DragonBaby and Board video sequences as examples, the target has a significant rotation, and most of the algorithms have tracking drift, but the proposed algorithm can track the target stably.
(5) Scale variation: Taking the Girl2 and Lemming video sequences as examples, there are obvious scale changes in the tracking process. The proposed algorithm can accurately track the target.

4.1.2 Quantitative Analysis

Table 2 shows the comparison between the proposed algorithm and the 9 mainstream tracking algorithms: SiameseFC, SiameseFC_3S [5], Staple [21], DSST [22], MEEM [23], KCF [24], SRDCF [26] and CFNet [8]. Among them, SiameseFC, SiameseFC_3S, CFNet is tracking algorithms based on deep Siamese network. Staple, SRDCF, KCF and DSST are tracking algorithms based on correlation filtering. MEEM considers the template update problem. The optimal result is red, the suboptimal result is green, and the third optimal result is blue.

The results show that the proposed algorithm has good tracking performance.

Table 2. Comparison results of tracking success rate of 10 different algorithms on OTB dataset

Tracker	OTB-2013	OTB-2015	Speed
SiameseFC	0.612	0.592	58
SiameseFC_3S	0.608	0.582	86
SRDCF	0.610	0.598	–
Staple	0.601	0.581	80
MEEM	0.566	0.530	–
DSST	0.554	0.511	23
KCF	0.514	0.477	20
CFNet	0.611	0.568	75
Ours	0.631	0.619	37

4.2 VOT Datasets

The proposed algorithm uses 7.0.1VOTToolkit to perform experiments on the VOT2016 [26] dataset containing 60 color video sequences. The evaluation index of the VOT2016 dataset has overlapping rate (Overlap) representing the average overlap rate of the tracker on a single test video sequence; the failure rate (Failures) is the performance of the algorithm from the perspective of robustness. The smaller the error rate, the more the algorithm Robustness; Expectation Average Overlay (EAO) is the expected value of non-reset overlap for each tracker over a short-term image sequence and is the most important indicator of the accuracy of the VOT evaluation tracking algorithm.

The comparison test results of the algorithm in this paper and 8 currently popular algorithms on the VOT2016 dataset are shown in Table 3. Among those trackers, our algorithm achieves the best EAO score of 0.299.

Figs. 5 and 6 shows an expected overlap scores and curves for baseline on VOT2016.

Table 3. VOT experimental results

Tracker	EAO	Failures	Overlap
SiamRN	0.277	23.996	0.549
SiamAN	0.236	29.802	0.531
Staple	0.294	23.895	0.540
Staple+	0.286	24.316	0.551
SRDCF	0.246	28.317	0.526
HCF [27]	0.220	23.857	0.436
DSST	0.181	44.814	0.525
KCF	0.194	38.082	0.492
Ours	0.299	22.678	0.553

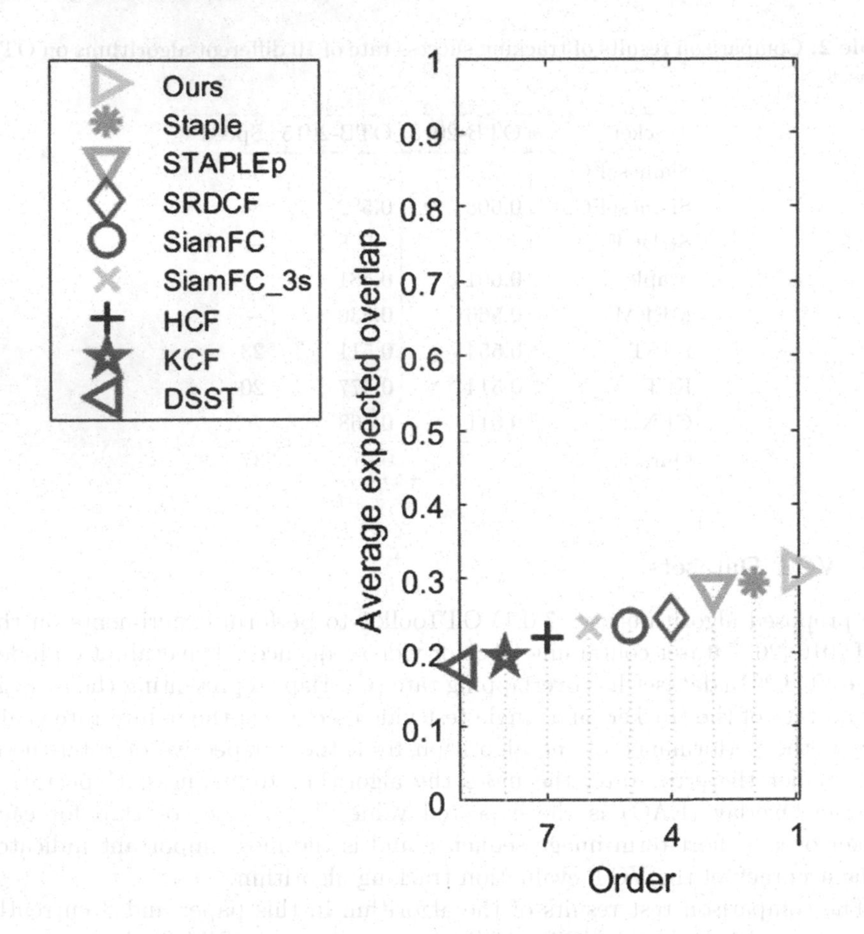

Fig. 5. Expected overlap scores for baseline on VOT2016

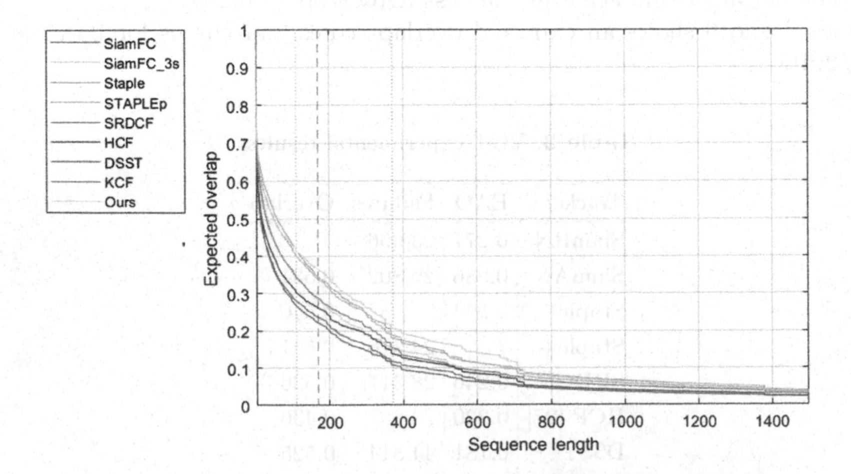

Fig. 6. Expected overlap curves for baseline on VOT2016

5 Conclusion

In this paper, a dual-template tracking algorithm based on Siamese network is proposed, in which difference hash algorithm is used to judge the update time of the template, and adaptive gaussian window is used to suppress the background of the target. The experimental results on the data sets of OTB-2013, OTB-2015 and VOT2016 show that the algorithm in this paper has stable and real-time performance.

The network structure used in proposed algorithm is a pair of relatively shallow shared weights AlexNet [28], only superficial appearance features can be obtained, so that the ability to distinguish foreground from semantic background needs to be improved. How to extract more robust features using deeper and wider networks will be the focus of research for the next step.

References

1. Hou, Z., Han, C.: Overview of visual tracking technology. IEEE/CAA J. Autom. Sinica (JAS). **32**(4), 603–617 (2006)
2. Wu, Y., Lim, J., Yang, M.: Object tracking benchmark. IEEE Trans. Pattern Anal. Mach. Intell. **37**(9), 1834–1848 (2015)
3. He, A., Luo, C., Tian, X., et al.: A twofold Siamese network for real-time object tracking. In: IEEE Conference on Computer Vision and Pattern Recognition, Salt Lake City, USA, pp. 4834–4843 (2018)
4. Tao, R., Gavves, E., Smeulders, A.W.M.: Siamese instance search for tracking. In: IEEE Conference on Computer Vision and Pattern Recognition, Las Vegas, USA, pp. 1420–1429 (2016)
5. Bertinetto, L., Valmadre, J., Henriques, J.F., Vedaldi, A., Torr, P.H.S.: Fully-convolutional siamese networks for object tracking. In: Hua, G., Jégou, H. (eds.) ECCV 2016. LNCS, vol. 9914, pp. 850–865. Springer, Cham (2016). https://doi.org/10.1007/978-3-319-48881-3_56
6. Wang, Q., Zhu, T., Xing, J., et al.: Learning attentions: Residual attentional Siamese network for high performance online visual tracking. In: IEEE Conference on Computer Vision and Pattern Recognition, Salt Lake City, USA, pp. 4854–4863 (2018)
7. Zhu, Z., Wu, W., Zou, W., et al.: End-to-end flow correlation tracking with spatial-temporal attention [OL] (2017). https://arxiv.org/abs/1711.01124v1
8. Valmadre, J., Bertinetto, L., Henriques, J.F., Vedaldi, A., Torr, P.H.S.: End-to-end representation learning for correlation filter based tracking. In: IEEE Conference on Computer Vision and Pattern Recognition, Hawaii, USA, pp. 2805–2813 (2017)
9. Guo, Q., Feng, W., Zhou, C., Huang, R., Wan, L., Wang, S.: Learning dynamic Siamese network for visual object tracking. In: IEEE International Conference on Computer Vision, Venice, Italy, pp. 1763–1771 (2017)
10. Wang, Q., Zhang, M., Xing, J., Gao, J., Hu, W., Maybank, S.: Do not lose the details: reinforced representation learning for high performance visual tracking. In: International Joint Conferences on Artificial Intelligence, Stockholm, Swedish (2018)

11. Li, B., Yan, J., Zhu, Z., Hu, X.: High performance visual tracking with Siamese region proposal network. In: IEEE Conference on Computer Vision and Pattern Recognition, Salt Lake City, USA, pp. 8971–8980 (2018)
12. Zhu, Z., Wang, Q., Li, B., et al.: Distractor-aware Siamese networks for visual object tracking. In: European Conference on Computer Vision, Munich, Germany, pp. 101–117 (2018)
13. Li, B., Wu, W., Wang, Q., et al.: SiamRPN++: evolution of Siamese visual tracking with very deep networks. In: IEEE Conference on Computer Vision and Pattern Recognition (2019)
14. Russakovsky, O., et al.: ImageNet large scale visual recognition challenge. Int. J. Comput. Vis. **115**, 211–252 (2015)
15. Real, E., Shlens, J., Mazzocchi, S., Pan, X.: YouTube-BoundingBoxes: a large high-precision human-annotated data set for object detection in video. In: IEEE Conference on Computer Vision and Pattern Recognition, Hawaii, USA, pp. 5296–5305 (2017)
16. Wu, Z., Yang, S., Wang, D., Sun, P.: Research on tracking and orientation of moving targets based on adaptive image enhanced difference hash algorithm. Glob. Position. Syst. **43**(05), 98–104 (2018)
17. Wang, J., Hou, Z., Yu, W., Liao, X., Chen, C.: Improved TLD algorithm using image perceptual hash algorithm. J. Air Force Eng. Univ. (Nat. Sci. Edn.) **19**(05), 58–64 (2018)
18. Wang, L., Huang, J., Sun, J., Wang, Q., Zhu, Y.: Improved FFT high-precision harmonic detection algorithm based on Hanning window. Power Syst. Protect. Control **40**(24), 28–33 (2012)
19. Hua, Y., Shi, Y., Yang, M., Liu, Z.: Multi-scale tracking algorithm based on background suppression and foreground anti-interference. Infrared Technol. **40**(11), 1098–1105 (2018)
20. Wu, Y., Lim, J., Yang, M.: Online object tracking: a benchmark. In: IEEE Conference on Computer Vision and Pattern Recognition, vol. 5, pp. 2411–2418 (2013)
21. Bertinetto, L., Valmadre, J., Golodetz, S., et al.: Staple: complementary learners for real-time tracking. In: IEEE Conference on Computer Vision and Pattern Recognition, Las Vegas, USA, pp. 1401–1409 (2016)
22. Danelljan, M., Hager, G., Khan, F.S.: Accurate scale estimation for robust visual tracking. In: British Machine Vision Conference, British pp. 65.1–65.11 (2014)
23. Zhang, J., Ma, S., Sclaroff, S.: MEEM: robust tracking via multiple experts using entropy minimization. In: Fleet, D., Pajdla, T., Schiele, B., Tuytelaars, T. (eds.) ECCV 2014. LNCS, vol. 8694, pp. 188–203. Springer, Cham (2014). https://doi.org/10.1007/978-3-319-10599-4_13
24. Henriques, J.F., Rui, C., Martins, P., et al.: High-speed tracking with kernelized correlation filters. IEEE Trans. Pattern Anal. Mach. Intell. **37**(3), 583–596 (2015)
25. Danelljan, M., Hager, G., Khan, F.S., et al.: Learning spatially regularized correlation filters for visual tracking. In: IEEE International Conference on Computer Vision, Santiago, Chile, pp. 4310–4318 (2015)
26. Kristan, M., Leonardis, A., Matas, J., Felsberg, M., Pflugfelder, R.: The visual object tracking VOT2016 challenge results. In: European Conference on Computer Vision WorkShop, vol. 9914, pp. 777–823 (2016)
27. Ma, C., Huang, J.B., Yang, X., et al.: Hierarchical convolutional features for visual tracking. In: IEEE International Conference on Computer Vision, Santiago, Chile, pp. 3074–3082 (2015)
28. Lee, K.M.: Locality-sensitive hashing techniques for nearest neighbor search. Int. J. Fuzzy Log. Intell. Syst. **12**(4), 300–307 (2012)

29. Xia, H., Wu, P., Hoi, S.C.H., et al.: Boosting multi-kernel locality-sensitive hashing for scalable image retrieval. In: Proceedings of the 35th International ACM SIGIR Conference on Research and Development in Information Retrieval, pp. 55–64. ACM (2012)
30. Guo, J., Li, J.: CNN based hashing for image retrieval. arXiv preprint arXiv:1509.01354 (2015)
31. Wang, Y., Guo, J., Zhou, L.: Compact image hashing algorithm based on data projection dimensionality reduction mechanism and symmetric local two value model. Laser Optoelectron. Progr. **54**(2), 416 (2017)
32. Yong, S.C., Park, J.H.: Image hash generation method using hierarchical histogram. Multimed. Tools Appl. **61**(1), 181–194 (2015)

Structure Function Based Transform Features for Behavior-Oriented Social Media Image Classification

Divya Krishnani[1], Palaiahnakote Shivakumara[2], Tong Lu[3], Umapada Pal[4], and Raghavendra Ramachandra[5](✉)

[1] International Institute of Information Technology, Naya Raipur, Naya Raipur, Chhattisgarh, India
divya16100@iiitnr.edu.in

[2] Faculty of Computer Science and Information Technology, University of Malaya, Kuala Lumpur, Malaysia
shiva@um.edu.my

[3] National Key Lab for Novel Software Technology, Nanjing University, Nanjing, China
lutong@nju.edu.cn

[4] Computer Vision and Pattern Recognition Unit, Indian Statistical Institute, Kolkata, India
umapada@isical.ac.in

[5] Faculty of Information Technology and Electrical Engineering, Norwegian University of Science and Technology, Trondheim, Norway
raghavendra.ramachandra@ntnu.no

Abstract. Social media has become an essential part of people to reflect their day to day activities including emotions, feelings, threatening and so on. This paper presents a new method for the automatic classification of behavior-oriented images like Bullying, Threatening, Neuroticism-Depression, Neuroticism-Sarcastic, Psychopath and Extraversion of a person from social media images. The proposed method first finds facial key points for extracting features based on a face detection algorithm. Then the proposed method labels face regions as foreground and other than face region as background to define context between foreground and background information. To extract context, the proposed method explores Structural Function based Transform (SFBT) features, which study variations on pixel values. To increase discriminating power of the context features, the proposed method performs clustering to integrate the strength of the features. The extracted features are then fed to Support Vector Machines (SVM) for classification. Experimental results on a dataset of six classes show that the proposed method outperforms the existing methods in terms of confusion matrix and classification rate.

Keywords: Social media images · Face detection · Structural features · Person behavior · Classification

1 Introduction

Since the usage of social media is growing exponentially, media has been used extensively for communication and broadcasting news in day to day human activities [1].

S. Palaiahnakote et al. (Eds.): ACPR 2019, LNCS 12046, pp. 594–608, 2020.
https://doi.org/10.1007/978-3-030-41404-7_42

Therefore, one can expect that messages or news posted in social media can influence environment or mind of targeted or concerned persons. For example, posting images on the social media, which may send messages of bullying, threatening, depression, sarcastic, psychopath and joyfulness (extraversion). It is true that the way a person upload images on social media reflects his/her behavior and mind, for example, committing crimes, suicide, etc. To prevent such crimes and social disharmony, there is a need for classifying behavior-oriented social media images uploaded on social media. It is evident from the news of Facebook that they are hiring a large number of people to watch and monitor unwanted images uploaded on Facebook. Hence, this work presents a method for classifying behavior-oriented social media images to assist automatic system for person behavior identification. In other words, the method can help to identify the normal and abnormal images uploaded on social media such that system can alert about unusual activities on website. Therefore, the proposed work focus on classification of normal and abnormal social media images. This work considers images of bullying, threatening, neuroticism-depressed, neuroticism-sarcastic, psychopathic and extraversion (as the shown sample images in Fig. 1) for classification. The classes of bullying, threatening, neuroticism-depression, neuroticism-sarcastic and psychopath are considered as abnormal classes and the extraversion as normal classes.

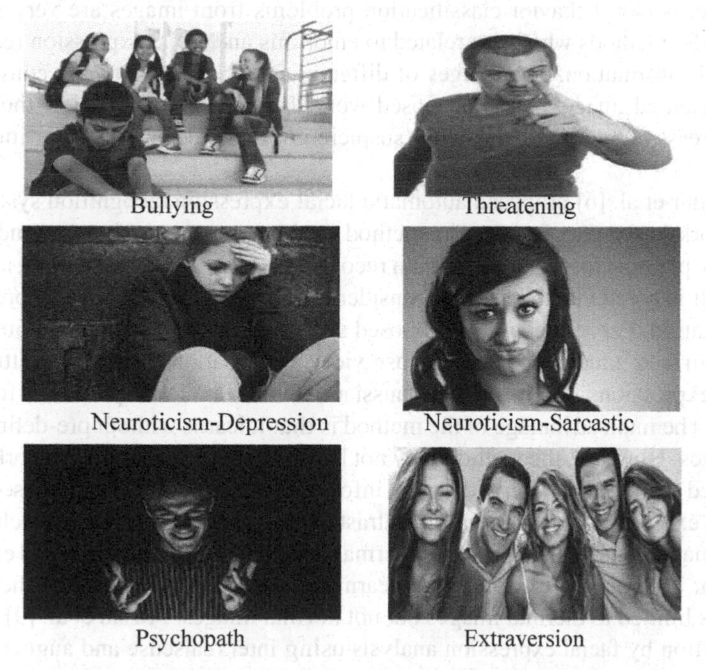

Fig. 1. Sample images of six behavior-oriented image classes.

Classification of images is not a new problem for the researchers in the field of image processing and pattern recognition. There are several methods proposed in the literature [2, 3]. However, their focus is to classify general images based on object shape and scene understanding, but not behavior-oriented social media images, where face and person posture are expected as prominent information. Similarly, there are methods [4] for person behavior identification, emotions recognition, posture recognition, etc., using face and other biometric features. These methods work well when images contain only one emotion but not for the images shown in Fig. 1, where it is noted that Bullying and Threatening can have multiple emotions in each single image. Therefore, inspired by the work in [5], where profile pictures posted on social media have been used for identifying person behaviors such as openness, extraversion and neuroticism, we propose to classify person behavior-oriented images, which include abnormal and normal behaviors, in this work. It is noted from the method [5] that profile alone is not sufficient for person behavior identification because the profile picture is not a reliable source for extracting features. The main challenge here is that it is hard to predict emotions, expression, posture and background variations in images. The presence of multiple emotions, expressions, actions in a single image makes the classification problem more complex and challenging.

2 Related Work

In literature, person behavior classification problems from images are very rare, thus we review the methods which are related to emotions and facial expression recognition using facial information. The images of different facial expressions are considered as behavior oriented images as the proposed work. Further, we also review the methods which addresses abnormal events and suspicious person detection using images and videos.

Majumder et al. [6] proposed automatic facial expression recognition system using deep network-based data fusion. The method explores geometric features and regional local binary patterns for facial expression recognition based on deep learning and fusion operation. It is noted that the method considers the images with uniform expression for experimentation. Perveen et al. [7] proposed spontaneous expression recognition using universal attribute model. The method use video information for learning attributes of the facial expressions. Then a large Gaussian mixture model is proposed for feature extraction. The main advantage of the method is that it learns without pre-defined labels of the images. However, the method may not be suitable for the proposed work because the proposed work does not provide video information. Wang et al. [8] proposed thermal augmented expression recognition. In contrast to conventional methods, which use visible facial images, this method proposes thermal infrared information for facial expression recognition. The method explores deep learning models for recognition. The scope of this work is limited to thermal images but not normal images. Prasad et al. [9] proposed fraud detection by facial expression analysis using intel realsense and augmented reality. The method develop a system to identify the fake expression by analyzing the facial features. The system requires not only facial features but also action information, which is not available in case of the proposed work. Arru et al. [10] proposed exploiting visual behavior for autism spectrum disorder identification. The method combines the image content as well as eyes fixation for feature extraction. The decision tree is proposed for identification. This method does not work for the proposed behavior oriented image classification because the data does not provide eyes fixation data. It is noted from the above-methods that the methods identify the images of different expression behavior. These methods work well for the images containing single expression in the images but not the images of multiple expression and action. Therefore, the scope of the methods is limited to the image of specific content but not the images of the proposed work.

There are methods, which explore video information for suspicious behavior identification based on image content. Beeck et al. [11] proposed abnormal behavior detection in long wavelength infrared (LWIR) surveillance of railway platforms. Cosar et al. [12] proposed abnormal trajectory and event detection in video surveillance. Liu et al. [13] proposed an accelerating vanishing point-based line sampling scheme for real-time people localization. Tiwari et al. [14] proposed suspicious face detection based on eye and other facial feature movement monitoring. The method explores facial features to classify persons as normal or abnormal. Hsu et al. [15] proposed video-based abnormal human behavior detection for psychiatric patient monitoring. The method uses person appearances and motion information for extracting abnormal behaviors.

In light of the above discussion, it is noted that none of the methods uses images uploaded on social media for classification. In addition, most of the methods depend on specific content of the images and video information for identifying expression or behaviors. In the case of the proposed work, the images can contain multiple expressions and actions and it does not provide video information. Therefore, we can conclude that the above facial expression behavior recognition methods and person behavior identification methods may not be suitable for the proposed classification problem. Hence, motivated by the method [5] where face information is useful for person behavior identification, the proposed method also uses face regions to extract features that are useful for classification.

One can observe from Fig. 1 that although the content of images of the same class changes, the context remains the same for respective classes. For example, in the case of bullying, low variations for face regions are expected (foreground components) and high variations for non-face regions (background components). This is due to the homogeneous skin regions of faces, and heterogeneous nature of non-face regions. Though faces and persons change in images, low and high variations remain the same for all the images in each class. This is the main basis to propose a new method for classifying behavior-oriented social media images. As stated in the method [16] that Structural Function based Transform (SFBT) features are robust in studying variations on pixel values for palmprint recognition, we explore the same SFBT features to find the relationship between foreground and background information, which defines context features. The proposed method uses clustering for fusing the strengths of features of foreground and background, which results in a feature vector. Furthermore, the extracted feature vector is fed to a Support Vector Machine (SVM) for classification.

3 Proposed Method

This work considers images of six classes, namely, Bullying, Threatening, Neuroticism-Depression, Neuroticism-Sarcastic, Psychopathic and Extraversion activities (normal) uploaded on social media such as Facebook, Instagram, YouTube and WhatsApp. The main reason to consider these six classes is that according to the study on social media images, the above five abnormal classes are real threats to society regardless of age and gender [17]. The proposed method uses the face detection method in [18] to find face regions, which are considered as foreground components and other than foreground regions considered as background components. To find the relationship between foreground and background components, we further propose to implement SFBT, which defines context features by studying variations on pixels of foreground and background information. It is true that all the extracted features may not contribute to discrimination. To select features which provide reliable discriminative power, we cluster the features into different groups. Further, for finding the resultant feature vector we propose a fusion technique to combine the features extracted from foreground and background based on weights that correspond to frequency of elements in the feature vectors. Finally, the feature vector is fed to an SVM for the classification of behavior-oriented social media images. The block diagram of the proposed method is shown in Fig. 2.

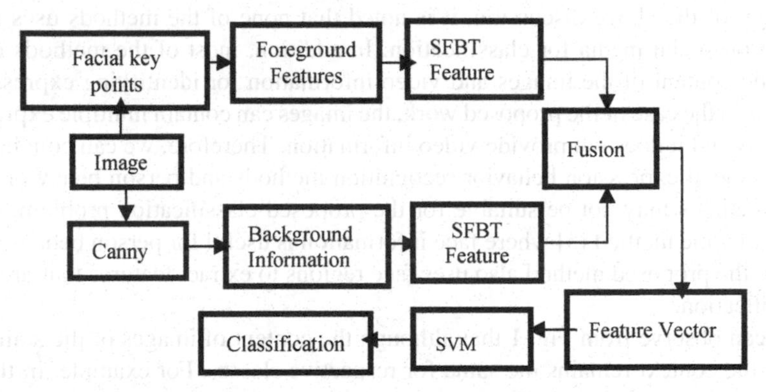

Fig. 2. The block diagram of the proposed method

3.1 Foreground and Background Region Detection

For the input image of each class, we propose to use the Multi-Task Cascaded Convolutional Network (MTCNN) for facial points detection [18]. MTCNN consists of three key steps for facial points detection. In the first step, MTCNN uses Proposal Networks (P-Net) to obtain candidate windows and their regression vectors. Regression vectors are then used for finding bounding boxes to calibrate candidates. In the second step, the best candidates are passed to Refine-Network (R-Net), which eliminates false candidates. In the third step, the method uses supervision for facial point detection in faces. We prefer to choose this method for detecting facial points because it works based on deep learning models that are robust to pose and contrast.

For the detected facial points, the proposed method fixes 8×8 bounding boxes as shown in Fig. 3 for feature extraction rather than using the whole face region. We believe that the 8×8 region contained facial points provides more prominent information compared to other regions of faces for feature extraction. In addition, it reduces a large number of computations. The size of the window is determined empirically based on predefined samples chosen randomly. The proposed method considers other than face region as background information as the shown samples in Fig. 4, while the (8 × 8) region of facial points are considered as foreground information. In order to obtain components for background information, the proposed method performs Canny edge operator over background information, which results in edge components. The proposed method restore the color information in input image corresponding to the edge components. This results in background components as shown in in Fig. 4.

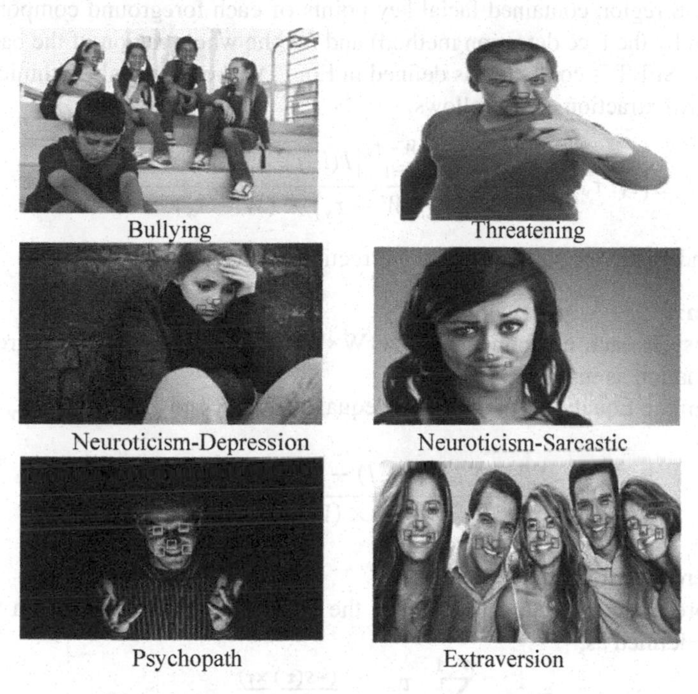

Fig. 3. Fixing 8 × 8 window for feature extraction

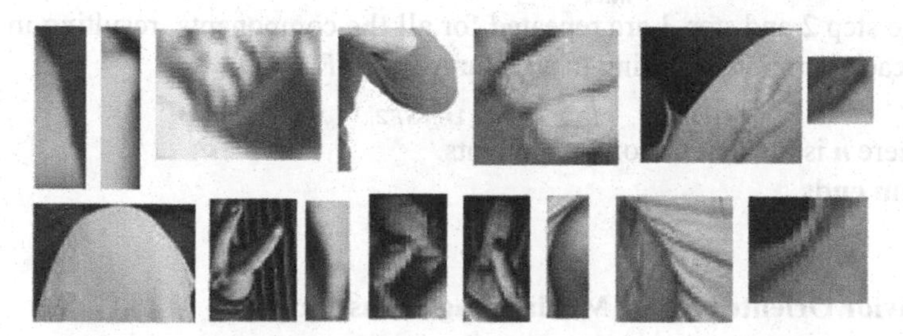

Fig. 4. Example of background regions for the images in Fig. 3.

3.2 Structural Function Based Transform (SFBT) for Feature Extraction

Inspired by the special property of SFBT, which extracts local variation in pixel values [16], we propose SFBT for feature extraction and classification. In other words, SFBT gives high values where there are uniform values such as plain regions, and low values where there are abrupt changes such as cluttered regions. In general, extracting variations on pixels values means studying edge properties, such as strength and sharpness. It is also true that edge information contributes to shapes of objects in images. This observation leads to use SFBT for feature extraction in this work.

For 8 × 8 region contained facial key points of each foreground component (face region given by the face detection method) and for the whole region of the background components, SFBT is computed as defined in Eq. (1). The formal algorithmic steps for SFBT feature extraction are as follows.

$$S(\tau_x, \tau_y) = \frac{\sum_{i=1}^{W-\tau_x} \sum_{j=1}^{W-\tau_y} \left| I(i, j) - I(i + \tau_x, j + \tau_y) \right|}{(W - \tau_y) \times (W - \tau_x)} \tag{1}$$

where τ_x and τ_y are the shifts in x and y direction respectively.

Algorithm:

1. Consider each component of size W×W of foreground and background information as input.
2. From the Equation (1), there is an equal shift in x and y, i.e, $\tau_x = \tau_y = \tau$,

$$S(\tau) = \frac{\sum_{i=1}^{W-\tau} \sum_{j=1}^{W-\tau} |I(i,j) - I(i + \tau, j + \tau)|}{(W - \tau) \times (W - \tau)} \tag{2}$$

   where τ varies from 1 to W-1
3. Representing structure function in the form of Hanman Transform function H_{SF} defined as,

$$H_{SF} = \sum_{\tau=1}^{W-1} \frac{\tau}{\tau_{max}} \cdot e^{\frac{(-S(\tau) \times \tau)}{\tau_{max}}} \tag{3}$$

   where τ_{max} is the maximum value of shift τ, i.e.

$$\tau_{max} = W - 1$$

4. The step 2 and step 3 are repeated for all the components, resulting in a H_{SF} , at each iteration, resulting in a feature vector F.

$$F = [H_{SF1}, H_{SF2}, \ldots H_{SFn}]$$

   where n is the number of components.

Algorithm ends.

3.3 Behavior Oriented Social Media Image Classification

Due to unpredictable foreground and background information, there are chances of detecting non-face regions as faces. This affects background information also because detection of background information depends on success of foreground information detection. As a result, extracted features may not be robust and discriminative. To overcome this problem, we propose to employ k-means clustering with k = 2 on feature vectors of foreground and background components, which classify high values into the Max cluster and low values into the Min cluster. As per our observations, high values represent facial points regions, while low values represent other face regions. This is valid because clutter regions can be seen at non-facial points compared to facial points regions. Therefore, the Max cluster contribute more compared to the Min cluster in case of foreground components. In the same way, for Max and Min clusters of background features, the Min cluster contributes more compared the Max cluster because the STBT gives low values for the objects in the background while high values for smooth regions (dark regions).

At the same time, the number of components of respective clusters also contribute to classification because the number varies according to the contribution of the components. We consider the number of components in respective clusters as weights. In order to increase the discriminative power and to utilize the strength of weights and clusters, the proposed method fuses the Max cluster of foreground components multiplied by its weight with the Min cluster of the background components multiplied by its weight as defined in Eq. (4). This results in feature vector A. In the same way, vector B is obtained for the Max cluster of background components and the Min cluster of foreground components with their weights as defined in Eq. (5). Please note that sometimes, especially for behaviors such as Neuroticism-Sarcastic, Neuroticism-Depression and Psychopathic, an image contains only one face. In this case, the face detection method gives one foreground component. Since we believe that it is a face region, the proposed approach fuses the features extracted from the facial key point region of the single face component with the Min cluster of background components without k-means clustering. This process results in two vectors A and B for the input image.

$$A = \left(max_f \times N_{maxf}\right) + \left(min_b \times N_{min_b}\right) \tag{4}$$

$$B = \left(min_f \times N_{min_f}\right) + \left(max_b \times N_{max_b}\right) \tag{5}$$

where min_f and max_f are the Min and Max clusters for the foreground, and min_b and max_b are the Min and Max clusters for background. N_{min_f}, N_{max_b} and N_{min_b}, N_{max_f} are the weights of Min and Max clusters of foreground and background components, respectively.

Motivated by the method in [19] where a fusion concept is proposed based on the variances of feature vectors to classify dominant information from other information in images, we propose to explore the same fusion for combining two feature vectors A and B of the input image. For each vector, the proposed approach finds variances and the same variances are used to determine weights with respect to the A and B feature vectors as defined in Eqs. (6) and (7), respectively. Finally, the weights are multiplied by respective feature vectors to generate a single feature vector as defined in Eq. (8).

$$W_A = \frac{Var_A}{Var_A + Var_B} \tag{6}$$

$$W_B = \frac{Var_B}{Var_A + Var_B} \tag{7}$$

where Var_A and Var_B denote the variance of the feature vectors of A and B, respectively, and W denotes the weight for the respective feature vectors.

$$F_{final} = [A \times W_A] + [B \times W_B] \tag{8}$$

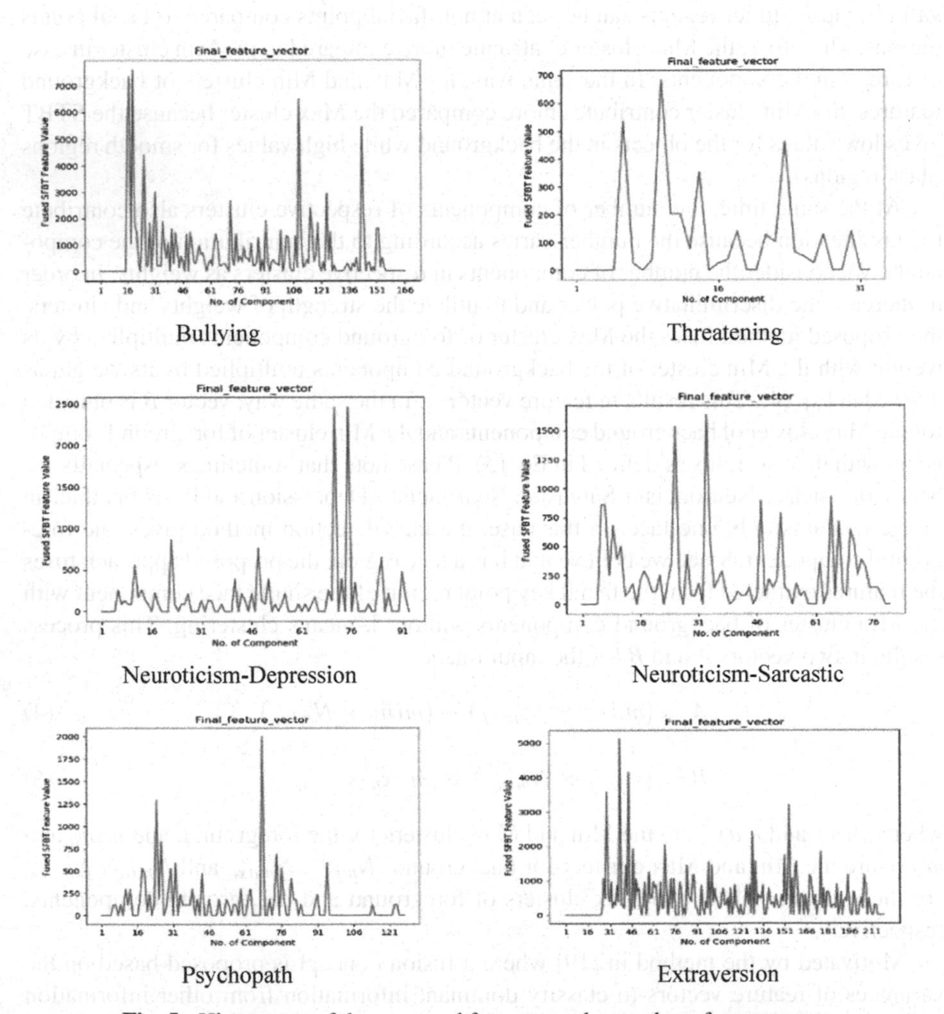

Fig. 5. Histograms of the proposed features vs the number of components

The effect of features for all the six classes can be seen in Fig. 5, where one can see that the behaviors of histograms are unique for each class. For the histograms, the number of components of the fusion results are considered on X axis, and feature values are on Y axis. For intra-class images, the behaviors of the histograms are almost similar for respective classes as we consider the context between foreground and background information. This is the advantage of the proposed method. Since the above feature extraction has the ability to discriminate behavior-oriented social media images, we propose to use SVM. For choosing the samples for training and testing, we follow the standard 10-fold cross-validation procedure in this work.

4 Experimental Results

Since there is no standard database for behavior-oriented social media image classification, we create our own dataset by collecting images from Facebook, Instagram, YouTube and WhatsApp. The classes considered in this work include: Bullying which contains photos of intimidation/teasing, Extraversion (normal) which contains photos of joyful, happy and positive behaviors, Neuroticism-Depression which contains photos of persons that are alone with sad faces, Neuroticism-Sarcastic which contains photos of faces with different expressions, e.g., mocking or cynical, Psychopathic which contains faces of unpredictable, abnormal or violent behaviors/expressions, and Threatening which contains photos of persons shouting or being hostile to others. For each of the six classes, we collected 200 images with different contents, which gives total 1200 images for experimentation. The above dataset is collected irrespective of age and gender from different sources for experimentation.

To measure the performance of the proposed and existing methods, we use Classification Rate (CR) through a confusion matrix for the classification of behavior-oriented social media images. For comparative study, we chose methods which are relevant to the proposed work. The method in [14] explores facial features for abnormal and normal person classification. This method is developed for video and considers the deviation between facial points of the current frame and other temporal frames. Since the proposed work considers individual images, we construct templates for normal and abnormal image classes by averaging the features of facial points of 100 images chosen randomly from respective normal and abnormal classes. We believe that the meaning deviation estimated using facial points of input images and templates is almost same as the deviation estimation of facial points between successive frames in the video. This is valid because the behavior of facial points region for normal and abnormal face images is almost same irrespective of persons. This results in template for normal and abnormal image classes. Therefore, the deviation between input images and templates of respective facial points are passed to an SVM classifier for classification. Similarly, the method in [15] extracts features using moments, N-cut, and conditional random fields from the full images for abnormal and normal behavior classification. Since the proposed work considers individual images, we ignore motion features and use spatial features for experimentation in this work. The main reason to consider the above two methods [14, 15] for comparative studies is that these two methods use general images (not the images posted on social media) for abnormal and normal behavior identification as in the proposed method.

The proposed method involves two key steps, namely, feature extraction using foreground and background components for classification. To assess the contribution of each step, we conduct experiments for the features of foreground and background separately as reported in Tables 1 and 2, respectively. It is observed from Tables 1 and 2 that Classification Rate (CR), which is the mean of diagonal elements of the confusion matrix, of background features (81.8%) is higher than that of the foreground features (81.3%). It is expected because background information provides more components, while foreground information sometimes lose components. It is also observed from Tables 1 and

2 that most misclassifications are with the Bullying class. This shows that the images of the Bullying class share the characteristics of other images. However, when we combine both the foreground and background features (the proposed method), CR is 88.3%, which is higher than that of foreground or background as reported in Table 3. Therefore, we can conclude that foreground and background contribute equally for achieving the best classification rate.

Table 1. CR using only foreground components (in %)

Class	Bullying	Depression	Sarcastic	Psychopath	Threatening	Extraversion
Bullying	**94.5**	0	0	0	0	5.5
Depression	15	**83.5**	0	0	0	1.5
Sarcastic	22	0	**76**	0	0	2
Psychopath	17	0	0	**80**	0	3
Threatening	19.5	0	0	0	**77.5**	3
Extraversion	20.5	0	0	0	0	**79.5**

Table 2. CR using only background components (in %)

Class	Bullying	Depression	Sarcastic	Psychopath	Threatening	Extraversion
Bullying	**94.5**	0	0	0	0	5.5
Depression	15	**83.5**	0	0	0	1.5
Sarcastic	22	0	**76**	0	0	2
Psychopath	17	0	0	**80**	0	3
Threatening	19.5	0	0	0	**77.5**	3
Extraversion	20.5	0	0	0	0	**79.5**

4.1 Experiments for Two Class Classification

To test the performance of the proposed method on two-class classification, namely, normal and abnormal, we consider Extraversion as a Normal class and all the other five classes are considered as Abnormal classes. The results of the proposed and the existing methods are reported in Table 4, where we can see that the proposed method achieves the best CR. This is due to the existing methods [14, 15], which are developed for general images but not the images posted on social media. On the other hand, the proposed method has the ability to extract context features and hence it gives the best classification rate. It is noted that the classification rates of the two classes are higher than those of the six classes. It is evident that for two-class classification, the complexity of the problem reduces compared to 6-class classification.

Table 3. CR of the proposed method (foreground + background features) (in %)

Class	Bullying	Depression	Sarcastic	Psychopath	Threatening	Extraversion
Bullying	**100**	0	0	0	0	0
Depression	10.5	**89.5**	0	0	0	0
Sarcastic	16.5	0	**83.5**	0	0	0
Psychopath	13.5	0	0	**86.5**	0	0
Threatening	13.5	0	0	0	**86.5**	0
Extraversion	13	0	0	0	0	**87**

Table 4. The CR of the proposed method for two classes: Abnormal vs. Normal classes (Extraversion is considered as normal class)

Methods	Proposed Method		Hsu et al. [15]		Tiwari et al. [14]	
Class	Abnormal	Normal	Abnormal	Normal	Abnormal	Normal
Abnormal	**100**	0	**100**	0	**100**	0
Normal	16.5	**83.5**	97	**3**	100	**0**
CR	**91.75%**		51.5%		50%	

4.2 Experiments for Multi-class Classification

For the dataset of 6 classes, quantitative results of the proposed method and existing methods are reported in Tables 3, 5 and 6, respectively. It is noted from Table 3 that the proposed method scores almost consistent results for all the classes. In addition, CR of the proposed method (88.3%) is higher than those of the existing methods, which scores 25.4% and 22.5%, respectively. Therefore, we can conclude that the proposed method is effective, robust and scalable for classification of person behavior-oriented social media images. It is noted from Tables 5 and 6 that the existing methods misclassify images as Extraversion class. This indicates that the existing methods are good for classifying Extraversion images but not abnormal images. The reason for the poor results of the existing methods is the same as the above discussed. It is evident from Fig. 6 that the proposed method misclassifies images as Bullying class. Therefore, there is a scope for the improvement in future.

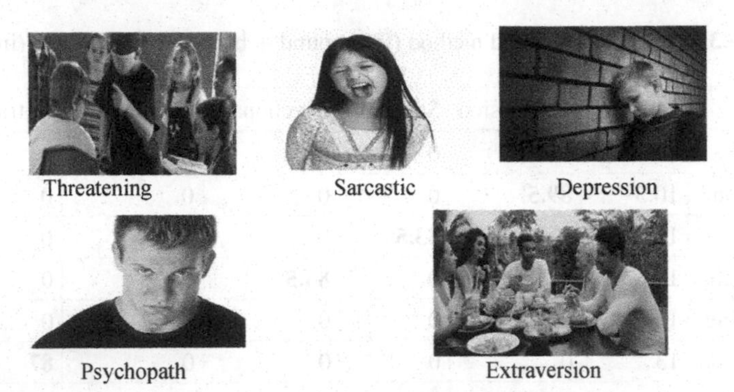

Fig. 6. Examples of unsuccessful classification of the proposed method. All the above images are misclassified as Bullying.

Table 5. The CR of the Hsu et al. [15] for multi-classes (in %)

Class	Bullying	Depression	Sarcastic	Psychopath	Threatening	Extraversion
Bullying	**15**	84.5	0	0	0	0.5
Depression	0	**100**	0	0	0	0
Sarcastic	0	93.5	**6.5**	0	0	0
Psychopath	0	85	0	**15**	0	0
Threatening	0	92	0	0	**8**	0
Extraversion	0	92	0	0	0	**8**

Table 6. The CR of the Tiwari et al. [14] for multi-classes (in %)

Class	Bullying	Depression	Sarcastic	Psychopath	Threatening	Extraversion
Bullying	**6**	92	1	0	0	1
Depression	0	**100**	0	0	0	0
Sarcastic	0	87	**13**	0	0	0
Psychopath	0	92	0	**8**	0	0
Threatening	0	95	1	0	**4**	0
Extraversion	1	94	1	0	0	**4**

5 Conclusion and Future Work

In this work, we have proposed a new method for behavior-oriented social media image classification. The proposed method detects facial points through a face detection method for separating foreground and background components. Our method introduce the Structural Function based Transform (SFBT) features for extracting context information given by foreground and background components. The extracted features are fed to an SVM for classification. Experimental results on the proposed and the existing methods on two as well as multiple classes show that the proposed method is superior to the existing methods in terms of classification rate. However, the proposed method still misclassifies images as Bullying class. Therefore, our future plan is to improve the performance of the proposed method such that it can be suitable for real-time monitoring of posted images on social media.

References

1. Xue, F., Sun, J., Liu, X., Liu, T., Lu, Q.: Social multi-modal event analysis via knowledge-based weighted topic model. J. Vis. Commun. Image Represent. **59**, 1–8 (2019)
2. Roy, S., et al.: Rough fuzzy based scene categorization for text detection and recognition in video. Pattern Recogn. **80**, 64–82 (2018)
3. Nogueria, K., Penatti, O.A.B., Santos, J.A.D.: Towards better exploiting convolutional neural networks for remote sensing scene classification. Pattern Recogn. **61**, 539–556 (2017)
4. Mabrouk, A.B., Zagrouba, E.: Abnormal behavior recognition for intelligent video surveillance systems: a review. Expert Syst. Appl. **91**, 480–491 (2018)
5. Liu, L., Pietro, D.P., Samani, Z.R., Moghadadam, M.E., Ungar, L.: Analyzing personality through social media profile picture choice. In: Proceedings of ICWSM (2016)
6. Majumder, A., Behera, L., Subramanian, V.K.: Automatic facial expression recognition system using deep network-based data fusion. IEEE Trans. Cybern. **48**, 103–114 (2018)
7. Perveen, N., Roy, D., Mohan, C.K.: Spontaneous expression recognition using universal attribute model. IEEE Trans. Image Process. **27**, 5575–5584 (2018)
8. Wang, S., Pan, B., Chen, H., Ji, Q.: Thermal augmented expression recognition. IEEE Trans. Cybern. **48**, 2203–2214 (2018)
9. Prasad, N., Unnikrishnan, K., Jayakrishnan, R.: Fraud detection by facial expression analysis using intel realsense and augmented reality. In: Proceedings of ICICCS, pp. 919–923 (2018)
10. Arru, G., Mazumdar, P., Battisti, F.: Exploiting visual behavior for autism spectrum disorder identification. In: Proceedings of ICMEM, pp. 637–640 (2019)
11. Beeck, K.V., Engeland, K.V., Vennekens, J., Goedeme, T.: Abnormal behavior detection in LWIR surveillance of railway platforms. In: Proceedings of AVSS (2017)
12. Cosar, S., Donatiello, G., Bogorny, V., Garate, C., Otavio, L., Bremond, F.: Toward abnormal trajectory and event detection in video surveillance. IEEE Trans. CSVT **27**, 683–695 (2017)
13. Liu, C.W., Chen, H.T., Lo, K.H., Wang, C.J., Chuang, J.H.: Accelerating vanishing point based line sampling scheme for real time people localization. IEEE Trans. CSVT **27**, 409–420 (2017)
14. Tiwari, C., Hanmandlu, M., Vasikarla, S.: Suspicious face detection based on eye and other facial features movement monitoring. In: Proceedings of AIPR, pp. 1–8 (2015)
15. Hsu, S.C., Chuang, C.H., Huang, C.L., Teng, P.R., Lin, M.J.: A video based abnormal human behavior detection for psychiatric patient monitoring. In: Proceedings of IWAIT, pp. 1–4 (2018)
16. Grover, J., Hanmandlu, M.: The fusion of multispectral palmprints using the information set based features and classifier. Eng. Appl. Artif. Intell. **67**, 111–125 (2018)
17. Farzindar, A., Inkpen, D.: Natural Language Processing for Social Media. Synthesis Lectures on Human Language Techniques. Morgan and Claypool Publishers, San Rafael (2015)

18. Zhang, K., Zhang, Z., Li, Z., Qiao, Y.: Joint face detection and alignment using multi-task cascaded convolutional networks. IEEE Signal Process. Lett. **23**, 1499–1503 (2016)
19. Xu, X., Wang, Y., Chen, S.: Medical image fusion using discrete fractional wavelet transform. Biomed. Signal Process. Control **27**, 103–111 (2016)

Single Image Reflection Removal Based on GAN with Gradient Constraint

Ryo Abiko(✉) and Masaaki Ikehara

Department of Electronics and Electrical Engineering,
Keio University, Yokohama, Kanagawa, Japan
{abiko,ikehara}@tkhm.elec.keio.ac.jp

Abstract. When we take a picture through glass windows, the photographs are often degraded by undesired reflections. To separate reflection layer and background layer is an important problem for enhancing image quality. However, single-image reflection removal is a challenging process because of the ill-posed nature of the problem. In this paper, we propose a single-image reflection removal method based on generative adversarial network. Our network is an end-to-end trained network with four types of losses. It includes pixel loss, feature loss, adversarial loss and gradient constraint loss. We propose a novel gradient constraint loss in order to separate the background layer and the reflection layer clearly. Gradient constraint loss is applied in a gradient domain and it minimize the correlation between the background and reflection layer. Owing to the novel loss and our new synthetic dataset, our reflection removal method outperforms state-of-the-art methods in PSNR and SSIM, especially in real world images.

Keywords: Deep learning · Reflection removal · Image separation · Generative adversarial network

1 Introduction

When taking photographs through transparent material such as glass or windows, undesired reflections often ruin the images. To obtain clear images, users may make dark situation or change the camera position but it is not effective for removing reflections because of the limitation on space. The reflection does not only degrade the image quality but also affects the results of applications such as segmentation. Thus, removing reflections from an image is an important task in computer vision. The example of single-image reflection removal task is shown in Fig. 1.

Separating background layer and reflection layer is an ill-posed problem because the photographing situation is not fixed. The thickness of the glass, the number of the glass, the transparent rate and the reflection rate could be change and we cannot model them in an appropriate manner. To work on this ill-posed problem, many previous methods use multiple input images [1,10,24,25]

S. Palaiahnakote et al. (Eds.): ACPR 2019, LNCS 12046, pp. 609–624, 2020.
https://doi.org/10.1007/978-3-030-41404-7_43

(a) Input image (b) Generated image (c) Reflection layer

Fig. 1. A visualization of single-image reflection removal. (a) is a synthetic input image which includes reflections. (b) is a generated background image of our method and (c) is a reflection layer.

or a video [29]. Inputting multiple images makes the ill-posed problem easier to solve but in actual cases, it is difficult to prepare multiple images so the study of single-image reflection removal is still important. Recently, some methods were proposed to remove reflection without using multiple images [2,11]. In particular, Convolutional Neural Network (CNN) based methods [3,5,7] showed good results in the past few years. Generative Adversarial Networks (GAN) have produced outstanding results in computer vision tasks such as inpainting [32] and super-resolution [15]. Reflection removal is not an exception and GAN-based methods [27,30,33] left good results.

In this paper, we propose a novel single-image reflection removal method based on generative adversarial networks as shown in Fig. 2. To preserve texture information effectively while separating background and reflection layer, four kinds of losses are adopted to train the network. The training loss is composed of pixel loss, feature loss, adversarial loss and gradient constraint loss. We propose a novel loss called gradient constraint loss, which keeps the correlation between background and reflection layer low. Since the background layer and reflection layer have no relevance, it is important not to share the information in these two layers. In addition, feature loss is applied to both background layer and reflection layer so it is possible to separate the image into two layers while retaining the image features. When training the networks, we used several reflection models and applied many conditions to the synthetic reflection image. It leads our network to remove real world reflection which has perplexing conditions.

The contributions of our paper are summarized below:

- We propose a new Gradient Constrained Network (GCNet) for single-image reflection removal. When training our network, we use four types of losses including pixel loss, feature loss, adversarial loss and gradient constraint loss.
- Since the gradient constraint keeps the correlation between background and reflection layer low, the output background layer preserves texture information well and the visual quality is high.
- We applied many kinds of terms to the training dataset, which enable our trained network to remove reflections in many challenging real conditions.

2 Related Work

Since reflection separation is an ill-posed problem, many methods use multiple images [1,9,10,20,21,24,25] or video [29] as an input. Multiple images make the ill-posed problem easier to solve but it is difficult to obtain and additional operation will be required. Thus, single-image reflection removal methods are mainly considered in this paper.

2.1 Optimization Based Methods

Several methods use optimization to suppress the reflection in a single image. To solve an optimization problem, additional prior such as gradient sparsity [2,31] or gaussian mixture models [22] is needed. These methods can suppress reflections effectively when the input image follow the assumption but when the assumption cannot be applied, the result will be catastrophic.

2.2 Deep Learning Based Methods

The first method which use deep convolutional neural networks for reflection removal was proposed by Fan et al. in [7]. Two networks are cascaded and they first predict edges of background layer by using the first CNN. The predicted edge is used for the guide when reconstructing background layer by using the second CNN. Since they only use pixel-wise loss function in the training process, the semantic structure is not considered. In particular, Generative Adversarial Networks (GAN)-based methods have produced outstanding results in reflection removing task, likewise in other computer vision tasks such as inpainting [32] and super-resolution [15]. Zhang et al. proposed PL Net [33] which is trained by loss function composed of feature loss, adversarial loss, and exclusion loss. The network architecture and loss function is tuned to focus on both low-level and high-level image information. The network is weak in processing overexposed images because their training method does not cope with those problem. Yang et al. [30] proposed a network which predicts the background layer and reflection layer alternately. They use L_2 loss and adversarial loss to train the networks. Wei et al. proposed ERR Net [27] which can be trained by misaligned data. The image features which are obtained by pre-trained VGG19 network [23] are used as input data and they are also used in calculating feature loss. Since these two methods do not focus on the correlation between background and reflection layer, they sometimes generate an image with unnatural color tone.

3 Supporting Methods

3.1 Synthetic Reflection Image

In this paper, we denote I as an image with reflections. The background layer is denoted as B and the reflection layer is denoted as R. In this case, I can be modeled as a linear combination of B and R as below:

$$I = B + R. \tag{1}$$

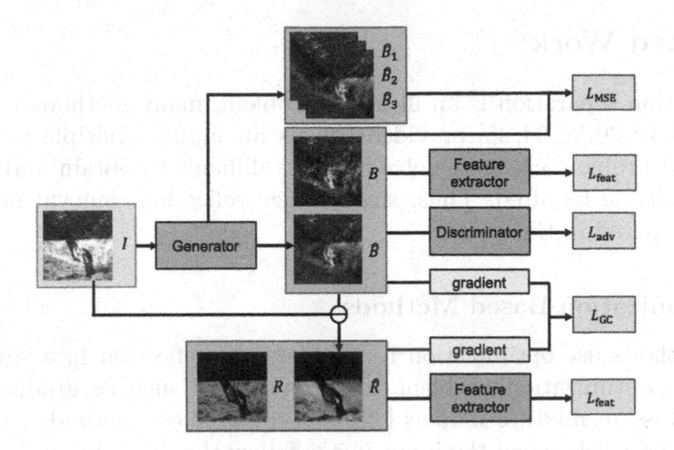

Fig. 2. The overview of our method.

In previous work, several reflection models are used to make R. In our training method, we use three of them. When we denote R_o as an original reflection image, first reflection model can be expressed as:

$$R_1 = \alpha K * R_o, \tag{2}$$

where R_1 is a synthetic reflection layer, K is a Gaussian kernel and α is a reflection rate. Second model can be expressed as:

$$R_2 = \beta K * H * R_o, \tag{3}$$

where R_2 is a synthetic reflection layer, H is a random kernel with two pulses and β is a reflection rate. Applying H represents the ghost effect which is caused by the thickness of the glass [5]. Third model can be expressed as:

$$R_3 = K * R_o - \gamma, \tag{4}$$

where R_3 is a synthetic reflection layer and γ is an amount of shift. In our method, γ is computed as the same way which is described in [7]. Restoring B from I is the final goal of single-image reflection removal methods but it is a difficult problem because solving B from I is an ill-posed problem.

3.2 Generative Adversarial Networks

Generative adversarial networks (GAN) [8] is a learning method which maps noise to an image. Generator G is trained to create a real-like image and discriminator D is trained to judge whether the discriminator input is real or not. When training GAN, min-maximizing process between generator and discriminator is applied and it can be expressed as:

$$\min_G \max_D V(G, D) = \mathbb{E}_x[logD(x)] + \mathbb{E}_z[log(1 - D(G(z)))], \tag{5}$$

where x is an image and z is a noise variable. When GAN is applied to image restoration tasks, z should be deteriorated image. Since GAN is good at solving inverse problem, it has shown remarkable results in image processing such as inpainting [32], colorization [18], denoising [4] and super-resolution [15].

4 Proposed Method

Our method removes reflection from a single image with a trained-based algorithm using GAN. We represent that our GAN based method with gradient constraint can remove reflection effectively. The overview of our method is shown in Fig. 2.

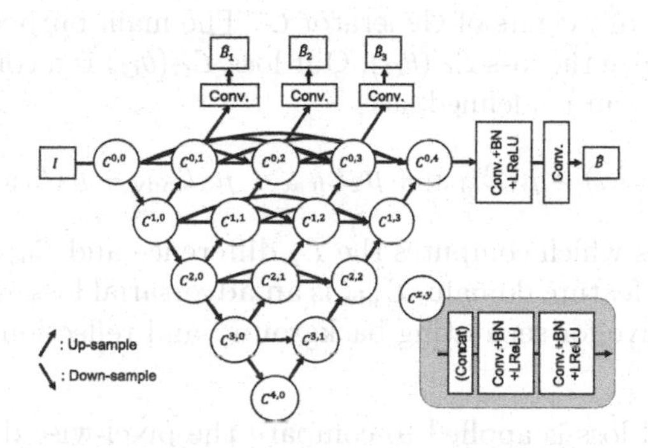

Fig. 3. The architecture of our proposed generator. It is based on UNet++ L^4 [34].

4.1 Network Model

We illustrate the proposed generator architecture in Fig. 3. The network structure of our proposed method is based on UNet++ L^4 [34]. It is a combination of convolutional layer, batch normalization layer [13], leaky ReLU layer [28], max pooling layer and bilinear interpolation layer. Since we adapt deep supervision structure [34], there are four outputs. We use $\hat{B}$ as the main output and the other outputs are used for computing pixel loss. The filter size of the convolutional layers are set to 3×3. The number of the channels in the convolutional layers in $C^{x,y}$ are set to 2^{x+5}.

Our discriminator is composed of the enumeration of convolutional layer, batch normalization layer and leaky ReLU layer. The stride of convolutional layers is set to 2 in every two convolutional layers. Since the final output size of our discriminator is 16×16, L_2 difference is applied to compute the adversarial loss.

4.2 Loss Functions for Generator

In our method, we applied four kinds of losses to separate background and reflection layer effectively. Let G, D, F be generator, discriminator, and feature extractor, respectively. Generated background image $\hat{B}_i$ can be obtained by inputting image I_i into generator G. In our method, we do not estimate reflection layer directly so the reflection layer $\hat{R}_i$ is estimated by subtracting generated background image from the input image. Thus, the estimation of $\hat{B}_i$ and $\hat{R}_i$ can be expressed as:

$$\begin{aligned} \hat{B}_i &= G(I_i; \theta_G) \\ \hat{R}_i &= I_i - \hat{B}_i \end{aligned} \tag{6}$$

where θ_G is the set of weights of Generator G. The main purpose in the training process is to minimize the loss $\mathcal{L}_G(\theta_G)$. Our loss $\mathcal{L}_G(\theta_G)$ is a combination of four kinds of losses and can be defined as:

$$\mathcal{L}_G(\theta_G) = \mu_1 \mathcal{L}_{\text{MSE}} + \mu_2 \mathcal{L}_{\text{feat}} + \mu_3 \mathcal{L}_{\text{adv}} + \mu_4 \mathcal{L}_{\text{GC}}. \tag{7}$$

$\mathcal{L}_{\text{MSE}}$ is a pixel loss which computes the L_2 difference and $\mathcal{L}_{\text{feat}}$ is a feature loss which is applied in feature domain. $\mathcal{L}_{\text{adv}}$ is an adversarial loss and $\mathcal{L}_{\text{GC}}$ is a novel loss which is effective for separating background and reflection layers.

Pixel Loss. Pixel loss is applied to compare the pixel-wise difference between generated image and ground truth image. Since minimizing the mean squared error (MSE) is effective for avoiding vanishing gradient problem in training GAN [17], we use MSE loss function to calculate the pixel loss. Our generator generates four images including one main generated image $\hat{B}$ and three supporting images $\hat{B}_1$, $\hat{B}_2$, and $\hat{B}_3$. $\hat{B}_1$, $\hat{B}_2$, and $\hat{B}_3$ are used only for calculating the pixel loss and it has a good influence in training process [34]. To emphasize the optimization of main generated image, the four output images are weight-averaged when the pixel loss is computed. The additional information is shown in Fig. 3. From the above, our pixel loss is computed by calculating L_2 difference and it is expressed as:

$$\begin{aligned} \hat{B}_{1i} = G_1(I_i; \theta_G), \hat{B}_{2i} &= G_2(I_i; \theta_G), \ \hat{B}_{3i} = G_3(I_i; \theta_G) \\ \mathcal{L}_{\text{MSE}} &= \sum_{i}^{N} || \frac{1}{8}(5 * \hat{B}_i + \hat{B}_{1i} + \hat{B}_{2i} + \hat{B}_{3i}) - B_i ||_2 \end{aligned} \tag{8}$$

where G_1, G_2, G_3 are the part of generator G and B_i is a ground truth background image.

Feature Loss. In the reflection removing task, it is important to preserve the structure of the image. Since the pixel loss cannot optimize the semantic feature of the image, we adopted feature loss in our method. Pretrained VGG-19 network [23] is applied for the feature extracting network and the output from the layer 'conv5_2' is used for the computation. We calculate the L_1 difference between the feature vector of generated image and ground truth image. Since background layer and reflection layer have different image structure, the feature loss is applied to both background and reflection layer. Our feature loss $\mathcal{L}_{\text{feat}}$ is expressed as:

$$\mathcal{L}_{\text{feat}} = \sum_{i}^{N}(||F(\hat{B}_i) - F(B_i)||_1 + ||F(\hat{R}_i) - F(R_i)||_1). \tag{9}$$

Adversarial Loss. It is known that simple CNN-based networks with MSE loss tend to generate blurry and unnatural images. It is because the images generated by those methods are the average of the several natural solutions [15]. To avoid this problem, adversarial loss was proposed in [8]. The adversarial loss is applied to encourage generator to generate images which follows natural image distribution. In the reflection removing task, the deterioration of color tone is a common problem but in our method, applying the adversarial loss restrained this problem. The adversarial loss in our method is expressed as:

$$\mathcal{L}_{\text{adv}} = \sum_{i}^{N} ||1 - D(\hat{B}_i; \theta_D)||_2. \tag{10}$$

Gradient Constraint Loss. The main task in a single-image reflection removal is to separate a single image into two layers including background layer and reflection layer. In most cases, background layer and reflection layer have no correlation so minimizing the correlation between two layers is effective in this task. To minimize the correlation, we applied a novel loss function called gradient constraint loss. It is applied in a gradient domain in order to make the task easier. Our gradient constraint loss is composed of two terms: $\mathcal{L}_{\text{GCM}}$ and $\mathcal{L}_{\text{GCS}}$. $\mathcal{L}_{\text{GCM}}$ is a term to keep the correlation between two layers low and $\mathcal{L}_{\text{GCS}}$ works as a constraint of $\mathcal{L}_{\text{GCM}}$. However, in the early stage of training, we find that the effect of gradient constraint loss is too strong and the network cannot be trained effectively. Thus, the gradient constraint loss is multiplied by the number of epochs in order to keep the effect of the loss low in the early stage of training. Finally, the gradient loss can be described as:

$$\mathcal{L}_{\text{GC}} = (\text{epoch} - 1) * (\mathcal{L}_{\text{GCM}} + \mathcal{L}_{\text{GCS}}). \tag{11}$$

Since the edge information of background layer and reflection layer should be independent, $\mathcal{L}_{\text{GCM}}$ calculates the element-wise product of these two edge layers. $\mathcal{L}_{\text{GCS}}$ is applied for giving a constraint to $\mathcal{L}_{\text{GCM}}$ and it helps network to separate layers effectively. $\mathcal{L}_{\text{GCM}}$ and $\mathcal{L}_{\text{GCS}}$ can be expressed as:

$$\hat{B}_{gi} = \text{Tanhshrink}(\nabla_x \hat{B}_i + \nabla_y \hat{B}_i)$$
$$\hat{R}_{gi} = \text{Tanhshrink}(\nabla_x \hat{R}_i + \nabla_y \hat{R}_i)$$
$$\mathcal{L}_{\text{GCM}} = \sum_{i}^{N} ||\hat{B}_{gi} \odot \hat{R}_{gi}||_1 \tag{12}$$
$$\mathcal{L}_{\text{GCS}} = \sum_{i}^{N} ||(\hat{B}_{gi} + \hat{R}_{gi}) - (\nabla_x I_i + \nabla_y I_i)||_1. \tag{13}$$

The basic idea of minimizing correlation between two layers are proposed in [33] but in our method, we applied a new active function and added a constraint. The main purpose of our gradient constraint loss is to focus on large edges and separate layers effectively. Since the input and ground truth images are normalized into the range $[-2.5, 2.5]$ in order to stabilize the training, the conventional Tanh function is not suitable for our network. In addition, to separate layers by mainly using large edges, we want to reduce the impact of small edge regions. Thus, we applied Tanhshrink function as an activation function. The formula of Tanh and Tanhshrink function can be described as:

$$\text{Tanh}(x) = \frac{\exp(x) - \exp(-x)}{\exp(x) + \exp(-x)}$$
$$\text{Tanhshrink}(x) = x - \text{Tanh}(x). \tag{14}$$

By using Tanhshrink, the robustness against blown out highlights is also obtained. When overexposure is occurred, the structure of the reflection layer will be corrupted with the background layer. In this case, the correlation between background and reflection layer does not become zero. Since Eq. 12 encourage the element-wise product of the gradient layers to be zero, the training will not perform well in this situation. To overcome this problem, Tanhshrink function is effective since it compresses small gradients. Owing to this effect, when Tanhshrink is applied as an activation function, the ground truth of element-wise product layer become close to zero even if overexposure is occurred. This is important when applying Eq. 12 during the training process.

We also apply $\mathcal{L}_{\text{GCS}}$ as a constraint of $\mathcal{L}_{\text{GCM}}$. Since we use Tanhshrink for the activation function, small gradients are compressed into even smaller values. The training process may be affected by this feature when a large gradient is wrongly divided into two small gradients. This problem often occurs when the global tone of the generated image are changed. Thus, we apply $\mathcal{L}_{\text{GCS}}$ in order to help generator to separate images not by deteriorating the color tone but by focusing on the structure of the image (Fig. 4).

The effectiveness of the gradient constraint loss in processing real image is shown in Sect. 5.2 and in Fig. 7.

(a) Ground truth image

(b) Gray-scaled reflection

(c) Color reflection

Fig. 4. A visualization of the types of synthetic reflection.

4.3 Loss Function for Discriminator

Since our method is based on GAN, discriminator has to be trained while generator is trained. The discriminator is trained by minimizing the loss $\mathcal{L}_D(\theta_D)$ and it is described as below:

$$\mathcal{L}_D(\theta_D) = \sum_i^N (||D(\hat{B}_i;\theta_D)||_2 + ||V - D(B_i;\theta_D)||_2), \tag{15}$$

where V is a random valued matrix which follows Gaussian distribution with an average of 1.

4.4 Training Dataset

To create the training dataset, we use PASCAL VOC 2012 dataset [6] which includes 17K images. We exclude grayscale and pale colored images since it affects the training. The images are first resized into 256×256 by using bicubic interpolation. After that, the images are randomly flipped and one image is used for the background layer B and another image is used for the reflection layer R. The background layer image is randomly shifted darker in order to deal with the dark real situations. The color reflection image is randomly converted into grayscale image and blurred with Gaussian filter ($\sigma \in [0.2, 7]$ in the case of grayscale, $\sigma \in [2, 4]$ in the case of RGB) and the tone is modified randomly. The reflection model is selected randomly from Eq. (2)–(4):

$$R = \begin{cases} R1 & \text{with probability } 0.1 \\ R2 & \text{with probability } 0.1. \\ R3 & \text{otherwise} \end{cases} \tag{16}$$

Finally, the synthetic reflection images I are generated by using Eq. (1) and clipped to the range $[0, 1]$.

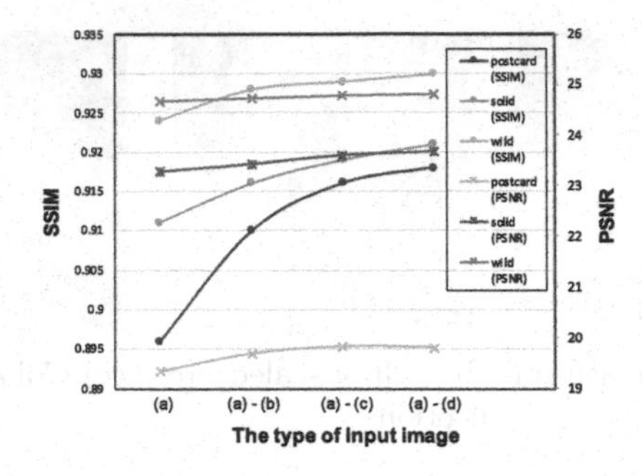

Fig. 5. The comparison of generated results in PSNR and SSIM. (a)–(c) means that we use (a), (b) and (c) as the input image of our network and we average all of the output images to get the final image.

4.5 Training

Since to remove gray-scaled reflection is easier than removing color reflection, we first trained our network by using the images only include gray-scaled reflection. After training the network for 50 epochs, we initialize a new network with the trained weights. The new network is trained for 100 epochs by using the dataset in Sect. 4.4. We train our generator by minimizing Eq. (7) where μ_1, μ_2, μ_3 and μ_4 is set to 2, 1, 0.001 and 0.01, respectively. The implementation of our model is based on PyTorch [19] and Adam solver [14] is used for the optimization. The initial learning rate is set to 0.0002 and the batch size is set to 8. It takes about 40 h to train the network on a single GeForce GTX 1080 Ti.

4.6 Rotate Averaging Process

Since the proposed network is not rotationally invariant, the results will change when the rotated image is processed. In our method, we propose a rotate averaging process, which averages the several output images generated from the rotated input images. Images in SIR^2 benchmark dataset [26] are used for the evaluation. We prepared four kinds of input images: (a) unprocessed image, (b) 90° rotated image, (c) 180° rotated image and (d) 270° rotated image. The comparison of generated results in PSNR and SSIM is shown in Fig. 5. We can see that when we use all the four images, the recovered image quality is the highest. Thus, in our method, we use four rotated images for the input and average all of the output images to get the final image.

5 Experimental Results

In this section, we compare our Gradient Constrained Network (GCNet) with other notable methods, including CEIL Net [7], BDN [30], PL [33], ERR [27]. Images in SIR^2 benchmark dataset [26] are used for the objective evaluation.

We used PSNR [12] and SSIM [12] to assess the performance. PSNR value provides the numerical differences between two images and SSIM value provides the structural differences between two images. Since reflection removal is an ill-posed problem and the transmittance rate cannot be decided, SSIM value is more important to measure the background image quality. We use real images provided by the authors of [7,16] for the subjective evaluation. All the comparison methods are implemented by the original authors.

Table 1. Comparison on restoration result in PSNR and SSIM. Images in SIR^2 benchmark dataset [26] are used for the benchmark.

Dataset	Methods				
	CEIL [7]	BDN [30]	PL [33]	ERR [27]	GCNet (ours)
Postcard	19.98/0.800	20.55/0.849	15.89/0.599	**21.86**/0.867	19.80/**0.918**
Solid	23.49/0.838	23.08/0.837	22.35/0.780	**24.74**/0.860	23.66/**0.921**
Wild	20.84/0.894	22.02/0.826	21.17/0.830	23.87/0.868	**24.80**/**0.930**

5.1 Results

Images in SIR^2 benchmark dataset [26] are used for the benchmark. SIR^2 includes two types of real reflection images: controlled scenes and wild scenes. Controlled scenes are collected in a controlled environment such as in a laboratory. Postcards and daily solid objects are selected as subjects for photography and the datasets includes 199 and 200 images, respectively. Images in wild scenes dataset are collected in a real world out of a lab. Since wild scenes dataset includes complex reflectance, various distance and different illumination, it is more difficult to remove reflections than the controlled scenes dataset.

Table 1 shows the comparison on restoration results in PSNR and SSIM. From Table 1, we can see that our proposed method achieves much higher SSIM than conventional methods in all datasets. In particular, our method shows good results when the wild scenes are processed. This is because our method uses various synthetic reflection image for the training. In addition, the high SSIM shows that the gradient constraint is effective for separating background layer and reflection layer while preserving the image structure. The subjective evaluation is performed in Fig. 6. We can see that BDN and ERR are not good at removing real reflections. CEIL Net and PL can remove some reflections effectively but the global tone of the images is changed.

5.2 The Effectiveness of Our Loss Function and Training Method

When we train our generator, a combination of four kinds of losses is minimized as remarked in Sect. 4.2. In addition, our proposed network is trained in two steps as remarked in Sect. 4.5. To show the effectiveness of our loss function and training method, we trained our network in several situations. As remarked in Sect. 4.5, we train our network by changing the dataset in the first step and

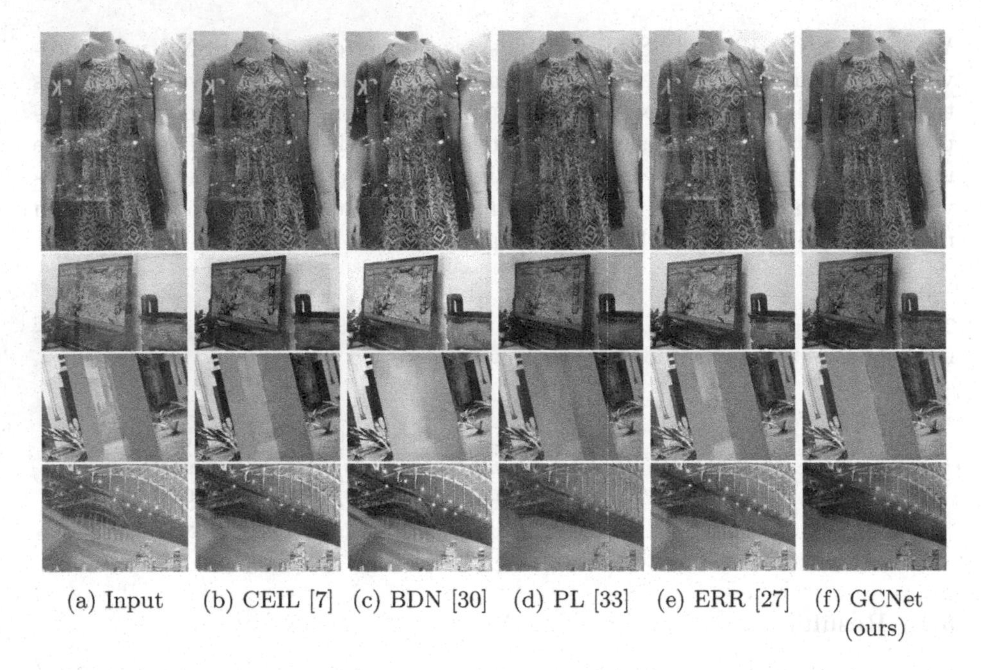

(a) Input (b) CEIL [7] (c) BDN [30] (d) PL [33] (e) ERR [27] (f) GCNet (ours)

Fig. 6. Reflection removal results on real images. Images are from [16,27], and [26]. Best viewed on screen with zoom.

the second step. Hence, we trained our network without dividing in two steps and used single dataset in order to validate the effectiveness of our training method. We show this restoration result as "Single training". We also trained our generator by ablating some loss functions. "No $\mathcal{L}_{\mathrm{GC}}$" indicates that gradient constraint loss is removed from the loss function when the training is performed. "No $\mathcal{L}_{\mathrm{GC}}$, $\mathcal{L}_{\mathrm{feat}}$" indicates that gradient constraint loss and feature loss are removed from the loss function. In the other words, loss function is composed of pixel loss and adversarial loss.

The comparison of the restoration result is shown in Table 2 and Fig. 7. We can see that the proposed training method achieves the highest PSNR and SSIM in most situation. By the visual result of "No $\mathcal{L}_{\mathrm{GC}}$" and "No $\mathcal{L}_{\mathrm{GC}}$, $\mathcal{L}_{\mathrm{feat}}$", we can say that the gradient constraint loss is effective to separate the background layer and the reflection layer. The texture of the background layer should not appear in the reflection layer but in Fig. 7g and i, we can recognize that the texture of the face is appeared in the reflection layer. Hence, we can say that minimizing the correlation between the background layer and the reflection layer by using gradient constraint loss is efficacious. By the result of "Single training", we can say that considering the character of the reflection is meaningful in the stage of training. In other words, when solving challenging problem by using learning-based method, finetuning of the network by considering the behavior of the problem is an effective way to train the network.

Table 2. Comparison on restoration result of our methods. Images in SIR^2 benchmark dataset [26] and synthetic reflection images generated by using Eq. (4) are used for the benchmark. (a) Our proposed method. (b) Trained without pre-training. (c) Trained without using $\mathcal{L}_{GC}$. (d) Trained without using $\mathcal{L}_{GC}$ and $\mathcal{L}_{feat}$.

Dataset	Methods			
	Proposed	Single training	No $\mathcal{L}_{GC}$	No $\mathcal{L}_{GC}$, $\mathcal{L}_{feat}$
Synthetic	**23.45/0.896**	19.82/0.872	19.29/0.867	16.12/0.824
Postcard	19.80/**0.918**	**21.60/0.918**	20.52/0.915	11.68/0.757
Solid	**23.66/0.921**	23.25/0.917	22.62/0.910	15.73/0.817
Wild	**24.80/0.930**	23.70/0.925	22.17/0.908	17.63/0.825

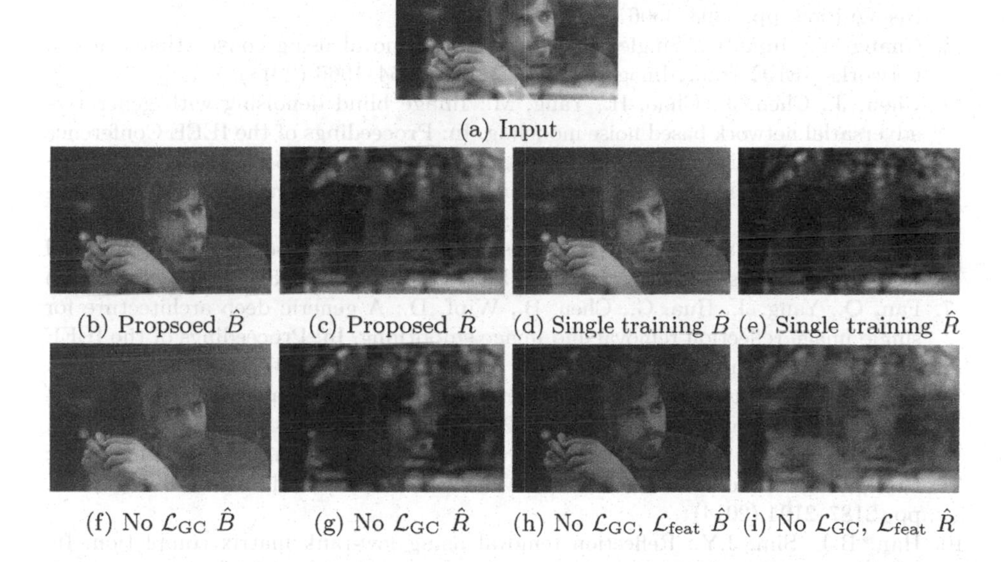

(a) Input

(b) Propsoed $\hat{B}$ (c) Proposed $\hat{R}$ (d) Single training $\hat{B}$ (e) Single training $\hat{R}$

(f) No $\mathcal{L}_{GC}$ $\hat{B}$ (g) No $\mathcal{L}_{GC}$ $\hat{R}$ (h) No $\mathcal{L}_{GC}$, $\mathcal{L}_{feat}$ $\hat{B}$ (i) No $\mathcal{L}_{GC}$, $\mathcal{L}_{feat}$ $\hat{R}$

Fig. 7. Comparison on reflection removal results. Background layers $\hat{B}$ and reflection layers $\hat{R}$ are shown. (a) Input image. (b–c) Our proposed method. (d–e) Trained without pre-training. (f–g) Trained without using $\mathcal{L}_{GC}$. (h–i) Trained without using $\mathcal{L}_{GC}$ and $\mathcal{L}_{feat}$.

6 Conclusion

In this paper, we have proposed a novel Gradient Constrained Network (GCNet) for single-image reflection removal. Four kinds of loss functions are combined to train the network and gradient constraint loss is a new loss function which we have proposed. Since the independence between background layer and reflection layer should be considered, the gradient constraint loss to minimize the correlation between these two layers improves the performance for reflection removal. Owing to the novel loss, new synthetic dataset and training method, our method can remove reflection more clearly than state-of-the-art methods. Both quantitative and qualitative evaluation results show that our proposed network preserves the background textures well and the image structure is not corrupted.

References

1. Agrawal, A., Raskar, R., Nayar, S.K., Li, Y.: Removing photography artifacts using gradient projection and flash-exposure sampling. ACM Trans. Graph. **24**, 828–835 (2005)
2. Arvanitopoulos, N., Achanta, R., Susstrunk, S.: Single image reflection suppression. In: Proceedings of the IEEE Conference on Computer Vision and Pattern Recognition, pp. 4498–4506 (2017)
3. Chang, Y., Jung, C.: Single image reflection removal using convolutional neural networks. IEEE Trans. Image Process. **28**(4), 1954–1966 (2018)
4. Chen, J., Chen, J., Chao, H., Yang, M.: Image blind denoising with generative adversarial network based noise modeling. In: Proceedings of the IEEE Conference on Computer Vision and Pattern Recognition, pp. 3155–3164 (2018)
5. Chi, Z., Wu, X., Shu, X., Gu, J.: Single image reflection removal using deep encoder-decoder network. arXiv preprint arXiv:1802.00094 (2018)
6. Everingham, M., Van Gool, L., Williams, C.K., Winn, J., Zisserman, A.: The pascal visual object classes (VOC) challenge. Int. J. Comput. Vis. **88**(2), 303–338 (2010)
7. Fan, Q., Yang, J., Hua, G., Chen, B., Wipf, D.: A generic deep architecture for single image reflection removal and image smoothing. In: Proceedings of the IEEE International Conference on Computer Vision, pp. 3238–3247 (2017)
8. Goodfellow, I., et al.: Generative adversarial nets. In: Advances in Neural Information Processing Systems, pp. 2672–2680 (2014)
9. Guo, X., Cao, X., Ma, Y.: Robust separation of reflection from multiple images. In: Proceedings of the IEEE Conference on Computer Vision and Pattern Recognition, pp. 2187–2194 (2014)
10. Han, B.J., Sim, J.Y.: Reflection removal using low-rank matrix completion. In: Proceedings of the IEEE Conference on Computer Vision and Pattern Recognition, pp. 5438–5446 (2017)
11. Heydecker, D., et al.: Mirror, mirror, on the wall, who's got the clearest image of them all?-a tailored approach to single image reflection removal. arXiv preprint arXiv:1805.11589 (2018)
12. Hore, A., Ziou, D.: Image quality metrics: PSNR vs. SSIM. In: 2010 20th International Conference on Pattern Recognition, pp. 2366–2369. IEEE (2010)
13. Ioffe, S., Szegedy, C.: Batch normalization: accelerating deep network training by reducing internal covariate shift. arXiv preprint arXiv:1502.03167 (2015)
14. Kingma, D.P., Ba, J.: Adam: a method for stochastic optimization. arXiv preprint arXiv:1412.6980 (2014)
15. Ledig, C., et al.: Photo-realistic single image super-resolution using a generative adversarial network. In: Proceedings of the IEEE Conference on Computer Vision and Pattern Recognition, pp. 4681–4690 (2017)

16. Li, Y., Brown, M.S.: Exploiting reflection change for automatic reflection removal. In: Proceedings of the IEEE International Conference on Computer Vision, pp. 2432–2439 (2013)
17. Mao, X., Li, Q., Xie, H., Lau, R.Y., Wang, Z., Paul Smolley, S.: Least squares generative adversarial networks. In: Proceedings of the IEEE International Conference on Computer Vision, pp. 2794–2802 (2017)
18. Nazeri, K., Ng, E., Ebrahimi, M.: Image colorization using generative adversarial networks. In: Perales, F.J., Kittler, J. (eds.) AMDO 2018. LNCS, vol. 10945, pp. 85–94. Springer, Cham (2018). https://doi.org/10.1007/978-3-319-94544-6_9
19. Paszke, A., et al.: Automatic differentiation in Pytorch (2017)
20. Punnappurath, A., Brown, M.S.: Reflection removal using a dual-pixel sensor. In: Proceedings of the IEEE Conference on Computer Vision and Pattern Recognition, pp. 1556–1565 (2019)
21. Sarel, B., Irani, M.: Separating transparent layers through layer information exchange. In: Pajdla, T., Matas, J. (eds.) ECCV 2004. LNCS, vol. 3024, pp. 328–341. Springer, Heidelberg (2004). https://doi.org/10.1007/978-3-540-24673-2_27
22. Shih, Y., Krishnan, D., Durand, F., Freeman, W.T.: Reflection removal using ghosting cues. In: Proceedings of the IEEE Conference on Computer Vision and Pattern Recognition, pp. 3193–3201 (2015)
23. Simonyan, K., Zisserman, A.: Very deep convolutional networks for large-scale image recognition. arXiv preprint arXiv:1409.1556 (2014)
24. Sinha, S.N., Kopf, J., Goesele, M., Scharstein, D., Szeliski, R.: Image-based rendering for scenes with reflections. ACM Trans. Graph. **31**(4), 100:1–100:10 (2012). https://doi.org/10.1145/2185520.2185596
25. Szeliski, R., Avidan, S., Anandan, P.: Layer extraction from multiple images containing reflections and transparency. In: Proceedings IEEE Conference on Computer Vision and Pattern Recognition. CVPR 2000 (Cat. No. PR00662), vol. 1, pp. 246–253, June 2000. https://doi.org/10.1109/CVPR.2000.855826
26. Wan, R., Shi, B., Duan, L.Y., Tan, A.H., Kot, A.C.: Benchmarking single-image reflection removal algorithms. In: Proceedings of the IEEE International Conference on Computer Vision, pp. 3922–3930 (2017)
27. Wei, K., Yang, J., Fu, Y., Wipf, D., Huang, H.: Single image reflection removal exploiting misaligned training data and network enhancements. In: Proceedings of the IEEE Conference on Computer Vision and Pattern Recognition, pp. 8178–8187 (2019)
28. Xu, B., Wang, N., Chen, T., Li, M.: Empirical evaluation of rectified activations in convolutional network. arXiv preprint arXiv:1505.00853 (2015)
29. Xue, T., Rubinstein, M., Liu, C., Freeman, W.T.: A computational approach for obstruction-free photography. ACM Trans. Graph. (TOG) **34**(4), 79 (2015)
30. Yang, J., Gong, D., Liu, L., Shi, Q.: Seeing deeply and bidirectionally: a deep learning approach for single image reflection removal. In: Ferrari, V., Hebert, M., Sminchisescu, C., Weiss, Y. (eds.) ECCV 2018. LNCS, vol. 11207, pp. 675–691. Springer, Cham (2018). https://doi.org/10.1007/978-3-030-01219-9_40
31. Yang, Y., Ma, W., Zheng, Y., Cai, J.F., Xu, W.: Fast single image reflection suppression via convex optimization. In: Proceedings of the IEEE Conference on Computer Vision and Pattern Recognition, pp. 8141–8149 (2019)

32. Yeh, R.A., Chen, C., Yian Lim, T., Schwing, A.G., Hasegawa-Johnson, M., Do, M.N.: Semantic image inpainting with deep generative models. In: The IEEE Conference on Computer Vision and Pattern Recognition (CVPR), July 2017
33. Zhang, X., Ng, R., Chen, Q.: Single image reflection separation with perceptual losses. In: Proceedings of the IEEE Conference on Computer Vision and Pattern Recognition. pp. 4786–4794 (2018)
34. Zhou, Z., Rahman Siddiquee, M.M., Tajbakhsh, N., Liang, J.: UNet++: a nested U-Net architecture for medical image segmentation. In: Stoyanov, D., et al. (eds.) DLMIA/ML-CDS -2018. LNCS, vol. 11045, pp. 3–11. Springer, Cham (2018). https://doi.org/10.1007/978-3-030-00889-5_1

SSA-GAN: End-to-End Time-Lapse Video Generation with Spatial Self-Attention

Daichi Horita and Keiji Yanai(✉)

The University of Electro-Communications, Tokyo, Japan
{horita-d,yanai}@mm.cs.uec.ac.jp

Abstract. We usually predict how objects will move in the near future in our daily lives. However, how do we predict? In this paper, to address this problem, we propose a GAN-based network to predict the near future for fluid object domains such as cloud and beach scenes. Our model takes one frame and predict future frames. Inspired by the self-attention mechanism [25], we propose introducing the spatial self-attention mechanism into the model. The self-attention mechanism calculates the reaction at a certain position as a weighted sum of the features at all positions, which enables us to learn the model efficiently in one-stage learning. In the experiment, we show that our model is comparable compared with the state-of-the-art method which performs two-stage learning.

Keywords: Video prediction · GAN · End-to-end training · Self-attention

1 Introduction

Human beings predict how objects will move in the near future in daily life. However, how do we predict? Generally, we have gained a visual experience by looking at the relationships between objects interacting in various scenes of life. Based on the wealth of experience and knowledge gained through the experience, we predict the future in a few seconds later. In addition, we utilize the experience and knowledge when we encounter new scenes, and predict future movements. Therefore, predicting future movements plays an important role in intelligent systems and automatic systems as it is necessary to decide and plan how objects will move in the future. To achieve this, we need to train a model that understands how scenes change and how objects move.

Recently, in the field of computer vision, there are many studies using images and videos. In particular, solving the video problems is beneficial for various applications, such as video prediction [5,16], action recognition [12,27], action localization [7,22], video understanding [3,23], and video captioning [14,18]. In unsupervised learning of images, Generative Adversarial Nets (GANs) [1,6] show excellent results, and success in producing high resolution and quality images such as people's faces [13,20]. In contrast, in unsupervised learning of video, there are still difficult problems compared to the field of image generation.

S. Palaiahnakote et al. (Eds.): ACPR 2019, LNCS 12046, pp. 625–638, 2020.
https://doi.org/10.1007/978-3-030-41404-7_44

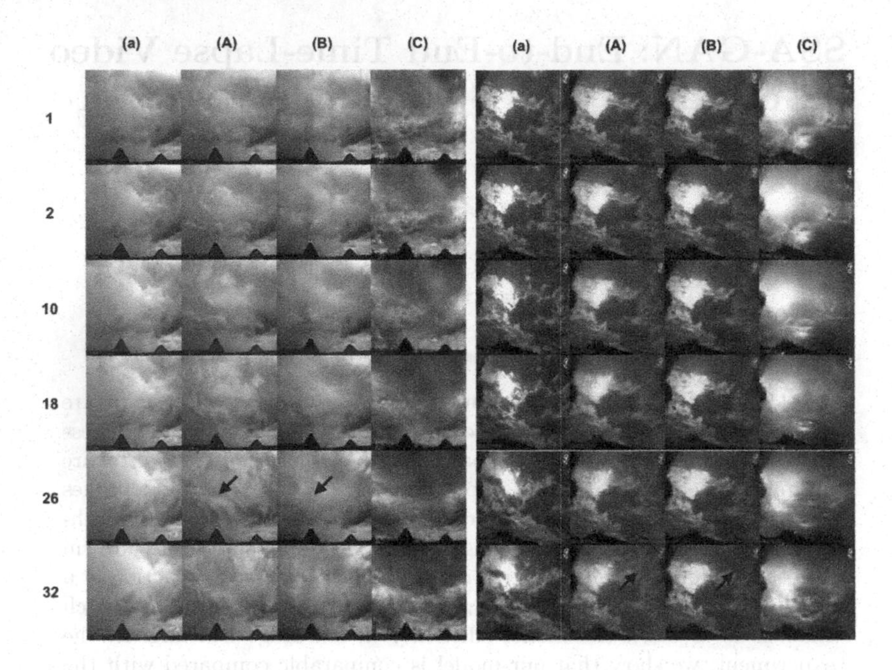

Fig. 1. Some example results of cloud motions generated by our proposed model trained with the cloud time-lapse dataset. From left to right: (a) the ground truth, (A) our model, (B) first stage of MD-GAN [29], and (C) second stage of MD-GAN, respectively. (B) and (C) are generated from official pre-trained models. (Color figure online)

If the model mistakenly learns the physical structure, the predicted motion may include movement which is physically impossible. In addition, the transition speed of scenes and movement speed of objects are also an important factor to make videos natural. Video prediction models have to predict appropriate speeds of objects and scenes as well as generate their appearances. Therefore, video prediction is a challenging problem and still needs much progress. In this paper, our goal is the future frame prediction of the video, which predicts natural movement according with human cognition.

Regarding video generation and prediction by neural networks, the studies started just four years ago. One of the representative works done in the early day is VGAN [26], which is a method that can generate moving images from large-scale unsupervised time-lapse video datasets. However, since VGAN generates the background and foreground of the image separately, the background is fixed, it has a problem that it can not generate the dynamic background. Therefore, it is necessary to learn a model that can generate not only the foreground but also the background at the same time. In addition, one of the biggest problems with video prediction is what we should focus on for training. The variation of motions in videos is very huge. It is unrealistic to generate many kinds of movements of any kind of object with the current techniques. Limiting video domains is a reasonable way to attack this problem. Even if one frame of consecutive moving images is given, it is difficult to set constraints to the model because there are multiple motion options for the future scene transition. As a result, frame prediction in unsupervised learning remains a very difficult problem. To achieve these issues, TemporalGAN [21] uses 2D convolution in the generator to handle temporal and spatial features separately. However, in contrast, we propose a method using 3D convolution to consider the problem of simultaneously dealing with temporal and spatial features.

Regarding learning methods, one-stage approaches are more efficient and elegant than two-stage methods because models are simple in general. However, in recent studies, two-stage training is prevailing. For example, MD-GAN [29] achieves excellent results with two-stages learning to predict future frames. In their method, they generate rough shapes and coarse dynamic movements in the first stage and add detailed appearances and motions to make the final video higher-quality in the second stage.

On the other hand, in this paper, we tackle a challenging problem with only one-stage learning. By introducing the spatial self-attention in the one-stage model in MD-GAN, we show that our model learns adequately in one-stage learning and predict more realistic future frames than MD-GAN, although the proposed model is simpler than existing two-stage methods.

Specifically, we propose the Spatial Self-Attention Generative Adversarial Network (SSA-GAN) model for future frame prediction. Our model consists of a generator and a discriminator. The generator has not a simple encoder-decoder architecture but the architecture like 3D U-Net [4] to avoid generating blurred images caused by losing content details. In addition, the generator has spacial self-attention layers based on [25] after each 3D convolutions and deconvolutions to preserve the spatial physical structure. Given a stationary input frame, the generator predicts future video frames which indicate how it will move in the future. In this way, our model keeps content details and predict as realistic dynamic scene transition as possible. We present a few example frames which are generated by our method and existing method. As shown in Fig. 1, the image frames generated by our model are realistic The red arrow indicates that our model can generate a more detailed image than the model before the introduction of this module.

Major contributions of this paper can be summarized as follows:

1. We propose the Spatial Self-Attention Generative Adversarial Networks (SSA-GAN) for video prediction.
2. We propose the spatial self-attention frameworks based on a self-attention mechanism [25], which enables our model to learn in one-stage while emphasizing spatial correlation between time series.
3. We introduce a model that sufficiently predicts future frames with an one-stage training and our model achieves comparable results with the state-of-the-art method.

2 Related Work

2.1 Generative Adversarial Networks

Generative adversarial networks (GANs) [1,6] have achieved impressive results in image generation [13,20] and image-to-image translation [11,34]. GANs consists of a generator and a discriminator. The discriminator learns to distinguish the produced fake samples from the real ones, while the generator learns to generate fake samples which are not distinguishable from the real ones. In this paper, we also leverage an adversarial loss to learn the mapping to generate future frames as realistic as possible.

2.2 Video Generation

There are two main approaches to the field of video generation using GAN. One of them is to produce plausible videos by limiting video datasets to specific areas such as human faces and poses [2,30,32]. The other is a study to deal without such constraints [21,24,26]. MoCoGAN [24] generates videos efficiently by decomposing the latent space into content and motion subspaces. TemporalGAN [21] uses 2D convolution to generate video in the generator in order to handle temporal and spatial features separately. In this paper, our study is close to the latter because our model generates video frames with free movement without such constraints.

2.3 Video Prediction

Video prediction has tasks different from the video generation and it is one of the major problems in the field of computer vision. In particular, the method of modeling the domain of videos is not unified, but in the existing research, the next frame is inferred using the recurrent neural networks like LSTM. In addition, a well-known approach is to estimate intermediate features of dynamic motion using optical flow and human bones [15,17]. However, our model architecture is different from other methods because our model does not use optical flow and the recurrent neural network. Also, our model is good at handling stationary images as our model learns without their additional information. The cutting-edge study is MD-GAN [29], which predicts future frames from a stationary image. However, there is a big difference between our model and MD-GAN. The first is that [29] learns in two-stage, but our model learns in one-stage. The second is that MD-GAN [29] leverage the Gram matrix to explicitly model dynamic motion, while our model leverages the spatial self-attention to model by the spatial average weight. In other words, our model is added to the self-spatial attention layer to the first stage structure of MD-GAN.

2.4 Self Attention Mechanism

Recently, there are many works that produced remarkable results using the self-attention mechanism [25,28,31]. The self-attention module [25] calculates the response at the position in the feature map by paying attention not only to the surroundings of an attending point but also to all the positions in the image and taking a weighted average of them. Non-local Neural Networks [28] proposes a non-local operator which handles global information in spatial and temporal directions using the self-attention method [25]. Similarly, our spatial self-attention is likewise based on a self-attention mechanism. However, in the case of frame prediction and generation, because all the frames are equally important, only the spatial direction is used without considering the time direction.

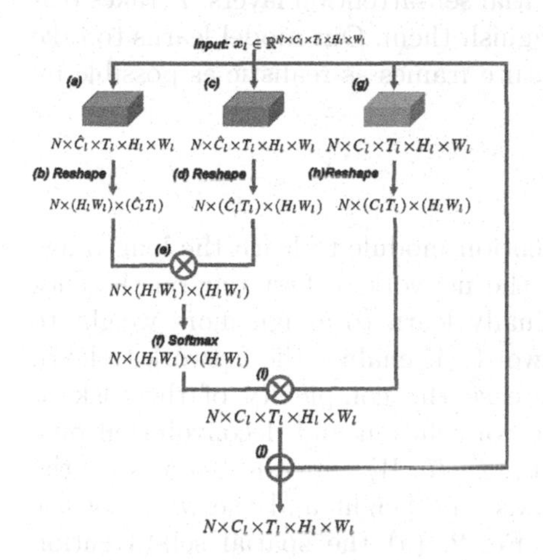

Fig. 2. The overview architecture of our spatial self-attention mechanism. The feature maps are shown as the shape of their tensors. "⊗" denotes a matrix multiplication, and "⊕" denotes element-wise sum. The softmax operations are calculated in each column. The blue box changes the matrix of channel size C_l to $\hat{C}_l$ and outputs it, but the orange box outputs a matrix with the channel size C_l. (Color figure online)

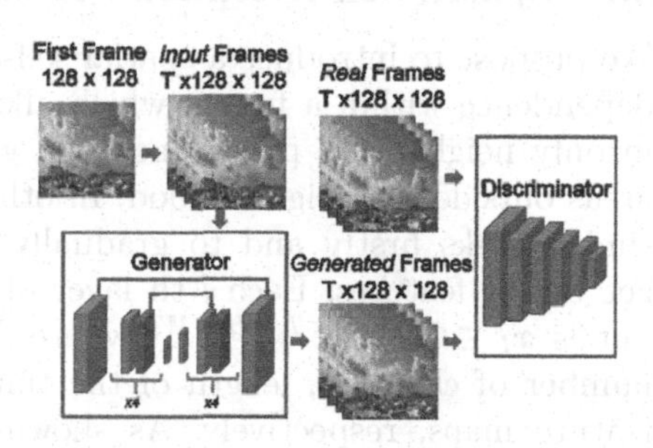

Fig. 3. The overview architecture of our SSA-VGAN. Blue layers indicate 3D convolutional layers and 3D deconvolutional layers, and orange layers indicate the spatial self-attention layers. The generator consists of an architecture like 3D U-Net, preventing skip connection from missing content. The input image is duplicated T times from the first frame of the ground truth. (Color figure online)

3 Our Approach

In this section, we first describe our proposed Spatial Self-Attention GAN, a framework to generate video samples in one-stage learning. Next, we describe the spatial self-attention module. Finally, we describe the objective function to learn our model.

3.1 Spatial Self-Attention GAN

As shown in Fig. 3, SSA-GAN is a generative adversarial network composed of the generator G and the discriminator D. G consists of 3D U-Net [4] with the skip connection which prevents future frames from blurring and losing content information. In addition, G has the spatial self-attention module based on self-attention [25] followed by each convolutional and deconvolutional layers. By using the module, it enables G to efficiently learn spatial features. D consists of the same structure as the encoder part of the generator and has a sigmoid function in the final layer except for the spatial self-attention layers. D takes real and fake videos as input and tries to distinguish them. Our model learns to take a single RGB frame and predict next T future frames as realistic as possible by one-stage learning.

3.2 Spatial Self-Attention Module

We propose to introduce a spatial self-attention module to learn the long-range dependence within a frame, which allows the network to first rely on the cues in only neighboring pixels and then gradually learn to assign more weight to areas outside the neighborhood. In other words, it enables the network to learn simple tasks firstly and to gradually increase the complexity of the task to get better features. Each l-th layer of the convolution and deconvolution output is $\boldsymbol{x}_l \in \mathbb{R}^{N\times C_l\times T_l\times H_l\times W_l}$ where (N, C_l, T_l, H_l, W_l) are the batch size, the number of channels, length of the time axis, the height and the width of the feature maps, respectively. As shown in Fig. 2, (a) the spatial self-attention layer firstly applies the 3D convolution to the input feature $\boldsymbol{x}_l$ and obtains $\boldsymbol{x}_{l_1} \in \mathbb{R}^{N\times \hat{C}_l\times T_l\times H_l\times W_l}$ and (b) resizes to $\hat{\boldsymbol{x}}_{l_1} \in \mathbb{R}^{N\times (H_l W_l)\times (\hat{C}_l T_l)}$. Next, (c) the layer gets $\boldsymbol{x}_{l_2} \in \mathbb{R}^{N\times \hat{C}_l\times T_l\times H_l\times W_l}$ by (a) the same operation and (d) resizes to $\hat{\boldsymbol{x}}_{l_2} \in \mathbb{R}^{N\times (\hat{C}_l T_l)\times (H_l W_l)}$. Furthermore, (e) after calculating the matrix multiplication of $\hat{\boldsymbol{x}}_{l_1}$ and $\hat{\boldsymbol{x}}_{l_2}$, (f) softmax calculate to obtain the attention $\hat{\boldsymbol{X}}_l \in \mathbb{R}^{N\times (H_l W_l)\times (H_l W_l)}$, defined as

$$\hat{\boldsymbol{X}}_l = \frac{\exp(\boldsymbol{X}_l)}{\sum \exp(\boldsymbol{X}_l)}, \text{where } \boldsymbol{X}_l = \boldsymbol{x}_{l_1} \otimes \boldsymbol{x}_{l_2}. \tag{1}$$

This represents the weighted average inside the feature map. Following, (g) the layer applies the 3D convolution to the input feature $\boldsymbol{x}_l$ and obtains $\boldsymbol{x}_{l_3} \in \mathbb{R}^{N\times C_l\times T_l\times H_l\times W_l}$ and (h) resizes to $\hat{\boldsymbol{x}}_{l_3} \in \mathbb{R}^{N\times (C_l T_l)\times (H_l W_l)}$.

Then, (i) the resized output of the layer is $\boldsymbol{o} \in \mathbb{R}^{N\times C_l\times T_l\times H_l\times W_l}$, defined as

$$\boldsymbol{o}_l = \hat{\boldsymbol{X}}_l \otimes \boldsymbol{x}_{l_3}. \tag{2}$$

Finally, (j) the layer multiplies the output o_l scale parameter γ and calculates the sum of it with the input feature map x_l. Therefore, the final output is y_l, defined as

$$\boldsymbol{y}_l = \gamma \boldsymbol{o}_l + \boldsymbol{x}_l, \tag{3}$$

where γ is a parameter initialized with 0. We leverage $\hat{C}_l = C_l$ for all experiments. We describe the role of the parameter γ in Sect. 5.4.

3.3 Spatial Self-Attention GAN Objectives

Our goal is to predict future frames from the stationary image in the one-stage learning model and to predict it as realistically as possible.

Adversarial Loss. In order to make the generated future frame more realistic, we adopt an adversarial loss

$$\mathcal{L}_{adv} = \min_{G} \max_{D} \mathop{\mathbb{E}}_{Y \sim \mathbb{P}_r} [\log D(Y)] + \mathop{\mathbb{E}}_{\bar{X} \sim \mathbb{P}_g} [\log (1 - D(\bar{X}))], \tag{4}$$

where Y is sampled from the data distribution $\mathbb{P}_r$ and $\bar{X}$ is sampled from the model distribution $\mathbb{P}_g$ implicitly defined by $\bar{X} = G(X), X \sim \mathbb{P}_r$. The generator predicts a future frame $\bar{X}$ from a stationary video X to fool the discriminator, while the discriminator tries to distinguish between real and fake frames.

Content Loss. Previous approach [19] indicates that it is more beneficial to combine traditional loss like $L1$ norm and $L2$ norm with the adversarial loss. Although the role of the discriminator remains unchanged, the role of the generator play a role not only to fool the discriminator but also to generate the fake images closer to the real ones. In addition, pix2pix [11] shows that the output images become less blurred at $L1$ norm than $L2$ norm. To ensure that the content of the generated frames is a pattern similar to the content of the real video, the content objective is defined as complementing the adversarial objective,

$$\mathcal{L}_{con} = \mathop{\mathbb{E}}_{Y \sim \mathbb{P}_r, \bar{X} \sim \mathbb{P}_g} [\| Y - \bar{X} \|], \tag{5}$$

where the generator tries to generate a frame similar to Y at the pixel level.

Full Objective. Finally, the loss objectives which optimize the generator and the discriminator are defined as

$$\mathcal{L}_D = -\mathcal{L}_{adv}, \tag{6}$$

$$\mathcal{L}_G = \mathcal{L}_{adv} + \lambda_{con} \mathcal{L}_{con}, \tag{7}$$

where λ_{con} is a hyperparameter that controls the relative importance of content loss compared to the adversarial loss. We leverage $\lambda_{con} = 1$ for all experiments.

4 Implementation Details

As shown in Fig. 3, SSA-GAN is composed of the generator of the 3D U-Net architecture [4] with the skip-connection and the discriminator to prevent future frames from blurring or losing content information. The skip connection is useful as identity mapping [9]. The generator network consists of a six convolution

Table 1. The architecture of the generator.

Layer	Filters	Kernel	Stride	Padding
conv1	32	(3, 4, 4)	(1, 2, 2)	(1, 1, 1)
conv2	64	(4, 4, 4)	(2, 2, 2)	(1, 1, 1)
conv3	128	(4, 4, 4)	(2, 2, 2)	(1, 1, 1)
conv4	256	(4, 4, 4)	(2, 2, 2)	(1, 1, 1)
conv5	512	(4, 4, 4)	(2, 2, 2)	(1, 1, 1)
conv6	512	(2, 4, 4)	(1, 1, 1)	(0, 0, 0)
deconv1	512	(2, 4, 4)	(1, 1, 1)	(0, 0, 0)
deconv2	256	(4, 4, 4)	(2, 2, 2)	(1, 1, 1)
deconv3	128	(4, 4, 4)	(2, 2, 2)	(1, 1, 1)
deconv4	64	(4, 4, 4)	(2, 2, 2)	(1, 1, 1)
deconv5	32	(4, 4, 4)	(2, 2, 2)	(1, 1, 1)
deconv6	3	(3, 4, 4)	(1, 2, 2)	(1, 1, 1)

layer, six transposed convolutions, and skip connection. In addition, the generator has the spatial self-attention module following each convolutional and deconvolutional layers. We apply Batch Normalization [10] to all 3D convolutional layers except the first and last layers, followed by Leaky ReLU and ReLU. The output layer exploits Tanh as an activation function for the generator. We adopt Adam as the optimizer with $\beta_1 = 0.5$ and $\beta_2 = 0.9$. The learning rate is fixed at 0.0002 during learning. We perform one generator update after five discriminator updates as in [8]. We set the batch size to 16 for all experiments. We used the same architecture as [29] regarding the architecture of the generator network, as shown in Table 1. The architecture of the discriminator is the same as the convolutional parts of the generator.

5 Experiments

In this section, we first describe two data sets used in the experiment. Next, we conduct to compare the models learned in those data sets with related studies.

Finally, we discuss the parameters *gamma* that manipulate our proposed spatial self-attention in Eq. 3.

5.1 Datasets

To evaluate the robustness and effectiveness of our approach, we compare our model with other approaches using two datasets, which are the cloud time-lapse dataset [29] and the beach dataset [26].

Cloud Time-Lapse Dataset. We leverage the time lapse video dataset[1] gathered from the Internet [29] for evaluation. The dataset includes over 5,000 time-lapse videos collected from Youtube. The videos are cut into short clips and

[1] https://sites.google.com/site/whluoimperial/mdgan.

Table 2. Quantitative comparison results on the cloud time-lapse dataset. The value range of POS is [0, 1000].

"Which is more realistic?"	POS
Prefer Ours over [29] Stage *I*	871
Prefer Ours over [29] Stage *II*	526
Prefer [29] Stage *I* over Real	286
Prefer [29] Stage *II* over Real	322
Prefer Ours over Real	334

Table 3. Experiment results on the cloud time-lapse dataset by MSE, PSNR, and SSIM. Ours (a) and Ours (b) are models which proposed layers are added to the first and second stages of MD-GAN [29], respectively.

Method	MSE↓	PSNR↑	SSIM↑
[29] *I*	0.0280	23.14	0.5997
[29] *II*	0.0245	23.8529	0.6327
Ours (a)	**0.0238**	**24.3512**	**0.6991**
Ours (b)	0.0259	23.5224	0.6460

include those containing dynamic sky scenes such as the cloudy sky with moving clouds, and the starry sky with moving stars. In addition, the dataset consists of 35,392 training video clips and 2,815 testing video clips each containing 32 frames. However, the original size of each frame is $3 \times 640 \times 360$, and we resize it into a square image size $3 \times 128 \times 128$. We duplicate the first frame of the input video 32 times to make it a static input video. We normalized the inputs by converting the color value to $[-1, 1]$.

Beach Dataset. We leverage the unlabeled video dataset which is released by [26][2], which do not contain any time-lapse video. We divide the dataset of 10% into training data and 90% into evaluation data.

5.2 Experiments on the Cloud Time-Lapse Dataset

In this section, we evaluate the performance of SSA-GAN for a quantitative evaluation. As a baseline model, we adopt MD-GAN, which is the method of performing the highest accuracy using the cloud time-lapse dataset. In addition, we also experiment with our model (a) to learn Stage *I* and our model (b) to learn Stage *II* that introduced our proposed layer at each stage of MD-GAN.

To evaluate whether the predicted future frames is more natural, we compare these models in each pair in the same way as [29]. We prepare 100 pairs of videos according to the five cases shown in Table 2, which is selected randomly from the evaluation dataset. We show ten subjects the pairs of generated video and ask them "which is more realistic?". Then, we count the answers of their evaluation, which means Preference Opinion Score (POS). The results generated from our model randomly appear in either left or right side in the test to get a more reliable evaluation. As shown in Table 2, our model achieved the better results than other models. We demonstrate that the spatial self-attention module generates dynamic cloud motion prediction from all spatial relationships in the image.

[2] http://www.cs.columbia.edu/~vondrick/tinyvideo/.

Table 4. Experiment results on the Beach dataset by MSE, PSNR, and SSIM.

Method	MSE↓	PSNR↑	SSIM↑
RNN-GAN	0.1849	7.7988	0.5143
VGAN	0.0958	11.5586	0.6035
MD-GAN Stage *II*	0.0422	16.1951	**0.8019**
Ours (a)	0.0379	23.6601	0.7320
Ours (b)	**0.0374**	**25.6432**	0.7346

Finally, for each approach, we calculate the Mean Squared Error (MSE), Peak Signal to Noise Ratio (PSNR), and Structural Similarity Index (SSIM) between the full of evaluation datasets. As shown in Table 3, our model (a) shows better performance than other methods.

5.3 Experiments on the Beach Dataset

In this section, we compare our model with MD-GAN, VGAN, and RNN-GAN [33] using the beach dataset in a quantitative evaluation. All models generate 32 future frames and are trained using the adversarial loss. VGAN and RNN-GAN take an image of 64×64 resolution and predict future frames of 64×64 resolution. In addition, MD-GAN takes also the same resolution image to satisfy these conditions. Therefore, for a fair comparison, our model is also adjusted to learning with a 64×64 resolution image. To learn this model, our model was removed the first convolutional and deconvolutional layer so that model can predict future frames of resolution 64×64. All models calculate MSE, PSNR, and SSIM using randomly sampled 1000 videos from the evaluation dataset. As shown in Table 4, our model showed the better scores than the other models regarding PSNR an MSE, although the MD-GAN Stage *II* achieved the best score in SSIM.

5.4 Discussion

We conduct ablation studies to verify the important role of the parameter *gamma* in Eq. 3. The parameter *gamma* is initialized to 0 and is the weight of the spatial self-attention module. Figure 4 shows the difference of the prediction result by (A) existence (B) non existence of gamma parameter for performing qualitative evaluation. In many cases, Method (B) fails to learn motion generation as the red arrows in Fig. 4. The issue is because the spatial self-attention module is affected by over-weighting the entire image. Thus, although the generator generates images with quality that can fool the discriminator, it fails to capture the movement of the cloud. Method (A) overcomes this problem by adjusting the influence while learning the overall weight of our module.

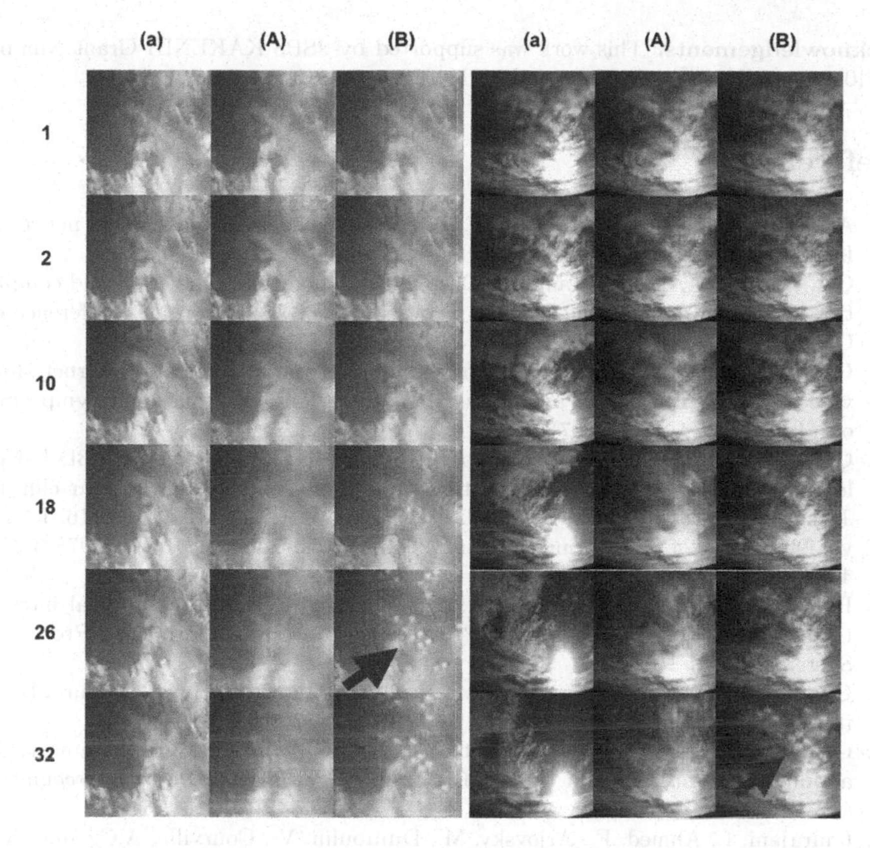

Fig. 4. Some example results of cloud motions generated by our proposed model. From left to right: (a) the ground truth, (A) existence, (B) non existence of *gamma* parameter in Eq. 3, respectively. The red arrow shows an example of failing to capture the movement of the cloud. (Color figure online)

6 Conclusion

We propose SSA-GAN with the spatial self-attention mechanism based on the self-attention. The spatial self-attention mechanism enables the models to represent features of real samples. In addition, the mechanism makes it possible to learn models efficiently in the one-stage of end-to-end learning. We demonstrate that our model achieves comparable results with the state-of-the-art method which performs a two-stage learning and predict future frames as realistically as possible.

However, our proposed model fails to generate cloud motion as much as ground truth video. In the future, we use temporal features to learn the model that can reproduce time-lapse video. More experimental results including generated videos can be seen at http://mm.cs.uec.ac.jp/horita-d/ssagan/.

Acknowledgements. This work was supported by JSPS KAKENHI Grant Number 15H05915, 17H01745, 17H06100 and 19H04929.

References

1. Arjovsky, M., Chintala, S., Bottou, L.: Wasserstein generative adversarial networks. In: International Conference on Machine Learning (ICML) (2017)
2. Cai, H., Bai, C., Tai, Y., Tang, C.: Deep video generation, prediction and completion of human action sequences. In: Proceedings of the European Conference on Computer Vision (ECCV) (2018)
3. Cheng, X., Dale, C., Liu, J.: Understanding the characteristics of internet short video sharing: Youtube as a case study. In: 2012 IEEE International Symposium on Multimedia (ISM) (2007)
4. Çiçek, Ö., Abdulkadir, A., Lienkamp, S.S., Brox, T., Ronneberger, O.: 3D U-Net: learning dense volumetric segmentation from sparse annotation. In: Ourselin, S., Joskowicz, L., Sabuncu, M.R., Unal, G., Wells, W. (eds.) MICCAI 2016. LNCS, vol. 9901, pp. 424–432. Springer, Cham (2016). https://doi.org/10.1007/978-3-319-46723-8_49
5. Finn, C., Goodfellow, I., Levine, S.: Unsupervised learning for physical interaction through video prediction. In: Proceedings of Neural Information Processing Systems (2016)
6. Goodfellow, I., et al.: Generative adversarial nets. In: Proceedings of Neural Information Processing Systems (2014)
7. Gu, C., et al.: AVA: a video dataset of spatio-temporally localized atomic visual actions. In: Proceedings of the IEEE Computer Vision and Pattern Recognition (CVPR) (2018)
8. Gulrajani, I., Ahmed, F., Arjovsky, M., Dumoulin, V., Courville, A.C.: Improved training of Wasserstein GANs. In: Proceedings of the Neural Information Processing Systems (2018)
9. He, K., Zhang, X., Ren, S., Sun, J.: Identity mappings in deep residual networks. In: Proceedings of the European Conference on Computer Vision (ECCV) (2016)
10. Ioffe, S., Szegedy, C.: Batch normalization: accelerating deep network training by reducing internal covariate shift. In: International Conference on Machine Learning (ICML) (2015)
11. Isola, P., Zhu, J.Y., Zhou, T., Efros, A.A.: Image-to-image translation with conditional adversarial networks. In: Proceedings of the IEEE Computer Vision and Pattern Recognition (CVPR) (2017)
12. Jhuang, H., Gall, J., Zuffi, S., Schmid, C., Black, M.J.: Towards understanding action recognition. In: Proceedings of the IEEE International Conference on Computer Vision (ICCV) (2013)
13. Karras, T., Aila, T., Laine, S., Lehtinen, J.: Progressive growing of GANs for improved quality, stability, and variation. In: Proceedings of the International Conference on Learning Representation (ICLR) (2017)
14. Krishna, R., Hata, K., Ren, F., Li, F., Niebles, J.C.: Dense-captioning events in videos. In: Proceedings of IEEE International Conference on Computer Vision (ICCV) (2017)

15. Li, Y., Fang, C., Yang, J., Wang, Z., Lu, X., Yang, M.: Flow-grounded spatial-temporal video prediction from still images. In: Proceedings of European Conference on Computer Vision (ECCV) (2018)
16. Mathieu, M., Couprie, C., LeCun, Y.: Deep multi-scale video prediction beyond mean square error. In: Proceedings of the International Conference on Learning Representation (ICLR) (2016)
17. Ohnishi, K., Yamamoto, S., Ushiku, Y., Harada, T.: Hierarchical video generation from orthogonal information: optical flow and texture. In: Proceedings of the AAAI Conference on Artificial Intelligence (AAAI) (2018)
18. Pan, P., Xu, Z., Yang, Y., Wu, F., Zhuang, Y.: Hierarchical recurrent neural encoder for video representation with application to captioning. In: Proceedings of IEEE Computer Vision and Pattern Recognition (CVPR) (2016)
19. Pathak, D., Krähenbühl, P., Donahue, J., Darrell, T., Efros, A.A.: Context encoders: feature learning by inpainting. In: Proceedings of IEEE Computer Vision and Pattern Recognition (CVPR) (2016)
20. Radford, A., Metz, L., Chintala, S.: Unsupervised representation learning with deep convolutional generative adversarial networks. In: Proceedings of the International Conference on Learning Representation (ICLR) (2016)
21. Saito, M., Matsumoto, E.: Temporal generative adversarial nets. In: Proceedings of the IEEE International Conference on Computer Vision (ICCV) (2017)
22. Shou, Z., Wang, D., Chang, S.: Action temporal localization in untrimmed videos via multi-stage CNNs. In: Proceeding of the IEEE Computer Vision and Pattern Recognition (CVPR) (2016)
23. Srivastava, N., Mansimov, E., Salakhutdinov, R.: Unsupervised learning of video representations using LSTMs. In: International Conference on Machine Learning (ICML) (2015)
24. Tulyakov, S., Liu, M., Yang, X., Kautz, J.: MoCoGAN: decomposing motion and content for video generation. In: Proceedings of the IEEE Computer Vision and Pattern Recognition (CVPR) (2018)
25. Vaswani, A., et al.: Attention is all you need. In: Proceedings of Neural Information Processing Systems (2017)
26. Vondrick, C., Pirsiavash, H., Torralba, A.: Generating videos with scene dynamics. In: Proceedings of the Neural Information Processing Systems (2016)
27. Wang, H., Schmid, C.: Action recognition with improved trajectories. In: Proceedings of the IEEE Computer Vision and Pattern Recognition (CVPR) (2013)
28. Wang, X., Girshick, R.B., Gupta, A., He, K.: Non-local neural networks. In: Proceedings of IEEE Computer Vision and Pattern Recognition (CVPR) (2018)
29. Xiong, W., Luo, W., Ma, L., Liu, W., Luo, J.: Learning to generate time-lapse videos using multi-stage dynamic generative adversarial networks. In: Proceedings of the IEEE Computer Vision and Pattern Recognition (CVPR) (2018)
30. Yang, C., Wang, Z., Zhu, X., Huang, C., Shi, J., Lin, D.: Pose guided human video generation. In: Proceedings of the European Conference on Computer Vision (ECCV) (2018)
31. Zhang, H., Goodfellow, I.J., Metaxas, D.N., Odena, A.: Self-attention generative adversarial networks. arXiv:1805.08318 (2018)
32. Zhao, L., Peng, X., Tian, Y., Kapadia, M., Metaxas, D.N.: Learning to forecast and refine residual motion for image-to-video generation. In: Proceedings of the European Conference on Computer Vision (ECCV) (2018)

33. Zhou, Y., Berg, T.L.: Learning temporal transformations from time-lapse videos. In: Leibe, B., Matas, J., Sebe, N., Welling, M. (eds.) ECCV 2016. LNCS, vol. 9912, pp. 262–277. Springer, Cham (2016). https://doi.org/10.1007/978-3-319-46484-8_16
34. Zhu, J.Y., Park, T., Isola, P., Efros, A.A.: Unpaired image-to-image translation using cycle-consistent adversarial networks. In: Proceedings of the IEEE International Conference on Computer Vision (ICCV) (2017)

Semantic Segmentation of Railway Images Considering Temporal Continuity

Yuki Furitsu[1(✉)], Daisuke Deguchi[1], Yasutomo Kawanishi[1], Ichiro Ide[1], Hiroshi Murase[1], Hiroki Mukojima[2], and Nozomi Nagamine[2]

[1] Nagoya University, Nagoya, Japan
furitsuy@murase.is.i.nagoya-u.ac.jp
[2] Railway Technical Research Institute, Tokyo, Japan

Abstract. In this paper, we focus on the semantic segmentation of images taken from a camera mounted on the front end of trains for measuring and managing rail-side facilities. Improving the efficiency and perhaps automating such tasks are crucial as they are currently done manually. We aim to realize this by capturing information about the railway environment through the semantic segmentation of train front-view camera images. Specifically, assuming that the lateral movement of trains are smooth, we propose a method to use information from multiple frames to consider temporal continuity during semantic segmentation. Based on the densely estimated optical flow between sequential frames, the weighted mean of class likelihoods of corresponding pixels of the focused frame are calculated. We also construct a new dataset consisting of train front-view camera images and its annotations for semantic segmentation. The proposed method outperforms a conventional single-frame semantic segmentation model, and the use of class likelihoods for the frame combination also proved effective.

Keywords: Semantic segmentation · Railway · Optical flow

1 Introduction

Railways are widely spread as a fast and mass transportation means, especially in Japan. Due to its nature, the impact of an accident once it occurs will be humanly, socially, and economically devastating, making the safety of railways a heavily emphasized issue. For such reasons, many rail-side facilities like railway signals, beacons for Automatic Train Stop system (ATS), and so on are installed. At the same time, some rail-side facilities like wire columns need daily maintenance to make sure they do not obstruct the trains' path. However, geological/geometrical positions of such facilities and objects are currently collected manually, which is a time-consuming and expensive task. Therefore, technological improvements in measuring the exact location of rail-side facilities and improving the efficiency of, perhaps fully automating, the maintenance of such facilities are essential.

S. Palaiahnakote et al. (Eds.): ACPR 2019, LNCS 12046, pp. 639–652, 2020.
https://doi.org/10.1007/978-3-030-41404-7_45

To meet such needs, some researches have been performed to apply Mobile Mapping System (MMS) to railways [7]. Dense 3D point clouds can be obtained from an MMS vehicle loaded on a railway bogie. Using such point clouds, it is possible to take close measurements of rail-side facilities like rail positions and station platforms. However, a specially designed and expensive equipment (MMS vehicle) is required in such approach, and also measurements cannot be taken during railway operation hours as a railway bogie must be pulled slowly. Meanwhile, since visible images cannot be taken during night time, texture information will be unavailable for maintenance tasks.

There is also an approach to combine semantic segmentation and 3D reconstruction to obtain a class-labeled 3D map [5]. However, this approach cannot be directly applied to the railway environment since the accuracy of semantic segmentation of such environment is insufficient for practical use.

To tackle this problem, we aim to improve the accuracy of semantic segmentation of the railway environment. We consider using train front-view camera images taken from a camera mounted in front of the driver's seat on a normally operated train. Such cameras can also be used for other purposes like obstacle detection, and also need little cost to introduce as it does not require large scale remodeling of trains or an expansion of ground facilities. Also, some recent trains already are equipped with driving recorders consisting of similar cameras. Combining train front-view cameras and the recent technology of semantic segmentation, a method of recognizing both the class of objects and their locations within an image, we aim to recognize the 3D space of railways including rail-side facilities. Specifically, we project the semantic segmentation result onto a 3D point cloud to obtain a class-labeled 3D map of the railway environment.

Semantic segmentation is a task of allocating labels to each pixel within an image. Many models have been developed for this purpose in recent years, with some prominent examples being the Fully Convolutional Network (FCN) [6], SegNet [1], and DeepLabv3+ [2]. Such state-of-the-art models have recorded high segmentation accuracies on the Cityscapes [3] dataset, consisting of in-vehicle camera images. In our research, we apply this technology to the railway environment.

In particular, we take into account that in sequential railway images, the same object tends to appear continuously and with small movement, and thus use semantic segmentation results of not only the current frame, but frames prior to and after it to better capture the information of objects. Our proposed model enhances the "raw" semantic segmentation outputs of state-of-the-art methods by considering the temporal continuity of such sequential frames using dense optical flow.

Also, to the authors' best of knowledge, there is no dataset available for the semantic segmentation of the railway environment. As a matter of fact, some researches have been performed on recognizing materials of objects that appear around rail tracks using semantic segmentation [4]. However, such research is insufficient for understanding the railway environment as a whole. Therefore, we build a novel dataset consisting of train front-view camera images, and its

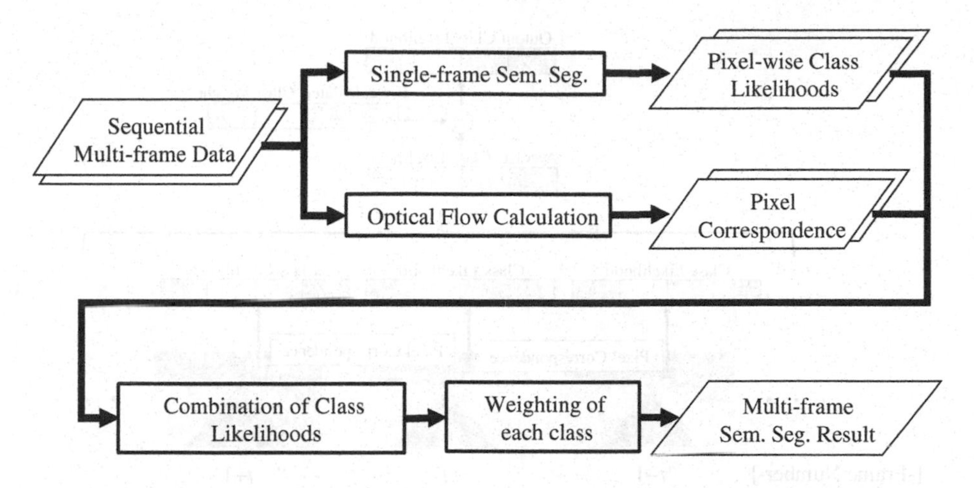

Fig. 1. Diagram showing the overview of the proposed method.

annotations for semantic segmentation. Though the dataset size is comparatively small, we show that the use of the dataset boosts the semantic segmentation accuracy of such environment.

Furthermore, we use the obtained semantic segmentation result and project it onto a 3D map. This map can be obtained by applying Structure from Motion (SfM) to train front-view camera images, and combining it with semantic labels will allow us to understand the railway environment at ease.

To summarize, the main contributions of this paper are:

1. A novel semantic segmentation method targeting train front-view camera images considering temporal continuity of the scene, improving the segmentation accuracy of the railway environment.
2. The construction of a new dataset containing train front-view camera images and its annotations for the semantic segmentation of the railway environment.
3. The automatic construction of a class-labeled 3D map of the railway environment only from monocular camera images to improve the efficiency of the maintenance of railway facilities.

Through experimental analysis, we demonstrate the effectiveness of our proposed framework using a dataset of train front-view camera images and show an improvement on the semantic segmentation of the railway environment.

2 Semantic Segmentation Considering Temporal Continuity

2.1 Overview of the Proposed Method

As trains generally move in one direction, we can observe objects of the same class continuously in sequential frames of train front-view camera images.

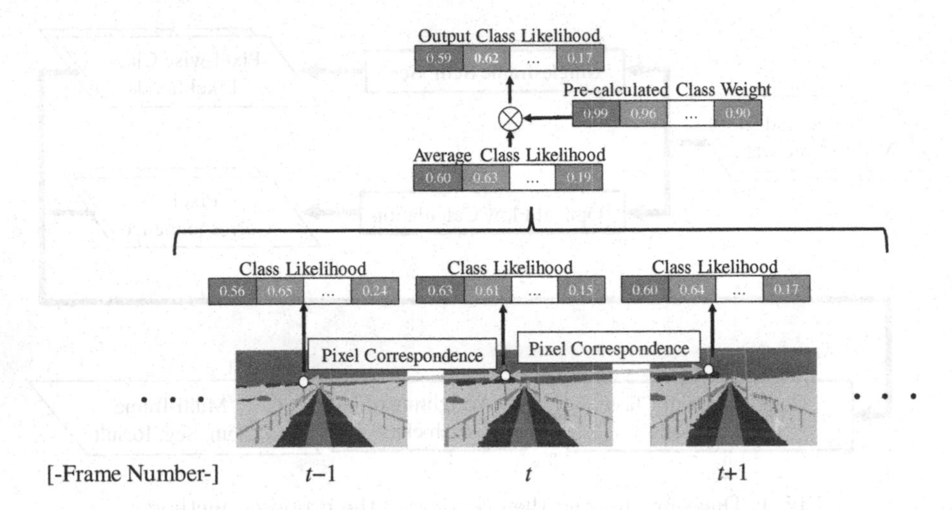

Fig. 2. Pixel-wise processing in the proposed method.

Accordingly, we extend a conventional single-frame semantic segmentation method into a method that considers the temporal continuity of multiple frames to improve the accuracy of semantic segmentation.

In addition, there tends to be far less moving objects in train front-view camera images compared to those taken from vehicles, where there are numerous pedestrians and oncoming vehicles. Furthermore, when compared to vehicles that often make sharp turns, the direction of movement of trains change much more gradually. From such characteristics, we can infer that the optical flow between sequential frames of train front-view camera images can be obtained with high accuracy and density.

When trying to understand the railway environment, the recognition of small rail-side facilities are important. However, as such objects occupy comparatively small areas in an image, their semantic segmentation seems difficult compared to classes with larger areas like "sky" or "building". To cope with this problem, we calculate each classes' pixel occupancy ratio from training data containing annotated ground truths, and set a suitable weight for frame combination beforehand. Based on this weight, we can correct the class likelihood of a small rail-side facility that takes up a small area in an image to improve the detection rate of the corresponding class.

Figure 1 shows the overall procedure of the proposed method. First, we apply conventional single-frame semantic segmentation to train front-view camera images and obtain likelihoods for each class per pixel. Then, we correspond each pixel in sequential frames, and by combining the class likelihoods of the corresponding pixels, output the multi-frame semantic segmentation results.

Figure 2 shows an example of the pixel-wise procedure of the proposed method. First, the optical flow of sequential frames is calculated. Based on this, corresponding pixels from sequential frames are estimated for each pixel within

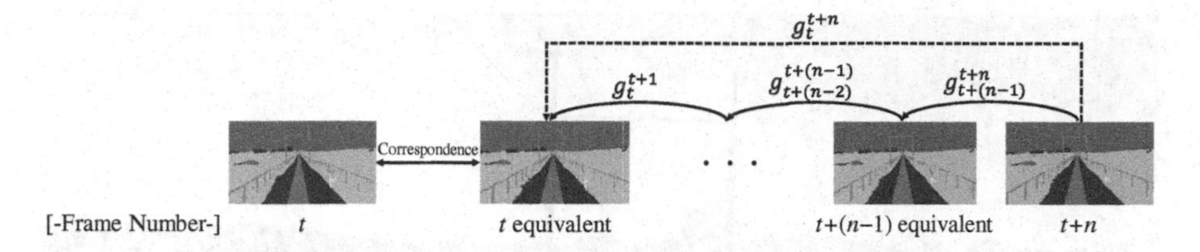

Fig. 3. Procedures for pixel correspondence between the focused frame and the n-th frame.

the focused frame by transforming the sequential frames. Next, we calculate the average class likelihood from single-frame semantic segmentation results of corresponding pixels in sequential frames. For each class value within the likelihood, we then multiply the pre-calculated weight for each class obtained from annotated training data. Finally, we select the class with the highest value within the weighted likelihood and output it as the result.

From here, we explain each step of the framework in detail.

2.2 Semantic Segmentation Using Multiple Frames

Correspondence of Pixels Using Optical Flow

In the proposed method, we correspond pixels between sequential frames by image transformation based on optical flow.

We consider a total of $2N+1$ frames between the $(t-N)$-th frame to the $(t+N)$-th frame when focusing on the t-th frame. From here, when we state that we use "M" frames, M refers to the total number of frames used ($M = 2N+1$).

To start with, we first apply PWC-Net [10] to calculate the optical flow of adjacent frames. PWC-Net is a CNN that enables fast and accurate optical flow calculation with the use of pyramidal processing, warping, and cost volume. For frames taken prior to the focused t-th frame (past frames), we calculate the forward optical flow (f) between two sequential frame pairs. For frames taken after the focused frame (future frames), we similarly calculate the backward optical flow (g) of frame pairs. After applying PWC-Net, pixel-wise dense optical flow ($f_{t-(N-1)}^{t-N}, ..., f_t^{t-1}, g_t^{t+1}, ..., g_{t+(N-1)}^{t+N}$) is obtained.

Next, we calculate pixel correspondences based on the dense optical flow. Figure 3 shows an overview of the process for finding pixel correspondence. To find out the correspondences of pixels to the pixel positions of the focused t-th frame, we transform past and future frames multiple times based on the calculated pixel movement vector (i.e. optical flow). For future frames, using the optical flow between the $(t+k)$-th frame and the $(t+k+1)$-th frame g_{t+k}^{t+k+1}, we can transform the pixel position vector of the $(t+n)$-th frame $\boldsymbol{x}_{t+n}$ to $\hat{\boldsymbol{x}}_{t+n}$ using the equation below, and correspond it with the focused t-th frame.

$$\hat{\boldsymbol{x}}_{t+n} = g_t^{t+n}(x_{t+n}) = g_t^{t+1} \circ g_{t+1}^{t+2} \circ \cdots \circ g_{t+n-2}^{t+n-1} \circ g_{t+n-1}^{t+n}(\boldsymbol{x}_{t+n}) \tag{1}$$

Fig. 4. Example of missing pixels around image rims.

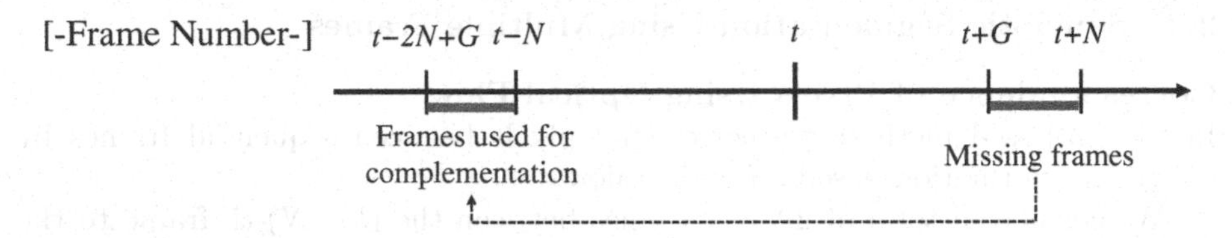

Fig. 5. Example of complementing the information for a missing pixel.

For past frames, similar procedures with the equation shown below can be used to convert the pixel position vector of the $(t-n)$-th frame $\boldsymbol{x}_{t-n}$ to $\hat{\boldsymbol{x}}_{t-n}$ to correspond it with the focused t-th frame.

$$\hat{\boldsymbol{x}}_{t-n} = f_t^{t-n}(x_{t-n}) = f_t^{t-1} \circ f_{t-1}^{t-2} \circ \cdots \circ f_{t-(n-2)}^{t-(n-1)} \circ f_{t-(n-1)}^{t-n}(\boldsymbol{x}_{t-n}) \tag{2}$$

Complementing the Information of Missing Pixels Around Image Rims

When transforming images based on optical flow, some corresponding pixels exit outside future frame image rims where camera vision does not overlap. Figure 4 shows examples of such cases. For such missing pixels, we complement the information with pixels from past frames to maintain the diversity of information and the denominator when calculating the average class likelihood. In particular, when corresponding pixels in future frames are missing from the $(t+G+1)$-th frame, we refer to the pixel information from the $(t-N-1)$-th frame to the $(t-N-(N-G) = t-2N+G)$-th frame to maintain $2N+1$ frames worth of information. An example of this process is show in Fig. 5.

Decision of Labels Using Pixel-Wise Class Likelihoods
Now, we have the pixel position correspondence of multiple sequential frames with regards to the focused frame. Combining this with the semantic segmentation result of each frame, we calculate the pixel-wise class likelihood of the focused frame.

Firstly, we decide the class label c of each pixel within the focused frame from corresponding pixels' class likelihoods as follows.

$$c = \arg\max_{k \in K} \omega_k \ell_k \tag{3}$$

The ω_k used here is a pre-set weight for each of the K classes. To be specific, because areas of rail-side facility classes within an image tend to be small, we pre-calculate the pixel sum ratio of each class labels within training data and decide the weight as follows.

$$\omega_k = 1 - \frac{\beta \alpha_i}{\sum_{k=0}^{K} \alpha_k} \tag{4}$$

Here, parameter α_i refers to the number of pixels that belong to class i in the training data, and β is a constant to adjust the sensitivity.

Meanwhile, $\bar{\ell}_k$, the class likelihood of class k, is calculated as the mean of class likelihoods of M number of frames. To be specific, it is calculated with the equation below referring to corresponding pixels from sequential frames.

$$\bar{\ell}_k = \frac{1}{M} \sum_{n=-N}^{+N} \ell_{t+n}^{k}(\hat{\boldsymbol{x}}_{t+n}) \tag{5}$$

Here, variable $\ell_{t+n}^{k}(\hat{\boldsymbol{x}}_{t+n})$ is the class likelihood of class k at pixel position vector $\hat{\boldsymbol{x}}_{t+n}$ at the $(t+n)$-th frame as calculated in Eq. (2). Thus, the output can be decided with the equation below.

$$c = \arg\max_{k \in K} \frac{\omega_k}{M} \sum_{n=-N}^{+N} \ell_{t+n}^{k}(\hat{\boldsymbol{x}}_{t+n}) \tag{6}$$

3 Experimental Evaluation

3.1 Class Settings of the Railway Environment

In the proposed method, we calculate the class label of each pixel for unannotated train-front view camera images using a neural network trained with small hand-annotated samples of such images. For the neural network, DeepLabv3+ [2] is used. This is a neural network for semantic segmentation, with main features including atrous convolution and encoder-decoder structure. Table 1 shows the list of all semantic segmentation class settings used for this research. This is based on the class structure of the Cityscapes dataset [3], a dataset including semantic segmentation labels of vehicle front-view camera images, and some classes are combined or added to conform to the railway environment.

Table 1. List of all semantic segmentation class settings.

Experimental class label	Corresponding Cityscapes [3] classes
flat	road, sidewalk, parking
building	building
construction	wall, guard rail, bridge, tunnel
fence	fence
pole	pole, pole group
traffic light	traffic light
traffic sign	traffic sign
nature	vegetation, terrain
sky	sky
human	person, rider
vehicle	car, truck, bus
train	train
two-wheel	motorcycle, bicycle
rail	—
track	—
level crossing	—
facility	—
crossing gate	—
overhead facility	—
railway light	—
railway sign	—

3.2 Datasets

In this research, we used images taken from a camera mounted in front of the driver's seat on a normally operated train. These images were taken by the Railway Technology Research Institute with the corporation of East Japan Railway Company. The train operated at a maximum of 85 km/h, which amounts to at most about 40 cm of forward movement as the video was taken at 60 frames per second. Furthermore, in addition to this train front-view camera image dataset, we used the Cityscapes dataset [3] for training neural networks for single-frame semantic segmentation (Fig. 6).

For the training of DeepLabv3+ and the evaluation of the proposed method, we built a dataset from train front-view camera images. First, we manually selected twelve frames from such images ($1,920 \times 1,080$ pixels) so that they contain a variety of different objects like crossings and signs. We then annotated semantic segmentation labels for each pixel in each frame by hand. An example of the annotation can be seen in Fig. 8.

Fig. 6. Annotation example of the train front-view camera image dataset.

3.3 Experiment

We conducted an experiment to evaluate the effectiveness of considering temporal continuity on semantic segmentation of train front-view images. We tested the following four methods:

City-1 Conventional single-frame semantic segmentation using Deeplabv3+, trained using only the Cityscapes dataset.

Rail-1 Conventional single-frame semantic segmentation using Deeplabv3+, pre-trained using the Cityscapes dataset and fine tuned using the train front-view camera image dataset.

Label Majority Multi-frame semantic segmentation that uses sequential frames' pixel correspondence and decides the output label as the majority of the corresponding pixels' class labels.

Weighted Mean Proposed multi-frame semantic segmentation that uses sequential frames' pixel correspondence and decides the output label according to the weighted mean of the corresponding pixels' class likelihoods.

On conducting the experiment, we set the number of frames used to 3, 5, or 7. Since the train front-view camera image dataset consists of only twelve images, we use transfer learning. After pre-training Deeplabv3+ with the Cityscapes dataset, we only initialize the weights between the last and the second to the last layer of the network, and re-train the network using the train front-view camera dataset. We also split the dataset into four sections, and apply cross validation to calculate the mean of the four results. When splitting the dataset, we try to contain each target class evenly within each section.

Table 2. Class IoU and mIoU for each method.

Method	City-1	Rail-1	Label majority			Weighted mean		
Frames used (M)	1	1	3	5	7	3	5	7
flat	*0.0195*	0.0259	0.0204	0.0244	0.0243	0.0363	**0.0776**	0.0578
building	*0.3482*	0.5684	0.5721	**0.5918**	0.5913	*0.5684*	0.5827	0.5845
construction	*0.0899*	0.1653	0.1690	0.1757	0.1807	0.1804	0.1844	**0.2181**
fence	*0.1153*	0.4639	0.4643	0.4590	0.4267	0.4829	**0.4896**	0.4705
pole	*0.3501*	0.4927	0.4905	0.4880	0.4541	**0.5007**	0.4741	0.4120
traffic light	—	—	—	—	—	—	—	—
traffic sign	—	—	—	—	—	—	—	—
nature	*0.5489*	0.7511	0.7531	0.7553	0.7516	0.7565	**0.7597**	0.7576
sky	*0.8945*	0.9258	0.9240	0.9233	0.9211	**0.9269**	0.9262	0.9229
human	—	—	—	—	—	—	—	—
vehicle	0.5246	0.5312	0.5306	0.5294	0.5298	**0.5334**	0.5292	*0.5244*
train	—	—	—	—	—	—	—	—
two-wheel	—	—	—	—	—	—	—	—
rail	*0.0000*	0.8837	0.8854	0.8770	0.8696	0.8869	**0.8887**	0.8853
track	*0.0000*	0.8283	0.8280	0.8253	0.8206	0.8312	0.8365	**0.8376**
level crossing	0.0000	0.0000	**0.0011**	0.0000	0.0000	0.0000	0.0000	0.0000
facility	*0.0000*	0.2185	0.2167	0.2363	0.2326	0.2316	**0.2406**	0.2164
crossing gate	*0.0000*	**0.1449**	0.0721	0.0489	0.0211	0.1305	0.0449	0.0153
overhead facility	*0.0000*	0.3115	0.2977	0.2830	0.2721	**0.3264**	0.3218	0.2894
railway light	*0.0000*	0.4646	0.4612	0.4808	**0.5123**	0.4848	0.5017	0.4936
railway sign	*0.0000*	0.2784	0.2780	0.2227	0.2761	**0.2855**	0.2431	0.2511
mIoU	*0.2041*	0.4917	0.4909	0.4898	0.4795	**0.4977**	0.4930	0.4785

For evaluation, we use mean intersection over union (mIoU) and class intersection over union (class IoU) as metrics. These are calculated using the area ρ_k of a given class k within an image. As our dataset is small in size, after splitting it into four, we may have cases where some classes only appear in the training data, and not appear in the testing data. To cope with such cases, we only calculate the class IoU of the classes that appear in both the training and the target data, and calculate mean IoU as the mean of all such class IoUs.

Table 2 shows the class IoU and the mIoU of the semantic segmentation results for each method. As the result of semantic segmentation considering temporal continuity, we can see that from the baseline single-frame method trained using only the Cityscapes dataset, the mIoU improved by about 28.7% when combining it with the train front-view camera image dataset. The mIoU further improved by about 0.6% in the proposed method which uses M = 3 frames and their class likelihoods. Note that in Table 2, classes without results did not appear in any of the ground-truth data for this experiment (Fig. 7).

Fig. 7. Output examples of semantic segmentation by the proposed method.

4 Discussion and Applications

4.1 Improvement of Semantic Segmentation Accuracy

First, we look at the experimental results shown in Table 2. The mIoU for the semantic segmentation improved from 20.4% in the baseline single-frame method (City-1) to 49.17% in the modified single-frame method (Rail-1); An improvement of 28.7%. This is simply due to the availability of an appropriate training data, since the Cityscapes dataset does not include any image of the railway environment. The mIoU also improved from the modified single-frame method to the proposed method 3 (Weighted Mean) with $M = 3$, by 0.6%, and by 0.1% with $M = 5$ frames. Such results may come from cases in class borders where the conventional single-frame semantic segmentation outputs incorrect labels, but using multiple frames considering temporal continuity helped stabilize the output. However, when $M = 7$, the mIoU actually decreased, which could suggest that simply increasing the number of frames does not correlate to improving the overall accuracy.

When looking at each class IoU result, we can see that the proposed method with $M = 3$, the results improved for all classes that were added for the railway environment other than "crossing gate". As stated before, we weighted classes that take up small areas in training images. This proved to be effective as class likelihoods of classes like "rail" and "track" are boosted. Also, for classes like "nature" and "sky" that take up large areas, there was no significant decrease in the class IoUs, suggesting that the class weights used in the proposed method effectively adjusted the class likelihoods of classes on small objects, while maintaining the results for those on large objects.

$(N + 1)$-th frame $(N + 3)$-th frame

Fig. 8. Visualized flow estimation results corresponding to the N-th frame. Each frame was warped to match the N-th frame using the estimated flow. Red and blue areas indicate pixels where the N-th frame and the warped image differ. (Color figure online)

4.2 Effects of Using Class Likelihoods

The proposed method outperformed a similar method that outputs the majority of class labels, especially in cases where the number of frames used was small. This result may have been influenced by sampling that occurs when images were taken. In particular, boundaries between two classes can become vague due to such sampling. In vague boundaries, both class likelihoods become small. However, by combining pixel information of multiple frames, we can use class likelihoods of corresponding pixels where class boundaries are clearer to estimate the semantic label. In such cases, the proposed method could comprehensively compare all class likelihoods of corresponding pixels and decide an appropriate output class label. Meanwhile, with the use of the majority of class labels, class labels are decided per frame even in vague class boundaries, which lead to a decrease in precision in such cases.

4.3 Accuracy of Flow Estimation

The proposed method used PWC-Net to estimate the flow between multiple frames, and used its output to correspond pixels among the frames. If the pixels were corresponded perfectly, the result scores of the proposed method should at least remain the same when more frames are used. However, the result in Table 2 shows that as more frames were used, the overall mIoU decreased. This result may be due to the limited accuracy of flow estimation. An example of flow estimation is visualized in Fig. 1. The estimated flow of the $(N + 3)$-th frame has more difference to the original frame compared to the flow of the $(N + 1)$-th frame, especially around edges of vertical objects like fences. As the number of used frames increases, flow estimation error will also accumulate, resulting in degraded overall performance of the proposed method. To alleviate the effects of flow estimation on overall IoU, better optical flow estimation methods that consider the characteristics of the railway environment are required.

Fig. 9. Combining SfM with semantic segmentation. (Color figure online)

4.4 Possible Applications to the Railway Environment

With the proposed method, we can obtain pixel-wise label information of images of the railway environment. For the purpose of railway environment recognition, we can apply methods like Structure from Motion (SfM) [9] to reconstruct 3D point clouds from a series of images. Combining the semantic segmentation results of 2D images and such 3D reconstruction enables us to build a class labeled 3D map of the railway environment. An example of such application is shown in Fig. 9. The pink points represent the "rail" class, and the red ones represent the "track" class. Other classes like "pole" (gray), "facility" (dark green), "fence" (light orange), and "nature" (light green) can also be seen. However, the accuracies of both semantic segmentation and SfM reconstruction are still insufficient for practical use. For the semantic segmentation side, using far more training data would likely improve the result. Meanwhile, SfM reconstruction of the railway environment is difficult as a monocular camera can only move forward, and the perspective of the images do not change dramatically. One idea to improve the SfM reconstruction would be to use extra information like semantic labels to post-process the 3D point clouds. This may give us more accurate labeled 3D point clouds, which we can then use for the maintenance of rail-side facilities in real-world environments.

5 Conclusion

In this paper, we proposed a method that improves the accuracy of semantic segmentation on train front-view camera images with the use of multiple frames and their optical flow to consider temporal continuity. Assuming that the lateral movement of trains are smooth, we used information from multiple frames to consider temporal continuity during semantic segmentation. We also constructed a new dataset consisting of train front-view camera images and its annotations for semantic segmentation.

Experimental results show that the proposed method outperforms the conventional single-frame semantic segmentation, as well as the effectiveness of the use of class likelihoods over class labels.

Future works include the mutual improvement of both semantic segmentation and SfM reconstruction accuracy, as well as experimenting the proposed method using a larger train front-view camera dataset.

Acknowledgement. Parts of this research were supported by MEXT, Grant-in-Aid for Scientific Research.

References

1. Badrinarayanan, V., Kendall, A., Cipolla, R.: SegNet: a deep convolutional encoder-decoder architecture for image segmentation. IEEE Trans. Pattern Anal. Mach. Intell. **39**(12), 2481–2495 (2017)
2. Chen, L.-C., Zhu, Y., Papandreou, G., Schroff, F., Adam, H.: Encoder-decoder with atrous separable convolution for semantic image segmentation. In: Ferrari, V., Hebert, M., Sminchisescu, C., Weiss, Y. (eds.) ECCV 2018. LNCS, vol. 11211, pp. 833–851. Springer, Cham (2018). https://doi.org/10.1007/978-3-030-01234-2_49
3. Cordts, M., et al.: The cityscapes dataset for semantic urban scene understanding. In: Proceedings of the 2016 IEEE Conference on Computer Vision and Pattern Recognition, pp. 3213–3223, June 2016
4. Gibert, X., Patel, V.M., Chellappa, R.: Material classification and semantic segmentation of railway track images with deep convolutional neural networks. In: Proceedings of the 2015 IEEE International Conference of Image Processing, pp. 621–625, September 2015
5. Kundu, A., Li, Y., Dellaert, F., Li, F., Rehg, J.M.: Joint semantic segmentation and 3D reconstruction from monocular video. In: Fleet, D., Pajdla, T., Schiele, B., Tuytelaars, T. (eds.) ECCV 2014. LNCS, vol. 8694, pp. 703–718. Springer, Cham (2014). https://doi.org/10.1007/978-3-319-10599-4_45
6. Long, J., Shelhamer, E., Darrell, T.: Fully convolutional networks for semantic segmentation. In: Proceedings of the 2015 IEEE Conference on Computer Vision and Pattern Recognition, pp. 3431–3440, June 2015
7. Niina, Y., Oketani, E., Yokouchi, H., Honma, R., Tsuji, K., Kondo, K.: Monitoring of railway structures by MMS. J. Jpn. Soc. Photogramm. Remote Sens. **55**(2), 95–99 (2016). https://doi.org/10.4287/jsprs.55.95
8. Ronneberger, O., Fischer, P., Brox, T.: U-Net: convolutional networks for biomedical image segmentation. In: Proceedings of the 2015 International Conference on Medical Image Computing and Computer-Assisted Intervention. pp. 234–241, November 2015
9. Schonberger, J.L., Frahm, J.M.: Structure-from-motion revisited. In: Proceedings of the 2016 IEEE Conference on Computer Vision and Pattern Recognition, pp. 4104–4113, June 2016
10. Sun, D., Yang, X., Liu, M.Y., Kautz, J.: PWC-Net: CNNs for optical flow using pyramid, warping, and cost volume. In: Proceedings of the 2018 IEEE Conference on Computer Vision and Pattern Recognition, pp. 8934–8943, June 2018

Real Full Binary Neural Network for Image Classification and Object Detection

Youngbin Kim(✉) and Wonjun Hwang

Department of Computer Engineering, Ajou University, Suwon, South Korea
{dudqls1994,wjhwang}@ajou.ac.kr

Abstract. We propose Real Full Binary Neural Network (RFBNN), a method that can reduce the memory and compute power of Deep Neural Networks. This method has similar performance to other BNNs in image classification and object detection, while reducing computation power and memory size. In RFBNN, the weight filters are approximated as a binary value by applying a sign function; we apply real binary weight to the whole layer. Therefore, RFBNN can be efficiently implemented on CPU, FPGA and GPU. Results of the all experiments show that the proposed method works successfully on various task such as image classification and object detection. All layers in our networks are composed of only {1, −1}, and unlike the other BNN, there is no scaling factor. Compared to recent network binarization methods, BC, BWN and BWRN, we have reduced the memory size and computation costs, but the performance is the same or better.

Keywords: Binary weight network · Quantization · Image classification and object detection

1 Introduction

Deep Neural Networks (DNNs) have achieved high performance in many fields such as Computer Vision, Speech recognition, Natural Language Processing, and so on. DNNs often requires a lot of parameters and high complexity. However, it needs to portability and real time performance. To solve this problem, many researchers focus on low rank decomposition [20, 24], network pruning [21–23], design compact network [8–10, 18] and low bit quantization [1, 3–5]. Among them, low bit quantization is the most essential study to apply deep network to embedded devices in the emerging Internet-of-Things (IoT) domain.

There are many works that use low-bit quantization to reduce the model parameters or even computation power in DNNs. In particular, binary weight filters instead of using full-precision weights filters have been reduced 32× memory savings and convolutions can be estimated by only addition and subtraction (without multiplication), resulting in ~2× speed up. In addition, binarization both input and weight filters allow use of XNOR operations, allowing convolution operations ~58× speed up (Table 1).

In this paper, we propose a simple and efficient low-bit network by binarizing whole weights and even remove scaling factor in BNNs. We aim to design an efficient BNNs

S. Palaiahnakote et al. (Eds.): ACPR 2019, LNCS 12046, pp. 653–662, 2020.
https://doi.org/10.1007/978-3-030-41404-7_46

Table 1. Comparison of Binary Neural Network architectures. All BNNs are composed of binary weight, but the weight filter of the first layer is full-precision except ours. Most BNNs borrow the common strategy called "straight through estimator" (STE) for updating the parameters.

Network	Weight	1st layer	Scaling factor	STE	Clipping	Activ
DCNNs	32-bits	32-bits	No	No	No	32-bits
BinaryNet	1-bit	32-bits	Yes	Yes	Weights & Gradients	1-bit
Xnor-Net [3]	1-bit	32-bits	Yes	Yes	Gradients	1-bit
BWN [3]	1-bit	32-bits	Yes	Yes	Gradients	32-bits
BWRN [5]	1-bit	32-bits	Yes	No	Gradients	32-bits
DoReFa-Net [4]	1-bit	32-bits	Yes	Yes	Gradients	≥1-bit
Ours	1-bit	1-bit	No	Yes	Gradients	32-bits

that has high accuracy and reduces memory and time complexity. We demonstrate that our way of BNNs is efficient by comparing performance and memory with other BNNs in image classification and object detection.

In Real Full Binary Neural Network all the weight values are composed of only $\{1, -1\}$. We even binarize the weight filter of 1st layer. As a result, RFBNN is 32$\times$ memory saving than full-precision networks. In addition, we remove the operation that multiplies the binary weight by scaling factor. Scaling factor plays an important role in approximate binary weight filters. In BNNs, however, it is more important to train by using the characteristics of the "straight through estimator" (STE) [2] than to approximate the weight filter using a scaling factor. All the weight values are binary and remove scaling factor, convolutions can be computed by addition and subtraction instead of a multiplication. This result we achieve 2$\times$ speed up. RFBNN can fit into the portable devices and embedded applications.

In general, BNNs experiments on simple networks like [14, 13]. Our Experiments show that RFBNN can apply on complex network like [7]. And we apply not only image classification task but also object detection task. Our main contributions are:

- We propose real binary weight $\{1, -1\}$ that reduce computation power while maintain accuracy. We remove the scaling factor to approximate the filters, but overcome the accuracy degradation using STE.
- We also binarize the weight filter of 1st layer to save memory than other BNNs. We use full precision weight to prevent loss of image features. First, train full precision model and fine tune RFBNN model.
- RFBNN is applicable to various DNN tasks besides image classification. Experiments show that RFBNN can apply on object detection task and get good performance.

2 Related Work

2.1 Design Efficient Model

Our goal is to design a model that reduces parameters and computational costs while preserving accuracy. GoogLeNet [8] and SqueezeNet [9] design a small network by replacing 3×3 convolutional kernel with 1×1 convolutional kernel. SqueezeNet has been shown to achieve $\times 50$ reduction in parameter size. Xception [10] and MobileNet [18] use depth-wise separable convolution to reduce computation power. MobileNet factorize a standard convolutional into a depth-wise convolution and 1×1 convolution called a point-wise convolution. ShuffleNet [11] propose channel shuffle, which achieves $\times 13$ speed up over AlexNet while maintaining accuracy. ResNet [7] also reduced the size of the model using a bottleneck structure. Recently, DNNs has been studied more effectively for efficient network design for mobile applications and embedded systems. However, only the design of the model structure is limited. In this paper, we design an efficient model using Quantized Neural Network.

2.2 Quantized Neural Network

Recently, Quantized Neural Network has become a necessity for applying deep learning models to mobile system or embedded systems. The first successful Quantized Neural Network is BinaryConnect [1]. They propose to quantize full precision weights using sign function. During the forward and backward path, they train deep neural networks with binary weights $\{-1, +1\}$. In weights update step, [1] employ [2] for gradient clipping and weight clipping. They did not work quantizing the activation function.

Previously, [1] applied the network only to small datasets such as MNIST, CIFAR-10 and SVHN, but [3] showed high performance even for large datasets such as ImageNet. They quantized the weight filter and input image. They approximated the binary weight and binary input by multiplying the scaling factor. By binarizing the input image, they able to use the bit operations, resulting in convolution operations that were $58\times$ faster and $32\times$ memory savings. [4, 5] improves [3]. [4] proposed a bit width activation function. It allows for low bit backpropagation as well. [4] obtained higher accuracy by using more bits than binary. [5] applied binary weights to a wide residual network. When approximating the binary weight, [3] is multiplied by a scaling factor for each channel, and [5] is multiplied by a scaling factor for each layer. [5] constructed a faster and more efficient Quantized Neural Network by reducing multiply operations.

Later in [6], describes how to effectively train Quantized Neural Network using [2]. They show gradient and weight clipping are only required the final stage of the training step and training a full-precision model first and fine-tune is more efficiently. They also suggested for efficient training of Binary models using ADAM for optimizing the objective and reducing the averaging rate in batch normalization layers. They can be achieved easily and found the best accuracy in training (Fig. 1).

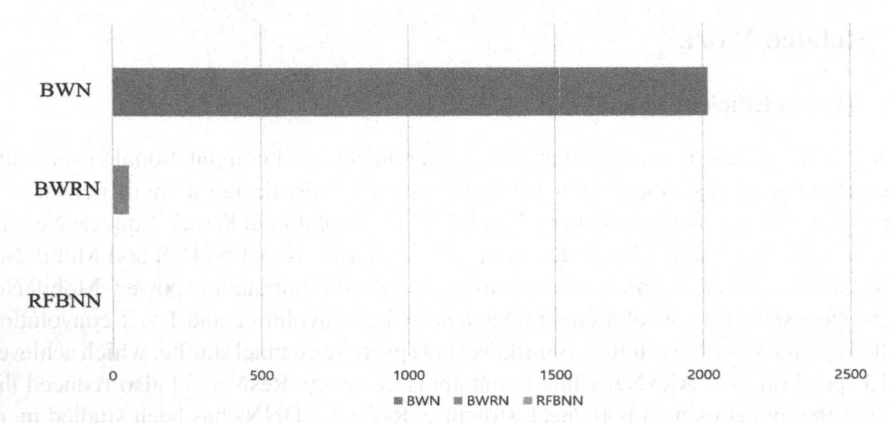

Fig. 1. Number of float scaling factors in ResNet56. RFBNN does not require float scaling factor multiplication. BWN calculate float scaling factors for each output channel and BWRN calculate float scaling factors for each layer.

3 Real Full Binary Neural Network

In this section we detail our formulation of Real Full Binary Neural Network, a method to train neural network with binary weights. Then we present details of our network. Finally, we analyse the computation power and memory size of the proposed model.

3.1 Binary Weight Filters

In order to efficiently train the Binary Neural Network, it is necessary to remove unnecessary operations. Recent Binary Neural Networks multiply weight filters by scaling factors to approximate weight filters.

In Binary-Weight-Networks, the filters are approximated with binary values. BWN introduces a real-valued scaling factor $\alpha \in \mathbb{R}^{+}$ along with B_i to approximate the full-precision weight W_i. They solve optimization problem by $\mathrm{J(B,}\ \alpha) = \|\mathrm{W} - \alpha\mathrm{B}\|^2$. They need to calculate scaling factor α for each output channel in each layer.

$$\mathrm{I} * \mathrm{W} \approx (\mathrm{I} \oplus B)\alpha \text{ and } \alpha = \frac{1}{d}\sum\nolimits_{j=1}^{d}\left|W_i^j\right| \tag{1}$$

Ternary-Weight-Networks are approximated with ternary value vector $\{-1, 0, 1\}$. TWN also multiply binary filters by scaling factors and 16× memory saving. It solves the optimization problem in the same way as BWN.

$$B_i^t = \begin{cases} +1\ if\ W_i > \Delta \\ 0\ if\ W_i \leq \Delta \\ -1\ if\ W_i < -\Delta \end{cases} \text{ and } \Delta = \frac{0.7}{d}\sum\nolimits_{j=1}^{d}\left|W_i^j\right| \text{ and } \alpha = \frac{1}{|I_\Delta|}\sum\left|W_i^j\right| \tag{2}$$

Binary Wide Residual Network is similar to the BWN method, but their scaling method is faster and less complex. They use the initialization method of He [12] for binarization. Their scaling method multiplies each layer.

$$B_i = \sqrt{\frac{2}{F_i^2 C_{i-1}}} \text{sign}(W_i) \tag{3}$$

RFBNN constructs binary filters by applying only sign function to the full-precision weight filters. Our weight filters are Eq. 4. Scaling factors approximate binary weight filters to full-precision weight filters. Figure 2 depicts our simple convolution weight filters creation process.

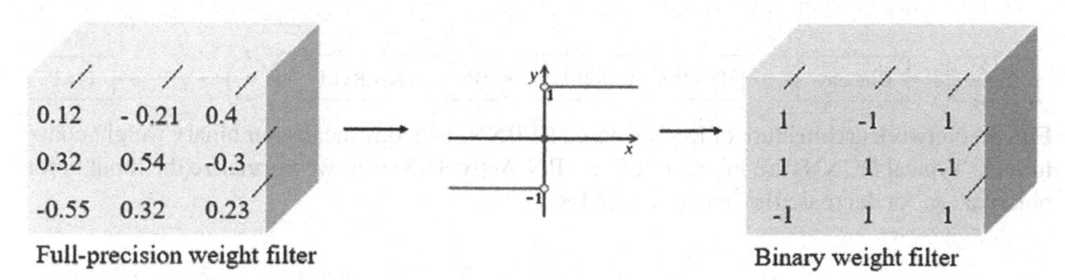

Fig. 2. The process of binarizing a convolution weight filter. We borrow sign function to binarize the weight filters.

$$B_i = \text{sign}(W_i) \tag{4}$$

We maximize BNNs training performance using STE instead of approximating the weight filters. STE preserves the gradient values and clips the gradient when the absolute value of the weight element is large, invoking the saturation effect. Equation 5 propagates gradient through hard tanh function.

$$\frac{\partial B}{\partial w} = w 1_{|w| \leq 1} \tag{5}$$

Therefore, when STE is applied to BNNs, parameter variations are too small and parameters can be updated slowly. For updating the parameters, we use full-precision weights. Our backward gradient of sign function is Eq. 6.

$$\frac{\partial C}{\partial W} = \frac{\partial C}{\partial B} \cdot w 1_{|w| \leq 1} \tag{6}$$

And we also binaries the weight filter of 1st layer to save memory. We use full-precision weight to prevent loss of image features. First, we train full precision models and fine tune RFBNN model. When fine tuning with RFBNN, learning rate is made smaller and the parameter is updated slowly. This training method helps the model converge faster and recover some accuracy.

3.2 Network Architecture

In image classification, we design a network architecture based ResNet. The difference from the existing ResNet is that it normalizes before passing through the convolution filters. When applying the normalization function first, there lead to less quantization error because of data to hold zero mean [3]. And we also replace the fully connected layer with global average pooling for reduce parameter size. Our network architecture is shown in Fig. 3.

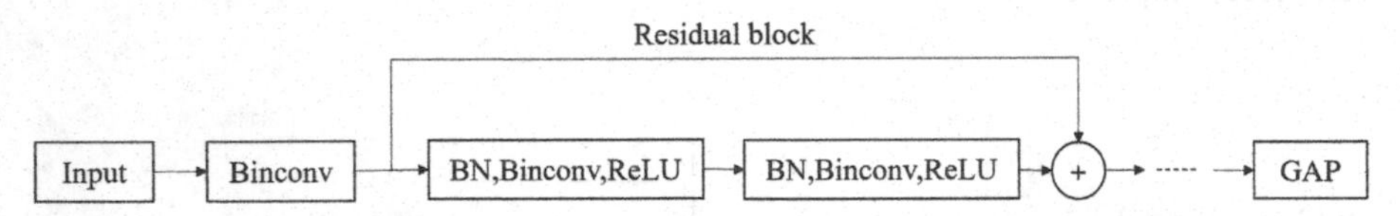

Fig. 3. Network architecture of ResNet based RFBNN. Binconv means our binary weight convolutions. Typical DCNNs are in order of Conv-BN-Activ. However, we normalize the input before binarization for decrease the image feature loss.

We present object detection experiment based on YOLO 9000 [15] network. Many real time detection methods have been proposed such as Faster R-CNN [16], SSD [17], YOLO 9000, and YOLOv3 [25]. We borrow the darknet19 and Tiny YOLO models of the smaller and faster YOLO 9000 to build the network architecture.

4 Experiments

In this section, we describe our experimental results. We apply the RFBNN method for image classification and object detection. To evaluate the performance of our RFBNN, we perform image classification on CIFAR-10 and CIFAR-100 dataset. We evaluate ResNet in our experiments. We compare our method with two works on BNNs; BWN and BWRN. In object detection experiments, we use PASCAL VOC dataset for evaluate our method. For all experimental studies, RFBNN reduces parameter and computational cost while preserving accuracy.

4.1 Image Classification

To validate the proposed method, we first evaluate our method on the benchmark image classification dataset, i.e., CIFAR-10 and CIFAR100 [19]. CIFAR-10 and CIFAR-100 consist of 50,000 training images and 10,000 test images with 32×32pixel color images. The only difference between Cifar-10 and Cifar-100 is the number of classes: 10 and 100 classes, respectively. We apply basic data augmentations for CIFAR-10,100 datasets. For instance, we use randomly cropped, zero padding with 4pixels, normalize and random horizontal flipping.

We implement our codes based on the PyTorch and TorchVision framework and make training and testing on Nvidia Titan Xp GPU. We make full experiments comparison between DCNNs, BWN, BWRN and RFBNN. We compare the results of DCNNs, BWN,

BWRN and RFBNN on ResNet. In this paper, the network is trained with SGD solver with momentum 0.9, weight decay 0.0005 and batch size of 128. The initial learning rate is set to 0.01, and it is decayed by a factor of 0.1 at 120, 200, 240, 280 epoch and terminate training at 320 epoch. We train a full-precision model first and fine-tune it in to RFBNN.

Table 2 shows the results on CIFAR-10 and CIFAR-100 datasets. In CIFAR-10, the BNNs model showed a 1%–2% error rates increase over DCNNs. However, in CIFAR-100, the error rates increase by 2%–4%. These result show that BNNs is less accuracy in complex datasets. And we also present that the accuracy of the RFBNN is similar to or higher than the accuracy of other BNNs. In particular, for the RFBNN-resnet20 model, CIFAR-10 improved 1.18% over BWRN-resnet20 and 3.86% for CIFAR-100. Hence our approach is an effective model that maintains accuracy and reduces memory size and computational complexity.

Table 2. Comparison of DCNNs, BWN, BWRN, RFBNN top-1 error rates on the CIFAR-10 and CIFAR-100 datasets. We implemented all the methods in PyTorch.

Dataset	CIFAR-10				CIFAR-100			
Layers	DCNNs	BWN	BWRN	**RFBNN**	DCNNs	BWN	BWRN	**RFBNN**
20	8.42%	10.96%	11.71%	**10.53%**	32.62%	38.42%	40.47%	**36.61%**
32	7.46%	9.32%	10.08%	**9.63%**	31.47%	34.31%	35.54%	**34.05%**
44	7.16%	9.02%	9.71%	**8.95%**	29.62%	32,74%	33,58%	**32.70%**
56	6.96%	8.13%	8.60%	**8.59%**	28.90%	31.57%	31.98%	**31.49%**
110	6.61%	7.32%	8.52%	**7.47%**	27.81%	29.61%	30.31%	**29.59%**

4.2 Detection Result

In object detection, the proposed method is evaluated on Pascal VOC 2007 dataset (4,952 images) and trained on Pascal VOC 2007 + 2012 (16,551 images). All input images are 416×416. We experimented with detection base on YOLO 9000. Here we used darknet 19 and Tiny YOLO network. Darknet19 is a 19-layer network architecture similar to VGG model, and Tiny YOLO network is small in memory size and fast, but not as good performance. We apply BWN, RFBNN method to darknet19, Tiny YOLO for evaluate our proposed method.

When training the network, we use the pre-trained model, which is fine-tune over the Pascal VOC dataset, as a darknet19 and Tiny YOLO. And we proceeded to train under the same condition as the existing YOLO 9000. In the evaluation phase, we use the mean average precision (mAP).

Figure 4 presents Tiny YOLO image detection results and RFBNN + Tiny YOLO image detection results. Comparing the two results, there was no significant performance difference on the example images. At the bottom of the Fig. 4, RFBNN + Tiny YOLO have some false detection. As shown in Table 3, shows object detection results compared to full-precision, BWN and RFBNN. BWN and RFBNN have reduced the model size by 30–32 times compared to full-precision model but have reduced 6–10 mAP. Our proposed RFBNN had smaller memory size than BWN and had some performance improvement. These results indicate that the proposed method has reduced computational complexity and memory size compared to other BNNs but the performance is similar or better.

Tiny YOLO RFBNN + Tiny YOLO

Fig. 4. Detection examples on images with Tiny YOLO and RFBNN + Tiny YOLO. We show detections with confidence higher than 0.5.

Table 3. Results of object detection on Pascal VOC 2007. We show mAP and model size results. In all experiments, input images size is 416 × 416. We measure the average precision of each class when the intersection over union (IoU) of the bounding box is 0.5.

Layer	Full-precision	BWN	RFBNN
Darknet19	76.8 (194 MB)	69.36 (6.46 MB)	70.75 (6.04 MB)
Tiny YOLO	57.1 (60 MB)	47.82 (2 MB)	48.23 (1.89 MB)

5 Conclusion

In this paper, we introduced the effective RFBNN that reduces memory size and computation power while maintaining or improving performance. We proposed a way to train without scaling factor in BNNs and designed the network by binarizing the first layer. We were able to construct simpler network than existing BNNs by fine-tuning full-precision weight and taking advantage of STE. Experiment results on CIFAR show that the proposed method outperforms the other BNNs. We applied our method to the YOLO 9000 to prove it effectiveness in object detection. In this experiment, we reduce 32× memory savings and offer the possibility of loading DNNs into embedded platform with limited memory. We expect that our approach proves the usefulness of design DNNs in many applications.

Acknowledgments. This research was supported by the MSIT(Ministry of Science and ICT), Korea, under the ITRC(Information Technology Research Center) support program(IITP-2018-2018-0-01431) supervised by the IITP(Institute for Information & communications Technology Promotion).

References

1. Courbariaux, M., Bengio, Y., David, J.P.: Binaryconnect: training deep neural networks with binary weights during propagations. In: Advances in Neural Information Processing Systems (NIPS) (2015)
2. Bengio, Y., Léonard, N., Courville, A.: Estimating or propagating gradients through stochastic neurons for conditional computation. arXiv preprint arXiv:1308.3432 (2013)
3. Rastegari, M., Ordonez, V., Redmon, J., Farhadi, A.: XNOR-Net: ImageNet classification using binary convolutional neural networks. In: Proceedings of the European Conference on Computer Vision (ECCV) (2016)
4. Zhou, S., Wu, Y., Ni, Z., Zhou, X., Wen, H., Zou, Y.: DoReFa-Net: training low bitwidth convolutional neural networks with low bitwidth gradients. In: Proceedings of the IEEE Conference on Computer Vision and Pattern Recognition (CVPR) (2016)
5. McDonnell, M.D.: Training wide residual networks for deployment using a single bit for each weight. In: International Conference of Learning Representation (ICLR) (2018)
6. Alizadeh, M., Fernández-Marqués, J., Lane, N., Gal, Y.: An empirical study of binary neural networks' optimization. In: International Conference of Learning Representation (ICLR) (2019)
7. He, K., Zhang, X., Ren, S., Sun, J.: Deep residual learning for image recognition. In: Proceedings of the IEEE Conference Computer Vision and Pattern Recognition (CVPR) (2016)
8. Szegedy, C., et al.: Going deeper with convolutions. In: Proceedings of the IEEE Conference on Computer Vision and Pattern Recognition (CVPR) (2015)
9. Iandola, F.N., Moskewicz, M.W., Ashraf, K., Han, S., Dally, W.J., Keutzer, K.: SqueezeNet: AlexNet-level accuracy with 50x fewer parameters and <0.5MB model size. arXiv preprint arXiv:1602.07360 (2016)
10. Chollet, F.: Xception: deep learning with depthwise separable convolutions. arXiv preprint arXiv:1610.02357 (2016)
11. Zhang, X., Zhou, X., Lin, M., Sun, J.: ShuffleNet: an extremely efficient convolutional neural network for mobile devices. In: Proceedings of the IEEE Conference on Computer Vision and Pattern Recognition (CVPR) (2018)
12. He, K., Zhang, X., Ren, S., Sun, J.: Delving deep into rectifiers: surpassing human-level performance on ImageNet classification. In: Proceedings of the IEEE International Conference on Computer Vision (ICCV) (2015)
13. Simonyan, K., Zisserman, A.: Very deep convolutional networks for large-scale image recognition. arXiv preprint arXiv:1409.1556 (2014)

14. Krizhevsky, A., Sutskever, I., Hinton, G.E.: Imagenet classification with deep convolutional neural networks. In: Advances in Neural Information Processing Systems (NIPS) (2012)
15. Redmon, J., Farhadi, A.: YOLO9000: better, faster, stronger. In: Proceedings of the IEEE Conference on Computer Vision and Pattern Recognition (CVPR) (2017)
16. Ren, S., He, K., Girshick, R., Sun, J.: Faster R-CNN: towards real-time object detection with region proposal networks. In: Advances in Neural Information Processing Systems (NIPS) (2015)
17. Liu, W., et al.: SSD: single shot multibox detector. In: Proceedings of the European Conference on Computer Vision (ECCV) (2016)
18. Howard, A.G., et al.: Mobilenets: efficient convolutional neural networks for mobile vision applications. arXiv preprint arXiv:1704.04861 (2017)
19. Krizhevsky, A.: Learning multiple layers of feature from tiny images. Technical report (2009)
20. Denton, E.L, Zaremba, W., Bruna, J., LeCun, Y., Fergus, R.: Exploiting linear structure within convolutional networks for efficient evaluation. In: Advances in Neural Information Processing Systems (NIPS) (2014)
21. Anwar, S., Sung, W.: Compact deep convolutional neural networks with coarse pruning. arXiv preprint arXiv:1610.09639 (2016)
22. Li, H., Kadav, A., Durdanovic, I., Samet, H., Graf, H.P.: Pruning filters for efficient ConvNets. In: International Conference of Learning Representation (ICLR) (2017)
23. Molchanov, P., Tyree, S., Karras, T., Aila, T., Kautz, J.: Pruning convolutional neural networks for resource efficient inference. In: International Conference of Learning Representation (ICLR) (2017)
24. Wen, W., Wu, C., Wang, Y., Chen, Y., Li, H.: Learning structured sparsity in deep neural networks. In: Advances in Neural Information Processing Systems (NIPS) (2016)
25. Redmon, J., Farhadi, A.: YOLOv3: an incremental improvement. In: Proceedings of the IEEE Conference on Computer Vision and Pattern Recognition (CVPR) (2018)

Progressive Scale Expansion Network with Octave Convolution for Arbitrary Shape Scene Text Detection

Shi Yan[1], Wei Feng[2,3], Peng Zhao[1], and Cheng-Lin Liu[2,3](✉)

[1] School of Computer Science and Technology, Anhui University, Hefei, China
{shi.yan,zhaopeng_ad}@ahu.edu.cn

[2] National Laboratory of Pattern Recognition (NLPR), Institute of Automation of Chinese Academy of Sciences, Beijing 100190, China
{wei.feng,liucl}@nlpr.ia.ac.cn

[3] School of Artificial Intelligence, University of Chinese Academy of Sciences, Beijing 100049, China

Abstract. Scene text detection is a challenging problem due to the image cluttering and high variability of text shape. Many methods have been proposed for multi-oriented and arbitrary shape text detection, in which the storage and computation costs of deep neural networks are still concerns. In this paper, we first introduce Octave Convolution into scene text detection for enlarging the receptive fields and reducing the spatial redundancy of networks. Then we combine Octave Convolution with a state-of-the-art arbitrary shape text detector PSENet, which predicts different scale of kernels for each text instance. Experimental results on several benchmarks show that the proposed method can improve both detection performance and speed in detecting multi-oriented and arbitrary shape texts. Furthermore, our method achieves state-of-the-art performances on these benchmarks.

Keywords: Scene text detection · Curved text · Octave Convolution · PSENet

1 Introduction

Text detection from natural scene images has attracted intensive attention in recent years, due to the potential of wide applications and the multitude of technical challenges. Except for the challenges of complex backgrounds and illumination change which exist in generic object detection, scene text detection also suffers from the challenges of variable aspect ratios, orientation, and arbitrary shape. Some examples are shown in Fig. 1. To cope with these challenges, many scene text detectors, based on deep neural networks (DNNs), try to improve

This work is supported by the National Natural Science Foundation of China (NSFC) Grants 61721004, 61733007 and 61602004.

S. Palaiahnakote et al. (Eds.): ACPR 2019, LNCS 12046, pp. 663–676, 2020.
https://doi.org/10.1007/978-3-030-41404-7_47

performance by enlarging the receptive fields. Some methods try to use a deeper backbone network to improve the performance, but this will slow down the inference speed of the detector. The recently proposed PSENet [27] is an example which tries to enlarge the receptive fields by deepening the backbone network for improving the performance. Alternatively, some methods try to change the way of convolution to enlarge the receptive fields. For example, Textboxes [11] modifies convolutional kernels to get larger receptive fields. Some methods [12,30] take Deformable Convolution [2] as an integral part of them to get flexible receptive fields. Although these methods enlarge the receptive fields, they also increase the number of parameters.

Fig. 1. Visualized explanation of the challenges scene text detectors suffer from. (a) and (b) show the variable aspect ratios and orientation of scene text. (c) and (d) show variable size and shape of scene text.

As a plug-and-play convolutional unit, Octave Convolution [1] aims to reduce the costs of memory and computation while enlarging the receptive fields of neural network. Comparing with Deformable Convolution, Octave Convolution does not increase the number of parameters. For enlarging the receptive fields and enhancing the ability of network to extract features, we adopt Octave Convolution instead of normal convolution to scene text detection for achieving high accuracy and speed in arbitrary shape text detection. PSENet can separate the adjacent text instances by predicting several scale kernels of text, and gets the full size of text by Progressive Scale Expansion Algorithm. By combining Octave Convolution with PSENet, we can achieve high detection performance while speeding up the process of inference. To the best of our knowledge, this is the first time to apply Octave Convolution to scene text detection.

The contributions of this paper are summarized as follows:

(1) To enlarge the receptive fields and enhance the ability of network to extract features, we combine Octave Convolution with PSENet. By utilizing the more contextual information, the detection performance can be boosted without increasing memory and computation costs.
(2) Our experiments on several datasets of both curved and multi-oriented texts show that the proposed method achieves state-of-the-art performances and runs faster than PSENet.

2 Related Work

In this section, we first review representative methods of scene text detection, then introduce some works on how to enlarge the receptive fields.

2.1 Scene Text Detection

Scene text detection methods proposed in recent years are mostly based on DNNs. They can be roughly categorized into two groups: regression-based and segmentation-based.

Regression-Based Methods. Regression-based methods often base on general object detection frameworks, such as Faster-RCNN [23], YOLO [22], SSD [15]. Seglink [24] adopts SSD to detect multi-oriented scene text by first detecting two locally detectable elements: segments and links. Textboxes [11] modifies convolutional kernels and anchor boxes to effectively capture various text shapes. RRD [13] is proposed to get more accurate bounding boxes. Inceptext [30] designs an Inception-Text Module to handle text with multiple scales, aspect ratios and orientations.

Different from the above methods, EAST [33], DeepReg [6] and FOTS [16] directly output the values for the position and size of text instance from a given point. These methods do not need complex anchor design, but they need the same size of receptive fields as the size of text instances and may fail to detect extremely long text.

Segmentation-Based Methods. Segmentation-based methods are mainly inspired by FCN [17], and have an advantage in detecting curved text. For these methods, they may fail to separate text instances which are close to each other. PixelLink [3] predicts pixel connections to separate adjacent texts. TextSnake [18] uses the text center line map to separate adjacent text instances. TextField [29] tries to learn a direction field to distinguish the adjacent text instances. PSENet [27] generates different scale of kernels for each text instance. By the minimal kernels, the close text instances can be distinguished. However, due to the pixel-wise prediction and time-consuming post-processing steps, the speed of it is quite slow.

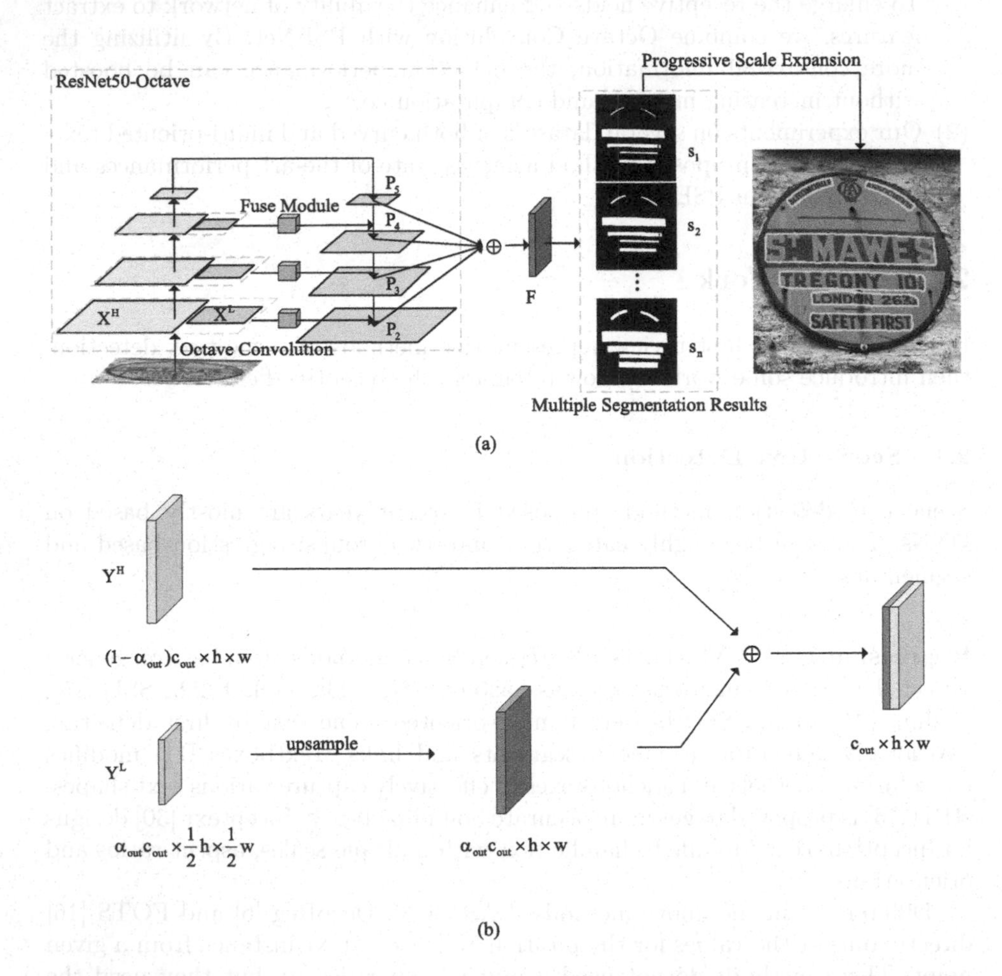

Fig. 2. Schematic illustration of our method. (a) The pipeline of our method. The backbone network is ResNet50 with Octave Convolution, and feature maps from each stage of it are firstly fed into the Fuse Module before inputting to FPN. (b) Details of the Fuse Module.

2.2 Methods for Enlarging Receptive Fields

Dilated Convolution [31] has been widely used in semantic segmentation and object detection. Its motivation is to increase the receptive fields without additional parameter cost by performing convolution at sparsely sampled locations. Different from the fixed sampling way, Deformable Convolution [2] adds 2D offsets to the regular grid sampling location in the standard convolution. These offsets are learned from the preceding feature maps via additional convolutional layers. Octave Convolution [1] is proposed to reduce the spatial redundancy in CNNs while enlarging the receptive fields. It enlarges the receptive fields by factorizing the feature maps along the channel dimension into high-frequency maps and low-frequency maps. The receptive fields are enlarged when convolution is applied on the compressed low-frequency feature maps. To cope with the variable aspect ratios and shape of scene text, it is intuitive to apply Octave Convolution to scene text detection.

3 Proposed Method

3.1 Overall Pipeline

An overview of our method is illustrated in Fig. 2. The pipeline utilizes a fully convolutional network (FCN) to produce different segmentation masks corresponding to different scale kernels of scene text. Octave Convolution is used as a direct replacement of normal convolution in the backbone network. Inspired by Feature Pyramid Network (FPN) [14], low-level feature maps and high-level feature maps are concatenated. As shown in Fig. 2(a), the outputs of each stage (except for the last stage) of the replaced backbone network are two feature maps, one high-frequency feature map X^H, and one low-frequency feature map X^L, which is the half size of the high-frequency feature map. Before used in FPN, the low-frequency feature map is up-sampled to the size of the high-frequency feature map, then the up-sampled feature map and the high-frequency feature map are concatenated for each stage (except for the last stage). This is illustrated in Fig. 2(b).

The feature maps from FPN are further fused in F to facilitate the generations of the kernels with various scales. We get four 256 channels feature maps (i.e. P_2, P_3, P_4, P_5) from the backbone. The function $\mathbf{C}$ is used for getting F with 1024 channels:

$$\begin{aligned} F &= \mathbf{C}(P_2, P_3, P_4, P_5) \\ &= P_2||Up_{\times 2}(P_3)||Up_{\times 4}(P_4)||Up_{\times 8}(P_5), \end{aligned} \tag{1}$$

where "||" refers to the concatenation and $Up_2(.)$, $Up_4(.)$, $Up_8(.)$ refer to $2, 4, 8$ times up-sampling, respectively. Subsequently, F is fed into Conv(3, 3)-BN-ReLU layers and is reduced to 256 channels. Next, it passes through n Conv(1, 1)-Up-Sigmoid layers and produces n segmentation results $S_1, S_2, ..., S_n$, the width and height of them is 1/1 of the input image. Here, BN and Up refer to batch normalization [7] and up-sampling.

Each S_i would be one segmentation mask for all text instances at a certain scale, which is decided by the hyper-parameters which will be introduced in later section. Among these masks, S_1 represents the minimal kernel among these predicted kernels, and S_n denotes for the maximal kernel. After obtaining these segmentation masks, the Progressive Scale Expansion Algorithm gradually makes use of these segmentation masks to get the full size of text instances.

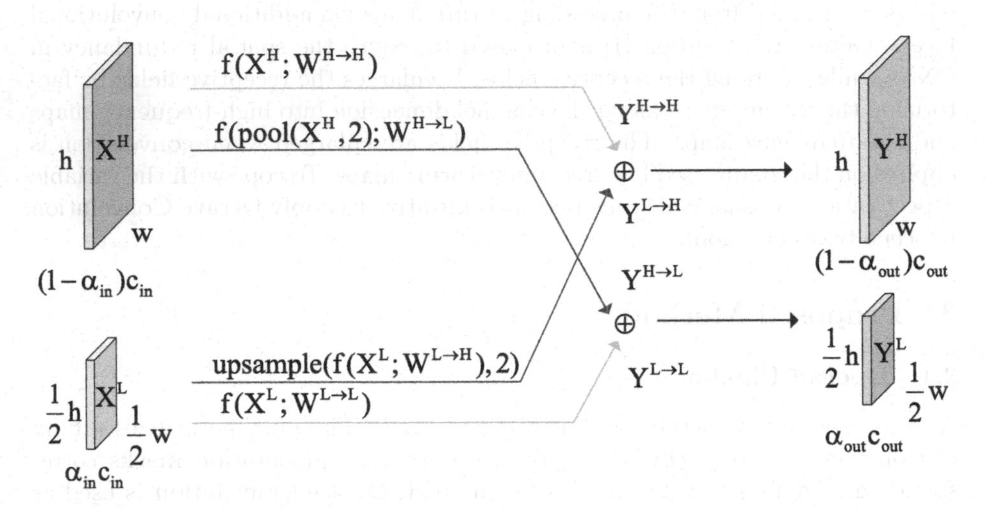

Fig. 3. The detailed process of Octave Convolution. At the first Octave Convolution layer, we set $\alpha_{in} = 0$, $\alpha_{out} = \alpha$, while we set $\alpha_{in} = \alpha$ and $\alpha_{out} = 0$ at the last Octave Convolution layer.

3.2 Octave Convolution

The advantages of Octave Convolution are enlarging the receptive fields and reducing the costs of memory and computation. The output feature maps of a convolution layer can be factorized along the channel dimension into high-frequency maps and low-frequency maps. The mentioned advantages are realized by reducing the resolution for low-frequency maps.

Let $X \in \mathbb{R}^{c \times h \times w}$ denotes the input feature tensor of a convolutional layer, where h and w denote the spatial dimensions and c the number of feature maps or channels. The input feature tensor X can be factorized along the channel dimension into $X = \{X^H, X^L\}$, where the high-frequency feature maps $X^H \in \mathbb{R}^{(1-\alpha)c \times h \times w}$ capture fine details and the low-frequency maps $X^L \in \mathbb{R}^{\alpha c \times \frac{h}{2} \times \frac{w}{2}}$ vary slower in the spatial dimensions. Here $\alpha \in [0, 1]$ denotes the ratio of channels allocated to the low-frequency part. The low-frequency feature maps are at half of the spatial resolution of the high frequency ones.

Let X, Y be the factorized input and output tensors. Similarly, the high- and low-frequency feature maps of the output tensors $Y = \{Y^H, Y^L\}$ will be obtained by $Y^H = Y^{H \to H} + Y^{L \to H}$ and $Y^L = Y^{L \to L} + Y^{H \to L}$, respectively, where $Y^{A \to B}$ denotes the convolutional update from feature map group A to group B. Specifically, $Y^{H \to H}, Y^{L \to L}$ denote intra-frequency information update, while $Y^{H \to L}, Y^{L \to H}$ denote inter-frequency communication. Figure 3 shows the detailed process of the Octave Convolution. The output $Y = Y^H, Y^L$ can be summarized as follows:

$$\begin{aligned} Y^H &= f(X^H; W^{H \to H}) + upsample(f(X^L; W^{L \to H}), 2), \\ Y^L &= f(X^L; W^{L \to L}) + f(pool(X^H, 2); W^{H \to L}), \end{aligned} \tag{2}$$

where $f(X; W)$ denotes a convolution with parameters W, $pool(X, k)$ is an average pooling operation with kernel size $k \times k$ and stride k. $upsample(X, k)$ is an up-sampling operation by a factor of k via nearest interpolation.

3.3 Label Generation

These corresponding ground truths with different kernel scales can be conducted by shrinking the original text instance. Subsequently, each shrunk polygon p_i is transferred into a 0/1 binary mask for segmentation label ground truth. These ground truth maps are denoted as $G_1, G_2, ..., G_n$ respectively. The scale ratio is defined as r_i, the margin d_i between p_n and p_i can be calculated as:

$$d_i = \frac{Area(p_n) \times (1 - r_i^2)}{Perimeter(p_n)}, \tag{3}$$

where $Area(.)$ is the function of computing the polygon area, $Perimeter(.)$ is the function of computing the polygon perimeter. The scale ratio r_i for ground truth map G_i is defined as:

$$r_i = 1 - \frac{(1 - m) \times (n - i)}{n - 1}, \tag{4}$$

where m is the minimal scale ratio, which is a value in $(0, 1]$. Based on the definition in Eq. (4), the values of scale ratios ($i.e.$, $r_1, r_2, ..., r_n$) are decided by two hyper-parameters n and m, and they increase linearly from m to 1.

3.4 Loss Function

The loss function is composed of two terms: the complete text instances loss L_c and the shrunk ones loss L_s. It can be formulated as:

$$L = \lambda L_c + (1 - \lambda) L_s, \tag{5}$$

where λ balances the importance between L_c and L_s. These two losses L_c and L_s are computed by dice coefficient loss. The dice coefficient D is formulated as:

$$D(S_i, G_i) = \frac{2 \sum_{x,y} (S_{i,x,y} \times G_{i,x,y})}{\sum_{x,y} S_{i,x,y}^2 + \sum_{x,y} G_{i,x,y}^2}, \tag{6}$$

where $S_{i,x,y}$ and $G_{i,x,y}$ refer to the value of pixel (x, y) in segmentation result S_i and ground truth G_i, respectively. To better distinguish many patterns similar to text strokes, Online Hard Example Mining (OHEM) [25] is adopted to L_c. The training mask given by OHEM is defined as M, and thus L_c can be formulated as:

$$L_c = 1 - D(S_n \cdot M, G_n \cdot M), \tag{7}$$

L_s is the loss for shrunk text instances. Since they are encircled by the original areas of the complete text instances, the pixels of the non-text region in the segmentation result S_n are ignored to avoid a certain redundancy. Therefore, L_s can be formulated as follows:

$$\begin{aligned} L_s &= 1 - \frac{\sum_{i=1}^{n-1} D(S_i \cdot W, G_i \cdot W)}{n-1}, \\ W_{x,y} &= \begin{cases} 1, & if\ S_{n,x,y} \geq 0.5; \\ 0, & otherwise. \end{cases} \end{aligned} \tag{8}$$

W is a mask which ignores the pixels of the non-text region in S_n, and $S_{n,x,y}$ refers to the value of pixel (x, y) in S_n.

3.5 Inference

During the inference stage, the outputs from the trained network are n segmentation results $S_1, S_2, ..., S_n$. We use Progressive Scale Expansion Algorithm [27] to obtain the final detection results. As mentioned before, S_1 is the minimal kernel which is used for separating the adjacent text instances. The Progressive Scale Expansion Algorithm is an iterative algorithm, and its central idea is brought from the Breadth-First-Search (BFS) algorithm.

In the first step, the central parts of texts in S_1 are the initial detection results. The next iteration steps are similar to progressively get the full size of scene texts. In the second step, the pixels in S_2 will be judged to belong to which text and are merged to the kernel of that text. Similarly, the pixels in $S_3, ..., S_n$ are merged to get the final detection results. The advantage of "progressively" is the detection results are not influenced by the margin between two close scene texts. Note that there may be conflicted pixels which are hard to be judged and this often happens for the margin pixels. In practice, these pixels are only be merged by one single kernel on a first-come-first-served basis.

4 Experimental Results

To validate the combination of Octave Convolution is beneficial to the detection performance and speed, we compare our method with other state-of-the-art methods on three challenging public datasets: CTW1500, ICDAR 2015 and ICDAR 2017 MLT.

Table 1. The single-scale results on CTW1500. "Ext" indicates external data. "1s" means the width and height of output map is 1/1 of the input test image.

Method	Ext	Precision	Recall	F-measure	FPS
CTPN [26]	–	60.4	53.8	56.9	7.14
SegLink [24]	–	42.3	40.0	40.8	10.7
EAST [33]	–	78.7	49.1	60.4	**21.2**
CTD+TLOC [32]	–	77.4	69.8	73.4	13.3
TextSnake [18]	✓	67.9	85.3	75.6	–
TextField [29]	✓	83.0	79.8	81.4	–
Wang et al. [28]	–	80.1	80.2	80.1	–
PSENet-1s [27]	–	80.57	75.55	78.0	3.9
PSENet-1s [27]	✓	84.84	79.73	82.2	3.9
Our method	–	85.25	78.19	81.57	6.0
Our method	✓	87.21	79.53	**83.19**	6.0

4.1 Datasets

CTW1500 [32] is a challenging dataset consisting of long curve texts. It consists of 1000 training images and 500 testing images. The text instances are labeled by 14 points at word-level.

ICDAR 2015 (IC15) [8] is a challenging dataset for multi-oriented text detection. It consists of 1000 training images and 500 testing images. The annotations are at word-level using quadrilateral boxes. There are many blurred text regions labeled Do Not Care.

ICDAR 2017 MLT (IC17-MLT) [21] is a large scale multi-lingual text dataset, which contains 7200 training images, 1800 validation images and 9000 testing images. This dataset is composed of complete scene images from 9 languages. Some languages like English are labeled at word-level, while other languages such as Chinese are labeled at line-level. Like IC15, text regions are also annotated by the 4 vertices of quadrilaterals and hard text instances are labeled as Do Not Care.

4.2 Implementation Details

We use the ResNet50 [5] with Octave Convolution pre-trained on ImageNet [4] as our backbone. The networks are optimized with stochastic gradient descent (SGD). We set α in Octave Convolution to 0.5, the kernel number n and the minimal kernel scale m are set to 7 and 0.4, respectively. And the λ of loss balance is set to 0.7.

Table 2. The single-scale results on IC15. "Ext" indicates external data. "1s" means the width and height of output map is 1/1 of the input test image.

Method	Ext	Precision	Recall	F-measure	FPS
EAST [33]	–	83.57	73.47	78.2	**13.2**
DeepReg [6]	–	82.0	80.0	81.0	–
PixelLink [3]	–	82.9	81.7	82.3	7.3
Lyu et al. [20]	✓	94.1	70.7	80.7	3.6
TextBoxes++ [10]	✓	87.2	76.7	81.7	11.6
RRD [13]	✓	85.6	79.0	82.2	6.5
IncepText [30]	–	90.5	80.6	85.3	–
TextSnake [18]	✓	84.9	80.4	82.6	1.1
FOTS(det only)[16]	✓	88.84	82.04	85.31	–
Mask TextSpotter [19]	✓	91.6	81.0	86.0	4.8
TextField [29]	✓	84.3	80.5	82.4	5.2
Wang et al. [28]	–	89.2	86.0	**87.6**	10.0
PSENet-1s [27]	–	81.49	79.68	80.57	1.6
PSENet-1s [27]	✓	86.92	84.5	85.69	1.6
Our method	–	85.15	80.64	82.83	2.45
Our method	✓	88.0	84.1	86.0	2.45

Data augmentation the same with PSENet is used during training. For IC17-MLT, we only use its dataset to train our model. But for CTW1500 and IC15, there are two strategies: (1) Training from scratch. (2) Fine-tuning on IC17-MLT model.

During test stage, we set the longer side of images to 1280 on CTW1500. And on IC15, the longer side of the input images is scaled to 2240. On IC17-MLT, the longer side of test images is set to 3200. The whole algorithm is implemented in PyTorch 1.0 and we conduct all experiments on a regular workstation whose CPU is Intel(R) Core(TM) i7-7700K and GPU is GeForce GTX 1080ti.

4.3 Comparisons with State-of-the-Art Methods

Detecting Curve Text. To test the effectiveness for curved text detection, we first evaluate our method on CTW1500. We report the single-scale performance of our method in Table 1. On CTW1500, our method surpasses all the counterparts. Without external data which means training from scratch, the F-measure of PSENet is 78.0%, and the speed of it is 3.9 FPS. The corresponding result of our method is 81.57%, which is 3.57% higher than PSENet. In addition, the speed of our method is about 2 FPS faster than PSENet. With external data, our method achieves 83.19% in F-measure and is about 1% higher than PSENet. The experiment demonstrates the effectiveness of enlarging receptive fields for detectors to handle curve texts. We show some test examples in Fig. 4(a).

Detecting Oriented Text. We evaluate the proposed model on IC15 to validate the effectiveness for oriented text detection. We compare our method with other state-of-the-art methods in Table 2. Without external data, PSENet achieves 80.57% in F-measure, and our method achieves 82.83% in F-measure. Also, our method is still faster than PSENet. With external data, our method still outperforms PSENet. Some detection results are shown in Fig. 4(b).

Table 3. The single-scale results on IC17-MLT. "Ext" indicates external data. "*" means the results are obtained in our experiments.

Method	Ext	Precision	Recall	F-measure	FPS
linkage-ER-Flow [21]		44.48	25.59	32.49	–
TH-DL [21]		67.75	34.78	45.97	–
TDN SJTU2017 [21]		64.27	47.13	54.38	–
SARI FDU RRPN v1 [21]		71.17	55.50	62.37	–
SCUT DLVClab1 [21]		80.28	54.54	64.96	–
Lyu et al. [20]	✓	83.8	55.6	66.8	–
FOTS(det only)[16]	✓	79.48	57.45	66.69	–
PSENet(ResNet50)[27]	–	73.77	68.21	70.88	0.56*
PSENet(ResNet152)[27]	–	75.35	69.18	72.13	0.50*
Our method	–	76.26	68.58	**72.22**	**0.80**

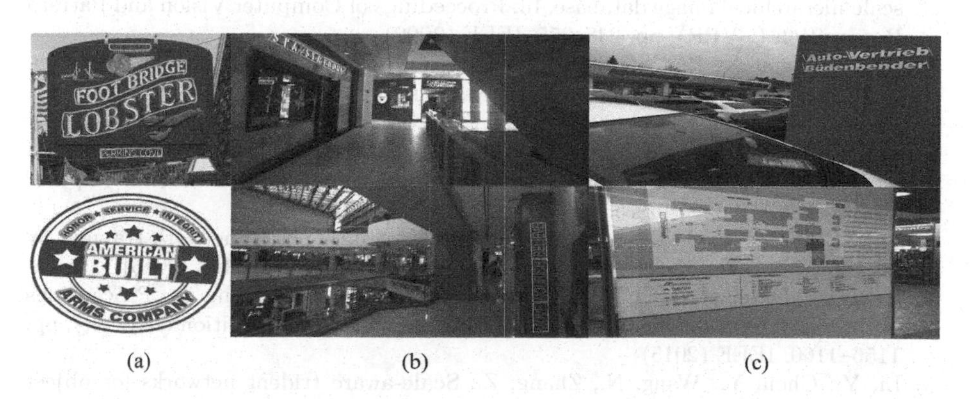

Fig. 4. Detection results on three benchmarks: CTW1500 (a), IC15 (b) and IC17-MLT (c).

Detecting Multi-Lingual Text. On IC17-MLT, our method achieves 72.22% in the F-measure, higher than PSENet which takes ResNet152 as the backbone network. In speed, our method is 0.3 FPS faster than PSENet whose backbone network is ResNet152 under the same condition. This experiment validates that the performance of scene text detector can be improved by enlarging the receptive fields for multi-lingual text detection. Some test examples are shown in Fig. 4(c).

5 Conclusion

In this paper, we first introduce Octave Convolution into scene text detection to expand the receptive fields of network for capturing more contextual information. With the larger receptive fields, the performance of detector can be highly improved. In addition, Octave Convolution can reduce both memory and computation cost, which is beneficial for the efficiency of scene text detectors. The experimental results on several datasets validate the effectiveness of our method. In the future, we will try other ways (e.g., [9]) to expand the receptive fields and further improve the speed of our method.

References

1. Chen, Y., et al.: Drop an octave: reducing spatial redundancy in convolutional neural networks with octave convolution. arXiv preprint arXiv:1904.05049 (2019)
2. Dai, J., et al.: Deformable convolutional networks. In: Proceedings of International Conference on Computer Vision (ICCV). pp. 764–773 (2017)
3. Deng, D., Liu, H., Li, X., Cai, D.: PixelLink: detecting scene text via instance segmentation. In: Proceedings of AAAI Conference on Artificial Intelligence (AAAI) (2018)
4. Deng, J., Dong, W., Socher, R., Li, L.J., Li, K., Fei-Fei, L.: ImageNet: a large-scale hierarchical image database. In: Proceedings of Computer Vision and Pattern Recognition (CVPR), pp. 248–255. IEEE (2009)
5. He, K., Zhang, X., Ren, S., Sun, J.: Identity mappings in deep residual networks. In: Leibe, B., Matas, J., Sebe, N., Welling, M. (eds.) ECCV 2016. LNCS, vol. 9908, pp. 630–645. Springer, Cham (2016). https://doi.org/10.1007/978-3-319-46493-0_38
6. He, W., Zhang, X.Y., Yin, F., Liu, C.L.: Deep direct regression for multi-oriented scene text detection. In: Proceedings of International Conference on Computer Vision (ICCV), pp. 745–753 (2017)
7. Ioffe, S., Szegedy, C.: Batch normalization: accelerating deep network training by reducing internal covariate shift. arXiv preprint arXiv:1502.03167 (2015)
8. Karatzas, D., et al.: ICDAR 2015 competition on robust reading. In: Proceedings of International Conference on Document Analysis and Recognition (ICDAR), pp. 1156–1160. IEEE (2015)
9. Li, Y., Chen, Y., Wang, N., Zhang, Z.: Scale-aware trident networks for object detection. arXiv preprint arXiv:1901.01892 (2019)
10. Liao, M., Shi, B., Bai, X.: TextBoxes++: a single-shot oriented scene text detector. IEEE Trans. Image Process. **27**(8), 3676–3690 (2018)
11. Liao, M., Shi, B., Bai, X., Wang, X., Liu, W.: TextBoxes: a fast text detector with a single deep neural network. In: Proceedings of AAAI Conference on Artificial Intelligence (AAAI) (2017)
12. Liao, M., et al.: Scene text recognition from two-dimensional perspective. arXiv preprint arXiv:1809.06508 (2018)

13. Liao, M., Zhu, Z., Shi, B., Xia, G.S., Bai, X.: Rotation-sensitive regression for oriented scene text detection. In: Proceedings of Computer Vision and Pattern Recognition (CVPR), pp. 5909–5918 (2018)
14. Lin, T.Y., Dollár, P., Girshick, R., He, K., Hariharan, B., Belongie, S.: Feature pyramid networks for object detection. In: Proceedings of Computer Vision and Pattern Recognition (CVPR), pp. 2117–2125 (2017)
15. Liu, W., et al.: SSD: single shot multibox detector. In: Leibe, B., Matas, J., Sebe, N., Welling, M. (eds.) ECCV 2016. LNCS, vol. 9905, pp. 21–37. Springer, Cham (2016). https://doi.org/10.1007/978-3-319-46448-0_2
16. Liu, X., Liang, D., Yan, S., Chen, D., Qiao, Y., Yan, J.: FOTS: fast oriented text spotting with a unified network. In: Proceedings of Computer Vision and Pattern Recognition (CVPR), pp. 5676–5685 (2018)
17. Long, J., Shelhamer, E., Darrell, T.: Fully convolutional networks for semantic segmentation. In: Proceedings of Computer Vision and Pattern Recognition (CVPR), pp. 3431–3440 (2015)
18. Long, S., Ruan, J., Zhang, W., He, X., Wu, W., Yao, C.: TextSnake: a flexible representation for detecting text of arbitrary shapes. In: Ferrari, V., Hebert, M., Sminchisescu, C., Weiss, Y. (eds.) ECCV 2018. LNCS, vol. 11206, pp. 19–35. Springer, Cham (2018). https://doi.org/10.1007/978-3-030-01216-8_2
19. Lyu, P., Liao, M., Yao, C., Wu, W., Bai, X.: Mask TextSpotter: an end-to-end trainable neural network for spotting text with arbitrary shapes. In: Ferrari, V., Hebert, M., Sminchisescu, C., Weiss, Y. (eds.) Computer Vision – ECCV 2018. LNCS, vol. 11218, pp. 71–88. Springer, Cham (2018). https://doi.org/10.1007/978-3-030-01264-9_5
20. Lyu, P., Yao, C., Wu, W., Yan, S., Bai, X.: Multi-oriented scene text detection via corner localization and region segmentation. In: Proceedings of Computer Vision and Pattern Recognition (CVPR), pp. 7553–7563 (2018)
21. Nayef, N., et al.: ICDAR 2017 robust reading challenge on multi-lingual scene text detection and script identification-RRC-MLT. In: Proceedings of International Conference on Document Analysis and Recognition (ICDAR), vol. 1, pp. 1454–1459. IEEE (2017)
22. Redmon, J., Divvala, S., Girshick, R., Farhadi, A.: You only look once: unified, real-time object detection. In: Proceedings of Computer Vision and Pattern Recognition (CVPR), pp. 779–788 (2016)
23. Ren, S., He, K., Girshick, R., Sun, J.: Faster R-CNN: towards real-time object detection with region proposal networks. In: Proceedings of Neural Information Processing Systems (NeurIPS), pp. 91–99 (2015)
24. Shi, B., Bai, X., Belongie, S.: Detecting oriented text in natural images by linking segments. In: Proceedings of Computer Vision and Pattern Recognition (CVPR), pp. 2550–2558 (2017)
25. Shrivastava, A., Gupta, A., Girshick, R.: Training region-based object detectors with online hard example mining. In: Proceedings of Computer Vision and Pattern Recognition (CVPR), pp. 761–769 (2016)
26. Tian, Z., Huang, W., He, T., He, P., Qiao, Y.: Detecting text in natural image with connectionist text proposal network. In: Leibe, B., Matas, J., Sebe, N., Welling, M. (eds.) ECCV 2016. LNCS, vol. 9912, pp. 56–72. Springer, Cham (2016). https://doi.org/10.1007/978-3-319-46484-8_4
27. Wang, W., et al.: Shape robust text detection with progressive scale expansion network. In: Proceedings of Computer Vision and Pattern Recognition (CVPR) (2019)

28. Wang, X., Jiang, Y., Luo, Z., Liu, C.L., Choi, H., Kim, S.: Arbitrary shape scene text detection with adaptive text region representation. In: Proceedings of Computer Vision and Pattern Recognition (CVPR), pp. 6449–6458 (2019)
29. Xu, Y., Wang, Y., Zhou, W., Wang, Y., Yang, Z., Bai, X.: TextField: learning a deep direction field for irregular scene text detection. IEEE Trans. Image Process. **28**, 5566–5579 (2019)
30. Yang, Q., et al.: IncepText: a new inception-text module with deformable PSROI pooling for multi-oriented scene text detection. arXiv preprint arXiv:1805.01167 (2018)
31. Yu, F., Koltun, V.: Multi-scale context aggregation by dilated convolutions. arXiv preprint arXiv:1511.07122 (2015)
32. Yuliang, L., Lianwen, J., Shuaitao, Z., Sheng, Z.: Detecting curve text in the wild: new dataset and new solution. arXiv preprint arXiv:1712.02170 (2017)
33. Zhou, X., et al.: EAST: an efficient and accurate scene text detector. In: Proceedings of Computer Vision and Pattern Recognition (CVPR), pp. 5551–5560 (2017)

SFLNet: Direct Sports Field Localization via CNN-Based Regression

Shuhei Tarashima(✉)

NTT Communications Corporation, Tokyo, Japan
tarashima@acm.org

Abstract. In this paper we propose a novel approach to build a single shot regressor, called *SFLNet*, that directly predicts a parameter set relating a sports field seen in an input frame to its metric model. This problem is challenging due to the huge intra-class variance of sports fields and the large number of free parameters to be predicted. To address these issues, we propose to train our regressor in combination with semantic segmentation in a multi-task learning framework. We also introduce an additional module to exploit the spacial consistency of sports fields, which boosts both regression and segmentation performances. SFLNet can be learned with a training dataset that can be semi-automatically built from human annotated point-to-point correspondences. To our knowledge, this work is the first attempt to solve this sports field localization problem relying only on an end-to-end deep learning framework. Experiments on our new dataset based on basketball games validate our approach over baseline methods.

Keywords: Homography · Semantic segmentation · Multi-task learning · Sports analytics

1 Introduction

Sports analytics have been extensively used to build competitive teams, improve scouting, predict match outcomes, and enhance the fan experience [1,2]. Among the techniques in sports analytics, computer vision plays a key role both in the automatic performance assessment of individual players and in the improvement of team formations and strategies. The majority of commercial systems like STATS[1] and TRACAB[2] collect visual data using static cameras with fixed intrinsic parameters, making analysis simple but requiring costly installation. One way to reduce the cost is to leverage alternative resources such as broadcast videos or consumer-generated media. However, it is challenging to analyze such data because camera parameters may be varied over time. To extract valuable statistics from these resources, we need to estimate frame-by-frame correspondence between the sports field seen by the camera and the metric model of the field.

[1] https://www.stats.com/.
[2] https://chyronhego.com/products/sports-tracking/tracab-optical-tracking/.

S. Palaiahnakote et al. (Eds.): ACPR 2019, LNCS 12046, pp. 677–690, 2020.
https://doi.org/10.1007/978-3-030-41404-7_48

Fig. 1. Our single shot regressor, SFLNet, directly regresses a set of parameters that corresponds the metric model of a sports field (shown in top right on the right image) to the court seen in an input frame. Best viewed in color.

In this work we tackle the automatic sports field localization problem, on which algorithms estimate a set of parameters that corresponds the sports field in a given frame to its metric model without any manual intervention. Specifically, we here aim at developing a single shot regressor that can directly predict the parameter set from an input frame (*cf.* Fig. 1). Existing algorithms [5–7] tailored to the same problem consist of several steps and have a tradeoff between accuracy and efficiency. Single shot regression has already been employed to solve related tasks (*e.g.* camera pose estimation [14–19]), but these approaches are difficult to be applied directly due to the different problem settings. To this end, we propose a novel approach to build a regressor based on a convolutional neural network (CNN), called *SFLNet*, that can directly predict the correspondence parameter. To our knowledge, this is the first attempt in the literature to solve the sports field localization problem relying only on an end-to-end deep learning framework. The contributions of this work can be summarized as follows:

1. We propose to build our parameter regressor in combination with a semantic segmentation module and train the whole model in an end-to-end multi-task learning framework. The semantic segmentation module is responsible for layout estimation of the input frame, and its intermediate feature map is used to regress correspondence parameters.
2. We introduce an additional module to exploit contextual information focusing on the property of sports fields. This module can exploit the spatial consistency of sports fields with a very low extra computational cost, and can efficiently boost both semantic segmentation and parameter regression performances. We will validate this module in our ablation studies.
3. We compile a novel dataset to evaluate sports field localization methods. This dataset is built on a number of basketball games held in different stadiums with various camera installations and moves. We use this dataset to demonstrate the superiority of our approach over several baseline methods. This dataset will be publicly available in the near future.

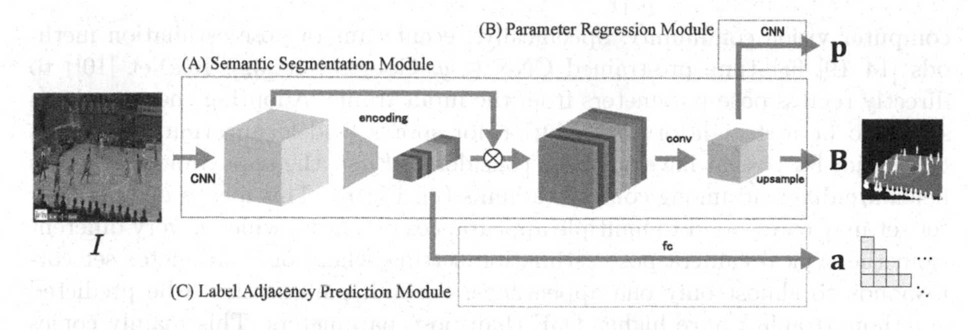

Fig. 2. The architecture of SFLNet. SFLNet takes a single frame as input, then generates a set of parameters $\mathbf{p}$, a label mask $\mathbf{B}$ and a label adjacency prediction $\mathbf{a}$. Best viewed in color.

2 Related Works

Assuming the sports field is planar, the transformation between its metric model and the field seen in an input frame can be defined by a homography matrix $H \in \mathbb{R}^{3\times3}$, which has 8 degrees of freedom (DoF). One of the simplest ways to estimate this homography is to first detect field markings (*e.g.* points, lines, intersections) in the frame and then associate them with corresponding markings in the model. Given these correspondences, the homography can be easily estimated by the closed form Direct Linear Transform (DLT) algorithm [31]. Unfortunately, this approach is difficult to be performed fully automatically: Field marking detection remains a non-trivial task because markings are usually small, textureless, and sometimes cannot be seen in the frame. Therefore, most existing sports field localization methods assume manual intervention [3,19–27], which make them less applicable within a real-time setting.

To our knowledge, relatively fewer works [5–7] focus on fully automatic approaches. For instance, Homayounfar *et al.* [5] formulate automatic sports field localization problem as a branch and bound inference in a Markov random field where an energy function is defined in terms of semantic cues such as the field surface, lines, and circles obtained from a semantic segmentation result. On the other hand, Sharma *et al.* [7] formulate the problem as a nearest neighbor search in a precomputed dictionary with known homographies. Chen *et al.* [6] improve Sharma's approach by adopting case-specific assumptions (*e.g.* PTZ camera and its position) to extend the dictionary and employing a GAN framework for better feature extraction. All the above methods consist of several steps and the whole pipelines cannot be optimized end-to-end. More importantly, they all suffer from a tradeoff between accuracy and efficiency: To improve accuracy, finer label spaces or dictionaries must be provided, which makes online procedure less efficient. This can be problematic especially when both accuracy and efficiency are highly demanded.

One alternative way to bypass the above issue is to directly predict a set of parameters in a single step. This approach has been employed in the camera pose estimation problem, which has been an active research topic in the computer vision community. Specifically, recent camera pose estimation methods [14–19] fine-tune pre-trained CNN (*e.g.* GoogLeNet [32], ResNet [10]) to directly regress pose parameters from the input frame. Adopting these methods seems to be a straightforward solution for sports field localization, but it has two major issues that have not been considered. First, the appearances of sports fields are different among courts/stadiums (*cf.* Fig. 6). This means one parameter set may correspond to multiple appearances of courts, which is very different from the typical camera pose estimation setting where one parameter set corresponds to almost only one appearance. Second, parameters to be predicted (*i.e.* homography) have higher DoF than pose parameters. This mainly comes from different camera settings: While intrinsic parameters are fixed (or known) in camera pose estimation, this does not hold in sports field localization due to different camera installations or some camera work like zooming. Regressors should deal with these issues, but they are not explicitly considered in existing camera pose estimation methods.

We develop our SFLNet based on these understandings. In the next section, we will detail SFLNet with respect to its architecture and training.

3 Proposed Approach

3.1 SFLNet Architecture

Figure 2 shows the architecture of our proposed SFLNet. Once a frame is fed into the network, SFLNet generates a parameter set $\mathbf{p}$, a segmentation mask $\mathbf{B}$ and a label adjacency prediction $\mathbf{a}$, where $\mathbf{B}$ and $\mathbf{a}$ are the by-products used in our model training. SFLNet consists of (A) semantic segmentation module, (B) parameter regression module, and (C) label adjacency prediction module, which will be described in the following.

(A) Semantic Segmentation Module. The semantic segmentation module assigns one of the pre-defined labels to every pixel in an input frame. This is helpful for a regressor to understand the spatial layout of a sports court under large intra-class variance. In our problem, we have several choices for defining labels. One of the simplest cases is to divide a frame into court, person, and background regions as shown in Fig. 3(a), which is a relatively easier setting for semantic segmentation but only coarser information remains for the following regression. On the contrary, we can also define more labels like Fig. 3(b)–(e) for finer layout representations, which is better for the regressor but is difficult settings for semantic segmentation. Note that we can use these label definitions with almost the same annotation cost by following an approach shown in Sect. 3.2. In this work we select the best label definition experimentally, as will be shown in our parameter studies (*cf.* Sect. 4.3).

We build this segmentation module based on the state-of-the-art semantic segmentation approaches [8,9]. Specifically, we use 50-layer ResNet [10] pre-trained on ImageNet as a backbone and build the Context Encoding module

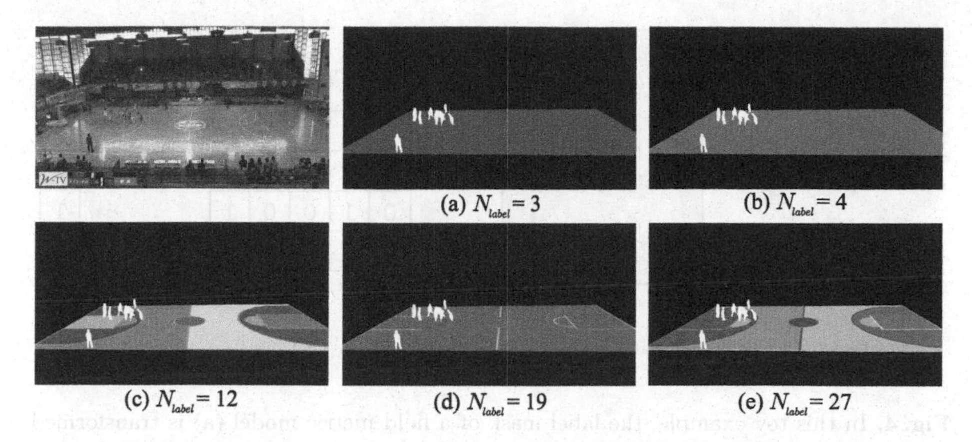

Fig. 3. We have several design choices about the label definition of a sport field. Examples (a)–(e) are ground truth segmentation masks of the top left image on different label definitions, where N_{label} is the number of labels used in each setting. Different colors represent different labels in each case. Best viewed in color.

[8] on top of the last convolutional layer right before the upsampling module to yield a per-pixel prediction. The output feature of the Context Encoding module is used as the input of the Label Adjacency Prediction module detailed later. To obtain higher resolution feature maps which preserve finer spatial information, we adopt Joint Pyramid Upsampling module [9] to our backbone network, which can approximate standard dilated convolution [28–30] while saving computation and memory overhead.

(B) Parameter Regression Module. This module regresses parameters that correspond a court metric model to the court seen in an input frame. In this work we define the parameter set as a 8-dimensional vector, each of which corresponds to a free parameter of a homography $H \in \mathbb{R}^{3\times3}$. Specifically, we relate a prediction $\mathbf{p} = [p_1, p_2, p_3, p_4, p_5, p_6, p_7, p_8]^{\mathrm{T}}$ to a homography H as follows:

$$H = \begin{bmatrix} p_1 + 1 & p_2 & p_3 \\ p_4 & p_5 + 1 & p_6 \\ p_7 & p_8, & 1 \end{bmatrix}. \tag{1}$$

Following [11], before computing the homography we normalize coordinate systems of both the model and the frame.

We build this module as a tiny CNN on top of the last convolutional layer of the semantic segmentation module. Specifically, we set this architecture as `C36-C48-C60-F8`, where `Ck` denotes a Convolution-BatchNorm-Relu-Maxpool block with `k` filters, `Fk` denotes a fc layer with `k` neurons. Every convolution layer has 3×3 filters and the stride of each maxpooling layer is set as 2.

Notice that we may have a choice to define $\mathbf{p}$ as a parameter set yielded via homography decomposition [19]: By introducing the natural camera assumption [31], we can break up a homography into a focal length, a rotation matrix and

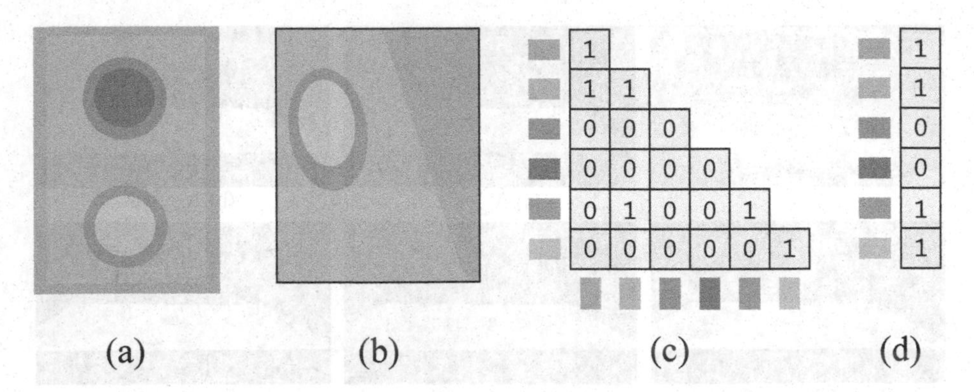

Fig. 4. In this toy example, the label mask of a field metric model (a) is transformed into a frame like (b). SE module of Zhang *et al.* [8] ideally predicts only the presence of each label like (d). In addition to the label presence, our proposed LAP module also predicts whether each label pair is adjacent or not like (c). Best viewed in color.

a translation vector, which in total have smaller degrees of freedom (7-DoF) than the homography itself. However, our preliminary experiments indicate that simply predicting the decomposed parameters does not work well for sports field localization. One reason is that errors are amplified when homographies are recovered, resulting in totally different results from ground truth. Therefore, in this work we regress homographies almost directly, and leave the above issue as a future work.

(C) Label Adjacency Prediction Module. In standard training process of semantic segmentation, the network is learned from isolated pixels and context (*e.g.* sizes, spatial relations) is not explicitly considered. Here we introduce Label Adjacency Prediction (LAP) module to regularize the model training via exploiting contextual information lying in the sport field localization problem. Specifically, LAP module predicts the adjacencies of label pairs in addition to their presence in an input frame. Figure 4 shows a toy example, in which the labels of this court are defined like (a). When the court is shown like (b) in a frame, the corresponding ground truth for the output of LAP module is (c), in which each orthogonal element represents the presence of the label (1 if the label exists and 0 otherwise) and the others represent adjacencies of label pairs (1 if the row-column pair is adjacent and 0 otherwise).

Note that LAP module can be seen as an extension of Semantic Encoding (SE) module [8] in the context of sports field localization. We can say almost all sports fields are not deformed and spatial relations between their parts (*i.e.* labels) are always consistent. While SE module makes predictions only for the presence of labels in the frame (*cf.* Fig. 4 (d)), LAP module can also exploit this problem-specific spatial consistency between labels, which makes LAP module a more efficient regularizer during the model training. We will validate LAP module in our ablation studies (*cf.* Sect. 4.3).

Fig. 5. Given a frame (b) and human annotated point-to-point correspondences to a field model (a), ground truth label mask $\mathbf{B}^*$ shown in (c) can be automatically generated by the approach described in Sect. 3.2. In (a) and (b), the markings of the same color are a correspondence. Best viewed in color.

Following [8], we implement LAP module as an additional fully connected layer with a sigmoid activation function on top of the encoding module in the semantic segmentation module. The output dimension depends on the label definition, which can be computed by $N_{label}(N_{label}+1)/2$. LAP module usually has higher computation cost than SE module due to larger output dimensions, but the overall cost is still very small.

3.2 SFLNet Training

Training Data. To learn model weights of SFLNet $\mathbf{\Theta}$, we need to provide a training data $\mathcal{D} = \{(I, \mathbf{p}^* \, \mathbf{B}^*, \mathbf{a}^*)\}$, consisting of the quadruplets of a frame I, a ground truth parameter set $\mathbf{p}^*$, a label mask $\mathbf{B}^*$ and a label adjacency indicator $\mathbf{a}^*$. Unfortunately, fully manual labeling of such a dataset is costly and cumbersome. So here we propose a semi-automatic approach to obtain the training data $\mathcal{D}$ from human annotated point-to-point correspondences. For each frame $I \in \mathcal{D}$ and its point-to-point correspondences, we first apply DLT algorithm to estimate a homography H^* that transforms a court model into the court seen in the frame. This homography can be used to project the label mask of the court model into the frame. Since players and referees are usually on the sports fields, we adopt a state-of-the-art person segmentation algorithm [13] and overlay the segmentation result to the projected court labels to obtain a label mask $\mathbf{B}^*$. An example generated through the above procedure is shown in Fig. 5. While segmentation results of [13] are almost correct in our test case, if the person segmentation clearly fails then we remove the frame from the dataset. Yielding the parameter set $\mathbf{p}^*$ from H^* is straightforward and the label adjacency indicator $\mathbf{a}^*$ can easily be computed from $\mathbf{B}^*$.

Loss Function. Given a training dataset $\mathcal{D} = \{(I, \mathbf{p}^*, \mathbf{B}^*, \mathbf{a}^*)\}$, model weights of SFLNet are learned by minimizing the following loss function:

$$L_{\mathcal{D}}(\Theta) = \sum_{i}^{|\mathcal{D}|} \tau(\mathbf{p}_i, \mathbf{p}_i^*) + w_\phi \sum_{i}^{|\mathcal{D}|} \phi(\mathbf{B}_i, \mathbf{B}_i^*) + w_\psi \sum_{i}^{|\mathcal{D}|} \psi(\mathbf{a}_i, \mathbf{a}_i^*), \quad (2)$$

where on the right side the first term is a parameter loss, the second term is a segmentation loss and the third term is a label adjacency prediction loss. Following [8], we use a per-pixel cross-entropy loss as ϕ and a binary cross-entropy as ψ. Since we have several choices for defining the parameter loss τ, we experimentally decide the best which is shown in Sect. 4.3.

To robustly learn the model, we use two-step approach to minimize the loss: We first train the semantic segmentation module and the label adjacent prediction module by considering the corresponding losses (*i.e.* first and second terms on the right side of Eq. (2)), then optimize the whole model by minimizing the loss $L_{\mathcal{D}}$.

4 Experimental Evaluation

As an evaluation protocol, we use the intersection-over-union (IoU) score between the model of a sports court and a predicted court: We first project a court in a given frame to a coordinate system of the metric model using the homography recovered from a parameter prediction $\mathbf{p}$, then compute the IoU score between the projected result and the model. If some field corners are not seen in the frame, we estimate their positions with a ground truth homography. We denote the score as $J_{\mathbf{p}}$. Additionally, in some ablations we evaluate the performance of semantic segmentation of our approach. We also use the IoU score between a predicted segmentation $\mathbf{B}$ and a ground truth, denoting the score as $J_{\mathbf{B}}$.

4.1 Dataset

In this work we create a new dataset for evaluating sport field localization methods using videos of basketball games. Basketball is challenging for this task because the appearances of basketball courts are varied between stadiums and different court regions are occluded by players or referees moving over time (*cf.* Fig. 6). We collected the videos of 22 games from a Japanese basketball league, each of which is held in a unique stadium. For each video we sequentially sampled 50–60 frames[3], and manually annotated point-to-point correspondences to each frame. Every frame size is 1024×720. Points to be annotated are defined like Fig. 5(a), and we specified the position only if it can be seen within the frame. After discarding frames in which less than 4 points are annotated (*i.e.* DLT cannot be performed), we obtained the whole dataset consisting of 1232 frames. This dataset can be used to automatically build the training data of SFLNet, following the procedure detailed in Sect. 4.1.

Note that we believe this dataset cannot be used to learn sequential models because our frame sampling is not so dense (*i.e.* about one frame per second). We are planning to extend this dataset for sequence learning, and leave it as a future work.

[3] We avoid sampling when the game is stopping in order not to sample duplicate frames.

Fig. 6. Example frames included in our dataset. Some frames have similar parameters but their appearances are different (first and second column). Also some frames from the same game are captured with different intrinsic parameters (third column).

4.2 Implementation Details

We implemented our algorithms with PyTorch[4], using the SGD optimizer with momentum of 0.9. The input frames are scaled to 448 × 448 pixels, and normalized by pixel mean subtraction and standard deviation division. In training we randomly crop training frames keeping its aspect ratio, and recompute the ground truth parameter $\mathbf{p}^*$ accordingly. Flipping and rotation are not performed since they degrade the performance. We use the mini-batch size of 16 during the training, and apply the approach of [30] to control the learning rate. We run 50 epochs on both steps in training, and use the final model for evaluating test data. Using a grid search, we set the hyperparameters w_ϕ and w_ψ in Eq. (2) as 1.0 and 0.2, respectively.

4.3 Ablation/Parameter Study

In this section we perform several ablation/parameter studies with respect to (i) architecture designs, (ii) label definitions and (iii) loss functions for parameter regression. In the following we used all the frames in one game (denoted as #1) as test data and all the remaining as training data.

[4] https://pytorch.org/.

Architecture Design. We first validate our architecture design of SFLNet, focusing on the semantic segmentation module and the label adjacency prediction module. To evaluate the semantic segmentation module, we built an alternative model that replaced the CNN backbone of SFLNet to vanilla ResNet-50 and introduced a fc layer with 2048 neurons after its global average pooling layer followed by ReLU and dropout with $p = 0.5$. This is followed by a final fc layer that outputs a parameter set $\mathbf{p}$. For label adjacency prediction module, we considered the following two alternatives: (1) simply removing the module from SFLNet, (2) replacing LAP module to SE module [8]. Loss functions are modified accordingly. Table 1 shows the results. From the first and second row, we can see $J_{\mathbf{P}}$ is significantly improved by introducing the semantic segmentation module. Also, the latter rows show that additional modules further boosts both parameter regression and semantic segmentation performances, especially when LAP module is employed. These results indicate the effectiveness of our architecture design.

Table 1. Ablation for different architectures.

Segmentation?	Context?	$J_{\mathbf{B}}$	$J_{\mathbf{P}}$
	None	–	0.855
✓	None	0.489	0.892
✓	SE-module [8]	0.504	0.909
✓	LAP-module	0.521	0.924

Label Definition. Here, we compare the performance of SFLNet on 5 different label definitions shown in Fig. 3. Table 2 shows the results. For $J_{\mathbf{P}}$, the best performance is achieved when $N_{label} = 27$ with LAP module, which is difficult case for semantic segmentation (*i.e.* $J_{\mathbf{B}}$ is low). Interestingly, when SE module [8] is used, $J_{\mathbf{P}}$ achieves the peak at $N_{label} = 12$, which is relatively an easier setting for semantic segmentation. One possible reason of this difference is that LAP module works better than SE module on the challenging setting of $N_{label} = 27$, making some positive effects to parameter regression. This result indicates our LAP module can achieve better tradeoffs between parameter regression and semantic segmentation.

Table 2. Comparison on different label definitions.

N_{label}	SE module [8]		LAP module	
	$J_{\mathbf{B}}$	$J_{\mathbf{P}}$	$J_{\mathbf{B}}$	$J_{\mathbf{P}}$
(a)3	0.860	0.855	0.864	0.875
(b)4	0.737	0.861	0.743	0.868
(c)12	0.685	0.913	0.712	0.919
(d)19	0.347	0.854	0.398	0.898
(e)27	0.498	0.909	0.521	0.924

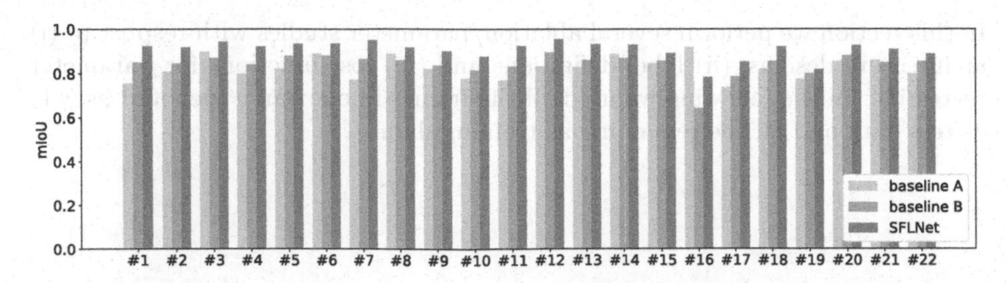

Fig. 7. Quantitative comparison between methods. #k represents the game id. Best viewed in color.

Loss Function for Parameter Regression. As discussed in Sect. 3.1, we have several choices for evaluating the parameter loss (*i.e.* τ in Eq. (2)). Here, we applied L1, L2 and smoothed L1 [12] losses to SFLNet and evaluate the performances. From the results shown in Table 3, we chose L1 loss for our parameter loss and used it in the following experiments.

Table 3. Comparison on different loss functions.

Loss	J_{p}
L2	0.912
L1	0.924
SmoothL1 [12]	0.887

4.4 Comparison to Baselines

Based on the above ablation results, we compared our approach to existing methods after tuning SFLNet to the best setting: We used both semantic segmentation and label adjacency prediction modules, and set $N_{label} = 27$ and τ as L1 norm. In the following evaluations we used our dataset in 1-vs-all manner. Specifically, we used all the frames from one game as a test set, and all the remaining as a training (or dictionary) set. Since to our knowledge existing works do not make their codes public, we implemented the following baselines for comparison:

- **Baseline A** This baseline extracts line parameters from semantic segmentation results and estimates a homography from line-to-line correspondences. We used segmentation results of SFLNet (setting $N_{label} = 27$) to estimate line parameters via the approach shown in [5] and used RANSAC for robust parameter estimation.
- **Baseline B** This baseline retrieves a dictionary (i.e. training data) based on a visual feature extracted from frames, and returns a homography corresponding to the nearest neighbor data. We used the intermediate feature map of SLFNet and used L2 norm for computing a similarity. We experimentally found that SFLNet feature works better than typical CNN feature extractors like ResNet.

Figure 7 shows the results with respect to $J_{\mathbf{p}}$. We can see that in most games SFLNet achieves best results. Compared to baseline B, SFLNet achieves better results on all the cases. Qualitative results shown in Fig. 8 also indicate SFLNet can correctly predict transformations between frames and the court model. However, in some cases (*i.e.* #16, #19) SFLNet does not perform well, and especially in the case of #16 the performance get worse results than baseline A. Some typical failure modes are shown in Fig. 9. One possible reason is a limited generalization power of our approach: Since in our dataset courts seen in frames like Fig. 9 are rare, SFLNet might fail to predict correct parameters. We may need to incorporate human supervision to address such unseen data.

Lastly, average running times per frame of methods are listed in Table 4. SFLNet is much faster than baselines and can be run over 30 FPS. Based on these results, we can say that our CNN-based single shot regressor is a reasonable choice with respect to both accuracy and efficiency for sports field localization.

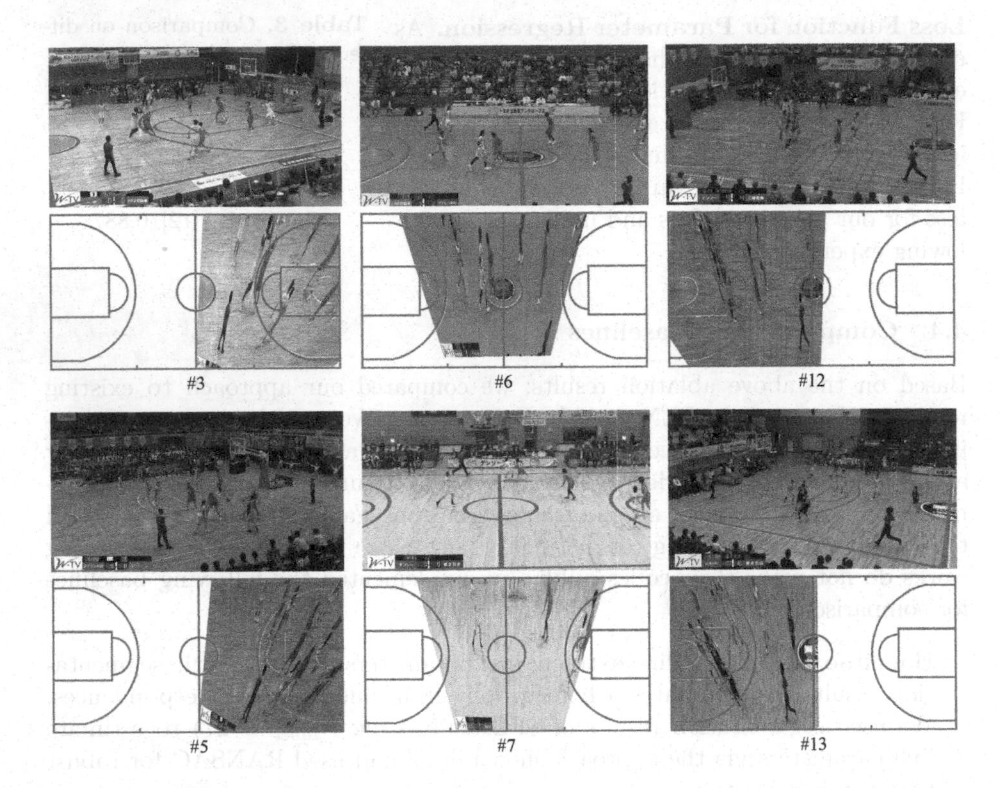

Fig. 8. Qualitative results of SFLNet. Odd rows show the projection of the model to the frame, and even rows show vice versa. #k represents the game id. Best viewed in color.

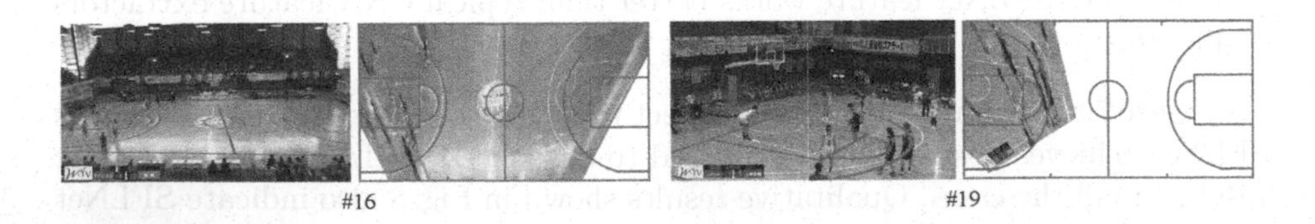

Fig. 9. Failure modes of SFLNet. #k represents the game id. Best viewed in color.

Table 4. Average running times per frame. We ran the algorithms on a standard desktop PC with a single GPU.

[ms]	Baseline A	Baseline B	SFLNet
	91.7	73.5	31.0

5 Conclusion

In this paper we proposed SFLNet, a CNN-based single shot regressor that predicts a parameter set relating a sports field in an input frame to its metric model. Experimental evaluations on our new dataset based on basketball games demonstrated that SFLNet can predict the parameter more precisely than baseline methods.

As a future work, we will evaluate our approach on different sports like soccer and hockey [4,5]. We also plan to extend SFLNet to sequential models, which can accept a video directly and produce temporally smooth results.

References

1. Theagarajan, R., Pala, F., Zhang, X., Bhanu, B.: Soccer: who has the ball? Generating visual analytics and player statistics. In: CVPR Workshop (2018)
2. Giancola, S., Amine, M., Dghaily, T., Ghanem, B.: SoccerNet: a scalable dataset for action spotting in soccer videos. In: CVPR Workshop (2018)
3. Gupta, A., Little, J.J., Woodham, R.J.: Using Line and Ellipse Features for Rectification of Broadcast Hockey Video, In: CRV (2011)
4. Chen, J., Zhu, F., Little, J.J.: A two-point method for PTZ camera calibration in sports. In: WACV (2018)
5. Homayounfar, N., Fidler, S., Urtasun, R.: Sports field localization via deep structured models. In: CVPR (2017)
6. Chen, J., Little, J.J.: Sports camera calibration via synthetic data. arXiv preprint (2018)
7. Sharma, R.A., Bhat, B., Gandhi, V., Jawahar, C.V.: Automated top view registration of broadcast football videos. In: WACV (2018)
8. Zhang, H., et al.: Context encoding for semantic segmentation. In: CVPR (2018)
9. Wu, H., Zhang, J., Huang, K.: FastFCN: rethinking dilated convolution in the backbone for semantic segmentation. arXiv preprint (2019)
10. He, K., Zhang, X., Ren, S., Sun, J.: Deep residual learning for image recognition. In: Proceedings of the CVPR (2016)
11. Lin, C.-H., Lucey, S.: Inverse compositional spatial transformer networks. In: CVPR (2017)
12. Girshick, R.: Fast R-CNN. In: ICCV (2015)
13. He, K., Gkioxari, G., Dollár, P., Girshick, R.: Mask R-CNN. In: ICCV (2017)
14. Kendall, A., Cipolla, R.: Modelling uncertainty in deep learning for camera relocalization. In: ICRA (2016)
15. Kendall, A., Cipolla, R.: Geometric loss functions for camera pose regression with deep learning. In: CVPR (2017)
16. Kendall, A., Grimes, M., Cipolla, R.: PoseNet: a convolutional network for real-time 6-DOF camera relocalization. In: ICCV (2015)
17. Brahmbhatt, B., Gu, J., Kim, K., Hays, J., Kautz, J.: Geometry-aware learning of maps for camera localization. In: CVPR (2018)
18. Sattler, T., Zhou, Q., Pollefeys, M., Leal-Taixé, L.: Understanding the limitations of CNN-based absolute camera pose regression. In: CVPR (2019)
19. Carr, P., Sheikh, Y., Matthews, I.: Point-less calibration: camera parameters from gradient-based alignment to edge images. In: WACV (2012)

20. Kim, H., Hong, K.S.: Soccer video mosaicing using self-calibration and line tracking. In: ICPR (200)
21. Yamada, A., Shirai, Y., Miura, J.: Tracking players and a ball in video image sequence and estimating camera parameters for 3D interpretation of soccer games. In: ICPR (2002)
22. Farin, D., Krabbe, S., With, P.H.N., de Effelsberg, W.: Robust camera calibration for sport videos using court models. In: Electronic Imaging (2004)
23. Watanabe, T., Haseyama, M., Kitajima, H.: A soccer field tracking method with wire frame model from TV images. In: ICIP (2004)
24. Wang, F., Sun, L., Yang, B., Yang, S.: Fast arc detection algorithm for play field registration in soccer video mining. In: ICSMC (2006)
25. Okuma, K., Little, J.J., Lowe, D.G.: Automatic rectification of long image sequences. In: ACCV (2004)
26. Dubrofsky, E., Woodham, R.J.: Combining line and point correspondences for homography estimation. In: Bebis, G., et al. (eds.) ISVC 2008. LNCS, vol. 5359, pp. 202–213. Springer, Heidelberg (2008). https://doi.org/10.1007/978-3-540-89646-3_20
27. Hess, R., Fern, A.: Improved video registration using nondistinctive local image features. In: CVPR (2007)
28. Chen, L.-C., Papandreou, G., Schroff, F., Adam, H.: Rethinking atrous convolution for semantic image segmentation. arXiv preprint (2017)
29. Yu, F., Koltun, V., Funkhouser, T.: Dilated residual networks. In: CVPR (2017)
30. Zhao, H., Shi, J., Qi, X., Wang, X., Jia, J.: Pyramid scene parsing network. In: CVPR (2017)
31. Hartley, R.I., Zisserman, A.: Multiple View Geometry in Computer Vision. Cambridge University Press, Cambridge (2004)
32. Szegedy, C., et al.: Going deeper with convolutions. In: CVPR (2015)

Trained Model Fusion for Object Detection Using Gating Network

Tetsuo Inoshita(✉), Yuichi Nakatani, Katsuhiko Takahashi, Asuka Ishii, and Gaku Nakano

NEC Corporation, Kawasaki, Japan
t-inoshita@ak.jp.nec.com, y-nakatani@da.jp.nec.com,
k-takahashi@fd.jp.nec.com, a-ishii@jg.jp.nec.com,
g-nakano@cq.jp.nec.com

Abstract. The major approaches of transfer learning in computer vision have tried to adapt the source domain to the target domain one-to-one. However, this scenario is difficult to apply to real applications such as video surveillance systems. As those systems have many cameras installed at each location regarded as source domains, it is difficult to identify the proper source domain. In this paper, we introduce a new transfer learning scenario that has various source domains and one target domain, assuming video surveillance system integration. Also, we propose a novel method for automatically producing a high accuracy model by fusing models trained at various source domains. In particular, we show how to apply a gating network to fuse source domains for object detection tasks, which is a new approach. We demonstrate the effectiveness of our method through experiments on traffic surveillance datasets.

1 Introduction

Along with the development of deep learning, the number of video surveillance systems with installations of hundreds of surveillance cameras is increasing. For improving recognition accuracy at new camera installation locations (target domain), for deep learning, it is helpful to use data at locations where cameras are already installed (source domains). However, as the data distribution is different at each camera installation location, finding the most suitable data from source domains is difficult.

Transfer learning aims to close the distribution gap between such different domains. These underlying technologies are to shift the data distribution of different domains so that models trained in the source domain can be used in the target domain. Fine-tuning is a simple and powerful way to use a pre-trained model [1]. The method is to fine-tune an existing network that was trained on a large dataset, such as the ImageNet [2], by continuing to train it (i.e., run back-propagation) on the smaller dataset we have.

In many typical approaches to transfer learning, a major assumption is that the source and target domain are transferred one-to-one by using an image classification task. Recently, as a more practical scenario, Cao [3, 4] proposed partial adversarial domain adaptation, which assumes that the source label space is a super space of the target label space. It can transfer knowledge from a big domain of many labels (e.g., ImageNet [2], Google Open Image [5]) to a small domain of few labels.

S. Palaiahnakote et al. (Eds.): ACPR 2019, LNCS 12046, pp. 691–704, 2020.
https://doi.org/10.1007/978-3-030-41404-7_49

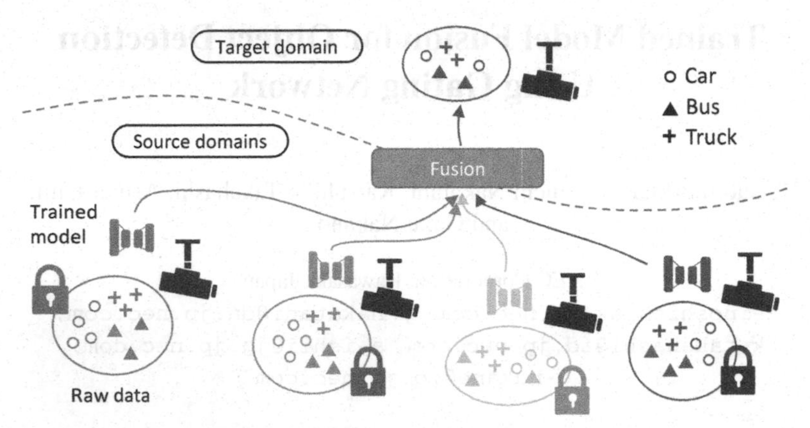

Fig. 1. Our transfer learning scenario supposes that the knowledge is transferred from various source domains to a target domain. Assuming that there is a video surveillance system, there are many source domains that consist of images from cameras installed at each location. However, due to privacy issues, we cannot use those images. Therefore, we handle the trained models that are generated by images and consist of parameters with a low privacy risk. Our proposed method produces a suitable model for a target domain by fusing trained models of these source domains.

However, in real applications, coping with the previous transfer learning scenarios is difficult. In the case of video surveillance systems, there are many live cameras that can be considered as multiple source domains. In this situation, transfer learning approaches require selecting suitable source domains for a target domain, but it is not easy. As each source domain consists of data generated by various camera locations, random selection from source domains may not be valid for a target domain and manual selection takes much time. Therefore, in this work, we focus on producing a good model for a target domain by using various source domains automatically, assuming the scenario of video surveillance system integration. Also, existing transfer learning approaches often deal with raw data, such as images or videos, as the source domain. However, storing these raw data is a high risk in terms of privacy. Instead, we utilize trained models that contain network parameters, not personal information. This trained model characteristic is effective in social implementation.

The challenge of this new scenario is to create a model suitable for a target domain with trained models that have various data distribution features that are generated in many environments (Fig. 1).

In this paper, we propose a fusing method for producing a high accuracy model for a target domain by using various trained models with different source domains. To accomplish this goal, we use the gating network, which was originally proposed using a mixture of experts [6, 7]. Basically, the previously proposed gating network aims to solve classification tasks. However, a method that applies to object detection tasks that estimate the location information of objects in an image has not been reported.

To summarize, our main contributions are as follows: we (1) introduce a new transfer learning scenario that assumes that there is video surveillance system integration and (2) design a method to optimally fuse various trained models that are trained in different source domains using the gating network, especially for object detection tasks.

Our experimental results show that our proposed method can achieve better detection accuracy than previous methods.

2 Related Work

2.1 Ensemble of Experts

Generally, an ensemble of multiple experts (e.g., pre-trained model, neural network, classifier, and detector) is a well-known technique to improve recognition accuracy [8–10]. Experts are used in many ways depending on the purpose. In this section, we define expert as three types (Fig. 2) as detailed below.

(1) detector-specific experts: These experts consist of various types of object detectors. In the studies of Bae et al. and Zhou et al. [11, 15], they provide a method for building an ensemble detection to combine different types of detectors (e.g., Faster R-CNN [12], SSD [13], DSSD [14], and YOLOv2 [16]). They demonstrate the effectiveness of their approach.
(2) class-specific experts: The target class of recognition is different for each expert. In [30], they design a multi-teacher knowledge distillation framework for the image classification task. Their purpose is to merge the knowledge from a lot of teachers (i.e., experts on cars, buses, trucks, birds, and flowers) into a single student model.
(3) bias-specific experts: We introduce a new definition of expert. The bias means the difference of data acquisition environment depending on the location, e.g. lighting, camera angles, and background. In video surveillance systems, for improving the accuracy, an expert is often trained by using the bias data of the installed location. Therefore, an expert becomes an expert specifically for the location. In this paper, our scenario defines the expert as the bias-specific expert.

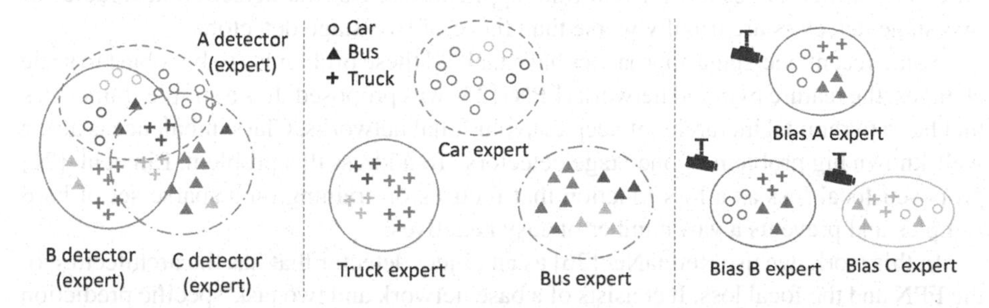

Fig. 2. (Left) detector-specific expert, (Center) class-specific expert, (Right) bias-specific expert. In this work, we deal with the bias-specific experts that are trained in different places. These experts have the same classes among experts, but differ from captured situations.

2.2 Gating Network

The gating network performs the important function of adjusting the fusion weights among the experts. The mixture of experts [6, 7] is one of the most popular methods that controls the activation of multiple experts using a gating network. This is achieved by training a gating network that maps each input to a distribution over the experts. These gating network architectures have been applied to various fields such as language models and machine translation [17–19].

In the field of computer vision, many applications using a gating network have been proposed [20]. Kim [21] introduced a deep fusion network that controls the amount of information coming from each modality through a gating network. Dodge et al. [22] proposed a visual saliency model that is formulated as a mixture of experts. The saliency map is computed as a weighted mixture of experts with weights determined by a gating network.

In our scenario, video surveillance system integration, due to the varieties of source domain, it is not easy to decide a source domain that is suitable for the target domain manually. Therefore, we design a method to optimally fuse various trained models that are trained in different source domains using a gating network automatically, especially for object detection tasks.

2.3 Object Detection

Current state-of-the-art object detectors have been classified into two types: (1) two-stage detectors (e.g., R-CNN [23], Faster R-CNN [12]) first generate a sparse set of candidate object region proposals and then refine the accurate object regions and the corresponding class labels by using CNN networks and (2) one-stage detectors (e.g., SSD [13], YOLOv3 [24]) are applied over a regular, dense sampling of object location that is called *anchor* [12]. The strength of one-stage detectors is high computational efficiency, which is desired for real time applications. But the detection accuracies of one-stage detectors are usually worse than those of two-stage detectors.

Some recent one-stage approaches have tackled these problems. To be robust to scale changes, the feature pyramid network (FPN) [25] was proposed. It is a simple framework that has a pyramidal hierarchy of deep convolutional networks. Class imbalance is also a well-known big problem of one-stage detectors. To address this problem, Lin et al. [26] proposed focal loss as a loss function that focuses on training on a sparse set of hard samples and prevents a vast number of easy negatives.

In this work, we use RetinaNet [26] as an object detector that has the architecture of the FPN and the focal loss. It consists of a base network and two task-specific prediction subnets. The role of the base network including the FPN is to extract features. The first subnet, the classification subnet, is used to classify objects and predict the probability of each anchor. The second subnet, the box regression subnet, is used to regress the bounding box position and the offset from each anchor box to the matched ground-truth object.

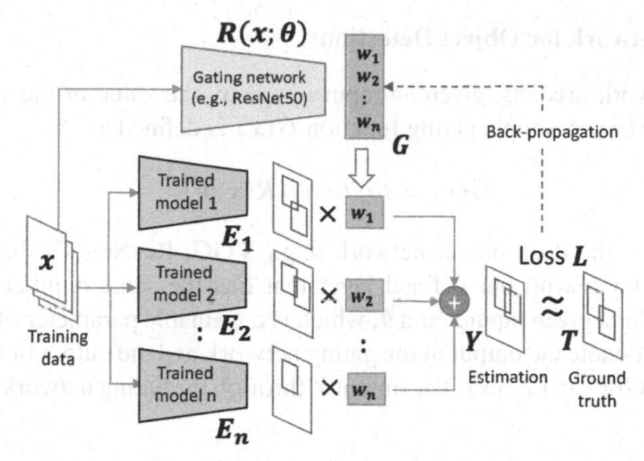

Fig. 3. The training framework of a gating network for object detection tasks. It has a function to fuse multiple trained models according to the weight. In the training phase, we calculate the weighted average of the output value of each trained model using the weight decided by the gating network. Then, we calculate the value of the loss function and re-train the gating network by simple back-propagation.

3 Proposed Method

3.1 Overall Structure

In this work, we treat the expert as a trained model that is learned by using data collected at each source domain. Our overall training framework is illustrated in Fig. 3. We aim to produce a high accuracy model for object detection tasks by fusing multiple trained models that had already been generated in various source domains. We use the gating network as the fusion function. The following two paragraphs summarize the training and inference phase.

Training Phase: A gating network is trained to decide the suitable weight for each trained model. First, we build a gating network that has the same number of outputs (w_n) as the number of experts. Second, to estimate object location in an image with trained models, we calculate the weighted average by using the output value of each trained model and the weight decided by the gating network. Finally, we calculate the value of the loss function and give feedback to the gating network by simple back-propagation.

Inference Phase: Object locations are predicted as bounding boxes in an image. First, an image is input to a gating network that has been already been trained, and then the fusion weights are acquired. Also, an image is input to each trained model, and then we stack the outputs that estimate the bounding boxes of objects. Second, we multiply the outputs by the weights, and then we apply non-maximum suppression (NMS) [27] for the outputs to remove overlapping boxes, which helps to reduce the number of unmerged false positives. After the NMS, we use the remaining boxes as final detections of the object.

3.2 Gating Network for Object Detection

Our gating network predicts, given an input image $\boldsymbol{x}$, the value of the weight of each trained model $\boldsymbol{E}(\boldsymbol{x})$. A simple gating function $\boldsymbol{G}(\boldsymbol{x})$ is defined as

$$\boldsymbol{G}(\boldsymbol{x}) = softmax(\boldsymbol{R}(\boldsymbol{x}; \boldsymbol{\theta})) \tag{1}$$

where $\boldsymbol{R}(\boldsymbol{x}; \boldsymbol{\theta})$ is the deep neural network (e.g., VGG, ResNet-50) that replaced the original output layer with our defined layer that has the same number of outputs of trained models for a given input $\boldsymbol{x}$ and $\boldsymbol{\theta}$, which is a trainable parameter of a deep neural network. Let us denote the output of the gating network and the output of the i-th trained model by using $\boldsymbol{G}(\boldsymbol{x})$ and $\boldsymbol{E}_i(\boldsymbol{x})$. The output $\boldsymbol{Y}$ through the gating network can be written as follows:

$$\boldsymbol{Y} = \sum_{i=1}^{n} \boldsymbol{G}(\boldsymbol{x})_i \boldsymbol{E}_i(\boldsymbol{x}) \tag{2}$$

As described in Sect. 2.3, RetinaNet consists of a box regression subnet that has the locations of the objects in the image and a classification subnet that has the classification score set for each object location. Both subnets weighted by the gating network can be denoted as

$$\boldsymbol{Y}_{reg} = \sum_{i}^{n} \boldsymbol{G}(\boldsymbol{x})_i \boldsymbol{E}_i(\boldsymbol{x})_{reg} \quad \boldsymbol{Y}_{cls} = \sum_{i}^{n} \boldsymbol{G}(\boldsymbol{x})_i \boldsymbol{E}_i(\boldsymbol{x})_{cls}$$

3.3 Training Gating Network

In the training phase on the gating network, our method minimizes the joint loss function that consists of regression loss and classification loss

$$\boldsymbol{l}_{reg} = l1\_smooth\left(\boldsymbol{Y}_{reg}, \boldsymbol{T}_{reg}\right) \tag{1}$$

$$\boldsymbol{l}_{cls} = focalweight \cdot BCE(\boldsymbol{Y}_{cls}, \boldsymbol{T}_{cls}) \tag{2}$$

$$\boldsymbol{L} = \boldsymbol{l}_{reg} + \boldsymbol{l}_{cls} \tag{3}$$

where the regression loss is the smooth L1 loss (l1_smooth) [28] between the prediction box $\boldsymbol{Y}$ and the ground-truth box $\boldsymbol{T}$.

Top-k Model Selection: If we have many trained models at the inference phase, we cannot apply these models to a real system due to a lack of computer resources. Therefore, we have to consider limiting the number of models used. We construct the gating network using the top k trained models instead of all of the trained models. Beforehand, we calculate the weight of the gating network using training data. Then, we select the top k trained models that have large weights. Finally, we re-train a gating network with selected models.

4 Experiments

Assuming traffic surveillance system integration, we evaluate the effectiveness of the proposed method by the detection accuracy of the vehicle. We consider the locations of the many surveillance cameras installed as source domains. Also, we consider the newly installed camera as the target domain.

4.1 Setup

Dataset: We use a part of the UA-DETRAC [29] dataset that contains 100 video sequences captured from real-world traffic scenes at different locations. In this work, we select 4 location videos as target domains (T1, T2, T3, and T4) for inference (Fig. 4). In this figure, for training, we are given a few target labeled data (T1′, T2′, T3′, and T4′). As source domains, we use 30 location videos (S1 to S30) (Fig. 5). Also, we set the detection target to the *car* class. The dataset pattern we used in this experiment is shown in Table 1, and more details are given in Appendix A.

Fig. 4. Upper row: target domain (inference dataset), T1, T2, T3, and T4. Lower row: training dataset, T1′, T2′, T3′, T4′ for fine-tuning and for training the gating network. When we fine-tune the model, we usually use data that is similar to the target domain as much as possible. Therefore, in these experiments, we use data obtained from different camera angles that is similar but not identical.

Fig. 5. A part of source domain dataset. Upper row: S1, S2, S3, and S4. Lower row: S27, S28, S29, and S30.

Table 1. Experimental datasets pattern

	Trained model	Fine-tuning	Average	Gating network
Training	S1, S2, ..., S30 (source domains)	T1′, T2′, T3′, T4′		
Inference	T1, T2, T3, and T4 (target domains)			

Trained Models: In total, we produce 30 trained models with RetinaNet architecture using a source domain dataset. For example, the trained model S1 is trained by using the S1 dataset in Appendix A. Most hyperparameters are set to be the same as those of the original RetinaNet.

Baseline: Fine-tuning: Fine-tuning is one of the effective methods of transfer learning. Generally, fine-tuning needs a lot of labeled data for training. However, it is not desirable due to the huge cost of data annotation. In view of the situation, we use few training data for fine-tuning. The number of each training data (T1′, T2′, T3′, and T4′) is 44, 80, 115, and 103, respectively. We fine-tune the same object detector, RetinaNet, as for the trained models above.

Baseline2: Average: We simply calculate an average of the outputs from 30 trained models (S1 to S30). We then apply NMS to these outputs and acquire the estimated object locations. This experimental condition can be considered as the uniform weight of the gating network. Therefore, when we evaluate this average method, we use a gating network in which all the weights are set to 1.

Proposed Method 1: Gating Network (all): The gating network architecture consists of ResNet-50 pre-trained on ImageNet as an initial value and an add output layer with the same number of outputs as the source domains. By using this architecture, we train the trainable weight of ResNet-50 with training data for the gating network. Under this condition, we use all the trained models as the elements of the gating network.

Proposed Method 2: Gating Network (top 5): The network architecture is the same as for the above condition, but the number of trained models used for the gating network is different. We use the top 5 trained models according to *top-k model selection* (Sect. 3.3). For example, the T1′ dataset is input into the gating network that consists of all the trained models (S1 to S30). Then, we choose the top 5 models with the highest weight value. Using these 5 models, we re-train the gating network with the T1′ dataset.

4.2 Results and Discussion

First, we evaluate the individual performance of the trained models considered as source domains. In Fig. 6, the accuracies for the T1, T2, T3, and T4 datasets are provided; more details are given in Appendix B. This shows that the trained models have their own strengths and weaknesses depending on the inference dataset. Thus, it is not easy to find one trained model (source domain) suitable for inference data.

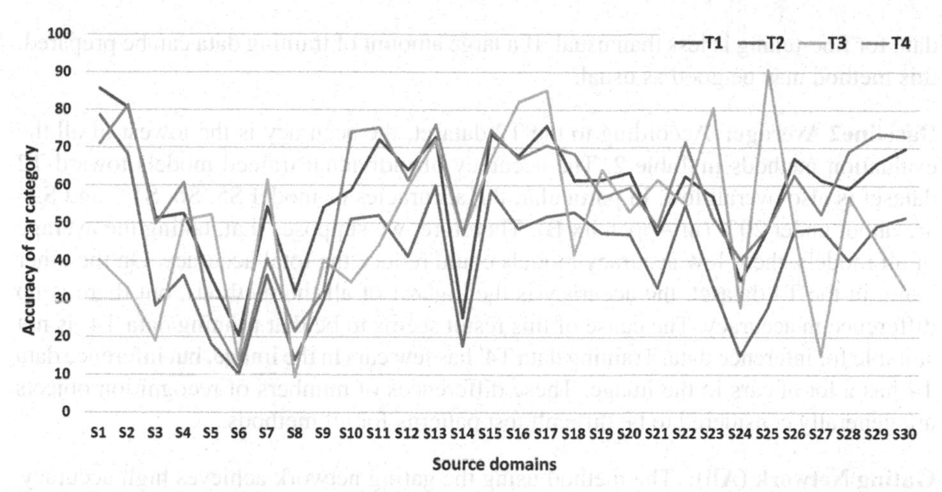

Fig. 6. Individual performance of 30 trained models. The accuracy of each source domain is different depending on the inference datasets (T1, T2, T3, and T4). Therefore, it is difficult to select one suitable trained model.

Next, we build a gating network using these trained models and compare the results with the results of the baselines with mean average precision (mAP) in Table 2. Judging the results of this experiment comprehensively, our proposed method (i.e., the gating network method) exceeds the baselines on several datasets. The following paragraphs discuss each individual method.

Maximum Accuracy of Trained Model: Trained models have the potential to achieve higher accuracy than baselines. But, as mentioned before at the beginning of this section, there is a large difference in accuracy between the trained models. It is difficult to choose the best trained model for the inference dataset. Therefore, selecting one trained model is not a realistic method for real applications.

Baseline Fine-Tuning: For inference data, the overall accuracy of the fine-tuning method is lower than that of other methods. However, the accuracy for all training datasets is 100% (not listed in Table 2). Therefore, the cause of this decrease in accuracy for inference data is considered to be over-fitting. In this scenario, the amount of training

Table 2. Mean average precision (mAP) of object detection task on UA-DETRAC (car)

Inference dataset	Max accuracy of trained model	Baseline: fine-tuning	Baseline2: average	Gating network: all (30 models)	Gating network: top 5 (5 models)
T1	85.6 (S1)	72.6	87.9	**90.4**	**91.0**
T2	78.6 (S1)	78.6	67.6	**80.5**	**81.6**
T3	90.7 (S25)	85.8	87.0	**94.1**	**93.7**
T4	81.3 (S2)	80.5	**82.1**	81.0	**82.0**

data for fine-tuning is less than usual. If a large amount of training data can be prepared, this method may be good as usual.

Baseline2 Average: According to the T2 dataset, the accuracy is the lowest of all the evaluation methods in Table 2. The accuracy of individual trained models toward T2 dataset is also overall low. In particular, the accuracies of model S5, S6, S14, and S24 are about under 20% (in Appendix B). Therefore, we supposes that, taking the average of all models, these low accuracy models could reduce the total accuracy. On the other hand, in the T4 dataset, the accuracy is the highest of all the methods, but there is no difference in accuracy. The cause of this result seems to be that training data T4' is not suitable for inference data. Training data T4′ has few cars in the image, but inference data T4 has a lot of cars in the image. These differences of numbers of recognition objects are generally considered to be difficult test patterns for all methods.

Gating Network (All): The method using the gating network achieves high accuracy. Gathering the knowledge of all the trained models seems to be effective for improving accuracy. It is considered that the optimal weight that is applied to all trained models is estimated for each inference data. Thus, even if there is few training data, we can increase the accuracy to utilize the existing trained models. Although not stated in Table 2, the accuracy for all training data (T1′, T2′, T3′, and T4′) is 92.75% on average. As mentioned in the result of fine-tuning section, in the case of fine-tuning, the accuracy for training data is 100% on average. This result is not considered to be over-fitting unlike with the fine-tuning results. Therefore, we assume that the gating network has a regularization effect.

Gating Network (Top 5): Once we train the gating network using all trained models, finally, we pick the top 5 trained models that have a large weight value manually (Table 3). That is to say, the trained model that is the most meaningful is selected for training data. As the training and inference data are similar, selected trained models are also suitable for inference data. Compared to the gating network (all) method, even the number of trained models has been reduced by 1/6, and the accuracy is almost the same or slightly improved. This result shows the accuracy remains good while suppressing the increase in computer resources.

Table 3. Top 5 selected trained models and their weight value of the gating network.

T1		T2		T3		T4	
Selected model	Weight value	Selected model	Weight value	Selected model	Weight value	Selected model	Weight value
S2	41.2	S1	44.6	S2	41.2	S1	44.6
S1	14.1	S2	14.1	S1	14.1	S2	14.1
S11	10.9	S15	8.1	S11	10.9	S15	8.1
S15	5.5	S10	6.6	S15	5.5	S10	6.6
S29	4.5	S19	4.0	S29	4.5	S19	4.0

Table 4. The accuracy (mAP) when increasing the number of models to be fused

Inference dataset	S1–S5 (5 models)	S1–S10 (10 models)	S1–S15 (15 models)	S1–S20 (20 models)	S1–S30 (30 models)
T1	87.9	87.1	89.0	**90.7**	**90.4**
T2	79.2	**81.7**	81.1	**81.3**	80.5
T3	66.5	70.0	81.7	**91.2**	**94.1**
T4	80.9	80.5	80.2	**81.3**	**81.0**

Effect of Number of Models on Accuracy: In the previous discussions, we chose the top 5 trained models according to the weight value. How does the accuracy change as the number of models is increased incrementally? In answering this question, we performed additional experiments. In Table 4, we show the results of adding the trained models. As an overall trend, adding the trained models tends to increase the accuracy. Focusing on the T3 dataset, the accuracy increases dramatically from 15 to 20 models. That is to say, the added models (S16, S17, S18, S19, and S20) contribute to the accuracy improvement. In particular, models S16 and S17 have accuracy within the top 3 of all the trained models in T3 (Appendix B). On the other hand, in the case of T2, adding the rest of the 10 models (from S21 to S30) has an adverse effect. The accuracies of the added models (from S21 to S30) are not good (Appendix B). Thus, adding a model with low accuracy will not contribute to improving the accuracy, but rather will lead to a bad result.

5 Conclusion

Existing transfer learning has focused on how to close the gap between a source domain and a target domain one-to-one. In this work, we have introduced and tackled a new scenario of transfer learning with various source domains. This scenario often arises in real applications, especially in video surveillance systems. In this situation, we propose a method to fuse many trained models using a gating network and apply these models to the object detection tasks. Our method is evaluated on the UA-DETRAC dataset and performs significantly better than the baseline methods. Safe and precise video surveillance system integration is one of the keys to social implementation. We have shown in this paper that it is possible. For future work, to further suppress the increase in the number of models, we will work on knowledge distillation technology.

Appendices

A UA-DETRAC Dataset

Model	File name	Model	File name	Model	File name
S1	mvi_20011 mvi_20012	S11	mvi_40141	S21	mvi_40752
S2	mvi_20051 mvi_20052	S12	mvi_40152	S22	mvi_40871
S3	mvi_39771	S13	mvi_40161 mvi_40162	S23	mvi_41073
S4	mvi_39781	S14	mvi_40181	S24	mvi_63525
S5	mvi_39801	S15	mvi_40191 mvi_40192	S25	mvi_63561 mvi_63562 mvi_63563
S6	mvi_39811	S16	mvi_40201	S26	mvi_39031
S7	mvi_39821	S17	mvi_40204	S27	mvi_39211
S8	mvi_39851	S18	mvi_40771 mvi_40772 mvi_40774 mvi_40775	S28	mvi_39371
S9	mvi_39931	S19	mvi_40732	S29	mvi_39401
S10	mvi_40131	S20	mvi_40751	S30	mvi_39501

Model	File name	Model	File name
T1	mvi_20034 mvi_20035	T1′	mvi_20032
T2	mvi_20063 mvi_20064 mvi_20065	T2′	mvi_20061
T3	mvi_63554	T3′	mvi_63352
T4	mvi_40714	T4′	mvi_40711

B Accuracy of Trained Model on Test Dataset

Model	T1	T2	T3	T4	Model	T1	T2	T3	T4
S1	85.6	78.6	40.3	71	S16	67.7	48.6	82.1	67
S2	80.6	68.1	32.8	81.3	S17	75.7	51.7	85.1	70.5
S3	51.3	28.2	18.9	49.8	S18	61.3	52.9	41.7	68.3
S4	52.5	36.1	50.8	60.7	S19	61.5	47.4	64.1	56.8
S5	35.4	18.1	52.2	24.7	S20	63.4	47.1	53	59.4
S6	20.3	10.1	13.7	11.6	S21	47.1	32.9	61.5	49.1
S7	54.3	36.3	61.4	40.6	S22	62.4	54.9	55.1	71.4
S8	31.7	13.9	9.3	21.5	S23	57	34	81	51
S9	54.2	29.7	40.2	32	S24	34.8	15.1	27.8	40.4
S10	58.7	51.1	34.4	74.1	S25	48.5	27.8	90.7	48.8
S11	72.1	52	44.3	75.2	S26	67.2	47.9	48.6	62.7
S12	64.1	41.2	59.6	61.3	S27	61.4	48.6	14.9	52.4
S13	72.8	59.9	72.1	76.1	S28	59.2	40.1	57.1	69.1
S14	25.1	17.6	47	47.1	S29	65.9	49.3	44.8	73.7
S15	73.6	58.7	66.8	74.7	S30	69.8	51.5	32.8	73

References

1. Chu, B., Madhavan, V., Beijbom, O., Hoffman, J., Darrell, T.: Best practices for fine-tuning visual classifiers to new domains. In: Hua, G., Jégou, H. (eds.) ECCV 2016. LNCS, vol. 9915, pp. 435–442. Springer, Cham (2016). https://doi.org/10.1007/978-3-319-49409-8_34
2. Russakovsky, O., et al.: ImageNet large scale visual recognition challenge. IJCV **115**, 211–252 (2015)
3. Cao, Z., Long, M., Wang, J., Jordan, M.I.: Partial transfer learning with selective adversarial networks. In: CVPR (2018)
4. Cao, Z., Ma, L., Long, M., Wang, J.: Partial adversarial domain adaptation. In: Ferrari, V., Hebert, M., Sminchisescu, C., Weiss, Y. (eds.) ECCV 2018. LNCS, vol. 11212, pp. 139–155. Springer, Cham (2018). https://doi.org/10.1007/978-3-030-01237-3_9
5. Krasin I., et al.: OpenImages: a public dataset for large-scale multi-label and multi-class image classification (2017). https://storage.googleapis.com/openimages/web/index.html
6. Jacobs, R.A., Jordan, M.I., Nowlan, S., Hinton, G.E.: Adaptive mixtures of local experts. Neural Comput. **3**, 1–12 (1991)
7. Jordan, M.I., Jacobs, R.A.: Hierarchical mixtures of experts and the EM algorithm. Neural Comput. **6**, 181–214 (1994)
8. Freund, Y.: Boosting a weak learning algorithm by majority. Inf. Comput. **121**(2), 256–285 (1995)
9. Opitz, D., Maclin, R.: Popular ensemble methods: an empirical study. J. Artif. Intell. Res. **11**, 169–198 (1999)
10. Hansen, L.K., Salamon, P.: Neural network ensembles. IEEE Trans. Pattern Anal. Mach. Intell. **12**(10), 993–1001 (1990)

11. Bae, S., Lee, Y., Jo, Y., Bae, Y., Hwang, J.: Rank of experts: detection network ensemble. CoRR, abs/1712.00185 (2017)
12. Ren, S., He, K., Girshick, R.B., Sun, J.: Faster R-CNN: towards real-time object detection with region proposal networks. IEEE Trans. Pattern Anal. Mach. Intell. **39**(6), 1137–1149 (2017)
13. Liu, W., et al.: SSD: single shot multibox detector. In: Leibe, B., Matas, J., Sebe, N., Welling, M. (eds.) ECCV 2016. LNCS, vol. 9905, pp. 21–37. Springer, Cham (2016). https://doi.org/10.1007/978-3-319-46448-0_2
14. Fu, C., Liu, W., Ranga, A., Tyagi, A., Berg, A.C.: DSSD: deconvolutional single shot detector. CoRR, abs/1701.06659 (2017)
15. Zhou, G., Dulloor, S., Andersen, D.G., Kaminsky, M.: EDF: ensemble, distill, and fuse for easy video labeling. CoRR, abs/1812.03626 (2018)
16. Redmon, J., Farhadi, A.: Yolo9000: better, faster, stronger. In: CVPR (2017)
17. Eigen, D., Ranzato, M., Sutskever, I.: Learning factored representations in a deep mixture of experts. In: ICLR Workshops (2014)
18. Dodge, S., Karam, L.: Quality resilient deep neural networks. CoRR, abs/1703.08119 (2017)
19. Aljundi, R., Chakravarty, P., Tuytelaars, T.: Expert gate: lifelong learning with a network of experts. In: CVPR (2017)
20. Tokunaga, H., Teramoto, Y., Yoshizawa, A., Bise, R.: Adaptive weighting multi-field-of-view CNN for semantic segmentation in pathology. In: CVPR (2019)
21. Kim, J., Koh, J., Kim, Y., Choi, J., Hwang, Y., Choi, J.W.: Robust deep multi-modal learning based on gated information fusion network. CoRR, abs/1807.06233 (2018)
22. Dodge, S., Karam, L.: Visual saliency prediction using a mixture of deep neural networks. IEEE Trans. Image Prosessing **27**(8), 4080–4090 (2018)
23. Girshick, R., Donahue, J., Darrel, T., Malik, J.: Rich feature hierarchies for accurate object detection and semantic segmentation. In: CVPR (2014)
24. Redmon, J., Farhadi, A.: YOLOv3: an incremental improvement. CoRR, abs/1804.02767 (2018)
25. Lin, T.Y., Dollar, P., Girshick, R., He, K., Hariharan, B., Belongie, S.: Feature pyramid networks for object detection. In: CVPR (2017)
26. Lin, T.Y., Goyal, P., Girshick, R., He, K., Dollar, P.: Focal loss for dense object detection. IEEE Trans. Pattern Anal. Mach. Intell. **42**(2), 318–327 (2020)
27. Felzenszwalb, P., Girshick, R., McAllester, D., Ramanan, D.: Object detection with discriminatively trained part based models. EEE Trans. Pattern Anal. Mach. Intell. **32**, 1627–1645 (2010)
28. Girshick, R.: Fast R-CNN. In: ICCV (2015)
29. L. Wen, et al.: UA-DETRAC: a new benchmark and protocol for multi-object detection and tracking. CoRR, abs/1511.04136 (2015)
30. Gao, J., Guo, Z., Li, Z., Nevatia, R.: Knowledge concentration: learning 100K object classifiers in a single CNN. CoRR, abs/1711.07607 (2017)

Category Independent Object Transfiguration with Domain Aware GAN

Kaori Kumagai(✉), Yukito Watanabe, Takashi Hosono, Jun Shimamura, and Atsushi Sagata

NTT Media Intelligence Laboratories, NTT Corporation,
1-1, Hikarinooka, Yokosuka-Shi, Kanagawa, Japan
kaori.kumagai.mw@hco.ntt.co.jp

Abstract. Object transfiguration aims to translate the domain of objects in an image. In this paper, we challenge a new task: category independent object transfiguration, which enables objects to be transfigured even for object categories not included in the training data. Conventional methods are based on the premise that the object categories in the test images are contained in the training images. Therefore, they can train transfer regions and magnitude implicitly, and they accurately estimate the transfer regions and magnitude in test images. However, when an image containing object categories not included in the training data is input, this premise breaks down. Consequently, undesired regions are converted with undesired magnitude. To tackle this problem, we propose a domain region and magnitude aware GAN that explicitly predicts transfer region and magnitude, and translates so that the predicted region and magnitude before and after translation are the same. Experimental results show that our method can more realistically and accurately translate the object domains than the state-of-the-art method.

Keywords: Generative adversarial networks · Image-to-image translation · Category independent object transfiguration

1 Introduction

Object transfiguration aims to translate object domains in an image and generate realistic images while preserving object identity information. For example, the upper part of Fig. 1 shows the results of our method. The left part shows the results converted from brown domain to stripe domain, and the right part shows the results converted from yellow domain to green, pink and blue domains. This task can be widely used as a fundamental processing method for various computer vision applications, such as object style translation [21] and face manipulation [3]. State-of-the-art methods often utilize Variational Auto Encoder (VAE) and Generative Adversarial Networks (GAN). They usually require a lot of training data that contain the same object category as the input data (Fig. 2(a)).

S. Palaiahnakote et al. (Eds.): ACPR 2019, LNCS 12046, pp. 705–719, 2020.
https://doi.org/10.1007/978-3-030-41404-7_50

Fig. 1. Category independent object transfiguration results obtained with our method and the conventional method (StarGAN [3]). Our method can convert only the object domain realistically while preserving object identity information. On the other hand, StarGAN converts background region or the face region of the bear. (Color figure online)

However, collecting a lot of training data is generally difficult when the object categories to be converted are not included in the public data.

To break through this limitation, we challenged a new task named category independent object transfiguration, which aims to transfer object categories not included in the training data (Fig. 2(b)). If the conventional method [3] is applied to this task, unexpected regions are translated. For example, as shown in the lower left part of Fig. 1, when converting to stripe domain, stripes appear in the background region. In addition, the face region is strongly translated into stripes. Namely, conventional methods translate images at inappropriate regions and magnitude and the object identity information disappears.

This problem is due to the fact that the conventional methods do not predict the transfer region and magnitude. The conventional methods are based on the premise that the object categories in the test images are contained in the training images. Thus, they can train transfer regions and magnitude implicitly, and they accurately estimate the transfer regions and magnitude in test images. However, when images containing object categories not included in training data are input, this premise breaks down and undesired regions are converted with undesired magnitude. For these reasons, the conventional methods do not work well for category independent object transfiguration.

In this paper, we tackle the problems by using domain region and magnitude aware GAN. In order to convert to realistic images, we assume that the domain region and domain magnitude should not change between before and after translation. For example, in Fig. 1 the brown domain should appear strongly in the torso of the bear that needed to be strongly converted. Furthermore, the brown domain should appear moderately in the eye that needed to be moderately converted. On the basis of this assumption, we introduced a domain segmentation network that predicts domain region, and consider the output probability of this

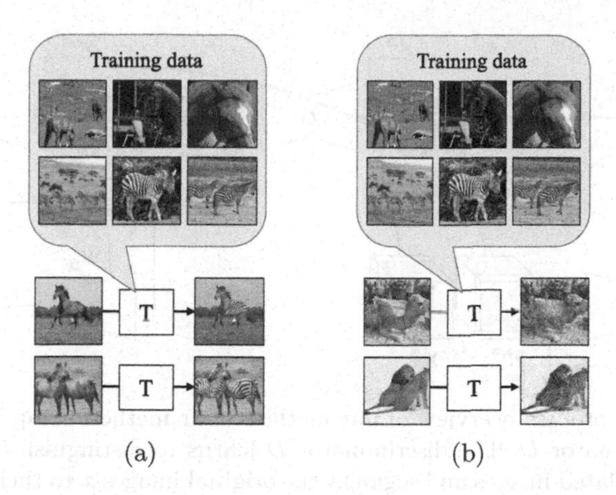

Fig. 2. Object transfiguration settings. Translating model T learned using training data transfers the test image to the target image. Under general object transfiguration setting (a), the object category in the test image is contained in the training images. In contrast, under category independent object transfiguration setting (b), the object category in the test image is not contained in the training images.

network as domain magnitude. We also tried to transfer it so that the domain probability distributions of object images before and after translation would not change. In particular, we introduced a domain magnitude consistency loss that calculates the difference between the probability distributions of object images before and after translation.

We conducted experiments using the Microsoft COCO dataset [9] and color dataset [20]. The experimental results show that our method can more realistically and accurately translate object domains while preserving object identity information than conventional method.

In short, the contributions of this paper are as follows:

- We challenge a new task: category independent object transfiguration.
- We propose a domain region and magnitude aware GAN that explicitly predicts transfer region and magnitude.

The remainder of this paper is organized as follows: In Sect. 2, we briefly review conventional methods for object transfiguration method. In Sect. 3, we explore in more detail the work most relevant to ours. In Sect. 4, we detail our method. We describe our implementation details in Sect. 5. In Sect. 6, we report on our experiment results that confirm our method's effectiveness through comparison with StarGAN [3] using the Microsoft COCO dataset [9] and color dataset [20]. In Sect. 7, we conclude the paper with a summary of key points and mention our future work.

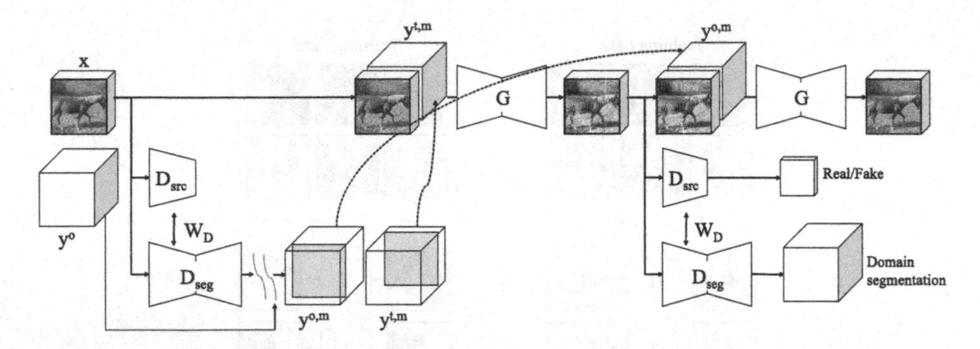

Fig. 3. Learning process overview of our method. Our method comprises a generator G and a discriminator D. The discriminator D learns to distinguish between original images and translated images and segment the original images x to their corresponding original domain binary mask y^o. G receives a matrix concatenated to the original image x and the target domain magnitude matrix $y^{t,m}$ and aims to generate a translated image $G(x, y^{t,m})$ that is indistinguishable from original images and segmented as the $y^{t,m}$ indicating the desired domain region and magnitude. G aims to reconstruct the original image x from a matrix concatenated from the translated image $G(x, y^{t,m})$ and the original domain magnitude matrix $y^{o,m}$.

2 Related Work

Object transfiguration has been developed as one of task in Image-to-Image translation [5–7,10,11,18,19,21]. We first briefly review recent image-to-image translation methods, and then review object transfiguration methods.

The pix2pix [6] is an image-to-image translation method that learns a mapping from input to output images using conditional GANs [12]. This method utilizes L_1 loss, which is Mean Absolute Error (MAE) between a target image that differs only in the object domain from the original image and a translated image. Thus, a paired data sequence that differs only in the object domain is required for training. Some methods [7,21] tackle unpaired settings. These methods reconstruct a translated image into a original image, and introduce cycle consistency loss, which calculates MAE between the original image and the reconstructed image. Therefore, these methods can learn in unpaired settings. These methods, however, can only handle one-to-one correspondence domain translation using a model, and they are inefficient in such multi-domain image-to-image translation tasks. StarGAN [3], which is the work most relevant to ours, can translate multiple domains with only one model. StarGAN [3] not only achieves efficient multi-domain image-to-image translation, but also improves translation quality. However, all these methods are based on the premise that the object categories in test images are contained in the training images. Thus, they cannot estimate transfer regions and magnitude accurately for category independent object transfiguration.

Several methods address the problem of object transfiguration in which only the object regions needs to be translated [2,13,14]. These methods utilize attention masks for blending translated images and original images. The translating models learn mapping between the object categories in the training data, like the generator of StarGAN [3]. These method cannot translate the object category not included in the training data.

3 Preliminaries

In this section, we explore in more detail about StarGAN [3] which is the most relevant work to ours. StarGAN comprises two networks, a generator G and a discriminator D. Their goal is to train the generator G, which learns the mappings among multiple domains. To achieve this, they introduce an auxiliary classifier for controlling multiple domains on top of D. The discriminator D, therefore, produces two probability distributions, $D_{src}(\cdot)$ and $D_{cls}(\cdot)$, when an image is given. $D_{src}(\cdot)$ represents the probability distribution over original images, and $D_{cls}(\cdot)$ represents the probability distribution over domain labels. D learns to minimize the following objective L_D, defined as

$$L_D = -L_{adv} + \lambda_{cls} L^o_{cls}, \tag{1}$$

where L_{adv} is the adversarial loss, L^o_{cls} is the domain classification loss and λ_{cls} is a hyper-parameter that controls the relative importance of domain classification loss compared to the adversarial loss. By maximizing L_{adv}, D learns to discriminate between original and translated images, and by minimizing L^o_{cls}, D learns to classify the image to a domain label. On the other hand, G learns to minimize the following objective L_G, defined as

$$L_G = L_{adv} + \lambda_{cls} L^g_{cls} + \lambda_{cyc} L_{cyc}, \tag{2}$$

where L^g_{cls} is the domain classification loss, L_{cyc} is the cycle consistency loss and λ_{cls} and λ_{cyc} are hyper-parameters that control the relative importance of domain classification and cycle consistency losses compared to the adversarial loss respectively. By minimizing L_{adv}, G learns to convert to an image that is indistinguishable from original images, and by minimizing L^g_{cls}, G learns to convert to an image that is classified to the target domain label. Moreover, by minimizing cycle consistency loss L_{cyc}, G learns to convert to an image preserving the content of its original image.

4 Domain Region and Magnitude Aware GAN

To address the issue of category independent object transfiguration, we propose domain region and magnitude aware GAN that explicitly predicts transfer region and magnitude. The learning process overview of our method is shown in Fig. 3. On the basis of our assumption that realistic images should be generated by converting images so that the domain region and magnitude before and after translation are the same, we introduce a domain segmentation network D_{seg}, that predicts the domain region, and consider the output probability of the network as domain magnitude. Moreover, for learning that domain region and magnitude do not change between before and after conversion, we introduce domain magnitude consistency loss L_{mag} that calculates the difference between the domain probability distributions before and after translation. D and G learn to minimize the objectives L_D and L_G, defined as

$$L_D = -L_{adv} + \lambda_{seg} L_{seg}, \tag{3}$$

$$L_G = L_{adv} + \lambda_{mag} L_{mag} + \lambda_{cyc} L_{cyc}, \tag{4}$$

where L_{adv} and L_{cyc} are the same as them in StarGAN [3]. L_{seg} is the domain segmentation loss. λ_{seg}, λ_{mag} and λ_{cyc} are hyper-parameters that control respectively the relative importance of domain segmentation, domain magnitude consistency and cycle consistency losses compared to the adversarial loss. By minimizing L_{seg}, D learns to segment an image to a domain mask. By minimizing L_{mag}, G learns to convert so as not to change the domain probability distributions before and after translation. Here, let us define $y^o \in \mathbb{R}^{H\times W\times N}$, $y^{t,m} \in \mathbb{R}^{H\times W\times N}$ and $y^{o,m} \in \mathbb{R}^{H\times W\times N}$. N is the number of domains that are trained at one time. y^o is the original domain binary mask which represents the domain of each region in original image. In particular, when domain n is located at (h, w) in original image, $y^o_{h,w,n} = 1$. $y^{o,m}$ is the original domain magnitude matrix which represents the domain region and magnitude of the original image. $y^{t,m}$ is the target domain magnitude matrix which represents the domain region and magnitude of the target image. $y^{o,m}$ and $y^{t,m}$ are created using y^o and $D_{seg}(x)$, which are the domain probability distribution of x predicted by D_{seg}. In particular, as shown in Fig. 4, $y^{o,m}$ is the product of $D_{seg}(x)$ and y^o. Specifically, when domain $\tilde{n}$ is located at $(\tilde{h}, \tilde{w})$ in x, $y^{o,m}_{\tilde{h},\tilde{w},\tilde{n}} = D_{seg}(x)_{\tilde{h},\tilde{w},\tilde{n}}$ and $y^{o,m}_{\tilde{h},\tilde{w},n\neq\tilde{n}} = 0$. Then, $y^{t,m}$ is the channel shifted $y^{o,m}$ that means a matrix for which the original domain channel in $y^{o,m}$ is replaced with the target domain channel. In this section, we first explain the network architecture and then the loss functions L_{seg} and L_{mag}.

4.1 Architecture

As input in the learning process, the network is given the original image $x \in \mathbb{R}^{H\times W\times 3}$ and the original domain binary mask y^o. $y^{o,m}$ and $y^{t,m}$ are created using x and $D_{seg}(x)$ in the above mentioned way. G generates the translated image $G(x, y^{t,m})$ from a matrix concatenated with x and $y^{t,m}$. Then, D is given $G(x, y^{t,m})$, and discriminates whether it is realistic using D_{src} and whether it has a domain in each region using D_{seg}. Finally, G is given the matrix concatenated with $G(x, y^{t,m})$ and $y^{o,m}$ and generates the reconstructed image $G(G(x, y^{t,m}), y^{o,m})$.

Note that, as input in test phase, the network is given only the original image x. And then, $y^{o,m}$ and $y^{t,m}$ are created using only $D_{seg}(x)$. In particular, about

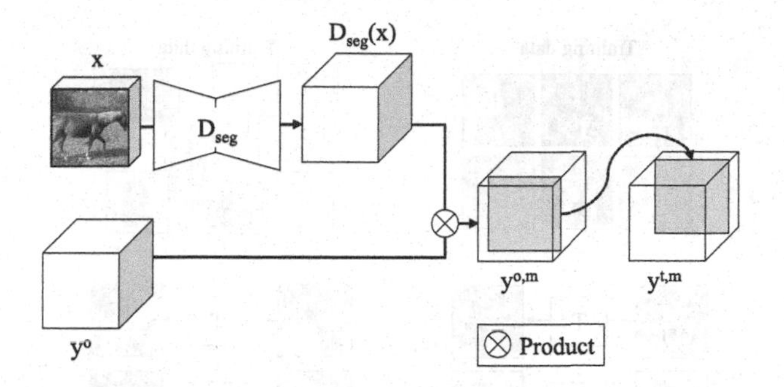

Fig. 4. Process of creating the domain matrices. The original domain magnitude matrix $y^{o,m}$ is the product of $D_{seg}(x)$ and the original domain binary mask y^o. The target domain magnitude matrix $y^{t,m}$ is the channel shifted $y^{o,m}$ that means a matrix which the original domain channel in $y^{o,m}$ is replaced with the target domain channel.

position $(\tilde{h}, \tilde{w})$ in $D_{seg}(x)$, when the domain with the largest probability value is $\tilde{n}$, $y^{o,m}_{\tilde{h},\tilde{w},\tilde{n}} = D_{seg}(x)_{\tilde{h},\tilde{w},\tilde{n}}$ and $y^{o,m}_{\tilde{h},\tilde{w},n \neq \tilde{n}} = 0$. And then, $y^{t,m}$ is a channel shifted $y^{o,m}$.

4.2 Loss Functions

Domain Segmentation Loss. In order to acquire a domain segmentation network D_{seg} that predicts domain region in images, we employ domain segmentation loss when optimizing D. Specifically, the former is defined as

$$L_{seg} = \mathbb{E}_{x,y^o}[-logD_{seg}(y^o|x)], \tag{5}$$

where the term $D_{seg}(y^o|x)$ represents a probability distribution that D_{seg} predicts y^o when x is input to D_{seg}. By minimizing this objective, D learns to segment a real image x to its corresponding original domain mask y^o.

Domain Magnitude Consistency Loss. To be able to translate so as not to change the domain probability values before and after conversion, we employ this loss function. Given $y^{t,m}$ indicating the target domain probability distribution, G is trained to generate an image that has the same probability distribution, defined as

$$L_{mag} = \mathbb{E}_{x,y}[-log(|D_{seg}(y^t|G(x, y^{t,m})) - y^{t,m}|)]. \tag{6}$$

where y^t is the target domain binary mask which is the channel shifted y^o. By minimizing this objective, G learns to generate images that can be segmented as the target domain magnitude matrix $y^{t,m}$.

5 Implementation Details

Our generator network architecture is the same as that for the network from CycleGAN [21] and StarGAN [3] which is composed of two stride-2 convolutions, five residual blocks [4] and two 1/2-strided convolutions. We use instance

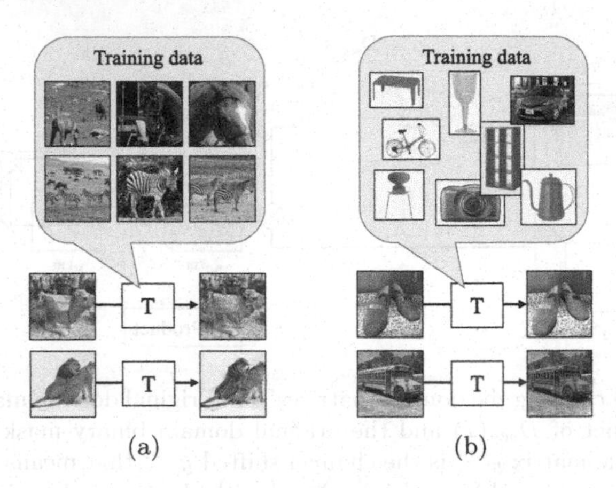

Fig. 5. Two kinds of training data. (a) One comprises few object categories. The domain to learn is unique for each object category. (b) The other comprises a wide variety of object categories. The domain to learn is the common domain among a wide variety of object categories.

normalization [17] for the generator. For the D_{src}, we leverage PatchGANs [6] which classifies whether local image patches are real or fake. For domain segmentation D_{seg}, we share the first five layers in D_{src} as an encoder, and add five 1/2-strided convolutions as a decoder. Finally, the output size becomes the same as that of the input image.

The learning settings were determined on the basis of [3]. All models were trained using Adam [8] with $\beta_1 = 0.5$ and $\beta_2 = 0.999$. We performed one generator update after five discriminator updates as reported by Arjovsky et al. [1]. The batch size was set to 16 for all experiments. We trained all models with a learning rate of 0.0001 for the first 10 epochs and linearly decayed the learning rate to 0 over the next 10 epochs. We used $\lambda_{seg} = 1$, $\lambda_{mag} = 1$ and $\lambda_{rec} = 10$ in all of our experiments. The training took about two days on a single NVIDIA Tesla P100 GPU.

6 Experiments

Training Data. As shown in Fig. 5, we performed our evaluations under two kinds of training data. One comprised few object categories (Fig. 5(a)), described in Subsect. 6.1. In this case, the domain to learn was unique for each object category. We conducted this experiment to confirm that our method is superior to the conventional method for category independent object transfiguration. The other training data comprised a wide variety of object categories (Fig. 5(b)), described in Subsect. 6.2. In this case, the domains to learn (e.g., color domain) was common to multiple object categories. This data type had not been used in experiments performed in conventional studies because the conventional methods implicitly learned the transfer region and magnitude using a large amount of training images for each object category. In contrast, our method explicitly predicts transfer region and magnitude using a domain segmentation network that learn to detect the domains. Therefore, the training images only need to have a domain, need not have a specific object category. In conducting this experiment, we demonstrate that object transfiguration is possible as long as images having the domain can be collected, even if sufficient object category images cannot be collected.

Evaluation Metrics. We qualitatively and quantitatively evaluated the translated images. In the qualitatively evaluation, we observed the translated images to determine whether our method's effectiveness could be seen in the translated images. In the quantitative evaluation, we used two evaluation values. One is to confirm that the desired region are converted to the desired domain with the desired magnitude, we used the Mean Squared Error (MSE) between the original domain channel in $D_{seg}(x)$ and the target domain channel in $D_{seg}(G(x, \cdot))$, called *segmentation MSE*. The smaller the *segmentation MSE* is, the generator can convert to the desired domain not to change the domain region and magnitude before and after translation. Another value is to confirm that the background region do not change, we used the MSE between the background region in the original image x and in the translated image $G(x, \cdot)$, called *background MSE*. In particular, given test samples comprised original images x and object masks m, to calculate the region other than object in x and $G(x, \cdot)$, we used the multiplication of $(1 - m)$ and those images. The smaller the *background MSE* is, the generator can convert not to change the background region.

Baselines. In order to validate the contribution of our method for category independent object transfiguration, using StarGAN [3] as an conventional image-to-image translation method, we conducted experiments with three methods: *StarGAN*, *StarGAN+domain region aware* and *StarGAN+domain region and magnitude aware (our method)*. The *StarGAN+*domain region aware method is the same as ours in terms of network architecture and domain segmentation loss. However, since it is not aware of the domain magnitude, as matrices concatenated to the image, it uses y^o instead of $y^{o,m}$ and y^t instead of $y^{t,m}$. Moreover, instead of the domain magnitude consistency loss (6), it uses the domain segmentation loss defined as

$$L^g_{seg} = \mathbb{E}_{x,y}[-log D_{seg}(y^t | G(x, y^t))]. \tag{7}$$

6.1 Few Object Categories Training Data

First, we conducted an experiment to train a model from data comprising few object categories. The training data we used were the sets of images and segmentation masks of the Horse and Zebra categories in Microsoft COCO [9], which comprised 2,941 sets for Horse, 1,916 sets for Zebra. The images were used for x and the segmentation masks were used for y^o. D_{seg} learns to segment the images to horse domain, zebra domain and background. G learns to translate among the horse domain and the zebra domain. All the training samples were first scaled as 513×513 and then randomly flipped and cropped as 256×256. As test data, we

Fig. 6. Example results obtained with few object categories training data. (Color figure online)

Table 1. Comparison of *segmentation MSE* and *background MSE* when using few object categories training data. *Segmentation MSE* is to confirm that the desired region are converted to the desired domain with the desired magnitude. *Background MSE* is to confirm that the background region do not change.

	StarGAN [3]	StarGAN+region	Ours
Segmentation MSE	0.1495	0.0958	**0.0628**
Background MSE	0.0308	0.0253	**0.0048**

used the other animal categories (Bear, Bird, Cat, Cow, Dog, Elephant, Giraffe and Sheep) in Microsoft COCO [9]. All the test samples were scaled as 513×513 and then cropped as 256×256. And we conducted the conversion experiments from horse domain to zebra domain.

Qualitative Evaluation. Figure 6 shows samples of translated images. The results obtained with *StarGAN* at the lower part show that there are some results that the object domains were not converted to zebra domain or that unexpected conversion occurred. For example, when converting the Cow image, the region of the object was not converted to zebra domain, and when converting the Giraffe image, the whole image was converted to grey scale image. Next, the results obtained with *StarGAN+region aware* at the middle row of the figure show that the transfer magnitude was constant and strong, so either the results were not realistic or the object identity information disappeared. For example, in the conversion results for Giraffe, the face region was converted strongly and parts of the face, such as eyes, disappeared. Finally, the results obtained with our method at the upper row of the figure look realistic while the object identity information was preserved. For example, in the conversion results obtained for Giraffe, the neck region was strongly translated and the face region was weakly translated so that the face parts, such as eyes, can be seen. As mentioned above, we consider that this indicates our method is effective for category independent object transfiguration.

Quantitative Evaluation. As seen in Table 1, by our method, the *segmentation MSE* and the *background MSE* are smaller than the other methods. These results lead us to consider that our method can convert more accurately the desired region to the desired domain with the desired magnitude while not to change the undesired region than other methods.

6.2 Wide Variety of Object Categories Training Data

We conducted an experiment to learn from data comprising a wide variety of object categories and to convert various object categories. As the training data comprised a wide variety object categories, we used the color dataset in [20]. The data comprised a set of images retrieved with the search word "colorname + object" in the web search engine. This data comprised object images in 11 colors (Black, Brown, Blue, Gray, Green, Orange, Pink, Purple, Red, White and Yellow), with about 200 images for each color. Those object images have masks which indicate 11 colors regions and we used them for y^o. We used the data to train a model that could transfer among the 11 color domains. The test data we used were the eight kinds of categories (Airplane, Train, Refrigerator, Clock, Teddy bear, Vase, Microwave and Bus) in Microsoft COCO [9]. All the test samples were conducted the same pre-processing as in Subsect. 6.1.

Moreover in quantitative evaluation, in addition to *segmentation and background MSE*, we computed category classification accuracy to evaluate whether the object identity information preserved in the translated images. Specifically, the category classifier we used was fine-tuned the final layers of the VGG16 [16] pretrained on ImageNet [15], as the classifier for above mentioned eight categories. The evaluation value we used was the ratio of translated images classified correctly into the corresponding category.

Qualitative Evaluation. Figure 7 shows samples of result images translated from blue domain. In the translated images obtained with *StarGAN* at the bottom of the figure, there are many examples in which not only the object but also the background regions were converted. See for instance the Teddy bear image conversion. Unexpected conversions also occurred. For example, when converting the Teddy bear image to the red domain it appeared as a yellow color region. Also, the results obtained with *StarGAN+region aware* in the middle row were

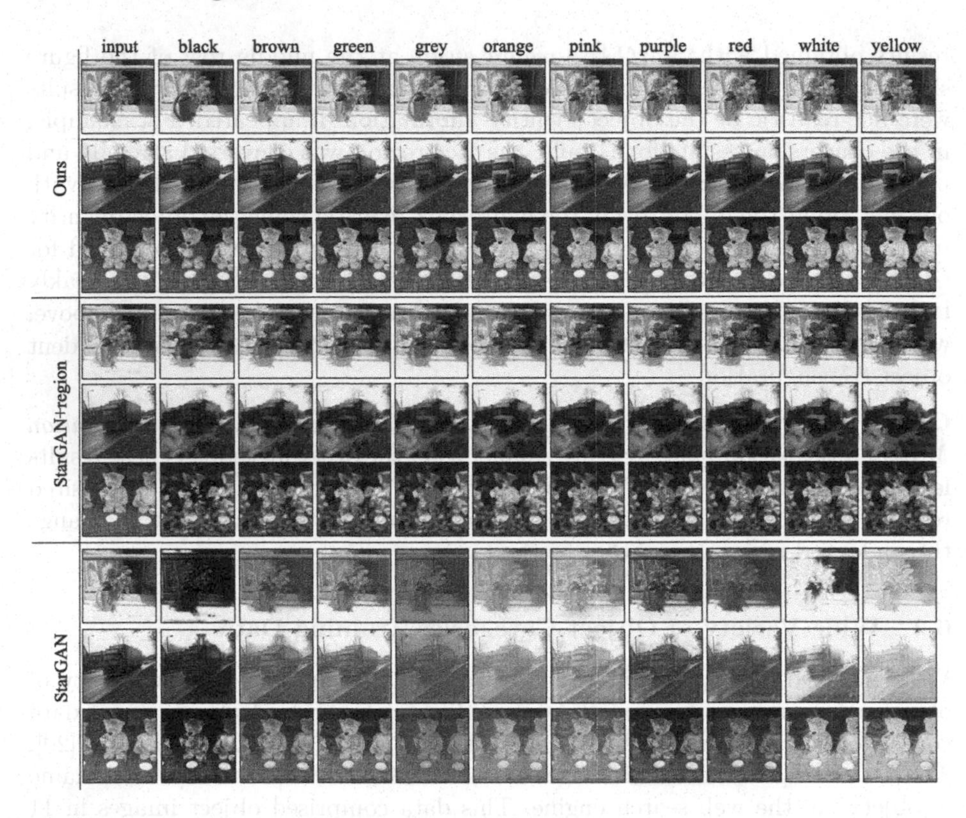

Fig. 7. Example results obtained with a wide variety of object categories training data.

not realistic and did not preserve object identity information because the transfer magnitude was constant and strong. For example, when converting the truck image, to distinguish the windows of truck is difficult. However, the translated images obtained with our method looked realistic and the object identity information was well preserved. For example, when converting the truck image, it was easy to distinguish the windows of truck. As mentioned before, when there were training domains that were common to a wide variety of object categories, we found that our method was effective.

Quantitative Evaluation. As seen in Table 2, by our method, the *segmentation MSE* and the *background MSE* are smaller than the other methods. These results lead us to consider that our method also can convert more accurately when training the common domain among various object categories. Table 3 indicates the our method categorized better than the other methods. It achieved 72.81% accuracy while *StarGAN* achieved only 27.53% and *StarGAN+region aware* achieved only 42.32%. These results lead us to consider that our method produces best preserves the object identity information under a setting containing a wide variety of object categories training data. Quantitative results

Table 2. Comparison of *segmentation MSE* and *background MSE* when using a wide variety of object categories training data.

	StarGAN [3]	StarGAN+region	Ours
Segmentation MSE	0.4722	0.1720	**0.0944**
Background MSE	0.0528	0.0357	**0.0107**

Table 3. Comparison of category classification accuracy (%) of original and translated images when using a wide variety of object categories training data.

Category	Original	StarGAN [3]	StarGAN+region	Ours
Airplane	93.94%	39.53%	44.77%	**88.29%**
Train	96.25%	79.32%	62.50%	**91.82%**
Refrigerator	76.19%	26.12%	27.71%	**65.22%**
Clock	82.61%	53.36%	31.54%	**73.91%**
Teddy bear	79.03%	42.67%	51.47%	**65.10%**
Vase	77.08%	62.50%	66.57%	**83.81%**
Microwave	24.32%	**18.67%**	2.95%	13.02%
Bus	78.26%	17.00%	19.37%	**60.67%**
Ave.	79.65%	27.53%	42.32%	**72.81%**

we obtained also confirmed that our method makes good object transfiguration when training common domains among a wide variety of object categories.

7 Conclusion

We challenged the new task of category independent object transfiguration and proposed a method to accomplish this task. Our method is a domain region and magnitude aware GAN that explicitly predicts transfer region and magnitude using a domain segmentation network and domain magnitude consistency loss. We qualitatively and quantitatively confirmed that our method outperforms conventional method in that it is able to translate object domains realistically and accurately while preserving object identity information well in category independent object transfiguration. A subject for future work will be for us to confirm scalability for the number of domain types that can be learned at one time using multiple training data.

References

1. Arjovsky, M., Chintala, S., Bottou, L.: Wasserstein generative adversarial networks. In: International Conference on Machine Learning (2017)
2. Chen, X., Xu, C., Yang, X., Tao, D.: Attention-GAN for object transfiguration in wild images. In: Ferrari, V., Hebert, M., Sminchisescu, C., Weiss, Y. (eds.) ECCV 2018. LNCS, vol. 11206, pp. 167–184. Springer, Heidelberg (2018). https://doi.org/10.1007/978-3-030-01216-8_11
3. Choi, Y., Choi, M., Kim, M., Ha, J., Kim, S., Choo, J.: StarGAN: unified generative adversarial networks for multi-domain image-to-image translation. In: IEEE Conference on Computer Vision and Pattern Recognition (2018)
4. Dai, J., He, K., Sun, J.: Instance-aware semantic segmentation via multi-task network cascades. In: Computer Vision and Pattern Recognition (2016)
5. Gan, Z., et al.: Triangle generative adversarial networks. In: Advances in Neural Information Processing Systems (2017)
6. Isola, P., Zhu, J.Y., Zhou, T., Efros, A.A.: Image-to-image translation with conditional adversarial networks. In: IEEE Conference on Computer Vision and Pattern Recognition (2017)
7. Kim, T., Cha, M., Kim, H., Lee, J.K., Kim, J.: Learning to discover cross-domain relations with generative adversarial networks. In: International Conference on Machine Learning (2017)
8. Kingma, D.P., Ba, J.: Adam: a method for stochastic optimization. In: International Conference on Learning Representations (2015)
9. Lin, T.Y., et al.: Microsoft COCO: Common objects in context. In: Fleet, D., Pajdla, T., Schiele, B., Tuytelaars, T. (eds.) ECCV 2014. LNCS, vol. 8693, pp. 740–755. Springer, Heidelberg (2014). https://doi.org/10.1007/978-3-319-10602-1_48
10. Liu, M.Y., Breuel, T., Kautz, J.: Unsupervised image-to-image translation networks. In: Advances in Neural Information Processing Systems (2017)
11. Liu, M.Y., Tuzel, O.: Coupled generative adversarial networks. In: Advances in Neural Information Processing Systems (2016)
12. Mirza, M., Osindero, S.: Conditional generative adversarial nets. arXiv preprint arXiv: 1411.1784 (2014)
13. Mo, S., Cho, M., Shin, J.: Instagan: instance-aware image-to-image translation. In: International Conference on Learning Representations (2019)
14. Pumarola, A., Agudo, A., Martinez, A.M., Sanfeliu, A., Moreno-Noguer, F.: Ganimation: anatomically-aware facial animation from a single image. In: Ferrari, V., Hebert, M., Sminchisescu, C., Weiss, Y. (eds.) ECCV 2018. LNCS, vol. 11214, pp. 835–851. Springer, Heidelberg (2018). https://doi.org/10.1007/978-3-030-01249-6_50
15. Russakovsky, O., et al.: Imagenet large scale visual recognition challenge. Int. J. Comput. Vis. **115**(3), 211–252 (2015)
16. Simonyan, K., Zisserman, A.: Very deep convolutional networks for large-scale image recognition. In: International Conference on Learning Representations (2015)
17. Ulyanov, D., Vedaldi, A., Lempitsky, V.S.: Instance normalization: The missing ingredient for fast stylization. arXiv preprint arXiv:1703.06868 (2016)
18. Wang, T.C., Liu, M.Y., Zhu, J.Y., Tao, A., Kautz, J., Catanzaro, B.: High-resolution image synthesis and semantic manipulation with conditional GANs. In: IEEE Conference on Computer Vision and Pattern Recognition (2018)

19. Yi, Z., Zhang, H., Tan, P., Gong, M.: DualGAN: unsupervised dual learning for image-to-image translation. In: International Conference on Computer Vision (2017)
20. Yu, l., Zhang, L., Weijer, J., Khan, F., Cheng, Y., Párraga, C.A.: Beyond eleven color names for image understanding. Mach. Vis. Appl. **29**(2), 361 (2017)
21. Zhu, J.Y., Park, T., Isola, P., Efros, A.A.: Unpaired image-to-image translation using cycle-consistent adversarial networks. In: IEEE International Conference on Computer Vision (2017)

New Moments Based Fuzzy Similarity Measure for Text Detection in Distorted Social Media Images

Soumyadip Roy[1], Palaiahnakote Shivakumara[2], Umapada Pal[1], Tong Lu[3](✉), and Michael Blumenstein[4]

[1] Computer Vision and Pattern Recognition Unit, Indian Statistical Institute, Kolkata, India
soumyadiproy58@gmail.com, umapada@isical.ac.in
[2] Faculty of Computer Science and Information Technology, University of Malaya, Kuala Lumpur, Malaysia
shiva@um.edu.my
[3] National Key Lab for Novel Software Technology, Nanjing University, Nanjing, China
lutong@nju.edu.cn
[4] Faculty of Engineering and Information Technology, University of Technology, Sydney, Australia
Michael.Blumenstein@uts.edu.au

Abstract. A trend towards capturing or filming images using cellphone and sharing images on social media is a part and parcel of day to day activities of humans. When an image is forwarded several times in social media it may be distorted a lot due to several different devices. This work deals with text detection from such distorted images. In this work, we consider images pass through three mobile devices on WhatsApp social media, which results in four images (including the original image) Unlike the existing methods that aim at developing new ways, we utilize the results detected by the existing ones to improve performances. The proposed method extracts Hu moments and fuzzy logic from detected texts of images. The similarity between text detection results given by three existing text detection methods is studied for determining the best pair of texts. The same similarity estimation is then used in a novel way to remove extra background or non-texts and restoring missing text information. Experimental results on own dataset and benchmark datasets of natural scene images, namely, MSRA-TD500, ICDAR2017-MLT, Total-Text, CTW1500 dataset and COCO datasets, show that the proposed method outperforms the existing methods.

Keywords: Social media images · Text detection · Moments · Correlation coefficient

1 Introduction

Social media is a huge platform for sharing and communicating data like images and videos [1]. For example, use of cellphone cameras for capturing selfie photos and its passing on social media mobile applications, such as YouTube, Snapchat, Instagram and

S. Palaiahnakote et al. (Eds.): ACPR 2019, LNCS 12046, pp. 720–734, 2020.
https://doi.org/10.1007/978-3-030-41404-7_51

Facebook is very popular now. It is common that most of the time images pass through several processing stages (devices or cellphones of different configuration) before reaching its destination. This process involves downloading and uploading the images but not forwarding the image to another person. During this process, one can expect variations in the quality of images due to different configurations of cellphone cameras and the use of social media. Besides, the process of rendering and transmission through the network creates more causes to image quality [2]. This work targets common cells or devices that are used widely. It is also true that one cannot decide exact configuration including resolution of camera and other parts of the devices as input image changes. Therefore, it is certain that the content of the image degrades. Since the process involves degradations due to different rotations, scaling and loss of quality due to other internal operations, we consider such effect as distortion rather than degradation, which covers the effect of both internal and external factors. As a result, the methods developed in the past for text detection in images may not work well for such images due to unpredictable variations in quality. It is expected inconsistent results for images of different quality. It is evident from the illustration shown in Fig. 1, where the text detection methods [3–5], namely, CTPN [3], EAST [4] and SegLink [5], which explore deep learning for text detection in natural scene images, do not detect texts accurately for all the images as shown in

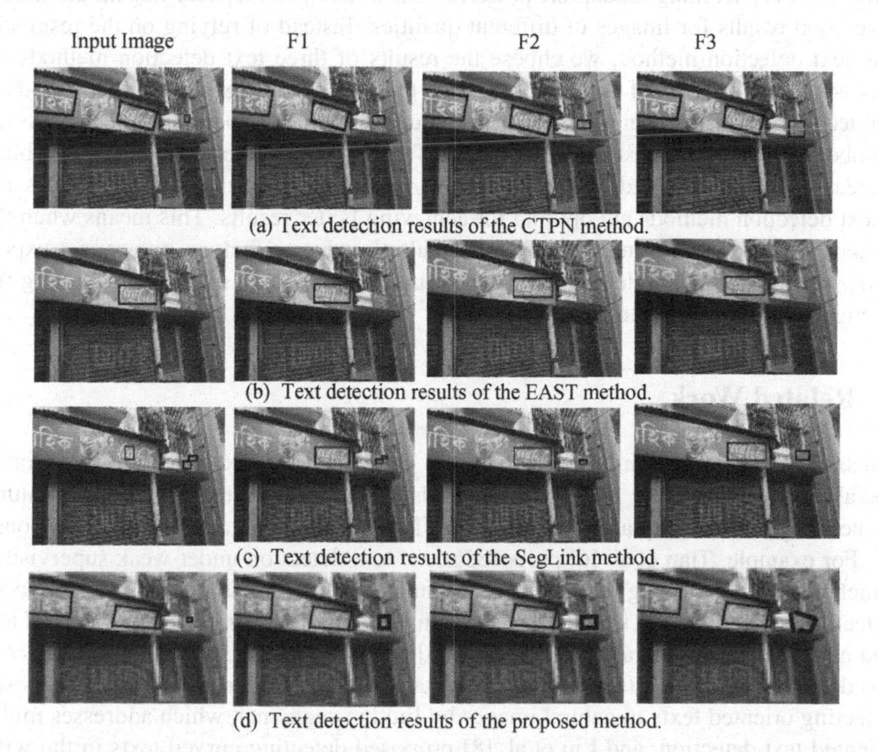

(a) Text detection results of the CTPN method.

(b) Text detection results of the EAST method.

(c) Text detection results of the SegLink method.

(d) Text detection results of the proposed method.

Fig. 1. Text detection of the proposed and different existing methods for the transmitted social media images on different mobile devices. F1, F2, F3 denote images passes through respective mobile devices.

Fig. 1(a)–(c), respectively. However, the proposed method detects texts well for all the images shown in Fig. 1. Figure 1 also shows that each text detection method reports different results for different images. Therefore, there is a gap for addressing this issue to improve text detection performance irrespective of a number of devices and social media.

In Fig. 1, the first is the original image (input image), F1 denotes the image which passes through cellphone camera with the configuration of 1 = Lenovo A7000 (Display-5.5, inch (720 × 1280), Processor-MediaTek MT6752m, rear camera-8MP, RAM-2 GB, Storage-8 GB, Battery Capacity-2900 mAh, OSAndroid-5.0). Similarly, for F2, we use Lenovo K8 Note (Display-5.50-in. (1080 × 1920), Processor-MediaTek Helio X23, rear camera-13MP, RAM-3 GB, Storage-32 GB, Battery Capacity 4000 mAh, OSAndroid-7.1.1). For F3, we use cellphone camera of 3 = MI Redmi 5 (Camera-12 MP Rear Display- 14.4 cm (5.7-in.) HD+ Full screen display with 720 × 1440 pixels, Memory-4 GB, Storage-64 GB, Operating System and Processor-Qualcomm Snapdragon 450 octa-core processor, Battery-3300 mA). For creating all the above three images, we use WhatsApp social media for sharing. In this work, we consider four images including the original one as the input and case study. For each image, the proposed method considers text detection results given by the respective three text detection methods. We believe that since deep learning models are powerful, one or another deep learning model should give good results for images of different qualities. Instead of relying on the results of one text detection method, we choose the results of three text detection methods. In this work, the number of devices as well as the number of text detection methods is limited to three. This is determined based on our preliminary experiments because as the number of devices and text detection methods increases, the complexity of the problem increases, which is beyond the scope of the work. Our result confirms that 3 devices and 3 text detection methods are optimal for achieving better results. This means when the images are affected by unpredictable and multiple adverse factors, one cannot expect better results by the single method. As a result, the challenge requires integrating the strengths of more than one methods.

2 Related Work

Since there are no existing methods that are developed for text detection in distorted social media images, we review the methods developed for text detection in natural scene images and low-quality images caused by poor light and affected by distortions.

For example, Tian et al. [6] proposed scene text detection under weak supervision, which aims at addressing the challenge of multi-orientation, Deng et al. [7] proposed detecting scene texts via instance segmentation, which focuses on the problem of text and non-text pixels separation, Zhou et al. [4] proposed an efficient and accurate scene text detector, which targets on arbitrary orientation text detection, Shi et al. [5] proposed detecting oriented texts in natural images by linking segments, which addresses multi-oriented text detection, and Liu et al. [8] proposed detecting curved texts in the wild, which finds a solution to complex curved text detection. He et al. [9] proposed multi-oriented and multi-lingual scene text detection with direct regression, which considers multi-lingual images for text detection. Xu et al. [10] proposed learning a deep direction field for irregular scene text detection, which considers irregularly shaped characters for detection in natural scene images. Raghunandan et al. [11] proposed multi-script-oriented text detection and recognition in video/scene/Born digital images, which focus on the causes of multi-type texts in images along with multi-oriented and multi-script. Tang et al. [12] proposed detecting dense and arbitrarily-shaped scene texts by instance-aware component grouping, which considers the challenges of thick texts written on bottles, tin and other objects, where we can expect irregularly shaped characters without spacing between text lines much. Most of the above methods explore deep learning for text detection in natural scene images and find solutions to complex issues of orientation, multi-script, multi-type, complex background and irregularly shaped character texts. However, the methods ignore low quality images obtained by low light and distortion. To overcome this limitation, the following methods are proposed.

Huang et al. [13] proposed an end to end vessel plate number detection and recognition using deep convolutional neural networks and LSTMs. Deep learning has been used for achieving results irrespective of light conditions. Panahi et al. [14] proposed accurate detection and recognition of dirty vehicle plate numbers of high-speed applications. The method is proposed to addresses challenges of images affected by weather and lighting conditions. Wahyono and Jo [15] proposed LED dot matrix text recognition in natural scenes. The method uses Canny edge operator for obtaining edge components. Then the method explores characteristics of connected component analysis for text LED dot matrix type text detection. Shemarry et al. [16] proposed an ensemble of AdaBoost cascades of 3L-LBPs classifiers for license plate detection with low quality images. The method explores Local Binary Patten features for detecting license plates including low light images. Lin et al. [17] proposed an efficient license plate recognition system using convolution neural networks. The method finds a solution to the challenge of low light or limited light images. Mohanty et al. [18] proposed an efficient system for hazy scene text detection using deep CNN and patch NMS. In this work, the method considers images affected by haziness as poor quality images. The method considers hazy scene text detection as a classification problem, and hence it classifies hazy scene images into one class. Then it proposes a method for text detection in hazy scene images. It is noted from the above review that none of the methods use social media images or images pass through devices of different configurations for text detection. In addition, the methods consider license plate images for text detection but not images considered in this work. Therefore, it is not sure the above text detection methods work for distorted social media images.

Hence this work aims at developing a new method for text detection in distorted social media images. It is noted that [2] as the number of passes increases through different devices, image quality changes. This is due to cellphone camera of different configurations, social media and limitation of communication network systems. It is also true from the above review that deep learning is a powerful model to solve complex issues. Therefore, the same deep learning models can be used in a different way for detecting texts in distorted social media images. In addition, since text detection is preprocessing steps for text recognition and understanding, the methods developed in the past focus in addressing different challenges of text detection. This motivates us to use text detection results given by three existing text detection methods to choose the best results rather than proposing a new method. For each input image, the proposed method compares the combination of results of three text detection methods for detecting texts in distorted social media images. In order to compare the results of combination, motivated by the method [19, 20] where it is shown that Hu moments are independent of character position, size or orientation and insensitive to variations in shapes, we explore the same Hu moments to tackle the challenges posed by images of different quality. It is true that due to variations in quality, it is not hard to find a match between the same pixels in text detection results. To handle this uncertainty, inspired by the method [21] where fuzzy logic based similarity measure is proposed for multimedia content recommendations, we explore the same with Hu moments for finding similarity between the results of the three combinations. The main contribution is exploring the combination of Hu moments and fuzzy logic based similarity for text detection to address challenges of distorted social media images. As per our knowledge, this is the first work for addressing such issues.

3 Proposed Method

For each input image, the proposed method obtains three combinations of text detection results by the three text detection methods, namely, Method-1 & Method-2, Method-1 & Method-3, Method-2 & Method-3. Since the same image is passing through different devices and social media, there is no need to choose all the possible combinations of the results. The pairs are decided based on the correspondence of text location in text detection result images. For each pair, the proposed method extracts Hu moment based features in column and row wise. Then the proposed method performs fuzzy logic similarity estimation through person coefficient calculation for each pair using Hu moments features. Based on similarity with a certain threshold, the proposed method finds the best pair out of three pairs, which is called a candidate pair. It is true that due to variations in the quality of images, text detection methods may not fix closed bounding boxes, resulting in extra background information, chances of missing text information and detecting non-texts as texts. To overcome these challenges, the proposed method explores the same similarity measure estimation for solving the above-mentioned issues. This is valid because if a candidate pair is the same, the similarity measure estimated for the columns from left to right and right to left converges to almost zero. It is verified by the similarity measure estimation for rows from top to bottom and bottom to up. The same idea is used for solving the other three issues, which will be discussed in the subsequent sections. The above process results in a text with a closed bounding box irrespective of orientation, script, font size, shape of the characters in text line.

3.1 Text Detection for Distorted Images

As mentioned in the previous section, for text detection in input images, we prefer to choose CTPN [3], EAST [4] and SegLink [5] methods. The reason to choose the above three methods is as follows. The method called CTPN proposes connectionist text proposal networks for text detection in natural images. The connectionist text proposal network explores rich context information of images, making it powerful to detect extremely ambiguous texts. In addition, CTPN is invariant to multi-scale and multi-language without further post processing. The method EAST proposes an Efficient and

Accurate Scene Text Detector (EAST) for text detection in natural scene images. The focus of the method is to detect text lines of arbitrary oriented text lines in images. For this, EAST proposes a single neural network. The method Selina proposes Segment Linking (SegLink) for oriented text detection in natural scene images. The main idea of SegLink is to divide each text into segments and links. A segment is an oriented box covering a part of a word or text line, and a link connects two adjacent segments after confirming two segments are belonging to the same line.

The above three methods are popular and the codes are available publicly. Besides, the scope of the above three methods covers challenges of the proposed work. Therefore, we prefer to choose the above three methods for text detection. Sample text detection results given by the three text detection methods are shown in Figs. 1, 2(a) and (c), respectively. It is observed from Fig. 3 that CTPN gives better results for the original image, F1, F2 and F3, while EAST misses text information as well as to detect non-texts as texts. In the same way, SegLink misses low quality texts. This shows that out of the three methods, there are chances of expecting good results at least by one method. At the same time, we can also note that the methods report inconsistent results for images of different quality.

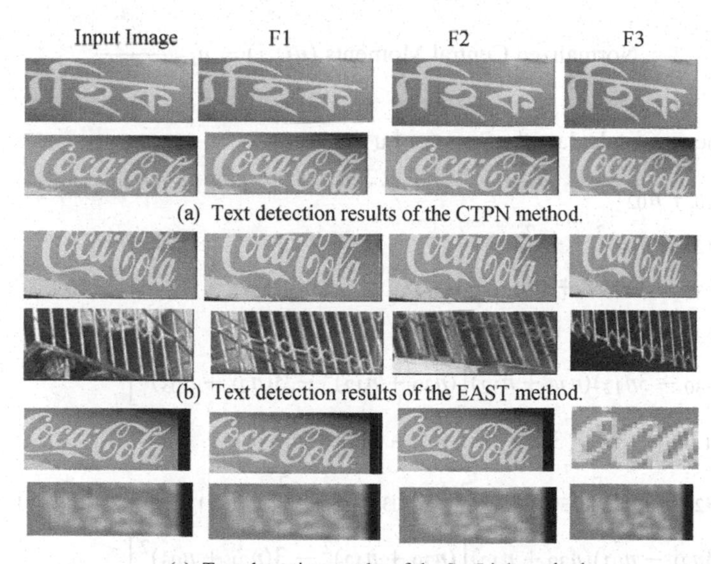

(a) Text detection results of the CTPN method.

(b) Text detection results of the EAST method.

(c) Text detection results of the SegLink method.

Fig. 2. Sample text detection results of different existing methods

3.2 Moments Based Fuzzy Logic Similarity Measure for Text Detection

For the text detection results obtained by the three text detection methods, to choose the best match, we explore Hu moments and Fuzzy logic similarity measure estimation. Hu moments as defined in Eq. (1) to Eq. (5), give 7 values for each column and row of input images. For Hu moments, the proposed method uses triangular rule of fuzzy to estimate the membership function defined in Eq. (6), where *a* denotes lower most value, *b* denotes upper most value, and *m* denotes midpoint. This results in a vector containing 7 fuzzy values. The vector containing fuzzy values are passed to Person coefficient as defined in Eq. (7), which estimates the similarity between two vectors of columns or rows of the pair results given by the three text detection methods.

$$M_{i,j} = \sum_x \sum_y x^i y^j I(x, y) \tag{1}$$

where *i* and *j* are integers (e.g., 0, 1, 2 ....). These moments ($m_{i,j}$) are often referred to as raw moments to distinguish them from the central moments mentioned later. Here *x* and *y* are image co-ordinates, $\bar{x}$ and $\bar{y}$ are the centroids of the group of connected pixels.

$$\bar{x} = \frac{M_{10}}{M_{00}} \quad \bar{y} = \frac{M_{01}}{M_{00}} \tag{2}$$

Central moments ($u_{i,j}$) is calculated by

$$u_{i,j} = \sum_x \sum_y (x - \bar{x})^i (y - \bar{y})^j I(x, y) \tag{3}$$

$$\text{Normalized Central Moments } (ni, j) = n_{i,j} \frac{u_{i,j}}{u_{00}^{\frac{i+j}{2}+1}} \tag{4}$$

From here we calculate the 7 vector hu moments-

$$\begin{aligned}
h_0 &= n_{20} + n_{02} \\
h_1 &= (n_{20} - n_{02})^2 + 4n_{11}^2 \\
h_2 &= (n_{30} - 3n_{12})^2 + (3n_{21} - n_{03})^2 \\
h_3 &= (n_{30} + n_{12})^2 + (n_{21} + n_{03})^2 \\
h_4 &= (n_{30} - 3n_{12})(n_{30} + n_{12})\left[(n_{30} + n_{12})^2 - 3(n_{21} + n_{03})^2\right] \\
&\quad + (3n_{21} - n_{03})\left[3(n_{30} + n_{12})^2 - (n_{21} + n_{03})^2\right] \\
h_5 &= (n_{20} - n_{02})\left[(n_{30} + n_{12})^2 - (n_{03} + n_{21})^2\right] + 4n_{11}(n_{30} + n_{12})^2(n_{21} + n_{03}) \\
h_6 &= (3n_{21} - n_{03})(n_{30} + n_{12})\left[(n_{30} + n_{12})^2 - 3(n_{21} + n_{03})^2\right] \\
&\quad + (n_{30} - 3n_{12})(n_{21} + n_{03})\left[3(n_{30} + n_{12})^2 - (n_{21} + n_{03})^2\right]
\end{aligned} \tag{5}$$

$$\begin{aligned}
u(X) &= (X - a)/(m - a)\, if\ X < mid \\
&\quad (b - X)/(b - m)\, if\ X >= mid
\end{aligned} \tag{6}$$

where, *X* is the Hu Mommment, *a* is the lower most value of Hu Mommment vector, and *b* is the upper most value of Hu Mommment vector and $mid = (a + b)/2$.

$$r_{x,y} = \frac{\frac{1}{n}\sum_{i=1}^{n}(x_i - \bar{x})(y_i - \bar{y})}{\left(\sqrt{\frac{\sum_{i=1}^{n}(x_i - \bar{x})^2}{n}}\right)\left(\sqrt{\frac{\sum_{i=1}^{n}(y_i - \bar{y})^2}{n}}\right)} \tag{7}$$

Where, x and y are two vectors containing n fuzzy values.

The effects of Hu moment for text and non-text results are shown in Fig. 3(a) and (b), where it is noted that the distribution of Hu moments for texts is smooth compared to the distribution of Hu moments of non-texts. This is the advantage of exploring Hu moments for text detection in this work.

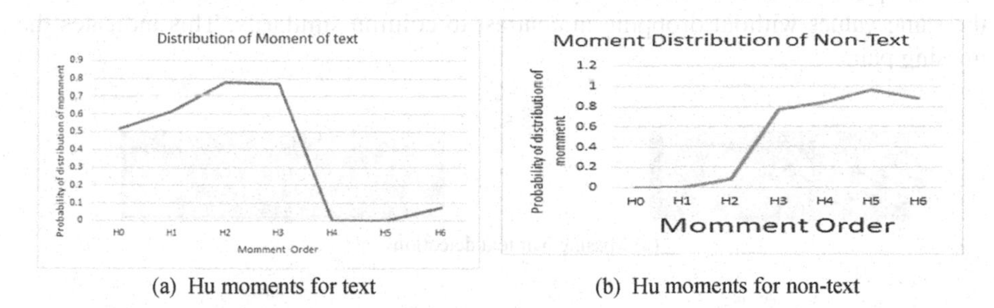

(a) Hu moments for text (b) Hu moments for non-text

Fig. 3. The effect of Hu moments for the text and non-text

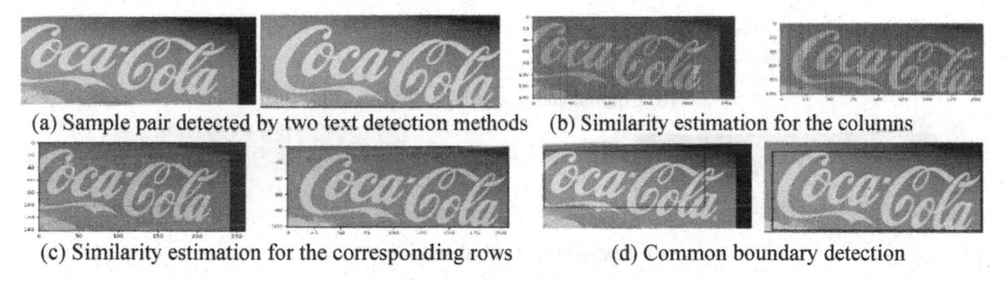

(a) Sample pair detected by two text detection methods (b) Similarity estimation for the columns

(c) Similarity estimation for the corresponding rows (d) Common boundary detection

Fig. 4. Candidate pair detection

For a sample pair given by text detection methods as shown in Fig. 4(a), the proposed method estimates the similarity measure for the columns corresponding to the first and the second images as shown in Fig. 4(b). Similarly, similarity estimation for the rows corresponding to the first and the second images is estimated as shown in Fig. 4(c). By analyzing the similarity values of columns and rows, the proposed method finds a common boundary for both the first and the second images as shown in Fig. 4(d). It is noted from Fig. 4(b) and (c) that the proposed method finds the columns and rows which indicate starting and ending texts in images respectively. This is valid because the similarity matches when both columns/rows have the same text information, else it does not match due to different information. This step outputs correct boundaries for texts, which is called a candidate pair out of three pairs. This step helps us to remove extra background in the pair of images. However, this step does not help us to detect missing text pairs and non-text pairs.

In each pair, if one contains the full text and another one misses a few characters as shown in Fig. 5(a), and if one is correct text and another result is non-text as shown in Fig. 5(c). For the above cases, the proposed method estimates similarity for columns and rows, namely, left-right, right-left for columns, and top-bottom, bottom-up for rows as shown in Fig. 5(b) for missing pair. It is observed from Fig. 5(b) that both the similarity score calculated for left-right (Series-1) and right-left (Series-2) is almost the same up to a certain point, and then there is a sudden drop at the similarity score of both. At the same time, the similarity scores calculated for rows from top-bottom (Series-1) and bottom-up (Series-2) in the same way as shown in Fig. 5(b), both the lines give almost the same values without dropping in contrast to column similarity. This indicates the missing pair.

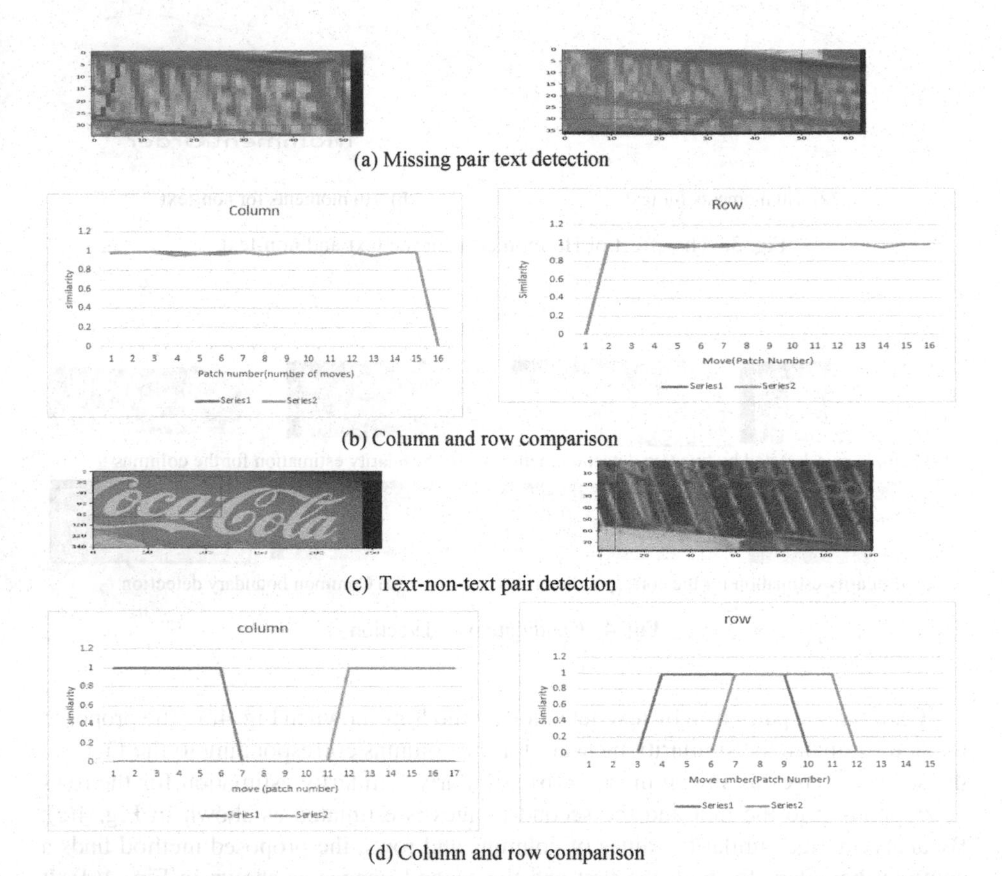

(a) Missing pair text detection

(b) Column and row comparison

(c) Text-non-text pair detection

(d) Column and row comparison

Fig. 5. Text restoration using column and row comparison. Series-1 represent the line for left to right and Series-2 represents the line from right to left in case of column graphs. In row graphs, Series-1 for top to bottom and Series-2 represents bottom-up operation.

For the case of text and non-text pair shown in Fig. 5(c), the similarity graphs obtained for columns and rows do not give any correlation as shown in Fig. 5(d), where we can see Series-1 and Series-2 of both graphs behave differently. This indicates that it is a non-text pair. To restore the missing text, the proposed method finds the image which has a shorter boundary compared to the other images of the pair. The proposed method expands columns and rows of short boundary images, and then similarity scores are estimated for corresponding columns and rows. As long as texts exist while expanding, the expanding process continues and terminates when there is a big difference, which indicates the end of a text. For a text-non-text pair, we use recognition results through edit distance to remove non-text images from the pair.

4 Experimental Results

As a new work, there are no standard datasets for evaluating our proposed method. Therefore, we create our own dataset collected by different natural scene images of arbitrarily oriented texts, multi-script and irregular shaped texts. This includes 2000 images for experimentation. All these images are used for testing the proposed and existing methods. However, for determining parameters and converging criteria, we choose 500 images randomly across databases, including a standard database of natural scene images. We divide 2000 images into four classes, namely, input image, F1 which passes through device-1, F2 which passes through device-2, and F3 which passes through device-3. In other words, each set contains 4 images. Details of the devices and configurations are described in the Introduction Section. As a result, our dataset consists of 500 sets of four classes. For this work, In order to evaluate the effectiveness and usefulness of the proposed method, we also consider the following standard datasets.

MSRA-TD500: This dataset provides 300 images for training and 200 images for testing. It includes multi-oriented texts of English and Chinese languages. **CTW1500**: This dataset provides 1000 images for training and 500 images for testing. It is created basically for evaluating curved text detection in scene images. **Total-Text**: This dataset provides 1255 images for training and 300 for testing. This is also the same as CTW1500 dataset but with more variations, which includes low resolution, low contrast and complex backgrounds. **ICDAR 2017 MLT**: This dataset provides multi-lingual text images, including 7200 training images, 1800 validation images and 9000 testing images. The dataset consists of images of 9 languages in arbitrary orientations. **COCO-Text**: This dataset is created not with the intention of text detection, hence texts in images are more realistic and there are a large number of variations compared to all the other datasets. As a result, this dataset is much more complex than the other datasets for text detection. It provides 43686 images for training, 20000 images for validation and 900 images for testing.

It is noted that in case of all the five benchmark datasets, there are no images which represent F1, F2 and F3. Therefore, we consider each image as the original one and then use the same image to create F1, F2, F3 images with the same above-mentioned devices. In this way, we create datasets for experimentation in this work. The size of testing samples for all the respective datasets is actually the number of testing samples multiplied by four. For evaluating the performance of the proposed and existing methods, we follow the standard instructions and evaluations discussed in [9]. More information about Recall (R), Precision (P) and F-Measures (F) can be found from [9]. The proposed method calculates the above measures for four classes, namely, Input image, F1, F2, F3 and Average. For Average, the proposed method considers the results of all the four type images as one image results for calculating Precision, Recall and F-measure. However, for our dataset, since there is no ground truth, we count manually for calculating measures. To show the objectiveness of the proposed method, we compare it with the sate-of-the art methods, namely, Tian et al. [3] which proposes Connectionist text Proposal Network (CTPN) for text detection in natural scene images, Zhou et al. [4] which proposes An Efficient and Accurate Scene Text Detector (EAST) for text detection in natural scene images, and Shi et al. [5] propose a Segment Linking (SegLink) based method for text detection in natural scene images. The codes of the above-methods are available publicly and popular for text detection in natural scene images because they address almost all the challenges of text detection in natural scene images.

4.1 Experiments on Distorted Social Media Images

As discussed in the previous section, quantitative results of the proposed and existing methods for Input, F1, F2 and F3 are reported in Table 1, where it is noted that the proposed method outperforms the existing methods in terms of Recall, Precision and F-measure for all the four type experiments. It is also noted from Table 1 that the existing methods are not consistent. This shows that the existing methods are not good enough to handle the distortion created by different devices, social media and networking. On the other hand, since the proposed method chooses the best results from the results of the three existing text detection methods through Hu moments based fuzzy logic similarity measures, the proposed method is capable of handling such issues. It is observed from Table 1 that as number of passes increases, the results of the existing methods change compared to the results of the input images. Some methods score better results for F2 and F3 compared to F1, while some methods do not. However, the proposed method is almost the same for all the four types of experiments. This is the advantage of the proposed method over the existing methods. In this work, we use the system with the following configuration, 8 gb Ram, Nvidia Ge force 940 m Graphics card and on Ubuntu 18.03 and Tensorflow 1.3 for all the experiments. Our experiments show that the average processing time of each image taken by the proposed method for the datasets, namely, MSRA TD500, CTW 1500, Total Text, ICDAR 2017 MLT and MS COCO dataset is between 3.3 to3.5 s.

Table 1. Performances of the proposed and existing methods on our dataset

Methods	Input			F1			F2			F3			Average		
	P	R	F	P	R	F	P	R	F	P	R	F	P	R	F
EAST [4]	65.0	60.0	62.4	63.0	65.0	63.9	62.0	66.0	63.9	64.5	66.5	65.4	60.0	64.5	62.1
Seglink [5]	81.0	75.0	77.8	83.0	74.0	78.2	85.0	76.0	80.2	86.0	76.5	80.9	80.0	74.2	77.0
CTPN [3]	83.0	85.0	83.9	83.0	82.0	82.5	83.5	81.0	82.2	81.0	84.0	82.4	80.0	83.0	81.4
Proposed method	**85.0**	**89.0**	**86.9**	**87.0**	**89.0**	**87.9**	**87.0**	**89.0**	**87.9**	**87.0**	**89.0**	**87.9**	**87.0**	**89.0**	**87.9**

4.2 Experiments on Benchmark Dataset of Natural Scene Images

Sample qualitative results of the proposed and existing methods for images of MSRA-TD500 dataset are shown in Fig. 6(a)–(d), respectively. It is observed from Fig. 6 that as discussed above, the existing method does not report consistent results for F1, F2 and F3 compared to the input, while the proposed method detects all the texts correctly. Quantitative results of the proposed and existing methods for natural scene text datasets, namely, MSRA-TD500, CTW1500, Total-Text, IDAR2017-MLT and COCO, are reported in Tables 2, 3, 4, 5 and 6, respectively. Tables 2, 3, 4, 5 and 6 show that the proposed method is better than the existing methods for all the four type experiments in terms of recall, precision and F-measure for all the datasets. This shows that the proposed idea can be used for solving still more complex issues by utilizing the existing methods results. However, it is noted from Tables 5 and 6, the existing methods report poor results compared to the other datasets. This is because the datasets, namely8, ICDAR2017-MLT and MS-COCO are much more complex than other datasets as pointed out earlier. This leads to obtaining poor results for the proposed method because the performance of the proposed method depends on the success of the existing methods. If all the three existing methods report poor results, obviously, the proposed method reports poor results. This indicates that choosing the existing methods is also important for achieving better results for complex issues. Overall, the proposed work gives a message that the combination of text detection results can cope with the distortion/challenges caused by different devices, social media and networks.

Table 2. Performance of the proposed and existing methods on MSRATD-500 dataset

Methods	Input			F1			F2			F3			Average		
	P	R	F	P	R	F	P	R	F	P	R	F	P	R	F
EAST [4]	87.3	67.4	76.0	90.0	60.0	72.0	85.0	62.0	71.7	89.0	61.0	72.3	88	61.4	72.3
Seglink [5]	86.0	70.0	77.0	86.5	74.0	79.7	83.0	76.0	79.3	85.0	75.0	79.6	86.5	73.0	79.1
CTPN [3]	83.0	73.2	77.8	80.0	79.0	79.4	83.5	80.0	81.7	82.0	81.0	81.5	80.5	77.5	78.9
Proposed method	**89**.0	**80**.0	**84.26**	**84**.0	**82**.0	**82.9**	**85**.0	**84**.0	84.4	**86**.0	**83**.0	84.4	**89**.0	**82**.0	85.3

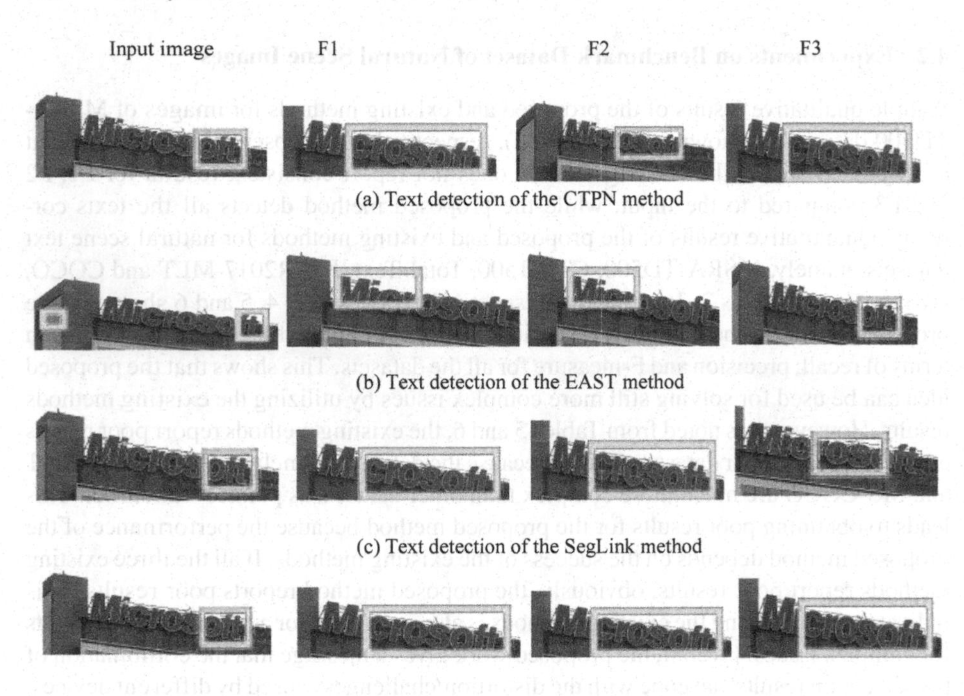

(a) Text detection of the CTPN method

(b) Text detection of the EAST method

(c) Text detection of the SegLink method

(d). Text detection of the proposed method

Fig. 6. Text detection for benchmark dataset of MSRATD-500 dataset

Table 3. Performance of the proposed and existing methods on CTW1500 dataset

Methods	Input			F1			F2			F3			Average		
	P	R	F	P	R	F	P	R	F	P	R	F	P	R	F
EAST [4]	78.7	49.1	60.4	79.0	55.0	64.8	77.0	53.5	63.1	79.5	55.5	65.3	78.0	53.5	63.4
Seglink [5]	42.3	40.0	40.8	50.0	50.0	50.0	49.0	53.0	50.9	49.0	51.0	49.8	49.0	50.0	49.4
CTPN [3]	70.0	**88**.0	77.9	75.0	88.0	80.9	75.5	89.0	81.7	76.0	86.0	80.6	73.0	88.0	79.8
Proposed method	**81**.0	**88**.0	**84.3**	**83**.0	**88**.0	**85.4**	**83.5**	**90**.0	86.6	**82**.0	**89**.0	85.3	**83**.0	**88**.0	85.4

Table 4. Performance of the proposed and existing methods on Total Text dataset.

Methods	Input			F1			F2			F3			Average		
	P	R	F	P	R	F	P	R	F	P	R	F	P	R	F
EAST [4]	50.0	36.2	42.0	55	32.0	40.4	55.5	31	39.7	53.0	35.0	42.1	53.7	33.0	40.8
Seglink [5]	30.3	23.8	26.7	30.5	25.0	27.4	30.0	25.5	27.5	32.0	26.0	28.6	30.0	25.0	27.2
CTPN [3]	82.7	74.5	78.4	82.7	76.0	79.2	84.0	76.0	79.8	83.0	77.0	79.8	81.0	75.0	77.8
Proposed method	**86.0**	**77.0**	**81.2**	**86**	**80**.0	**82.8**	**87**.0	**79**.0	82.8	**85**.0	**80.5**	82.6	**86**.0	**80**.0	82.8

Table 5. Performance of the proposed and existing methods on ICDAR 2017 MLT dataset.

Methods	Input			F1			F2			F3			Average		
	P	R	F	P	R	F	P	R	F	P	R	F	P	R	F
EAST [4]	44.4	25.5	32.4	46.0	27.0	34.0	45.0	26.0	32.9	45.0	26.0	33.0	45.5	26.5	33.4
Seglink [5]	67.7	34.7	45.9	66.0	36.0	46.5	66.0	35.5	46.1	66.0	37.0	47.1	66.0	35.5	46.1
CTPN [3]	71.1	55.5	62.3	73.0	56.0	63.3	71.0	55.5	62.3	71.0	55.5	63.7	72.5	55.0	62.5
Proposed method	**74.0**	**56.0**	**63.7**	**76.0**	**59.0**	**66.4**	**76.5**	**58.0**	65.9	**76.5**	**60.0**	67.6	**76.0**	**59.0**	66.4

Table 6. Performance of the proposed and existing methods on MS-COCO dataset

Methods	Input			F1			F2			F3			Average		
	P	R	F	P	R	F	P	R	F	P	R	F	P	R	F
EAST [4]	30.0	30.0	30.0	32.0	26.0	28.6	32.5	26.5	29.1	33.0	25.0	28.4	31.0	27.0	28.8
Seglink [5]	60.0	55.0	51.4	62.0	60.0	60.9	61.0	59.0	59.9	60.0	60.0	60.0	59.0	58.0	58.5
CTPN [3]	55.0	55.0	59.5	59.0	60.0	59.4	57.0	59.0	57.9	58.0	61.0	59.4	58.0	58.5	58.2
Proposed method	**62.0**	**60.0**	**63.7**	**61.0**	**61.0**	**61.0**	**62.0**	**61.5**	61.7	**63.0**	**62.0**	62.5	**62.0**	**61.0**	61.5

5 Conclusion and Future Work

In this work, we have proposed a new idea of exploring the combination of text detection results of the existing methods for overcoming the problems of distortion created by different devices, social media and networks. To choose the best pair from the results of the existing text detection methods, we have combined Hu moments and fuzzy logic similarity measure in a new way for solving the issues. Similarity measure estimation is used for removing excessive background, restoring missing text information and eliminating false positives. Experimental results on our datasets and different datasets of natural scene images show that the proposed method is better than the existing methods, and it is consistent for four type experiments in contrast to the existing methods. However, it is noted from the experimental results that choosing the number of devices, social media, and existing text detection methods are important in achieving better results. Therefore, our future work shall be providing a roadmap for choosing an optimal number for the above.

References

1. Ghadiyaram, D., Pan, J., Bovik, A.C., Moorthy, A.K., Panda, P., Yang, K.C.: In-capture mobile video distortions: a study of subjective behaviour and objective algorithms. IEEE Trans. CSVT **28**, 2061–2077 (2018)

2. Ghadiyaram, D., Pan, J., Bovik, A.C.: A subjective and objective study stalling events in mobile streaming videos. IEEE Trans. CSVT **29**, 183–197 (2019)
3. Tian, Z., Huang, W., He, T., He, P., Qiao, Yu.: Detecting text in natural image with connectionist text proposal network. In: Leibe, B., Matas, J., Sebe, N., Welling, M. (eds.) ECCV 2016. LNCS, vol. 9912, pp. 56–72. Springer, Cham (2016). https://doi.org/10.1007/978-3-319-46484-8_4
4. Zhou, X., et al.: East: an efficient and accurate scene text detector. In: Proceedings of the CVPR, pp. 2642–2651 (2017)
5. Shi, B., Bai, X., Belongie, S.: Detecting oriented text in natural images by linking segments. In: Proceedings of the CVPR, pp. 3482–3490 (2017)
6. Tian, S., Lu, S., Li, C.: WeText: scene text detection under weak supervision. In: Proceedings of the CVPR, pp. 1501–1509 (2017)
7. Deng, D., Liu, H., Li, X., Cai, D.: PixelLink: detecting scene text via instance segmentation. In: Proceedings of the AAAI (2018)
8. Liu, Y., Jin, L., Zhang, S., Zhang, S.: Detecting curve text in the wild: new dataset and new solution. arXiv:1712.02170 (2017)
9. He, W., Zhang, X.-Y., Yin, F., Liu, C.-L.: Multi-oriented and multi-lingual scene text detection with direct regression. IEEE Trans. IP **27**, 5406–5419 (2018)
10. Xu, Y., Wang, Y., Zhou, W., Wang, Y., Yang, Z., Bai, X.: TextField: learning a deep direction field for irregular scene text detection. IEEE Trans. IP **28**, 5566–5579 (2019)
11. Raghunandan, K.S., Shivakumara, P., Roy, S., Hemantha Kumar, G., Pal, U., Lu, T.: Multi-script-oriented text detection and recognition in video/scene/born digital images. IEEE Trans. CSVT **29**, 1145–1162 (2019)
12. Tang, J., Yang, Z., Wang, Y., Zheng, Q., Xu, Y., Bai, X.: Detecting dense and arbitrary-shaped scene text by instance-aware component grouping. Pattern Recognit. (2019, to appear)
13. Huang, S., Xu, H., Xia, X., Zhang, Y.: End-to-end vessel plate number detection and recognition using deep convolutional neural networks and LSTMs. In: Proceedings of the ISCID, pp 195–199 (2018)
14. Panahi, R., Gholampour, I.: Accurate detection and recognition of dirty vehicle plate numbers for high speed applications. IEEE Trans. ITS **18**, 767–779 (2017)
15. Wahyono, Jo, K.: LED dot matrix text recognition method in natural scene. Neurocomputing **151**, 1033–1041 (2015)
16. Shemarry, M.S.A., Li, Y., Abdulla, S.: Ensemble of adaboost cascades of 3L-LBPs classifiers for license plated detection with low quality images. ESWA **92**, 216–235 (2018)
17. Lin, C.H., Lin, Y.S., Liu, W.C.: An efficient license plate recognition system using convolutional neural networks. In: Proceedings of the ICASI, pp 224–227 (2018)
18. Mohanty, S., Dutta, T., Gupta, H.P.: An efficient system for hazy scene text detection using a deep CNN and patch-NMS. In: Proceedings of the ICPR, pp. 2588–2593 (2018)
19. Nawali, M., Liao, S.: A new fast algorithm to compute continuous moments defined in a rectangular region. Pattern Recognit. **89**, 151–160 (2019)
20. Hu, M.-K.: Visual pattern recognition by moment invariants. IRE Trans. Inf. Theory **8**, 179–187 (1962)
21. Kant, S., Mahara, T., Jain, V.K., Jain, D.K.: Fuzzy logic similarity measure for multimedia contents recommendation. Multimed. Tools Appl. **78**, 4107–4130 (2019)

Fish Detection Using Convolutional Neural Networks with Limited Training Data

Shih-Lun Tseng and Huei-Yung Lin(✉)

Department of Electrical Engineering, National Chung Cheng University, Chiayi 621, Taiwan
shih.lun1208@gmail.com, lin@ee.ccu.edu.tw

Abstract. Due to the effect of global climate changes to marine biology and aquaculture, researchers start to investigate the deep ocean environment and living circumstances of rare fish species. One major issue of the related research is the difficulty of sufficient image data acquisition. This paper presents a method for underwater fish detection using limited training data. Current convolutional neural network based techniques have good performance on object detection and segmentation but require a large collection of image data. The proposed network structure is based on the U-Net model, modified with various encoders, convolutional layers, and residual blocks, to achieve high accuracy detection and segmentation results. It is able to provide better mIoU compared to other improved U-Net variants with a small amount of training data. Experiments carried out on fish tank scenes and the underwater environment have demonstrated the effectiveness of the proposed technique compared to other state-of-the-art detection networks.

Keywords: CNN · Semantic segmentation · Fish detection · U-Net

1 Introduction

Nowadays, a large variety of ecology studies on monitoring fish populations in the ocean are emphasized by fish producers, scientific researchers and biologists. The objectives include monitoring the types of habitats [4] and the distribution of animal species and trophic chains, evaluating the ecosystems differences before and after natural events or human disturbances, and investigating specific characteristics of species. While the rapid development of technologies, the marine ecosystem is also changing. Natural disasters and artificial pollution have caused the habitat change of fish [6,17]. The water pollution such as oil toxic has destroyed the food chain. Some fish die from eating the poisoned fish, while others survive and are eaten by other animals [16]. To prevent such threats of diseases and accidents have draw much attentions by researchers.

One of the important studies is the length-weight relation analysis of deep sea fishes. It aims to investigate the trophic relations and food web dynamics of

S. Palaiahnakote et al. (Eds.): ACPR 2019, LNCS 12046, pp. 735–748, 2020.
https://doi.org/10.1007/978-3-030-41404-7_52

deep sea fishes, and observe whether deep sea fish grows at an abnormal rate [2,3]. In order to determine the species distribution, species data and appropriate habitat changes of rare fish species, obtaining distribution maps are helpful to promote global conservation actions [32]. Taking the hippocampus conservation as an example, sea horses are rare animals and usually have a higher extinction risk than other animals. In addition to observing the rare animals in the wildlife, large aquariums also have equipments to monitor fishes. Different fish adapt to different pH values, and the water quality also affects the living conditions and disease infections. Therefore, the study of fish detection and recognition is a way to help the researchers to resolve some problems, and developing a fish monitoring system will be able to maintain the fish living quality.

For fish detection in the wild, there are several challenges due to the impact of the ocean environment. The underwater images may be blurred due to the illumination condition. Furthermore, the light is absorbed or reflected by water many times, the color of the fish might be changed, or the fish could hide in some complicated coral environments. Most object detection techniques are developed for the living environment of human beings such as natural or man-made objects. They cannot be applied directly for fish detection due to their highly deformable body shapes and the sudden speed change in any directions. Traditional object detection and recognition methods which adopt feature descriptors such as SIFT or SURF have very low accuracies on the underwater creatures.

In recent years, convolutional neural networks (CNN) have great progress on image classification and recognition. Deep and large networks for object detection and pattern recognition have shown impressive results when using with a large amount of training data and scalable computation resources [19]. Krizhevsky *et al.* trained AlexNet on ImageNet database to classify 1.2 million images and achieved top-1 and top-5 error rates of 37.5% and 17.0% [9]. After the impact of AlexNet, CNNs are used in many research fields and spread exponentially in the applications of computer vision. Architectures such as VGG [25], Resnet [7], Inceptionv4, Inception Resnet v2 [28] achieve better and better classification accuracy. These networks generally require a large amount of training data, which are not suitable for the situation when the cost of data collection is extremely high. In this work, we adopt U-Net as the framework for semantic segmentation. It has an impressive capability on medical image segmentation using a small amount of training data. We improve the model architecture, compare with other U-Net variants, and change the backbone structure to incorporate with other encoders. In the experiments and evaluation, the proposed technique is compared with two popular end-to-end deep models for object detection, SSD [14] and YOLO [22], using the same amount of fish datasets. The results have demonstrated the effectiveness and feasibility of our approach on rare fish detection with very limited training data.

2 Related Work

Currently there are two major fish detection approaches, one is based on background subtraction and the other uses convolutional neural networks.

The background subtraction methods are often adopted for a fixed scene to generate foreground masks, followed by post-processing steps for fish detection and position calculation. Convolutional neural networks are widely used for image classification by learning invariant features of images on large-scale datasets. In general, domain-specific training data are required for fish detection and recognition.

2.1 Background Subtraction

For low visibility underwater fish detection, Shevchenko *et al.* present a framework based on adaptive Gaussian mixture model (GMM), kernel density estimation and visual background extractor [23]. Background subtraction is first applied on the input images, followed by a post-processing stage to reduce the misdetection of foreground pixels and noise. Optical flow is then used to trace the fish motion. The results show that GMM is capable of motion detection even when the color of foreground and background is similar. Verschae *et al.* present a fish detection system based on multi-view silhouettes matching [29]. The proposed method first segments the foreground objects using a background subtraction technique. The silhouette model is then integrated to generate 3D fish candidates using triangulation. Their work is able to detect and track 3D fish locations in real-time. Zhao *et al.* propose a two-stage algorithm for multiple fish tracking [33]. The first detection stage uses Otsu's adaptive method for background subtraction and fish target segmentation. The latter tracking stage applies Kalman filter to estimate the motion state, and the cost is calculated from the position of the target body and movement direction.

More recently, Malik *et al.* propose a combined technique to extract features using FAST, PCA and neural network, and use it to identify the fish with EUS disease [15]. Their system starts with image acquisition and pre-processing, and adopts various edge detection techniques to enhance and preserve useful information. Several feature extraction methods are then applied, followed by machine learning algorithms for classification. In SeaCLEF 2016 fish recognition competition, Jağer *et al.* proposed a method that generated bounding box proposals using background subtraction [8]. The bounding box proposals are classified to fish and background by binary support vector machine with a confidence level higher than 0.5. It greatly reduces the false detection of the median image background subtraction method adopted by the participants in the past years.

2.2 Convolutional Neural Network

For CNN based fish detection methods, the YOLO network has been adopted in many papers. Wang *et al.* point out that the original YOLOv2 is unable to detect small objects. They modify the architecture and change the grid of the last convolutional layer for fish detection tasks [30]. Liu *et al.* combine the parallel correlation filter with YOLOv3 for fish tracking [13]. Since fish frequently hide in the seabed with colors similar to them for camouflage and protection, Sung *et al.* present a method to prevent false positive detection by taking the training data with various seabed images [27]. Shi *et al.* present FFDet which consists of an improved SSD-based backbone structure [24]. Their work indicates that six convolutional layers in the SSD backbone are not capable of predicting fish at different scales. A feature fusion module is proposed to aggregate adjacent prediction layers for feature representation. The experiments on SeaCLEF dataset show that YOLOv3 has much faster processing speed but with moderate mAP performance. Compared to SSD, the mAPs of FFDet and YOLOv3 are 6% and 3% higher, respectively.

In [10], Li *et al.* apply Fast R-CNN for fish detection. Due to the imbalance data in ImageCLEF, they ignore the fish class which has less than 600 images. Compared to DPM, their model achieves an mAP of 81.4%. For the later redesign of Faster R-CNN feature extract architecture by combining high-level semantic feature map, they have achieved 89% mAP with the processing speed of 89 ms per image [11]. Olsvik *et al.* are the first using squeeze-and-excitation(SE) architecture for fish recognition task [18]. With the knowledge of transfer learning, they use Fish4Knowledge dataset (which contains mainly tropical species) to learn fish features, and the pre-trained weights are adopted for further training on their custom dataset. It is necessary since CNN trains on specific species will not be able to classify fish species in other marine ecosystems. The authors also show that data augmentation makes a big different on fish classification accuracy.

The literature review shows that background subtraction methods usually work for specific circumstances. As the underwater scenes cannot be predicted, this kind of techniques might not be suitable for deep sea fish recognition. Alternatively, CNN for fish detection can achieve high accuracy if sufficient training data are provided. However, the public datasets are mostly outdated and imbalanced. Most collected fish images belong to tropical species, which only cover a very small part of fish species in the ocean. Thus, the development of a learning based fish detection algorithm which requires only very limited training data will benefit the related marine research.

3 Approach

The proposed method mainly includes the improved network architecture based on U-Net, as well as several pre- and post-processing steps for more accurate classification.

3.1 Network Architecture

U-Net is built on the FCN structure for medical image segmentation. Due to the limited biomedical samples, it aims to use small datasets to yield better segmentation results. Apart from the high accuracy with a small number of samples, U-Net can hardly segment well for challenging case or with complex background. There are several improved network architectures based on U-Net in recently years [26,31,34]. Some of the concepts are adopted with further modifications to

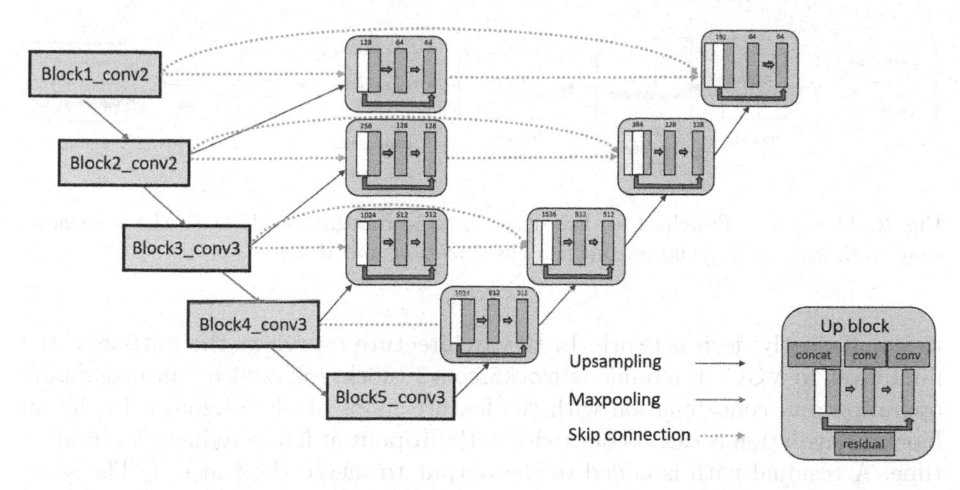

Fig. 1. The proposed network model changes the encoder path to VGG16 and includes more convolutional layers. The residual blocks are adopted to improve the detection accuracy. The input and output are both 512 × 512 images.

design our networks for underwater fish detection with limited training samples. The proposed architecture is much deeper by adding more convolutional layers. Since the size of our training data is small, the over-fitting problem is mitigated by data augmentation and adding dropout layers to the model. The learning rate is set empirically to 0.0001 as the initial parameter for training. Furthermore, we replace the ReLU activation function with Swish, and a better accuracy is obtained in the experiments [20]. The detailed network architecture is shown in Fig. 1.

To deal with the tasks provided only limited training data by transfer learning, the knowledge from previously trained models is used to train newer models with less data. In this work, our encoder path is based on the ImageNet-trained VGG16 with pre-trained weights. Fine-tuning the whole network shows a better performance, and the results are shown in the experiment section. Figure 2 shows the system flowchart for fish detection and recognition. Since the network is also for segmentation, mask images instead of ROI locations are used as the input. The same data augmentation process is carried out for the original image and the associated mask file before training the network. The training process terminates when the loss stops decreasing. Finally, the network output goes through a post-processing stage to eliminate false predictions and calculate the fish locations.

The main idea of the nested network architecture in UNet++ is to bridge the semantic gap between the feature maps of encoder and decoder paths. However, changing the encoder structure to other state-of-the-art network structures leads to a lower performance due to the following nested structure. Our model adopts the idea of the nested structure of UNet++, but reduces the number of convolutional layers. It slightly improves the detection accuracy as expected, since the residual module has been proved to provide a better accuracy when added

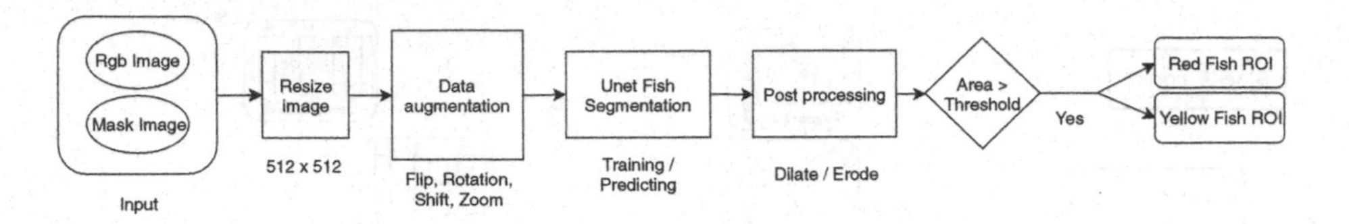

Fig. 2. The system flowchart for fish detection and recognition. It takes the segmentation mask for training and output fish classification and ROIs.

to a sufficiently deep network. In the architecture overview, the output of the final layer in VGG-16 module is block5_conv3 block, followed by an upsamping operation and concatenation with the feature maps of block4_conv3. In the up block, convolution is carried out twice with dropout at 0.3 to reduce the training time. A residual path is added to the output to merge the features. The same process is performed on all other blocks, and the output goes through a softmax layer and predicts the pixel class of the image at the resolution of 512×512.

3.2 Data Augmentation Pre-processing

When the training dataset is extremely small, it is essential to apply data augmentation for deep learning based object detection techniques. In addition to reducing the over-fitting problem, it generates new training data from the existing data. We apply shift, rotation, horizontal flip, zooming to our fish data. We also observe that doing too much transformation causes the accuracy drop. The rotation angles from -10 to 10° are the best values applied on the dataset for data augmentation. Different directions of fish body created with horizontal flip for training data is useful as shown in our experiments, while most fish detection works only apply shift and rotation transforms.

3.3 Activation Function and Loss Function

The most well-known and commonly used activation function for deep neural networks is the Rectified Linear Unit (ReLU). Recently, Google Brain proposed a new activation function Swish [21]. The difference between Swish and ReLU is that, when the input is less 0 Swish keeps updating while ReLU stops and leads to dead neurons. It is shown that, compared to ReLU, Swish takes more time to converge but achieves a higher test accuracy. Table 1 tabulates the 3 times comparison of our fish detection implementation with different network structures, and Swish does slightly improve the accuracy.

In addition to the activation function, our model also tests on two loss functions, focal loss [12] and focal Tversky loss [1], to address the data imbalance issue and improve the training performance. These loss functions have a great ability to contribute lower loss while learning is focused on hard samples. However, the modification does not provide improvement as shown in Table 2, and thus the widely used cross entropy is adopted in our detection framework.

Table 1. The comparison of mIoU between ReLU and Swish for different U-Net structures.

Network model	U-Net VGG16	U-Net VGG16	UNet++ VGG16	Ours
Activation function	ReLU	Swish	Swish	Swish
1st	92.33%	92.33%	92.00%	92.33%
2nd	91.33%	92.00%	92.00%	92.00%
3rd	91.00%	92.67%	92.00%	92.33%
Average mIoU	91.53%	92.33%	92.00%	92.22%

Table 2. The comparison of different loss functions for the U-Net VGG16 structure with various rotation angles.

Network model	U-Net VGG16	U-Net VGG16
Loss function	Cross entropy	Focal loss
Rotation = 10	92.33%	92.33%
Rotation = 20	91.67%	91.67%
Rotation = 30	91.67%	91.00%

3.4 Post-processing

The output mask of our model is a grayscale image with 512 × 512 resolution and the class scores at each pixel. In general, most semantic segmentation tasks use the largest score for class assignment. In this work, a pixel is assigned to a class only if the score is greater than a threshold (say, 0.5), otherwise the default background is given. This definition performs better in the experiments. It should be noted that the threshold might need to change to an appropriate value for different training datasets. Finally, we use the erosion and dilation operations to remove noise, and draw a bounding box if its size is over 400 pixels (Fig. 3).

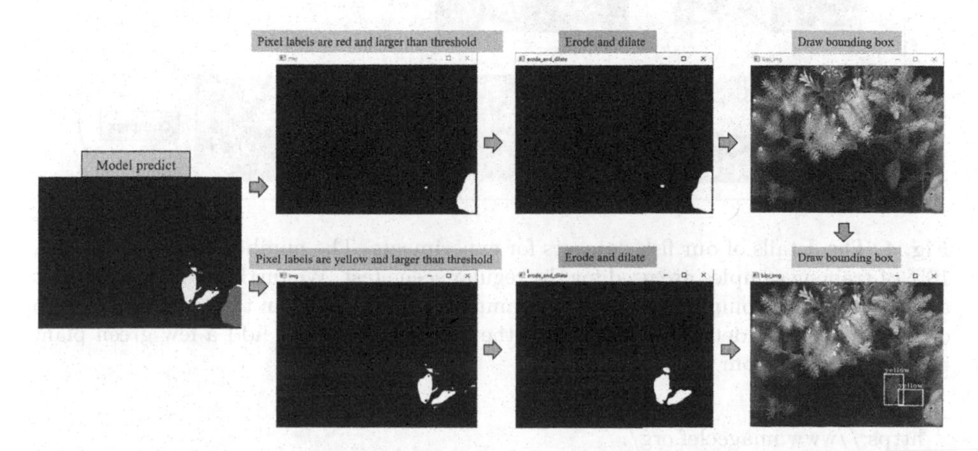

Fig. 3. The post-processing flowchart. This example shows a false positive on the tree trunk. It could be due to the lack of similar objects in our training data.

4 Experiments

4.1 Data Collection

In general object detection and classification research, most public datasets are created with the scenes in our daily life. There are only very limited public datasets for fish recognition. At present, ImageCLEF and SeaCLEF are the most important resources in fish recognition[1]. Other datasets such as Fish Recognition Ground-Truth data [5] and Labeled Fishes in the Wild image dataset[2] are also used by fish recognition research. However, they are not updated for a long period of time, the image resolution is worse than general object classification datasets, and the imbalance data issue has never been solved. Since these public datasets also have labeling problem and are not suitable for this research, we have created our own with the images of a fish tank. Our dataset contains two Amphilophus citrinellus with different colors (see Fig. 4). We also test our model in real ocean scenes with the videos from BlueWorldTV YouTube channel for cavefish detection. The videos are cut into frames for training and testing. There are totally 422 images in the training data, and 100 images are used as the testing video. It should be noted that the image background and environment in the training data are different from those in the testing video.

Fig. 4. The details of our fish datasets for experiments. The number of samples is 400. 10% of training samples are used for the regular scene test. We further add green plants and woods to the complex scene testing samples, which are not in the training data. To deal with the miss detection problem in the complex scene, we add a few green plant images obtained from the Internet.

[1] https://www.imageclef.org/.

[2] https://swfscdata.nmfs.noaa.gov/labeled-fishes-in-the-wild/.

4.2 Results

Table 3 shows the average mIoU performance tested in a regular scene three times with different encoder, fine-tuning, and data augmentation. Without data augmentation, U-Net VGG19 performs the best, while Inception Resnet v2 structure is the worse. This might be due to insufficient training data since the network is much deeper with more convolutional layers. After data augmentation is applied, U-Net VGG16 reaches the best mIoU performance, and the accuracy of Inception Resnet v2 is also increased. The result also indicates that the original U-Net model performs better than the network without fine-tuning.

Table 3. The comparison of the U-Net structures with different encoders and the use of data augmentation.

Network model (U-Net)	Original	VGG16	VGG16	VGG19	Inception Resnet v2
Fine-tuning	x	No	Yes	Yes	Yes
1st	89.00%	86.67%	91.33%	92.00%	86.67%
2nd	90.67%	88.33%	89.00%	91.67%	85.67%
3rd	89.00%	x	91.00%	91.33%	91.00%
Average mIoU	89.56%	87.5%	90.44%	**91.67%**	88.78%
Data augmentation	85.67%	x	**92.33%**	91.33%	91.67%

To deal with complex underwater scenes, we add the images with green plants to the training data to reduce the false positives. Table 4 shows the result of three tests for the complex scene, and our model achieves the highest mIoU scores. As indicated in the table, the original U-Net can barely handle the diverse situations, and several improved U-Net models using pre-training weight perform better and better with more convolutional layers. Figure 5 shows the result images of different network outputs.

Table 4. The mIoU performance comparison of different network models. Our UNet+Residual VGG16 has the best mIoU score in the complex scene.

Network model	U-Net	U-Net VGG16	Stack U-Net VGG16	UNet++ VGG16	UNet+Residual VGG16
Activation function	ReLU	Swish	Swish	Swish	Swish
Regular scene	87.67%	92.00%	92.00%	91.67%	92.00%
Complex scene 1	42.67%	72.00%	75.00%	72.67%	79.00%
Complex scene 2	49.33%	66.00%	66.33%	71.67%	75.67%
Complex scene 3	53.67%	72.67%	71.33%	72.67%	76.00%
Average mIoU	48.56%	70.22%	70.87%	72.34%	**76.89%**
No. of parameters	31M	25M	28M	30M	30M

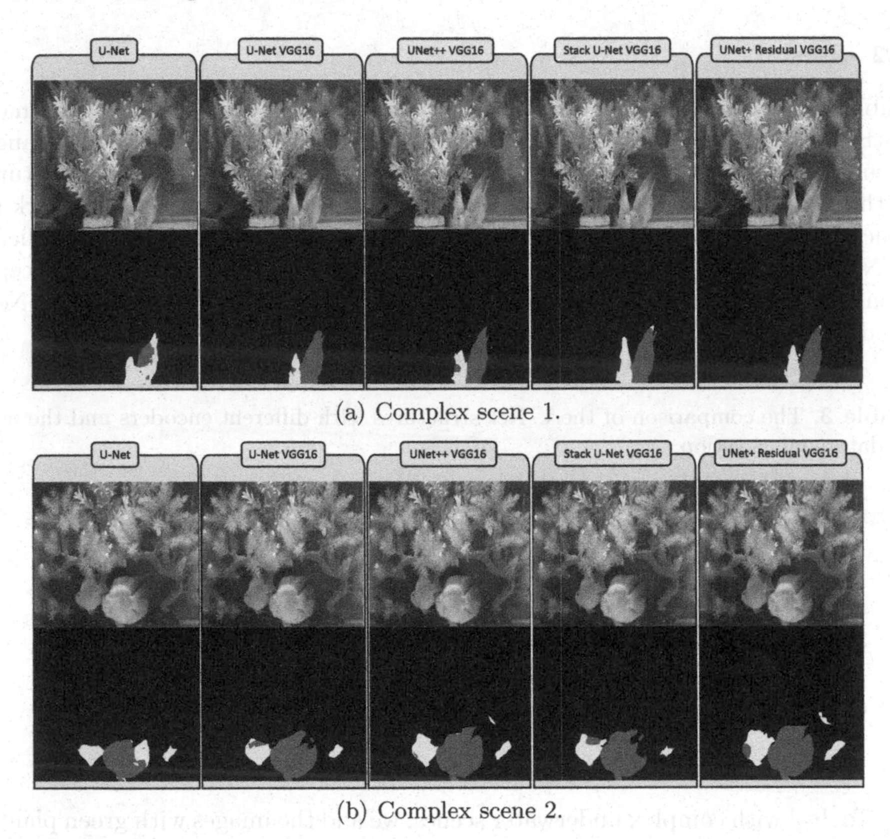

(a) Complex scene 1.

(b) Complex scene 2.

Fig. 5. The results of different network outputs, from left to right: U-Net, U-Net VGG16, UNet++ VGG16, Stack U-Net VGG16, UNet+ Residual VGG16. The original U-Net is not able to distinguish the fish correctly in the complex scenes, Our model performs well in both detection and segmentation compared to other network models.

We compare our model with SSD and YOLOv3 using 100 and 500 images as training samples. With only a small amount of training data, SSD and YOLOv3 have larger false positives and false negatives even tested in a fish tank scene (with one red and one yellow fish) as shown in Table 5. We then test these algorithms for underwater cavefish detection using 422 training samples and 100 testing samples. Our model only fails on one image, which is due to the overlapping of the bounding boxes is less than 70%. Figure 6 shows some cavefish detection results and failed cases. SSD and YOLOv3 perform poorly in the natural scene. As a result, the mAPs are quite low (35.32% and 13.70%) compared to our 98.57% (see Table 5). Finally we test the algorithms on the original cavefish videos with 1775 image frames. The result shows that our model outperforms SSD and YOLOv3 at the mAPs of 82.31% vs. 31.00% and 24.25%. Our method is also capable of handling the tough case when the cavefish is very small and covered by seaweed as shown in Fig. 7.

(a) Cavefish detection with the proposed model.

(b) Cavefish detection with SSD.

(c) Cavefish detection with YOLOv3.

Fig. 6. The cavefish detection results and failed cases of our model, SSD, and YOLOv3. The red and green boxes indicate the false and true positives, and the blue box is the ground truth. (Color figure online)

Table 5. The mAP performance comparison of our model, SSD and YOLOv3 in the fish tank scene (with one red and one yellow fish) and underwater cavefish detection. Two different numbers of training samples are used for the fish tank scene. The cavefish detection is tested on individual images and a video sequence.

Network model	Ours	SSD	YOLOv3
Fish tank scene - 100 training samples	**93.94%**	37.67%	71.15%
Fish tank scene - 500 training samples	**96.15%**	39.36%	79.97%
Cavefish image (100 frames) - 422 training samples	**98.57%**	35.32%	13.70%
Cavefish video (1775 frames) - 422 training samples	**82.31%**	31.00%	24.25%

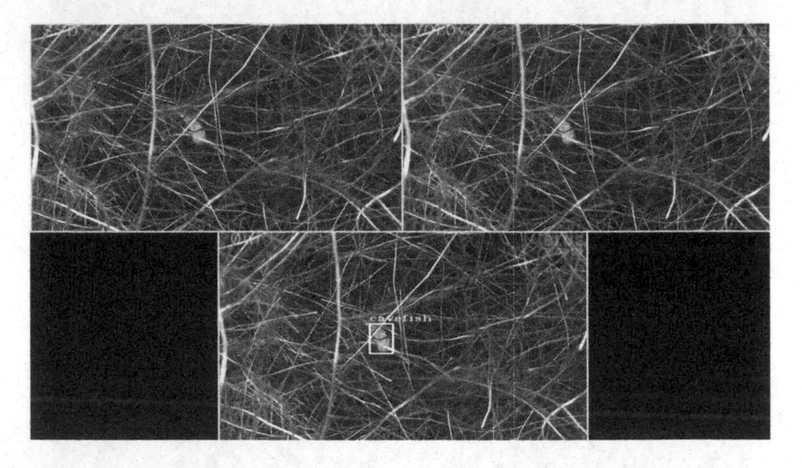

Fig. 7. The cavefish detection results of a challenging scene where the target is very small and covered by seaweed. Our method (bottom image) is able to successfully detect the small object. Top-left: SSD, top-right: YOLOv3.

5 Conclusion

This paper presents a network structure for fish detection. It aims for the application of rare fish detection, where the training data are very difficult to acquire. In this work, the original U-Net model for semantic segmentation is modified to incorporate various encoders, more convolutional layers, and residual blocks. Data augmentation and post-processing are adopted to improved the overall performance. Our model is able to provide better mIoU compared to other improved U-Net variants. Experiments are carried out on fish tank scenes and underwater cavefish detection using a small amount of training data. The results demonstrate that our method provides much better mAP performance compared to SSD and YOLOv3.

Acknowledgment. The support of this work in part by the Ministry of Science and Technology of Taiwan under Grant MOST 106-2221-E-194-004 is gratefully acknowledged.

References

1. Abraham, N., Khan, N.M.: A novel focal Tversky loss function with improved attention U-Net for lesion segmentation. arXiv preprint arXiv:1810.07842 (2018)
2. Aneesh Kumar, K., Nikki, R., Oxona, K., Hashim, M., Sudhakar, M.: Relationships between fish and otolith size of nine deep-sea fishes from the Andaman and Nicobar waters, North Indian Ocean. J. Appl. Ichthyol. **33**(6), 1187–1195 (2017)
3. Aneesh Kumar, K., Thomy, R., Manjebrayakath, H., Sudhakar, M.: Length-weight relationships of 11 deep-sea fishes from the western Bay of Bengal and Andaman waters, India. J. Appl. Ichthyol. **34**(4), 1048–1051 (2018)
4. Beauxis-Aussalet, E., He, J., Spampinato, C., Boom, B., van Ossenbruggen, J., Hardman, L.: Fish4knowledge deliverable d2. 3 component-based prototypes and evaluation criteria
5. Boom, B.J., Huang, P.X., He, J., Fisher, R.B.: Supporting ground-truth annotation of image datasets using clustering. In: Proceedings of the 21st International Conference on Pattern Recognition (ICPR 2012), pp. 1542–1545, November 2012
6. Brown, C.J., Broadley, A., Adame, M.F., Branch, T.A., Turschwell, M.P., Connolly, R.M.: The assessment of fishery status depends on fish habitats. Fish Fish. **20**(1), 1–14 (2019)
7. He, K., Zhang, X., Ren, S., Sun, J.: Deep residual learning for image recognition. In: Proceedings of the IEEE Conference on Computer Vision and Pattern Recognition, pp. 770–778 (2016)
8. Jäger, J., Rodner, E., Denzler, J., Wolff, V., Fricke-Neuderth, K.: SeaCLEF 2016: object proposal classification for fish detection in underwater videos. In: CLEF (Working Notes), pp. 481–489 (2016)
9. Krizhevsky, A., Sutskever, I., Hinton, G.E.: Imagenet classification with deep convolutional neural networks. In: Advances in Neural Information Processing Systems, pp. 1097–1105 (2012)
10. Li, X., Shang, M., Qin, H., Chen, L.: Fast accurate fish detection and recognition of underwater images with fast R-CNN. In: OCEANS 2015-MTS/IEEE Washington, pp. 1–5. IEEE (2015)
11. Li, X., Tang, Y., Gao, T.: Deep but lightweight neural networks for fish detection. In: OCEANS 2017-Aberdeen, pp. 1–5. IEEE (2017)
12. Lin, T.Y., Goyal, P., Girshick, R., He, K., Dollár, P.: Focal loss for dense object detection. In: Proceedings of the IEEE International Conference on Computer Vision, pp. 2980–2988 (2017)
13. Liu, S., et al.: Embedded online fish detection and tracking system via YOLOv3 and parallel correlation filter. In: OCEANS 2018 MTS/IEEE Charleston, pp. 1–6. IEEE (2018)
14. Liu, W., et al.: SSD: single shot multibox detector. In: Leibe, B., Matas, J., Sebe, N., Welling, M. (eds.) ECCV 2016. LNCS, vol. 9905, pp. 21–37. Springer, Heidelberg (2016). https://doi.org/10.1007/978-3-319-46448-0_2
15. Malik, S., Kumar, T., Sahoo, A.: Image processing techniques for identification of fish disease. In: 2017 IEEE 2nd International Conference on Signal and Image Processing (ICSIP), pp. 55–59. IEEE (2017)
16. McConville, M.M., et al.: The sensitivity of a deep-sea fish species (anoplopoma fimbria) to oil-associated aromatic compounds, dispersant, and Alaskan North Slope crude oil. Environ. Toxicol. Chem. **37**(8), 2210–2221 (2018)
17. Muhling, B., Lindegren, M., Clausen, L.W., Hobday, A., Lehodey, P.: Impacts of climate change on pelagic fish and fisheries. Climate Change Impacts Fish. Aquac.: Glob. Anal. **2**, 771–814 (2017)

18. Olsvik, E., et al.: Biometric fish classification of temperate species using convolutional neural network with squeeze-and-excitation. arXiv preprint arXiv:1904.02768 (2019)
19. Qin, H., Li, X., Liang, J., Peng, Y., Zhang, C.: Deepfish: accurate underwater live fish recognition with a deep architecture. Neurocomputing **187**, 49–58 (2016)
20. Ramachandran, P., Zoph, B., Le, Q.V.: Searching for activation functions. CoRR abs/1710.05941 (2017). http://arxiv.org/abs/1710.05941
21. Ramachandran, P., Zoph, B., Le, Q.V.: Searching for activation functions. arXiv preprint arXiv:1710.05941 (2017)
22. Redmon, J., Divvala, S., Girshick, R., Farhadi, A.: You only look once: Unified, real-time object detection. In: Proceedings of the IEEE Conference on Computer Vision and Pattern Recognition, pp. 779–788 (2016)
23. Shevchenko, V., Eerola, T., Kaarna, A.: Fish detection from low visibility underwater videos. In: 2018 24th International Conference on Pattern Recognition (ICPR), pp. 1971–1976. IEEE (2018)
24. Shi, C., Jia, C., Chen, Z.: FFDet: a fully convolutional network for coral reef fish detection by layer fusion. In: 2018 IEEE Visual Communications and Image Processing (VCIP), pp. 1–4. IEEE (2019)
25. Simonyan, K., Zisserman, A.: Very deep convolutional networks for large-scale image recognition. arXiv preprint arXiv:1409.1556 (2014)
26. Sun, T., Chen, Z., Yang, W., Wang, Y.: Stacked U-Nets with multi-output for road extraction. In: 2018 IEEE/CVF Conference on Computer Vision and Pattern Recognition Workshops (CVPRW), pp. 187–1874. IEEE (2018)
27. Sung, M., Yu, S.C., Girdhar, Y.: Vision based real-time fish detection using convolutional neural network. In: OCEANS 2017, Aberdeen, pp. 1–6. IEEE (2017)
28. Szegedy, C., Ioffe, S., Vanhoucke, V., Alemi, A.A.: Inception-v4, inception-resnet and the impact of residual connections on learning. In: Thirty-First AAAI Conference on Artificial Intelligence (2017)
29. Verschae, R., Kawashima, H., Nobuhara, S.: A multi-camera system for underwater real-time 3D fish detection and tracking. In: OCEANS 2017, Anchorage, pp. 1–5. IEEE (2017)
30. Wang, M., Liu, M., Zhang, F., Lei, G., Guo, J., Wang, L.: Fast classification and detection of fish images with YOLOv2. In: 2018 OCEANS-MTS/IEEE Kobe Techno-Oceans (OTO), pp. 1–4. IEEE (2018)
31. Xiao, X., Lian, S., Luo, Z., Li, S.: Weighted Res-UNet for high-quality retina vessel segmentation. In: 2018 9th International Conference on Information Technology in Medicine and Education (ITME), pp. 327–331. IEEE (2018)
32. Zhang, X., Vincent, A.: Predicting distributions, habitat preferences and associated conservation implications for a genus of rare fishes, seahorses (Hippocampus spp.). Diversity and Distributions (2018). https://doi.org/10.1111/ddi.12741
33. Zhao, X., Yan, S., Gao, Q.: An algorithm for tracking multiple fish based on biological water quality monitoring. IEEE Access **7**, 15018–15026 (2019)
34. Zhou, Z., Siddiquee, M.M.R., Tajbakhsh, N., Liang, J.: Unet++: a nested u-net architecture for medical image segmentation. In: Stoyanov, D. et al. (eds.) DLMIA 2018, ML-CDS 2018. LNCS, vol. 11045, pp. 3–11. Springer, Heidelberg (2018). https://doi.org/10.1007/978-3-030-00889-5_1

A New U-Net Based License Plate Enhancement Model in Night and Day Images

Pinaki Nath Chowdhury[1], Palaiahnakote Shivakumara[2], Ramachandra Raghavendra[3](✉), Umapada Pal[1], Tong Lu[4], and Michael Blumenstein[5]

[1] Computer Vision and Pattern Recognition Unit, Indian Statistical Institute, Kolkata, Kolkata, India
pinakinathc@gmail.com, umapada@isical.ac.in
[2] Faculty of Computer Science and Information Technology, University of Malaya, Kuala Lumpur, Malaysia
shiva@um.edu.my
[3] Faculty of Information Technology and Electrical Engineering, IIK, NTNU, Gjøvik, Norway
raghavendra.ramachandra@ntnu.no
[4] National Key Lab for Novel Software Technology, Nanjing University, Nanjing, China
lutong@nju.edu.cn
[5] Faculty of Engineering and Information Technology, University of Technology, Sydney, Ultimo, Australia
Michael.Blumenstein@uts.edu.au

Abstract. A new trend of smart city development opens up many challenges. One such issue is that automatic vehicle driving and detection for toll fee payment in night or limited light environments. This paper presents a new work for enhancing license plates captured in limited or low light conditions such that license plate detection methods can be expanded to detect images at night. Due to the popularity of Convolutional Neural Network (CNN) in solving complex issues, we explore U-Net-CNN for enhancing contrast of license plate pixels. Since the difference between pixels that represent license plates and pixels that represent background is too due to low light effect, the special property of U-Net that extracts context and symmetric of license plate pixels to separate them from background pixels irrespective of content. This process results in image enhancement. To validate the enhancement results, we use text detection methods and based on text detection results we validate the proposed system. Experimental results on our newly constructed dataset which includes images captured in night/low light/limited light conditions and the benchmark dataset, namely, UCSD, which includes very poor quality and high quality images captured in day, show that the proposed method outperforms the existing methods. In addition, the results on text detection by different methods show that the proposed enhancement is effective and robust for license plate detection.

Keywords: Text detection · License plate detection · U-Net · Convolutional neural networks · Low quality license plate detection

S. Palaiahnakote et al. (Eds.): ACPR 2019, LNCS 12046, pp. 749–763, 2020.
https://doi.org/10.1007/978-3-030-41404-7_53

1 Introduction

The era of smart city development for developing countries poses several research challenges. One such challenge is to develop systems for automatic driving, transportation, delivering goods and toll fee regardless of day and night. In this work, we focus on license plate detection in images captured at night, low light or limited light conditions [1]. This is essential for making toll fee systems automatic for 24 h, especially for Malaysia and India to accommodate high-density traffics. There are several powerful methods for license plate detection and recognition in literature [2, 3]. However, most of the methods work well for images captured in day but not night and low light. Due to the lack of sufficient light illumination, the captured images suffer from low contrast, loss of visibility, blur, noise and the effect of non-uniform street light, headlight and moonlight illumination as shown sample images in Fig. 1(a), where it can be seen the effects of the above threats.

(a) Text detection (EAST) for the input night and day license plate images

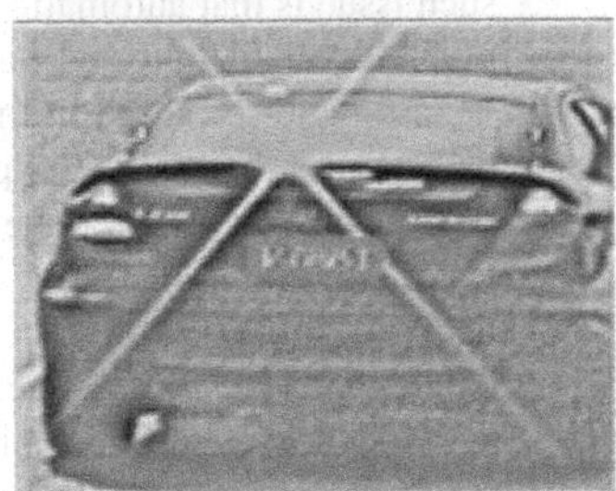

(b) Text detection (EAST) for the proposed enhanced night and day license plate images

Fig. 1. Illustrating the importance of enhancement for license plate detection.

It is noted from the literature that there are many sophisticated methods for license plate detection and recognition for day images. For example, the method in [1] is used for detecting dirty license plate images for high speed applications, the method in [2] is proposed for end to end car license plate detection and recognition with a deep neural network, which focuses on detecting accurate license plates by fixing exact bounding boxes, and the method in [3] deals with an efficient license plate recognition system using convolutional neural networks, which addresses the challenge of low light images. However, as mentioned above, these methods work well for day images with good contrast but not night images that suffer from poor quality. It is evident from the illustration shown in Fig. 1, where one can notice that for the input night and day images with poor quality shown in Fig. 1(a), the text detection method in [4], which explores a powerful deep learning model for text detection in natural scene images, does not detect text for the input images, while for the enhanced images, the same text detection method detects texts well. This observation motivates us to propose a new method for enhancement such that the same text detection or license plate detection methods can be used for license plate detection in night images.

2 Related Work

This section reviews the methods for license plate detection in low quality images and the methods of image enhancement. Asif et al. [5] proposed multinational vehicle license plate detection in complex backgrounds. Rather than dealing with license plates directly, the method finds rare lights as regions of interest, which include license plates. It proposes a heuristic energy map based on vertical edge information for regions of interest. Dense edge areas are extracted for detecting license plates in images. Xie et al. [6] proposed a new CNN based method for multi-directional car license plate detection. The method presents an idea for addressing the challenges caused by different rotations. Therefore, the method explores CNN for detecting license plates by estimating degree of rotation. Yuan et al. [7] proposed a robust and efficient method for license plate detection. The method explores a line density filter approach for extracting candidate regions, which significantly reduces area of localization of license plates. The method used the combination of a cascaded classifier and support vector machines for eliminating false candidate regions. Li et al. [2] proposed an end-to-end car license plate detection and recognition with deep neural networks. Instead of developing two separate models for detection and recognition, the method proposed a unified model for both detection and recognition in license plate images. It is noted from the review on these license plate detection methods that the methods consider images with high quality (day images) because the main target of the methods is to achieve the best results for license plate detection irrespective of challenges posed by day images. This shows that the scope is limited today images but not low quality and night images.

There are also methods, which aim at addressing the challenges of low quality images for license plate detection. Shemarry et al. [8] proposed an ensemble of adaboost cascades of 3L-LBPs classifiers for license plate detection with low quality images. The method combines adaboost classifiers and local binary patterns based features for detecting license plate regions. The method is tuned for addressing issues of low contrast, dusk, dirt, and fogy. Lin et al. [3] proposed an efficient license plate detection system using convolutional neural networks. The method extracts conventional features such as histogram oriented gradients based features and then an SVM classifier for license plate detection in low quality images. Panahi et al. [1] proposed accurate detection and recognition of dirty vehicle plate numbers for high-speed applications. To solve the issues of day and night images, the method proposes adaptive thresholding for gray images. The method finds initially key points for images, with these key points it then detects license plate regions through adaptive thresholding. Since thresholds are determined based on empirical results, the method may not be effective for different applications and datasets.

In the light of the above discussions on license plate detection of low quality images, it is not sure how the methods work for night or low light images, where one can expect not only poor quality but also low contrast, blur, and noises.

There are several methods developed for image enhancement in the past. For instance, Dong et al. [9] proposed a fast-efficient algorithm for enhancement of low lighting video. The method explores the idea of de-hazing for enhancing details of images. Jiang et al. [10] proposed night video enhancement using improved dark channel prior. The method uses an improved dark channel prior model and integrates it with local smoothing and image Gaussian pyramid operators. Sharma et al. [11] proposed contrast enhancement using a pixel-based image fusion in wavelet domain. The method proposes wavelet decomposition to obtain high-frequency sub-bands. Rui and Guoyu [12] proposed a medical X-ray image enhancement method based on TV-Homomorphic filter. The method explores the total variation model as transfer function, which balances the brightness in images by increasing high frequency coefficients in Fourier domain. Ravishankar et al. [13] proposed acoustic image enhancement using Gaussian and Laplacian pyramids. The method uses the combination of Gaussian and Laplacian pyramid levels with histogram equalization for enhancing noisy images. Raghunandan et al. [14] proposed a Riesz fractional based model for enhancing license plate detection and recognition. The method focuses on improving edge strength to improve the visibility of low contrast images. Zhang et al. [15] proposed a new fusion-based enhancement for text detection in night video footage. The method combines color information in spatial domain and high-frequency coefficients in frequency domain for enhancing information. It is noted from the above license plate detection methods and enhancement methods that none of the method provide reasonable detection accuracy for night images.

Hence, in this work, we propose a new method based on the U-Net-CNN for enhancing fine details in night images such that license plate detection performance improves. Inspired by the deep learning model proposed for complex medical image segmentation, we explore the same for exploiting the exclusive property of U-Net for image enhancement in this work. It is true that text exhibits symmetrical patterns, such as the uniform color of character pixels, constant stroke width for characters in license plates, the uniform character size, and the uniform spacing between characters. These patterns are invariant to rotation, scaling, color, illumination effect and contrast variations because the patterns are unique, which do not depend on individual pixel values. To extract such context and symmetric patterns, we propose U-Net as it is a special property of U-Net [16].

3 Proposed Model

The proposed work consists of two sub-sections, namely, exploring U-Net for image enhancement and text detection methods to validate the output of image enhancement. As mentioned in the previous section, U-Net helps us to extract context and symmetrical properties of text information. The training of U-Net network is done using an adversarial loss from the EAST network. Therefore, the EAST network along with its loss function becomes the objective function or the empirical risk function for the enhancement network. Further, the proposed method is optimized using Adam Optimization technique.

Hence intuitively we can expect the enhancer network to modify low-quality images in such a way that the task of text detection becomes easier for algorithms like EAST. To verify the results of U-Net, we propose to use the EAST method [4] which works based on deep learning for text detection in complex natural scene images. The block diagram of the proposed work is presented in Fig. 2, where we can notice the architecture of U-Net and the enhancement results.

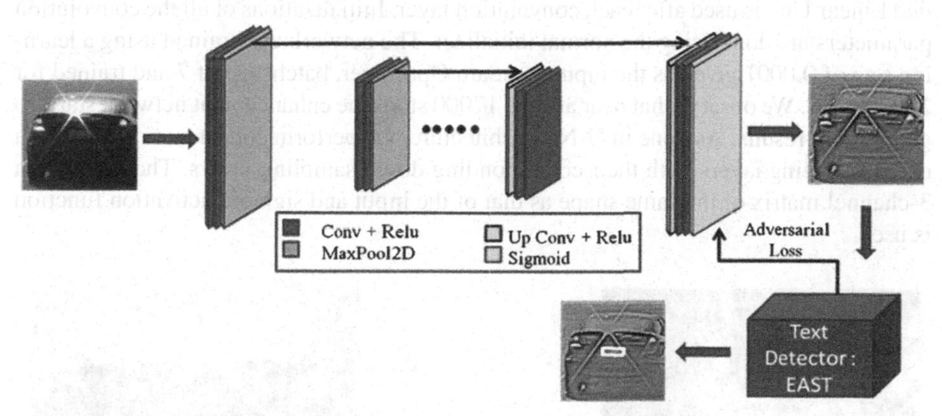

Fig. 2. Proposed architecture for the enhancement (a) Text detection (EAST) for the input night and day license plate images

3.1 The Proposed U-Net Based Enhancement Model

Motivated by the method [16] where U-Net has been proposed for medical image segmentation, we explore the same property with modifications for enhancing images in this work. The architecture used in [16] uses a single input channel, while the proposed U-Net uses three-channel input. The process of U-Net can be described as follows. Let us assume the encoder-decoder to be represented by a function $\boldsymbol{f_{unet}}$ and the network parameters be represented by $\boldsymbol{\theta_{unet}}$. We first evaluate:

$$Z_i = f_{unet}(X_i, \theta_{unet}) \quad (1)$$

where $\boldsymbol{X_i}$ is the input image, $\boldsymbol{Z_i}$ is the output image, f_{unet} is the function which represents the encoder-decoder network, θ_{unet} is the parameters. As mentioned before, the entire EAST network and its loss function is the objective function for U-Net like enhancement network. If f_{EAST} represents EAST network along with its loss function, then we would expect f_{EAST} (Z_i) to be a scalar value (as we mentioned that f_{EAST} not only represents the EAST network but also its loss function which essentially always returns a scalar value).

Hence the loss function for the enhancement network can be represented by the following equation:

$$Loss = f_{EAST}(f_{unet}(X_i, \theta_{unet})) \quad (2)$$

From Eq. (2) we know the optimization function, which we want to solve in order to find the optimal θ^*_{unet} as shown below:

$$\theta^*_{unet} = \underset{\theta_{unet}}{\operatorname{argmin}}(f_{EAST}(f_{unet}(X_i, \theta_{unet}))) \tag{3}$$

The U-Net architecture used two convolution layers followed by a Max Pooling layer, which essentially performs the down-sampling operation. The activation function Rectified Linear Unit is used after each convolution layer. Initializations of all the convolution parameters are done using the normal initializer. The network was trained using a learning rate of 0.0001 given as the input to Adam Optimizer, batch size of 7 and trained for 27000 steps. We observe that near around 17000 steps the enhancement network starts to give decent results. As done in U-Net architecture, we perform concatenation operation of up-sampling layers with their corresponding down-sampling layers. The output is a 3-channel matrix of the same shape as that of the input and sigmoid activation function is used.

(a) Input night and day license plate images

(b) The result of the proposed enhancement model

Fig. 3. The effectiveness of the proposed enhancement model

The U-Net integrates the local information through down sampling path and up sampling path, which results in extracting context information (pattern). Since the kernel used in U-Net is independent of input image size, the model does not need dense layer and works well for any size of input images [16]. The effect of the proposed U-Net for image enhancement is shown in Fig. 3, where it is seen that for the poor quality images affected by lights in case of nigh image and non-uniform illumination effect in case of day image as shown in Fig. 3(a), the proposed model enhances text details as shown in Fig. 3(b). It is observed from Fig. 3(b) that one can guess the presence of texts compared to the texts in input images. This is the advantage of the proposed U-Net.

3.2 Text Detection for the Enhancement Images

To validate the output of the previous step, we implement the state-of-the-art methods, which address almost all the challenges of text detection in natural scene images, such as low contrast, complex background, multi-script, and orientation. If a text detection method detects texts correctly for an enhanced image, it is said that the proposed enhancement steps are effective and useful. The EAST method [4] proposes an efficient and accurate scene text detector, which explores a single neural network. The main reason to choose the above method is that it is addressing the issues which are part of license plate detection in night images. In addition, the codes of the method are available publicly for supporting research reducibility. Sample license plate detection for the input and output of the proposed enhancement is shown in Fig. 4(a) and (b), respectively. It is observed from Fig. 4 that the EAST method does not detect any text in the input images, while for the enhanced image the same method detects the license plate, accurately. Therefore, we can argue that the proposed enhancement is effective for both night images and day images with poor quality.

(a) Text detection (EAST) for night day license plate images before enhancement

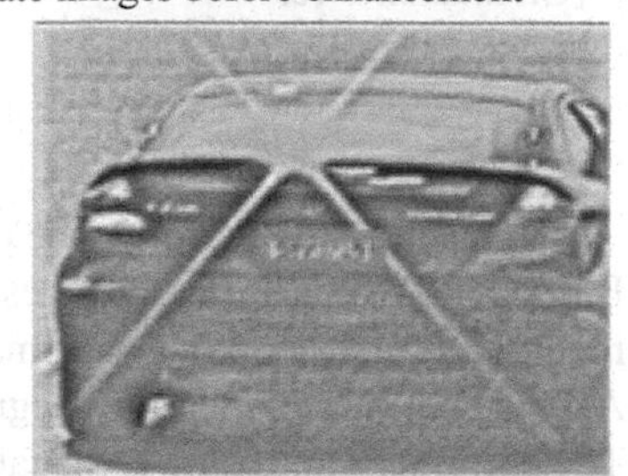

(b) Text detection (EAST) for the night and day license plate images after enhancement

Fig. 4. Validating the enhancement results through text detection performance.

4 Experimental Results

To evaluate the proposed enhancement model, we create a new dataset by capturing license plate images in night, low light and limited light conditions. This dataset includes 200 images for experimentation with a large variation, such as low contrast, poor quality, affected lights, and multiple vehicles in images affected by headlights of vehicles, etc. At the same time, we also test the proposed enhancement model on the benchmark dataset called UCSD [17], which includes low quality as well as high quality images to show that the proposed method is effective for enhancing not only night images but also day images affected by poor quality. The UCSD dataset is further divided into three sub-categories, namely, UCSD-1 which consists of images with blur and low-resolution images, UCSD-2 which consists of images of severe blur with noises, and UCSD-3 which comprises images with good focus and quality. The details of our dataset and the benchmark dataset are reported in Table 1. In summary, the proposed enhancement model is evaluated on both night and day images to show that the proposed enhancement is useful for improving license plate detection performance.

Table 1. The details of our dataset and benchmark datasets of license plate images

Dataset	Night-Our-LPR	Day-LPR UCSD-1	Day-LPR UCSD-2	Day-LPR UCSD-3
Testing	200	1290	114	291
Resolution	Min: 2067 × 2066 Max: 3120 × 4160	Min: 463 × 685 Max: 463 × 685	Min: 241 × 241 Max: 241 × 241	Min: 480 × 640 Max: 480 × 640
Blur	Yes	Yes	Yes	No
Script	Yes	No	No	No
Imbalanced illumination	Yes	No	No	No
Orientation	Yes	No	No	No
Perspective	Yes	No	No	No

To measure the performance of the enhancement, we use quality measures, namely, BRISQUE (Blind/Reference Less Image Spatial Quality Evaluator) which measures naturalness and smoothness of images, and NRIQA (Blind No Reference Image Quality Assessment) which measures degradations caused by blur, noise and distortion artifacts. The definitions and more explanation can be found in [18], where the quality measure is defined. The reason to choose these two measures for evaluating the proposed enhanced results is that unlike MLE, PSNR measures, these two do not require ground truth for measuring the quality of enhanced images. In addition, these two measures smoothness (fine details of the image) and degradations affected by illumination, distortion, noise, etc. The low value of BRISQUE indicates an image is enhanced, while a high value of NRIQA indicates better quality. Similarly, for measuring text detection results, we use standard metrics, namely, Recall (R), Precision (P) and F-measure (F). We calculate these measures before enhancement and after enhancement to assess the contribution of the enhancement model. In case of before enhancement experiments, text detection methods consider input images directly for text detection. In case of after enhancement, text detection methods consider the enhanced images as input for text detection.

To show the objectiveness of the proposed method, we implement three enhancement methods to compare with the results of the proposed enhancement model in terms of quality measures. Jiang et al. [10] proposed night video enhancement using improved dark channel prior, which explores color values in spatial domain for enhancement. Rui and Guoyu [12] proposed a medical X-ray image enhancement method on TV homomorphic filter, which explores frequency coefficients in frequency domain for enhancement. Zhang et al. [15] proposed a new fusion-based enhancement for text detection in night video footage, which combines both spatial and frequency domain-based features for enhancement. The reason to choose the above methods for comparative

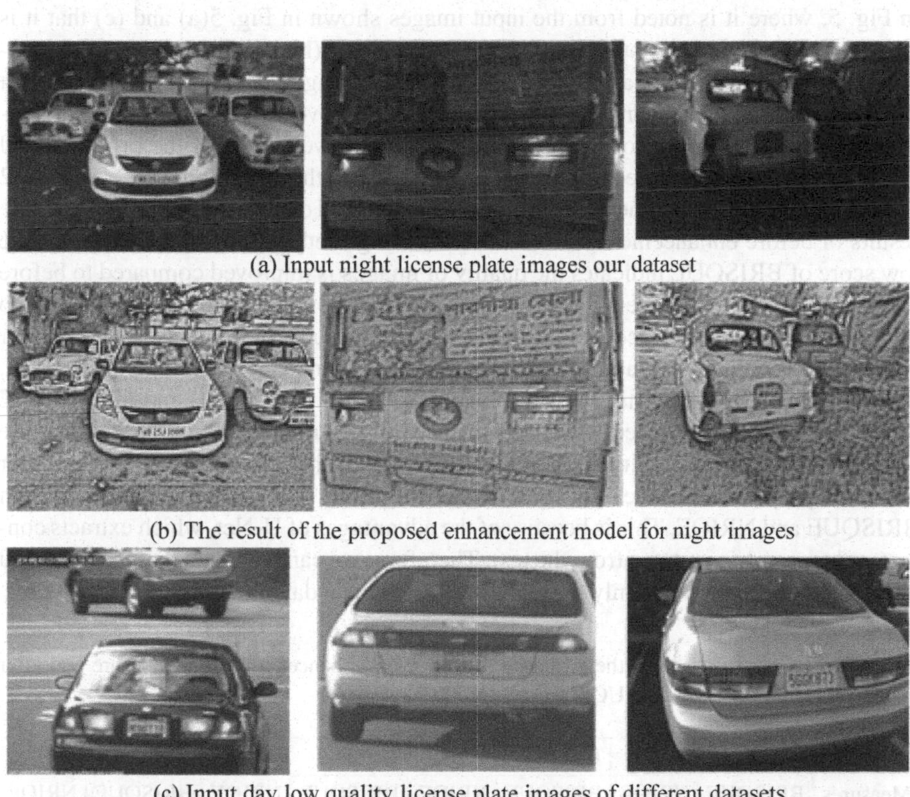

(a) Input night license plate images our dataset

(b) The result of the proposed enhancement model for night images

(c) Input day low quality license plate images of different datasets.

(d) The result of the proposed enhancement model for different day low quality images.

Fig. 5. Sample results of the proposed enhancement model for day and night datasets.

study is that the objective of all the methods was similar to the objective of the proposed work. For text detection experiments, we use codes of EAST [4] and PixelLink [19], which explore different deep learning models for text detection in natural scene images. The reason to choose these methods for validating the proposed enhanced results is that the methods are robust and addressed almost all the challenges of text detection in natural scene images.

4.1 Evaluating the Proposed Enhancement Model

Qualitative results of the proposed enhancement for both night and day images are shown in Fig. 5, where it is noted from the input images shown in Fig. 5(a) and (c) that it is hard to read the number plates. On the other hand, Fig. 5(b) and (d) show that the number plates are visible compared to those in the input images. Therefore, one can assert that the proposed enhancement is robust, and can improve license plate detection performance for night and poor quality images. Quantitative results of the proposed and existing methods are reported in Table 2 for our night and three standard datasets. Table 2 shows that the BRISQUE measure is low for the proposed enhancement compared to the results of before enhancement as well as the existing methods for all the datasets. The low score of BRISQUE indicates the quality of images is improved compared to before enhancement. Similarly, the NRIQE is high for the proposed enhancement compared to the results of before enhancement and the existing methods for all datasets. The higher score of NRIQE indicates that the quality is improved compared to before enhancement. It is expected that the existing methods should give low BRISQUE and high NRIQE after enhancement compared to before enhancement. But due to the limitations of the existing methods, the results are not consistent for all the four datasets. On the other hand, the proposed enhancement is consistent for all the four datasets in terms of both BRISQUE and NRIQE. This is because of the advantages of U-Net, which extracts context and symmetric patterns from the text. Therefore, we can conclude that the proposed enhancement is robust not only for night images but also day images with poor quality.

Table 2. The performance of the proposed and existing enhancement models before and after enhancement on our UCSD-1, UCSD-2 and UCSD-3 datasets

Datasets	Our-Night		UCSD-1		UCSD-2		UCSD-3	
Measures	BRISQUE	NRIQE	BRISQUE	NRIQE	BRISQUE	NRIQE	BRISQUE	NRIQE
Before	37.99	3.27	46.01	3.59	37.06	5.12	45.74	3.80
Proposed	21.48	5.48	44.85	6.98	33.80	8.32	29.29	4.49
Jinag et al. [10]	40.56	3.37	54.79	3.94	68.34	4.91	39.72	2.41
Rui and Guoyu [12]	39.77	3.57	54.43	4.35	74.32	5.16	40.95	3.18
Zhang et al. [15]	37.52	3.17	52.28	3.75	64.18	4.39	35.52	2.31

4.2 Validating the Proposed Enhancement Model Through Text Detection

To test the usefulness of the proposed enhancement compared to the existing enhancement methods, we conduct text detection experiments for the outputs of the proposed and existing enhancement methods on all the four datasets. Qualitative results of the EAST and PixelLink text detection methods for the input and enhanced images of all the four datasets are shown in Fig. 6(a)–(d). It is noted from Fig. 6 that the text detection methods do not detect texts accurately in the input images as shown in Fig. 6(a) and (b).

Night UCSD-1 UCSD-2 UCSD-3

(a) The text detection result of the EAST method before enhancement.

(b) The text detection result of the PixelLink method before enhancement.

(c) The text detection result of the EAST method after enhancement.

(d) The text detection result of the PixelLink method after enhancement.

Fig. 6. Text detection performance before after enhancement.

This indicates that the input images are complex and suffer from poor quality and other adverse factors. However, the results in Fig. 6(b) and (d) show that the same methods detect almost all the texts in the input images correctly. Therefore, it is concluded that the proposed enhancement is effective and useful for improving text detection performance for night images and day image with poor quality.

Quantitative results of text detection methods before and after enhancement for all the four datasets are reported in Tables 3, 4, 5 and 6, respectively. It is observed from Tables 3, 4, 5 and 6 that the proposed enhancement is the best at F-measure calculated according to text detection methods compared to the existing enhancement methods as well as before enhancement for all the four datasets. However, due to limitations of the existing enhancement methods, text detection results are not consistent for enhanced images compared to before enhancement and the proposed enhancement. There is a significant improvement in the text detection result after enhancement compared to before enhancement and the existing methods. With this analysis, we can argue that the proposed enhancement is effective and useful for improving text detection performance for night and day with poor quality images.

Table 3. Text detection performance on the proposed and existing enhancement results before and after enhancement for our dataset

Methods	EAST [8]			PixelLink [9]		
	P	R	F	P	R	F
Before enhancement	0.97	0.26	0.41	0.93	0.23	0.37
Jiang et al. [10]	0.97	0.26	0.41	0.98	0.27	0.42
Rui and Guoyu [12]	0.95	0.23	0.37	0.96	0.42	0.58
Zhang et al. [15]	0.98	0.27	0.42	0.95	0.43	0.59
Proposed method	0.92	0.27	**0.43**	0.95	0.45	**0.61**

Table 4. Text detection performance on the proposed and existing enhancement results before and after enhancement for UCSD-1 dataset

Methods	EAST [8]			PixelLink [9]		
	P	R	F	P	R	F
Before enhancement	1.0	0.32	0.49	1.0	0.38	0.55
Jiang et al. [10]	1.0	0.30	0.46	1.0	0.42	0.59
Rui and Guoyu [12]	1.0	0.28	0.43	0.99	0.43	0.60
Zhang et al. [15]	1.0	0.29	0.45	0.98	0.43	0.60
Proposed method	1.0	0.34	**0.51**	1.0	0.43	**0.60**

Table 5. Text detection performance on the proposed and existing enhancement results before and after enhancement for UCSD-2 dataset

Methods	EAST [8]			PixelLink [9]		
	P	R	F	P	R	F
Before enhancement	1.0	0.58	0.74	1.0	0.51	0.68
Jiang et al. [10]	1.0	0.35	0.52	0.98	0.66	0.79
Rui and Guoyu [12]	1.0	0.53	0.70	0.8	0.62	0.70
Zhang et al. [15]	0.96	0.31	0.47	0.89	0.68	0.77
Proposed method	0.93	0.82	**0.87**	0.81	0.81	**0.81**

Table 6. Text detection performance on the proposed and existing enhancement results before and after enhancement for UCSD-3 dataset

Methods	EAST [8]			PixelLink [9]		
	P	R	F	P	R	F
Before enhancement	0.98	0.37	0.54	1.0	0.39	0.56
Jiang et al. [10]	1.0	0.38	0.55	1.0	0.39	0.56
Rui and Guoyu [12]	1.0	0.37	0.54	1.0	0.41	0.59
Zhang et al. [15]	1.0	0.37	0.55	1.0	0.41	0.58
Proposed method	1.0	0.39	**0.56**	0.99	0.42	**0.59**

To show that the scaling operation does not affect much for the overall performance of the proposed enhancement method, we conduct experiments for estimating quality and text detection measures for the randomly scaled up and down images using our night dataset. The results of text detection by the methods [8, 9] for the input and output of the proposed and existing enhancement methods, and quality measures for the input and enhanced images are reported in Table 7. It is observed from Table 7 that there is no significant difference in quality measures for the input and the enhanced results but the text detection methods [8, 9] report better results for the enhanced results compared to input images (before enhancement). This shows that the proposed enhancement is capable of handling the effects of different scaling. It is evident from the results reported in Tables 3 and 7 that the text detection methods achieve almost same results in terms of recall, precision and F-measure. However, it is not true for the existing enhancement methods when we compare before and after enhancement. This is due to limitation of the existing enhancement methods. Therefore, we can conclude that the proposed enhancement method is invariant to scaling effect to some extent.

Table 7. Proposed enhancement and text detection performance for randomly scaled up and down images using our night dataset.

Methods	Text enhancement		Text detection using [8]			Text detection using [9]		
Measures	BRISQUE	NRIQE	P	R	F	P	R	F
Before enhancement	37.99	3.27	0.97	0.25	0.40	0.94	0.24	0.38
Jiang et al. [10]	21.48	5.48	0.97	0.26	0.41	0.99	0.27	0.42
Rui and Guoyu [12]	40.56	3.37	0.95	0.23	0.37	0.97	0.42	0.59
Zhang et al. [15]	39.77	3.57	0.98	0.27	0.42	0.95	0.43	0.59
After proposed enhancement	37.52	3.17	0.92	0.27	**0.42**	0.95	**0.45**	**0.61**

5 Conclusion and Future Work

In this work, we have proposed a new method for enhancing license plate image captured at night, low light and limited light conditions. The proposed method explores the special property of U-Net, which extracts context and symmetric patterns with the minimum number of samples, for enhancing fine details of license plates in images. In case of text or number plates, one can expect the uniform color, and symmetric patters such as constant stroke width of characters and regular spacing between characters. To verify enhancement results, we have performed text detection on enhanced images and on the original input images to test the contribution of the proposed enhancement. Text detection results on our own night license plate images and day images with poor quality show that the proposed enhancement method is better compared to the existing enhancement methods. However, when we look at number plates in enhanced images, it is not easy to recognize characters by OCR. Therefore, our plan is to extend the work for improving recognition results in the near future.

References

1. Panahi, R., Gholampour, I.: Accurate detection and recognition of dirty vehicle plate numbers for high speed applications. IEEE Trans. ITS **18**, 767–779 (2017)
2. Li, H., Wang, P., Shen, C.: Toward end to end car license plate detection and recognition with deep neural networks. IEEE Trans. ITS **20**, 1126–1136 (2019)
3. Lin, C.H., Lin, Y.S., Liu, W.C.: An efficient license plate recognition system using convolutional neural networks. In: Proceedings of the ICASI, pp. 224–227 (2018)
4. Zhou, X., et al.: East: an efficient and accurate scene text detector. In: Proceedings of the CVPR, pp. 2642–2651 (2017)
5. Asif, M.R., Chun, Q., Hussain, S., Fareed, M.S., Khan, S.: Multinational vehicle license plate detection in complex backgrounds. J. Vis. Commun. Image Represent. **46**, 176–186 (2017)
6. Xie, L., Ahmad, W., Jin, L., Liu, Y., Zhang, S.: A new CNN based method for multi-directional car license plate detection. IEEE Trans. ITS **19**, 507–517 (2018)
7. Yuan, Y., Zou, W., Zhao, Y., Wang, X., Hu, X., Komodakis, N.: A robust and efficient approach to license plate detection. IEEE Trans. IP **26**, 1102–1114 (2017)

8. Shemarry, M.S.A., Li, Y., Abdulla, S.: Ensemble of adaboost cascades of 3L-LBPs classifiers for license plated detection with low quality images. ESWA **92**, 216–235 (2018)
9. Dong, X., et al.: Fast efficient algorithm for enhancement of low lighting video. In: Proceedings of the ICME, pp. 1–6 (2011)
10. Jiang, X., Yao, H., Zhang, S., Lu, X., Zeng, W.: Night video enhancement using improved dark channel prior. In: Proceedings of the ICIP, pp. 553–557 (2013)
11. Sharma, S., Zuo, J.J., Fang, G.: Contrast enhancement using pixel based image fusion in wavelet domain. In: Proceedings of the FC3I, pp. 285–290 (2016)
12. Rui, W., Guoyu, W.: Medical X-ray image enhancement method based on TV-homomorphic filter. In: Proceeding of the ICIVC, pp. 315–318 (2017)
13. Ravishankar, P., Sharmila, R.S., Rajendran, V.: Acoustic image enhancement using Gaussian and Laplacian pyramid – a multiresolution based technique. Multimedia Tools Appl. **77**, 5547–5561 (2018)
14. Raghunandan, K.S., et al.: Riesz fractional based model for enhancing license plate detection and recognition. IEEE Trans. CSVT **28**, 2276–2288 (2018)
15. Zhang, C., Shivakumara, P., Xue, M., Zhu, L., Lu, T., Pal, U.: New fusion based enhancement for text detection in night video footage. In: Hong, R., Cheng, W.-H., Yamasaki, T., Wang, M., Ngo, C.-W. (eds.) PCM 2018. LNCS, vol. 11166, pp. 46–56. Springer, Cham (2018). https://doi.org/10.1007/978-3-030-00764-5_5
16. Ronneberger, O., Fischer, P., Brox, T.: U-Net: convolutional networks for biomedical image segmentation. In: Navab, N., Hornegger, J., Wells, W.M., Frangi, A.F. (eds.) MICCAI 2015. LNCS, vol. 9351, pp. 234–241. Springer, Cham (2015). https://doi.org/10.1007/978-3-319-24574-4_28
17. Zamberletti, A., Gallo, I., Noce, L.: Augmented text character proposals and convolutional neural networks for text spotting from scene images. In: Proceedings of the ACPR, pp. 196–200 (2015)
18. Khare, V., Shivakumara, P., Kumar, A., Chan, C.C., Lu, T., Blumenstein, M.: A quad tree based method for blurred and non-blurred video text frame classification through quality measures. In: Proceedings of the ICPR, pp. 4012–4017 (2016)
19. Deng, D., Liu, H., Li, X., Cai, D.: PixelLink: detecting scene text via instance segmentation. In: Proceedings of the AAAI (2018)

Integration of Biologically Inspired Pixel Saliency Estimation and IPDA Filters for Multi-target Tracking

Daniel Griffiths[1](✉), Laleh Badriasl[1], Tony Scoleri[2], Russell S. A. Brinkworth[1], Sanjeev Arulampalam[2], and Anthony Finn[1]

[1] Defence and Systems Institute, University of South Australia, Adelaide, Australia
Daniel.Griffiths@unisa.edu.au

[2] Defence Science and Technology Group, Canberra, Australia

Abstract. The ability to visually locate and maintain targets is fundamental to modern autonomous systems. By augmenting a novel biologically-inspired target saliency estimator with Integrated Probability Data Association (IPDA) filters and linear prediction techniques, this paper demonstrates the reliable detection and tracking of small and weak-signature targets in cluttered environments. The saliency estimator performs an adaptive, spatio-temporal tone mapping and directional filtering that enhances local contrast and extracts consistent motion, strengthened by the IPDA mechanism which incrementally confirms targets and further removes stochastic false alarms. This joint technique was applied to mid-wave infra-red imagery of maritime scenes where heavy sea clutter distracts significantly from true vessels. Once initialised, the proposed method is shown to successfully maintain tracks of dim targets as small as 2×1 pixels with 100% accuracy and zero false positives. On average, this method scored a sensitivity of 93.2%, with 100% precision, which surpasses well-established techniques in the literature. These results are very encouraging, especially for applications that require no misses in highly cluttered environments.

Keywords: Tone mapping · Visual saliency · Small target detection · Target tracking · Weak signature · Infra-red

1 Introduction

The visual detection and tracking of targets is a task performed by human observers to this day. Practical examples of this problem include the monitoring of maritime waters for vessel traffic, and search and rescue applications. The challenge is also to operate reliably across multiple atmospheric conditions and sea states. Automating vision tasks such as these will require image processing techniques to perform at or above human visual capabilities, while suppressing visual clutter, adapting to large dynamic range shifts, and isolating small and weak-signature targets.

S. Palaiahnakote et al. (Eds.): ACPR 2019, LNCS 12046, pp. 764–778, 2020.
https://doi.org/10.1007/978-3-030-41404-7_54

This work considers the use of biologically inspired (bio-inspired) processing techniques given their intrinsic nature relating closer to human vision than pure computer-vision algorithms. In particular, we propose a novel method which combines pre-processing and target extraction, with proven tracking and filtering techniques. The inclusion of a bio-inspired pre-processing stage readily enables the use of full sensor dynamic range—preventing the significant information loss found with standard 8-bit data [9]—and bypassing the numerous issues that come with porting techniques designed for 8-bit data to the High Dynamic Range (HDR) space [19]. This culminates in a sensitive system resistant to drop-out and false alarms while maintaining temporal coherency.

1.1 Target Detection via Bio-inspired Vision

The Biologically Inspired Vision (BIV) model for target enhancement consists of four distinct processing stages. These stages are based on known and assumed neuronal stages in the target detection pathway of insect visual systems: Photoreceptor Cell (PRC), Laminar Monopolar Cell (LMC), Rectified Transient Cell (RTC), and Elementary Small Target Motion Detector (ESTMD). There is strong neurophysiological evidence that a model similar to this exists in the brain of insects [17,24]. Over the years, elements of this model have been applied in simulation [23] and reduced versions employed in low-dynamic range natural conditions [1] and recently in the context of HDR infra-red imagery [10].

The photoreceptor model is based on a parametric model for the dynamics of fly phototransduction [22] that has been modified to better account for the operation at different light levels [14]. In biology, there is evidence that it is the role of the sensors themselves (i.e. the PRC) to compensate for difficult lighting (such as backlit objects, or looking into shadows cast by sporadic lighting) and accurately encode the information within a limited neuronal bandwidth, essentially tone mapping incoming images [21]. The processing for the PRC operates only in the temporal domain, that is, it works independently on each pixel within the image, to optimise the signal-to-noise ratio (SNR) and enhance the dynamic components of the scene. It has been shown that this processing alone, even without the subsequent stages of the model, has a significant effect on the detectability of targets in environments that have large dynamic range, clutter and/or high contrast [5].

The laminar monopolar cells in flies are second order neurons and are similar in operation to bipolar cells in vertebrate eyes [13]. They perform spatio-temporal high-pass filtering that is adjusted based on the SNR of the incoming information [20]. In the BIV model, this filtering is relaxed to allow a proportion of the DC component of the signal to still propagate depending on the light levels observed on a per-pixel level [12]. Modifications have also been made to the spatial kernel used to generate the high-pass filter from literature [6] to account for the difference between the hexagonal pixel packing in the fly being different to the rectangular arrangement used in current digital imaging technology. The parameter values for the gains and time constants in the model were taken from literature [8] and modified to account for the lower temporal and higher spatial resolution of the incoming data compared to that seen in the fly.

Rectified transient cells are a class of cells found in the fly brain with responses that make them well suited to be on the target processing pathway [24]. These cells perform full-wave rectification of the incoming signals from the LMC with two classes of cell that adapt differently to rising (on) and falling (off) stimuli. The purpose of this processing step is to highlight the leading and trailing edges of targets of interest.

Unlike the other three processing stages, elementary small target motion detectors have not been directly recorded from within the brain of an insect, but rather represent a theoretical input to the Small Target Motion Detector (STMD) [18]. ESTMDs are based on the elementary motion detector [11], however rather than correlating the delayed response of one pixel with an adjacent one, it compares the two outputs of the RTC for the same pixel. In this way it compares a delayed version of the expected leading edge of a target (falling for dark targets, rising for bright targets) with the expected trailing edge of a target (rising for dark targets, falling for bright targets). This means the model confounds speed and target width and can only detect small targets (or parts of larger targets) that move into and then out of a pixel in the image. It has been shown that the spatio-temporal profiles generated by small targets, and detected by this target detection model, are sufficiently rare in natural scenes so as to serve as a good discriminator [24]. The derived saliency map is real-valued, only requiring a thresholding operation to produce a binary map of target presence (Fig. 1).

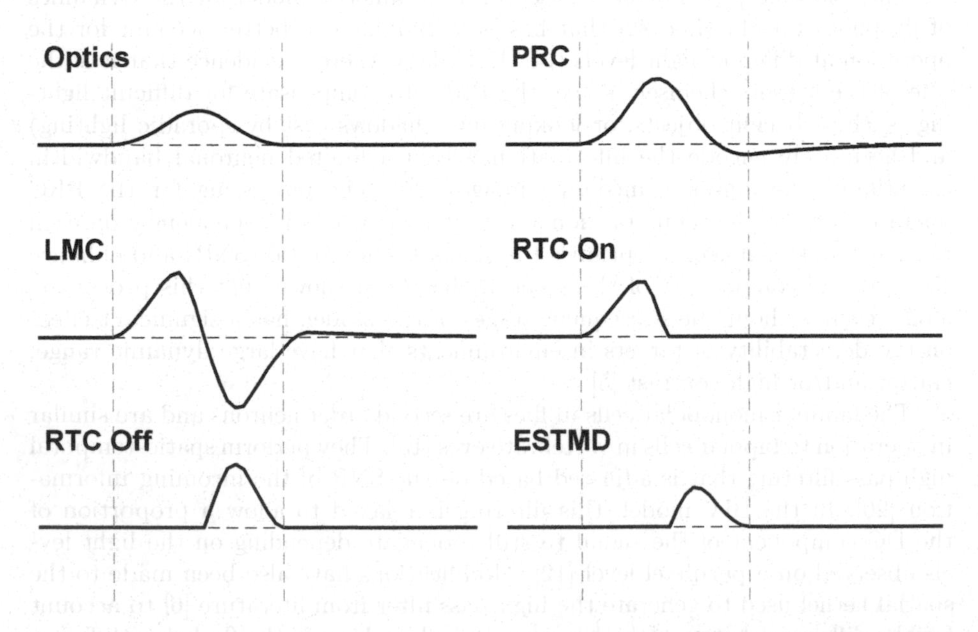

Fig. 1. Idealised responses of the BIV stages for a single pixel and an impulse target. Time is along the x-axis, response on the y-axis. The horizontal dashed line is a reference to a zero response, and the blue vertical lines denote when the target first enters then exits the field of view of a pixel.

1.2 Multi-target Tracking in Cluttered Environments

This paper also addresses the two-dimensional (2D) multi-target tracking problem in the presence of clutter when the probability of detection is less than one. Note that the standard tracking methods, such as Kalman or particle filter, cannot fully solve the multi-target tracking problem. This requires an algorithm that can perform data association (target-measurement assignment) and distinguish measurements received from different targets and clutter. Different data association techniques have been proposed in the literature for this purpose. For instance, the Nearest Neighbour (NN) method [3] is the simplest form of data association for single target tracking in clutter. In this approach, the measurement that is closest to a predicted state of a track is associated with the track. However, in practice, the closest measurement may not always be the correct one to assign to the track, which implies that in a highly cluttered environment, this strategy may yield poor performance.

An alternative approach for single target tracking in the presence of clutter is the Probabilistic Data Association (PDA) [4]. The PDA is a simple and fast association algorithm, which significantly outperforms the NN technique [2]. Furthermore, Integrated Probabilistic Data Association (IPDA) [16] is a version of PDA, where an existence probability is associated with each track. This track existence probability, which is updated at each time step, is used to autonomously initiate and terminate tracks. The IPDA has the ability to identify the origin of different targets in a multi-target tracking problem. Moreover, it can discriminate temporally inconsistent false alarms from true measurements of the targets. The IPDA is also able to track manoeuvring targets using a nearly-constant velocity model by modelling the small perturbations in velocity through a process noise term in the target dynamics. Note that, in our implementation, the Kalman filter has been used in the IPDA in order to update the state vector and covariance matrix of different tracks. Kalman filter provides an optimal solution as the tracking problem under investigation has a linear state-space model.

Given its relatively low computational complexity, multi-target capability and good performance, the IPDA approach was selected in this paper to address the tracking problem in the presence of clutter.

1.3 The Tracking Filter: Integrated Probabilistic Data Association

In this section, the IPDA tracking algorithm is summarised. The measurements in this problem are the centre locations of bounding boxes, which are identified at each frame at evenly spaced time instants $t_k = kT$, where $k = 1, 2, \ldots$, is the measurement time index and T is the time between consecutive measurements. These measurements may include targets of interest or false measurements from clutter. We assume that targets follow a nearly constant velocity model given by

$$\boldsymbol{x}_{k+1}^t = \boldsymbol{F}\boldsymbol{x}_k^t + \boldsymbol{w}_k^t,$$

where $\boldsymbol{x}_k^t = [x_k^t, y_k^t, \dot{x}_k^t, \dot{y}_k^t]^T$ is the state vector of the tth target consisting of its location and velocity at time k and

$$\boldsymbol{F} = \begin{bmatrix} \boldsymbol{I}_2 & T\boldsymbol{I}_2 \\ \boldsymbol{0}_2 & \boldsymbol{I}_2 \end{bmatrix}.$$

Here $\boldsymbol{I}_2$ is the 2×2 identity matrix and $\boldsymbol{0}_2$ is the 2×2 zero matrix. The vector $\boldsymbol{w}_k^t$ is a zero-mean white Gaussian process noise sequence with covariance matrix $\boldsymbol{Q}_k^t$.

Since the camera is considered stationary in this setting, the linear measurement model for target t corresponds to the location of the target and is given by

$$\boldsymbol{z}_k^t = \boldsymbol{H}\boldsymbol{x}_k^t + \boldsymbol{v}_k^t, \qquad k = 1, 2, \ldots,$$

where $\boldsymbol{H} = [\boldsymbol{I}_2\ \boldsymbol{0}_2]$ and $\boldsymbol{v}_k^t$ is the measurement noise with covariance $\boldsymbol{R}_k^t$. At each time epoch k, the sensor returns a set of measurements $\boldsymbol{Z}_k$ which consists of false alarms and target-originated measurements with detection probability P_D. The aim is to estimate the state vector $\boldsymbol{x}_k^t$ of the detected targets as well as their associated covariance matrices $\boldsymbol{P}_k^t$ given the set of measurements $\boldsymbol{Z}^k = \{\boldsymbol{Z}_1, \cdots, \boldsymbol{Z}_k\}$.

Judgement of Track Existence. Track existence is modeled as a two-state Markov process where E_k^t and $\bar{E}_k^t$ denote the events that target t exists or does not exist at time k, respectively. The probability matrix of transition between the two states is

$$\boldsymbol{p} = \begin{bmatrix} p_{11} & p_{12} \\ p_{21} & p_{22} \end{bmatrix},$$

where $0 \le p_{ij} \le 1$ and $\sum_{j=1}^{2} p_{ij} = 1, i = 1, 2$. Denoting $\boldsymbol{Z}^{k-1}$ as the set of accumulated measurements within the tracking gate up to time $k-1$ and assuming that the probability that target t exists at time $k-1$, i.e., $\Pr\left\{E_{k-1}^t|\boldsymbol{Z}^{k-1}\right\}$ is known, the predicted probability of track existence can be calculated as

$$\Pr\left\{E_k^t|\boldsymbol{Z}^{k-1}\right\} = p_{11}\Pr\left\{E_{k-1}^t|\boldsymbol{Z}^{k-1}\right\} + p_{12}\left(1 - \Pr\left\{E_{k-1}^t|\boldsymbol{Z}^{k-1}\right\}\right).$$

Let m_k^t and $\hat{m}_k^t$ respectively denote the number of validated measurements and expected number of false measurements within the tracking gate of the target t at time k, V_k^t the area (volume) of the gate at time k, given as $V_k^t = \pi\gamma|\boldsymbol{S}_k^t|^{\frac{1}{2}}$. Here $\boldsymbol{S}_k^t$ is the innovation covariance associated with target t and γ is 25 for the gate probability equal to one. Since in this work the prior distribution of the number of false measurements is unknown, $\hat{m}_k^t = m_k^t$. Then the updated probability of track existence is given by

$$\Pr\left\{E_k^t|\boldsymbol{Z}^k\right\} = \frac{1-\delta_k}{1-\delta_k \Pr\left\{E_k^t|\boldsymbol{Z}^{k-1}\right\}} \Pr\left\{E_k^t|\boldsymbol{Z}^{k-1}\right\},$$

where

$$\delta_k = \begin{cases} P_D P_G & m_k^t = 0, \\ P_D P_G - P_D P_G \frac{V_k^t}{\hat{m}_k^t} \sum_{i=1}^{m_k^t} \Lambda_i^t(k), \, m_k^t > 0, \end{cases}$$

and $\Lambda_i^t(k) = P_G^{-1}\mathcal{N}[\boldsymbol{\nu}_k^i; 0, \boldsymbol{S}_k^t]$. Here P_G is the gate probability (probability of detected measurements falling in the gate), which is considered one in this paper and $\boldsymbol{\nu}_k^i$ is the measurement residual corresponding to the ith measurement. The updated probability $\Pr\left\{E_k^t|\boldsymbol{Z}^k\right\}$ is used to confirm or terminate a track. In the IPDA, initially a number of tracks are generated and their existence probability is updated at each frame. After few iterations, confirmed tracks provide an indication of the state of targets.

Data Association. The association probability that the ith measurement $\boldsymbol{z}_k^i$ within the tracking gate originated from target t at time k is

$$\beta_{k,0} = \frac{1 - P_D P_G}{1-\delta_k}, \quad \beta_{k,i} = \frac{P_D P_G \frac{V_k^t}{\hat{m}_k^t} \Lambda_i^t(k)}{1-\delta_k}.$$

State Update. The state and covariance update equations of target t are

$$\hat{\boldsymbol{x}}_{k|k} = \sum_{i=0}^{m_k^t} \beta_k^i \hat{\boldsymbol{x}}_{k|k}^i, \; \boldsymbol{P}_{k|k} = \sum_{i=0}^{m_k^t} \beta_k^i \left(\boldsymbol{P}_{k|k}^i + (\hat{\boldsymbol{x}}_{k|k}^i - \hat{\boldsymbol{x}}_{k|k})(\hat{\boldsymbol{x}}_{k|k}^i - \hat{\boldsymbol{x}}_{k|k})^T\right),$$

where $\hat{\boldsymbol{x}}_{k|k}^0 = \hat{\boldsymbol{x}}_{k|k-1}$, $\hat{\boldsymbol{P}}_{k|k}^0 = \hat{\boldsymbol{P}}_{k|k-1}$, and $\hat{\boldsymbol{x}}_{k|k}^i$ and $\boldsymbol{P}_{k|k}^i$ are the updated target state and covariance, respectively, corresponding to the ith measurement.

1.4 Statement of Contribution

This paper presents a novel integration of two previously published technologies: the BIV target enhancement model and IPDA tracking filters. A novel handover strategy for interfacing the BIV with a tracking technique has been developed, including the morphological filtering and binarisation of a saliency map into target centroids. Additionally, this study is the first instance of the BIV target extraction pipeline being applied to non-synthetic, infra-red imagery.

2 Data Collection

This study exclusively uses Mid-Wave Infra-Red (MWIR) imagery captured using a FLIR X8400sc camera. This camera records images with a 14 bits-per-pixel dynamic range and a spatial resolution of 1280×1024 pixels. The image in Fig. 2a shows the data gathering location where sequences were taken at a port in the Northern Territory of Australia at various times of day, over several days. A small boat—a Stabicraft 759 (Fig. 2b)—was hired to navigate the harbour throughout these trials.

Fig. 2. Trial components. (a) View of the littoral environment; (b) Hired Stabicraft 759.

Three individual sequences and one particular frame (Table 1) were chosen from the overall data set to provide representative examples of target extraction capabilities. This selection was made to cover a variety of times of day, sea conditions, target types, and background complexities (Fig. 3a–c). The chosen targets (Fig. 3d–g) were manually tagged using key-frames and linear interpolation to provide ground-truth bounding boxes.

Table 1. Description of example scenes used in this study. The contrast quality was assessed by calculating the Global Contrast Factor [15]. *As a point-tracker, the BIV model only detected the hotter engine, the full size of the boat was 4×8 pixels.

	Frames	Description	Targets		
			Name	Pixels	Contrast
Scene 1	300	Clear background, calm water	Shark Fin	2×3	Weak
			Boat 1	14×12	Very strong
Scene 2	220	Port in background, active ocean	Boat 2	6×4	Medium
Scene 3	250	Foreground clutter, calm ocean	Boat 3	2×1*	Weak
Scene 4	1	Clear background, sky	Insect	2×2	Weak

Fig. 3. Full-view of elected scenes (top row) and cropped targets (bottom row), without processing applied. Targets are highlighted by the red rectangles. Bottom row, from left to right: Shark Fin, Boat 1, Boat 2, and Boat 3. (Color figure online)

3 Methodology

Five processing pipelines were evaluated, two as variations of the proposed method:

1. Multi-scale Local Contrast Method (MLCM)
2. Multi-scale Top Hat (MTH)
3. BIV
4. BIV & IPDA tracker
5. BIV, IPDA tracker & Linear predictor

The MLCM [7] and MTH [25] target extraction algorithms were chosen to provide a comparison to techniques in the literature. Both of these methods are applied to 8-bit representations of the infra-red data, linear rescaling was used for methods 1–2, and the BIV pre-processing stages for methods 3–5.

3.1 Target Extraction

For each tested method the target centroids are extracted from the computed saliency or detection map using binary thresholding and morphological filters. Upper and lower threshold bounds were empirically chosen for each individual scene and method to maximise performance. A 2×2 square structuring element is used to perform identical dilate, bridge, and then erode operations on the produced binary map, clustering detected pixels and reducing false positives. Lastly, each continuous pixel cluster is converted into an object, and the centroid location calculated.

3.2 Dropout Reduction via Linear Prediction

To reduce the rate of target drop-out in confirmed tracks, a velocity-based linear predictor has been incorporated. To remain temporally coherent, this predictor uses the target's previous state vector $\hat{\boldsymbol{x}}^i_{k-n|k-n}$ at time-step $k-n$ to estimate the current state vector $\hat{\boldsymbol{x}}^i_{k|k-n}$ at time k given measurements up to time $k-n$:

$$\hat{\boldsymbol{x}}^i_{k|k-n} = [\hat{x}^i_{k-n|k-n} + nT\hat{\dot{x}}^i_{k-n|k-n}, \hat{y}^i_{k-n|k-n} + nT\,\hat{\dot{y}}^i_{k-n|k-n}, \hat{\dot{x}}^i_{k-n|k-n}, \hat{\dot{y}}^i_{k-n|k-n}]^T,$$

where n samples have passed without reacquiring the target. In application, n was bound at 2 to limit error accumulation from prolonged estimation of an undetected target. The predictor is only applied to confirmed tracks, and does not interact with the track confirmation or termination processes.

4 Experimental Validation

Figure 4 demonstrates the BIV model's ability for target enhancement, in both the PRC and ESTMD stages. In the unprocessed images, Fig. 4a and b, the target has a very weak-signature, with little contrast to the background, making extraction difficult. Applying the BIV's PRC and ESTMD stages, Fig. 4(b) and (c) respectively, significantly increases the target's contrast, the latter giving near binary extraction.

Fig. 4. Example extraction of a small, weak-signature target. Left: Original frame (target highlighted in red); Right: Cropped representations of target, without processing, and with PRC and ESTMD respectively (top to bottom). (Color figure online)

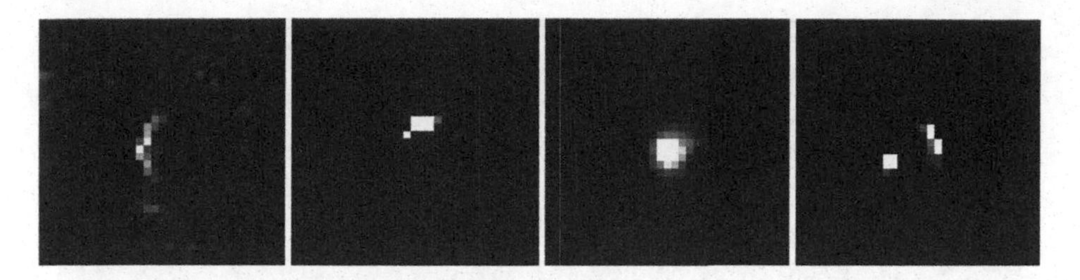

Fig. 5. Cropped views of the targets, as represented by the ESTMD. From left to right: Shark Fin, Boat 1, Boat 2, and Boat 3.

Similar results are achieved for the targets in Table 1, as demonstrated in Fig. 5. Since the BIV is a small-target detector, larger targets were reduced to individual edges, when compared with their original representations (Fig. 3).

Figure 6 below provides a complete view of a sample scene considered in this study, and resulting track visualisation for the proposed method. Detections (cyan tracks) appended with magenta arrows correspond to tracked objects. The arrow direction indicates the estimated motion direction whereas the arrow length is proportional to target's track confidence.

As can be seen, the far target has a shorter arrow because its distance makes it perceptually move slower for the observer. The other target, a shark fin, is moving more rapidly, hence its longer arrow. Note also several false alarms in the bottom of the viewpoint, caused by the motion of the ocean. While they are detected, the IPDA method discards them correctly, as noted by the absence of a magenta arrow.

To quantify the performance of the different five target extraction pipelines run on the three scenes, detected targets were compared to the ground truth, and the statistical sensitivity and specificity measures calculated. The accumulation of errors—false positives and false negatives—over time was modelled to demonstrate the frame-to-frame capability of the tested methods (Fig. 7). This highlights the initialisation process of all methods and the latency to confirm tracks, as well as demonstrates the BIV's ability to produce minimal false positives by default, without the addition of IPDA filters and linear prediction.

Applying the IPDA filters suppress all false positives, while the linear predictor removes false negatives. Once the complete pipeline has initialised, the proposed method (BIV, IPDA & Predictor) demonstrates an absence of false negatives. The BIV takes 3 frames to initialise, and the IPDA filter 12 and 26 frames to confirm tracks for "Shark Fin" and "Boat 1", respectively. Other methods show a steady accumulation of false alarms.

Since a target vessel was present for the entire length of all three scenes, we were unable to model true negatives for the data set. Instead, scenes have been characterised using the True Positive Rate (TPR) and Positive Predictive Value (PPV). The TPR—or sensitivity—of a system indicates the probability

Fig. 6. Example output of the proposed method when applied to Scene 1, with annotations accumulated to visualise target paths. The red circle indicates the location of an anchored boat, without an arrow, since it is static and therefore not tracked. The top-left target is a boat moving towards the camera, and the centre target, a shark fin, is moving rapidly to the left. The motion of the sea causes increased saliency in the foreground, however does not have constant motion and is excluded by the IPDA tracker. (Color figure online)

of a true target being located, and the PPV—or precision—the trustworthiness of any detection the system reports. Notably, the combination BIV, IPDA & Predictor performs the best by far, consistently scoring the highest TPR and PPV, as shown in Table 2.

Figure 8 demonstrates the per-frame error for each tracked target, when using the proposed BIV, IPDA & Predictor method. A constant offset was applied to the detected centroid of targets located by the BIV model. This offset was half the size of the target in the relevant axis, and was performed because the BIV is designed for single pixels, and thus would always locate the strongest edge of a target and not necessarily its centroid.

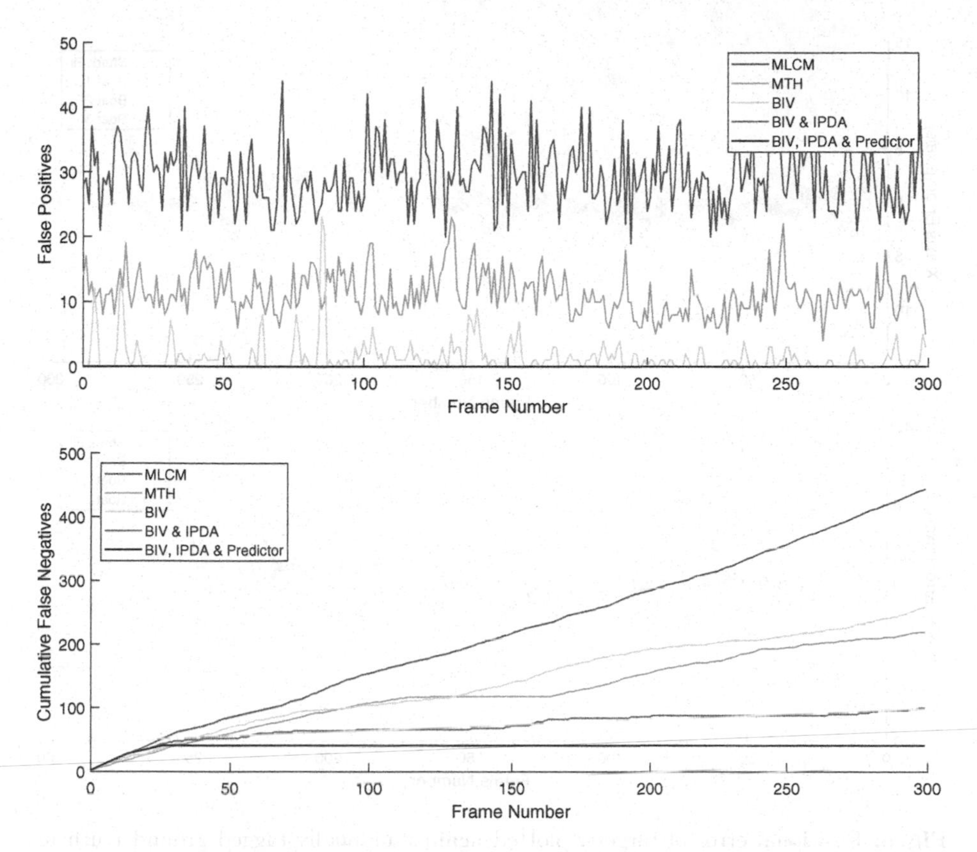

Fig. 7. Results of five target detection methods applied to Scene 1. Top: False positives/alarms per frame. Bottom: Cumulative false negatives over the frame sequence. This result is representative of all three scenes, and thus the underlying techniques. Note the absence of any false positives in the BIV & IPDA and BIV, IPDA & Predictor models. In addition no false negatives were present in the IPDA & Predictor results after initialisation as evidenced by the horizontal line after frame number 26

Table 2. Summary of statistical results for the target extraction. The True Positive Rate (TRP), Positive Predictive Value (PPV), and Error as the mean absolute pixel distance (and standard deviation thereof) between a detected target and ground truth centroid.

	Scene 1			Scene 2			Scene 3		
	TPR	PPV	Error	TPR	PPV	Error	TPR	PPV	Error
MLCM	26.0%	3.4%	2.7 ± 0.90	33.1%	1.4%	1.0 ± 0.54	50.3%	3.6%	1.8 ± 1.11
MTH	63.5%	11.4%	3.6 ± 2.63	9.9%	0.6%	0.6 ± 0.28	0.3%	22.5%	3.3 ± 0.04
BIV	56.8%	66.7%	2.8 ± 1.37	78.2%	86.9%	5.3 ± 1.92	98.8%	16.0%	4.7 ± 1.35
BIV & IPDA	83.3%	100%	2.7 ± 1.44	80.9%	100%	4.7 ± 2.51	96.8%	100%	1.9 ± 1.16
BIV, IPDA & Predictor	93.2%	100%	2.7 ± 1.48	89.6%	100%	4.9 ± 2.65	96.8%	100%	1.9 ± 1.16

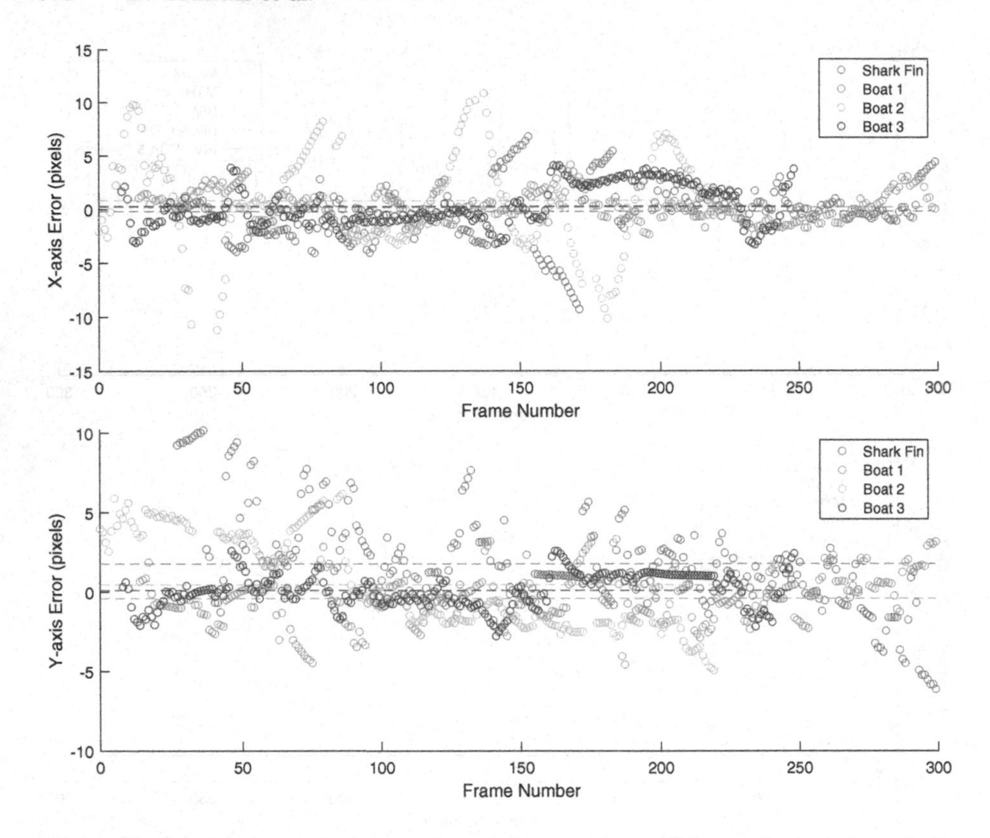

Fig. 8. Positional error of targets, plotted against manually-tagged ground truth for the BIV, IPDA & Predictor method. The dashed lines represent the mean error.

5 Conclusion

This paper presented a novel method for small target detection, using a bio-inspired extraction pipeline augmented by more traditional IPDA filters and a linear predictor based on target location and velocity. Compared to existing techniques in the literature, the BIV model's temporally-aware extraction was able to significantly reduce false positives in high clutter environments. The IPDA filtering approach was able to eliminate all remaining false alarms and accurately track target location and velocity. Overall, the proposed technique managed to track the target for 93% of frames, with initialisation responsible for the 7% deficiency. Comparatively, the highest performing technique from literature averaged a 63.5% success rate, with one-tenth the precision. Notably, the presented system is temporally coherent and thus capable of online operation.

To expand upon this work, future development will include processing additional videos from the presented data set as well as other trial videos in both the maritime and aerial domains. This will strengthen the statistical analysis on a greater variety of targets, backgrounds and environmental conditions. Additionally, implementing modern foreground extraction techniques, such as Convolutional Neural Networks, will demonstrate their capacity and enable comparison to our method. Lastly, utilising the recorded GPS data will create 3-dimensional ground truth for the system, which can be projected in images to assess against the tracker's predicted locations and velocities.

Acknowledgements. The authors would like to thank the Sensor Processing and Algorithms Group (SPA) in the Weapons and Combat Systems Division (WCSD) of the Defence Science and Technology Group (DSTG) for providing the Northern Territory data set. Additionally, we wish to thank the DSTG for the collaborative project agreement funding this work.

References

1. Bagheri, Z.M., Wiederman, S.D., Cazzolato, B.S., Grainger, S., O'Carroll, D.C.: Performance of an insect-inspired target tracker in natural conditions. Bioinspir. Biomim. **12**(2), 025006 (2017)
2. Bar-Shalom, Y., Daum, F., Huang, J.: The probabilistic data association filter. IEEE Control Syst. Mag. **29**(6), 82–100 (2010)
3. Bar-Shalom, Y., Li, X.R.: Multitarget-Multisensor Tracking: Principles and Techniques, vol. 16. YBS, Storrs (1996)
4. Bar-Shalom, Y., Tse, E.: Tracking in a cluttered environment with probabilistic data association. Automatica **11**(5), 451–460 (1975)
5. Brinkworth, R.S., Mah, E.L., Gray, J.P., O'Carroll, D.C.: Photoreceptor processing improves salience facilitating small target detection in cluttered scenes. J. Vis. **8**(11), 1–17 (2008)
6. Brinkworth, R.S., O'Carroll, D.C.: Robust models for optic flow coding in natural scenes inspired by insect biology. PLoS Comput. Biol. **5**, e1000555 (2009)
7. Chen, C.P., Li, H., Wei, Y., Xia, T., Tang, Y.Y.: A local contrast method for small infrared target detection. IEEE Trans. Geosci. Remote Sens. **52**(1), 574–581 (2014)
8. Dubs, A.: The spatial integration of signals in the retina and lamina of the fly compound eye under different conditions of luminance. J. Comp. Physiol. **146**(3), 321–343 (1982)
9. Geronimo, D., Lopez, A.M., Sappa, A.D., Graf, T.: Survey of pedestrian detection for advanced driver assistance systems. IEEE Trans. Pattern Anal. Mach. Intell. **32**(7), 1239–1258 (2010)
10. Griffiths, D., Scoleri, T., Brinkworth, R.S., Finn, A.: Bio-inspired filtering on infrared data for persistent vessel detection despite adverse maritime visibility conditions. In: Safeguarding Australia Summit, pp. 1–10, May 2019
11. Hassenstein, B., Reichardt, W.: Systemtheoretische analyse der zeit-, reihenfolgen- und vorzeichenauswertung bei der bewegungsperzeption des rüsselkäfers chlorophanus. Zeitschrift für Naturforschung B **11**(9–10), 513–524 (1956)
12. Juusola, M., French, A.S., Uusitalo, R.O., Weckström, M.: Information processing by graded-potential transmission through tonically active synapses. Trends Neurosci. **19**(7), 292–297 (1996)
13. Laughlin, S.B., Hardie, R.C.: Common strategies for light adaptation in the peripheral visual systems of fly and dragonfly. J. Comp. Physiol. **128**(4), 319–340 (1978)
14. Mah, E.L., Brinkworth, R.S., O'Carroll, D.C.: Implementation of an elaborated neuromorphic model of a biological photoreceptor. Biol. Cybern. **98**(5), 357–369 (2008)

15. Matkovic, K., Neumann, L., Neumann, A., Psik, T., Purgathofer, W.: Global contrast factor - a new approach to image contrast. In: Conference on Computational Aesthetics in Graphics, Visualization and Imaging, pp. 159–167, May 2005
16. Musicki, D., Evans, R., Stankovic, S.: Integrated probabilistic data association. IEEE Trans. Autom. Control **39**(6), 1237–1241 (1994)
17. Nordström, K., Barnett, P.D., O'Carroll, D.C.: Insect detection of small targets moving in visual clutter. PLoS Biol. **4**(3), e54 (2006)
18. O'Carroll, D.: Feature-detecting neurons in dragonflies. Nature **362**(6420), 541 (1993)
19. Reinhard, E., Heidrich, W., Debevec, P., Pattanaik, S., Ward, G., Myszkowski, K.: High Dynamic Range Imaging: Acquisition, Display, and Image-Based Lighting. Morgan Kaufmann, Burlington (2010)
20. Van Hateren, J.: A theory of maximizing sensory information. Biol. Cybern. **68**(1), 23–29 (1992)
21. Van Hateren, J.: Processing of natural time series of intensities by the visual system of the blowfly. Vision. Res. **37**(23), 3407–3416 (1998)
22. Van Hateren, J., Snippe, H.: Information theoretical evaluation of parametric models of gain control in blowfly photoreceptor cells. Vision. Res. **41**(14), 1851–1865 (2001)
23. Wiederman, S., Brinkworth, R.S., O'Carroll, D.C., et al.: Performance of a bio-inspired model for the robust detection of moving targets in high dynamic range natural scenes. J. Comput. Theor. Nanosci. **7**(5), 911–920 (2010)
24. Wiederman, S.D., Shoemaker, P.A., O'Carroll, D.C.: A model for the detection of moving targets in visual clutter inspired by insect physiology. PLoS ONE **3**(7), e2784 (2008)
25. Zeng, M., Li, J., Peng, Z.: The design of top-hat morphological filter and application to infrared target detection. Infrared Phys. Technol. **48**(1), 67–76 (2006)

The Effectiveness of Noise in Data Augmentation for Fine-Grained Image Classification

Nanyu Sun, Xianjie Mo, Tingting Wei, Dabin Zhang, and Wei Luo(✉)

College of Mathematics and Informatics, South China Agricultural University, Guangzhou 510000, GD, People's Republic of China
sunnanyu@foxmail.com, cedricmo.cs@gmail.com, {weitingting,zdbff}@scau.edu.cn, cswluo@gmail.com

Abstract. Recognizing images from subcategories with subtle differences remains a challenging task due to the scarcity of quantity and diversity of training samples. Existing data augmentation methods either rely on models trained with fully annotated data or involve human in the loop, which is labor-intensive. In this paper, we propose a simple approach that leverages large amounts of noisy images from the Web for fine-grained image classification. Beginning with a deep model taken as input image patches for feature representation, the maximum entropy learning criterion is first introduced to improve the score-based patch selection. Then a noise removal procedure is designed to verify the usefulness of noisy images in the augmented data for classification. Extensive experiments on standard, augmented, and combined datasets with and without noise validate the effectiveness of our method. Generally, we achieve comparable results on benchmark datasets, e.g., *CUB-Birds, Stanford Dogs,* and *Stanford Cars*, with only 50 augmented noisy samples for every category.

Keywords: Fine-grained image classification · Data augmentation · Maximum entropy learning

1 Introduction

Fine-grained image classification (FGIC) refers to classifying images from subord-inate-level categories that belong to one base-level category. Current methods for FGIC are almost all relying on deep convolutional neural networks (DCNNs) [8,20,23,31], which require large quantities of labeled training samples. However, the subtle difference between fine-grained categories makes correct classifying them with high accuracy become impossible by solely collecting more training samples with image-level labels. On the other hand, collecting samples with rich annotations, e.g., part locations, bounding boxes, becomes increasingly difficult with the number of samples and categories increasing.

Existing studies tackle the deficiency of training data in FGIC either by augmenting data through geometrical transformation, i.e., rotating, cropping, and

S. Palaiahnakote et al. (Eds.): ACPR 2019, LNCS 12046, pp. 779–792, 2020.
https://doi.org/10.1007/978-3-030-41404-7_55

color jitter et al. [16], or by selecting highly relevant samples from a corresponding large-scale datasets based on similarity scores [4,30], or by enlarging the training set with filtered Web images [5,26]. Although these methods achieve success in some certain degree, inefficiency limits their large-scale applications. Selecting samples relies on an effective similarity measurement, which usually requires a feature learning model pretrained on the original dataset, and an available large-scale dataset. Collecting images from the Web presumes that a strongly trained model pre-exists so that it can filter out noisy images. They both augment data by utilizing a model pretrained on small-scale datasets, which may cause suboptimal problems—augmented samples are model dependent.

In this paper, we blindly trust the quality of images returned by current image search engines, e.g., Google image search, and propose to augment benchmark datasets with these returned images for FGIC, thus circumventing the suboptimal problem in previous methods. Our proposal is clearly different from previous methods in two aspects: (1) no pretrained model on small-scale dataset is needed to enlarge the training set; (2) allowing noisy images to be incorporated into the training of FGIC models. We believe that enlarging training set through a pretrained model may cause suboptimal problems, which means the newly incorporated images are model dependent. This problem could become serious especially when the available training data on benchmark datasets is scarce. In contrast, we circumvent this problem by directly including the search engine returned images, which is model independent. Such operation may take an adventure to incorporate noisy data into the model training, which is a major concern in previous data augmentation studies. However, we argue that given the advantage of current text-based image search engines, we can believe that the returned images are with reliable quality. Even noisy images might be included, they could present weakly semantic relationships to the search input, thus augmenting the training set with diversity. To verify the effectiveness of the returned noisy images, a noise removal method based on three-sigma rule of thumb is designed and corresponding comparison tests are conducted. Experiments validate our proposal that noisy images returned by current text-based search engines have a positive effect to FGIC and can bring significant performance improvement. In our work, we further study the maximum entropy learning for FGIC. Since the appearance of objects from different subcategories is very similar in FGIC, it is reasonable to make the output predictions to have a relatively high entropy to make sure the top-K outputs include the ground-truth category. Experiments on three datasets verified our proposal and showed a better or comparable performance compared to related studies in previous works. Generally, we make the following contributions in this paper:

- We investigate the feasibility of learning an FGIC model by extending existing training set using samples directly collected from current image search engines, in which the returned noisy images, had a weak semantic relationship and defined in terms of visual similarity to the search, contribute the performance of FGIC.

- We incorporate the maximum entropy criterion to regularize the learning of an FGIC model, in which a patch selection for feature presentation is optimized to provide more informative and discriminative patches.
- We construct augmented and combined training sets for three fine-grained datasets, and conduct comprehensive experiments to verify the feasibility of data augmentation with noise for FGIC. Experimental results validate the effectiveness of our method.

The reminder of this work is organized as follows: A brief review of related work is presented in Sect. 2. Steps of data augmentation, noise removal, a DCNN learning model, and maximum entropy learning are detailed in Sect. 3. Section 4 demonstrates our experimental results and ablation analysis. We conclude our work in Sect. 5.

2 Related Work

Fine-Grained Image Classification. There have been many methods proposed to distinguish objects from different fine-grained categories. Since the pioneering work of [16], deep convolution neural networks (DCNNs) have made great progress on large-scale image classification tasks [8,20,21,23,28,31]. State-of-the-art FGIC methods usually extracts local discriminative features from images of fine-grained categories, and then utilize these local parts to achieve fine-grained image classification. [10,19] adopt image-processing methods to generate object proposals and perform category classification and bounding box regression based on object detection. [1–3,9,17,24,29] utilize fine-grained human annotations to train fine-grained classification models. However, fine-grained human annotations are so expensive to acquire that it is not applicable in practice. [27] proposes NTS-Net (Navigator-Teacher-Scrutinizer Network), which employs a multi-agent cooperative learning scheme to effectively localize the discriminative informative regions of the target object without bounding-box/part-annotations. While these works have made great progress, They are approaching a limit since there is very few training data available for each category. In order to alleviate this difficulty, a better solution is to apply transfer learning [18] to FGIC, i.e. pre-training on a rich set of auxiliary data (e.g. ImageNet [6]) and transferring the weights of the pre-trained model to a specific FGIC task. The weights of the network are fine-tuned on the target dataset to get the final classification model. This strategy alleviates the problem of overfitting, but the goal of pre-training does not take the target FGIC task into account, resulting in a suboptimal model.

Data Augmentation. Some works tackle the deficiency of training data in FGIC by augmenting data through geometrical transformation, i.e., rotating, cropping, and color jitter et al. [16]. However, these methods are difficult to introduce the diversity of training sample. And other methods identify and leverage auxiliary data beyond the ImageNet [6]. For example, [14] leverages free, noisy data from the web and simple, generic methods of recognition train effective models of fine-grained recognition without manually-annotated training label. [25] augments the FGIC dataset with hyper-class-labeled Web images from online search engines, and proposes the hyper-class augmented and regularized deep learning framework that exploits a regularization between the fine-grained recognition model and the hyper-class recognition model. [26] utilizes a training set augmented by collecting a large number of part patches from weakly supervised web images, and uses a multi-instance learning algorithm jointly to learn a more robust object classifier on the strong and weak datasets. In our work, we blindly trust the quality of images returned by Google image search, and propose to augment benchmark datasets with these returned images for FGIC, thus circumventing the suboptimal problem in previous methods.

3 Methods

We present the data augmentation and noise removal in Sect. 3.1. Section 3.2 briefly describes the NTS-Net [27] architecture. Section 3.3 introduces regularization methods that penalize minimum entropy predictions. Figure 1 is the flowchart of our work in this paper.

3.1 Data Augmentation from the Web

By training a DCNN, it usually requires a large quantity of training data to ensure it has a good generalization [4,5,26,30]. However, it is difficult to collect large numbers of samples for fine-grained categories. To address this problem, data augmentation is usually employed to alleviate the deficiency of training examples. Typical data augmentation methods include flip, random cropping, rotation, etc. [16]. However, these methods are difficult to introduce the diversity of training samples. In this paper, we study the data augmentation by collecting images from the Web through a currently high-performance image search engine.

Data Acquisition. Generally, there are two ways to augment the dataset. The first way, we can use the existing large-scale dataset to expand the original relative small dataset. There are three small datasets: CUB-Birds [22], Stanford Dogs [13], and Stanford Cars [15], the corresponding three large datasets are NaBirds [12], CompCars, and Dogs-in-the-Wild. But through verifying, we do not find that the categories in the small datasets all exsit in the corresponding large datasets. Therefore we take an alternative approach, we expand our datasets by collecting images from the Web. At the very first place, we download images for every category in the datasets via Google Image Search Engine. In our implementation, we use a simple python script called Google-images-download[1] to download Google images automatically in batches by setting keywords or key phrases. On keyword settings, query keywords are the academic names of the corresponding categories for CUB-Birds and Stanford Dogs, e.g. *Black footed*

[1] Google-images-download: https://github.com/hardikvasa/google-images-download.

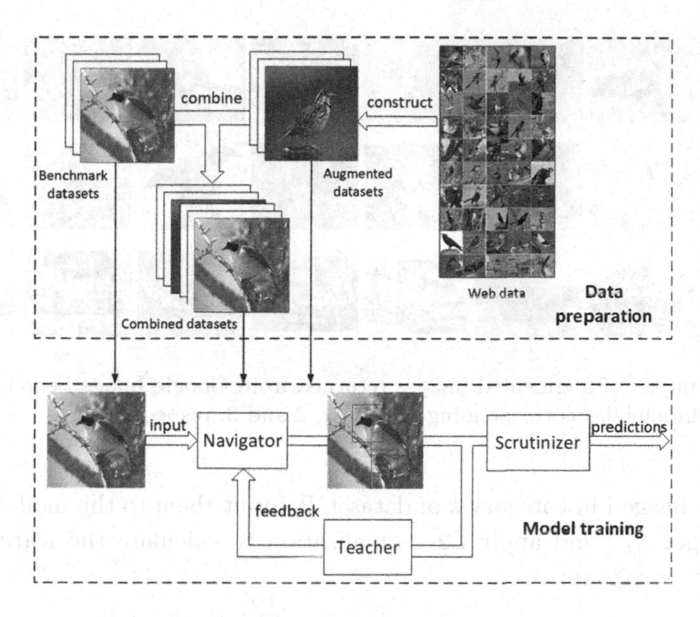

Fig. 1. Flowchart of our method. The augmented dataset is collected by downloading images from the Web. It then combines the benchmark dataset to form the combined dataset. Then benchmark, augmented, and combined datasets are used to train fine-grained classification models, respectively. The navigator agent computes the informativeness of all regions and proposes the most informative regions (denoted by red rectangles). The teacher agent evaluates the confidence that the proposed regions belongs to ground-truth class and provides feedback. The scrutinizer agent scrutinizes the proposed regions from navigator and makes predictions. (Color figure online)

Albatross (birds) or *affenpinscher* (dogs), and meta category names are used as query keywords for Stanford Cars, e.g. *the 2012 Tesla Model S* (automobiles). In addition, the number of images downloaded for every category is set to 150 in our experiments. Figure 2 shows some augmented images for the three datasets.

Noise Removal. Though large numbers of images are freely available for fine-grained categories, we can not ignore a key issue: the noise in the augmented data. To this end, we propose a simple yet effective noise removal method. Suppose for image i from category k of the benchmark dataset B, we denote parameters of the vector after average-pooling layer as $z_{bk}^{(i)}$ and apply it L2 normalization as feature vector of the image, denoted as $\tilde{z_{bk}}^{(i)}$. We calculate the clustering center of all N images from category k of dateset B as $\bar{z_{bk}}$ and the distance from the normalized feature vector $\tilde{z_{bk}}^{(i)}$ to the clustering center $\bar{z_{bk}}$ as $d_{bk}^{(i)}$. In the same way, we can get the distance $d_{ak}^{(j)}$ for image j from category k of the augmented dataset A. The steps are as follows:

Step 1: Train a network on the original benchmark dataset B.
Step 2: Remove noisy images for each class of the augmented dataset A:

Fig. 2. Examples of augmented images returned from Google Image Search for birds, dogs and automobiles corresponding to Line 1, 2 and 3, respectively.

- For image i in category k of dataset B, input them to the model of *Step* 1 to get $z_{bk}^{(i)}$, and apply L2 normalization to calculate the feature vector $\tilde{z_b}^{(i)}$ as follows:

$$\tilde{z_{bk}}^{(i)} = \frac{z_{bk}^{(i)}}{\sqrt{{z_{bk}^{(i)}}^T \cdot z_{bk}^{(i)}}} \tag{1}$$

- Calculate the clustering center of all N normalized feature vectors as follows:

$$\bar{z_{bk}} = \frac{1}{N_{bk}} \sum \tilde{z_{bk}}^{(i)} \tag{2}$$

- Calculate the distance $d_{bk}^{(i)}$ from the normalized feature vector $\tilde{z_{bk}}$ to the clustering center $\bar{z_{bk}}$ as follows:

$$d_{bk}^{(i)} = \sqrt{\left(\tilde{z_{bk}}^{(i)} - \bar{z_{bk}}\right)^T \cdot \left(\tilde{z_{bk}}^{(i)} - \bar{z_{bk}}\right)} \tag{3}$$

- Then we calculate the mean $\bar{d_b}$ and variance σ^2 of the distance $d_{bk}^{(i)}$ as follows:

$$\bar{d_{bk}} = \frac{1}{N_{bk}} \sum d_{bk}^{(i)}, \sigma_{bk}^2 = \frac{1}{N_{bk}} \sum \left(d_{bk}^{(i)} - \bar{d_{bk}}\right)^2 \tag{4}$$

- Repeat the above steps, we can get the distance $d_{ak}^{(j)}$ for image j from category k of the augmented dataset A. Finally we filter images if:

$$\bar{d_{bk}} - 3\sigma_{bk} < d_{ak}^{(j)} < \bar{d_{bk}} + 3\sigma_{bk} \tag{5}$$

In our implementation, we construct two augmented datasets—one is constructed by randomly selecting 50 images from the augmented dataset before noise removal, and the other is with the same number of images from the augmented dataset after noise removal. We respectively train classification networks on these two datasets to validate the effectiveness of noise in FGIC.

3.2 NTS Network

NTS-Net [27] is a FGIC network, which can automatically infer discriminative regions via a self-supervised mechanism from images without part/bbox annotations. It consists of three agents—a Navigator agent, a Teacher agent, and a Scrutinizer agent. For completeness, we briefly review NTS-Net in this section. Please refer to [27] for details.

Navigator and Teacher Agents. In [27], to evaluate the informativeness of a region and the confident of it to belonging to the ground-truth class, a navigator and a teacher agents are built correspondingly. Both agents are implemented in ResNet-50 [11]. Specifically, the navigator agent computes the informativeness of regions, and predicts the top-M informative regions as $\{I_1, I_2, \cdots, I_M\}$. Then these regions are fed into the teacher agent to evaluate the confidence that M regions belong to the ground-truth class $\{C_1, C_2, \cdots, C_M\}$. Under the consistency of regions with more information should have higher confidence, the teacher agent guides the navigator agent to make $\{I_1, I_2, \cdots, I_M\}$ and $\{C_1, C_2, \cdots, C_M\}$ have the same order. The navigation loss is thus defined as:

$$L_I(I, C) = \sum_{(i,s):C_i<C_s} f(IF_s - IF_i), \tag{6}$$

where IF_i is the informativeness of region I_i from the navigator agent, $f(x)$ is hinge loss function $f(x) = \max\{1 - x, 0\}$ that encourages $IF_s > IF_i$ if $C_s > C_i$ in our experiment. The teaching loss is defined as follows:

$$L_C = -\sum_{i=1}^{M} \log C(R_i) - \log C(X), \tag{7}$$

where C is the confidence output from a softmax classifier, the first term is the sum of cross-entropy loss of all regions, the second term is the cross-entropy loss of the full image.

In our implementation, we employ the maximum entropy learning to regularize the learning of the navigator and teacher agent, thus affecting the scores of the agents outputs, which are used to measure the informativeness and confidence of regions in the navigator and teacher agent, respectively. Referring to Sect. 3.3 for the maximum entropy learning.

Scrutinizer Agent. Scrutinizer agent scrutinizes the Top-K informative regions from the navigator agent, extracts their features and generates K feature vectors. Then these K features are concatenated with the feature of the full image to form the final fine-grained features for categorization. When the navigator agent navigates to the most informative regions $\{R_1, R_2, \cdots, R_M\}$, the scrutinizer agent predicts the fine-grained classification result $P = S(X, R_1, R_2, \cdots, R_K)$. Cross-entropy is used as the loss function:

$$L_S = -\log S(X, R_1, R_2, \cdots, R_K). \tag{8}$$

The algorithm jointly deals with the navigation loss, teaching loss and scrutinizing loss, and the total loss is defined as:

$$L_{total} = L_I + \lambda \cdot L_S + \mu \cdot L_C, \tag{9}$$

where λ and μ are hyper-parameters, we set $\lambda = \mu = 1$ and employ stochastic gradient descent (SGD) to optimize L_{total}.

3.3 Maximum Entropy Learning

We usually can obtain significant performance gains from fine-tuning models pre-trained on a rich set of auxiliary data (e.g. ImageNet [6]). In this fine-tuning process, the cross-entropy is used to measure the loss between the predicted outputs and the ground-truth labels. But for FGIC, in which objects from different sub-categories are very similar in appearance and share almost the same structure, it is unreasonable for the classifier to output too high confidence for a particular class and low confidence for the other classes, and minimizing cross-entropy may cause biased prediction outputs. So in this paper, we propose maximum entropy learning criterion to improve the score-based patch selection. We can make sure that the output predictions have a relatively high entropy and the predicted top-K classes contain the ground-truth category with a very high probability. We regularize the cross-entropy loss function to improve its performance. Formally, the rectified loss can be written as [7]:

$$\theta^* = \arg\min_{\theta} E_{x \sim D} \left[\bar{y}(x) \log(\hat{y} \mid x, \theta) - \gamma H(\hat{y} \mid x, \theta) \right], \tag{10}$$

where θ represents the model parameters, and is initialized using a pre-trained model. D is the dataset, $\bar{y}$ and $\hat{y}$ are the predicted and ground-truth labels respectively, γ is a hyper-parameter.

In our work, we incorporate the maximum entropy learning into NTS-Net to guide the learning of the teacher agent, thus affecting the region selection proposed by the navigator agent. In addition, we also employ this learning criterion on the scrutinizer agent for concatenated feature learning.

4 Experiments

4.1 Datasets

In addition to the three existing benchmark datasets, in this section, we also construct the augmented and combined datasets to validate the effectiveness of noise. Figure 3 shows the total number of images for training and validation on benchmark, augmented and combined datasets respectively.

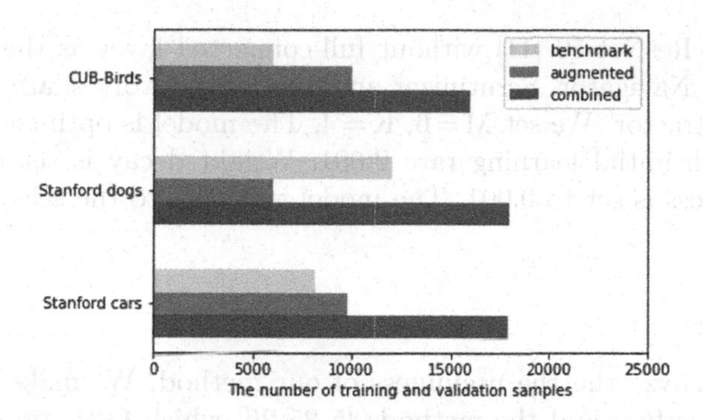

Fig. 3. The total number of training and validation samples on benchmark, augmented, and combined datasets.

Benchmark Datasets. The CUB-Birds dataset contains 200 bird species, 11,788 bird images, of which 5994 are training images and 5794 are test images. The Stanford dogs dataset contains 120 categories of dog images, 12,000 images for training and 8,580 images for testing. The Stanford Cars dataset contains 16185 automobile images of 196 different models, and the images of each category is divided into training set and test set in a ratio of approximately 1:1. In this paper, 10% training images are taken from the training set as the validation set of the benchmark dataset.

Augmented Datasets. We obtain about 150 augmented images for each category of the benchmark datasets. We randomly select 50 images in each category and divide them into training set and validation set in a ratio of 8:2. We set the corresponding benchmark test sets as the augmented test sets. Thus, we get three augmented datasets of three different domains.

Combined Datasets. We combine the augmented datasets without noise removal with the corresponding benchmark training sets as the combined training sets. Validation sets and test sets of benchmark datasets are used as validation sets and test sets of the combined datasets respectively. We also get three combined datasets of these three domains.

4.2 Implementations

In [27], NTS-Net is trained on training set of a fine-grained dataset, validated on test set and tested on test set. Different from [27], we train a fine-grained classification model and fit parameters of the model on the training set. In order to avoid overfitting, it is necessary to have a validation set to tune hyper-parameters of the model in addition to the training and test set. Finally, we test the final model on the test set to get the classification result and evaluate generalization ability of the model. And we just train networks for 50 epochs, which is different from the implementation of 500 epochs in [27].

We choose ResNet-50 [11] without full-connected layer as the CNN feature extractor, and Navigator, Scrutinizer and Teacher network share parameters of the feature extractor. We set M = 6, K = 4. The model is optimized by momentum SGD with initial learning rate 0.001. Weight decay is set to 1e−4, γ in max-entropy loss is set to 0.001. The model is robust to the selection of hyper-parameters.

4.3 Results

In order to analyze the the usefulness of our method, We make a comparison between our method and the methods [5,25,26] which focus on data augmentation as well. [25] augments the FGIC dataset with hyper-class-labeled Web images from online search engines. [26] utilizes a training set augmented by collecting a large number of part patches from weakly supervised web images. [5] adopts data augmentation by deep metric learning with humans in the loop. We also compare our classification accuracy with NTS-Net [27] results. The results indicate that our proposed methods perform extremely well on these tasks.

Results on CUB-Birds. The performance comparison on CUB-Birds is shown in Table 1, The benchmark classification accuracy of our method is 85.3%, training on the combined dataset further improves the benchmark results to 87.9%, which generates a obvious improvement over CUB-Birds. The experimental results verifies our conception and shows better and comparable performance. After applying maximum entropy learning, our method gives an accuracy of 88.2%. And our Top-1 accuracy on CUB-BIrds is better than NTS-net 0.7%.

Table 1. Comparison of different methods on the CUB-Birds dataset.

Methods	Accuracy		
	Benchmark	Augmented	Combined
Re-fine-tuned-part-CNN [26]	84.6%	–	–
Triplet-A (64) [5]	80.7%	–	–
NTS-Net [27]	87.5%	–	–
Augmentation	85.3%	83.7%	87.9%
Augmentation w. max-entropy	85.7%	84.9%	**88.2%**

Results on Stanford Dogs. Table 2 shows the comparative results on Stanford dogs. Our method outperforms the comparative method substantially. Due to small inter-class variance, large intra-class variance and more chaotic background of dog images returned by Google Image Search, the classification task of this augmented dataset is a great challenge, but overall, we can also use augmented data to train an effective fine-grained image classification model.

Table 2. Comparison of different methods on the Stanford Dogs dataset.

Methods	Accuracy		
	Benchmark	Augmented	Combined
HAR-CNN [25]	49.4%	–	–
Augmentation	83.6%	71.2%	84.1%
Augmentation w. max-entropy	83.9%	71.7%	**84.3%**

Results on Stanford Cars. Comparative studies of different methods on Stanford Cars is shown in Table 3. Our results on Stanford cars are slightly lower than NTS results due to different experimental settings from [27], but we also yield comparable results in our comparative experiments, which can prove the effectiveness of our proposed method. The classification accuracy of the model trained on the combined dataset increased by 2.1% compared with the benchmark result, which also indicates that combined data can enhance the robustness of the fine-grained classification model. The use of max-entropy learning enjoys a clear advantage for fine-grained recognition, Especially on the augmented dataset, the classification accuracy is improved from 76.9% to 81.1%.

Table 3. Comparison of different methods on the Stanford Cars dataset.

Methods	Accuracy		
	Benchmark	Augmented	Combined
HAR-CNN [25]	80.8%	–	–
FT-HAR-CNN [25]	86.3%	–	–
NTS-Net [27]	93.9%	–	–
Augmentation	90.6%	76.9%	92.7%
Augmentation w. max-entropy	90.9%	81.1%	**93.0%**

Table 4. Results on augmented datasets with and without noise.

Datasets	Augmented w. noise	Augmented w/o noise
CUB-Birds	83.7%	82.1%
Stanford dogs	71.2%	70.6%
Stanford cars	76.9%	76.2%

We also compare their performance via validation loss or validation accuracy. In Fig. 4, we plot both validation accuracy curve of the model trained on CUB-Birds and its combined dataset and validation loss curve on Stanford Cars and its

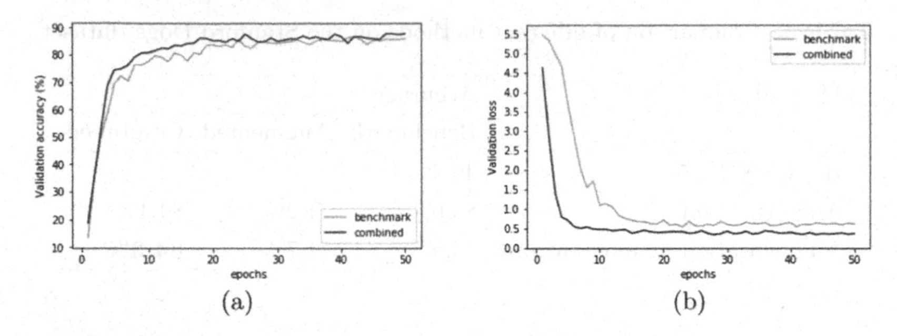

Fig. 4. Left is validation accuracy curves of the model trained on CUB-Birds and its combined dataset; Right is validation loss curve of the model trained on Stanford Cars and its combined dataset.

combined dataset. When we add training data to benchmark datasets, validation accuracy curve converges to a higher classification accuracy, validation loss curve converges to a lower loss, which can verify that the system can be trained to a better scheme when there is more training data, even noisy images might be included, they could present weakly semantic relationships to the search input, thus augmenting the training set with diversity.

4.4 Ablation Studies

Table 4 shows comparison tests with and without noise removal in our experiments. We find that when we apply the noise removal method on augmented datasets, the models do not become more efficient as a result. For three benchmark datasets, the accuracy drops from 83.7%, 71.2% and 76.9% to 82.1%, 70.6% and 76.2% respectively, which validates that noisy images returned by image search engines have a positive effect to FGIC and can bring a performance improvement. Figure 5 presents the noisy images from three augmented datasets by our proposed noise removal scheme.

Fig. 5. Examples of noisy images selected by noise removal for birds (top-row), dogs (mid-row) and automobiles (bottom-row), respectively.

5 Conclusion

In this paper, we propose a simple method that leverages a large amount of noisy data from the Web for fine-grained image classification. Analysis on models trained on datasets with and without noise removal demonstrates the advantage of noise in collected samples for FGIC, which implies the enhancement of diversity in training sets introduced by noisy images. Experiments on benchmark, augmented, and combined datasets further validate the improvement of directly collected data from the Web for FCIC.

Acknowledgements. This work was supported in part by the National Natural Science Foundation of China under Grant 61702197, in part by the Natural Science Foundation of Guangdong Province under Grant 2017A030310261.

References

1. Berg, T., Belhumeur, P.N.: Part-based one-vs.-one features for fine-grained categorization, face verification, and attribute estimation. In: CVPR (2013)
2. Branson, S., Van Horn, G., Belongie, S., Perona, P.: Bird species categorization using pose normalized deep convolutional nets. In: arXiv preprint arXiv:1406.2952 (2014)
3. Chai, Y., Lempitsky, V.S., Zisserman, A.: Symbiotic segmentation and part localization for fine-grained categorization. In: ICCV, pp. 321–328 (2013)
4. Cui, Y., Song, Y., Sun, C., Howard, A., Belongie, S.: Large scale fine-grained categorization and domain-specific transfer learning. In: CVPR (2018)
5. Cui, Y., Zhou, F., Lin, Y., Belongie, S.: Fine-grained categorization and dataset bootstrapping using deep metric learning with humans in the loop. In: CVPR (2016)
6. Deng, J., Dong, W., Socher, R., Li, L.J., Li, K., Li, F.F.: ImageNet: a large-scale hierarchical image database. In: CVPR (2009)
7. Dubey, A., Gupta, O., Raskar, R., Naik, N.: Maximum entropy fine-grained classification. In: NIPS (2018)
8. Fu, J., Zheng, H., Mei, T.: Recurrent attention convolutional neural network for fine-grained image recognition. In: CVPR (2017)
9. Gavves, E., Fernando, B., Snoek, C.G.M., Smeulders, A.W.M., Tuytelaars, T.: Fine-grained categorization by alignments. In: ICCV, pp. 1713–1720 (2013)
10. Girshick, R., Donahue, J., Darrell, T., Malik, J.: Rich feature hierarchies for accurate object detection and semantic segmentation. In: CVPR (2014)
11. He, K., Zhang, X., Ren, S., Sun, J.: Deep residual learning for image recognition. In: CVPR (2016)
12. Horn, G.V., et al.: Building a bird recognition app and large scale dataset with citizen scientists: the fine print in fine-grained dataset collection. In: CVPR (2015)
13. Khosla, A., Jayadevaprakash, N., Yao, B., Li, F.F.: Novel dataset for fine-grained image categorization. In: First Workshop on Fine-Grained Visual Categorization (FGVC) at CVPR (2011)
14. Krause, J., et al.: The unreasonable effectiveness of noisy data for fine-grained recognition. In: Leibe, B., Matas, J., Sebe, N., Welling, M. (eds.) ECCV 2016. LNCS, vol. 9907, pp. 301–320. Springer, Cham (2016). https://doi.org/10.1007/978-3-319-46487-9_19

15. Krause, J., Stark, M., Deng, J., Li, F.F.: 3D object representations for fine-grained categorization. In: 4th IEEE Workshop on 3D Representation and Recognition at ICCV (2013)
16. Krizhevsky, A., Sutskever, I., Hinton, G.E.: ImageNet classification with deep convolutional neural networks. In: NIPS (2012)
17. Liu, J., Kanazawa, A., Jacobs, D., Belhumeur, P.: Dog breed classification using part localization. In: Fitzgibbon, A., Lazebnik, S., Perona, P., Sato, Y., Schmid, C. (eds.) ECCV 2012. LNCS, vol. 7572, pp. 172–185. Springer, Heidelberg (2012). https://doi.org/10.1007/978-3-642-33718-5_13
18. Pan, S.J., Yang, Q.: A survey on transfer learning. IEEE Trans. Knowl. Data Eng. **22**, 1345–1359 (2010)
19. Sermanet, P., Eigen, D., Zhang, X., Mathieu, M., Fergus, R., LeCun, Y.: OverFeat: integrated recognition, localization and detection using convolutional networks. In: ICLR (2014)
20. Sun, M., Yuan, Y., Zhou, F., Ding, E.: Multi-attention multi-class constraint for fine-grained image recognition. In: Ferrari, V., Hebert, M., Sminchisescu, C., Weiss, Y. (eds.) ECCV 2018. LNCS, vol. 11220, pp. 834–850. Springer, Cham (2018). https://doi.org/10.1007/978-3-030-01270-0_49
21. Szegedy, C., et al.: Going deeper with convolutions. In: CVPR (2015)
22. Wah, C., Branson, S., Welinder, P., Perona, P., Belongie, S.: The caltech-UCSD birds-200-2011 dataset. Technical report, California Institute of Technology (2011)
23. Wang, Y., Morariu, V.I., Davis, L.S.: Learning a discriminative filter bank within a CNN for fine-grained recognition. In: CVPR (2018)
24. Xie, L., Tian, Q., Hong, R., Yan, S., Zhang, B.: Hierarchical part matching for fine-grained visual categorization. In: ICCV, pp. 1641–1648 (2013)
25. Xie, S., Yang, T., Wang, X., Lin, Y.: Hyper-class augmented and regularized deep learning for fine-grained image classification. In: CVPR (2015)
26. Xu, Z., Huang, S., Zhang, Y., Tao, D.: Augmenting strong supervision using web data for fine-grained categorization. In: ICCV (2015)
27. Yang, Z., Luo, T., Wang, D., Hu, Z., Gao, J., Wang, L.: Learning to navigate for fine-grained classification. In: Ferrari, V., Hebert, M., Sminchisescu, C., Weiss, Y. (eds.) Computer Vision – ECCV 2018. LNCS, vol. 11218, pp. 438–454. Springer, Cham (2018). https://doi.org/10.1007/978-3-030-01264-9_26
28. Zeiler, M.D., Fergus, R.: Visualizing and understanding convolutional networks. In: Fleet, D., Pajdla, T., Schiele, B., Tuytelaars, T. (eds.) ECCV 2014. LNCS, vol. 8689, pp. 818–833. Springer, Cham (2014). https://doi.org/10.1007/978-3-319-10590-1_53
29. Zhang, N., Donahue, J., Girshick, R., Darrell, T.: Part-based R-CNNs for fine-grained category detection. In: Fleet, D., Pajdla, T., Schiele, B., Tuytelaars, T. (eds.) ECCV 2014. LNCS, vol. 8689, pp. 834–849. Springer, Cham (2014). https://doi.org/10.1007/978-3-319-10590-1_54
30. Zhang, Y., Tang, H., Jia, K.: Fine-grained visual categorization using meta-learning optimization with sample selection of auxiliary data. In: Ferrari, V., Hebert, M., Sminchisescu, C., Weiss, Y. (eds.) ECCV 2018. LNCS, vol. 11212, pp. 241–256. Springer, Cham (2018). https://doi.org/10.1007/978-3-030-01237-3_15
31. Zheng, H., Fu, J., Mei, T., Luo, J.: Learning multi-attention convolutional neural network for fine-grained image recognition. In: ICCV (2017)

Attention Recurrent Neural Networks for Image-Based Sequence Text Recognition

Guoqiang Zhong(✉) and Guohua Yue

Department of Computer Science and Technology,
Ocean University of China, Qingdao, China
gqzhong@ouc.edu.cn, 15053241153@163.com

Abstract. Image-based sequence text recognition is an important research direction in the field of computer vision. In this paper, we propose a new model called Attention Recurrent Neural Networks (ARNNs) for the image-based sequence text recognition. ARNNs embed the attention mechanism seamlessly into the recurrent neural networks (RNNs) through an attention gate. The attention gate generates a gating signal that is end-to-end trainable, which empowers the ARNNs to adaptively focus on the important information. The proposed attention gate can be applied to any recurrent networks, e.g., standard RNN, Long Short-Term Memory (LSTM), and Gated Recurrent Unit (GRU). Experimental results on several benchmark datasets demonstrate that ARNNs consistently improves previous approaches on the image-based sequence text recognition tasks.

Keywords: Attention gate · Recurrent Neural Networks (RNNs) · Image-based sequence text recognition

1 Introduction

RNNs are very powerful neural network models for processing sequence data. The recurrent structure overcomes many limitations of traditional machine learning methods, such as long-term dependency and unequal sizes of the sequences. RNNs and its variant networks have been successfully applied to a variety of tasks, such as speech recognition [14], machine translation [4], language models [39], text classification [31], word vector generation [43], and information retrieval [29]. In this paper, we are concerned with a classic problem in computer vision: image-based sequence text recognition. In the field of sequence text recognition, text images can be transformed to feature sequences, and the recognition result

Supported by the Major Project for New Generation of AI under Grant No. 2018AAA0100400, the National Natural Science Foundation of China (NSFC) under Grant No. 41706010, the Joint Fund of the Equipments Pre-Research and Ministry of Education of China under Grand No. 6141A020337, the Graduate Education Reform and Research Project of Ocean University of China under Grand No. HDJG19001, and the Fundamental Research Funds for the Central Universities of China.

S. Palaiahnakote et al. (Eds.): ACPR 2019, LNCS 12046, pp. 793–806, 2020.
https://doi.org/10.1007/978-3-030-41404-7_56

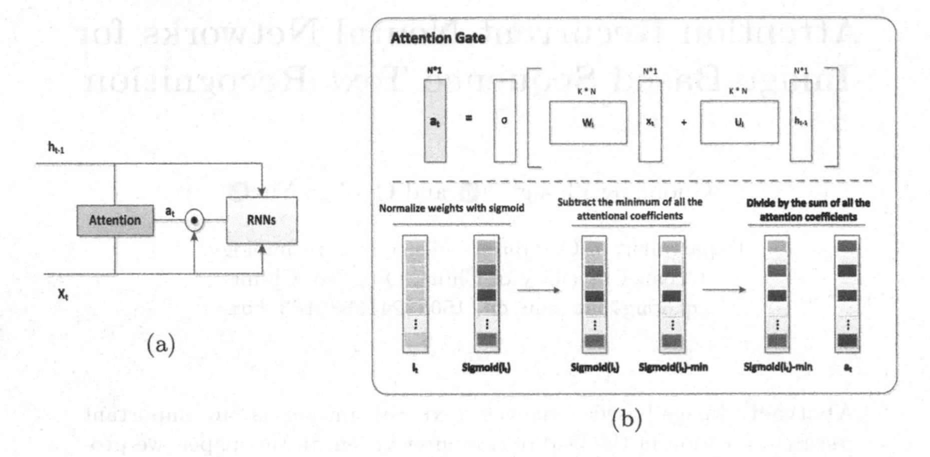

Fig. 1. (a): Illustration of the attention gate (marked in green) for a generic RNN unit. The input sequence $\mathbf{x}_t$ and the hidden information $\mathbf{h}_{t-1}$ are passed to the attention gate. An attention vector $\mathbf{a}_t$ is generated. The updated input of RNN includes the input vector with attention ($\mathbf{a}_t \odot \mathbf{x}_t$) and the original input vector ($\mathbf{x}_t$), where $\odot$ denotes the element-wise product. **(b)**: The process for calculating the attention coefficients. The input information is activated by σ to get the attention vector $\mathbf{a}_t$, where σ contains three steps as shown below the dotted line, which will increase the attention coefficients implying important information (the deeper the blue color, the larger the attention coefficients). (Color figure online)

is also a series of characters. Therefore, the sequence text recognition problem can be considered as a sequence-to-sequence learning problem.

Although RNNs are originally designed to learn long-term dependencies, many practical experiences have shown that the standard RNN is often difficult to achieve long-term information preservation. Bengio *et al.* [2] demonstrate that a standard RNN has problems with gradient vanishing and gradient exploding, which are caused by the multi-step iterations of RNN. In order to solve the problem of long-term dependence, Hochreiter *et al.* [15] propose a long short-term memory (LSTM) network, which alleviates the problem of gradient vanishing by adding three internal gates. Another widely used RNN variant is the gated recurrent unit (GRU) [8], which is a simplified structure of the LSTM that reduces the number of gates to two. Both LSTM and GRU cell cope with gradient vanishing through the gate mechanism. The gate mechanism provides a selective way for information to enter or remove, which contains the input information of the current time step and the hidden state of the last step. However, existing recurrent networks lack a gate mechanism that determines the importance of each element of the input. In other words, the existing recurrent networks take the input as a whole, without exploring the effect of each element of the input.

Recently, the attention mechanisms have been widely used in many applications, such as image caption [43], text classification [22], machine translation [1,4,23,37,40], action recognition [35,38,45] and text recognition [5,32]. The attention mechanism in machine learning is very similar to the human visual attention mechanism. It is a way to quickly select key points from a large amount of information, eliminate useless information and complete tasks efficiently. In the field of natural language processing, the attention mechanism is mainly combined with encoder-decoder architecture. The attention mechanism helps the encoder calculate a better intermediate code vector for the decoder as its inputs [1]. Inspired by this, we apply the attention mechanism to the interior of RNN to select the information related to the next output as input. More specifically, we have designed an attention gate to adaptively focus on the important elements in the input vector as shown in Fig. 1. Furthermore, we use the residual connection method to ensure that the input information is not lost. To the end, we call the RNN with an attention gate as attention RNN (ARNN). Such an architecture can bring us the following benefits:

(a) Compared with traditional RNNs, due to the consideration of the useful information for the next time step, the input adjusted with the attention mechanism is more informative, so that ARNNs can lead to better learning results than traditional RNNs.
(b) The attention mechanism proposed in this paper is an independent operation. Such an attention mechanism can also be applied to other recurrent networks, such as LSTM and GRU. Correspondingly, they can be called attention LSTM (ALSTM) and attention GRU (AGRU).
(c) ARNN can be used to replace the original RNN cell, and stacked in multiple layers. Therefore, similar with RNN, LSTM and GRU, it can be applied to any sequence learning tasks.

We demonstrate the effectiveness of the proposed ARNNs by applying it to image-based text sequence recognition. The text recognition task can be seen as a special translation process: translating image signals into "natural language". In recent years, with the development of research on the image-based text sequence recognition, the text recognition network based on CNN + RNN has become the mainstream architecture [10,20,33]. Based on this, the text recognition system of this paper consists of an encoder module and a decoder module. Given an input image, the encoder module generates a sequence feature representation, which is a sequence of feature vectors. The decoder module recurrently generates a character sequence based on RNNs. We apply the ARNNs proposed in this paper to the decoder module instead of RNNs. Further, we evaluate our proposed ARNNs on the SVHN, IAM Off-Line Handwriting and some natural scene text (III5K, SVT) datasets. The results show that ARNNs bring significant benefits.

2 Related Work

In this section, we introduce some related work, which mainly contains the following two aspects: attention based RNNs and attention models for image-based sequence text recognition.

2.1 Attention Based RNNs

RNNs can be used to solve sequence-to-sequence problems, where both input and output have a sequential structure. There are usually some implicit relationships between the structures of the input and output sequences. For RNNs, the attention mechanism can be used to explore these implicit relationships and represent important information under the condition of limited coding length [1,6,7,26].

In machine translation tasks, Bahdanau *et al.* [1] used the attention mechanism in the encoder-decoder architecture. It explores how each word in the input sentence affects the generation of the target word. On this basis, Luong *et al.* [23] proposed the global attention mechanism and the local attention mechanism. In the field of computer vision, Mnih *et al.* [26] proposed a new recurrent model that applies the attention mechanism to image classification. It mimics the human visual attention mechanism to give more attention to the target area, while it pays less attention to the surrounding area, and dynamically adjusts its attention position. Fu *et al.* [9] proposed a recurrent attention convolutional neural network in a fine-grained image classification. According to the processing from coarse to fine, the recurrent network was used to extract important regions according to attention.

In essence, attention mechanism is an intuitive methodology by giving different weights to different parts of the input (sequence information or images). However, the aforementioned attention based RNNs are only applied at the network architecture level, not at the RNN cell level. This inspires us to design a more efficient RNN cell with the attention mechanism.

Santoro *et al.* [30] explored the interaction of memories in LSTM by embedding the multi-headed self-attention mechanism [40] into it. The self-attention mechanism endows LSTM with the ability of reasoning. Therefore, it combines reinforcement learning to achieve good results in relational reasoning problems. Li *et al.* [21] proposed an independent recurrent neural network (IndRNN). It replaces the matmul product by Hadamard product in the recurrent input, and uses the unsaturated function, such as ReLU, to handle longer sequences. Zhang *et al.* [45] proposed to add an element-wise-attention gate (EleAttG) to RNN unit (EleAttG-RNN). They used EleAttG-RNN to solve the task of action detection and achieved good results. However, such an EleAttG has the problem of losing information, which is a disadvantage for sequence text recognition tasks that require precise semantic information. The experimental results in Sect. 5 demonstrate this fact.

In this work, we construct an attention gate to explore the relationship between the current input and hidden state, and pay more attention to important element of the input vector. At the same time, we use the residual connection method to ensure that the input information is preserved. Therefore, ARNN is more effective to represent the predicted character in the problem of image-based sequence text recognition.

2.2 Attention Models for Image-Based Sequence Text Recognition

In practice, text tends to appear in sequential form rather than in isolation, such as scene text, handwritten documents, and house numbers. Unlike general object recognition, identifying such objects as sequence-like objects typically requires the system to predict a series of object labels rather than a single label.

The traditional method is mainly based on character recognition, where individual characters are firstly detected using sliding windows [41,42], connected components [28], over-segmentation [3] or Hough voting [44], and then the detected characters are integrated into words by passed dynamic programming, lexicon search and so on. These methods deal with isolated character classification and subsequent word recognition, respectively. The potential semantic information and connections of the text content are not explored during the recognition process.

Recently, text recognition takes words as a whole instead of detecting and recognizing individual characters. The representative work of such methods is proposed by [17]. It used a deep convolutional neural network to directly classify words. Su *et al.* [36] extracted image sequence features based on the histogram of oriented gradient (HOG) features and then used RNN to predict the corresponding character sequences. Shi *et al.* [33] proposed an end-to-end sequence recognition network, which first combined CNN and RNN for feature representation, then applied the connectionist temporal classification (CTC) [13] loss to RNN outputs for calculating the conditional probability between the predicted and the target sequences. Later, Shi *et al.* [34] introduced a spatial transformation model [18] to preprocess the input image, and the encoder-decoder model completed the text recognition, which further improved the accuracy of text recognition. Since then, the overall framework of text recognition based on sequence has gradually yielded stable results.

Particularly, attention based approaches have achieved substantial performance improvement [10,11,20]. Gao *et al.* [10] proposed an end-to-end attention convolutional network for scene text recognition. The CNN with attention mechanism replaced the original RNN for sequence modeling. Lee *et al.* [20] proposed a recursive CNN for image feature extraction, then applied attention-based decoder for sequence generation. Cheng *et al.* [11] proposed a focusing attention network (FAN), which greatly improved the accuracy of scene text recognition.

In summary, the encoder-decoder architecture is widely used in text recognition tasks at present. Standard attention mechanism is mainly used in the decoding process, which helps the encoder calculate a better intermediate code vector for the RNN decoder. Based on this, we replace RNNs in the decoder with ARNNs that contain an internal attention mechanism. ARNNs are more powerful to represent the input sequence information, such that the text recognition accuracy is significantly improved.

3 ARNNS

In this section, we introduce the attention gate and the ARNNs in detail.

3.1 The Attention Gate

For ARNNs, we design an attention gate to make it pay more attention to the important elements in the input vectors. We also use the residual connection method to ensure that the original input information can be preserved. Figure 1 (a) illustrates the attention gate. With the attention mechanism, the updated input vector to RNNs, $\hat{\mathbf{x}}_t$, can be expressed as:

$$\hat{\mathbf{x}}_t = \mathbf{a}_t \odot \mathbf{x}_t + \mathbf{x}_t. \tag{1}$$

The activation output of an attention gate is a vector $\mathbf{a}_t$ with the input $\mathbf{h}_{t-1}$ and $\mathbf{x}_t$,

$$\mathbf{a}_t = \sigma(\mathbf{W}_l \mathbf{h}_{t-1} + \mathbf{U}_l \mathbf{x}_t), \tag{2}$$

where $\mathbf{W}_l, \mathbf{U}_l \in \mathbb{R}^{N \times N}$ are weight matrices, $\mathbf{x}_t$ is the N dimensional input vector at time t, and $\mathbf{h}_{t-1}$ is the N-dimensional hidden state at the last moment. The output of the attention gate, $\mathbf{a}_t$, is with the same dimension as the input $\mathbf{x}_t$ of RNNs. For the convenience of explanation, we set $\mathbf{l_t} = \mathbf{W}_l \mathbf{h}_{t-1} + \mathbf{U}_l \mathbf{x}_t$, which has the same dimension with $\mathbf{a}_t$.

About the Activation Function σ: In order to normalize the attention coefficient, the softmax operation commonly used in the attention mechanism [1,23,43] may not be the best method for ARNNs, because many elements of the softmax output may be very close to 0, which results in the loss of information. Hence, we consider to use a modified sigmiod function as the activation function. We first subtract the $min_i(\mathbf{l_t}^i)_{i=1}^N$ from all attention coefficients to align the minimum value to be 0. Then, we divide each element by the updated $\sum_i(\mathbf{l_t}^i)$. This is similar to softmax but can to some extent avoid the activation outputs being close to 0. And more, it increases the attention coefficient of important information as illustrated in Fig. 1 (b) .

Through such a simple gate mechanism, we can integrate the attention mechanism into RNNs. It has a strong ability to model information at the cost of increasing a small amount of parameters.

3.2 Attention Recurrent Neural Networks

The attention gate is an independent structure. As shown in Fig. 2, it can be easily integrated into any recurrent networks, such as standard RNN, GRU and LSTM.

For ARNNs, the attention mechanism is seamlessly added using the attention gate, which enhances the memory of important information in the input sequence. We do not change the recurrent structure of RNNs, but update the input of its recurrent unit to $\hat{\mathbf{x}}_t$ given in Eq. 1. Therefore, its recurrent unit is calculated as follows:

$$\mathbf{h}_t = tanh(\mathbf{W}[\hat{\mathbf{x}}_t, \mathbf{h}_{t-1}] + \mathbf{b}), \tag{3}$$

where $\mathbf{W}$ and $\mathbf{b}$ are the weight matrix and bias term.

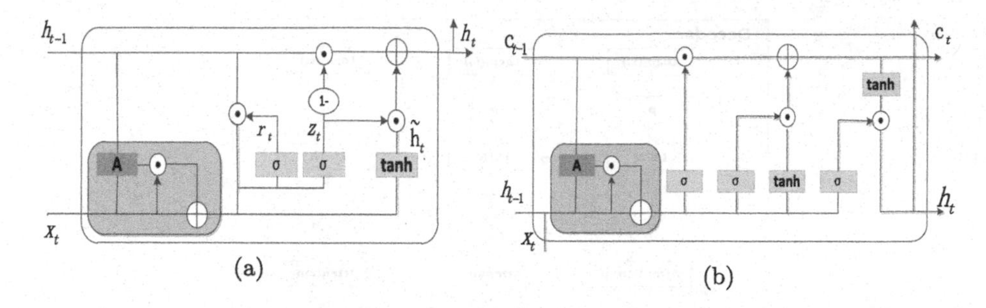

Fig. 2. (a) The structure of AGRU; (b) The structure of ALSTM. The embedded attention gate is marked in blue. (Color figure online)

Similarly, for ALSTM, the gates and memory cell can be updated as:

$$\begin{pmatrix} \mathbf{i_t} \\ \mathbf{f_t} \\ \mathbf{o_t} \\ \mathbf{g_t} \end{pmatrix} = \begin{pmatrix} \psi \\ \psi \\ \psi \\ tanh \end{pmatrix} * \mathbf{T} * \begin{pmatrix} \mathbf{\hat{x}_t} \\ \mathbf{h_{t-1}} \end{pmatrix}, \tag{4}$$

$$\mathbf{c_t} = \mathbf{f_t} \odot \mathbf{c_{t-1}} + \mathbf{i_t} \odot \mathbf{g_t}, \tag{5}$$

$$\mathbf{h_t} = \mathbf{o_t} \odot tanh(\mathbf{c_t}), \tag{6}$$

where $\mathbf{T}$ is the weight matrix, $\mathbf{i_t}$, $\mathbf{f_t}$ and $\mathbf{o_t}$ denotes the input, forget and output gate of the ALSTM, $\mathbf{c_t}$ is the memory state, and $\mathbf{h_t}$ is the hidden state of ALSTM, and ψ represents the conventional sigmoid activation function.

Here, Eqs. (1), (2) and (3) present the learning process of ARNNs, while Eqs. (1), (2), (4), (5) and (6) specify that of ALSTM. Similarly, we can get the equations for AGRU. Due to the excellent modeling capabilities of LSTM in many sequence learning applications, we use ALSTM to model the image-based sequence text recognition problem in the following.

4 ARNNs for Image-Based Sequence Text Recognition

Our text recognition approach is based on an encode-decoder architecture for sequence to sequence learning. An overall architecture is illustrated in Fig. 3.

Encoder: The encoder is composed of CNN for extracting features from images. In particular, we use CNN proposed by [12] for text recognition. The CNN encodes the image into a sequence of convolutional features. Thus, given an input image, the encoder produces a set of feature vectors:

$$\phi = \{\mathbf{x}_1, \mathbf{x}_2, \cdots, \mathbf{x}_k\}. \tag{7}$$

Decoder: The decoder is composed of ALSTM. It produces a character from the given character set L at every step. The output of ALSTM is the probability

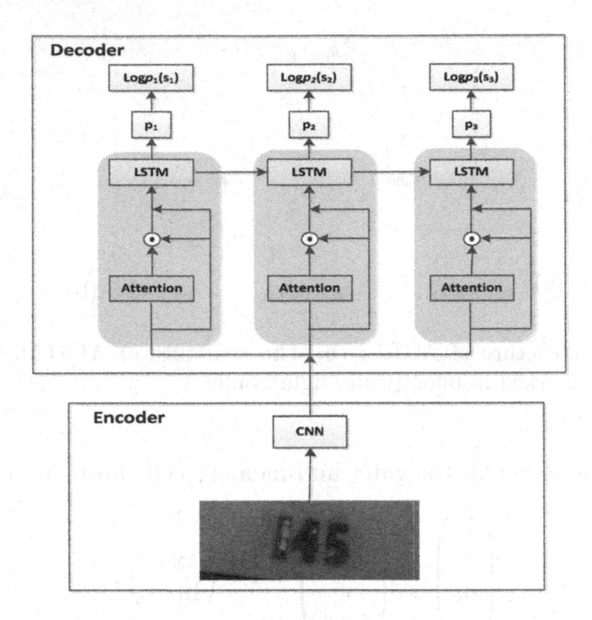

Fig. 3. The proposed encoder-decoder framework with ALSTM. The ALSTM is marked in blue color. (Color figure online)

distribution $\{p_1, p_2, \cdots, p_k\}$, where k is the length of the output sequence. This is the probability that the model predicts the next character. The log likelihood probabilities are $\{\log p_1(s_1), \log p_2(s_2), \cdots, \log p_k(s_k)\}$, where $\{s_1, \cdots, s_k\}$ are character embedding sequences.

ARNNs: As shown in Fig. 3, the attention gate is embedded in the ALSTM module of the decoder. The input of the attention gate is a sequence of features extracted by CNN. The attention gate can adaptively focus on the important information, which can alleviate the problem of fixed length representation. Hence, the ALSTM is more powerful than traditional LSTM to represent the predicted character. In addition, this model can be easily optimized using standard back propagation algorithm.

5 Experiments and Results

In this section, we evaluate the performance of ARNNs on three tasks: (1) House number recognition on the SVHN dataset; (2) Handwritten word recognition on the IAM Off-Line dataset; (3) Scene text recognition based on the convolutional recurrent neural network (CRNN) architecture [29].

Table 1. The results obtained by ALSTM and other compared methods on the SVHN dataset.

Models	Test accuracy (%)
Goodfellow *et al.* [12]	96.03
LSTM	93.26
EleAttG-LSTM [45]	96.01
ALSTM	***96.34***

5.1 House Number Recognition on the SVHN Dataset

The Street View House Numbers (SVHN) dataset [27] is a dataset containing approximately 200,000 street numbers, as well as a bounding box of individual numbers, giving a total of approximately 600,000 digits. As far as we know, most previous publications cut out individual numbers and tried to identify them. In this paper, we put together the original images containing multiple numbers and concentrate on identifying them at the same time as the practice in [12]. We also use the data enhancement technique in [12] to randomly crop $54 * 54$ pixels from $64 * 64$ images to increase the size of the dataset.

We use the encoder-decoder architecture mentioned in Sect. 4 in this experiment, where the encoder consists of eight convolutional layers, one locally connected hidden layer, and two densely connected hidden layers. Each convolutional layer includes max pooling and normalization. All convolutions are padded with zeros on the input to preserve the representation size. Convolutional kernels are of size 5×5. The fully connected layers contain 3,072 units. The output of the fully connected layer is converted into a vector as input to the decoder. The ALSTM is applied, whose output is the probability distribution that predicts the output of the next number. We implement our model with Tensorflow and train the model for about three days with an NVIDIA Geforce GTX 1080Ti GPU.

Table 1 shows the comparison results between ALSTM and the compared approaches. From Table 1, we can see that ALSTM achieves the best performance among the compared approaches. ALSTM obtains an accuracy of 96.34%, while that of LSTM is only 93.26%. Compared to the EleAttG-LSTM model [45], ALSTM improve its accuracy by 0.33%. Hence, we can infer that the Element-Attention Gate in EleAttG-LSTM has the problem of information loss, and the missing information is those with small attention coefficient. This to some extent affects the expressiveness of the input vectors to the LSTM cells.

5.2 Handwritten Word Recognition on the IAM Off-Line Dataset

The IAM Off-Line handwriting dataset [24] (IAM) contains scanned pages of handwritten text passages, which were written by 500 different writers. We use the word-level data in the IAM dataset, which contains 115320 isolated and labeled words. They are extracted from the page of scanned text using an automatic segmentation scheme and validated manually [46].

Table 2. The results obtained by ALSTM and the compared methods on the IAM dataset. The "Character accuracy" refers to the accuracy rate of character prediction; the "Word accuracy" refers to the accuracy rate of word prediction.

Models	Character accuracy (%)	Word accuracy(%)
LSTM	87.99	70.99
EleAttG-LSTM [45]	88.23	71.54
ALSTM	***89.56***	***74.30***

We use the encoder-decoder architecture and the CTC loss [13] for the model training. For concreteness, we first resize the image to 128 $\times$ 32. A five-layer CNN is used to extract image feature sequences with size 32 $\times$ 256. Each layer consists of convolutional operation, non-linear ReLU activation and the pooling operation. Then, a two-layer ALSTM is used to process 256-dimensional feature sequences. The ALSTM output sequence is mapped to a matrix of size 32 $\times$ 80. The IAM dataset consists of 79 different characters, and the CTC operations require an additional character (CTC blank label), so that each of the 32 time steps has 80 entries. Finally, the CTC loss is fed with the RNN output matrix and the ground truth text and it is used to train the network.

In order to verify the effectiveness of the proposed attention gate, we compare ALSTM with the baseline method as shown in Table 2. The word prediction accuracy of our proposed method is 3.31% higher than LSTM. We use a predictive difference analysis method [47] that visualizes the response of a deep neural network to a particular input. Neural network decisions are made interpretable through visualization. From Fig. 4, we can observe the effect of each single pixel to the prediction results. We can see some key areas (dark red/dark blue) in the image to get an idea of which image features are important for making decisions to the neural network. For example, when the neural network performs text recognition of the picture "again", it focuses on the position of the topmost point in the letter "i" in the picture (this is highlighted in red in the first set of pictures in Fig. 4). This is very important for the correct prediction "i". Therefore, our network has learned some features that have an impact on prediction. This helps the neural network to recognize the text in the images.

5.3 Scene Text Recognition Based on the CRNN Architecture

Since our purpose is to evaluate whether the proposed ARNNs can generally improve text recognition accuracy, we embed ARNNs directly into the CRNN architecture proposed by [33]. CRNN is a convolutional recurrent neural network structure, which is used to solve the problem of image-based sequence recognition, especially scene recognition. The CRNN architecture consists of CNN layers, bidirectional LSTM layers and CTC transcription layers. We replace the Bidirectional-LSTM with Bidirectional-ALSTM and keep the overall architecture of CRNN consistent with the original one.

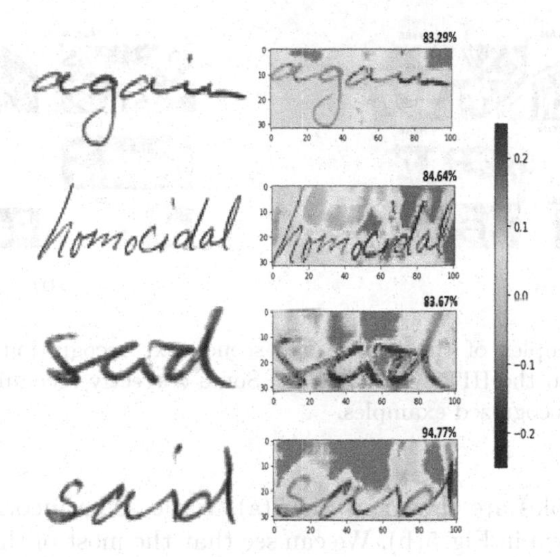

Fig. 4. Left: Input images. Right: The correlation between the predicted results and each pixel. Red color represents high correlation, while blue color represents low correlation. The prediction accuracy is given in the upper right corner of each image. (Color figure online)

Following the work of [33], we only use the synthetic dataset (Synth) released by [16] for training. The dataset contains 8-million training images and their corresponding ground truth words. We test our proposed method on the III5K and SVT datasets without any fine-tuning.

III5K-Words [25] (IIIT5K) is collected from the Internet. The test set contains 3000 cropped word images. Each image has been associated to a 50-words lexicon and a 1K-words lexicon.

Street View Text [19] (SVT) is collected from Google Street View. The test set contains 249 images, from which 647 word images are cropped. Each word image has a 50 words lexicon defined by Wang *et al.* [41].

Table 3. The recognition accuracy (%) obtained by ALSTM and the compared methods on the III5K and SVT datasets.

Models	III5K-50	III5K-1K	III5K	SVT-50	SVT
CRNN with B-LSTM [33]	97.6	94.4	78.2	96.4	80.8
CRNN with B-ALSTM	***97.8***	***94.9***	***78.6***	***96.5***	***81.2***

The results obtained based on traditional LSTM and ALSTM on the used datasets are shown in Table 3. From Table 3, we can see that ALSTM achieves better performance compared with LSTM on both the III5K and the SVT datasets. Some examples of the lexicon-free scene text recognition by the proposed ALSTM method on the IIIT5K test set are shown in Fig. 5. Some correctly

Fig. 5. Some examples of the lexicon-free scene text recognition by the proposed ALSTM method on the IIIT5K test set. (a) Some correctly recognized examples. (b) Some incorrectly recognized examples.

recognized examples are shown in Fig. 5(a), while some incorrectly recognized examples are shown in Fig. 5(b). We can see that the most of the incorrectly recognized samples have problems with text warping, special characters or blurry.

6 Conclusion

In this work, we propose a new model called ARNNs, which have strong information representation capabilities for image-based sequence text recognition. ARNNs integrate the attention mechanism seamlessly into the RNN cells by adding an attention gate. With the attention gate, ARNNs are able to adaptively pay attention to the part containing important information. Experimental results on several benchmark datasets demonstrate that ARNNs greatly improve previous approaches on the image-based sequence text recognition problem.

References

1. Bahdanau, D., Cho, K., Bengio, Y.: Neural machine translation by jointly learning to align and translate. In: ICLR (2015)
2. Bengio, Y., Simard, P.Y., Frasconi, P.: Learning long-term dependencies with gradient descent is difficult. IEEE Trans. Neural Netw. **5**(2), 157–166 (1994)
3. Bissacco, A., Cummins, M., Netzer, Y., Neven, H.: PhotoOCR: reading text in uncontrolled conditions. In: ICCV, pp. 785–792 (2013)
4. Britz, D., Goldie, A., Luong, M., Le, Q.V.: Massive exploration of neural machine translation architectures. CoRR abs/1703.03906 (2017)
5. Cheng, Z., Bai, F., Xu, Y., Zheng, G., Pu, S., Zhou, S.: Focusing attention: towards accurate text recognition in natural images. In: ICCV, pp. 5086–5094 (2017)
6. Chevalier, G.: LARNN: linear attention recurrent neural network. CoRR abs/1808.05578 (2018)
7. Cho, K., et al.: Learning phrase representations using RNN encoder-decoder for statistical machine translation. In: EMNLP, pp. 1724–1734 (2014)
8. Chung, J., Gülçehre, Ç., Cho, K., Bengio, Y.: Empirical evaluation of gated recurrent neural networks on sequence modeling. CoRR abs/1412.3555 (2014)

9. Fu, J., Zheng, H., Mei, T.: Look closer to see better: recurrent attention convolutional neural network for fine-grained image recognition. In: CVPR, pp. 4476–4484 (2017)
10. Gao, Y., Chen, Y., Wang, J., Lu, H.: Reading scene text with attention convolutional sequence modeling. CoRR abs/1709.04303 (2017)
11. Ghosh, S.K., Valveny, E., Bagdanov, A.D.: Visual attention models for scene text recognition. In: ICDAR, pp. 943–948 (2017)
12. Goodfellow, I.J., Bulatov, Y., Ibarz, J., Arnoud, S., Shet, V.D.: Multi-digit number recognition from street view imagery using deep convolutional neural networks. In: ICLR (2014)
13. Graves, A., Fernández, S., Gomez, F.J., Schmidhuber, J.: Connectionist temporal classification: labelling unsegmented sequence data with recurrent neural networks. In: ICML, pp. 369–376 (2006)
14. Graves, A., Mohamed, A., Hinton, G.E.: Speech recognition with deep recurrent neural networks. In: ICASSP, pp. 6645–6649 (2013)
15. Hochreiter, S., Schmidhuber, J.: Long short-term memory. Neural Comput. **9**(8), 1735–1780 (1997)
16. Jaderberg, M., Simonyan, K., Vedaldi, A., Zisserman, A.: Synthetic data and artificial neural networks for natural scene text recognition. CoRR abs/1406.2227 (2014)
17. Jaderberg, M., Simonyan, K., Vedaldi, A., Zisserman, A.: Reading text in the wild with convolutional neural networks. IJCV **116**(1), 1–20 (2016)
18. Jaderberg, M., Simonyan, K., Zisserman, A., Kavukcuoglu, K.: Spatial transformer networks. In: NIPS, pp. 2017–2025 (2015)
19. Wang, K., Babenko, B., Belongie, S.: End-to-end scene text recognition. In: ICCV, pp. 1457–1464 (2011)
20. Lee, C., Osindero, S.: Recursive recurrent nets with attention modeling for OCR in the wild. In: CVPR, pp. 2231–2239 (2016)
21. Li, S., Li, W., Cook, C., Zhu, C., Gao, Y.: Independently recurrent neural network (indrnn): building a longer and deeper RNN. In: CVPR, pp. 5457–5466 (2018)
22. Liu, G., Guo, J.: Bidirectional LSTM with attention mechanism and convolutional layer for text classification. Neurocomputing **337**, 325–338 (2019)
23. Luong, M., Pham, H., Manning, C.D.: Effective approaches to attention-based neural machine translation. CoRR abs/1508.04025 (2015)
24. Marti, U.V., Bunke, H.: The IAM-database: an english sentence database for offline handwriting recognition. IJDAR **5**(1), 39–46 (2002)
25. Mishra, A., Alahari, K., V. Jawahar, C.: Scene text recognition using higher order language priors. In: BMVC, September 2012
26. Mnih, V., Heess, N., Graves, A., Kavukcuoglu, K.: Recurrent models of visual attention. In: NIPS, pp. 2204–2212 (2014)
27. Netzer, Y., Wang, T., Coates, A., Bissacco, A., Wu, B., Ng, A.Y.: Reading digits in natural images with unsupervised feature learning. In: NIPS (2011)
28. Neumann, L., Matas, J.: Real-time scene text localization and recognition. In: CVPR, pp. 3538–3545 (2012)
29. Palangi, H., et al.: Deep sentence embedding using the long short term memory network: Analysis and application to information retrieval. CoRR abs/1502.06922 (2015)
30. Santoro, A., et al.: Relational recurrent neural networks. In: NIPS, pp. 7310–7321 (2018)
31. Shang, L., Lu, Z., Li, H.: Neural responding machine for short-text conversation. In: ACL, pp. 1577–1586 (2015)

32. Shi, B., Yang, M., Wang, X., Lyu, P., Yao, C., Bai, X.: ASTER: an attentional scene text recognizer with flexible rectification. TPAMI **41**(9), 2035–2048 (2018)
33. Shi, B., Bai, X., Yao, C.: An end-to-end trainable neural network for image-based sequence recognition and its application to scene text recognition. TPAMI **39**(11), 2298–2304 (2017)
34. Shi, B., Wang, X., Lyu, P., Yao, C., Bai, X.: Robust scene text recognition with automatic rectification. In: CVPR, pp. 4168–4176 (2016)
35. Song, S., Lan, C., Xing, J., Zeng, W., Liu, J.: An end-to-end spatio-temporal attention model for human action recognition from skeleton data. In: AAAI, pp. 4263–4270 (2017)
36. Su, B., Lu, S.: Accurate scene text recognition based on recurrent neural network. In: ACCV, pp. 35–48 (2014)
37. Sutskever, I., Vinyals, O., Le, Q.V.: Sequence to sequence learning with neural networks. In: NIPS, pp. 3104–3112 (2014)
38. Tian, Y., Hu, W., Jiang, H., Wu, J.: Densely connected attentional pyramid residual network for human pose estimation. Neurocomputing **347**, 13–23 (2019)
39. Tran, K.M., Bisazza, A., Monz, C.: Recurrent memory networks for language modeling. In: NAACL HLT, pp. 321–331 (2016)
40. Vaswani, A., et al.: Attention is all you need. In: NIPS, pp. 6000–6010 (2017)
41. Wang, K., Babenko, B., Belongie, S.J.: End-to-end scene text recognition. In: ICCV, pp. 1457–1464 (2011)
42. Wang, K., Belongie, S.J.: Word spotting in the wild. In: ECCV, pp. 591–604 (2010)
43. Xu, K., et al.: Show, attend and tell: neural image caption generation with visual attention. In: ICML, pp. 2048–2057 (2015)
44. Yao, C., Bai, X., Shi, B., Liu, W.: Strokelets: a learned multi-scale representation for scene text recognition. In: CVPR, pp. 4042–4049 (2014)
45. Zhang, P., Xue, J., Lan, C., Zeng, W., Gao, Z., Zheng, N.: Adding attentiveness to the neurons in recurrent neural networks. In: ECCV, pp. 136–152 (2018)
46. Zimmermann, M., Bunke, H.: Automatic segmentation of the IAM off-line database for handwritten English text. In: Object Recognition Supported by User Interaction for Service Robots, vol. 4, pp. 35–39, August 2002
47. Zintgraf, L.M., Cohen, T.S., Adel, T., Welling, M.: Visualizing deep neural network decisions: Prediction difference analysis. CoRR abs/1702.04595 (2017)

Nighttime Haze Removal with Glow Decomposition Using GAN

Beomhyuk Koo and Gyeonghwan Kim(✉)

Sogang University, 35, Baekbeom-ro, Mapo-gu, Seoul, Republic of Korea
llamakoo9@gmail.com, gkim@sogang.ac.kr

Abstract. In this paper, we investigate the problem of a single image haze removal in the nighttime. Glow effect is inherently existing in nighttime scenes due to multiple light sources with various colors and prominent glows. As the glow obscures the color and the shape of objects nearby light sources, it is important to handle the glow effect in the nighttime haze image. Even the convolutional neural network has brought impressive improvements for daytime haze removal, it has been hard to train the network in supervised manner in the nighttime because of difficulty in collecting training samples. Towards this end, we propose a nighttime haze removal algorithm with a glow decomposition network as a learning-based layer separation technique. Once the generative adversarial network removes the glow effect from the input image, the atmospheric light and the transmission map are obtained, then eventually the haze-free image. To verify the effectiveness of the proposed method, experiments are conducted on both real and synthesized nighttime haze images. The experiment results show that our proposed method produces haze-removed images that have better quality and less artifacts than ones from previous studies.

Keywords: Nighttime image haze removal · Generative adversarial network · Perceptual losses · Glow decomposition · Fully convolutional structure

1 Introduction

Haze is an atmospheric phenomenon that particulates obscure the visibility and clarity of scenes. Scattering effect, in which moisture particles scatter an incident light reflected from objects, is the main cause of the haze. As the light passes through the atmosphere filled with particles, the light is attenuated in proportion to the distance between a camera and objects [13]. As a result, images captured in bad weather have characteristics of low contrast and shifted colors. These corrupted images bring adverse effects on many applications of computer vision and image processing. In nighttime, the problem becomes more serious due to various active light sources in the scene. For instance, headlights of vehicles yield atmospheric light spatially variant and consequently the glow effect. An

S. Palaiahnakote et al. (Eds.): ACPR 2019, LNCS 12046, pp. 807–820, 2020.
https://doi.org/10.1007/978-3-030-41404-7_57

objective of the nighttime haze removal is to obtain images with clear visibility and least artifacts. Especially, appropriate handling of the glow effect is a key to the success.

Most previous studies of haze removal follow the optical haze model that is represented by a linear equation composed of the transmission map and the atmospheric light. To get a haze-free image in daytime, therefore, the transmission map and the atmospheric light need to be predicted. The haze removal, however, is an ill-posed problem because it has to estimate various unknown parameters in the single formula. To solve the problem, many classic methods used to take multiple images or polarizing filters. Narasimhan et al. [12] proposed a method of estimating the atmospheric light chromaticity using multiple images of the same scene taken in different haze density. Schechmer et al. [19] introduced a polarization-based method according to the principle that the atmospheric light scattered by particles is partially polarized.

Recently, there have been various studies of haze removal using a single image. He et al. [8] introduced an algorithm using dark channel prior (DCP). DCP is a statistical property that founded from the observation that most outdoor objects in clear weather have a significant low intensity at least one color channel. The atmospheric light and the transmission map are estimated based on the DCP. There have been many DCP-based dehaze algorithms because of its simplicity and effectiveness. Moreover DCP is applied to other applications such as deblurring [15]. Fattal [4] introduced a haze removal method employing color-lines. The method assumes that pixels of small image patches generally exhibit a 1D distribution in RGB color space (aka color-line), and haze is removed based on the lines' offset from the origin. With recent breakthroughs in deep learning techniques, learning-based haze removal approaches have emerged and show great performance. Cai et al. [3] proposed a haze removal algorithm based on a supervised learning framework of convolutional neural network (CNN). Zhang et al. [24] suggested an end-to-end densely connected pyramid dehazing network (DCPDN). DCPDN is a haze removal method based on a generative adversarial network (GAN) trained with synthetic daytime haze images.

The nature of nighttime haze images hinders direct application of the dehaze algorithms developed for daytime images. Li et al. [10] defined a nighttime optical haze model that describes physics of the night haze scene and glow effect. To get a haze-free image, they removed the glow effect with layer separation technique, then estimates a transmission map using DCP. The algorithm produces a haze-free image with acceptable quality, but noise and halo artifacts are often amplified. Ancuti et al. [2] suggested a method of estimating the atmospheric light using multi-scale fusion. In an algorithm proposed by Park et al. [16], the glow effects from an input image are removed based on a notion of relative smoothness and the transmission map is estimated using the weighted entropy. Zhang et al. [25] suggested a heuristic assumption, maximum reflectance prior (MRP), to estimates the ambient illumination of the nighttime haze image. The prior is based on the observation that each color channel has high intensity in most daytime haze-free image patches. MRP is employed to estimate the ambient illumination and the transmission map. However, indirect handling of the glow effect results in limited success in dehazing. In an algorithm offered by Yang et al. [22], the glow effect is handled with layer separation technique. To estimate the atmospheric light, the input image is divided into super-pixels and the brightest intensity is selected in each of the super-pixels. Though some morphological artifacts are effectively removed when compared with the patch-based methods, the glow and the flare effects are not completely removed because the operation mainly relies on the gradient.

In this paper, we introduce a nighttime dehazing method by efficient handling of the glow effect, mainly consisting of the glow decomposition. In the implementation, the nighttime optical model in [10] is assumed. It needs to be noted that a generative adversarial learning technique [5] is employed to recover clear and perceptually natural glow-removed images, and then eventually haze-free images. In the first stage, the input image is decomposed into the glow image and the glow-free image by the generator. Then, in training session, the discriminator judges the authenticity of the glow-removed image estimated by the generator, and the judgement is to make the generator decompose more accurately. In the second stage, the glow-removed image is divided into super-pixels with simple linear iterative clustering (SLIC) [1] for estimating the atmospheric light and the transmission map, and both are refined by a guided image filter (GIF) [7]. DCP is adopted in estimating the transmission map. The final haze-free image is obtained with the atmospheric light and the transmission map based on the optical haze model.

Our main contribution can be summarized as active application of adversarial learning in glow removal for nighttime dehazing. Experiment results indicate that the GAN based approach significantly reduces halo artifacts and color distortion, comparing to the previous glow removal methods.

2 Preliminary Knowledge

2.1 Conditional Generative Adversarial Network

The generative adversarial network (GAN), introduced by Goodfellow et al. [5], is composed of two network modules, the generator and the discriminator. The generator produces a fake data that is identical with the real data. The discriminator judges the authenticity of the fake data. These network modules are trained simultaneously until the generator is able to consistently produce results that the discriminator cannot distinguish the real and the fake. Mathematically, this can be expressed as:

$$\min_{G}\max_{D} V(G,D) = \mathbb{E}_x[logD(x)] + \mathbb{E}_z[log(1-D(G(z)))] \tag{1}$$

where G, D indicate the generator and the discriminator, respectively. V is the value function and x is a discriminator input. z indicates a generator input that uniformly distributed noise variable. However, in our task, the input z is a color image, not just a noise. So, the generator input z is treated as a latent variable conditioned with the color image y. Therefore, (1) is rewritten as:

$$\min_{G}\max_{D} V(G,D) = \mathbb{E}_x[logD(x|y)] + \mathbb{E}_z[log(1 - D(G(z|y)))] \tag{2}$$

2.2 Atrous Convolution

To integrate knowledge of the global context, people often use a spatial pooling. However, the spatial pooling losses some detailed information. To address the problem, Yu et al. [23] introduced the atrous convolution that is also called "dilated convolution." Atrous convolution enables a network to solve multi-scale problems without increasing the number of parameters. Atrous convolution between signal f and kernel k is expressed as (3):

$$(k \oplus_l f)_t = \sum_{\tau=-\infty}^{\infty} k_\tau \cdot f_{t-l\tau} \tag{3}$$

where $\oplus_l$ indicates the atrous convolution with dilation rate l and the standard convolution $f_{t-\tau}$ is modified to $f_{t-l\tau}$. A dilation rate l defines size of receptive field. In the atrous convolution, the kernel only touches the signal at every l^{th} entry. The size of the receptive field expressed as $(l*(k-1)+k)^2$.

3 Single Image Nighttime Haze Removal

3.1 Nighttime Haze Optical Model

As previously mentioned, an atmospheric particle scatters an incident light then the intensity of the light is attenuated. Based on the optical phenomenon, Narasimhan et al. [13] expressed a daytime optical haze model as:

$$I_c(\mathbf{x}) = R_c(\mathbf{x})t(\mathbf{x}) + A_c(1 - t(\mathbf{x})) \tag{4}$$

where $c \in \{r, g, b\}$ indicates rgb color channels, I_c is an observed haze image, R_c is a haze-free image, t is a transmission map that represents the portion of a light go through the haze, and A_c is an atmospheric light. $R_c(\mathbf{x})t(\mathbf{x})$ and $A_c(1-t(\mathbf{x}))$ is called the direct transmission and the airlight, respectively. On the other hand, Li et al. [10] expressed a nighttime optical haze model as:

$$I_c(\mathbf{x}) = R_c(\mathbf{x})t(\mathbf{x}) + A_c(\mathbf{x})(1 - t(\mathbf{x})) + A_a(\mathbf{x}) * APSF \tag{5}$$

In nighttime, as previously mentioned, the atmospheric light is no longer globally constant because of various light sources, such as street lights. Therefore A_c in (5) has matrix form. A_a indicates the intensity of active light sources and APSF(atmospheric point spread function) reveals the analytical expression for the glow effect derived by Narasimhan et al. [14].

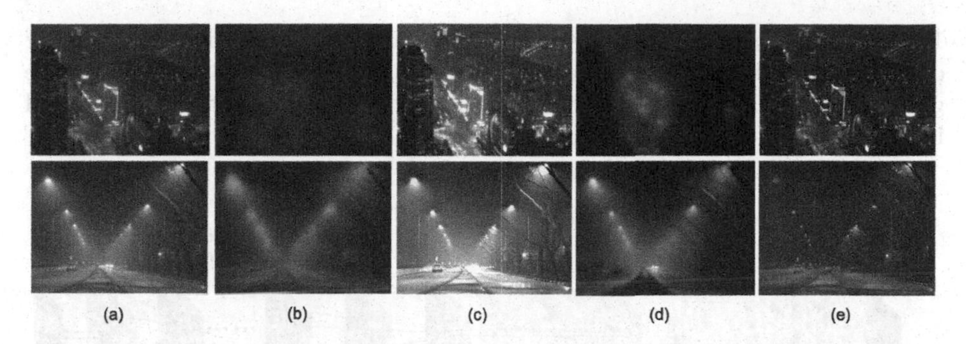

Fig. 1. Results of glow decomposition: For the input image pair in (a), the glow and the glow-removed images, respectively; (b, c) by [10] and (d, e) by the proposed algorithm. In (b, c), the glow effect is boosted and the color is unnatural due to the wrongly predicted glow layer. However, in (d, e), the shape and the color of the glow images are close to the input images and the glow-removed images is more natural. (Color figure online)

3.2 Glow Removal with Generative Adversarial Network

The glow effect is a significant problem should be taken care of in nighttime dehaze. The glow obscures the color and the shape of objects that nearby light sources. Consequently, the glow should be handled properly in order to produce the result image with great visibility. We regard the glow removal as a layer separation problem and thus (5) is rewritten as:

$$I_c(\mathbf{x}) = J_c(\mathbf{x}) + G_c(\mathbf{x}) \tag{6}$$

where, $J_c(\mathbf{x}) = R_c(\mathbf{x})t(\mathbf{x}) + A_c(\mathbf{x})(1 - t(\mathbf{x}))$ and $G_c(\mathbf{x}) = A_a(\mathbf{x}) * APSF$ represent the glow-removed night haze image and the glow image, respectively. Li et al. [10] applied a glow removal algorithm on the basis that the glow effect of nighttime haze has "short tail" distribution. However, when the shape and the color of the illuminants are complex, it is insufficient for separating glow layer by just considering in gradient domain, as can be seen in Fig. 1(c). It indicates that high-level information needs to be involved. Since the glow effect is influenced by the shape, color and location of the illuminants, it needs to consider not only low-level information but also high-level semantic information of the glow effect.

Our glow decomposition network is devised to separate layer with fine glows and handle some image degradation problems, including noise, halo artifacts, and color distortion. The network is designed based on the structure of Zhang et al. [28], in which the network is composed of fully convolutional layers. In the initial stage, features are extracted from five convolutional layers of VGG-19 network [20] pre-trained with ImageNet dataset [18]. The extracted feature maps are resized as the same size as the input image. And the resized feature maps are concatenated in channel-wise, and the concatenated feature maps are called hypercolumn features [6]. Through the hypercolumn features, the network extracts multi-level information of the glow and the illuminants. Performing

1×1 convolution to the condensed hypercolumn features to reduce the number of channels is followed by the continuous atrous convolution [23] to produce the glow layer and the glow-removed layer. The network's architecture is described in Fig. 2.

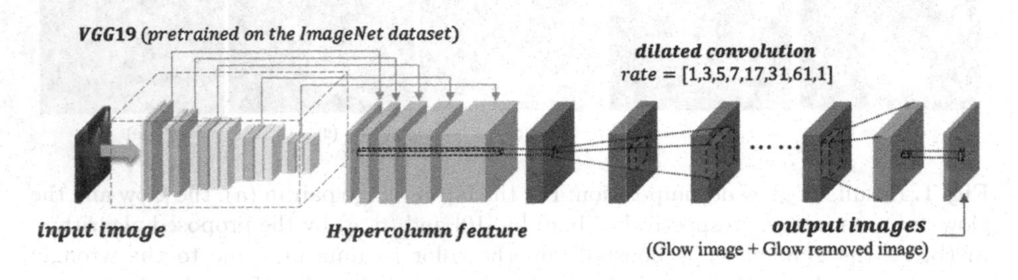

Fig. 2. Architecture of the generator

To train the network, we need a large number of glow and glow-free image pairs of the same spatiotemporal scenes. Based on our observation, structural property of the glow in feature level is similar to that of the corresponding reflection image which can be taken from glass. A reflection image is composed of brightest spots which produces high contrast and large gradients due to illuminant. In addition, the image is blurred with low intensity and thus consists of small gradients. By taking into account these aspects, we train the network with refection images synthesized by Zhang's method [28]. About 13,000 nighttime images, consisting of diverse environments, were collected from Youtube and Flicker.

In the generative adversarial network, the generator produces a fake glow-removed image, $\hat{J}_c$. The generated image is fed into a discriminator alongside a stream of images taken from the ground-truth image, J_c^{gt}. The discriminator judges the authenticity of the generated image by returning the probability. The generator is to produce realistic fake glow-removed images, and the discriminator is to identify the image coming from the generator.

The Fig. 1 shows the glow-removed images by [10] and the proposed method. The network extracts multi-level features of the glow image and thus predict the shape and colors of the glow layer perceptually well. The figure shows that the proposed network excels at comprehensively disassembling the glow layer near the light sources.

In order to train the glow decomposition network effectively, we adopt the objective function by combining several loss terms as follows.

$$L_{glow} = \lambda_1 L_1 + \lambda_p L_p + \lambda_a L_a + \lambda_e L_e + \lambda_{dh} L_{dh} \tag{7}$$

We adopt perceptual loss (L_p), adversarial loss (L_a), and exclusion loss (L_e), which are used in state-of-the-art approaches [5,9,28] In addition, we include dense haze loss (L_{dh}) motivated from [27]. We also simply add L_1 loss defined as $L_1 = \sum_{(I_c, J_c^{gt}) \in \mathfrak{D}} \left\| \hat{J}_c - J_c^{gt} \right\|_1$. For simplicity, we denote $J_c(\mathbf{x})$ and $G_c(\mathbf{x})$ as J_c and G_c, respectively. We build a dataset $\mathfrak{D} = (I_c, J_c^{gt}, G_c^{gt})$, where I_c is the input image synthesized by Zhang's method [28], J_c^{gt} is the glow-removed image, and G_c^{gt} is the reflection image of I_c. λ represents the weight of each loss. Each term in (7) is briefly described as following:

Perceptual loss (L_p): As mentioned earlier, the network has to be trained with not only low-level features but also high-level features of the glow image. Therefore, we use a perceptual loss:

$$L_p = \sum_{I_c, J_c^{gt} \in \mathfrak{D}} \sum_{l} \lambda_l \left\| \Phi_l(J_c^{gt}) - \Phi_l(\hat{J}_c) \right\|_1 \tag{8}$$

The perceptual loss is computed by comparing the multi-level representations of ground-truth glow-removed image, J_c^{gt}, and the predicted glow-removed image, $\hat{J}_c$. In the equation, Φ represents the pretrained VGG-19 network and l indicates layer of the network. λ_l is a hyperparameter used as a weight.

Adversarial loss (L_a): The adversarial loss is used to show the distance between two different distributions of $P(\hat{J}_c)$ and $P(J_c^{gt})$. The role of the adversarial loss is to make the two probability distributions similar so that it makes the generator to produce photo-realistic glow-removed image and to handle some artifacts.

$$L_a = \sum_{I_c \in \mathfrak{D}} -logD(J_c^{gt}, \hat{J}_c) \tag{9}$$

In the equation, D indicates the discriminator of the glow decomposition network. We use $-logD(J_c^{gt}, \hat{J}_c)$ instead of $log(1 - D(J_c^{gt}, \hat{J}_c))$ due to the gradient problem [5].

Exclusion loss (L_e): The exclusion loss, introduced by Zhang et al. [28], helps to separate different layers well in gradient domain. As there is little correlation between the edges of the glow layer and the edges of the glow-removed layer, we use the exclusion loss to minimize correlation of the two different layers in gradient domain.

$$L_e = \sum_{I_c \in \mathfrak{D}} \sum_{n=1}^{N} \left\| \Psi(\hat{J_c^n}, \hat{G_c^n}) \right\|_F \tag{10}$$

$$\Psi(J_c, G_c) = tanh(\lambda_J \left| \nabla J_c \right|) \odot tanh(\lambda_G \left| \nabla G_c \right|) \tag{11}$$

where, $\|\cdot\|_F$ is Frobenius norm, $\odot$ indicates element-wise multiplication, n is the image downsampling factor, and λ_J and λ_G mean normalization factors. In our implementation, we set $N = 3$.

Dense haze loss (L_{dh}): Color ambiguity problem can be expected when objects are seen through dense haze, which causes object color saturation. Motivated by Zhang et al. [27], we introduced a loss term to deal with the color ambiguity problem, by expecting the network takes care of overall color tone of the image and produces vibrant and realistic colorizations.

$$L_{dh} = \frac{1}{3} \sum_{(I_c, J_c^{gt}) \in \mathfrak{D}} \sum_{l=1}^{3} \left\| h_{gray}(J_c^{gt})^l - h_{Lab}(J_c^{gt})^l \right\| \tag{12}$$

In the equation, $h_{gray}(J_c^{gt})$ means the transition to grayscale image from ground truth glow-removed image J_c^{gt}, and $h_{Lab}(J_c^{gt})$ means the transition to CIE Lab color space from the image J_c^{gt}. Each 3 channel of the grayscale image is identical. l indicates channels of CIE Lab color space. As shown in Fig. 3, it turns out to be effective when the network predicts the saturated object colors in dense haze.

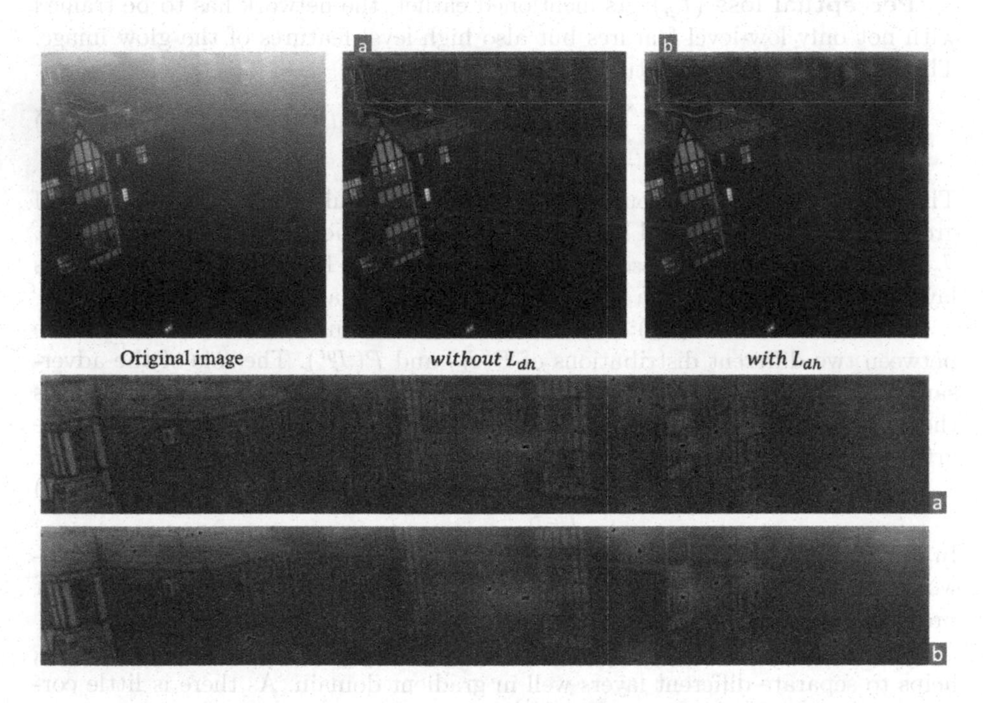

Fig. 3. Role of the *dense haze loss*, L_{dh}: the network can predict effectively the colors of objects in dense haze, which are seriously saturated. (Color figure online)

3.3 Computation of Atmospheric Light

Once the glow effect is removed from the night haze image, the glow-removed night haze image, $J_c(\mathbf{x})$, is obtained. As shown in (13), we find the atmospheric light, $A_c(\mathbf{x})$, and the transmission map, $t(\mathbf{x})$, in order to get the haze-free image, $R_c(\mathbf{x})$.

$$J_c(\mathbf{x}) = R_c(\mathbf{x})t(\mathbf{x}) + A_c(\mathbf{x})(1 - t(\mathbf{x})) \tag{13}$$

Yang et al. [22] exploit a way to compute the atmospheric light with fine preserved structure based on super-pixel representation. Therefore, the method in [22] can be applied to get the atmospheric light from the glow-removed image by rewriting (13) as (14) on the basis of image formation model.

$$J_c(\mathbf{x}) = A_c(\mathbf{x})R_c^r(\mathbf{x})t(\mathbf{x}) + A_c(\mathbf{x})(1 - t(\mathbf{x})) \tag{14}$$

The scene radiance $R_c(\mathbf{x})$ is decomposed into the illumination, $A_c(\mathbf{x})$, and the reflectance, $R_c^r(\mathbf{x})$.

We begin the decomposition by segmenting $J_c(\mathbf{x})$ via SLIC algorithm [1]. The intensity of the atmospheric light and the transmission values are assumed to be constant in the super-pixel Ω. Then (14) can be derived as:

$$\begin{aligned}\max_{\mathbf{x}'\in\Omega(\mathbf{x})}\{J_c(\mathbf{x}')\} &= \max_{\mathbf{x}'\in\Omega(\mathbf{x})}\{A_c(\mathbf{x}')R_c(\mathbf{x}')t(\mathbf{x}')) + A_c(\mathbf{x}')(1-t(\mathbf{x}'))\} \\ &= \max_{\mathbf{x}'\in\Omega(\mathbf{x})} A_c(\mathbf{x})\{R_c(\mathbf{x}')\}\, t(\mathbf{x}) + A_c(\mathbf{x})(1-t(\mathbf{x}))\end{aligned} \tag{15}$$

Based on the maximum reflectance prior [25], we assume that $\max_{\mathbf{x}'\in\Omega(\mathbf{x})}\{R_c^r(\mathbf{x}')\} = 1$. Therefore, the atmospheric light can be computed as:

$$A_c(\mathbf{x}) = \max_{\mathbf{x}'\in\Omega(\mathbf{x})}\{R_c(\mathbf{x}')\} \tag{16}$$

After the computation of the atmospheric light, we apply the guided image filter (GIF) [7] to remove the morphological artifacts and to make result image smooth.

3.4 Estimation of Transmission Map

To estimate the transmission map of a glow-removed image, we adopt dark channel prior (DCP) [8] defined as (17).

$$\min_{c\in\{r,g,b\}}\left(\min_{\mathbf{x}'\in\Omega(\mathbf{x})} J_c(\mathbf{x}')\right) \approx 0 \tag{17}$$

Then the transmission map computed as:

$$\min_{\mathbf{x}'\in\Omega(\mathbf{x})}\min_{c}\frac{J_c(\mathbf{x}')}{A_c(\mathbf{x}')} = t(\mathbf{x})\min_{\mathbf{x}'\in\Omega(\mathbf{x})}\min_{c}\left(\frac{R_c(\mathbf{x}')}{A_c(\mathbf{x}')}\right) + (1-t(\mathbf{x})) \tag{18}$$

$$t(\mathbf{x}) = 1 - \min_{\mathbf{x}'\in\Omega(\mathbf{x})}\min_{c}\frac{J_c(\mathbf{x}')}{A_c(\mathbf{x}')} \tag{19}$$

3.5 Scene Recovery

We need to introduce the lower bound of the transmission, t_0, since noise exists in the result image when the transmission value is close to zero. We set the value of t_0 as 0.15, in our implementation.

$$R_c(\mathbf{x}) = \frac{J_c(\mathbf{x}) - A_c(\mathbf{x})}{\max(t(\mathbf{x}), t_0)} + A_c(\mathbf{x}) \tag{20}$$

Normally, the atmospheric light is darker than the scene reflection as removed haze reduces the overall brightness of the image. So we increase the intensity of $R_c(\mathbf{x})$ multiplying by a ratio of C. Therefore the average intensity of $R_c(\mathbf{x})$ is equal to the average intensity of $J_c(\mathbf{x})$.

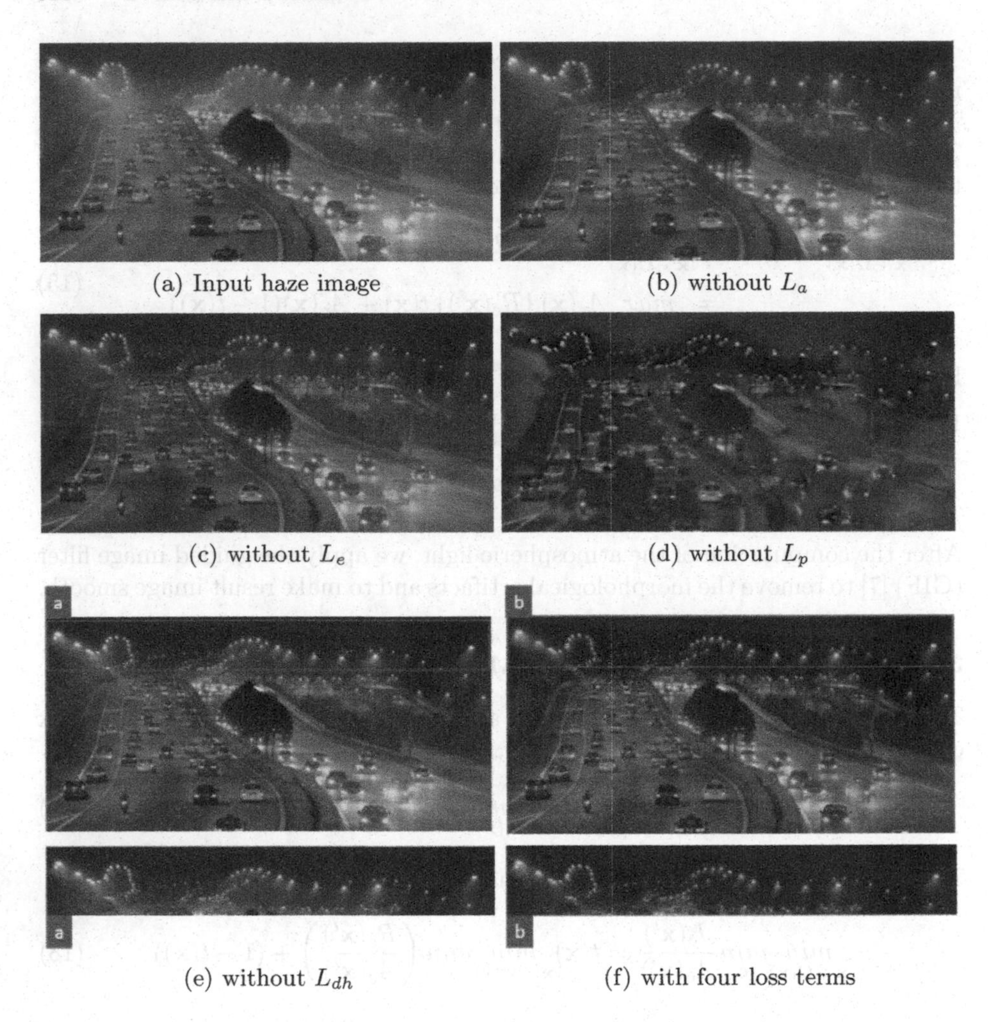

(a) Input haze image (b) without L_a

(c) without L_e (d) without L_p

(e) without L_{dh} (f) with four loss terms

Fig. 4. Ablation experiment results with four loss terms: (b) the glow effect is still remaining, (c) illumination of the image is unnatural and the glow effect is not separated well, (d) heavy color distortion and artifacts are observed, (e) the glow effect at far distance are still remaining, and (f) image obtained with four loss terms. (Color figure online)

4 Experiment Results

To prove the effectiveness of the proposed algorithm, we conduct qualitative and quantitative analyses.

4.1 Qualitative Analysis

Ablation study: To figure out the role of each term in the objective function defined in (7), a set of experiments has been carried out. In each experiment, a

(a) Input haze image (b) He et al.[7] (c) Zhang et al.[26]

(d) Li et al.[10] (e) Yang et al.[22] (f) Proposed method

Fig. 5. Comparison with other methods: (a) input haze image; (b, c, d, e) dehazed images by the method in [7], [26], [10], [22], respectively, and (f) dehazed image by the proposed method.

loss term is eliminated and the generator network is re-trained, and we analyze how the term affects to the over quality of the result image.

Figure 4 shows the ablation experiment results. Without L_a, the glow effect is not removed completely. Without L_e, illumination of the image is unnatural and color distortion appears. Without L_p, the output image suffers from heavy color distortion. The dense haze loss, L_{dh}, helps removing the glow at far distance and making the result cleaner.

Comparison with Other Methods. The performance of the proposed algorithm is compared with four other methods of [7], [26], [10], [22] as shown in Fig. 5. The method by He et al. [7], devised for daytime haze removal, is not working properly to the nighttime scene. The glow and haze aren't removed. Even though the remaining three algorithms were designed for the nighttime scenes, different kinds of defects are observed in the result images. The method in [26] removed the glow, but strong halo artifact is observed. Li's method [10] decomposed the glow better than the method in [26], but halo artifact and noise are observed. The method in [22] suppressed the halo artifact well, however, the shifted color make the result image unnatural. The result image of the proposed method, on the other hand, suppressed noise and halo artifact in the sky region. In addition, our method is able to maintain realistic colors with better glow removing.

4.2 Quantitative Analysis

We also made comparison with other methods in quantitative manner in terms of the structural similarity index (SSIM [21]). For the comparison, we use a synthetic image generated using PBRT [17] as the ground truth is needed. Fig. 6 shows the ground truth image, the synthesized haze image, and the dehazed image by our method, respectively. Table 1 shows the quantitative results against the other methods. Higher SSIM value means the haze-free image is more similar to the ground-truth image. The result proves that our haze removal method works better in nighttime than the other methods.

Table 1. SSIM for the dehazing results on synthetic hazy images generated using PBRT

Methods	SSIM
Zhang et al.'s [26]	0.9952
He et al.'s [8]	0.9978
Meng et al.'s [11]	0.9984
Li et al.'s [10]	0.9987
Park et al.'s [16]	0.9989
Our method	0.9989

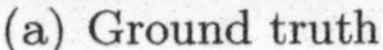

(a) Ground truth

(b) Synthetic haze image

(c) Dehazed image

Fig. 6. Quantitative evaluation using SSIM [21] on a synthetic image generated using Photorealistic Rendering and the Ray-Tracing Algorithm(PBRT)[17].

5 Conclusion

This paper presented a novel glow decomposition method using GAN for the nighttime haze removal. The generative adversarial network is devised to handle the glow effect by decomposing the input image into the glow image and the glow-free image. In addition, a way to train the network by data synthesized from night images collected. Significantly reduced halo artifact and noise in the result image brought perceptually better quality comparing to the state-of-the-art methods. Experiment results prove that the effectiveness of the proposed method in both qualitatively and quantitatively.

Acknowledgements. This research was supported by a grant(19PQWO-B153369-01) from Smart road lightning platform development and empirical study on test-bed Program funded by Ministry of the Interior and Safety of Korean government.

References

1. Achanta, R., Shaji, A., Smith, K., Lucchi, A., Fua, P., Süsstrunk, S.: SLIC superpixels compared to state-of-the-art superpixel methods. IEEE Trans. Pattern Anal. Mach. Intell. **34**(11), 2274–2282 (2012)
2. Ancuti, C., Ancuti, C.O., De Vleeschouwer, C., Bovik, A.C.: Night-time dehazing by fusion. In: 2016 IEEE International Conference on Image Processing, pp. 2256–2260. IEEE (2016)
3. Cai, B., Xu, X., Jia, K., Qing, C., Tao, D.: Dehazenet: an end-to-end system for single image haze removal. IEEE Trans. Image Process. **25**(11), 5187–5198 (2016)
4. Fattal, R.: Dehazing using color-lines. ACM Trans. Graph. **34**(1), 13 (2014)
5. Goodfellow, I., et al.: Generative adversarial nets. In: Advances in Neural Information Processing Systems, pp. 2672–2680 (2014)
6. Hariharan, B., Arbeláez, P., Girshick, R., Malik, J.: Hypercolumns for object segmentation and fine-grained localization. In: Proceedings of the IEEE Conference on Computer Vision and Pattern Recognition, pp. 447–456 (2015)
7. He, K., Sun, J., Tang, X.: Guided image filtering. In: Daniilidis, K., Maragos, P., Paragios, N. (eds.) ECCV 2010. LNCS, vol. 6311, pp. 1–14. Springer, Heidelberg (2010). https://doi.org/10.1007/978-3-642-15549-9_1
8. He, K., Sun, J., Tang, X.: Single image haze removal using dark channel prior. IEEE Trans. Pattern Anal. Mach. Intell. **33**(12), 2341–2353 (2010)
9. Johnson, J., Alahi, A., Fei-Fei, L.: Perceptual losses for real-time style transfer and super-resolution. In: Leibe, B., Matas, J., Sebe, N., Welling, M. (eds.) ECCV 2016. LNCS, vol. 9906, pp. 694–711. Springer, Cham (2016). https://doi.org/10.1007/978-3-319-46475-6_43
10. Li, Y., Tan, R.T., Brown, M.S.: Nighttime haze removal with glow and multiple light colors. In: Proceedings of the IEEE Conference on Computer Vision and Pattern Recognition, pp. 226–234 (2015)
11. Meng, G., Wang, Y., Duan, J., Xiang, S., Pan, C.: Efficient image dehazing with boundary constraint and contextual regularization. In: Proceedings of the IEEE Conference on Computer Vision and Pattern Recognition, pp. 617–624 (2013)
12. Narasimhan, S.G., Nayar, S.K.: Chromatic framework for vision in bad weather. In: Proceedings of the IEEE Conference on Computer Vision and Pattern Recognition, pp. 598–605. IEEE (2000)

13. Narasimhan, S.G., Nayar, S.K.: Vision and the atmosphere. Int. J. Comput. Vis. **48**(3), 233–254 (2002)
14. Narasimhan, S.G., Nayar, S.K.: Shedding light on the weather. In: Proceedings of the IEEE Conference on Computer Vision and Pattern Recognition. IEEE (2003)
15. Pan, J., Sun, D., Pfister, H., Yang, M.H.: Blind image deblurring using dark channel prior. In: Proceedings of the IEEE Conference on Computer Vision and Pattern Recognition, pp. 1628–1636 (2016)
16. Park, D., Han, D.K., Ko, H.: Nighttime image dehazing with local atmospheric light and weighted entropy. In: 2016 IEEE International Conference on Image Processing, pp. 2261–2265. IEEE (2016)
17. Pharr, M., Jakob, W., Humphreys, G.: Physically Based Rendering: From Theory to Implementation. Morgan Kaufmann, Burlington (2016)
18. Russakovsky, O., et al.: Imagenet large scale visual recognition challenge. Int. J. Comput. Vis. **115**(3), 211–252 (2015)
19. Schechner, Y.Y., Narasimhan, S.G., Nayar, S.K.: Instant dehazing of images using polarization. In: Proceedings of the IEEE Conference on Computer Vision and Pattern Recognition, pp. 325–332 (2001)
20. Simonyan, K., Zisserman, A.: Very deep convolutional networks for large-scale image recognition. In: International Conference on Learning Representations (2015)
21. Wang, Z., Bovik, A.C., Sheikh, H.R., Simoncelli, E.P., et al.: Image quality assessment: from error visibility to structural similarity. IEEE Trans. Image Process. **13**(4), 600–612 (2004)
22. Yang, M., Liu, J., Li, Z.: Superpixel-based single nighttime image haze removal. IEEE Trans. Multimed. **20**(11), 3008–3018 (2018)
23. Yu, F., Koltun, V.: Multi-scale context aggregation by dilated convolutions. In: 4th International Conference on Learning Representations (2016)
24. Zhang, H., Patel, V.M.: Densely connected pyramid dehazing network. In: Proceedings of the IEEE Conference on Computer Vision and Pattern Recognition, pp. 3194–3203 (2018)
25. Zhang, J., Cao, Y., Fang, S., Kang, Y., Wen Chen, C.: Fast haze removal for nighttime image using maximum reflectance prior. In: Proceedings of the IEEE Conference on Computer Vision and Pattern Recognition, pp. 7418–7426 (2017)
26. Zhang, J., Cao, Y., Wang, Z.: Nighttime haze removal based on a new imaging model. In: 2014 IEEE International Conference on Image Processing, pp. 4557–4561. IEEE (2014)
27. Zhang, R., Isola, P., Efros, A.A.: Colorful image colorization. In: Leibe, B., Matas, J., Sebe, N., Welling, M. (eds.) ECCV 2016. LNCS, vol. 9907, pp. 649–666. Springer, Cham (2016). https://doi.org/10.1007/978-3-319-46487-9_40
28. Zhang, X., Ng, R., Chen, Q.: Single image reflection separation with perceptual losses. In: Proceedings of the IEEE Conference on Computer Vision and Pattern Recognition, pp. 4786–4794 (2018)

Finding Logo and Seal in Historical Document Images - An Object Detection Based Approach

Sukalpa Chanda[1,2(✉)], Prashant Kumar Prasad[4], Anders Hast[2], Anders Brun[2], Lasse Martensson[3], and Umapada Pal[5]

[1] Faculty of Computer Science, Østfold University College, Halden, Norway
[2] Centre for Image Analysis, Uppsala University, Uppsala, Sweden
{sukalpa.chanda,anders.hast,anders.brun}@it.uu.se
[3] Department of Scandinavian Languages, Uppsala University, Uppsala, Sweden
lasse.martensson@nordiska.uu.se
[4] RCC Institute of Information Technology, Kolkata, India
prashant.rcciit@acm.org
[5] CVPR Unit, Indian Statistical Institute, Kolkata, India
umapada@isical.ac.in

Abstract. Logo and Seal serves the purpose of authenticating and referring to the source of a document. This strategy was also prevalent in the medieval period. Different algorithm exists for detection of logo and seal in document images. A close look into the present state-of-the-art methods reveals that those methods were focused toward detection of logo and seal in contemporary document images. However, such methods are likely to underperform while dealing with historical documents. This is due to the fact that historical documents are attributed with additional challenges like extra noise, bleed-through effect, blurred foreground elements and low contrast. The proposed method frames the problem of the logo and seals detection in an object detection framework. Using a deep-learning technique it counters earlier mentioned problems and evades the need for any pre-processing stage like layout analysis and/or binarization in the system pipeline. The experiments were conducted on historical images from 12th to the 16th century and the results obtained were very encouraging for detecting logo in historical document images. To the best of our knowledge, this is the first attempt on logo detection in historical document images using an object-detection based approach.

Keywords: Logo detection · Logo detection in historical document image · Historical document image analysis · Deep learning for logo and seal detection · YOLOv3 logo detection

1 Introduction

Logo (Notarial symbol) and seal in a document could assert the source of a document. Even in the medieval period this notion was prevalent and practised.

S. Palaiahnakote et al. (Eds.): ACPR 2019, LNCS 12046, pp. 821–834, 2020.
https://doi.org/10.1007/978-3-030-41404-7_58

It has been observed that many historical documents (in particular documents pertaining to administrative activities) consist of a hand-drawn logo to denote the one specific writer /scribe who has written/recorded that administrative activity. Researchers from the digital humanities domain are often interested in asserting scribe authorship by looking into the logo and seal. A lot of work has been done on Logo/Seal detection in contemporary document images, but the area is rather un-touched in historical document image perspective. Though it might be noted that historical document image can be retrieved and indexed in a digital archive on the basis of the presence of a logo and seal. According to [2], logos are primarily of three types:- only with text, only with a diagram, and a mixture of two. However, in case of historical document image (in context of the SDHK dataset), a logo is mainly a hand-drawn picture and in most of the case such a logo image does not contain any text (though right top image exhibits some text inside it). See Fig. 1 for an illustration.

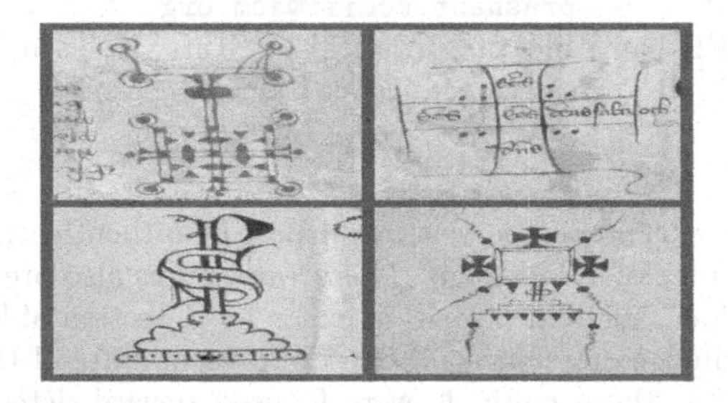

Fig. 1. Example of four different type of logo in SDHK dataset.

Over the last half-decade, an incredible advancement is evident in the field of object detection and recognition. This is mainly due to improvement in deep-learning based methodologies. However, using a standard convolutional network is not very convenient for the logo and seal detection purpose. Here, a sliding window needs to be glided over different regions of the image, and then a CNN can be used to classify the presence of the object within that region. But, it can be easily noted that the objects of interest might have spread into two spatial locations (divided between two consecutive sliding window regions) within the image and could be of different aspect ratio as well. To combat this drawback some algorithms evolved in the recent past and R-CNN was the first of those type of algorithms [10]. Later over the years more advanced versions like [9,16] have evolved. The objective of this article is to explore how we can leverage such state-of-the-art object detectors for the purpose of the logo and seal detection in degraded historical document images, to the best of our knowledge this has never been explored before.

It is worth mentioning that the appearance of logo and seal in formal/contemporary documents differ a lot in comparison to a logo and seal found in historical document images. In particular, logo in a contemporary administrative document is much brighter/colourful and is printed in nature, whereas in a historical document image the logo is mostly hand-drawn thus making it very challenging. Hence, the earlier proposed methods would not work well in the context of the logo and seal detection in the historical document images. This article investigates the problem of the logo and seal detection in historical document image using a very advanced state-of-the-art object-detector algorithm called "Yolo".

2 Related Work

Logo and Seal detection in document images have been explored extensively within a span of two decades or a bit more. Some of the early attempts are due to [4–6,14,24], those were proposed more than a decade back and more recently in [7,8,11–13,15,19–21,25,26]. The research as stated in [6] can be termed as one of the first attempts in performing logo detection. Here the logos were decomposed to a set of graphical structures like lines, circles, rectangles, triangles, later using those a logo signature is composed which was then matched against a logo database. In [4], a method termed as spot-backpropagation (S-BP) has been proposed and it performs well even in case of partial noise occluded logo images. Neumann et al. [14] uses the local, global and a combination of the local and global method for logo detection. The local method computes a number of statistical and perceptual shape features for each connected component of an image and its background. The global method uses a wavelet decomposition of the horizontal and vertical projections of the whole image, and the mixed approach combines both using an adaptive weighting scheme based on relative performance. In [5] logos were represented by line segment drawings and later a modified Hausdorff distance has been used to match those line segments. A segmentation free and layout independent approach for logo detection is due to [24]. It operates in multiple stages where in the first stage a trained Fisher classifier classifies logo using features from document context and connected components. Then a cascade of simple classifiers is used so that each logo candidate region could be further classified at successively finer scales, thus allowing a lesser number of false alarms and the detected region to be refined [24]. An advanced method on query by example logo retrieval is discussed in [20], where Logos are compactly described by a variant of the shape context descriptor. Later those descriptors were indexed using a locality-sensitive hashing data structure. In [23] a dynamic approach to logo detection and recognition in document images has been proposed using a Bayesian Belief Network. Roy et al. [19] proposed a method which uses Generalized Hough Transform (GHT) where to find possible location of the seal in a document the proposed method used spatial feature descriptor of neighbouring component pairs. In [15], logo detection has been solved using a two-stage approach. In the first stage, a set of Outer Contour Strings (OCSs) describing each graphics and text parts of the documents were generated. In the second stage, the logo detection problem is defined as a region scoring regression problem where those OCS were evaluated to be a part of a logo or not. Using a bag-of-visual-words model and a by a sliding-window technique of blurred shape model descriptor within documents an attempt has been made to sort similar administrative documents in [21]. There exists some Key-point descriptor-based approach for logo detection and recognition [11–13]. Jain et al. [11] proposed the use of the SURF feature for logo retrieval and a method to filter results using the orientation of local features and geometric constraints. In [12], SIFT key points from both the query document images and a given set of logos (logo gallery) were matched. Consequently, logo segmentation is performed using spatial density-based clustering. In the final stage, a homography is used to filter the matched key points as a post-processing and logo classification is performed using an accumulating histogram. Using SIFT and BRISK keypoint descriptors a logo detection and retrieval system has been proposed in [13].

From the literature review, it is evident that though logo and seal detection have been explored for two decades, such published methods do not focus on the logo and seal detection problem in historical document images. Hence this article tries to address that unexplored area of the logo and seal detection in historical document images.

3 Motivation and Dataset

During the medieval period in Scandinavia, notarial symbols were used as a means of confirming the authenticity of the document on which they were placed, as an alternative or complement to the seals. The form of the symbol was unique to the specific scribe (a Notarius Publicus), and it was accompanied by a notarial text, stating that the scribe behind the notarial symbol vouches for the authenticity of the document, either by stating that he/she has written with his own hand ("propria manu scripsi" or similar) or that he/she has given the task to someone else ("per alium fideliter scriptum" or similar). These charters are important for the philological and palaeographical research, as they contain explicit statements as to who has written the document in question. Thus, they represent ground truth regarding the scribal identity. In most cases, the medieval documents are anonymous as to who has written them, and the few cases we have where the scribes themselves make themselves known are thus very valuable. The extraction of the charters containing notarial texts is therefore an important task to provide empirical material to the philological research. Henceforth, these notarial symbols are referred to as "Logos".

The dataset (SDHK dataset) for the present investigation consists of the digitized medieval charters in the card index of Diplomatarium Suecanum, comprising a total number of approximately 11,000 charters. (A substantial number of charters is not yet digitized.) Charters are legal documents, containing various types of transactions, such as purchases, exchanges of property and similar. The date of the charter images in this corpus ranges from the 12th century to the beginning of the 16th century, with only a few from the beginning of this period but with a considerable increase towards the end. The languages represented are mainly Latin and old Swedish, but some charters in German are also present in this corpus. In the oldest charters, the language is Latin, and the oldest charter in Swedish date from 1330. Later, especially in the 15th century, there are more charters in Swedish. To verify the authenticity of the content of the charter, seals were used. They were primarily made of wax or clay, and they were fastened to a strip below the charter. See an example of such seals hanging from the bottom part of a charter image in Fig. 2.

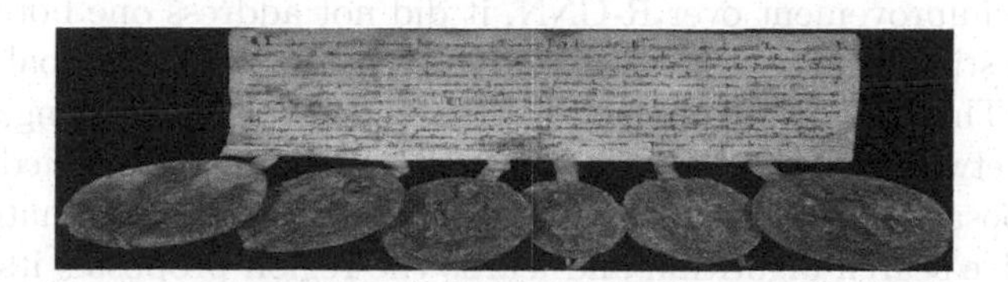

Fig. 2. Example of a charter-image with 6 seals hanging from the bottom.

3.1 Data Aquisitition and Annotation

29 Logo images and 141 Seal images out of 11k images in the corpus was used for training. Out of those 170 images (141 + 29), 38 images were used as validation data during the training process. Images from both classes were cropped and the bounding box information along with the respective class labels were stored in a text file to be used during training of the network.

4 Methodology

Detection of logo and seal could also be performed without a deep-learning framework as done previously on many occassions. But that traditional road map demands additional pre-processing steps like layout analysis or binarization. This could be detrimental to the performance of the system as those pre-processing steps are itself challenging in the context of a historical document image. Hence to evade that problem we opted for this object detection-based approach.

4.1 Object Detection - Brief Overview

A regular CNN is good enough for image classification, where generally an image is presented to the network and the task is to say what that image is! On the other hand, the real human vision looks at the world around and carries out far more complex classification by classifying multiple objects present simultaneously in one frame of sight. A CNN is unable to perform such a task. The idea of adapting CNN's to identify the different objects in the image and their boundaries gave rise to a set of algorithms like "R-CNN" [10], "Fast-R-CNN" [9], "Faster-R-CNN" [18] and their advanced counterpart like "Yolo" [16] and its most sophisticated successor "YOLOv3" [17]. In "R-CNN" [10], object detection is essentially performed in three steps: (a) propose bounding boxes using a selective search method; (b) use a pre-trained AlexNet and an SVM to classify object type inside the bounding box region; (c) use a linear regression model to refine bounding box coordinates. However the algorithm lacks in speed as it needs to train three different models - CNN to generate image features, the SVM classifier for classification, and the regression model to tighten the bounding boxes. In "Fast-R-CNN" [9] this 3 steps were amalgamated to jointly train the CNN, classifier, and bounding box regressor in a single model. Though "Fast-R-CNN" [9] displayed improvement over R-CNN, it did not address one bottleneck of R-CNN, which still requires a selective search step to generate probable bounding box regions. This has been addressed in "Faster-R-CNN" by adding a Fully Convolutional Network on top of the features of the CNN and termed that as the Region Proposal Network. This Region Proposal Network eliminates the usage of the selective search algorithm and learns the region proposals itself.

All of those algorithms from the "R-CNN" family does not look at the complete image. Those algorithms look into parts of the image which has high probabilities of containing the object. "YOLO" or You Only Look Once on the other hand is an object detection algorithm much different from the region based algorithms discussed above. In "YOLO" the bounding boxes and the class probabilities for these boxes were predicted using a single convolutional network. "YOLO" network comprises of 24 convolutional layers followed by 2 fully connected layers (FC). Some convolution layers use 1×1 reduction layers alternatively and this reduces the feature map depth. The basic steps in "YOLO" are as follows:

- Divide an image into $S \times S$ grids
- In every grid cell,
  - it predicts 'B' number of boundary boxes and each of those boxes has one confidence score
  - Regardless of the number of boxes, it detects one object
  - Predicts conditional class probabilities for each possible class object

In our case with two classes (Logo and Seal), if the images were divided into 13×13 grid then with 5 bounding boxes the final output tensor gets of dimension $13 \times 13 \times (5 \times (2 + 5))$. Since each Bounding box will have 7 elements namely: $x, y, w_d, h_t, \mathbb{C}_*, p_0(*), p_1(*)$ representing coordinates of the centre of the bounding box, width and height of the bounding box, confidence score and probability associated with each of the two classes, respectively.

The objective function L_f as shown in Eq. 1 of "YOLO" is a convex combination of 4 factors [16][1], see Eq. 1: (a) Difference between Centre coordinates GT and Predicted Centre coordinates- The 1st expression computes a sum over each bounding box predictor ($j = 0..B$) of each grid cell ($i = 0..S^2$); (b) Difference between bounding box width and height of GT and predicted bounding box width and height is expressed in 2nd expression; (c) The third expression represents the difference between bounding box confidence score GT and predicted bounding box confidence score; (d) Finally the fourth expression represents the difference between classification score GT - predicted classification

[1] https://hackernoon.com/understanding-yolo-f5a74bbc7967.

score. Here "GT" denotes "Ground Truth". It can be noted from the 4th expression that "YOLO" uses a mean square error in calculating the classification loss. In above-mentioned expressions $\hat{x_i}$ and $\hat{y_i}$ denotes x and y coordinate of the predicted bounding box centre, $\hat{w_i}$ and $\hat{h_i}$ denotes width and height of the predicted bounding box. The reason why the algorithm uses the square root of the bounding box width and height instead of the width and height directly is due to the fact that small deviations in large boxes matter less than in small boxes, this has been partially achieved by using the square root term.

$$\begin{aligned} L_f = \lambda_{coord} \sum_{i=0}^{S^2} \sum_{j=0}^{B} \mathbb{I}_{ij}^{obj} (x_i - \hat{x_i}) + (y_i - \hat{y_i}) + \\ \lambda_{coord} \sum_{i=0}^{S^2} \sum_{j=0}^{B} \mathbb{I}_{ij}^{obj} (\sqrt{w_i} - \sqrt{\hat{w_i}})^2 + (\sqrt{h_i} - \sqrt{\hat{h_i}})^2 + \\ \left(\sum_{i=0}^{S^2} \sum_{j=0}^{B} \mathbb{I}_{ij}^{obj} (\mathbb{C}_i - \hat{\mathbb{C}}_i)^2 + \lambda_{noobj} \sum_{i=0}^{S^2} \sum_{j=0}^{B} \mathbb{I}_{ij}^{obj} (\mathbb{C}_i - \hat{\mathbb{C}}_i)^2 \right) + \\ \sum_{i=0}^{S^2} \mathbb{I}_{i}^{obj} \sum_{c \in classes} (p_i(c) - \hat{p_i}(c))^2 \end{aligned} \tag{1}$$

$$\lambda_{coord} \sum_{i=0}^{S^2} \sum_{j=0}^{B} \mathbb{I}_{ij}^{obj} (x_i - \hat{x_i}) + (y_i - \hat{y_i}) \tag{2}$$

$$\lambda_{coord} \sum_{i=0}^{S^2} \sum_{j=0}^{B} \mathbb{I}_{ij}^{obj} (\sqrt{w_i} - \sqrt{\hat{w_i}})^2 + (\sqrt{h_i} - \sqrt{\hat{h_i}})^2 \tag{3}$$

$$\sum_{i=0}^{S^2} \sum_{j=0}^{B} \mathbb{I}_{ij}^{obj} (\mathbb{C}_i - \hat{\mathbb{C}}_i)^2 + \lambda_{noobj} \sum_{i=0}^{S^2} \sum_{j=0}^{B} \mathbb{I}_{ij}^{obj} (\mathbb{C}_i - \hat{\mathbb{C}}_i)^2 \tag{4}$$

$$\sum_{i=0}^{S^2} \mathbb{I}_{i}^{obj} \sum_{c \in classes} (p_i(c) - \hat{p_i}(c))^2 \tag{5}$$

Where $\mathbb{I}_{*}^{obj}, \lambda_{coord}, \lambda_{noobj}$ are the indicator functions corresponding to the object *obj*, regularization for coordinates and number of objects, respectively. However, "Yolo" cannot always detect small objects. In [16] it has been mentioned that the algorithm has a problem with new or unusual aspect ratios or configurations and most of the errors incurred are due to erroneous localization. An advanced and a much sophisticated member of the "YOLO" family of algorithm is "YOLOv3" [17]. In this article, experiments were done with "YOLOv3". This "YOLOv3" [17] is different from its base version "Yolo" mainly in three aspects[2]. They are as follows:

[2] https://mc.ai/yolo3-a-huge-improvement/.

- Bounding Box Predictions - clustering technique to generate anchor boxes (also known as priors). It calculates the objective function value using logistic regression, a complete overlap of bounding box prior over the ground truth object denotes zero loss.
- Class Predictions - are performed using independent logistic classifiers for each class instead of a regular softmax layer as done in "Yolo". This is how multi-label classification is achieved.
- Multi-scales Predictions: It predicts boxes at 3 different scales.

4.2 YOLOv3-A Fully Connected Network

"YOLOv3" is a feature-learning based network that adopts 53 convolutional layers and no fully-connected layer is used. This structure makes it possible to deal with images of any sizes. Also, no pooling layers are used. Instead, a convolutional layer with stride 2 is used to downsample the feature map, passing size-invariant feature forward "YOLOv3" uses binary cross-entropy loss for each label. In addition, a ResNet-like structure and FPN-like structure is also a key to its accuracy improvement."YOLOv3" makes prediction across 3 different scales. The detection layer is used to make detection at feature maps of three different sizes, having strides 32, 16, 8 respectively. For example, with an input image of 416×416, detections were performed on scales 13×13, 26×26 and 52×52. The network downsamples the input image until the first detection layer, where a detection is made using feature maps of a layer with stride 32. Further, layers are upsampled by a factor of 2 and concatenated with feature maps of a previous layers having identical feature map sizes. The second detection is now made at layer with stride 16. On further upsampling, a final detection is made at the layer of stride 8. At each scale, each cell predicts 3 bounding boxes using 3 anchors, making the total number of anchors used 9. (The anchors are different for different scales).

Determining Bounding Box Dimension. In many application scenarios the dimensions of boundary boxes exhibit strong patterns. To identify the top-K boundary box dimensions that have the best coverage for the training data. To determine those bounding-box priors (anchors), "YOLOv3" applies k-means cluster. Then it pre-select 9 clusters. For our dataset, it turned out that the width and height of the anchors are as follows: $(38 \times 41), (44 \times 60), (69 \times 43), (58 \times 74), (79 \times 61), (54 \times 105), (73 \times 101), (99 \times 115), (161 \times 152)$. These 9 priors are grouped into three different groups according to their scale. Each group is assigned to a specific feature map in detecting objects.

4.3 Experimental Framework

Altogether 170 document images (with 29 Logo images and 141 Seal images) were selected from the corpus consisting of ≈11k images. Out of those 170 images, we randomly selected 138 images for training and rest 32 images for validation during the training process of the "YOLOv3" network. It is worth mentioning that many images consist of more than one Seal whereas there was only one Logo per image. We deployed initially the basic algorithm of "Yolo", and noticed that in a small pilot-test dataset it performed a bit less than the "YOLOv3". It was being observed that in some occasions the "Yolo" was not able to detect a Logo if that Logo is small in size. Taking this factor into consideration, "YOLOv3" was chosen for all further experiment. Later, a miniature version of "YOLOv3" known as "YOLOv3-Tiny" was also used and its performance was compared with "YOLOv3". Networks were fed with input training images, along with precise bounding-box information of each labelled object (Logo and Seal) present in the image. All input images were size normalized to 416 × 416. That image was divided into 13 × 13 grids and a stride of 32 was used. "YOLOv3" makes prediction across 3 different scales. The network performs detection at feature maps of three different sizes, having strides 32, 16, 8 respectively. This means, with an input of 416, detections on scales 13 × 13, 26 × 26 and 52 × 52 were performed. We have used the implementation from [3].

5 Experimental Results and Discussions

5.1 YOLOv3 Network Learning Details and Obtained Results

The network in YOLOv3 was trained from the scratch using a "TITAN-X" GPU card with 12 GB memory, while the batch size was 64 and mini-batch size was set to 16, the learning rate was set to 0.001 with momentum set to 0.9. From Fig. 5(a) it can be easily noted that the loss function value dropped substantially at around 2k iteration and then it kept on dwindling till the end. Considering the fact that the loss function did not reduce/vary much after 10k of training iteration, we opted to use the network model after 21k iteration. From a paleographer point of view precise detection of the logo is crucial, hence we have reported the accuracy of Logo detection at the instance level. Note that in some test pages there was more than one logo. In our test images, there were 95 instances of logo in total, out of those 80 were correctly detected. A miniature version of YOLOv3 termed as YOLOv3-Tiny is comprised of a much shallow network with only 16 convolutional layers. However, while using YOLOv3-Tiny network, the number of correct hits dropped hugely, and hence we are not reporting that result in details. It is worth mentioning here that detecting such hand-drawn logo in a degraded historical document image is an extremely challenging task and has not been investigated before. Seal detection was not very crucial from palaeography perspective. Hence the accuracy has been calculated at the page level, where the classification is considered correct if majority of the number of seals were detected correctly in a page, and misclassification otherwise. Also, about 590 images from the corpus were discarded from being considered into this evaluation since the seal object present in those images were extremely small and debatable to be considered as a legible seal. From Table 2 it can be noted that seal detection accuracy was 93.53%.

Table 1. Logo detection accuracy

Class	Accuracy		
	Total number of Logo instances	True hits	False hits
Logo	95	80 (84.21%)	15 (15.78%)

Table 2. Seal detection accuracy using YOLOv3 network

Page level detection accuracy for seal		
Total number of pages with seal	Correct identification	Wrong identification
≈6650	≈6220 (93.53%)	≈430 (6.47%)

Some Observations. It was being noticed that the network could detect logo perfectly even if the image is wrongly oriented. Another striking incident is that the network is capable of identifying Logos which are shape-wise alike to a Seal like object. Note that the network was not trained with huge number of Logo samples, still, its accuracy is high. For an illustration see Fig. 3. Here the text of the document image is in an inverted orientation (text going from right to left in this case), and also the shape of the Logo (both are circular) is very similar to a Seal type, (see Fig. 3) which is common in the SDHK images.

Fig. 3. (Left) Logo similar to Seal in shape, yet correctly identified as Logo. Also note that the direction of the text beside the Logo is from right to left in this particular image, even then it is not detrimental for Logo detection. (Right) A circular shaped Seal.

Error Analysis. Some errors (in 3 occasions) while detecting Logo occurred due to the presence of big embellished text present in those charter images. See Fig. 4 for illustration. Most of the errors incurred while detecting Seals were due to blurred Seal objects, see Fig. 5, here the seal is almost invisible due to its low contrast with respect to the surroundings.

5.2 Results on Tobacco800 Dataset

The Tobacco800 dataset [25] is the most popular dataset used for benchmarking performance of a Logo detection system for almost a decade now. However, there

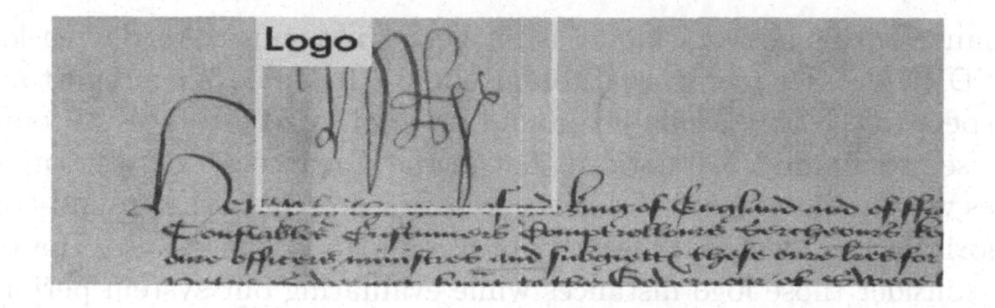

Fig. 4. Embellished text identified as Logo.

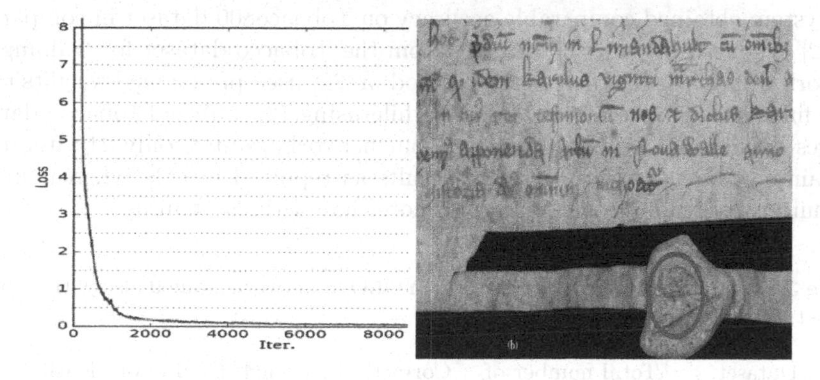

Fig. 5. (Left) Loss function value of YOLOv3 with respect to number of iterations. (Right) Seal (marked with red circle) not detected due to faded foreground appearance. (Color figure online)

is no defined train-test split in the dataset that has been uniformly used by other published research that used this dataset. For example, in [1], the system was trained using 100 images from the Tobacco800 dataset, whereas in a very recent endeavour [22], the system was trained with (20–50)% images of the dataset. Under these circumstances, it is quite impossible to make a fair comparison between our proposed method and other published experimental results. Since it is not possible to know exactly which images were used for training and which were used for testing. It is also worth mentioning that there is a difference in the form of Logos that is observed in Tobacco dataset in comparison to the Logos found in the SDHK dataset. In Tobacco800 dataset, a logo is always a printed material, not hand-drawn as it is seen in SDHK images (see Fig. 6). Moreover, some Logos are completely textual in nature. Another difference between the SDHK dataset and Tobacco dataset is the absence of Seal and the presence of Signature object type in tobacco dataset. Due to such differences, initially the network used for detection of Logo in SDHK images could not detect any logo from the tobacco dataset images. To adapt the YOLOv3 network with Tobacco dataset logo images, only 30 logo samples (20 for training and 10 for validation) from the tobacco dataset were additionally used to train a YOLOv3 network from scratch. The results are quite fascinating and depicted in Table 3. Note that the performance of this network model is bit better in terms of retrieving logo also on the SDHK dataset (compare Tables 1 and 3). In Table 3, we report accuracy with respect to the only available ground truth of Logo instances of tobacco800 dataset, see results in[3]. We noticed that in the Tobacco800 dataset, many logo instances were not annotated and hence were not present in the ground-truth list. Our algorithm has identified majority of those logo instances also. However, we did not consider those logo instances while evaluating our system performance. To make a tentative idea about the efficacy of our proposed system, we compare its performance with a very recently published research [22]. It is evident that our system obtained comparable accuracy on Tobacco800 dataset in comparsion to [22] despite using only 30 samples from the Tobacco dataset for training the network from scratch, whereas the method in [22] used pre-trained weights those were fine-tuned in the last few layers while using (20–50)% of tobacco dataset images during the training. Moreover, our network requires only 21k iterations of training to generate very similar results as reported in [22], whereas in [22] the number of training iterations was more than 4 times than us.

Table 3. Accuracy on Logo detection with YOLOv3 network trained also with Tobacco dataset.

Dataset	Total number of Logo instances	Correctly identified	Could not identify
Tobacco800	431	383 (89%)	48 (11%)
SDHK	95	84 (88.42%)	11 (11.58%)

Fig. 6. (Left) Textual logo in tobacco800 dataset. (Right) Printed logo from tobacco dataset.

6 Conclusion and Future Work

Detection of logo and seal found in historical document images has been addressed in this article using an Object-Detection algorithm "YOLOv3". The proposed method exhibits robust performance despite dealing with challenging data and low amount of training samples. Moreover, it does not require any pre-processing step like layout-analysis or binarization. The proposed method has

[3] https://drive.google.com/file/d/1Ux-HoK5DavJ-6LA8OwG6jurWRXL1hrfn/view?usp=sharing.

also perform equally well on a public dataset (Tobacco800 dataset), which consists of completely different logo types. Future research could be in the direction of classifying different types of logo and making a logo catalogue.

Acknowledgment. This research has been carried out under the aegis of "New Eyes on Sweden's Medieval Scribes. Scribal Attribution using Digital Palaeography in the Medieval Gothic Script" by virtue of the grant number NHS14-2068:1, from Riksbankens Jubileumsfond.

References

1. Alaei, A., Delalandre, M.: A complete logo detection/recognition system for document images, April 2014. https://doi.org/10.1109/DAS.2014.79
2. Alaei, A., Roy, P.P., Pal, U.: Logo and seal based administrative document image retrieval: a survey. Comput. Sci. Rev. **22**, 47–63 (2016)
3. Alexey: DarkNet-YoloV3 (2018). https://github.com/AlexeyAB. Accessed 25 March 2019
4. Cesarini, F., Francesconi, E., Gori, M., Marinai, S., Sheng, J.Q., Soda, G.: A neural-based architecture for spot-noisy logo recognition. In: Proceedings of the 4th ICDAR, vol. 1, pp. 175–179 (1997)
5. Chen, J., Leung, M.K.H., Gao, Y.: Noisy logo recognition using line segment hausdorff distance. Pattern Recogn. **36**, 943–955 (2003)
6. Doermann, D., Rivlin, E., Weiss, I.: Applying algebraic and differential invariants for logo recognition. Mach. Vision Appl. **9**(2), 73–86 (1996)
7. En, S., Nicolas, S., Petitjean, C., Jurie, F., Heutte, L.: New public dataset for spotting patterns in medieval document images. J. Electron. Imaging **26**(1), 11010 (2017). https://doi.org/10.1117/1.JEI.26.1.011010
8. En, S., Petitjean, C., Nicolas, S., Heutte, L.: A scalable pattern spotting system for historical documents. Pattern Recogn. **54**, 149–161 (2016)
9. Girshick, R.: Fast R-CNN. In: Proceedings of the 2015 IEEE International Conference on Computer Vision (ICCV), pp. 1440–448 (2015)
10. Girshick, R.B., Donahue, J., Darrell, T., Malik, J.: Rich feature hierarchies for accurate object detection and semantic segmentation. In: 2014 IEEE Conference on Computer Vision and Pattern Recognition, CVPR, pp. 580–587 (2014)
11. Jain, R., Doermann, D.: Logo retrieval in document images. In: 2012 10th IAPR International Workshop on Document Analysis Systems, pp. 135–139, March 2012
12. Le, V.P., Visani, M., Tran, C.D., Ogier, J.: Improving logo spotting and matching for document categorization by a post-filter based on homography. In: 2013 12th International Conference on Document Analysis and Recognition, pp. 270–274 (2013)
13. Le, V.P., Nayef, N., Visani, M., Ogier, J.M., Tran, C.D.: Document retrieval based on logo spotting using key-point matching. In: Proceedings of the 22nd International Conference on Pattern Recognition, ICPR 2014, pp. 3056–3061 (2014)
14. Neumann, J., Samet, H., Soffer, A.: Integration of local and global shape analysis for logo classification. Pattern Recogn. Lett. **23**(12), 1449–1457 (2002)
15. Pham, T.A., Delalandre, M., Barrat, S.: A contour-based method for logo detection. 2011 International Conference on Document Analysis and Recognition, pp. 718–722 (2011)

16. Redmon, J., Divvala, S.K., Girshick, R.B., Farhadi, A.: You only look once: unified, real-time object detection. In: 2016 IEEE Conference on Computer Vision and Pattern Recognition, CVPR, pp. 779–788 (2016)
17. Redmon, J., Farhadi, A.: Yolov3: an incremental improvement. CoRR abs/1804.02767 (2018). http://arxiv.org/abs/1804.02767
18. Ren, S., He, K., Girshick, R.B., Sun, J.: Faster R-CNN: towards real-time object detection with region proposal networks. In: Annual Conference on Neural Information Processing Systems (NIPS), pp. 91–99 (2015)
19. Roy, P.P., Pal, U., Lladós, J.: Document seal detection using GHT and character proximity graphs. Pattern Recogn. **44**(6), 1282–1295 (2011)
20. Rusiñol, M., Lladós, J.: Efficient logo retrieval through hashing shape context descriptors. In: Proceedings of the 9th IAPR International Workshop on Document Analysis Systems, DAS 2010, pp. 215–222. ACM, New York (2010)
21. Rusiñol, M., Poulain D'Andecy, V., Karatzas, D., Lladós, J.: Classification of administrative document images by logo identification. In: Kwon, Y.-B., Ogier, J.-M. (eds.) GREC 2011. LNCS, vol. 7423, pp. 49–58. Springer, Heidelberg (2013). https://doi.org/10.1007/978-3-642-36824-0_5
22. Sharma, N., Mandal, R., Sharma, R., Pal, U., Blumenstein, M.: Signature and logo detection using deep CNN for document image retrieval. In: 16th International Conference on Frontiers in Handwriting Recognition, ICFHR 2018, Niagara Falls, NY, USA, 5–8 August 2018, pp. 416–422 (2018)
23. Wang, H.: Document logo detection and recognition using Bayesian model. In: 2010 20th International Conference on Pattern Recognition, pp. 1961–1964 (2010)
24. Zhu, G., Doermann, D.: Automatic document logo detection. In: Proceedings of the 9th ICDAR (ICDAR 2007), vol. 2, pp. 864–868 (2007)
25. Zhu, G., Doermann, D.: Logo matching for document image retrieval. In: 2009 10th International Conference on Document Analysis and Recognition, pp. 606–610, July 2009
26. Zhu, Q., Keogh, E.: Mother fugger: mining historical manuscripts with local color patches. In: 2010 IEEE International Conference on Data Mining, pp. 699–708, December 2010

KIL: Knowledge Interactiveness Learning for Joint Depth Estimation and Semantic Segmentation

Ling Zhou, Chunyan Xu(✉), Zhen Cui, and Jian Yang

Key Lab of Intelligent Perception and Systems for High-Dimensional Information of Ministry of Education, School of Computer Science and Engineering, Nanjing University of Science and Technology, Nanjing, China
cyx@njust.edu.cn

Abstract. Depth estimation and semantic segmentation are two important yet challenging tasks in the field of pixel-level scene understanding. Previous works often solve the two tasks as the parallel decoding/modeling process, but cannot well consider strongly correlated relationships between these tasks. In this paper, given an input image, we propose to learn knowledge interactiveness of depth estimation and semantic segmentation for jointly predicting results in an end-to-end way. Especially, the key Knowledge Interactiveness Learning (KIL) module can mine and leverage the connections/complementations of these two tasks effectively. Furthermore, the network parameters can be jointly optimized for boosting the final predictions of depth estimation and semantic segmentation with the coarse-to-fine strategy. Extensive experiments on SUN-RGBD and NYU Depth-V2 datasets demonstrate state-of-the-art performance of the proposed unified framework for both depth estimation and semantic segmentation tasks.

Keywords: Depth estimation · Semantic segmentation · Knowledge interactiveness

1 Introduction

With the rapid development of deep learning (especially CNNs), great progress has been made on the study of computer vision, especially in depth estimation [8, 13,21,34,42] and semantic segmentation [28,41,45,49]. These are two important and challenging tasks which have many potential applications in autonomous driving [19], simultaneous localization and mapping (SLAM) [30] and so on. For example, it is essential to analyze accurate semantic information in front of the vehicle by semantic segmentation.

Most methods used to predict depth and semantic segmentation follow such a model: a separate model needs to be trained for each new task. This single-task model emphasizes the learning of robust regression, but rarely consider the interactions among tasks. Actually, many tasks can share information with each

S. Palaiahnakote et al. (Eds.): ACPR 2019, LNCS 12046, pp. 835–848, 2020.
https://doi.org/10.1007/978-3-030-41404-7_59

other. For example, depth estimation and semantic segmentation are both pixel-level tasks which deal with high-level semantic information. They own some common information like object boundaries. Mining intrinsic connections and using them appropriately can give each task extra information and improve their performance. Meanwhile, it is worth considerating the case of single task without enough data. Single-task learning is difficult to obtain sufficient data feature information through training, which results in the decline of the learning efficiency in different degrees. What's more, a increasing number of datasets, such as SUN-RGBD [38] and NYU Depth-v2 [32], contain segmentation and depth labels at the same time. Thus, multi-task learning has gradually attracted people's attention and achieved great success [32,46] [58,62]. There are different forms of multi-task learning, such as joint task learning and learning to learn. In our work, we propose an end-to-end network to address depth estimation and semantic segmentation based on joint learning which can collaborate two tasks for advancing the performance.

Due to the fact that these two joint tasks can share information with each other during the learning process, it is difficult yet valuable to learn and utilize the relationship of information between tasks. Positive relationships learning can benefit each task, bring them extra information and make them more robust while negative learning has no beneficial rewarding and even lead to noise. Motivated by SENet [20], we propose a Knowledge Interactiveness Learning(KIL) module to address this problem. KIL can learn how to find relationships between tasks and interactive information adaptively.

In summary, our contributions are in three aspects:

- We propose an end-to-end network to address depth estimation and semantic segmentation based on joint learning which can mutually collaborate two tasks for advancing the performance.
- Motivated by SENet, we propose a knowledge interactiveness leanring module to enclose the two tasks information. What's more, the block has been packaged and can be used in conventional networks generally.
- We implement and validate the effectiveness of the proposed block. Also, some state-of-the-art results have been reported for the dual tasks of depth estimation and semantic segmentation on SUN-RGBD [38] and NYU Depth-V2 datasets [32].

This paper is divided into five parts. Related work on multi-task learning, semantic segmentation and depth estimation will be introduced in Sect. 2 The framework is illustrated in Sect. 3. And Sect. 4 reports the details of the experiment and the analysis of the experiments' results. We summarize and put forward some prospects for the existing work in Sect. 5.

2 Related Work

According to the relevance of our work, we review related work in the following three aspects: semantic segmentation, depth estimation and multi-task learning.

Semantic Segmentation: Before deep network achieving such great success, traditional methods for semantic segmentation are typically based on clustering [10,11,35]. Despite improvement and development of methods based on clustering, segmentation algorithms with deep learning have achieved more state-of-the-art results and been more widely accepted. As increasingly large segmentation datasets are born, more and more methods [28,45] conduct semantic segmentation from single RGB images. Long *et al.* [28] first proposed to use a full convolutional neural network (FCN) for semantic image segmentation. This method converts the fully connected layers in the previous classification network into convolutional layers, so that a rough probability score map can be generated, which can be upsampled to the original image size. Qi *et al.* [41] proposed a 3D graph neural network. They used depth maps and RGB images to generate a graph for better segmentation results. Recently, Chen *et al.* [46] propose to use depth information to predict segmentation.

Depth Estimation: Monocular depth estimation has been studied for a long history [21,34], previous work on it generally utilized Markov Random Field (MRF) to solve the problem of depth prediction [4,5]. However, these methods lack flexibility. With the success of CNN architectures, several works are carried out based on a single CNN. Eigen *et al.* [12,13] proposed a multi-stage CNN, merged the coarse and fine cues to solve the monocular depth estimation. Besides, Liu *et al.* [15] proposed CRF model based on approximation methods to deal with the connection between superpixels. Recently, Xu *et al.* [8] employ multi-scale continuous CRFs as sequential deep networks. All of these methods are trained only to predict depth. Unlike these methods, we propose to make use of segmentation cues to improve the performance of depth estimation.

Multi-task Learning: It has been a long time since multi-task learning caused widely-spread attention, a lot of relevant studies in different research fields [2,23,24,40] have sprung up. Most of methods falls into two categories: hard and soft parameters sharing [7,27,39,44]. Recently, there are some researchers focus on good multi-task learning mechanisms in deep neural networks. Long and Wang [31] proposed a network that can learn the deep relationship between tasks through matrix priors on the fully connected layers. Recently, Liu *et al.* [37] propose a novel end-to-end multi-task learning architecture, which allows learning of task-specific feature-level attention. Different from these methods, we devote to promote and refine depth estimation and semantic segmentation in our network architecture.

3 Framework

3.1 Network Arichtecture

The overview of our proposed network architecture is shown in Fig. 1. The whole network arichitecture is composed of the shared encoder part and two-stream

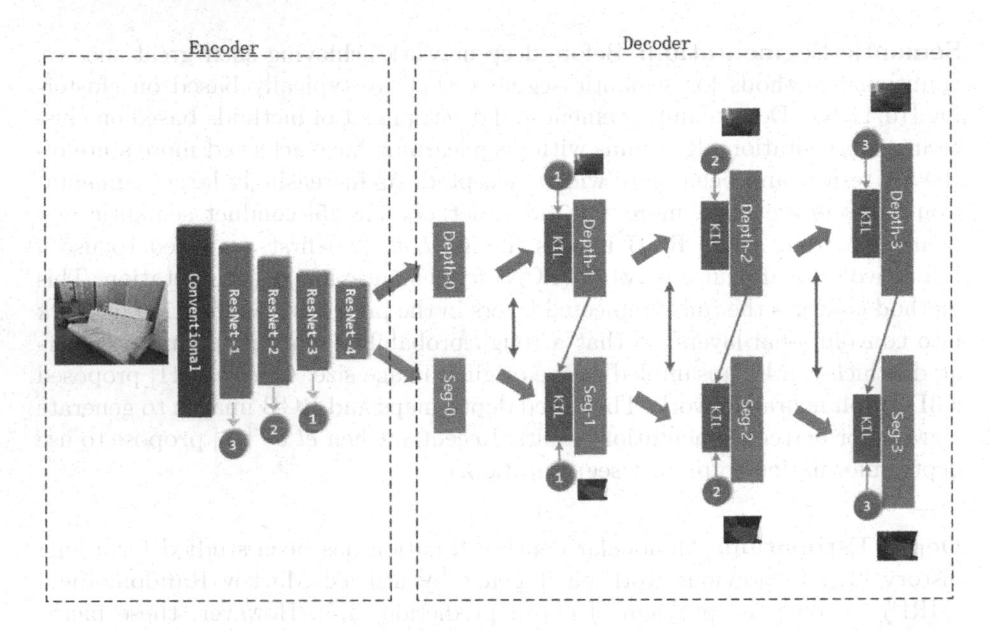

Fig. 1. An overview of our proposed network architecture. It can address tasks jointly and boost the performance in an end-to-end way. The encoder part is composed of one conventional layer and some residual-blocks. The decoder part has a two-stream network to deal with the dual tasks. Each layer has a KIL block before except Depth-0 and Seg-0 to enhance the common information. For producing fine-gained predictions, we adopt a coarse-to-fine strategy on the dual tasks.

decoder networks. The encoder is based on the ResNet-50 [29] and its residual blocks are pretrained on the ImageNet classification task [25]. Multi-scale response maps from residual blocks (ResNet1-ResNet4 in the Fig. 1) are feeded to the following decoder part. In the decoder part, a two-stream network composed of residual blocks and KIL modules is used to predict the pixel-level results. Obviously, from Depth-0 to Depth-3 are engaged in the prediction of depth while the rest parts for semantic segmentation. Each sub-stream network has three different scale layers and a prediciton layer, and a knowledge interactiveness learning module before each layer except Depth-0 and Seg-0. We choose the same residual-blocks as corresponding ones in the encoder part. Therefore, different responses from the encoder are able to be introduced to the corresponding blocks for more original semantic features. For each sub-stream network, each layer feeds the features to the corresponding layer of the other sub-stream network before the next layer accepts the features. For example, the output of Depth-1 is fed to the KIL modules before Seg-1 and Depth-2. In addition, it will exchange with the output of Seg-1 before it arrives Depth-2. The KIL module is designed to learn and leverage the connection between the information of depth estimation and semantic segmentation. Specifically, feature maps of the dual tasks will interactive in the module, where the common information will be enhanced selectively and be more adaptive for the current tasks.

Furthermore, a coarse-to-fine strategy is taken for rebuilding fine-grained details and predcitions. So, we predict the results after every scale layer and use multi-scale loss.

3.2 Knowledge Interactiveness Learning Module

As mentioned in Sect. 1, depth estimation and semantic segmentation are both high-level tasks of and they have some common information like object boundaries. The point is finding and utilizing the relationship between two tasks' information. Therefore, we design a module and use it before each residual-block except Depth-0 and Seg-0 for learning the interactiveness between tasks and also enhance the important semantic information. As illustrated in Fig. 2, depth features and segmentation features are firstly concatenated and then fed to an average-pooling layer. Here we use H, W, C represents the height, the width and the number of channels. It squeezes the input feature from the size of $H \times W \times C$ to $1 \times 1 \times C$ one-dimensional vector, from which we can get the global receptive field. We use D to represent depth feature, S represent segmentation feature and P is the average pooling layer:

$$F = P(concat(D, S)) \tag{1}$$

where $F \in 1 \times 1 \times C$ is the vector containing global information. Then, we put F through two linear layers Θ_1, Θ_2 with parameters W_1, W_2. In order to reduce the cost of computing, just like SENet [20], we scale the number of channels. Specifically, the input channel of Θ_1 is k times of output channel while the input channel of Θ_2 is $\frac{1}{k}$ times of output channel. From that, a high response attentional map M is achieved:

$$\begin{aligned} F' &= ReLu(\Theta_1(F, W_1)) \\ M &= Sigmoid(\Theta_2(F', W_2)) \end{aligned} \tag{2}$$

Next we use two fully-connected layers, represented by FC_1, FC_2, to do the non-linear operation. The goal is to resize the shape of attentional map M. Therefore, we can get two weights $w1$, $w2$ and the sizes of them fit the depth and segmentation features. They also keep global information. Formally:

$$\begin{aligned} w_1 &= FC_1(M) \\ w_2 &= FC_2(M) \end{aligned} \tag{3}$$

Finally, $w1$, $w2$ are used to generate the gated depth and segmentation features. Thus, we can get the enhanced feature D' and S':

$$\begin{aligned} D' &= (1 + w1) \bullet D \\ S' &= (1 + w2) \bullet S \end{aligned} \tag{4}$$

where D', S' are enhanced features through the learned weights, $\bullet$ means the matrix multiplication. After achieving D' and S', we connect them and pass the

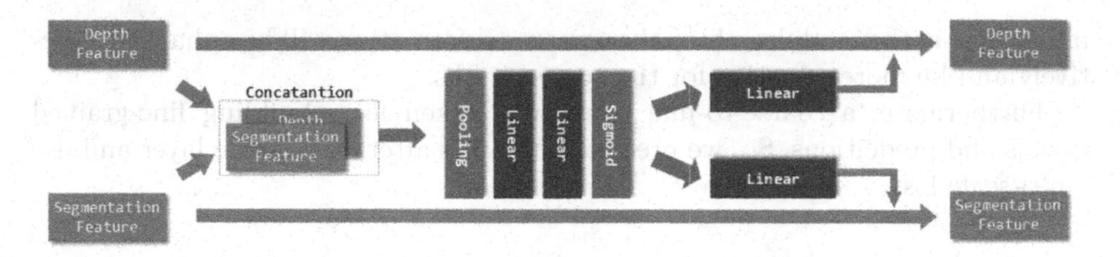

Fig. 2. The overview of our knowledge interactiveness learning module. It can mine and leverage the connections/complementations of these two tasks effectively. For find correlated relationships, depth features and segmentation features are firstly concatenated. Then, the concatenated features are fed to an average-pooling layer to integrate global information. After squeezing and extending, we obtain two weights for depth and segmentation information respectly. Thus, the common information has been enhanced.

concatenation through one convolutional layer. The analysis of the module can benefit dual tasks is shown in Sect. 4.

3.3 Network Training

Due to our two-stream network architecture, we adapt different loss function for depth estimation and semantic segmentation. Also, in order to achieve multi-scale predictions, we use supervised loss function.

For depth estimation, we use Huber Loss defined in [22], formally:

$$L^D(x_i, x_i') = \begin{cases} |x_i - x_i'|, |x_i - x_i'| \leq \delta \\ \frac{(x_i - x_i')^2 + \delta^2}{2\delta}, otherwise \end{cases} \tag{5}$$

where L^D is the loss for depth, x_i, x_i' represent the prediction results and ground truth respectively. In our experiment, $\delta = 0.2max|x_i - x_i'|$. Huber loss contains the advantages of MSE and MAE, thus it can benifit the network training. As to semantic segmentaion, we use the cross-entropy loss represented by L^S:

$$L^S(y_i, y_i') = -\log \frac{e^{y_i}}{e^{y_i'}} \tag{6}$$

Finally, suppose there are N scales of depth and segmentation predict-maps, the total loss can be defined as:

$$L(\theta_1, \theta_2) = \frac{1}{\theta_1^2} \sum_N L^D + \frac{1}{\theta_2^2} \sum_N L^S + \log(\theta_1^2) + \log(\theta_2^2) \tag{7}$$

where θ_1, θ_2 are weights to the two tasks. Actually, there may be a case where one of θ_1, θ_2 is zero in the experimental operation. In order to avoid this, we make $\mu = log(\theta)$ to eliminate the logarithmic function in the formula. So, we can get the finally loss function as following:

$$L(\mu_1, \mu_2) = \exp(-\mu_1) \sum_N L^D + \exp(-\mu_2) \sum_N L^S + \mu_1 + \mu_2 \tag{8}$$

4 Experiment

Datasets: SUN-RGBD dataset [38] is a very large and challenging dataset containing 10355 RGB-D images of indoor scenes. These images are divided into 37 classes including wall, table, floor etc. All these images have both segmentation and depth labels. Because of various shapes and poses of object classes, it is hard to complete this task. We use 5285 images for training and 5050 for testing according to the official documents. To increase the diversity of data, we have taken the same data augmentation strategy as [18]: scaling, flipping, cropping and rotating. NYU Depth-v2 dataset [32] is a popular dataset with RGB-D images of natural indoor scenes. It contains both segmentation and depth labels. However, only 1449 selected frames from 40 classes are labeled for segmentation labels. Thus, we use the standard training/testing split with 795 images and 654 images. We take the data augmentation strategy as SUN-RGBD dataset too. Due to the lack of training data, we then attempt to pre-train depth subnetwork on 4205 images with only depth estimation label and freeze segmentation subnetwork before training the dual tasks.

Implementation Details: We implement the proposed network using the Pytorch framework. The whole training procedure costs 30 hours on a single Nvidia P40 GPU. ReLU activating function and Batch Normalization are applied behind every convolutional layers except the final layers before the predictions. Our training process is divided into two parts for SUN-RGBD and NYU Depth-V2 dataset. First, we train our network with the learning rate of 0.01. Meanwhile, we fine-tune the encoder with the learning rate of 1e-4. After 50 epochs, we move on to the next stage with the decoder's learning rate of 0.001 and encoder's learning rate of 1e-5 for 20 epochs. During every step, the Optimizer is SGD and its momentum is 0.9. The batchSize is set to 16.

To evaluate our segmentation prediction results, We follow the previous work [13,22], use three methods: pixel-accuracy(pix-acc), mean accuracy(mean-acc) and mean class intersection over union (IoU). For prediction results of depth estimation, we evaluate them with the following methods just as [1, 43]:average relative error (rel): $\frac{1}{n}\sum_i \frac{|x_i' - x_i|}{x_i}$, root mean squared error (rms): $\sqrt{\frac{1}{n}\sum_i (x_i' - x_i)^2}$, accuracy with threshold (δ):% of x_i', s.t. $\max(\frac{x_i'}{x_i}, \frac{x_i}{x_i'}) = \delta$ where δ takes a value of 1.25^3, x_i' represents predictions of depth at pixel i and x_i is the ground truth.

4.1 Ablation Study

For the purpose of validating the effectiveness of our proposed KIL network, we set up experiments of different network architectures. In these architectures, they all have the same encoder part but different decoder. ResNet-50 is an infrastructure for all these ablation experiments. First, we set the baseline work. The interaction of depth and segmentation information in its decoder is replaced

Table 1. Comparisons of different network architectures and the baseline on SUN-RGBD dataset

Method	Pix-acc	Mean-acc	IoU	rmse	$\delta = 1.25^3$
Baseline	81.9	50.4	44.6	0.535	0.989
KIL with d1& s1	82.0	51.5	45.6	0.478	0.990
KIL with d2& s2	81.9	52.0	45.7	0.484	0.989
KIL with d3& s3	81.8	51.6	44.8	0.488	0.989
KIL-ResNet50	84.0	57.6	51.5	0.436	0.992

by concatenating dual tasks directly. As shown in Table. 1, compared with the baseline, the network architecture with our proposed KIL module performs better on both depth and segmentation tasks. Specifically, for segmentation metric, the network with KIL improves the performance of the baseline by 2.1% on pixel accuracy, 7.2% on mean-accuracy and 6.9% on IoU. Apart from this, we also achieve a lower value on rmse, decreasing 9.9% compared with the baseline network and also gain 3% on $\delta = 1.25^3$.

We also attempt to verify if KIL works on each scale layer. Therefore, we set up it separately before each scale of the network layer. We can easily find that no matter which layer we add the module to, the performance of the network is improved to varying degrees. For example, the statistics of network with KIL only in Depth-0 and Seg-0 are 1.1% more than the baseline and in Depth-2 and Seg-2 are 1.6% more than the baseline network. This can prove that it has a good effect on dealing with high-level and low-level semantic information.

Table 2. Our final evaluation results comparing with the state-of-the-art semantic segmentation approaches on SUN-RGBD dataset.

Method	data	Pixel-acc	Mean-acc	IoU
B-SegNet [1]	RGB	71.2	45.9	30.7
Context [18]	RGB	78.4	53.4	42.3
RefineNet-101 [17]	RGB	80.4	57.8	45.7
TRL-ResNet50 [49]	RGB	83.6	58.9	50.3
PAP [48]	RGB	83.8	58.4	50.5
LSTM-cf. [47]	RGBD	–	48.1	–
Cheng *et al.* [43]	RGBD	–	58.0	–
RDF-152 [36]	RGBD	81.5	**60.1**	47.7
3D-GNN [41]	RGBD	–	57.0	45.9
CFN [14]	RGBD	–	–	48.1
Ours-ResNet50	RGB	**84.0**	57.6	**51.5**
Ours-ResNet101	RGB	84.8	58.0	52.0

4.2 Comparisions with the State-of-the-Art Methods

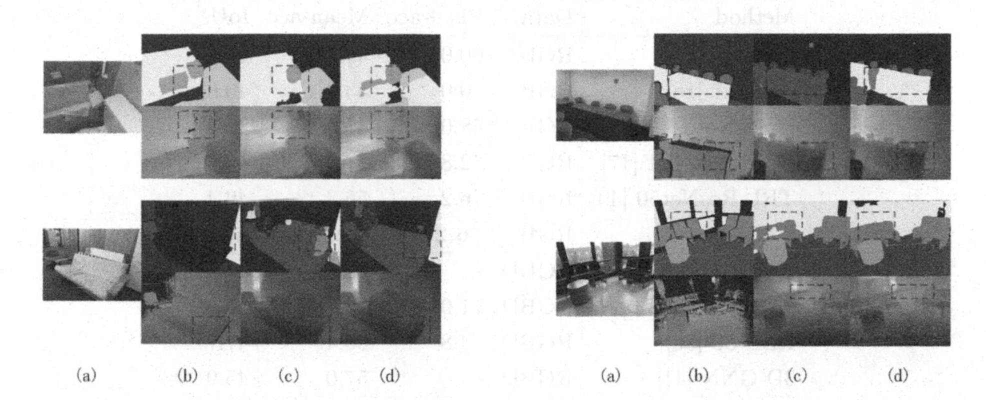

Fig. 3. visualizations of segmentation and depth prediction on SUN-RGBD dataset. (a) input RGB image; (b) ground truth; (c) result of [49]; (d) results of our KIL based on ResNet-50 architecture. We can easily find that the predictions of ours contain more details and are more precise.

Semantic Segmentaion: We compare our proposed KIL with the state-of-the-art methods on SUN-RGBD and NYU Depth-V2 dataset. As to SUN-RGBD dataset, evaluations of different models are displayed in Table 2. As quantitative results show that although using only RGB as input, the performance of our proposed KIL is competitive. Statistic results show that our work achieves the best pixel accuracy and class mean IoU, but slightly poor on class mean accuracy than RDF-152 [36]. Specifically, for instance, our KIL outperforms TRL [49] by 1.2% on pixel accuracy, 1.7% on class mean IoU and achieves a total 5.6% gain comparing with RDF-152 based on ResNet-101. It is worth mentioning that the input of RDF-152 in [36] is more than RGB images, they use depth ground truth as input too. What's more, they choose the stronger network architecture: ResNet-152. So, despite that the results of our method are slightly poor on mean accuracy but is still comparable.

To show the results of our method are more intuitively, we show some visual comparison examples on SUN-RGBD dataset in Fig. 3. It is easily to find that the predictions of ours contain more details than the method [49]. Specifically, the boundaries of objects like chairs in the result images are more clear.

For NYU Depth-V2 dataset, we focus on working with ResNet-101. As illustrated in the Table 3, although our work hasn't obtained the state-of-the-art results, ours is still good. Our slightly poor results may due to the reason that PAP [48] consider depth, surface normal and segmentation information simultaneously. Therefore, each task can get more comprehensive information that usually makes the model more robust.

Table 3. Our final evaluation results comparing with the state-of-the-art semantic segmentation approaches on NYU Depth-V2 dataset.

Method	Data	Pixel-acc	Mean-acc	IoU
FCN	RGB	60.0	49.2	29.2
Context [18]	RGB	70.0	53.6	40.6
B-SegNet [1]	RGB	68.0	45.8	32.4
RefineNet-101 [17]	RGB	72.8	57.8	44.9
TRL-ResNet50 [49]	RGB	76.2	56.3	46.4
PAP [48]	RGB	**76.2**	**62.5**	**50.4**
LSTM-cf. [47]	RGBD	–	49.4	–
Cheng *et al.* [43]	RGBD	71.9	60.7	45.9
RDF-50 [36]	RGBD	74.8	60.4	47.7
3D-GNN [41]	RGBD	–	57.0	45.9
Ours-ResNet101	RGB	75.1	58.4	50.2

Table 4. Comparisons with the state-of-the-art depth estimation approaches on NYU Depth-V2 dataset.

Method	Data	Lower is better↓		Higher is better↑
		rmse	rel	$\delta = 1.25^3$
HCRF [6]	795	0.821	0.232	0.968
DCNF [16]	795	0.824	0.230	0.971
Wang [33]	795	0.745	0.220	0.970
NR forest [3]	795	0.744	0.187	–
Xu *et al.* [8]	795	0.593	0.125	0.986
PAD-Net [9]	795	0.582	0.120	0.987
Eigen *et al.* 2014 [12]	120k	0.877	0.214	0.971
Eigen *et al.* 2015 [13]	120k	0.641	0.158	0.988
FCRN [22]	12k	0.573	0.127	0.988
AdaD-S [26]	100k	0.506	**0.114**	0.991
TRL-ResNet50 [49]	12k	0.501	0.144	0.992
PAP [48]	12k	**0.497**	0.121	**0.994**
Our-ResNet101	795	0.554	0.167	0.987
Ours with more data	5K	0.511↓	0.141↓	0.991↑

Depth Estimation: To evaluate our work on depth estimation, we mainly focus on experiments with ResNet-101 on the NYU Depth-V2 dataset. We benchmark the proposed method against several other well-adopted architectures for depth estimation. From the Table. 4, ours are slightly poor in metrics. The main reason is the lack of data. Just as mentioned before, the NYU Depth-V2 dataset only contains 765 images with both semantic and depth labels for training and 654 for testing. The number of input images is much less than other competitive methods shown in the table. Such as AdaD-S [26] used 120k images as input and PAP [48] use 12k. After we increase the input images, the performance of our work becomes better. Specifically, in comparison with our work with 795 images as input, we decrease rmse 3.9% and rel 2.3% while gain 3% in $\delta = 1.25^3$ after using 5k images as input. There are enough reasons for us to believe that we can achieve better performance if we use more data.

5 Conclusion

In this paper, we tend to design a module to fuse the information between tasks flexibly and adaptively. Thus, we proposed an end-to-end network to solve depth estimation and semantic segmentation synchronously and a knowledge interactieness leanring module which can be used as a general layer. This module can learn how to deal with feature maps from the dual tasks and strengthen the information which is helpful for the learning of another task. Extensive experiments display our KIL network is able to learn adaptively and enhance the valuable information. We also demonstrate some state-of-the-art results on SUN-RGBD and NYU Depth-V2 dataset in this paper. In the future, we will attempt to improve the performance of our work and also generalize it on more challenging tasks in computer vision.

Acknowlegdement. This work was supported by the National Natural Science Foundation of China (Grants Nos. 61972204, 61772276, 61906094), the Natural Science Foundation of Jiangsu Province (Grant No. BK20191283), the fundamental research funds for the central universities (No. 30919011232).

References

1. Kendall, A., Badrinarayanan, V., Cipolla, R.: Bayesian segNet: model uncertainty in deep convolutional encoder-decoder architectures for scene understanding. arXiv preprint arXiv:1511.02680 (2015)
2. Jalali, A., Sanghavi, S., Ruan, C., Ravikumar, P.K.: A dirty model for multi-task learning. In: Advances in Neural Information Processing Systems, pp. 964–972 (2010)
3. Roy, A., Todorovic, S.: Monocular depth estimation using neural regression forest. In: Proceedings of the IEEE Conference on Computer Vision and Pattern Recognition, pp. 5506–5514 (2016)
4. Saxena, A., Sun, M., Ng, A.Y.: Make3D: learning 3d scene structure from a single still image. IEEE Trans. Pattern Anal. Mach. Intell. **31**(5), 824–840 (2008)
5. Saxena, A., Chung, S.H., Ng, A.Y.: Learning depth from single monocular images. In: Advances in Neural Information Processing Systems, pp. 1161–1168 (2006)
6. Li, B., Shen, C., Dai, Y., Van Den Hengel, A., He, M.: Depth and surface normal estimation from monocular images using regression on deep features and hierarchical CRFs. In: Proceedings of the IEEE Conference on Computer Vision and Pattern Recognition, pp. 1119–1127 (2015)

7. Caruana, R.: Multitask learning. Mach. Learn. **28**(1), 41–75 (1997)
8. Xu, D., Ricci, E., Ouyang, W., Wang, X., Sebe, N.: Multi-scale continuous crfs as sequential deep networks for monocular depth estimation. In: Proceedings of the IEEE Conference on Computer Vision and Pattern Recognition, pp. 5354–5362 (2017)
9. Xu, D., Ouyang, W., Wang, X., Sebe, N.: Pad-Net: multi-tasks guided prediction-and-distillation network for simultaneous depth estimation and scene parsing. In: Proceedings of the IEEE Conference on Computer Vision and Pattern Recognition, pp. 675–684 (2018)
10. Ilea, D.E., Whelan, P.F.: Image segmentation based on the integration of colour-texture descriptors-a review. Pattern Recogn. **44**(10–11), 2479–2501 (2011)
11. Daniel, W., Remi, R., Edmond, B.: A survey of vision-based methods for action representation, segmentation and recognition. Comput. Vis. Image Understand. **115**(2), 224–241 (2011)
12. Eigen, D., Puhrsch, C., Fergus, R.: Depth map prediction from a single image using a multi-scale deep network. In: Advances in Neural Information Processing Systems, pp. 2366–2374 (2014)
13. Eigen, D., Fergus, R.: Predicting depth, surface normals and semantic labels with a common multi-scale convolutional architecture. In: Proceedings of the IEEE International Conference on Computer Vision, pp. 2650–2658 (2015)
14. Lin, D., Chen, G., Cohen-Or, D., Heng, P.A., Huang, H.: Cascaded feature network for semantic segmentation of RGB-D images. In: Proceedings of the IEEE International Conference on Computer Vision, pp. 1311–1319 (2017)
15. Liu, F., Shen, C., Lin, G.: Deep convolutional neural fields for depth estimation from a single image. In: Proceedings of the IEEE Conference on Computer Vision and Pattern Recognition, pp. 5162–5170 (2015)
16. Liu, F., Shen, C., Lin, G., Reid, I.: Learning depth from single monocular images using deep convolutional neural fields. IEEE Trans. Pattern Anal. Mach. Intell. **38**(10), 2024–2039 (2015)
17. Lin, G., Milan, A., Shen, C., Reid, I.: RefineNet: multi-path refinement networks for high-resolution semantic segmentation. In: Proceedings of the IEEE Conference on Computer Vision and Pattern Recognition, pp. 1925–1934 (2017)
18. Lin, G., Shen, C., Van Den Hengel, A., Reid, I.: Efficient piecewise training of deep structured models for semantic segmentation. In: Proceedings of the IEEE Conference on Computer Vision and Pattern Recognition, pp. 3194–3203 (2016)
19. Hadsell, R., et al.: Learning long-range vision for autonomous off-road driving. J. Field Robot. **26**, 120–144 (2009)
20. Hu, J., Shen, L., Sun, G.: Squeeze-and-excitation networks. In: Proceedings of the IEEE Conference on Computer Vision and Pattern Recognition, pp. 7132–7141 (2018)
21. Fu, H., Gong, M., Wang, C., Batmanghelich, K., Tao, D.: Deep ordinal regression network for monocular depth estimation. In: Proceedings of the IEEE Conference on Computer Vision and Pattern Recognition, pp. 2002–2011 (2018)
22. Laina, I., Rupprecht, C., Belagiannis, V., Tombari, F., Navab, N.: Deeper depth prediction with fully convolutional residual networks. In: 2016 Fourth International Conference on 3D Vision (3DV), pp. 239–248 (2016)
23. Misra, I., Shrivastava, A., Gupta, A., Hebert, M.: Cross-stitch networks for multi-task learning. In: Proceedings of the IEEE Conference on Computer Vision and Pattern Recognition, pp. 3994–4003 (2016)

24. Yosinski, J., Clune, J., Bengio, Y., Lipson, H.: How transferable are features in deep neural networks? In: Advances in Neural Information Processing Systems, pp. 3320–3328 (2014)
25. Deng, J., Dong, W., Socher, R., Li, L.J., Li, K., Fei-Fei, L.: ImageNet: a large-scale hierarchical image database. In: Proceedings of the IEEE Conference on Computer Vision and Pattern Recognition, pp. 248–255 (2009)
26. Nath Kundu, J., Krishna Uppala, P., Pahuja, A., Venkatesh Babu, R.: AdaDepth: unsupervised content congruent adaptation for depth estimation. In: Proceedings of the IEEE Conference on Computer Vision and Pattern Recognition, pp. 2656 2665 (2018)
27. Baxter, J.: A Bayesian/information theoretic model of learning to learn via multiple task sampling. Mach. Learn. **28**(1), 7–39 (1997)
28. Long, J., Shelhamer, E., Darrell, T.: Fully convolutional networks for semantic segmentation. In: Proceedings of the IEEE Conference on Computer Vision and Pattern Recognition, pp. 3431–3440 (2015)
29. He, K., Zhang, X., Ren, S., Sun, J.: Deep residual learning for image recognition. In: Proceedings of the IEEE Conference on Computer Vision and Pattern Recognition, pp. 770–778 (2016)
30. Tateno, K., Tombari, F., Laina, I., Navab, N.: CNN-SLAM: real-time dense monocular slam with learned depth prediction. In: Proceedings of the IEEE Conference on Computer Vision and Pattern Recognition, pp. 6243–6252 (2017)
31. Long, M., Wang, J.: Learning multiple tasks with deep relationship networks. arXiv preprint arXiv:1506.02117 2 (2015)
32. Silberman, N., Hoiem, D., Kohli, P., Fergus, R.: Indoor segmentation and support inference from RGBD images. In: Fitzgibbon, A., Lazebnik, S., Perona, P., Sato, Y., Schmid, C. (eds.) ECCV 2012. LNCS, vol. 7576, pp. 746–760. Springer, Heidelberg (2012). https://doi.org/10.1007/978-3-642-33715-4_54
33. Wang, P., Shen, X., Lin, Z., Cohen, S., Price, B., Yuille, A.L.: Towards unified depth and semantic prediction from a single image. In: Proceedings of the IEEE Conference on Computer Vision and Pattern Recognition, pp. 2800–2809 (2015)
34. Jarvis, R.A.: A perspective on range finding techniques for computer vision. IEEE Trans. Pattern Anal. Mach. Intell. **PAMI–5**(2), 122–139 (1983)
35. Geman, S., Geman, D.: Stochastic relaxation, Gibbs distribution and tlle Bayesian restoration of images. IEEE Trans. Pattern Anal. Machine Intell. 721–741
36. Park, S.J., Hong, K.S. and Lee, S.: RDFNet: RGB-D multi-level residual feature fusion for indoor semantic segmentation. In: Proceedings of the IEEE International Conference on Computer Vision, pp. 4980–4989 (2017)
37. Liu, S., Johns, E., Davison, A.J.: End-to-end multi-task learning with attention. In: Proceedings of the IEEE Conference on Computer Vision and Pattern Recognition, pp. 1871–1880 (2019)
38. Song, S., Lichtenberg, S.P., Xiao, J.: SUN RGB-D: A RGB-D scene understanding benchmark suite. In: Proceedings of the IEEE Conference on Computer Vision and Pattern Recognition, pp. 567–576 (2015)
39. Evgeniou, T., Micchelli, C.A., Pontil, M.: Learning multiple tasks with kernel methods. J. Mach. Learn. Res. **6**(Apr), 615–637 (2005)
40. Gebru, T., Hoffman, J., Fei-Fei, L.: Fine-grained recognition in the wild: a multitask domain adaptation approach. In: Proceedings of the IEEE International Conference on Computer Vision, pp. 1349–1358 (2017)
41. Qi, X., Liao, R., Jia, J., Fidler, S., Urtasun, R.: 3d graph neural networks for RGBD semantic segmentation. In: Proceedings of the IEEE International Conference on Computer Vision, pp. 5199–5208 (2017)

42. Yang, X., Gao, Y., Luo, H., Liao, C., Cheng, K.T.: Bayesian DeNet: monocular depth prediction and frame-wise fusion with synchronized uncertainty. IEEE Trans. Multimed. **21**(11), 2701–2713 (2019)
43. Cheng, Y., Cai, R., Li, Z., Zhao, X., Huang, K.: Locality-sensitive deconvolution networks with gated fusion for RGB-D indoor semantic segmentation. In: Proceedings of the IEEE Conference on Computer Vision and Pattern Recognition, pp. 3029–3037 (2017)
44. Yang, Y., Hospedales, T.M.: Trace norm regularised deep multi-task learning. arXiv preprint arXiv:1606.04038 (2016)
45. Liu, Y., Guo, Y., Lew, M.S.: On the exploration of convolutional fusion networks for visual recognition. In: International Conference on Multimedia Modeling, pp. 277–289 (2017)
46. Chen, Y., Li, W., Chen, X., Gool, L.V.: Learning semantic segmentation from synthetic data: a geometrically guided input-output adaptation approach. In: Proceedings of the IEEE Conference on Computer Vision and Pattern Recognition, pp. 1841–1850 (2019)
47. Li, Z., Gan, Y., Liang, X., Yu, Y., Cheng, H., Lin, L.,: LSTM-CF: unifying context modeling and fusion with LSTMs for RGB-D scene labeling. In: European Conference on Computer Vision, pp. 541–557 (2016)
48. Zhang, Z., Cui, Z., Xu, C., Yan, Y., Sebe, N., Yang, J.: Pattern-affinitive propagation across depth, surface normal and semantic segmentation. In: Proceedings of the IEEE Conference on Computer Vision and Pattern Recognition, pp. 4106–4115 (2019)
49. Zhang, Z., Cui, Z., Xu, C., Jie, Z., Li, X., Yang, J.: Joint task-recursive learning for semantic segmentation and depth estimation. In: Proceedings of the European Conference on Computer Vision, pp. 235–251 (2018)

Road Scene Risk Perception for Intelligent Vehicles Using End-to-End Affordance Learning and Visual Reasoning

Jayani Withanawasam[1(✉)], Ehsan Javanmardi[2], Kelvin Wong[2], Mahdi Javanmardi[2], and Shunsuke Kamijo[1,2]

[1] Department of Information and Communication Engineering, The University of Tokyo, Tokyo, Japan
withanawasamjayani@kmj.iis.u-tokyo.ac.jp, kamijo@iis.u-tokyo.ac.jp
[2] Institute of Industrial Science, The University of Tokyo, Tokyo, Japan
{ehsan,kelvinwong,mahdi}@kmj.iis.u-tokyo.ac.jp

Abstract. A key goal of intelligent vehicles is to provide a safer and more efficient method of transportation. One important aspect of intelligent vehicles is to understand the road scene using vehicle-mounted camera images. Perceiving the level of driving risk of a given road scene enables intelligent vehicles to drive more efficiently without compromising on safety. Existing road scene understanding methods, however, do not explicitly nor holistically model this notion of driving risk. This paper proposes a new perspective on scene risk perception by modeling end-to-end road scene affordance using a weakly supervised classifier. A subset of images from BDD100k dataset was relabeled to evaluate the proposed model. Experimental results show that the proposed model is able to correctly classify three different levels of risk. Further, saliency maps were used to demonstrate that the proposed model is capable of visually reasoning about the underlying causes of its decision. By understanding risk holistically, the proposed method is intended to be complementary to existing advanced driver assistance systems and autonomous vehicles.

Keywords: Road scene understanding · Scene understanding · Road safety

1 Introduction

Recently there has been an unprecedented interest both in academia and in the industry towards intelligent vehicles. Achieving the optimal efficiency without compromising the safety is not merely a favorable outcome of intelligent vehicles, but a key requirement which necessitates them. Perceiving the potentially dangerous situations earlier helps both human drivers and intelligent vehicles to remain more vigilant and preempt hazardous situations. Human drivers make

S. Palaiahnakote et al. (Eds.): ACPR 2019, LNCS 12046, pp. 849–862, 2020.
https://doi.org/10.1007/978-3-030-41404-7_60

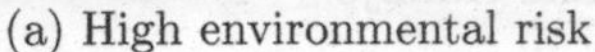

(a) High environmental risk (b) Low environmental risk

Fig. 1. Imagine you are a driver. Can you guess which scene you should be more vigilant than the other just by looking at the scene? (i.e., which scene is safe to accelerate and which scene should you stay on alert?) Can you reason about what makes one scene potentially riskier than the other? Can intelligent vehicles understand the same way?

both safe and efficient driving maneuver by simultaneously considering multiple risk factors in the environment effortlessly. While collision avoidance is one such factor, the right amount of driving action (e.g., acceleration or deceleration, steering) and the level of environmental risk depends on multiple scene attributes such as pedestrians, distance to the nearby vehicles, road layout, time of the day (e.g., daytime or night) and weather conditions (e.g., rain or snow). For example, drivers should be more vigilant during a rainy night in a congested road than during a sunny day having few vehicles around. Human drivers are capable of grasping this conceptual scene gist (the high-level meaning of the scene)[13] intuitively, instantly and more holistically by looking at the driving scene. Having an intuitive sense of potential danger helps human drivers to drive more vigilantly without compromising efficiency.

Recent progress on modular road scene understanding methods such as pedestrian and vehicle detection and drivable area segmentation largely contributes towards collision avoidance for safe navigation.

While these semantic recognition based methods (i.e., what is where?) are appealing, as the first step towards road scene understanding, reaching higher levels of visual intelligence requires functional scene understanding that goes beyond recognition to effectively interact with the environment. Scene affordance (i.e., what can I do?) [5] that models the opportunities for interactions with the environment (instead of merely modeling the semantics of the scene), has gained recent attention in the computer vision community as the next level towards a better understanding of a scene [12]. Even though learning visual affordance is useful for safe navigation, it is not widely used in holistic road scene understanding [6].

In this work, we explore an alternative paradigm to complement the environment perception in intelligent vehicles by providing them with the aforementioned intuitive sense of potential danger.

We ask the following research question in our study. *How can we computationally perceive the intuitive sense of potential danger in a road scene and visually reason about the underlying risk factors involved?* We define three levels of risk (high, medium, low) to represent the intuitive sense of potential danger. They are based on the presence of different environmental risk factors (e.g., pedestrians on the cross-walk, moving close to near-by vehicles). The environmental risk factors are selected from different sources on road safety such as factors that contribute to road accidents.

Further, when learning an abstract semantic concept such as risk (e.g., high risk), that is caused by multiple concrete concepts (e.g., night, traffic congestion, bad weather), a naive way to achieve this is to explicitly label the underlying concrete concepts and use them along with abstract concepts to train the model. However, this involves a high labeling effort.

Instead, we propose a more intelligent, reverse engineered, weakly supervised approach to train the model to learn the abstract concept of risk. A more intelligent model is a model that can learn the underlying concrete concepts on its own, given only the abstract label per scene. However, an autonomous vehicle is a safety-critical application, so we need to ensure that the model actually learns the relevant concrete concepts given only the abstract labels. Consequently, we train the model only using abstract labels and localize the regions that contribute towards its decision using saliency maps to reason if they include the right concrete concepts. The risk caused by the mispredictions of this model is asymmetric. In other words, predicting a given road scene as low risk in an actual high-risk scenario is more dangerous than predicting as high risk when it is actually low risk. Accordingly, in addition to standard accuracy, we evaluate our model against a different evaluation metric that takes the said aspect into consideration as well.

Our contributions in this paper are given below.

1. Different perspective on holistic road scene understanding to perceive environmental risk in weakly supervised manner
2. Different evaluation strategy to assess both safety and efficiency of the proposed model

2 Related Work on Road Scene Understanding

Recent advances in road scene understanding for autonomous vehicles are primarily twofold. The first line of work operate on multiple modules such as pedestrian detection, vehicle detection, and drivable road area segmentation separately and then integrate them later using rule based methods for total road scene understanding. The second line of work follows end-to-end learning (e.g., imitation learning) to map the raw camera sensor input directly to the required actuator output. Additionally, there are emerging road scene understanding methods based on affordance learning and visual reasoning.

2.1 Modular Methods

Modular methods (also stated as 'mediated perception' [2]) such as obstacle detection and drivable area segmentation are largely inspired by the recent successes in deep learning algorithms for object detection and semantic segmentation. Recognition tasks focus on detecting, localizing and semantically classifying individual road object instances such as vehicles and pedestrians one by one. Improvements on these tasks were proposed to predict their future behavior as well, for example, by analyzing the intent of the pedestrians and predicting the future path they may navigate [15]. Recent holistic road scene understanding methods [22] are typically based on semantic segmentation where each pixel of a given road scene is assigned to a predefined semantic category such as road, building or sky. Above tasks implicitly model the notion of risk as a collision avoidance problem. While avoiding collisions is paramount for the safe and convenient path planning and motion control decisions, there are other factors such as weather, time of the day, and road conditions (e.g., merging lanes or bends), traffic congestion level that need to be collectively considered when intuitively perceiving risk of any situation. Such global contextual information along with other spatial information in the scene (e.g., spatial relationships, spatial layout) is lost at different processing stages of these modules. For example, when segmenting a road scene to predefined semantic categories (e.g., vehicle, tree, sky) the expectation is set beforehand on the possible observations in the environment, preventing models learning the ambient context that those categories have to offer (e.g., weather, time of the day). Further, the cumulative error of the system due to open research problems in different modules may lead to severe accuracy degradation, hence affecting the overall safety. Also, the processing time becomes a bottleneck in real time operation as the outcomes of these individual modules needs to be integrated to reason about a given traffic situation. Moreover, high labeling cost is involved to train these modules in terms of bounding boxes or pixel level labels. However, these methods are relatively semantically interpretable as opposed to end-to-end learning based methods.

2.2 End-to-End Learning

Recently there is a surge of interest on end-to-end learning methods that directly map the input road scene to required driving action. Current end-to-end learning methods either map the input road scene to steering angle (imitation learning) [1,23] or to one particular aspect of the driving task such as lane change (block or free) [8] or brake decision (stop or go) [26]. Even though these methods also implicitly address risk as a collision avoidance problem in a more holistic manner by avoiding dangerous maneuver, it is challenging to semantically interpret the rationale behind the control decision. Further, end-to-end learning based methods are not semantically guided by human experts during the labeling process. Even though the imitation learning based methods ease the process of data collection, they avoid manually designing the complex intermediate representations that require human design.

2.3 Affordance Learning

Recently, a third new paradigm (more task-driven) is proposed in scene understanding to learn visual affordance [5]. Visual affordance models possible interactions with the environment (human-scene interactions). While the majority of them focus on perceiving the functionality of objects, not many research available on outdoor scene understanding [6]. In [2], visual affordance is modeled for individual object instances relevant for the driving task (e.g., distance to the preceding car, availability of right lanc) in highways. In [17], it is extended to urban setting (e.g., traffic light, speed sign information). Even though having an intuitive sense of potential danger is useful to know when to interact with the environment more vigilantly (i.e., safe maneuver), such global situational context is largely ignored in these methods.

2.4 Visual Reasoning

Visual reasoning is a key aspect of visual intelligence in making rational decisions. Visual common sense reasoning is an emerging area in scene understanding [25]. Currently, Visual Question Answering (VQA), using both images and language is the most widely used method of accommodating visual common sense reasoning. However, an accurate textual explanation may incur an additional overhead rather than an advantage in autonomous vehicles due to their time-critical operation. In [14], environmental causes of different driving actions (e.g., make a stop because the front car stopped) are identified and localized using bounding boxes. However, the environmental risk and the potential underlying risk factors (e.g., the scene is dangerous because there are pedestrians in the road) are not yet accommodated explicitly and holistically to incorporate the intuitive sense of potential danger.

3 Proposed Method

According to affordance theory, learning scene affordance demands to have an understanding of the possible interactions with the environment. When it comes to controlling locomotion (e.g., walking, driving an automobile), having awareness and distinguishing the possible beneficial situations from situations that might be injurious (positive and negative affordances) is essential for safe and efficient navigation [5].

3.1 Road Scene Risk Perception Using End-to-End Affordance Learning

Our goal is to encompass intelligent vehicles with an intuitive sense of potential danger when perceiving a road scene.

We represent the intuitive sense of potential danger quantitatively by specifying three levels of risk. A risky situation is a potentially dangerous situation that might lead to hazardous events in the future. Since human risk perception is subjective [20], we need a systematic way to define objective risk in our method. For that, we use the following aspects to define a potentially dangerous situation.

- Environmental factors that contribute to road accidents (e.g., poor weather conditions such as rain, snow) [16]
- Tricky road situations for autonomous vehicles that necessitate strict human driver monitoring (e.g., moving too close to other vehicles) [4]
- Road situations that human drivers should be more vigilant while driving (e.g., parked vehicles) [10]

Based on the above aspects, we define a set of environmental risk factors along with potential hazards that can cause due to those environmental risk factors. In order to avoid subjective measurement while determining a reliable ground truth, we specify the criteria for three risk levels (low, medium, high) using the identified risk factors as given in Table 1.

Table 1. Risk level of the road scene and underlying risk factors.

Risk level	Environmental risk factors
High risk	• Pedestrians on the road • Vehicle immediately ahead/ moving too close • Complex road layout (bend/ merging lanes/ intersections) • Road-side parked cars • Cross walk • Poor weather conditions such as rain, snow • Traffic complexity (More than three vehicles around in the visible range)
Medium risk	• Less than or equal to three vehicles around (Mid traffic complexity) • No vehicles around (night time)
Low risk	• No vehicles around in day time (Low traffic complexity)

We process input road scenes from a vehicle-mounted monocular camera. To process the scene holistically without ignoring the contextual information, we use an end-to-end learning mechanism as opposed to modular methods using scene-parsing techniques. Example images for each category are given in Fig. 2.

BDD100k dataset [24] has images taken in different environmental conditions such as different times of the day (e.g., day time or night time), different weather conditions (e.g., sunny, snow, rain), and different nature of roads (e.g., urban, highway, residential). The image dimension in pixels is 1280*720. We use a subset of the BDD100k dataset. To avoid selection bias, we select the first 1500 images. We exclude 26 of them due to poor quality such as blurriness. The remaining images are used with the new annotation scheme given in Table 1. The number of training and test images for each category are given in Table 2.

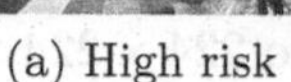
(a) High risk

(b) Medium risk

(c) Low risk

Fig. 2. Example road scenes for each risk level

Table 2. Dataset statistics

Type of images	High risk	Medium risk	Low risk
Number of train images	605	320	223
Number of test images	222	70	34
Total (Class-wise)	827	390	257

Achieving a good accuracy using the proposed method is challenging due to high intra-class variance and low inter-class variance. Inspired by the recent advances in deep neural networks, we use a convolutional neural network (CNN) for scene affordance classification. We use ResNet-18 [7], an image classifier with relatively small model capacity that has outperformed other classifiers. Further, we use transfer learning to alleviate the limited number of training examples (with pre-trained weights using ImageNet dataset [3]).

3.2 Weakly Supervised Visual Reasoning of Underlying Risk Factors

Risk is an intangible abstract concept, where as the underlying risk factors form tangible concrete semantic concepts. Even though we give image labels for each risk level, we do not give any explicit labels for the underlying risk factors that constitute those risk levels. However, since an intelligent vehicle is a safety-critical application, we need to ensure that the model is capable of providing a rationale for its decision. Accordingly, the model should be able to answer the question on 'why a given road scene belongs to a given risk category?' by reasoning about the underlying risk factors (e.g., the road scene is risky because there is a vehicle immediately ahead). To demonstrate that, we re-purpose deriving saliency maps using Grad-cam [18] to visually reason if the classification decision is made upon correct underlying risk factors for the predicted risk level.

4 Experimental Results and Evaluation

We evaluate the test accuracy based on the following configurations.

1. ResNet-18 Fixed: Use fixed pre-trained weights and fine-tune only fully connected layer (using Adam)
2. ResNet-18 Trained from scratch: Train the network from the scratch (without using pre-trained weights, using Adam)
3. ResNet-18 Finetune: use pre-trained weights for initialization and fine-tune all the layers (SGD + momentum, Adam, Weighted loss with Adam)

We resize our input images of dimension $1280 \times 720 \times 3$ to $224 \times 224 \times 3$ to fit the network architecture. The network is trained using Adam optimization algorithm with a learning rate of 0.0001. Cross entropy loss is used as the loss function. The network is trained on a GPU with mini-batch size of 4.

Results are given in Table 3. Class-wise recall is given in Table 4.

Table 3. Test accuracy

Trained model	Test accuracy (%)
ResNet-18: Fixed (Adam)	74
ResNet-18: Trained from scratch (Adam)	75
ResNet-18: Finetune (SGD+Momentum)	77
ResNet-18: Finetune (Adam)	**79**
ResNet-18: Finetune (Weighted loss with Adam)	78

Table 4. Class-wise recall

Trained model	High risk	Medium risk	Low risk
ResNet-18: Fixed (Adam)	0.80	0.48	0.75
ResNet-18: Trained from scratch (Adam)	0.83	0.45	0.81
ResNet-18: Finetune (SGD+Momentum)	0.80	0.66	0.87
ResNet-18: Finetune (Adam)	0.81	0.64	**0.84**
ResNet-18: Finetune (weighted loss with Adam)	0.83	0.62	**0.93**

The preliminary results in Table 3 on test accuracy show that when the model is trained from the scratch, it performs slightly better than fine-tuning only the final fully-connected layers (while using pre-trained weights for other layers). However, fine-tuning all the layers further improves the test accuracy. Overall, even though there are high inter-class similarity and a varying number of scene risk factors involved for each class, the model is capable of achieving reasonable success in distinguishing between three different levels of risk.

'High risk' class contains the highest number of scene risk factors (7 risk factors as given in Table 1), hence the highest appearance variation in terms of color, texture, and scale. Still, 'high risk' class has a relatively high accuracy in most cases than the classes with lesser scene risk factors such as 'medium risk' as shown in Table 4. One possible explanation for this observation could be the imbalanced nature of the data set. The number of training examples available for each class is approximately proportional to the number of scene risk factors for each class. Further, there is class-wise recall degradation in the 'medium risk' class, probably due to the inter-class similarity between 'high risk' (e.g., presence of vehicles) and 'low risk' (e.g., ample free road space). Further, even though, applying weighted loss function has a small accuracy degradation (from 79% to 78%) in the overall test accuracy, it has improved the class-wise recall of 'low risk' class (from 0.84 to 0.93), which has a low number of training examples.

The processing latency of our model is less than 28ms on average on Nvidia GeForce GTX 1080. That falls well within the real-time constraint of 100ms for intelligent vehicles [11].

4.1 Using Saliency Maps for Visual Reasoning

The saliency maps for some road scenes from each risk level are given in Fig. 3. The model is able to correctly pick the relevant concrete concepts (i.e., underlying risk factors) that cause the road scene to belong to a given risk level. The concrete concepts for 'high risk' such as 'vehicle immediately ahead', 'crosswalk', 'pedestrian on the road' and 'parked vehicles' are understood collectively irrespective of their scale, color or viewpoint. Also, it is important to note that in addition to the most prominent concrete concepts, the surrounding background (e.g., daytime or night, weather) is also considered, with lower significance, for the classification decision. The model is able to recognize the concrete concepts such as 'fewer vehicles around' for the 'medium risk' class. Also, 'free road space available during day time' is correctly captured for the 'low risk' class. However, the model poorly performs with the snow-covered road scenes and bends, probably due to the less number of training examples available.

4.2 Different Evaluation Strategy to Assess Safety and Efficiency of the Model

The risk of misprediction of the proposed classifier is asymmetric. In other words, given a pair of predicted class and actual class, the risk of misprediction is either higher or lower for the misprediction with same class pair conversely. For example, if the model predicts as 'low risk' for an actual 'high risk' road scene, the result can be fatal, whereas if the model predicts 'low' for an actual 'high risk' it will cause inefficiency and slight inconvenience for the passengers in the vehicle as well as for the surrounding vehicles, yet it cannot cause fatal accidents as the former misprediction. We propose a different evaluation strategy, in addition to the standard accuracy measure, to validate this effect for a given model.

In the classification context, accuracy can be measured as a combination of true positives and true negatives over the total number of predictions. Precision and recall measures are necessary to evaluate the relevance of the model.

(a) Risk level: High, Reason: Pedestrian on the road

(b) Risk level: High, Reason: Vehicle immediately ahead

(c) Risk level: High, Reason: High traffic complexity

(d) Risk level: High, Reason: Road side parked vehicles

(e) Risk level: Medium, Reason: Few vehicles around

(f) Risk level: Low, Reason: No vehicles around (free road space)

Fig. 3. Saliency maps to visually reason about the underlying risk factors for each risk level

Safety Precision. The standard precision measure for a multi-class problem measures the positive prediction value, in other words, given all the predicted pairs for a given class i, (both true positives and false positive) how many of them were correctly predicted (true positives). In our context, the risk of increasing the mispredictions in terms of **false positives for 'low risk' class** is higher than the other cases. Accordingly, we redefine the precision measure, that we coin as safety-precision as given in the Eq. 1.

$$Safety\_Precision = \frac{TP_{ii}}{TP_{ii} + \Sigma_{j \in [0,1]} FP_{ji}} \tag{1}$$

where i = 2, (0: high risk, 1: medium risk, 2:low risk)

Safety Recall. Recall measures the sensitivity, in other words, given all the prediction pairs that should have been correct (both true positives and false negatives), how many of them were correctly predicted. In our context, the risk of increasing the **false negatives for the class 'high risk'** causes a higher risk than the other misprediction pairs. Accordingly, we redefine the recall measure as safety-recall in the Eq. 2.

$$Safety\_Recall = \frac{TP_{ii}}{TP_{ii} + \Sigma_{j\in[1,2]} FN_{ij}} \tag{2}$$

where i = 0, (0: high risk, 1: medium risk, 2:low risk)

Then, we consider the harmonic mean of the safety-recall and safety-precision to calculate the safety score of the model as given in Eq. 3.

$$Safety\_Score = 2 * \frac{Safety\_Precision * Safety\_Recall}{Safety\_Precision + Safety\_Recall} \tag{3}$$

Efficiency. Efficiency measures based on precision and recall measures the convenience of the ride. In other words, does the vehicle slow down when it is possible to speed up, causing other vehicles also stranded behind? It is the opposite of the safety measure. Efficiency precision and efficiency recall are given in Eq. 4 and Eq. 5 respectively. Efficiency score is given in Eq. 6.

$$Efficiency\_Precision = \frac{TP_{ii}}{TP_{ii} + \Sigma_{j\in[1,2]} FP_{ji}} \tag{4}$$

where i = 0 (0: high risk, 1: medium risk, 2:low risk)

$$Efficiency\_Recall = \frac{TP_{ii}}{TP_{ii} + \Sigma_{j\in[1,2]} FN_{ij}} \tag{5}$$

where i = 2 (0: high risk, 1: medium risk, 2:low risk)

$$Efficiency\_Score = 2 * \frac{Efficiency\_Precision * Efficiency\_Recall}{Efficiency\_Precision + Efficiency\_Recall} \tag{6}$$

The experimental results for safety and efficiency are given in Table 5 and Table 6 respectively. The results show that the model is capable of achieving high efficiency with a reasonable level of safety. Safety precision is relatively lower than safety recall, probably due to the mispredictions caused by appearance similarity between complex road layouts such as bends without vehicles (high risk) and free roads with no vehicles around (low risk).

4.3 Comparison with Other Studies

We propose a new paradigm for scene understanding that goes 'beyond recognition', so it is challenging for us to directly compare with the other existing road

Table 5. Safety evaluation

Trained model	Safety precision	Safety recall	Safety score
ResNet-18: Fixed (Adam)	0.52	0.80	0.63
ResNet-18: Trained from scratch (Adam)	0.52	0.83	0.63
ResNet-18: Finetune (SGD+Momentum)	0.46	0.80	0.58
ResNet-18: Finetune (Adam)	0.53	0.81	**0.64**
ResNet-18: Finetune (weighted loss with Adam)	0.50	0.83	0.61

Table 6. Efficiency evaluation

Trained model	Efficiency precision	Efficiency recall	Efficiency score
ResNet-18: Fixed (Adam)	0.85	0.75	0.79
ResNet-18: Trained from scratch (Adam)	0.85	0.81	0.82
ResNet-18: Finetune (SGD+Momentum)	0.92	0.87	0.89
ResNet-18: Finetune (Adam)	0.89	0.84	0.86
ResNet-18: Finetune (weighted loss with Adam)	0.92	0.93	**0.92**

scene understanding methods. However, we can roughly compare some aspects such as the labeling effort and computation time. For example, road semantic segmentation, the most widely used method for holistic scene understanding requires pixel-level labeling for each region and takes 62.5 ms (around 3 times slower than our proposed method) on average [19]. So, our method is suitable to acquire a quick scene gist, before detailed semantic understanding.

Further, even though, understanding abstract concepts of the scene such as an intuitive sense of potential danger are not common for road scenes, there are other studies for general holistic scene understanding to understand abstract concepts such as communicative intent [9] or affective scene understanding for movies [21]. However, in such cases, the underlying low-level aspects require explicit labels or modular level processing, whereas in our case we use explicit labels only at high-level. So, this kind of saliency map-based approach (to verify the low-level aspects) may be generalizable in such cases to provide weak supervision.

5 Applications of Road Scene Risk Perception

Understanding the environmental risk helps intelligent vehicles to be aware of the level of vigilance required in any given driving situation. It is useful for human driver distraction monitoring systems in advanced driver assistance systems (ADAS). The level of damage that can cause by driver distraction is proportional to the level of environmental risk (i.e., if the driver is distracted when there are other vehicles closely around, it can be more dangerous than when driving on a road with ample of free space without any vehicles around). Having an understanding of the level of environmental risk helps to provide different levels of warnings (e.g., beep sounds). This way of scene understanding is also useful for monitoring the human driver vigilance in semi-autonomous vehicles during tricky situations (for automated take-over requests based on scene context).

6 Conclusion and Future Work

We proposed an end-to-end weakly supervised classifier to learn road scene affordance for risk perception. Given the road scenes from a monocular camera mounted on the vehicle, the goal was to acquire an intuitive sense of potential danger to achieve optimal efficiency without compromising safety. We defined three levels of risks with underlying environmental risk factors for each level. Instead of densely annotating the low-level risk factors, we used saliency maps for visual reasoning and localization of underlying low-level risk factors. Further, we used different evaluation criteria to measure the asymmetric risk of misprediction. Future work includes extending the proposed method to video understanding.

References

1. Bojarski, M., et al.: End to end learning for self-driving cars. http://arxiv.org/abs/1604.07316
2. Chen, C., Seff, A., Kornhauser, A., Xiao, J.: DeepDriving: learning affordance for direct perception in autonomous driving. In: 2015 IEEE International Conference on Computer Vision (ICCV), pp. 2722–2730. IEEE. https://doi.org/10.1109/ICCV.2015.312, http://ieeexplore.ieee.org/document/7410669/
3. Deng, J., Dong, W., Socher, R., Li, L.J., Li, K., Fei-Fei, L.: ImageNet: a large-scale hierarchical image database. In: CVPR09 (2009)
4. Fridman, L., Brown, D.E., Kindelsberger, J., Angell, L., Mehler, B., Reimer, B.: Human side of tesla autopilot: Exploration of functional vigilance in real-world human-machine collaboration
5. Gibson, J.J.: The Ecological Approach to Visual Perception: classic edition. Psychology Press (2014)
6. Hassanin, M., Khan, S., Tahtali, M.: Visual affordance and function understanding: a survey (2018). arXiv preprint, arXiv:1807.06775
7. He, K., Zhang, X., Ren, S., Sun, J.: Deep residual learning for image recognition. CoRR abs/1512.03385 (2015). http://arxiv.org/abs/1512.03385
8. Jeong, S.G., Kim, J., Kim, S., Min, J.: End-to-end learning of image based lane-change decision. http://arxiv.org/abs/1706.08211
9. Joo, J., Li, W., Steen, F.F., Zhu, S.C.: Visual persuasion: inferring communicative intents of images. In: 2014 IEEE Conference on Computer Vision and Pattern Recognition, pp. 216–223. IEEE. https://doi.org/10.1109/CVPR.2014.35, http://ieeexplore.ieee.org/lpdocs/epic03/wrapper.htm?arnumber=6909429

10. Kokubun, M., Konishi, H., Higuchi, K., Kurahashi, T., Umemura, Y., Nishi, H.: Assessment of drivers' risk perception using a simulator. R&D Rev. Toyota CRDL **39**(2), 9–15 (2004)
11. Lin, S.C., et al.: The architectural implications of autonomous driving: constraints and acceleration. In: Proceedings of the Twenty-Third International Conference on Architectural Support for Programming Languages and Operating Systems, pp. 751–766. ACM (2018)
12. Lüddecke, T., Wörgötter, F.: Scene affordance: inferring actions from household scenes. In: Workshop on Action and Anticipation for Visual Learning, European Conference on Computer Vision (2016)
13. Oliva, A.: Gist of the scene. In: Neurobiology of attention, pp. 251–256. Elsevier (2005)
14. Ramanishka, V., Chen, Y.T., Misu, T., Saenko, K.: Toward driving scene understanding: a dataset for learning driver behavior and causal reasoning. In: Proceedings of the IEEE Conference on Computer Vision and Pattern Recognition, pp. 7699–7707 (2018)
15. Rasouli, A., Kotseruba, I., Tsotsos, J.K.: Are they going to cross? A benchmark dataset and baseline for pedestrian crosswalk behavior. In: 2017 IEEE International Conference on Computer Vision Workshops (ICCVW), pp. 206–213. IEEE. https://doi.org/10.1109/ICCVW.2017.33, http://ieeexplore.ieee.org/document/8265243/
16. Rolison, J.J., Regev, S., Moutari, S., Feeney, A.: What are the factors that contribute to road accidents? an assessment of law enforcement views, ordinary drivers' opinions, and road accident records. Accid. Anal. Prev. **115**, 11–24 (2018)
17. Sauer, A., Savinov, N., Geiger, A.: Conditional affordance learning for driving in urban environments. arXiv preprint arXiv:1806.06498 (2018)
18. Selvaraju, R.R., Cogswell, M., Das, A., Vedantam, R., Parikh, D., Batra, D.: Grad-CAM: Visual explanations from deep networks via gradient-based localization. http://arxiv.org/abs/1610.02391
19. Siam, M., Gamal, M., Abdel-Razek, M., Yogamani, S., Jagersand, M., Zhang, H.: A comparative study of real-time semantic segmentation for autonomous driving. In: Proceedings of the IEEE Conference on Computer Vision and Pattern Recognition Workshops, pp. 587–597 (2018)
20. Sjöberg, L., Moen, B.E., Rundmo, T.: Explaining risk perception. an evaluation of the psychometric paradigm in risk perception research. Rotunde publikasjoner Rotunde 84, 55–76 (2004)
21. Wang, H.L., Cheong, L.F.: Affective understanding in film. IEEE Trans. Circuits Syst. Video Technol. **16**(6), 689–704 (2006)
22. Wang, S., Fidler, S., Urtasun, R.: Holistic 3d scene understanding from a single geo-tagged image. In: 2015 IEEE Conference on Computer Vision and Pattern Recognition (CVPR), pp. 3964–3972. IEEE. https://doi.org/10.1109/CVPR.2015.7299022, http://ieeexplore.ieee.org/document/7299022/
23. Xu, H., Gao, Y., Yu, F., Darrell, T.: End-to-end learning of driving models from large-scale video datasets. http://arxiv.org/abs/1612.01079
24. Yu, F., et al.: BDD100K: A diverse driving video database with scalable annotation tooling. CoRR abs/1805.04687 (2018). http://arxiv.org/abs/1805.04687
25. Zellers, R., Bisk, Y., Farhadi, A., Choi, Y.: From recognition to cognition: visual commonsense reasoning. In: Proceedings of the IEEE Conference on Computer Vision and Pattern Recognition, pp. 6720–6731 (2019)
26. Čermák, J., Angelova, A.: Learning with proxy supervision for end-to-end visual learning. In: 2017 IEEE Intelligent Vehicles Symposium (IV), pp. 1–6 (2018)

Image2Height: Self-height Estimation from a Single-Shot Image

Kei Shimonishi[1(✉)], Tyler Fisher[2], Hiroaki Kawashima[3], and Kotaro Funakoshi[1]

[1] Kyoto University, Kyoto, Kyoto, Japan
{shimonishi,funakoshi.k}@i.kyoto-u.ac.jp
[2] University of Victoria, Victoria, BC, Canada
fisher.tyler2@gmail.com
[3] University of Hyogo, Kobe, Hyogo, Japan
kawashima@sis.u-hyogo.ac.jp

Abstract. This paper analyzes a self-height estimation method from a single-shot image using a convolutional architecture. To estimate the height where the image was captured, the method utilizes object-related scene structure contained in a single image in contrast to SLAM methods, which use geometric calculation on sequential images. Therefore, a variety of application domains from wearable computing (e.g., estimation of wearer's height) to the analysis of archived images can be considered. This paper shows that (1) fine tuning from a pretrained object-recognition architecture contributes also to self-height estimation and that (2) not only visual features but their location on an image is fundamental to the self-height estimation task. We verify these two points through the comparison of different learning conditions, such as preprocessing and initialization, and also visualization and sensitivity analysis using a dataset obtained in indoor environments.

Keywords: Self-height estimation · Convolutional neural network · Interpretation · Visualization

1 Introduction

Given a single photo of scenery, a person can roughly estimate the height where the picture was captured. With information of a scene's structure, one can easily recognize that a picture was captured from lower height (e.g., by a small kid) or from the top of a staircase. This estimation may be based not on precise geometric calculation but on "knowledge" of scene, such as size of objects and their location in a scene. In a room, for example, the appearance of furniture (e.g., which surface of a table is observable) provides a clue to infer the height. The goal of this work is to mimic this process: Given a single-shot image, we address the problem of estimating the height of the camera/viewpoint where the image was captured.

S. Palaiahnakote et al. (Eds.): ACPR 2019, LNCS 12046, pp. 863–877, 2020.
https://doi.org/10.1007/978-3-030-41404-7_61

In this paper, we analyze a self-height estimation method from a single-shot image using a convolutional network. In contrast to visual simultaneous location and mapping (SLAM) methods [1,5,6], the proposed approach does not depend on a video sequence but exploits scene structure inside a single image. Therefore, even from a piece of photo in an album, the method can infer the height level of the camera when the image was captured. It is also applicable in a situation when the ground or floor is not visible in an image because the method utilizes the information of objects in a captured scene. That is, the proposed method tries to learn links between object information (e.g., categories, appearance, and location) and the height level of a camera.

We hypothesize that "visual features obtained through an object recognition task are also useful in our height-estimation task." Here, we define "self-height" as vertical distance of a camera from ground or floor, and we assume the camera is facing horizontally (not downward), i.e., the optical axis of the camera is almost parallel to the floor or ground surface. Under this situation, we verify the hypothesis from the following aspects:

1. We show that fine tuning from a pretrained convolutional network model for a standard object recognition task/dataset is also effective for a self-height estimation task.
2. We show that standard preprocessing used in object recognition is not necessarily appropriate for self-height estimation.
3. We visualize important regions in input images and analyze the sensitivity of network response on positional change of visual features.

Specifically, for the last aspect, we first utilize a popular visualization technique for a convolutional network model, gradient-weighted class activation mapping (Grad-CAM) [7], and then change the position of the visual feature found by the Grad-CAM map to investigate which information the trained networks exploit for the self-height estimation task.

To focus on the verification of the basic concept of our approach, we conduct experimental evaluation in indoor situations in particular in office rooms, while this is not a limitation of the proposed approach.

In the next section, we briefly discuss the novelty of our method compared to existing methods and also some related studies on visualization. In Sect. 3, we explain our approach, and in Sect. 4, we show experimental results, which are followed by discussion in Sect. 5. The work is concluded in Sect. 6.

2 Related Work

In the following sections, we summarize two types of self-height estimation methods: (1) geometric approach and (2) recognition-based approach. Then, we briefly explain a visualization technique called Grad-CAM and its related work.

2.1 Geometric Approach with Dynamic Scene Information

Stereo vision is a standard approach to estimate distance from an object to a camera given a sequence of images. From corresponding points on the ground appeared in multiple images captured with a moving camera, the height of the camera can be calculated using the information of camera pose and translation. This approach is mainly used when the camera is facing downward, multiple images are available, and an additional sensor for camera pose and motion is attached. Internal sensors are not necessarily required when the horizontal ground plane can be assumed, because the camera rotation/translation or its instantaneous velocities can be solved by a homography-based method [3].

Visual SLAM has been widely used recently in many application domains including robotics and wearable cameras for its simplicity of configuration, i.e., no additional sensors are required. By using sequential images captured by a monocular camera, visual SLAM approach simultaneously estimates the camera trajectory and reconstructs the 3D environment map [1,5,6]. In this approach, it is essential to capture images that have enough visual overlaps to solve camera calibration (extrinsic parameter estimation) and 3D reconstruction problems.

While the above mentioned techniques are promising to estimate camera location precisely, configuration assumed in our method is different, since we assume that only a single image is given, and the ground needs not necessarily be observable.

2.2 Recognition-Based Approach

Image-recognition techniques are now widely used for egocentric, or first-person vision applications. In particular, in the context of wearable devices, wearer's pose and identity is important to be inferred for many applications including daily-living activity monitoring and biometrics. Jiang and Grauman [4] proposed a learning-based approach to estimate wearer's invisible pose using video captured by an egocentric camera. They utilized homographies obtained from optical flows as dynamic features, trained a random-forest pose classifier, and compared it with other types of classifiers including convolutional neural networks (CNNs). They also combined static cues obtained by fine-tuned AlexNet to classify sitting and standing poses (i.e., two classes) to compensate situations with little motion.

Finocchiaro et al. [2] proposed to use a two stream network [8], consists of two CNNs with a late-integration architecture, where spatial information (pixel intensities of grey images) and temporal information (optical flows) are combined to estimate self-height from egocentric video. While the objective of the research is similar to ours, they assume to use not a single-shot image but video data since their focus is on wearable/egocentric cameras; that is, an image sequence is used as input not only in the temporal network but also in the spatial network.

Our motivation is different from the above mentioned related works. First, we only use a single-shot image as input to infer self-height to focus on situations when SLAM cannot be applied. Second, we evaluate the accuracy of self-height estimation using "leave-one-place-out," i.e., test data do not include images captured in the same places where training data obtained; this has not been clearly considered in the related studies. Third, we interpret the trained CNN architectures by visualizing class activation maps and also analyzing sensitivity to the change of visual-feature locations. Through the analysis, we reveal which information the trained CNNs utilize to estimate self-height.

2.3 Visualization Techniques for CNNs

While many visualization techniques try to obtain visual explanation of filters in trained CNNs (e.g., Deconvnet [11], Guided Backprop [10]), a technique called class activation mapping (CAM) [12] can be used to highlight discriminative regions for a specific class. This technique has been generalized by Selvaraju et al. as Grad-CAM [7].

Grad-CAM uses the gradients of the target-class score with respect to feature maps of the last convolutional layer. These gradients are linearly combined with the weights calculated by global average pooling of the gradients, and a ReLU is finally applied to the combined map to extract class-discriminative regions. Since Grad-CAM does not need any architectural change unlike CAM, which requires retraining with a fully-convolutional architecture, the technique can be used for a wide variety of CNN architectures. Grad-CAM can be further combined with Guided Backprop [10] to create Guided Grad-CAM for higher-resolution class-discriminative visualization [7].

3 Approach

3.1 Model

We consider an end-to-end simple architecture to achieve a single-shot self-height estimation. Given a single color image, we do minimum preprocessing and enter the pixel values to a CNN. As for the output, either a discrete class set of height levels or continuous values with regression-based network can be used. We here adopt a classification-based network, where each class corresponds to a range of height level.

Pretrained models of popular CNN architectures are expected to be useful for the self-height estimation task because of the following reason. When we manually estimate the height level where the image was captured, it is well known that a so-called "eye-level line" (also known as an eye line or horizon line) is useful. An eye-level line can be estimated from a single image by drawing a line that passes any vanishing point(s) found in the given image. Since the eye-level line corresponds to the height level where the image was captured, one can infer the self-height level by recognizing what kind of objects are above (or below) the eye-level line in the image. Therefore, the information found from objects in a scene is essential to self-height estimation.

We use a VGG16 as a standard object-recognition architecture, and utilize a model pretrained by ImageNet. As shown in many existing studies including the original work of VGG [9], the model has been proven to be useful for other tasks such as object localization. Another reason we use VGG16 is its simplicity, which can be an advantage for visualization purpose. Since other architectures can also be used, we later compare the accuracy of popular architectures including AlexNet and ResNet (see Sect. 4.2).

3.2 Fine Tuning and Preprocessing

Similar to standard manners of fine tuning [9], we swap the last fully-connected (FC) layer with randomly initialized linear layer whose output dimensionality corresponds to the number of height classes. All the remaining layers including fully-connected layers up to the second-last layer are initialized by the weights of the original model trained by the ImageNet dataset. Since we use five classes in the experiments, the last FC layer has 4096 inputs and 5 outputs.

In the fine-tuning step, we do not randomly crop partial images, because the location of objects must be important cues to estimate self-height, as discussed in Sect. 3.1.

In particular, we assume that the optical axis of the camera used for data capturing is parallel to the ground/floor (see Sect. 4.1 for details) and the image screen is not rotated around the optical axis (see Sect. 5 for discussions on more general configuration).

3.3 Visualization and Sensitivity Analysis

In addition to accuracy-based evaluation, we introduce several analyses to better understand why self-height can be estimated by trained CNNs (i.e., which information contributes to the self-height estimation).

As a qualitative analysis to interpret the trained model, we visualize important regions for the prediction of each height class using Grad-CAM [7]. Then, we quantitatively analyze the sensitivity of location of visual features using typical example images.

To conduct the analysis of location sensitivity, we first utilize Grad-CAM to find one of the most important regions in an image for the target-class classification. Once the maximum point of a Grad-CAM map is obtained, we crop a rectangle region around the point, and overlay the region on a grey image to generate a masked image; that is, the surrounding region except the overlaid region has grey color. We here call the grey region as *background*, and the overlaid region as *foreground*. Then, the sensitivity of the class output (before softmax) is examined by moving the foreground region vertically or horizontally.

Our hypothesis is that "the trained self-height estimation model is highly sensitive to the change of vertical position of the foreground compared to the change of horizontal position." As explained in the previous section, the eye-level line crosses horizontally on the center of the image in an ideal situation of our capturing configuration. Therefore, when a specific object (e.g., a door knob) is appeared vertically in the middle of an image, the height where the image was captured is almost the same as the actual object height (e.g., one meter or so for the door knob case).

In spite that semantic labels of objects in scenes are not given in the training phase, we expect that CNNs can learn the importance of *which objects/features located where* for height-level prediction. Of course, some objects or visual features are difficult to observe from some height levels (e.g., objects under the table). While such specific objects may have large importance independent of their position, for general objects/features, the importance should also depend on the objects' position in an image.

To simplify the analysis, we do not deal with combinatorial importance of multiple objects/features in the sensitivity analysis but only focus on the positional influence of a single fixed-size region around the point that yields the highest activation. However, the visualization of Grad-CAM heatmaps also tell us how multiple objects/features contribute to self-height estimation. Therefore, we also visualize averaged activation distribution of each height class (for each trained model) to understand which location in general is important to predict each height level.

4 Experiments

For the analysis of self-height estimation in this pilot study, we were especially interested in small-sized datasets of indoor scenes, because we wanted to evaluate the effect of fine tuning general object-recognition models using a limited number of images. A moderate variety of objects in indoor scenes is also preferable compared to outside scenes. Moreover, such indoor datasets can be easily divided based on "rooms," which allows us to conduct a what we call "leave-one-room-out (LORO)" test for generalization evaluation of trained models.

4.1 Data Collection

A Point Grey Research[1] Flea camera (1280 × 1024, color) was integrated with a SICK laser-based height sensor (DT35-B15851) to capture images with ground-truth height. Four rooms were captured continuously with 30 Hz for the camera and 5 Hz for the height sensor, and later the captured images were sampled randomly to obtain training and test datasets. Each ground-truth height of an image was selected from the sensor data within 50 ms the image was captured. The camera had a little rotation in tilt and roll angles, but was not completely adjusted and had non-negligible deviation in the both angles.

The captured four rooms were named as Room A, B, C, and D, where each pair of (A, B) and (C, D) were located in the same building, respectively. All the rooms were used for meetings; Room D also had a private office space separated by a white board but was not included in the captured data.

While more than 2k images were captured in each room, we manually checked the image quality and selected 748 to 750 images (depending on rooms) for

[1] Currently, FLIR Systems.

Table 1. Five class height-level categories (height range) used in the evaluation, and the sample size of each class used for training (tr.) and validation (val.).

Class	Range (mm)	Sample size (tr. + val.)
0	200–350	380 + 26
1	500–650	518 + 35
2	800–950	564 + 38
3	1100–1250	864 + 57
4	1400–1550	669 + 44

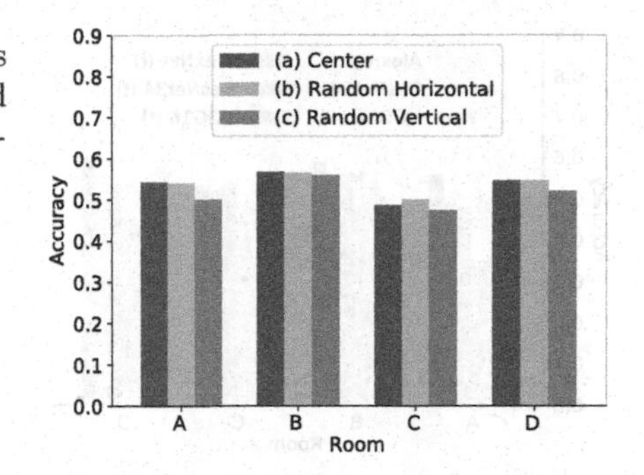

Fig. 1. Comparison of three cropping methods in each room (chance level: 0.2).

training, 49 to 51 images for validation in the training, and 250 images (50 for each class) for test.

Five height-level ranges were defined as height classes (categories), where each class had a range of 150 mm (see Table 1 for details including each sample size). To avoid intermediate data overlap between classes, a 150 mm gap was added between adjacent class ranges where no images were used.

4.2 Accuracy Evaluation

In the leave-one-room-out (LORO) test, data captured in three rooms were used for training and data from the remaining one room were used for test. Weighted sampling was used for training with different sample size among the classes.

Influence of Cropping Position. To compare the influence of cropping positions, we first show the result of the following three cropping: (a) center crop, (b) horizontal crop, and (c) vertical crop. Each method cropped a 800 × 800 partial image from an original 1280 × 1024 image and then resized it to 224 × 224 size. Each cropping position was however decided differently: (a) fixed position in the center of each image, (b) random horizontal position with fixed vertical position, (b) random vertical position with fixed horizontal position. There was no additional preprocessing except normalization of pixel values.

Because of the limited size of validation data, accuracy values may have some variance. For each room, we therefore conducted LORO ten times to reduce the parameter estimation variance. Figure 1 shows the mean accuracy of each room. The accuracy of (a) and (b) are almost same, while (c) shows slightly lower accuracy. This result suggests that vertical position of an image frame influences the result of self-height prediction, as discussed in Sect. 3.

In what follows, we adopt a variant of the cropping method (a): We do not crop a partial image but utilize the full region of an image frame and resize it to 224 × 224. Note that this changes the aspect ratio, but because we do the same resizing method for both training and test images, this change is expected to be accommodated by the fine-tuning step.

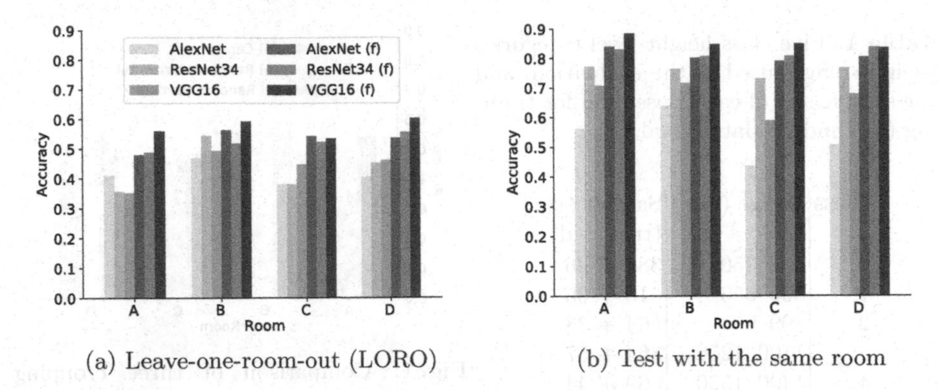

(a) Leave-one-room-out (LORO) (b) Test with the same room

Fig. 2. Comparison of CNN models in terms of both architecture types and initialization methods. The legend in (a) is shared by (b). The marks "(f)" in the legend denote that "fine tuning" had been applied to the models.

Comparison of CNN Architectures. We compared three CNN architectures (AlexNet, ResNet34, and VGG16) with two initialization methods (random and pretrained). Regarding preprocessing, standard random rotation (10 degree), color jitter, and horizontal flips were also applied in addition to the resize operation explained in the previous paragraph.

Figure 2a shows the result of these six cases for each room. Note that we conducted LORO tests, and thus data from a room for test was excluded from the corresponding training data. Similar to the previous experiment, we trained all the 24 (= 6 × 4 rooms) cases ten times each to reduce the variance of accuracy. All the accuracy scores were much higher than chance rate (20 %). As shown in the figure, VGG16 (pretrained) outperformed other architectures except for Room C, while its difference was small. It can also be found that the pretrained models had much better accuracy than the randomly initialized models. This suggests that visual features for object recognition contribute a lot even for self-height estimation from captured scenes, as discussed in Sect. 3.

For reference, we also tested room-specific models on the same-room data (i.e., non-LORO case), where the size of test data in each room was 200 to 202, where the test data were not included in the training data. From the results shown in Fig. 2b, the accuracy values of the same-room test were more than 80 % for VGG16 (pretrained). This result suggests that we need more variety of training data captured in many places for model generalization.

4.3 Visualization of Important Regions

Following the discussion in Sect. 3.3, we analyzed the trained models using visualization and sensitivity analysis to understand what is actually trained in the CNNs for self-height estimation. Note that all the VGG16 models used in this visualization were trained by LORO, i.e., data from the room used for test were excluded from the training data.

Class Activation Mapping. To visualize class-specific important regions, we utilized the Grad-CAM and Guided Grad-CAM [7] (see also Sect. 2.3). Figure 3 shows the visualization results of typical input data of class 0 (the lowest-height category) in each room[2]. For the visualization, the original 14 × 14 Grad-CAM maps were up-sampled to 224 × 224 using the Lanczos filter. In the third column, each Grad-CAM heatmap is visualized on the corresponding input image to show which parts were class discriminative.

As can be seen in Fig. 3, class 0 (the lowest-height category) tends to have high activation for specific objects on the floor. For example, the lower parts of furniture (e.g., legs or casters of chairs, sofas, and tables). Bottom corners of doors or walls seem to be important to predict lower-height categories, especially class 0. Figure 4 shows the visualization results of typical input data of each class (except class 0) in Room A. For example, one can see that the bottom of window frame had high activation in class 1 (Fig. 4a), whereas the top part of the window was high in class 4 (Fig. 4d). In addition, high activation regions for target class 1 to 3 (middle-height categories) widely spread inside an image frame.

What is suggested in this experiment is that multiple objects or visual features may contribute to the prediction of those middle-height classes. On the other hand, class 0 and 4 basically have high activation in bottom and top regions of an image frame, respectively (e.g., class 4 has activation in many parts on the ceiling of a room).

Spatial Distribution of Class-Specific Activation. To see the difference of Grad-CAM's spatial distribution statistically, we averaged Grad-CAM maps computed from the test images of each category in each room. Let $L_{ij}^{(k,r,c)}$ $(i, j \in \{1, ..., 14\})$ be the value of Grad-CAM activation for target class $c \in \{0, ..., 4\}$ on grid (i, j), where the grid corresponds to the last convolutional feature map of VGG16. The model was trained by data except those of Room $r \in \{A, B, C, D\}$. Then, we take mean $\bar{L}_{ij}^{(r,c)} = \frac{1}{K}\sum_{k=1}^{K} L_{ij}^{(k,r,c)}$, where $K = 50$ in our setting (see Sect. 4.1). The visualization of those mean distribution in Fig. 5 supports the findings discussed in the previous paragraph.

4.4 Sensitivity Analysis

To show the sensitivity of class outputs to the location of visual features, we conducted the analysis introduced in Sect. 3.3. The third and fourth columns of Fig. 6 respectively show typical examples of VGG16 output values with respect to vertical and horizontal displacement of each foreground region, where the region size was 80 × 80. Each image in the second column shows an example of created masked input (at the original position), where the most activated foreground region was cropped and moved vertically or horizontally.

[2] https://github.com/utkuozbulak/pytorch-cnn-visualizations was modified and used for the implementation.

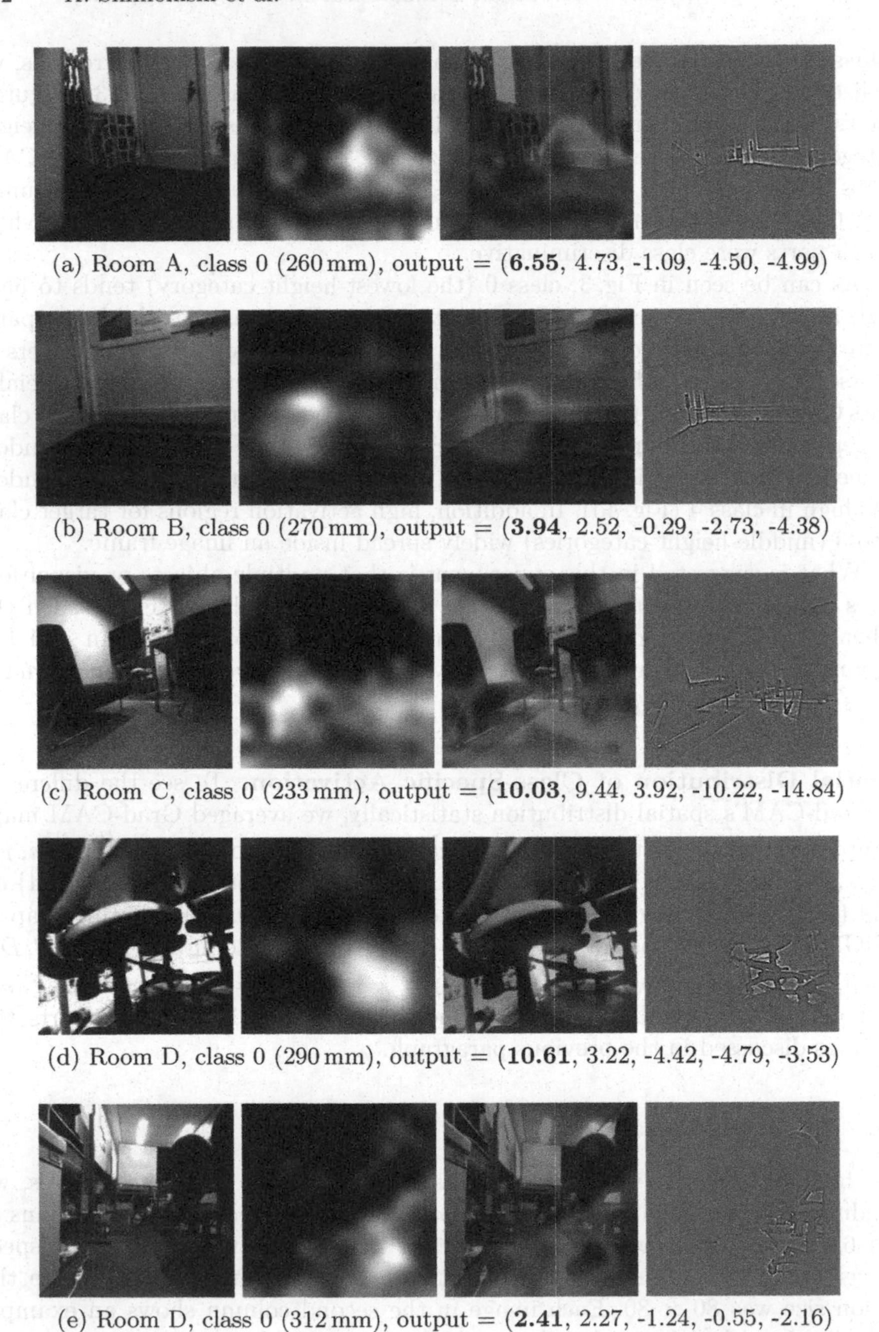

(a) Room A, class 0 (260 mm), output = (**6.55**, 4.73, -1.09, -4.50, -4.99)

(b) Room B, class 0 (270 mm), output = (**3.94**, 2.52, -0.29, -2.73, -4.38)

(c) Room C, class 0 (233 mm), output = (**10.03**, 9.44, 3.92, -10.22, -14.84)

(d) Room D, class 0 (290 mm), output = (**10.61**, 3.22, -4.42, -4.79, -3.53)

(e) Room D, class 0 (312 mm), output = (**2.41**, 2.27, -1.24, -0.55, -2.16)

Fig. 3. Visualization of class activation maps (class 0). From left to right: input image, Grad-CAM, its heatmap on the image, Guided Grad-CAM. Output values of VGG16 were also shown in each subcaption. Under the LORO evaluation, four VGG16 models (weights) were used for the visualization above (one for each room's input); each of the models was trained by three rooms' data except the room of input data.

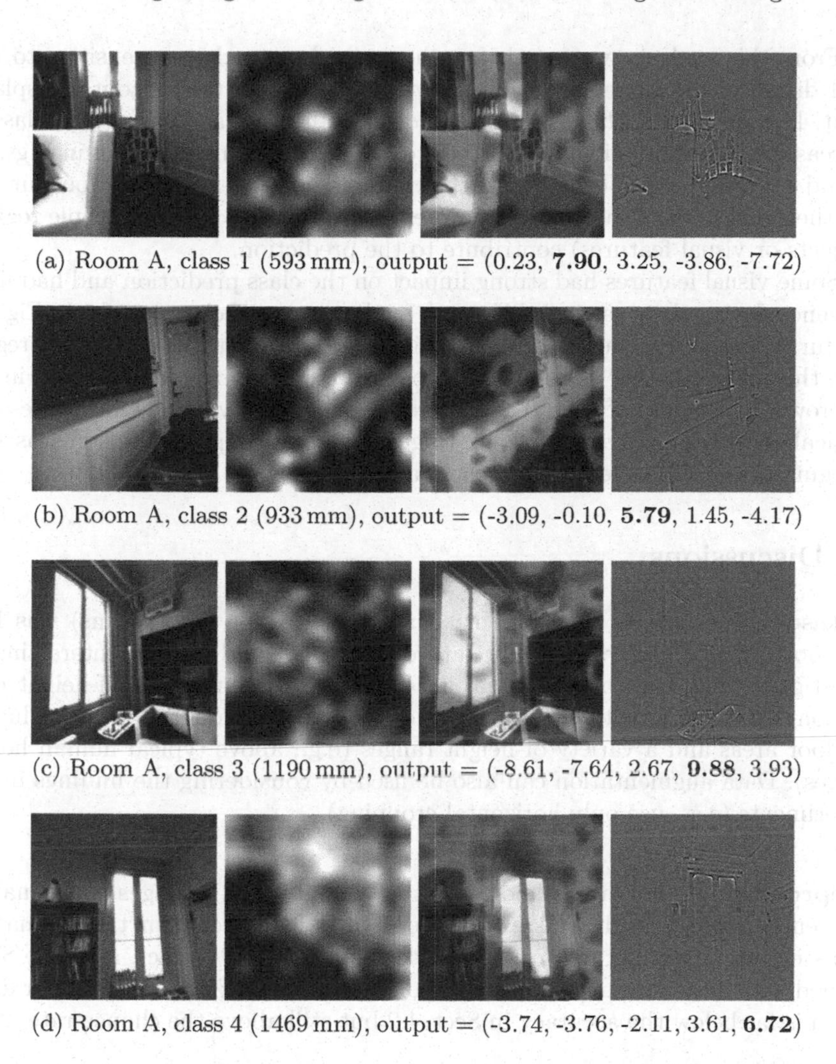
(a) Room A, class 1 (593 mm), output = (0.23, **7.90**, 3.25, -3.86, -7.72)

(b) Room A, class 2 (933 mm), output = (-3.09, -0.10, **5.79**, 1.45, -4.17)

(c) Room A, class 3 (1190 mm), output = (-8.61, -7.64, 2.67, **9.88**, 3.93)

(d) Room A, class 4 (1469 mm), output = (-3.74, -3.76, -2.11, 3.61, **6.72**)

Fig. 4. Visualization of class activation maps (Room A). From left to right: input image, Grad-CAM, its heatmap on the image, Guided Grad-CAM. One VGG16 model (weights) trained by Room {B, C, D} data was used for the visualization above.

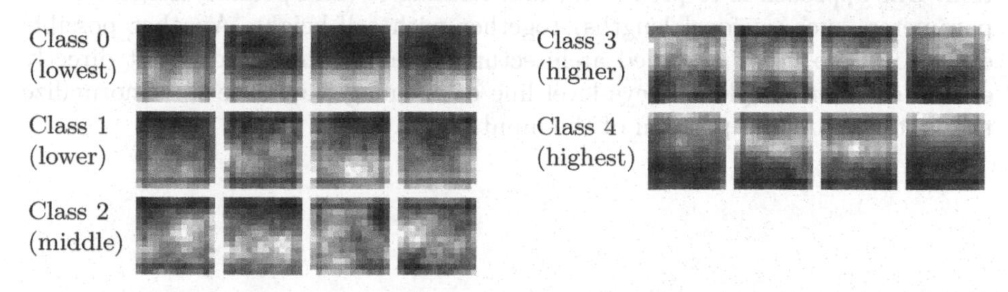

Fig. 5. Mean Grad-CAM of target class 0–4, test room A, B, C, D (from left to right).

From this analysis, we found that the trained networks are sensitive to vertical displacement of region, while they are insensitive to horizontal displacement. In many cases, the class outputs of lower-height categories (e.g., class 0) decreased when the region was moved from top to bottom as shown in Figs. 6a, b, and c. Note that, in each input, the class of the highest network output was not the same as the final classification result, particularly when multiple regions (objects or visual features) contribute to the prediction.

Some visual features had strong impact on the class prediction and had little influence during their vertical shift, such as the output of class 0 and 1 in Fig. 6d. We further replaced the foreground region in Fig. 6d with non-textured region with the averaged color of the original foreground. As shown in the result in the last row, the outputs of class 0 and 1 dropped drastically, and some classes had vertical sensitivity (class 4), which suggests that the replaced region was now recognized as a visual feature of other categories.

5 Discussions

Dataset. The dataset used in this study (i.e., indoor, four rooms) was limited both in size and variety. For future work, it would also be interesting to investigate what kind of additional general visual features for self-height estimation can be obtained by collecting and using large amount of data, including outdoor areas and a variety of height ranges (e.g., above typical human height ranges). Data augmentation can also be used by considering the findings in the experiments (e.g., use only horizontal cropping).

Preprocessing. For a method robust to illumination changes, illumination differences among height classes also need to be considered in the normalization step; usually, lower classes have darker illumination. In fact, a simple SVM trained with only illumination distributions got about 30% accuracy in our data, which is far below the accuracy in Sect. 4.2 but still above the chance rate, 20%.

Extensions. To apply the proposed approach to more general configuration and different cameras, a classifier needs to deal with general camera configuration. One approach is to predict tilt and roll angles (and possibly other camera parameters such as focal lengths) together with self-height. Another possible extension is to use a cascaded architecture: train another model that directly estimates, for example, the eye-level line of an image, and use it to normalize the vertical cropping position of the input image.

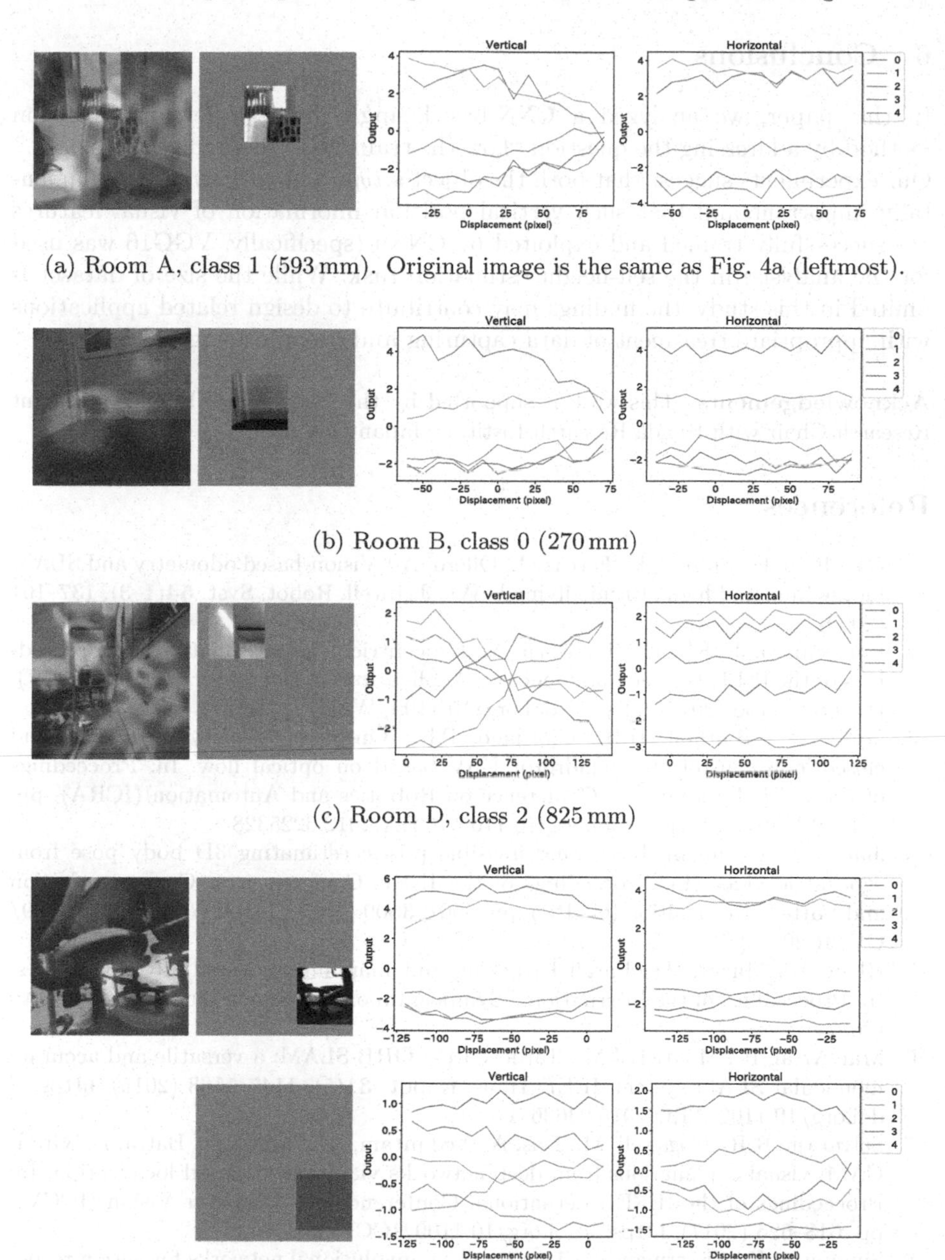

(a) Room A, class 1 (593 mm). Original image is the same as Fig. 4a (leftmost).

(b) Room B, class 0 (270 mm)

(c) Room D, class 2 (825 mm)

(d) Room D, class 0 (290 mm). Original image is the same as Fig. 3d (leftmost).

Fig. 6. Sensitivity analysis of VGG16 outputs to the displacement of the highest Grad-CAM region with masked background. From left to right: Grad-CAM heatmap on the image, input image (with the original foreground position), vertical sensitivity, horizontal sensitivity. Each line depicts a class output value from corresponding VGG16. The result on an artificial foreground (averaged color of the original foreground with no texture) is also shown in the second row of (d).

6 Conclusions

In this paper, we analyzed a CNN-based single-shot self-height estimation method by addressing the question "how the trained CNNs predict self-height." Our experiments suggest that both the object's *type* and *position* are fundamentally important and that such vertical position information of visual features are successfully trained and exploited by CNNs (specifically, VGG16 was used for the analysis) in the self-height estimation task. While the size of dataset is limited in this study, the findings may contribute to design related applications with appropriate treatment of data capturing and preprocessing.

Acknowledgements. This work is supported by the Cooperative Intelligence Joint Research Chair with Honda Research Institute Japan Co., Ltd.

References

1. Caballero, F., Merino, L., Ferruz, J., Ollero, A.: Vision-based odometry and SLAM for medium and high altitude flying UAVs. J. Intell. Robot. Syst. **54**(1–3), 137–161 (2009)
2. Finocchiaro, J., Khan, A.U., Borji, A.: Egocentric height estimation. In: Proceedings of the IEEE Winter Conference on Applications of Computer Vision (WACV), pp. 1142–1150 (2017). https://doi.org/10.1109/WACV.2017.132
3. Grabe, V., Bülthoff, H.H., Giordano, P.R.: On-board velocity estimation and closed-loop control of a quadrotor UAV based on optical flow. In: Proceedings of the IEEE International Conference on Robotics and Automation (ICRA), pp. 491–497 (2012). https://doi.org/10.1109/ICRA.2012.6225328
4. Jiang, H., Grauman, K.: Seeing invisible poses: estimating 3D body pose from egocentric video. In: Proceedings of the IEEE Conference on Computer Vision and Pattern Recognition (CVPR), pp. 3501–3509 (2017). https://doi.org/10.1109/CVPR.2017.373
5. Klein, G., Murray, D.: Parallel tracking and mapping for small AR workspaces. In: Proceedings of the International Symposium on Mixed and Augmented Reality (2007)
6. Mur-Artal, R., Montiel, J.M., Tardos, J.D.: ORB-SLAM: a versatile and accurate monocular SLAM system. IEEE Trans. Robot. **31**(5), 1147–1163 (2015). https://doi.org/10.1109/TRO.2015.2463671
7. Selvaraju, R.R., Cogswell, M., Das, A., Vedantam, R., Parikh, D., Batra, D.: Grad-CAM: visual explanations from deep networks via gradient-based localization. In: Proceedings of the IEEE International Conference on Computer Vision (ICCV), pp. 618–626 (2017). https://doi.org/10.1109/ICCV.2017.74
8. Simonyan, K., Zisserman, A.: Two-stream convolutional networks for action recognition in videos. In: Proceedings of the International Conference on Neural Information Processing Systems (NIPS), pp. 568–576 (2014)
9. Simonyan, K., Zisserman, A.: Very deep convolutional networks for large-scale image recognition. In: Proceeding of the International Conference on Learning Representations (ICLR) (2015)
10. Springenberg, J.T., Dosovitskiy, A., Brox, T., Riedmiller, M.: Striving for simplicity: the all convolutional net. In: Proceedings of the International Conference on Learning Representations (ICLR) (2014)

11. Zeiler, M.D., Fergus, R.: Visualizing and understanding convolutional networks. In: Fleet, D., Pajdla, T., Schiele, B., Tuytelaars, T. (eds.) ECCV 2014, Part I. LNCS, vol. 8689, pp. 818–833. Springer, Cham (2014). https://doi.org/10.1007/978-3-319-10590-1_53
12. Zhou, B., Khosla, A., Lapedriza, A., Oliva, A., Torralba, A.: Learning deep features for discriminative localization. In: Proceedings of the IEEE Conference on Computer Vision and Pattern Recognition (CVPR), pp. 1–9 (2016)

Segmentation of Foreground in Image Sequence with Foveated Vision Concept

Kwok Leung Chan(✉)

Department of Electrical Engineering, City University of Hong Kong, Hong Kong, China
itklchan@cityu.edu.hk

Abstract. The human visual system has no difficulty to detect moving object. To design an automated method for detecting foreground in videos captured in a variety and complicated scenes is a challenge. The topic has attracted much research due to its wide range of video-based applications. We propose a foveated model that mimics the human visual system for the detection of foreground in image sequence. It is a two-step framework simulating the awareness of motion followed by the extraction of detailed information. In the first step, region proposals are extracted based on similarity of intensity and motion features with respect to the pre-generated archetype. Through integration of the similarity measures, each image frame is segregated into background and foreground points. Large foreground regions are preserved as region proposals (RPs). In the second step, analysis is performed on each RP in order to obtain the accurate shape of moving object. Photometric and textural features are extracted and matched with another archetype. We propose a probabilistic refinement scheme. If the RP contains a point initially labeled as background, it can be converted to a foreground point if its features are more similar to neighboring foreground points than neighboring background points. Both archetypes are updated immediately based on the segregation result. We compare our method with some well-known and recently proposed algorithms using various video datasets.

Keywords: Foreground detection · Background subtraction · Flux tensor · Local ternary pattern · Foveated vision

1 Introduction

In human vision system, the first level of visual processing starts with the eye. The retina contains light-sensing photoreceptors, each of which converts visual information to neural signals. The distribution of photoreceptors differs across the retina, with the highest density located at the center of the retina, called the fovea. The density of photoreceptors slowly decreases towards the peripheral part of the retina. Parvocellular cells (P-cells) are mostly present at fovea and magnocellular cells (M-cells) are mostly outside the fovea. P-cells have higher spatial resolution but lower temporal resolution than M-cells. The parvocellular neurons are sensitive to color. They can sense fine details better than the magnocellular neurons.

S. Palaiahnakote et al. (Eds.): ACPR 2019, LNCS 12046, pp. 878–888, 2020.
https://doi.org/10.1007/978-3-030-41404-7_62

With the same sensor and processing system, human has no difficulty to know what he sees, whether it is a static or a moving object. To gain high-level understanding from images or videos with computer (computer vision) is a challenging research field. It has attracted much attention because a system capable of inferring meaning from image can have many applications such as anomaly event identification in video surveillance. One approach to imitate the human vision system is to use a space-variant image sensor with a retina-like distribution of pixels. However, a space-variant sensing device is expensive and difficult to produce. Another approach is to transform the resolution of the image into a log-polar visual field in software. This requires post-processing and downgrading resolution may result in information loss. In [1], a foveated object detector is developed that processes the scene with varying resolution. Foveated method achieves nearly the same performance as the non-foveated method (homogeneous spatial resolution processing). In [2], retina model is applied for motion analysis. Two channels of information are obtained. The parvocellular channel provides detail extraction and the magnocellular channel extracts motion information.

The detection of moving objects in video has found many applications, for instances, human motion recognition [3], anomaly event detection [4], video indexing and retrieval [5], etc. Video-based object detection can be formulated as a background subtraction problem. Pixels in each image frame are identified as background if they are similar to the background model. The pixels that are not similar to the background model are labeled as foreground. As a result, foreground and background are segregated by classifying the pixels in each image frame of the video. Many methods had been proposed for background/foreground segmentation in video acquired by a fixed camera. More recent researches tackle complex scenes and non-stationary camera. A background subtraction framework contains background modeling, joint background/foreground classification, and background model updating. Sobral and Vacavant [6] presented a recent review and evaluation of 29 background subtraction methods. The background scene can be represented by statistical model [7]. Elgammal et al. [8] proposed an algorithm for estimating the pdf of the background directly from previous pixels using kernel estimator. Recently, more researches employ background model generated using real observed pixel values. Barnich et al. [9] proposed a fast sample-based background subtraction algorithm called ViBe. Background model is initialized by randomly sampling of pixels on the first image frame. Pixel of the new image frame is classified as background when there are sufficient background samples similar to the new pixel. Heikkilä and Pietikäinen [10] proposed to model the background of a pixel by local binary pattern (LBP) histograms estimated around that pixel. Liao et al. [11] proposed the scale invariant local ternary pattern (SILTP) which can tackle illumination variations.

Moving object detection can be very difficult under various complex circumstances – camouflage, illumination changes, background motions, intermittent object motion, shadows, camera jitter, etc. Camouflage can produce false negative error. Background motions (e.g. waving trees and rippling water) and shadows can produce false positive error. Object detection can be improved via background model updating. Many background subtraction methods update parameters of matched background model with a fixed learning factor. In [9], a random policy is employed for updating the background model at the pixel location and its neighbor. Van Droogenbroeck and Paquot [12] introduced some modifications, such as inhibiting the update of neighboring background model across the background-foreground border, for improving ViBe. The detected foreground often suffers from distorted shape and holes. Kim et al. [13] proposed a PID tracking control system for foreground segmentation refinement.

In this paper, we have two contributions. First, we propose a two-step foreground segmentation framework with foveated vision concept. In the first step, intensity and motion features are extracted from the visual information and matched with the pre-generated archetype to identify region proposals. In the following step, photometric and textural features are extracted and matched with the second archetype to refine the foreground region. Our second contribution is to propose a novel local ternary pattern for characterizing the background texture.

2 Foreground Detection Framework

The two-step foreground detection framework is shown in Fig. 1. In stage I, intensity and motion features are computed from a short image sequence and stored in archetype I. In each new image frame, the same features are extracted and matched with the archetype. Through integration of the similarity measures, each image frame is segregated into background and foreground points. The foreground points, which are close enough to form a sufficiently large blob, are grouped to form a region proposal (RP). Features of the background points are employed for updating of archetype I. The RP may have defects such as holes or distortions on the boundary. In stage II, analysis will be performed on the RP in order to obtain the accurate shape of moving object. Photometric and textural features are extracted and matched with the pre-generated archetype II via a probabilistic refinement scheme. If the RP has a point initially labeled as background, it can be converted to a foreground point if its features are more similar to neighboring foreground points than neighboring background points. Archetype II is updated immediately with a random mechanism.

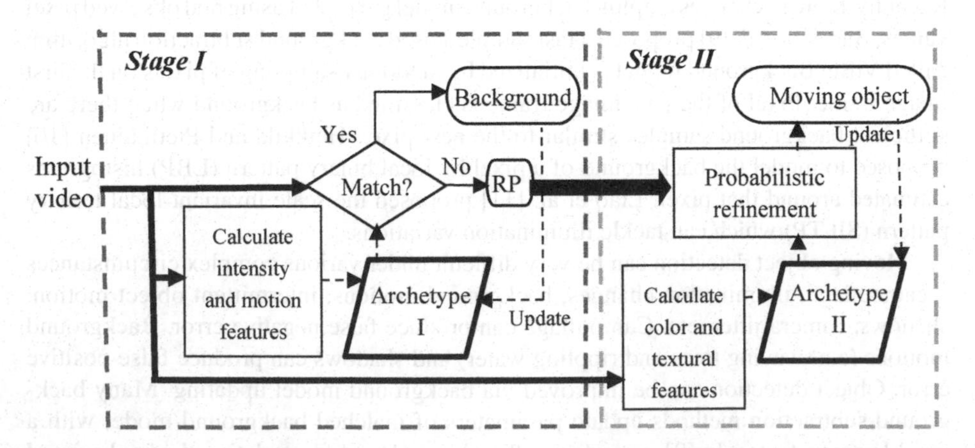

Fig. 1. Overview of foreground detection framework.

3 Intensity and Motion Features

At each point of the initialization image sequence, the mean, minimum and maximum intensities are found. For a long image sequence, the background intensity can fall outside the range of (minimum, maximum). Therefore, the lower and upper bounds of the intensity range are computed and used for identifying those genuine background pixels. The extended intensity range is controlled by two parameters. If it is too wide, more false negative errors will be produced. Through thorough experimentation, we set α_I and β_I as 0.8 and 1.2 respectively.

$$I_{lower} = \alpha_I * I_{min} \tag{1}$$

$$I_{upper} = \beta_I * I_{max} \tag{2}$$

In each new image frame, intensity of each pixel is matched with the corresponding intensity features in archetype I. Normalized similarity measure is computed. Background pixel should have S_I close to one, while object pixel close to zero.

$$S_I = \begin{cases} 1.0 - min\left(1.0, \dfrac{I_{new} - I_{mean}}{I_{upper} - I_{mean}}\right), \\ if\ I_{new} \geq I_{mean} \\ max\left(0, \frac{I_{new} - I_{lower}}{I_{mean} - I_{lower}}\right), \\ otherwise \end{cases} \tag{3}$$

Motion of the background is characterized by flux tensor. It computes the temporal variation of the optical flow field in the spatio-temporal domain.

$$J_F = \begin{bmatrix} \int_\Omega \left\{\frac{\partial^2 I}{\partial x \partial t}\right\}^2 dy & \int_\Omega \frac{\partial^2 I}{\partial x \partial t}\frac{\partial^2 I}{\partial y \partial t} dy & \int_\Omega \frac{\partial^2 I}{\partial x \partial t}\frac{\partial^2 I}{\partial t^2} dy \\ \int_\Omega \frac{\partial^2 I}{\partial y \partial t}\frac{\partial^2 I}{\partial x \partial t} dy & \int_\Omega \left\{\frac{\partial^2 I}{\partial y \partial t}\right\}^2 dy & \int_\Omega \frac{\partial^2 I}{\partial y \partial t}\frac{\partial^2 I}{\partial t^2} dy \\ \int_\Omega \frac{\partial^2 I}{\partial t^2}\frac{\partial^2 I}{\partial x \partial t} dy & \int_\Omega \frac{\partial^2 I}{\partial t^2}\frac{\partial^2 I}{\partial y \partial t} dy & \int_\Omega \left\{\frac{\partial^2 I}{\partial t^2}\right\}^2 dy \end{bmatrix} \tag{4}$$

We adopt the neighborhood Ω of 9×9 pixels. Trace of J_F is then employed as a compact representation of background motion.

$$M = \int_\Omega \left\| \frac{\partial}{\partial t} \nabla I \right\|^2 dy \tag{5}$$

At each point of the initialization image sequence, the mean, minimum and maximum motion features are found. Similar to the intensity range, the lower and upper bounds of the motion feature range are computed and controlled by two parameters. We also set α_M and β_M as 0.8 and 1.2 respectively.

$$M_{lower} = \alpha_M * M_{min} \tag{6}$$

$$M_{upper} = \beta_M * M_{max} \tag{7}$$

Motion feature of each new pixel is matched with archetype I and normalized similarity measure is computed. Background pixel should have S_M close to one, while object pixel close to zero.

$$S_M = 1.0 - \frac{M_{diff}}{M_{upper} - M_{lower}} \tag{8}$$

$$M_{diff} = \begin{cases} M_{upper} - M_{lower}, & if\ M_{new} > M_{upper} \\ 0, & elseif\ M_{new} < M_{lower} \\ M_{new} - M_{lower}, & otherwise \end{cases} \tag{9}$$

Through integration of the similarity measures, each image frame is segregated into background (*BG*) and foreground (*FG*) points. Through experimentation, we set τ_I as 0.4.

$$x_{label} = \begin{cases} BG, if\ S > \tau_I \\ FG, otherwise \end{cases} \tag{10}$$

$$S = \rho S_I + (1 - \rho) S_M \tag{11}$$

Small foreground regions are eliminated via component analysis. The filter size depends on the similarity of motion feature.

$$filter_{size} = \begin{cases} 30\ pixels, if\ S_M < \tau_f \\ 15\ pixels,\ otherwise \end{cases} \tag{12}$$

Archetype I is updated gradually based on the features of the identified background.

$$I^{new}_{mean} = \begin{cases} I^{old}_{mean} + \sigma\left(I_{new} - I^{old}_{mean}\right), if\ I_{new} > I^{old}_{mean} \\ I^{old}_{mean} - \sigma\left(I^{old}_{mean} - I_{new}\right), if\ I_{new} < I^{old}_{mean} \end{cases} \tag{13}$$

$$I^{new}_{min} = I^{old}_{min} - \sigma\left(I^{old}_{min} - I_{new}\right), if\ I_{new} < I^{old}_{min} \tag{14}$$

$$I^{new}_{max} = I^{old}_{max} + \sigma\left(I_{new} - I^{old}_{max}\right), if\ I_{new} > I^{old}_{max} \tag{15}$$

$$M^{new}_{min} = M^{old}_{min} - \sigma\left(M^{old}_{min} - M_{new}\right), if\ M_{new} < M^{old}_{min} \tag{16}$$

$$M^{new}_{max} = M^{old}_{max} + \sigma\left(M_{new} - M^{old}_{max}\right), if\ M_{new} > M^{old}_{max} \tag{17}$$

4 Photometric and Textural Features

The original color values of the initialization image sequence are saved as photometric features in archetype II. The similarity between the current pixel color and the color of the archetype sample is computed by

$$s_C = \frac{C^i \cdot C^B}{\left\|C^i\right\|_2 \cdot \left\|C^B\right\|_2} \tag{18}$$

where C^i is color the current pixel, C^B is color of an archetype sample, $\|\cdot\|_2$ denotes the Euclidean length of a vector.

We propose a local ternary pattern for characterizing the background texture. A pattern, with multiple pixels, can characterize the local texture more effectively than individual pixel. Also, our perception-based local ternary pattern makes full use of color information which is better than other texture-based methods that use only grey values. At each image pixel, patterns can be generated from the same color channels and different color channels. For a block of 3 × 3 pixels, neighbors n_k are compared with the confidence interval (*CI*) of the center pixel *b*. *CI*(*b*) is defined by (CI_l, CI_u) where CI_l and CI_u are the lower bound and upper bound of *CI* respectively.

$$CI_l = b - 0.1087b \tag{19}$$

$$CI_u = b + 0.122b \tag{20}$$

The pattern value is set according to the following equation.

$$p_k = \begin{cases} 00, & CI_l \le n_k \le CI_u \\ 01, & n_k > CI_u \\ 10, & n_k < CI_l \end{cases}, 1 \le k \le 8 \tag{21}$$

If the center pixel *b* and neighbors n_1 to n_8 are from the same color channel, the Same-Channel Pattern (*SCP*) is generated as follows:

$$SCP_k = \oplus\{p_k^c\}, c = \{R, G, B\}, 1 \le k \le 8 \tag{22}$$

where p_k^c is the binary pattern value for color channel *c* at position *k*, and $\oplus$ is the concatenation of the corresponding binary pattern values for all color channels. If the center pixel *b* and neighbors n_1 to n_8 are from different color channels, the Cross-Channel Pattern (*CCP*) is generated as follows:

$$CCP_k = \oplus\{p_k^{c_b:c_n}\},$$

$$c_b{:}c_n = \{R{:}B, G{:}R, B{:}G\}, 1 \le k \le 8 \tag{23}$$

where $p_k^{c_b:c_n}$ is the binary pattern value at position *k* estimated with center pixel *b* from color channel c_b and neighbor n_k from color channel c_n, and $\oplus$ is the concatenation of the corresponding cross-channel binary pattern values. *SCP* and *CCP* are combined into a 12-bit string:

$$CP_k = SCP_k \oplus CCP_k, 1 \le k \le 8 \tag{24}$$

For convenient of storage, CP_k is transformed into a single value:

$$F_k = \sum\nolimits_{p=1}^{12} CP_k(p) \cdot 2^p, 1 \le k \le 8 \tag{25}$$

where $CP_k(p)$ is bit *p* of CP_k. Therefore, at each image pixel location, the local ternary patterns are transformed into an 8-dimensional feature vector F_k and saved in archetype

II as one sample. The similarity between patterns of the current pixel and the background model can be computed by measuring the Hamming distance between two bit strings

$$d_p = \sum_{k=1}^{8} \left| CP_k^i \otimes CP_k^B \right| \quad (26)$$

where CP_k^i is CP_k of the current pixel, CP_k^B is CP_k of a background sample, $\otimes$ is the XOR operator, $|\cdot|_2$ is the cardinality.

The RP obtained in stage I is refined via a probabilistic scheme. Let x be a foreground point (*FG*). Its neighboring background points (*BG*) y are defined by

$$y \,|\, dist(x, y) < D, x = FG, y = BG \quad (27)$$

where $dist(\cdot)$ is the city-block distance and D is fixed as 1. y are changed to *FG* when they have image features more similar to neighboring *FG* pixels than neighboring *BG* pixels. To analyze the local ternary pattern feature

$$y_i = FG \text{ if} log\frac{P(y_i = FG)}{P(y_i = BG)} > \tau_{IIp} \quad (28)$$

$$P(y_i = FG) = exp\left(-\sum\nolimits_j \left|d_p^{y_j} - d_p^{y_i}\right|\right), dist\left(y_i, y_j\right) < D, y_j = FG \quad (29)$$

$$P(y_i = BG) = exp\left(-\sum\nolimits_j \left|\mu(d_p^{y_j}) - d_p^{y_i}\right|\right), dist\left(y_i, y_j\right) < D, y_j = FG \quad (30)$$

where $\mu(\cdot)$ is the mean of the local ternary pattern features in archetype II. To analyze the photometric feature

$$y_i = FG \text{ if} log\frac{P(y_i = BG)}{P(y_i = FG)} > \tau_{IIc} \quad (31)$$

$$P(y_i = FG) = exp\left(-\sum\nolimits_j \left|s_c^{y_j} - s_c^{y_i}\right|\right), dist\left(y_i, y_j\right) < D, y_j = FG \quad (32)$$

$$P(y_i = BG) = exp\left(-\sum\nolimits_j \left|\mu(s_c^{y_j}) - s_c^{y_i}\right|\right), dist\left(y_i, y_j\right) < D, y_j = FG \quad (33)$$

where $\mu(\cdot)$ is the mean of the photometric features in archetype II. A false negative pixel will be corrected when both Eqs. (28) and (31) are satisfied.

Archetype II is updated based on the segregation result with a random mechanism similar to ViBe [9]. For each identified background point, the chance to employ it for updating is 1 out of 16. If selected, its photometric and textural features will replace a randomly selected archetype II sample.

5 Result

We implemented our two-step foreground detection method using MATLAB and run on a 2.1 GHz PC with 1 Gbyte memory. We evaluated and compared its performance with four well-known and recently proposed background subtraction algorithms quantitatively in terms of F-Measure (F1). Based on sample consensus, ViBe [9] can achieve very good results with very few tunable parameters. ViBe uses only RGB values and keeps 20 samples in the background model. A new pixel is identified as background when it matches with 2 background samples. SILTP [11] employs scale invariant local patterns.

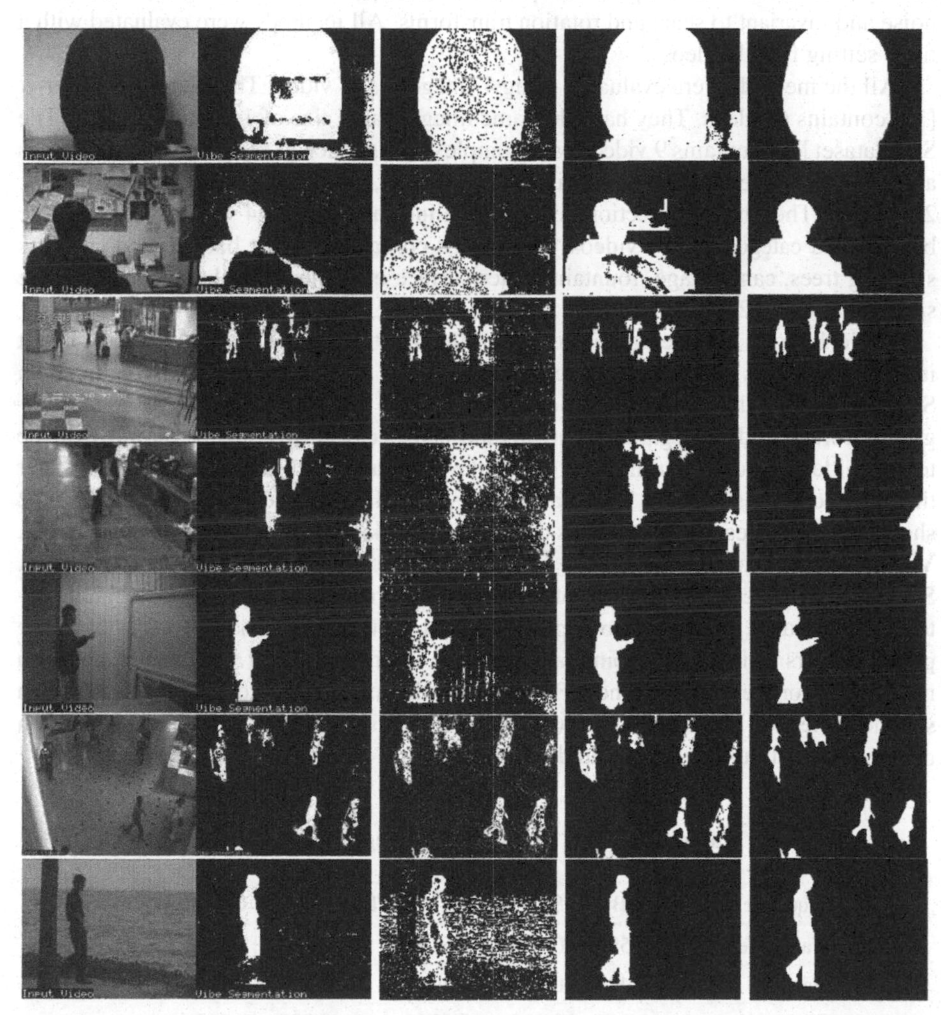

Fig. 2. Foreground detection results – original image frames (first column), results obtained by ViBe (second column), results obtained by SILTP (third column), results obtained by our method (fourth column), ground truths (last column).

It was showed that it performs better other LBP based methods [10, 14]. We implemented SILTP using MATLAB with the same set of parameters as reported in [11]. Ma and Sang [15] proposed the multi-channel SILTP (MC-SILTP) which can perform better than SILTP with pattern obtained by cross-computation on RGB color channels. Recently, a method (PSD) for the detection of moving objects in video based on color and local ternary pattern features was proposed [16]. The local pattern feature is robust to random noise and invariant to scale and rotation transforms. All methods were evaluated with a fixed setting for all videos.

All the methods were evaluated using 4 categories of video. The Wallflower dataset [17] contains 6 videos. They have the same image frame size of 160 × 120 pixels. The Star dataset [18] contains 9 videos with complex scenes such as busy human flows, trees and water etc. They have different image frame size, from 160 × 120 pixels to 320 × 256 pixels. The ChangeDetection.net [19] baseline category has 4 videos. The dynamic background category has 6 videos. The videos contain complex backgrounds such as swaying trees, camouflage, fountain, water surface etc. They have larger image frame size, from 320 × 240 pixels to 720 × 576 pixels.

Table 1 shows the average F1 results of the 4 categories of videos. The best result in a given row is highlighted. It can be seen that MC-SILTP performs better than SILTP. PSD, which is a recent method with powerful features, produces accurate background/foreground segregation. Our method can perform even better on most of the testing videos. Overall, our method can achieve average F1 result more than 3% higher than the second best method PSD. Table 2 shows the F1 results of some videos. Figure 2 shows the visual results. The videos contain various kinds of complications. Generally, ViBe produces more false negative errors (see Camouflage and ForegroundAperture). SILTP can produce large amount of false positive errors, especially in the ChangeDetection.net videos like canoe, overpass, etc. Our method can produce much less false positive errors whilst also keeping false negative errors low. It can achieve highest F1 on most videos or the second highest F1 on a few others. The superiority of our method in saliency detection is the consequence of the foveated vision framework and the utilization of effective features for background representation.

Table 1. Average F1 results of 4 categories of videos.

Sequence	ViBe	SILTP	MC-SILTP	PSD	Our method
Wallflower	0.590	0.669	0.685	0.600	**0.734**
Star	0.483	0.420	0.493	0.573	**0.602**
CD baseline	0.866	0.406	0.704	**0.881**	0.802
CD dynamic background	0.459	0.041	0.160	0.472	**0.538**
Average	0.600	0.384	0.511	0.632	**0.669**

Table 2. F1 results of individual videos.

Sequence	ViBe	SILTP	MC-SILTP	PSD	Our method
Camouflage	0.931	0.927	0.901	0.942	**0.944**
ForegroundAperture	0.644	**0.837**	0.680	0.635	0.834
AirportHall	0.496	0.566	0.610	0.553	**0.645**
Bootstrap	0.514	0.519	**0.621**	0.503	0.616
Curtain	0.775	0.687	0.654	0.833	**0.854**
ShoppingMall	0.522	0.566	0.525	0.620	**0.684**
WaterSurface	0.801	0.333	0.462	0.866	**0.950**
Highway	0.855	0.378	0.677	**0.862**	0.852
Canoe	0.783	0.101	0.395	0.865	**0.883**
Fountain02	0.563	0.016	0.068	0.211	**0.581**
Overpass	0.685	0.062	0.146	0.627	**0.756**

6 Conclusion

In summary, we propose a two-step foreground detection framework that mimics the human foveated vision system. In the first stage, intensity and motion features are computed for identifying the region proposal. In the second stage, photometric and textural features are extracted from the initial region. Moving object is refined with a probabilistic scheme by referring to the pre-generated archetype. We compare our method with some background subtraction algorithms. Testing is performed on various datasets, containing simple videos with small image frame size as well as challenging videos with large image frame size. The quantitative and visual results show the consistency and superiority of our method.

References

1. Akbas, E., Eckstein, M.P.: Object detection through search with a foveated visual system. PLOS Comput. Biol. **13**(10), e1005743 (2017)
2. Benoit, A., Caplier, A., Durette, B., Herault, J.: Using human visual system modeling for bio-inspired low level image processing. Comput. Vis. Image Underst. **114**(7), 758–773 (2010)
3. Hsieh, J.-W., Hsu, Y.-T., Liao, H.-Y.M., Chen, C.-C.: Video-based human movement analysis and its application to surveillance systems. IEEE Trans. Multimedia **10**(3), 372–384 (2008)
4. Lu, W., Tan, Y.-P.: A vision-based approach to early detection of drowning incidents in swimming pools. IEEE Trans. Circuits Syst. Video Technol. **14**(2), 159–178 (2004)
5. Visser, R., Sebe, N., Bakker, E.: Object recognition for video retrieval. In: Lew, M.S., Sebe, N., Eakins, John P. (eds.) CIVR 2002. LNCS, vol. 2383, pp. 262–270. Springer, Heidelberg (2002). https://doi.org/10.1007/3-540-45479-9_28
6. Sobral, A., Vacavant, A.: A comprehensive review of background subtraction algorithms evaluated with synthetic and real videos. Comput. Vis. Image Underst. **122**, 4–21 (2014)

7. Stauffer, C., Grimson, W.E.L.: Learning patterns of activity using real-time tracking. IEEE Trans. Pattern Anal. Mach. Intell. **22**(8), 747–757 (2000)
8. Elgammal, A., Duraiswami, R., Harwood, D., Davis, L.S.: Background and foreground modeling using nonparametric kernel density estimation for visual surveillance. Proc. IEEE **90**(7), 1151–1163 (2002)
9. Barnich, O., Van Droogenbroeck, M.: ViBe: a powerful random technique to estimate the background in video sequences. In: Proceedings of International Conference on Acoustics, Speech and Signal Processing, pp. 945–948 (2009)
10. Heikkilä, M., Pietikäinen, M.: A texture-based method for modeling the background and detecting moving objects. IEEE Trans. Pattern Anal. Mach. Intell. **28**(4), 657–662 (2006)
11. Liao, S., Zhao, G., Kellokumpu, V., Pietikäinen, M., Li, S.Z.: Modeling pixel process with scale invariant local patterns for background subtraction in complex scenes. In: Proceedings of IEEE Conference on Computer Vision and Pattern Recognition, pp. 1301–1306 (2010)
12. Van Droogenbroeck, M., Paquot, O.: Background subtraction: experiments and improvements for ViBe. In: Proceedings of IEEE Workshop on Change Detection at IEEE Conference on Computer Vision and Pattern Recognition, pp. 32–37 (2012)
13. Kim, S.W., Yun, K., Yi, K.M., Kim, S.J., Choi, J.Y.: Detection of moving objects with a moving camera using non-panoramic background model. Mach. Vis. Appl. **24**, 1015–1028 (2013)
14. Heikkilä, M., Pietikäinen, M., Heikkilä, J.: A texture-based method for detecting moving objects. In: Proceedings of British Machine Vision Conference, pp. 187–196 (2004)
15. Ma, F., Sang, N.: Background subtraction based on multi-channel SILTP. In: Park, J.-I., Kim, J. (eds.) ACCV 2012. LNCS, vol. 7728, pp. 73–84. Springer, Heidelberg (2013). https://doi.org/10.1007/978-3-642-37410-4_7
16. Chan, K.L.: Saliency detection in video sequences using perceivable change encoded local pattern. SIViP **12**(5), 975–982 (2018)
17. Toyama, K., Krumm, J., Brumitt, B., Meyers, B.: Wallflower: principles and practice of background maintenance. In: Proceedings of International Conference on Computer Vision, pp. 255–261 (1999)
18. Li, L., Huang, W., Gu, I.Y.-H., Tian, Q.: Statistical modelling of complex backgrounds for foreground object detection. IEEE Trans. Image Process. **13**(11), 1459–1472 (2004)
19. Goyette, N., Jodoin, P.-M., Porikli, F., Konrad, J., Ishwar, P.: Changedetection.net: a new change detection benchmark dataset. In: Proceedings of IEEE Workshop on Change Detection at IEEE Conference on Computer Vision and Pattern Recognition, pp. 16–21 (2012)

Bi-direction Feature Pyramid Temporal Action Detection Network

Jiang He, Yan Song(✉), and Haiyu Jiang

Nanjing University of Science and Technology, Nanjing, China
songyan@njust.edu.cn

Abstract. Temporal action detection in long-untrimmed videos is still a challenging task in video content analysis. Many existing approaches contain two stages, which firstly generate action proposals and then classify them. The main drawback of these approaches is that there are repeated operations in the proposal extraction and the classification stages. In this paper, we propose a novel Bi-direction Feature Pyramid Temporal Action Detection (BFPTAD) Network based on 1D temporal convolutional and deconvolutional layers to detect action instances directly in long-untrimmed videos. We use the top-down pathway to add semantic information to the shallow feature maps, and then use the bottom-up pathway to add location information to the deep feature maps. We evaluate our network on THUMOS14 and ActivityNet benchmarks. Our approach significantly outperforms other state-of-the-art methods by increasing mAP@IoU = 0.5 from 44.2% to 52.2% on THUMOS14.

Keywords: Video content analysis · Action detection · Feature Pyramid Network

1 Introduction

With the popularity of mobile devices and cameras, more and more video data are generated, most of which are about human activities. This brings a great demands to the automatic video content analysis. An important branch of video content analysis is action recognition. Many satisfactory progress [3,21,22] has been made in this area. However, in the real world, videos are usually untrimmed, and the actions of interest are often embedded in a background of irrelevant scenes. Therefore, recent research attention has shifted to temporal action detection in untrimmed videos. Compared to action recognition, which only classifies the categories of trimmed video clips, temporal action detection not only identifies the type of actions instances, but also detects the start and the end time of action instances in long-untrimmed videos.

Most of current works [5,19,20,26,28] are two-stage approaches. First, they use the sliding windows or other proposal extraction methods to generate temporal proposals. And then, they apply temporal action classifiers to each proposal to predict its category. The main drawbacks of these two-stage approaches are that

S. Palaiahnakote et al. (Eds.): ACPR 2019, LNCS 12046, pp. 889–901, 2020.
https://doi.org/10.1007/978-3-030-41404-7_63

they have slow computational speed and there may be repeated calculations in the proposal extraction and classification stages. On the contrary, the one-stage approaches directly detect actions in one step. For example, SSAD [14] utilizes 1D convolution to generate multiple temporal anchor action instances for action classification and boundary box regression. However, the feature maps contain insufficient information to detect actions and locate accurately.

To solve the above problems, we propose a Bidirectional Feature Pyramid Temporal Action Detection (BFPTAD) Network. Our BFPTAD network skips the proposal generation step and directly predicts the temporal boundaries and confidence scores for multiple action categories. As illustrated in Fig. 1, we extract I3D feature, and then adopt 1D temporal convolutions to obtain a series of feature layers. Next, we utilize top-down pathway and lateral connections to merge the semantic information into the shallow feature maps. We then use the bottom-up pathway to add location information to the deep feature maps. Finally, we obtain a fixed set of detection predictions by the classification and the location branches.

The main contributions of this paper are: (1) we propose a new network for temporal action detection in one stage; (2) we demonstrate that the top-down pathway and the bottom-up pathway can effectively enhance feature

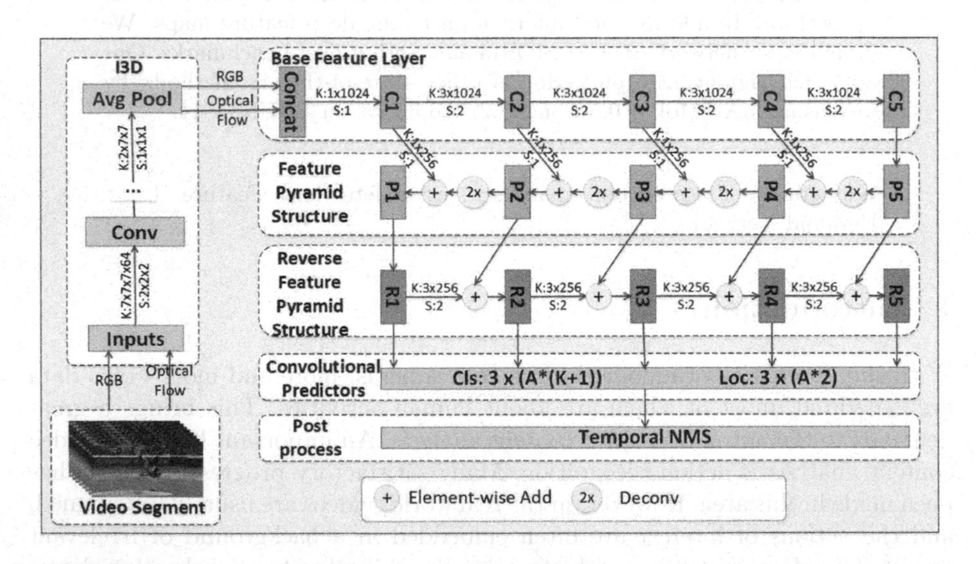

Fig. 1. Our BFPTAD network architecture. We extract I3D RGB and optical flow features, and then concatenate them. Next, we adopt temporal Conv1d to extract rich feature hierarchies. We use temporal Conv1d and deconvolution to incorporate the rich semantic information of deep feature maps to shallow feature maps. Also, we use temporal Conv1d to integrate the rich location information of shallow feature maps into deep feature maps. The $R1$–$R5$ are used to detect actions. For each feature map R_i, we associate a set of anchors with each feature map cell. During test, we use temporal NMS to process the detection results.

representation; (3) we conduct experiments on the standard benchmark THUMOS14, and achieve the state-of-the-art performance.

2 Related Work

Here, we review relevant works in action recognition, object detection, and temporal action detection.

Action Recognition. Action recognition is an important research area in video content analysis. Earlier methods used hand-crafted visual features. Such as improved Dense Trajectory (iDT) [23,24]. IDT feature consisted of MBH, HOF and HOG features extracted from dense trajectories. With the successes of deep learning methods, most recent works have been done with deep learning methods, such as two-stream networks [21] used network to learn both spatial and temporal features on single frame and stacked optical flow field respectively. And C3D network [22] utilized 3D convolutions to capture spatio-temporal feature directly from video streams. These works adopted deep neural networks and improved the performance. Just like image classification networks can be used in image object detection, action recognition models can also be used in temporal action detection for feature extraction.

Object Detection. There are two main sets of object detection methods proposed in recent years. One set is R-CNN and its variation. R-CNN [9] consisted of selective search, CNN feature extractions, SVM classifiers and bounding box regression. Fast R-CNN [8] reshaped R-CNN into a single-stage by using multi-loss, and also had a RoI Pooling layer to share the computation of one image in ConvNets. Faster R-CNN [18] adopted a RPN network to generate region proposals instead of selective search. Another set of object detection methods are single shot detection methods, which means detecting object directly without generating proposals. There are two representative models, YOLO and SSD. YOLO [17] used the whole topmost feature map to predict probabilities of multiple categories and corresponding confidence scores and location offsets. SSD [16] used multiple scales anchor to predict on multiple feature maps. Our network is inspired by SSD and uses the same design mentality on temporal action detection.

Temporal Action Detection. As mentioned above, the current temporal action detection works can be divided into two types: two-stage methods and one-stage methods. The two-stage methods include the proposal extraction stage and the classification stage. CDC [19] network performed temporal upsampling and spatial downsampling operations simultaneously to generate per-frame classification scores which were used to refine temporal boundaries. Gao *et al.* [6] proposed to use Cascaded Boundary Regression model to adjust temporal boundaries in a regression cascade, which outperformed other state-of-the-art temporal action localization methods. SSN [28] adopted temporal pyramid pooling to model the complicated temporal structures. However, these approaches need to get temporal proposals in advance. The one-stage methods don't need the explicit proposal extraction step and can detect actions in one single stage. S^3D [27] used three-dimensional convolutions to generate multiple instances of temporal anchor actions for action classification and bounding box regression. Single Stream Temporal Action Detection (SS-TAD) [1] used RNN-based architecture to jointly learn action recommendations and classifications. In this paper, we eliminate the proposal generation step and directly predict the temporal boundaries and the classification scores of multiple actions in one stage.

3 Methods

We propose a Bi-direction Feature Pyramid Temporal Action Detection Network based on 1D temporal convolutional and deconvolutional layers to detect action instances directly in long-untrimmed videos. The network generates a fixed-size set of temporal anchors (temporal anchor indicates that the anchor is only used in temporal dimension) and their scores of action instances in those anchors. Finally, we use a temporal NMS to remove redundant results to obtain the final detection results.

3.1 Network

Our framework is illustrated in Fig. 1, consists of four major components: base feature layers, feature pyramid structure, reverse feature pyramid structure and convolutional predictors. The *base feature layers* are used to generate high-level features. We then use the *feature pyramid structure* to add semantic information to the shallow feature maps. Next, we adopt the *reverse feature pyramid structure* to add location information to the deep feature maps. Finally, the *convolutional predictors* utilizes 1D temporal convolutions with temporal kernel size of 3 to predict the location offsets and the classification scores.

Base Feature Layers. We extract I3D [3] feature and adopt 1D temporal convolutions to extract rich feature hierarchies. Specifically, we extract the 1024-dimensional output of the average pooling layer by stacking every 16 RGB/optical flow frames in each clip, and then concatenate the RGB and the optical flow features. Next, we adopt N_l temporal Conv1d layers to extract rich feature hierarchies. The first layer uses a 1D temporal convolution with temporal kernel size 1 and the stride is 1 to reduce the number of channels. And the rest use 1D temporal convolutions with temporal kernel size 3 and the strides are 2 to extend the temporal receptive field.

Feature Pyramid Structure. In order to enhance the feature representation of feature maps, we consider applying Feature Pyramid Network (FPN)

[15]. FPN combines the deep semantically-strong feature maps with shallow semantically-weak but location-strong maps by using top-down pathway and lateral connection. Particularly, the feature map P_i in the i-th layer is given by

$$P_i = \begin{cases} Conv_{k3}(C_{N_l}), & i = N_l \\ Conv_{k3}(De_{s2}(P_{i+1}) \oplus Conv_{k1}(C_i)), & 1 \leq i < N_l \end{cases} \tag{1}$$

where De_{s2} denotes the deconvolution operation for feature map up-sampling with the stride 2 and $\oplus$ denotes the element-wise summation. Both $Conv_{k3}$ and $Conv_{k1}$ indicate the 1D temporal convolution with the stride of 1. Among them, $Conv_{k3}$ uses a temporal kernel size of 3 while $Conv_{k1}$ uses a temporal kernel of 1.

Reverse Feature Pyramid Structure. We use the FPN structure to enhance the feature representation. However, the FPN structure can only enhance the semantic information of the shallow feature maps, which is helpful for detecting short actions. We find that the aggregation feature in the reverse direction is also important. Therefore, we propose a *reverse feature pyramid structure* that combines the location information of the shallow feature maps to the deep feature maps. Specifically, the feature map R_i in the i-th layer is given by

$$R_i = \begin{cases} P_i, & i = 1 \\ Conv_{k3s2}(R_{i-1}) \oplus P_i, & 1 < i \leq N_l \end{cases} \tag{2}$$

where $Conv_{k3s2}$ indicates the 1D temporal convolution with temporal kernel size 3 and the stride of 2.

Convolutional Predictors. Each temporal feature layer can produce a fixed set of detection predictions by using a set of Conv1D filters. As shown in Fig. 1, the $R1$–$R5$ feature maps are used for detection. For a feature map $R_i \in \mathbb{R}^{t \times c}$, the basic operation for predicting action instances is to use 1D temporal convolution with temporal kernel size 3 to generate the classification scores and the temporal location offsets, where t represents the temporal dimension size and c represents the number of channels. Specifically, for each anchor at a given temporal location, we calculate K classification scores (including background) and two temporal location offsets, respectively. We use 1D temporal convolution with temporal kernel size of $3 \times (K * A)$ to produce classification scores, where A denotes the number of anchor scales around each location in the feature map R_i. Similarly, we use 1D temporal convolution with temporal kernel size of $3 \times (2 * A)$ to generate temporal location offsets relative to the default location. For an illustration of anchors, please refer to Fig. 2. Therefore, the temporal feature map R_i can generate $t \times (K * A)$ classification scores and $t \times (2 * A)$ temporal location offsets.

3.2 Train

Training Data Construction. Given an untrimmed video, we divide the clips of length S_l on the frames sequence with 75% overlap rate. The overlap of the clips is for the case where the action instances are located at the boundary of the clips. If the number of video frames are less than S_l, we fill background image to S_l frames and treat it as a clip. In the training phase, if there is no action in a clip, we discard the clip.

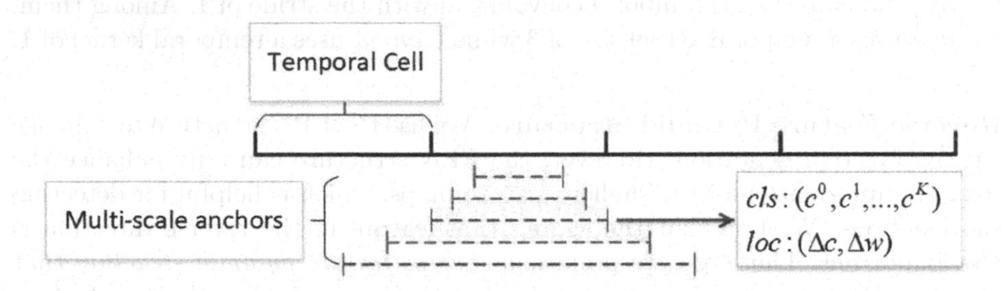

Fig. 2. We evaluate a set of multi-scale anchors at each temporal cell in several feature maps with different temporal resolution. Here, we show the *R4* feature map with temporal resolution 4 using five ratios $\{0.5, 0.75, 1.0, 1.5, 2.0\}$. For each anchor, we predict K +1 classification scores and 2 temporal location offsets, respectively.

Matching Strategy. During training, we need to determine which anchor corresponds to which ground truth instance, and then train the network. More specifically, for each anchor, we need to calculate its Intersection-over-Union (IoU) with all ground truth. If the highest IoU score of an anchor is greater than 0.5, the anchor will match the corresponding ground truth instance and be considered as positive. Otherwise, the anchor is treated as negative. Therefore, a ground truth instance can match multiple anchors but an anchor can only match one ground truth instance.

Hard Negative Mining. After matching, only a small part of the anchors are positive, and most of the anchors are negative. This causes a serious imbalance between positive and negative instances. So we use the hard negative mining method to reduce the number of negative instances. We sort all anchors that belong to negative instances according to the background confidence. Next, we pick the N anchors with the lowest background confidences so that the ratio between the negative and positive instances is 3:1. This ratio is chosen by empirical validation.

Training Objective. The training objective of our network is to solve a multi-task optimizer problem. The whole loss function includes two parts, the classification loss and the location loss:

$$L = L_{cls} + \alpha L_{loc}, \tag{3}$$

where α is the weight term used for balancing each part of the loss function.

The classification loss is a standard multi-class cross-entropy loss:

$$L_{cls} = -\frac{1}{N}(\sum_{i \in Pos}^{N} x_{ij}^{c} log(p_i^c) + \sum_{i \in Neg} log(p_i^0)), \tag{4}$$

where N is the number of total positive anchors in a batch, x_{ij}^{p} denotes whether the i-th anchor matches the j-th ground truth for category c, and if it matches, $x_{ij}^{c} = 1$, otherwise $x_{ij}^{c} = 0$. p_i^c denotes the classification score of the c-th category of the i-th anchor, and p_i^0 is the background score of the i-th anchor.

The location loss is a Smooth L1 loss [8] between the predicted action offsets and the ground truth instance. The location loss is defined as:

$$L_{loc} = \frac{1}{N} \sum_{i \in Pos}^{N} \sum_{m \in \{c,w\}} x_{ij} smooth_{L1}(l_i^m - gt_j^m), \tag{5}$$

where x_{ij} indicates whether the i-th anchor matches the j-th ground truth instance, and if it matches, $x_{ij} = 1$, otherwise $x_{ij} = 0$. l_i^m denotes the center/length prediction offset of the i-th anchor, and gt_j^m indicates the center/width offset of the j-th ground truth instance.

3.3 Inference

We follow the data generation method in the training phase for the testing phase except for two aspects. First, the overlap rate between clips is changed to 50%, in order to increase the detection speed. Second, the clip without annotation will not be removed. Given a clip, we generate all anchors with the classification scores and the temporal location offsets. The temporal location offsets are applied to the anchor in the form of a relative displacement of the center point and the length of each instance as described in Eq. 5 to predict accurate start time and end time. Next, we filter out the anchors below a certain threshold according to the classification scores, and use NMS with a threshold of 0.3 on the remaining anchors.

4 Experiments

In this section, we evaluate the effectiveness of our network on the THUMOS14 and ActivityNet action detection benchmark dataset. As shown in the experiments, our approach obtain the state-of-the-art performance on THUMOS14.

4.1 Dataset and Setup

THUMOS 2014. We conduct the experiments on the THUMOS Challenge 2014 dataset [12]. The dataset contains videos from 20 types of sports action for temporal action detection. Following the standard practice, we train our model on the 200 untrimmed validations videos, and evaluate on the 213 test videos.

ActivityNet. ActivityNet v1.2 [2] includes a total of 9682 untrimmed videos with 100 activity classes. This dataset is officially split into training, validation, and testing subsets. We use the training subset (4819 videos) to train and the validation subset (2383 videos) to test the performance of our model.

Evaluation Metrics. We follow the conventional metrics used in THUMOS 2014, which calculates the Average Precision (AP) for each action class and calculates the mean AP for evaluation. When a prediction action instance has the correction category and its temporal IoU with the ground truth instance is larger than the overlap threshold, it can be marked as correct. On THUMOS14, the tIoU thresholds we report range from 0.1 to 0.7, and we use the mAp at tIoU threshold of 0.5 to compare with other methods. On ActivityNet v1.2, the tIoU thresholds are {0.5, 0.75, 0.95}. The average of mAP values of IoU thresholds [0.5:0.05:0.95] is used to compare the performance of different methods.

I3D Features. We use the I3D feature extracted from the Kinetics pre-trained I3D [3] network. The model takes a stack of 16 RGB/optical flow frames as input. The output is passed through a 3D average pooling layer of kernel size $2 \times 7 \times 7$ to obtain feature of dimension 1024 each from RGB and optical flow. Next, we concatenate the RGB and optical flow features, and get a 2048-dimension feature. We extract RGB and optical flow frames at 25 frames per second (fps) and input them into the pre-trained I3D network.

Implementation Details. We implement our model by Tensorflow and use the Adam [13] optimizer to train the network. We set the location loss weight α to 1. The batch size and learning rate are set as 4 and 0.0001, respectively. For all layers in the *base feature layers*, we set the number of filters to 1024 and the number of filters in the remaining layers to 256. On THUMOS14, we set the clip length C_l to 512. We use $R1$–$R5$ layers as the anchor layers, where the anchor ratios of the $R1$–$R4$ layers are $[0.5, 0.75, 1, 1.5, 2]$, and the anchor ratios of $R5$ layer are $[0.5, 0.75, 1]$. On ActivityNet v1.2, we set the clip length C_l to 8192. Therefore, the *base feature layers* has a total of 9 layers, namely $C1$–$C9$. Next, we use the *feature pyramid structure* and the *reverse feature pyramid structure* on $C5$–$C9$ and get $R5$–$R9$ layers. Finally, we use $C1$–$C4$ and $R5$–$R9$ layers as the anchor layers, the anchor ratios of $R9$ layer are $[0.5, 0.75, 1]$, remainings are $[0.5, 0.75, 1, 1.5, 2]$.

4.2 Ablation Study

We conduct an ablation study to analyse the impacts of different components in our model on THUMOS14: (1) w/o rFP: we remove the *reverse feature pyramid structure* and only use $P_1 - P_5$; (2) w/o FP: we remove the *feature pyramid structure* and the *reverse feature pyramid structure* and only use C_1–C_5; (3) ALL: we keep all components and use R_1–R_5. We list the results in Table 1. We can see that each component plays an important role in improving performance. We also compare the influence of RGB and flow features. Particularly, we only use the RGB feature or the optical flow feature to train our network, respectively. The results are shown in Table 2.

Table 1. Effects of different components of our proposed model.

tIoU	0.1	0.2	0.3	0.4	0.5	0.6	0.7
w/o rFP	66.6	65.4	62.6	58.1	50.0	37.3	23.0
w/o FP	62.8	61.5	59.5	55.5	48.1	36.9	21.1
ALL	70.4	69.7	67.2	60.4	52.2	38.9	24.4

Table 2. Effects of the RGB or the optical flow features.

tIoU	0.1	0.2	0.3	0.4	0.5	0.6	0.7
RGB	57.6	55.8	53	48.2	40.3	28.5	15.9
Flow	59.4	57.9	55.9	52.5	44.9	33.6	20.7
RGB + flow	70.4	69.7	67.2	60.4	52.2	38.9	24.4

In our experiments, we use 5 anchors at each temporal location on the feature maps $R1$–$R4$, and 3 anchors at each temporal location on the $R5$ feature map. As shown in Table 3, if we remove the anchors with ratio 2 and the mAP drops by 1.4%. We then delete the anchors with ratio 1.5, the mAP drops another 2.1%. By further removing the anchors with ratios 0.75 and 0.5, the mAP drops another 2.7%. Because different layers are responsible for predicting temporal actions of different lengths, our network still has a strong performance (mAP 46.0%) when the anchors are only kept at ratio 1.0. Using multiple ratios makes the task of predicting anchor easier and the performance better.

4.3 Compare with State-of-the-Art

Finally, we compare our approach with other action detection methods on THUMOS14 [12] and ActivityNet v1.2 [2] using the above metrics.

Table 3. Effects of using different ratios on multiple temporal feature maps, and $R5$ layer does not use ratios 1.5 and 2.

Ratio	Performance				
1.0	✓	✓	✓	✓	✓
2.0	✓				
1.5	✓	✓			
0.75	✓	✓	✓		
0.5	✓	✓	✓	✓	
mAP@0.5 (%)	52.2	50.8	48.7	48.2	46.0

THUMOS14. We compare our method with other state-of-the-art approaches of temporal action detection on THUMOS14 in Table 4. The results indicate that our method outperforms other state-of-the-art approaches. In particular, the TRI-3D [10], TAL-net [4] and Two-stage CBR [25] all use I3D feature, and they achieve 37.4%, 42.8%, and 44.2% of mAP@0.5, respectively. Our method also uses the I3D feature, and the effect has been significantly improved. Compared to the best method Two-stage CBR [25], we obtain an achievement of 8%. For all the tIoU thresholds, our method achieves the highest mAP, which indicates that it can locate the boundary more accurately.

Table 4. Temporal action localization performance (mAP %) comparison at different tIoU threshold on THUMOS 2014.

tIoU	0.1	0.2	0.3	0.4	0.5	0.6	0.7
S-CNN [20]	47.7	43.5	36.3	28.7	19.0	10.3	5.3
CDC [19]	49.1	46.1	40.1	29.4	23.3	13.1	7.9
SSAD [14]	50.1	47.8	43.0	35.0	24.6	15.4	7.7
TURN [7]	54.0	50.9	44.1	34.9	25.6	–	–
R-C3D [26]	54.5	51.5	44.8	35.6	28.9	–	–
SSN [28]	60.3	56.2	50.6	40.8	29.1	–	–
SS-TAD [1]	–	–	45.7	–	29.2	–	9.6
CBR [6]	60.1	56.7	50.1	41.3	31.0	19.1	9.9
TRI-3D [10]	52.1	51.4	49.7	46.1	37.4	26.2	15.2
TAL-net [4]	59.8	57.1	53.2	48.5	42.8	33.8	20.8
Two-stage CBR [25]	–	–	53.5	50.2	44.2	33.9	22.7
Decouple-SSAD [11]	–	–	60.2	54.1	44.2	32.3	19.1
Ours	**70.4**	**69.7**	**67.2**	**60.4**	**52.2**	**38.9**	**24.4**

ActivityNet. The results on the validation set of ActivityNet v1.2 are shown in Table 5. Our approach is a one-stage approach that can detect actions directly on sliding window of length S_l in a single shot. Compared to the SSN-SW [28] method that uses the sliding window to generate temporal proposals, our method has achieved significant improvement. Although SSN-TAG [28] performs a little better than ours, it needs the TAG algorithm to obtain high-quality temporal proposals.

Table 5. Action detection results on ActivityNet v1.2, measured by mean average precision (mAP) for different tIoU thresholds and the average mAP of IoU thresholds from 0.5 to 0.95.

Method	0.5	0.75	0.95	Average
SSN-SW [28]	–	–	–	18.1
SSN-TAG [28]	–	–	–	**25.9**
Ours	37.6	21.8	2.4	21.9

5 Conclusion

In this paper, we have proposed a Bi-direction Feature Pyramid Temporal Action Detection (BFPTAD) Network in long-untrimmed videos. Our BFPTAD network does not need the explicit proposal extraction step and is able to detect actions in one single stage. Our research shows that top-down pathway combined with semantic information of the deep feature maps can enhance feature representation of the shallow feature maps. Similarly, rich location information from shallow feature maps is integrated into deep feature maps through the bottom-up pathway. In addition, we use multi-scale temporal anchors to obtain detection results from multiple temporal feature maps. We achieve the state-of-the-art performance for temporal action location on THUMOS14 detection benchmark.

Acknowledgments. This work was supported by the National Nature Science Foundation of China under Grants 61672285, U1611461, and 61732007.

References

1. Buch, S., Escorcia, V., Ghanem, B., Fei-Fei, L., Niebles, J.C.: End-to-end, single-stream temporal action detection in untrimmed videos. In: Proceedings of the British Machine Vision Conference (BMVC), vol. 1, p. 2 (2017)
2. Caba Heilbron, F., Escorcia, V., Ghanem, B., Carlos Niebles, J.: ActivityNet: a large-scale video benchmark for human activity understanding. In: Proceedings of the IEEE Conference on Computer Vision and Pattern Recognition, pp. 961–970 (2015)

3. Carreira, J., Zisserman, A.: Quo vadis, action recognition? a new model and the kinetics dataset. In: Proceedings of the IEEE Conference on Computer Vision and Pattern Recognition, pp. 6299–6308 (2017)
4. Chao, Y.W., Vijayanarasimhan, S., Seybold, B., Ross, D.A., Deng, J., Sukthankar, R.: Rethinking the faster R-CNN architecture for temporal action localization. In: Proceedings of the IEEE Conference on Computer Vision and Pattern Recognition, pp. 1130–1139 (2018)
5. Dai, X., Singh, B., Zhang, G., Davis, L.S., Chen, Y.Q.: Temporal context network for activity localization in videos. In: 2017 IEEE International Conference on Computer Vision (ICCV), pp. 5727–5736. IEEE (2017)
6. Gao, J., Yang, Z., Nevatia, R.: Cascaded boundary regression for temporal action detection. arXiv preprint arXiv:1705.01180 (2017)
7. Gao, J., Yang, Z., Sun, C., Chen, K., Nevatia, R.: Turn tap: temporal unit regression network for temporal action proposals. In: 2017 IEEE International Conference on Computer Vision (ICCV), pp. 3648–3656. IEEE (2017)
8. Girshick, R.: Fast R-CNN. Computer Science (2015)
9. Girshick, R., Donahue, J., Darrell, T., Malik, J.: Rich feature hierarchies for accurate object detection and semantic segmentation. In: Proceedings of the IEEE Conference on Computer Vision and Pattern Recognition, pp. 580–587 (2014)
10. Gleason, J., Ranjan, R., Schwarcz, S., Castillo, C., Chen, J.C., Chellappa, R.: A proposal-based solution to spatio-temporal action detection in untrimmed videos. In: 2019 IEEE Winter Conference on Applications of Computer Vision (WACV), pp. 141–150. IEEE (2019)
11. Huang, Y., Dai, Q., Lu, Y.: Decoupling localization and classification in single shot temporal action detection. arXiv preprint arXiv:1904.07442 (2019)
12. Jiang, Y.G., et al.: THUMOS challenge: action recognition with a large number of classes (2014). http://crcv.ucf.edu/THUMOS14/
13. Kingma, D.P., Ba, J.: Adam: a method for stochastic optimization. arXiv preprint arXiv:1412.6980 (2014)
14. Lin, T., Zhao, X., Shou, Z.: Single shot temporal action detection. In: Proceedings of the 25th ACM International Conference on Multimedia, pp. 988–996. ACM (2017)
15. Lin, T.Y., Dollár, P., Girshick, R., He, K., Hariharan, B., Belongie, S.: Feature pyramid networks for object detection. In: Proceedings of the IEEE Conference on Computer Vision and Pattern Recognition, pp. 2117–2125 (2017)
16. Liu, W., et al.: SSD: single shot multibox detector. In: Leibe, B., Matas, J., Sebe, N., Welling, M. (eds.) ECCV 2016. LNCS, vol. 9905, pp. 21–37. Springer, Cham (2016). https://doi.org/10.1007/978-3-319-46448-0_2
17. Redmon, J., Divvala, S., Girshick, R., Farhadi, A.: You only look once: unified, real-time object detection (2015)
18. Ren, S., He, K., Girshick, R., Sun, J.: Faster R-CNN: towards real-time object detection with region proposal networks. In: Advances in Neural Information Processing Systems, pp. 91–99 (2015)
19. Shou, Z., Chan, J., Zareian, A., Miyazawa, K., Chang, S.F.: CDC: convolutional-de-convolutional networks for precise temporal action localization in untrimmed videos. In: 2017 IEEE Conference on Computer Vision and Pattern Recognition (CVPR), pp. 1417–1426. IEEE (2017)
20. Shou, Z., Wang, D., Chang, S.F.: Temporal action localization in untrimmed videos via multi-stage CNNs. In: Proceedings of the IEEE Conference on Computer Vision and Pattern Recognition, pp. 1049–1058 (2016)

21. Simonyan, K., Zisserman, A.: Two-stream convolutional networks for action recognition in videos. In: Advances in Neural Information Processing Systems, pp. 568–576 (2014)
22. Tran, D., Bourdev, L., Fergus, R., Torresani, L., Paluri, M.: Learning spatiotemporal features with 3D convolutional networks. In: Proceedings of the IEEE International Conference on Computer Vision, pp. 4489–4497 (2015)
23. Wang, H., Kläser, A., Schmid, C., Liu, C.L.: Action recognition by dense trajectories. In: 2011 IEEE Conference on Computer Vision and Pattern Recognition (CVPR), pp. 3169–3176. IEEE (2011)
24. Wang, H., Schmid, C.: Action recognition with improved trajectories. In: Proceedings of the IEEE International Conference on Computer Vision, pp. 3551–3558 (2013)
25. Xie, T., Yang, X., Zhang, T., Xu, C., Patras, I.: Exploring feature representation and training strategies in temporal action localization. arXiv preprint arXiv:1905.10608 (2019)
26. Xu, H., Das, A., Saenko, K.: R-C3D: region convolutional 3D network for temporal activity detection. In: IEEE International Conference on Computer Vision (ICCV), pp. 5794–5803 (2017)
27. Zhang, D., Dai, X., Wang, X., Wang, Y.F.: S3D: single shot multi-span detector via fully 3D convolutional networks. arXiv preprint arXiv:1807.08069 (2018)
28. Zhao, Y., Xiong, Y., Wang, L., Wu, Z., Tang, X., Lin, D.: Temporal action detection with structured segment networks. In: ICCV, 2 October 2017

Hand Segmentation for Contactless Palmprint Recognition

Yusei Suzuki[1(✉)], Hiroya Kawai[1], Koichi Ito[1], Takafumi Aoki[1], Masakazu Fujio[2], Yosuke Kaga[2], and Kenta Takahashi[2]

[1] Graduate School of Information Sciences, Tohoku University, 6-6-05, Aramaki Aza Aoba, Sendai 9808579, Japan
yusei@aoki.ecei.tohoku.ac.jp

[2] Hitachi Ltd., 292, Yoshida-cho, Totsuka-ku, Yokohama 2440817, Japan

Abstract. Extracting a palm region with fixed location from an input hand image is a crucial task for palmprint recognition to realize reliable person authentication under unconstrained conditions. A palm region can be extracted from the fixed position using the gaps between fingers. Hence, an accurate and robust hand segmentation method is indispensable to extract a palm region from an image with complex background taken under various environments. This paper proposes a hand segmentation method for contactless palmprint recognition. The proposed method employs a new CNN architecture consisting of an encoder-decoder model of CNN with a pyramid pooling module. Through a set of experiments using a hand image dataset, we demonstrate that the proposed method exhibits efficient performance on hand segmentation.

Keywords: Palmprint · Segmentation · Biometrics · CNN · Hand

1 Introduction

Biometrics has attracted much attention with the needs for efficient and convenient person authentication compared with the conventional approach using password, PIN, card, etc [6]. A biometric authentication system identifies a person using his/her biological or behavioral characteristics such as face, fingerprint, iris, palmprint, signature, voice, gait, etc. Among biometric traits, this paper focuses on a palmprint. A palm is a large inner surface of a hand with many features such as principle lines, ridges, minutiae, texture, etc., and is expected to be one of the distinctive biometric traits [7,15]. In addition, a hand image can be acquired using a camera under contactless and unconstrained conditions so that we can develop a user-friendly and contactless person authentication system using palmprints.

A palmprint recognition system, in general, consists of 4 processes: (i) image acquisition, (ii) palm region extraction, (iii) feature extraction and (iv) matching. Among the above processes, palm region extraction is one of the most important processes, since the accuracy and reliableness of extracted palm region have a

S. Palaiahnakote et al. (Eds.): ACPR 2019, LNCS 12046, pp. 902–912, 2020.
https://doi.org/10.1007/978-3-030-41404-7_64

significant impact on recognition performance. Especially in contactless recognition systems, a palm region has to be extracted from a palm image with taking into consideration a variety of hand poses. Most of palmprint recognition algorithms employed the Zhang's method [16] to extract the central part of a palm for accurate matching, which consists of 5 steps: (i) binarizing the image, (ii) extracting the contour of the hand, (iii) detecting keypoints, (iv) building a coordinate system and (v) extracting the central part. This method assumes that a hand is fixed on the palmprint recognition system and the background has a simple such as uniform color. Therefore, the problem to be considered is how to extract a hand region from an input image to utilize the Zhang's method in the contactless situation as well as in the contact situation.

The accuracy of image segmentation methods has been dramatically improved because of the recent development in deep learning technology. Among them, encoder-decoder networks have been successful at an image segmentation task. U-Net [11] is a standard and well-known encoder-decoder network for image segmentation. TernausNet [5] replaced the encoder into VGG11 [13] pre-trained using ImageNet [3] to improve the accuracy of feature extraction in U-Net. PSPNet [17] introduced Pyramid Pooling Module (PPM) to extract features having the global and local information. DeepLab v3 [2] introduced the atrous convolution into the encoder and PPM to control the resolution of features and modified the structure of the decoder. The conventional methods considered to extract multi-class segments simultaneously from a scene. Hence, such methods are not always effective in hand segmentation for contactless palmprint recognition.

This paper proposes a hand segmentation method using the encoder-decorder network for contactless palmprint recognition. The network architecture of the proposed CNN is inspired by PSPNet, which consists of the encoder, PPM and the decoder. We employs ResNet18 with dilated convolution layers for the encoder and find the best skip connections from the encoder to the decoder. We also introduce the Intersection over Union (IoU) loss [10] to improve the quality of hand segmentation in addition to the cross-entropy loss. Through a set of experiments using a hand image dataset, we demonstrate that the proposed method exhibits efficient performance on hand segmentation compared with conventional methods: U-Net, TernausNet, PSPNet and DeepLab v3 in terms of the accuracy and IoU.

2 Related Work

This section describes the brief summary of conventional image segmentation methods using the encoder-decoder network.

2.1 U-Net [11]

U-Net has been proposed to extract segments from biomedical images. The network architecture of U-Net is inspired by Fully-Convolutional Network (FCN) [12] and has symmetric architectures between the encoder and decoder, resulting in a U-shaped architecture. Figure 1(a) shows the architecture of U-Net.

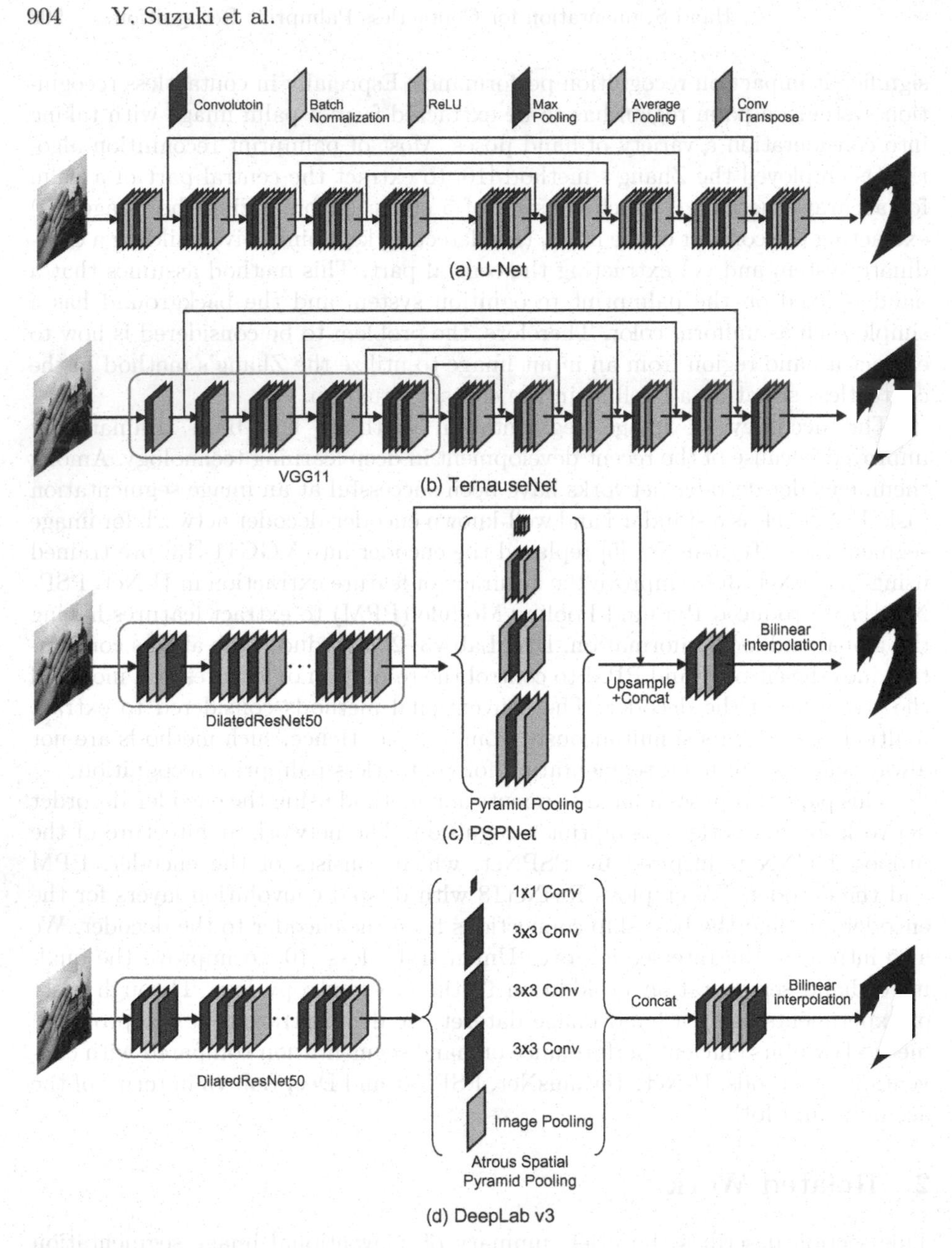

Fig. 1. Network architecture of conventional methods: (a) U-Net, (b) TernausNet, (c) PSPNet and (d) DeepLab v3.

2.2 TernausNet [5]

TernausNet has the same architecture as U-Net. The difference from U-Net is to employ VGG11 pretrained on ImageNet for the encoder. The accuracy of TernausNet is higher than U-Net, since fine-tuning was applied to weights for the encoder, which are initialized by training on ImageNet. Figure 1(b) shows the architecture of TernausNet.

2.3 PSPNet [17]

PSPNet introduced PPM to extract the global and local features from the encoder. PPM has a hierarchical structure so as to extract features containing information with different scales and varying among different sub-regions. PPM combines features extracted from four different pyramid scales. The coarsest level outputs a single bin by global pooling. The following level outputs the feature map from different sub-regions. The output of PPM is obtained by concatenating feature maps from each level and the feature map from the encoder. The final prediction map is generated by a convolution layer as well as FCN. PSPNet employed ResNet50 pretrained on ImageNet as the encoder. Figure 1(c) shows the architecture of PSPNet.

2.4 DeepLab v3 [2]

DeepLab v3 introduced the atrous convolution, which is also known as the dilated convolution, to prevent from decreasing the resolution of feature maps by pooling and striding. The use of the atrous convolution makes it possible to extract features from wide range depending on the atrous rate. DeepLab v3 employed the Atrous Spatial Pyramid Pooling (ASPP) module, which consists of PPM with atrous convolutions. In addition, ResNet used in the encoder was improved so as to control the resolution of feature maps. Figure 1(d) shows the architecture of DeepLab v3.

3 Proposed Method

This section describes the hand segmentation method using CNN for contactless palmprint recognition. The proposed method is based on the encoder-decoder network with PPM. The encoder-decoder network like U-Net can extract the reliable structure of segments compared with FCN. Figure 2 shows the network architecture of the proposed method. The detail configuration for the decoder and the encoder shown in Tables 1 and 2.

3.1 Encoder

The encoder of the proposed method is based on ResNet18 [4] pretrained on ImageNet, which consists of 1 convolution layer and 4 convolution blocks. The difference from ResNet18 is to employ the dilated convolution layer [14] in Block 3 and Block 4. In the case of 3×3 kernel size, the receptive filed of the common convolution is adjacent 3×3 pixels, while that of the dilated convolution is sampled 3×3 pixels at intervals of the parameter *dilation*. Note that the common convolution is the same as the dilated convolution with $dilation = 1$. The receptive fields can be expanded without losing resolution or coverage by replacing the convolutions into the dilated convolutions. The use of dilated convolutions makes it possible to reduce the size of feature map by 1/8 and to contain the loss of positional information.

3.2 PPM

The feature map extracted by the encoder is input to PPM. The network structure of PPM used in the proposed method is the same in PSPNet [17]. PPM applies pooling with the different size of kernels to the feature map extracted from the encoder so as to obtain the global and local information.

3.3 Decoder

The pooling process in PPM may remove the information of object boundaries. Such boundary information is significantly important to extract objects having complex structure like a hand. Therefore, the proposed method introduces the decoder like U-Net [11] and RefineNet [8] to PSPNet so as to reconstruct the object boundary using the feature map from PPM and the intermediate features from the encoder. It is not always optimal to use the intermediate features from the same resolution layers in the encoder, although the intermediate features from the same resolution layers in the encoder are usually used in the decoder of the U-Net based approaches. Hence, we find which resolution of intermediate features in the encoder is optimal for the decoder.

3.4 Loss Function for Hand Segmentation

Most image segmentation methods using CNN employed the cross-entropy loss function in training, since such methods produce segments for each class such as human, chair, table, car, bike, etc. On the other hand, this paper focuses on only one class, that is, a hand. We also emphasize the accuracy in terms of IoU to obtain the precise hand segment. For this purpose, we introduce the IoU loss function to optimize our network in training. IoU is an evaluation criterion for image segmentation and is defined by

$$IoU = \frac{|X \cap Y|}{|X \cup Y|}, \tag{1}$$

where X and Y indicate the output of the network and the ground-truth, respectively. It is easy to understand that back propagation cannot be defined for Eq. (1), since this equation is not differentiable. Addressing this problem, the

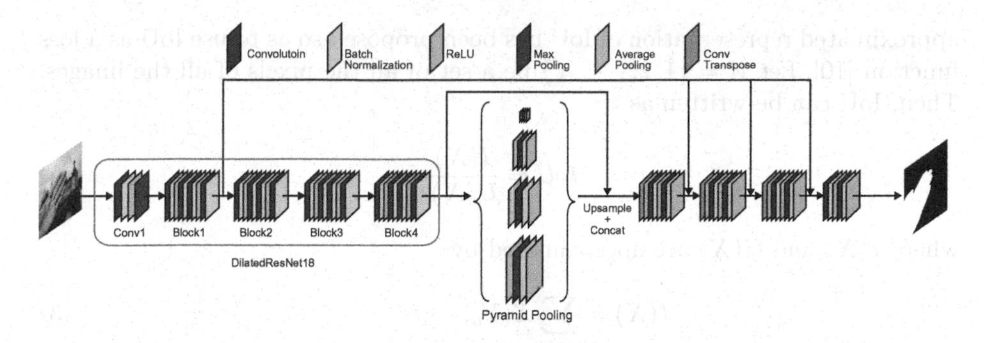

Fig. 2. Network architecture of the proposed method.

Table 1. Configuration of the encoder in the proposed method.

Layer	Output size	Configuration of layers
Conv1	240 × 240	7 × 7, 64, stride = 2
Block1	120 × 120	3 × 3 maxpool, stride = 2
		[3 × 3 64, 3 × 3 64]×2
Block2	60 × 60	[3 × 3 128, 3 × 3 128]×2
Block3	60 × 60	[3 × 3 256, 3 × 3 256]
		[3 × 3 256 dilation = 2,
		3 × 3 256 dilation = 2]
Block4	60 × 60	[3 × 3 512, 3 × 3 512]
		[3 × 3 512 dilation = 4,
		3 × 3 512 dilation = 4]
PPM	60 × 60	

Table 2. Configuration of the decoder in the proposed method.

Layer	Output size	Configuration of layers
upConv1	120 × 120	2 × 2 ConvTranspose, stride = 2
		[3 × 3 512, 3 × 3 512]
upConv2	240 × 240	2 × 2 ConvTranspose, stride = 2
		[3 × 3 256, 3 × 3 256]
upConv3	480 × 480	2 × 2 ConvTranspose, stride = 2
		[3 × 3 128, 3 × 3 128]
Conv	480 × 480	[3 × 3 2, 3 × 3 2]

approximated representation of IoU has been proposed so as to use IoU as a loss function [10]. Let $V = \{1, 2, \cdots, N\}$ be a set of all the pixels of all the images. Then, IoU can be written as

$$IoU = \frac{I(X)}{U(X)}, \tag{2}$$

where $I(X)$ and $U(X)$ are approximated by

$$I(X) = \sum_{v \in V} X_v Y_v, \tag{3}$$

$$U(X) = \sum_{v \in V} (X_v + Y_v - X_v Y_v). \tag{4}$$

The IoU loss is defined as follows:

$$L_{IoU} = 1 - IoU = 1 - \frac{I(x)}{U(x)}. \tag{5}$$

4 Experiments and Discussion

This section discribes experiments to evaluate the performance of the proposed method using the hand image dataset.

The experiments use three image datasets: 11k Hands, Places365 and ours. The 11k Hands dataset provided by Afifi [1] consists of 189 subjects and about 58 images per person as shown in Fig. 3(a). The total number of hand images is 11,076 and the image size is $1,600 \times 1,200$ pixels. All the images are taken with the white background, resulting in easily extracting a hand region from the image. Therefore, we use the 11k Hands dataset for training. The Places365 dataset consists of 1,825,000 scene images with 365 categories as shown in Fig. 3(b), where the image size is 256×256 pixels. This dataset is used as a background of hand images. Our dataset consists of 180 images taken from 5 subjects with a wide variety of hand pose as shown in Fig. 3(c), where the image size is $2,272 \times 1,704$ pixels and the images are taken with the blue-color background. The images in this dataset are used in test.

We use the synthetic images for training and test in the experiments. We randomly select 2 images for each subject from the 11k Hands dataset and extract a hand segment from each image by simple thresholding. The total number of hand segments is 378. We apply data augmentation of random rotation and random crop to hand segments to have 1,890 images with $1,200 \times 1,200$ pixels. All the images are resized to 480×480 pixels and then are combined with the background image from the Places365 dataset as shown in Fig. 4(a), where the size of background images is resized to 480×480 pixels. The resultant images are used in training. 80% of training data is used for training and the remaining 20% is used for validation to check the overfitting. The images in our dataset are resized to $1,600 \times 1,600$ pixels after center cropping and then hand segments are extracted by simple thresholding. The hand segments are resized to 480 × 480 pixels and are combined with the background image from the Places365 dataset as well as the training data as shown in Fig. 4(b). The resultant images are used in test.

The loss is calculated by cross entropy and the initial learning rate is 0.001. We use Nesterov Accelerated Gradients Optimizer [9]. We train the network the maximum 100 epochs and use a batch size of 4. We randomly change the pixel intensity and contrast of the training data for data augmentation in training. We use the evaluation criteria of IoU [%] and the accuracy [%] in the experiments, where the accuracy is defined by the pixel accuracy.

Fig. 3. Example of images in each dataset: (a) 11k Hands, (b) Places365 and (c) ours.

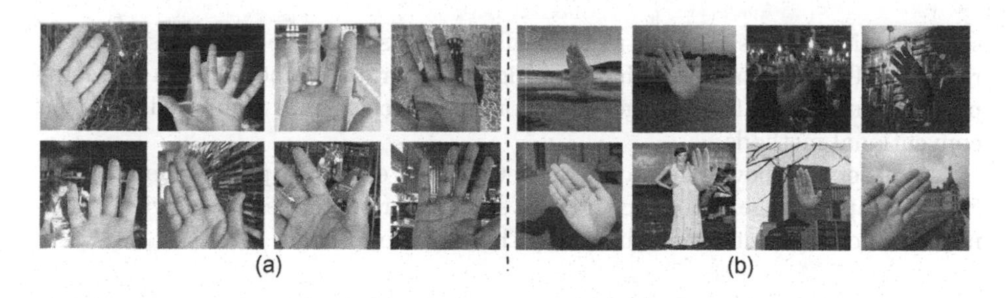

Fig. 4. Example of synthesized training data and test data: (a) training data generated from images in 11k Hands and (b) test data generated from images in our dataset.

At first, we find the optimal skip connections for the proposed method. We consider 6 patters of skip connections as shown in Fig. 5. Table 3 shows the experimental results for finding optimal skip connections. The upper row indicates the proposed method trained by the cross-entropy loss and the lower row indicates the proposed method trained by the cross-entropy loss and the IoU loss. the pattern (iii) trained by the cross-entropy loss and the IoU loss exhibits the best result in terms of IoU and accuracy.

Next, we compare the accuracy of the proposed method with the conventional methods: U-Net, TernausNet, PSPNet and DeepLab v3. Table 4 show the experimental results for each method and Fig. 6 shows the example of hand

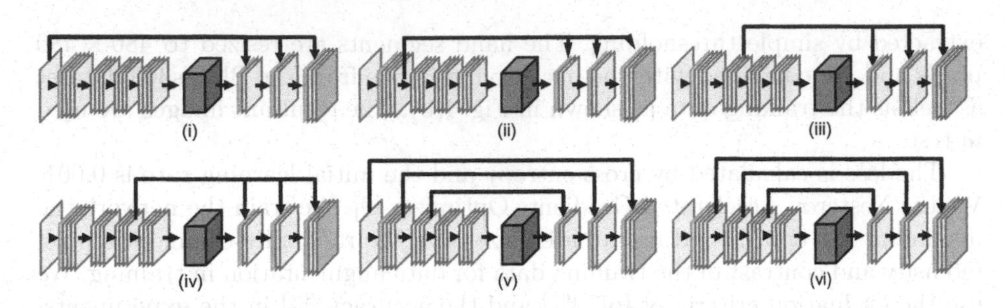

Fig. 5. Variations of skip connection for the proposed method.

Table 3. Experimental results for finding the best skip connections from the encoder to the decoder in the proposed method. The upper row indicates the proposed method with cross-entropy loss and the lower row indicates the proposed method with cross-entropy and IoU loss.

Method	(i)	(ii)	(iii)	(iv)	(v)	(vi)
IoU [%]	81.51	76.34	89.64	83.16	88.83	87.95
	89.40	86.39	**93.2**	87.57	90.46	89.83
Accuracy [%]	97.34	96.44	98.56	97.65	98.45	98.05
	98.21	97.62	**98.90**	98.30	98.51	98.26

segmentation results for each method. The proposed method exhibits the best result in all the methods. As shown in Fig. 6, the proposed method can extract a precise hand region from images with complex backgrounds compared with the conventional methods.

As observed above, the proposed method can extract a precise hand region from an input image, whose accuracy is enough for contactless palmprint recognition, since segmentation results keep the shape of a hand.

Table 4. Experimental results for each method.

Method	U-Net [11]	TernausNet [5]	PSPNet [17]	DeepLab v3 [2]	Proposed
IoU [%]	57.26	66.39	80.27	88.35	**93.20**
Accuracy [%]	92.11	93.99	96.26	98.14	**98.90**

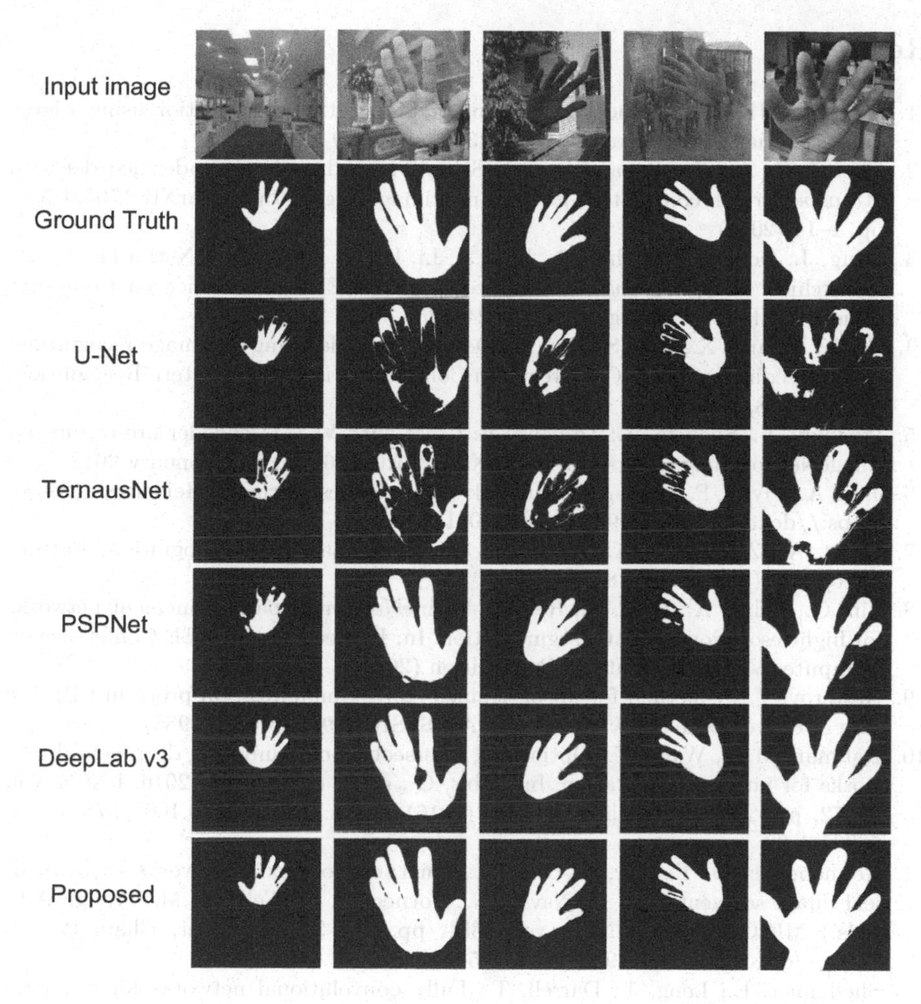

Fig. 6. Example of hand segmentation results for each method.

5 Conclusion

This paper proposed a hand segmentation method using the encoder-decorder network for contactless palmprint recognition. We developed the architecture inspired by PSPNet, which consists of the encoder, PPM and the decoder. We employed ResNet18 with dilated convolution layers for the encoder and introduced the IoU loss to improve the quality of hand segmentation. Through a set of experiments using a hand image dataset, we demonstrated that the proposed method exhibited efficient performance on hand segmentation compared with conventional methods: U-Net, TernausNet, PSPNet and DeepLab v3. We will develop a contactless palmprint recognition system using the proposed hand segmentation method in the future work.

References

1. Afifi, M.: 11K hands: gender recognition and biometric identification using a large dataset of hand images. arXiv:1711.04322, pp. 1–19 (2017)
2. Chen, L.C., Zhu, Y., Papandreou, G., Schroff, F., Adam, H.: Encoder-decoder with atrous separable convolution for semantic image segmentation. arXiv:1706.05587, pp. 1–14 (2017)
3. Deng, J., Dong, W., Socher, R., Li, L.J., Li, K., Li, F.F.: ImageNet: a large-scale hierarchical image database. In: Proceedings of IEEE Conference on Computer Vision and Pattern Recognition, pp. 248–255, June 2009
4. He, K., Zhang, X., Ren, S., Sun, J.: Deep residual learning for image recognition. In: Proceedings of IEEE Conference on Computer Vision and Pattern Recognition, pp. 770–778, June 2016
5. Iglovikiv, V., Shebets, A.: TernausNet: U-net with VGG11 encoder pre-trained on ImageNet for image segmentation. arXiv:1801.05746, pp. 1–5, January 2018
6. Jain, A., Flynn, P., Ross, A.: Handbook of Biometrics. Springer, Heidelberg (2008). https://doi.org/10.1007/978-0-387-71041-9
7. Kong, A., Zhang, D., Kamel, M.: A survey of palmprint recognition. Pattern Recogn. **42**(7), 1408–1418 (2009)
8. Lin, G., Milan, A., Shen, C., Reid, I.: RefineNet: multi-path refinement networks for high-resolution semantic segmentation. In: Proceedings of IEEE Conference on Computer Vision and Pattern Recognition (2017)
9. Nesterov, Y.: A method for unconstrained convex minimization problem with the rate of convergence $o(1/k^2)$. Doklady AN SSSR **269**, 543–547 (1983)
10. Rahman, M.A., Wang, Y.: Optimizing intersection-over-union in deep neural networks for image segmentation. In: Bebis, G., et al. (eds.) ISVC 2016. LNCS, vol. 10072, pp. 234–244. Springer, Cham (2016). https://doi.org/10.1007/978-3-319-50835-1_22
11. Ronneberger, O., Fischer, P., Brox, T.: U-net: convolutional networks for biomedical image segmentation. In: Navab, N., Hornegger, J., Wells, W.M., Frangi, A.F. (eds.) MICCAI 2015. LNCS, vol. 9351, pp. 234–241. Springer, Cham (2015). https://doi.org/10.1007/978-3-319-24574-4_28
12. Shelhamer, E., Long, J., Darrell, T.: Fully convolutional networks for semantic segmentation. IEEE Trans. Pattern Anal. Mach. Intell. **39**(4), 640–651 (2017)
13. Simonyan, K., Zisserman, A.: Very deep convolutional networks for large-scale image recognition. arXiv:1409.1556, September 2014
14. Yu, F., Koltun, V.: Multi-scale context aggregation by dilated convolutions. In: Proceedings of International Conference on Learning Representation (2016)
15. Zhang, D.: Palmprint Authentication. Kluwer Academic Publication, Dordrecht (2004)
16. Zhang, D., Kong, W.K., You, J., Wong, M.: Online palmprint identification. IEEE Trans. Pattern Anal. Mach. Intell. **25**(9), 1041–1050 (2003)
17. Zhao, H., Shi, J., Qi, X., Wang, X., Jia, J.: Pyramid scene parsing network. In: Proceedings of IEEE Conference on Computer Vision and Pattern Recognition, pp. 2881–2890 (2017)

Selecting Discriminative Features for Fine-Grained Visual Classification

Qin Xu(✉), Linyang Li, Qian Chen, and Bin Luo

Key Laboratory of Intelligent Computing and Signal Processing of Ministry of Education, School of Computer Science and Technology, Anhui University, Hefei 230601, China
{xuqin,luobin}@ahu.edu.cn, linyanglly@163.com, cqchenqianqc@163.com

Abstract. Fine-grained visual classification is a challenging task because of intra-class variation and inter-class similarity. Most fine-grained models predominantly focus on discriminative region localization which can effectively solve the intra-class variation, but ignore global information and the problem of inter-class similarity which easily leads to overfitting on specific samples. To address these issues, we develop an end-to-end model based on selecting discriminative features for fine-grained visual classification without the help of part or bounding box annotations. In order to accurately select discriminative features, we integrate effective information from different receptive fields to enhance the quality of features, then the features of discriminative regions detected by anchors and the whole image's feature are jointly processed for classification. Besides, we propose a new loss function to optimize the model to find discriminative regions and prevent overfitting in the particular sample, which can simultaneously solve the problems of intra-class variation and inter-class similarity. Comprehensive experiments show that the proposed approach is superior to the state-of-the-art methods on CUB-200-2011, Stanford Cars and FGVC-Aircraft datasets.

Keywords: Fine-grained visual classification · Feature pyramid networks · Selective kernel networks

1 Introduction

Fine-grained visual classification has recently emerged as a hot topic in the field of computer vision. It aims to classify different subordinate categories within a general category, such as species of birds [16], types of aircrafts [27] and models of vehicles [20]. Compared with the coarse-grained classification tasks, the fine-grained visual classification is more difficult, because it focuses on capturing subtle differences between fine-grained categories. These marginal visual differences within subordinate categories are too hard to be discovered for people who don't have relevant professional knowledge. Objects that belong to the same subordinate category usually show significantly different due to many uncertain factors such as illumination, pose and background interference, etc. These factors

S. Palaiahnakote et al. (Eds.): ACPR 2019, LNCS 12046, pp. 913–926, 2020.
https://doi.org/10.1007/978-3-030-41404-7_65

are easy to interfere with the learning of effective features in training. Moreover, fine-grained datasets have many subordinate categories that require experts to collect and mark, thus it is difficult to expand. Although the fine-grained visual classification task faces formidable challenges, it has a wide range of application prospects such as damage identification of vehicle and flower recognition. Accurately identifying fine-grained images can greatly reduce labor costs and improve production rate.

The majority of efforts in the fine-grained visual classification focus on how to effectively localize discriminative regions and learn powerful feature representation. Some works [10,12,31,35] learn fine-grained features by relying on extra part or bounding box annotations, but the additional human cost is too high to be widely used in practice. Therefore, fine-grained visual classification only depends on image-level annotations has received more and more attention and makes significant progress in recent research. For example, TLAN [11] performs spectral clustering on a large number of alternative regions from the input image and regards each cluster as a region detector to find discriminative regions. In contrast, [22] uses convolutional neural networks to generate neural activation maps, chooses the larger response as key points for fine-grained classification. Lin et al. [7] design an end-to-end bilinear model which compute the pairwise feature interactions by two independent CNNs. Later, RA-CNN [13] proposes a novel recurrent attention convolutional neural network which enables to localize discriminative regions and learn high-quality features in a mutually enhanced manner. However, this method can only locate the most discriminative regions, while [14] can generate multiple discriminative regions by clustering spatially related channels, and zoom in those critical regions to learn fine-grained features. The OSME module [25] consists of multiple SEnets [23] can also learn multiple detailed features of fine-grained images, and uses the multi-attention multi-class constraint to pull the features of the same attention and same class closer, which has achieved the state-of-the-art results in fine-grained visual classification.

A large number of fine-grained visual classification methods [7,11,13,14,22, 25] show that the key of fine-grained classification lies on discriminative regions localization and the learning of fine-grained features. In order to meet these demands, we adopt the idea of SKnet [29], which could adaptively adjust the size of the receptive field according to multiple scales of the input information, to fuse useful information in different receptive fields for localization and feature learning. However, discriminative regions localization only tackles the problem of intra-class variance, we also solve the issue of inter-class similarity by a novel loss function that can prevent overfitting on specific samples.

Specifically, we utilize a pre-trained model ResNet-50 [1] to acquire the feature map from an input image, then fuse the useful information of different receptive fields by convolutional kernels of different size to obtain a powerful feature map, which combines global and detailed information in the image for localization and feature learning. Anchors of different size are used to generate multiple part regions, which can predict the informativeness of these regions and the region's probability belongs to the real category. Our method zooms in discriminative regions to extract fine-grained features and concatenates these part features with image's feature for fine-grained classification. The effective features can further boost the classification performance in various fine-grained classification tasks. A novel loss function is used to supervise the selected regions, it not only encourages that the informativeness of regions and their probability being true class is in the same order, but also prevents overfitting on specific samples by adding the Euclidean Confusion loss [17] so that the generalization ability of our model is improved.

In short, the main contributions of our work can be summarized as follows: Firstly, we accurately localize discriminative regions and learn fine-grained features for fine-grained visual classification by fusing useful information of different receptive fields without the need of additional part annotations. The effective discriminative regions localization solves the problem of intra-class variance. Secondly, we propose a new loss function to help the model localize discriminative regions and prevent overfitting on specific samples that can deal with the issue of inter-class similarity.

2 Related Work

2.1 Fine-Grained Visual Classification

With the rapid development of deep neural networks, deep convolutional features that have replaced traditional features by its powerful advantages become one of the key factors to improve the performance of fine-grained visual classification. Earlier works [10,12,18,19,21] extract convolutional features based on extra part or bounding box annotations. Although it achieves better classification accuracy than previous works, additional part or bounding box annotations that require a large amount of manual cost are unpractical to solve large-scaled problems. Therefore, fine-grained visual classification relies on the category labels [3,4,17,24,26,28] which show its superior performance has attracted more and more attention. Different from [11] and [14] determine key regions by clustering, NTS-Net [26] introduces the Feature Pyramid Networks [6] into fine-grained visual classification, which detects informative regions and learns the corresponding fine-grained features. WS-DAN [28] uses data augmentation to generate discriminative object's parts by dropping and cropping the part regions of images. Besides, Recurrent Attention Convolutional Neural Network [13] utilizes an inter-scale ranking loss and an intra-scale classification loss to jointly optimize the network, so that discriminative region detection and fine-grained feature learning can reinforce each other. Lin et al. [7] employs parallel CNNs for bilinear feature extraction, and the work in [25] adopts multiple SEnets [23] and multi-attention multi-class constraint to achieve significantly performance in fine-grained classification. Unlike the above approaches, in [15], a measure is designed to estimate the visual similarity between source and target domains, while [17] and [24] perform fine-grained classification by introducing confusion in activations and learning a set of convolutional filters, respectively.

2.2 Part Localization

Due to the interference of different poses and viewpoints, fine-grained images that belong to the same category usually present significantly different. Discriminative part localization is beneficial for fine-grained models to focus on key details that overcome the intra-class variance in fine-grained images. Accurate positioning of multiple parts by image-level labels become a new challenge in the field of fine-grained visual classification. Therefore, some methods of fine-grained visual classification based on attention mechanism have emerged. MA-CNN [14] that extends the classification performance of RA-CNN [13] enables the network to simultaneously localize multiple attention areas with strong discrimination ability by clustering spatially-correlated channels, it achieves superior performance over the RA-CNN on three different fine-grained datasets. When the most discriminative regions is hidden, Hide-and-Seek [30] can find other relevant parts. Therefore, Hu et al. [28] utilize attention-guided data augmentation to acquire discriminative parts of the object. Besides, picking deep filter responses [33] and multiple granularity descriptors [32] analyze filter response to acquire a set of part detectors, and then [24] proposes to learn a group of convolutional filters to capture minor differences of different objects. Compared with them, our work has significant advantages. First, the performance of the feature map is improved by reducing the interference of useless information in the preprocessing stage, thus it can promote the accuracy of discriminative part localization among different objects. Second, it conducts all-round information detection on multi-scale regions, which can efficiently localize multiple discriminative regions at the same time, so that the model concentrates on the parts that are easy to distinguish the object. Fine-grained feature learning and region localization can reinforce each other, it is possible to acquire representative regions and achieve better performance in fine-grained tasks.

3 Proposed Method

Our proposed method learns multiple discriminative features quickly and efficiently without additional part or bounding box annotations. It can fuse effective information of different receptive fields to improve the quality of the extracted feature maps. Then part regions are scored by using different scale anchors, and regions get higher scores on the correct label are selected as discriminative regions to further improve the classification accuracy. Finally, we design a loss function to ensure that our model extracts more discriminative features from the object and prevents overfitting effectively. Our framework is shown in Fig. 1.

3.1 Feature Augmentation

Given an input image, we put it into ResNet-50 to obtain a feature map $\mathbf{X} \in \mathbb{R}^{H' \times W' \times C'}$. In the deep neural networks, the larger receptive field means the more global features can be learned, on the contrary, the smaller receptive field is

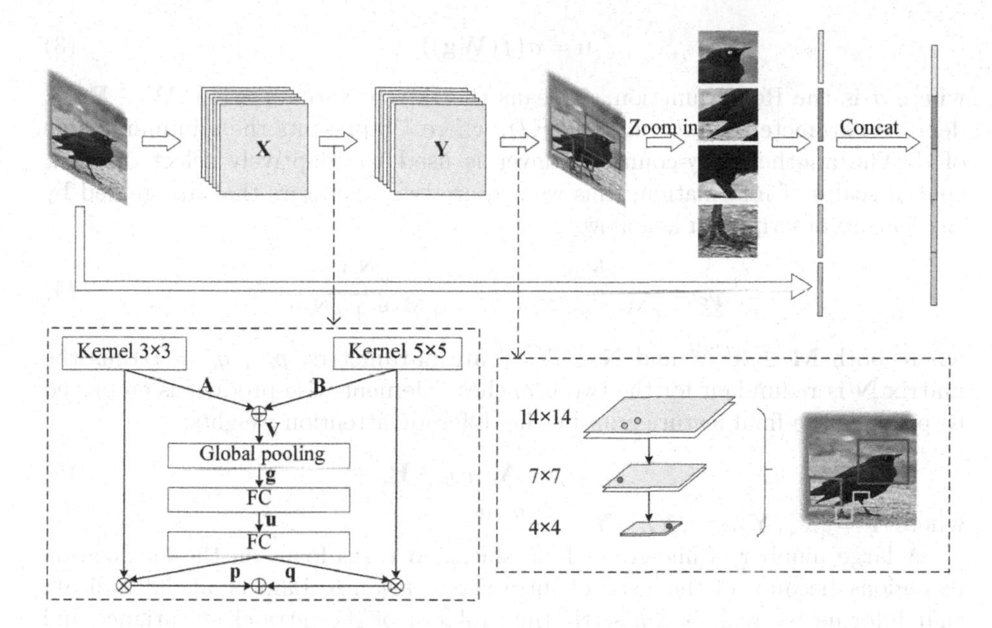

Fig. 1. Overview of our network architecture. Given an input image, we first extract its deep feature map by a feature extractor. Aggregating the feature maps of differently sized kernels via attention weights to optimize the feature map. After that, part regions with different scales are constructed with a score denoting the informativeness of the region, the four part regions with the highest score are retained and enlarged. Concatenating the features of those regions with input image's feature into a fully-connected layer for the final classification.

easier to grasp some detailed features. In order to fuse the useful information of different receptive fields and improve the quality of the feature map, we use a set of operations which are composed of grouped convolutions, Batch Normalization [2] and ReLU [5] function in sequence with convolutional kernels of different size, thus we get two new feature maps, a feature map $\mathbf{A} \in \mathbb{R}^{H \times W \times C}$ with a 3×3 convolutional kernel and another feature map $\mathbf{B} \in \mathbb{R}^{H \times W \times C}$ with kernel sizes 5×5, respectively. In order to integrate the information of different branches, we merge the results of feature maps through element-wise summation:

$$\mathbf{V} = \mathbf{A} + \mathbf{B} \tag{1}$$

To enhance the useful information and suppress the useless information in the feature map, we use global average pooling to compress the information of each channel into a channel descriptor, thus a vector $\mathbf{g} \in \mathbb{R}^{C}$ is obtained by:

$$g_c = \frac{1}{H \times W} \sum_{i=1}^{H} \sum_{j=1}^{W} \mathbf{V}_c(i, j) \tag{2}$$

Then two fully-connected layers are utilized to filter the useless information from different scales. First, we apply a fully-connected layer to compress $\mathbf{g}$ into a compact feature $\mathbf{u} \in \mathbb{R}^{d \times 1}$:

$$\mathbf{u} = \sigma(f(\mathbf{Wg})) \tag{3}$$

where σ is the ReLU function, f means the Batch Normalization, $\mathbf{W} \in \mathbb{R}^{d\times C}$ denotes parameter and $d = \max(C/r, l)$, where l represents the minimum value of d. The another fully-connected layer is used to adaptively select different spatial scales of information, thus we acquire two operators that are guided by the feature descriptor $\mathbf{u}$ as follows:

$$p_c = \frac{e^{\mathbf{M}_c\mathbf{u}}}{e^{\mathbf{M}_c\mathbf{u}} + e^{\mathbf{N}_c\mathbf{u}}}, q_c = \frac{e^{\mathbf{N}_c\mathbf{u}}}{e^{\mathbf{M}_c\mathbf{u}} + e^{\mathbf{N}_c\mathbf{u}}} \tag{4}$$

where both $\mathbf{M} \in \mathbb{R}^{C\times d}$ and $\mathbf{N} \in \mathbb{R}^{C\times d}$ are parameters. $p_c + q_c = 1$ thus the matrix $\mathbf{N}$ is redundant for the two branches. Element-wise product is employed to produce the final feature map by the different attention weights:

$$\mathbf{Y}_c = p_c \cdot \mathbf{A}_c + q_c \cdot \mathbf{B}_c \tag{5}$$

where $\mathbf{Y} = [\mathbf{Y}_1, \mathbf{Y}_2, \cdots, \mathbf{Y}_C]$, $\mathbf{Y}_c \in \mathbb{R}^{H\times W}$.

A large number of fine-grained classification tasks focus on the localization of regions because of the issue of intra-class variance. Lam et al. [9] indicate that informative regions can settle the problem of the intra-class variance and may generate a higher confidence score on the true label. Therefore, discriminative regions must be abundant in useful information, the performance of the fine-grained classification task can be effectively improved by finding the most informative regions and concatenating the features of these regions and the whole image.

Inspired by the introduced Feature Pyramid Networks [6] into the fine-grained classification by Yang et al. [26], we consider to use anchors to predict multiple regions and extract discriminative features from selected regions to carry out fine-grained classification. Inputting the feature map of an image, we utilize convolutional layers to calculate feature hierarchy and then obtain a series of multi-scale feature maps, which can generate informativeness of regions of different scale. The sizes of the feature maps are 14 × 14, 7 × 7 and 4 × 4, which corresponds to scales 48 × 48, 96 × 96 and 192 × 192 in the image, respectively.

Multiple regions are marked with scores, the region with a higher score means its informativeness is richer, which is beneficial to enhance the classification performance of the whole image. In order to reduce the redundancy of regions and the computational cost of the network, we use non-maximum suppression (NMS) to pick out T region proposals with higher scores and zoom in them to extract the fine-grained features. These features are fed into the network to predict the image's probability that belongs to the real category. The loss function is utilized to optimize the informativeness of region proposals to acquire discriminative features for fine-grained classification.

We select the top F discriminative regions from region proposals and concatenate their features with the whole image's feature, so that the network can obtain both global information and detailed information of the object, which is beneficial to further improve the classification accuracy.

3.2 Optimization

In the fine-grained visual classification tasks, the richer informativeness the selected region has, the better classification performance we will acquire. The role of L_{ipre} ensures that the order of the informativeness of each selected region and probability of real category is consistent, otherwise the penalty is imposed. For the tth region proposal, the informativeness of the region is R_t, and its probability being real category is P_t, then L_{ipre} is defined as follows:

$$L_{ipre} = \sum_{P_i < P_j} f(R_j - R_i) - \sum_{i=1}^{T} logP_i \quad (6)$$

where i and j respectively represent different region proposals, and $f(x) = \max(1 - x, 0)$ is a hinge loss function. If $P_j > P_i$, then $R_j > R_i$. The second term is the sum of cross entropy loss of region proposals.

Using the anchors to detect informative regions in the image only solves the intra-class variance problem, but can't get over the inter-class similarity. Different objects usually have similar content in fine-grained images, it is easy to force the network to learn the unique features based on specific samples, which may cause overfitting and weaken the generalization capability of the network.

Therefore, we prevent the overfitting of the network on particular samples by minimizing the distance between the predicted probability distribution of random sample pairs. Specifically, images are divided into two groups on average, the first group and the second group are corresponding one by one. If the labels of corresponding data are same, the value of L_{dl} is 0, otherwise, it is calculated:

$$L_{dl} = \|P_i - P_j\|_2^2 \quad (7)$$

where P_i denotes the predicted probability distribution of image i, P_j is the predicted probability distribution of image j in another group. The most discriminative regions are enlarged to extract fine-grained features. We concatenate these features with the entire image's feature into a fully-connected layer. Then the concatenate feature loss is defined as:

$$L_{concate} = -logP_0 - logP_{concate} \quad (8)$$

the first half part is the cross entropy loss of the original image, and the second half part represents the cross entropy loss of the concatenate feature.

In summary, our total loss is given by:

$$L_{total} = L_{concate} + L_{ipre} + \alpha \cdot L_{dl} \quad (9)$$

where α is a hyperparameter. The proposed loss function L_{total} not only ensures that the region with richer information has higher predicted probability, but also prevents the overfitting on specific samples and improves the generalization ability of our network. We optimize L_{total} via the stochastic gradient method.

4 Experiments

To verify the proposed approach, we compare experimental results with seven methods on three challenging datasets which are widely used for fine-grained visual classification, including CUB-200-2011 [16], Stanford Cars [20] and FGVC-Aircraft [27] datasets. In our experiments, we only use image-level labels without any additional manual annotations.

4.1 Datasets

The CUB-200-2011 dataset consists of 11,788 images from 200 bird species, the Stanford Cars dataset contains 16,185 images over 196 categories and the FGVC-Aircraft dataset has 10,000 images across 100 classes. Detailed statistics of each dataset is summarized in Table 1, including the number of categories and the split of data.

Table 1. The statistics of fine-grained datasets used in this paper.

Datasets	#Category	#Training	#Testing
CUB-200-2011	200	5,994	5,794
Stanford Cars	196	8,144	8,041
FGVC-Aircraft	100	6,667	3,333

4.2 Implementation Details

We use Pytorch to perform all experiments without any pre-trained detection model on TITAN Xp GPUs. The model is trained using Stochastic Gradient Descent (SGD) with momentum 0.9, weight decay of 0.0001, Batch Normalization as regularizer. The initial learning rate is set to 0.001 and multiplied by 0.1 after 60 epochs. The threshold of the NMS is 0.25, α and r are set to 10 and 16, respectively. The input images are resized to 448×448, then image's features are extracted by the Resnet-50 model pre-trained on ImageNet. $T = 6$ and $F = 4$ mean that top-6 region proposals are selected from all regions and then zoom in top-4 discriminative regions from region proposals to extract their fine-grained features. We concatenate these discriminative features with the image's feature as the final representation. Top-1 accuracy is regarded as the evaluation metric.

4.3 Comparison with State-of-the-Art Methods

We conduct experiments that rely on image-level labels, thus all compared methods do not use any part or bounding box annotations. Our experiments show that our approach achieves better performance on these fine-grained datasets. In particular, we significantly improve the accuracy compared with the backbone ResNet-50, it indicates the effectiveness of our method.

Table 2. Comparison results on CUB-200-2011.

Method	Accuracy
B-CNN [7]	84.1
Resnet-50 [1]	84.5
HIHCA [34]	85.3
RA-CNN [13]	85.3
GP-256 [8]	85.8
MA-CNN [14]	86.5
PC [17]	86.9
Ours	**87.6**

The classification accuracy on the CUB-200-2011 dataset is summarized in Table 2. Compared with B-CNN, we achieve a 3.5% improvement, it shows that discriminative feature learning achieves better performance in fine-grained visual classification. Our model surpasses RA-CNN [13] which can localize the most discriminative part of the object at a time with 2.3% relative accuracy gains and exceeds MA-CNN [14] that can simultaneously obtain multiple key parts with a clear margin 1.1%, indicating that rich information from multiple parts can further improve the classification accuracy. Compared with the previous fine-grained classification method without additional annotation, our approach is able to efficiently localize multiple regions with discriminative information and achieve superior classification performance on the CUB-200-2011 dataset.

As can be seen from the Table 3, compared with the other state-of-the-art methods on Stanford Cars, our model acquires the relative accuracy gain of 2% at most and 0.4% at least. The experimental results show that our method not only can preferably localize subtle discriminative regions, but also can effectively integrate the global information and local details of the car to learn higher quality features. Exact region localization and fine-grained feature learning are mutually reinforced to improve the fine-grained classification accuracy.

Table 4 shows our experimental results on the FGVC-Aircraft dataset. Compared to B-CNN [7] and RA-CNN, we achieve a significant increase of 8% and 3.9% respectively. While for PC [17], our algorithm improves the classification accuracy by 2.9% which shows that discriminative features contribute to distinguishing different aircrafts. The valid classification of similar aircraft means that our method overcomes the difficulty of inter-class similarity in the fine-grained visual classification, in a way it prevents overfitting on specific samples and improves the generalization ability of the model. The classification accuracy of MA-CNN on the FGVC-Aircraft dataset is 89.9% while our accuracy reaches to 92.1%, indicating that our approach localizes discriminative regions more accurately. A more precise localization forces our model to focus on discriminative features in the image, thus it is beneficial to improve the accuracy of fine-grained visual classification.

Table 3. Comparison results on Stanford Cars.

Method	Accuracy
B-CNN [7]	91.3
HIHCA [34]	91.7
Resnet-50 [1]	91.7
RA-CNN [13]	92.5
GP-256 [8]	92.8
MA-CNN [14]	92.8
PC [17]	92.9
Ours	**93.3**

Table 4. Comparison results on FGVC-Aircraft.

Method	Accuracy
B-CNN [7]	84.1
RA-CNN [13]	88.2
HIHCA [34]	88.3
Resnet-50 [1]	88.5
PC [17]	89.2
GP-256 [8]	89.8
MA-CNN [14]	89.9
Ours	**92.1**

We perform some experiments to demonstrate the effectiveness of each component, as shown in Table 5. Compared with the classification results which are obtained by NTS-Net [26], we acquire minor improvements by adding the proposed loss function L_{total} to NTS-CNN. However, the performance of discriminative region localization can be further improved in the third row via fusing different scales useful information, with the relative accuracy gain of 0.7% and 0.5% compared with the first row and the second row, respectively. This phenomenon indicates that each component of our model plays a key role in capturing discriminative features among fine-grained images.

To demonstrate the efficiency of our model, we visualize the most discriminative region that be used to fine-grained classification on three datasets, as shown in Fig. 2. The size of birds is small, thus it is too hard to discover subtle differences among birds. However, our method can grasp the most discriminative features to distinguish the species of birds, such as the shape of beak and the color of feather. The model also finds out the most discriminative features on Stanford Cars and FGVC-Aircraft datasets, it means that our approach achieves significantly better performance in discriminative region localization. Exact region

Table 5. Ablation analysis of our model on FGVC-Aircraft.

Method	Accuracy
NTS-Net [26]	91.4
NTS-Net + L_{total}	**91.6**
Ours	**92.1**

Fig. 2. The visualized results of discriminative region localization on CUB-200-2011, Stanford Cars and FGVC-Aircraft datasets.

localization is helpful to learn finer features so that it can further improve the fine-grained classification results.

5 Conclusions

This paper has proposed a new method for fine-grained classification in an end-to-end manner. The proposed method can jointly learn discriminative region localization and fine-grained feature representation via image-level labels. In order to pick out discriminative regions and learn better features, we fuse the useful information of different receptive fields of the fine-grained image. Besides, we have presented a new loss function to optimize the model, so that our model can find discriminative regions and prevent overfitting in the particular sample, which can simultaneously solve the problems of intra-class variation and inter-class similarity. A large number of experiments have shown that our method can learn high-quality discriminative features and achieve better performance in fine-grained image classification.

Acknowledgments. The authors would like to thank the anonymous referees for their constructive comments which have helped improve the paper. This work is supported by National Natural Science Foundation of China (61502003, 71501002, 71701001, 61860206004); Natural Science Foundation of Anhui Province (1608085QF133); Key Research Project of Humanities and Social Sciences in Colleges and Universities of Anhui Province (SK2019A0013).

References

1. He, K., Zhang, X., Ren, S., Sun, J.: Deep residual learning for image recognition. In: Proceedings of the IEEE Conference on Computer Vision and Pattern Recognition, pp. 770–778 (2016)
2. Ioffe, S., Szegedy, C.: Batch normalization: accelerating deep network training by reducing internal covariate shift. arXiv preprint arXiv: 1502.03167 (2015)
3. Li, Z., Yang, Y., Liu, X., Zhou, F., Wen, S., Xu, W.: Dynamic computational time for visual attention. In: Proceedings of the IEEE International Conference on Computer Vision Workshops, pp. 1199–1209 (2017)
4. Lai, D., Tian, W., Chen, L.: Improving classification with semi-supervised and fine-grained learning. Pattern Recogn. **88**, 547–556 (2019)
5. Nair, V., Hinton, G.E.: Rectified linear units improve restricted Boltzmann machines. In: Proceedings of the 27th International Conference on Machine Learning, pp. 807–814 (2010)
6. Lin, T.Y., Dollar, P., Girshick, R., He, K., Hariharan, B., Belongie, S.: Feature pyramid networks for object detection. In: Proceedings of the IEEE Conference on Computer Vision and Pattern Recognition, pp. 2117–2125 (2017)
7. Lin, T.Y., RoyChowdhury, A., Maji, S.: Bilinear CNN models for fine-grained visual recognition. In: Proceedings of the IEEE International Conference on Computer Vision, pp. 1449–1457 (2015)
8. Wei, X., Zhang, Y., Gong, Y., Zhang, J., Zheng, N.: Grassmann pooling as compact homogeneous bilinear pooling for fine-grained visual classification. In: Proceedings of the European Conference on Computer Vision, pp. 355–370 (2018)
9. Lam, M., Mahasseni, B., Todorovic, S.: Fine-grained recognition as hsnet search for informative image parts. In: Proceedings of the IEEE Conference on Computer Vision and Pattern Recognition, pp. 2520–2529 (2017)
10. Branson, S., Van Horn, G., Belongie, S., Perona, P.: Bird species categorization using pose normalized deep convolutional nets. arXiv preprint arXiv: 1406.2952 (2014)
11. Xiao, T., Xu, Y., Yang, K., Zhang, J., Peng, Y., Zhang, Z.: The application of two-level attention models in deep convolutional neural network for fine-grained image classification. In: Proceedings of the IEEE Conference on Computer Vision and Pattern Recognition, pp. 842–850 (2015)
12. Zhang, N., Donahue, J., Girshick, R., Darrell, T.: Part-based R-CNNs for fine-grained category detection. In: Fleet, D., Pajdla, T., Schiele, B., Tuytelaars, T. (eds.) ECCV 2014. LNCS, vol. 8689, pp. 834–849. Springer, Cham (2014). https://doi.org/10.1007/978-3-319-10590-1_54
13. Fu, J., Zheng, H., Mei, T.: Look closer to see better: recurrent attention convolutional neural network for fine-grained image recognition. In: Proceedings of the IEEE Conference on Computer Vision and Pattern Recognition, pp. 4438–4446 (2017)

14. Zheng, H., Fu, J., Mei, T., Luo, J.: Learning multi-attention convolutional neural network for fine-grained image recognition. In: Proceedings of the IEEE International Conference on Computer Vision, pp. 5209–5217 (2017)
15. Cui, Y., Song, Y., Sun, C., Howard, A., Belongie, S.: Large scale fine-grained categorization and domain-specific transfer learning. In: Proceedings of the IEEE Conference on Computer Vision and Pattern Recognition, pp. 4109–4118 (2018)
16. Wah, C., Branson, S., Welinder, P., Perona, P., Belongie, S.: The Caltech-UCSD birds-200-2011 dataset. Computation Neural Systems Technical Report CNS-TR-2011-001, California Institute of Technology (2011)
17. Dubey, A., Gupta, O., Guo, P., Raskar, R., Farrell, R., Naik, N.: Pairwise confusion for fine-grained visual classification. In: Proceedings of the European Conference on Computer Vision, pp. 70–86 (2018)
18. Krause, J., Jin, H., Yang, J., Fei-Fei, L.: Fine-grained recognition without part annotations. In: Proceedings of the IEEE Conference on Computer Vision and Pattern Recognition, pp. 5546–5555 (2015)
19. Lin, D., Shen, X., Lu, C., Jia, J.: Deep LAC: deep localization, alignment and classification for fine-grained recognition. In: Proceedings of the IEEE Conference on Computer Vision and Pattern Recognition, pp. 1666–1674 (2015)
20. Krause, J., Stark, M., Deng, J., Fei-Fei, L.: 3D object representations for fine-grained categorization. In: Proceedings of the IEEE International Conference on Computer Vision Workshops, pp. 554–561 (2013)
21. Zhang, H., et al.: SPDA-CNN: unifying semantic part detection and abstraction for fine-grained recognition. In: Proceedings of the IEEE Conference on Computer Vision and Pattern Recognition, pp. 1143–1152 (2016)
22. Simon, M., Rodner, E.: Neural activation constellations: unsupervised part model discovery with convolutional networks. In: Proceedings of the IEEE International Conference on Computer Vision, pp. 1143–1151 (2015)
23. Hu, J., Shen, L., Sun, G.: Squeeze-and-excitation networks. In: Proceedings of the IEEE Conference on Computer Vision and Pattern Recognition, pp. 7132–7141 (2018)
24. Wang, Y., Morariu, V.I., Davis, L.S.: Learning a discriminative filter bank within a CNN for fine-grained recognition. In: Proceedings of the IEEE Conference on Computer Vision and Pattern Recognition, pp. 4148–4157 (2018)
25. Sun, M., Yuan, Y., Zhou, F., Ding, E.: Multi-attention multi-class constraint for fine-grained image recognition. In: Proceedings of the European Conference on Computer Vision, pp. 805–821 (2018)
26. Yang, Z., Luo, T., Wang, D., Hu, Z., Gao, J., Wang, L.: Learning to navigate for fine-grained classification. In: Proceedings of the European Conference on Computer Vision, pp. 420–435 (2018)
27. Maji, S., Rahtu, E., Kannala, J., Blaschko, M., Vedaldi, A.: Fine-grained visual classification of aircraft. arXiv preprint arXiv:1306.5151 (2013)
28. Hu, T., Qi, H., Huang, Q., Lu, Y.: See better before looking closer: weakly supervised data augmentation network for fine-grained visual classification. arXiv preprint arXiv: 1901.09891 (2019)
29. Li, X., Wang, W., Hu, X., Yang, J.: Selective kernel networks. In: Proceedings of the IEEE Conference on Computer Vision and Pattern Recognition, pp. 510–519 (2019)
30. Singh, K.K., Lee, Y.J.: Hide-and-seek: forcing a network to be meticulous for weakly-supervised object and action localization. In: 2017 IEEE International Conference on Computer Vision, pp. 3544–3553 (2017)

31. Wei, X. S., Xie, C. W., Wu, J.: Mask-CNN: localizing parts and selecting descriptors for fine-grained image recognition. arXiv preprint arXiv: 1605.06878 (2016)
32. Wang, D., Shen, Z., Shao, J., Zhang, W., Xue, X., Zhang, Z.: Multiple granularity descriptors for fine-grained categorization. In: Proceedings of the IEEE International Conference on Computer Vision, pp. 2399–2406 (2015)
33. Zhang, X., Xiong, H., Zhou, W., Lin, W., Tian, Q.: Picking deep filter responses for fine-grained image recognition. In: Proceedings of the IEEE Conference on Computer Vision and Pattern Recognition, pp. 1134–1142 (2016)
34. Cai, S., Zuo, W., Zhang, L.: Higher-order integration of hierarchical convolutional activations for fine-grained visual categorization. In: Proceedings of the IEEE International Conference on Computer Vision, pp. 511–520 (2017)
35. Donahue, J., et al.: DeCAF: a deep convolutional activation feature for generic visual recognition. In: International Conference on Machine Learning, pp. 647–655 (2014)

Author Index

Printed in the United States
By Bookmasters